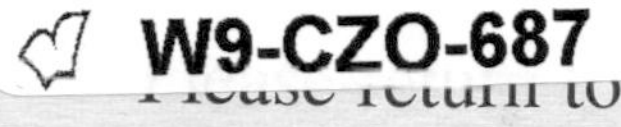

The Complete BIBLICAL LIBRARY

The Complete
BIBLICAL
LIBRARY

THE NEW TESTAMENT STUDY BIBLE

JOHN

The Complete BIBLICAL LIBRARY

The Complete Biblical Library, part 1, a 16-volume study series on the New Testament. Volume 5: STUDY BIBLE, JOHN. World copyright ©1986 by Thoralf Gilbrant and Tor Inge Gilbrant.
© Published 1988 by THE COMPLETE BIBLICAL LIBRARY, Springfield, Missouri 65802, U.S.A.

Printed in the United States of America 1987 by R.R. Donnelley and Sons Company, Chicago, Illinois 60606. Library of Congress Catalog Card Number 88-071159
International Standard Book Number 0-88243-365-X.

THE NEW TESTAMENT
Study Bible, Greek-English Dictionary, Harmony of the Gospels

THE OLD TESTAMENT
Study Bible, Hebrew-English Dictionary

THE BIBLE ENCYCLOPEDIA

INTERNATIONAL AND INTERDENOMINATIONAL BIBLE STUDY SYSTEM

THE NEW TESTAMENT STUDY BIBLE JOHN

Executive Editor: Ralph W. Harris, M.A.

Editor: Stanley M. Horton, Th.D.

Managing Editor: Gayle Garrity Seaver, J.D.

THE COMPLETE BIBLICAL LIBRARY
Springfield, Missouri, U.S.A.

Table of Contents

	Page
Personnel	**5**
Introduction	**6**
Features of the Study Bible	6
Translation of Greek Words	7
How the New Testament Came to Us	7
Literary and Biblical Standards	10
Study Helps	10
Greek and Hebrew Alphabets	12
Relationship of the Interlinear and the Textual Apparatus	13
Interlinear and Commentary	**18**
Overview	**565**
Manuscripts	**616**
Egyptian Papyri	616
Major Codices	618
Majuscules and Minuscules	619
Early Versions	619
Early Church Fathers	**620**
Books of the New and Old Testament and the Apocrypha	**621**
Bibliography	**622**
Acknowledgments	**626**

VERSE-BY-VERSE COMMENTARY
ROBERT E. TOURVILLE, M.A.

VARIOUS VERSIONS
GERARD FLOKSTRA, JR. Ph.D.

BOARD OF REVIEW

Zenas Bicket, Ph.D.
Jesse Moon, D.Min.
Charles Harris, Ed.D.
Opal Reddin, D.Min.

STAFF

Senior Editors: Gary Leggett, M.A.; Dorothy Morris

Editorial Team: Patrick Alexander, M.A. (research); Lloyd Anderson; Ken Barney; Betty Bates; Faye Faucett; Cynthia Riemenschneider; Wesley Smith, M.Div.; Denis Vinyard, M.Div.

Art Director: Terry Van Someren, B.F.A.

Word Processing and Secretarial: Charlotte Gribben; Sonja Jensen; Don Williams, B.A.; Rachel Wisehart

Introduction

This volume of the *Study Bible* is part of a 16-volume set titled *The Complete Biblical Library*. It is an ambitious plan to provide all the information one needs for a basic understanding of the New Testament—useful for scholars but also for students and lay people.

In addition to the Harmony, *The Complete Biblical Library* provides a 9-volume *Study Bible* and a 6-volume *Greek-English Dictionary*. They are closely linked. You will find information about the *Study Bible*'s features later in the Introduction. The *Greek-English Dictionary* lists all the Greek words of the New Testament in their alphabetic order, provides a concordance showing each place the words appear in the New Testament, and includes an article explaining the background, significance, and meaning of the words.

FEATURES OF THE STUDY BIBLE

The *Study Bible* is a unique combination of study materials which will help both the scholar and the layman achieve a better understanding of the New Testament and the language in which it was written. All of these helps are available in various forms but bringing them together in combination will save many hours of research. Most scholars do not have in their personal libraries all the volumes necessary to provide the information so readily available here.

The editors of *The Complete Biblical Library* are attempting an unusual task: to help scholars in their research but also to make available to laymen the tools by which to acquire knowledge which up to this time has been available only to scholars.

Following are the major divisions of the *Study Bible*:

Overview

Each volume contains an encyclopedic survey of the New Testament book. It provides a general outline, discusses matters about which there may be a difference of opinion, and provides background information regarding the history, culture, literature, and philosophy of the era covered by the book.

Interlinear

Following the overall principle of providing help for both the scholar and the layman, we supply a unique *Interlinear*. Most interlinears, if not all, give merely the Greek text and the meanings of the words. Our *Interlinear* contains *five* parts:

1. *Greek Text*. Our Greek text is a comparative text which includes both the traditional text type and the text which is common in modern textual editions.

2. *Grammatical Forms*. These are shown above each Greek word, alongside its assigned number. This information is repeated, along with the Greek word, in the *Greek-English Dictionary* where more details may be found.

3. *Transliteration*. No other interlinears provide this. Its purpose is to familiarize laymen with the proper pronunciation of Greek words so they will feel comfortable when using them in teaching situations. Complete information on pronunciation is found on the page showing the Greek and Hebrew alphbets.

4. *Translation*. The basic meaning of each Greek word is found beneath it. Rather than merely accepting the work of past interlinears, we have assigned scholars to upgrade words to a more modern description. See a later section for the principles we have followed in translation of the Greek words in our *Interlinear*.

5. *Assigned Numbers*. The unique numbering system of *The Complete Biblical Library* makes cross-reference study between the *Study Bible* and the *Greek-English Dictionary* the ultimate in simplicity. Each Greek word has been assigned a number. *Alpha* is the first word in alphabetic order as well as the first letter of the Greek alphabet, so the number *1* has been assigned to it. The rest of the almost 5,000 words follow in numerical and alphabetic sequence.

The *Greek-English Dictionary* follows the same plan with each word listed in alphabetic sequence. If a student desires further study on a certain word, he can find its number above it and locate it in the dictionary. In moments he has access to all the valuable information he needs for a basic understanding of that word.

Textual Apparatus

As said above, our Greek text is a comparative text. A text based only upon the *Textus Receptus* is not adequate for today's needs. Also, an eclectic text—using the "best" from various text types—will not be satisfactory, because such an approach may be quite subjective, with decisions influenced by the personal viewpoint of the scholar. Our text is a combination of both the main types of the Greek New Testament text. We have the *Textus Receptus*, a Stephanus text, based on the Byzantine text type. When there are important variants which differ from the *Textus Receptus*, they are included within brackets in the text. In the narrow column to the left of the *Interlinear*, the sources of the variants are listed. This will provide a fascinating study for a scholar and student, and will save him innumerable hours of research.

Verse-by-Verse Commentary

Many Bible-loving scholars have combined their knowledge, study, and skills to provide this. It is not an exhaustive treatment (many other commentaries are available for that), but again it provides a basic understanding of every verse in the New Testament. It does not usually deal with textual criticism (that can be dealt with in another arena), but it opens up the nuances of the Greek New Testament as written by the inspired writers.

Various Versions

This offers a greatly amplified New Testament. Each verse is broken down into its phrases; the King James Version is shown in boldface type; then from more than 60 other versions we show various ways the Greek of that phrase may be translated. The Greek of the First Century was such a rich language that to obtain the full meaning of words, several synonyms may be needed.

TRANSLATION OF GREEK WORDS

No word-for-word translation can be fully "literal" in the sense of expressing all the nuances of the original language. Rather, our purpose is to help the student find the English word which most correctly expresses the original Greek word in that particular context. The Greek language is so rich in meaning that the same word may have a slightly different meaning in another context.

In any language idioms offer a special translation problem. According to the dictionary, this is an expression which has "a meaning which cannot be derived from the conjoined meanings of its elements." The Greek language abounds in such phrases which cannot be translated literally.

We have come to what we consider a splendid solution to the problem, whether the translation should be strictly literal or abound in a plethora of idiomatic expressions. From more than 60 translations, the *Various Versions* column presents the various ways phrases have been translated. Here the student will find the translations of the idioms. This enables us to make our English line in the *Interlinear* strictly literal. The student will have available both types of translation—and will have a fresh appreciation for the struggles through which translators go.

HOW THE NEW TESTAMENT CAME TO US

Volume 1 of *The Complete Biblical Library*, the *Harmony of the Gospels*, contains information on how the four Gospels came into being. The preponderance of proof points to the fact that the rest of the New Testament was written before A.D. 100. Like the Gospels, it was written in Greek, the universal language of that era. It was qualified in a special way for this purpose. Probably no other language is so expressive and able to provide such fine nuances of meaning.

Yet the New Testament Greek is not the perfectly structured form of the language from the old classical period. It is the more simple Koine Greek from the later Hellenistic age. This had become the lingua franca of the Hellenistic and Roman world. The Egyptian papyri have shown that the language which the New Testament writers used was the common language of the people. It seems as though God accomodated himself to a form of communication which would make His Word most readily accepted and easily understood.

At the same time we should recognize that the language of the Greek New Testament also is a *religious language*, with a tradition going back a couple of centuries to the Septuagint, the Greek translation of the Old Testament.

The Manuscripts

None of the original manuscripts (handwritten documents) still exist. Even in the First Century they must have often been copied so as to share their treasured truths with numerous congregations of believers. The original documents then soon became worn out through use. Evidently, only copies of the New Testament still exist.

Over 5,000 manuscripts of the New Testament have been discovered up to the present time. Most of them are small fragments of verses or chapters, a few books of the New Testament, some copies of the Gospels. Very few contain all or nearly all of the New Testament.

The manuscripts have come to us in various forms: (1) Egyptian papyri, (2) majuscules, (3) minuscules, (4) writings of the Early Church fathers, (5) lectionaries, and (6) early versions.

The Egyptian Papyri

These are the oldest copies of parts of the Greek New Testament. The earliest are dated about A.D. 200, a few even earlier, and the youngest are from the Seventh Century. Most of them date back to the Third, Fourth and Fifth Centuries of the Christian Era.

They were found in the late 1800s in Egypt. The dry climatic conditions of that country enabled them to be preserved. The largest fragments contain only a few dozen pages, while the smallest are the size of a postage stamp.

The papyri are listed in the back of this volume under the heading "Manuscripts."

The Majuscules

These are the second oldest kind of copies of New Testament manuscripts. They received this description because they were written in majuscules; that is, large letters (the uncials are a form of majuscules). Three major majuscules are the following:

1. Codex Aleph, also called Codex Sinaiticus, because it was discovered in the mid-1840s by the great scholar Tischendorf at St. Catharine's Monastery, located at the foot of Mount Sinai. Numbered 01, it contains all the New Testament and is dated in the Fourth Century.

2. Codex A, numbered 02, is named Alexandrinus, because it came from Alexandria in Egypt. In the Gospels, this manuscript is the foremost witness to the Byzantine text type.

3. Codex B, 03, is called Codex Vaticanus, because it is in the Vatican library. Along with the Sinaiticus, it is the main witness for the Egyptian text type. However, it is important to realize there are more than 3,000 differences between these 2 manuscripts in the Gospels alone (Hoskier).

See the list of majuscules in the back of this volume, under "Manuscripts."

The Minuscules

This is a kind of manuscript written in small letters. They are only a few hundred years old, beginning with the Ninth Century. Most come from the 12th to the 14th Century A.D. They form, by far, the greatest group of the New Testament manuscripts, numbering almost 2,800.

The minuscules represent the unbroken text tradition in the Greek Orthodox Church, and about 90 percent of them belong to the Byzantine text group. They are numbered 1, 2, 3, etc.

Lectionaries and Church Fathers

Lectionaries include manuscripts which were not Scripture themselves but contain Scripture quotations, used for the scheduled worship services of the annual church calendar. These are numbered consecutively and are identified by *lect.*

Practically all the New Testament could be retrieved from the writings of early Christian leaders, called church fathers. These lists are located in the back of this volume.

Early Versions

Translations of the New Testament from Greek are also of value. They are listed under "Manuscripts" in the back of this volume. The best known is the Latin Vulgate by Jerome.

Major Greek Texts

From the manuscripts which have just been described, various types of Greek texts have been formed:

The Western text can possibly be traced back to the Second Century. It was used mostly in Western Europe and North Africa. It tends to add to the text and makes long paraphrases of it. Today some scholars do not recognize it as a special text type.

The Caesarean text may have originated in Egypt and was brought, it is believed, to the city of Caesarea in Palestine. Later, it was carried to Jerusalem, then by Armenian missionaries into a province in the kingdom of Georgia, now a republic of the U.S.S.R. Some scholars consider it a mixture of other text types.

The two most prominent text types, however, are the Egyptian (also called the Alexandrian) and the Byzantine. These are the major ones considered in our *Interlinear* and *Textual Apparatus*. Except for the papyrus texts which are highly varied, these are the only text families which have any degree of support. References to numerous text groups which were so common a few decades ago must now probably be considered out of date. At any rate, out of practical considerations, we have kept the Byzantine and Egyptian (Alexandrian) as fixed text groups in our *Textual Apparatus*. Following is historical information about them.

The Byzantine Text

Many titles have been applied to this text type. It has been called the *K* (Koine), Syrian, Antiochian, and Traditional. It is generally believed to have been produced at Antioch in Syria, then taken to Byzantium, later known as Constantinople. For about 1,000 years, while the Byzantine Empire ruled the Middle East, this was the text used by the Greek Orthodox Church. It also influenced Europe.

Because of this background it became the basis for the first printed text editions, among others the famous *Textus Receptus*, called "the acknowledged text."

The Byzantine text form is also called the Majority text, since 80 to 90 percent of all existing manuscripts are represented in this text, though most of them are quite recent and evidently copies of earlier manuscripts. Like the Egyptian text, the Byzantine text can be traced back to the Fourth Century. It also contains some readings which seem to be the same as some papyri which can be traced back to a much earlier time. Among the oldest majuscules the Byzantine is, among others, represented by Codex Alexandrinus (02, A), 07, 08, 09, 010, 011, 012, 013, 015, and others.

The Egyptian Text

This text type originated in Egypt and is the one which gained the highest recognition and acceptance there in the Fourth Century. It was produced mainly by copyists in Alexandria, from which it received the name *Alexandrian*. This text form is represented mostly by two codices: Sinaiticus (01, Aleph) and Vaticanus (03, B) from the Fourth Century, also from Codex Ephraemi (04, C) from the Fifth Century. The use of this text type ceased about the year 450 but lived on in the Latin translation, the Vulgate version.

Printed Greek Texts

The invention of printing about 1450 opened the door for wider distribution of the Scriptures. In 1516 Erasmus, a Dutch scholar, produced the first *printed* Greek New Testament. It was based on the Byzantine text type, with most of the New Testament coming from manuscripts dated at about the 12th Century. He did his work very hurriedly, finishing his task in just a few months. His second edition, produced in 1519 with some of the mistakes corrected, became the basis for translations into German by Luther and into English by Tyndale.

A printed Greek New Testament was produced by a French printer, Stephanus, in 1550. His edition and those produced by Theodore Beza, of Geneva, between 1565 and 1604, based on the Byzantine text, have been entitled the *Textus Receptus*. That description, however, originated with the text produced by Elzevir. He described his second edition of 1633 by the Latin phrase *Textus Receptus*, or the "Received Text"; that is, the one accepted generally as the correct one.

A list of the printed editions of the Greek text is found in the section describing the relationship of the *Interlinear* and the *Textual Apparatus*.

Contribution of Westcott and Hort

Two British scholars, Westcott and Hort, have played a prominent role in deciding which text type should be used. They (especially Hort) called the Byzantine text "corrupt," because of the young age of its supporting manuscripts and proceeded to develop their own text (1881-86). It was really a restoration of the Egyptian text from the Fourth Century. It depended mainly on two codices, Sinaiticus and Vaticanus, but was also supported by numerous majuscules such as 02, 04, 019, 020, 025, 032, 033, 037, and 044.

Westcott and Hort opposed the *Textus Receptus* because it was based on the Byzantine text form. Most scholars agreed with their contention, and the *Textus Receptus* fell into disrepute. However, Westcott and Hort made their assumptions before the Greek papyri were discovered, and in recent years some scholars have come to the defense of the Byzantine text and the *Textus Receptus*. They have learned that some of the readings in the Byzantine text are the same as those found in the earliest papyri, dated about A.D. 200 and even earlier (p45, p46, p64 and p66, for example). This seems to take the Byzantine text back at least as far as the Egyptian.

Two important statements must be made: (1) We should always remember there are good men and scholars on both sides of the controversy, and their major concern is to obtain as pure a text as possible, to reassure Bible students that the New Testament we now possess conforms to that written in the First Century. (2) Since it was the original writings which were inspired by the Holy Spirit, it is important for us to ascertain as closely as possible how well our present-day text agrees with the original writings. It should alleviate the fears some may have as to whether we have the true gospel enunciated in the First Century to know that most of the differences in the Greek text (about 1 percent of the total) are minor in nature and do not affect the great Christian doctrines we hold dear. Significant differences may be found in only a very few cases.

We have consciously avoided polemics in the area of textual criticism. There is legitimacy for such discussion, but *The Complete Biblical Library* is not the arena for such a conflict. (1) Often the opposing views are conjectural. (2) There is insufficient space to treat subjects adequately and to raise questions without answering them fully leads to confusion.

LITERARY AND BIBLICAL STANDARDS

Several hundred people, highly qualified scholars and specialists in particular fields have participated in producing *The Complete Biblical Library*. Great care has been taken to maintain high standards of scholarship and ethics. By involving scholars in Boards of Review for the *Study Bible* and the *Greek-English Dictionary*, we added an extra step to the editorial process. We have been particularly concerned about giving proper credit for citations from other works and have instructed our writers to show care in this regard. Any deviation from this principle has been inadvertent and not intentional.

Obviously, with writers coming from widely differing backgrounds, there are differences of opinion as to how to interpret certain passages.

We have tried to be just. When there are strong differences on the meaning of a particular passage, we have felt it best to present the contrasting viewpoints.

STUDY HELPS

As you come to the Scripture section of this volume, you will find correlated pages for your study. The facing pages are designed to complement each other, so you will have a better understanding of the Word of God than ever before. Each two-page spread will deal with a group of verses.

On the left-hand page is the *Interlinear* with its fivefold helps: (1) the Greek text in which the New Testament was written; (2) the transliteration, showing how to pronounce each word; (3) the basic meaning of each word; (4) next to Greek words an assigned number (you will need this number to learn more about the word in the *Greek-English Dictionary*, companion to the *Study Bible*); and (5) the grammatical forms of each Greek word. The left-hand page also contains a column called the *Textual Apparatus*. This column is explained later.

The right-hand page contains two features. The *Verse-by-Verse Commentary* refers to each verse, except when occasionally it deals with some closely related verses. The *Various Versions* column provides an expanded understanding of the various ways Greek words or phrases can be translated. The phrase from the King James Version appears first in boldface print, then other meaningful ways the Greek language has been translated. This feature will bring to you the riches of the language in which the New Testament first appeared.

General Abbreviations

In a work of this nature it is necessary to use some abbreviations in order to conserve space. In deference to the Scriptures it is our custom not to abbreviate the titles of the books of the Bible, but abbreviations are used elsewhere. Becoming familiar with them will enable you to pursue in-depth study more effectively.

The following are general abbreviations which you will find used throughout the book:

cf.	compared to or see
ibid.	in the same place
id.	the same
idem	the same
i.e.	that is
e.g.	for example
f. ff.	and following page or pages
sic	intended as written
MS(S)	manuscript(s)
ET	editor's translation

Greek and Hebrew Alphabets with Pronunciation Guide

Some readers may want to become better acquainted with the Greek and Hebrew alphabets (the latter the language of the Old Testament). If so, the following lists will be of service to you.

Greek

Α	α	alpha	a	(father)
Β	β	beta	b	
Γ	γ	gamma	g	(got)
Δ	δ	delta	d	
Ε	ε	epsilon	e	(get)
Ζ	ζ	zeta	z	dz (leads)
Η	η	eta	e	(ate)
Θ	θ	theta	th	(thin)
Ι	ι	iota	i	(sin or machine)
Κ	κ	kappa	k	
Λ	λ	lambda	l	
Μ	μ	mu	m	
Ν	ν	nu	n	
Ξ	ξ	x i	x	
Ο	ο	omicron	o	(lot)
Π	π	pi	p	
Ρ	ρ	rho	r	
Σ	σ,ς[1]	sigma	s	
Τ	τ	tau	t	
Υ	υ	upsilon	u	German ü
Φ	φ	phi	ph	(philosophy)
Χ	χ	chi	ch	(chaos)
Ψ	ψ	psi	ps	(lips)
Ω	ω	omega	o	(ocean)

Hebrew

א	aleph	’ [2]	
ב	beth	b, bh	(v)[3]
ג	gimel	g, gh	
ד	daleth	d, dh	(they)[3]
ה	he	h	
ו	waw	w	
ז	zayin	z	
ח	heth	h	(kh)
ט	teth	t	
י	yod	y	
כ ך	kaph	k, kh	
ל	lamed	l	
מ ם	mem	m	
נ ן	nun	n	
ס	samekh	s	
ע	ayin	‘	
פ ף	pe	p, ph	
צ ץ	sadhe	s	(ts)
ק	qoph	q	
ר	resh	r	
שׂ	sin	s	
שׁ	shin	sh	
ת	taw	t, th	(thing)[3]

Greek Pronunciation Rules

Before another *g*, or before a *k* or a *ch*, *g* is pronounced and spelled with an *n*, in the transliteration of the Greek word.

In the Greek, ς is written at the end of a word, elsewhere it appears as σ. The rough breathing mark (‛) indicates that an *h*-sound is to be pronounced before the initial vowel or diphthong. The smooth breathing mark (’) indicates that no such *h*-sound is to be pronounced.

There are three accents, the acute (—́), the circumflex (—̂) and the grave (—̀). These stand over a vowel and indicate that stress in pronunciation is to be placed on the syllable having any one of the accents.

Pronouncing Diphthongs

ai is pronounced like *ai* in aisle
ei is pronounced like *ei* in eight
oi is pronounced like *oi* in oil
au is pronounced like *ow* in cow
eu is pronounced like *eu* in feud
ou is pronounced like *oo* in food
ui is pronounced like *ui* in suite (sweet)

1. Where two forms of a letter are given, the one at the right is used at the end of a word.
2. Not represented in transliteration when the initial letter.
3. Letters underscored represent pronunciation of the second form only.

Old and New Testament Books and Apocrypha

As a service to you, we have listed the books of the Bible in their order. The Apocrypha is a series of books which were included in the Vulgate version (the Latin translation of the Bible endorsed by the Roman Catholic Church). Though not considered part of the canon by either the Jews or Protestants, they give interesting insights, on occasion, concerning the times with which they deal. They are not on the same level as the 66 books of our canon. These lists are located in the back of the book.

Bibliographic Citations

The Complete Biblical Library has adopted a system of coordinated citations in the text and bibliography material which accommodates every type of reader. For the sake of simplicity and space, information given in the text to document a source is minimal, often including only the last name of the writer, or a shortened title and a page number.

Those who would like to research the subject more deeply can easily do so by looking in the Bibliography in the back of the book under the last name or shortened title. The Bibliography lists complete information necessary to locate the source in a library, supplemented by the page number given in the citation in the text.

RELATIONSHIP OF THE INTERLINEAR AND THE TEXTUAL APPARATUS

The Greek text of the *Study Bible* provides a means of collating the traditional texts with modern text editions; that is, comparing them critically to discover their degree of similarity or divergence. The *Textual Apparatus* column provides information as to which manuscripts or groups of manuscripts support certain readings. Some scholarly works use an eclectic text, selecting from various sources the text they consider to be the best. In our view, our comparative text provides a better system for considering the relative merits of the major texts.

The *Textual Apparatus* refers to many different manuscripts but to just two text groups, the Byzantine and the Egyptian, also known as Alexandrian. Except for the papyri texts, which are highly varied, these two text families are the only ones which have a significant degree of support. Reference to many different text groups is now becoming passé. Using only the byz (Byzantine) and eg (Egyptian) text groups makes the work of the researcher less complicated and provides an adequate system of reference.

The *Interlinear* uses the Stephanus text as its basis but is not confined to it. Actually, most of the Greek text is the same in all the text types. For easy comparison variants are inserted in the text and are then considered in the *Textual Apparatus* column, which provides their background in the major and minor manuscripts.

Abbreviations and Signs Used in the Textual Apparatus

Using the information which follows you will be able to identify the variants and their sources and to compare them with the basic text and other variants.

Txt	The Greek text used, the TR
byz	Byzantine text form
eg	Egyptian text form
p 1, etc.	Papyrus manuscripts
01, etc.	Majuscule manuscripts
1, etc.	Minuscule manuscripts
lect	Lectionaries
org	Reading of original copier
corr 1, etc.	Change by another person
( )	Supports in principle
sa	Sahidic
bo	Bohairic

Printed Editions of the Greek Text (with abbreviations)

Steph	Stephanus, 1550
Beza	Beza, 1564-1604
Elzev	Elzevir, 1624
Gries	Griesbach, 1805
Lach	Lachmann, 1842-50
Treg	Tregelles, 1857-72
Alf	Alford, 1862-71
Tisc	Tischendorf, 1865-95
Word	Wordsworth, 1870
We/Ho	Westcott and Hort, 1881-86
Wey	Weymouth, 1885
Weis	Weiss, 1894-1900
Sod	von Soden, 1902-10
H/Far	Hodges and Farstad (Majority text)
☆	various modern text editions
UBS	United Bible Society

Understanding the Codes in the Greek Text and the Textual Apparatus

Definitions:

TR. The *Textus Receptus,* the basic text of this *Interlinear.*

Reading. A word or phrase from a Greek text.

Variant. A reading which differs from the TR.

The *Textual Apparatus* contains two divisions for analyzing the text when variants occur: *Txt,* meaning the TR (*Textus Receptus*); and *Var,* meaning variants, readings which differ from the TR. Under these two headings are listed the manuscripts which support either the TR or the variant.

Illustrations:

The following examples from Luke 10:19-21 show how to understand the relationship between the Greek text and the *Textual Apparatus.*

The half-parenthesis indicates that the next word begins a TR reading for which a variant is shown. See example A.

The variant itself is enclosed in brackets (note the example of this at the beginning of verse 19). The text (TR) reads, "I give . . . , " but the variant reads, "I have given . . . ." See example B.

The small *a* at the beginning of the bracket refers back to the *Textual Apparatus* column, showing it is the first variant in that particular verse. See example C. Only those variants identified by *a, b, c,* etc., are considered in the *Textual Apparatus.*

The star following the *a* means that the variant is used in some modern text editions, such as the UBS text. See example D.

Note that in variant *b* of verse 19 the star appears before the TR word. This means that in this case UBS and/or others do not follow the variant but read the same as the TR. See example E.

In verse 20, variant *a* appears between two half-parentheses, showing *mallon* ("rather") is not included in some texts. The TR reads, "Rejoice but rather that . . . ," while the variant (without *mallon*) reads, "Rejoice but that . . . ." See example F.

It is important to recognize that the star in the *Textual Apparatus* for verse 20 means that UBS and other modern texts support the variant reading. If the UBS supported the TR, the star would have appeared under the *Txt* heading. See example G.

Sometimes there is more than one variant reading, as in variant *b* of verse 20. In such cases they are numbered in order (see the *2* before the star in the second reading). This shows the difference and also provides an easy reference in the *Textual Apparatus.* See example H.

In verse 21, variant *a* presents a case where the word *en* ("in") is not a part of the TR but appears in other texts. The + sign indicates this. See example I.

Understanding the Codes in the Greek Text and the Textual Apparatus

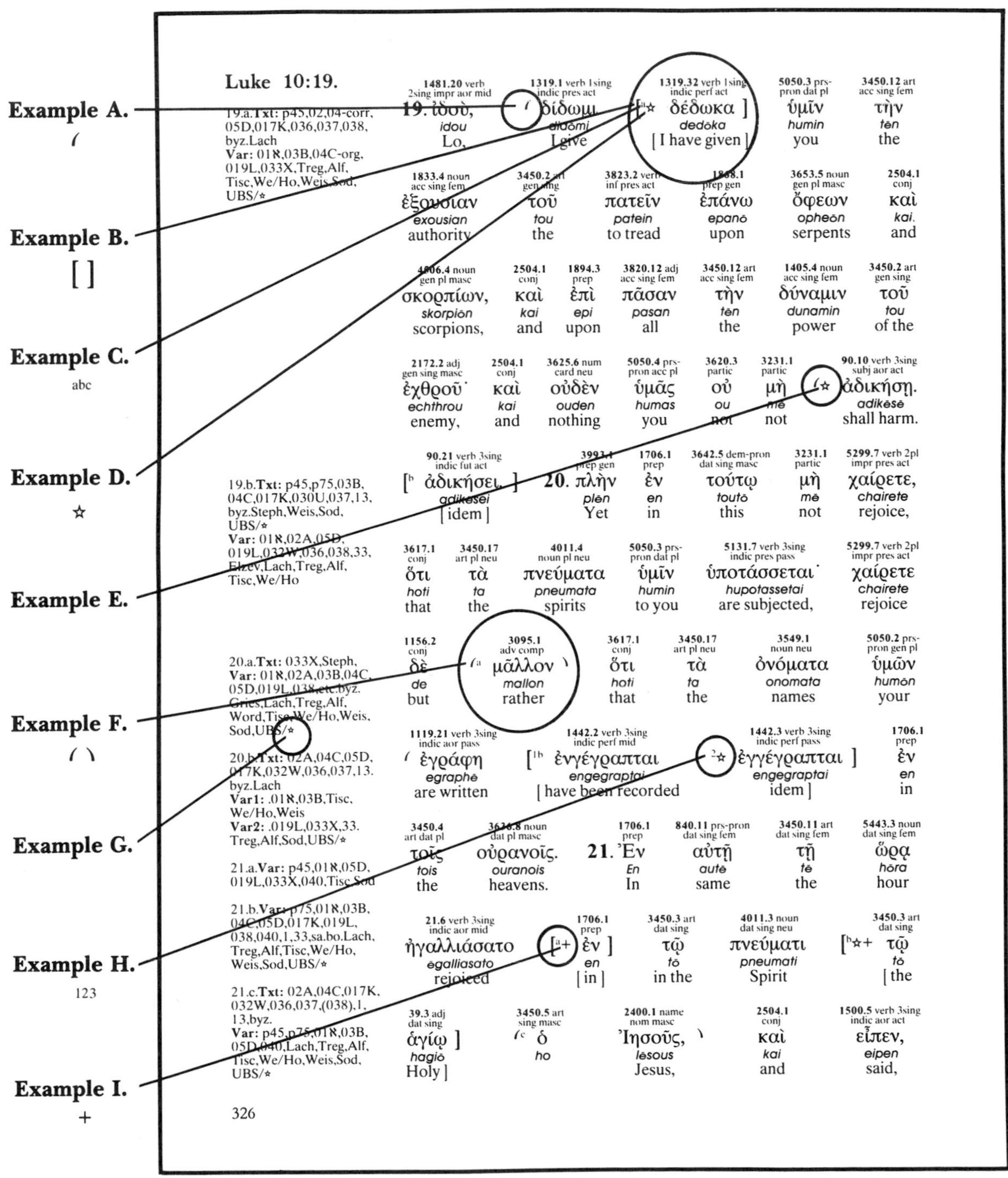

Luke 10:19.

1481.20 verb 2sing impr aor mid	1319.1 verb 1sing indic pres act	1319.32 verb 1sing indic perf act	5050.3 prs-pron dat pl	3450.12 art acc sing fem
19. ἰδοὺ,	⸀ δίδωμι	[ᵃ☆ δέδωκα]	ὑμῖν	τὴν
idou	*didōmi*	*dedōka*	*humin*	*tēn*
Lo,	I give	[I have given]	you	the

1833.4 noun acc sing fem	3450.2 art gen sing	3823.2 verb inf pres act	1868.1 prep gen	3653.5 noun gen pl masc	2504.1 conj
ἐξουσίαν	τοῦ	πατεῖν	ἐπάνω	ὄφεων	καὶ
exousian	*tou*	*patein*	*epanō*	*opheōn*	*kai*
authority	the	to tread	upon	serpents	and

4506.4 noun gen pl masc	2504.1 conj	1894.3 prep	3820.12 adj acc sing fem	3450.12 art acc sing fem	1405.4 noun acc sing fem	3450.2 art gen sing
σκορπίων,	καὶ	ἐπὶ	πᾶσαν	τὴν	δύναμιν	τοῦ
skorpiōn	*kai*	*epi*	*pasan*	*tēn*	*dunamin*	*tou*
scorpions,	and	upon	all	the	power	of the

2172.2 adj gen sing masc	2504.1 conj	3625.6 num card neu	5050.4 prs-pron acc pl	3620.3 partic	3231.1 partic	90.10 verb 3sing subj aor act
ἐχθροῦ·	καὶ	οὐδὲν	ὑμᾶς	οὐ	μὴ	⸀☆ ἀδικήσῃ.
echthrou	*kai*	*ouden*	*humas*	*ou*	*mē*	*adikēsē*
enemy,	and	nothing	you	not	not	shall harm.

90.21 verb 3sing indic fut act	3993.1 prep gen	1706.1 prep	3642.5 dem-pron dat sing masc	3231.1 partic	5299.7 verb 2pl impr pres act
[ᵇ ἀδικήσει]	**20.** πλὴν	ἐν	τούτῳ	μὴ	χαίρετε,
adikēsei	*plēn*	*en*	*toutō*	*mē*	*chairete*
[idem]	Yet	in	this	not	rejoice,

3617.1 conj	3450.17 art pl neu	4011.4 noun pl neu	5050.3 prs-pron dat pl	5131.7 verb 3sing indic pres pass	5299.7 verb 2pl impr pres act
ὅτι	τὰ	πνεύματα	ὑμῖν	ὑποτάσσεται·	χαίρετε
hoti	*ta*	*pneumata*	*humin*	*hupotassetai*	*chairete*
that	the	spirits	to you	are subjected,	rejoice

1156.2 conj	3095.1 adv comp	3617.1 conj	3450.17 art pl neu	3549.1 noun neu	5050.2 prs-pron gen pl
δὲ	⸂ᵃ μᾶλλον ⸃	ὅτι	τὰ	ὀνόματα	ὑμῶν
de	*mallon*	*hoti*	*ta*	*onomata*	*humōn*
but	rather	that	the	names	your

1119.21 verb 3sing indic aor pass	1442.2 verb 3sing indic perf mid	1442.3 verb 3sing indic perf pass	1706.1 prep
⸀ ἐγράφη	[¹ᵇ ἐνγέγραπται	²☆ ἐγγέγραπται]	ἐν
egraphē	*engegraptai*	*engegraptai*	*en*
are written	[have been recorded	idem]	in

3450.4 art dat pl	3636.8 noun dat pl masc	1706.1 prep	840.11 prs-pron dat sing fem	3450.11 art dat sing fem	5443.3 noun dat sing fem
τοῖς	οὐρανοῖς.	**21.** Ἐν	αὐτῇ	τῇ	ὥρᾳ
tois	*ouranois*	*En*	*autē*	*tē*	*hōra*
the	heavens.	In	same	the	hour

21.6 verb 3sing indic aor mid	1706.1 prep	3450.3 art dat sing	4011.3 noun dat sing neu	3450.3 art dat sing
ἠγαλλιάσατο	[ᵃ+ ἐν]	τῷ	πνεύματι	[ᵇ☆+ τῷ
ēgalliasato	*en*	*tō*	*pneumati*	*tō*
rejoiced	[in]	in the	Spirit	[the

39.3 adj dat sing	3450.5 art sing masc	2400.1 name nom masc	2504.1 conj	1500.5 verb 3sing indic aor act
ἁγίῳ]	⸂ᶜ ὁ	Ἰησοῦς, ⸃	καὶ	εἶπεν,
hagiō	*ho*	*Iēsous*	*kai*	*eipen*
Holy]		Jesus,	and	said,

19.a.**Txt:** p45,02,04-corr, 05D,017K,036,037,038, byz.Lach
Var: 01ℵ,03B,04C-org, 019L,033X,Treg,Alf, Tisc,We/Ho,Weis,Sod, UBS/☆

19.b.**Txt:** p45,p75,03B, 04C,017K,030U,037,13, byz.Steph,Weis,Sod, UBS/☆
Var: 01ℵ,02A,05D, 019L,032W,036,038,33, Elzev,Lach,Treg,Alf, Tisc,We/Ho

20.a.**Txt:** 033X,Steph,
Var: 01ℵ,02A,03B,04C, 05D,019L,038,etc.byz. Gries,Lach,Treg,Alf, Word,Tisc,We/Ho,Weis, Sod,UBS/☆

20.b.**Txt:** 02A,04C,05D, 017K,032W,036,037,13, byz.Lach
Var1: .01ℵ,03B,Tisc, We/Ho,Weis
Var2: .019L,033X,33, Treg,Alf,Sod,UBS/☆

21.a.**Var:** p45,01ℵ,05D, 019L,033X,040,Tisc,Sod

21.b.**Var:** p75,01ℵ,03B, 04C,05D,017K,019L, 038,040,1,33,sa.bo.Lach, Treg,Alf,Tisc,We/Ho, Weis,Sod,UBS/☆

21.c.**Txt:** 02A,04C,017K, 032W,036,037,(038),1, 13,byz.
Var: p45,p75,01ℵ,03B, 05D,040,Lach,Treg,Alf, Tisc,We/Ho,Weis,Sod, UBS/☆

326

THE GOSPEL OF JOHN

Expanded Interlinear
Textual Critical Apparatus
Verse-by-Verse Commentary
Various Versions

The Overview for John is placed at the back of this volume.

2077.1 noun sing neu	2567.3 prep	2464.4 name acc masc
Εὐαγγέλιον	κατὰ	Ἰωάννην.
Euangelion	*kata*	*Iōannēn*
Gospel	according	to John.

1706.1 prep	741.3 noun dat sing fem	1498.34 verb sing indic imperf act	3450.5 art sing masc	3030.1 noun nom sing masc	2504.1 conj
1:1. Ἐν	ἀρχῇ	ἦν	ὁ	λόγος,	καὶ
En	*archē*	*ēn*	*ho*	*logos*	*kai*
In	beginning	was	the	Word,	and

3450.5 art sing masc	3030.1 noun nom sing masc	1498.34 verb sing indic imperf act	4242.1 prep	3450.6 art acc sing masc	2296.4 noun acc sing masc
ὁ	λόγος	ἦν	πρὸς	τὸν	θεόν,
ho	*logos*	*ēn*	*pros*	*ton*	*theon*
the	Word	was	with		God,

2504.1 conj	2296.1 noun nom sing masc	1498.34 verb sing indic imperf act	3450.5 art sing masc	3030.1 noun nom sing masc	3642.4 dem-pron nom sing masc
καὶ	θεὸς	ἦν	ὁ	λόγος.	2. οὗτος
kai	*theos*	*ēn*	*ho*	*logos*	*houtos*
and	God	was	the	Word.	This

1498.34 verb sing indic imperf act	1706.1 prep	741.3 noun dat sing fem	4242.1 prep	3450.6 art acc sing masc	2296.4 noun acc sing masc
ἦν	ἐν	ἀρχῇ	πρὸς	τὸν	θεόν.
ēn	*en*	*archē*	*pros*	*ton*	*theon*
was	in	beginning	with		God.

3820.1 adj	1217.1 prep	840.3 prs-pron gen sing	1090.33 verb 3sing indic aor mid	2504.1 conj
3. Πάντα	δι'	αὐτοῦ	ἐγένετο,	καὶ
Panta	*di'*	*autou*	*egeneto*	*kai*
All things	through	him	came into being,	and

5400.1 prep gen	840.3 prs-pron gen sing	1090.33 verb 3sing indic aor mid	3624.1 adv	1518.9 num card neu	3614.16 rel-pron sing neu
χωρὶς	αὐτοῦ	ἐγένετο	οὐδὲ	ʻ ἕν	ὃ
chōris	*autou*	*egeneto*	*oude*	*hen*	*ho*
without	him	came into being	not even	one	which

4.a.**Txt:** 01ℵ-corr,017K, 038,041,044,13,565,byz. bo.Tisc,WeisSod,UBS/⋆
Var: p75-corr,04C,019L, 032W,sa.Treg,We/Ho

4.b.**Var:** 01ℵ,05D,it.sa. Tisc

1090.3 verb 3sing indic perf act	1706.1 prep	1518.9 num card neu	3614.16 rel-pron sing neu	1090.3 verb 3sing indic perf act
γέγονεν.	4. ἐν	[[a] ἕν.	Ὃ	γέγονεν
gegonen	*en*	*hen*	*Ho*	*gegonen*
has come into being.	In	[one thing.	Which	has become

1706.1 prep	840.4 prs-pron dat sing	2205.1 noun nom sing fem	1498.34 verb sing indic imperf act	1498.4 verb 3sing indic pres act	2504.1 conj
ἐν]	αὐτῷ	ζωὴ	ʻ ἦν,	[[b] ἐστιν,]	καὶ
en	*autō*	*zōē*	*ēn*	*estin*	*kai*
in]	him	life	was,	[is,]	and

3450.9 art nom sing fem	2205.1 noun nom sing fem	1498.34 verb sing indic imperf act	3450.16 art sing neu	5295.1 noun sing neu	3450.1 art gen pl
ἡ	ζωὴ	ἦν	τὸ	φῶς	τῶν
hē	*zōē*	*ēn*	*to*	*phōs*	*tōn*
the	life	was	the	light	of the

THE GOSPEL OF JOHN

1:1,2. The subject of the statements made in verse 1 is "the Word" (*ho logos*). By placing the words "in the beginning" (*en archē*) first in the sentence, this fact about "the Word" is stressed.

"And the Word was with God" gives the second fact or truth concerning "the Word." "And" links the two traits as equal. The preposition "with" (*pros*) is translated hundreds of times in the King James Version as "to, unto, or towards." It always implies mutual fellowship and intercommunication. Thus the Son was with God in a close personal relationship.

"And the Word was God" expresses the third preexistent quality of "the Word," with "and" connecting the second and third attributes as equal. Though the definite article *the* (*ton*) is not found with "God" (as it was in the preceding phrase), the meaning is still that the Word was deity.

1:3. "All things" (*panta*) includes all created beings and things. This is parallel to Genesis 1:1: "God created." "The Word" (*ho logos*) was the one Mediator in creation, through whom God the Father spoke the worlds into existence and formed man. This is John's fourth statement as to who the Logos is. First he states the Logos' eternality, next His equality with God, then His deity, and in this verse His creativity. Like the first three statements this signifies the Logos as God by essential nature, for "create" is always used in the Bible with God as the subject. Man can only rearrange what is already there. God alone can create.

1:4. This verse is the most amazing one in John's Gospel, for it takes the Logos of eternity and makes Him available to human beings.

"In him was life" constitutes a statement of inconceivable magnitude. The kind of life indicated by the Greek word *zōē* specifies the highest form of life known in Scripture. "The Word" is the author of our life. John indicates not only spiritual life but also all forms of life.

The life principle exists in the Logos (cf. 5:26) and life's source came originally from Him. A beautiful analogy is noted in creation. The sun's rays caress the earth with light. The leaves of plants bud and absorb the warm life-giving light.

Various Versions

1. In the beginning was the Word: The Logos existed in the very beginning, *Moffatt*... From the first the Word was in being, *BB*... When all things began, the Word already was, *NEB*... The WORD existed, *Fenton.*

and the Word was with God: ...was face to face with God, *Montgomery*... in fellowship, *Wuest.*

and the Word was God: The Message was deity, *SEB*... And God was the Logos, *Klingensmith* ...was God Himself, *Williams* ...what God was, the Word was, *NEB* ...God was thatt worde, *Tyndale.*

2. The same was in the beginning with God:... was originally with God, *Rotherham*... He was with God from the first, *BB* ...was present with God at the beginning, *Fenton*... From eternity, *ALBA.*

3. All things were made by him: Through him all things came into being, *TCNT*... All creation took place through him, *Phillips* ...everything was by his hand, *Murdock*... came into existence, *Williams*... did happen, *Young* ...all things came to be, *JB.*

and without him was not any thing made that was made:... not a single creature, *Campbell* ...not a single thing, *TCNT* ...came into existence not even one thing, *Rotherham*... no existence came into being apart from him, *Moffatt.*

4. In him was life: In him appeared life, *Phillips*... It was by Him that life began to exist, *Williams*... What originated in Him was Life, *Fenton*... the Source of life, *SEB.*

442.7 noun gen pl masc	2504.1 conj	3450.16 art sing neu	5295.1 noun sing neu	1706.1 prep	3450.11 art dat sing fem
ἀνθρώπων·	5. καὶ	τὸ	φῶς	ἐν	τῇ
anthrōpōn	*kai*	*to*	*phōs*	*en*	*tē*
men.	And	the	light	in	the

4508.3 noun dat sing fem	5154.2 verb 3sing indic pres act	2504.1 conj	3450.9 art nom sing fem	4508.1 noun nom sing fem	840.15 prs-pron sing neu
σκοτίᾳ	φαίνει,	καὶ	ἡ	σκοτία	αὐτὸ
skotia	*phainei*	*kai*	*hē*	*skotia*	*auto*
darkness	appears,	and	the	darkness	it

3620.3 partic	2608.1 verb 3sing indic aor act	1090.33 verb 3sing indic aor mid	442.1 noun nom sing masc	643.29 verb nom sing masc part perf pass
οὐ	κατέλαβεν.	6. Ἐγένετο	ἄνθρωπος	ἀπεσταλμένος
ou	*katelaben*	*Egeneto*	*anthrōpos*	*apestalmenos*
not	apprehended.	There was	a man	sent

3706.2 prep	2296.2 noun gen sing masc	3549.2 noun sing neu	840.4 prs-pron dat sing	2464.1 name nom masc	3642.4 dem-pron nom sing masc
παρὰ	θεοῦ,	ὄνομα	αὐτῷ	Ἰωάννης.	7. οὗτος
para	*theou*	*onoma*	*autō*	*Iōannēs*	*houtos*
from	God,	name	his	John.	This one

2048.3 verb 3sing indic aor act	1519.1 prep	3114.3 noun acc sing fem	2419.1 conj	3113.20 verb 3sing subj aor act
ἦλθεν	εἰς	μαρτυρίαν,	ἵνα	μαρτυρήσῃ
ēlthen	*eis*	*marturian*	*hina*	*marturēsē*
came	for	a witness,	that	he might witness

3875.1 prep	3450.2 art gen sing	5295.2 noun gen sing neu	2419.1 conj	3820.7 adj pl masc	3961.27 verb 3pl subj aor act
περὶ	τοῦ	φωτός,	ἵνα	πάντες	πιστεύσωσιν
peri	*tou*	*phōtos*	*hina*	*pantes*	*pisteusōsin*
concerning	the	light,	that	all	might believe

1217.1 prep	840.3 prs-pron gen sing	3620.2 partic	1498.34 verb sing indic imperf act	1552.3 dem-pron nom sing masc	3450.16 art sing neu
δι'	αὐτοῦ.	8. οὐκ	ἦν	ἐκεῖνος	τὸ
di'	*autou*	*ouk*	*ēn*	*ekeinos*	*to*
through	him.	Not	was	that one	the

5295.1 noun sing neu	233.1 conj	2419.1 conj	3113.20 verb 3sing subj aor act	3875.1 prep	3450.2 art gen sing
φῶς,	ἀλλ'	ἵνα	μαρτυρήσῃ	περὶ	τοῦ
phōs	*all'*	*hina*	*marturēsē*	*peri*	*tou*
light,	but	that	he might witness	concerning	the

5295.2 noun gen sing neu	1498.34 verb sing indic imperf act	3450.16 art sing neu	5295.1 noun sing neu	3450.16 art sing neu	226.1 adj sing
φωτός.	9. Ἦν	τὸ	φῶς	τὸ	ἀληθινόν
phōtos	*Ēn*	*to*	*phōs*	*to*	*alēthinon*
light.	Was	the	light	the	true

3614.16 rel-pron sing neu	5297.1 verb 3sing indic pres act	3820.1 adj	442.4 noun acc sing masc	2048.42 verb sing part pres	1519.1 prep
ὃ	φωτίζει	πάντα	ἄνθρωπον	ἐρχόμενον	εἰς
ho	*phōtizei*	*panta*	*anthrōpon*	*erchomenon*	*eis*
which	lightens	every	man	coming	into

3450.6 art acc sing masc	2862.4 noun acc sing masc	1706.1 prep	3450.3 art dat sing	2862.3 noun dat sing masc	1498.34 verb sing indic imperf act
τὸν	κόσμον.	10. ἐν	τῷ	κόσμῳ	ἦν,
ton	*kosmon*	*en*	*tō*	*kosmō*	*ēn*
the	world.	In	the	world	he was,

1:5. Basic truth is revealed in these terms (*light* and *darkness*). The Greek verb for "comprehended" (*katalambanō*) is translated in various ways, such as, "comprehend," "apprehend," "overtake," "perceive," etc., but it was used most commonly to mean "to seize, grasp, or win over" in order to make something one's own or in order to overcome it. Both meanings may be included here. In the physical area the idea would be that darkness cannot master the light either in the sense of understanding it or putting it out. The light resists the darkness and will overcome it in the end.

1:6. "There was a man" introduces the introducer. When the Logos condescended, He did so not only in coming to the earth in the Incarnation, but also by yielding to an introduction by one of His creatures. John the Baptist was the one God selected to speak for Jesus.

1:7. God used a man to introduce himself to man. The verb "came" (*ēlthen*) of this verse is different from the "came" (NIV) (*egeneto*) of verse 6. In verse 6 "came" carries the thought of "happened," but here the idea of man's action.

In the phrase "for a witness" (*eis marturian*), the preposition *eis* indicates purpose. "Bear witness" refers to the action of the witness. He came to testify about the Light. "The Light" directs our consideration back to verses 4 and 5. "Might believe" is a concise statement of John's witness. This clause sums up the purpose of John's Gospel (20:31).

1:8. John was not that light but a lamp from which that light shone. Lamps are important only insofar as they are bearers of the light. "Bear witness" again points to John's prime task. No man is the light. Only Jesus the Logos could reveal the Almighty.

1:9. "The true (real, original, genuine, dependable, perfect, steady, worthy-of-confidence) Light" refers to verses 4 and 5. God cannot be known fully from partial light such as creation, nor any light source except the Logos.

"Cometh into the world" refers to the true Light and not to man. The context indicates that the Light is the focus of attention. "The true Light" then is modified by the participle "coming." The object to be enlightened is man. "Lighteth" is the action of the true Light on every person.

and the life was the light of men: . . . this Life was the Light of men, *Norlie* . . . of human beings, *Adams.*

5. And the light shineth in darkness: . . . goes on shining, *BB* . . . continues to shine, *Williams* . . . is constantly shining, *Wuest.*

and the darkness comprehended it not: . . . has not put it out, *Beck* . . . has not extinguished it, *HistNT* . . . did not absorb it, *Fenton* . . . did not overwhelm it, *Berkeley* . . . was not penetrated by it, *Norton.*

6. There was a man sent from God: . . . arose a man, *Rotherham* . . . appeared a man, *NEB* . . . commissioned by God, *Concordant* . . . sent off as an ambassador, *Wuest.*

whose name was John:

7. The same came for a witness: . . . for testimony, *RSV* . . . for the purpose of witnessing, *Moffatt.*

to bear witness of the Light: He came to tell the truth, *Beck* . . . give evidence concerning, *Fenton.*

that all men through him might believe: . . . everyone through him might come to believe, *Williams* . . . so that all men might have faith through him, *BB.*

8. He was not that Light: He was not himself the Light, *Berkeley.*

but was sent to bear witness of that Light: . . . came to tell the truth about the light, *SEB* . . . as a personal witness to that light, *Phillips.*

9. That was the true Light, which lighteth every man that cometh into the world: . . . the real light, *Rotherham* . . . which illumines, *Weymouth* . . . which shines upon every man, *Phillips* . . . into the universe, *Klingensmith.*

2504.1 conj	3450.5 art sing masc	2862.1 noun nom sing masc	1217.1 prep	840.3 prs-pron gen sing	1090.33 verb 3sing indic aor mid
καὶ	ὁ	κόσμος	δι'	αὐτοῦ	ἐγένετο,
kai	*ho*	*kosmos*	*di'*	*autou*	*egeneto*
and	the	world	through	him	came into being,

2504.1 conj	3450.5 art sing masc	2862.1 noun nom sing masc	840.6 prs-pron acc sing masc	3620.2 partic	1091.17 verb 3sing indic aor act
καὶ	ὁ	κόσμος	αὐτὸν	οὐκ	ἔγνω.
kai	*ho*	*kosmos*	*auton*	*ouk*	*egnō*
and	the	world	him	not	knew.

1519.1 prep	3450.17 art pl neu	2375.13 adj pl neu	2048.3 verb 3sing indic aor act	2504.1 conj	3450.7 art pl masc	2375.7 adj nom pl masc
11. εἰς	τὰ	ἴδια	ἦλθεν,	καὶ	οἱ	ἴδιοι
eis	*ta*	*idia*	*ēlthen*	*kai*	*hoi*	*idioi*
To	the	his own	he came,	and	the	his own

840.6 prs-pron acc sing masc	3620.3 partic	3741.4 verb indic aor act	3607.2 rel-pron nom pl masc	1156.2 conj	2956.12 verb indic aor act
αὐτὸν	οὐ	παρέλαβον·	12. ὅσοι	δὲ	ἔλαβον
auton	*ou*	*parelabon*	*hosoi*	*de*	*elabon*
him	not	received;	as many as	but	received

840.6 prs-pron acc sing masc	1319.14 verb 3sing indic aor act	840.2 prs-pron dat pl	1833.4 noun acc sing fem	4891.4 noun pl neu	2296.2 noun gen sing masc
αὐτόν	ἔδωκεν	αὐτοῖς	ἐξουσίαν	τέκνα	θεοῦ
auton	*edōken*	*autois*	*exousian*	*tekna*	*theou*
him	he gave	to them	authority	children	of God

1090.63 verb inf aor mid	3450.4 art dat pl	3961.3 verb 3pl pres act	1519.1 prep	3450.16 art sing neu	3549.2 noun sing neu
γενέσθαι,	τοῖς	πιστεύουσιν	εἰς	τὸ	ὄνομα
genesthai	*tois*	*pisteuousin*	*eis*	*to*	*onoma*
to be,	to the	believing	on	the	name

840.3 prs-pron gen sing	3614.7 rel-pron nom pl masc	3620.2 partic	1523.1 prep gen	129.4 noun gen pl neu	3624.1 adv	1523.2 prep gen
αὐτοῦ·	13. οἳ	οὐκ	ἐξ	αἱμάτων	οὐδὲ	ἐκ
autou	*hoi*	*ouk*	*ex*	*haimatōn*	*oude*	*ek*
his;	who	not	of	bloods	nor	of

2284.2 noun gen sing neu	4418.2 noun gen sing fem	3624.1 adv	1523.2 prep gen	2284.2 noun gen sing neu	433.2 noun gen sing masc
θελήματος	σαρκὸς	οὐδὲ	ἐκ	θελήματος	ἀνδρὸς
thelēmatos	*sarkos*	*oude*	*ek*	*thelēmatos*	*andros*
will	of flesh	nor	of	will	of man

233.1 conj	1523.2 prep gen	2296.2 noun gen sing masc	1074.15 verb 3pl indic aor pass	2504.1 conj	3450.5 art sing masc
ἀλλ'	ἐκ	θεοῦ	ἐγεννήθησαν.	14. Καὶ	ὁ
all'	*ek*	*theou*	*egennēthēsan*	*Kai*	*ho*
but	of	God	were born.	And	the

3030.1 noun nom sing masc	4418.1 noun nom sing fem	1090.33 verb 3sing indic aor mid	2504.1 conj	4492.3 verb 3sing indic aor act	1706.1 prep
λόγος	σὰρξ	ἐγένετο,	καὶ	ἐσκήνωσεν	ἐν
logos	*sarx*	*egeneto*	*kai*	*eskēnōsen*	*en*
Word	flesh	became,	and	tabernacled	among

2231.3 prs-pron dat 1pl	2504.1 conj	2277.3 verb 1pl indic aor mid	3450.12 art acc sing fem	1385.4 noun acc sing fem	840.3 prs-pron gen sing
ἡμῖν,	καὶ	ἐθεασάμεθα	τὴν	δόξαν	αὐτοῦ,
hēmin	*kai*	*etheasametha*	*tēn*	*doxan*	*autou*
us,	and	we beheld	the	glory	his,

1:10. The verb "was" (*ēn*) reminds one of His continuing existence prior to the time of creation (verses 1 and 2). The mention of the world, however, places the time after creation. "Knew him not" implies they did not acknowledge Him because they did not realize who He was.

1:11. "He came unto his own" is literally "into His own things He came." The things (and the place) belonged to Him and He came to them. "His own" in the second part of the sentence means the Jewish people.

1:12. *Hosoi* translated "as many as" occurs frequently in the New Testament. It is sometimes rendered "whosoever," and it opens the floodgate of salvation. "Received him" means received Him as the Logos. The Logos is God's revelation of light and truth.

What they receive is "power" (the authority or the right) to become the sons (children) of God. "To become" should not be understood as referring to a future time. As soon as one believes, he is born into God's family.

1:13. Those "which were born" are those who believe. The two terms assert the corresponding experience. Believing is an active commitment. "Born" refers to a passive experience on the part of the individual but an active participation on the part of God.

"Not of blood" (not out of the mingling of bloods; not out of the union of human ancestries) is the first of three negative ways that relate to "born." "Nor of the will of the flesh" asserts the second impossible way to become a child of God. "Nor of the will of man" (e.g., not out of the will of a husband) sets forth the third impossible way to become a child of God. "But of God" means that God is the source of life in the new birth of the believer.

1:14. When Jesus became flesh, He did not cease to be God. How can the infinite God cease to be infinite? Flesh carries the idea of being frail and vulnerable. When "flesh" is assumed by God, it implies humility (Philippians 2:7,8).

The Logos (deity) "became" (NASB) and "dwelt" (tabernacled, camped; as God dwelt with Israel in the tabernacle in the wilderness). The disciples "beheld," observed the Logos in manifestation. The glory refers to the revelation of God. It speaks of the total essence and activities of God.

"Only begotten" refers to the unique being of the Logos-God. All the Heavenly Father has in the way of attributes and nature

10. He was in the world, and the world was made by him: . . . he entered the world, *Moffatt* . . . came into existence through him, *Weymouth*.

and the world knew him not: . . . and did not recognize him, *Moffatt* . . . did not acknowledge him, *SEB*.

11. He came unto his own: . . . unto his own possessions, *Alford* . . . to his own creation, *Montgomery* . . . his own land, *Campbell*.

and his own received him not: . . . those who were His own, *Worrell* . . . his own people, *Rotherham* . . . his own inheritance, *Scarlett* . . . his peculiar people, *Norton* . . . did not take him to their hearts, *BB* . . . didn't welcome Him, *Beck*.

12. But as many as received him: But to those who did accept Him, *Berkeley* . . . who welcomed him, *Beck*.

to them gave he power to become the sons of God: . . . he granted, *Campbell* . . . authority, *Rotherham* . . . the privilege of becoming, *Weymouth* . . . the prerogative, *Murdock* . . . a legal right, *Wuest*.

even to them that believe on his name: . . . to those who trust, *Montgomery* . . . who had faith, *BB*.

13. Which were born, not of blood, nor of the will of the flesh: . . . nor of the inclination, *HistNT* . . . not of the blood of parents or of a sexual desire, *Beck* . . . or from an impulse of the flesh, *BB* . . . the pleasure of the flesh, *Murdock*.

nor of the will of man, but of God: . . . through the will of a human father, *Weymouth* . . . from the design of man; but from God Himself, *Fenton*.

14. And the Word was made flesh: . . . became human, *SEB* . . . became a man, *Norton*.

and dwelt among us: . . . and tarried among us, *Moffatt* . . . and tabernacled, *Murdock* . . . lived temporarily among us, *Adams*.

John 1:15

1385.4 noun acc sing fem	5453.1 conj	3302.2 adj gen sing masc	3706.2 prep	3824.2 noun gen sing masc	3994.1 adj sing
δόξαν	ὡς	μονογενοῦς	παρὰ	πατρός,	πλήρης
doxan	*hōs*	*monogenous*	*para*	*patros*	*plērēs*
a glory	as	of an only begotten	with	a father,	full

5322.2 noun gen sing fem	2504.1 conj	223.2 noun gen sing fem	2464.1 name nom masc	3113.3 verb 3sing indic pres act
χάριτος	καὶ	ἀληθείας.	**15.** Ἰωάννης	μαρτυρεῖ
charitos	*kai*	*alētheias*	*Iōannēs*	*marturei*
of grace	and	truth.	John	witnesses

3875.1 prep	840.3 prs-pron gen sing	2504.1 conj	2869.16 verb 3sing indic perf act	2978.15 verb sing masc part pres act
περὶ	αὐτοῦ,	καὶ	κέκραγεν,	λέγων,
peri	*autou*	*kai*	*kekragen*	*legōn*
concerning	him,	and	cried,	saying,

3642.4 dem-pron nom sing masc	1498.34 verb sing indic imperf act	3614.6 rel-pron acc sing masc	1500.3 verb indic aor act	3450.5 art sing masc	3557.1 adv
Οὗτος	ἦν	ὃν	εἶπον,	Ὁ	ὀπίσω
Houtos	*ēn*	*hon*	*eipon*	*Ho*	*opisō*
This	was he	of whom	I said,	The	after

1466.2 prs-pron gen 1sing	2048.44 verb nom sing masc part pres	1699.1 prep gen	1466.2 prs-pron gen 1sing	1090.3 verb 3sing indic perf act
μου	ἐρχόμενος,	ἔμπροσθέν	μου	γέγονεν·
mou	*erchomenos*	*emprosthen*	*mou*	*gegonen*
me	coming,	precedence	of me	has,

16.a.**Txt:** 02A,04C-corr, 017K,032W,036,037, 038,1,13,byz.
Var: p66,p75,01ℵ,03B, 04C-org,05D,019L, 033X,33,sa.Lach,Treg Alf,Tisc,We/Ho,Weis, Sod,UBS/☆

3617.1 conj	4272.5 num ord nom sing masc	1466.2 prs-pron gen 1sing	1498.34 verb sing indic imperf act	2504.1 conj	3617.1 conj
ὅτι	πρῶτός	μου	ἦν.	**16.** ʼ Καὶ	[a☆ ὅτι]
hoti	*prōtos*	*mou*	*ēn*	*Kai*	*hoti*
for	before	me	he was.	And	[because]

1523.2 prep gen	3450.2 art gen sing	3998.2 noun gen sing neu	840.3 prs-pron gen sing	2231.1 prs-pron nom 1pl	3820.7 adj pl masc
ἐκ	τοῦ	πληρώματος	αὐτοῦ	ἡμεῖς	πάντες
ek	*tou*	*plērōmatos*	*autou*	*hēmeis*	*pantes*
of	the	fullness	his	we	all

2956.15 verb 1pl indic aor act	2504.1 conj	5322.4 noun acc sing fem	470.2 prep gen	5322.2 noun gen sing fem	3617.1 conj
ἐλάβομεν,	καὶ	χάριν	ἀντὶ	χάριτος·	**17.** ὅτι
elabomen	*kai*	*charin*	*anti*	*charitos*	*hoti*
received,	and	grace	upon	grace.	For

3450.5 art sing masc	3414.1 noun nom sing masc	1217.2 prep	3337.2 name gen masc	3338.2 name gen masc
ὁ	νόμος	διὰ	ʼ Μωσέως	[☆ Μωϋσέως]
ho	*nomos*	*dia*	*Mōseōs*	*Mōuseōs*
the	law	through	Moses	[idem]

1319.44 verb 3sing indic aor pass	3450.9 art nom sing fem	5322.1 noun nom sing fem	2504.1 conj	3450.9 art nom sing fem	223.1 noun nom sing fem
ἐδόθη,	ἡ	χάρις	καὶ	ἡ	ἀλήθεια
edothē	*hē*	*charis*	*kai*	*hē*	*alētheia*
was given;	the	grace	and	the	truth

1217.2 prep	2400.2 name masc	5382.2 name gen masc	1090.33 verb 3sing indic aor mid	2296.4 noun acc sing masc
διὰ	Ἰησοῦ	Χριστοῦ	ἐγένετο.	**18.** θεὸν
dia	*Iēsou*	*Christou*	*egeneto*	*theon*
through	Jesus	Christ	came.	God

belongs to the unique, one-of-a-kind Son of God. "Only begotten" (*monogenous*) is used of Isaac as the special, unique son of Abraham (Hebrews 11:17,18).

"Truth" (including uprightness, fidelity, and reality) is connected to "grace" (unmerited favor, including gracious help that is the outflow of divine life and love) by the conjunction "and" showing they are inseparable. Truth and grace are the basic qualities of God revealed by what the disciples saw in the glory of the Logos.

(and we beheld his glory, the glory as of the only begotten of the Father,): . . . the splendor, *Phillips* . . . gazed upon His majesty, *Fenton.*

full of grace and truth: . . . completely filled with, *Klingensmith* . . . abounding in, *Berkeley* . . . full of gracious love, *SEB.*

1:15. John the Baptist did no miracle (10:41); his whole life was a miracle. His "witness" was of (concerning) Jesus Christ.

John did not compare himself with Deity but with the office of the Messiah. The comparison is that of the announcer with the main event. "He was before me" also implies "He was my chief, my Lord."

15. John bare witness of him, and cried, saying: . . . gave testimony...cried aloud, *Weymouth.*

This was he of whom I spake: This is he of whom I spoke, *Norlie.*

He that cometh after me is preferred before me: . . . takes rank above me, *Fenton* . . . in existence before me, *BB* . . . ranks ahead of me, *Berkeley.*

for he was before me: . . . because He existed before me, *Williams* . . . he existed before I was born, *Phillips* . . . he was prior, *Murdock* . . . has already superseded me, *Torrey* . . . he was my superior, *Norton.*

1:16. "And of his fulness" continues the thought of verse 14, "full of grace and truth." We know the incarnate Word is full of grace and truth because we have received of His fullness.

"And grace for grace" is an interesting assertion. To the thought of receiving out of His fullness, grace upon grace is added. Each blessing becomes the means of receiving a new, fresh, increasing blessing.

16. And of his fulness have all we received: . . . from His abundance, *Berkeley* . . . his plenitude, *Murdock* . . . out of His fulness we were all supplied, *Fenton* . . . of the plente of him, *Wycliffe* . . . his inexhaustible store, *Norton.*

and grace for grace: . . . one grace after another, *Berkeley* . . . with gift heaped upon gift, *Fenton.*

1:17. The mediatorship of Jesus Christ is contrasted with that of Moses. Furthermore, grace and truth (reality) through Jesus Christ is contrasted with the partial grace and truth received through the Law (cf. Hebrews 10:1).

Here John uses the personal name of the Logos for the first time in his Gospel. The name "Jesus Christ" was the name He called himself when He prayed to the Father (17:3). "Jesus" (from the Greek form of Joshua or Jeshua, "the Lord is salvation") indicates His human given name. "Christ" (anointed One) was the title of the long-awaited Messiah.

17. For the law was given by Moses:

but grace and truth came by Jesus Christ: . . . spiritual blessing, *Williams* . . . but Jesus Christ brought love and truth, *Beck.*

1:18. The "fulness" of God as stated in verse 16 could not be known through any ordinary man. It must come through the One who possesses the nature of God. The word "God" is stated first and is without the definite article. This indicates first, that the emphasis is on the word "God," and second, the nature of God

John 1:19

18.a.**Txt:** p75,01ℵ-corr, 02A,04C-corr,017K, 032W,036,037,038,1,13, etc.byz.it.bo.Lach,Tisc, Sod
Var: p66,01ℵ-org,03B, 04C-org,019L,Treg, We/HoWeis,UBS/☆

18.b.**Txt:** 02A,04C-corr, 017K,032W,036,037, 038,1,13,byz.it.Lach, Tisc,Sod
Var: p66,p75,01ℵ,03B, 04C-org,019L,bo.Treg, We/Ho,Weis,UBS/☆

19.a.**Var:** 03B,04C-org, 33,bo.Lach,Treg,Alf, We/Ho,Weis,Sod,UBS/☆

3625.2 num card nom masc	**3571.11** verb 3sing indic perf act	**4312.1** adv	**3450.5** art sing masc	**3302.1** adj nom sing
οὐδεὶς	ἑώρακεν	πώποτε·	(a ὁ \	μονογενὴς
oudeis	*heōraken*	*pōpote*	*ho*	*monogenēs*
no one	has seen	at any time;	the	only begotten

5048.1 noun nom sing masc	**2296.1** noun nom sing masc	**3450.5** art sing masc	**1498.21** verb sing masc part pres act	**1519.1** prep	**3450.6** art acc sing masc
ʻ υἱός,	[b☆ θεὸς]	ὁ	ὢν	εἰς	τὸν
huios	*theos*	*ho*	*ōn*	*eis*	*ton*
Son,	[God]	the	being	in	the

2831.2 noun acc sing masc	**3450.2** art gen sing	**3824.2** noun gen sing masc	**1552.3** dem-pron nom sing masc	**1817.2** verb 3sing indic aor mid	**2504.1** conj
κόλπον	τοῦ	πατρὸς,	ἐκεῖνος	ἐξηγήσατο.	**19.** Καὶ
kolpon	*tou*	*patros*	*ekeinos*	*exēgēsato*	*Kai*
bosom	of the	Father,	that	declared.	And

3642.9 dem-pron nom sing fem	**1498.4** verb 3sing indic pres act	**3450.9** art nom sing fem	**3114.1** noun nom sing fem	**3450.2** art gen sing
αὕτη	ἐστὶν	ἡ	μαρτυρία	τοῦ
hautē	*estin*	*hē*	*marturia*	*tou*
this	is	the	witness	

2464.2 name gen masc	**3616.1** conj	**643.9** verb 3pl indic aor act	**4242.1** prep	**840.6** prs-pron acc sing masc
Ἰωάννου,	ὅτε	ἀπέστειλαν	[a☆+ πρὸς	αὐτὸν]
Iōannou	*hote*	*apesteilan*	*pros*	*auton*
of John,	when	sent	[to	him]

3450.7 art pl masc	**2428.2** name-adj pl masc	**1523.1** prep gen	**2389.2** name gen pl neu	**2385.4** noun pl masc	**2504.1** conj
οἱ	Ἰουδαῖοι	ἐξ	Ἱεροσολύμων	ἱερεῖς	καὶ
hoi	*Ioudaioi*	*ex*	*Hierosolumōn*	*hiereis*	*kai*
the	Jews	from	Jerusalem	priests	and

2993.2 name acc pl masc	**2419.1** conj	**2049.12** verb 3pl subj aor act	**840.6** prs-pron acc sing masc	**4622.1** prs-pron nom 2sing	**4949.3** intr-pron nom sing
Λευίτας,	ἵνα	ἐρωτήσωσιν	αὐτόν,	Σὺ	τίς
Leuitas	*hina*	*erōtēsōsin*	*auton*	*Su*	*tis*
Levites,	that	they might ask	him,	You	who

1498.3 verb 2sing indic pres act	**2504.1** conj	**3533.8** verb 3sing indic aor act	**2504.1** conj	**3620.2** partic	**714.7** verb 3sing indic aor mid
εἶ;	**20.** Καὶ	ὡμολόγησεν	καὶ	οὐκ	ἠρνήσατο,
ei	*Kai*	*hōmologēsen*	*kai*	*ouk*	*ērnēsato*
are you?	And	he confessed	and	not	denied,

2504.1 conj	**3533.8** verb 3sing indic aor act	**3617.1** conj	**3620.2** partic	**1498.2** verb 1sing indic pres act	**1466.1** prs-pron nom 1sing
καὶ	ὡμολόγησεν,	Ὅτι	ʻ οὐκ	εἰμὶ	Ἐγὼ
kai	*hōmologēsen*	*Hoti*	*ouk*	*eimi*	*Egō*
and	confessed,		Not	am	I

1466.1 prs-pron nom 1sing	**3620.2** partic	**1498.2** verb 1sing indic pres act	**3450.5** art sing masc	**5382.1** name nom masc	**2504.1** conj
[☆ Ἐγὼ	οὐκ	εἰμὶ]	ὁ	Χριστός.	**21.** Καὶ
Egō	*ouk*	*eimi*	*ho*	*Christos*	*Kai*
[I	not	am]	the	Christ.	And

2049.10 verb 3pl indic aor act	**840.6** prs-pron acc sing masc	**4949.9** intr-pron sing neu	**3631.1** conj	**2226.1** name nom masc	**1498.3** verb 2sing indic pres act
ἠρώτησαν	αὐτόν,	ʻ Τί	οὖν;	Ἡλίας	εἶ
ērōtēsan	*auton*	*Ti*	*oun*	*Hēlias*	*ei*
they asked	him,	What	then?	Elijah	are

should be the object of our attention. The statement is not referring to the impossibility of a vision of God (a theophany), but rather to His qualities.

"Hath seen" (*heōraken*) is in the Greek perfect tense indicating a past action of seeing which is held in the mind so that it may be related to others. God's nature cannot be seen or held and revealed to others by any ordinary man. The utter inability of "no man" is stressed in opposition to God who revealed himself in the Only Begotten. (Many ancient manuscripts read "God only begotten" indicating that Jesus is both God and only begotten or unique, one of a kind.)

John's Gospel begins with the Logos who has eternality and equality with God. The Logos then assumed human nature and was introduced by the Baptist. Then John's Gospel proclaims that the fullness of truth and grace was in Jesus Christ. Verse 18 is related to verses 1 and 2 by this assertion that the Logos, who is Jesus Christ, retained His deity when He came to earth. Since He is God, He had the ability to give the full revelation of God.

"In the bosom of the Father" refers to the truth of His deity and shows the reason the only begotten God could be the full revelation of all that God is. He, the Logos, and now known as Jesus Christ, "is in the bosom" of God the Father. The evidence indicates that not only in eternity but even while He was on earth in the flesh His existence was in the bosom of the Father. This is the closest relationship to God. His position is not merely *beside* (*para*) God, but He is the *heart* of God.

The Son of God is God's interpreter. God did not entrust His full revelation to be given by men; He took the initiative to declare it for himself.

18. No man hath seen God at any time: No human eye, *Weymouth.*

the only begotten Son: . . . the only begotten God, *Murdock* . . . who is God, *Beck* . . . God the Only Son, *TCNT* . . . the unique God, *Adams.*

which is in the bosom of the Father: . . . and close to the Father's heart, *Beck* . . . in the intimate presence of the Father, *Norlie* . . . Deity Himself, *Williams* . . . Who exists in union, *Fenton* . . . on the breast, *BB* . . . Who is closest of all to the Father, *Adams* . . . lives in the intimacy, *ALBA* . . . in the closest intimacy with the Father, *Phillips.*

he hath declared him: He interpreted him, *Rotherham* . . . he has made him known, *RSV* . . . He unfolds Him, *Concordant* . . . that One fully explained deity, *Wuest.*

1:19. "And this is the record (witness, testimony) of John" introduces a rough desert preacher. He was totally unlike the religious leaders of Jerusalem in appearance and demeanor. But he stirred the common people to such an extent that some thought he could be the promised Messiah. The priests and Levites came to find out if John considered himself the Messiah and if not, who was he?

19. And this is the record of John: . . . the testimony, *RSV.*

when the Jews sent priests and Levites from Jerusalem to ask him, Who art thou?: . . . dispatch to him priests and Levites, *Concordant* . . . to ask him who he was, *Weymouth.*

1:20. Notice the threefold negative of his answer—"confessed," "denied not," and "confessed." Here the emphasis is raised to a superlative degree.

20. And he confessed, and denied not: He admitted without denial, *Berkeley* . . . he frankly stated, *Fenton* . . . and sayde playnly, *Tyndale* . . . with complete candor, *TCNT* . . . and did not refuse to answer, *Norton.*

but confessed, I am not the Christ: . . . but declared, *Scarlett* . . . he frankly admitted, *Williams* . . . He said quite openly and straightforwardly, *BB* . . . but acknowledged, *Montgomery* . . . I'm not the promised Savior, *Beck* . . . not the Messiah, *Campbell.*

1:21. Those from Jerusalem were not content to receive an answer as to who John the Baptist was not. They wanted to know who he was. John's great anointing from God drew multitudes of

21. And they asked him, What then? Art thou Elias?:

John 1:22

21.a.**Txt:** 02A,04C-corr, 017K,033X,037,038,1, 13,etc.byz.Lach,Sod, UBS/☆
Var1: .01ℵ,019L,Tisc
Var2: .p75,04C-org,044, 33,Treg,We/Ho

4622.1 prs-pron nom 2sing	**4949.9** intr-pron sing neu	**3631.1** conj	**2226.10** name nom	**1498.3** verb 2sing indic pres act	**4949.9** intr-pron sing neu
σύ;	[[1a] τί	οὖν;	Ἡλείας	εἶ;	[2] τί
su	*ti*	*oun*	*Hēleias*	*ei*	*ti*
you?	[what	then?	Elijah	you are?	what

3631.1 conj	**4622.1** prs-pron nom 2sing	**2226.1** name nom masc	**1498.3** verb 2sing indic pres act	**2504.1** conj	**2978.5** verb 3sing indic pres act
οὖν;	σὺ	Ἠλίας	εἶ;]	Καὶ	λέγει,
oun	*su*	*Hēlias*	*ei*	*Kai*	*legei*
then?	You	Elijah	are?]	And	he says,

3620.2 partic	**1498.2** verb 1sing indic pres act	**3450.5** art sing masc	**4254.1** noun nom sing masc	**1498.3** verb 2sing indic pres act	**4622.1** prs-pron nom 2sing
Οὐκ	εἰμί.	Ὁ	προφήτης	εἶ	σύ;
Ouk	*eimi*	*Ho*	*prophētēs*	*ei*	*su*
Not	I am.	The	prophet	are	you?

22.a.**Txt:** 01ℵ,02A, 04C-corr,019L,038,etc. byz.Sod
Var: 03B,04C-org,037, Lach,Treg,Alf,Tisc, We/Ho,Weis,UBS/☆

2504.1 conj	**552.6** verb 3sing indic aor pass	**3620.3** partic	**1500.3** verb indic aor act	**1500.28** verb 3pl indic aor act	**3631.1** conj
Καὶ	ἀπεκρίθη,	Οὔ.	22. ⸀ Εἶπον	[[a]☆ εἶπαν]	οὖν
Kai	*apekrithē*	*Ou*	*Eipon*	*eipan*	*oun*
And	he answered,	No.	They said	[idem]	therefore

840.4 prs-pron dat sing	**4949.3** intr-pron nom sing	**1498.3** verb 2sing indic pres act	**2419.1** conj	**606.2** noun acc sing fem	**1319.21** verb 1pl subj aor act
αὐτῷ,	Τίς	εἶ;	ἵνα	ἀπόκρισιν	δῶμεν
autō	*Tis*	*ei*	*hina*	*apokrisin*	*dōmen*
to him,	Who	are you?	that	an answer	we may give

3450.4 art dat pl	**3854.16** verb dat pl masc part aor act	**2231.4** prs-pron acc 1pl	**4949.9** intr-pron sing neu	**2978.4** verb 2sing indic pres act	**3875.1** prep
τοῖς	πέμψασιν	ἡμᾶς·	τί	λέγεις	περὶ
tois	*pempsasin*	*hēmas*	*ti*	*legeis*	*peri*
to the	having sent	us:	what	do you say	about

4427.1 prs-pron gen 2sing masc	**5183.4** verb 3sing indic act	**1466.1** prs-pron nom 1sing	**5292.1** noun nom sing fem	**987.1** verb gen sing masc part pres act
σεαυτοῦ;	23. ἔφη,	Ἐγὼ	φωνὴ	βοῶντος
seautou	*ephē*	*Egō*	*phōnē*	*boōntos*
yourself?	He said,	I	a voice	crying

1706.1 prep	**3450.11** art dat sing fem	**2031.2** noun dat sing fem	**2096.2** verb 2pl impr aor act	**3450.12** art acc sing fem	**3461.4** noun acc sing fem
ἐν	τῇ	ἐρήμῳ,	Εὐθύνατε	τὴν	ὁδὸν
en	*tē*	*erēmō*	*Euthunate*	*tēn*	*hodon*
in	the	wilderness,	Make straight	the	way

2935.2 noun gen sing masc	**2503.1** conj	**1500.5** verb 3sing indic aor act	**2246.1** name nom masc	**3450.5** art sing masc	**4254.1** noun nom sing masc
κυρίου·	καθὼς	εἶπεν	Ἠσαΐας	ὁ	προφήτης.
kuriou	*kathōs*	*eipen*	*Hēsaias*	*ho*	*prophētēs*
of Lord,	as	said	Isaiah	the	prophet.

24.a.**Txt:** 01ℵ-corr, 02A-corr,04C-corr, 032W,036,037,038,1,13, etc.byz.Lach
Var: 01ℵ-org,02A-org, 03B,04C-org,019L,bo. Treg,AlfTisc,We/Ho, Weis,Sod,UBS/☆

2504.1 conj	**3450.7** art pl masc	**643.30** verb nom pl masc part perf pass	**1498.37** verb 3pl indic imperf act	**1523.2** prep gen
24. Καὶ	⸂[a] οἱ ⸃	ἀπεσταλμένοι	ἦσαν	ἐκ
Kai	*hoi*	*apestalmenoi*	*ēsan*	*ek*
And	the	had been sent	were	from among

3450.1 art gen pl	**5168.5** name gen pl masc	**2504.1** conj	**2049.10** verb 3pl indic aor act	**840.6** prs-pron acc sing masc	**2504.1** conj
τῶν	Φαρισαίων.	25. καὶ	ἠρώτησαν	αὐτὸν	καὶ
tōn	*Pharisaiōn*	*kai*	*ērōtēsan*	*auton*	*kai*
the	Pharisees.	And	they asked	him	and

people. They asked, "Art thou Elijah?" The delegation may have been asking in accord with the promise made in Malachi 4:5. It was predicted that Elijah would come before "the great and dreadful day of the Lord." John's answer seems somewhat perplexing in the light of Christ's remark in Matthew 11:14 that John the Baptist "is Elijah." However, Jesus was saying that John had the ministry of Elijah, though he was not Elijah in person.

The next question as to who John was also shows a misconception. Deuteronomy 18:15 foretells a prophet like Moses. In the New Testament "the prophet" is interpreted as Christ (Acts 3:22; 7:37). John was quite correct in saying, "No."

And he saith, I am not: Of course, I am not, *Williams.*
Art thou that prophet?: Are you the prophet we await, *NEB* . . . the promised prophet? *ALBA.*
And he answered, No:

1:22. The priests and Levites persisted by probing yet further: "Who art thou?" They needed an answer to take back to Jerusalem. They had received only negative responses. The Baptist had no desire to emphasize his person or identity. His mission was to point to Christ. John's example should be followed by all ministers and followers of Jesus Christ.

22. Then said they unto him, Who art thou?: So they pressed the question, *Weymouth* . . . They therefore asked him, *Fenton* . . . Tell, then, who you are, *Campbell.*
that we may give an answer to them that sent us: We have to give an answer to those who, *Adams.*
What sayest thou of thyself?: What have you to say about yourself? *BB, Berkeley* . . . What do you say about yourself? *Norlie* . . . Who do you claim to be? *ALBA.*

1:23. Note the humility of John when he finally gives a positive reply: "I am the voice of one crying in the wilderness." John pointed to the prophecy concerning his mission (Isaiah 40:3). According to Matthew 3:3, Mark 1:3, and Luke 3:4, John the Baptist fulfilled the Isaiah 40:3 passage. John paralleled his environment "in the wilderness" with the desert condition of the people of Israel. The wilderness was a difficult place in which to travel. In the days of John, rulers had road crews going before them to prepare the way so that their travel would be made easier. John heralded the coming of the King; therefore the road had to be made ready. To "make straight" with reference to a road has a spiritual parallel. The crooked has the figurative connotation of the Old Serpent.

23. He said, I am the voice of one crying in the wilderness: . . . imploring, *Concordant* . . . he whose voice proclaims, *Campbell* . . . one shouting, *Williams* . . . in the wasteland, *BB* . . . in the desert, *TCNT.*
Make straight the way of the Lord: Make the road straight for the Lord, *Williams* . . . Make ready the highway for the Lord, *Fenton* . . . Make ready the way, *ALBA* . . . Straighten the road by which the Lord will come, *Barclay.*
as said the prophet Esaias:

1:24. "Of (or 'from') the Pharisees" tells us more about the delegation from the Jews. The religious leaders who were interested in the Scriptures and prophecy were Pharisees, not Sadducees. Though the Sadducees controlled the temple government, the Pharisees were more numerous and possessed greater influence directly over the multitudes.

24. And they which were sent were of the Pharisees: The messengers belonged to, *Williams* . . . This deputation, *TCNT* . . . of the Orthodox, *Klingensmith.*

1:25. The reason the Pharisees came to John, that is, to find out who he was, now broadened into criticism. John was calling *Jews,*

John 1:26

25.a.**Txt:** 01א,02A, 04C-corr,036,037,038, byz.Sod
Var: 03B,04C-org,019L, 033X,33,Lach,Treg,Alf, Tisc,We/HoWeis,UBS/*

25.b.**Txt:** 017K,036,037, byz.
Var: 01א,02A,03B,04C, 019L,033X,33,Lach, TregAlf,Tisc,We/Ho, Weis,Sod,UBS/*

25.c.**Txt:** 017K,036,037, byz.
Var: 01א,02A,03B,04C, 019L,033X,33,Lach, TregAlf,Tisc,We/Ho, Weis,Sod,UBS/*

26.a.**Txt:** 02A,04C-corr, 017K,032W,036,037, 038,1,13,byz.it.bo.Lach
Var: p59,p66,p75,01א, 03B,04C-org,019L,Treg, Alf,Tisc,We/Ho,Weis, Sod,UBS/*

26.b.**Txt:** p66,02A,04C, 017K,032W,036,037, 038,13,33,byz.Lach
Var: 03B,019L,1,Treg, AlfTisc,We/Ho,Weis,Sod, UBS/*

27.a.**Txt:** 02A,04C-corr, 017K,036,037,1,byz. Lach
Var: 01א,03B,04C-org, 019L,038,33,bo.Gries Treg,Alf,Tisc,We/Ho, Weis,Sod,UBS/*

27.b.**Txt:** 02A,04C-corr, 017K,036,037,(038),13, byz.it.Lach
Var: 01א,03B,04C-org, 019L,33,bo.Gries,Treg, AlfTisc,We/Ho,Weis,Sod, UBS/*

27.c.**Txt:** 02A,017K,036, 037,038,1,byz.Lach
Var: p66,p75,01א,03B, 04C,019L,032W,033X, 011G3,13,TregAlf,Tisc, We/Ho,Weis,Sod,UBS/*

27.d.**Var:** p66-corr,03B, 032W,033X,011G3,13, Treg,Alf,Tisc,We/Ho, Weis,Sod,UBS/*

1500.3 verb indic aor act	**1500.28** verb 3pl indic aor act	**840.4** prs-pron dat sing	**4949.9** intr-pron sing neu	**3631.1** conj	**901.2** verb 2sing indic pres act
⸂ εἶπον	[a* εἶπαν]	αὐτῷ,	Τί	οὖν	βαπτίζεις,
eipon	*eipan*	*autō*	*Ti*	*oun*	*baptizeis*
said	[idem]	to him,	Why	then	baptize you,

1479.1 conj	**4622.1** prs-pron nom 2sing	**3620.2** partic	**1498.3** verb 2sing indic pres act	**3450.5** art sing masc	**5382.1** name nom masc
εἰ	σὺ	οὐκ	εἶ	ὁ	Χριστὸς,
ei	*su*	*ouk*	*ei*	*ho*	*Christos*
if	you	not	are	the	Christ,

3641.1 conj	**3624.1** adv	**2226.1** name nom masc	**3641.1** conj	**3624.1** adv	**3450.5** art sing masc
⸂ οὔτε	[b* οὐδὲ]	Ἠλίας	⸂ οὔτε	[c* οὐδὲ]	ὁ
oute	*oude*	*Hēlias*	*oute*	*oude*	*ho*
nor	[idem]	Elijah,	nor	[idem]	the

4254.1 noun nom sing masc	**552.6** verb 3sing indic aor pass	**840.2** prs-pron dat pl	**3450.5** art sing masc	**2464.1** name nom masc
προφήτης;	26. Ἀπεκρίθη	αὐτοῖς	ὁ	Ἰωάννης
prophētēs	*Apekrithē*	*autois*	*ho*	*Iōannēs*
prophet?	Answered	them		John

2978.15 verb sing masc part pres act	**1466.1** prs-pron nom 1sing	**901.1** verb 1sing indic pres act	**1706.1** prep	**5045.3** noun dat sing neu	**3189.2** adj nom sing masc
λέγων,	Ἐγὼ	βαπτίζω	ἐν	ὕδατι·	μέσος
legōn	*Egō*	*baptizō*	*en*	*hudati*	*mesos*
saying,	I	baptize	with	water;	in midst

1156.2 conj	**5050.2** prs-pron gen 2pl	**2449.18** verb 3sing indic perf act	**4590.2** verb 3sing indic pres act	**3614.6** rel-pron acc sing masc
⸂a δὲ ⸃	ὑμῶν	⸂* ἕστηκεν	[b στήκει]	ὃν
de	*humōn*	*hestēken*	*stēkei*	*hon*
but	of you	stands	[is standing]	whom

5050.1 prs-pron nom 2pl	**3620.2** partic	**3471.6** verb 2pl indic perf act	**840.5** prs-pron nom sing masc	**1498.4** verb 3sing indic pres act	**3450.5** art sing masc
ὑμεῖς	οὐκ	οἴδατε·	27. ⸂a αὐτός	ἐστιν ⸃	ὁ
humeis	*ouk*	*oidate*	*autos*	*estin*	*ho*
you	not	know;	he	it is	the

3557.1 adv	**1466.2** prs-pron gen 1sing	**2048.44** verb nom sing masc part pres	**3614.5** rel-pron nom sing masc	**1699.1** prep gen
ὀπίσω	μου	ἐρχόμενος,	⸂b ὃς	ἔμπροσθέν
opisō	*mou*	*erchomenos*	*hos*	*emprosthen*
after	me	coming,	who	precedence

1466.2 prs-pron gen 1sing	**1090.3** verb 3sing indic perf act	**3614.2** rel-pron gen sing	**1466.1** prs-pron nom 1sing	**3620.2** partic	**1498.2** verb 1sing indic pres act
μου	γέγονεν· ⸃	οὗ	⸂c ἐγὼ ⸃	οὐκ	εἰμὶ
mou	*gegonen*	*hou*	*egō*	*ouk*	*eimi*
of me	has,	of whom	I	not	am

1466.1 prs-pron nom 1sing	**510.2** adj nom sing masc	**2419.1** conj	**3061.7** verb 1sing subj aor act	**840.3** prs-pron gen sing
[d*+ ἐγὼ]	ἄξιος	ἵνα	λύσω	αὐτοῦ
egō	*axios*	*hina*	*lusō*	*autou*
[I]	worthy	that	I should loose	his

3450.6 art acc sing masc	**2414.1** noun acc sing masc	**3450.2** art gen sing	**5104.1** noun gen sing neu	**3642.18** dem-pron pl neu
τὸν	ἱμάντα	τοῦ	ὑποδήματος.	28. Ταῦτα
ton	*himanta*	*tou*	*hupodēmatos*	*Tauta*
the	thong	of the	sandal.	These things

including Pharisees, to the baptism of repentance for the remission of sins (Matthew 3:1-9; Mark 1:5; Luke 3:8). This was something new in Israel. The Talmud specified the rite by which *Gentiles* might become identified with Jews as proselytes.

Usually proselytes went into the water and stood while elders recited the Law which would thenceforth be binding on them. They then dipped in the water; males were also circumcised. By this ceremony Gentiles were accepted as belonging to Israel.

The Pharisees taught most dogmatically that no prophet after Moses, except the Messiah himself, had a right to introduce any new rite for Israelites. The delegation saw no reason for John to initiate a new system. Why not allow the One he introduced to do that job? John, however, viewed his ministry as one that would prepare the hearts of people to receive the Messiah's message.

In mentioning Elijah, the Pharisees showed that they knew the prophecy of Malachi that God would send Elijah before the great Day of the Lord (Malachi 4:5,6). They also knew of "that Prophet" who was foretold by Moses (Deuteronomy 18:15,18).

Like the scribes with whom Herod consulted about Messiah's birthplace (Matthew 2:4-6), the Pharisees were intellectually prepared for the coming of the Christ. They were not spiritually perceptive, however. If they had been, they would have known that John, in the spirit and power of Elijah, was preparing the way of the Messiah (Matthew 11:14).

1:26. John passed over the explanation as to why he baptized. He, rather, indirectly answered by contrasting his ministry with that of the "one (who is) among you, whom ye know not." John wisely sidestepped the possibility of disputation concerning ritual washings and water baptism. His mission was not to argue but to point to the Christ. "Whom ye know not" informed them of their ignorance of the Messiah's presence. John had baptized the Lord Jesus over 40 days before this time. It was then that special revelation came to John. The Spirit, like a dove, descended on Christ after John baptized Him. This manifestation confirmed to John that Jesus was the Christ.

1:27. This assertion pointed out that John's arrival was before Christ's arrival. John's birth was prior to Christ's. John pointed to his place as a servant. He even indicated that he was unworthy to do a slave's task of unloosing the sandal thong of the coming One.

1:28. Bethabara ("house of the crossing"), also called Bethany beyond Jordan, was probably the ford of Abarah about 12 miles

25. And they asked him, and said unto him, Why baptizest thou then: They questioned him again, *Norlie* . . . and they put this further question to him, *JB* . . . Why, then, do you immerse, *Worrell* . . . art thou immersing, *Rotherham* . . . why are you immersing people, *SEB* . . . What is the reason, then, *Phillips* . . . Why then are you baptizing since you are not the Christ, *Wuest* . . . if you're not the promised Savior, *Beck.*

if thou be not that Christ, nor Elias, neither that prophet?: . . . the promised savior, *Beck* . . . nor yet the Prophet? *Fenton.*

26. John answered them, saying: . . . and John responded, *Adams* . . . In reply, *Fenton.*

I baptize with water: . . . baptizing only in water, *Williams.*

but there standeth one among you, whom ye know not: . . . but my successor, *Moffatt* . . . with whom you are not acquainted, *Williams* . . . unknown to you, *JB* . . . whom you do not recognize, *Montgomery, Berkeley* . . . In your midst, *Wuest* . . . of Whom you are not aware, *Concordant.*

27. He it is, who coming after me is preferred before me: He comes after me, it is true, *Phillips* . . . taketh place before me, *Alford* . . . is put before me, *Norlie* . . . the One coming after me, *Worrell* . . . to become my successor, *Williams.*

whose shoe's latchet I am not worthy to unloose: I am not good enough even to, *TEV* . . . I am not fit to undo his sandal-strap, *JB* . . . to unfasten his sandal, *TCNT* . . . to undo his shoes, *BB* . . . I am not fit to untie, *Moffatt, Berkeley* . . . whose shoe-string, *Campbell.*

John 1:29

28.a.**Txt:** 04C-corr,017K, 1,13,33,1079,(byz.),sa. **Var:** p75,01ℵ-org,02A, 03B,04C-org,019L, 032W,036,037,038,565, 700,(byz.),Gries,Lach, Treg,Alf,Word,Tisc, We/Ho,WeisSod,UBS/☆

28.b.**Var:** 01ℵ,03B,04C, Lach,Treg,Alf,Tisc, We/Ho,Sod,UBS/☆

1706.1 prep	**955.1** name fem	**956.3** name dat fem	**1090.33** verb 3sing indic aor mid	**3871.1** adv
ἐν	⸀ Βηθαβαρᾶ	[a☆ Βηθανίᾳ]	ἐγένετο	πέραν
en	*Bēthabara*	*Bēthania*	*egeneto*	*peran*
in	Bethabara	[Bethany]	took place	across

3450.2 art gen sing	**2422.1** name gen masc	**3562.1** adv	**1498.34** verb sing indic imperf act	**3450.5** art sing masc
τοῦ	Ἰορδάνου,	ὅπου	ἦν	[b☆+ ὁ]
tou	*Iordanou*	*hopou*	*ēn*	*ho*
the	Jordan,	where	was	

2464.1 name nom masc	**901.4** verb nom sing masc part pres act	**3450.11** art dat sing fem	**1872.1** adv	**984.4** verb 3sing indic pres act
Ἰωάννης	βαπτίζων.	**29.** Τῇ	ἐπαύριον	βλέπει
Iōannēs	*baptizōn*	*Tē*	*epaurion*	*blepei*
John	baptizing.	On the	next day	sees

29.a.**Txt:** 04C-corr,036, Steph **Var:** 01ℵ,02A,03B, 04C-org,017K,019L,037, 038,bo.Gries,LachTreg, Alf,Word,Tisc,We/Ho, Weis,Sod,UBS/☆

3450.5 art sing masc	**2464.1** name nom masc	**3450.6** art acc sing masc	**2400.3** name acc masc	**2048.42** verb sing part pres	**4242.1** prep
⸂a ὁ	Ἰωάννης ⸃	τὸν	Ἰησοῦν	ἐρχόμενον	πρὸς
ho	*Iōannēs*	*ton*	*Iēsoun*	*erchomenon*	*pros*
	John		Jesus	coming	to

840.6 prs-pron acc sing masc	**2504.1** conj	**2978.5** verb 3sing indic pres act	**1481.14** verb 2sing impr aor act	**3450.5** art sing masc	**284.1** noun nom sing masc
αὐτόν,	καὶ	λέγει,	Ἴδε	ὁ	ἀμνὸς
auton	*kai*	*legei*	*Ide*	*ho*	*amnos*
him,	and	says,	Behold	the	Lamb

3450.2 art gen sing	**2296.2** noun gen sing masc	**3450.5** art sing masc	**142.6** verb nom sing masc part pres act	**3450.12** art acc sing fem	**264.4** noun acc sing fem
τοῦ	θεοῦ,	ὁ	αἴρων	τὴν	ἁμαρτίαν
tou	*theou*	*ho*	*airōn*	*tēn*	*hamartian*
	of God,	the	taking away	the	sin

3450.2 art gen sing	**2862.2** noun gen sing masc	**3642.4** dem-pron nom sing masc	**1498.4** verb 3sing indic pres act	**3875.1** prep
τοῦ	κόσμου.	**30.** οὗτός	ἐστιν	⸀ περὶ
tou	*kosmou*	*houtos*	*estin*	*peri*
of the	world.	This	it is	concerning

30.a.**Txt:** 01ℵ-corr,02A, 04C-corr,017K,019L, 036,037,038,1,13,byz. **Var:** p5,p66,p75, 01ℵ-org,03B,04C-org, Lach,TregAlf,Tisc, We/Ho,Weis,Sod,UBS/☆

5065.1 prep	**3614.2** rel-pron gen sing	**1466.1** prs-pron nom 1sing	**1500.3** verb indic aor act	**3557.1** adv	**1466.2** prs-pron gen 1sing
[a☆ ὑπὲρ]	οὗ	ἐγὼ	εἶπον,	Ὀπίσω	μου
huper	*hou*	*egō*	*eipon*	*Opisō*	*mou*
[idem]	whom	I	said,	After	me

2048.34 verb 3sing indic pres	**433.1** noun nom sing masc	**3614.5** rel-pron nom sing masc	**1699.1** prep gen	**1466.2** prs-pron gen 1sing
ἔρχεται	ἀνὴρ,	ὃς	ἔμπροσθέν	μου
erchetai	*anēr*	*hos*	*emprosthen*	*mou*
comes	a man,	who	precedence	of me

1090.3 verb 3sing indic perf act	**3617.1** conj	**4272.5** num ord nom sing masc	**1466.2** prs-pron gen 1sing	**1498.34** verb sing indic imperf act
γέγονεν,	ὅτι	πρῶτός	μου	ἦν.
gegonen	*hoti*	*prōtos*	*mou*	*ēn*
has,	because	before	me	he was.

2476.3 conj	**3620.2** partic	**3471.9** verb 1sing indic plperf act	**840.6** prs-pron acc sing masc	**233.1** conj	**2419.1** conj
31. κἀγὼ	οὐκ	ᾔδειν	αὐτόν·	ἀλλ'	ἵνα
kagō	*ouk*	*ēdein*	*auton*	*all'*	*hina*
And I	not	knew	him;	but	that

south of the Sea of Galilee 20 miles from Cana where Jesus went next. Another tradition places it east of Jericho at the Jordan River.

28. These things were done in Bethabara beyond Jordan, where John was baptizing: These things occurred, *Berkeley* . . . This happened in the town of Bethany, *SEB* . . . This interview took place, *Fenton* . . . This happened at Bethany, *JB* . . . where John was engaged in baptizing, *Wuest.*

1:29. "The next day" speaks of the day following the delegation's inquiry.

"Behold the Lamb of God" is a forceful declaration. The indication is that it had been revealed to John the Baptist that the Saviour's death was to be a fulfillment of Isaiah 53 and the Passover lamb of Exodus 12. Any Jew would connect a lamb (especially the word used here which speaks of a sacrificial lamb without blemish) with the Passover. Not all Jews looked for a suffering Messiah. Yet some did (Luke 2:35). How else could John say "which taketh away the sin of the world" if not by the shed blood? All Jews knew that without shedding of blood there was no forgiveness (Leviticus 17:11).

The Atonement is brilliantly depicted in Leviticus chapter 16. Two goats were presented before the Lord as a sin offering. One was slain, the other dismissed or sent away (Septuagint, *apopempō*). Christ fulfilled both aspects of the Atonement. First, He shed His life's blood as a propitiation for sin. Second, Christ "takes away" the penalty, power, and guilt of sin.

"The sin" (*tēn hamartian*) is interesting because of the definite article and the singular number. This speaks of the root source and nature of sin, not merely of the symptoms called sins (plural).

"The sin" may also refer to the totality of the sins of the world in a collective sense. Christ's work was potentially efficacious for every human being. Since God loves the world, He was willing to give His Son so that those who believe in Him might not perish but have everlasting life (3:16).

29. The next day John seeth Jesus coming unto him, and saith: John was looking on as Jesus approached him, *ALBA* . . . approaching him, *Berkeley* . . . seeing Jesus coming toward him, *JB.*

Behold the Lamb of God, which taketh away the sin of the world: Here is God's Lamb, *Adams* . . . who is to take away, *Weymouth* . . . who takes and bears away the sin of the world, *Montgomery* . . . that beareth, *Murdock.*

1:30. "This is he" refers to the prior verses. The Baptist had been explaining the chief work of Jesus. When he saw Jesus coming, he lifted his voice and cried, "This is He!" How fascinating that in the first 30 verses of this Gospel the Christ is called "God" (verses 1,2) and "man" (*anēr*). "(He) is preferred before me" implies His humanity. "He was (NASB, 'existed') before me" implies His deity. John was 6 months older than Jesus (Luke 1:36). The reference is to the preincarnate life of Jesus as the eternal Son of God. (See 1:1,2; 8:58.)

30. This is he of whom I said: He is the One I meant, *Beck* . . . He is the One about Whom, *Adams* . . . This is the one I was talking about, *SEB* . . . This is the man I meant, *Phillips* . . . concerning whom I said, *Wuest.*

After me cometh a man which is preferred before me: for he was before me: There follows me a man, *Fenton* . . . Behind me, *Concordant* . . . is preferred to me, *Campbell* . . . who ranks ahead of me, *Berkeley* . . . A man is coming after me who ranks before me because he existed before me, *JB* . . . one who is greater than I, because he already existed before me, *ALBA* . . . he was my superior, *Norton* . . . for he existed before I was born! *Phillips, Barclay* . . . because He antedated me, *Wuest.*

1:31. The Baptist was not saying that he had never met Jesus. He may have gone with his mother, Elisabeth, to visit Joseph and Mary on occasion. What John was saying was that he had not rec-

31. And I knew him not: I did not know him myself, *JB* . . . And I myself didn't know, *Adams* . . . I did not recognize Him, *Berkeley.*

5157.12 verb 3sing subj aor pass	**3450.3** art dat sing	**2447.1** name masc	**1217.2** prep	**3642.17** dem-pron sing neu
φανερωθῇ	τῷ	Ἰσραὴλ,	διὰ	τοῦτο
phanerōthē	*tō*	*Israēl*	*dia*	*touto*
he might be manifested		to Israel,	because of	this

31.a.**Txt:** 02A,017K,036,037,13,byz.Alf,Sod
Var: 01ℵ,03B,04C,019L,038,33,Lach,TregTisc,We/Ho,Weis,UBS/☆

2048.1 verb indic aor act	**1466.1** prs-pron nom 1sing	**1706.1** prep	**3450.3** art dat sing	**5045.3** noun dat sing neu	**901.4** verb nom sing masc part pres act
ἦλθον	ἐγὼ	ἐν	⸂a τῷ ⸃	ὕδατι	βαπτίζων.
ēlthon	*egō*	*en*	*tō*	*hudati*	*baptizōn*
came	I	with	the	water	baptizing.

2504.1 conj	**3113.16** verb 3sing indic aor act	**2464.1** name nom masc	**2978.15** verb sing masc part pres act	**3617.1** conj
32. Καὶ	ἐμαρτύρησεν	Ἰωάννης	λέγων,	Ὅτι
Kai	*emarturēsen*	*Iōannēs*	*legōn*	*Hoti*
And	bore witness	John	saying,	

2277.12 verb 1sing indic perf	**3450.16** art sing neu	**4011.1** noun sing neu	**2568.10** verb sing neu part pres act	**5448.1** adv
τεθέαμαι	τὸ	πνεῦμα	καταβαῖνον	⸂ ὡσεὶ
tetheamai	*to*	*pneuma*	*katabainon*	*hōsei*
I have beheld	the	Spirit	descending	as

32.a.**Txt:** p66,017K,024P,037,1,13,byz.
Var: 01ℵ,02A,03B,04C,019L,036,038,Gries,LachTreg,Alf,Word,Tisc,We/Ho,Weis,Sod,UBS/☆

5453.1 conj	**3918.1** noun acc sing fem	**1523.1** prep gen	**3636.2** noun gen sing masc	**2504.1** conj	**3176.16** verb 3sing indic aor act
[a☆ ὡς]	περιστερὰν	ἐξ	οὐρανοῦ,	καὶ	ἔμεινεν
hōs	*peristeran*	*ex*	*ouranou*	*kai*	*emeinen*
[idem]	a dove	out of	heaven,	and	it stayed

1894.2 prep	**840.6** prs-pron acc sing masc	**2476.3** conj	**3620.2** partic	**3471.9** verb 1sing indic plperf act	**840.6** prs-pron acc sing masc
ἐπ'	αὐτόν.	33. κἀγὼ	οὐκ	ᾔδειν	αὐτόν·
ep'	*auton*	*kagō*	*ouk*	*ēdein*	*auton*
upon	him.	And I	not	knew	him;

233.1 conj	**3450.5** art sing masc	**3854.11** verb nom sing masc part aor act	**1466.6** prs-pron acc 1sing	**901.6** verb inf pres act	**1706.1** prep
ἀλλ'	ὁ	πέμψας	με	βαπτίζειν	ἐν
all'	*ho*	*pempsas*	*me*	*baptizein*	*en*
but	the	having sent	me	to baptize	with

5045.3 noun dat sing neu	**1552.3** dem-pron nom sing masc	**1466.4** prs-pron dat 1sing	**1500.5** verb 3sing indic aor act	**1894.1** prep	**3614.6** rel-pron acc sing masc
ὕδατι,	ἐκεῖνός	μοι	εἶπεν,	Ἐφ'	ὃν
hudati	*ekeinos*	*moi*	*eipen*	*Eph'*	*hon*
water,	that	to me	said,	Upon	whom

300.1 partic	**1481.9** verb 2sing subj aor act	**3450.16** art sing neu	**4011.1** noun sing neu	**2568.10** verb sing neu part pres act	**2504.1** conj
ἂν	ἴδῃς	τὸ	πνεῦμα	καταβαῖνον	καὶ
an	*idēs*	*to*	*pneuma*	*katabainon*	*kai*
	you shall see	the	Spirit	descending	and

3176.14 verb sing neu part pres act	**1894.2** prep	**840.6** prs-pron acc sing masc	**3642.4** dem-pron nom sing masc	**1498.4** verb 3sing indic pres act	**3450.5** art sing masc
μένον	ἐπ'	αὐτόν,	οὗτός	ἐστιν	ὁ
menon	*ep'*	*auton*	*houtos*	*estin*	*ho*
staying	on	him,	this	it is	the

901.4 verb nom sing masc part pres act	**1706.1** prep	**4011.3** noun dat sing neu	**39.3** adj dat sing	**2476.3** conj	**3571.9** verb 1sing indic perf act
βαπτίζων	ἐν	πνεύματι	ἁγίῳ.	34. κἀγὼ	ἑώρακα,
baptizōn	*en*	*pneumati*	*hagiō*	*kagō*	*heōraka*
baptizing	with	Spirit	Holy.	And I	have seen,

ognized Jesus for what He was. Knowing Christ for who He is is a work of the Holy Spirit. The recognition of who Christ was was not to be John's alone. He said, "But in order that He might be manifested to Israel" (NASB).

"Manifest" (*phanerōthē*) is an absorbing word occurring 9 times in John and 49 times in the New Testament. The denotation is "to reveal," "make known," and "to know by revelation." The last meaning fits this context. John declared that the reason he "(came) baptizing with (or 'in') water" was that Christ might be manifested in Israel.

but that he should be made manifest to Israel: . . . yet it was in order to reveal Him, *Adams* . . . that he might be openly shown, *Montgomery* . . . be revealed to, *ET* . . . that He may be made known to Israel, *Berkeley.*

therefore am I come baptizing with water: . . . for this reason, *Confraternity* . . . but the very reason why, *Barclay* . . . and yet the reason I came, *ALBA.*

1:32. Jesus did not receive the Holy Spirit at the time of His baptism in water. He possesses the fullness of the Spirit, for He is God. The sign was a confirmation of God's revelation as to the messiahship of Jesus. The physical form of a dove was clearly visible. The dove was a fitting symbol of the Spirit because it was *harmless* (Matthew 10:16), a word which also means "pure" both in purpose and in character. The Law also allowed the poor to use the dove as a substitute for the sacrificial lamb. Thus, the dove also revealed Jesus as God's Lamb for mankind, all of whom are poor sinners in God's sight.

The visible form of the dove did not light upon Him and then fly away. It stayed until it became invisible. The Spirit remained upon Jesus in contrast to most Old Testament manifestations of the Spirit which were temporary or which came from time to time.

32. And John bare record, saying: Then John gave this testimony, *Williams* . . . testified further, *Berkeley* . . . gave further evidence, *AmpB.*

I saw the Spirit descending from heaven like a dove: I have gazed upon, *Concordant* . . . from the sky, *TCNT* . . . like a pigeon, *Klingensmith.*

and it abode upon him: . . . and it remained upon him, *Alford* . . . and rest, *Concordant* . . . and alighting upon, *Fenton* . . . and dwellinge on him, *Wycliffe* . . . and settling on him, *Barclay* . . . and stay on Him, *Beck.*

1:33. John did not say that the sign meant anything to Jesus' ministry. But it certainly confirmed to John that Jesus was the Messiah. Jesus himself used this contrast in Acts 1:5 where His reminder reconfirmed the promise made here. John's baptism in water prepared the hearts of the people and instructed them to look for the full realities in Jesus Christ. Christ's ministry brought life into the dead forms and monotonous rituals. It is the Spirit who gives life. Then Jesus baptizes and fills individual believers with the Holy Spirit to empower them.

The only sign of Messiah listed in all four Gospels is that He baptizes in the Holy Spirit. Several terms are used in the New Testament which are parallel to the baptism in the Spirit. Some are "filled with the Spirit," "the Spirit coming upon," and "being clothed with the Spirit."

33. And I knew him not: For my part, *Campbell.*

but he that sent me to baptize with water, the same said unto me: . . . told me Himself, *Berkeley.*

Upon whom thou shalt see the Spirit descending, and remaining on him: . . . the Spirit come down to rest, *ALBA* . . . and settling, *Barclay* . . . and tary styll on hym, *Tyndale.*

the same is he which baptizeth with the Holy Ghost: . . . immerseth in the Holy Spirit, *HBIE.*

1:34. A witness tells what he knows. He knows by what he sees and hears. John summed up what he "saw" with the perfect tense

2504.1 conj	**3113.25** verb 1sing indic perf act	**3617.1** conj	**3642.4** dem-pron nom sing masc	**1498.4** verb 3sing indic pres act
καὶ	μεμαρτύρηκα	ὅτι	οὗτός	ἐστιν
kai	*memarturēka*	*hoti*	*houtos*	*estin*
and	have borne witness	that	this	is

3450.5 art sing masc	**5048.1** noun nom sing masc	**3450.2** art gen sing	**2296.2** noun gen sing masc	**3450.11** art dat sing fem	**1872.1** adv
ὁ	υἱὸς	τοῦ	θεοῦ.	**35.** Τῇ	ἐπαύριον
ho	*huios*	*tou*	*theou*	*Tē*	*epaurion*
the	Son		of God.	On the	next day

35.a.**Txt:** 01א,02A,04C, 017K,036,037,038,etc. byz.Gries,TiscWeis,Sod, UBS/☆
Var: p75,03B,019L, Lach,Treg,Alf,We/Ho

3687.1 adv	**2449.22** verb 3sing indic plperf act	**3450.5** art sing masc	**2464.1** name nom masc	**2504.1** conj	**1523.2** prep gen
πάλιν	εἱστήκει	(a☆ ὁ)	Ἰωάννης,	καὶ	ἐκ
palin	*heistēkei*	*ho*	*Iōannēs*	*kai*	*ek*
again	was standing		John,	and	of

3450.1 art gen pl	**3073.6** noun gen pl masc	**840.3** prs-pron gen sing	**1411.3** num card	**2504.1** conj	**1676.4** verb nom sing masc part aor act
τῶν	μαθητῶν	αὐτοῦ	δύο,	**36.** καὶ	ἐμβλέψας
tōn	*mathētōn*	*autou*	*duo*	*kai*	*emblepsas*
the	disciples	his	two.	And	looking at

3450.3 art dat sing	**2400.2** name masc	**3906.14** verb dat sing masc part pres act	**2978.5** verb 3sing indic pres act	**1481.14** verb 2sing impr aor act
τῷ	Ἰησοῦ	περιπατοῦντι,	λέγει,	Ἴδε
tō	*Iēsou*	*peripatounti*	*legei*	*Ide*
	Jesus	walking,	he says,	Behold

36.a.**Var:** p66-org, 04C-org,Lach

3450.5 art sing masc	**284.1** noun nom sing masc	**3450.2** art gen sing	**2296.2** noun gen sing masc	**3450.5** art sing masc	**142.6** verb nom sing masc part pres act
ὁ	ἀμνὸς	τοῦ	θεοῦ.	[a+ ὁ	αἴρων
ho	*amnos*	*tou*	*theou*	*ho*	*airōn*
the	Lamb		of God!	[the	taking away

3450.12 art acc sing fem	**264.4** noun acc sing fem	**3450.2** art gen sing	**2862.2** noun gen sing masc	**2504.1** conj	**189.24** verb 3pl indic aor act
τὴν	ἁμαρτίαν	τοῦ	κόσμου.]	**37.** Καὶ	ἤκουσαν
tēn	*hamartian*	*tou*	*kosmou*	*Kai*	*ēkousan*
the	sin	of the	world.]	And	heard

840.3 prs-pron gen sing	**3450.7** art pl masc	**1411.3** num card	**3073.5** noun nom pl masc	**3450.7** art pl masc	**1411.3** num card
(αὐτοῦ	οἱ	δύο	μαθηταὶ	[☆ οἱ	δύο
autou	*hoi*	*duo*	*mathētai*	*hoi*	*duo*
him	the	two	disciples	[the	two

3073.5 noun nom pl masc	**840.3** prs-pron gen sing	**2953.13** verb gen sing masc part pres act	**2504.1** conj	**188.13** verb 3pl indic aor act
μαθηταὶ	αὐτοῦ]	λαλοῦντος,	καὶ	ἠκολούθησαν
mathētai	*autou*	*lalountos*	*kai*	*ēkolouthēsan*
disciples	his]	speaking,	and	followed

3450.3 art dat sing	**2400.2** name masc	**4613.8** verb nom sing masc part aor pass	**1156.2** conj	**3450.5** art sing masc	**2400.1** name nom masc
τῷ	Ἰησοῦ.	**38.** στραφεὶς	δὲ	ὁ	Ἰησοῦς,
tō	*Iēsou*	*strapheis*	*de*	*ho*	*Iēsous*
	Jesus.	Having turned	but		Jesus,

2504.1 conj	**2277.7** verb nom sing masc part aor mid	**840.8** prs-pron acc pl masc	**188.9** verb acc pl masc part pres act	**2978.5** verb 3sing indic pres act
καὶ	θεασάμενος	αὐτοὺς	ἀκολουθοῦντας,	λέγει
kai	*theasamenos*	*autous*	*akolouthountas*	*legei*
and	beheld	them	following,	says

verb "have seen" (*heōraka*), asserting past action with a present result.

The content of his witness was put into a short, powerful statement of fact "that this is the Son of God." John did not speak of His nature this time but of His identity as God's Son because John used the definite article with both Son and God (*ho huios tou theou*). John's last few words are most important. The title "Son of God" is recorded in the New Testament over 40 times, in the Gospels nearly 30 times, and in the Gospel of John 10 times. The term emphasized the unique relationship of the Father and the Son. Jesus never included anyone else when He said "my Father." He never included himself when He told others to pray "Our Father." By way of comparison, "Son of man" (1:51), a term more often used by Christ himself, is a term meaning His messiahship.

34. And I saw, and bare record that this is the Son of God: I did see it, *Williams* . . . I have seen it with my own eyes; I therefore testify, *ALBA* . . . have testified, *HBIE* . . . testified that the same is, *Rotherham* . . . have declared my belief, *TCNT* . . . and I declare publicly before you all that, *Phillips* . . . have given my evidence, *Fenton* . . . and I testify, *Adams* . . . I have seen with discernment, *Wuest* . . . I have seen this myself, *TCNT* . . . Now I did see it, *Moffatt* . . . I actually did see it, *AmpB* . . . I am telling you the truth. He is the Son of God! *SEB* . . . This is God's Chosen One, *NEB* . . . he is the Chosen One of God, *JB*.

1:35. "The next day" points to the day after the Baptist introduced Jesus as the Lamb of God (verse 29), 2 days after the delegation came from Jerusalem and about 6 weeks after His baptism. John's position is important as the bridge between the Messiah and His followers-to-be.

"Stood" is a picture of expectant waiting.

35. Again the next day after John stood, and two of his disciples: The following day, *TCNT* . . . Again, on the day after that, *Fenton*.

1:36. They were "looking upon" Jesus with a long penetrating glance as He walked by or away. Jesus was not walking toward John as He was in verse 29. The disciples' opportunity was slipping away. "Behold the Lamb of God" asserted again John's declaration of verse 29. This time he omitted "which taketh away the sin of the world," though this would be implied.

36. And looking upon Jesus as he walked: After gazing intently on, *Montgomery* . . . he saw Jesus passing by, *Beck* . . . and John stared hard at him, *JB*.

he saith, Behold the Lamb of God!: Look at, *Beck* . . . There is the, *NEB* . . . There is God's Lamb! *Adams*.

1:37. This was the beginning of Christ's obtaining disciples upon whom He exerted 3½ years of the most intense and valuable training ever imparted to a human being. A disciple (*mathētēs*) is a learner, one who really wants to learn and who first, shows he has learned by his conduct and second, teaches the truth to others. The word "followed" has a literal and figurative meaning here. By walking with Jesus, the disciples became followers of His way of life.

37. And the two disciples heard him speak, and they followed Jesus: . . . heard his exclamation, *Montgomery*.

1:38. From this verse forward, the account of the early earthly ministry of Jesus begins. John's Gospel gives some of the events in

38. Then Jesus turned, and saw them following, and saith unto them, What seek ye?: . . . noticing that they followed Him ...What are you looking for, *Berkeley* . . . and when he observed them

John 1:39

38.a.**Txt:** 01ℵ,02A, 04C-corr,019L,038,etc. byz.Sod
Var: 03B,04C-org,Lach, Treg,AlfTisc,We/Ho, Weis,UBS/☆

38.b.**Txt:** 01ℵ-org,017K, 036,037,038,byz.Tisc
Var: p66,p75,01ℵ-corr, 02A,03B,04C,019L, 032W,033X,Lach,Treg, Alf,We/HoWeis,Sod, UBS/☆

39.a.**Txt:** 01ℵ,02A, 04C-corr,017K,036,037, 038,13,byz.Lach
Var: 03B,04C-org,019L, 1,33,Treg,Tisc,We/Ho, Weis,Sod,UBS/☆

39.b.**Txt:** 01ℵ,02A, 03B-corr,017K,019L, 036,037,038,byz.Weis, Sod
Var: 03B-org,04C,Treg, Alf,TiscWe/Ho,UBS/☆

39.c.**Var:** 01ℵ,02A,03B, 04C,019L,033X,038,33, bo.Lach,Treg,Alf,Tisc, We/HoWeis,Sod,UBS/☆

39.d.**Txt:** 01ℵ,02A, 03B-corr,017K,019L, 036,037,038,byz.Weis, Sod
Var: 03B-org,04C,Treg, Alf,TiscWe/Ho,UBS/☆

39.e.**Txt:** (byz.),bo.Steph
Var: 01ℵ,02A,03B,04C, 017K,019L,036,037,038, (byz.)Gries,Lach,Treg, Alf,Word,Tisc,We/Ho, WeisSod,UBS/☆

840.2 prs-pron dat pl	**4949.9** intr-pron sing neu	**2195.1** verb 2pl pres act	**3450.7** art pl masc	**1156.2** conj	**1500.3** verb indic aor act
αὐτοῖς,	Τί	ζητεῖτε;	Οἱ	δὲ	ʻ εἶπον
autois	*Ti*	*zēteite*	*Hoi*	*de*	*eipon*
to them,	What	seek you?	The	and	said

1500.28 verb 3pl indic aor act	**840.4** prs-pron dat sing	**4318.1** noun sing masc	**3614.16** rel-pron sing neu	**2978.28** verb 3sing indic pres pass
[a☆ εἶπαν]	αὐτῷ,	ʽΡαββί,	ὃ	λέγεται
eipan	*autō*	*Rhabbi*	*ho*	*legetai*
[idem]	to him,	Rabbi,	which	is to say

2043.3 verb nom sing neu part pres pass	**3148.2** verb nom sing neu part pres pass	**1314.3** noun voc sing masc
ʻ ἑρμηνευόμενον	[b☆ μεθερμηνευόμενον]	Διδάσκαλε,
hermēneuomenon	*methermēneuomenon*	*Didaskale*
being interpreted	[being translated]	Teacher,

4085.1 adv	**3176.4** verb 2sing indic pres act	**2978.5** verb 3sing indic pres act	**840.2** prs-pron dat pl	**2048.41** verb 2pl impr pres
ποῦ	μένεις;	**39.** λέγει	αὐτοῖς,	Ἔρχεσθε
pou	*meneis*	*legei*	*autois*	*Erchesthe*
where	do you reside?	He says	to them,	Come

2504.1 conj	**1481.15** verb 2pl impr aor act	**3571.33** verb 2pl indic fut mid	**2048.1** verb indic aor act	**2048.64** verb 3pl indic aor act
καὶ	ʻ ἴδετε.	[a☆ ὄψεσθε.]	ʻ Ἦλθον	[b☆ ἦλθαν]
kai	*idete*	*opsesthe*	*Ēlthon*	*ēlthan*
and	see.	[you will see.]	They went	[idem]

3631.1 conj	**2504.1** conj	**1481.1** verb indic aor act	**1481.7** verb 3pl indic aor act	**4085.1** adv	**3176.1** verb 3sing indic act
[c☆+ οὖν]	καὶ	ʻ εἶδον	[d εἶδαν]	ποῦ	μένει·
oun	*kai*	*eidon*	*eidan*	*pou*	*menei*
[therefore]	and	saw	[idem]	where	he stays;

2504.1 conj	**3706.1** prep	**840.4** prs-pron dat sing	**3176.18** verb 3pl indic aor act	**3450.12** art acc sing fem	**2232.4** noun acc sing fem
καὶ	παρ'	αὐτῷ	ἔμειναν	τὴν	ἡμέραν
kai	*par'*	*autō*	*emeinan*	*tēn*	*hēmeran*
and	with	him	they stayed	the	day

1552.12 dem-pron acc sing fem	**5443.2** noun nom sing fem	**1156.2** conj	**1498.34** verb sing indic imperf act	**5453.1** conj	**1176.3** num ord nom sing fem
ἐκείνην·	ὥρα	ʻe δὲ ʼ	ἦν	ὡς	δεκάτη.
ekeinēn	*hōra*	*de*	*ēn*	*hōs*	*dekatē*
that.	Hour	now	was	about	tenth.

1498.34 verb sing indic imperf act	**404.1** name nom masc	**3450.5** art sing masc	**79.1** noun nom sing masc	**4468.2** name gen masc	**3935.2** name gen masc
40. Ἦν	Ἀνδρέας	ὁ	ἀδελφὸς	Σίμωνος	Πέτρου
Ēn	*Andreas*	*ho*	*adelphos*	*Simōnos*	*Petrou*
Was	Andrew	the	brother	of Simon	Peter

1518.3 num card nom masc	**1523.2** prep gen	**3450.1** art gen pl	**1411.3** num card	**3450.1** art gen pl	**189.33** verb gen pl masc part aor act	**3706.2** prep
εἷς	ἐκ	τῶν	δύο	τῶν	ἀκουσάντων	παρὰ
heis	*ek*	*tōn*	*duo*	*tōn*	*akousantōn*	*para*
one	of	the	two	the	having heard	from

2464.2 name gen masc	**2504.1** conj	**188.17** verb gen pl masc part aor act	**840.4** prs-pron dat sing	**2128.3** verb 3sing indic pres act
Ἰωάννου,	καὶ	ἀκολουθησάντων	αὐτῷ·	**41.** εὑρίσκει
Iōannou	*kai*	*akolouthēsantōn*	*autō*	*heuriskei*
John,	and	followed	him.	Finds

Judea during the first year of ministry that are not found in the other Gospels.

Note the progress of the action of Jesus—He turned suddenly; He beheld (studying them with a long look); then He spoke to them.

The question He asked, He also asks of every human being. Our activities reveal our search for meaning in life. Our desires motivate our conduct. The two disciples of John were seekers as all men are seekers. Notice, Jesus did not ask "Who?"; He asked, "What?" Nevertheless, the "what?" comes with the "who?" when the "who" is Christ. In the Sermon on the Mount, Jesus taught His disciples to seek first His kingdom and His righteousness (Matthew 6:33). This is the "what" they were to seek, and this "what" came in the person of Jesus Christ, the King of the kingdom.

"Rabbi" is interpreted as "Master" (literally, "Teacher") showing that John's Gospel is directed primarily to Gentiles who did not know the Aramaic or Hebrew.

coming after him, *Moffatt* . . . looked at them attentively, *Wuest* . . . What do you want, *Moffatt* . . . What do you seek? *Fenton* . . . what is it you wish? *AmpB.*

They said unto him, Rabbi, (which is to say, being interpreted, Master,) where dwellest thou?: . . . (which, being construed, is termed "Teacher"), *Concordant* . . . where are you staying, *ALBA* . . . where do you dwell, *Campbell* . . . where are you living? *BB* . . . where abidest thou? *Alford, Rotherham, Worrell* . . . where do you stay? *Berkeley.*

1:39. Jesus' answer was appropriate to their question, but it was not a direct answer. So many of Jesus' answers invite people to investigate.

"Come and see" was the Lord's gracious invitation for John's disciples to become His disciples. "Come and see" was both the summons and the assurance. Doubtless the two stayed with Him that night. The principle of following and experiencing holds good in all discipleship. Much of our ignorance is a result of our lack of involvement.

They "saw where he dwelt." This may have been a temporary brush shelter.

"It was about the tenth hour" tells us two things. First, "the tenth hour" was 4 o'clock, therefore the day was coming to a close. The disciples would not travel during the night. They would wait until morning. Second, "the tenth hour" was the hour the first two disciples would long remember. It was when they first became acquainted with Jesus.

39. He saith unto them, Come and see: "Come," he replied, "and you will see, *NIV.*

They came and saw where he dwelt, and abode with him that day: They accordingly went and saw where He was staying, *Fenton* . . . and spent the day with him, *TCNT* . . . and spent the remainder of the day with him, *ALBA* . . . remained with him, *Alford.*

for it was about the tenth hour: . . . about ten o'clock in the morning, *Weymouth* . . . then about four in the afternoon, *Berkeley* . . . about four in the afternoon, *Williams* . . . about ten in the forenoon, *Beck.*

1:40. "One of the two . . . was Andrew, Simon Peter's brother." *Andrew* is a Greek name meaning "manly." A reference to his name occurs 13 times in the New Testament. Many times his name occurs in association with his brother Simon Peter as if we could not know him apart from his connection with Peter. At the time the apostle John wrote these words, the Church among the Gentiles was well acquainted with Simon Peter.

There is an interesting fact to allude to at this point. In the Old Testament creation Adam's name meant "man." The Church be-

40. One of the two which heard John speak, and followed him, was Andrew, Simon Peter's brother: . . . who heard the remark of John, *Fenton.*

John 1:42

41.a.**Txt:** 01ℵ-org,017K,019L,032W,036,037,28,565,700,byz.Tisc
Var: p66,p75,01ℵ-corr,02A,03B,038,1,13,it.Lach,Treg,Alf,We/Ho,Weis,Sod,UBS/☆

41.b.**Txt:** bo.Steph
Var: 01ℵ,02A,03B,017K,019L,036,037,038,byz.Gries,LachTreg,Alf,Tisc,We/Ho,Weis,Sod,UBS/☆

42.a.**Txt:** 02A,017K,032W,036,037,038,13,byz.Lach
Var: 01ℵ,03B,019L,bo.Treg,Alf,Tisc,We/Ho,Weis,Sod,UBS/☆

42.b.**Txt:** p75,033X,037,038,13,Steph,Lach
Var: 01ℵ,02A,03B,017K,019L,036,Gries Treg,Alf,Word,Tisc,We/Ho,Weis,Sod,UBS/☆

42.c.**Txt:** 02A,03B-corr,017K,036,037,1,13,565,700,byz.
Var: p66,p75,01ℵ,019L,032W,33,sa.bo.Lach,Alf,Tisc,We/Ho,Weis,Sod,UBS/☆

43.a.**Txt:** 07E,036,038,Steph
Var: 01ℵ,02A,03B,017K,019L,037,038,byz.it.bo.GriesLach,Treg,Alf,Tisc,We/Ho,Weis,Sod,UBS/☆

3642.4 dem-pron nom sing masc	**4272.5** num ord nom sing masc	**4270.1** adv	**3450.6** art acc sing masc	**79.4** noun acc sing masc
οὗτος	⸀ πρῶτος	[a☆ πρῶτον]	τὸν	ἀδελφὸν
houtos	*prōtos*	*prōton*	*ton*	*adelphon*
this	first	[idem]	the	brother

3450.6 art acc sing masc	**2375.4** adj acc sing	**4468.4** name acc masc	**2504.1** conj	**2978.5** verb 3sing indic pres act	**840.4** prs-pron dat sing
τὸν	ἴδιον	Σίμωνα,	καὶ	λέγει	αὐτῷ,
ton	*idion*	*Simōna*	*kai*	*legei*	*autō*
the	his own	Simon,	and	says	to him,

2128.23 verb 1pl indic perf act	**3450.6** art acc sing masc	**3193.2** name acc masc	**3614.16** rel-pron sing neu	**1498.4** verb 3sing indic pres act
Εὑρήκαμεν	τὸν	Μεσσίαν,	ὅ	ἐστιν
Heurēkamen	*ton*	*Messian*	*ho*	*estin*
We have found	the	Messiah,	which	is

3148.2 verb nom sing neu part pres pass	**3450.5** art sing masc	**5382.1** name nom masc	**2504.1** conj
μεθερμηνευόμενον	⸂b ὁ ⸃	Χριστός·	**42.** ⸂a καὶ ⸃
methermēneuomenon	*ho*	*Christos*	*kai*
being interpreted	the	Christ.	And

70.8 verb 3sing indic aor act	**840.6** prs-pron acc sing masc	**4242.1** prep	**3450.6** art acc sing masc	**2400.3** name acc masc	**1676.4** verb nom sing masc part aor act
ἤγαγεν	αὐτὸν	πρὸς	τὸν	Ἰησοῦν.	ἐμβλέψας
ēgagen	*auton*	*pros*	*ton*	*Iēsoun*	*emblepsas*
he led	him	to		Jesus.	Looking at

1156.2 conj	**840.4** prs-pron dat sing	**3450.5** art sing masc	**2400.1** name nom masc	**1500.5** verb 3sing indic aor act	**4622.1** prs-pron nom 2sing
⸂b δὲ ⸃	αὐτῷ	ὁ	Ἰησοῦς	εἶπεν,	Σὺ
de	*autō*	*ho*	*Iēsous*	*eipen*	*Su*
and	him		Jesus	said,	You

1498.3 verb 2sing indic pres act	**4468.1** name masc	**3450.5** art sing masc	**5048.1** noun nom sing masc	**2468.2** name gen masc
εἶ	Σίμων	ὁ	υἱὸς	⸀ Ἰωνᾶ·
ei	*Simōn*	*ho*	*huios*	*Iōna*
are	Simon	the	son	of Jona;

2464.2 name gen masc	**4622.1** prs-pron nom 2sing	**2535.51** verb 2sing indic fut pass	**2758.1** name nom masc	**3614.16** rel-pron sing neu
[c☆ Ἰωάννου·]	σὺ	κληθήσῃ	Κηφᾶς	ὅ
Iōannou	*su*	*klēthēsē*	*Kēphas*	*ho*
[of John;]	you	shall be called	Cephas,	which

2043.1 verb 3sing indic pres pass	**3935.1** name nom masc	**3450.11** art dat sing fem	**1872.1** adv	**2286.22** verb 3sing indic aor act
ἑρμηνεύεται	Πέτρος.	**43.** Τῇ	ἐπαύριον	ἠθέλησεν
hermēneuetai	*Petros*	*Tē*	*epaurion*	*ēthelēsen*
is interpreted	Stone.	On the	next day	desired

3450.5 art sing masc	**2400.1** name nom masc	**1814.20** verb inf aor act	**1519.1** prep	**3450.12** art acc sing fem	**1049.4** name acc sing fem
⸂a ὁ	Ἰησοῦς ⸃	ἐξελθεῖν	εἰς	τὴν	Γαλιλαίαν·
ho	*Iēsous*	*exelthein*	*eis*	*tēn*	*Galilaian*
	Jesus	to go forth	into		Galilee,

2504.1 conj	**2128.3** verb 3sing indic pres act	**5213.4** name acc masc	**2504.1** conj	**2978.5** verb 3sing indic pres act	**840.4** prs-pron dat sing
καὶ	εὑρίσκει	Φίλιππον	καὶ	λέγει	αὐτῷ,
kai	*heuriskei*	*Philippon*	*kai*	*legei*	*autō*
and	he finds	Philip	and	says	to him,

gins with the first disciple, Andrew, whose name also means "man." God began the old and new creations with a man.

41. He first findeth his own brother Simon and saith unto him: In the morning, *Moffatt* . . . The first thing Andrew did, *NIV* . . . The first thing he did was to find his brother, *NEB, ALBA* . . . sought out his own brother, *Fenton.*

We have found the Messias, which is, being interpreted, the Christ: . . . made a discovery! *BB* . . . when translated, *Fenton* . . . which means Christ, the Anointed One, *Montgomery* . . . the promised Savior, *Beck* . . . a name equivalent to Christ, *Campbell* . . . whych ys be interpretacion Announted, *Tyndale* . . . or 'Consecrated,' *TCNT.*

1:41. "First" indicates three ideas. First, Andrew put the priority where it belonged, on his brother's welfare. Second, Andrew was the first of the Christian soulwinners. Third, by inference John, the other of the two disciples, also found his brother James.

"Findeth" (from *heuriskō*) has the emphatic first place in the sentence. It emphasizes the action from the human vantage point. True theology is that God takes the initiative in finding man.

42. And he brought him to Jesus: . . . led him to Jesus, *Norlie, Berkeley.*

And when Jesus beheld him, he said: Jesus gazed at Him, *Moffatt* . . . fixing his eyes on him, *TCNT* . . . looked steadily at him, *Phillips.*

Thou art Simon the son of Jona: "You are Simon Johnson," *Klingensmith* . . . the son of John, *Fenton.*

thou shalt be called Cephas, which is by interpretation, A stone: From now on your name shall be Cephas (which means Peter, or Rock), *Williams* . . . which denotes the same as Peter, *Campbell.*

1:42. "Brought" has the place of emphasis in this verse. John was impressed by Andrew's action. Andrew exhibited a beautiful Christian trait in his desire to share with his brother.

"Jesus 'beheld' (*emblepsas*) him" means He gave him one penetrating glance. The prefix (*em*) on the verb expresses intensification of looking. Jesus' look penetrated the character of His third disciple.

"Simon" is another spelling of Simeon, "hearing." (See Genesis 49:5.) The Jews did not use family names, so the name of his father was added to distinguish him. "Jona" in many ancient manuscripts is found as *Iōannou*, "John," the Greek form of the Hebrew *Yohanan*, "the Lord has been gracious."

"Thou shalt be called Cephas"; that which he would become, he would be called. Among the Hebrew people, names had a great significance. The name was to conform to the character. At times God changed the names of certain people: Abram to Abraham, Jacob to Israel, etc., to indicate a change in character or relationship. *Cephas* is the Aramaic for the Greek translation *Petros*; the transliteration is *Peter*. As "Simon" he was unstable. He would become Peter, "a stone rock, a boulder" equaling "stable."

Thus far in the narrative four men have become disciples of Jesus Christ. Andrew and John (John is implied) are the first two. Andrew brought his brother (it is implied that John brought his brother James). It seems that all the early followers had been the Baptist's disciples.

43. The day following Jesus would go forth into Galilee: At a subsequent time, *Fenton* . . . Next day Jesus decided, *ALBA* . . . Jesus decided to leave, *Williams* . . . he wished to go forth, *HBIE* . . . determined to depart, *Norton* . . . Jesus intended to leave, *Barclay* . . . He purposed to go forth, *NASB* . . . Jesus planned to go out, *Berkeley* . . . he resolved to go to, *Campbell.*

1:43. "The day following" indicates that the four came to Jesus within one day. The day after, the five left the region of Peraea or Gilead on the east side of the Jordan and went into Galilee. From what Jesus did in Galilee, we can assume His desire was to go there to add disciples. Philip is a Greek name meaning "fond of horses."

John 1:44

43.b.**Var:** 01ℵ,02A,03B, 07E,019L,037,038,byz. Lach,Treg,Alf,Tisc We/Ho,Weis,Sod,UBS/☆

3450.5 art sing masc	2400.1 name nom masc	188.3 verb 2sing impr pres act	1466.4 prs-pron dat 1sing	1498.34 verb sing indic imperf act
[b☆+ ὁ	Ἰησοῦς,]	Ἀκολούθει	μοι.	44. Ἦν
ho	*Iēsous*	*Akolouthei*	*moi*	*En*
	[Jesus,]	Follow	me.	Was

1156.2 conj	3450.5 art sing masc	5213.1 name nom masc	570.3 prep gen	959.2 name fem	1523.2 prep gen	3450.10 art gen sing fem
δὲ	ὁ	Φίλιππος	ἀπὸ	Βηθσαϊδά,	ἐκ	τῆς
de	*ho*	*Philippos*	*apo*	*Bēthsaida*	*ek*	*tēs*
now		Philip	from	Bethsaida,	of	the

4032.2 noun gen sing fem	404.2 name gen masc	2504.1 conj	3935.2 name gen masc	2128.3 verb 3sing indic pres act
πόλεως	Ἀνδρέου	καὶ	Πέτρου.	45. Εὑρίσκει
poleōs	*Andreou*	*kai*	*Petrou*	*Heuriskei*
city	of Andrew	and	Peter.	Finds

5213.1 name nom masc	3450.6 art acc sing masc	3345.1 name masc	2504.1 conj	2978.5 verb 3sing indic pres act	840.4 prs-pron dat sing
Φίλιππος	τὸν	Ναθαναὴλ	καὶ	λέγει	αὐτῷ,
Philippos	*ton*	*Nathanaēl*	*kai*	*legei*	*autō*
Philip		Nathanael	and	says	to him,

3614.6 rel-pron acc sing masc	1119.8 verb 3sing indic aor act	3337.1 name nom masc	3338.1 name nom masc	1706.1 prep
Ὃν	ἔγραψεν	⸂ Μωσῆς	[☆ Μωϋσῆς]	ἐν
Hon	*egrapsen*	*Mōsēs*	*Mōusēs*	*en*
Whom	wrote of	Moses	[idem]	in

3450.3 art dat sing	3414.3 noun dat sing masc	2504.1 conj	3450.7 art pl masc	4254.4 noun pl masc	2128.23 verb 1pl indic perf act
τῷ	νόμῳ	καὶ	οἱ	προφῆται,	εὑρήκαμεν,
tō	*nomō*	*kai*	*hoi*	*prophētai*	*heurēkamen*
the	law	and	the	prophets,	we have found,

45.a.**Txt:** 02A,017K, 019L,032W,036,037, 038,1,13,etc.byz.Treg, Sod
Var: p66,p75,01ℵ,03B, 33,Lach,Tisc,We/Ho, Weis,UBS/☆

2400.3 name acc masc	3450.6 art acc sing masc	5048.4 noun acc sing masc	3450.2 art gen sing	2473.1 name masc	3450.6 art acc sing masc
Ἰησοῦν	⸂a τὸν ⸃	υἱὸν	τοῦ	Ἰωσὴφ	τὸν
Iēsoun	*ton*	*huion*	*tou*	*Iōsēph*	*ton*
Jesus	the	son		of Joseph	the

45.b.**Txt:** 01ℵ,02A,03B, 019L,033X,Steph,Lach Tisc,We/Ho,Weis,Sod
Var: 017K,036,bo.Elzev, Gries,Word,UBS/☆

570.3 prep gen	3341.1 name fem	3341.3 name fem	2504.1 conj	1500.5 verb 3sing indic aor act
ἀπὸ	⸂☆ Ναζαρέτ.	[b Ναζαρέθ.]	46. Καὶ	εἶπεν
apo	*Nazaret*	*Nazareth*	*Kai*	*eipen*
from	Nazareth.	[idem]	And	said

46.a.**Txt:** 01ℵ,02A,03B, 019L,033X,037,Steph, Lach,Tisc,We/Ho,Weis, Sod
Var: 017K,036,Elzev, GriesWord,UBS/☆

840.4 prs-pron dat sing	3345.1 name masc	1523.2 prep gen	3341.1 name fem	3341.3 name fem
αὐτῷ	Ναθαναήλ,	Ἐκ	⸂☆ Ναζαρὲτ	[a Ναζαρέθ.]
autō	*Nathanaēl*	*Ek*	*Nazaret*	*Nazareth*
to him	Nathanael,	Out of	Nazareth	[idem]

1404.4 verb 3sing indic pres	4948.10 indef-pron sing neu	18.3 adj sing	1498.32 verb inf pres act	2978.5 verb 3sing indic pres act
δύναταί	τι	ἀγαθὸν	εἶναι;	Λέγει
dunatai	*ti*	*agathon*	*einai*	*Legei*
can	any	good thing	to be?	Says

46.b.**Var:** p66-corr,03B, 019L,33,Lach,Treg,Alf, We/HoWeis,UBS/☆

840.4 prs-pron dat sing	3450.5 art sing masc	5213.1 name nom masc	2048.39 verb 2sing impr pres	2504.1 conj	1481.14 verb 2sing impr aor act
αὐτῷ	[b+ ὁ]	Φίλιππος,	Ἔρχου	καὶ	ἴδε.
autō	*ho*	*Philippos*	*Erchou*	*kai*	*ide*
to him		Philip,	Come	and	see.

"Follow me." Without any previous introduction of Philip, John recorded Jesus' invitation for Philip to join His company. The call Jesus made to Philip is the call He makes to all. It is a call to discipleship. The word is used literally, but contains strong spiritual connotations. One who follows literally, doubtless learns spiritually.

and findeth Philip, and saith unto him, Follow me: So He found Philip, *Adams* . . . Start following with me, *Wuest.*

1:44. Bethsaida, "house of fishing," was situated on the northern coast of the Sea of Galilee. The town is referred to seven times in the New Testament.

"The city of Andrew and Peter" was the same as that of Philip. It is very likely that Andrew, in his zeal for others to know Jesus (1:41), had been telling Philip about Him. This can explain Philip's ready response to Jesus. Philip emulated Andrew in promptly becoming an effective witness. He took the initiative to find another friend: Nathanael. It seems that there was a special rapport between Philip and Andrew (6:5-9; 12:21,22).

A year later Peter had a house in Capernaum (Mark 1:21,29). According to Luke 9:10, on at least one occasion, Jesus took His disciples privately to Bethsaida. This indicates His purpose may have been that they might relax from their rigorous labors.

44. Now Philip was of Bethsaida, the city of Andrew and Peter: . . . belonged to Bethsaida, the native town of, *Fenton* . . . Philip came from the same town, Bethsaida, *JB* . . . out of the city, *Wuest.*

45. Philip findeth Nathanael, and saith unto him: Philip meets Nathanael, *Campbell* . . . Philip found Nathanael and told him, *ALBA* . . . sought out Nathanael, *Fenton.*

We have found him, of whom Moses in the law, and the prophets, did write: We have met the man spoken of by, *NEB* . . . found (discovered), *AmpB* . . . the person described by, *Campbell* . . . referred in the law, *Fenton* . . . and whom the prophets foretold, *Barclay.*

Jesus of Nazareth, the son of Joseph: . . . the [legal] son, *AmpB.*

1:45,46. Nathanael's name means "God's gift." His other name may have been Bartholomew (Mark 3:18). Philip's testimony to Nathanael revealed the depth of his spiritual understanding. He realized that Jesus was at the same time the long-awaited Messiah and "the son of Joseph." He recognized Him as the One of whom Moses wrote (Deuteronomy 18:15,18) and the One of whom the prophets spoke.

We see in Philip's recognition of Him the principle of *faith.* Those Israelites who were "going about to establish their own righteousness" by good works (Romans 10:2,3) could not know Him (John 1:10). They eventually rejected Him. Those walking humbly in faith (Simeon, Anna, and others) recognized Him immediately. His response was somewhat different from that of the other disciples as to whether Nazareth could be the place from which the Messiah would come. Philip's reply was, "Come and see." Nathanael was a skeptic. The invitation was brief. It was the one Jesus gave to Andrew and John (verse 39). Philip presented the invitation, but Nathanael would have to act upon it. Knowledge of God's Word and an experiential relationship with the Lord give rise to a true disciple. Skepticism disappears through knowledge and experience in the Lord.

46. And Nathanael said unto him, Can there any good thing come out of Nazareth?: "From Nazareth!" said Nathanael. "Do you mean to say there's something good, *ALBA* . . . is any good thing able to come? *Wuest* . . . Is it possible for anything good, *SEB* . . . retorted Nathanael, *Phillips.*

Philip saith unto him, Come and see: . . . see for yourself, *SEB.*

1:47. The verb "saw" (*eiden*) has the emphasis in the sentence, but it does not denote the strong prolonged seeing as that of verse

John 1:47

47.a.**Txt:** p66,p75,01ℵ, 02A,017K,019L,032W, 038,1,13,etc.byz.Weis, Sod
Var: 03B,036,Lach,Treg Alf,Tisc,We/Ho,UBS/☆

1481.3 verb 3sing indic aor act	**3450.5** art sing masc	**2400.1** name nom masc	**3450.6** art acc sing masc	**3345.1** name masc
47. Εἶδεν	⸂a ὁ ⸃	Ἰησοῦς	τὸν	Ναθαναὴλ
Eiden	*ho*	*Iēsous*	*ton*	*Nathanaēl*
Saw		Jesus		Nathanael

2048.42 verb sing part pres	**4242.1** prep	**840.6** prs-pron acc sing masc	**2504.1** conj	**2978.5** verb 3sing indic pres act
ἐρχόμενον	πρὸς	αὐτὸν,	καὶ	λέγει
erchomenon	*pros*	*auton*	*kai*	*legei*
coming	to	him,	and	says

3875.1 prep	**840.3** prs-pron gen sing	**1481.14** verb 2sing impr aor act	**228.1** adv	**2448.1** name nom sing masc
περὶ	αὐτοῦ,	Ἴδε	ἀληθῶς	Ἰσραηλίτης,
peri	*autou*	*Ide*	*alēthōs*	*Israēlitēs*
concerning	him,	Behold	truly	an Israelite,

1706.1 prep	**3614.3** rel-pron dat sing	**1382.1** noun nom sing masc	**3620.2** partic	**1498.4** verb 3sing indic pres act	**2978.5** verb 3sing indic pres act
ἐν	ᾧ	δόλος	οὐκ	ἔστιν.	**48.** Λέγει
en	*hō*	*dolos*	*ouk*	*estin*	*Legei*
in	whom	deceit	not	is.	Says

840.4 prs-pron dat sing	**3345.1** name masc	**4019.1** adv	**1466.6** prs-pron acc 1sing	**1091.2** verb 2sing indic pres act
αὐτῷ	Ναθαναήλ,	Πόθεν	με	γινώσκεις;
autō	*Nathanaēl*	*Pothen*	*me*	*ginōskeis*
to him	Nathanael,	From where	me	know you?

48.a.**Txt:** 01ℵ,07E-org, 038,Steph
Var: 02A,03B,07E-corr, 017K,019L,036,037,byz. Gries,Lach,Treg,AlfTisc, We/Ho,Weis,Sod,UBS/☆

552.6 verb 3sing indic aor pass	**3450.5** art sing masc	**2400.1** name nom masc	**2504.1** conj	**1500.5** verb 3sing indic aor act	**840.4** prs-pron dat sing
Ἀπεκρίθη	⸂a ὁ ⸃	Ἰησοῦς	καὶ	εἶπεν	αὐτῷ,
Apekrithē	*ho*	*Iēsous*	*kai*	*eipen*	*autō*
Answered		Jesus	and	said	to him,

4112.1 prep	**3450.2** art gen sing	**4622.4** prs-pron acc 2sing	**5213.4** name acc masc	**5291.11** verb inf aor act	**1498.18** verb part pres act
Πρὸ	τοῦ	σε	Φίλιππον	φωνῆσαι,	ὄντα
Pro	*tou*	*se*	*Philippon*	*phōnēsai*	*onta*
Before	the	you	Philip	called,	being

5097.3 prep	**3450.12** art acc sing fem	**4659.4** noun acc sing fem	**1481.1** verb indic aor act	**4622.4** prs-pron acc 2sing	**552.6** verb 3sing indic aor pass
ὑπὸ	τὴν	συκῆν,	εἶδόν	σε.	**49.** Ἀπεκρίθη
hupo	*tēn*	*sukēn*	*eidon*	*se*	*Apekrithē*
under	the	fig tree,	I saw	you.	Answered

49.a.**Var:** 01ℵ,03B,019L, 33,Lach,Treg,Alf,Tisc, We/HoWeis,Sod,UBS/☆

49.b.**Txt:** 02A,017K,038, 041,1,13,byz.
Var: 03B,019L,33,Treg, Alf,Tisc,We/Ho,Weis, UBS/☆

840.4 prs-pron dat sing	**3345.1** name masc	**2504.1** conj	**2978.5** verb 3sing indic pres act	**840.4** prs-pron dat sing
[a☆+ αὐτῷ]	Ναθαναὴλ	⸂b καὶ	λέγει	αὐτῷ, ⸃
autō	*Nathanaēl*	*kai*	*legei*	*autō*
[him]	Nathanael	and	says	to him,

4318.1 noun sing masc	**4622.1** prs-pron nom 2sing	**1498.3** verb 2sing indic pres act	**3450.5** art sing masc	**5048.1** noun nom sing masc	**3450.2** art gen sing
Ῥαββί,	σὺ	εἶ	ὁ	υἱὸς	τοῦ
Rhabbi	*su*	*ei*	*ho*	*huios*	*tou*
Rabbi,	you	are	the	Son	

2296.2 noun gen sing masc	**4622.1** prs-pron nom 2sing	**1498.3** verb 2sing indic pres act	**3450.5** art sing masc	**928.1** noun nom sing masc
θεοῦ,	σὺ	⸂ εἶ	ὁ	βασιλεὺς
theou	*su*	*ei*	*ho*	*basileus*
of God,	you	are	the	King

38. It implies a casual looking. It did not take a lengthy time for Jesus to determine Nathanael's character.

A casual observer might have taken Nathanael's question in the previous verse as evidence of prejudice or of calloused skepticism. Jesus, however, saw it was an honest question from a seeker after truth.

The Jewish scholars had placed great emphasis on Messiah's coming as the Seed of David, and rightly so. They expected Him then to come from Judea, not from Galilee. The concept of Messiah's coming from Nazareth would seem preposterous.

Nathanael's inquiry came from no ulterior motives such as those displayed by other Jewish leaders (7:41,42,52). He was ready to walk in the light as God revealed it. Any doubts he had were dispelled by Jesus' greeting.

"An Israelite indeed" directs our attention to the first Israelite (Jacob). "Guile" includes deceit, treachery, and craftiness. The word was used to translate Jacob's "subtilty" in taking Esau's blessing (Genesis 27:35).

Jesus' words point out three things. First, Nathanael's character was guileless. Second, Jesus knows the character of every person. Third, Jesus implies that the true order of Israelites is to be without deceit. The last implication will be seen more clearly as the passage unfolds. The parallel between Jacob and his descendants, the Israelites, and Jesus and His disciples is clearly indicated in this passage.

1:48. Nathanael asked how Jesus knew about him. Seeing Nathanael under the fig tree was the exercise of omniscience which only God has. If He so desired, Jesus could have told Nathanael what he was thinking when Philip called him.

Something intimately personal, by way of revelation, was communicated to Nathanael by Jesus' remark.

1:49. "Rabbi" is the same word Andrew and John used in verse 38. It means "my lord, my master" and was used as an honorary title to show great respect to outstanding teachers.

Next, Nathanael confessed that he now believed Jesus was indeed the King of Israel, the Son of God as John the Baptist had presented Him (verse 34).

The One who fulfilled the prophecies of the Son of God was to be the King of Israel. Psalm 2:6 presents the Messiah as the King of Israel.

1:50. Nathanael was assured that what he had heard from the Lord would be only a beginning of the evidence as to Christ's identity.

47. Jesus saw Nathanael coming to him, and saith of him: Jesus perceived Nathanael, *Concordant* . . . noticed Nathanael approaching Him, *Berkeley* . . . and said concerning him, *AmpB.*

Behold an Israelite indeed: . . . a true son of Israel, *BB* . . . a real Israelite, *Murdock* . . . a genuine Israelite, *Williams* . . . There is an Israelite who deserves the name, *JB* . . . worthy of the name, *NEB.*

in whom is no guile!: . . . there is no duplicity, *Fenton* . . . there is nothing false, *BB* . . . no deceitfulness! *Weymouth* . . . is no trickery, *Klingensmith* . . . incapable of deceit, *JB* . . . is genuine all through, *Barclay* . . . in whom guile does not exist, *Wuest.*

48. Nathanael saith unto him, Whence knowest thou me?: Where did You get to know me, *Beck* . . . How is it that You know these things about me? *AmpB* . . . How do you know me? *ALBA* . . . From what source do you have an experiential knowledge of me? *Wuest.*

Jesus answered and said unto him, Before that Philip called thee, when thou wast under the fig tree, I saw thee: Philip summons you, *Concordant* . . . at your quiet time, *Barclay* . . . Before ever, *AmpB* . . . When you were under that fig tree . . . I saw you, *Moffatt.*

49. Nathanael answered and saith unto him, Rabbi, thou art the Son of God; thou art the King of Israel: You are Israel's King! *Adams.*

John 1:50

49.c.**Txt:** p66,01ℵ,017K, 036,037,038,13,byz.
Var: p75,02A,03B,019L, 032W,33,Treg,AlfTisc, We/Ho,Weis,Sod,UBS/☆

928.1 noun nom sing masc	**1498.3** verb 2sing indic pres act	**3450.2** art gen sing	**2447.1** name masc	**552.6** verb 3sing indic aor pass
[c☆ βασιλεὺς	εἶ]	τοῦ	Ἰσραήλ.	**50.** Ἀπεκρίθη
basileus	*ei*	*tou*	*Israēl*	*Apekrithē*
[King	you are]		of Israel.	Answered

2400.1 name nom masc	**2504.1** conj	**1500.5** verb 3sing indic aor act	**840.4** prs-pron dat sing	**3617.1** conj	**1500.3** verb indic aor act
Ἰησοῦς	καὶ	εἶπεν	αὐτῷ,	Ὅτι	εἶπόν
Iēsous	*kai*	*eipen*	*autō*	*Hoti*	*eipon*
Jesus	and	said	to him,	Because	I said

50.a.**Var:** p66,p75,01ℵ, 02A,03B,019L,032W, Lach,Treg,Alf,Tisc, We/Ho,WeisSod,UBS/☆

4622.3 prs-pron dat 2sing	**3617.1** conj	**1481.1** verb indic aor act	**4622.4** prs-pron acc 2sing	**5108.1** prep gen	**3450.10** art gen sing fem
σοι,	[a☆+ ὅτι]	Εἶδόν	σε	ὑποκάτω	τῆς
soi	*hoti*	*Eidon*	*se*	*hupokatō*	*tēs*
to you,		I saw	you	under	the

4659.2 noun gen sing fem	**3961.5** verb 2sing indic pres act	**3157.5** adj comp acc	**3642.2** dem-pron gen pl	**3571.29** verb 2sing indic fut mid
συκῆς,	πιστεύεις;	μείζω	τούτων	ʼ ὄψει.
sukēs	*pisteueis*	*meizō*	*toutōn*	*opsei*
fig tree,	believe you?	Greater things	than these	you shall see.

50.b.**Txt:** 030U,036,(byz.)
Var: 01ℵ,02A,03B, 017K,019L,037,038, (byz.)Gries,Lach,Treg, Alf,Tisc,We/HoWeis,Sod, UBS/☆

3571.39 verb 2sing indic fut mid	**2504.1** conj	**2978.5** verb 3sing indic pres act	**840.4** prs-pron dat sing	**279.1** partic
[b☆ ὄψη.]	**51.** Καὶ	λέγει	αὐτῷ,	Ἀμὴν
opsē	*Kai*	*legei*	*autō*	*Amēn*
[idem]	And	he says	to him,	Truly

51.a.**Txt:** 02A,017K, 033X,036,037,038,1,13, etc.byz.Gries,Word,Sod
Var: p66,p75,01ℵ,03B, 019L,032W,1241,sa.bo. Lach,Treg,AlfTisc, We/Ho,Weis,UBS/☆

279.1 partic	**2978.1** verb 1sing pres act	**5050.3** prs-pron dat 2pl	**570.2** prep gen	**732.1** adv	**3571.33** verb 2pl indic fut mid
ἀμὴν	λέγω	ὑμῖν,	ʼa ἀπʼ	ἄρτι ʽ	ὄψεσθε
amēn	*legō*	*humin*	*ap'*	*arti*	*opsesthe*
truly	I say	to you,	From	now on	you shall see

3450.6 art acc sing masc	**3636.4** noun acc sing masc	**453.13** verb acc sing masc part perf act	**2504.1** conj	**3450.8** art acc pl masc	**32.8** noun acc pl masc
τὸν	οὐρανὸν	ἀνεῳγότα,	καὶ	τοὺς	ἀγγέλους
ton	*ouranon*	*aneōgota*	*kai*	*tous*	*angelous*
the	heaven	opened,	and	the	angels

3450.2 art gen sing	**2296.2** noun gen sing masc	**303.9** verb acc pl masc part pres act	**2504.1** conj	**2568.7** verb acc pl masc part pres act
τοῦ	θεοῦ	ἀναβαίνοντας	καὶ	καταβαίνοντας
tou	*theou*	*anabainontas*	*kai*	*katabainontas*
	of God	ascending	and	descending

1894.3 prep	**3450.6** art acc sing masc	**5048.4** noun acc sing masc	**3450.2** art gen sing	**442.2** noun gen sing masc	**2504.1** conj
ἐπὶ	τὸν	υἱὸν	τοῦ	ἀνθρώπου.	**2:1.** Καὶ
epi	*ton*	*huion*	*tou*	*anthrōpou*	*Kai*
on	the	Son		of man.	And

1.a.**Var:** 03B,030U,038, 13,Treg,Alf,Weis

3450.11 art dat sing fem	**2232.3** noun dat sing fem	**3450.11** art dat sing fem	**4995.6** num ord dat sing fem	**3450.11** art dat sing fem	**4995.6** num ord dat sing fem
ʼ τῇ	ἡμέρᾳ	τῇ	τρίτῃ	[a τῇ	τρίτῃ
tē	*hēmera*	*tē*	*tritē*	*tē*	*tritē*
on the	day	the	third	[on the	third

2232.3 noun dat sing fem	**1055.1** noun nom sing masc	**1090.33** verb 3sing indic aor mid	**1706.1** prep	**2551.2** name fem	**3450.10** art gen sing fem
ἡμέρᾳ]	γάμος	ἐγένετο	ἐν	Κανὰ	τῆς
hēmera	*gamos*	*egeneto*	*en*	*Kana*	*tēs*
day]	a marriage	took place	in	Cana	

There is a parallel between Jacob and Nathanael. The experience of both these men happened in a solitary place. Jacob's vision was only the beginning of his encounters with his God. The "greater things" which Jesus told Nathanael he would see would be the unfolding glory of God. Nathanael did indeed see a multitude of miracles. He heard the truth expounded as no other man ever gave it. Nathanael was a witness of the resurrection and ascension of the Son of God. He was the recipient of the glorious baptism in the Holy Spirit on the Day of Pentecost. He "saw" God at work throughout his life and ministry.

50. Jesus answered and said unto him, Because I said unto thee, I saw thee under the fig tree, believest thou?: Is this the ground of your faith, *NEB* . . . You believe because I told you, *Beck* . . . You have faith because I said to you, *BB* . . . "Do you really believe," asked Jesus, *Fenton.*

thou shalt see greater things than these: You should be viewing greater things, *Concordant.*

1:51. The word "verily" (*amēn*) is a Hebrew word of response meaning "truly," and is also rendered "indeed." John's Gospel is the only one that records Jesus' double use of it. The repetition gives emphasis.

"I say unto you" (*legō humin*) carries the ring of authority. In some places where Jesus used these words, as in the Sermon on the Mount (Matthew chapters 5 to 7), He presented His interpretation of the Old Testament as the only valid one.

The declaration "ye shall see heaven open" affirmed that great disclosures were about to be given. Heaven was only partly opened for man to view under the Old Testament disclosures. God was behind the veil. The people could see "good things to come" only by shadows cast by rituals, events, and holy men who spoke and represented the ideal Shepherd, King, Prophet, Priest, etc. In Jesus the heavens are opened.

"And the angels of God ascending and descending" brings to mind the vision of Jacob (Genesis 28:12). The allusion to Jacob's dream of a great, wide ladder is clear, but with Jesus there is no ladder. When Jesus said, "Ye shall see . . . ," He used the plural word for "you" (*opsesthe*). He no longer was speaking solely to Nathanael, but to all the disciples. Christ was not making a prediction of special angelic appearances. He was predicting the unfolding of God in the full revelation contained in himself. The ladder showed Jacob that heaven was open and God is accessible. Jesus is the "new and living (resurrected) way" to God (Hebrews 10:20). By Him we have free access to the very throne of God.

51. And he saith unto him, verily, verily, I say unto you, Hereafter ye shall see heaven open: Amen, amen, *Confraternity* . . . Most assuredly, *Campbell, Wuest* . . . I most solemnly say to you all, *Williams* . . . This is the truth I tell you, you will see heaven standing wide open, *Barclay* . . . the sky open, *Adams* . . . opened wide, *Weymouth* . . . heaven wide open, *TCNT.*

and the angels of God ascending and descending upon the Son of man: . . . the messengers of God, *Young, Klingensmith* . . . going up and coming down upon, *Williams* . . . coming down and going up from me, *SEB* . . . upon the Son of Mankind, *Concordant.*

2:1,2. It was at a wedding that Jesus entered upon His public ministry. Weddings were special occasions. Betrothals were sometimes years before the wedding. The wedding itself lasted as many as 7 days.

The most likely location of this Cana was 9 miles north of Nazareth. Nathanael was from this village. It is interesting that the fulfillment of the promise of "greater things" was begun in Nathanael's own town.

1. And the third day there was a marriage in Cana of Galilee: Two days afterwards, *Knox* . . . there was a wedding, *TCNT* . . . a marriage festival took place, *Wuest* . . . a wedding occurred, *Concordant.*

John 2:2

1049.2 name gen sing fem	2504.1 conj	1498.34 verb sing indic imperf act	3450.9 art nom sing fem	3251.1 noun nom sing fem	3450.2 art gen sing
Γαλιλαίας·	καὶ	ἦν	ἡ	μήτηρ	τοῦ
Galilaias	*kai*	*ēn*	*hē*	*mētēr*	*tou*
of Galilee,	and	was	the	mother	

2400.2 name masc	1550.1 adv	2535.37 verb 3sing indic aor pass	1156.2 conj	2504.1 conj	3450.5 art sing masc	2400.1 name nom masc
Ἰησοῦ	ἐκεῖ·	**2.** ἐκλήθη	δὲ	καὶ	ὁ	Ἰησοῦς
Iēsou	*ekei*	*eklēthē*	*de*	*kai*	*ho*	*Iēsous*
of Jesus	there.	Was invited	and	also		Jesus

2504.1 conj	3450.7 art pl masc	3073.5 noun nom pl masc	840.3 prs-pron gen sing	1519.1 prep	3450.6 art acc sing masc	1055.3 noun acc sing masc
καὶ	οἱ	μαθηταὶ	αὐτοῦ	εἰς	τὸν	γάμον.
kai	*hoi*	*mathētai*	*autou*	*eis*	*ton*	*gamon*
and	the	disciples	his	to	the	marriage.

3.a.**Var:** 01א-org,it.Tisc

2504.1 conj	5139.7 verb gen sing masc part aor act	3494.2 noun gen sing masc	3494.4 noun acc sing masc	3620.2 partic
3. καὶ	⸀ ὑστερήσαντος	οἴνου	[a οἶνον	οὐκ
kai	*husterēsantos*	*oinou*	*oinon*	*ouk*
And	lacking	wine	[wine	not

2174.42 verb indic imperf act	3617.1 conj	4783.7 verb 3sing indic aor pass	3450.5 art sing masc	3494.1 noun nom sing masc	3450.2 art gen sing
εἶχον,	ὅτι	συνετελέσθη	ὁ	οἶνος	τοῦ
eichon	*hoti*	*sunetelesthē*	*ho*	*oinos*	*tou*
they had,	because	was given out	the	wine	of the

1055.2 noun gen sing masc	1520.1 adv	2978.5 verb 3sing indic pres act	3450.9 art nom sing fem	3251.1 noun nom sing fem	3450.2 art gen sing
γάμου.	εἶτα]	λέγει	ἡ	μήτηρ	τοῦ
gamou	*eita*	*legei*	*hē*	*mētēr*	*tou*
wedding.	Then]	says	the	mother	

2400.2 name masc	4242.1 prep	840.6 prs-pron acc sing masc	3494.4 noun acc sing masc	3620.2 partic	2174.6 verb 3pl indic pres act
Ἰησοῦ	πρὸς	αὐτόν,	⸀ Οἶνον	οὐκ	ἔχουσιν.
Iēsou	*pros*	*auton*	*Oinon*	*ouk*	*echousin*
of Jesus	to	him,	Wine	not	they have.

3.b.**Var:** 01א-org,Tisc

4.a.**Var:** p66,01א-corr, 02A,03B,017K,019L, 032W,037,038,13,bo. LachTreg,Alf,We/Ho, Weis,Sod,UBS/☆

3494.1 noun nom sing masc	3620.2 partic	1498.4 verb 3sing indic pres act		2504.1 conj	2978.5 verb 3sing indic pres act
[b οἶνος	οὐκ	ἔστιν.]	**4.** [a☆+	καὶ]	Λέγει
oinos	*ouk*	*estin*		*kai*	*Legei*
[wine	not	there is.]		[and]	Says

840.11 prs-pron dat sing fem	3450.5 art sing masc	2400.1 name nom masc	4949.9 intr-pron sing neu	1466.5 prs-pron dat 1sing	2504.1 conj
αὐτῇ	ὁ	Ἰησοῦς,	Τί	ἐμοὶ	καὶ
autē	*ho*	*Iēsous*	*Ti*	*emoi*	*kai*
to her		Jesus,	What	to me	and

4622.3 prs-pron dat 2sing	1129.5 noun voc sing fem	3632.1 adv	2223.2 verb 3sing indic pres act	3450.9 art nom sing fem	5443.2 noun nom sing fem
σοί,	γύναι;	οὔπω	ἥκει	ἡ	ὥρα
soi	*gunai*	*oupō*	*hēkei*	*hē*	*hōra*
to you,	woman?	not yet	is come	the	hour

1466.2 prs-pron gen 1sing	2978.5 verb 3sing indic pres act	3450.9 art nom sing fem	3251.1 noun nom sing fem	840.3 prs-pron gen sing
μου.	**5.** Λέγει	ἡ	μήτηρ	αὐτοῦ
mou	*Legei*	*hē*	*mētēr*	*autou*
my.	Says	the	mother	his

Mary is never called by name in this Gospel. She was probably a relative or intimate friend of the bridegroom's family and was already there assisting in the preparations. Jesus and His disciples had received no previous invitation but were invited at this point because of His mother.

2:3. Mary knew more about the provisions for the wedding than did the other guests. She knew Eastern hospitality would consider a shortage of wine a disgraceful calamity. She also knew where to find the solution to the problem which faced them. She could have had in mind one of two solutions. First, she might have asked Jesus and His disciples to pool their money and go for wine in nearby villages. Or, second, she might have asked Him to supernaturally supply the wine. She had pondered many things in her heart ever since Jesus' supernatural birth. Doubtless she heard John the Baptist's announcement of Jesus as the Messiah. She was also aware that Jesus' ministry had begun.

2:4. The Lord's answer to Mary seems to be either a denial or a test of her confidence that He would do something to remedy the situation. What Jesus says is never a wall to faith, but it is sometimes a hurdle to overcome. Jesus wanted Mary to learn that her faith in Him was the only means by which she might initiate His action.

"Woman" is not a disrespectful term, but it does seem to keep her claim as His mother at a distance. "What have I to do with thee?" is a phrase of refusal or protest, possibly a protest against the reasons or motives in her mind.

Several meanings are possible as to what Jesus meant by "mine hour." First, Jesus might have meant that at His wedding feast, He will be responsible to supply the refreshment, but this feast in Cana was not His obligation. We know the Marriage Supper of the Lamb is coming (Revelation 19:7-9). Second, Jesus might have been indicating His hour of crucifixion. The reference to His "hour" often meant His hour of suffering (7:30; 8:20). The third meaning is the most probable; it was that the hour of His public manifestation had not come.

2:5. Obviously Mary was satisfied with Jesus' answer concerning His "hour." It was probably the word "yet" (verse 4) that caused her to proceed as she did. Mary left the solution in the hands of Jesus. She believed He would remedy the situation. True faith wants only the will of the Lord to be done. Faith, furthermore,

and the mother of Jesus was there: . . . was present, *Fenton.*

2. And both Jesus was called, and his disciples, to the marriage: Jesus was invited, *HBIE* . . . with his disciples, *BB* . . . were also guests, *ET* . . . to the festivities, *Phillips.*

3. And when they wanted wine, the mother of Jesus saith unto him, They have no wine: . . . the supply of wine gave out, *Phillips* . . . The wine ran out, *ALBA* . . . the wine ran short, *Fenton* . . . the wine fell short, *Murdock* . . . the supply of wine having failed, *Wuest* . . . "They have no more wine," *NIV.*

4. Jesus saith unto her:

Woman, what have I to do with thee?: You must not try to tell me what to do, *Barclay* . . . Of what concern, *Adams* . . . What do you want with me, *SEB* . . . this is not your business, *BB* . . . why turn to me? *JB* . . . what business is that of mine? *Klingensmith* . . . why do you involve me? *NIV* . . . Is that your concern, or mine, *Phillips* . . . why concern ourselves? *Clementson.*

mine hour is not yet come: My time to act, *Williams* . . . My time is not here yet, *Berkeley* . . . It isn't the right time yet, *Beck* . . . I am not yet ready to act, *Weymouth.*

5. His mother saith unto the servants, Whatsoever he saith unto you, do it: . . . to the attendants, *Fenton* . . . the waiters,

3450.4 art dat pl	1243.4 noun dat pl masc	3614.16 rel-pron sing neu	4948.10 indef-pron sing neu	300.1 partic	2978.7 verb 3sing subj pres act
τοῖς	διακόνοις,	Ὅ	τι	ἂν	λέγῃ
tois	*diakonois*	*Ho*	*ti*	*an*	*legē*
to the	servants,	What	ever		he may say

5050.3 prs-pron dat 2pl	4020.36 verb 2pl impr aor act	1498.37 verb 3pl indic imperf act	1156.2 conj	1550.1 adv	5042.2 noun nom pl fem
ὑμῖν,	ποιήσατε.	6. Ἦσαν	δὲ	ἐκεῖ	⸂ ὑδρίαι
humin	*poiēsate*	*Esan*	*de*	*ekei*	*hudriai*
to you,	do.	There were	and	there	water vessels

6.a.**Txt:** 02A,036,037, 038,041,1,byz.Lach **Var:** p66,p75,01ℵ,03B, 019L,032W,33,Treg,Alf, Tisc,We/Ho,Weis,Sod, UBS/☆

3009.1 adj nom pl fem	3009.1 adj nom pl fem	5042.2 noun nom pl fem	1787.1 num card	2719.8 verb nom pl fem part pres
λίθιναι	[☆ λίθιναι	ὑδρίαι]	ἓξ	⸂[a] κείμεναι ⸃
lithinai	*lithinai*	*hudriai*	*hex*	*keimenai*
of stone	[stone	water vessels]	six	standing

2567.3 prep	3450.6 art acc sing masc	2484.2 noun acc sing masc	3450.1 art gen pl	2428.3 name-adj gen pl masc
κατὰ	τὸν	καθαρισμὸν	τῶν	Ἰουδαίων,
kata	*ton*	*katharismon*	*tōn*	*Ioudaiōn*
according to	the	purification	of the	Jews,

6.b.**Var:** p66,p75, 01ℵ-corr,03B,019L, 032W,Treg,Alf,Tisc, We/Ho,Weis,Sod,UBS/☆

2719.8 verb nom pl fem part pres	5397.4 verb nom pl fem part pres act	301.1 adv	3225.1 noun acc pl masc	1411.3 num card	2211.1 conj
[b☆+ κείμεναι,]	χωροῦσαι	ἀνὰ	μετρητὰς	δύο	ἢ
keimenai	*chōrousai*	*ana*	*metrētas*	*duo*	*ē*
[standing,]	holding	each	firkins	two	or

4980.1 num card nom	2978.5 verb 3sing indic pres act	840.2 prs-pron dat pl	3450.5 art sing masc	2400.1 name nom masc	1065.3 verb 2pl impr aor act
τρεῖς.	7. λέγει	αὐτοῖς	ὁ	Ἰησοῦς,	Γεμίσατε
treis	*legei*	*autois*	*ho*	*Iēsous*	*Gemisate*
three.	Says	to them		Jesus,	Fill

3450.15 art acc pl fem	5042.3 noun acc pl fem	5045.2 noun gen sing neu	2504.1 conj	1065.2 verb 3pl indic aor act	840.13 prs-pron pl fem
τὰς	ὑδρίας	ὕδατος.	Καὶ	ἐγέμισαν	αὐτὰς
tas	*hudrias*	*hudatos*	*Kai*	*egemisan*	*autas*
the	water vessels	with water.	And	they filled	them

2175.1 conj	504.1 adv	2504.1 conj	2978.5 verb 3sing indic pres act	840.2 prs-pron dat pl	498.2 verb 2pl impr aor act	3431.1 adv
ἕως	ἄνω.	8. Καὶ	λέγει	αὐτοῖς,	Ἀντλήσατε	νῦν
heōs	*anō*	*Kai*	*legei*	*autois*	*Antlēsate*	*nun*
unto	brim.	And	he says	to them,	Draw out	now

8.a.**Txt:** 02A,036,037, 038,13,byz.it.Gries,Lach **Var:** 01ℵ,03B,017K, 019L,041,1,33,bo.Treg, Alf,Tisc,We/Ho,Weis, Sod,UBS/☆

2504.1 conj	5179.1 verb 2pl pres act	3450.3 art dat sing	750.2 noun dat sing masc	2504.1 conj	3450.7 art pl masc
καὶ	φέρετε	τῷ	ἀρχιτρικλίνῳ.	⸂ Καὶ	[a☆ οἱ
kai	*pherete*	*tō*	*architriklinō*	*Kai*	*hoi*
and	carry	to the	master of the feast.	And	[the

1156.2 conj	5179.15 verb 3pl indic aor act	5453.1 conj	1156.2 conj	1083.1 verb 3sing indic aor mid	3450.5 art sing masc
δὲ]	ἤνεγκαν.	9. ὡς	δὲ	ἐγεύσατο	ὁ
de	*ēnenkan*	*hōs*	*de*	*egeusato*	*ho*
and]	they carried.	When	but	had tasted	the

750.1 noun nom sing masc	3450.16 art sing neu	5045.1 noun sing neu	3494.4 noun acc sing masc	1090.66 verb acc sing neu part perf pass
ἀρχιτρίκλινος	τὸ	ὕδωρ	οἶνον	γεγενημένον,
architriklinos	*to*	*hudōr*	*oinon*	*gegenēmenon*
master of the feast	the	water	wine	that had become,

acquiesces to God's own means and methods to perform His will. The servants were slaves who poured the wine.

We see here a striking example of proper recognition of authority. Jesus knew at age 12 who He was, but He subjected himself to the authority of Mary and Joseph (Luke 2:51). Now the time had come that He was subject only to the Father (5:30). Mary recognized that she was under Jesus' authority. She was then free to exercise her authority over the servants.

Berkeley . . . do it with dispatch, *Wuest* . . . Do whatever he shall bid you, *Campbell.*

2:6. John's Gospel records details in order to show the extent of the miracles. This is the first of seven selected miracles in the book.

The stone jars were empty inasmuch as the guests' feet had been washed by the water the jars had contained. The jars may have varied in size from 18 to 27 gallons. Thus, the total amount of water changed to wine may have been about 135 gallons. From this we gather that Jesus supplied more than enough. The wine left over was surely a gracious gift to the newlyweds. What Jesus achieved, He did in a grand fashion. His gifts proceed from His grace which is boundless.

God's "exceeding abundantly above all that we ask" (Ephesians 3:20) was seen also in the 12 baskets of bread and fish left over after the multitude had eaten (John 6:13) and in the 153 fish in the net when the apostles obeyed (John 21:11).

6. And there were set there six water pots of stone, after the manner of the purifying of the Jews: . . . meant for the ablutions that are customary among the Jews, *JB* . . . used for the ritualistic ablutions, *Wuest* . . . for the Jewish ceremonial cleansing, *Phillips* . . . for the religious washings, *Beck.*

containing two or three firkins apiece: . . . large enough to hold twenty gallons or more, *Weymouth.*

2:7,8. Jesus gave the servants (verse 5) a natural, menial task to perform. They little realized the miracle in which they were becoming involved.

Jesus' commands are sometimes strange to human nature. First, He said, "Fill." Second, He asserted, "Draw." Third, He ordered, "Bear unto the governor of the feast." These three imperative verbs stating Jesus' commands were obeyed. Somewhere between the drawing and the taking to the governor of the feast, the water was changed into wine.

7. Jesus saith unto them, Fill the waterpots with water: . . . the water jars at once, *Wuest.*

And they filled them up to the brim: . . . them even to the top, *Wuest.*

8. And he saith to them, Draw out now, and bear unto the governor of the feast: Now take a dip and carry it to the table manager! *Berkeley* . . . Draw a sample now, *ALBA* . . . Now pour out, and take it to the master of the festival, *Fenton* . . . and carry it to the table-manager! *Berkeley* . . . dip out some and bring it to the head steward, *Norlie* . . . the director, *Campbell* . . . the feast-ruler, *Panin* . . . to the supervisor, *Wuest* . . . chief of the dining room, *Concordant* . . . to the president of the feast, *Rotherham* . . . of the banquet, *NIV.*

And they bare it: So they took him some, *Williams.*

2:9. The governor of the feast was usually a slave who superintended the arrangements for the wedding party and saw to the comfort and well-being of the guests. He was like a butler or cupbearer who protected the health of those invited. Contaminated food or wine would cause embarrassment and possible harm to the marriage family.

9. When the ruler of the feast had tasted the water that was made wine: . . . the water now become wine, *Alford* . . . which had now become wine, *TCNT.*

2:10. Was it good wine? The governor of the feast was elated at its quality. He expressed his surprise that the groom had reversed

2504.1 conj	**3620.2** partic	**3471.11** verb 3sing indic plperf act	**4019.1** adv	**1498.4** verb 3sing indic pres act	**3450.7** art pl masc	**1156.2** conj
καὶ	οὐκ	ᾔδει	πόθεν	ἐστίν·	οἱ	δὲ
kai	*ouk*	*ēdei*	*pothen*	*estin*	*hoi*	*de*
and	not	knew	from where	it is,	the	but

1243.3 noun nom pl masc	**3471.13** verb 3pl indic plperf act	**3450.7** art pl masc	**498.4** verb nom pl masc part perf act	**3450.16** art sing neu	**5045.1** noun sing neu
διάκονοι	ᾔδεισαν	οἱ	ἠντληκότες	τὸ	ὕδωρ·
diakonoi	*ēdeisan*	*hoi*	*ēntlēkotes*	*to*	*hudōr*
servants	knew	the	had drawn	the	water,

5291.1 verb 3sing indic pres act	**3450.6** art acc sing masc	**3429.3** noun acc sing masc	**3450.5** art sing masc	**750.1** noun nom sing masc
φωνεῖ	τὸν	νυμφίον	ὁ	ἀρχιτρίκλινος
phōnei	*ton*	*numphion*	*ho*	*architriklinos*
calls	the	bridegroom	the	master of the feast

2504.1 conj	**2978.5** verb 3sing indic pres act	**840.4** prs-pron dat sing	**3820.6** adj sing masc	**442.1** noun nom sing masc	**4270.1** adv
10. καὶ	λέγει	αὐτῷ,	Πᾶς	ἄνθρωπος	πρῶτον
kai	*legei*	*autō*	*Pas*	*anthrōpos*	*prōton*
and	says	to him,	Every	man	first

3450.6 art acc sing masc	**2541.1** adj sing	**3494.4** noun acc sing masc	**4935.2** verb 3sing indic pres act	**2504.1** conj	**3615.1** conj
τὸν	καλὸν	οἶνον	τίθησιν,	καὶ	ὅταν
ton	*kalon*	*oinon*	*tithēsin*	*kai*	*hotan*
the	good	wine	sets on,	and	when

10.a.**Txt:** 01א-corr,02A, 017K,036,037,038,1,13, byz.LachTreg,Alf,Weis, Sod
Var: p66,p75,01א-org, 03B,019L,sa.bo.Tisc, We/Ho,UBS/*

3155.6 verb 3pl subj aor pass	**4966.1** adv	**3450.6** art acc sing masc	**1629.2** adj comp acc sing masc
μεθυσθῶσιν	⸂a τότε⸃	τὸν	ἐλάσσω·
methusthōsin	*tote*	*ton*	*elassō*
they may have gotten drunk	then	the	inferior;

4622.1 prs-pron nom 2sing	**4931.23** verb 2sing indic perf act	**3450.6** art acc sing masc	**2541.1** adj sing	**3494.4** noun acc sing masc	**2175.1** conj
σὺ	τετήρηκας	τὸν	καλὸν	οἶνον	ἕως
su	*tetērēkas*	*ton*	*kalon*	*oinon*	*heōs*
you	have kept	the	good	wine	until

11.a.**Txt:** 01א,017K, 032W,036,037,13,byz.
Var: p66-corr,p75,02A, 03B,019L,038,33,Lach, Treg,Alf,Tisc,We/Ho, WeisSod,UBS/*

732.1 adv	**3642.12** dem-pron acc sing fem	**4020.24** verb 3sing indic aor act	**3450.12** art acc sing fem	**741.4** noun acc sing fem
ἄρτι.	**11.** Ταύτην	ἐποίησεν	⸂a τὴν⸃	ἀρχὴν
arti	*Tautēn*	*epoiēsen*	*tēn*	*archēn*
now.	This	did	the	beginning

3450.1 art gen pl	**4447.3** noun gen pl neu	**3450.5** art sing masc	**2400.1** name nom masc	**1706.1** prep	**2551.2** name fem	**3450.10** art gen sing fem
τῶν	σημείων	ὁ	Ἰησοῦς	ἐν	Κανὰ	τῆς
tōn	*sēmeiōn*	*ho*	*Iēsous*	*en*	*Kana*	*tēs*
of the	signs		Jesus	in	Cana	

1049.2 name gen sing fem	**2504.1** conj	**5157.3** verb 3sing indic aor act	**3450.12** art acc sing fem	**1385.4** noun acc sing fem	**840.3** prs-pron gen sing
Γαλιλαίας,	καὶ	ἐφανέρωσεν	τὴν	δόξαν	αὐτοῦ·
Galilaias	*kai*	*ephanerōsen*	*tēn*	*doxan*	*autou*
of Galilee,	and	manifested	the	glory	his;

2504.1 conj	**3961.23** verb 3pl indic aor act	**1519.1** prep	**840.6** prs-pron acc sing masc	**3450.7** art pl masc	**3073.5** noun nom pl masc	**840.3** prs-pron gen sing
καὶ	ἐπίστευσαν	εἰς	αὐτὸν	οἱ	μαθηταὶ	αὐτοῦ.
kai	*episteusan*	*eis*	*auton*	*hoi*	*mathētai*	*autou*
and	believed	on	him	the	disciples	his.

the usual custom. At the beginning of a feast the host wished to impress the guests by giving the very best. The governor of the feast attested to the superior taste of the wine Jesus produced from only water. The Creator who produces wine from sunshine, air, soil, and water can, as well, omit some of the ingredients or speed up the process.

The question of what wine is good wine will not be settled for everyone. The word is used of unfermented wine at times, such as in Matthew 9:17. The word can also mean fermented wine as in Ephesians 5:18 and Revelation 17:2. Since its purpose was to show Christ's creative power, it seems more likely that it was unfermented, for fermentation is a process of decay.

The point to be remembered is that John's Gospel presents evidence of a supernatural miracle attested to by an accredited witness who was unaware of the source of the wine.

2:11. "This beginning of miracles" points to this sign as the first in Jesus' public manifestation as the Messiah. It also shows that the miracles described in the Second Century A.D. "Infancy Gospels" are false.

The indication is that more signs will follow. A sign (*sēmeion*) is a miracle which marks an evidence of the reality in Christ as the Logos (1:14). John's Gospel emphasizes eight signs or miracles as testimonials to its theme—the deity of Christ.

"Did . . . in Cana of Galilee" refers to the little, obscure village in which Jesus chose to begin His ministry of universal import. His first miracle was done in the district of His residence. John regularly used the same Greek word for *miracle* (sign). There are other synonyms which are translated in the King James Version as "miracle." The second one is *teras*, "wonders" (John 4:48; Acts 2:22). The third word is *dunamis*, "mighty works" (Mark 6:2; 9:39). The last is more numerous and general in meaning. Thus John pointed to this sign as a manifestation of Jesus' glory.

Jesus manifested His glory revealing who He was by the deeds He performed. When His person and nature were seen by His action, the disciples believed (and trusted) in Him. What He had declared in word was now demonstrated by His deed. Their faith ("believed on him") was expanded because their understanding increased with each gleam of glory from the Sunrise ("dayspring," Luke 1:78, KJV). Notice it was the disciples who believed, not the guests, not the wedding party or the servants.

2:12. A number of reasons may be assumed for Jesus changing His residence from Nazareth to Capernaum. First, Nazareth was in a small side valley, somewhat off the caravan route, with a limited

and knew not whence it was: . . . not knowing its source, *NEB.*

(but the servants which drew the water knew;) the governor of the feast called the bridegroom: He rebuked the groom, *ET.*

10. And saith unto him, Every man at the beginning doth set forth good wine; and when men have well drunk: The normal practice, *ALBA* . . . A man usually serves out the best, *Fenton* . . . People generally serve the best wine first, *JB* . . . serve the fine wine first, *Adams* . . . as a rule...after people have drunk freely, *Williams* . . . when men have had plenty to drink, *Phillips* . . . drank plentifully, *Scarlett* . . . whensoever they may be well-supplied, *Rotherham* . . . when the guests have drunk freely, *Norton* . . . as soon as the guests have drunk deeply, *TCNT.*

then that which is worse: . . . the inferior, *Rotherham* . . . the cheaper sort, *JB* . . . the poor stuff, *Phillips.*

but thou hast kept the good wine until now: . . . but you have retained, *Berkeley.*

11. This beginning of miracles did Jesus in Cana of Galilee: He thereby revealed His greatness, *Norlie* . . . That was how Jesus inaugurated his, *ALBA* . . . gave this first demonstration of the power of God in action, *Barclay* . . . this earliest of his signs, *Berkeley* . . . of His wonder-works, *Williams* . . . of His evidences, *Fenton* . . . displaying his glory, *Campbell.*

and manifested forth his glory: His glorious power, *Williams* . . . and displayed His majesty, *Fenton* . . . and manifested his glory, *Alford.*

and his disciples believed on him: . . . his disciples put their faith in him, *BB* . . . led his disciples to believe, *NEB* . . . his students, *Klingensmith.*

John 2:12

12.a.**Txt:** p66-corr,01ℵ, 02A,017K,032W,036, 037,038,1,13,byz.it.sa. bo.Gries,Lach,AlfTisc
Var: p66-org,p75,03B, 019L,016I2,Treg,We/Ho Weis,Sod,UBS/☆

3196.3 prep	**3642.17** dem-pron sing neu	**2568.14** verb 3sing indic aor act	**1519.1** prep	**2555.1** name fem
12. Μετὰ	τοῦτο	κατέβη	εἰς	ʼ Καπερναοὺμ,
Meta	*touto*	*katebē*	*eis*	*Kapernaoum*
After	this	he went down	to	Capernaum,

2555.2 name fem	**840.5** prs-pron nom sing masc	**2504.1** conj	**3450.9** art nom sing fem	**3251.1** noun nom sing fem
[☆ Καφαρναοὺμ]	αὐτὸς	καὶ	ἡ	μήτηρ
Kapharnaoum	*autos*	*kai*	*hē*	*mētēr*
[idem]	he	and	the	mother

840.3 prs-pron gen sing	**2504.1** conj	**3450.7** art pl masc	**79.6** noun pl masc	**840.3** prs-pron gen sing	**2504.1** conj	**3450.7** art pl masc
αὐτοῦ	καὶ	οἱ	ἀδελφοὶ	ʼa αὐτοῦ ˎ	καὶ	οἱ
autou	*kai*	*hoi*	*adelphoi*	*autou*	*kai*	*hoi*
his	and	the	brothers	his	and	the

3073.5 noun nom pl masc	**840.3** prs-pron gen sing	**2504.1** conj	**1550.1** adv	**3176.18** verb 3pl indic aor act	**3620.3** partic	**4044.15** adj acc pl fem
μαθηταὶ	αὐτοῦ,	καὶ	ἐκεῖ	ἔμειναν	οὐ	πολλὰς
mathētai	*autou*	*kai*	*ekei*	*emeinan*	*ou*	*pollas*
disciples	his,	and	there	they remained	not	many

2232.1 noun fem	**2504.1** conj	**1445.1** adv	**1498.34** verb sing indic imperf act	**3450.16** art sing neu	**3818.1** noun sing neu
ἡμέρας.	**13.** Καὶ	ἐγγὺς	ἦν	τὸ	πάσχα
hēmeras	*Kai*	*engus*	*ēn*	*to*	*pascha*
days.	And	near	was	the	passover

3450.1 art gen pl	**2428.3** name-adj gen pl masc	**2504.1** conj	**303.13** verb 3sing indic aor act	**1519.1** prep	**2389.1** name
τῶν	Ἰουδαίων,	καὶ	ἀνέβη	εἰς	Ἱεροσόλυμα
tōn	*Ioudaiōn*	*kai*	*anebē*	*eis*	*Hierosoluma*
of the	Jews,	and	went up	to	Jerusalem

3450.5 art sing masc	**2400.1** name nom masc	**2504.1** conj	**2128.8** verb 3sing indic aor act	**1706.1** prep	**3450.3** art dat sing
ὁ	Ἰησοῦς.	**14.** καὶ	εὗρεν	ἐν	τῷ
ho	*Iēsous*	*kai*	*heuren*	*en*	*tō*
	Jesus.	And	he found	in	the

2387.2 adj dat sing neu	**3450.8** art acc pl masc	**4310.5** verb acc pl masc part pres act	**1009.4** noun acc pl masc	**2504.1** conj	**4122.3** noun pl neu
ἱερῷ	τοὺς	πωλοῦντας	βόας	καὶ	πρόβατα
hierō	*tous*	*pōlountas*	*boas*	*kai*	*probata*
temple	the	selling	oxen	and	sheep

2504.1 conj	**3918.4** noun acc pl fem	**2504.1** conj	**3450.8** art acc pl masc	**2744.1** noun acc pl masc
καὶ	περιστερὰς,	καὶ	τοὺς	κερματιστὰς
kai	*peristeras*	*kai*	*tous*	*kermatistas*
and	doves,	and	the	money changers

2493.12 verb acc pl masc part pres	**2504.1** conj	**4020.37** verb nom sing masc part aor act	**5252.1** noun acc sing neu	**1523.2** prep gen
καθημένους·	**15.** καὶ	ποιήσας	φραγέλλιον	ἐκ
kathēmenous	*kai*	*poiēsas*	*phragellion*	*ek*
sitting;	and	having made	a scourge	of

4831.1 noun gen pl neu	**3820.8** adj acc pl masc	**1531.11** verb 3sing indic aor act	**1523.2** prep gen	**3450.2** art gen sing	**2387.1** adj gen sing neu
σχοινίων	πάντας	ἐξέβαλεν	ἐκ	τοῦ	ἱεροῦ,
schoiniōn	*pantas*	*exebalen*	*ek*	*tou*	*hierou*
cords	all	he drove out	from	the	temple,

population. Second, many of Jesus' disciples lived near Capernaum. Third, Capernaum was a hub of human activity, affording a rich field for His ministry. Fourth, Nazareth had rejected Jesus' claim as Messiah.

Jesus seems to be the head of the family now, since His mother and His brothers accompanied Him to Capernaum. His brothers were sons of Mary and Joseph after Jesus' virgin birth. Mary probably had four sons after Jesus: James the Just, Joseph (Joses), Simon, and Jude (Judas) (Matthew 13:55).

12. After this he went down to Capernaum, he, and his mother, and his brethren, and his disciples: and they continued there not many days: He descended down into, *Concordant* . . . Subsequently he went down, *ALBA* . . . accompanied by his mother, *Phillips* . . . but they stayed there only a few days, *JB* . . . for a few days, *Berkeley, SEB.*

2:13. After a short stay in Capernaum Jesus went to Jerusalem. The Passover celebrated the Jews' deliverance from bondage in Egypt nearly 15 centuries before. At this Passover the nation was to view God's Lamb. Jesus inaugurated His institutional claims as the Messiah at the temple. There also His ministry ended 3 years later.

From Capernaum to Jerusalem would be a rise of about 3,000 feet in elevation, yet Jerusalem was considered "up" figuratively speaking also. Malachi had predicted that the Lord "whom ye seek" would suddenly come to His temple (Malachi 3:1). The Lord asserted His authority over the temple by cleansing it.

13. And the Jews' passover was at hand, and Jesus went up to Jerusalem: . . . was shortly to be observed, *Barclay* . . . was about to be observed, *Wuest* . . . when it was almost time for, *NIV.*

14. And found in the temple those that sold oxen and sheep and doves, and the changers of money sitting: . . . on the Temple grounds, *Adams* . . . In the Temple Courts...and the bankers seated there, *TCNT* . . . seated in the outer courts...who were in the habit...and those who for a fee exchanged one type of money for another, *Wuest* . . . seated inside the temple, dealers in cattle, *Moffatt* . . . seated at their tables, *NEB* . . . transacting their business, *Fenton.*

2:14. The temple had three courts: the Court of the Gentiles, the Court of Israel, and the Court of the Priests. The first was the one in which "those that sold oxen and sheep and doves" transacted their sordid business. One can imagine the haggling accompanying the sales and the general confusion.

The worshiper was not permitted to give a Roman coin in support of the temple because such a coin was considered unholy. He must change his foreign money for sanctified coins. Jesus intimated this kind of money changing had become a fraud (Matthew 21:13).

15. And when he had made a scourge of small cords: . . . a rough whip, *Phillips* . . . So he plaited a scourge of rushes, *Montgomery* . . . made a lash out of cords, *Williams* . . . making a whip, *Concordant* . . . He plaited a whip, *Weymouth.*

he drove them all out of the temple, and the sheep, and the oxen: He forced all of them to leave the courtyard, *SEB* . . . He

2:15. Two cleansings of the temple are recorded. John's Gospel records the one at the outset of Jesus' ministry, and the Synoptics narrate the second cleansing during the Passion Week.

The "scourge," which is not mentioned in the second cleansing, is indicative of Jesus' holy zeal. His quickly improvising it of small cords showed that His righteous anger was motivating Him to lose no time.

Jesus dealt with each class of intruders according to its nature. He drove the oxen and sheep with the scourge. He scattered the coins to show the money-changers that speculating in mammon was

3450.17 art pl neu	4885.1 conj	4122.3 noun pl neu	2504.1 conj	3450.8 art acc pl masc	1009.4 noun acc pl masc	2504.1 conj	3450.1 art gen pl
τά	τε	πρόβατα	καὶ	τοὺς	βόας.	καὶ	τῶν
ta	*te*	*probata*	*kai*	*tous*	*boas*	*kai*	*tōn*
the	both	sheep	and	the	oxen;	and	of the

15.a.**Txt:** p66-org,01א,02A,017K,024P,036,037,038,13,byz.Lach,Tisc,Sod
Var: p66-corr,p75,03B,019L,032W,033X,016I2,33,bo.Treg,AlfWe/Ho,Weis,UBS/☆

2829.1 noun gen pl masc	1618.1 verb 3sing indic aor act	3450.16 art sing neu	2743.1 noun acc sing neu	3450.17 art pl neu
κολλυβιστῶν	ἐξέχεεν	⸂☆ τὸ	κέρμα	[a τα
kollubistōn	*execheen*	*to*	*kerma*	*ta*
money changers	he poured out	the	coin	[the

2743.2 noun pl neu	2504.1 conj	3450.15 art acc pl fem	4971.5 noun acc pl fem	388.1 verb 3sing indic aor act
κέρματα]	καὶ	τὰς	τραπέζας	⸂ ἀνέστρεψεν,
kermata	*kai*	*tas*	*trapezas*	*anestrepsen*
coins]	and	the	tables	turned.

15.b.**Txt:** p75,02A,017K,019L,024P,036,037,1,byz.Lach,Tisc,Sod
Var: p66,03B,032W,033X,038,016I2,We/Ho,Weis,UBS/☆

394.2 verb 3sing indic aor act	2504.1 conj	3450.4 art dat pl	3450.15 art acc pl fem	3918.4 noun acc pl fem
[b☆ ἀνέτρεψεν,]	**16.** καὶ	τοῖς	τὰς	περιστερὰς
anetrepsen	*kai*	*tois*	*tas*	*peristeras*
[idem]	And	to the	the	doves

4310.4 verb dat pl masc part pres act	1500.5 verb 3sing indic aor act	142.15 verb 2pl impr aor act	3642.18 dem-pron pl neu	1766.1 adv
πωλοῦσιν	εἶπεν,	Ἄρατε	ταῦτα	ἐντεῦθεν·
pōlousin	*eipen*	*Arate*	*tauta*	*enteuthen*
having sold	he said,	Take	these things	from here;

3231.1 partic	4020.2 verb 2pl pres act	3450.6 art acc sing masc	3486.4 noun acc sing masc	3450.2 art gen sing	3824.2 noun gen sing masc
μὴ	ποιεῖτε	τὸν	οἶκον	τοῦ	πατρός
mē	*poieite*	*ton*	*oikon*	*tou*	*patros*
not	make	the	house	of the	father

17.a.**Txt:** 02A,017K,024P,036,037,038,1,13,byz.Gries,Lach
Var: 01א,03B,019L,033X,bo.Treg,Alf,Tisc,We/HoWeis,Sod,UBS/☆

1466.2 prs-pron gen 1sing	3486.4 noun acc sing masc	1696.1 noun gen sing neu	3279.4 verb 3pl indic aor pass	1156.2 conj
μου	οἶκον	ἐμπορίου.	**17.** Ἐμνήσθησαν	⸂a δὲ ⸃
mou	*oikon*	*emporiou*	*Emnēsthēsan*	*de*
my	a house	of merchandise.	Remembered	and

3450.7 art pl masc	3073.5 noun nom pl masc	840.3 prs-pron gen sing	3617.1 conj	1119.29 verb sing neu part perf pass	1498.4 verb 3sing indic pres act
οἱ	μαθηταὶ	αὐτοῦ	ὅτι	γεγραμμένον	ἐστίν,
hoi	*mathētai*	*autou*	*hoti*	*gegrammenon*	*estin*
the	disciples	his	that	written	it is,

3450.5 art sing masc	2188.1 noun sing neu	3450.2 art gen sing	3486.2 noun gen sing masc	4622.2 prs-pron gen 2sing	2688.6 verb 3sing indic aor act
Ὁ	ζῆλος	τοῦ	οἴκου	σου	⸂ κατέφαγέν
Ho	*zēlos*	*tou*	*oikou*	*sou*	*katephagen*
The	zeal	of the	house	your	has eaten up

17.b.**Txt:** 13,Steph
Var: 01א,02A,03B,017K,019L,024P,036,037,038,041,Gries,Lach,Treg,Alf,Word,Tisc We/Ho,Weis,Sod,UBS/☆

2688.10 verb 3sing indic fut mid	1466.6 prs-pron acc 1sing	552.8 verb 3pl indic aor pass	3631.1 conj
[b☆ καταφάγεταί]	με.	**18.** Ἀπεκρίθησαν	οὖν
kataphagetai	*me*	*Apekrithēsan*	*oun*
[will consume]	me.	Answered	therefore

18.a.**Txt:** 01א,02A,017K,024P,036,037,038,byz.Sod
Var: 03B,019L,33,Lach,Treg,Alf,Tisc,We/Ho,Weis,UBS/☆

3450.7 art pl masc	2428.2 name-adj pl masc	2504.1 conj	1500.3 verb indic aor act	1500.28 verb 3pl indic aor act
οἱ	Ἰουδαῖοι	καὶ	⸂ εἶπον	[a☆ εἶπαν]
hoi	*Ioudaioi*	*kai*	*eipon*	*eipan*
the	Jews	and	said	[idem]

"out of order" in the house of God. Our Lord cleansed His house physically as a symbol of spiritual purification. "All" is a masculine word signifying those who sold as well as the animals they bought. Jesus demonstrated God's attitude toward those who hinder others from coming to and worshiping God in Spirit and in truth.

ejected from the outer courts, *Wuest* . . . he thrust all forth out, *Rotherham* . . . with the sheep and oxen, *BB.*

and poured out the changers' money, and overthrew the tables: He turned the money-exchangers' tables over, *SEB* . . . He pours out the change of the brokers, *Concordant* . . . knocked their tables over, *JB* . . . he poured out their money, *Murdock* . . . He scattered the coins, *Beck* . . . sending in all directions, *BB.*

2:16. Jesus did not say "our Father" but "my Father" because He was aware of His own special relationship with God. Jesus was not gentle with regard to sin. His position was identical with that of the Law. The Law was a disclosure of God's very attitude, revealed at Mount Sinai.

No one opposed Him in His action. The reason may be attributed to the authority expressed by His majestic demeanor, the authority of His words, and the persuasiveness of the deed. Surely some priests may have desired to do what Jesus did, and the majority of the godly people who came to the temple resented walking through something resembling a barn lot in approaching the true God whose name and nature is holy. Perhaps the authorities were fearful of a riot if they intervened.

16. And said unto them that sold doves, Take these things hence: . . . said to the pigeon-dealers, *Fenton* . . . Take away all these, *ALBA* . . . Take these things away, *RSV* . . . "Get these out of here! *NIV.*

make not my Father's house a house of merchandise: . . . a house of trade, *Montgomery* . . . a market-house, *TCNT* . . . a merchant's store, *Concordant* . . . a business place, *Adams* . . . a sales shop, *Berkeley* . . . a trading post, *Klingensmith.*

2:17. Notice how familiar the disciples were with the Scriptures. The quotation they remembered is from Psalm 69:9. The Messiah's zeal caused Him to be hated by His enemies, but He would have been negligent if He had not demonstrated by His actions God's attitude against flagrant abuses.

17. And his disciples remembered that it was written, The zeal of thine house hath eaten me up: . . . remembered these words, *Campbell* . . . I am on fire, *BB* . . . Concern for God's House will be My undoing! *LivB* . . . shall consume me, *Berkeley* . . . be devouring Me, *Concordant* . . . hath devoured me, *Murdock* . . . did eat me up, *Young* . . . burns within me! *SEB* . . . will destroy me, *NEB.*

2:18. We may rightly assume that the Levitical police of the temple reported Jesus' action to the captain of the guard, who in turn sought orders from the leaders of the Sanhedrin. Before long Jesus was confronted by "the Jews."

Throughout the Gospel of John, the term *Jew* has the meaning of "opposition" and refers to Jewish leaders, not to the mass of the people. From simple hostility, the attitudes and deeds of these leaders led them to the murder of the Messiah.

18. Then answered the Jews and said unto him, What sign shewest thou unto us, seeing that thou doest these things?: The Jews intervened and said, *JB* . . . What sign of authority do you

2:19. The verb "destroy" (*lusate*) is an aorist imperative of *luō* meaning "to loose" or "to break up into component parts," which in many cases means to destroy. The imperative mood of this verb

840.4 prs-pron dat sing	4949.9 intr-pron sing neu	4447.1 noun sing neu	1161.2 verb 2sing indic pres act	2231.3 prs-pron dat 1pl	3617.1 conj
αὐτῷ,	Τί	σημεῖον	δεικνύεις	ἡμῖν	ὅτι
autō	*Ti*	*sēmeion*	*deiknueis*	*hēmin*	*hoti*
to him,	What	sign	show you	to us	that

19.a.**Txt:** 01ℵ,017K,33, Steph
Var: 02A,03B,019L, 024P,036,037,038,byz. Lach,Treg,AlfWord,Tisc, We/Ho,Weis,Sod,UBS/⋆

3642.18 dem-pron pl neu	4020.4 verb 2sing indic pres act	552.6 verb 3sing indic aor pass	3450.5 art sing masc	2400.1 name nom masc
ταῦτα	ποιεῖς;	19. Ἀπεκρίθη	⸂a ὁ ⸃	Ἰησοῦς
tauta	*poieis*	*Apekrithē*	*ho*	*Iēsous*
these things	you do?	Answered		Jesus

2504.1 conj	1500.5 verb 3sing indic aor act	840.2 prs-pron dat pl	3061.12 verb 2pl impr aor act	3450.6 art acc sing masc	3348.4 noun acc sing masc
καὶ	εἶπεν	αὐτοῖς,	Λύσατε	τὸν	ναὸν
kai	*eipen*	*autois*	*Lusate*	*ton*	*naon*
and	said	to them,	Destroy	the	temple

3642.6 dem-pron acc sing masc	2504.1 conj	1706.1 prep	4980.3 num card dat	2232.7 noun dat pl fem	1446.11 verb 1sing indic fut act
τοῦτον,	καὶ	ἐν	τρισὶν	ἡμέραις	ἐγερῶ
touton	*kai*	*en*	*trisin*	*hēmerais*	*egerō*
this,	and	in	three	days	I will raise up

20.a.**Txt:** 01ℵ,02A,017K, 019L,024P,036,037,038, byz.Lach,Sod
Var: 03B,Treg,Alf,Tisc, We/HoWeis,UBS/⋆

840.6 prs-pron acc sing masc	1500.3 verb indic aor act	1500.28 verb 3pl indic aor act	3631.1 conj	3450.7 art pl masc
αὐτόν.	20. ⸀ Εἶπον	[a⋆ εἶπαν]	οὖν	οἱ
auton	*Eipon*	*eipan*	*oun*	*hoi*
it.	Said	[idem]	therefore	the

2428.2 name-adj pl masc	4910.2 num card	4910.1 num card	2504.1 conj
Ἰουδαῖοι,	⸀ Τεσσαράκοντα	[⋆ Τεσσεράκοντα]	καὶ
Ioudaioi	*Tessarakonta*	*Tesserakonta*	*kai*
Jews,	Forty	[idem]	and

20.b.**Txt:** 02A,03B-corr, 019L,024P,036,037,038, etc.byz.Lach,Sod
Var: 01ℵ,03B-org,33, Tisc,We/HoWeis,UBS/⋆

1787.1 num card	2073.5 noun dat pl neu	3481.18 verb 3sing indic aor pass	3481.23 verb 3sing indic aor pass	3450.5 art sing masc
ἓξ	ἔτεσιν	⸀ ᾠκοδομήθη	[b⋆ οἰκοδομήθη]	ὁ
hex	*etesin*	*ōkodomēthē*	*oikodomēthē*	*ho*
six	years	was building	[was built]	the

3348.1 noun nom sing masc	3642.4 dem-pron nom sing masc	2504.1 conj	4622.1 prs-pron nom 2sing	1706.1 prep	4980.3 num card dat	2232.7 noun dat pl fem
ναὸς	οὗτος,	καὶ	σὺ	ἐν	τρισὶν	ἡμέραις
naos	*houtos*	*kai*	*su*	*en*	*trisin*	*hēmerais*
temple	this,	and	you	in	three	days

1446.12 verb 2sing indic fut act	840.6 prs-pron acc sing masc	1552.3 dem-pron nom sing masc	1156.2 conj	2978.26 verb 3sing indic imperf act
ἐγερεῖς	αὐτόν;	21. Ἐκεῖνος	δὲ	ἔλεγεν
egereis	*auton*	*Ekeinos*	*de*	*elegen*
will raise up	it?	That one	but	spoke

3875.1 prep	3450.2 art gen sing	3348.2 noun gen sing masc	3450.2 art gen sing	4835.2 noun gen sing neu	840.3 prs-pron gen sing
περὶ	τοῦ	ναοῦ	τοῦ	σώματος	αὐτοῦ.
peri	*tou*	*naou*	*tou*	*sōmatos*	*autou*
concerning	the	temple	of the	body	his.

3616.1 conj	3631.1 conj	1446.20 verb 3sing indic aor pass	1523.2 prep gen	3361.2 adj gen pl
22. ὅτε	οὖν	ἠγέρθη	ἐκ	νεκρῶν
hote	*oun*	*ēgerthē*	*ek*	*nekrōn*
When	therefore	he was raised up	from among	dead

is a possible condition which edges toward an ironical command. In other words, Jesus was saying "you" (plural) "destroy this temple." Later the false witnesses against Jesus testified that Jesus claimed He would destroy the temple (Matthew 26:61; Mark 14:58). At the Crucifixion the passers-by repeated what the false witnesses had said (Matthew 27:40; Mark 15:29). But Jesus did not say "I"; He said, "(You) destroy this temple."

Our Lord was clearly foretelling His own resurrection. "In three days" means literally "in" or "during," i.e., within the space of 3 days.

Jesus asserted with all the authority of God himself that He possessed the power of His own resurrection. No man could make this claim. Jesus Christ is by nature and action God! This is not an isolated assertion, for He also said He had authority to lay down His life and take it again.

show us, *Norlie* . . . What authority can you show us, *Weymouth* . . . What proof do You show us, *Fenton* . . . What sign can you show us, to justify this action of yours? *ALBA* . . . your title to do these things? *Campbell* . . . for acting in this way, *Moffatt* . . . do you exhibit to us, *Weymouth* . . . to justify what you have done? *JB* . . . show us to back up your actions? *Adams* . . . since you act in this way? *TCNT.*

19. Jesus answered and said unto them, Destroy this temple, and in three days I will raise it up: Demolish this Sanctuary, *Weymouth* . . . Raze this temple, *Concordant* . . . in three days I will restore it, *Norlie* . . . erect it, *Murdock.*

2:20. "Forty and six years" was the time the temple had been in the process of being built, and the work was still in progress in the days of the Saviour. This temple, called Herod's temple, replaced the temple of Zerubbabel which was a rebuilding of Solomon's Temple and was finished in 516 B.C.

The Jews either misunderstood or misapplied Jesus' words. They pointed out the absurdity of raising the temple in 3 days as compared with 46 years. Their ignorance was surely a willful twisting of the Messiah's prophecy.

20. Then said the Jews, Forty and six years was this temple in building, and wilt thou rear it up in three days?: It has taken forty-six years to build this sanctuary, *JB.*

2:21. John's Gospel clears any possible misconception readers might have by stating what Jesus was talking about. "The temple of his body" indicated the temple God actually dwelt in. In Solomon's time the temple became God's earthly house. The temple rebuilt by Zerubbabel became God's house (Ezra 6:14). However, it had no ark, no cherubim, no glory cloud, and the Holy of Holies was totally empty. The same was true of Herod's magnificent temple. Jesus' body was the true temple of God on earth at that time.

Their destruction of His body-temple was His crucifixion. Jesus predicted that the Jews would kill Him. The prophecy was made early in His ministry (see 3:14).

21. But he spake of the temple of his body: . . . the temple Jesus had in mind, *ALBA* . . . But He meant the sanctuary of His body, *Williams* . . . that holy building, *BB* . . . His bodily temple, *Berkeley.*

2:22. The Father is said to raise the Son and Jesus said He would raise himself. What the Son does, the Father does. What the Father does, the Son does. God is triune: the three Persons in One work together. What is attributed to One can be attributed likewise to any Person in the Godhead.

22. When therefore he was risen from the dead: Afterwards, when he had, *TCNT* . . . Later on, when he had been raised, *ALBA* . . . had been raised from among, *Rotherham.*

John 2:23

3279.4 verb 3pl indic aor pass	3450.7 art pl masc	3073.5 noun nom pl masc	840.3 prs-pron gen sing	3617.1 conj	3642.17 dem-pron sing neu
ἐμνήσθησαν	οἱ	μαθηταὶ	αὐτοῦ	ὅτι	τοῦτο
emnēsthēsan	*hoi*	*mathētai*	*autou*	*hoti*	*touto*
remembered	the	disciples	his	that	this

22.a.**Txt:** 017K,041, Steph
Var: 01ℵ,02A,03B,019L, 024P,036,037,038,byz.it. bo.Gries,Lach,Treg,Alf, Word,Tisc,We/HoWeis, Sod,UBS/☆

2978.26 verb 3sing indic imperf act	840.2 prs-pron dat pl	2504.1 conj	3961.23 verb 3pl indic aor act	3450.11 art dat sing fem
ἔλεγεν	⸂a αὐτοῖς, ⸃	καὶ	ἐπίστευσαν	τῇ
elegen	*autois*	*kai*	*episteusan*	*tē*
he had said	to them,	and	believed	the

22.b.**Txt:** 02A,017K, 032W,036,037,038,1,13, etc.byz.Sod
Var: 01ℵ,03B,019L, Lach,TregAlf,Tisc, We/Ho,Weis,UBS/☆

1118.3 noun dat sing fem	2504.1 conj	3450.3 art dat sing	3030.3 noun dat sing masc	3614.3 rel-pron dat sing	3614.6 rel-pron acc sing masc
γραφῇ	καὶ	τῷ	λόγῳ	⸀ ᾧ	[b☆ ὃν]
graphē	*kai*	*tō*	*logō*	*hō*	*hon*
scripture	and	the	word	which	[idem]

1500.5 verb 3sing indic aor act	3450.5 art sing masc	2400.1 name nom masc		5453.1 conj	1156.2 conj	1498.34 verb sing indic imperf act
εἶπεν	ὁ	Ἰησοῦς.	23.	Ὡς	δὲ	ἦν
eipen	*ho*	*Iēsous*		*Hōs*	*de*	*ēn*
had spoken		Jesus.		When	but	he was

23.a.**Var:** 01ℵ,02A,03B, 017K,019L,024P,036, 037,038,Gries,LachTreg, Alf,Tisc,We/Ho,Weis, Sod,UBS/☆

1706.1 prep	3450.4 art dat pl	2389.3 name dat pl neu	1706.1 prep	3450.3 art dat sing	3818.1 noun sing neu
ἐν	[a☆+ τοῖς]	Ἱεροσολύμοις	ἐν	τῷ	πάσχα,
en	*tois*	*Hierosolumois*	*en*	*tō*	*pascha*
in		Jerusalem	at	the	passover,

1706.1 prep	3450.11 art dat sing fem	1844.3 noun dat sing fem	4044.7 adj nom pl masc	3961.23 verb 3pl indic aor act	1519.1 prep
ἐν	τῇ	ἑορτῇ,	πολλοὶ	ἐπίστευσαν	εἰς
en	*tē*	*heortē*	*polloi*	*episteusan*	*eis*
at	the	feast,	many	believed	on

3450.16 art sing neu	3549.2 noun sing neu	840.3 prs-pron gen sing	2311.11 verb nom pl masc part pres act	840.3 prs-pron gen sing	3450.17 art pl neu
τὸ	ὄνομα	αὐτοῦ,	θεωροῦντες	αὐτοῦ	τὰ
to	*onoma*	*autou*	*theōrountes*	*autou*	*ta*
the	name	his,	beholding	his	the

24.a.**Txt:** 01ℵ,02A,017K, 024P,032W,036,037, 038,1,13,etc.byz.Sod
Var: p66,p75,03B,019L, Lach,Treg,Alf,Tisc, We/HoWeis,UBS/☆

4447.2 noun pl neu	3614.17 rel-pron pl neu	4020.57 verb 3sing indic imperf act		840.5 prs-pron nom sing masc	1156.2 conj	3450.5 art sing masc
σημεῖα	ἃ	ἐποίει·	24.	αὐτὸς	δὲ	⸂a ὁ ⸃
sēmeia	*ha*	*epoiei*		*autos*	*de*	*ho*
signs	which	he was doing.		Himself	but	

24.b.**Txt:** p66,01ℵ-corr, 02A-corr,017K,024P, 032W,036,037,038,1,13, byz.Gries,Weis,Sod
Var: 01ℵ-org,02A-org, 03B,019L,Lach,Treg, Alf,Tisc,We/Ho,UBS/☆

2400.1 name nom masc	3620.2 partic	3961.53 verb 3sing indic imperf act	1431.6 prs-pron acc 3sing masc	1431.15 prs-pron acc sing masc
Ἰησοῦς	οὐκ	ἐπίστευεν	⸀ ἑαυτὸν	[b☆ αὐτὸν]
Iēsous	*ouk*	*episteuen*	*heauton*	*hauton*
Jesus	not	did trust	himself	[him]

840.2 prs-pron dat pl	1217.2 prep	3450.16 art sing neu	840.6 prs-pron acc sing masc	1091.14 verb inf pres act	3820.8 adj acc pl masc
αὐτοῖς,	διὰ	τὸ	αὐτὸν	γινώσκειν	πάντας,
autois	*dia*	*to*	*auton*	*ginōskein*	*pantas*
to them,	because of	the	his	knowing	all,

	2504.1 conj	3617.1 conj	3620.3 partic	5367.3 noun acc sing fem	2174.44 verb 3sing indic imperf act	2419.1 conj	4948.3 indef-pron nom sing
25.	καὶ	ὅτι	οὐ	χρείαν	εἶχεν	ἵνα	τις
	kai	*hoti*	*ou*	*chreian*	*eichen*	*hina*	*tis*
	and	that	no	need	he had	that	any

Many of the teachings and prophecies of Jesus were not understood until after the Resurrection and the Day of Pentecost. The fullness of the Spirit's activities illuminated what Jesus said and did (14:26). The Scripture passage referred to here is probably Psalm 16:10. (See Acts 2:27; 13:35.)

The apostles of the New Testament insisted that the Old Testament prophecies and Jesus' own prophecies emphatically declare that Jesus arose from the dead (1 Corinthians 15:4). This message is the vital point of all New Testament preaching. There would not be the gospel or the believers' resurrection without His resurrection.

his disciples remembered that he had said this unto them: . . . his disciples recalled these words, *ALBA* . . . his disciples recollected that he had said this, *TCNT.*

and they believed the scripture, and the word which Jesus had said: . . . trusted in and relied, *AmpB* . . . the writings, *Klingensmith* . . . in the words he had spoken, *ALBA.*

2:23. Previously, John associated the cleansing of the temple with the response of hostility from the Jewish leaders. Also he stated the positive results with regard to Jesus' disciples. In this verse John sets forth how Jesus' ministry affected the pilgrims who came to the Feast.

"Day" is in italics in the King James Version indicating the word is not in the Greek but was added by the translators. Actually, the "feast" here included the 7 days of the Feast of Unleavened Bread which immediately followed the Passover. The Jews referred to all 8 days as "Passover."

The "many" believed or trusted as far as they understood what the signs meant. Jesus performed signs to attest His messiahship. They trusted these signs as true indications that He was the Messiah. John tells us that Jesus did many miracles which are not recorded (21:25).

23. Now when he was in Jerusalem at the passover, in the feast day: While he was in, *ALBA* . . . During his stay in, *JB.*

many believed in his name: . . . many came to trust in him, *TCNT* . . . many became believers, *Weymouth* . . . trusted in Him as the Christ, *Williams* . . . many gave their allegiance to him, *NEB* . . . many put faith in his name, *Rotherham.*

when they saw the miracles which he did: . . . observed the signs which he wrought, *Berkeley* . . . viewing his signs which he was doing, *Rotherham* . . . carefully observing with a purposeful interest...which He was constantly performing, *Wuest* . . . which He wrought, *Weymouth* . . . giving of his mission, *TCNT* . . . were visible demonstrations, *Barclay.*

2:24. The reason He did not commit or trust himself to them is contained in the words "because he knew all men." The belief of the "many" was superficial for it rested on the signs, and the "many" inadequately understood them. Jesus did commit himself to the six early disciples because their commitment to Him was sufficient to entrust them with a further revelation of His person and mission.

"Because he knew all men" states another clear proof of His omniscience. The Gospel of John abounds with sparkling gems of this sort. The Lord's knowledge of Peter and Nathanael emphasized the same truth (1:42,47,48). Jesus knew Nicodemus and the Samaritan woman better than they knew themselves (chapters 3 and 4). He "knew (*to auton ginōskein*) all men" because He had created them and observed and worked with them through the centuries (Genesis, chapters 1 to 3; John 1:1-11).

24. But Jesus did not commit himself unto them: But for His part, *Montgomery* . . . would not trust, *Moffatt* . . . did not confide himself, *Murdock* . . . did not trust Himself to them, *Norlie.*

because he knew all men: Because he knew them all, *TEV* . . . he saw through all men, *ALBA* . . . Jesus knew what people were like, *SEB* . . . since he could read every heart, *TCNT.*

2:25. Jesus knew the secrets within the thinking of each man. The Book of Hebrews puts it this way, "For the word (*Logos,* as

25. And needed not that any should testify of man: . . . about human nature, *Barclay* . . . should give Him evidence about man,

John 3:1

3113.20 verb 3sing subj aor act	**3875.1** prep	**3450.2** art gen sing	**442.2** noun gen sing masc	**840.5** prs-pron nom sing masc
μαρτυρήσῃ	περὶ	τοῦ	ἀνθρώπου·	αὐτὸς
marturēsē	*peri*	*tou*	*anthrōpou*	*autos*
should testify	concerning	the	man,	he

1056.1 conj	**1091.38** verb 3sing indic imperf act	**4949.9** intr-pron sing neu	**1498.34** verb sing indic imperf act	**1706.1** prep	**3450.3** art dat sing
γὰρ	ἐγίνωσκεν	τί	ἦν	ἐν	τῷ
gar	*eginōsken*	*ti*	*ēn*	*en*	*tō*
for	knew	what	was	in	the

442.3 noun dat sing masc	**1498.34** verb sing indic imperf act	**1156.2** conj	**442.1** noun nom sing masc	**1523.2** prep gen	**3450.1** art gen pl
ἀνθρώπῳ.	3:1. Ἦν	δὲ	ἄνθρωπος	ἐκ	τῶν
anthrōpō	*En*	*de*	*anthrōpos*	*ek*	*tōn*
man.	There was	but	a man	of	the

5168.5 name gen pl masc	**3392.1** name nom masc	**3549.2** noun sing neu	**840.4** prs-pron dat sing	**752.1** noun nom sing masc
Φαρισαίων,	Νικόδημος	ὄνομα	αὐτῷ,	ἄρχων
Pharisaiōn	*Nikodēmos*	*onoma*	*autō*	*archōn*
Pharisees,	Nicodemus	name	his,	a ruler

3450.1 art gen pl	**2428.3** name-adj gen pl masc	**3642.4** dem-pron nom sing masc	**2048.3** verb 3sing indic aor act	**4242.1** prep	**3450.6** art acc sing masc
τῶν	Ἰουδαίων·	2. οὗτος	ἦλθεν	πρὸς	˹ τὸν
tōn	*Ioudaiōn*	*houtos*	*ēlthen*	*pros*	*ton*
of the	Jews;	this	came	to	

2.a.**Txt:** 07E,021M,036, bo.Steph
Var: 01ℵ,02A,03B, 017K,019L,037,038,byz. Gries,Lach,Treg,Alf, Word,Tisc,We/HoWeis, Sod,UBS/☆

2400.3 name acc masc	**840.6** prs-pron acc sing masc	**3433.2** noun gen sing fem	**2504.1** conj	**1500.5** verb 3sing indic aor act	**840.4** prs-pron dat sing
Ἰησοῦν	[a☆ αὐτὸν]	νυκτός,	καὶ	εἶπεν	αὐτῷ,
Iēsoun	*auton*	*nuktos*	*kai*	*eipen*	*autō*
Jesus	[him]	by night,	and	said	to him,

4318.1 noun sing masc	**3471.5** verb 1pl indic perf act	**3617.1** conj	**570.3** prep gen	**2296.2** noun gen sing masc	**2048.25** verb 2sing indic perf act
Ῥαββί,	οἴδαμεν	ὅτι	ἀπὸ	θεοῦ	ἐλήλυθας
Rhabbi	*oidamen*	*hoti*	*apo*	*theou*	*elēluthas*
Rabbi,	we know	that	from	God	you have come

1314.1 noun nom sing masc	**3625.2** num card nom masc	**1056.1** conj	**3642.18** dem-pron pl neu	**3450.17** art pl neu	**4447.2** noun pl neu
διδάσκαλος·	οὐδεὶς	γὰρ	˹ ταῦτα	τὰ	σημεῖα
didaskalos	*oudeis*	*gar*	*tauta*	*ta*	*sēmeia*
a teacher,	no one	for	these	the	signs

1404.4 verb 3sing indic pres	**1404.4** verb 3sing indic pres	**3642.18** dem-pron pl neu	**3450.17** art pl neu	**4447.2** noun pl neu	**4020.20** verb inf pres act
δύναται	[☆ δύναται	ταῦτα	τὰ	σημεῖα]	ποιεῖν
dunatai	*dunatai*	*tauta*	*ta*	*sēmeia*	*poiein*
is able	[is able	these	the	signs]	to do

3614.17 rel-pron pl neu	**4622.1** prs-pron nom 2sing	**4020.4** verb 2sing indic pres act	**1430.1** partic	**3231.1** partic	**1498.10** verb 3sing subj pres act
ἃ	σὺ	ποιεῖς,	ἐὰν	μὴ	ᾖ
ha	*su*	*poieis*	*ean*	*mē*	*ē*
which	you	do	if	not	be

3.a.**Txt:** 01ℵ,02A,030U, 037,038,Steph
Var: p66,03B,07E,017K, 019L,036,Lach,TregAlf, Tisc,We/Ho,Weis,Sod, UBS/☆

3450.5 art sing masc	**2296.1** noun nom sing masc	**3196.2** prep	**840.3** prs-pron gen sing	**552.6** verb 3sing indic aor pass	**3450.5** art sing masc
ὁ	θεὸς	μετ'	αὐτοῦ.	3. Ἀπεκρίθη	˹a ὁ ˺
ho	*theos*	*met'*	*autou*	*Apekrithē*	*ho*
	God	with	him.	Answered	

in John 1:1) of God is . . . able to judge the thoughts and intentions of the heart. And there is no creature hidden from His sight, but all things are open and laid bare to the eyes of Him with whom we have to do" (Hebrews 4:12,13, NASB). John repeats this truth in several passages (John 5:42; 6:61,64; Revelation 2:23). Jesus knew the inward character of Peter and the guilelessness of Nathanael, but He did not find in the multitude at the Feast a man to whom He could commit himself or rely on. If the multitude had heard more, they might have believed more. In that case, Jesus could have entrusted himself to them. Thus, for Him to entrust himself to believers, there must be progress in their knowledge of Him.

Fenton . . . had no need to be informed about any man, *ALBA* . . . not need any one's evidence, *Berkeley*.

for he knew what was in man: . . . he understood human nature, *Phillips* . . . for He knew mankind to the core, *LivB* . . . what was to be known about the human heart, *ALBA*.

3:1. John next introduces an example of the kind of superficial belief and limited knowledge that characterized the crowd at the Feast. While most of the Jewish leaders were hostile to Jesus from His first ministry in Judea, Nicodemus shows some were not. Nicodemus was an honored Pharisee among his people. The term "ruler of the Jews" is also given in John 7:26 and Acts 3:17 where it refers to members of the Sanhedrin. We may assume that Nicodemus was a Sanhedrin member. But, unlike the crowd as a whole, Nicodemus was going to show progress toward believing in Jesus. We note progress in the two other scenes in which Nicodemus had a key role (7:50; 19:39). Doubtless, he and Joseph of Arimathea, also a Sanhedrin member, became disciples of Jesus. They showed their love by caring for His body.

1. There was a man of the Pharisees, named Nicodemus, a ruler of the Jews: . . . who belonged to the school of the Pharisees, and who was a member of the Sanhedrin, *Barclay* . . . a leading man among the Jews, *TCNT* . . . a leading Jew, *JB* . . . an outstanding man in authority, *Wuest* . . . Among the Pharisees, *Norlie* . . . one of the Judean princes, *Fenton* . . . a Jewish ruler, *Adams* . . . Belonged to the Pharisee party and was a member of the supreme Council, *ALBA* . . . a member of the Jewish court, *Beck*.

3:2. Nicodemus "came to Jesus by night" for this was an advantageous time for a lengthy, private interview. Jesus was encircled during the day. Night studies of the Law were held in high esteem by the rabbis. There is also the possibility that Nicodemus chose the night because of fear of the Jews and regard for his reputation. Nicodemus may have represented a group within the high court of Israel. His address to Jesus as "Rabbi" was indeed correct. Yet, all he saw was a good teacher worthy of that respectful title because God was with Him.

2. The same came to Jesus by night, and said to him, Rabbi, we know that thou art a teacher come from God: . . . we know positively, *Wuest* . . . you have come from God to teach us, *Moffatt*.

for no man can do these miracles that thou doest, except God be with him: Obviously no one could show the signs, *Phillips* . . . can perform, *Sawyer* . . . is able to keep on constantly performing, *Wuest* . . . which you are continually doing, *Montgomery* . . . are so obviously demonstrations of divine power, *Barclay* . . . except perchance God, *Rotherham*.

3:3. "Jesus answered and said unto him" is a reiteration which is typical Hebrew idiom. In our words we could paraphrase it "Jesus responded by saying to him." Nicodemus had not asked a question, but he had numerous problems for which he needed solutions.

"I say unto thee" is personal to Nicodemus. Jesus displayed mar-

2400.1 name nom masc	2504.1 conj	1500.5 verb 3sing indic aor act	840.4 prs-pron dat sing	279.1 partic	279.1 partic	2978.1 verb 1sing pres act
Ἰησοῦς	καὶ	εἶπεν	αὐτῷ,	Ἀμὴν	ἀμὴν	λέγω
Iēsous	*kai*	*eipen*	*autō*	*Amēn*	*amēn*	*legō*
Jesus	and	said	to him,	Truly	truly	I say

4622.3 prs-pron dat 2sing	1430.1 partic	3231.1 partic	4948.3 indef-pron nom sing	1074.16 verb 3sing subj aor pass	505.1 adv	3620.3 partic
σοι,	ἐὰν	μή	τις	γεννηθῇ	ἄνωθεν,	οὐ
soi	*ean*	*mē*	*tis*	*gennēthē*	*anōthen*	*ou*
to you,	If	not	anyone	be born	again,	not

1404.4 verb 3sing indic pres	1481.19 verb inf aor act	3450.12 art acc sing fem	926.4 noun acc sing fem	3450.2 art gen sing	2296.2 noun gen sing masc
δύναται	ἰδεῖν	τὴν	βασιλείαν	τοῦ	θεοῦ.
dunatai	*idein*	*tēn*	*basileian*	*tou*	*theou*
he can	to see	the	kingdom		of God.

2978.5 verb 3sing indic pres act	4242.1 prep	840.6 prs-pron acc sing masc	3450.5 art sing masc	3392.1 name nom masc	4316.1 adv
4. Λέγει	πρὸς	αὐτὸν	ὁ	Νικόδημος,	Πῶς
Legei	*pros*	*auton*	*ho*	*Nikodēmos*	*Pōs*
Says	to	him		Nicodemus,	How

1404.4 verb 3sing indic pres	442.1 noun nom sing masc	1074.21 verb inf aor pass	1082.1 noun nom sing masc	1498.21 verb sing masc part pres act
δύναται	ἄνθρωπος	γεννηθῆναι	γέρων	ὤν;
dunatai	*anthrōpos*	*gennēthēnai*	*gerōn*	*ōn*
can	a man	to be born	old	being?

3231.1 partic	1404.4 verb 3sing indic pres	1519.1 prep	3450.12 art acc sing fem	2809.4 noun acc sing fem	3450.10 art gen sing fem	3251.2 noun gen sing fem
μὴ	δύναται	εἰς	τὴν	κοιλίαν	τῆς	μητρὸς
mē	*dunatai*	*eis*	*tēn*	*koilian*	*tēs*	*mētros*
not	can he	into	the	womb	of the	mother

840.3 prs-pron gen sing	1202.8 num ord sing neu	1511.21 verb inf aor act	2504.1 conj	1074.21 verb inf aor pass
αὐτοῦ	δεύτερον	εἰσελθεῖν	καὶ	γεννηθῆναι;
autou	*deuteron*	*eiselthein*	*kai*	*gennēthēnai*
his	a second time	to enter	and	to be born?

5.a.**Txt:** 03B,019L,030U, 13,Steph,Treg,Alf, We/Ho
Var: 01ℵ,02A,017K, 021M,036,037,038, Gries,Lach,Tisc,Weis, Sod,UBS/⋆

552.6 verb 3sing indic aor pass	3450.5 art sing masc	2400.1 name nom masc	279.1 partic	279.1 partic	2978.1 verb 1sing pres act
5. Ἀπεκρίθη	⸂[a] ὁ ⸃	Ἰησοῦς,	Ἀμὴν	ἀμὴν	λέγω
Apekrithē	*ho*	*Iēsous*	*Amēn*	*amēn*	*legō*
Answered		Jesus,	Truly	truly	I say

4622.3 prs-pron dat 2sing	1430.1 partic	3231.1 partic	4948.3 indef-pron nom sing	1074.16 verb 3sing subj aor pass	1523.1 prep gen	5045.2 noun gen sing neu
σοι,	ἐὰν	μή	τις	γεννηθῇ	ἐξ	ὕδατος
soi	*ean*	*mē*	*tis*	*gennēthē*	*ex*	*hudatos*
to you,	If	not	anyone	be born	of	water

2504.1 conj	4011.2 noun gen sing neu	3620.3 partic	1404.4 verb 3sing indic pres	1511.21 verb inf aor act	1519.1 prep	3450.12 art acc sing fem
καὶ	πνεύματος	οὐ	δύναται	εἰσελθεῖν	εἰς	τὴν
kai	*pneumatos*	*ou*	*dunatai*	*eiselthein*	*eis*	*tēn*
and	of Spirit	not	he can	to enter	into	the

5.b.**Var:** 01ℵ-org,Tisc

926.4 noun acc sing fem	3450.2 art gen sing	2296.2 noun gen sing masc	3450.1 art gen pl	3636.7 noun gen pl masc
βασιλείαν	⸀ τοῦ	θεοῦ.	[[b] τῶν	οὐρανῶν.]
basileian	*tou*	*theou*	*tōn*	*ouranōn*
kingdom		of God.	[of the	heavens.]

velous understanding of this man who was laboring under false impressions. Evidently he saw no need for a change in himself. Like other Pharisees he probably thought he could obtain entrance to the Kingdom by his own merit and his natural descent from Abraham.

"Except a man" is not just to Nicodemus but is all-inclusive. "Born again" is also to be translated "born from above" (*anōthen*). "Again" is inferred because a spiritual birth is a second birth. The term *anōthen*, "from above, from heaven," is used only here and in verse 7 in connection with "born" (*gennaō*). Note how *anōthen* is used in John 3:31; 19:11; James 1:17; 3:15,17. Note also a similar analogy to being born from above in 1 John 3:9; 2:29; 4:7; 5:1,4,18.

Terms that express aspects of the same wonderful truth of His grace are "repentance," "salvation," "faith," "receiving Christ," etc. The analogy of being born from above is more complex and suggestive. Nicodemus surely had abundant truth on which to meditate.

Nicodemus was not merely a Jew, but a ruler of the most religious people on earth. The shock of hearing that "birth" was a prerequisite to "seeing" could have sent him from Jesus in disgust. But he did not leave. He stayed to learn more. To see the kingdom of God is equivalent to experience by observing. The temple in which Nicodemus observed the things of God was outward, formal, ritualistic, and lacked life. Jesus told Nicodemus that everyone who would "see" must be born with eyes to see the things of God.

3:4. Nicodemus was figuratively stating the impossibility of a physical rebirth to parallel the ridiculousness of Jews having to be born from above. He felt he was already a child of the Kingdom, a subject under the rule of God. His second question was stated in such a way as to expect a negative answer.

3:5. Jesus replied by telling him that unless a man is "born of water and of the Spirit, he cannot enter into (share in and enjoy) the kingdom (rule, power, and authority) of God." Some interpret "born of water" as natural birth. Others take it as water baptism. Many, however, note that Jesus did not mean literal water in 4:10,13,14, and 7:37-39. The emphasis of this passage is on the effectual work of the Holy Spirit. Since the basic Greek word for *and* also means "even," it is possible to take the meaning here to be "water, *even* the Spirit." Others take the water to signify spiritual cleansing through the Word rather than through outward forms. (See John 15:3; 17:17; Ephesians 5:26; Titus 3:5; 1 Peter 1:23.)

The fact that water baptism is not a condition of salvation nor results in regeneration is demonstrated by the experience of the

3. Jesus answered and said unto him, Verily, verily, I say unto thee: In truth I tell you, *TCNT* . . . I most solemnly say, *Williams* . . . Most assuredly I tell you, *Fenton* . . . Truly I assure you, *Berkeley.*

Except a man be born again: . . . unless one is born anew, *RSV* . . . born from above, *Rotherham, Berkeley* . . . without a new birth, *BB* . . . born over again, *TCNT.*

he cannot see the kingdom of God: . . . no one can see God's Realm, *Moffatt* . . . he cannot perceive, *Concordant* . . . he cannot behold, *Murdock* . . . can not discern the Reign of God, *Campbell* . . . God's empire, *Adams.*

4. Nicodemus saith unto him, How can a man be born when he is old?: But how is it possible, *NEB* . . . being a veteran be begotten, *Concordant* . . . a grown man, *Campbell* . . . being an old man? *Panin* . . . When a man is already old, how can he be reborn? *SEB* . . . How can a grown man be born? *JB.*

can he enter the second time into his mother's womb, and be born?: It is obviously impossible, *Barclay* . . . Can he be conceived of his mother a second time, *Fenton* . . . and be born a second time? *ALBA.*

5. Jesus answered, Verily, verily, I say unto thee: I assure you, *Phillips* . . . this is true, *Norlie.*

Except a man be born of water and of the Spirit: . . . be begotten, *Concordant* . . . unless a man owes his birth to Water and Spirit, *TCNT* . . . unless a person is born again, *Wuest* . . . unless he is reborn, *ALBA* . . . is due to, *Berkeley* . . . the Holy Ghost, *Douay.*

he cannot enter into the kingdom of God: . . . he can't get into God's kingdom, *Beck* . . . it is not possible for him to go, *BB.*

3450.16 art sing neu	**1074.25** verb sing part perf	**1523.2** prep gen	**3450.10** art gen sing fem	**4418.2** noun gen sing fem	**4418.1** noun nom sing fem
6. τὸ	γεγεννημένον	ἐκ	τῆς	σαρκὸς	σάρξ
to	*gegennēmenon*	*ek*	*tēs*	*sarkos*	*sarx*
The	having been born	of	the	flesh	flesh

1498.4 verb 3sing indic pres act	**2504.1** conj	**3450.16** art sing neu	**1074.25** verb sing part perf	**1523.2** prep gen	**3450.2** art gen sing
ἐστιν·	καὶ	τὸ	γεγεννημένον	ἐκ	τοῦ
estin	*kai*	*to*	*gegennēmenon*	*ek*	*tou*
is;	and	the	having been born	of	the

4011.2 noun gen sing neu	**4011.1** noun sing neu	**1498.4** verb 3sing indic pres act	**3231.1** partic	**2273.12** verb 2sing subj aor act	**3617.1** conj
πνεύματος	πνεῦμά	ἐστιν.	**7.** μὴ	θαυμάσῃς	ὅτι
pneumatos	*pneuma*	*estin*	*mē*	*thaumasēs*	*hoti*
Spirit	spirit	is.	Not	do marvel	that

1500.3 verb indic aor act	**4622.3** prs-pron dat 2sing	**1158.1** verb 3sing indic pres act	**5050.4** prs-pron acc 2pl	**1074.21** verb inf aor pass
εἶπόν	σοι,	Δεῖ	ὑμᾶς	γεννηθῆναι
eipon	*soi*	*Dei*	*humas*	*gennēthēnai*
I said	to you,	It is needful for	you	to be born

505.1 adv	**3450.16** art sing neu	**4011.1** noun sing neu	**3562.1** adv	**2286.3** verb 3sing indic pres act
ἄνωθεν.	**8.** τὸ	πνεῦμα	ὅπου	θέλει
anōthen	*to*	*pneuma*	*hopou*	*thelei*
again.	The	wind	where	it wills

4014.1 verb 3sing indic pres act	**2504.1** conj	**3450.12** art acc sing fem	**5292.4** noun acc sing fem	**840.3** prs-pron gen sing	**189.4** verb 2sing indic pres act
πνεῖ,	καὶ	τὴν	φωνὴν	αὐτοῦ	ἀκούεις,
pnei	*kai*	*tēn*	*phōnēn*	*autou*	*akoueis*
blows,	and	the	sound	its	you hear,

233.1 conj	**3620.2** partic	**3471.3** verb 2sing indic perf act	**4019.1** adv	**2048.34** verb 3sing indic pres	**2504.1** conj
ἀλλ'	οὐκ	οἶδας	πόθεν	ἔρχεται	καὶ
all'	*ouk*	*oidas*	*pothen*	*erchetai*	*kai*
but	not	know	from where	it comes	and

4085.1 adv	**5055.3** verb 3sing indic pres act	**3643.1** adv	**1498.4** verb 3sing indic pres act	**3820.6** adj sing masc	**3450.5** art sing masc
ποῦ	ὑπάγει	οὕτως	ἐστὶν	πᾶς	ὁ
pou	*hupagei*	*houtōs*	*estin*	*pas*	*ho*
where	it goes:	thus	is	everyone	the

1074.26 verb nom sing masc part perf pass	**1523.2** prep gen	**3450.2** art gen sing	**4011.2** noun gen sing neu	**552.6** verb 3sing indic aor pass
γεγεννημένος	ἐκ	τοῦ	πνεύματος.	**9.** Ἀπεκρίθη
gegennēmenos	*ek*	*tou*	*pneumatos*	*Apekrithē*
having been born	of	the	Spirit.	Answered

3392.1 name nom masc	**2504.1** conj	**1500.5** verb 3sing indic aor act	**840.4** prs-pron dat sing	**4316.1** adv	**1404.4** verb 3sing indic pres
Νικόδημος	καὶ	εἶπεν	αὐτῷ,	Πῶς	δύναται
Nikodēmos	*kai*	*eipen*	*autō*	*Pōs*	*dunatai*
Nicodemus	and	said	to him,	How	can

3642.18 dem-pron pl neu	**1090.63** verb inf aor mid	**552.6** verb 3sing indic aor pass	**3450.5** art sing masc	**2400.1** name nom masc
ταῦτα	γενέσθαι;	**10.** Ἀπεκρίθη	⸂a ὁ ⸃	Ἰησοῦς
tauta	*genesthai*	*Apekrithē*	*ho*	*Iēsous*
these things	to be?	Answered		Jesus

10.a.**Txt:** 01א,Steph
Var: 02A,03B,017K, 019L,036,037,038,Gries, Lach,Treg,Alf,Word,Tisc We/Ho,Weis,Sod,UBS/⋆

dying thief (Luke 23:43) and by the fact that Cornelius and his household were regenerated and filled with the Spirit before water baptism (Acts 10). Water baptism is not a condition of regeneration, but rather a testimony to an inward spiritual work of grace that has already taken place (Romans 6:3,4,11; 1 Peter 3:21). By it the believer declares his identification with Christ in His death and commits himself to walk in newness of life.

6. That which is born of the flesh is flesh: Flesh gives birth to flesh, *Phillips* . . . of the physical is physical, *Williams.*

and that which is born of the Spirit is spirit: . . . whatever is born of the Spirit is spiritual, *Williams.*

3:6,7. Nicodemus had stated the absurdity of a second physical birth, so Jesus put the emphasis once again on the fact that the new birth from above is the work of the Spirit. If all we have is physical birth, we are merely flesh and are limited to what the flesh can perceive. Thus the flesh profits nothing toward one's relationship with God. But the second birth by the Spirit makes it possible for us to perceive what the Spirit can perceive. (See 1 Corinthians 2:14.)

7. Marvel not that I said unto thee, Ye must be born again: Do not be astonished, *BB* . . . It is necessary, *Clementson* . . . It behoveth you to, *Young* . . . have a second birth, *BB.*

8. The wind bloweth where it listeth: The Spirit where He willeth breathes, *Clementson* . . . breathes where he pleases, *Campbell* . . . brethith where it wole, *Wycliffe* . . . where it will, *Alford* . . . wherever it pleases, *Beck* . . . where it chooseth, *Murdock.*

and thou hearest the sound thereof: . . . and you hear its voice, *Montgomery* . . . and thou heerist his vois, *Wycliffe* . . . the report, *Campbell.*

but canst not tell whence it cometh, and whither it goeth: . . . but you do not know, *TCNT* . . . where it comes from and where it goes, *BB* . . . whither he goeth, *Douay.*

so is every one that is born of the Spirit: It is the same with everyone, *Berkeley.*

3:8. Jesus chose to give Nicodemus an example of the mystery of the new birth from the inexplicable activity of the wind. "Wind" translates the same Greek word (*pneuma*) that may also be translated "breath, spirit, and Spirit." The identical word is also translated "Spirit" in this verse. Since the Greek word "sound" (*phōnē*) usually means "voice," it is also possible to translate this: "The Spirit breathes where He wills, and you hear His voice." But with either translation it is clear that though the operation of the Spirit is mysterious and beyond human analysis we can still experience those operations. The movement of the wind is real to us and its effect may be observed. So it is with the work of the Spirit in the life of everyone who is born of the Spirit. (See Galatians 5:22,23; Acts 2:3,4; 1 Corinthians 12:7.)

This does not limit the Spirit's effect to outward spectacular manifestations. Manifestations of the fruit of the Spirit are as important to indicate the Spirit's activity as manifestations of His gifts.

9. Nicodemus answered and said unto him, How can these things be?: How is all this possible? asked Nicodemus, *Weymouth* . . . How can that be possible? *JB.*

3:9. Nicodemus began to show a change here. His words no longer indicate mere amazement or bewilderment. Instead, his question seems to indicate an earnest, sincere desire to know by what means these things can be brought to pass.

3:10. Jesus answered him with a mild rebuke for his spiritual ignorance. "A master of Israel" is literally "the teacher of Israel."

John 3:11

2504.1 conj	1500.5 verb 3sing indic aor act	840.4 prs-pron dat sing	4622.1 prs-pron nom 2sing	1498.3 verb 2sing indic pres act	3450.5 art sing masc
καὶ	εἶπεν	αὐτῷ,	Σὺ	εἶ	ὁ
kai	*eipen*	*autō*	*Su*	*ei*	*ho*
and	said	to him,	You	are	thc

1314.1 noun nom sing masc	3450.2 art gen sing	2447.1 name masc	2504.1 conj	3642.18 dem-pron pl neu	3620.3 partic
διδάσκαλος	τοῦ	Ἰσραήλ,	καὶ	ταῦτα	οὐ
didaskalos	*tou*	*Israēl*	*kai*	*tauta*	*ou*
teacher		of Israel,	and	these things	not

1091.2 verb 2sing indic pres act	279.1 partic	279.1 partic	2978.1 verb 1sing pres act	4622.3 prs-pron dat 2sing	3617.1 conj
γινώσκεις;	**11.** ἀμὴν	ἀμὴν	λέγω	σοι,	ὅτι
ginōskeis	*amēn*	*amēn*	*legō*	*soi*	*hoti*
know?	Truly	truly	I say	to you,	That

3614.16 rel-pron sing neu	3471.5 verb 1pl indic perf act	2953.4 verb 1pl indic pres act	2504.1 conj	3614.16 rel-pron sing neu	3571.12 verb 1pl indic perf act
ὃ	οἴδαμεν	λαλοῦμεν,	καὶ	ὃ	ἑωράκαμεν
ho	*oidamen*	*laloumen*	*kai*	*ho*	*heōrakamen*
which	we know	we speak,	and	that which	we have seen

3113.4 verb 1pl indic pres act	2504.1 conj	3450.12 art acc sing fem	3114.3 noun acc sing fem	2231.2 prs-pron gen 1pl
μαρτυροῦμεν·	καὶ	τὴν	μαρτυρίαν	ἡμῶν
marturoumen	*kai*	*tēn*	*marturian*	*hēmōn*
we bear witness of;	and	the	witness	our

3620.3 partic	2956.1 verb 2pl pres act	1479.1 conj	3450.17 art pl neu	1904.3 adj pl neu	1500.3 verb indic aor act
οὐ	λαμβάνετε.	**12.** εἰ	τὰ	ἐπίγεια	εἶπον
ou	*lambanete*	*ei*	*ta*	*epigeia*	*eipon*
not	you receive.	If	the	earthly things	I said

5050.3 prs-pron dat 2pl	2504.1 conj	3620.3 partic	3961.2 verb 2pl pres act	4316.1 adv	1430.1 partic	1500.6 verb 1sing subj aor act
ὑμῖν,	καὶ	οὐ	πιστεύετε,	πῶς	ἐὰν	εἴπω
humin	*kai*	*ou*	*pisteuete*	*pōs*	*ean*	*eipō*
to you,	and	not	you believe,	how	if	I say

5050.3 prs-pron dat 2pl	3450.17 art pl neu	2016.7 adj pl neu	3961.50 verb 2pl indic fut act	2504.1 conj
ὑμῖν	τὰ	ἐπουράνια	πιστεύσετε;	**13.** καὶ
humin	*ta*	*epourania*	*pisteusete*	*kai*
to you	the	heavenly things	will you believe?	And

3625.2 num card nom masc	303.22 verb 3sing indic perf act	1519.1 prep	3450.6 art acc sing masc	3636.4 noun acc sing masc	1479.1 conj
οὐδεὶς	ἀναβέβηκεν	εἰς	τὸν	οὐρανὸν	εἰ
oudeis	*anabebēken*	*eis*	*ton*	*ouranon*	*ei*
no one	has gone up	into	the	heaven	if

3231.1 partic	3450.5 art sing masc	1523.2 prep gen	3450.2 art gen sing	3636.2 noun gen sing masc	2568.20 verb nom sing masc part aor act
μὴ	ὁ	ἐκ	τοῦ	οὐρανοῦ	καταβάς,
mē	*ho*	*ek*	*tou*	*ouranou*	*katabas*
not	the	out of	the	heaven	having come down,

13.a.**Txt:** 02A,017K,036,037,038,1,13,byz.it.Lach,Tisc
Var: p66,p75,01ℵ,03B,019L,032W,011G3,33,We/Ho,Weis,Sod,UBS/⋆

3450.5 art sing masc	5048.1 noun nom sing masc	3450.2 art gen sing	442.2 noun gen sing masc	3450.5 art sing masc	1498.21 verb sing masc part pres act
ὁ	υἱὸς	τοῦ	ἀνθρώπου	(a ὁ	ὢν
ho	*huios*	*tou*	*anthrōpou*	*ho*	*ōn*
the	Son		of man	the	being

The definite article points to Nicodemus' office and prominence. When he came to Jesus, he called Jesus "a teacher." By calling Nicodemus "the teacher," Jesus recognized that Nicodemus claimed to sit in the chair of Moses, Samuel, and Ezra. But his culture and traditions blinded him to the realities of spiritual truth.

The word "knowest" (*ginōskeis*) means "to know by experience." Nicodemus was the zenith of all the old economy could produce, yet he did not understand. Nowhere else does Jesus speak of the new birth in the way He does here. It is because Nicodemus should have been able to understand.

10. Jesus answered and said unto him, Art thou a master of Israel, and knowest not these things?: Are you the famous teacher, *Barclay* . . . yet unable to discern this? *Fenton* . . . and ignorant of this? *Berkeley.*

3:11. This is the third time during the interview that Jesus used the authoritative affirmation "verily, verily" (see verses 3 and 5).

"We speak" refers to the witness of Christ and John the Baptist. "We do know" (*oidamen*) means we know as a fact, but is a knowledge which does not necessarily come through experience. It may come by revelation. The prophets, John the Baptist, and Jesus testified (bore witness) by revelation, but the people did not accept the witness. "Ye" (plural) refers to the group Nicodemus represented.

11. Verily, verily, I say unto thee, We speak that we do know: What we know we speak, *Rotherham.*

and testify that we have seen: . . . and witness only to what we have seen, *JB.*

and ye receive not our witness: . . . yet you all reject our evidence, *Weymouth* . . . are all rejecting, *Williams* . . . yet you refuse our testimony, *Moffatt* . . . but you do not accept our testimony, *ALBA.*

3:12. "If I have told you" is a statement of fact expressed as a condition so that the conclusion "and ye believe not" can be drawn. The "earthly things" are the things Jesus related to Nicodemus. They are the essentials, rudiments, the ABC's of salvation including spiritual experiences like the new birth from above which must take place on earth. The new birth is the transitional experience from "earthly things" into the "heavenly things." If Nicodemus did not enter into the sacred realm by regeneration, he would never know heavenly things.

"How shall ye believe?" The action of believing is a requisite of heavenly things. Spiritual eyes are not opened except by believing. Nicodemus had said, "How can these things be?" (verse 9). Jesus now said, "How shall ye believe?" Nicodemus' "how" was countered by Jesus' "how." The "ye" in this sentence is plural, referring to more than Nicodemus. Nicodemus would possibly report the complete interview to other members of the Sanhedrin.

12. If I have told you earthly things: I mention to you, *Berkeley* . . . things which happen on this earth, *Phillips* . . . of the terrestrial, *Concordant* . . . about worldly things, *ET.*

and ye believe not: . . . none of you believe me, *Montgomery* . . . If your faith falls short, *ALBA.*

how shall ye believe, if I tell you of heavenly things?: . . . how can you credit, *Fenton* . . . I might tell you, *Berkeley* . . . of the celestial? *Concordant.*

3:13. Jesus continued the thought of "heavenly things." Since man has not ascended into heaven, he cannot know about heavenly things. It is the Spirit that reveals heavenly things (1 Corinthians 2:10).

13. And no man hath ascended up to heaven, but he that came down from heaven: And yet the Son of man, descended from heaven, is the only one who has ever ascended into heaven, *Moffatt* . . . No one has gone up to heaven, *JB.*

even the Son of man which is in heaven: . . . whose abode, *Campbell.*

1706.1 prep	3450.3 art dat sing	3636.3 noun dat sing masc	2504.1 conj	2503.1 conj	3337.1 name nom masc
ἐν	τῷ	οὐρανῷ˙ ˎ	14. καὶ	καθὼς	ˏ Μωσῆς
en	*tō*	*ouranō*	*kai*	*kathōs*	*Mōsēs*
in	the	heaven.	And	even as	Moses

3338.1 name nom masc	5150.2 verb 3sing indic aor act	3450.6 art acc sing masc	3653.3 noun acc sing masc	1706.1 prep	3450.11 art dat sing fem
[☆ Μωϋσῆς]	ὕψωσεν	τὸν	ὄφιν	ἐν	τῇ
Mōusēs	*hupsōsen*	*ton*	*ophin*	*en*	*tē*
[idem]	lifted up	the	serpent	in	the

2031.2 noun dat sing fem	3643.1 adv	5150.10 verb inf aor pass	1158.1 verb 3sing indic pres act	3450.6 art acc sing masc
ἐρήμῳ,	οὕτως	ὑψωθῆναι	δεῖ	τὸν
erēmō	*houtōs*	*hupsōthēnai*	*dei*	*ton*
wilderness,	thus	to be lifted up	it is necessary	the

5048.4 noun acc sing masc	3450.2 art gen sing	442.2 noun gen sing masc	2419.1 conj	3820.6 adj sing masc	3450.5 art sing masc
υἱὸν	τοῦ	ἀνθρώπου˙	15. ἵνα	πᾶς	ὁ
huion	*tou*	*anthrōpou*	*hina*	*pas*	*ho*
Son		of man,	that	everyone	the

15.a.**Txt:** 01ℵ,017K,037, 038,1,13,28,33,byz. GriesWord,Sod
Var1: .02A,Lach
Var2: .p75,03B,032W, 011G3,Treg,Alf,Tisc, We/HoWeis,UBS/☆

15.b.**Txt:** p63,02A,017K, 036,037,038,13,byz.it. Lach
Var: 01ℵ,03B,019L,1, 33,bo.Treg,Alf,Tisc, We/Ho,WeisSod,UBS/☆

3961.10 verb nom sing masc part pres act	1519.1 prep	840.6 prs-pron acc sing masc	1894.2 prep	840.6 prs-pron acc sing masc	1706.1 prep
πιστεύων	ˏ εἰς	αὐτὸν	[1a ἐπ’	αὐτὸν	2☆ ἐν
pisteuōn	*eis*	*auton*	*ep’*	*auton*	*en*
believing	on	him	[upon	him	in

840.4 prs-pron dat sing	3231.1 partic	616.24 verb 3sing subj aor mid	233.1 conj	2174.7 verb 3sing subj pres act	2205.4 noun acc sing fem
αὐτῷ]	ˏb μὴ	ἀπόληται,	ἀλλ’ ˎ	ἔχῃ	ζωὴν
autō	*mē*	*apolētai*	*all’*	*echē*	*zōēn*
him]	not	may perish,	but	may have	life

164.1 adj sing	3643.1 adv	1056.1 conj	25.14 verb 3sing indic aor act	3450.5 art sing masc	2296.1 noun nom sing masc
αἰώνιον.	16. Οὕτως	γὰρ	ἠγάπησεν	ὁ	θεὸς
aiōnion	*Houtōs*	*gar*	*ēgapēsen*	*ho*	*theos*
eternal.	Thus	for	loved		God

16.a.**Txt:** p63,01ℵ-corr, 02A,017K,019L,036, 037,038,etc.byz.Lach, Sod
Var: p66,p75,01ℵ-org, 03B,032W,Tisc,We/Ho Weis,UBS/☆

3450.6 art acc sing masc	2862.4 noun acc sing masc	5452.1 conj	3450.6 art acc sing masc	5048.4 noun acc sing masc	840.3 prs-pron gen sing
τὸν	κόσμον	ὥστε	τὸν	υἱὸν	ˏa αὐτοῦ ˎ
ton	*kosmon*	*hōste*	*ton*	*huion*	*autou*
the	world	that	the	Son	his

3450.6 art acc sing masc	3302.3 adj acc sing masc	1319.14 verb 3sing indic aor act	2419.1 conj	3820.6 adj sing masc	3450.5 art sing masc
τὸν	μονογενῆ	ἔδωκεν,	ἵνα	πᾶς	ὁ
ton	*monogenē*	*edōken*	*hina*	*pas*	*ho*
the	only begotten	he gave,	that	everyone	the

3961.10 verb nom sing masc part pres act	1519.1 prep	840.6 prs-pron acc sing masc	3231.1 partic	616.24 verb 3sing subj aor mid	233.1 conj
πιστεύων	εἰς	αὐτὸν	μὴ	ἀπόληται,	ἀλλ’
pisteuōn	*eis*	*auton*	*mē*	*apolētai*	*all’*
believing	on	him	not	may perish,	but

2174.7 verb 3sing subj pres act	2205.4 noun acc sing fem	164.1 adj sing	3620.3 partic	1056.1 conj	643.8 verb 3sing indic aor act
ἔχῃ	ζωὴν	αἰώνιον.	17. οὐ	γὰρ	ἀπέστειλεν
echē	*zōēn*	*aiōnion*	*ou*	*gar*	*apesteilen*
may have	life	eternal.	Not	for	sent

By the words "but he that came down from heaven," Jesus unfolded to Nicodemus a most glorious heavenly truth. A contrast is presented between "no man" and "He" and between "ascended" and "descended" (see NASB). The "no man" is excluded from the knowledge of heavenly things because he has not ascended from the earth into heaven to observe them. The "He" is the One who is a part of heaven itself, and His "descended" action brings heaven down so heaven can be experienced by mankind on earth.

3:14. In this verse Jesus unfolded how the Son of Man would accomplish "life" for everyone who would believe. Jesus illustrated the "how" of the new birth by pointing to an episode found in Numbers 21:5-9 as a type of His own crucifixion. The serpent was also a type of God's judgment on sin. "Must" indicates the necessity of being lifted up on the cross. John uses "lifted up" of the Cross, never of the Ascension.

3:15. "That whosoever" (*pas*) is stated also in the next verse. It is an all-inclusive word. "Believeth in him" reveals the "how" to Nicodemus. The "him" refers to the Son of Man who is lifted up (verse 14). To believe in Him is to commit oneself entirely into His care. "Believeth" also implies obedience.

3:16. The verb "loved" (*ēgapēsen*) has the prominent position in the sentence. Jesus wanted all to know that it was God's love that was bringing eternal life to the world. The Son of Man who descended from heaven and is in heaven has brought to us the truth of this assertion (3:13; 1:18).

God's motive (love), action ("gave"), and gift (His Son) are one inseparable unit. Love could not be love without its expression and its gift. Love such as this is a high, holy love that is a noble expression of God's nature and will. Such love must be expressed in a tangible sense. It is constant in God, less often in man. Love brought heaven to man and will carry man to heaven. By love, God was manifested in Jesus Christ. All man's graces and gifts flow from God's love. Love is that supreme quality which is the means to the end and an enduring end in itself (1 Corinthians 13). It does not deny the holiness and justice of God, for behind them lies a longing and loving heart. God's love provides the most excellent plan for the object of His love.

Both verb forms, "loved" and "gave," are in the historical aorist tense to emphasize the act as a definite fact. The result of His love was "that he gave." Giving must have a gift to bestow.

14. And as Moses lifted up the serpent in the wilderness: . . . elevated the serpent, *Murdock* . . . the snake, *Beck* . . . placed on high, *Campbell* . . . on the pole, *Williams* . . . in the desert, *TCNT.*

even so must the Son of man be lifted up: . . . so it is necessary for the, *Fenton.*

15. That whosoever believeth in him should not perish: . . . everyone who trusts in Him, *Williams* . . . who commits himself to me, *SEB.*

but have eternal life: . . . may have enduring Life, *TCNT.*

16. For God so loved the world: . . . had such love for the world, *BB* . . . loved the world so dearly, *Moffatt* . . . the world so much, *Williams* . . . so greatly, *Weymouth.*

that he gave his only begotten Son: . . . he sacrificed, *ALBA* . . . His only-begotten (unique) Son, *AmpB* . . . His only born Son, *Norlie.*

that whosoever believeth in him should not perish: . . . everyone who has faith may not die, *ALBA* . . . for the entent that, *Tyndale* . . . so that anyone, *Williams* . . . whoever trusts in him, *Montgomery* . . . may not be lost, *TCNT* . . . shall not die, *Norlie* . . . not come to destruction, *BB* . . . need not be destroyed, *Klingensmith.*

but have everlasting life: . . . but have eonian life, *Concordant* . . . but obtain, *Campbell* . . . life eternal, *Murdock.*

John 3:18

17.a.**Txt:** 02A,017K,036,037,(038),13,byz.Gries,Lach,Treg,Alf
Var: 01ℵ,03B,019L,1,Tisc,We/Ho,Weis,Sod,UBS/⋆

3450.5 art	2296.1 noun	3450.6 art	5048.4 noun	840.3 prs-pron	1519.1
sing masc	nom sing masc	acc sing masc	acc sing masc	gen sing	prep
ὁ	θεὸς	τὸν	υἱὸν	(a αὐτοῦ)	εἰς
ho	*theos*	*ton*	*huion*	*autou*	*eis*
	God	the	Son	his	into

3450.6 art	2862.4 noun	2419.1	2892.2 verb	3450.6 art	2862.4 noun
acc sing masc	acc sing masc	conj	3sing subj act	acc sing masc	acc sing masc
τὸν	κόσμον	ἵνα	κρίνῃ	τὸν	κόσμον,
ton	*kosmon*	*hina*	*krinē*	*ton*	*kosmon*
the	world	that	he might judge	the	world,

233.1	2419.1	4834.26 verb 3sing	3450.5 art	2862.1 noun	1217.1
conj	conj	subj aor pass	sing masc	nom sing masc	prep
ἀλλ'	ἵνα	σωθῇ	ὁ	κόσμος	δι'
all'	*hina*	*sōthē*	*ho*	*kosmos*	*di'*
but	that	might be saved	the	world	through

840.3 prs-pron	3450.5 art	3961.10 verb nom sing	1519.1	840.6 prs-pron	3620.3
gen sing	sing masc	masc part pres act	prep	acc sing masc	partic
αὐτοῦ.	18. ὁ	πιστεύων	εἰς	αὐτὸν	οὐ
autou	*ho*	*pisteuōn*	*eis*	*auton*	*ou*
him.	The	believing	on	him	not

18.a.**Txt:** p66,p75,02A,017K,019L,036,037,038,1,13,etc.byz.Lach,Treg,Sod
Var: 01ℵ,03B,Alf,Tisc,We/HoWeis,UBS/⋆

2892.29 verb 3sing	3450.5 art	1156.2	3231.1	3961.10 verb nom sing	2218.1
indic pres pass	sing masc	conj	partic	masc part pres act	adv
κρίνεται·	ὁ	(a δὲ)	μὴ	πιστεύων	ἤδη
krinetai	*ho*	*de*	*mē*	*pisteuōn*	*ēdē*
is judged;	the	but	not	believing	already

2892.38 verb 3sing	3617.1	3231.1	3961.39 verb 3sing	1519.1	3450.16 art
indic perf pass	conj	partic	indic perf act	prep	sing neu
κέκριται,	ὅτι	μὴ	πεπίστευκεν	εἰς	τὸ
kekritai	*hoti*	*mē*	*pepisteuken*	*eis*	*to*
has been judged,	because	not	he has believed	on	the

3549.2 noun	3450.2 art	3302.2 adj	5048.2 noun	3450.2 art	2296.2 noun
sing neu	gen sing	gen sing masc	gen sing masc	gen sing	gen sing masc
ὄνομα	τοῦ	μονογενοῦς	υἱοῦ	τοῦ	θεοῦ.
onoma	*tou*	*monogenous*	*huiou*	*tou*	*theou*
name	of the	only begotten	Son		of God.

3642.9 dem-pron	1156.2	1498.4 verb 3sing	3450.9 art	2893.1 noun	3617.1
nom sing fem	conj	indic pres act	nom sing fem	nom sing fem	conj
19. αὕτη	δέ	ἐστιν	ἡ	κρίσις,	ὅτι
hautē	*de*	*estin*	*hē*	*krisis*	*hoti*
This	and	is	the	judgment,	that

3450.16 art	5295.1 noun	2048.26 verb 3sing	1519.1	3450.6 art	2862.4 noun
sing neu	sing neu	indic perf act	prep	acc sing masc	acc sing masc
τὸ	φῶς	ἐλήλυθεν	εἰς	τὸν	κόσμον,
to	*phōs*	*elēluthen*	*eis*	*ton*	*kosmon*
the	light	has come	into	the	world,

2504.1	25.16 verb 3pl	3450.7 art	442.6 noun	3095.1	3450.16 art
conj	indic aor act	pl masc	nom pl masc	adv comp	sing neu
καὶ	ἠγάπησαν	οἱ	ἄνθρωποι	μᾶλλον	τὸ
kai	*ēgapēsan*	*hoi*	*anthrōpoi*	*mallon*	*to*
and	loved	the	men	rather	the

4510.1	2211.1	3450.16 art	5295.1 noun	1498.34 verb sing	1056.1	4050.10
noun sing	conj	sing neu	sing neu	indic imperf act	conj	adj
σκότος	ἢ	τὸ	φῶς·	ἦν	γὰρ	(πονηρὰ
skotos	*ē*	*to*	*phōs*	*ēn*	*gar*	*ponēra*
darkness	than	the	light;	were	for	evil

The term "only begotten Son" (*ton huion ton monogenē*) has appeared in this Gospel in John 1:14,18 and also in Hebrews 11:17 and indicates a unique, special relationship.

"In him" asserts the simplest relationship by the preposition "in" (*eis*). The word *eis* means "into" or "toward" confidence and commitment. This leaves plenty of room for progress "toward" relationship with the total reality of who Jesus Christ is.

"But" (*alla*) places in contrast the words "perish" and "everlasting life." *Eternal* (*aiōnion*) emphasizes quality rather than duration. It is eternal because it is Christ's life in us, not because we cannot lose it. It begins here and now with believing in the Lord Jesus Christ. Its source and origin is in the life of God himself.

17. For God sent not his Son into the world to condemn the world: . . . dispatch, *Concordant* . . . to pass sentence on it, *Moffatt.*

but that the world through him might be saved: . . . but to save it-through him, *Phillips* . . . might live by means of him, *Murdock* . . . by him, *Campbell.*

3:17. "For" (*gar*) links the previous verse with this one and provides the reason for the sending. God "gave" by "sending." God "sent" not that He might judge the world, but that He might save the world.

18. He that believeth on him is not condemned: When a man has faith in him, *ALBA* . . . shall not be condemned, *TCNT* . . . does not come up for judgement, *Weymouth* . . . escape condemnation, *TCNT.*

but he that believeth not is condemned already: . . . but whoever refuses to believe, *JB* . . . has already received his sentence, *Williams.*

because he hath not believed in the name of the only begotten Son of God: . . . on the ground of their not having believed, *TCNT* . . . God's Only Son, *Norlie* . . . he has refused faith in God's only Son, *ALBA* . . . he has refused to believe, *JB* . . . the name of God's unique Son, *Adams.*

3:18. "Believeth on him." "Believeth" (*pisteuōn*) is a present participle and indicates continuous action. Those who keep on believing and trusting in Jesus are not condemned, are not under judgment.

"Hath not believed" (*pepisteuken*) is a perfect tense meaning they did not and still do not believe.

19. And this is the condemnation: The ground of his condemnation, *TCNT* . . . the indictment is this, *Fenton* . . . And the judgement is this, *ALBA* . . . Sothli this is the dom, *Wycliffe* . . . On these grounds is sentence pronounced, *JB* . . . the sentence, *Berkeley.*

that light is come into the world: . . . that though the light has come, *JB.*

and men loved darkness rather than light: . . . men preferred the darkness, *TCNT* . . . people have loved the darkness more, *Berkeley.*

3:19. The Lord himself reveals the cause of the condemnation, the basis of their judgment. He does not say they are very wicked, though some are. Light is the revelation of what God is (1:4). To reject the Light is to reject God. Excluding oneself from God severs unbelievers from the source of life. Their love of darkness leads to their rejection of the revelation (light) of God as manifested in the only begotten (unique, one-of-a-kind) Son. The love (*ēgapēsan*) men have for darkness is a steadfast sort of love. It is a love to which they are completely devoted.

"Because their deeds were evil" renders proof of the darkness they loved. Evil (wicked, vile, vicious, evil-intentioned, degenerate) deeds proceed from darkness (see 1:5). Conduct is the evidence of character. The greatest of all deeds of darkness is unbelief. Sin thrives in darkness. To receive Christ is to receive light, and to reject Christ is to remain in darkness.

3:20. "For" (*gar*) clarifies Jesus' reason for the statement in verse 19, just as verse 19 gives the reason for men's rejecting the light.

840.1 prs-pron gen pl	840.1 prs-pron gen pl	4050.10 adj	3450.17 art pl neu	2024.4 noun pl neu	3820.6 adj sing masc
αὐτῶν	[☆ αὐτῶν	πονηρὰ]	τὰ	ἔργα.	20. πᾶς
autōn	autōn	ponēra	ta	erga	pas
their	[their	evil]	the	works.	Everyone

1056.1 conj	3450.5 art sing masc	5175.2 adj acc pl neu	4097.7 verb nom sing masc part pres act	3268.3 verb 3sing indic pres act	3450.16 art sing neu
γὰρ	ὁ	φαῦλα	πράσσων	μισεῖ	τὸ
gar	ho	phaula	prassōn	misei	to
for	the	evil	doing	hates	the

5295.1 noun sing neu	2504.1 conj	3620.2 partic	2048.34 verb 3sing indic pres	4242.1 prep	3450.16 art sing neu	5295.1 noun sing neu
φῶς,	καὶ	οὐκ	ἔρχεται	πρὸς	τὸ	φῶς,
phōs	kai	ouk	erchetai	pros	to	phōs
light,	and	not	comes	to	the	light,

2419.1 conj	3231.1 partic	1638.12 verb 3sing subj aor pass	3450.17 art pl neu	2024.4 noun pl neu	840.3 prs-pron gen sing	3450.5 art sing masc
ἵνα	μὴ	ἐλεγχθῇ	τὰ	ἔργα	αὐτοῦ·	21. ὁ
hina	mē	elenchthē	ta	erga	autou	ho
that	not	may be exposed	the	works	his;	the

1156.2 conj	4020.15 verb sing masc part pres act	3450.12 art acc sing fem	223.4 noun acc sing fem	2048.34 verb 3sing indic pres	4242.1 prep
δὲ	ποιῶν	τὴν	ἀλήθειαν	ἔρχεται	πρὸς
de	poiōn	tēn	alētheian	erchetai	pros
but	practicing	the	truth	comes	to

3450.16 art sing neu	5295.1 noun sing neu	2419.1 conj	5157.12 verb 3sing subj aor pass	840.3 prs-pron gen sing	3450.17 art pl neu
τὸ	φῶς,	ἵνα	φανερωθῇ	αὐτοῦ	τὰ
to	phōs	hina	phanerōthē	autou	ta
the	light,	that	may be manifested	his	the

2024.4 noun pl neu	3617.1 conj	1706.1 prep	2296.3 noun dat sing masc	1498.4 verb 3sing indic pres act	2021.17 verb nom pl neu part perf pass
ἔργα	ὅτι	ἐν	θεῷ	ἐστιν	εἰργασμένα.
erga	hoti	en	theō	estin	eirgasmena
works	that	in	God	they are	worked.

3196.3 prep	3642.18 dem-pron pl neu	2048.3 verb 3sing indic aor act	3450.5 art sing masc	2400.1 name nom masc	2504.1 conj
22. Μετὰ	ταῦτα	ἦλθεν	ὁ	Ἰησοῦς	καὶ
Meta	tauta	ēlthen	ho	Iēsous	kai
After	these things	came		Jesus	and

3450.7 art pl masc	3073.5 noun nom pl masc	840.3 prs-pron gen sing	1519.1 prep	3450.12 art acc sing fem	2424.4 name acc fem
οἱ	μαθηταὶ	αὐτοῦ	εἰς	τὴν	Ἰουδαίαν
hoi	mathētai	autou	eis	tēn	Ioudaian
the	disciples	his	into		Judea

1087.4 noun acc sing fem	2504.1 conj	1550.1 adv	1298.5 verb 3sing indic imperf act	3196.2 prep	840.1 prs-pron gen pl	2504.1 conj
γῆν.	καὶ	ἐκεῖ	διέτριβεν	μετ'	αὐτῶν	καὶ
gēn	kai	ekei	dietriben	met'	autōn	kai
land of;	and	there	he stayed	with	them	and

901.10 verb 3sing indic imperf act	1498.34 verb sing indic imperf act	1156.2 conj	2504.1 conj	3450.5 art sing masc	2464.1 name nom masc
ἐβάπτιζεν.	23. ἦν	δὲ	καὶ	ὁ	Ἰωάννης
ebaptizen	ēn	de	kai	ho	Iōannēs
was baptizing.	Was	and	also		John

"The light" is the revelation of God in the Son. Since man has chosen darkness, he "doeth evil" (*ho phaula prassōn*), he practices evil; that is, he makes evil his life-style. *Phaula* indicates actions with low or worthless motives. Verse 19 speaks of active evil deeds. They are a moral cancer. Verse 20 speaks of base and worthless things and includes those things that may seem good but are not motivated by love. A selfish motive reveals the darkness in which the motive was born. The person who does these worthless things does not want his deeds reproved by being exposed and rebuked.

because their deeds were evil: . . . their actions, *Williams* . . . their practices, *Fenton* . . . have been wicked, *Weymouth.*

20. For every one that doeth evil hateth the light: . . . every wrongdoer hates the light, *Weymouth* . . . For every one who practices evil, *Berkeley* . . . that doeth abominable things, *Murdock* . . . acts vilely, *Fenton.*

neither cometh to the light: . . . and keeps away from the light, *Berkeley* . . . shrinks from it, *Fenton* . . . and shun it, *ALBA.*

lest his deeds should be reproved: . . . else his activities would be exposed, *Berkeley* . . . be effectually rebuked, *Wuest* . . . be detected, *Rotherham.*

3:21. The one who has made his decision for Christ keeps coming to "the light." He lives the truth. He keeps on putting the truth into practice. He is able to do this because he comes to "the light" and wants his practice to conform to the truth revealed in Jesus Christ. Thus, the blood of Jesus cleanses him continuously (1 John 1:7).

Such a one compares his conduct with that which is revealed in Christ. He studies the Holy Word and prays to be conformed to the image of Christ (James 1:23; 2 Corinthians 3:18; Romans 8:29). He comes to "the light" because he wants his deeds to be revealed, for it is in God (emphatic) that they have been accomplished or carried out. This does not mean that the believer never makes mistakes or that he never sins. But when he does, he comes to "the light" in search of forgiveness and guidance (1 John 1:7 to 2:1).

21. But he that doeth truth cometh to the light: . . . of living the truth, *Williams.*

that his deeds may be made manifest: . . . so that his works may be seen, *Beck.*

that they are wrought in God: . . . are agreeable, *Campbell* . . . the origin of his conduct is in God, *Fenton* . . . working in union with God, *Berkeley* . . . in reliance upon God, *TCNT.*

3:22. Jerusalem was in Judea, but Jesus now went into the rural area surrounding Jerusalem. "His disciples" who were close followers and learners, were His constant companions. John does not relate how many disciples were with Jesus; however, at least six were with Him, including John.

"And baptized" leads us to conclude that Jesus was teaching and preaching to the people who gathered. The scene was the Jordan River. The Jordan was a natural memorial of God's past work in behalf of Israel when Joshua led the nation into the new land. Jesus began His ministry at this memorial that brought an end to the old life and initiated a new order.

22. After these things came Jesus and his disciples into the land of Judaea: . . . the Judean district, *Berkeley* . . . the territory, *Wilson.*

and there he tarried with them, and baptized: . . . he stayed there with them and kept baptizing people, *Williams.*

3:23. The action words "was baptizing" gives a vivid picture of activity which took place before their eyes. At the scene people were descending into the water of the river and ascending to the bank while friends extended a helping hand.

The location of "Aenon near to Salim" is not definitely known today, but John tells us there was much water there. "Water" is

23. And John also was baptizing in Aenon near to Salim: . . . immersing in Aenon, *HBIE.*

John 3:24

901.4 verb nom sing masc part pres act	1706.1 prep	137.1 name fem	1445.1 adv	3450.2 art gen sing	4387.1 name neu
βαπτίζων	ἐν	Αἰνὼν	ἐγγὺς	τοῦ	⸂☆ Σαλείμ,
baptizōn	*en*	*Ainōn*	*engus*	*tou*	*Saleim*
baptizing	in	Aenon,	near		Salim,

4387.2 name neu	3617.1 conj	5045.4 noun pl neu	4044.17 adj pl neu	1498.34 verb sing indic imperf act	1550.1 adv
[Σαλίμ,]	ὅτι	ὕδατα	πολλὰ	ἦν	ἐκεῖ·
Salim	*hoti*	*hudata*	*polla*	*ēn*	*ekei*
[idem]	because	waters	many	were	there;

2504.1 conj	3716.12 verb 3pl indic imperf	2504.1 conj	901.28 verb 3pl indic imperf pass	3632.1 adv	1056.1 conj
καὶ	παρεγίνοντο	καὶ	ἐβαπτίζοντο·	**24.** οὔπω	γὰρ
kai	*pareginonto*	*kai*	*ebaptizonto*	*oupō*	*gar*
and	they were coming	and	being baptized.	Not yet	for

24.a.**Txt:** p66,p75, 01ℵ-corr,02A,017K, 019L,032W,036,037, 038,1,13,etc.byz.Gries, Lach,Treg,Alf,Sod
Var: 01ℵ-org,03B,Tisc, We/HoWeis,UBS/☆

1498.34 verb sing indic imperf act	900.39 verb nom sing masc part perf pass	1519.1 prep	3450.12 art acc sing fem	5274.4 noun acc sing fem	3450.5 art sing masc
ἦν	βεβλημένος	εἰς	τὴν	φυλακὴν	⸂a ὁ ⸃
ēn	*beblēmenos*	*eis*	*tēn*	*phulakēn*	*ho*
was	cast	into	the	prison	

2464.1 name nom masc	1090.33 verb 3sing indic aor mid	3631.1 conj	2197.1 noun nom sing fem	1523.2 prep gen	3450.1 art gen pl
Ἰωάννης.	**25.** Ἐγένετο	οὖν	ζήτησις	ἐκ	τῶν
Iōannēs	*Egeneto*	*oun*	*zētēsis*	*ek*	*tōn*
John.	Arose	then	a question	of	the

25.a.**Txt:** p66,01ℵ-org, 038,1,13,565,bo.Steph
Var: p75,01ℵ-corr,02A, 03B,017K,019L,032W, 037,33,700,byz.Gries, Lach,Treg,Alf,Tisc, We/Ho,Weis,Sod,UBS/☆

3073.6 noun gen pl masc	2464.2 name gen masc	3196.3 prep	2428.3 name-adj gen pl masc	2428.7 name-adj gen masc
μαθητῶν	Ἰωάννου	μετὰ	⸀ Ἰουδαίων	[a☆ Ἰουδαίου]
mathētōn	*Iōannou*	*meta*	*Ioudaiōn*	*Ioudaiou*
disciples	of John	with	Jews	[a Jew]

26.a.**Txt:** 01ℵ,02A, 03B-corr,019L,038,etc. byz.Lach,Tisc,Weis,Sod, UBS/☆
Var: 03B-org,Treg,Alf, We/Ho

26.b.**Txt:** 01ℵ,02A, 03B-corr,017K,019L, 036,037,038,etc.byz. Lach,Tisc,Sod
Var: 03B-org,Treg,Alf, We/Ho,Weis,UBS/☆

3875.1 prep	2484.1 noun gen sing masc	2504.1 conj	2048.1 verb indic aor act	2048.64 verb 3pl indic aor act
περὶ	καθαρισμοῦ·	**26.** καὶ	⸀ ἦλθον	[a ἦλθαν]
peri	*katharismou*	*kai*	*ēlthon*	*ēlthan*
about	purification.	And	they came	[idem]

4242.1 prep	3450.6 art acc sing masc	2464.4 name acc masc	2504.1 conj	1500.3 verb indic aor act	1500.28 verb 3pl indic aor act
πρὸς	τὸν	Ἰωάννην	καὶ	⸀ εἶπον	[b☆ εἶπαν]
pros	*ton*	*Iōannēn*	*kai*	*eipon*	*eipan*
to		John	and	said	[idem]

840.4 prs-pron dat sing	4318.1 noun sing masc	3614.5 rel-pron nom sing masc	1498.34 verb sing indic imperf act	3196.3 prep	4622.2 prs-pron gen 2sing
αὐτῷ,	Ῥαββί,	ὃς	ἦν	μετὰ	σοῦ
autō	*Rhabbi*	*hos*	*ēn*	*meta*	*sou*
to him,	Rabbi,	who	was	with	you

3871.1 adv	3450.2 art gen sing	2422.1 name gen masc	3614.3 rel-pron dat sing	4622.1 prs-pron nom 2sing
πέραν	τοῦ	Ἰορδάνου,	ᾧ	σὺ
peran	*tou*	*Iordanou*	*hō*	*su*
beyond	the	Jordan,	to whom	you

3113.26 verb 2sing indic perf act	1481.14 verb 2sing impr aor act	3642.4 dem-pron nom sing masc	901.3 verb 3sing indic pres act	2504.1 conj
μεμαρτύρηκας,	ἴδε	οὗτος	βαπτίζει,	καὶ
memarturēkas	*ide*	*houtos*	*baptizei*	*kai*
have borne witness,	behold	this	baptizes,	and

plural (as it always is in Hebrew). Some wish to translate this "many springs," but the plural is also used of water in a river and the emphasis is clearly on a depth of water necessary for baptism by immersion.

because there was much water there: . . . many streams there, *Montgomery* . . . an abundance of water, *Norton.*

and they came, and were baptized: People were coming to him, *ALBA* . . . and people were constantly coming, *NEB* . . . and they were coming and being immersed, *Rotherham* . . . kept coming to receive baptism, *Montgomery* . . . and he was baptizing them, *TEV.*

3:24. This verse tells us that John the Baptist had not yet been thrown into prison. The Baptist continued his ministry by preparing people's hearts for the Messiah's kingdom, but his ministry was waning. The narrative indicates that the work of the forerunner overlapped the ministry of Christ. This Gospel puts the relationship between Jesus and John in clear perspective.

24. For John was not yet cast into prison: This was before John had been put, *JB* . . . hadn't yet been thrown into, *Adams* . . . not yet fallen into, *Murdock* . . . as yet been imprisoned, *Fenton* . . . before John's imprisonment, *NEB.*

3:25. There came about a discussion or a questioning between John's disciples and the Jews about ceremonial purifying. We are not told what the discussion was about, but we know the Jews had varying legalistic rites stemming from the traditions of the elders.

"About purifying" (*peri katharismou*) referred to rites of ceremonial purification, but whether they were discussing water baptism or other ritual washings of parts of the body is not specified. Again, "the Jews" indicates opposition. It is possible that the Jews were attempting to stir up discord between the disciples of John and Jesus.

25. Then there arose a question between some of John's disciples and the Jews: . . . had a dispute with a Jew, *Campbell* . . . had opened a discussion, *JB* . . . A discussion accordingly took place, *Fenton* . . . Then there was an argument, *ALBA* . . . on the part of John's disciples with a Jew, *Alford* . . . an argument developed, *NIV* . . . A dispute about cleansing then arose, *Norlie.*

about purifying: . . . about the whole matter of being cleansed, *Phillips* . . . about religious cleansing, *Beck* . . . about proper purification, *ET* . . . concerning purification, *Fenton* . . . about a matter of ritual washing, *TEV.*

3:26. John's disciples brought their problem to their teacher. They were envious of Jesus' success. Perhaps the Jews' questions had borne fruit. "Rabbi" was a title for an outstanding teacher as in 1:38 and 3:2. "To whom thou barest witness" is a self-inflicted reproach on John's disciples. Since they knew John had borne witness to Christ, why were they not following their Messiah?

The next statement, "the same baptizeth," implies that they thought Jesus had stolen the Baptist's technique of ministry. The third comment, "and all men come to him," reveals some envy on behalf of their beloved teacher, John. These disciples were more attached to the powerful personality of John than they were to the message he proclaimed. What did they do when John the Baptist left the scene? John's personality, methods, and power were means by which the message of Christ was introduced. They were to fade when Jesus' message was received.

John had performed his mission exceedingly well. But some of John's disciples would not separate themselves from the man who brought new hope to the nation. Perhaps John knew the message he proclaimed must do its own work in the lives of his followers.

26. And they came unto John, and said unto him, Rabbi, he that was with thee beyond Jordan, to whom thou bearest witness: "Teacher, you remember the man, *TEV* . . . the man you have endorsed, *SEB* . . . so great a character, *Campbell* . . . for whom you have testified, *ALBA* . . . concerning Whom you have yourself given evidence, *Fenton.*

3820.7 adj pl masc	2048.36 verb 3pl indic pres	4242.1 prep	840.6 prs-pron acc sing masc	552.6 verb 3sing indic aor pass
πάντες	ἔρχονται	πρὸς	αὐτόν.	27. Ἀπεκρίθη
pantes	*erchontai*	*pros*	*auton*	*Apekrithē*
all	come	to	him.	Answered

2464.1 name nom masc	2504.1 conj	1500.5 verb 3sing indic aor act	3620.3 partic	1404.4 verb 3sing indic pres	442.1 noun nom sing masc
Ἰωάννης	καὶ	εἶπεν,	Οὐ	δύναται	ἄνθρωπος
Iōannēs	*kai*	*eipen*	*Ou*	*dunatai*	*anthrōpos*
John	and	said,	Not	is able	a man

2956.10 verb inf pres act	3625.6 num card neu	1430.1 partic	3231.1 partic	1498.10 verb 3sing subj pres act	1319.56 verb nom sing neu part perf pass
λαμβάνειν	οὐδὲν	ἐὰν	μὴ	ᾖ	δεδομένον
lambanein	*ouden*	*ean*	*mē*	*ē*	*dedomenon*
to receive	nothing	if	not	it be	given

840.4 prs-pron dat sing	1523.2 prep gen	3450.2 art gen sing	3636.2 noun gen sing masc	840.7 prs-pron nom pl masc	5050.1 prs-pron nom 2pl
αὐτῷ	ἐκ	τοῦ	οὐρανοῦ.	28. αὐτοὶ	ὑμεῖς
autō	*ek*	*tou*	*ouranou*	*autoi*	*humeis*
to him	from	the	heaven.	You	yourselves

1466.4 prs-pron dat 1sing	3113.5 verb 2pl indic pres act	3617.1 conj	1500.3 verb indic aor act	3620.2 partic	1498.2 verb 1sing indic pres act
μοι	μαρτυρεῖτε	ὅτι	εἶπον,	Οὐκ	εἰμὶ
moi	*martureite*	*hoti*	*eipon*	*Ouk*	*eimi*
to me	bear witness	that	I said,	Not	am

1466.1 prs-pron nom 1sing	3450.5 art sing masc	5382.1 name nom masc	233.1 conj	3617.1 conj	643.29 verb nom sing masc part perf pass
ἐγὼ	ὁ	Χριστός,	ἀλλ'	ὅτι	Ἀπεσταλμένος
egō	*ho*	*Christos*	*all'*	*hoti*	*Apestalmenos*
I	the	Christ,	but	that	being sent

1498.2 verb 1sing indic pres act	1699.1 prep gen	1552.2 dem-pron gen sing	3450.5 art sing masc	2174.17 verb nom sing masc part pres act
εἰμὶ	ἔμπροσθεν	ἐκείνου.	29. ὁ	ἔχων
eimi	*emprosthen*	*ekeinou*	*ho*	*echōn*
I am	before	him.	The	having

3450.12 art acc sing fem	3428.3 noun acc sing fem	3429.1 noun nom sing masc	1498.4 verb 3sing indic pres act	3450.5 art sing masc	1156.2 conj
τὴν	νύμφην,	νυμφίος	ἐστίν·	ὁ	δὲ
tēn	*numphēn*	*numphios*	*estin*	*ho*	*de*
the	bride	bridegroom	is;	the	but

5224.1 adj nom sing masc	3450.2 art gen sing	3429.2 noun gen sing masc	3450.5 art sing masc	2449.27 verb nom sing masc part perf act	2504.1 conj
φίλος	τοῦ	νυμφίου,	ὁ	ἑστηκὼς	καὶ
philos	*tou*	*numphiou*	*ho*	*hestēkōs*	*kai*
friend	of the	bridegroom,	the	having stood	and

189.11 verb nom sing masc part pres act	840.3 prs-pron gen sing	5315.3 noun dat sing fem	5299.2 verb 3sing indic pres act	1217.2 prep
ἀκούων	αὐτοῦ,	χαρᾷ	χαίρει	διὰ
akouōn	*autou*	*chara*	*chairei*	*dia*
hearing	him,	with joy	rejoices	because of

3450.12 art acc sing fem	5292.4 noun acc sing fem	3450.2 art gen sing	3429.2 noun gen sing masc	3642.9 dem-pron nom sing fem	3631.1 conj
τὴν	φωνὴν	τοῦ	νυμφίου·	αὕτη	οὖν
tēn	*phōnēn*	*tou*	*numphiou*	*hautē*	*oun*
the	voice	of the	bridegroom,	this	then

At any rate, he did not force those who were devoted to him to depart. Surely, it was not easy for John who had spent about 30 years in preparation for his ministry and only about 1 year in its activity to give up his ministry suddenly.

behold, the same baptizeth, and all men come to him: . . . behold, he immerses, and all are coming, *HBIE* . . . notice, he baptizes, and they all flock to him, *Berkeley* . . . is baptizing, and everybody is going to him, *TCNT*.

3:27. John's answer again reveals the sense of his mission. He was a finger pointing to Jesus. It was his gift from God to be the powerful voice of one crying aloud in the desert. His anointing was not his own, but His whose message he brought. He was the messenger sent before the presence of the Lord himself. This had been "given him from heaven."

It may have seemed humiliating to John's disciples for him to tell them they belonged to a waning movement. John was content in his subordinate role. He reminded both them and himself that he must never aspire above his God-given commission.

27. John answered and said, A man can receive nothing, except it be given him from heaven: A man can claim nothing, *Norlie* . . . A man cannot receive a grace, *ALBA* . . . A man can lay claim only to what is given him from heaven, *JB* . . . can get only what Heaven has given him, *Beck* . . . can obtain no success, *Fenton* . . . can assume nothing, *Norton* . . . but what he derives from heaven, *Campbell* . . . unless it has been granted, *Montgomery* . . . as enabled to do so, *TCNT*.

3:28. John reminded his disciples that he had said, "I am not the Christ." Disciples are to follow Christ, not the minister who points to Him. John's message several months before had been the same as at this time (1:19-36).

28. Ye yourselves bear me witness, that I said, I am not the Christ: You can bear me out, *Moffatt* . . . you personally bear me out, *Berkeley*.

but that I am sent before him: . . . but I have been sent as his forerunner, *Phillips* . . . I am dispatched in front of, *Concordant* . . . I have been sent to prepare for him, *ALBA* . . . as His announcer, *Williams* . . . His appointed forerunner, *BB* . . . sent to precede that man, *Norton* . . . ahead of him, *Berkeley*.

3:29. John explained to his disciples that he and the Christ were not competitors. Christ was the bridegroom and he (John) was a friend of the groom. "He that hath the bride is the bridegroom." The groomsman was always near the groom during the marriage negotiations, the ceremony, and the vows. As he heard the joyful voice of the bridegroom, he too was happy. The apostle Paul expanded this analogy into a beautiful relationship (2 Corinthians 11:2; Ephesians 5:23). As "the friend of the bridegroom," John the Baptist rejoiced that he had a part in bringing the Church to her Lord. The Hebrew wedding was a joyful time. The Baptist here parallels the two, the analogy with the reality. He had shared his joy in wooing the Bride for Christ. His ministry was similar to Abraham's servant who presented the invitation to Rebekah in behalf of Isaac. No image is so intimate as a wedding. Jesus began His ministry at a wedding (John 2). He will complete His work at His own wedding banquet (Revelation 19:1-7).

29. He that hath the bride is the bridegroom: Only the bridegroom can claim the bride, *ALBA* . . . The bride is only for the bridegroom, *JB*.

but the friend of the bridegroom, which standeth and heareth him, rejoiceth greatly because of the bridegroom's voice: . . . stands by his side, *Weymouth* . . . who stands listening to him, *Fenton* . . . who assists him, *Campbell*.

3:30. "He must increase, but I must decrease." "He" obviously refers to Christ. "Must" (*dei*) indicates it is necessary for Him to

3450.9 art nom sing fem	5315.1 noun sing fem	3450.9 art nom sing fem	1684.6 adj nom 1sing fem	3997.29 verb 3sing indic perf pass
ἡ	χαρὰ	ἡ	ἐμὴ	πεπλήρωται.
hē	*chara*	*hē*	*emē*	*peplērōtai*
the	joy	the	my	is fulfilled.

	1552.5 dem-pron acc sing masc	1158.1 verb 3sing indic pres act	831.6 verb inf pres act	1466.7 prs-pron acc 1sing	1156.2 conj
30.	ἐκεῖνον	δεῖ	αὐξάνειν,	ἐμὲ	δὲ
	ekeinon	*dei*	*auxanein*	*eme*	*de*
	That	it is necessary	to increase,	me	but

1628.2 verb inf pres		3450.5 art sing masc	505.1 adv	2048.44 verb nom sing masc part pres	1868.1 prep gen
ἐλαττοῦσθαι.	**31.**	Ὁ	ἄνωθεν	ἐρχόμενος	ἐπάνω
elattousthai		*Ho*	*anōthen*	*erchomenos*	*epanō*
to decrease.		The	from above	coming,	above

3820.4 adj gen pl	1498.4 verb 3sing indic pres act	3450.5 art sing masc	1498.21 verb sing masc part pres act	1523.2 prep gen	3450.10 art gen sing fem
πάντων	ἐστίν.	ὁ	ὢν	ἐκ	τῆς
pantōn	*estin*	*ho*	*ōn*	*ek*	*tēs*
all	is.	The	being	from	the

1087.2 noun gen sing fem	1523.2 prep gen	3450.10 art gen sing fem	1087.2 noun gen sing fem	1498.4 verb 3sing indic pres act	2504.1 conj	1523.2 prep gen
γῆς	ἐκ	τῆς	γῆς	ἐστιν,	καὶ	ἐκ
gēs	*ek*	*tēs*	*gēs*	*estin*	*kai*	*ek*
earth	from	the	earth	is,	and	from

3450.10 art gen sing fem	1087.2 noun gen sing fem	2953.2 verb sing indic pres act	3450.5 art sing masc	1523.2 prep gen	3450.2 art gen sing
τῆς	γῆς	λαλεῖ·	ὁ	ἐκ	τοῦ
tēs	*gēs*	*lalei*	*ho*	*ek*	*tou*
the	earth	speaks.	The	from	the

31.a.**Txt:** p66,01א-corr, 02A,03B,017K,019L, 032W,037,038,etc.byz. Lach,We/Ho,Weis,Sod, UBS/⋆
Var: p75,01א-org,05D,1, 565,sa.Tisc

32.a.**Txt:** 02A,017K,036, 037,038,13,byz.Gries, Lach
Var: p66,p75,01א,03B, 05D,019L,032W,1,33,bo. Treg,Alf,Tisc,We/Ho Weis,Sod,UBS/⋆

3636.2 noun gen sing masc	2048.44 verb nom sing masc part pres	1868.1 prep gen	3820.4 adj gen pl	1498.4 verb 3sing indic pres act
οὐρανοῦ	ἐρχόμενος	⸂a ἐπάνω	πάντων	ἐστίν, ⸃
ouranou	*erchomenos*	*epanō*	*pantōn*	*estin*
heaven	coming	above	all	is,

	2504.1 conj	3614.16 rel-pron sing neu	3571.11 verb 3sing indic perf act	2504.1 conj	189.21 verb 3sing indic aor act
32. ⸂a	καὶ ⸃	ὃ	ἑώρακεν	καὶ	ἤκουσεν
	kai	*ho*	*heōraken*	*kai*	*ēkousen*
	and	what	he has seen	and	heard

3642.17 dem-pron sing neu	3113.3 verb 3sing indic pres act	2504.1 conj	3450.12 art acc sing fem	3114.3 noun acc sing fem	840.3 prs-pron gen sing
τοῦτο	μαρτυρεῖ·	καὶ	τὴν	μαρτυρίαν	αὐτοῦ
touto	*marturei*	*kai*	*tēn*	*marturian*	*autou*
this	he testifies;	and	the	testimony	his

3625.2 num card nom masc	2956.4 verb 3sing indic pres act		3450.5 art sing masc	2956.25 verb nom sing masc part aor act	840.3 prs-pron gen sing
οὐδεὶς	λαμβάνει.	**33.**	ὁ	λαβὼν	αὐτοῦ
oudeis	*lambanei*		*ho*	*labōn*	*autou*
no one	receives.		The	having received	his

3450.12 art acc sing fem	3114.3 noun acc sing fem	4824.2 verb 3sing indic aor act	3617.1 conj	3450.5 art sing masc	2296.1 noun nom sing masc
τὴν	μαρτυρίαν	ἐσφράγισεν	ὅτι	ὁ	θεὸς
tēn	*marturian*	*esphragisen*	*hoti*	*ho*	*theos*
the	testimony	has set to his seal	that		God

continue to multiply numbers of believers. The word "increase" (*auxanein*) occurs once in this Gospel and 22 times in the New Testament, and in all instances it is translated by either "increase" or "grow." The word "decrease" (*elattousthai*) is used but once in John's Gospel and twice elsewhere in the New Testament. *LSJ* under *elattoō* defines the word as "to cut down," "shorten," "make smaller," and "to reduce." The words are nearly the last words of John the Baptist given to his disciples, recorded in Holy Scripture. They were fitting words for John's epitaph, for they had been the motto of his life. John was imprisoned and became the last Old Testament prophet to suffer martyrdom. His last known preaching reached a zenith few preachers attain. John demonstrated two great traits in his life and ministry; first, he made Jesus his preeminent message, and second, he minimized himself.

this my joy therefore is fulfilled: . . . such is my joy, and it is complete, *BB* . . . I have experienced to the full, *TCNT* . . . is running over, *Williams.*

30. He must increase, but I must decrease: He must go on from strength to strength; I must fade out of the picture, *Barclay* . . . He must grow greater and greater, *Norlie* . . . He must grow greater, but I must grow less, *Weymouth* . . . He must be growing, yet I am to be inferior, *Concordant* . . . grow greater, I must grow smaller, *JB* . . . To him must be increase, *Murdock* . . . to become greater, *BB* . . . He must wax, *Moffatt* . . . and I must wane, *Berkeley.*

3:31. The first "he" is Jesus. John's desire was that his disciples become followers of Jesus. The second "he" refers to John himself. Jesus had referred to "earthly things" (3:12). He could do this because He became man. But He was also from above. He brought the revelation of heavenly things with Him. Like Jesus, the Baptist pointed away from earthly things to the revelation of heavenly things.

31. He that cometh from above is above all: . . . is greater than all others, *BB* . . . stands above all, *ALBA* . . . is over all, *Adams.*

he that is of the earth is earthly, and speaketh of the earth: . . . who originates, *Fenton* . . . springs from earth, *Williams* . . . has his origin in this world, *Barclay* . . . is earth-minded and speaks from an earthly standpoint, *Berkeley.*

he that cometh from heaven is above all: . . . is far above all others, *Williams* . . . is the most important, *SEB.*

3:32. John the Baptist continued to speak of Jesus. John said what He (Jesus) "hath seen," indicating the heavenly things by the use of the perfect tense verb. John changed the tense for the next verb "heard" (aorist), indicating a historical fact. That is to say, the revelation of God was based on historical knowledge. True testimony must stand on this kind of truth.

"And no man receiveth his testimony" is not meant in an absolute sense, as the next verse indicates.

32. And what he hath seen and heard, that he testifieth: He states what he has seen and what he heard, *TCNT.*

and no man receiveth his testimony: . . . yet no one accepts his testimony, *Moffatt, ALBA* . . . yet no one believes His witness, *Norlie.*

3:33. John was speaking of himself as one of those who received the witness of Jesus. The revelation God gave to John made him sure of his office as the herald of the Messiah. By receiving the witness of Jesus, John set his seal that God is true. The seal was a sign of acceptance.

33. He that hath received his testimony hath set to his seal that God is true: . . . has sealed, *Sawyer* . . . has certified, *Williams* . . . vouches the veracity of God, *Campbell* . . . attest the fact, *TCNT* . . . is acknowledging the

3:34. "He whom God hath sent" gives the reason for accepting the witness of Jesus. He is the great "Sent One," heaven's own

225.2 adj nom sing	**1498.4** verb 3sing indic pres act	**3614.6** rel-pron acc sing masc	**1056.1** conj	**643.8** verb 3sing indic aor act	**3450.5** art sing masc
ἀληθής	ἐστιν.	**34.** ὃν	γὰρ	ἀπέστειλεν	ὁ
alēthēs	*estin*	*hon*	*gar*	*apesteilen*	*ho*
true	is;	he whom	for	sent	

2296.1 noun nom sing masc	**3450.17** art pl neu	**4343.4** noun pl neu	**3450.2** art gen sing	**2296.2** noun gen sing masc	**2953.2** verb sing indic pres act
θεὸς	τὰ	ῥήματα	τοῦ	θεοῦ	λαλεῖ·
theos	*ta*	*rhēmata*	*tou*	*theou*	*lalei*
God	the	words		of God	speaks;

34.a.**Txt:** 02A,04C-corr, 05D,017K,036,037,038, 13,byz.sa.bo.Lach
Var: 01ℵ,03B,04C-org, 019L,33,Alf,Tisc,We/Ho, WeisSod,UBS/*

3620.3 partic	**1056.1** conj	**1523.2** prep gen	**3228.1** noun gen sing neu	**1319.2** verb 3sing indic pres act	**3450.5** art sing masc	**2296.1** noun nom sing masc
οὐ	γὰρ	ἐκ	μέτρου	δίδωσιν	⸂a ὁ	θεὸς ⸃
ou	*gar*	*ek*	*metrou*	*didōsin*	*ho*	*theos*
not	for	by	measure	gives		God

3450.16 art sing neu	**4011.1** noun sing neu	**3450.5** art sing masc	**3824.1** noun nom sing masc	**25.2** verb 3sing pres act	**3450.6** art acc sing masc
τὸ	πνεῦμα.	**35.** ὁ	πατὴρ	ἀγαπᾷ	τὸν
to	*pneuma*	*ho*	*patēr*	*agapa*	*ton*
the	Spirit.	The	Father	loves	the

5048.4 noun acc sing masc	**2504.1** conj	**3820.1** adj	**1319.33** verb 3sing indic perf act	**1706.1** prep	**3450.11** art dat sing fem
υἱόν,	καὶ	πάντα	δέδωκεν	ἐν	τῇ
huion	*kai*	*panta*	*dedōken*	*en*	*tē*
Son,	and	all things	has given	into	the

5331.3 noun dat sing fem	**840.3** prs-pron gen sing	**3450.5** art sing masc	**3961.10** verb nom sing masc part pres act	**1519.1** prep	**3450.6** art acc sing masc
χειρὶ	αὐτοῦ.	**36.** ὁ	πιστεύων	εἰς	τὸν
cheiri	*autou*	*ho*	*pisteuōn*	*eis*	*ton*
hand	his.	The	believing	on	the

5048.4 noun acc sing masc	**2174.4** verb 3sing indic pres act	**2205.4** noun acc sing fem	**164.1** adj sing	**3450.5** art sing masc	**1156.2** conj
υἱὸν	ἔχει	ζωὴν	αἰώνιον·	ὁ	δὲ
huion	*echei*	*zōēn*	*aiōnion*	*ho*	*de*
Son	has	life	eternal;	the	and

540.2 verb nom sing masc part pres act	**3450.3** art dat sing	**5048.3** noun dat sing masc	**3620.2** partic	**3571.31** verb 3sing indic fut mid	**2205.4** noun acc sing fem
ἀπειθῶν	τῷ	υἱῷ	οὐκ	ὄψεται	ζωήν,
apeithōn	*tō*	*huiō*	*ouk*	*opsetai*	*zōēn*
not being subject	to the	Son	not	shall see	life,

233.1 conj	**3450.9** art nom sing fem	**3572.1** noun nom sing fem	**3450.2** art gen sing	**2296.2** noun gen sing masc	**3176.1** verb 3sing indic act	**1894.2** prep
ἀλλ'	ἡ	ὀργὴ	τοῦ	θεοῦ	μένει	ἐπ'
all'	*hē*	*orgē*	*tou*	*theou*	*menei*	*ep'*
but	the	wrath		of God	stays	on

840.6 prs-pron acc sing masc	**5453.1** conj	**3631.1** conj	**1091.17** verb 3sing indic aor act	**3450.5** art sing masc	**2935.1** noun nom sing masc
αὐτόν.	**4:1.** Ὡς	οὖν	ἔγνω	ὁ	⸀ Κύριος
auton	*Hōs*	*oun*	*egnō*	*ho*	*Kurios*
him.	When	therefore	knew	the	Lord

1.a.**Var:** 01ℵ,05D,038,1, 565,1241,bo.Tisc

2400.1 name nom masc	**3617.1** conj	**189.24** verb 3pl indic aor act	**3450.7** art pl masc	**5168.4** name pl masc	**3617.1** conj
[a Ἰησοῦς]	ὅτι	ἤκουσαν	οἱ	Φαρισαῖοι,	ὅτι
Iēsous	*hoti*	*ēkousan*	*hoi*	*Pharisaioi*	*hoti*
[Jesus]	that	heard	the	Pharisees,	that

Apostle (Hebrews 3:1). His words are the very words of God. In contrast to the Old Testament saints and prophets, God did not give Him the Spirit "by measure." (Some scholars believe it was John the Baptist who had this kind of anointing that brought the words of God through him.)

fact, *Phillips* . . . stamped with his seal of approval, *Beck* . . . attests his belief that God is true, *Norton* . . . definitely certifies that God is true, *Berkeley* . . . it is Divine truth, *Fenton.*

3:35. "Loveth" (*agapa*) is the same verb as that used to indicate God's love for the world. An interesting parallel occurs in 5:20. In this verse the word *love* is not *agapa* as here, but *philei* which at times indicates the love in a family relationship.

"And hath given all things into his hand" refers to an outgrowth of the Father's love for the Son. This is not an indication that Jesus is less than God. It means that Jesus in His work of redemption has the love and resources of His Father under His authority. Our Lord claims the same power in Matthew 11:27 and 28:18.

34. For he whom God hath sent speaketh the words of God: . . . has commissioned, *Campbell.*

for God giveth not the Spirit by measure unto him: God does not give the Spirit sparingly, *Montgomery* . . . He did not grant the Spirit with limitation, *Fenton* . . . only in a limited way, *Adams* . . . does not limit the gift of the Spirit, *TCNT . . . limited way, Adams* . . . does not limit the gift of the Spirit, *TCNT* . . . without limit, *Norlie.*

3:36. This verse is a summary of all the witness to Christ. The Baptist was still teaching his disciples. It is clear that they must turn from John and believe on the Son. All Christ's previous teaching is condensed in these few comprehensive words. The simple act of receiving the revelation of God in Christ and a commitment to that truth brings untold benefits to the believer. "On the Son" is again the simplest beginning of faith, but it is necessary for a journey that will end in blessedness for eternity. The verb indicates the one who believes now has life now. It also indicates continuous action so that those who keep on believing keep on having eternal life. The moment we believe the seed of eternal life sprouts and, as we keep believing, it grows. One who receives the gift of Jesus Christ receives eternal life. The gift and eternal life are inherently bonded together. In Jesus is salvation! In Him is eternal life! Outside of Him is darkness, death, and gloom.

This verse concludes all that the Baptist witnessed concerning Christ. These last two verses are an essence of sweetness for the believer and an extract of wormwood for the unbeliever.

35. The Father loveth the Son, and hath given all things into his hand: . . . has given him control over everything, *Moffatt* . . . has entrusted him with all authority, *NEB.*

36. He that believeth on the Son hath everlasting life: Whoever trusts...possesses eternal life, *Williams* . . . He who has faith, *BB.*

and he that believeth not the Son shall not see life: . . . but he that disbelieves the Son, *HBIE* . . . but he who disobeys the Son, *Montgomery.*

but the wrath of God abideth on him: . . . he lives under the anger of God, *Phillips* . . . the vengeance, *Campbell* . . . God's anger broods over him, *Moffatt.*

4:1,2. "Knew" is a verb for *knowing* which comes from either divine or human experience. Jesus had both divine and human knowledge.

The Pharisees took pride in thinking they were spiritual. They could not tolerate anyone whose popularity detracted from their own. The multitudes were drawn to both John the Baptist and Jesus. This was not pleasing to the Pharisees. Jesus' amazing success

1. When therefore the Lord knew how the Pharisees had heard that Jesus made and bap-

John 4:2

2400.1 name nom masc	3979.4 adj comp acc pl	3073.8 noun acc pl masc	4020.5 verb 3sing indic pres act	2504.1 conj	901.3 verb 3sing indic pres act
Ἰησοῦς	πλείονας	μαθητὰς	ποιεῖ	καὶ	βαπτίζει
Iēsous	*pleionas*	*mathētas*	*poiei*	*kai*	*baptizei*
Jesus	more	disciples	makes	and	baptizes

2211.1 conj	2464.1 name nom masc	2515.1 conj	2400.1 name nom masc	840.5 prs-pron nom sing masc
ἢ	Ἰωάννης·	**2.** καίτοιγε	Ἰησοῦς	αὐτὸς
ē	*Iōannēs*	*kaitoige*	*Iēsous*	*autos*
than	John	although indeed	Jesus	himself

3620.2 partic	901.10 verb 3sing indic imperf act	233.1 conj	3450.7 art pl masc	3073.5 noun nom pl masc	840.3 prs-pron gen sing
οὐκ	ἐβάπτιζεν,	ἀλλ'	οἱ	μαθηταὶ	αὐτοῦ·
ouk	*ebaptizen*	*all'*	*hoi*	*mathētai*	*autou*
not	was baptizing	but	the	disciples	his,

856.10 verb 3sing indic aor act	3450.12 art acc sing fem	2424.4 name acc fem	2504.1 conj	562.2 verb 3sing indic aor act	3687.1 adv
3. ἀφῆκεν	τὴν	Ἰουδαίαν,	καὶ	ἀπῆλθεν	πάλιν
aphēken	*tēn*	*Ioudaian*	*kai*	*apēlthen*	*palin*
he left		Judea,	and	went away	again

1519.1 prep	3450.12 art acc sing fem	1049.4 name acc sing fem	1158.6 verb 3sing indic imperf act	1156.2 conj	840.6 prs-pron acc sing masc
εἰς	τὴν	Γαλιλαίαν.	**4.** ἔδει	δὲ	αὐτὸν
eis	*tēn*	*Galilaian*	*edei*	*de*	*auton*
into		Galilee.	It was necessary	and	for him

1324.14 verb inf pres	1217.2 prep	3450.10 art gen sing fem	4397.2 name gen fem	2048.34 verb 3sing indic pres
διέρχεσθαι	διὰ	τῆς	Σαμαρείας.	**5.** ἔρχεται
dierchesthai	*dia*	*tēs*	*Samareias*	*erchetai*
to pass	through		Samaria.	He comes

3631.1 conj	1519.1 prep	4032.4 noun acc sing fem	3450.10 art gen sing fem	4397.2 name gen fem	2978.35 verb acc sing fem part pres pass
οὖν	εἰς	πόλιν	τῆς	Σαμαρείας	λεγομένην
oun	*eis*	*polin*	*tēs*	*Samareias*	*legomenēn*
therefore	to	a city		of Samaria	called

5.a.**Var:** p66,04C-org, 05D,019L,021M,032W, 038,1,28,33,Gries,Lach

4817.1 name fem	3999.1 adv	3450.2 art gen sing	5399.1 noun gen sing neu	3614.16 rel-pron sing neu	3614.2 rel-pron gen sing
Συχὰρ,	πλησίον	τοῦ	χωρίου	⸀ ὃ	[a οὗ]
Suchar	*plēsion*	*tou*	*chōriou*	*ho*	*hou*
Sychar,	near	the	land	which	[idem]

5.b.**Var:** p66,p75,01ℵ, 03B,We/Ho,Weis,UBS/☆

1319.14 verb 3sing indic aor act	2361.1 name masc	3450.3 art dat sing	2473.1 name masc	3450.3 art dat sing	5048.3 noun dat sing masc
ἔδωκεν	Ἰακὼβ	[b☆+ τῷ]	Ἰωσὴφ	τῷ	υἱῷ
edōken	*Iakōb*	*tō*	*Iōsēph*	*tō*	*huiō*
gave	Jacob		to Joseph	the	son

840.3 prs-pron gen sing	1498.34 verb sing indic imperf act	1156.2 conj	1550.1 adv	3938.1 noun nom sing fem	3450.2 art gen sing	2361.1 name masc
αὐτοῦ.	**6.** ἦν	δὲ	ἐκεῖ	πηγὴ	τοῦ	Ἰακώβ.
autou	*ēn*	*de*	*ekei*	*pēgē*	*tou*	*Iakōb*
his.	Was	now	there	spring		Jacob's;

3450.5 art sing masc	3631.1 conj	2400.1 name nom masc	2844.16 verb nom sing masc part perf act	1523.2 prep gen	3450.10 art gen sing fem
ὁ	οὖν	Ἰησοῦς	κεκοπιακὼς	ἐκ	τῆς
ho	*oun*	*Iēsous*	*kekopiakōs*	*ek*	*tēs*
	therefore	Jesus,	being tired	from	the

irritated the self-righteous, self-centered, and self-exalting religious bigots.

tized more disciples than John: Now the Pharisees had heard that, *ALBA* . . . Jesus is securing, *Fenton* . . . that He was winning, *Williams* . . . was constantly making and baptizing more disciples, *Wuest.*

4:3. The Lord left Judea to go to Galilee in order to avoid a conflict with the Pharisees, as verse 1 indicates. His ministry would be hindered by the Pharisees' strong opposition. The Baptist also was a target of their hostility.

The most fruitful period of His ministry was in Galilee. Nearly all of His disciples and especially the apostles came from Galilee. His journey led northward along the ridge of the Judean mountains toward Galilee.

2. (Though Jesus himself baptized not: . . . although Jesus himself was not in the habit of baptizing at all, *Barclay* . . . was not accustomed, *Montgomery.*

but his disciples): . . . but only His disciples, *Fenton.*

3. He left Judaea, and departed again into Galilee: Because of this, He left, *ET* . . . He abruptly went away from Judaea, *Wuest* . . . went back to Galilee, *JB.*

4:4. "He" is obviously Jesus, yet His disciples were in His company. "Must needs" points out a necessity. First, there was the physical necessity because Samaria was located between Judea and Galilee. The Jews had no dealings with the Samaritans. Second, Jesus "must" go through Samaria because of a spiritual necessity. Jesus' going "through" the area brought the gospel to many Samaritans. Jesus also set an example for the Church after Pentecost to reach other Samaritans (Acts 8:4-25).

4. And he must needs go through Samaria: He had to pass through Samaria, *RSV* . . . This meant that he had to cross Samaria, *JB* . . . To get there he had to travel through, *ALBA* . . . he had occasion, *Murdock* . . . Being obliged, *Campbell* . . . he was of necessity, *Douay.*

4:5. The Samaritans lived in only a part of Samaria. Sychar may have been their chief village. The city's location was near old Shechem.

The area had historical roots reaching back to the patriarchs. The Samaritans had a rich heritage. The promises, the people, and the land were uniquely interwoven. This place was their connection with the one true God. God had commanded the Law to be read from this location (Joshua 8:33). The Samaritans who occupied this area felt they had an unusual claim on God who had worked so wonderfully there in the past.

5. Then cometh he to a city of Samaria, which is called Sychar, near to the parcel of ground that Jacob gave to his son Joseph: . . . close to the piece of ground, *ALBA* . . . near the plot of land, *TCNT* . . . piece of land, *HBIE* . . . the historic plot, *Phillips* . . . the heritage, *Campbell* . . . the estate, *Fenton* . . . Jacob had presented, *Berkeley.*

4:6. Jacob's well is really a cistern (*pēgē*) dug so deep that spring water feeds it. Its depth has been estimated to be up to 100 feet. Jacob had it dug when he lived near Shechem. Genesis 33:18 through chapter 34 contains the background for the period in which Jacob dug the well. The well was a meeting site and a resting place for travelers.

6. Now Jacob's well was there: Jacob's spring, *Concordant, Barclay* . . . the one which had belonged to Jacob, *Wuest.*

Jesus therefore, being wearied with his journey: . . . so Jesus, tired out, *Weymouth* . . . exhausted by the journey, *Moffatt*

3460.1 noun gen sing fem	2488.5 verb 3sing indic imperf	3643.1 adv	1894.3 prep	3450.11 art dat sing fem	3938.3 noun dat sing fem
ὁδοιπορίας	ἐκαθέζετο	οὕτως	ἐπὶ	τῇ	πηγῇ.
hodoiporias	*ekathezeto*	*houtōs*	*epi*	*tē*	*pēgē*
journey,	sat	thus	at	the	fountain.

6.a.**Txt:** 01ℵ-corr,017K, 036,037,byz.
Var: 01ℵ-org,02A,03B, 04C,05D,019L,038,33, LachTreg,Alf,Word,Tisc, We/Ho,Weis,Sod,UBS/☆

5443.2 noun nom sing fem	1498.34 verb sing indic imperf act	5448.1 adv	5453.1 conj	1608.3 num ord nom sing fem	2048.34 verb 3sing indic pres
ὥρα	ἦν	ˊ ὡσεὶ	[a☆ ὡς]	ἕκτη.	7. Ἔρχεται
hōra	*ēn*	*hōsei*	*hōs*	*hektē*	*Erchetai*
Hour	was	about	[idem]	sixth.	Comes

1129.1 noun nom sing fem	1523.2 prep gen	3450.10 art gen sing fem	4397.2 name gen fem	498.3 verb inf aor act	5045.1 noun sing neu
γυνὴ	ἐκ	τῆς	Σαμαρείας	ἀντλῆσαι	ὕδωρ.
gunē	*ek*	*tēs*	*Samareias*	*antlēsai*	*hudōr*
a woman	out of		Samaria	to draw	water.

2978.5 verb 3sing indic pres act	840.11 prs-pron dat sing fem	3450.5 art sing masc	2400.1 name nom masc	1319.25 verb 2sing impr aor act
λέγει	αὐτῇ	ὁ	Ἰησοῦς,	Δός
legei	*autē*	*ho*	*Iēsous*	*Dos*
Says	to her		Jesus,	Give

7.a.**Txt:** 01ℵ-corr,02A, 03B-corr,017K,036,037, 038,byz.Lach,Sod
Var: 03B-org,04C-org, 05D,019L,Treg,Alf,Tisc, We/Ho,Weis,UBS/☆

1466.4 prs-pron dat 1sing	3956.23 verb inf aor act	3956.29 verb inf aor act	3450.7 art pl masc	1056.1 conj	3073.5 noun nom pl masc
μοι	ˊ πιεῖν·	[a☆ πεῖν·]	8. οἱ	γὰρ	μαθηταὶ
moi	*piein*	*pein*	*hoi*	*gar*	*mathētai*
me	to drink;	[idem]	the	for	disciples

840.3 prs-pron gen sing	562.14 verb 3pl indic plperf act	1519.1 prep	3450.12 art acc sing fem	4032.4 noun acc sing fem	2419.1 conj
αὐτοῦ	ἀπεληλύθεισαν	εἰς	τὴν	πόλιν,	ἵνα
autou	*apelēlutheisan*	*eis*	*tēn*	*polin*	*hina*
his	had gone away	into	the	city,	that

5001.4 noun acc pl fem	58.9 verb 3pl subj aor act	2978.5 verb 3sing indic pres act	3631.1 conj	840.4 prs-pron dat sing
τροφὰς	ἀγοράσωσιν.	9. Λέγει	οὖν	αὐτῷ
trophas	*agorasōsin*	*Legei*	*oun*	*autō*
provisions	they might buy.	Says	therefore	to him

3450.9 art nom sing fem	1129.1 noun nom sing fem	3450.9 art nom sing fem	4399.1 name nom sing fem	4399.3 name nom sing fem
ἡ	γυνὴ	ἡ	ˊ Σαμαρεῖτις,	[☆ Σαμαρῖτις,]
hē	*gunē*	*hē*	*Samareitis*	*Samaritis*
the	woman		Samaritan,	[idem]

4316.1 adv	4622.1 prs-pron nom 2sing	2428.6 name-adj nom masc	1498.21 verb sing masc part pres act	3706.1 prep	1466.3 prs-pron gen 1sing
Πῶς	σὺ	Ἰουδαῖος	ὢν	παρ'	ἐμοῦ
Pōs	*su*	*Ioudaios*	*ōn*	*par'*	*emou*
How	you	a Jew	being	from	me

9.a.**Txt:** 01ℵ-corr, 03B-corr,04C-corr,017K, 036,037,038,byz.Sod
Var: 03B-org,04C-org, 05D,Treg,Alf,Tisc, We/Ho,Weis,UBS/☆

3956.23 verb inf aor act	3956.29 verb inf aor act	153.4 verb 2sing indic pres act	1498.27 verb gen sing fem part pres act	1129.2 noun gen sing fem
ˊ πιεῖν	[a☆ πεῖν]	αἰτεῖς,	ˊ οὔσης	γυναικὸς
piein	*pein*	*aiteis*	*ousēs*	*gunaikos*
to drink	[idem]	do ask,	being	a woman

4399.2 name gen sing fem	1129.2 noun gen sing fem	4399.4 name gen sing fem	1498.27 verb gen sing fem part pres act
Σαμαρείτιδος;	[☆ γυναικὸς	Σαμαρίτιδος	οὔσης;]
Samareitidos	*gunaikos*	*Samaritidos*	*ousēs*
Samaritan?	[a woman	Samaritan	being?]

The word *houtōs* means "thus" and may modify the verb "sat," in which case it would mean "He sat right down," or it could modify the adjective "tired" meaning "tired as He was," or it could simply mean "thus as He was." The Early Church Father Chrysostom explains it as, "Not upon a throne, not upon a cushion, but simply, as He was, upon the ground" (Morris, *New International Commentary*, 4:258). He had an appointment in the plan of God. The woman was a part of the plan, but the larger design was for the entire population: the gospel of the Kingdom was to be presented to them.

John's description is vivid: a beautiful, historical well and a weary Jesus sitting upon its curbstone. The time, John says, was about the sixth hour or, according to Jewish counting the sixth hour from sunrise, noon. The sun was high and hot. In the distance the Lord's disciples were strolling toward the village. A woman with a large pitcher came toward the well. The day was an ordinary one, yet on this day many Samaritans would drink of the water of life. The *Logos* (Word, manifestation) was sitting on their doorstep—waiting!

. . . having become wearied to the point of exhaustion, *Wuest* . . . being fatigued with travelling, *Sawyer* . . . with the toil of travelling, *Murdock* . . . was tired because of traveling, *SEB.*

sat thus on the well: . . . sat down beside it, *Phillips* . . . dropped down just as He was by the well, *Berkeley* . . . wearily sat down beside the well, *Adams.*

and it was about the sixth hour: It was then about mid-day, *TCNT* . . . It was then about noon, *Fenton.*

7. There cometh a woman of Samaria to draw water: . . . then coming along, *Fenton.*

Jesus saith unto her, Give me to drink: Let me have a drink, *Berkeley* . . . Please, give me a drink of water, *SEB.*

4:7. Water for drinking, washing, etc., was carried in pitchers from a community well to the homes. Bits of detail enable us to see why the woman came alone at noon. She had been married five times, and at the time of this incident she was living in open adultery. She came alone because she was not welcomed by the women who came to the well at sundown.

Jesus said, "Give me to drink." Can you imagine the giver of the water of life asking for a drink? He was naturally thirsty. The day was hot and He had walked for some hours. His wearied and thirsty condition showed His humanity. The woman would not have opened the conversation with Jesus. Women did not talk to men unless the man began the dialogue. Furthermore, she was a Samaritan, and He was a Jew. Except for business reasons, Samaritans and Jews had no social contacts.

8. (For his disciples were gone away unto the city to buy meat.): . . . to buy food, *ASV* . . . to buy provisions, *Weymouth* . . . be buying nourishment, *Concordant* . . . in order that they might buy, *Wuest.*

9. Then saith the woman of Samaria unto him, How is it that thou, being a Jew: What? You are a Jew, *Moffatt* . . . You are a Jewish man, *SEB.*

askest drink of me, which am a woman of Samaria?: Why are you asking me for a drink of water? *SEB.*

4:8. "To buy meat" (*hina trophas agorasōsin*) is literally "that they might buy food at the open marketplace." More than bread or meat is included in the word "food" (*trophas*). The term carries the basic meaning of nourishment.

4:9. For the first time in the narrative we learn that the woman was a Samaritan. Samaritans were a mixed race, descendants of

3620.3 partic	1056.1 conj	4649.1 verb 3pl indic pres	2428.2 name-adj pl masc	4398.4 name dat pl masc
οὐ	γὰρ	συγχρῶνται	Ἰουδαῖοι	⸀ Σαμαρείταις.
ou	gar	sunchrōntai	Ioudaioi	Samareitais
No	for	associate	Jews	with Samaritans.

4398.8 name dat pl masc	552.6 verb 3sing indic aor pass	2400.1 name nom masc	2504.1 conj	1500.5 verb 3sing indic aor act
[☆ Σαμαρίταις.]	10. Ἀπεκρίθη	Ἰησοῦς	καὶ	εἶπεν
Samaritais	Apekrithē	Iēsous	kai	eipen
[idem]	Answered	Jesus	and	said

840.11 prs-pron dat sing fem	1479.1 conj	3471.10 verb 2sing indic plperf act	3450.12 art acc sing fem	1424.4 noun acc sing fem	3450.2 art gen sing
αὐτῇ,	Εἰ	ᾔδεις	τὴν	δωρεὰν	τοῦ
autē	Ei	ēdeis	tēn	dōrean	tou
to her,	If	you had known	the	gift	

2296.2 noun gen sing masc	2504.1 conj	4949.3 intr-pron nom sing	1498.4 verb 3sing indic pres act	3450.5 art sing masc	2978.15 verb sing masc part pres act
θεοῦ,	καὶ	τίς	ἐστιν	ὁ	λέγων
theou	kai	tis	estin	ho	legōn
of God,	and	who	it is	the	saying

10.a.**Txt:** 01ℵ-corr,02A, 03B-corr,04C-corr,017K, 036,037,038,byz.Lach, Sod
Var: 03B-org,04C-org, 05D,019L,Treg,Alf,Tisc, We/Ho,Weis,UBS/☆

4622.3 prs-pron dat 2sing	1319.25 verb 2sing impr aor act	1466.4 prs-pron dat 1sing	3956.23 verb inf aor act	3956.29 verb inf aor act
σοι,	Δός	μοι	⸀ πιεῖν,	[a☆ πεῖν,]
soi	Dos	moi	piein	pein
to you,	Give	me	to drink,	[idem]

4622.1 prs-pron nom 2sing	300.1 partic	153.11 verb 2sing indic aor act	840.6 prs-pron acc sing masc	2504.1 conj
σὺ	ἂν	ᾔτησας	αὐτὸν,	καὶ
su	an	ētēsas	auton	kai
you		would have asked	him,	and

1319.14 verb 3sing indic aor act	300.1 partic	4622.3 prs-pron dat 2sing	5045.1 noun sing neu	2180.10 verb sing part pres act
ἔδωκεν	ἂν	σοι	ὕδωρ	ζῶν.
edōken	an	soi	hudōr	zōn
he would have given		to you	water	living.

11.a.**Txt:** p66,01ℵ-corr, 02A,04C,05D,017K, 019L,032W,036,037, 038,1,13,28,33,565,700, etc.byz.Gries,Lach,Treg, Tisc,Sod
Var: p75,03B,We/Ho Weis,UBS/☆

2978.5 verb 3sing indic pres act	840.4 prs-pron dat sing	3450.9 art nom sing fem	1129.1 noun nom sing fem	2935.5 noun voc sing masc	3641.1 conj
11. Λέγει	αὐτῷ	⸂a ἡ	γυνή, ⸃	Κύριε,	οὔτε
Legei	autō	hē	gunē	Kurie	oute
Says	to him	the	woman,	Sir,	nothing

499.1 noun acc sing neu	2174.3 verb 2sing indic pres act	2504.1 conj	3450.16 art sing neu	5257.1 noun sing neu	1498.4 verb 3sing indic pres act
ἄντλημα	ἔχεις,	καὶ	τὸ	φρέαρ	ἐστὶν
antlēma	echeis	kai	to	phrear	estin
to draw with	you have,	and	the	well	is

895.3 adj nom sing neu	4019.1 adv	3631.1 conj	2174.3 verb 2sing indic pres act	3450.16 art sing neu	5045.1 noun sing neu
βαθύ·	πόθεν	οὖν	ἔχεις	τὸ	ὕδωρ
bathu	pothen	oun	echeis	to	hudōr
deep;	from where	then	have you	the	water

3450.16 art sing neu	2180.10 verb sing part pres act	3231.1 partic	4622.1 prs-pron nom 2sing	3157.2 adj comp nom sing	1498.3 verb 2sing indic pres act
τὸ	ζῶν;	12. μὴ	σὺ	μείζων	εἶ
to	zōn	mē	su	meizōn	ei
the	living?	Not	you	greater	are

the imported Gentiles and poor Jews left in Palestine from the Assyrian (722 B.C.) and the Babylonian (586 B.C.) conquests. Intermarriages between these two groups produced the Samaritans. They were hated by the Jews and despised by the Gentiles.

In addition, considering them to be half-breeds, the Jews also disdained the Samaritans for religious reasons. The Samaritans refused to worship at Jerusalem, preferring instead their own temple on Mount Gerizim. Also, the Samaritans recognized only the first five books of Moses as canonical, while the Jews included the Prophets and Writings in their canon of inspired Scriptures.

Jesus told one of His most thought-provoking parables about the good Samaritan (Luke 10:33-36).

for the Jews have no dealings with the Samaritans: (For Jews do not associate with Samaritans), *Wuest* . . . don't want to associate, *SEB* . . . are not beholden, *Concordant* . . . have no familiarity, *Murdock* . . . medle not, *Tyndale* . . . do not communicate, *Douay* . . . are not on good terms, *TCNT* . . . do not use vessels in common, *NEB* . . . do not get on together, *ALBA.*

4:10. By this time Jesus intimated that the woman could expect more from Him than a mere dipper of water. He pointed out her ignorance and turned her thoughts from national prejudice and racial hostility. His statement awakened her interest and appealed to her curiosity. "The gift of God" is the same as the gift Jesus revealed to Nicodemus (3:16). God's gift is the only begotten Son through whom we may receive eternal life (3:16) and the gift of the "living water." Jesus is the gift and the source of all that salvation brings. Note that Jesus spoke of the Holy Spirit as the wind to Nicodemus and as living water to the Samaritan woman.

How extensive was her ignorance! Yet, she surpassed many of the religious Jews of Jerusalem for she was unhindered by formalism and hypocrisy. Christ asked for a drink. He took the initiative to bring her to salvation.

"Living water" (*hudōr zōn*) occurs three times in the New Testament (4:10,11; 7:38). In 7:38,39 John interprets living water as the fullness of the Holy Spirit whose coming is recorded in Acts chapter 2.

10. Jesus answered and said unto her, If thou knewest the gift of God: If you had known the free gift of God, *Montgomery* . . . If you were aware of the gratuity of God, *Concordant* . . . If you had recognised the gift of, *Fenton* . . . If you only knew what God is offering, *JB* . . . the gratuitous gift, *Wuest* . . . the bounty of God, *Campbell.*

and who it is that saith to thee, Give me to drink: . . . and who is asking you for a drink, *Moffatt.*

thou wouldest have asked of him: . . . you would have been the one to ask, *JB* . . . you would have requested of Him, *Berkeley.*

and he would have given thee living water: . . . the water of lyfe, *Tyndale* . . . quyk watir, *Wycliffe* . . . fresh running water, *ET* . . . water which is alive, *Wuest.*

4:11. "Sir" is a title of respect. The woman had called Jesus by the racial designation "Jew" in verse 9, but now her hostility was disappearing. The Lord's declaration that He would give her living water was like the first breeze before a rain. She became alert, curious, and inquisitive. She saw that He had "nothing to draw with." The well was deep and there was no water for miles to compare with that of Jacob's well. Why did He speak of living water? Such thoughts must have gone through her mind.

Nicodemus had asked, "How can these things be?" The Samaritan woman asked, "Whence then hast thou that living water?" Nicodemus was interested in the theological process of "how." The Samaritan woman was concerned with the practical source, "where."

11. The woman saith unto him, Sir, thou hast nothing to draw with, and the well is deep: You have no draw-bucket, *Fenton* . . . You have no bucket, sir, *JB* . . . Mister, you don't even have a bucket, *SEB* . . . a pail, *Adams.*

from whence then hast thou that living water?: . . . where will you obtain the living water, *Norlie* . . . Where are you going to get, *SEB* . . . How can you secure, *ET* . . . where have you got that 'living water' from? *TCNT* . . . the Water of Life? *Fenton.*

4:12. Jacob, the early patriarch, gave the best water; how could He give water that was better? The words "our father Jacob" re-

John 4:13

3450.2 art gen sing	3824.2 noun gen sing masc	2231.2 prs-pron gen 1pl	2361.1 name masc	3614.5 rel-pron nom sing masc	1319.14 verb 3sing indic aor act
τοῦ	πατρὸς	ἡμῶν	Ἰακώβ,	ὃς	ἔδωκεν
tou	*patros*	*hēmōn*	*Iakōb*	*hos*	*edōken*
the	father	our	Jacob,	who	gave

2231.3 prs-pron dat 1pl	3450.16 art sing neu	5257.1 noun sing neu	2504.1 conj	840.5 prs-pron nom sing masc	1523.1 prep gen
ἡμῖν	τὸ	φρέαρ,	καὶ	αὐτὸς	ἐξ
hēmin	*to*	*phrear*	*kai*	*autos*	*ex*
us	the	well,	and	himself	of

840.3 prs-pron gen sing	3956.11 verb 3sing indic aor act	2504.1 conj	3450.7 art pl masc	5048.6 noun pl masc	840.3 prs-pron gen sing
αὐτοῦ	ἔπιεν	καὶ	οἱ	υἱοὶ	αὐτοῦ
autou	*epien*	*kai*	*hoi*	*huioi*	*autou*
it	drank,	and	the	sons	his

13.a.**Txt:** Steph
Var: 01ℵ,02A,03B,04C,05D,017K,019L,036,037,038,byz.Gries,Lach Treg,Alf,Word,Tisc,We/Ho,Weis,Sod,UBS/⋆

2504.1 conj	3450.17 art pl neu	2330.1 noun nom pl neu	840.3 prs-pron gen sing	552.6 verb 3sing indic aor pass	3450.5 art sing masc
καὶ	τὰ	θρέμματα	αὐτοῦ;	13. Ἀπεκρίθη	⌈a ὁ ⌉
kai	*ta*	*thremmata*	*autou*	*Apekrithē*	*ho*
and	the	cattle	his?	Answered	

2400.1 name nom masc	2504.1 conj	1500.5 verb 3sing indic aor act	840.11 prs-pron dat sing fem	3820.6 adj sing masc	3450.5 art sing masc
Ἰησοῦς	καὶ	εἶπεν	αὐτῇ,	Πᾶς	ὁ
Iēsous	*kai*	*eipen*	*autē*	*Pas*	*ho*
Jesus	and	said	to her,	Everyone	the

3956.8 verb nom sing masc part pres act	1523.2 prep gen	3450.2 art gen sing	5045.2 noun gen sing neu	3642.1 dem-pron gen sing	1366.10 verb 3sing indic fut act
πίνων	ἐκ	τοῦ	ὕδατος	τούτου	διψήσει
pinōn	*ek*	*tou*	*hudatos*	*toutou*	*dipsēsei*
drinking	of	the	water	this	will thirst

3687.1 adv	3614.5 rel-pron nom sing masc	1156.1 conj	300.1 partic	3956.15 verb 3sing subj aor act	1523.2 prep gen	3450.2 art gen sing
πάλιν·	14. ὃς	δ'	ἂν	πίῃ	ἐκ	τοῦ
palin	*hos*	*d'*	*an*	*piē*	*ek*	*tou*
again;	who	but		may drink	of	the

5045.2 noun gen sing neu	3614.2 rel-pron gen sing	1466.1 prs-pron nom 1sing	1319.36 verb 1sing indic fut act	840.4 prs-pron dat sing	3620.3 partic
ὕδατος	οὗ	ἐγὼ	δώσω	αὐτῷ,	οὐ
hudatos	*hou*	*egō*	*dōsō*	*autō*	*ou*
water	which	I	will give	him	not

14.a.**Txt:** p66,04C-corr,017K,032W,13,byz.Gries
Var: 01ℵ,02A,03B,05D,019L,021M,036,038,28,Lach,Treg,Alf,Tisc,We/HoWeis,Sod,UBS/⋆

14.b.**Var:** 01ℵ,05D,021M,032W,33,Tisc

3231.1 partic	1366.9 verb 3sing subj aor act	1366.10 verb 3sing indic fut act	1519.1 prep	3450.6 art acc sing masc	163.3 noun acc sing masc
μὴ	⌈ διψήσῃ	[a⋆ διψήσει]	εἰς	τὸν	αἰῶνα·
mē	*dipsēsē*	*dipsēsei*	*eis*	*ton*	*aiōna*
not	shall thirst	[idem]	for	the	age,

233.2 conj	3450.16 art sing neu	5045.1 noun sing neu	3614.16 rel-pron sing neu	1466.1 prs-pron nom 1sing	1319.36 verb 1sing indic fut act
ἀλλὰ	τὸ	ὕδωρ	ὃ	[b+ ἐγὼ]	δώσω
alla	*to*	*hudōr*	*ho*	*egō*	*dōsō*
but	the	water	which	[I]	I will give

840.4 prs-pron dat sing	1090.69 verb 3sing indic fut mid	1706.1 prep	840.4 prs-pron dat sing	3938.1 noun nom sing fem	5045.2 noun gen sing neu
αὐτῷ	γενήσεται	ἐν	αὐτῷ	πηγὴ	ὕδατος
autō	*genēsetai*	*en*	*autō*	*pēgē*	*hudatos*
to him	shall become	in	him	a spring	of water

ferred to the Samaritans' claim that they (not the Jews) were the true descendants of Jacob. The Samaritans possessed the well and claimed the promises God made to Jacob. The woman's statement was a half-truth because the Samaritans were a mixed nationality. Jacob, she said, "gave us the well." Actually Jacob left the well soon after digging it and moved south with his family. The woman's claim of Jacob's gift to them as Samaritans was plain fancy. She pointed out that no better water was possible. The water was good enough for Jacob, his sons, and his cattle. Jacob was materially and spiritually prosperous because of the water of the well. Her implication was that what was good enough for Jacob was excellent for her.

12. Art thou greater than our father Jacob, which gave us the well: Surely you are not greater, *TCNT* . . . are not superior, *Berkeley* . . . You don't claim to be greater than Jacob, do you? *TEV* . . . and superior to, *AmpB* . . . our forefather Jacob, *Weymouth* . . . our ancestor Jacob, *Phillips.*

and drank thereof himself, and his children, and his cattle?: . . . and used to drink from it himself, *Montgomery* . . . and drank from it himself, *JB* . . . who used to drink from it himself, *AmpB* . . . and what was nurtured by him? *Concordant* . . . and his flocks, *Rotherham* . . . and herds, *NIV.*

4:13. "Drinketh" (*ho pinōn*) indicates one who continues to drink. Jesus progressively unfolded truth as she was able to understand it.

13. Jesus answered and said unto her, Whosoever drinketh of this water shall thirst again: . . . everyone who drinks, *ET* . . . who keeps on drinking of this water, *Wuest* . . . will get thirsty again, *Beck* . . . will be in need of it again, *BB.*

4:14. The waters of Jacob's well gave a temporary refreshment along the way. To thirst again revealed the insufficiency of natural water. Thus Jesus declared His gift superior to Jacob's gift. "Drinketh" (*piē*) in this verse refers to a once and for all drinking. Observe that Jesus was leading the woman to see eternal truth by comparing natural water with the living water He could give her. Natural things, of which the water was symbolic, will never give man the satisfaction for which his soul longs. Jesus further explained that the living water He gives would be within the believer; therefore there would be no need to yearn for it, since it is resident within.

"In him a well" is distinguished from the well of Jacob, a source of temporal satisfaction which must be sought after daily. The living water within the believer becomes the well.

"Water springing up" is a delightful, refreshing expression. Jesus promises a gushing, springing up, artesian well within the believer. The water is not labored for, but received, for its origin is from grace.

The verb *hallomenou* ("springing up") is also significant because of Jesus' comparison of water and the Holy Spirit in John's Gospel. It looks forward to Jesus' words that "out of his belly shall flow rivers of living water" (7:38) which Jesus said in reference to the Holy Spirit who had not yet been given (7:39). Another connection between water and the Holy Spirit is that in John 4:10 water is called a "gift" and four times in Acts the Holy Spirit is called a "gift" (Acts 2:38; 8:20; 10:45; 11:17).

The word *zōē* ("life") appears more than 130 times in the New

14. But whosoever drinketh of the water that I shall give him shall never thirst: . . . shall never thirst any more, *Montgomery* . . . shall under no circumstances, *Concordant* . . . will never be thirsty, *ALBA* . . . shall positively not thirst, no, never, *Wuest* . . . will never, no never, be thirsty again, *Williams* . . . shall not thirst eternally, *Berkeley* . . . to the remotest age, *Rotherham.*

but the water that I shall give him shall be in him a well of water springing up into everlasting life: . . . leaping up, *Concordant* . . . that bubbles up for eternal life, *Berkeley* . . . a fountain of water ...eternal life, *Alford* . . . welling up into eternal life, *Phillips*

John 4:15

240.2 verb gen sing neu part pres	1519.1 prep	2205.4 noun acc sing fem	164.1 adj sing	2978.5 verb 3sing indic pres act	4242.1 prep
ἁλλομένου	εἰς	ζωὴν	αἰώνιον.	**15.** Λέγει	πρὸς
hallomenou	*eis*	*zōēn*	*aiōnion*	*Legei*	*pros*
springing up	into	life	eternal.	Says	to

840.6 prs-pron acc sing masc	3450.9 art nom sing fem	1129.1 noun nom sing fem	2935.5 noun voc sing masc	1319.25 verb 2sing impr aor act
αὐτὸν	ἡ	γυνή,	Κύριε,	δός
auton	*hē*	*gunē*	*Kurie*	*dos*
him	the	woman,	Sir,	give

15.a.**Txt:** 02A,04C,05D, 036,037,byz.Gries,Lach **Var:** p66,01ℵ-org,Alf, Tisc,We/HoWeis,UBS/☆

1466.4 prs-pron dat 1sing	3642.17 dem-pron sing neu	3450.16 art sing neu	5045.1 noun sing neu	2419.1 conj	3231.1 partic
μοι	τοῦτο	τὸ	ὕδωρ,	ἵνα	μὴ
moi	*touto*	*to*	*hudōr*	*hina*	*mē*
me	this	the	water,	that	not

16.a.**Txt:** 01ℵ-corr, 04C-corr,017K,019L, 032W,036,037,byz.sa.bo. Sod **Var:** p66,p75,01ℵ-org, 02A,03B,04C-org,038,1, 13,33,Lach,AlfTisc, We/Ho,Weis,UBS/☆

1366.1 verb 1sing pres act	3234.1 adv	2048.37 verb 1sing subj pres mid	1324.18 verb 1sing pres mid	1743.1 adv
διψῶ	μηδὲ	⸀ ἔρχωμαι	[a☆ διέρχωμαι]	ἐνθάδε
dipsō	*mēde*	*erchōmai*	*dierchōmai*	*enthade*
I may thirst	nor	come	[idem]	here

16.b.**Txt:** 01ℵ,02A, 04C-corr,017K,019L, 032W,036,037,038,1,13, byz.sa.bo.Lach,Sod **Var:** p66,p75,03B, 04C-org,33,Alf,Tisc, We/Ho,Weis,UBS/☆

498.1 verb inf pres act	2978.5 verb 3sing indic pres act	840.11 prs-pron dat sing fem	3450.5 art sing masc	2400.1 name nom masc
ἀντλεῖν.	**16.** Λέγει	αὐτῇ,	⸂a ὁ ⸃	⸂b Ἰησοῦς, ⸃
antlein	*Legei*	*autē*	*ho*	*Iēsous*
to draw.	Says	to her		Jesus,

5055.6 verb 2sing impr pres act	5291.8 verb 2sing impr aor act	3450.6 art acc sing masc	433.4 noun acc sing masc	4622.2 prs-pron gen 2sing	2504.1 conj
Ὕπαγε,	φώνησον	τὸν	ἄνδρα	σου	καὶ
Hupage	*phōnēson*	*ton*	*andra*	*sou*	*kai*
Go,	call	the	husband	your	and

2048.10 verb 2sing impr aor act	1743.1 adv	552.6 verb 3sing indic aor pass	3450.9 art nom sing fem	1129.1 noun nom sing fem
ἐλθὲ	ἐνθάδε.	**17.** Ἀπεκρίθη	ἡ	γυνὴ
elthe	*enthade*	*Apekrithē*	*hē*	*gunē*
come	here.	Answered	the	woman

17.a.**Var:** p66,03B,04C, 07E,it.Lach,Alf,We/Ho, Sod

2504.1 conj	1500.5 verb 3sing indic aor act	840.4 prs-pron dat sing	3620.2 partic	2174.1 verb 1sing pres act	433.4 noun acc sing masc
καὶ	εἶπεν,	[a+ αὐτῷ,]	Οὐκ	ἔχω	ἄνδρα.
kai	*eipen*	*autō*	*Ouk*	*echō*	*andra*
and	said,	[to him,]	Not	I have	a husband.

2978.5 verb 3sing indic pres act	840.11 prs-pron dat sing fem	3450.5 art sing masc	2400.1 name nom masc	2544.1 adv	1500.2 verb 2sing aor act
Λέγει	αὐτῇ	ὁ	Ἰησοῦς,	Καλῶς	⸀ εἶπας,
Legei	*autē*	*ho*	*Iēsous*	*Kalōs*	*eipas*
Says	to her		Jesus,	Well	you did say,

17.b.**Txt:** 02A,03B-corr, 04C,05D,017K,019L, 036,037,038,byz.Lach, Weis,Sod **Var:** 01ℵ,03B-org,Tisc, We/Ho,UBS/☆

1500.27 verb 2sing indic aor act	3617.1 conj	433.4 noun acc sing masc	3620.2 partic	2174.1 verb 1sing pres act	3864.1 num card
[b☆ εἶπες]	Ὅτι	Ἄνδρα	οὐκ	ἔχω·	**18.** πέντε
eipes	*Hoti*	*Andra*	*ouk*	*echō*	*pente*
[idem]		A husband	not	I have;	five

1056.1 conj	433.9 noun acc pl masc	2174.31 verb 2sing indic aor act	2504.1 conj	3431.1 adv	3614.6 rel-pron acc sing masc	2174.3 verb 2sing indic pres act
γὰρ	ἄνδρας	ἔσχες.	καὶ	νῦν	ὃν	ἔχεις
gar	*andras*	*esches*	*kai*	*nun*	*hon*	*echeis*
for	husbands	you have had,	and	now	whom	you have

Testament, and about half of these occurrences are in the writings of John (his Gospel, his epistles, and the Book of Revelation). In addition, the expression *zōē aiōnios* ("eternal life") appears nearly 20 times in John's Gospel. With these frequent references to life or eternal life in John's writings, it is understandable that this book has been called the Gospel of Life (Filson, "Gospel of Life," pp.111-123). This is true, not only because the word appears so frequently but because John's stated purpose for writing is "that ye might believe that Jesus is the Christ, the Son of God; and that believing ye might have life through his name" (20:31). Just as man received natural life when God breathed into the dust of the earth (Genesis 2:7), so eternal life can only be received from Jesus, who is life himself (John 11:25; 14:6) and whose words are life (John 6:63). Most importantly, it is only by believing in Jesus that one can receive this gift of life (3:16; 5:24; 20:31).

. . . within him, welling up for enduring Life, *TCNT* . . . gushing up as a fountain of eternal life, *Norton* . . . flowing into life eternal, *Fenton.*

15. The woman saith unto him, Sir, give me this water, that I thirst not: . . . this water at once, sir, *Williams* . . . so that I may never again be thirsty, *Norlie* . . . that I suffer not thirst, *Torrey* . . . so that I may not get thirsty, *Fenton.*

neither come hither to draw: . . . nor have to come all the way for drawing water, *Berkeley* . . . so far, *Williams* . . . and never have to come here again to draw water, *JB* . . . never again have to come way out here to draw water, *Norlie.*

4:15. The woman had little understanding of the words "eternal life." But Jesus suited His soul winning to the person and circumstances. Compare His dialogue with Nicodemus in John chapter 3. Jesus reached through their known to their unknown in order to draw them to His truth.

The woman understood two things which Jesus related: (1) that if she drank the water He would give, she would not be thirsty again, and (2) that she would have a water supply for which she need not work. Her mind was still centered on natural pursuits. She did not understand the spiritual connection. She realized she was continually thirsty. Jacob's gift of the well provided temporary satisfaction. But there was within her a thirst which had not been quenched.

16. Jesus saith unto her, Go, call thy husband, and come hither: Go home...Call your husband and come back here, *ALBA* . . . and return here, *Fenton.*

17. The woman answered and said, I have no husband:

Jesus said unto her, Thou hast well said, I have no husband: You put it well when, *Adams* . . . So true! *SEB* . . . All too true! Jesus said, *LivB* . . . You answer well, *Fenton.*

4:16,17. "Go, call thy husband" introduced the woman to the personal pertinency of His message to her. She could never receive what she failed to see she needed. Jesus proceeded to probe her moral condition that she might know her spiritual need. Look at the three verbs in this verse. "Go" was the easy command (*hupage,* present imperative) for she was going, and He did not have to insist that she do it. "Call" (*phōnēson,* aorist imperative) means "to voice it." "Come" (*elthe,* aorist imperative) stands for the command which involved obedience and faith. He gave such words of command to arouse her conscience. Observe the gentle and indirect method of Jesus' approach to her openly sinful life. Neither Jesus nor John ever mentions the woman by her personal name. How wonderfully He protects the person and exposes the sin!

18. For thou hast had five husbands; and he whom thou now hast is not thy husband: The fact is, you have had, *NIV* . . . you have been married to five men, *TEV* . . . the man with whom you are now living is not, *NEB* . . . the

3620.2 partic	1498.4 verb 3sing indic pres act	4622.2 prs-pron gen 2sing	433.1 noun nom sing masc	3642.17 dem-pron sing neu	225.5 adj sing neu
οὐκ	ἔστιν	σου	ἀνήρ·	τοῦτο	ἀληθὲς
ouk	estin	sou	anēr	touto	alēthes
not	is	your	husband:	this	truly

2029.2 verb 2sing indic perf act	2978.5 verb 3sing indic pres act	840.4 prs-pron dat sing	3450.9 art nom sing fem	1129.1 noun nom sing fem
εἴρηκας.	19. Λέγει	αὐτῷ	ἡ	γυνή,
eirēkas	Legei	autō	hē	gunē
you have spoken.	Says	to him	the	woman,

2935.5 noun voc sing masc	2311.2 verb 1sing indic pres act	3617.1 conj	4254.1 noun nom sing masc	1498.3 verb 2sing indic pres act	4622.1 prs-pron nom 2sing
Κύριε,	θεωρῶ	ὅτι	προφήτης	εἶ	σύ.
Kurie	theōrō	hoti	prophētēs	ei	su
Sir,	I perceive	that	a prophet	are	you.

3450.7 art pl masc	3824.6 noun pl masc	2231.2 prs-pron gen 1pl	1706.1 prep	3642.5 dem-pron dat sing masc	3450.3 art dat sing	3598.3 noun dat sing neu
20. οἱ	πατέρες	ἡμῶν	ἐν	ʻ τούτῳ	τῷ	ὄρει
hoi	pateres	hēmōn	en	toutō	tō	orei
The	fathers	our	in	this	the	mountain

3450.3 art dat sing	3598.3 noun dat sing neu	3642.5 dem-pron dat sing masc	4210.10 verb 3pl indic aor act	2504.1 conj	5050.1 prs-pron nom 2pl
[☆ τῷ	ὄρει	τούτῳ]	προσεκύνησαν·	καὶ	ὑμεῖς
tō	orei	toutō	prosekunēsan	kai	humeis
[the	mountain	this]	worshiped,	and	you

2978.2 verb 2pl pres act	3617.1 conj	1706.1 prep	2389.3 name dat pl neu	1498.4 verb 3sing indic pres act	3450.5 art sing masc
λέγετε	ὅτι	ἐν	Ἱεροσολύμοις	ἐστὶν	ὁ
legete	hoti	en	Hierosolumois	estin	ho
say	that	in	Jerusalem	is	the

4964.1 noun nom sing masc	3562.1 adv	1158.1 verb 3sing indic pres act	4210.8 verb inf pres act	4210.8 verb inf pres act
τόπος	ὅπου	ʻ δεῖ	προσκυνεῖν.	[☆ προσκυνεῖν
topos	hopou	dei	proskunein	proskunein
place	where	it is necessary	to worship.	[to worship

1158.1 verb 3sing indic pres act	2978.5 verb 3sing indic pres act	840.11 prs-pron dat sing fem	3450.5 art sing masc	2400.1 name nom masc
δεῖ.]	21. Λέγει	αὐτῇ	ὁ	Ἰησοῦς,
dei	Legei	autē	ho	Iēsous
it is ncessary.]	Says	to her		Jesus,

21.a.**Txt:** 02A,04C-corr, 017K,036,037,038,byz. **Var:** 01ℵ,03B,04C-org, 019L,Treg,Alf,Tisc, We/Ho,Weis,UBS/☆

1129.5 noun voc sing fem	3961.28 verb 2sing impr aor act	1466.4 prs-pron dat 1sing	3961.9 verb 2sing impr pres act	1466.4 prs-pron dat 1sing
ʻ Γύναι,	πίστευσόν	μοι,	[a☆ Πίστευέ	μοι,
Gunai	pisteuson	moi	Pisteue	moi
Woman,	believe	me,	[Believe	me,

1129.5 noun voc sing fem	3617.1 conj	2048.34 verb 3sing indic pres	5443.2 noun nom sing fem	3616.1 conj	3641.1 conj	1706.1 prep
γύναι,]	ὅτι	ἔρχεται	ὥρα	ὅτε	οὔτε	ἐν
gunai	hoti	erchetai	hōra	hote	oute	en
woman,]	that	is coming	an hour	when	neither	in

3450.3 art dat sing	3598.3 noun dat sing neu	3642.5 dem-pron dat sing masc	3641.1 conj	1706.1 prep	2389.3 name dat pl neu
τῷ	ὄρει	τούτῳ	οὔτε	ἐν	Ἱεροσολύμοις
tō	orei	toutō	oute	en	Hierosolumois
the	mountain	this	nor	in	Jerusalem

4:18. Because of His divine omniscience Jesus knew of the five "husbands" and of the one she now had! Because she had former companions still alive, she was living in adultery and the present mate was not really her husband.

one you are now living with, *Berkeley* . . . he whom you have now espoused, *Moffatt* . . . and the man you have at present is not, *Weymouth.*

in that saidst thou truly: You have spoken the truth, *Weymouth* . . . What you have just said is quite true, *NIV* . . . What you have said is true, *ALBA.*

4:19. Each time the woman called Jesus "Sir," there was a rising respect for Jesus (note 11, 15, and 19).

Nicodemus came to Jesus, referring to Him as Rabbi (teacher). This woman's designation of Jesus was that of a prophet. Both titles were correct.

19. The woman saith unto him, Sir, I perceive that thou art a prophet: . . . as I am carefully observing you, I am coming to the place where I see that, *Wuest* . . . understand that You, *AmpB.*

4:20. After the woman stated she perceived Jesus was a prophet, she followed it by stating there was a difference between the Samaritans and Jews as to "where" to worship. Jesus answered her as though she was interested in the truth about "where" to worship.

"This mountain" refers to Mount Gerizim, a twin to Mount Ebal. They were separated by a small valley. Mount Ebal was called the mount of cursing and Mount Gerizim was called the mount of blessing (see Deuteronomy 27:1-26; Joshua 8:30-35). The Samaritans had built a temple on Mount Gerizim when they were barred from helping to rebuild the temple in Jerusalem during the days of Ezra and Nehemiah (Ezra 4:1-3). John Hyrcanus destroyed the Gerizim temple in 129 B.C. It was not rebuilt, but the Samaritans continued to offer sacrifices at the site.

"In Jerusalem" brings to the foreground the difference between the Jews and the Samaritans. Not even the synagogues were worship places; they were for instruction.

20. Our fathers worshipped in this mountain: "My Samaritan ancestors worshipped, *TEV* . . . that our ancestors worshipped, *TCNT* . . . on this mountain, *ET.*

and ye say, that in Jerusalem is the place where men ought to worship: . . . and yet you Jews say, *TCNT* . . . say that the temple, *NEB* . . . the proper place for worship, *Moffatt, Berkeley* . . . it is proper to worship, *Murdock* . . . is the spot, *Fenton* . . . it is necessary in the nature of the case, *Wuest* . . . where it is necessary and proper, *AmpB* . . . where it is necessary to worship, *Clementson* . . . where God must be worshipped, *ALBA.*

21. Jesus saith unto her, Woman, believe me, the hour cometh: . . . trust me, *Tyndale* . . . the time is coming, *Phillips* . . . the time approaches, *Campbell* . . . the day is coming, *ALBA.*

when ye shall neither in this mountain nor yet at Jerusalem, worship the Father: . . . nor merely in, *Berkeley.*

4:21. Normally Jesus declared who He was by the signs, wonders, and miracles which He performed. The credentials of His messiahship abounded throughout His ministry. However, on occasion Jesus plainly spoke of His messianic identity. Strangely enough, Jesus revealed His office as Messiah during private interviews.

Jesus addressed the Samaritan harlot, "Woman." The term was one of respect. Jesus called His earthly mother by the same title. Thus we see the level of respect He showed to even this fallen woman. She called Him a prophet; therefore Jesus joined His message to her acknowledgment. The imperative "believe me" is quite unusual among the commands of Jesus. Notice a similar statement Jesus made to His disciples during His farewell discourse (14:11).

The Lord spoke of the Samaritans' future. He predicted that the

John 4:22

4210.21 verb 2pl indic fut act	3450.3 art dat sing	3824.3 noun dat sing masc	5050.1 prs-pron nom 2pl	4210.3 verb 2pl indic pres act
προσκυνήσετε	τῷ	πατρί.	22. ὑμεῖς	προσκυνεῖτε
proskunēsete	*tō*	*patri*	*humeis*	*proskuneite*
shall you worship	the	Father.	You	worship

3614.16 rel-pron sing neu	3620.2 partic	3471.6 verb 2pl indic perf act	2231.1 prs-pron nom 1pl	4210.2 verb 1pl indic pres act
ὃ	οὐκ	οἴδατε·	ἡμεῖς	προσκυνοῦμεν
ho	*ouk*	*oidate*	*hēmeis*	*proskunoumen*
what	not	you know:	we	worship

3614.16 rel-pron sing neu	3471.5 verb 1pl indic perf act	3617.1 conj	3450.9 art nom sing fem	4843.1 noun nom sing fem	1523.2 prep gen	3450.1 art gen pl
ὃ	οἴδαμεν·	ὅτι	ἡ	σωτηρία	ἐκ	τῶν
ho	*oidamen*	*hoti*	*hē*	*sōtēria*	*ek*	*tōn*
what	we know;	for	the	salvation	of	the

2428.3 name-adj gen pl masc	1498.4 verb 3sing indic pres act	233.1 conj	233.2 conj	2048.34 verb 3sing indic pres
Ἰουδαίων	ἐστίν.	23. (ἀλλ'	[☆ ἀλλὰ]	ἔρχεται
Ioudaiōn	*estin*	*all'*	*alla*	*erchetai*
Jews	is.	But	[idem]	is coming

5443.2 noun nom sing fem	2504.1 conj	3431.1 adv	1498.4 verb 3sing indic pres act	3616.1 conj	3450.7 art pl masc	226.4 adj nom pl masc
ὥρα	καὶ	νῦν	ἐστιν,	ὅτε	οἱ	ἀληθινοὶ
hōra	*kai*	*nun*	*estin*	*hote*	*hoi*	*alēthinoi*
an hour	and	now	is,	when	the	true

4211.1 noun nom pl masc	4210.22 verb 3pl indic fut act	3450.3 art dat sing	3824.3 noun dat sing masc	1706.1 prep
προσκυνηταὶ	προσκυνήσουσιν	τῷ	πατρὶ	ἐν
proskunētai	*proskunēsousin*	*tō*	*patri*	*en*
worshipers	will worship	the	Father	in

4011.3 noun dat sing neu	2504.1 conj	223.3 noun dat sing fem	2504.1 conj	1056.1 conj	3450.5 art sing masc
πνεύματι	καὶ	ἀληθείᾳ·	καὶ	γὰρ	ὁ
pneumati	*kai*	*alētheia*	*kai*	*gar*	*ho*
spirit	and	truth;	also	for	the

3824.1 noun nom sing masc	4955.8 dem-pron acc pl masc	2195.5 verb 3sing indic pres act	3450.8 art acc pl masc	4210.6 verb acc pl masc part pres act
πατὴρ	τοιούτους	ζητεῖ	τοὺς	προσκυνοῦντας
patēr	*toioutous*	*zētei*	*tous*	*proskunountas*
Father	such	seeks	the	worshiping

840.6 prs-pron acc sing masc	4011.1 noun sing neu	3450.5 art sing masc	2296.1 noun nom sing masc	2504.1 conj	3450.8 art acc pl masc
αὐτόν.	24. Πνεῦμα	ὁ	θεός·	καὶ	τοὺς
auton	*Pneuma*	*ho*	*theos*	*kai*	*tous*
him.	A spirit		God,	and	the

24.a.**Txt:** p66,p75, 01ℵ-corr,02A,03B,04C, 05D-corr,017K,019L, 032W,036,037,038,1,13, etc.byz.sa.bo.Gries,Lach, We/Ho,Sod
Var: 01ℵ-org,05D-org, TiscWeis,UBS/☆

4210.6 verb acc pl masc part pres act	840.6 prs-pron acc sing masc	1706.1 prep	4011.3 noun dat sing neu	2504.1 conj
προσκυνοῦντας	(a αὐτὸν)	ἐν	πνεύματι	καὶ
proskunountas	*auton*	*en*	*pneumati*	*kai*
worshiping	him,	in	spirit	and

223.3 noun dat sing fem	1158.1 verb 3sing indic pres act	4210.8 verb inf pres act	2978.5 verb 3sing indic pres act	840.4 prs-pron dat sing
ἀληθείᾳ	δεῖ	προσκυνεῖν.	25. Λέγει	αὐτῷ
alētheia	*dei*	*proskunein*	*Legei*	*autō*
truth	must	to worship.	Says	to him

woman and the townspeople would truly worship the Father. Jesus offered the woman a fresh, close, and intimate relation to God as Father.

22. Ye worship ye know not what: You pay homage without knowledge, *Fenton* . . . One of whom you know nothing, *Weymouth* . . . in ignorance, *ALBA* . . . you are worshiping with your eyes shut, *Phillips.*

we know what we worship:

for salvation is of the Jews: . . . the Deliverer, *Norton* . . . for the salvation of mankind is to come from our race, *Phillips* . . . salvation belongs to, *ALBA* . . . the Jews as a source, *Wuest.*

4:22. "Ye know not what" speaks about the error of their worship. It is in contrast to the words "we know what." The Samaritans had received only the first five books of Moses. This limited their conception of the fulfillment of the promises of God, especially the promise of the Messiah. The prophets were the interpreters of the Law. The Samaritans lacked inspired interpretation of the Scriptures.

Jesus used the word "salvation" (*sōtēria*) but twice, and in both occurrences He meant himself (here and Luke 19:9). He is His own commentary on salvation. He is salvation's text, and all about Him is salvation's commentary.

23. But the hour cometh, and now is, when the true worshippers shall worship the Father in spirit and in truth: . . . and now is near, *Norlie* . . . in fact it is here already, *JB* . . . when genuine worshipers, *Berkeley* . . . in Spirit and in reality, *Moffatt* . . . in the true way of the spirit, *BB* . . . as His worshipers, *Berkeley* . . . spiritually, with true insight, *TCNT* . . . in the true, spiritual way, *SEB* . . . a truly spiritual worship, *Barclay* . . . and reality, *Williams.*

for the Father seeketh such to worship him: . . . the Father is looking for such people, *Beck* . . . the Father wants, *Norlie* . . . that is the kind of worshiper, *JB* . . . requireth that, *Murdock.*

4:23. "True worshippers" are those who worship in spirit and truth. The temple in Jerusalem served the limited revelation of the old economy. Ceremonies, rites, and sacrifices help the worshiper only insofar as a shadow or symbol are rightfully interpreted, but the reality of God is seen clearly in the revelation of Christ.

"Worship . . . in spirit" could mean either in the Holy Spirit or in human spirit. Translators render *spirit* with a small *s*, not a capital *S*, to denote the human spirit. In Matthew chapter 5 Jesus said, "Blessed are the poor in spirit: for theirs is the kingdom of heaven." It is the human spirit Jesus speaks of that must feel its poverty. To worship the Father is to see oneself in the child-father relationship, with all the aspirations and emotions a child has toward his father. Except one becomes as a little child, he cannot enter the Kingdom. When a worshiper approaches God in worship, it is by way of the childlike attitude.

It is not sufficient to worship with one's entire spirit for the spirit may be misdirected. Truth is what Jesus is and what He came to reveal to the world. To worship in "truth" is to adore God as the Father in accordance with the Living Word (Jesus) and the written Word (the Scriptures). The Father earnestly desires and is in the process of seeking true worshipers.

24. God is a Spirit: God is Spirit, *HBIE, Campbell, ALBA* . . . is a spiritual Being, *Williams* . . . as to His nature is spirit, *Wuest.*

and they that worship him must worship him in spirit and in truth: . . . and it is necessary, *Clementson* . . . to be worshipping in a spiritual sphere, and in the sphere of truth, *Wuest.*

4:24. The word "Spirit" has the position of emphasis in the statement. "God is Spirit" means that God by His very nature is spirit.

In verse 23 Jesus stated the twin requirements of worship. Now He adds the "must" (*dei*) as a genuine necessity. Whoever comes

3450.9 art nom sing fem	1129.1 noun nom sing fem	3471.2 verb 1sing indic perf act	3617.1 conj	3193.1 name nom masc	2048.34 verb 3sing indic pres
ἡ	γυνή,	Οἶδα	ὅτι	Μεσσίας	ἔρχεται,
hē	*gunē*	*Oida*	*hoti*	*Messias*	*erchetai*
the	woman,	I know	that	Messiah	is coming,

3450.5 art sing masc	2978.30 verb nom sing masc part pres pass	5382.1 name nom masc	3615.1 conj	2048.8 verb 3sing subj aor act
ὁ	λεγόμενος	Χριστός·	ὅταν	ἔλθῃ
ho	*legomenos*	*Christos*	*hotan*	*elthē*
the	being called	Christ;	when	comes

25.a.**Txt:** 02A,04C-corr, 05D,017K,019L,036, 037,038,13,byz.Gries, Lach,Sod
Var: p66,p75,01ℵ,03B, 04C-org,032W,1,Treg Alf,Tisc,We/Ho,Weis, UBS/☆

1552.3 dem-pron nom sing masc	310.9 verb 3sing indic fut act	2231.3 prs-pron dat 1pl	3820.1 adj	533.1 adj
ἐκεῖνος	ἀναγγελεῖ	ἡμῖν	ʿ πάντα.	[a☆ ἅπαντα.]
ekeinos	*anangelei*	*hēmin*	*panta*	*hapanta*
that	he will tell	us	all things.	[idem]

2978.5 verb 3sing indic pres act	840.11 prs-pron dat sing fem	3450.5 art sing masc	2400.1 name nom masc	1466.1 prs-pron nom 1sing	1498.2 verb 1sing indic pres act
26. Λέγει	αὐτῇ	ὁ	Ἰησοῦς,	Ἐγώ	εἰμι,
Legei	*autē*	*ho*	*Iēsous*	*Egō*	*eimi*
Says	to her		Jesus,	I	am

3450.5 art sing masc	2953.12 verb nom sing masc part pres act	4622.3 prs-pron dat 2sing	2504.1 conj	1894.3 prep	3642.5 dem-pron dat sing masc
ὁ	λαλῶν	σοι.	27. Καὶ	ἐπὶ	τούτῳ
ho	*lalōn*	*soi*	*Kai*	*epi*	*toutō*
the	speaking	to you.	And	upon	this

27.a.**Txt:** 01ℵ-corr,02A, 03B-corr,04C,05D,019L, 038,etc.byz.Lach,Weis Sod
Var: 03B-org,Treg,Tisc, We/Ho,UBS/☆

2048.1 verb indic aor act	2048.64 verb 3pl indic aor act	3450.7 art pl masc	3073.5 noun nom pl masc	840.3 prs-pron gen sing	2504.1 conj
ʿ ἦλθον	[a☆ ἦλθαν]	οἱ	μαθηταὶ	αὐτοῦ,	καὶ
ēlthon	*ēlthan*	*hoi*	*mathētai*	*autou*	*kai*
came	[idem]	the	disciples	his,	and

27.b.**Txt:** 07E,030U,036, 037,byz.
Var: 01ℵ,02A,03B,04C, 05D,017K,019L,021M, 038,041,it.bo.GriesLach, Treg,Alf,Word,Tisc, We/Ho,Weis,Sod,UBS/☆

2273.11 verb 3pl indic aor act	2273.17 verb 3pl indic imperf act	3617.1 conj	3196.3 prep	1129.2 noun gen sing fem
ʿ ἐθαύμασαν	[b☆ ἐθαύμαζον]	ὅτι	μετὰ	γυναικὸς
ethaumasan	*ethaumazon*	*hoti*	*meta*	*gunaikos*
marveled	[were marveling]	that	with	a woman

2953.45 verb 3sing indic imperf act	3625.2 num card nom masc	3175.1 conj	1500.5 verb 3sing indic aor act	4949.9 intr-pron sing neu
ἐλάλει·	οὐδεὶς	μέντοι	εἶπεν,	Τί
elalei	*oudeis*	*mentoi*	*eipen*	*Ti*
he was speaking;	no one	however	said,	What

2195.4 verb 2sing indic pres act	2211.1 conj	4949.9 intr-pron sing neu	2953.3 verb 2sing indic pres act	3196.2 prep	840.10 prs-pron gen sing fem
ζητεῖς;	ἤ,	Τί	λαλεῖς	μετ’	αὐτῆς;
zēteis	*ē*	*Ti*	*laleis*	*met'*	*autēs*
seek you?	or	Why	speak you	with	her?

856.10 verb 3sing indic aor act	3631.1 conj	3450.12 art acc sing fem	5042.1 noun acc sing fem	840.10 prs-pron gen sing fem	3450.9 art nom sing fem
28. Ἀφῆκεν	οὖν	τὴν	ὑδρίαν	αὐτῆς	ἡ
Aphēken	*oun*	*tēn*	*hudrian*	*autēs*	*hē*
Left	then	the	water jar	her	the

1129.1 noun nom sing fem	2504.1 conj	562.2 verb 3sing indic aor act	1519.1 prep	3450.12 art acc sing fem	4032.4 noun acc sing fem	2504.1 conj
γυνὴ	καὶ	ἀπῆλθεν	εἰς	τὴν	πόλιν,	καὶ
gunē	*kai*	*apēlthen*	*eis*	*tēn*	*polin*	*kai*
woman	and	went away	into	the	city,	and

to God to worship must worship according to the truth of God's revelation of himself.

25. The woman saith unto him, I know that Messias cometh, which is called Christ: . . . the Christ, the Anointed One, *AmpB* . . . called Consecrated, *Fenton* . . . I know positively that Messiah comes, *Wuest.*

when he is come, he will tell us all things: . . . when once he has come, he will tell us everything, *TCNT* . . . He will make everything plain to us, *Berkeley* . . . make everything clear to us, *Adams.*

4:25. The woman believed (1) there was a coming One called Christ, (2) Christ would make plain many things, and (3) the Messiah would declare all things.

26. Jesus saith unto her, I that speak unto thee am he: I am He, *Norlie, ALBA* . . . the very One, *Adams* . . . I am the Messiah, *TCNT.*

4:26. "I that speak unto thee am he." *Ho lalōn soi* means "the one speaking to you." Jesus thus implied that He was doing just what she said the Messiah would do. Compare the Jewish conception of Messiah as the coming King with the woman's belief that the Messiah was the coming Teacher. The woman was nearer to the truth than the Jews were in believing the Messiah to be a Prophet-Teacher.

"I . . . am he" (*egō eimi*) is very informative (John 4:26; 6:20,35,41,48,51; 8:12,24; 10:7,9,11,14; 11:25; 14:6; 15:1,5; 18:37; also see Revelation 1:8).

Jesus' assertion, "I am," is highly significant because it is a direct statement that He is God himself. In the Old Testament the expression "I am" (Hebrew, *'ani hu*; Septuagint, *egō eimi*) is reserved exclusively by God to reveal His essence. In Exodus 3:14,15 and six times in Isaiah (Isaiah 41:4; 43:10,25; 46:4; 51:12; 52:6) God refers to himself as "I am," signifying that Yahweh is God alone; that He is Lord of history; and that He is the Redeemer of Israel (cf. Harner, *Facet Books Biblical Series*, 26:7). Thus, when Jesus said "I am," He was making the direct claim that He is Lord and Redeemer just as God the Father is.

27. And upon this came his disciples, and marvelled that he talked with the woman: At this point, *Fenton, ALBA* . . . At this juncture, *Berkeley, Wuest* . . . his disciples returned, *JB* . . . were surprised to find Him talking with a woman, *Weymouth* . . . kept on wondering because with a woman, *Wuest.*

yet no man said, What seekest thou?: What is your purpose, *BB* . . . What is your wish? *Weymouth.*

or, Why talkest thou with her?: What are You discussing? *Fenton* . . . converse with her? *Scarlett* . . . or talking about, *ALBA.*

4:27. "Marveled" (*ethaumasan*) indicates a continuous wondering as to why He would speak to a woman in public. The authorities tell us that Jewish men did not speak to women in public for fear of being seduced. The disciples wondered "what" and "why." They did not question His integrity; therefore, they refrained from asking either.

28. The woman then left her water pot, and went her way into the city, and saith to the men: As for the woman, she left, *Barclay* . . . left her water-jar behind, *ALBA* . . . thereupon went off to the town, *Fenton* . . . set off to town, *Norlie.*

4:28. In her excitement temporal things gave way to life's most important priorities. The gospel of eternal life will cause a woman to leave her waterpot and a man to forget his hunger. The woman's

2978.5 verb 3sing indic pres act	3450.4 art dat pl	442.8 noun dat pl masc	1199.1 adv	1481.15 verb 2pl impr aor act
λέγει	τοῖς	ἀνθρώποις,	29. Δεῦτε,	ἴδετε
legei	*tois*	*anthrōpois*	*Deute*	*idete*
says	to the	men,	Come,	see

442.4 noun acc sing masc	3614.5 rel-pron nom sing masc	1500.5 verb 3sing indic aor act	1466.4 prs-pron dat 1sing	3820.1 adj
ἄνθρωπον	ὃς	εἶπέν	μοι	πάντα
anthrōpon	*hos*	*eipen*	*moi*	*panta*
a man	who	told	me	all things

29.a.**Txt:** p66,p75,02A, 04C-corr,05D,017K, 019L,032W,036,037, 038,1,13,byz.Gries,Lach **Var:** 01ℵ,03B,04C-org, sa.bo.Tisc,We/Ho,Weis, Sod,UBS/☆

3607.8 rel-pron pl neu	3614.17 rel-pron pl neu	4020.22 verb 1sing indic aor act	3252.1 partic	3642.4 dem-pron nom sing masc
⌐☆ ὅσα	[a ἃ]	ἐποίησα·	μήτι	οὗτός
hosa	*ha*	*epoiēsa*	*mēti*	*houtos*
whatsoever	[what]	I did:	could	this

30.a.**Txt:** p66,01ℵ,1,13, sa.Steph **Var:** 02A,03B,017K, 019L,037,038,byz.Gries, Lach,Treg,Alf,Word, Tisc,We/HoWeis,Sod, UBS/☆

1498.4 verb 3sing indic pres act	3450.5 art sing masc	5382.1 name nom masc	1814.1 verb indic aor act	3631.1 conj
ἐστιν	ὁ	Χριστός;	30. Ἐξῆλθον	⌐a οὖν ˥
estin	*ho*	*Christos*	*Exēlthon*	*oun*
be	the	Christ!	They went forth	therefore

1523.2 prep gen	3450.10 art gen sing fem	4032.2 noun gen sing fem	2504.1 conj	2048.60 verb 3pl indic imperf	4242.1 prep	840.6 prs-pron acc sing masc
ἐκ	τῆς	πόλεως,	καὶ	ἤρχοντο	πρὸς	αὐτόν.
ek	*tēs*	*poleōs*	*kai*	*ērchonto*	*pros*	*auton*
out of	the	city,	and	came	unto	him.

31.a.**Txt:** p75,02A, 04C-corr,017K,036,037, 038,1,13,byz.bo.Lach **Var:** 01ℵ,03B,04C-org, 05D,019L,Treg,Alf,Tisc, We/HoWeis,Sod,UBS/☆

1706.1 prep	1156.2 conj	3450.3 art dat sing	3212.1 adv	2049.17 verb 3pl indic imperf act	840.6 prs-pron acc sing masc
31. Ἐν	⌐a δὲ ˥	τῷ	μεταξὺ	ἠρώτων	αὐτὸν
En	*de*	*tō*	*metaxu*	*ērōtōn*	*auton*
In	but	the	meantime	were asking	him

3450.7 art pl masc	3073.5 noun nom pl masc	2978.16 verb pl masc part pres act	4318.1 noun sing masc	2052.22 verb 2sing impr aor act
οἱ	μαθηταὶ,	λέγοντες,	Ῥαββί,	φάγε.
hoi	*mathētai*	*legontes*	*Rhabbi*	*phage*
the	disciples,	saying,	Rabbi,	eat.

3450.5 art sing masc	1156.2 conj	1500.5 verb 3sing indic aor act	840.2 prs-pron dat pl	1466.1 prs-pron nom 1sing	1028.4 noun acc sing fem
32. Ὁ	δὲ	εἶπεν	αὐτοῖς,	Ἐγὼ	βρῶσιν
Ho	*de*	*eipen*	*autois*	*Egō*	*brōsin*
The	but	said	to them,	I	food

2174.1 verb 1sing pres act	2052.25 verb inf aor act	3614.12 rel-pron acc sing fem	5050.1 prs-pron nom 2pl	3620.2 partic	3471.6 verb 2pl indic perf act
ἔχω	φαγεῖν	ἣν	ὑμεῖς	οὐκ	οἴδατε.
echō	*phagein*	*hēn*	*humeis*	*ouk*	*oidate*
have	to eat	which	you	not	know.

2978.25 verb indic imperf act	3631.1 conj	3450.7 art pl masc	3073.5 noun nom pl masc	4242.1 prep	238.3 prs-pron acc pl masc
33. Ἔλεγον	οὖν	οἱ	μαθηταὶ	πρὸς	ἀλλήλους,
Elegon	*oun*	*hoi*	*mathētai*	*pros*	*allēlous*
Said	therefore	the	disciples	to	one another,

3231.1 partic	4948.3 indef-pron nom sing	5179.14 verb 3sing indic aor act	840.4 prs-pron dat sing	2052.25 verb inf aor act	2978.5 verb 3sing indic pres act
Μή	τις	ἤνεγκεν	αὐτῷ	φαγεῖν;	34. Λέγει
Mē	*tis*	*ēnenken*	*autō*	*phagein*	*Legei*
Not	anyone	did bring	him	to eat?	Says

first impulse did not concern the water or her waterpot, but that others should meet the Messiah.

"Saith" (*legei*) is a present tense verb signifying she "continuously is saying." This refers to the thrill she had in telling others about Jesus. She would not be silent. What an evidence of her new birth!

29. Come, see a man, which told me all things that ever I did: is not this the Christ?: He is not the Christ, is he, *Williams* . . . revealed to me my whole past, *ALBA* . . . I wonder if he is the Christ, *JB.*

4:29. What the woman said to the men in the village is very similar to the invitation Jesus gave to Andrew and John (1:39) and the first disciples who summoned their friends (1:46). What better witness could one give than to call others to experience new life.

The relevant proof to her was the message that pierced her conscience. Jesus gave her ample evidence to convince her that He could have told her "all (the) things" she had ever done. Compare that which persuaded Nathanael that Jesus was the Messiah (1:48). Christ uncovers the secrets of one's innermost being.

30. Then they went out of the city, and came unto him: So they left the town and went to see Jesus, *TEV* . . . they left the town and started to come to Jesus, *Phillips* . . . They left town and made their way to see Him, *Weymouth* . . . and rushed out to see Him, *Williams* . . . proceeded in a steady stream toward, *Wuest.*

4:30. John describes a rush out of the city by using the aorist verb "went," and a graphic continuing procession in the imperfect verb *ērchonto,* literally "were coming." The possibility that the long expected Messiah had come aroused the men to action. The woman's words brought a ready response.

31. In the mean while his disciples prayed him, saying, Master, eat: . . . the disciples kept urging him, *Montgomery* . . . were entreating Him, *Worrell* . . . In the meantime His disciples pressed Him, saying, "Master, take something to eat, *Fenton* . . . encouraged Him, "Rabbi, eat, *Adams* . . . Teacher, eat something, *Williams* . . . have something to eat, *NEB.*

4:31. "In the mean while" expresses the interval between the woman's departure and the return of the Samaritans with her. The disciples returned as the woman was leaving.

They had bought food in the village. It had been several hours since the party had eaten. They knew Jesus needed food. They revealed a concern for Jesus by insisting that He eat. "Rabbi" (*rhabbi*) is the Greek transliteration of the Aramaic word for "teacher" (see 1:38).

32. But he said unto them, I have meat to eat that ye know not of: I have food, *Rotherham* . . . But he assured them, I have nourishment of which ye have no idea! *Berkeley* . . . of which you have no knowledge, *BB* . . . of which you are not aware, *Concordant* . . . you know nothing about, *Phillips* . . . that you don't know anything about, *Adams.*

33. Therefore said the disciples one to another, Hath any man brought him ought to eat?: They began to wonder, *ALBA* . . . Has anyone brought him anything to eat, *HBIE.*

4:32. On many occasions Jesus used material objects to teach spiritual truths. The disciples were thinking in terms of the noon meal, but Jesus wanted them to be more sensitive to eternal values. Jesus' food was to fulfill His mission. To walk in the perfect will of His Father was His utmost desire; it surpassed His desire for food.

To reach the woman and the Samaritans was Jesus' reason for going through Samaria (see 4:4). As yet the disciples had not the

John 4:35

840.2 prs-pron dat pl	3450.5 art sing masc	2400.1 name nom masc	1684.1 adj 1sing	1026.1 noun sing neu	1498.4 verb 3sing indic pres act
αὐτοῖς	ὁ	Ἰησοῦς,	Ἐμὸν	βρῶμά	ἐστιν
autois	*ho*	*Iēsous*	*Emon*	*brōma*	*estin*
to them		Jesus,	My	food	is

34.a.**Var:** p66,p75,03B, 04C,05D,017K,019L, 032W,038,Lach,Treg, Alf,We/HoSod

2419.1 conj	4020.1 verb 1sing pres act	4020.21 verb 1sing act	3450.16 art sing neu	2284.1 noun sing neu	3450.2 art gen sing
ἵνα	⸀ ποιῶ	[a ποιήσω]	τὸ	θέλημα	τοῦ
hina	*poiō*	*poiēsō*	*to*	*thelēma*	*tou*
that	I should do	[I shall do]	the	will	of the

3854.12 verb gen sing masc part aor act	1466.6 prs-pron acc 1sing	2504.1 conj	4896.3 verb 1sing subj aor act	840.3 prs-pron gen sing
πέμψαντός	με,	καὶ	τελειώσω	αὐτοῦ
pempsantos	*me*	*kai*	*teleiōsō*	*autou*
having sent	me,	and	should finish	his

3450.16 art sing neu	2024.1 noun sing neu	35. 3620.1 partic	5050.1 prs-pron nom 2pl	2978.2 verb 2pl pres act	3617.1 conj
τὸ	ἔργον.	35. οὐχ	ὑμεῖς	λέγετε,	ὅτι
to	*ergon*	*ouch*	*humeis*	*legete*	*hoti*
the	work.	Not	you	say,	that

35.a.**Txt:** 032W,Steph
Var: 01ℵ,02A,03B,04C, 05D,017K,019L,036, 037,038,Gries,Lach, Treg,AlfWord,Tisc, We/Ho,Weis,Sod,UBS/☆

2068.1 adv	4920.1 adj nom sing neu	4920.2 adj nom sing masc	1498.4 verb 3sing indic pres act	2504.1 conj
Ἔτι	⸀ τετράμηνόν	[a☆ τετράμηνός]	ἐστιν	καὶ
Eti	*tetramēnon*	*tetramēnos*	*estin*	*kai*
yet	four months	[idem]	it is	and

3450.5 art sing masc	2303.1 noun nom sing masc	2048.34 verb 3sing indic pres	1481.20 verb 2sing impr aor mid	2978.1 verb 1sing pres act
ὁ	θερισμὸς	ἔρχεται;	ἰδοὺ	λέγω
ho	*therismos*	*erchetai*	*idou*	*legō*
the	harvest	comes?	Behold,	I say

5050.3 prs-pron dat 2pl	1854.4 verb 2pl impr aor act	3450.8 art acc pl masc	3652.8 noun acc pl masc	5050.2 prs-pron gen 2pl	2504.1 conj
ὑμῖν,	Ἐπάρατε	τοὺς	ὀφθαλμοὺς	ὑμῶν	καὶ
humin	*Eparate*	*tous*	*ophthalmous*	*humōn*	*kai*
to you,	Lift up	the	eyes	your	and

2277.6 verb 2pl impr aor mid	3450.15 art acc pl fem	5396.1 noun fem	3617.1 conj	2996.7 adj nom pl fem	1498.7 verb 3pl indic pres act
θεάσασθε	τὰς	χώρας,	ὅτι	λευκαί	εἰσιν
theasasthe	*tas*	*chōras*	*hoti*	*leukai*	*eisin*
see	the	fields,	for	white	they are

4242.1 prep	2303.3 noun acc sing masc	2218.1 adv	2303.3 noun acc sing masc	2218.1 adv
πρὸς	⸀ θερισμόν	ἤδη.	[☆ θερισμόν.	ἤδη]
pros	*therismon*	*ēdē*	*therismon*	*ēdē*
to	harvest	already.	[harvest.	Already]

36.a.**Txt:** 02A,04C-corr, 017K,036,037,038,1,13, byz.bo.Lach
Var: 01ℵ,03B,04C-org, 05D,019L,33,Gries, Treg,AlfTisc,We/Ho, Weis,Sod,UBS/☆

36. 2504.1 conj	3450.5 art sing masc	2302.4 verb nom sing masc part pres act	3272.3 noun acc sing masc	2956.4 verb 3sing indic pres act
36. ⸂a καὶ ⸃	ὁ	θερίζων	μισθὸν	λαμβάνει,
kai	*ho*	*therizōn*	*misthon*	*lambanei*
And	the	reaping	a reward	receives,

2504.1 conj	4714.2 verb 3sing indic pres act	2561.3 noun acc sing masc	1519.1 prep	2205.4 noun acc sing fem	164.1 adj sing	2419.1 conj
καὶ	συνάγει	καρπὸν	εἰς	ζωὴν	αἰώνιον·	ἵνα
kai	*sunagei*	*karpon*	*eis*	*zōēn*	*aiōnion*	*hina*
and	gathers	fruit	unto	life	eternal,	that

intense desire for winning souls which Jesus had. The next verse helps to explain their insensitivity to the needs of the Samaritans.

34. Jesus saith unto them, My meat is to do the will of him that sent me, and to finish his work: ... to complete his work, *Rotherham* ... My nourishment comes from doing the will of God, *LivB* ... do the pleasure, *Murdock* ... will of My Sender, *Fenton, Berkeley* ... make his work complete, *BB* ... and fully to accomplish, *Weymouth* ... to do what he wants, *Beck.*

4:33. The disciples questioned among themselves. They were confused as to why Jesus was not eating. Could someone have brought Him food while they were gone?

4:34. Because of the disciples' lack of understanding, Jesus told them plainly what His food was. "My meat is to do the will of him that sent me." Food gives nourishment, refreshment, and energy. Jesus found His nourishment in His communion with the Father. The word "will" (*thelēma*) carries the idea of the Father's good pleasure. What pleased the Father, pleased the Son.

"And to finish his work." These words are in agreement with the words "to do" of the first part of the statement. Thus "to do" is parallel with "to accomplish" (NASB), and "the will" and "the work" are analogous. The purpose for which the Father sent Jesus was to do His will and purpose. By "to do" and "to accomplish" the Saviour would fulfill His messianic mission. All other hungers came under the control of the Father's will and work.

35. Say not ye, There are yet four months and then cometh harvest?: You have a saying, have you not, *Moffatt* ... In four months more the harvest comes, *Williams* ... with the fourth month? *Fenton* ... time of the grain-cutting, *BB* ... No harvest without waiting for it, *ALBA.*

behold, I say unto you, Lift up your eyes, and look on the fields: ... raise your eyes and observe the fields, *Berkeley* ... Look around, *JB* ... and view attentively the fields, *Wuest* ... upon the grounds, *Murdock* ... and survey the fields, *Campbell* ... scan the fields, *Williams* ... see the countries, *Douay.*

for they are white already to harvest: ... they are already golden, *ALBA* ... gleaming white, *Phillips* ... ripe for the sickle, *Weymouth* ... ready to be cut, *Beck.*

4:35. Jesus had taught the Samaritan woman about her approach to God. Now, the Lord taught the disciples a lesson in spiritual harvest. He wanted His chosen apostles to become skillful harvesters.

Jesus encouraged them to have more eagerness for the spiritual harvest than men do for the natural harvest. "Four months" probably refers to the period between His saying and wheat harvest. He may have pointed to the green wheat as He spoke. Perhaps He also pointed out the Samaritan harvest of souls who were by now making their way up the path toward Him. The Samaritans were like ripe wheat ready for the harvest.

Note the parallels of food in verses 32 and 33 with harvest (natural) and harvest (spiritual) of verse 35.

36. And he that reapeth receiveth wages: The reaper is already getting his wages, *Moffatt.*

and gathereth fruit unto life eternal: ... and gathering in sheaves for Immortal Life, *TCNT* ... is gathering a crop for eternal life, *Williams* ... gathering grain for everlasting life, *Beck.*

4:36. Those who reap the wheat have a double reward: (1) the joy of knowing food will be available until the next harvest, and (2) pay for the day's labor. Those who reap the spiritual harvest

John 4:37

36.b.**Txt:** 01א,02A,05D,017K,036,037,038,13,byz.Lach,Tisc
Var: 03B,04C,019L,030U,33,bo.Treg,We/Ho Weis,Sod,UBS/☆

2504.1 conj	3450.5 art sing masc	4540.5 verb nom sing masc part pres act	3537.1 adv	5299.4 verb 3sing subj pres act	2504.1 conj
(b καὶ)	ὁ	σπείρων	ὁμοῦ	χαίρῃ	καὶ
kai	*ho*	*speirōn*	*homou*	*chairē*	*kai*
both	the	sowing	together	may rejoice	and

3450.5 art sing masc	2302.4 verb nom sing masc part pres act	1706.1 prep	1056.1 conj	3642.5 dem-pron dat sing masc	3450.5 art sing masc
ὁ	θερίζων.	**37.** ἐν	γὰρ	τούτῳ	ὁ
ho	*therizōn*	*en*	*gar*	*toutō*	*ho*
the	reaping.	In	for	this	the

37.a.**Txt:** p66,02A,04C-corr,05D,036,038,13,byz.Lach,Alf
Var: 01א,03B,04C-org,017K,019L,037,33,Treg,Tisc,We/Ho,Weis,Sod,UBS/☆

3030.1 noun nom sing masc	1498.4 verb 3sing indic pres act	3450.5 art sing masc	226.2 adj sing masc	3617.1 conj	241.4 adj nom sing masc
λόγος	ἐστὶν	(a ὁ)	ἀληθινὸς,	ὅτι	Ἄλλος
logos	*estin*	*ho*	*alēthinos*	*hoti*	*Allos*
saying	is	the	true,	That	one

1498.4 verb 3sing indic pres act	3450.5 art sing masc	4540.5 verb nom sing masc part pres act	2504.1 conj	241.4 adj nom sing masc	3450.5 art sing masc
ἐστὶν	ὁ	σπείρων,	καὶ	ἄλλος	ὁ
estin	*ho*	*speirōn*	*kai*	*allos*	*ho*
it is	the	sowing,	and	another	the

38.a.**Var:** 01א,05D,Tisc

2302.4 verb nom sing masc part pres act	1466.1 prs-pron nom 1sing	643.6 verb 1sing indic aor act	643.16 verb 1sing indic perf act
θερίζων.	**38.** ἐγὼ	(ἀπέστειλα	[a ἀπέσταλκα]
therizōn	*egō*	*apesteila*	*apestalka*
reaping.	I	sent	[idem]

5050.4 prs-pron acc 2pl	2302.5 verb inf pres act	3614.16 rel-pron sing neu	3620.1 partic	5050.1 prs-pron nom 2pl	2844.14 verb 2pl indic perf act
ὑμᾶς	θερίζειν	ὃ	οὐχ	ὑμεῖς	κεκοπιάκατε·
humas	*therizein*	*ho*	*ouch*	*humeis*	*kekopiakate*
you	to reap	which	not	you	have labored;

241.6 adj nom pl masc	2844.15 verb 3pl indic perf act	2504.1 conj	5050.1 prs-pron nom 2pl	1519.1 prep	3450.6 art acc sing masc
ἄλλοι	κεκοπιάκασιν,	καὶ	ὑμεῖς	εἰς	τὸν
alloi	*kekopiakasin*	*kai*	*humeis*	*eis*	*ton*
others	have labored,	and	you	into	the

2845.4 noun acc sing masc	840.1 prs-pron gen pl	1511.24 verb 2pl indic perf act	1523.2 prep gen	1156.2 conj	3450.10 art gen sing fem
κόπον	αὐτῶν	εἰσεληλύθατε.	**39.** Ἐκ	δὲ	τῆς
kopon	*autōn*	*eiselēluthate*	*Ek*	*de*	*tēs*
labor	their	have entered.	Out of	but	the

4032.2 noun gen sing fem	1552.10 dem-pron gen sing fem	4044.7 adj nom pl masc	3961.23 verb 3pl indic aor act	1519.1 prep	840.6 prs-pron acc sing masc
πόλεως	ἐκείνης	πολλοὶ	ἐπίστευσαν	εἰς	αὐτὸν
poleōs	*ekeinēs*	*polloi*	*episteusan*	*eis*	*auton*
city	that	many	believed	on	him

3450.1 art gen pl	4398.3 name gen pl masc	4398.7 name gen pl masc	1217.2 prep
τῶν	(Σαμαρειτῶν,	[☆ Σαμαριτῶν]	διὰ
tōn	*Samareitōn*	*Samaritōn*	*dia*
of the	Samaritans,	[idem]	because of

3450.6 art acc sing masc	3030.4 noun acc sing masc	3450.10 art gen sing fem	1129.2 noun gen sing fem	3113.12 verb gen sing fem part pres act
τὸν	λόγον	τῆς	γυναικὸς	μαρτυρούσης,
ton	*logon*	*tēs*	*gunaikos*	*marturousēs*
the	word	of the	woman	testifying,

have great benefits. First, there is opportunity to labor in the work that satisfies the purpose of life. Second, there is promise of abundant results from the toil, and third, the Lord of harvest rewards His laborers. If reaping of the natural harvest brings earthly joy, then the labors of spiritual harvest will result in eternal ecstasy.

"He that soweth and he that reapeth may rejoice together" indicates that the reapers are not the only workers rewarded. The sowers and the reapers share the wages of the harvest. Both kinds of workers are necessary for the Master's service. Jesus pointed out that all laborers will share the joy of the harvest.

Jesus was thinking of much more than monetary rewards here; the proper motivation of the reaper is to gather fruit "unto life eternal." "The man who wins souls for Christ is at work on something with lasting consequences. His work is for eternity" (Morris, *New International Commentary*, 4:280). This is why the reaper will one day rejoice, even though harvesting may be difficult work.

Jesus frequently used the image of sowing and reaping to characterize the work of evangelism. In Matthew 13:3-9,18-23 there is the promise that the harvest will bring "forth fruit, some a hundredfold, some sixtyfold, some thirtyfold" (Matthew 13:8).

4:37. Jesus stated that in spiritual harvest the saying, "One soweth, and another reapeth," is especially true. Often a laborer who sows the field does not reap the grain and therefore has no joy in the grain harvest, but in His harvest Jesus stressed that sowers and reapers will rejoice together. The apostle Paul used the same analogy of harvest and its rewards. He wrote to the Corinthians, "I have planted, Apollos watered; but God gave the increase" (1 Corinthians 3:6).

4:38. Jesus told the disciples that He "sent" (*apesteila*, the word for "commission") them. They had been called and commissioned to baptize disciples for Him (4:2). He reveals here that He had commissioned them before this time. Now, Jesus wanted them to realize their first priority in the work of the Kingdom was to be soul winners.

Jesus spoke of the labor of the others before them. Moses and the patriarchs each had a part in the harvest of souls. The spiritual road had been prepared so that the apostles could enter into the harvest. Jesus' words to the disciples go beyond the Samaritan harvest. The principle He spoke of here is universal for all laborers in the Lord's harvest. Jesus claims the authority as the Lord of the harvest (Luke 10:2).

4:39. The Samaritan woman possessed two characteristics which affected the conversion of her fellow villagers: wisdom in what she

that both he that soweth and he that reapeth may rejoice together: . . . and harvesters, *Klingensmith* . . . may be jointly glad, *Berkeley.*

37. And herein is that saying true, One soweth, and another reapeth: For here the proverb holds good, *JB* . . . In this respect the proverb is true, *ALBA* . . . is verified here, *Berkeley* . . . One does the planting...another gets in the grain, *BB.*

38. I sent you to reap that whereon ye bestowed no labour: . . . where you had not worked before, *Beck* . . . I sent you to reap a crop on which you had not toiled, *Montgomery* . . . that which you have not cultivated, *Fenton* . . . where you had not sown, *Norlie* . . . a harvest you had not worked for, *JB.*

other men laboured, and ye are entered into their labours: Others have sown, and you have come in for the reaping, *Norlie* . . . you step in to benefit from their work, *Berkeley* . . . you get possession, *Campbell* . . . you have reaped the benefit, *Montgomery* . . . you are having the benefit, *TCNT.*

39. And many of the Samaritans of that city believed on him for the saying of the woman, which testified: Samaritans though they were, *TCNT* . . . on account of the statement of the woman, asserting, *Fenton* . . . on the strength of the woman's testimony, *JB.*

John 4:40

39.a.**Txt:** p66,02A, 04C-corr,05D,017K, 032W,036,037,038,1,13, byz.Gries,Lach
Var: p75,01ℵ,03B, 04C-org,019L,bo.Treg, AlfTisc,We/Ho,Weis,Sod, UBS/☆

3617.1 conj	1500.5 verb 3sing indic aor act	1466.4 prs-pron dat 1sing	3820.1 adj	3607.8 rel-pron pl neu	3614.17 rel-pron pl neu
῞Οτι	Εἶπέν	μοι	πάντα	⸂☆ ὅσα	[a ἃ]
Hoti	*Eipen*	*moi*	*panta*	*hosa*	*ha*
	He told	me	all things	whatsoever	[idem]

4020.22 verb 1sing indic aor act	5453.1 conj	3631.1 conj	2048.1 verb indic aor act	4242.1 prep	840.6 prs-pron acc sing masc
ἐποίησα.	40. ῾Ως	οὖν	ἦλθον	πρὸς	αὐτὸν
epoiēsa	*Hōs*	*oun*	*ēlthon*	*pros*	*auton*
I did.	When	therefore	came	to	him

3450.7 art pl masc	4398.2 name nom pl masc	4398.6 name nom pl masc	2049.17 verb 3pl indic imperf act	840.6 prs-pron acc sing masc
οἱ	⸀ Σαμαρεῖται,	[☆ Σαμαρῖται,]	ἠρώτων	αὐτὸν
hoi	*Samareitai*	*Samaritai*	*ērōtōn*	*auton*
the	Samaritans,	[idem]	they asked	him

3176.25 verb inf aor act	3706.1 prep	840.2 prs-pron dat pl	2504.1 conj	3176.16 verb 3sing indic aor act	1550.1 adv	1411.3 num card
μεῖναι	παρ'	αὐτοῖς·	καὶ	ἔμεινεν	ἐκεῖ	δύο
meinai	*par'*	*autois*	*kai*	*emeinen*	*ekei*	*duo*
to stay	with	them,	and	he stayed	there	two

2232.1 noun fem	2504.1 conj	4044.3 adj dat sing	3979.3 adj comp pl	3961.23 verb 3pl indic aor act	1217.2 prep
ἡμέρας.	41. καὶ	πολλῷ	πλείους	ἐπίστευσαν	διὰ
hēmeras	*kai*	*pollō*	*pleious*	*episteusan*	*dia*
days.	And	many	more	believed	because of

3450.6 art acc sing masc	3030.4 noun acc sing masc	840.3 prs-pron gen sing	3450.11 art dat sing fem	4885.1 conj	1129.3 noun dat sing fem
τὸν	λόγον	αὐτοῦ·	42. τῇ	τε	γυναικὶ
ton	*logon*	*autou*	*tē*	*te*	*gunaiki*
the	word	his;	to the	and	woman

2978.25 verb indic imperf act	3617.1 conj	3629.1 adv	1217.2 prep	3450.12 art acc sing fem	4528.7 adj acc 2sing fem
ἔλεγον,	῞Οτι	Οὐκέτι	διὰ	τὴν	σὴν
elegon	*Hoti*	*Ouketi*	*dia*	*tēn*	*sēn*
they said,		No longer	because of	the	your

2954.2 noun acc sing fem	3961.7 verb 1pl indic pres act	840.7 prs-pron nom pl masc	1056.1 conj	189.38 verb 1pl indic perf act
λαλιὰν	πιστεύομεν·	αὐτοὶ	γὰρ	ἀκηκόαμεν,
lalian	*pisteuomen*	*autoi*	*gar*	*akēkoamen*
saying	we believe,	ourselves	for	have heard,

2504.1 conj	3471.5 verb 1pl indic perf act	3617.1 conj	3642.4 dem-pron nom sing masc	1498.4 verb 3sing indic pres act	228.1 adv
καὶ	οἴδαμεν	ὅτι	οὗτός	ἐστιν	ἀληθῶς
kai	*oidamen*	*hoti*	*houtos*	*estin*	*alēthōs*
and	we know	that	this	is	truly

42.a.**Txt:** 02A,04C-corr, 05D,017K,019L,036, 037,038,1,13,byz.Gries, Word
Var: 01ℵ,03B,04C-org, LachTreg,Alf,Tisc, We/Ho,Weis,Sod,UBS/☆

3450.5 art sing masc	4842.1 noun nom sing masc	3450.2 art gen sing	2862.2 noun gen sing masc	3450.5 art sing masc	5382.1 name nom masc
ὁ	σωτὴρ	τοῦ	κόσμου,	⸂a ὁ	χριστός. ⸃
ho	*sōtēr*	*tou*	*kosmou*	*ho*	*christos*
the	Saviour	of the	world,	the	Christ.

3196.3 prep	1156.2 conj	3450.15 art acc pl fem	1411.3 num card	2232.1 noun fem	1814.3 verb 3sing indic aor act
43. Μετὰ	δὲ	τὰς	δύο	ἡμέρας	ἐξῆλθεν
Meta	*de*	*tas*	*duo*	*hēmeras*	*exēlthen*
After	but	the	two	days	he went forth

said (verse 29), and a genuine conversion herself. They knew of her immoral life. Her testimony was so convincing that they believed "on Him" as the Messiah.

Jesus' supernatural knowledge of the woman's past life provided the messianic credentials which they needed to believe. While Jesus was teaching His disciples about harvesting the lost, the woman was reaping the souls of her neighbors (see verse 29).

He told me all that ever I did: . . . that he had revealed her whole past, *ALBA.*

4:40. "So when the Samaritans were come unto him" affirms how advantageous it was that the woman had prepared her neighbors' hearts to receive Christ's message.

The barriers of race and prejudice were destroyed by the faith of the Samaritans. The wall that divided the Samaritans from their Jewish neighbors crumbled. Jesus was a Jew, but He was also their Messiah.

40. So when the Samaritans were come unto him:

they besought him that he would tarry with them: . . . they begged him to stay with them, *TCNT* . . . they asked Him to stay with them, *Beck* . . . they invited Him to stay, *Berkeley* . . . they began asking him to remain with them, *Montgomery.*

and he abode there two days: He stayed for two days, *ALBA.*

4:41. Notice the "And" indicates the continuation of the narrative as did the "and" before "he abode" of verse 40.

This verse points out the foundation of their belief. "His own word" gave them the basis for believing. The next verse (42) reveals the content of their faith. "Believed," *episteusan*, an aorist tense historical fact, has no need of a preposition as in verse 39 where they believed in Him. Believing toward Him was based on another's testimony, that He told her all things that she had done. They "believed because of his own word" which produced a firmer foundation for faith than seeing His miracles or believing the testimony of a witness.

41. And many more believed because of his own word: . . . a far larger number, *Weymouth* . . . Far more believed when they heard him for themselves, *Barclay* . . . Then a much larger number believed, *Williams* . . . of His personal message, *Berkeley.*

4:42,43. The woman's neighbors had believed her testimony, but that progressive form of believing gave way to a better ground for their faith. They as much as said, "Thank you for your testimony. Now we know firsthand by His teaching." That which brought greater assurance had replaced the need for her testimony. They now had a testimony of their own.

They had "heard" (*akēkoamen*) is a perfect tense verb meaning that they had an abiding experience. It began some time in the past and remained. What they "know" (*oidamen*) is grounded in the truths of what they heard; what they "know," they now reveal.

They now saw Jesus as the world's Saviour. Their experience extended beyond their villages and beyond the nation of the Jews. To them He was now universal. They placed no limit on His saving power. Did He teach them some of the truths He shared with

42. And said unto the woman:

Now we believe, not because of thy saying: Now we have faith, but not because of your story, *BB* . . . We no longer believe in Him simply because of your statement, *Weymouth* . . . not merely because of, *Williams* . . . Our faith no longer rests on what you say, *ALBA* . . . through your assertion, *Fenton.*

for we have heard him ourselves, and know that this is indeed the Christ, the Saviour of the world: . . . this is certainly, *Montgomery* . . . this is in truth the Saviour of the world, *HBIE* . . . the Life-Giver, *Murdock.*

43. Now after two days he departed thence, and went into Gal-

John 4:44

43.a.**Txt:** 02A,017K,036,037,038,1,33,byz.Lach
Var: 01ℵ,03B,04C,05D,bo.Treg,Alf,Tisc,We/Ho,Weis,Sod,UBS/☆

1551.1 adv	2504.1 conj	562.2 verb 3sing indic aor act	1519.1 prep	3450.12 art acc sing fem	1049.4 name acc sing fem
ἐκεῖθεν,	(a καὶ	ἀπῆλθεν \	εἰς	τὴν	Γαλιλαίαν.
ekeithen	*kai*	*apelthen*	*eis*	*tēn*	*Galilaian*
from there,	and	went away	into		Galilee;

44.a.**Txt:** 019L,021M,byz.
Var: 01ℵ,02A,03B,04C,05D,017K,036,037,038,Gries,Lach,Treg,Alf,Word,Tisc,We/HoWeis,Sod,UBS/☆

840.5 prs-pron nom sing masc	1056.1 conj	3450.5 art sing masc	2400.1 name nom masc	3113.16 verb 3sing indic aor act	3617.1 conj
44. αὐτὸς	γὰρ	(a ὁ \	Ἰησοῦς	ἐμαρτύρησεν,	ὅτι
autos	*gar*	*ho*	*Iēsous*	*emarturēsen*	*hoti*
himself	for		Jesus	testified,	that

4254.1 noun nom sing masc	1706.1 prep	3450.11 art dat sing fem	2375.10 adj dat sing fem	3830.1 noun dat sing fem	4940.4 noun acc sing fem
προφήτης	ἐν	τῇ	ἰδίᾳ	πατρίδι	τιμὴν
prophētēs	*en*	*tē*	*idia*	*patridi*	*timēn*
a prophet	in	the	his own	country	honor

45.a.**Var:** 01ℵ-org,05D,Tisc

3620.2 partic	2174.4 verb 3sing indic pres act	3616.1 conj	5453.1 conj	3631.1 conj	2048.3 verb 3sing indic aor act
οὐκ	ἔχει.	**45.** (Ὅτε	[a ὡς]	οὖν	ἦλθεν
ouk	*echei*	*Hote*	*hōs*	*oun*	*ēlthen*
not	has.	When	[as]	therefore	he came

1519.1 prep	3450.12 art acc sing fem	1049.4 name acc sing fem	1203.8 verb 3pl indic aor mid	840.6 prs-pron acc sing masc	3450.7 art pl masc
εἰς	τὴν	Γαλιλαίαν	ἐδέξαντο	αὐτὸν	οἱ
eis	*tēn*	*Galilaian*	*edexanto*	*auton*	*hoi*
into		Galilee	received	him	the

45.b.**Txt:** 01ℵ-org,05D,017K,036,037,it.Steph,Tisc
Var: 01ℵ-corr,02A,03B,04C,019L,038,Lach,Treg,Alf,We/HoWeis,Sod,UBS/☆

1050.3 name-adj pl masc	3820.1 adj	3571.17 verb nom pl masc part perf act	3614.17 rel-pron pl neu	3607.8 rel-pron pl neu
Γαλιλαῖοι,	πάντα	ἑωρακότες	(ἃ	[b☆ ὅσα]
Galilaioi	*panta*	*heōrakotes*	*ha*	*hosa*
Galileans,	all things	having seen	which	[idem]

4020.24 verb 3sing indic aor act	1706.1 prep	2389.3 name dat pl neu	1706.1 prep	3450.11 art dat sing fem
ἐποίησεν	ἐν	Ἱεροσολύμοις	ἐν	τῇ
epoiēsen	*en*	*Hierosolumois*	*en*	*tē*
he did	in	Jerusalem	during	the

1844.3 noun dat sing fem	2504.1 conj	840.7 prs-pron nom pl masc	1056.1 conj	2048.1 verb indic aor act	1519.1 prep	3450.12 art acc sing fem
ἑορτῇ·	καὶ	αὐτοὶ	γὰρ	ἦλθον	εἰς	τὴν
heortē	*kai*	*autoi*	*gar*	*ēlthon*	*eis*	*tēn*
feast,	also	they	for	went	to	the

46.a.**Txt:** Steph
Var: 01ℵ,02A,03B,04C,05D,017K,019L,036,037,038,1,13,byz.it.bo.Gries,Lach,Treg,Alf Word,Tisc,We/Ho,Weis,Sod,UBS/☆

1844.4 noun acc sing fem	2048.3 verb 3sing indic aor act	3631.1 conj	3450.5 art sing masc	2400.1 name nom masc
ἑορτήν.	**46.** Ἦλθεν	οὖν	(a ὁ	Ἰησοῦς \
heortēn	*Ēlthen*	*oun*	*ho*	*Iēsous*
feast.	Came	therefore		Jesus

46.b.**Var:** 02A,017K,036,037,038,1,13,byz.Word

3687.1 adv	3450.5 art sing masc	2400.1 name nom masc	1519.1 prep	3450.12 art acc sing fem	2551.2 name fem
πάλιν	[b+ ὁ	Ἰησοῦς]	εἰς	τὴν	Κανὰ
palin	*ho*	*Iēsous*	*eis*	*tēn*	*Kana*
again		[Jesus]	to		Cana

3450.10 art gen sing fem	1049.2 name gen sing fem	3562.1 adv	4020.24 verb 3sing indic aor act	3450.16 art sing neu	5045.1 noun sing neu
τῆς	Γαλιλαίας,	ὅπου	ἐποίησεν	τὸ	ὕδωρ
tēs	*Galilaias*	*hopou*	*epoiēsen*	*to*	*hudōr*
	of Galilee,	where	he made	the	water

Nicodemus, such as in 3:14-16? How did they know such terms as "Saviour of the world"? The arm of one born of love extended to embrace the world. Love includes, it never excludes. "Saviour of the world" occurs only here and in 1 John 4:14. An equivalent expression "Saviour of all men" is found written by the apostle Paul to Timothy (1 Timothy 4:10). The word "Saviour" (*sōtēr*) appears in the New Testament 24 times. The word means "savior," "deliverer" and "preserver." Often the term means to save in the physical sense, but as applied to Christ, it means the spiritual and eternal Saviour.

Galilee was the destination according to 4:3. The "two days" of verses 40 and 43 are those during which Jesus stayed with the Samaritans. His disciples were with Him. His 2-day visit in Sychar provided a break in the long trek from Judea to Galilee, and it afforded a copious field of harvest.

ilee: After spending two days there, *TEV* . . . at the end of, *Berkeley*.

4:44. "For Jesus himself testified" speaks of the contrast between His ministry among the Samaritans and His reception already mentioned in Judea. His presence had stirred hostility among the Pharisees (4:1,2). Jesus had left Judea so that the opposition might subside.

"His own country" refers to Judea. Jesus was of the tribe of Judah. He was born in Bethlehem, Judea, but was brought up in Nazareth.

44. For Jesus himself testified, that a prophet hath no honour in his own country: . . . although Jesus had Himself declared, *Fenton* . . . Jesus Himself affirmed, *Berkeley* . . . Jesus Himself had pointed out, *NIV* . . . that there is no respect for a, *JB* . . . a prophet has no honor in his own fatherland, *Norlie* . . . is not honored in his own city, *Murdock* . . . is not regarded, *Campbell* . . . is not accepted in his own home town, *SEB* . . . country of his birth, *BB* . . . in his native town, *Berkeley* . . . is not correctly evaluated, and is therefore not treated with the respect and deference which is his due, *Wuest* . . . in his native country, *Sawyer* . . . in his own fatherland, *Rotherham*.

4:45. "The Galileans received him." It was because of the miracles Jesus performed at the Passover (see 2:23). They were proud that one of their own number had gained such popularity. Galileans were usually treated as inferior citizens by the religious community of Judea. But the Galileans did not receive Him because of their faith in Him as the Saviour. Their reception was because of His miracles and popularity, not because of His teaching.

45. Then when he was come into Galilee, the Galilaeans received him: So, on His arrival in, *Berkeley* . . . when He arrived in Galilee, *Fenton* . . . gave him a reception, *ALBA* . . . entertained him, *Scarlett* . . . with open arms, *Phillips*.

having seen all the things that he did at Jerusalem at the feast: . . . seen with a discerning eye, *Wuest*.

for they also went unto the feast: . . . which they too had attended, *JB* . . . had attended the feast, *Berkeley* . . . to the festival, *Fenton*.

4:46. We should note the many levels of society Jesus touched from the first chapter of this Gospel to this point. Jesus won the peasant workers from Galilee (1:29-51). He ministered to the wedding guests (chapter 2). A ruler of the Pharisees by the name of Nicodemus came to Him (chapter 3). The Samaritan harlot became a soul winner (chapter 4). And now a royal officer came to seek healing for his son.

Cana is referred to four times in the New Testament and each time in John (twice in chapter 2, here, and 21:2). This was the second time Jesus visited Cana.

46. So Jesus came again into Cana of Galilee, where he made the water wine: Jesus went once more, *Berkeley* . . . He returned then to, *Fenton*.

46.c.**Var:** 01א,05D,019L, 33,it.bo.Tisc

3494.4 noun acc sing masc	2504.1 conj	1498.34 verb sing indic imperf act	1498.34 verb sing indic imperf act	1156.2 conj	4948.3 indef-pron nom sing
οἶνον.	⸀ καὶ	ἦν	[ᶜ ☆Ἦν	δέ]	τις
oinon	kai	ēn	Ēn	de	tis
wine.	And	there was	[There was	and]	a certain

930.1 adj nom sing masc	3614.2 rel-pron gen sing	3450.5 art sing masc	5048.1 noun nom sing masc	764.16 verb 3sing indic imperf act
βασιλικὸς,	οὗ	ὁ	υἱὸς	ἠσθένει
basilikos	hou	ho	huios	ēsthenei
court official,	whose	the	son	was sick

1706.1 prep	2555.1 name fem	2555.2 name fem	3642.4 dem-pron nom sing masc
ἐν	⸀ Καπερναούμ.	[☆ Καφαρναούμ·]	47. οὗτος
en	Kapernaoum	Kapharnaoum	houtos
in	Capernaum.	[idem]	This

189.31 verb nom sing masc part aor act	3617.1 conj	2400.1 name nom masc	2223.2 verb 3sing indic pres act	1523.2 prep gen	3450.10 art gen sing fem
ἀκούσας	ὅτι	Ἰησοῦς	ἥκει	ἐκ	τῆς
akousas	hoti	Iēsous	hēkei	ek	tēs
having heard	that	Jesus	had come	out of	

2424.2 name gen fem	1519.1 prep	3450.12 art acc sing fem	1049.4 name acc sing fem	562.2 verb 3sing indic aor act	4242.1 prep
Ἰουδαίας,	εἰς	τὴν	Γαλιλαίαν	ἀπῆλθεν	πρὸς
Ioudaias	eis	tēn	Galilaian	apēlthen	pros
Judea	into		Galilee,	went	to

47.a.**Txt:** 02A,017K,036, 037,038,1,byz.Gries, Lach
Var: 01א,03B,04C,05D, 019L,33,Treg,Alf,Tisc, We/HoWeis,Sod,UBS/☆

840.6 prs-pron acc sing masc	2504.1 conj	2049.16 verb 3sing indic imperf act	840.6 prs-pron acc sing masc	2419.1 conj
αὐτὸν,	καὶ	ἠρώτα	⸂ᵃ αὐτὸν ⸃	ἵνα
auton	kai	ērōta	auton	hina
him,	and	asked	him	that

2568.16 verb 3sing subj aor act	2504.1 conj	2367.9 verb 3sing subj aor mid	840.3 prs-pron gen sing	3450.6 art acc sing masc
καταβῇ	καὶ	ἰάσηται	αὐτοῦ	τὸν
katabē	kai	iasētai	autou	ton
he would come down	and	heal	his	the

5048.4 noun acc sing masc	3165.21 verb 3sing indic imperf act	1056.1 conj	594.8 verb inf pres act	1500.5 verb 3sing indic aor act
υἱόν·	ἤμελλεν	γὰρ	ἀποθνήσκειν.	48. εἶπεν
huion	ēmellen	gar	apothnēskein	eipen
son;	he was about	for	to die.	Said

3631.1 conj	3450.5 art sing masc	2400.1 name nom masc	4242.1 prep	840.6 prs-pron acc sing masc	1430.1 partic
οὖν	ὁ	Ἰησοῦς	πρὸς	αὐτόν,	Ἐὰν
oun	ho	Iēsous	pros	auton	Ean
therefore		Jesus	to	him,	If

3231.1 partic	4447.2 noun pl neu	2504.1 conj	4907.1 noun pl neu	1481.12 verb 2pl subj aor act	3620.3 partic	3231.1 partic
μὴ	σημεῖα	καὶ	τέρατα	ἴδητε,	οὐ	μὴ
mē	sēmeia	kai	terata	idēte	ou	mē
not	signs	and	wonders	you see	not	not

3961.1 verb 2pl subj act	2978.5 verb 3sing indic pres act	4242.1 prep	840.6 prs-pron acc sing masc	3450.5 art sing masc
πιστεύσητε.	49. Λέγει	πρὸς	αὐτὸν	ὁ
pisteusēte	Legei	pros	auton	ho
will you believe.	Says	to	him	the

"There was a certain nobleman" indicates the man was connected to King Herod the tetrarch of Galilee either by birth or office. One's blood line often procured a man his military or civil office; therefore, both are likely (compare Luke 8:3 and Acts 13:1). The man's court was probably at Tiberias on the western shore of the Sea of Galilee. The reference to Capernaum reminds us that Jesus had made that city His headquarters (Matthew 4:13; Luke 4:31). Capernaum was located on the northwest shore of the lake about 12 miles from Cana.

"Sick" (*ēsthenei*) is an imperfect tense verb meaning he was in a condition of weakness, feebleness, frailness, and sickness. This verb occurs eight times in John (4:46; 5:3,7; 6:2; 11:1,2,3,6). John uses the noun twice (5:5; 11:4). It is the word describing Lazarus' sickness.

And there was a certain nobleman, whose son was sick at Capernaum: . . . a certain officer, *Norlie* . . . a king's servant, *Murdock* . . . a Certain Courtier, *Wilson* . . . one of the king's officers, *Montgomery* . . . government official, *TEV, SEB* . . . an official of the imperial government, *Barclay* . . . royal officer, *ALBA* . . . lay ill in, *Berkeley* . . . with a chronic ailment, *Wuest.*

4:47. When the royal officer's son became sick, there was naturally a hope for his son's healing. The father thought it was necessary for Jesus to come to Capernaum to perform the miracle. But Jesus often surprises us.

47. When he heard that Jesus was come out of Judaea into Galilee: . . . having heard, *Weymouth* . . . had arrived in, *NIV* . . . had come back from Judea, *AmpB.*

he went unto him, and besought him that he would come down, and heal his son: . . . begging that He would go down and cure his son, *Fenton* . . . and commenced begging Him, *Wuest.*

for he was at the point of death: . . . who was close to death, *NIV* . . . who was about to die, *TEV.*

4:48. "Then" (*oun*) indicates that Jesus took into consideration the urgency of the circumstances.

The critics of Jesus often confronted Him by asking for miracles. Christ sometimes used a negative response when seekers came to Him. For example, the Syrophoenician woman came to Him with an urgent request for Him to cast a demon out of her daughter. At that interview Jesus said, "It is not good to take the children's bread and throw it to the dogs" (Mark 7:27, NASB). Jesus sometimes utilizes unusual means to burn the dross from faith.

The word "signs" (*sēmeion*) is highly significant in the Gospel of John. It occurs 17 times in John, almost always in a positive sense. Signs are miracles which point beyond themselves, beyond the mere physical event, to highlight the deity of Christ. When Jesus multiplied the bread (6:1-15), it was not just to give people physical food to eat, but to illustrate that He is the Bread of Life (6:35-58). Signs, therefore, reveal the glory of God (2:11; 11:4,40).

The reason Jesus was disappointed in the official's request was that he wanted only some physical demonstration of Jesus' power without seeing beyond it to the Person who performed the sign and then believing in Him. Jesus did not perform "signs and wonders" to please people's fancy or to give them something to marvel at. He did so to lead people to belief in Him as the Son of God (20:31), and to reveal His glory.

The lesson that Jesus wished to impart to the nobleman was that he needed not to believe in signs and wonders for themselves but

48. Then said Jesus unto him, Except ye see signs and wonders, ye will not believe: None of you will ever believe, *TEV* . . . Unless you see signs and portents you will not have faith, *ALBA* . . . you see visible and astonishing displays of the, *Barclay* . . . and miracles happen, you [people] never will believe (trust, have faith) at all, *AmpB* . . . nothing will induce you to believe, *Weymouth* . . . they just won't believe, *Adams* . . . believe at all, *Berkeley.*

930.1 adj nom sing masc	2935.5 noun voc sing masc	2568.17 verb 2sing impr aor act	4109.1 adv	594.20 verb inf aor act
βασιλικός,	Κύριε,	κατάβηθι	πρὶν	ἀποθανεῖν
basilikos	Kurie	katabēthi	prin	apothanein
court official,	Sir,	come down	before	dies

3450.16 art sing neu	3676.1 noun sing masc	1466.2 prs-pron gen 1sing	2978.5 verb 3sing indic pres act	840.4 prs-pron dat sing
τὸ	παιδίον	μου.	50. Λέγει	αὐτῷ
to	paidion	mou	Legei	autō
the	little child	my.	Says	to him

50.a.**Txt:** 02A,04C,017K, 036,037,038,1,13,byz.bo. Gries,Lach,Treg
Var: 01ℵ,03B,05D,Alf, TiscWe/Ho,Weis,Sod, UBS/*

3450.5 art sing masc	2400.1 name nom masc	4057.4 verb 2sing impr pres	3450.5 art sing masc	5048.1 noun nom sing masc	4622.2 prs-pron gen 2sing
ὁ	Ἰησοῦς,	Πορεύου·	ὁ	υἱός	σου
ho	Iēsous	Poreuou	ho	huios	sou
	Jesus,	Go,	the	son	your

50.b.**Txt:** p66,05D,017K, 032W,036,037,1,13,byz. Gries,Sod
Var: p75,01ℵ-corr,02A, 03B,04C,019L,038,Lach Treg,Alf,Tisc,We/Ho, Weis,UBS/*

2180.1 verb sing indic pres	2504.1 conj	3961.20 verb 3sing indic aor act	3450.5 art sing masc	442.1 noun nom sing masc
ζῇ.	⸂ᵃ καὶ ⸃	ἐπίστευσεν	ὁ	ἄνθρωπος
zē	kai	episteusen	ho	anthrōpos
lives.	And	believed	the	man

50.c.**Var:** 02A,03B,04C, 05D,017K,019L,036, 037,038,byz.Lach,Treg Alf,Tisc,We/Ho,Weis, Sod,UBS/*

3450.3 art dat sing	3030.3 noun dat sing masc	3614.3 rel-pron dat sing	3614.6 rel-pron acc sing masc	1500.5 verb 3sing indic aor act	840.4 prs-pron dat sing
τῷ	λόγῳ	⸀ ᾧ	[ᵇ* ὃν]	εἶπεν	αὐτῷ
tō	logō	hō	hon	eipen	autō
the	word	which	[idem]	said	to him

51.a.**Txt:** p66,p75,02A, 03B,04C,017K,036,037, 038,13,byz.Lach,We/Ho
Var: 01ℵ,05D,019L,Tisc Weis,Sod,UBS/*

3450.5 art sing masc	2400.1 name nom masc	2504.1 conj	4057.36 verb 3sing indic imperf	2218.1 adv	1156.2 conj
[ᶜ*+ ὁ]	Ἰησοῦς,	καὶ	ἐπορεύετο.	51. ἤδη	δὲ
ho	Iēsous	kai	eporeueto	ēdē	de
	Jesus,	and	went away.	Already	but

51.b.**Txt:** 02A,036,037, byz.
Var: 01ℵ,03B,04C,05D, 017K,019L,038,Lach Treg,Alf,Tisc,We/Ho, Weis,Sod,UBS/*

840.3 prs-pron gen sing	2568.3 verb gen sing masc part pres act	3450.7 art pl masc	1395.6 noun pl masc	840.3 prs-pron gen sing
αὐτοῦ	καταβαίνοντος	οἱ	δοῦλοι	⸂ᵃ αὐτοῦ ⸃
autou	katabainontos	hoi	douloi	autou
he	going down	the	slaves	his

51.c.**Txt:** p66,02A,04C, 032W,036,037,038,13, byz.Lach,TregAlf
Var: p75,03B,019L,bo. We/Ho,Weis,Sod,UBS/*

524.2 verb 3pl indic aor act	5059.2 verb 3pl indic aor act	840.4 prs-pron dat sing	2504.1 conj
⸀ ἀπήντησαν	[ᵇ* ὑπήντησαν]	αὐτῷ,	⸂ᶜ καὶ
apēntēsan	hupēntēsan	autō	kai
met	[idem]	him,	and

514.8 verb 3pl indic aor act	2978.16 verb pl masc part pres act	3617.1 conj	3450.5 art sing masc	3679.3 noun sing fem	4622.2 prs-pron gen 2sing
ἀπήγγειλαν ⸃	λέγοντες,	Ὅτι	ὁ	παῖς	⸀ σου
apēngeilan	legontes	Hoti	ho	pais	sou
reported,	saying,		The	child	your

51.d.**Txt:** p66-corr,05D, 017K,019L,036,037,038, 1,byz.sa.bo.
Var: p66-org,p75,01ℵ, 02A,03B,04C,032W, LachTreg,Alf,Tisc, We/Ho,Weis,Sod,UBS/*

840.3 prs-pron gen sing	2180.1 verb sing indic pres	4299.3 verb 3sing indic aor mid	3631.1 conj	3706.1 prep
[ᵈ* αὐτοῦ]	ζῇ.	52. Ἐπύθετο	οὖν	⸀ παρ'
autou	zē	Eputheto	oun	par'
[his]	lives.	He inquired	therefore	from

840.1 prs-pron gen pl	3450.12 art acc sing fem	5443.4 noun acc sing fem	3450.12 art acc sing fem	5443.4 noun acc sing fem	3706.1 prep
αὐτῶν	τὴν	ὥραν	[* τὴν	ὥραν	παρ'
autōn	tēn	hōran	tēn	hōran	par'
them	the	hour	[the	hour—	from

to believe in the One who performed them. The official was able to realize this and believed in Jesus (4:53).

49. The nobleman saith unto him, Sir, come down ere my child die: The king's officer pleaded, *Williams* . . . pleaded with Him, Sir, do come down at once before my little child is dead! *AmpB* . . . Come down, sir, before my boy is dead, *Moffatt* . . . Lord, come down...before my little boy dies, *Beck.*

4:49. "Sir" speaks of the respect the nobleman had for Jesus. He might have been turned away by Jesus' response to his plea for help, but Jesus' statement only served to intensify the nobleman's efforts.

Note the anguish of the father's heart. There was tender affection expressed in the term "my child."

By saying "ere my child die," the man placed a limit on Jesus' healing power. As in the case of Lazarus' death, Martha and Mary said, "Lord, if thou hadst been here, my brother had not died" (11:21,32). Jesus was implored to come down and to do it very soon. If He did not, the child's death would end all the nobleman's hope. The man did not answer Jesus' seeming rebuke, nor did he have time to argue the facts. His heart was filled with love and concern for his child.

50. Jesus saith unto him, Go thy way; thy son liveth: Be proceeding on your way, *Wuest* . . . Go yourself, your son is alive, *Moffatt* . . . Go away...your son lives, *Fenton* . . . Your boy is going to live, *Williams* . . . you can go ...your son is alive and well, *TCNT.*

And the man believed the word that Jesus had spoken unto him, and he went his way: He took Jesus at his word and left, *SEB* . . . and started on his way, *JB* . . . and set out for home, *ALBA.*

4:50. Jesus put the nobleman's faith to the test (verse 48). He gave him a command and a promise. "Go" (*poreuou*) is a present imperative verb meaning "be going" on your way. The verb "went" is an imperfect tense verb meaning he "was going." Thus the command was followed by progressive obedience. "Thy son liveth" (*ho huios sou zē*) is an ambiguous statement. It can mean "your son is still living," therefore be satisfied, or "your son is living," meaning that he is healed. The assertion Jesus made attracted the officer to deepen his trust in His authority and power. The Lord gave no indication, except His bare word, that the healing would happen.

"Believed" was an act of his volition. "Went" was an action of his person. The second action was a result of his conviction.

There is an interesting parallel to this healing in Matthew chapter 8. These two healings revealed a faith that would later become necessary for all believers, for Jesus' bodily presence would one day be absent from the earth.

51. And as he was now going down, his servants met him, and told him, saying: And, when he was even now going down, *Rotherham* . . . On his way home his servants met him with the news, *TEV* . . . his bondservants met him, *Clementson* . . . the slaves, *Concordant* . . . and informed him, *Campbell* . . . and announced that, *Berkeley.*

Thy son liveth: Your boy is going to live! *TEV.*

4:51. "And as he was now going down" signifies continuation of his obedience. Cana was situated among the hills southwest of Capernaum.

52. Then enquired he of them the hour when he began to amend: What time it was when his son got better, *TEV* . . . at what time the crisis had passed, *Norlie*

4:52. "Then inquired he" speaks of the father's desire to confirm the fact that Jesus had healed his child. "Began to amend" has the

840.1 prs-pron gen pl	1706.1 prep	3614.11 rel-pron dat sing fem	2838.1 adv comp	2174.32 verb 3sing indic aor act
αὐτῶν]	ἐν	ᾗ	κομψότερον	ἔσχεν.
autōn	en	hē	kompsoteron	eschen
them]	in	which	better	he got.

52.a.**Txt:** 01ℵ,02A,017K,036,037,038,13,byz.Gries,Lach
Var: (03),(04),(019),Tisc,We/Ho,Weis,UBS/☆

2504.1 conj	1500.3 verb indic aor act	1500.28 verb 3pl indic aor act	3631.1 conj	840.4 prs-pron dat sing	3617.1 conj
⸀ καὶ	εἶπον	[a☆ εἶπαν	οὖν]	αὐτῷ,	⸀Ὅτι
kai	eipon	eipan	oun	autō	Hoti
And	they said	[They said	therefore]	to him,	

52.b.**Txt:** 03B-corr,036,037,byz.
Var: 01ℵ,02A,03B-org,04C,05D,017K,019L,038,Lach,Treg,Alf,Word,Tisc,We/Ho,Weis,Sod,UBS/☆

5340.1 adv	2170.1 adv	5443.4 noun acc sing fem	1436.5 num ord acc sing fem	856.10 verb 3sing indic aor act
⸀ Χθὲς	[b☆ Ἐχθὲς]	ὥραν	ἑβδόμην	ἀφῆκεν
Chthes	Echthes	hōran	hebdomēn	aphēken
Yesterday	[idem]	hour	seventh	left

840.6 prs-pron acc sing masc	3450.5 art sing masc	4304.1 noun nom sing masc	1091.17 verb 3sing indic aor act	3631.1 conj	3450.5 art sing masc
αὐτὸν	ὁ	πυρετός.	53. Ἔγνω	οὖν	ὁ
auton	ho	puretos	Egnō	oun	ho
him	the	fever.	Knew	therefore	the

53.a.**Txt:** p66,01ℵ-corr,02A,05D,017K,019L,032W,036,037,038,byz.Lach
Var: 01ℵ-org,03B,04C,TiscWe/Ho,Weis,Sod,UBS/☆

3824.1 noun nom sing masc	3617.1 conj	1706.1 prep	1552.11 dem-pron dat sing fem	3450.11 art dat sing fem	5443.3 noun dat sing fem
πατὴρ	ὅτι	⸂a ἐν ⸃	ἐκείνῃ	τῇ	ὥρᾳ
patēr	hoti	en	ekeinē	tē	hōra
father	that	at	that	the	hour

1706.1 prep	3614.11 rel-pron dat sing fem	1500.5 verb 3sing indic aor act	840.4 prs-pron dat sing	3450.5 art sing masc	2400.1 name nom masc
ἐν	ᾗ	εἶπεν	αὐτῷ	ὁ	Ἰησοῦς,
en	hē	eipen	autō	ho	Iēsous
in	which	said	to him		Jesus,

53.b.**Txt:** 05D,017K,032W,036,037,038,13,byz.
Var: 01ℵ,02A,03B,04C,019L,33,Lach,Treg,Alf,Tisc,We/HoWeis,Sod,UBS/☆

3617.1 conj	3450.5 art sing masc	5048.1 noun nom sing masc	4622.2 prs-pron gen 2sing	2180.1 verb sing indic pres	2504.1 conj
⸂b Ὅτι ⸃	ὁ	υἱός	σου	ζῇ.	Καὶ
Hoti	ho	huios	sou	zē	Kai
	The	son	your	lives.	And

3961.20 verb 3sing indic aor act	840.5 prs-pron nom sing masc	2504.1 conj	3450.9 art nom sing fem	3477.2 noun nom sing fem	840.3 prs-pron gen sing
ἐπίστευσεν	αὐτὸς	καὶ	ἡ	οἰκία	αὐτοῦ
episteusen	autos	kai	hē	oikia	autou
he believed	himself	and	the	house	his

54.a.**Var:** p66,p75,03B,04C-org,032W,13,Treg,Alf,We/Ho,Weis,Sod,UBS/☆

3513.6 adj nom sing fem	3642.17 dem-pron sing neu	1156.2 conj	3687.1 adv	1202.8 num ord sing neu
ὅλη.	54. Τοῦτο	[a☆+ δὲ]	πάλιν	δεύτερον
holē	Touto	de	palin	deuteron
whole.	This	[and]	again	a second

4447.1 noun sing neu	4020.24 verb 3sing indic aor act	3450.5 art sing masc	2400.1 name nom masc	2048.13 verb nom sing masc part aor act
σημεῖον	ἐποίησεν	ὁ	Ἰησοῦς,	ἐλθὼν
sēmeion	epoiēsen	ho	Iēsous	elthōn
sign	did		Jesus,	having come

1523.2 prep gen	3450.10 art gen sing fem	2424.2 name gen fem	1519.1 prep	3450.12 art acc sing fem	1049.4 name acc sing fem
ἐκ	τῆς	Ἰουδαίας	εἰς	τὴν	Γαλιλαίαν.
ek	tēs	Ioudaias	eis	tēn	Galilaian
out of		Judea	into		Galilee.

historical aorist verb as its tense. The action is a completed one. There is no idea of progressively mending in the statement. Jesus healed the boy by His word instantly. The servants would not have brought the father the news of the boy's recovery if the healing had not been complete. They would have feared a relapse. The father understood his servants to mean his child was healed.

"The seventh hour the fever left him." The verb "left" (*aphēken*) also is the historical aorist indicating a definite point of the action, not a continued action. The time was important to the father because it was at the seventh hour (1 p.m.) that Jesus spoke the healing word.

... during which he was getting better, *Wuest* ... at what hour he had shown improvement, *Weymouth* ... the hour when he became better, *BB* ... began to improve, *Berkeley.*

And they said unto him, Yesterday at the seventh hour the fever left him: Yesterday at one o'clock the fever left him, *Berkeley* ... on the previous day, *ALBA.*

4:53. The father "knew" because the time Jesus spoke to him, "thy son liveth," was the time his child was healed.

The healing of the lad was instrumental in bringing the nobleman to the Saviour, for he "believed" (*episteusen*), indicating a recorded fact. His household believed by hearing the father's testimony and seeing the miracle performed on the son. The growth of the officer's faith spread through his entire family.

53. So the father knew that it was at the same hour, in the which Jesus said unto him: Then the Father remembered, *TEV* ... Then the father realized, *Barclay* ... So the father observed, *Rotherham* ... The father then recognised that that was the very time, *Fenton* ... at the exact time, *ET* ... about the exact time, *SEB* ... realized that it had left him at the very time, *Moffatt.*

Thy son liveth: and himself believed:

and his whole house: ... and he and his whole household became believers, *Weymouth* ... his entire household, *Berkeley* ... So he and all his family, *TEV* ... and his whole family believed, *SEB.*

4:54. "This is again the second miracle" points back to chapter 2 in which Jesus turned the water into wine. John's Gospel positions this miracle beside the first (John 2) to give evidence as to who Jesus is: the Son of God.

A major theme found in chapters 2 to 4 is the reaction of different individuals to the message of Jesus and the degree of faith they had in Him. John records that after Jesus turned the water into wine, "his disciples believed on him" (2:11). In contrast to this, many in Jerusalem believed because of Jesus' signs, but perhaps their faith was inadequate since "Jesus did not commit himself unto them, because he knew all men" (2:24). Then follows the story concerning Nicodemus (3:1-21) who did not yet fully believe. In chapter 4, both the Samaritan woman and the whole village of Sychar believed (4:29,42). Finally, the nobleman and his household believed in Jesus because of the healing He performed (4:53). (Cf. Brown, *Anchor Bible*, 29:cxliii, 197.)

The second theme found in this passage is that of Jesus giving life. In His talk with Nicodemus, Jesus had told him that God sent His only Son in order that the world might have eternal life (3:16,36). Jesus had also told the Samaritan woman that He could give water that produces life (4:14). Finally, with the healing of the official's son, Jesus proved that He can give life, as He did again by raising Lazarus from the dead (11:25).

"Out of Judea into Galilee" indicates the second journey from Judea into Galilee, the first implied by chapter 2, verse 1 (see also 2:11).

54. This is again the second miracle that Jesus did: ... the second occasion on which Jesus gave a sign, *TCNT* ... a second attesting miracle, *Wuest* ... the second proof, *SEB.*

when he was come out of Judaea into Galilee: ... while passing from Judea into Galilee, *Fenton.*

1.a.**Var:** 01ℵ,04C,019L, 037,044,1,sa.bo.Tisc,Sod

3196.3 prep	**3642.18** dem-pron pl neu	**1498.34** verb sing indic imperf act	**3450.9** art nom sing fem	**1844.1** noun nom sing fem
5:1. Μετὰ	ταῦτα	ἦν	[a+ ἡ]	ἑορτὴ
Meta	*tauta*	*ēn*	*hē*	*heortē*
After	these things	was	[the]	a feast

1.b.**Txt:** 01ℵ,04C,030U, 032W,037,038,012G5,1, 13,byz.Sod
Var: p66,p75,02A,03B, 05D,017K,019L,036, Lach,Treg,Alf,Word, Tisc,We/HoWeis,UBS/☆

3450.1 art gen pl	**2428.3** name-adj gen pl masc	**2504.1** conj	**303.13** verb 3sing indic aor act	**3450.5** art sing masc	**2400.1** name nom masc
τῶν	Ἰουδαίων,	καὶ	ἀνέβη	(b ὁ)	Ἰησοῦς
tōn	*Ioudaiōn*	*kai*	*anebē*	*ho*	*Iēsous*
of the	Jews,	and	went up		Jesus

1519.1 prep	**2389.1** name	**1498.4** verb 3sing indic pres act	**1156.2** conj	**1706.1** prep	**3450.4** art dat pl
εἰς	Ἱεροσόλυμα.	2. ἔστιν	δὲ	ἐν	τοῖς
eis	*Hierosoluma*	*estin*	*de*	*en*	*tois*
to	Jerusalem.	There is	and	in	

2389.3 name dat pl neu	**1894.3** prep	**3450.11** art dat sing fem	**4121.1** adj dat sing fem	**2833.1** noun nom sing fem
Ἱεροσολύμοις	ἐπὶ	τῇ	προβατικῇ	κολυμβήθρα,
Hierosolumois	*epi*	*tē*	*probatikē*	*kolumbēthra*
Jerusalem	at	the	sheepgate	a pool,

2.a.**Var:** 01ℵ-org,Tisc

3450.9 art nom sing fem	**1937.1** verb nom sing fem part pres pass	**3450.16** art sing neu	**2978.29** verb acc sing part pres pass	**1440.1** name-adv
(ἡ	ἐπιλεγομένη	[a+ τὸ	λεγόμενον]	Ἑβραϊστὶ
hē	*epilegomenē*	*to*	*legomenon*	*Hebraisti*
the	being called	[the	being called]	in Hebrew

2.b.**Txt:** 02A,04C,017K, 036,037,038,1,13,byz. LachWeis
Var: 01ℵ,(019),33,Tisc, We/Ho,Sod,UBS/☆

957.1 name fem	**957.2** name fem	**3864.1** num card	**4596.2** noun acc pl fem	**2174.22** verb nom sing fem part pres act
(Βηθεσδά,	[b☆ Βηθζαθά,]	πέντε	στοὰς	ἔχουσα.
Bēthesda	*Bēthzatha*	*pente*	*stoas*	*echousa*
Bethesda,	[idem]	five	porches	having.

3.a.**Txt:** 02A,017K,036, 037,038,1,13,byz.Lach
Var: 01ℵ,03B,04C,05D, 019L,33,sa.bo.TregAlf, Tisc,We/Ho,Weis,Sod, UBS/☆

1706.1 prep	**3642.14** dem-pron dat pl fem	**2591.5** verb 3sing indic imperf	**3988.1** noun sing neu	**4044.16** adj sing neu
3. ἐν	ταύταις	κατέκειτο	πλῆθος	(a πολὺ)
en	*tautais*	*katekeito*	*plēthos*	*polu*
In	these	were lying	a multitude	great

3450.1 art gen pl	**764.8** verb gen pl masc part pres act	**5026.7** adj gen pl masc	**5395.5** adj gen pl masc	**3446.1** adj gen pl masc
τῶν	ἀσθενούντων,	τυφλῶν,	χωλῶν,	ξηρῶν,
tōn	*asthenountōn*	*tuphlōn*	*chōlōn*	*xērōn*
of the	being sick,	blind,	lame,	withered,

3.b.**Txt:** 02A-corr, 04C-corr,017K,(032), 036,037,038,1,13,byz. Lach
Var: p66,p75,01ℵ, 02A-org,03B,04C-org, 019L,sa.Treg,Alf,Tisc, We/Ho,Weis,Sod,UBS/☆

1538.6 verb gen pl masc part pres mid	**3450.12** art acc sing fem	**3450.2** art gen sing	**5045.2** noun gen sing neu	**2768.1** noun acc sing fem
(b ἐκδεχομένων	τὴν	τοῦ	ὕδατος	κίνησιν.)
ekdechomenōn	*tēn*	*tou*	*hudatos*	*kinēsin*
awaiting	the	of the	water	moving.

4.a.**Txt:** 02A,04C-corr, 017K,019L,036,037,038, 1,13,byz.Lach
Var: p66,p75,01ℵ,03B, 04C-org,05D,032W, 012G5,33,sa.Treg,Alf Tisc,We/Ho,Weis,Sod, UBS/☆

32.1 noun nom sing masc	**1056.1** conj	**2567.3** prep	**2511.4** noun acc sing masc	**2568.27** verb 3sing indic imperf act
4. (a ἄγγελος	γὰρ	κατὰ	καιρὸν	κατέβαινεν
angelos	*gar*	*kata*	*kairon*	*katebainen*
An angel	for	throughout	time	descended

1706.1 prep	**3450.11** art dat sing fem	**2833.3** noun dat sing fem	**2504.1** conj	**4866.5** verb 3sing indic imperf act	**3450.16** art sing neu
ἐν	τῇ	κολυμβήθρᾳ,	καὶ	ἐτάρασσεν	τὸ
en	*tē*	*kolumbēthra*	*kai*	*etarassen*	*to*
in	the	pool,	and	agitated	the

5:1. "After this" marks an unknown space of time. The phrase is John's way of going to the next sign in unfolding the identity of the Son of God.

We are not told which feast this was. The Sinaiticus manuscript has an article before the word "feast," possibly identifying it as the Passover. John's Gospel definitely mentions three Passovers (2:13; 6:4; 11:55).

Jesus kept the three major annual feasts: the Feast of Passover, Pentecost, and Tabernacles (Exodus 34:22,23). It is nearly certain this feast was one of these three and probably the Passover of A.D. 28.

1. After this there was a feast of the Jews: Some time later came one of the Jewish feast days, *Phillips.*

and Jesus went up to Jerusalem:

5:2. The Gospel of John singles out one of Jesus' miracles in Jerusalem because it confirmed the identity of Christ, and because this sign brought heated controversy from the Jews (verse 16).

The focus of our attention is settled on the scene at "the sheep market (gate), a pool." This place was northeast of the temple area, where sheep were brought before they were sacrificed. The Hebrew or Aramaic name of the place was "Bethesda." This name occurs only here in the New Testament. "Bethesda" means "house of mercy." By associating the Good Shepherd of chapter 10 with this sheepgate, pool, and sheep marketplace, we discover the reason Jesus spoke of the analogy of the Good Shepherd. The shepherd-sheep concept permeated the fabric of Jewish religion and culture.

John relates a bit of physical detail by describing the place as having five porticoes. These were porches built for shelter from the hot sun and inclement weather.

2. Now there is at Jerusalem by the sheep market a pool: . . . by the slaughter housse, *Tyndale* . . . a bath, *Campbell* . . . a public bath, *Fenton* . . . a bathing pool, *Berkeley.*

which is called in the Hebrew tongue Bethesda, having five porches: . . . with five colonnades round it, *TCNT* . . . with five porticoes, *ALBA.*

5:3. The five porches were filled with a "great multitude" of those who were "blind, halt, withered." *Tōn asthenountōn*, literally "the sick," (used 35 times in the New Testament) is a general term meaning "ailing, sick, weak, and diseased." The "blind" (*tuphlōn*) (used 50 times in the New Testament) is the usual term used for those who cannot see. The "halt" (*chōlōn*) (used 15 times in the New Testament) means "cripple, lame." The "withered" (*xērōn*) occurs seven times in the New Testament and describes anything that is dry. It is applied to dry land as found in Hebrews 11:29, and Jesus speaks of a "dry" tree in Luke 23:31. The word refers to people whose muscles had dwindled so that they were paralyzed.

3. In these lay a great multitude of impotent folk, of blind, halt, withered, waiting for the moving of the water: . . . and under these were crowds of sick people, *JB* . . . large number of suffering people, *ALBA* . . . languishinge men, blynde, krokid, drye, *Wycliffe* . . . and the withered, *Murdock* . . . in which a crowd of invalids...shriveled-up patients, *Berkeley* . . . paralyzed, *Fenton* . . . with different diseases. . .some with wasted bodies, *BB* . . . with shrivelled limbs, *Confraternity* . . . the motion, *Wilson* . . . waiting for the water to bubble, *Moffatt.*

5:4. A number of early manuscripts, such as papyri 66 and 75, Aleph, B, C, D, W, and others, omit this verse, but they all have

4. For an angel went down at a certain season into the pool, and troubled the water: . . . for a messenger at times descended, *Campbell* . . . for at intervals, *Berkeley, JB* . . . bathed in the pool, *Concordant* . . . descended into the baptistry, *Murdock* . . . put the water in motion, *Norlie.*

5045.1 noun sing neu	3450.5 art sing masc	3631.1 conj	4272.5 num ord nom sing masc	1671.3 verb nom sing masc part aor act	3196.3 prep
ὕδωρ·	ὁ	οὖν	πρῶτος	ἐμβὰς	μετὰ
hudōr	*ho*	*oun*	*prōtos*	*embas*	*meta*
water.	The	therefore	first	having entered	after

3450.12 art acc sing fem	4867.1 noun acc sing fem	3450.2 art gen sing	5045.2 noun gen sing neu	5040.1 adj nom sing	1090.72 verb 3sing indic imperf
τὴν	ταραχὴν	τοῦ	ὕδατος,	ὑγιὴς	ἐγίνετο,
tēn	*tarachēn*	*tou*	*hudatos*	*hugiēs*	*egineto*
the	agitation	of the	water,	well	became,

3614.3 rel-pron dat sing	1215.1 adv	2692.11 verb 3sing indic imperf pass	3416.1 noun dat sing neu	1498.34 verb sing indic imperf act
ᾧ	δήποτε	κατείχετο	νοσήματι. ⸌	5. Ἦν
hō	*dēpote*	*kateicheto*	*nosēmati*	*En*
which	whatever	he was held by	disease.	Was

1156.2 conj	4948.3 indef-pron nom sing	442.1 noun nom sing masc	1550.1 adv	4985.1 num card
δέ	τις	ἄνθρωπος	ἐκεῖ	⸂ τριάκονταοκτὼ
de	*tis*	*anthrōpos*	*ekei*	*triakontaoktō*
but	a certain	man	there	thirty-eight

5.a.**Txt:** 03B,017K,036,038,041,byz.sa.bo.Treg **Var:** 01ℵ,02A,04C,05D,019L,037,28,33,Gries,Lach,Alf,Word,Tisc,We/Ho,Weis,Sod,UBS/☆

4984.1 num card	2504.1 conj	3501.1 num card	2073.3 noun pl neu	2174.17 verb nom sing masc part pres act
[a☆ τριάκοντα	καὶ	ὀκτὼ]	ἔτη	ἔχων
triakonta	*kai*	*oktō*	*etē*	*echōn*
[thirty	and	eight]	years	being

5.b.**Var:** 01ℵ,03B,04C-org,05D,019L,038,sa.bo.Lach,Treg,AlfTisc,We/Ho,Weis,Sod,UBS/☆

1706.1 prep	3450.11 art dat sing fem	763.3 noun dat sing fem	840.3 prs-pron gen sing	3642.6 dem-pron acc sing masc
ἐν	τῇ	ἀσθενείᾳ.	[b☆+ αὐτοῦ·]	6. τοῦτον
en	*tē*	*astheneia*	*autou*	*touton*
in	the	sickness.	[his.]	This

1481.16 verb nom sing masc part aor act	3450.5 art sing masc	2400.1 name nom masc	2591.2 verb acc sing masc part pres	2504.1 conj
ἰδὼν	ὁ	Ἰησοῦς	κατακείμενον,	καὶ
idōn	*ho*	*Iēsous*	*katakeimenon*	*kai*
seeing		Jesus	lying,	and

1091.26 verb nom sing masc part aor act	3617.1 conj	4044.6 adj acc sing masc	2218.1 adv	5385.4 noun acc sing masc	2174.4 verb 3sing indic pres act
γνοὺς	ὅτι	πολὺν	ἤδη	χρόνον	ἔχει,
gnous	*hoti*	*polun*	*ēdē*	*chronon*	*echei*
knowing	that	a long	already	time	he has been,

2978.5 verb 3sing indic pres act	840.4 prs-pron dat sing	2286.2 verb 2sing indic pres act	5040.1 adj nom sing	1090.63 verb inf aor mid
λέγει	αὐτῷ,	Θέλεις	ὑγιὴς	γενέσθαι;
legei	*autō*	*Theleis*	*hugiēs*	*genesthai*
says	to him,	Desire you	well	to become?

552.6 verb 3sing indic aor pass	840.4 prs-pron dat sing	3450.5 art sing masc	764.6 verb nom sing masc part pres act	2935.5 noun voc sing masc
7. ἀπεκρίθη	αὐτῷ	ὁ	ἀσθενῶν,	Κύριε,
apekrithē	*autō*	*ho*	*asthenōn*	*Kurie*
Answered	him	the	sick,	Sir,

442.4 noun acc sing masc	3620.2 partic	2174.1 verb 1sing pres act	2419.1 conj	3615.1 conj	4866.9 verb 3sing subj aor pass
ἄνθρωπον	οὐκ	ἔχω	ἵνα	ὅταν	ταραχθῇ
anthrōpon	*ouk*	*echō*	*hina*	*hotan*	*tarachthē*
a man	not	I have,	that	when	has been agitated

verse 7 which refers back to it. The people hoped to find healing when they saw the waters stirred up in the pool. Some writers try to find a naturalistic explanation by saying the agitation of the water was caused by an intermittent spring. But the only such spring in the area is Gihon which is some distance away. This was probably filled by rain. God can use any means He chooses. The focus of the incident is upon the miracle wrought by Jesus.

whosoever then first after the troubling of the water stepped in was made whole of whatsoever disease he had: . . . after the agitation, *Campbell* . . . enjoyed healing, *Berkeley* . . . whatever disease had gotten possession of him and was holding him down, *Wuest* . . . no matter what sickness he had, *Norlie.*

5:5. "A certain man was there." He had been paralyzed for "thirty and eight years." He was poor, for he could not hire anyone to help him into the pool. He was friendless, for a friend would have helped him. Perhaps he crawled from place to place, and coming to this pool may very well have been his last effort to be healed. The extreme case was an opportunity for the manifestation of the mercy and authority of the man's Saviour and the nation's Messiah.

5. And a certain man was there, which had an infirmity thirty and eight years: One particular man had been there, *Phillips* . . . who had been an invalid for thirty-eight years, *Weymouth* . . . in feeble health, *Wilson* . . . who had been diseased, *Murdock.*

5:6. Here John focuses our attention on the one miserable man. Of the multitude it was "him" Jesus saw. This particular man was singled out by Jesus in order to display His power over physical life.

Jesus "saw" and "knew" about the man. He had no need for people to tell Him of the man's 38-year condition. His omniscience made Him aware of the man's need. He knows all men (2:24,25).

Jesus' question, "Wilt thou be made whole?" was designed to get the man's attention so that He could cure him. "Be made whole" (*hugiēs genesthai*) literally means to become instantly whole. There was no thought of a progressive cure contained in the words because the term is an aorist infinitive.

6. When Jesus saw him lie: . . . noticing him prostrate, *Fenton* . . . him as he lie there, *ET.*

and knew that he had been now a long time in that case: . . . and knew that he had been there a long time, *Montgomery.*

he saith unto him, Wilt thou be made whole?: Do you want to get well? *TCNT* . . . Do you want to become well, *Berkeley* . . . do you have a longing to become well? *Wuest* . . . Do you want your health restored? *Moffatt.*

5:7. "Sir" (*kurie*) is a respectful title meaning "sir" or "mister." When the Greek word is used of Jesus with a knowledge of who He is, it means "Lord." At this point the man did not know who Jesus was.

"I have no man." He was alone and must have crawled to his place beside the pool. He was helpless and friendless, but Jesus supplied what he did not find in others.

"When the water is troubled" indicates that at times a bubbling of the water occurred. At such times the people believed the water had curative properties or that God pinpointed the time of an underground spring releasing water into the pool as a time for healing provisions brought by an angel. The Old Testament taught that God was His people's healer (Exodus 15:26; Psalms 103:3; 107:20; Isaiah 53:5).

7. The impotent man answered him, Sir, I have no man, when the water is troubled, to put me into the pool: The sick man answered, *SEB* . . . The ailing man, *Young* . . . Yes, my lord, *Murdock* . . . replied the sick man to Him, *Fenton* . . . into the pond, *Douay* . . . when the water bubbles up, *Klingensmith* . . . whenever the water is stirred, *ALBA* . . . he might throw me at once into, *Wuest.*

7.a.**Txt:** Steph
Var: 01ℵ,02A,03B,04C-corr,05D,017K,019L,036,037,038,byz.Gries,LachTreg,Alf,Word,Tisc,We/Ho,Weis,Sod,UBS/☆

3450.16 art sing neu	**5045.1** noun sing neu	**900.5** verb 3sing subj pres act	**900.13** verb 3sing subj aor act	**1466.6** prs-pron acc 1sing	**1519.1** prep
τὸ	ὕδωρ	⸀ βάλλῃ	[a☆ βάλῃ]	με	εἰς
to	*hudōr*	*ballē*	*balē*	*me*	*eis*
the	water	he may put	[idem]	me	into

3450.12 art acc sing fem	**2833.2** noun acc sing fem	**1706.1** prep	**3614.3** rel-pron dat sing	**1156.2** conj	**2048.32** verb 1sing indic pres
τὴν	κολυμβήθραν·	ἐν	ᾧ	δὲ	ἔρχομαι
tēn	*kolumbēthran*	*en*	*hō*	*de*	*erchomai*
the	pool;	in	the	but	coming

1466.1 prs-pron nom 1sing	**241.4** adj nom sing masc	**4112.1** prep	**1466.3** prs-pron gen 1sing	**2568.1** verb 3sing indic pres act
ἐγὼ	ἄλλος	πρὸ	ἐμοῦ	καταβαίνει.
egō	*allos*	*pro*	*emou*	*katabainei*
I	another	before	me	descends.

2978.5 verb 3sing indic pres act	**840.4** prs-pron dat sing	**3450.5** art sing masc	**2400.1** name nom masc	**1446.28** verb 2sing mid
8. Λέγει	αὐτῷ	ὁ	Ἰησοῦς,	⸀ Ἔγειραι,
Legei	*autō*	*ho*	*Iēsous*	*Egeirai*
Says	to him		Jesus,	Arise,

8.a.**Var:** 02A,05D,017K,041,it.Lach

1446.34 verb 2sing impr pres act	**2504.1** conj	**142.13** verb 2sing impr aor act	**3450.6** art acc sing masc	**2868.2** noun acc sing masc
[☆ Ἔγειρε]	[a+ καὶ]	ἆρον	τὸν	⸀ κράββατόν
Egeire	*kai*	*aron*	*ton*	*krabbaton*
[idem]	[and]	take up	the	bed

2868.7 noun acc sing masc	**4622.2** prs-pron gen 2sing	**2504.1** conj	**3906.9** verb 2sing impr pres act	**2504.1** conj
[☆ κράβαττόν]	σου,	καὶ	περιπάτει.	**9.** Καὶ
krabatton	*sou*	*kai*	*peripatei*	*Kai*
[idem]	your,	and	walk.	And

9.a.**Txt:** p66,p75,01ℵ-corr,02A,03B,04C,017K,019L,036,037,038,1,13,etc.byz.Gries,Lach,We/Ho,WeisSod,UBS/☆
Var: 01ℵ-org,05D,032W,Tisc

2091.1 adv	**1090.33** verb 3sing indic aor mid	**5040.1** adj nom sing	**3450.5** art sing masc	**442.1** noun nom sing masc
⸂a εὐθέως ⸃	ἐγένετο	ὑγιὴς	ὁ	ἄνθρωπος,
eutheōs	*egeneto*	*hugiēs*	*ho*	*anthrōpos*
immediately	became	well	the	man,

2504.1 conj	**142.8** verb 3sing indic aor act	**3450.6** art acc sing masc	**2868.2** noun acc sing masc	**2868.7** noun acc sing masc
καὶ	ἦρεν	τὸν	⸀ κράββατον	[☆ κράβαττον]
kai	*ēren*	*ton*	*krabbaton*	*krabatton*
and	took up	the	bed	[idem]

840.3 prs-pron gen sing	**2504.1** conj	**3906.28** verb 3sing indic imperf act	**1498.34** verb sing indic imperf act	**1156.2** conj	**4378.1** noun sing neu
αὐτοῦ,	καὶ	περιεπάτει·	Ἦν	δὲ	σάββατον
autou	*kai*	*periepatei*	*En*	*de*	*sabbaton*
his,	and	walked;	it was	and	sabbath

1706.1 prep	**1552.11** dem-pron dat sing fem	**3450.11** art dat sing fem	**2232.3** noun dat sing fem	**2978.25** verb indic imperf act	**3631.1** conj
ἐν	ἐκείνῃ	τῇ	ἡμέρᾳ.	**10.** Ἔλεγον	οὖν
en	*ekeinē*	*tē*	*hēmera*	*Elegon*	*oun*
on	that	the	day.	Said	therefore

3450.7 art pl masc	**2428.2** name-adj pl masc	**3450.3** art dat sing	**2300.17** verb dat sing masc part perf pass	**4378.1** noun sing neu
οἱ	Ἰουδαῖοι	τῷ	τεθεραπευμένῳ,	Σάββατόν
hoi	*Ioudaioi*	*tō*	*tetherapeumenō*	*Sabbaton*
the	Jews	to the	had been healed,	Sabbath

5:8. By these three imperatives, "Rise, take up . . . , and walk," Jesus exercised His authority as God. The One who created and granted our wonderful human bodies can by His word heal them. We could call these three commands "three thunder bolts of healing power."

but while I am coming, another steppeth down before me: . . . somebody else gets there first, *TEV* . . . another steps in right ahead of me, *Norlie.*

5:9. This sign of Christ's divinity was instantaneous, miraculous, and defiant of normal reasons. Literally the man became "whole." Jesus' question (verse 6) concerned the man's desired condition of wholeness (*hugiēs,* "whole"). The pallet was a thin mat on which he stretched out for reclining. It would normally be rolled up or folded in order to facilitate carrying it. Thirty-eight years of sickness were destroyed by three simple words of the Master. What euphoria must have filled the man's total being!

Jesus' command to carry the pallet and His healing on the Sabbath brought Him powerful hostility from the Jews. Jesus' conception of God's purpose for the Sabbath drastically affected His acceptance as the Jews' Messiah.

8. Jesus saith unto him, Rise, take up thy bed, and walk: Stand up! *ALBA* . . . Get up, take your bed and go, *BB* . . . Rise to your feet, *NEB* . . . pick up your pallet, *Concordant* . . . take up your rug, *Fenton* . . . Pick up your bedroll, *Klingensmith* . . . Snatch up your pallet, *Wuest* . . . go walking away, *Montgomery* . . . and go to walking, *Williams.*

9. And immediately the man was made whole: Instantly the man became well, *Montgomery* . . . There and then the man was cured, *Barclay* . . . At once the man recovered, *Phillips* . . . was at once restored, *Fenton* . . . became strong and well, *ALBA* . . . recovered his strength, *AmpB.*

and took up his bed, and walked: . . . and took his mat, *TCNT* . . . picked up his bed, *ALBA* . . . picked up his mat, *Berkeley* . . . took up his stretcher, *NEB* . . . and began to walk, *Rotherham* . . . and went to walking, *Williams* . . . began walking around, *SEB* . . . and went walking about, *Wuest.*

and on the same day was the sabbath: This happened on a Sabbath day, *Phillips* . . . Now this day happened to be a sabbath, *ALBA* . . . That day was the Sabbath, *Barclay* . . . The day this happened was a Sabbath, *TEV.*

5:10. How strange that the "Jews" had no words of appreciation for the sick man's welfare. What a bizarre silence! They chose to accuse Jesus indirectly through the healed man. The Pharisaical Jews interpreted a great number of Scriptures (Exodus 20:8-11; 23:12; 31:13-17; 35:2,3; Numbers 15:32-36; Nehemiah 13:15-22) with hairsplitting distinctions insomuch that the people were under great legal bondage.

Let us look at the Sabbath as Jesus interprets the spirit of its law. First, Jesus taught the Sabbath was not meant to be a means of slavery but an aid to life. Jesus asserted that "the sabbath was made for man, and not man for the sabbath" (Mark 2:27). His statement gave the reason for the institution of the Sabbath.

Second, Jesus taught that the priests and Levites performed their duties on the Sabbath as an act of ministry. Why should He not heal on the same day?

Third, if the day of a child's birth necessitates circumcision on the Sabbath, on the eighth day, the Law permitted the work to be done (7:22). If therefore the ceremonial law was kept on the Sabbath Day, why not an act of mercy?

Fourth, if a man's sheep fell into a pit on the Sabbath, rather than allow the beast to die, its removal was permitted (Luke 14:5). Furthermore, even the superspiritual hypocrites untied their own oxen and donkeys and led them to the water holes on the Sabbath (Luke 13:15).

Fifth, in Mark 3:4 Jesus asked the Jews if it was lawful to do good or to do evil on the Sabbath. The Lord implied that by re-

10. The Jews therefore said unto him that was cured, It is the sabbath day: The Jewish leaders, *SEB* . . . remarked to the healed man, *Berkeley* . . . Today is the day of rest, *Beck.*

John 5:11

10.a.**Var:** 01ℵ,02A,03B, 04C-org,05D,019L,036, sa.bo.Lach,Treg,Alf,Tisc, We/HoWeis,Sod,UBS/☆

10.b.**Var:** p66,p75,01ℵ, 04C-org,05D,019L, 032W,038,13,Lach

11.a.**Var:** p75,02A,03B, (038),Lach,Treg,We/Ho, Weis,UBS/☆

12.a.**Txt:** p75,02A,04C, 017K,019L,036,037,038, 1,13,byz.Lach,Treg,Sod **Var:** p66,01ℵ,03B,05D, Alf,Tisc,We/Ho,Weis, UBS/☆

12.b.**Txt:** 02A,04C-corr, 05D,017K,036,037,038, byz.it.bo.Lach **Var:** 01ℵ,03B,04C-org, 019L,sa.Tisc,We/Ho, Weis,UBS/☆

13.a.**Var:** 05D,Tisc

1498.4 verb 3sing indic pres act ἐστιν· *estin* it is, **2504.1** conj [a☆+ καὶ] *kai* [and] **3620.2** partic οὐκ *ouk* not **1815.1** verb 3sing indic pres act ἔξεστίν *exestin* it is lawful **4622.3** prs-pron dat 2sing σοι *soi* for you

142.18 verb inf aor act ἆραι *arai* to take up **3450.6** art acc sing masc τὸν *ton* the **2868.2** noun acc sing masc ⸀ κράββατόν. *krabbaton* bed. **2868.7** noun acc sing masc [☆ κράβαττόν] *krabatton* [idem]

4622.2 prs-pron gen 2sing [b+ σου.] *sou* [your.]

11. **3450.5** art sing masc [a☆+ ὁ *ho* [The **1156.2** conj δὲ] *de* and] **552.6** verb 3sing indic aor pass Ἀπεκρίθη *Apekrithē* He answered **840.2** prs-pron dat pl αὐτοῖς, *autois* them,

3450.5 art sing masc Ὁ *Ho* The **4020.37** verb nom sing masc part aor act ποιήσας *poiēsas* having made **1466.6** prs-pron acc 1sing με *me* me **5040.2** adj acc sing masc ὑγιῆ, *hugiē* well, **1552.3** dem-pron nom sing masc ἐκεῖνός *ekeinos* that

1466.4 prs-pron dat 1sing μοι *moi* to me **1500.5** verb 3sing indic aor act εἶπεν, *eipen* said, **142.13** verb 2sing impr aor act Ἆρον *Aron* Take up **3450.6** art acc sing masc τὸν *ton* the **2868.2** noun acc sing masc ⸀ κράββατόν *krabbaton* bed

2868.7 noun acc sing masc [☆ κράβαττόν] *krabatton* [idem] **4622.2** prs-pron gen 2sing σου *sou* your **2504.1** conj καὶ *kai* and **3906.9** verb 2sing impr pres act περιπάτει. *peripatei* walk.

12. **2049.10** verb 3pl indic aor act Ἠρώτησαν *Erōtēsan* They asked

3631.1 conj ⸂a οὖν ⸃ *oun* therefore **840.6** prs-pron acc sing masc αὐτόν, *auton* him, **4949.3** intr-pron nom sing Τίς *Tis* Who **1498.4** verb 3sing indic pres act ἐστιν *estin* is **3450.5** art sing masc ὁ *ho* the

442.1 noun nom sing masc ἄνθρωπος *anthrōpos* man **3450.5** art sing masc ὁ *ho* the **1500.15** verb nom sing masc part aor act εἰπών *eipōn* having said **4622.3** prs-pron dat 2sing σοι, *soi* to you, **142.13** verb 2sing impr aor act Ἆρον *Aron* Take up

3450.6 art acc sing masc ⸂b τὸν *ton* the **2868.2** noun acc sing masc κράββατόν *krabbaton* bed **4622.2** prs-pron gen 2sing σου ⸃ *sou* your **2504.1** conj καὶ *kai* and **3906.9** verb 2sing impr pres act περιπάτει; *peripatei* walk?

13. **3450.5** art sing masc Ὁ *Ho* The

1156.2 conj δὲ *de* but **2367.11** verb nom sing masc part aor pass ⸀ ἰαθεὶς *iatheis* having been healed **764.6** verb nom sing masc part pres act [a ἀσθενῶν] *asthenōn* [healing] **3620.2** partic οὐκ *ouk* not **3471.11** verb 3sing indic plperf act ᾔδει *ēdei* knew

4949.3 intr-pron nom sing τίς *tis* who **1498.4** verb 3sing indic pres act ἐστιν· *estin* it is, **3450.5** art sing masc ὁ *ho* **1056.1** conj γὰρ *gar* for **2400.1** name nom masc Ἰησοῦς *Iēsous* Jesus **1580.1** verb 3sing indic aor act ἐξένευσεν, *exeneusen* had moved away,

fraining from doing good, one is actually doing evil.

Sixth, Jesus taught that the Father works even on the Sabbath Day. God upholds, maintains, and sustains His creatures even on the holy day. If the Father's will was to work through the Son on the Sabbath, Jesus would work (5:17).

Seventh, the Saviour claimed the authority of being the Lord of the Sabbath (Mark 2:28; Luke 6:5). The reference to the healing taking place on the Sabbath is important not only because it has theological significance, but because it was the catalyst which prompted the Jews to kill Jesus (5:16,18). From the time of the healing until the time of Jesus' actual arrest, the Gospel of John is replete with references to the fact that the Jewish leaders were constantly trying to arrest and kill Jesus (e.g., 7:1,25,30,32,44; 8:59; 10:31-33,39; 11:47-54).

In connection with this, note that with the exception of chapter 6, the rest of Jesus' ministry in the Gospel of John takes place in and around Jerusalem, and it is here above all that the authorities wished to kill Jesus. In John, "Judaism, which had decided against Jesus, and its metropolis, in which Jesus was crucified, become the symbol of unbelief and hostility towards the Son of God and the event of Christ's death becomes a conflict of fundamental importance between belief and unbelief or between God and the 'world' (15:18ff.)" (Schnackenburg, *Gospel According to St. John*, 2:90).

The conflict between Jesus and "his own" who would not receive him, which was announced at the outset of the Gospel (1:11), found its culmination in Jerusalem. What was true in the time of Jesus is true in every age; one either receives Jesus as Son of God or else is guilty (like Jerusalem) of participating in His death.

5:11,12. The "same" (*ekeinos*) who had healed him was the One who had told him to pick up his bed and walk. If He could heal, He could also command!

The Jews' question in verse 12 implies a contempt for anyone who would command another to break their Law.

5:13,14. The Jewish leaders knew more of the One who healed the man than the man did. The crowd of people around the pool must have looked on in awe as they watched the drama unfold. But Jesus quietly moved away from the scene.

But Jesus had not finished His saving work in the man. A short time later He found the man in the temple and said to him, "Sin no more" (*mēketi hamartane*). We find these words in Jesus' command to the woman caught in adultery (8:11). The words mean "do not continue to sin." But the Lord does not teach that all disease is because of personal sin. We must compare the Lord's total teach-

it is not lawful for thee to carry thy bed: It is not right for you, *SEB* . . . you have no right to carry, *Berkeley* . . . You are not allowed, *ALBA* . . . the law forbids you to carry, *NIV*. . . to carry the couch, *Campbell* . . . it is against the law, *BB* . . . you must not carry your mat, *TCNT* . . . it is not allowable for you to carry your rug about, *Fenton*.

11. He answered them, He that made me whole: The man who healed me, *Montgomery* . . . He Who makes me sound, *Concordant*.

the same said unto me, Take up thy bed, and walk: But I was told to, *ALBA* . . . told me to take up my bed and walk, *Moffatt* . . . and start walking and keep on walking, *Wuest*.

12. Then asked they him, What man is that which said unto thee, Take up thy bed, and walk?: Who ordered you, *Torrey*.

13. And he that was healed wist not who it was: . . . had no idea who he was, *NIV*.

for Jesus had conveyed himself away: . . . evades him, *Concordant* . . . had slipped away, *Campbell, ALBA, Norlie* . . . turned aside, *Rotherham* . . . withdrawn among, *Berkeley* . . . escaped his notice, *Alford* . . . had withdrawn to avoid a crowd, *Adams*. . . since Jesus had disappeared into the crowd, *JB* . . . had withdrawn Himself, *Fenton* . . . for Jesus moved away, *Clementson*.

John 5:14

3657.2 noun gen sing masc	1498.19 verb gen sing part pres act	1706.1 prep	3450.3 art dat sing	4964.3 noun dat sing masc	3196.3 prep
ὄχλου	ὄντος	ἐν	τῷ	τόπῳ.	**14.** Μετὰ
ochlou	*ontos*	*en*	*tō*	*topō*	*Meta*
a crowd	being	in	the	place.	After

3642.18 dem-pron pl neu	2128.3 verb 3sing indic pres act	840.6 prs-pron acc sing masc	3450.5 art sing masc	2400.1 name nom masc	1706.1 prep
ταῦτα	εὑρίσκει	αὐτὸν	ὁ	Ἰησοῦς	ἐν
tauta	*heuriskei*	*auton*	*ho*	*Iēsous*	*en*
these things	finds	him		Jesus	in

3450.3 art dat sing	2387.2 adj dat sing neu	2504.1 conj	1500.5 verb 3sing indic aor act	840.4 prs-pron dat sing	1481.14 verb 2sing impr aor act
τῷ	ἱερῷ,	καὶ	εἶπεν	αὐτῷ,	Ἴδε
tō	*hierō*	*kai*	*eipen*	*autō*	*Ide*
the	temple,	and	said	to him,	Behold,

5040.1 adj nom sing	1090.2 verb 2sing indic perf act	3239.1 adv	262.3 verb 2sing impr pres act	2419.1 conj	3231.1 partic
ὑγιὴς	γέγονας·	μηκέτι	ἁμάρτανε,	ἵνα	μὴ
hugiēs	*gegonas*	*mēketi*	*hamartane*	*hina*	*mē*
well	you have become:	no more	sin,	that	not

5337.3 adj comp sing neu	4949.9 intr-pron sing neu	4622.3 prs-pron dat 2sing	4622.3 prs-pron dat 2sing	4948.10 indef-pron sing neu
χεῖρόν	‹ τί	σοι	[☆ σοί	τι]
cheiron	*ti*	*soi*	*soi*	*ti*
worse	something	to you	[to you	something]

1090.40 verb 3sing subj aor mid	562.2 verb 3sing indic aor act	3450.5 art sing masc	442.1 noun nom sing masc	2504.1 conj
γένηται.	**15.** Ἀπῆλθεν	ὁ	ἄνθρωπος	καὶ
genētai	*Apēlthen*	*ho*	*anthrōpos*	*kai*
happens.	Went away	the	man	and

15.a.**Txt:** p66,p75,02A, 03B,017K,032W,036, 037,038,1,Gries,Lach, Weis,Sod
Var: 01ℵ,04C,019L,bo. Tisc,We/Ho,UBS/☆

310.4 verb 3sing indic aor act	1500.5 verb 3sing indic aor act	3450.4 art dat pl	2428.4 name-adj dat pl masc	3617.1 conj
‹☆ ἀνήγγειλεν	[a εἶπεν]	τοῖς	Ἰουδαίοις	ὅτι
anēngeilen	*eipen*	*tois*	*Ioudaiois*	*hoti*
told	[idem]	the	Jews	that

2400.1 name nom masc	1498.4 verb 3sing indic pres act	3450.5 art sing masc	4020.37 verb nom sing masc part aor act	840.6 prs-pron acc sing masc
Ἰησοῦς	ἐστιν	ὁ	ποιήσας	αὐτὸν
Iēsous	*estin*	*ho*	*poiēsas*	*auton*
Jesus	it is	the	having made	him

5040.2 adj acc sing masc	2504.1 conj	1217.2 prep	3642.17 dem-pron sing neu	1371.20 verb indic imperf act	3450.6 art acc sing masc
ὑγιῆ.	**16.** Καὶ	διὰ	τοῦτο	ἐδίωκον	‹ τὸν
hugiē	*Kai*	*dia*	*touto*	*ediōkon*	*ton*
well.	And	because of	this	persecuted	

2400.3 name acc masc	3450.7 art pl masc	2428.2 name-adj pl masc	3450.7 art pl masc	2428.2 name-adj pl masc	3450.6 art acc sing masc
Ἰησοῦν	οἱ	Ἰουδαῖοι,	[☆ οἱ	Ἰουδαῖοι	τὸν
Iēsoun	*hoi*	*Ioudaioi*	*hoi*	*Ioudaioi*	*ton*
Jesus	the	Jews,	[the	Jews	

16.a.**Txt:** 02A,017K,036, 037,038,byz.Lach
Var: 01ℵ,03B,04C,05D, 019L,33,Gries,Treg,Alf, Tisc,We/HoWeis,Sod, UBS/☆

2400.3 name acc masc	2504.1 conj	2195.26 verb 3pl indic imperf act	840.6 prs-pron acc sing masc	609.12 verb inf aor act
Ἰησοῦν,]	‹a καὶ	ἐζήτουν	αὐτὸν	ἀποκτεῖναι, ›
Iēsoun	*kai*	*ezētoun*	*auton*	*apokteinai*
Jesus,]	and	sought	him	to kill,

ing on the subject. Notice what Jesus taught His disciples concerning the man who was born blind (9:1-3).

Jesus' words not to sin are surprising, however, because nothing had yet been said about sin on the man's part. Jesus' words, though, indicate that the source of healing for the paralytic is God, the One who also forgives sins. This is what Jesus means when He says, "My Father worketh hitherto, and I work" (5:17). "The will of the Father that the man should be forgiven also obliges the Son (who knows this) to 'work' " (Schnackenburg, *Gospel According to St. John,* 2:97). As the Gospel of John makes so clear, it is through Jesus Christ that God mediates forgiveness (cf. 3:16).

God's healing of the physical body, then, is an indication of what He wishes to do internally to man's soul. On the other hand, Jesus' warning to the man about "something worse" (*cheiron ti*) stands in contrast to the "greater works" of 5:20. Jesus' physical healing of the man thus poses both a greater promise and a greater threat. "His work of healing the man externally and physically is a sign pointing to the greater work of transmitting eternal life, while the threat of an even greater evil points to the judgment that has been handed over by the Father to the Son" (Schnackenburg, *Gospel According to St. John,* 2:98).

5:15. The man attempted to be cooperative with his religious leaders and made known his great benefactor. His motive was unknown, but though he was undoubtedly grateful to Jesus, he perhaps desired to reinforce the truthfulness of his prior statement to the authorities by providing the information they originally sought. He may have hoped to influence the Jews through the great miracle of his healing.

5:16. "And therefore" (KJV) signifies the cause for the Jews' hostility. They did not refer to the miracle, for that would point to evidence which would incriminate them.

The continued action of persecuting is brought out by the imperfect tense verb *ediōkon.* "They kept it up" is the meaning. Their habit of persecuting Jesus was based on His habit of healing poor, suffering, miserable, and tormented people on the Sabbath.

5:17. "My Father worketh hitherto." The last verse indicates a continued harassment of Jesus by the Jewish authorities; therefore Jesus responded by saying that it is because the Father is working

a multitude being in that place: . . . since there was a crowd at the place, *Williams* . . . in the dense crowd, *Phillips* . . . in the great multitude, *Murdock.*

14. Afterward Jesus findeth him in the temple, and said unto him: Jesus found the man in the Temple Courts, *TCNT.*

Behold, thou art made whole: Now that you have been made well, *Norlie, ALBA* . . . See, you are well again, *Adams* . . . Lo! you have become sound, *Concordant* . . . Reflect! you have been made well, *Fenton* . . . you have become well, *Wuest.*

sin no more, lest a worse thing come unto thee: Do not go on sinning, lest a worse thing befall you, *Montgomery* . . . From now on stop sinning, *Barclay* . . . leave your sinful ways, *NEB* . . . quit sinning, *Berkeley* . . . Stop sinning, *SEB* . . . take care not to sin again, lest something worse should happen you, *ALBA* . . . or something worse might happen to you, *Phillips.*

15. The man departed, and told the Jews that it was Jesus, which had made him whole: Then the man went off, *ALBA.*

16. And therefore did the Jews persecute Jesus: And, on this account, *Worrell* . . . that stirred the Jews to persecute, *NEB* . . . therefore began to persecute, *ALBA.*

and sought to slay him: . . . came in pursuit of Jesus, *Norton.*

John 5:17

3617.1 conj	3642.18 dem-pron pl neu	4020.57 verb 3sing indic imperf act	1706.1 prep	4378.3 noun dat sing neu	3450.5 art sing masc
ὅτι	ταῦτα	ἐποίει	ἐν	σαββάτῳ.	**17.** ὁ
hoti	*tauta*	*epoiei*	*en*	*sabbatō*	*ho*
because	these things	he did	on	a sabbath.	

17.a.**Txt:** p66,02A,05D, 017K,019L,036,037,038, 1,13,33,etc.byz.sa.bo. Gries,LachTreg,Sod **Var:** p75,01ℵ,03B, 032W,892,1241,Tisc, We/Ho,Weis,UBS/☆

1156.2 conj	2400.1 name nom masc	552.7 verb 3sing indic aor mid	840.2 prs-pron dat pl	3450.5 art sing masc	3824.1 noun nom sing masc
δὲ	(a Ἰησοῦς)	ἀπεκρίνατο	αὐτοῖς,	Ὁ	πατήρ
de	*Iēsous*	*apekrinato*	*autois*	*Ho*	*patēr*
But	Jesus	answered	them,	The	Father

1466.2 prs-pron gen 1sing	2175.1 conj	732.1 adv	2021.4 verb 3sing indic pres	2476.3 conj	2021.2 verb 1sing indic pres
μου	ἕως	ἄρτι	ἐργάζεται,	κἀγὼ	ἐργάζομαι.
mou	*heōs*	*arti*	*ergazetai*	*kagō*	*ergazomai*
my	until	now	works,	and I	work.

18.a.**Txt:** 02A,03B,04C, 017K,019L,036,037,038, etc.byz.Lach,We/Ho, Weis,Sod,UBS/☆ **Var:** 01ℵ,05D,it.Tisc

1217.2 prep	3642.17 dem-pron sing neu	3631.1 conj	3095.1 adv comp	2195.26 verb 3pl indic imperf act	840.6 prs-pron acc sing masc
18. Διὰ	τοῦτο	(a οὖν)	μᾶλλον	ἐζήτουν	αὐτὸν
Dia	*touto*	*oun*	*mallon*	*ezētoun*	*auton*
Because of	this	therefore	the more	sought	him

3450.7 art pl masc	2428.2 name-adj pl masc	609.12 verb inf aor act	3617.1 conj	3620.3 partic	3303.1 adv
οἱ	Ἰουδαῖοι	ἀποκτεῖναι,	ὅτι	οὐ	μόνον
hoi	*Ioudaioi*	*apokteinai*	*hoti*	*ou*	*monon*
the	Jews	to kill,	because	not	only

3061.16 verb 3sing indic imperf act	3450.16 art sing neu	4378.1 noun sing neu	233.2 conj	2504.1 conj	3824.4 noun acc sing masc
ἔλυεν	τὸ	σάββατον,	ἀλλὰ	καὶ	πατέρα
eluen	*to*	*sabbaton*	*alla*	*kai*	*patera*
did he break	the	sabbath,	but	also	Father

2375.4 adj acc sing	2978.26 verb 3sing indic imperf act	3450.6 art acc sing masc	2296.4 noun acc sing masc	2443.1 adj acc sing masc	1431.6 prs-pron acc 3sing masc
ἴδιον	ἔλεγεν	τὸν	θεόν,	ἴσον	ἑαυτὸν
idion	*elegen*	*ton*	*theon*	*ison*	*heauton*
his own	called		God,	equal	himself

4020.15 verb sing masc part pres act	3450.3 art dat sing	2296.3 noun dat sing masc	552.7 verb 3sing indic aor mid	3631.1 conj
ποιῶν	τῷ	θεῷ.	**19.** Ἀπεκρίνατο	οὖν
poiōn	*tō*	*theō*	*Apekrinato*	*oun*
making		to God.	Answered	therefore

19.a.**Txt:** 02A,05D,017K, 032W,036,037,038,13, byz.Gries,Lach,Treg **Var:** 01ℵ,03B,019L,Tisc, We/HoWeis,Sod,UBS/☆

3450.5 art sing masc	2400.1 name nom masc	2504.1 conj	1500.5 verb 3sing indic aor act	2978.26 verb 3sing indic imperf act	840.2 prs-pron dat pl
ὁ	Ἰησοῦς	καὶ	(εἶπεν	[a☆ ἔλεγεν]	αὐτοῖς,
ho	*Iēsous*	*kai*	*eipen*	*elegen*	*autois*
	Jesus	and	said	[idem]	to them,

279.1 partic	279.1 partic	2978.1 verb 1sing pres act	5050.3 prs-pron dat 2pl	3620.3 partic	1404.4 verb 3sing indic pres	3450.5 art sing masc
Ἀμὴν	ἀμὴν	λέγω	ὑμῖν,	οὐ	δύναται	ὁ
Amēn	*amēn*	*legō*	*humin*	*ou*	*dunatai*	*ho*
Truly	truly	I say	to you,	not	is able	the

5048.1 noun nom sing masc	4020.20 verb inf pres act	570.1 prep gen	1431.4 prs-pron gen 3sing	3625.6 num card neu	1430.1 partic
υἱὸς	ποιεῖν	ἀφ'	ἑαυτοῦ	οὐδὲν,	(ἐὰν
huios	*poiein*	*aph'*	*heautou*	*ouden*	*ean*
Son	to do	from	himself	nothing,	if

that He works. In other words, Jesus cooperates with the Father's work. God worked in creation and continues to work in sustaining His creation. Jesus pointed out to the Jews that He was continuing to work through His words and work.

"And I work" signifies that He and His Father work in conjunction with each other. Jesus does the miracles, yet the Father performs miracles on the Sabbath also. Later, Jesus told the Jews that He did that which He saw the Father do (10:32,37; 8:28,38).

because he had done these things on the sabbath day: . . . because He persisted in doing such things on the sabbath, *Williams* . . . because he did things like this on, *TCNT* . . . habitually acted like this, *Barclay.*

17. But Jesus answered them, My Father worketh hitherto: He replied, *ALBA* . . . My Father worketh even until now, *Alford* . . . has continued working until now, *Montgomery* . . . is working until now, *Fenton.*

and I work: . . . and so I am working, *Beck* . . . and I also work, *ALBA.*

5:18. The Jews' unbelief led them to opposition, hostility, and persecution, and finally they sought to kill Jesus. When their unbelief was allowed to grow, the result was murder.

The Jews understood perfectly what Jesus was saying. Jesus did not assume merely a relationship to the Father equal to that of His followers. He never said, "Our Father" (except when He taught the disciples to pray). He always referred to "My Father" in a unique sense, indicating a relationship which cannot be applied to any other being in the universe.

"Equal" (*ison*) occurs eight times in the New Testament (Matthew 20:12; Mark 14:56; Luke 6:34; John 5:15; Acts 11:17; Philippians 2:6; Revelation 21:16). Jesus claimed to be the Son of God in the sense that no other believer is of God's essence. As the result of this man's healing, the Jews came face-to-face with their God. But they did not bow before Him.

It is amazing how the Saviour and God of their fathers could stand before them in calmness and longsuffering. The majesty of His person and His love in the presence of His antagonists were evidence that He possessed the glory of His Father.

18. Therefore the Jews sought the more to kill him: This made the Jews all the more eager, *TCNT* . . . their desire to kill him was only whetted, *ALBA* . . . the Judeans sought to murder Him, *Fenton.*

because he not only had broken the sabbath: . . . did he not keep the Sabbath, *BB* . . . He not only annulled, *Concordant* . . . He wasn't only abolishing the Sabbath, *Beck.*

but said also that God was his Father: . . . kept on saying, *Williams* . . . was calling God his own Father, *Rotherham* . . . his real Father, *Campbell* . . . in a special sense His Father, *Weymouth* . . . speaking of God as his own Father, *Montgomery* . . . as particularly his Father, *Norton.*

making himself equal with God: . . . had equaled himself, *Campbell* . . . putting himself on an equality, *TCNT* . . . putting himself on the same level with God, *SEB* . . . equal to God, *ALBA.*

5:19. "Verily, verily" indicates an important statement is forthcoming. It is a characteristic quotation of Jesus recorded by John alone.

The Son does not act independently of the Father. What the Jews accused the Son of must apply also to God the Father. Jesus used a well-known analogy in stating that the Son does what the Father does. Many sons are like and act like their fathers. Yet, Jesus claims His relationship with His Father is on a higher level than the natural son-father relationship. He as the Son acts in conjunction with the Father.

"What he seeth the Father do" means Jesus knows perfectly the will of His Father, for that is His will also. The Son has no contrary will of His own. The Father has no contrary will of His own. They are in perfect harmony in their nature, plans, and actions. The implication is clear. When the Jews opposed Jesus the Son, they were opposing God His Father. The Father worked the miracle on

19. Then answered Jesus and said unto them, Verily, verily, I say unto you, The Son can do nothing of himself: . . . the Son can do nothing of his own accord, *Moffatt* . . . nothing on his own account, *ALBA* . . . on his own initiative, *Barclay.*

John 5:20

19.b.**Txt:** p66,p75,02A, 05D,017K,019L,032W, 036,037,038,1,13,etc. byz.Lach,Sod
Var: 01ℵ,03B,Tisc, We/Ho,Weis,UBS/☆

300.1 partic	**3231.1** partic	**4948.10** indef-pron sing neu	**984.8** verb 3sing subj pres act	**3450.6** art acc sing masc	**3824.4** noun acc sing masc
[b☆ ἂν]	μή	τι	βλέπῃ	τὸν	πατέρα
an	*mē*	*ti*	*blepē*	*ton*	*patera*
	not	anything	he may see	the	Father

4020.13 verb part pres act	**3614.17** rel-pron pl neu	**1056.1** conj	**300.1** partic	**1552.3** dem-pron nom sing masc	**4020.8** verb 3sing subj pres act
ποιοῦντα·	ἃ	γὰρ	ἂν	ἐκεῖνος	ποιῇ,
poiounta	*ha*	*gar*	*an*	*ekeinos*	*poiē*
doing:	what	for		that	does,

3642.18 dem-pron pl neu	**2504.1** conj	**3450.5** art sing masc	**5048.1** noun nom sing masc	**3532.1** adv	**4020.5** verb 3sing indic pres act
ταῦτα	καὶ	ὁ	υἱὸς	ὁμοίως	ποιεῖ.
tauta	*kai*	*ho*	*huios*	*homoiōs*	*poiei*
these things	also	the	Son	in like manner	does.

3450.5 art sing masc	**1056.1** conj	**3824.1** noun nom sing masc	**5205.3** verb 3sing indic pres act	**3450.6** art acc sing masc	**5048.4** noun acc sing masc
20. ὁ	γὰρ	πατὴρ	φιλεῖ	τὸν	υἱὸν,
ho	*gar*	*patēr*	*philei*	*ton*	*huion*
The	for	Father	loves	the	Son,

2504.1 conj	**3820.1** adj	**1161.3** verb 3sing indic pres act	**840.4** prs-pron dat sing	**3614.17** rel-pron pl neu	**840.5** prs-pron nom sing masc
καὶ	πάντα	δείκνυσιν	αὐτῷ	ἃ	αὐτὸς
kai	*panta*	*deiknusin*	*autō*	*ha*	*autos*
and	all things	shows	to him	which	himself

4020.5 verb 3sing indic pres act	**2504.1** conj	**3157.1** adj comp acc	**3642.2** dem-pron gen pl	**1161.12** verb 3sing indic fut act	**840.4** prs-pron dat sing
ποιεῖ·	καὶ	μείζονα	τούτων	δείξει	αὐτῷ
poiei	*kai*	*meizona*	*toutōn*	*deixei*	*autō*
he does;	and	greater	than these	he will show	him

20.a.**Var:** 01ℵ,019L,Tisc

2024.4 noun pl neu	**2419.1** conj	**5050.1** prs-pron nom 2pl	**2273.3** verb 2pl subj pres act	**2273.1** verb 2pl pres act
ἔργα,	ἵνα	ὑμεῖς	ʼ θαυμάζητε.	[a θαυμάζετε]
erga	*hina*	*humeis*	*thaumazēte*	*thaumazete*
works,	that	you	may wonder.	[wonder]

5450.1 adv	**1056.1** conj	**3450.5** art sing masc	**3824.1** noun nom sing masc	**1446.1** verb 3sing indic pres act	**3450.8** art acc pl masc
21. ὥσπερ	γὰρ	ὁ	πατὴρ	ἐγείρει	τοὺς
hōsper	*gar*	*ho*	*patēr*	*egeirei*	*tous*
Even as	for	the	Father	raises up	the

3361.7 adj acc pl masc	**2504.1** conj	**2210.1** verb 3sing indic pres act	**3643.1** adv	**2504.1** conj	**3450.5** art sing masc	**5048.1** noun nom sing masc
νεκροὺς	καὶ	ζῳοποιεῖ,	οὕτως	καὶ	ὁ	υἱὸς
nekrous	*kai*	*zōopoiei*	*houtōs*	*kai*	*ho*	*huios*
dead	and	makes alive,	thus	also	the	Son

3614.8 rel-pron acc pl masc	**2286.3** verb 3sing indic pres act	**2210.1** verb 3sing indic pres act	**3624.1** adv	**1056.1** conj	**3450.5** art sing masc
οὓς	θέλει	ζῳοποιεῖ.	**22.** οὐδὲ	γὰρ	ὁ
hous	*thelei*	*zōopoiei*	*oude*	*gar*	*ho*
whom	he will	makes alive;	neither	for	the

3824.1 noun nom sing masc	**2892.5** verb 3sing indic pres act	**3625.3** num card acc masc	**233.2** conj	**3450.12** art acc sing fem	**2893.4** noun acc sing fem
πατὴρ	κρίνει	οὐδένα,	ἀλλὰ	τὴν	κρίσιν
patēr	*krinei*	*oudena*	*alla*	*tēn*	*krisin*
Father	judges	no one,	but	the	judgment

the Sabbath. The Jews therefore were warring against the God of the Law they claimed to be defending.

but what he seeth the Father do: . . . unless He sees the Father doing it, *Fenton* . . . he does only what, *TCNT* . . . is always modeled on, *Phillips.*

for what things soever he doeth, these also doeth the Son likewise: . . . whatever the Father does the Son does it in the same way, *BB* . . . also persists in doing, *Williams* . . . the Son similarly does, *Berkeley* . . . in like manner is doing, *Wuest.*

5:20. "For" (*gar*) can be translated "because" which binds together the affection of the Father to the Son and the Son to the Father. *Love* (*philei*) is the word for natural family feelings. We might have expected Jesus to use the word *agape.* In 3:35 Jesus used the term *agapē* love, indicating the strongest love in the unity of purpose of the Father and Son in bringing salvation to mankind. Here Jesus is stressing the close bond He and the Father have for each other. Therefore He used the word for love which expresses this kinship affection, the word *phileō.*

"And showeth him all things that himself doeth" pinpoints the reason for Jesus' healing the sick on the Sabbath. Jesus' work corresponds to the Father's work because the Father shows the Son. This statement corresponds to verse 19 where Jesus claims that the Son does what He sees the Father doing. What a beautiful way to express the absolute harmony between the Son and the Father.

"And he will show him greater works than these, that ye may marvel." The next verse reveals the greater works which the Son will do; namely, Jesus will raise the dead. The Jews may marvel, but marveling is not believing, trusting, and committing, that which God seeks from the sinner.

What Jesus has done before this time reveals the unique relationship He has with the Father. This kind of relationship means that the two share each other's plans and activities.

20. For the Father loveth the Son, and sheweth him all things that himself doeth: . . . and is constantly showing Him, *Wuest* . . . shows Him everything He is doing, *Beck* . . . and shows him all his works, *ALBA.*

and he will shew him greater works than these: . . . will he show him, *Sawyer.*

that ye may marvel: . . . may be marveling, *Concordant* . . . that you may be amazed, *Torrey* . . . to make you wonder, *Norlie, ALBA* . . . to your astonishment, *Norton* . . . to fill you with wonder, *Barclay* . . . so that you will keep on wondering, *Williams.*

5:21. Jesus explained the greater works than the healing of the sick man. "For as the" parallels the Father and Son's work. The gift of life is from the Father, yet Jesus gave life to the impotent man because the Father showed Him to do so. "For as" the Father gives life, so does the Son. The general statement of "raiseth up the dead, and quickeneth them" applies both to the spiritual birth and the final resurrection. Through the following verses Jesus spoke of three prerogatives which reveal His true identity. The first is life (21,24), the second is judgment (24,27), and the third is the final resurrection (28,29). Life is the prerogative of deity.

21. For as the Father raiseth up the dead, and quickeneth them: . . . wakes up the dead, *Rotherham* . . . makes them alive, *HBIE* . . . and makes them live, *ALBA* . . . and vivifieth them, *Murdock* . . . Even as the Father awakens the dead, *Norlie.*

even so the Son quickeneth whom he will: . . . the Son also giveth life, *ASV* . . . whom he chooses, *Moffatt.*

5:22. This verse states the second prerogative of deity, namely, judgment. The prerogative of "judgment" (*tēn krisin*) has been given to the Son inasmuch as the Son brought to the world the revelation of the Father. Jesus' work was to bring life to men and judgment to those who reject life. The apostle Paul asserts the same fact of judgment in Romans 14:9-12 (see also Philippians 2:10,11).

22. For the Father judgeth no man: For the Father decides nothing, *Fenton* . . . does not pass judgment on anyone, *Barclay.*

3820.12 adj acc sing fem	1319.33 verb 3sing indic perf act	3450.3 art dat sing	5048.3 noun dat sing masc		2419.1 conj	3820.7 adj pl masc
πᾶσαν	δέδωκεν	τῷ	υἱῷ,	23.	ἵνα	πάντες
pasan	*dedōken*	*tō*	*huiō*		*hina*	*pantes*
all	has given	to the	Son,		that	all

4939.1 verb 3pl pres act	3450.6 art acc sing masc	5048.4 noun acc sing masc	2503.1 conj	4939.1 verb 3pl pres act	3450.6 art acc sing masc
τιμῶσιν	τὸν	υἱὸν	καθὼς	τιμῶσιν	τὸν
timōsin	*ton*	*huion*	*kathōs*	*timōsin*	*ton*
may honor	the	Son	even as	they honor	the

3824.4 noun acc sing masc	3450.5 art sing masc	3231.1 partic	4939.6 verb nom sing masc part pres act	3450.6 art acc sing masc	5048.4 noun acc sing masc
πατέρα.	ὁ	μὴ	τιμῶν	τὸν	υἱὸν
patera	*ho*	*mē*	*timōn*	*ton*	*huion*
Father.	The	not	honoring	the	Son

3620.3 partic	4939.3 verb 3sing indic pres act	3450.6 art acc sing masc	3824.4 noun acc sing masc	3450.6 art acc sing masc	3854.14 verb acc sing masc part aor act
οὐ	τιμᾷ	τὸν	πατέρα	τὸν	πέμψαντα
ou	*tima*	*ton*	*patera*	*ton*	*pempsanta*
not	honors	the	Father	the	having sent

840.6 prs-pron acc sing masc		279.1 partic	279.1 partic	2978.1 verb 1sing pres act	5050.3 prs-pron dat 2pl	3617.1 conj
αὐτόν.	24.	Ἀμὴν	ἀμὴν	λέγω	ὑμῖν,	ὅτι
auton		*Amēn*	*amēn*	*legō*	*humin*	*hoti*
him.		Truly	truly	I say	to you,	that

3450.5 art sing masc	3450.6 art acc sing masc	3030.4 noun acc sing masc	1466.2 prs-pron gen 1sing	189.11 verb nom sing masc part pres act	2504.1 conj
ὁ	τὸν	λόγον	μου	ἀκούων,	καὶ
ho	*ton*	*logon*	*mou*	*akouōn*	*kai*
the	the	word	my	hearing,	and

3961.10 verb nom sing masc part pres act	3450.3 art dat sing	3854.13 verb dat sing masc part aor act	1466.6 prs-pron acc 1sing	2174.4 verb 3sing indic pres act
πιστεύων	τῷ	πέμψαντί	με,	ἔχει
pisteuōn	*tō*	*pempsanti*	*me*	*echei*
believing	the	having sent	me,	has

2205.4 noun acc sing fem	164.1 adj sing	2504.1 conj	1519.1 prep	2893.4 noun acc sing fem	3620.2 partic	2048.34 verb 3sing indic pres
ζωὴν	αἰώνιον,	καὶ	εἰς	κρίσιν	οὐκ	ἔρχεται,
zōēn	*aiōnion*	*kai*	*eis*	*krisin*	*ouk*	*erchetai*
life	eternal,	and	into	judgment	not	comes,

233.2 conj	3197.6 verb 3sing indic perf act	1523.2 prep gen	3450.2 art gen sing	2265.2 noun gen sing masc	1519.1 prep
ἀλλὰ	μεταβέβηκεν	ἐκ	τοῦ	θανάτου	εἰς
alla	*metabebēken*	*ek*	*tou*	*thanatou*	*eis*
but	has passed	out of	the	death	into

3450.12 art acc sing fem	2205.4 noun acc sing fem		279.1 partic	279.1 partic	2978.1 verb 1sing pres act	5050.3 prs-pron dat 2pl
τὴν	ζωήν.	25.	Ἀμὴν	ἀμὴν	λέγω	ὑμῖν,
tēn	*zōēn*		*Amēn*	*amēn*	*legō*	*humin*
the	life.		Truly	truly	I say	to you,

3617.1 conj	2048.34 verb 3sing indic pres	5443.2 noun nom sing fem	2504.1 conj	3431.1 adv	1498.4 verb 3sing indic pres act	3616.1 conj
ὅτι	ἔρχεται	ὥρα	καὶ	νῦν	ἐστιν,	ὅτε
hoti	*erchetai*	*hōra*	*kai*	*nun*	*estin*	*hote*
that	is coming	an hour	and	now	is,	when

Those who reject Christ reject life, and judgment is an inevitable consequence of one's rejection of Christ.

but hath committed all judgment unto the Son: He has entrusted, *Knox* . . . committed the power of judging entirely, *Campbell* . . . given all decisions, *BB* . . . has deputed every decision to, *Fenton* . . . entirely into the Son's hands, *Phillips* . . . the right to judge everything, *SEB.*

5:23. Since these three prerogatives of deity are in the possession of the Son of God, they require for Him the honor due God. Throughout this Gospel the Holy Spirit stresses the equality of Jesus Christ with the Father as to (1) person, (2) works, and (3) honor which are due both.

On a human level if an ambassador of a king is dishonored, the king is dishonored also. But, Jesus is equal with the Father; an ambassador is not equal with a king. Our Lord's authority to give life proves His almighty power as deity. His authority to judge establishes His divine attribute of omniscience. The possession of omnipotence and omniscience attest to His deity.

23. That all men should honour the Son:

even as they honour the Father:

He that honoureth not the Son honoureth not the Father which hath sent him: . . . who withholds honour, *Weymouth* . . . Whoever refuses honour, *ALBA.*

5:24. The word of Jesus ("my word") equals the manifestation of the Father which imparts life to those who believe. Notice "hath" (*echei*) is a present reality. In fact, one of the main themes of the Gospel of John is what is called "realized eschatology." Numerous times it is made clear that salvation, which the Jews believed would not be available until the end times, is present even now. In His incarnation and earthly ministry Jesus made both salvation and judgment a present reality (3:18; 12:31-33).

The present possession with the future combine together in the present tense verb. The believer does not come into eternal life at death, but continues his eternal life through death into eternity. To hear and believe brings "everlasting (eternal) life." This is the only means of averting "judgment." Eternal life is contrasted with "condemned already" (3:18). The spiritual conversion of a person guarantees his not coming into judgment.

24. Verily, verily, I say unto you, He that heareth my word, and believeth on him that sent me: Truly—or doubly, *Berkeley* . . . a most solemn truth, *Norlie* . . . my doctrine, *Campbell* . . . has faith in him who sent me, *BB.*

hath everlasting life: . . . has eternal life, *RSV* . . . possesses eternal life, *Fenton.*

and shall not come into condemnation: . . . and does not come under judgment, *Weymouth* . . . he will incur no sentence of judgment, *Moffatt* . . . does not have to face judgment, *Phillips* . . . under no sentence, *Berkeley.*

but is passed from death unto life: . . . for he has already come, *Norlie* . . . out of death, *Fenton* . . . but has already passed from death, *ALBA.*

5:25,26. Another momentous statement is indicated by "Verily, verily." "The hour is coming, and now is" identifies this hearing of the voice of the Son of God as a present reality. The same "and now is" was stated in chapter 4 concerning worship (4:23). Apparently, verse 25 refers to a present spiritual raising of those who are dead in sin (Ephesians 2:1,5; 5:14).

The dead are those who are under judgment in the world. Jesus claims full authority as "the Son of God" whose voice (revelation of the Father) awakens the dead conscience of the lost. Jesus mingles the spiritual resurrection with the physical resurrection figures because the two are inseparably intertwined.

25. Verily, verily, I say unto you, The hour is coming, and now is, when the dead shall hear the voice of the Son of God: Indeed, *ALBA* . . . the dead shall hearken unto, *Rotherham* . . . will listen to, *Moffatt.*

John 5:26

25.a.**Txt:** 02A,05D,017K, 036,037,038,byz.Gries, Lach
Var: p75,03B,Treg,Tisc, We/HoWeis,UBS/☆

3450.7 art pl masc	**3361.5** adj nom pl masc	**189.54** verb 3pl indic fut mid	**189.44** verb 3pl indic fut act
οἱ	νεκροὶ	' ἀκούσονται	[a☆ ἀκούσουσιν]
hoi	*nekroi*	*akousontai*	*akousousin*
the	dead	shall hear	[idem]

3450.10 art gen sing fem	**5292.2** noun gen sing fem	**3450.2** art gen sing	**5048.2** noun gen sing masc	**3450.2** art gen sing	**2296.2** noun gen sing masc
τῆς	φωνῆς	τοῦ	υἱοῦ	τοῦ	θεοῦ,
tēs	*phōnēs*	*tou*	*huiou*	*tou*	*theou*
the	voice	of the	Son		of God,

25.b.**Txt:** 02A,017K,036, 037,038,byz.
Var: 01ℵ,03B,05D,019L, 33,Lach,Treg,Alf,Tisc, We/Ho,WeisSod,UBS/☆

2504.1 conj	**3450.7** art pl masc	**189.32** verb nom pl masc part aor act	**2180.32** verb 3pl indic fut mid	**2180.35** verb 3pl indic fut act
καὶ	οἱ	ἀκούσαντες	' ζήσονται.	[b☆ ζήσουσιν.]
kai	*hoi*	*akousantes*	*zēsontai*	*zēsousin*
and	the	having heard	shall live.	[idem]

	5450.1 adv	**1056.1** conj	**3450.5** art sing masc	**3824.1** noun nom sing masc	**2174.4** verb 3sing indic pres act	**2205.4** noun acc sing fem
26.	ὥσπερ	γὰρ	ὁ	πατὴρ	ἔχει	ζωὴν
	hōsper	*gar*	*ho*	*patēr*	*echei*	*zōēn*
	Even as	for	the	Father	has	life

1706.1 prep	**1431.5** prs-pron dat 3sing masc	**3643.1** adv	**1319.14** verb 3sing indic aor act	**2504.1** conj	**3450.3** art dat sing	**5048.3** noun dat sing masc
ἐν	ἑαυτῷ,	οὕτως	' ἔδωκεν	καὶ	τῷ	υἱῷ
en	*heautō*	*houtōs*	*edōken*	*kai*	*tō*	*huiō*
in	himself,	so	he gave	also	to the	Son

2504.1 conj	**3450.3** art dat sing	**5048.3** noun dat sing masc	**1319.14** verb 3sing indic aor act	**2205.4** noun acc sing fem	**2174.29** verb inf pres act
[☆ καὶ	τῷ	υἱῷ	ἔδωκεν]	ζωὴν	ἔχειν
kai	*tō*	*huiō*	*edōken*	*zōēn*	*echein*
[also	to the	Son	he gave]	life	to have

1706.1 prep	**1431.5** prs-pron dat 3sing masc		**2504.1** conj	**1833.4** noun acc sing fem	**1319.14** verb 3sing indic aor act	**840.4** prs-pron dat sing
ἐν	ἑαυτῷ.	**27.**	καὶ	ἐξουσίαν	ἔδωκεν	αὐτῷ
en	*heautō*		*kai*	*exousian*	*edōken*	*autō*
in	himself,		and	authority	gave	to him

27.a.**Txt:** 05D,017K,036, 037,038,1,13,byz.
Var: 01ℵ-corr,02A,03B, 019L,33,bo.Lach,Treg, AlfTisc,We/Ho,Weis,Sod, UBS/☆

2504.1 conj	**2893.4** noun acc sing fem	**4020.20** verb inf pres act	**3617.1** conj	**5048.1** noun nom sing masc	**442.2** noun gen sing masc
'a καὶ '	κρίσιν	ποιεῖν,	ὅτι	υἱὸς	ἀνθρώπου
kai	*krisin*	*poiein*	*hoti*	*huios*	*anthrōpou*
also	judgment	to execute,	because	Son	of man

1498.4 verb 3sing indic pres act		**3231.1** partic	**2273.1** verb 2pl pres act	**3642.17** dem-pron sing neu	**3617.1** conj	**2048.34** verb 3sing indic pres
ἐστίν.	**28.**	μὴ	θαυμάζετε	τοῦτο·	ὅτι	ἔρχεται
estin		*mē*	*thaumazete*	*touto*	*hoti*	*erchetai*
he is.		Not	marvel at	this,	for	is coming

5443.2 noun nom sing fem	**1706.1** prep	**3614.11** rel-pron dat sing fem	**3820.7** adj pl masc	**3450.7** art pl masc	**1706.1** prep	**3450.4** art dat pl
ὥρα	ἐν	ᾗ	πάντες	οἱ	ἐν	τοῖς
hōra	*en*	*hē*	*pantes*	*hoi*	*en*	*tois*
an hour	in	which	all	the	in	the

28.a.**Txt:** 02A,05D,017K, 036,037,1,13,byz.Gries, Lach
Var: p75,03B,Treg,Tisc, We/HoWeis,UBS/☆

3283.6 noun dat pl neu	**189.54** verb 3pl indic fut mid	**189.44** verb 3pl indic fut act	**3450.10** art gen sing fem
μνημείοις	' ἀκούσονται	[a☆ ἀκούσουσιν]	τῆς
mnēmeiois	*akousontai*	*akousousin*	*tēs*
graves	shall hear	[idem]	the

"Hath he given to the Son." This affirmation concerns not the Son as deity, but the office that the Son was commissioned to execute. "Gave" (*edōken*; KJV, "hath given") is an aorist tense verb stating a historical fact.

and they that hear shall live: . . . and all who hear it will live, *ALBA.*

26. For as the Father hath life in himself: . . . who is the source of life, *JB* . . . the fountain of life, *Norton.*

so hath he given to the Son to have life in himself: In the same way, *SEB* . . . he granted to the Son, *Montgomery* . . . the possession of life within Himself, *Fenton* . . . by the Father's gift, *ALBA* . . . has made the Son the source of life, *JB.*

5:27. Not only life and the power of life were granted the Son due to His mission, but the right of judgment was given also ("gave" in the Greek, *edōken*, a historical aorist verb). "To execute judgment" means to render the sentence of judgment in a formal way. Literally, "to execute judgment" (*krisin poiein*) is to render judgment, that is, the act of judging.

The Son of God speaks (verse 25) and the Son of Man executes judgment. The Son of God refers to His relationship with God which qualifies Him to bring God to man. As the Son of Man He is qualified to represent man to God. The action called for on man's part is to believe the revelation of God in the Son of God, so that the Son of Man may present the believer faultless before God.

Verses 19-25 speak of Jesus' power to give life and to judge in terms of realized eschatology; namely, He both gives life and pronounces judgment now, in the present. Verses 26-30, however, restate both of these themes in terms of final eschatology; namely, that Jesus will dispense the gift of eternal life, and also damnation, at the final judgment.

Verse 25, for instance, speaks of the hour which "now is" when the spiritually dead can receive life; verse 28 speaks of the hour which "is coming" when the physically dead will hear Jesus' voice pronouncing eternal life or judgment.

One key to this interpretation is found in verse 27 where Jesus speaks of himself as the Son of Man. The Son of Man, according to Daniel 7:13, is the One who will dispense the final judgment at the end of the world. Jesus explicitly draws on Daniel 7:13 in Mark 14:62, Matthew 26:64, and Luke 22:69.

27. And hath given him authority to execute judgment also: . . . to act as Judge, *Berkeley* . . . invested Him with authority, *Fenton* . . . appointed him supreme judge, *JB* . . . He granted Him authority to pass judgment, *Adams* . . . the right to execute judgement, *ALBA* . . . to pronounce judgment, *Montgomery.*

because he is the Son of man: . . . because he is man, *TCNT* . . . seeing that He is a son of mankind, *Concordant.*

5:28. In verse 25 the present spiritual resurrection of those who believe is indicated. In this verse the time for physical resurrection is yet future.

"In the which all that are in the graves shall hear his voice" specifies this future resurrection of the body. Jesus, the Son of God, has power to raise the bodies of the dead (see 11:25). The Pharisees believed the greatest act of the power of God was to take place at the physical resurrection. Our Lord thereby claims this outstanding evidence as proof of His deity.

The Lord said, "All that . . ." (*pantes hoi*) without exception. These words refer to all the dead. One is struck with the enormous claims of Jesus. His titles, assertions, and demands are given with

28. Marvel not at this: This should not surprise you, *Beck* . . . Stop being surprised at this, *Williams* . . . Stop marvelling at this, *Wuest* . . . You should not wonder at this, *ALBA* . . . Don't be amazed at this, *Norlie.*

for the hour is coming, in the which all that are in the graves shall hear his voice: . . . because the time comes, *Fenton* . . . there comes an hour in which all who are in the tombs, *Wuest* . . . when all who are buried in the tombs, *Barclay* . . . will hear Him calling, *Beck* . . . will listen, *Williams.*

5292.2 noun gen sing fem	840.3 prs-pron gen sing	2504.1 conj	1594.15 verb 3pl indic fut mid	3450.7 art pl masc	3450.17 art pl neu
φωνῆς	αὐτοῦ,	29. καὶ	ἐκπορεύσονται,	οἱ	τὰ
phōnēs	*autou*	*kai*	*ekporeusontai*	*hoi*	*ta*
voice	his,	and	shall come forth,	the	the

18.14 adj pl neu	4020.39 verb nom pl masc part aor act	1519.1 prep	384.4 noun acc sing fem	2205.2 noun gen sing fem	3450.7 art pl masc
ἀγαθὰ	ποιήσαντες	εἰς	ἀνάστασιν	ζωῆς,	οἱ
agatha	*poiēsantes*	*eis*	*anastasin*	*zōēs*	*hoi*
good	having practiced	to	a resurrection	of life,	the

29.a.**Txt:** p75,01ℵ,02A, 05D,017K,019L,036, 037,038,1,13,byz.Lach, Sod
Var: p66-corr,03B,Alf, Tisc,We/Ho,Weis,UBS/⋆

1156.2 conj	3450.17 art pl neu	5175.2 adj acc pl neu	4097.20 verb nom pl masc part aor act	1519.1 prep	384.4 noun acc sing fem
⸂a δὲ ⸃	τὰ	φαῦλα	πράξαντες	εἰς	ἀνάστασιν
de	*ta*	*phaula*	*praxantes*	*eis*	*anastasin*
and	the	evil	having done	to	a resurrection

2893.2 noun gen sing fem	3620.3 partic	1404.1 verb 1sing indic pres	1466.1 prs-pron nom 1sing	4020.20 verb inf pres act	570.2 prep gen
κρίσεως.	30. Οὐ	δύναμαι	ἐγὼ	ποιεῖν	ἀπ'
kriseōs	*Ou*	*dunamai*	*egō*	*poiein*	*ap'*
of judgment.	Not	am able	I	to do	from

1670.1 prs-pron gen 1sing masc	3625.6 num card neu	2503.1 conj	189.1 verb 1sing pres act	2892.1 verb 1sing act	2504.1 conj
ἐμαυτοῦ	οὐδέν·	καθὼς	ἀκούω	κρίνω,	καὶ
emautou	*ouden*	*kathōs*	*akouō*	*krinō*	*kai*
myself	nothing;	even as	I hear	I judge,	and

3450.9 art nom sing fem	2893.1 noun nom sing fem	3450.9 art nom sing fem	1684.6 adj nom 1sing fem	1337.10 adj nom sing fem	1498.4 verb 3sing indic pres act
ἡ	κρίσις	ἡ	ἐμὴ	δικαία	ἐστίν·
hē	*krisis*	*hē*	*emē*	*dikaia*	*estin*
the	judgment	the	my	just	is,

3617.1 conj	3620.3 partic	2195.3 verb 1sing indic pres act	3450.16 art sing neu	2284.1 noun sing neu	3450.16 art sing neu	1684.1 adj 1sing
ὅτι	οὐ	ζητῶ	τὸ	θέλημα	τὸ	ἐμὸν,
hoti	*ou*	*zētō*	*to*	*thelēma*	*to*	*emon*
because	not	I seek	the	will	the	my,

233.2 conj	3450.16 art sing neu	2284.1 noun sing neu	3450.2 art gen sing	3854.12 verb gen sing masc part aor act	1466.6 prs-pron acc 1sing
ἀλλὰ	τὸ	θέλημα	τοῦ	πέμψαντός	με
alla	*to*	*thelēma*	*tou*	*pempsantos*	*me*
but	the	will	of the	who sent	me

30.a.**Txt:** 07E,021M, 030U,036,038,13,byz.it.
Var: 01ℵ,02A,03B,05D, 017K,019L,037,Gries, LachTreg,Alf,Word,Tisc, We/Ho,Weis,Sod,UBS/⋆

3824.2 noun gen sing masc	1430.1 partic	1466.1 prs-pron nom 1sing	3113.1 verb 1sing pres act	3875.1 prep
⸂a πατρός. ⸃	31. Ἐὰν	ἐγὼ	μαρτυρῶ	περὶ
patros	*Ean*	*egō*	*marturō*	*peri*
Father.	If	I	bear witness	concerning

1670.1 prs-pron gen 1sing masc	3450.9 art nom sing fem	3114.1 noun nom sing fem	1466.2 prs-pron gen 1sing	3620.2 partic	1498.4 verb 3sing indic pres act
ἐμαυτοῦ,	ἡ	μαρτυρία	μου	οὐκ	ἔστιν
emautou	*hē*	*marturia*	*mou*	*ouk*	*estin*
myself,	the	witness	my	not	is

225.2 adj nom sing	241.4 adj nom sing masc	1498.4 verb 3sing indic pres act	3450.5 art sing masc	3113.7 verb nom sing masc part pres act
ἀληθής.	32. ἄλλος	ἐστὶν	ὁ	μαρτυρῶν
alēthēs	*allos*	*estin*	*ho*	*marturōn*
true.	Another	it is	the	bearing witness

clarity, conviction, and authority. All that He said was supported by His powerful deeds and absolute authority.

29. And shall come forth: . . . and out they will come, *Phillips.*

they that have done good, unto the resurrection of life: . . . shall arise to enjoy life, *Campbell.*

and they that have done evil, unto the resurrection of damnation: But they who the corrupt things have practised, *Rotherham* . . . practiced evil, *Berkeley* . . . to the resurrection of judgment, *ASV* . . . will rise again to be judged, *Norlie* . . . of condemnation, *Murdock.*

5:29. Those who do good things are contrasted with those who commit evil deeds. The Lord Jesus discloses only two destinies for the human race: the resurrection to life or the resurrection to judgment (a thousand years later). These are indeed solemn declarations: for the believer, life; for the unbeliever, death.

The final judgment and its consequences are so important that almost every writer of the New Testament writes of it. Matthew, Mark, and Luke all incorporate the words of Jesus relating to the final judgment (cf. among many other passages, Matthew 25:31-46; Mark 16:16; Luke 21:25-36). The apostle Paul also writes extensively about the final judgment (cf. Romans 2:6-9; 1 Thessalonians 4:13-18). The apostle Peter likewise writes of Christ's return and judgment (2 Peter 3).

John, in addition to the statements found in his Gospel, wrote an entire book, the Revelation, devoted to describing Christ's second coming and the destiny of eternal life or judgment that awaits all humanity. Those who believe in Jesus as Saviour have the blessed assurance that He is even now preparing a place for His followers, who will one day dwell with Him in those prepared mansions (14:1-3).

30. I can of mine own self do nothing: as I hear, I judge: and my judgment is just: I can never act on my own, *ALBA* . . . I judge as I am informed and My judgment is fair, *Berkeley* . . . a single thing, *Rotherham.*

because I seek not mine own will: . . . for I am not trying to do my own will, *Williams* . . . because my aim is not to do, *TCNT* . . . not seek My own purpose, *Fenton* . . . I do not live to please myself, *Phillips.*

but the will of the Father which hath sent me:

5:30. The Son does not act independently of the Father. What the Father does, the Son does; what the Son does, the Father does also. The same is true of the Holy Spirit. The Godhead works in cooperation and harmony. What the Son did in healing on the Sabbath was done by the Father.

31. If I bear witness of myself: If I alone testify about Myself, *Beck.*

my witness is not true: My testimony is not valid, *Norlie* . . . my evidence cannot be accepted, *Weymouth* . . . My testimony is not reliable, *Berkeley* . . . would not be valid, *Murdock* . . . is not to be regarded, *Campbell* . . . is not trustworthy, *TCNT* . . . isn't dependable, *Beck.*

5:31-33. If He were a private person with no authority to back His claims, He would not demand that His testimony be believed. He does not stand on individual testimony alone, but He has a number of witnesses. Jesus' mission originated with God (verses 19,30). It was sustained and maintained by the Father (verse 26). It was guided by the will of God (verse 30).

"There is another." The other is evidently the Father, though Jesus does not here name Him as the other. According to verse 34 the witness of the other is not man; therefore He is God the Father.

"Beareth witness of me" refers to the Father. This is the first of the seven witnesses to Jesus as the Christ.

32. There is another that beareth witness of me: . . . to bear testimony to me, *Moffatt.*

(1) The Father's witness to the Son (verses 32,37). Compare the three times the Father's voice was heard from heaven. First, at the Saviour's baptism in water (Matthew 3:17; Mark 1:11; Luke 3:22;

John 5:33

32.a.**Var:** 01א-org,05D, Tisc

3875.1 prep	1466.3 prs-pron gen 1sing	2504.1 conj	3471.2 verb 1sing indic perf act	3471.6 verb 2pl indic perf act	3617.1 conj
περὶ	ἐμοῦ,	καὶ	‛ οἶδα	[ᵃ οἴδατε]	ὅτι
peri	*emou*	*kai*	*oida*	*oidate*	*hoti*
concerning	me,	and	I know	[you know]	that

225.2 adj nom sing	1498.4 verb 3sing indic pres act	3450.9 art nom sing fem	3114.1 noun nom sing fem	3614.12 rel-pron acc sing fem
ἀληθής	ἐστιν	ἡ	μαρτυρία	ἣν
alēthēs	*estin*	*hē*	*marturia*	*hēn*
true	is	the	witness	which

3113.3 verb 3sing indic pres act	3875.1 prep	1466.3 prs-pron gen 1sing	5050.1 prs-pron nom 2pl	643.19 verb 2pl indic perf act
μαρτυρεῖ	περὶ	ἐμοῦ.	33. Ὑμεῖς	ἀπεστάλκατε
marturei	*peri*	*emou*	*Humeis*	*apestalkate*
he witnesses	concerning	me.	You	have sent

4242.1 prep	2464.4 name acc masc	2504.1 conj	3113.27 verb 3sing indic perf act	3450.11 art dat sing fem	223.3 noun dat sing fem
πρὸς	Ἰωάννην	καὶ	μεμαρτύρηκεν	τῇ	ἀληθείᾳ·
pros	*Iōannēn*	*kai*	*memarturēken*	*tē*	*alētheia*
unto	John	and	he has borne witness	to the	truth.

1466.1 prs-pron nom 1sing	1156.2 conj	3620.3 partic	3706.2 prep	442.2 noun gen sing masc	3450.12 art acc sing fem
34. ἐγὼ	δὲ	οὐ	παρὰ	ἀνθρώπου	τὴν
egō	*de*	*ou*	*para*	*anthrōpou*	*tēn*
I	but	not	from	man	the

3114.3 noun acc sing fem	2956.2 verb 1sing indic pres act	233.2 conj	3642.18 dem-pron pl neu	2978.1 verb 1sing pres act	2419.1 conj
μαρτυρίαν	λαμβάνω,	ἀλλὰ	ταῦτα	λέγω	ἵνα
marturian	*lambanō*	*alla*	*tauta*	*legō*	*hina*
witness	receive,	but	these things	I say	that

5050.1 prs-pron nom 2pl	4834.24 verb 2pl aor pass	1552.3 dem-pron nom sing masc	1498.34 verb sing indic imperf act	3450.5 art sing masc
ὑμεῖς	σωθῆτε.	35. ἐκεῖνος	ἦν	ὁ
humeis	*sōthēte*	*ekeinos*	*ēn*	*ho*
you	may be saved.	That	was	the

3060.1 noun nom sing masc	3450.5 art sing masc	2516.3 verb nom sing masc part pres pass	2504.1 conj	5154.5 verb nom sing masc part pres act	5050.1 prs-pron nom 2pl
λύχνος	ὁ	καιόμενος	καὶ	φαίνων,	ὑμεῖς
luchnos	*ho*	*kaiomenos*	*kai*	*phainōn*	*humeis*
lamp	the	burning	and	shining,	you

35.a.**Txt:** 019L,Steph **Var:** 01א,02A,03B,05D, 017K,036,037,(038), Gries,Lach,Treg,Alf, Tisc,We/HoWeis,Sod, UBS/☆

1156.2 conj	2286.24 verb 2pl indic aor act	21.7 verb inf aor pass	21.9 verb inf aor pass
δὲ	ἠθελήσατε	‛ ἀγαλλιασθῆναι	[ᵃ☆ ἀγαλλιαθῆναι]
de	*ēthelēsate*	*agalliasthēnai*	*agalliathēnai*
and	were willing	to rejoice	[idem]

4242.1 prep	5443.4 noun acc sing fem	1706.1 prep	3450.3 art dat sing	5295.3 noun dat sing neu	840.3 prs-pron gen sing
πρὸς	ὥραν	ἐν	τῷ	φωτὶ	αὐτοῦ.
pros	*hōran*	*en*	*tō*	*phōti*	*autou*
for	an hour	in	the	light	his.

1466.1 prs-pron nom 1sing	1156.2 conj	2174.1 verb 1sing pres act	3450.12 art acc sing fem	3114.3 noun acc sing fem	3157.5 adj comp acc
36. ἐγὼ	δὲ	ἔχω	τὴν	μαρτυρίαν	‛ μείζω
egō	*de*	*echō*	*tēn*	*marturian*	*meizō*
I	but	have	the	witness	greater

2 Peter 1:17). The second time the Father's voice was heard from heaven was at the Transfiguration (Mark 9:7; Luke 9:35). The third time the Father spoke in witness to the Son occurred during the final week of the Son's ministry on earth (12:28).

(2) The witness of John the Baptist provided credible testimony as to the person and work of the Messiah (5:33-35). Although John was not the light of the world, he did come to "bear witness of the light" (1:7).

(3) Jesus' witness of himself is a valid and necessary testimony when accompanied by other credible witnesses. If He did not know himself to be Christ and God, one could reasonably doubt that He was, even if others claimed it for Him. He did know and testified to His personal identity and mission.

(4) The ministry of Jesus by His miracles attested to His office as Messiah as given in the Old Testament (Isaiah 61:1-3).

(5) The Scriptures foretold the Messiah's coming and the events accompanying His ministry (5:39,40).

(6) The Holy Spirit witnessed to the person and activities of the Lord Jesus Christ (15:26).

(7) The disciples of Jesus were reliable witnesses (15:27).

The seven witnesses provide many bona fide, credible proofs. The Law demanded two or three; God gave seven.

"Ye sent unto John." The Jews were aware of John the Baptist's preaching. Jesus reminded them that they sought the witness of John for they valued his ministry and witness. Yet they did not follow his testimony to accept the Messiah.

Jesus said John was a credible witness to the truth. Thus, Jesus implied, "Why did you not believe him?"

5:34. Jesus asserted that "man" is not His most important evidence, even though John's identification of Him as the Messiah had great significance. Jesus' purpose in displaying the evidence as to who He is is revealed in "that ye might be saved." His defense is neither selfish nor self-glorifying. He presented the truth in order that the Jews might come to Him for salvation. To believe on Him was the only way to be saved (Acts 4:12).

5:35. "He was a burning and a shining light" refers to John the Baptist. It was the light of John's ministry that revealed the path of salvation through the Messiah.

The Lord testifies of John as a light bearer. He does not mean to divest John of his great ministry by saying His witness was not from man; therefore, He corrected any misunderstanding of His comment that the Jews might have. John's ministry stirred the people to an awakened spiritual condition. The Jews rejoiced in the light for awhile, but that rejoicing did not endure. His message

and I know that the witness which he witnesseth of me is true: . . . the testimony which he bears to me it trustworthy, *TCNT* . . . the evidence he bears for me is valid, *Moffatt* . . . absolutely true, *Phillips.*

33. Ye sent unto John, and he bare witness unto the truth: You yourselves sent delegates, *ALBA* . . . and he has given evidence, *Fenton.*

34. But I receive not testimony from man: Not that I rely on human testimony, *NEB* . . . I do not rest My claim, *Berkeley* . . . Not that human testimony is adequate, *ALBA* . . . accept mere human testimony, *Williams.*

but these things I say, that ye might be saved: . . . for your salvation, *TCNT* . . . so that you may have salvation, *BB* . . . I only mention this, *Montgomery* . . . in order that even you may be saved, *Fenton.*

35. He was a burning and a shining light: . . . the blazing, *Campbell* . . . He was the Lamp, *TCNT* . . . he was a lanterne, *Wycliffe* . . . and appearing, *Concordant* . . . a lamp, burning for all to see, *ALBA.*

and ye were willing for a season to rejoice in his light: . . . and for a while you wanted to enjoy his light, *Beck* . . . will exult an hour in its light, *Concordant* . . . pleased to exult, for an hour, *Rotherham.*

36. But I have greater witness that that of John: I rely on weightier testimony, *Norlie* . . . a higher testimony, *Phillips* . . . is weightier, *Weymouth* . . . more proof, *SEB.*

John 5:37

36.a.**Var:** p66,02A,03B,07E,021M,032W,13,LachTreg,Alf,Sod

3157.2 adj comp nom sing	3450.2 art gen sing	2464.2 name gen masc	3450.17 art pl neu	1056.1 conj	2024.4 noun pl neu
[a μείζων]	τοῦ	Ἰωάννου·	τὰ	γὰρ	ἔργα
meizōn	*tou*	*Iōannou*	*ta*	*gar*	*erga*
[idem]		John's	the	for	works

36.b.**Txt:** 02A,05D,017K,037,038,byz.Gries,Lach **Var:** 01ℵ,03B,019L,036,33,Treg,Alf,Tisc,We/Ho Weis,Sod,UBS/☆

3614.17 rel-pron pl neu	1319.14 verb 3sing indic aor act	1319.33 verb 3sing indic perf act	1466.4 prs-pron dat 1sing	3450.5 art sing masc
ἃ	⸀ ἔδωκέν	[b☆ δέδωκεν]	μοι	ὁ
ha	*edōken*	*dedōken*	*moi*	*ho*
which	gave	[has given]	me	the

3824.1 noun nom sing masc	2419.1 conj	4896.3 verb 1sing subj aor act	840.16 prs-pron pl neu	840.16 prs-pron pl neu	3450.17 art pl neu
πατὴρ	ἵνα	τελειώσω	αὐτά,	αὐτὰ	τὰ
patēr	*hina*	*teleiōsō*	*auta*	*auta*	*ta*
Father	that	I should complete	them,	themselves	the

36.c.**Txt:** 017K,036,037,038,13,byz. **Var:** 01ℵ,02A,03B,05D,019L,33,bo.Lach,Treg Alf,Tisc,We/Ho,Weis,Sod,UBS/☆

2024.4 noun pl neu	3614.17 rel-pron pl neu	1466.1 prs-pron nom 1sing	4020.1 verb 1sing pres act	3113.3 verb 3sing indic pres act	3875.1 prep
ἔργα	ἃ	⸂c ἐγὼ ⸃	ποιῶ,	μαρτυρεῖ	περὶ
erga	*ha*	*egō*	*poiō*	*marturei*	*peri*
works	which	I	do,	bear witness	concerning

1466.3 prs-pron gen 1sing	3617.1 conj	3450.5 art sing masc	3824.1 noun nom sing masc	1466.6 prs-pron acc 1sing	643.17 verb 3sing indic perf act
ἐμοῦ	ὅτι	ὁ	πατήρ	με	ἀπέσταλκεν.
emou	*hoti*	*ho*	*patēr*	*me*	*apestalken*
me	that	the	Father	me	has sent.

2504.1 conj	3450.5 art sing masc	3854.11 verb nom sing masc part aor act	1466.6 prs-pron acc 1sing	3824.1 noun nom sing masc	840.5 prs-pron nom sing masc
37. καὶ	ὁ	πέμψας	με	πατὴρ	⸀ αὐτὸς
kai	*ho*	*pempsas*	*me*	*patēr*	*autos*
And	the	having sent	me	Father,	himself

37.a.**Txt:** p66,02A,017K,036,037,038,1,13,byz.it. bo.Gries,Lach,Sod **Var:** p75,01ℵ,03B,019L,032W,Treg,Alf,Tisc,We/HoWeis,UBS/☆

1552.3 dem-pron nom sing masc	3113.27 verb 3sing indic perf act	3875.1 prep	1466.3 prs-pron gen 1sing	3641.1 conj
[a☆ ἐκεῖνος]	μεμαρτύρηκεν	περὶ	ἐμοῦ.	οὔτε
ekeinos	*memarturēken*	*peri*	*emou*	*oute*
[that]	has borne witness	concerning	me.	Neither

5292.4 noun acc sing fem	840.3 prs-pron gen sing	189.39 verb 2pl indic perf act	4312.1 adv	4312.1 adv
φωνὴν	αὐτοῦ	⸀ ἀκηκόατε	πώποτε,	[☆ πώποτε
phōnēn	*autou*	*akēkoate*	*pōpote*	*pōpote*
voice	his	have you heard	at any time,	[at any time

189.39 verb 2pl indic perf act	3641.1 conj	1482.1 noun sing neu	840.3 prs-pron gen sing	3571.13 verb 2pl indic perf act	2504.1 conj
ἀκηκόατε]	οὔτε	εἶδος	αὐτοῦ	ἑωράκατε,	**38.** καὶ
akēkoate	*oute*	*eidos*	*autou*	*heōrakate*	*kai*
you have heard]	nor	form	his	have you seen.	And

3450.6 art acc sing masc	3030.4 noun acc sing masc	840.3 prs-pron gen sing	3620.2 partic	2174.2 verb 2pl pres act	3176.12 verb acc sing masc part pres act
τὸν	λόγον	αὐτοῦ	οὐκ	ἔχετε	⸀ μένοντα
ton	*logon*	*autou*	*ouk*	*echete*	*menonta*
the	word	his	not	you have	residing

1706.1 prep	5050.3 prs-pron dat 2pl	1706.1 prep	5050.3 prs-pron dat 2pl	3176.12 verb acc sing masc part pres act	3617.1 conj
ἐν	ὑμῖν,	[☆ ἐν	ὑμῖν	μένοντα,]	ὅτι
en	*humin*	*en*	*humin*	*menonta*	*hoti*
in	you,	[in	you	residing,]	for

demanded a change in their character and conduct, so they resisted his truth (Matthew 3:7,8) and rejected the Messiah (John 1:11).

5:36. "But I have greater witness" refers to Jesus' works as His messianic credentials. This statement is not intended to be derogatory to John and is probably best understood as " 'greater than the testimony John *gave*,' rather than 'greater than the testimony John *had*' " (Brown, *Anchor Bible*, 29:224). John's testimony as such did not reveal the full magnitude of Jesus' glory. He considered these miracles and fulfilled prophecies as "greater . . . than that of John." The imperative of the Messiah was to reveal His mission by the works which were to accompany that commission. The Lord pointed to His works as the beginning place for one's faith.

"The same works that I do, bear witness of me." The works proved His identity. "Jesus always appeals to his works when it is a matter of proving his divine mission (10:25,32,37-38; 14:10-11; 15:24); they are one and the same as his 'signs,' which, as 'revelatory deeds,' are simply another aspect of the 'works' " (Schnackenburg, *Gospel According to St. John*, 2:123).

"That the Father hath sent (*apestalken*) me" calls attention to the Father's commission. Jesus was sent with a continuing commission (the perfect tense verb indicates the permanence of the authority), and the accomplishment of it bore greater witness than John's testimony.

5:37. The Father "sent" and "hath borne witness." Here Jesus used the ordinary word for "sent" (*pempsas*), but "hath borne witness" (*memarturēken*) is a perfect tense verb indicating an action in the past and continuing to the time of the statement. The Father was continuing to bear witness in many direct and indirect ways. The direct means of witness included His voice from heaven (see verse 32 for comments). The Father's indirect testimony was in His confirmations of His Word, the miracles Jesus performed, and the prophets whom He sent who were apparent to all men.

"Ye have neither heard his voice at any time, nor seen his shape." No direct means of testimony person to person was possible by the Father. The voice from heaven was heard by believers. The unbelievers thought they heard thunder (12:29).

Jesus indicated later that believing is a prerequisite for experiencing the glories of His kingdom (11:40).

5:38. "Abiding in you" refers to the Spirit's witness to the inward man. The apostle Paul speaks of the witness of the Spirit to the

for the works which the Father hath given me to finish: . . . the deeds that I do, *SEB* . . . to bring to completion, *Montgomery* . . . given Me to accomplish, *Berkeley* . . . has empowered me to perform, *Campbell* . . . gave me power to do, *Barclay* . . . to achieve, *ALBA*.

the same works that I do: . . . the activities in which I am engaged, *Berkeley* . . . the very work which I am now doing, *BB*.

bear witness of me, that the Father hath sent me: . . . there is sufficient testimony, *Norlie* . . . give evidence about Me, *Fenton* . . . these are my testimony that, *ALBA* . . . these are My evidence, *Berkeley* . . . are proof that I have come with a message from the Father, *TCNT*.

37. And the Father himself, which hath sent me, hath borne witness of me: He testified about Me, *Beck* . . . testified on My behalf, *Berkeley* . . . has commissioned Me, *Concordant* . . . has himself attested me, *Campbell* . . . has himself given evidence on my behalf, *Barclay*.

Ye have neither heard his voice at any time, nor seen his shape: . . . you have never listened, *ET* . . . nor seen his form, *ASV* . . . seen His appearance, *Concordant* . . . looked upon His Ideal, *Fenton* . . . his form you have not seen, *BB* . . . nor seen his face, *ALBA*.

38. And ye have not his word abiding in you: . . . have not kept his word in your hearts, *BB* . . . Nor do you really believe his Word, *Phillips* . . . have his word rooted in your hearts, *ALBA*.

3614.6 rel-pron acc sing masc	643.8 verb 3sing indic aor act	1552.3 dem-pron nom sing masc	3642.5 dem-pron dat sing masc	5050.1 prs-pron nom 2pl
ὃν	ἀπέστειλεν	ἐκεῖνος,	τούτῳ	ὑμεῖς
hon	*apesteilen*	*ekeinos*	*toutō*	*humeis*
whom	sent	that,	this	you

39.a.**Var:** p66,01ℵ, 03B-org,Treg,Alf,Tisc, We/Ho,Weis

3620.3 partic	3961.2 verb 2pl pres act	2028.2 verb 2pl impr pres act	2020.1 verb 2pl pres act	3450.15 art acc pl fem
οὐ	πιστεύετε.	**39.** ʻ Ἐρευνᾶτε	[a ἐραυνᾶτε]	τὰς
ou	*pisteuete*	*Ereunate*	*eraunate*	*tas*
not	believe.	You search	[idem]	the

1118.8 noun acc pl fem	3617.1 conj	5050.1 prs-pron nom 2pl	1374.1 verb 2pl pres act	1706.1 prep	840.14 prs-pron dat pl fem
γραφάς,	ὅτι	ὑμεῖς	δοκεῖτε	ἐν	αὐταῖς
graphas	*hoti*	*humeis*	*dokeite*	*en*	*autais*
scriptures,	for	you	think	in	them

2205.4 noun acc sing fem	164.1 adj sing	2174.29 verb inf pres act	2504.1 conj	1552.13 dem-pron nom pl fem	1498.7 verb 3pl indic pres act
ζωὴν	αἰώνιον	ἔχειν,	καὶ	ἐκεῖναί	εἰσιν
zōēn	*aiōnion*	*echein*	*kai*	*ekeinai*	*eisin*
life	eternal	to have,	and	those	are they

3450.13 art pl fem	3113.13 verb nom pl fem part pres act	3875.1 prep	1466.3 prs-pron gen 1sing	2504.1 conj
αἱ	μαρτυροῦσαι	περὶ	ἐμοῦ·	**40.** καὶ
hai	*marturousai*	*peri*	*emou*	*kai*
the	bearing witness	concerning	me;	and

3620.3 partic	2286.5 verb 2pl indic pres act	2048.23 verb inf aor act	4242.1 prep	1466.6 prs-pron acc 1sing	2419.1 conj
οὐ	θέλετε	ἐλθεῖν	πρός	με,	ἵνα
ou	*thelete*	*elthein*	*pros*	*me*	*hina*
not	you are willing	to come	to	me,	that

2205.4 noun acc sing fem	2174.9 verb 2pl subj pres act	1385.4 noun acc sing fem	3706.2 prep	442.7 noun gen pl masc
ζωὴν	ἔχητε.	**41.** Δόξαν	παρὰ	ἀνθρώπων
zōēn	*echēte*	*Doxan*	*para*	*anthrōpōn*
life	you may have.	Glory	from	men

3620.3 partic	2956.2 verb 1sing indic pres act	233.1 conj	233.2 conj	1091.30 verb 1sing indic perf act
οὐ	λαμβάνω·	**42.** ʻ ἀλλ'	[☆ ἀλλὰ]	ἔγνωκα
ou	*lambanō*	*all'*	*alla*	*egnōka*
not	I receive;	but	[idem]	I have known

5050.4 prs-pron acc 2pl	3617.1 conj	3450.12 art acc sing fem	26.4 noun acc sing fem	3450.2 art gen sing	2296.2 noun gen sing masc	3620.2 partic
ὑμᾶς	ὅτι	τὴν	ἀγάπην	τοῦ	θεοῦ	οὐκ
humas	*hoti*	*tēn*	*agapēn*	*tou*	*theou*	*ouk*
you	that	the	love		of God	not

2174.2 verb 2pl pres act	1706.1 prep	1431.7 prs-pron dat pl masc	1466.1 prs-pron nom 1sing	2048.24 verb 1sing indic perf act	1706.1 prep
ἔχετε	ἐν	ἑαυτοῖς.	**43.** ἐγὼ	ἐλήλυθα	ἐν
echete	*en*	*heautois*	*egō*	*elēlutha*	*en*
you have	in	yourselves.	I	have come	in

3450.3 art dat sing	3549.4 noun dat sing neu	3450.2 art gen sing	3824.2 noun gen sing masc	1466.2 prs-pron gen 1sing	2504.1 conj	3620.3 partic
τῷ	ὀνόματι	τοῦ	πατρός	μου,	καὶ	οὐ
tō	*onomati*	*tou*	*patros*	*mou*	*kai*	*ou*
the	name		of Father	my,	and	not

believer: "The Spirit itself beareth witness with our spirit, that we are the children of God" (Romans 8:16).

for whom he hath sent, him ye believe not: . . . for you refuse to believe Him, *Weymouth* . . . whom He personally sent, *Berkeley* . . . give not credit to him, *Norton.*

5:39. "You search" (*ereunate*) has the position of emphasis. It makes little difference whether we take *ereunate* as imperative or indicative. It may be best to consider the statement as a challenge for the Jews to study God's Word because Jesus had been explaining the Father's witness to Him. In the Word of God, the Father witnesses to Jesus' messiahship. The many Old Testament prophecies confirm this to be true.

"The Scriptures" (*tas graphas*) corresponds with "his word" of verse 38. Jesus based His argument on the authority of the Father's witness.

Jesus' command for the Jews to examine the Scriptures is followed by the reasons they should do so. The Scriptures had given the Jews their only hope, but nowhere did the Scriptures promise eternal life by observance of the Law. Jesus challenged them to find it anywhere.

The second reason to search the Scriptures is "and they are they which testify of me." There is an emphasis on the word "they" (*ekeinai*, literally "those very ones"). The Jews did see the Messiah in the Scriptures; however, they did not understand the kind of Messiah Jesus was. They expected a political, military deliverer, not the gentle, meek, miracle-working teacher. They desired a second King David with earthly power. This will indeed happen after the return of Christ, during the Millennium.

39. Search the scriptures: You keep on searching, *Williams* . . . You study the Scriptures, *ALBA* . . . You investigate, *Berkeley* . . . You pore over the scriptures, *Phillips.*

for in them ye think ye have eternal life: . . . in the belief that through them you get eternal life, *BB* . . . for you imagine that you will find, *Phillips* . . . you are supposing, *Concordant* . . . for you yourselves suppose, *Williams* . . . you think by them to obtain, *Wilson* . . . imagining you possess eternal life in their pages, *Moffatt* . . . a means to eternal life, *ALBA.*

and they are they which testify of me: . . . they are the very writings, *Norlie* . . . yet they testify about Me! *Beck* . . . are giving proof about me! *SEB.*

5:40. Life is contained in Jesus Christ, not in observance of the Law on which they depended. Eternal life is a gift in Christ (3:15,16). No one has ever kept the Law; therefore he cannot be justified by it, nor granted life through it. "Come to me" is the invitation of hope, one's only hope of life.

40. And ye will not come to me, that ye might have life: . . . you refuse to come to me to have Life, *TCNT* . . . in order to have life, *Berkeley.*

5:41. In this verse the Lord pointed out that the witness of the Father far outweighs any glory that could be attributed to Him from men; men's glory is accounted as nothing. Furthermore, Jesus indicated that He did not need glory from men as a conquering king to fulfill His mission and bring eternal life.

41. I receive not honour from men: I do not, in any case, *TCNT* . . . I accept no credit from men, *Moffatt* . . . I do not crave human honour, *Fenton* . . . I reach for no human fame, *Berkeley* . . . I catch at no credit from men, *HistNT.*

5:42. "I know" (*egnōka*, perfect tense verb) indicates His past experience of the Jews. The reason they would not come to Him was their lack of love for God, His Father. The Jews had an inward, personal unwillingness to search the Scriptures for the truth.

42. But I know you, that ye have not the love of God in you: . . . that in your hearts you do not really love God, *Weymouth* . . . you are strangers, *Campbell.*

43. I am come in my Father's name: I have come, *HBIE, Berkeley* . . . I have come on the authority of, *ALBA* . . . as the representative of, *Barclay.*

2956.1 verb 2pl pres act	1466.6 prs-pron acc 1sing	1430.1 partic	241.4 adj nom sing masc	2048.8 verb 3sing subj aor act	1706.1 prep
λαμβάνετέ	με·	ἐὰν	ἄλλος	ἔλθῃ	ἐν
lambanete	*me*	*ean*	*allos*	*elthē*	*en*
you receive	me;	if	another	should come	in

3450.3 art dat sing	3549.4 noun dat sing neu	3450.3 art dat sing	2375.3 adj dat sing	1552.5 dem-pron acc sing masc	2956.41 verb 2pl indic fut mid
τῷ	ὀνόματι	τῷ	ἰδίῳ,	ἐκεῖνον	ʼ λήψεσθε.
tō	*onomati*	*tō*	*idiō*	*ekeinon*	*lēpsesthe*
the	name	the	his own,	him	you will receive.

2956.47 verb 2pl indic fut mid	4316.1 adv	1404.6 verb 2pl indic pres	5050.1 prs-pron nom 2pl	3961.36 verb inf aor act
[☆ λήμψεσθε.]	**44.** πῶς	δύνασθε	ὑμεῖς	πιστεῦσαι,
lēmpsesthe	*pōs*	*dunasthe*	*humeis*	*pisteusai*
[idem]	How	are able	you	to believe,

1385.4 noun acc sing fem	3706.2 prep	238.1 prs-pron gen pl	2956.9 verb nom pl masc part pres act	2504.1 conj	3450.12 art acc sing fem
δόξαν	παρὰ	ἀλλήλων	λαμβάνοντες,	καὶ	τὴν
doxan	*para*	*allēlōn*	*lambanontes*	*kai*	*tēn*
glory	from	one another	who receive,	and	the

44.a.**Txt:** 01ℵ,02A,05D, 017K,019L,036,037,038, 1,13,28,33,565,byz.syr. it.Lach,Treg,Alf,Tisc, We/Ho,Weis,Sod,UBS/☆ **Var:** p66,p75,03B,032W, sa.

1385.4 noun acc sing fem	3450.12 art acc sing fem	3706.2 prep	3450.2 art gen sing	3304.3 adj gen sing masc	2296.2 noun gen sing masc	3620.3 partic
δόξαν	τὴν	παρὰ	τοῦ	μόνου	ʼa θεοῦ ʽ	οὐ
doxan	*tēn*	*para*	*tou*	*monou*	*theou*	*ou*
glory	the	from	the	only	God	not

2195.1 verb 2pl pres act	3231.1 partic	1374.1 verb 2pl pres act	3617.1 conj	1466.1 prs-pron nom 1sing	2693.11 verb 1sing indic fut act
ζητεῖτε;	**45.** μὴ	δοκεῖτε	ὅτι	ἐγὼ	κατηγορήσω
zēteite	*mē*	*dokeite*	*hoti*	*egō*	*katēgorēsō*
you seek?	Not	think	that	I	will accuse

5050.2 prs-pron gen 2pl	4242.1 prep	3450.6 art acc sing masc	3824.4 noun acc sing masc	1498.4 verb 3sing indic pres act	3450.5 art sing masc
ὑμῶν	πρὸς	τὸν	πατέρα·	ἔστιν	ὁ
humōn	*pros*	*ton*	*patera*	*estin*	*ho*
you	to	the	Father:	there is	the

2693.5 verb nom sing masc part pres act	5050.2 prs-pron gen 2pl	3337.1 name nom masc	3338.1 name nom masc	1519.1 prep
κατηγορῶν	ὑμῶν,	ʼ Μωσῆς,	[☆ Μωϋσῆς,]	εἰς
katēgorōn	*humōn*	*Mōsēs*	*Mousēs*	*eis*
accusing	you,	Moses,	[idem]	in

3614.6 rel-pron acc sing masc	5050.1 prs-pron nom 2pl	1666.11 verb 2pl indic perf act	1479.1 conj	1056.1 conj	3961.54 verb 2pl indic imperf act
ὃν	ὑμεῖς	ἠλπίκατε.	**46.** εἰ	γὰρ	ἐπιστεύετε
hon	*humeis*	*ēlpikate*	*ei*	*gar*	*episteuete*
whom	you	have hoped.	If	for	you believed

3337.4 name dat masc	3338.3 name dat masc	3961.54 verb 2pl indic imperf act	300.1 partic	1466.5 prs-pron dat 1sing
ʼ Μωσῇ,	[☆ Μωϋσεῖ,]	ἐπιστεύετε	ἂν	ἐμοί·
Mōsē	*Mousei*	*episteuete*	*an*	*emoi*
Moses,	[idem]	you would have believed		me,

3875.1 prep	1056.1 conj	1466.3 prs-pron gen 1sing	1552.3 dem-pron nom sing masc	1119.8 verb 3sing indic aor act	1479.1 conj
περὶ	γὰρ	ἐμοῦ	ἐκεῖνος	ἔγραψεν.	**47.** εἰ
peri	*gar*	*emou*	*ekeinos*	*egrapsen*	*ei*
concerning	for	me	that	wrote.	If

5:43. "If another" refers to those who come without witness and with an objective of self-glorification. The Antichrist is the ultimate one meant, though the Jews had received political saviors, to their destruction (2 Thessalonians 2:8-13; 1 John 2:18).

and ye receive me not: . . . and you refuse to accept me, *JB* . . . and yet you do not welcome Me, *Norlie* . . . and you will not accept me, *Phillips.*

if another shall come in his own name: . . . as the representative of no one but himself, *Barclay* . . . with no other authority but himself, *BB.*

him ye will receive: . . . you will accept him! *Moffatt, Berkeley* . . . you will give him your approval, *BB.*

5:44. The seeking of human acclaim is a form of self-idolatry. John 12:37-43 points out that it is precisely this love for the praise of men which prevented the Sanhedrin from believing in Jesus. The vanity which drives men to prefer the glory of human praise to the humility which accepts Jesus' love is captured in John Milton's words, "Better to reign in hell, than serve in Heaven" (Milton, *Paradise Lost,* I.263). No one can love God who is infatuated with himself. The desire for man's approval and praise cannot be reconciled with the love one should have for God. The Old Testament plainly asserts, "I command you today to love the Lord your God" (NASB, Deuteronomy 30:16; cf. Micah 6:8).

"That cometh from God only" implies that the Jews had made for themselves gods by seeking glory from men. Their attitude and conduct should have been to walk humbly before God, not to walk proudly before men!

44. How can ye believe, which receive honour one of another: How on earth can you believe, while you are for ever looking for one another's approval, *Phillips* . . . when you welcome the praise of others, *Berkeley.*

and seek not the honour that cometh from God only?: . . . while you do not try to obtain, *TCNT* . . . and do not desire the honour which comes from the only God, *TCNT* . . . the rectification which comes, *Fenton* . . . from the one God? *JB.*

5:45. Jesus told the Jews the Law condemned both their attitude and life. "The one who accuses you is Moses" (NASB). The Law as given by Moses doomed all who were guilty of idolatry (Exodus 20:3-7). The people's opinion and their self-glorying were more important to them than God's approval. The Law in which they sought refuge pointed out their guilt.

"In whom ye trust" referred to their supposed safe resting place; yet it was their plot of condemnation. "In whom ye trust" (*ēlpikate*) is a perfect tense verb specifying a settled situation of hope. Jesus unveiled the fallacy of that kind of thinking.

45. Do not think that I will accuse you to the Father: Do not imagine that I will, *Berkeley.*

there is one that accuseth you, even Moses, in whom ye trust: . . . there is your accuser, Moses, *Panin* . . . your accuser will be Moses, *ALBA* . . . on whom ye rely, *Murdock* . . . you confide, *Campbell* . . . on whom ye have set your hope, *PNT* . . . you place your hopes on Moses, *JB* . . . the very one in whom you have hoped! *Adams.*

5:46. "For had ye believed Moses" points to the reason for the last statement. Moses would have no occasion to accuse them if they had believed him. Their unbelief in Christ showed they did not believe Moses. "Ye would have believed me" is a natural consequence of believing Moses. The law of Moses made clear the coming of the Christ as well as His nature and work.

"For he wrote of me" gives the reason they would have believed Him. "Me" is an emphatic word to lay emphasis on the fact that Moses wrote with the objective of declaring the Messiah (Exodus 3:13,14; Deuteronomy 18:15-18).

46. For had ye believed Moses, ye would have believed me: for he wrote of me: He personally wrote, *Berkeley* . . . for it was about me that he wrote, *Barclay.*

John 6:1

1156.2 conj	3450.4 art dat pl	1552.2 dem-pron gen sing	1115.5 noun dat pl neu	3620.3 partic	3961.2 verb 2pl pres act
δὲ	τοῖς	ἐκείνου	γράμμασιν	οὐ	πιστεύετε,
de	*tois*	*ekeinou*	*grammasin*	*ou*	*pisteuete*
but	the	that	writings	not	you believe,

4316.1 adv	3450.4 art dat pl	1684.14 adj dat 1pl neu	4343.6 noun dat pl neu	3961.50 verb 2pl indic fut act	3196.3 prep
πῶς	τοῖς	ἐμοῖς	ῥήμασιν	πιστεύσετε;	**6:1.** Μετὰ
pōs	*tois*	*emois*	*rhēmasin*	*pisteusete*	*Meta*
how	the	my	words	shall you believe?	After

3642.18 dem-pron pl neu	562.2 verb 3sing indic aor act	3450.5 art sing masc	2400.1 name nom masc	3871.1 adv	3450.10 art gen sing fem
ταῦτα	ἀπῆλθεν	ὁ	Ἰησοῦς	πέραν	τῆς
tauta	*apēlthen*	*ho*	*Iēsous*	*peran*	*tēs*
these things	went away		Jesus	over	the

2258.2 noun gen sing fem	3450.10 art gen sing fem	1049.2 name gen sing fem	3450.10 art gen sing fem	4933.1 name gen fem
θαλάσσης	τῆς	Γαλιλαίας	τῆς	Τιβεριάδος·
thalassēs	*tēs*	*Galilaias*	*tēs*	*Tiberiados*
sea		of Galilee		of Tiberias,

2.a.**Txt:** 02A,017K,036,037,038,byz.
Var: 01ℵ,03B,05D,019L,33,bo.Lach,Treg,Alf,Tisc,We/HoWeis,Sod,UBS/☆

2.b.**Var:** p66-corr,03B,05D,019L,022N,044,LachTreg,Alf,We/Ho,Sod

2504.1 conj	188.21 verb 3sing indic imperf act	188.21 verb 3sing indic imperf act	1156.2 conj	840.4 prs-pron dat sing
2. ⸀ καὶ	ἠκολούθει	[a☆ ἠκολούθει	δὲ]	αὐτῷ
kai	*ēkolouthei*	*ēkolouthei*	*de*	*autō*
and	followed	[followed	and]	him

3657.1 noun nom sing masc	4044.5 adj nom sing masc	3617.1 conj	3571.19 verb 3pl indic imperf act	2311.20 verb indic imperf act
ὄχλος	πολύς,	ὅτι	⸀ ἑώρων	[b ἐθεώρουν]
ochlos	*polus*	*hoti*	*heōrōn*	*etheōroun*
a crowd	great,	because	they saw	[idem]

2.c.**Txt:** 07E,021M,036,037,byz.
Var: 01ℵ,02A,03B,05D,017K,019L,038,041,it.bo.Gries,Lach,TregAlf,Tisc,We/Ho,Weis,Sod,UBS/☆

840.3 prs-pron gen sing	3450.17 art pl neu	4447.2 noun pl neu	3614.17 rel-pron pl neu	4020.57 verb 3sing indic imperf act	1894.3 prep
⸂c αὐτοῦ ⸃	τὰ	σημεῖα	ἃ	ἐποίει	ἐπὶ
autou	*ta*	*sēmeia*	*ha*	*epoiei*	*epi*
of him	the	signs	which	he performed	upon

3450.1 art gen pl	764.8 verb gen pl masc part pres act	422.2 verb 3sing indic aor act	1156.2 conj	1519.1 prep	3450.16 art sing neu
τῶν	ἀσθενούντων.	**3.** ἀνῆλθεν	δὲ	εἰς	τὸ
tōn	*asthenountōn*	*anēlthen*	*de*	*eis*	*to*
the	being sick.	Went up	and	into	the

3.a.**Txt:** 01ℵ-corr,02A,017K,019L,036,038,1,13,etc.byz.Gries,Weis,Sod
Var: p66,01ℵ-org,03B,05D,032W,Lach,Treg,Alf,TiscWe/Ho,UBS/☆

3.b.**Var:** 01ℵ,(05),Tisc

3598.1 noun sing neu	3450.5 art sing masc	2400.1 name nom masc	2504.1 conj	1550.1 adv	2493.17 verb 3sing indic imperf
ὄρος	⸂a ὁ ⸃	Ἰησοῦς,	καὶ	ἐκεῖ	⸀ ἐκάθητο
oros	*ho*	*Iēsous*	*kai*	*ekei*	*ekathēto*
mountain		Jesus,	and	there	sat

2488.5 verb 3sing indic imperf	3196.3 prep	3450.1 art gen pl	3073.6 noun gen pl masc	840.3 prs-pron gen sing	1498.34 verb sing indic imperf act
[b ἐκαθέζετο]	μετὰ	τῶν	μαθητῶν	αὐτοῦ.	**4.** ἦν
ekathezeto	*meta*	*tōn*	*mathētōn*	*autou*	*ēn*
[was sitting]	with	the	disciples	his;	was

1156.2 conj	1445.1 adv	3450.16 art sing neu	3818.1 noun sing neu	3450.9 art nom sing fem	1844.1 noun nom sing fem	3450.1 art gen pl
δὲ	ἐγγὺς	τὸ	πάσχα	ἡ	ἑορτὴ	τῶν
de	*engus*	*to*	*pascha*	*hē*	*heortē*	*tōn*
and	near	the	passover,	the	feast	of the

5:47. The reverse of the preceding is found in this verse. The negative is stated here while the positive is given in verse 46. Repetition is an effective technique for instruction and emphasis. Parallels are brought out in this verse. Moses and Christ are compared ("his" and "my"). The one who wrote was inferior to the One he wrote about. Moses was a faithful servant in the house of God's Son (Hebrew 3:5,6). "Believe not" is contrasted with "believe." The present tense of believing Moses' writing is compared with the future tense of believing Christ. Lastly, Moses' "writings" are analogous with Christ's words. Christ's words here have the same importance as Moses "writings." Both "writings" (*grammasin*) and "words" (*rhēmasin*) indicate the vehicle for the communication.

Jesus established His claims to messiahship on the prophecies of Moses in whose writings the Jews claimed to believe. He called on the Jews to believe Moses. If they would, they could also believe that Jesus was who He said.

6:1. "After these things" reaffirms what has taken place previously. Jesus disclosed to the Jews the great truths of who He is by declaring that He possesses the authority of life, judgment, and resurrection. The claim to these three prerogatives of deity was revealed as a result of the healing of the impotent man (5:5-9). In chapter 6 Jesus reveals that He supports life by providing bread. His provision of natural bread illustrates the truth that He gives spiritual bread to sustain the inward person.

"Jesus went over." John identified the Sea of Galilee as the Sea of Tiberias. Tiberias was the Roman name given in honor of Caesar. The sea is about 14 miles long and 9 miles wide. It has been a freshwater lake from ancient times.

6:2. Some of these people had gathered because of the Passover. The last part of the verse states the reason they followed Him. "Were diseased" (*asthenountōn*) indicates a wide variety of diseases as in 5:3 where the same word is used.

6:3. A chain of hills surrounds the Sea of Galilee. Jesus sought time to teach the disciples because the multitudes often prevented Him from teaching the Twelve. This time of rest was spent profitably. The disciples needed to be instructed, and they were awaiting the approaching crowds.

6:4. The term "the passover" (*to pascha*) occurs in the New Testament 29 times, of which 10 are found in John's Gospel. The word

47. But if ye believe not his writings, how shall ye believe my words?: . . . there is no possibility that, *Barclay* . . . How can you rely upon My statements? *Fenton.*

1. After these things Jesus went over the sea of Galilee, which is the sea of Tiberias: Later on Jesus went to the further side, *Berkeley* . . . crossed over to the other side, *Beck* . . . otherwise called the Lake of Tiberias, *TCNT.*

2. And a great multitude followed him: A vast multitude, *Weymouth* . . . a vast crowd, *Williams* . . . a great throng, *Wuest.*

because they saw his miracles which he did on them that were diseased: . . . they had been viewing with a discerning eye, *Wuest* . . . because they recognized the power of God in action, *Barclay* . . . the signs of his mission, *TCNT* . . . the signs, *Murdock* . . . the wonderful cures that He had worked upon the ailing, *Norlie* . . . on account of the miraculous cures, *Norton* . . . he was continually performing, *Montgomery* . . . in his dealings with the sick, *Phillips* . . . effected upon the sick people, *Fenton.*

3. And Jesus went up into a mountain, and there he sat with his disciples: . . . into the hill country, *Barclay.*

4. And the passover, a feast of the Jews, was nigh: Now the passover was near, *Rotherham* . . . It was shortly before, *JB* . . . near the date, *Barclay* . . . The Jewish festival of the Passover, *Beck* . . . the great Jewish festival, *Norlie.*

2428.3 name-adj gen pl masc	1854.5 verb nom sing masc part aor act	3631.1 conj	3450.5 art sing masc	2400.1 name nom masc	3450.8 art acc pl masc
Ἰουδαίων.	5. ἐπάρας	οὖν	⸀ ὁ	Ἰησοῦς	τοὺς
Ioudaiōn	*eparas*	*oun*	*ho*	*Iēsous*	*tous*
Jews.	Having lifted up	then		Jesus	the

3652.8 noun acc pl masc	3450.8 art acc pl masc	3652.8 noun acc pl masc	3450.5 art sing masc	2400.1 name nom masc
ὀφθαλμοὺς,	[☆ τοὺς	ὀφθαλμοὺς	ὁ	Ἰησοῦς]
ophthalmous	*tous*	*ophthalmous*	*ho*	*Iēsous*
eyes,	[the	eyes		Jesus]

2504.1 conj	2277.7 verb nom sing masc part aor mid	3617.1 conj	4044.5 adj nom sing masc	3657.1 noun nom sing masc	2048.34 verb 3sing indic pres
καὶ	θεασάμενος	ὅτι	πολὺς	ὄχλος	ἔρχεται
kai	*theasamenos*	*hoti*	*polus*	*ochlos*	*erchetai*
and	having seen	that	a great	crowd	is coming

5.a.**Txt:** 02A,017K,036, 038,041,1,13,etc.byz. Gries,Word **Var:** 01ℵ,03B,05D,019L, 037,33,Lach,TregAlf, Tisc,We/Ho,Weis,Sod, UBS/☆

4242.1 prep	840.6 prs-pron acc sing masc	2978.5 verb 3sing indic pres act	4242.1 prep	3450.6 art acc sing masc	5213.4 name acc masc
πρὸς	αὐτὸν,	λέγει	πρὸς	⸀a τὸν ⸌	Φίλιππον,
pros	*auton*	*legei*	*pros*	*ton*	*Philippon*
to	him,	he says	to		Philip,

5.b.**Txt:** 017K,030U, Steph **Var:** 01ℵ,02A,03B,05D, 019L,021M,036,037, 038,byz.LachTreg,Alf, Tisc,We/Ho,Weis,Sod, UBS/☆

4019.1 adv	58.16 verb 1pl indic fut act	58.8 verb 1pl subj aor act	735.8 noun acc pl masc
Πόθεν	⸀ ἀγοράσομεν	[b☆ ἀγοράσωμεν]	ἄρτους
Pothen	*agorasomen*	*agorasōmen*	*artous*
From where	shall we buy	[may we buy]	loaves

2419.1 conj	2052.20 verb 3pl subj aor act	3642.7 dem-pron nom pl masc	3642.17 dem-pron sing neu	1156.2 conj	2978.26 verb 3sing indic imperf act
ἵνα	φάγωσιν	οὗτοι;	6. Τοῦτο	δὲ	ἔλεγεν
hina	*phagōsin*	*houtoi*	*Touto*	*de*	*elegen*
that	may eat	these?	This	but	he said

3847.4 verb nom sing masc part pres act	840.6 prs-pron acc sing masc	840.5 prs-pron nom sing masc	1056.1 conj	3471.11 verb 3sing indic plperf act	4949.9 intr-pron sing neu
πειράζων	αὐτόν·	αὐτὸς	γὰρ	ᾔδει	τί
peirazōn	*auton*	*autos*	*gar*	*ēdei*	*ti*
testing	him,	he	for	knew	what

7.a.**Var:** 01ℵ-org,05D, Tisc

3165.22 verb 3sing indic imperf act	4020.20 verb inf pres act	552.6 verb 3sing indic aor pass	552.2 verb 3sing indic pres
ἔμελλεν	ποιεῖν.	7. ⸀ ἀπεκρίθη	[a ἀποκρίνεται]
emellen	*poiein*	*apekrithē*	*apokrinetai*
he was about	to do.	Answered	[answering]

7.b.**Var:** p66,01ℵ,019L, 032W,Tisc,Weis,UBS/☆

840.4 prs-pron dat sing	3450.5 art sing masc	5213.1 name nom masc	1244.1 num card gen masc	1214.3 noun gen pl neu
αὐτῷ	[b☆+ ὁ]	Φίλιππος,	Διακοσίων	δηναρίων
autō	*ho*	*Philippos*	*Diakosiōn*	*dēnariōn*
him		Philip,	For two hundred	denarii

7.c.**Txt:** 05D,017K,036, 037,1,13,byz.Gries,Word **Var:** 01ℵ,02A,03B,019L, 038,041,33,it.bo.Lach, Treg,Alf,Tisc,We/Ho, WeisSod,UBS/☆

735.5 noun nom pl masc	3620.2 partic	708.2 verb 3pl indic pres act	840.2 prs-pron dat pl	2419.1 conj	1524.3 adj nom sing masc
ἄρτοι	οὐκ	ἀρκοῦσιν	αὐτοῖς	ἵνα	ἕκαστος
artoi	*ouk*	*arkousin*	*autois*	*hina*	*hekastos*
loaves	not	are sufficient	for them	that	each

7.d.**Txt:** 01ℵ,02A,017K, 019L,036,037,038,etc. byz.Lach,Alf,Tisc,Weis, Sod,UBS/☆ **Var:** p75,03B,05D,it.bo. Treg,We/Ho

840.1 prs-pron gen pl	1017.2 adj acc sing neu	4948.10 indef-pron sing neu	2956.18 verb 3sing subj aor act	2978.5 verb 3sing indic pres act
⸀c αὐτῶν ⸌	βραχύ	⸀d τι ⸌	λάβῃ.	8. Λέγει
autōn	*brachu*	*ti*	*labē*	*Legei*
of them	little	some	may receive.	Says

comes from the verb *paschō* meaning "to suffer." The origin of the Feast can be found in Exodus 12, when the Passover lamb was slain, and its flesh was roasted and eaten. The Feast celebrated the deliverance of the Jews from Egyptian bondage. The Passover of this verse was (A.D. 29) 1 year before the Passover at which Jesus was crucified. This is the third Passover of our Lord's ministry (see 2:13; 5:1).

The Passover Feast "was nigh" and accounts for the gathering of great crowds on their way to Jerusalem.

5. When Jesus then lifted up his eyes, and saw a great company come unto him: On looking up and seeing a large crowd approach, *Moffatt* . . . Looking up and observing a vast host coming, *Berkeley* . . . Jesus looked around and, seeing the great crowd, *Norlie* . . . raising his eyes, *NEB* . . . and having looked attentively, *Wuest* . . . vast throng, *Concordant* . . . an immense crowd, *Weymouth* . . . was flocking to him, *Campbell.*

he saith unto Philip, Whence shall we buy bread, that these may eat?: Where are we going to buy, *Adams* . . . for all these people, *BB.*

6:5. "Lifted up his eyes, and saw" is a typical Hebrew way of stressing Jesus' intense compassion for the multitude. We learn from Luke 9:12 and Mark 6:37 that the Lord tested the disciples by questioning them about the feeding of the multitude. Yet He knew what He would do. Jesus turned to Philip with a question (see 1:43 for Philip's background). In essence Jesus asked, "Where are we to buy bread on such short notice?" Perhaps Philip was in charge of provisions, though Judas was the treasurer for the apostles. Jesus' question also produces a number of parallels with Numbers 11 in the Old Testament. It is similar to Moses' question in Numbers 11:13. Other parallels between Numbers 11 and John 6 are: Numbers 11:1 and John 6:41,43; Numbers 11:7-9 and John 6:31ff.; Numbers 11:13 and John 6:51ff.; Numbers 11:22 and John 6:9,12 (cf. Brown, 29:233).

6. And this he said to prove him: for he himself knew what he would do: He said this to test him...what he intended to do, *Montgomery* . . . actually he already knew, *TEV* . . . for He well knew what He was about to do, *AmpB* . . . for he had determined what to do, *Norton* . . . had in mind, *NIV* . . . knew exactly what he was going to do, *JB.*

6:6. "To prove him" (i.e., Philip) discloses the reason Jesus asked the question. The Lord knew what He was going to do about the difficulty. The question to Philip called attention to their natural inability to provide food for such a great crowd.

When the Lord tests His people it is for their good. He strengthens by testing as a tree is made more fruitful by pruning (15:2,3).

7. Philip answered him, Two hundred pennyworth of bread is not sufficient for them: . . . 200 silver coins' worth, *SEB* . . . A year's wages would not buy enough, *Barclay.*

that every one of them may take a little: . . . for everybody to get even a morsel, *Moffatt* . . . for each of them to get just a little, *Beck* . . . have each receive a tiny bit, *Berkeley* . . . each person had only a small amount, *SEB* . . . get a bit, *Concordant* . . . take but a little, *Murdock* . . . to give each one even a bite, *Norlie* . . . even a scanty meal apiece, *Williams* . . . take a morsel, *Montgomery* . . . to have a scrap, *Adams.*

6:7. "Two hundred pennyworth" seems to be the total amount of their treasury (about $25–$30). A penny was the amount a laborer received for a day's work. Mark's Gospel gives the parallel to this miracle (Mark 6:37-44).

"Not sufficient for them" was the obvious conclusion drawn by Philip. According to verse 10 the number of men was about 5,000. It was no wonder that the money was not enough even if ample food could be found. Natural resources are always inadequate. No matter how much man has, a few more dollars seem to be needed. One should recall that man does not live by bread alone, but by every word that proceeds from the mouth of God (Deuteronomy 8:3).

John 6:9

840.4 prs-pron dat sing	1518.3 num card nom masc	1523.2 prep gen	3450.1 art gen pl	3073.6 noun gen pl masc	840.3 prs-pron gen sing
αὐτῷ	εἷς	ἐκ	τῶν	μαθητῶν	αὐτοῦ,
autō	*heis*	*ek*	*tōn*	*mathētōn*	*autou*
to him	one	of	the	disciples	his,

404.1 name nom masc	3450.5 art sing masc	79.1 noun nom sing masc	4468.2 name gen masc	3935.2 name gen masc
Ἀνδρέας	ὁ	ἀδελφὸς	Σίμωνος	Πέτρου,
Andreas	*ho*	*adelphos*	*Simōnos*	*Petrou*
Andrew	the	brother	of Simon	Peter,

9.a.**Txt:** 02A,017K,036,037,038,byz.Lach,Alf
Var: 01ℵ,03B,05D,019L,Treg,Tisc,We/Ho,Weis,Sod,UBS/⋆

1498.4 verb 3sing indic pres act	3671.1 noun nom sing neu	1518.9 num card neu	5436.1 adv	3614.16 rel-pron sing neu
9. Ἔστιν	παιδάριον	⸂a ἓν ⸃	ὧδε,	⸀ ὃ
Estin	*paidarion*	*hen*	*hōde*	*ho*
Is	little boy	one	here,	who

9.b.**Txt:** 01ℵ,05D-corr,017K,019L,036,037,038,byz.
Var: 02A,03B,05D-org,030U,Lach,Treg,Alf,Word,Tisc,We/HoWeis,Sod,UBS/⋆

3614.5 rel-pron nom sing masc	2174.4 verb 3sing indic pres act	3864.1 num card	735.8 noun acc pl masc	2889.2 adj acc pl masc	2504.1 conj
[b⋆ ὃς]	ἔχει	πέντε	ἄρτους	κριθίνους	καὶ
hos	*echei*	*pente*	*artous*	*krithinous*	*kai*
[idem]	has	five	loaves	barley	and

1411.3 num card	3659.3 noun acc pl neu	233.2 conj	3642.18 dem-pron pl neu	4949.9 intr-pron sing neu	1498.4 verb 3sing indic pres act
δύο	ὀψάρια·	ἀλλὰ	ταῦτα	τί	ἐστιν
duo	*opsaria*	*alla*	*tauta*	*ti*	*estin*
two	small fishes;	but	these	what	are

10.a.**Txt:** 02A,017K,032W,036,037,038,1,13,byz.GriesLach,Sod
Var: p75,01ℵ,03B,019L,Treg,Alf,Tisc,We/Ho,Weis,UBS/⋆

1519.1 prep	4965.5 dem-pron acc pl masc	1500.5 verb 3sing indic aor act	1156.2 conj	3450.5 art sing masc	2400.1 name nom masc
εἰς	τοσούτους;	**10.** Εἶπεν	⸂a δὲ ⸃	ὁ	Ἰησοῦς,
eis	*tosoutous*	*Eipen*	*de*	*ho*	*Iēsous*
for	so many?	Said	and		Jesus,

4020.36 verb 2pl impr aor act	3450.8 art acc pl masc	442.9 noun acc pl masc	375.5 verb inf aor act	1498.34 verb sing indic imperf act
Ποιήσατε	τοὺς	ἀνθρώπους	ἀναπεσεῖν.	ἦν
Poiēsate	*tous*	*anthrōpous*	*anapesein*	*ēn*
Make	the	men	to recline.	Was

1156.2 conj	5363.1 noun nom sing masc	4044.5 adj nom sing masc	1706.1 prep	3450.3 art dat sing	4964.3 noun dat sing masc	375.2 verb 3pl indic aor act
δὲ	χόρτος	πολὺς	ἐν	τῷ	τόπῳ.	⸀ ἀνέπεσον
de	*chortos*	*polus*	*en*	*tō*	*topō*	*anepeson*
now	grass	much	in	the	place:	reclined

10.b.**Txt:** 017K,030U,038,041,byz.
Var: 01ℵ,02A,03B,05D,019L,036,037,LachTreg,Alf,Tisc,We/Ho,Weis,Sod,UBS/⋆

375.7 verb 3pl indic aor act	3631.1 conj	3450.7 art pl masc	433.6 noun pl masc	3450.6 art acc sing masc
[b⋆ ἀνέπεσαν]	οὖν	οἱ	ἄνδρες	τὸν
anepesan	*oun*	*hoi*	*andres*	*ton*
[idem]	therefore	the	men,	the

10.c.**Txt:** p66,02A,017K,036,037,038,1,13,byz.Gries,LachWord
Var: 01ℵ,03B,05D,019L,Treg,Alf,Tisc,We/Ho,Weis,Sod,UBS/⋆

700.4 noun acc sing masc	5448.1 adv	5453.1 conj	3861.2 num card nom masc	2956.14 verb 3sing indic aor act
ἀριθμὸν	⸀ ὡσεὶ	[c⋆ ὡς]	πεντακισχίλιοι.	**11.** ἔλαβεν
arithmon	*hōsei*	*hōs*	*pentakischilioi*	*elaben*
number	about	[idem]	five thousand.	Took

11.a.**Txt:** 01ℵ-org,017K,036,037,byz.
Var: 01ℵ-corr,02A,03B,05D,019L,bo.Lach,Treg,Alf,Tisc,We/HoWeis,Sod,UBS/⋆

1156.2 conj	3631.1 conj	3450.8 art acc pl masc	735.8 noun acc pl masc	3450.5 art sing masc	2400.1 name nom masc
⸀ δὲ	[a⋆ οὖν]	τοὺς	ἄρτους	ὁ	Ἰησοῦς,
de	*oun*	*tous*	*artous*	*ho*	*Iēsous*
and	[therefore]	the	loaves		Jesus,

6:8. "Andrew, Simon Peter's brother" brought his brother Simon to Jesus (1:41). John also tells us in 1:44 that Andrew was of the same city as Philip. This probably indicates a close friendship between the two.

8. One of his disciples, Andrew, Simon Peter's brother, saith unto him:

9. There is a lad here, which hath five barley loaves, and two small fishes: There is a boy right here, *ET* . . . There is a servant here, *Moffatt* . . . a couple of fishes, *Weymouth.*

but what are they among so many?: . . . they won't be of much help, *Adams* . . . but what's the good of that for such a crowd, *Phillips* . . . But what use is that for a crowd like this? *Barclay* . . . but how long would that last, *SEB* . . . But they will certainly not be enough for all these people, *TEV.*

6:9. "There is a lad here." Who the lad was and why he had the small supply, we are not told. The lad here is called a *paidarion* which is a double diminutive of *pais. Paidarion* is rarely used, but it does recall the story of Elisha in 2 Kings 4 where his servant Gehazi is called a *paidarion.* This is of further significance because "boy" and "barley loaves" recalls Elisha's miracle of feeding the prophets in 2 Kings 4:38-44. This is one of several instances where Elisha may be considered a type of Christ.

Five loaves and two fish were an adequate supply for a small boy, who must have carried provisions while following the Lord. Barley loaves were not as tasty as wheat bread and were less expensive. Barley bread was the bread of the poor. The 5,000 men would be content to eat as poor people that day. The "loaves" were not as our loaves, but rather like flat pancakes.

"But what are these for so many people?" (NASB). First, the money supply was not sufficient. Now, the food the lad brought was totally inadequate. The two fish were small ones. But it is interesting to note that Jesus delights in making little boys feel so important by using their meager talents and supplies to satisfy the multitudes.

10. And Jesus said, Make the men sit down: Make the people recline, *Rotherham* . . . Get the people to lie down, *Moffatt* . . . lean back, *Concordant.*

Now there was much grass in the place: . . . plenty of grass at that spot, *Fenton* . . . The ground was covered with thick grass, *Weymouth.*

So the men sat down, in number about five thousand: . . . threw themselves down, *Williams.*

6:10. "Have the people sit down" (NASB). In the spring (6:4) the grass grew on the hillsides. The men literally reclined on the grass. The usual way one ate his meals was not in a chair, but by resting on the elbow with his head toward a low table. Here there was no table, for it was a picnic on the hillside.

"The men" (*tous anthrōpous*) could here include women also, but in Mark 6:44 the Greek word *andres* is used, indicating only the men. (Sometimes New Testament references follow the Old Testament custom of enumerating only men. This practice was likely repeated because censuses were taken of men for the purpose of war.) Therefore we may conclude that perhaps as many as 10,000 may have been fed from the 5 loaves and 2 fish.

11. And Jesus took the loaves; and when he had given thanks, he distributed to the disciples,

6:11. "Jesus took the loaves." "Took" is the word emphasized. Jesus took the offering of the lad though it was extremely small. No matter how meager the supply, He can make up the difference.

John 6:12

11.b.**Var:** 01ℵ,(05),it.Tisc

2504.1 conj	**2149.11** verb nom sing masc part aor act	**1233.2** verb 3sing indic aor act	**2149.9** verb 3sing indic aor act
καὶ	ʿ εὐχαριστήσας	διέδωκεν	[b εὐχαρίστησεν
kai	*eucharistēsas*	*diedōken*	*eucharistēsen*
and	having given thanks	distributed	[gave thanks

11.c.**Txt:** 01ℵ-corr,05D, 017K,036,037,038,13, byz.
Var: 01ℵ-org,02A,03B, 019L,041,33,bo.Lach Treg,Alf,Tisc,We/Ho, Weis,Sod,UBS/☆

2504.1 conj	**1319.14** verb 3sing indic aor act	**3450.4** art dat pl	**3073.7** noun dat pl masc	**3450.7** art pl masc	**1156.2** conj
καὶ	ἔδωκεν]	ʿc τοῖς	μαθηταῖς,	οἱ	δὲ
kai	*edōken*	*tois*	*mathētais*	*hoi*	*de*
and	gave]	to the	disciples,	the	and

3073.5 noun nom pl masc	**3450.4** art dat pl	**343.5** verb dat pl masc part pres	**3532.1** adv	**2504.1** conj	**1523.2** prep gen
μαθηταὶ ˎ	τοις	ἀνακειμένοις˙	ὁμοίως	καὶ	ἐκ
mathētai	*tois*	*anakeimenois*	*homoiōs*	*kai*	*ek*
disciples	to the	reclining;	in like manner	and	of

3450.1 art gen pl	**3659.2** noun gen pl neu	**3607.1** rel-pron sing	**2286.30** verb indic imperf act	**5453.1** conj	**1156.2** conj
τῶν	ὀψαρίων	ὅσον	ἤθελον.	**12.** ὡς	δὲ
tōn	*opsariōn*	*hoson*	*ēthelon*	*hōs*	*de*
the	small fishes	as much as	they wished.	When	and

1689.3 verb 3pl indic aor pass	**2978.5** verb 3sing indic pres act	**3450.4** art dat pl	**3073.7** noun dat pl masc	**840.3** prs-pron gen sing
ἐνεπλήσθησαν	λέγει	τοῖς	μαθηταῖς	αὐτοῦ,
eneplēsthēsan	*legei*	*tois*	*mathētais*	*autou*
they were filled	he says	to the	disciples	his,

4714.10 verb 2pl impr aor act	**3450.17** art pl neu	**3915.17** verb acc pl neu part aor act	**2774.2** noun acc pl neu	**2419.1** conj
Συναγάγετε	τὰ	περισσεύσαντα	κλάσματα,	ἵνα
Sunagagete	*ta*	*perisseusanta*	*klasmata*	*hina*
Gather together	the	over and above	fragments,	that

3231.1 partic	**4948.10** indef-pron sing neu	**616.24** verb 3sing subj aor mid	**4714.8** verb 3pl indic aor act	**3631.1** conj
μή	τι	ἀπόληται.	**13.** Συνήγαγον	οὖν
mē	*ti*	*apolētai*	*Sunēgagon*	*oun*
not	anything	may be lost.	They gathered together	therefore

2504.1 conj	**1065.2** verb 3pl indic aor act	**1420.1** num card	**2867.2** noun acc pl masc	**2774.1** noun gen pl neu
καὶ	ἐγέμισαν	δώδεκα	κοφίνους	κλασμάτων
kai	*egemisan*	*dōdeka*	*kophinous*	*klasmatōn*
and	filled	twelve	hand-baskets	of fragments

1523.2 prep gen	**3450.1** art gen pl	**3864.1** num card	**735.6** noun gen pl masc	**3450.1** art gen pl	**2889.1** adj gen pl masc
ἐκ	τῶν	πέντε	ἄρτων	τῶν	κριθίνων
ek	*tōn*	*pente*	*artōn*	*tōn*	*krithinōn*
from	the	five	loaves	the	barley

13.a.**Txt:** 01ℵ,02A,017K, 019L,1,13,etc.byz.Sod
Var: p75,03B,05D, 032W,Lach,Treg,Alf, Tisc,We/HoWeis,UBS/☆

3614.17 rel-pron pl neu	**3915.13** verb 3sing indic aor act	**3915.21** verb 3pl indic aor act	**3450.4** art dat pl
ἃ	ʿ ἐπερίσσευσεν	[a☆ ἐπερίσσευσαν]	τοῖς
ha	*eperisseusen*	*eperisseusan*	*tois*
which	were over and above	[idem]	to the

970.1 verb dat pl masc part perf act	**3450.7** art pl masc	**3631.1** conj	**442.6** noun nom pl masc	**1481.17** verb nom pl masc part aor act
βεβρωκόσιν.	**14.** Οἱ	οὖν	ἄνθρωποι	ἰδόντες
bebrōkosin	*Hoi*	*oun*	*anthrōpoi*	*idontes*
having eaten.	The	therefore	men	having seen

And having "given thanks" places Jesus' approval on the giving of thanks to God at mealtime (Deuteronomy 6:7; 8:10). "Thanks" (*eucharisteō*) is used 3 times in John's Gospel and 39 times in the New Testament. Mark uses *eulogeō*, "blessed." In His humanity Jesus gave thanks for their food; because of His deity He blessed the food.

"As much as they would" indicates that Jesus did not merely supply enough to sustain life. He gave them an abundance of bread and fish.

and the disciples to them that were set down: . . . and had them served to, *Berkeley* . . . distributed it to those reclining, *Sawyer* . . . to those who were resting on the ground, *Weymouth.*

and likewise of the fishes as much as they would: And the same, *Berkeley* . . . the fish was served in the same way, *Norlie* . . . so also the fish, as much as they wanted, *RSV* . . . as they desired, *Weymouth.*

6:12. "When they were filled" indicates that some lapse of time occurred so that the very hungry ate until they were satisfied.

"Gather up the fragments." The Jews broke their bread, they did not slice it. All the food not eaten would be in fragments. Jesus satisfied all the people, but He did not waste anything. By this gathering the disciples were taught the economy of God's provisions: not a crumb was to be "lost." Believers are to be good stewards of natural blessings and supernatural gifts. The entire narrative is one of a great sign performed by the Lord; it is done orderly, completely, and with conservation. Jesus did not often supply the needs of people in this supernatural way. His own needs were supplied in the usual way (see Luke 4:3,4).

12. When they were filled, he said unto his disciples: And when they had had enough, *BB* . . . When all were fully satisfied, *Weymouth.*

Gather up the fragments that remain, that nothing be lost: Collect the pieces that are left over, *Phillips* . . . Pick up the pieces, *Williams* . . . the surplus, *Concordant* . . . the broken pieces, *Fenton* . . . the leftovers, *Norlie* . . . so that nothing will be wasted, *Beck.*

6:13. The disciples acted in accord with the Lord's command. Each apostle had a basket, for the basket was standard traveling gear. "Baskets" (*kophinous*) occurs six times in the New Testament, and only here in John. It was made of wicker-work and used for carrying food. The other word for "basket" (*spuridas*) indicates a flexible mat-basket. The latter word is used in the parallel accounts of the feeding of the 4,000 (Mark 8:8; Matthew 15:37). "Twelve baskets" were filled with fragments of food. The size of the baskets is not given; yet the measure must have been considerable. The size may have varied according to the individual's needs. After the great multitude (between 5,000 and 10,000 people) were fed, more fragments were gathered than the amount with which Jesus started. The 12 baskets filled with fragments of bread are proof of the miracle. No one of the multitude objected when the 12 apostles gathered up the leftovers. The people knew Jesus had multiplied the food and given it to them.

13. Therefore they gathered them together: And they collected them, *Rieu* . . . So they did as he suggested, *Phillips.*

and filled twelve baskets with the fragments of the five barley loaves: . . . with the broken pieces, *Phillips* . . . and filled twelve handbaskets, *Norlie* . . . twelve bags, *Fenton* . . . twelve traveling-baskets, *Sawyer.*

which remained over and above unto them that had eaten: . . . which were left over by them who had eaten, *Rotherham* . . . which were more than the eaters wanted, *Williams* . . . left uneaten by the people, *ALBA* . . . after all had eaten, *Norlie.*

6:14. This effect of the miracle of feeding the multitude is recorded by John only. The purpose of this Gospel is to reveal the

John 6:15

14.a.**Txt:** 02A,017K, 019L,036,037,038,1,13, 33,byz.Gries,Lach
Var: p75,01ℵ,03B,05D, 032W,it.sa.Treg,AlfTisc, We/Ho,Weis,Sod,UBS/☆

3614.16 rel-pron sing neu	**4020.24** verb 3sing indic aor act	**4447.1** noun sing neu	**3450.5** art sing masc	**2400.1** name nom masc
ὃ	ἐποίησεν	σημεῖον	˹a ὁ	Ἰησοῦς, ˺
ho	*epoiēsen*	*sēmeion*	*ho*	*Iēsous*
what	had done	sign		Jesus,

2978.25 verb indic imperf act	**3617.1** conj	**3642.4** dem-pron nom sing masc	**1498.4** verb 3sing indic pres act	**228.1** adv	**3450.5** art sing masc
ἔλεγον,	Ὅτι	Οὗτός	ἐστιν	ἀληθῶς	ὁ
elegon	*Hoti*	*Houtos*	*estin*	*alēthōs*	*ho*
said,		This	is	truly	the

4254.1 noun nom sing masc	**3450.5** art sing masc	**2048.44** verb nom sing masc part pres	**1519.1** prep	**3450.6** art acc sing masc	**2862.4** noun acc sing masc
προφήτης	ὁ	ἐρχόμενος	εἰς	τὸν	κόσμον.
prophētēs	*ho*	*erchomenos*	*eis*	*ton*	*kosmon*
prophet	the	coming	into	the	world.

2400.1 name nom masc	**3631.1** conj	**1091.26** verb nom sing masc part aor act	**3617.1** conj	**3165.6** verb 3pl indic pres act
15. Ἰησοῦς	οὖν	γνοὺς	ὅτι	μέλλουσιν
Iēsous	*oun*	*gnous*	*hoti*	*mellousin*
Jesus	therefore	knowing	that	they are about

15.a.**Txt:** 05D,017K,036, 037,038,13,byz.
Var: p75,01ℵ-corr,02A, 03B,019L,032W,1,Lach Treg,Alf,Tisc,We/Ho, Weis,Sod,UBS/☆

2048.53 verb inf pres	**2504.1** conj	**720.4** verb inf pres act	**840.6** prs-pron acc sing masc	**2419.1** conj	**4020.32** verb 3pl subj aor act
ἔρχεσθαι	καὶ	ἁρπάζειν	αὐτὸν,	ἵνα	ποιήσωσιν
erchesthai	*kai*	*harpazein*	*auton*	*hina*	*poiēsōsin*
to come	and	to seize	him,	that	they may make

15.b.**Var:** 01ℵ-org,Dia. Tisc,ert.Tisc

840.6 prs-pron acc sing masc	**928.4** noun acc sing masc	**400.2** verb 3sing indic aor act	**5180.1** verb 3sing indic pres act	**3687.1** adv
˹a αὐτὸν ˺	βασιλέα,	˹ ἀνεχώρησεν	[b φεύγει]	πάλιν
auton	*basilea*	*anechōrēsen*	*pheugei*	*palin*
him	king,	withdrew	[flees]	again

1519.1 prep	**3450.16** art sing neu	**3598.1** noun sing neu	**840.5** prs-pron nom sing masc	**3304.2** adj nom sing masc	**5453.1** conj
εἰς	τὸ	ὄρος	αὐτὸς	μόνος.	**16.** Ὡς
eis	*to*	*oros*	*autos*	*monos*	*Hōs*
to	the	mountain	himself	alone.	When

1156.2 conj	**3662.1** adj nom sing fem	**1090.33** verb 3sing indic aor mid	**2568.15** verb 3pl indic aor act	**3450.7** art pl masc	**3073.5** noun nom pl masc
δὲ	ὀψία	ἐγένετο	κατέβησαν	οἱ	μαθηταὶ
de	*opsia*	*egeneto*	*katebēsan*	*hoi*	*mathētai*
and	evening	it became	went down	the	disciples

840.3 prs-pron gen sing	**1894.3** prep	**3450.12** art acc sing fem	**2258.4** noun acc sing fem	**2504.1** conj	**1671.7** verb nom pl masc part aor act
αὐτοῦ	ἐπὶ	τὴν	θάλασσαν,	**17.** καὶ	ἐμβάντες
autou	*epi*	*tēn*	*thalassan*	*kai*	*embantes*
his	to	the	sea,	and	having entered

17.a.**Txt:** 02A,05D,017K, 032W,036,038,1,13,byz. LachWeis
Var: p75,01ℵ,03B,019L, 037,33,Treg,AlfTisc, We/Ho,Sod,UBS/☆

1519.1 prep	**3450.16** art sing neu	**4003.1** noun sing neu	**2048.60** verb 3pl indic imperf	**3871.1** adv	**3450.10** art gen sing fem
εἰς	˹a τὸ ˺	πλοῖον	ἤρχοντο	πέραν	τῆς
eis	*to*	*ploion*	*ērchonto*	*peran*	*tēs*
into	the	boat	they were going	over	the

2258.2 noun gen sing fem	**1519.1** prep	**2555.1** name fem	**2555.2** name fem
θαλάσσης	εἰς	˹ Καπερναούμ.	[☆ Καφαρναούμ.]
thalassēs	*eis*	*Kapernaoum*	*Kapharnaoum*
sea	to	Capernaum.	[idem]

deity of Jesus; therefore John tells us the people were aware of the sign. The people even stated Jesus was "that Prophet that should come into the world" (see Deuteronomy 18:15-18). God had used Moses to feed the people with manna in the wilderness. The prophet like Moses surely would do a similar miracle. The people saw the parallel between the manna and the miracle bread, thus concluding that Jesus was "the prophet" like Moses. The popular interpretation of "the prophet" was that He was the Messiah.

14. Then those men, when they had seen the miracle that Jesus did, said: . . . saw the evidence which He had produced, they exclaimed, *Fenton* . . . the sign, *Berkeley* . . . he had performed, *Weymouth.*

This is of a truth that prophet that should come into the world: . . . this is indeed, *Weymouth* . . . Truly, this is the Prophet who was to come, *Norlie.*

6:15. The people became excited with the prospect that Jesus might yet fulfill their expectations of a political Messiah. After all, one who could feed over 5,000 could sustain an army with miracle rations. Even Moses was a semi-military leader. If the Prophet was like Moses, perhaps they thought they might yet drive out the Romans.

"They would come and take him by force." The kingship of Messiah had roots in the promises God made to King David that his seed would rule the nation forever (2 Samuel 7). Yet it was the Father who would bring the King and kingdom together in His own time. Even the disciples asked Jesus, after the Resurrection, the same question (Acts 1:6).

"He departed again into a mountain." "Again" refers to verse 3 which states that Jesus went up on the mountain. Jesus sent the apostles by boat toward the western shore. He then sent the multitude away. Mark and Matthew tell us that Jesus went up on the mountain to pray (Mark 6:46; Matthew 14:23). John omits telling us Jesus' prayer time, but gives the reason Jesus went up on the mountain. He knew it was not yet time for Him to become Israel's king: therefore He withdrew.

15. When Jesus therefore perceived that they would come and take him by force, to make him a king: Since Jesus knew that they were about, *Norlie* . . . So having discovered that they were intending to come, *TCNT* . . . aware that they intended, *Berkeley* . . . that they were about to come and carry him off by force, *Weymouth* . . . for the purpose, *Fenton* . . . to crown Him king, *Williams.*

he departed again into a mountain himself alone: . . . he fled again, *Confraternity* . . . withdrew again into, *ASV* . . . retired once more, *Phillips* . . . the hills by himself, *RSV* . . . alone by Himself, *Norlie.*

16. And when even was now come, his disciples went down unto the sea: But when evening came, *Rotherham* . . . Meanwhile, as it got late, *Beck.*

6:16. "Even was now come" speaks of a time beginning at sunset and extending to about 9 o'clock.

The "sea" was the Sea of Galilee. Mark tells us that Jesus had sent the disciples across the sea toward Bethsaida, on the northeast shore (Mark 6:45). John tells us that they were going toward Capernaum, on the northwest shore (verse 17). Perhaps the wind blew them off course.

17. And entered into a ship, and went over the sea toward Capernaum: . . . they got on board, *Weymouth* . . . boarded a boat, *Berkeley* . . . and embarking in a boat they started, *Moffatt* . . . returning over the lake, *Fenton* . . . and sat in a ship, *Murdock* . . . in a vessel, *Scarlett.*

6:17. The darkness was due in part to the storm. Usual occurrences are sometimes intensified by unusual events. One's life is occasionally upset by a compounding of circumstances. At such times, rely on Jesus.

John 6:18

17.b.**Var:** 01ℵ,05D,Tisc

2504.1 conj	4508.1 noun nom sing fem	2218.1 adv	1090.65 verb 3sing indic plperf mid	2608.1 verb 3sing indic aor act	1156.2 conj
ʻ καὶ	σκοτία	ἤδη	ἐγεγόνει,	[b κατέλαβεν	δὲ
kai	*skotia*	*ēdē*	*egegonei*	*katelaben*	*de*
And	dark	already	it had become,	[came upon	and

17.c.**Txt:** p28,02A,017K, 036,037,038,1,byz.sa. **Var:** p75,01ℵ,03B,05D, 019L,032W,33,it.bo. Lach,Treg,Alf,Tisc, We/Ho,WeisSod,UBS/☆

840.8 prs-pron acc pl masc	3450.9 art nom sing fem	4508.1 noun nom sing fem	2504.1 conj	3620.2 partic	3632.1 adv
αὐτοὺς	ἡ	σκοτία]	καὶ	ʻ οὐκ	[c☆ οὔπω]
autous	*hē*	*skotia*	*kai*	*ouk*	*oupō*
them	the	darkness]	and	not	[not yet]

17.d.**Var:** 01ℵ,(05),Tisc

2048.27 verb 3sing indic plperf act	4242.1 prep	840.8 prs-pron acc pl masc	3450.5 art sing masc	2400.1 name nom masc	2400.1 name nom masc
ἐληλύθει	ʻ πρὸς	αὐτοὺς	ὁ	Ἰησοῦς,	[d Ἰησοῦς
elēluthei	*pros*	*autous*	*ho*	*Iēsous*	*Iēsous*
had come	to	them		Jesus,	[Jesus

4242.1 prep	840.8 prs-pron acc pl masc	3614.9 rel-pron nom sing fem	4885.1 conj	2258.1 noun nom sing fem	415.2 noun gen sing masc
πρὸς	αὐτούς,]	18. ἡ	τε	θάλασσα	ἀνέμου
pros	*autous*	*hē*	*te*	*thalassa*	*anemou*
to	them,]	which	and	sea	by a wind

18.a.**Var:** 03B,019L, 030U,Treg,Alf,We/Ho, Weis

3144.3 adj gen sing masc	4014.3 verb gen sing masc part pres act	1320.6 verb 3sing indic imperf pass	1320.7 verb 3sing indic imperf pass
μεγάλου	πνέοντος	ʻ διηγείρετο.	[a διεγείρετο.]
megalou	*pneontos*	*diēgeireto*	*diegeireto*
strong	blowing	was rough.	[idem]

19.a.**Var:** 01ℵ-org,05D, it.Tisc

1630.2 verb nom pl masc part perf act	3631.1 conj	5453.1 conj	4563.3 noun acc pl masc	4563.4 noun pl neu
19. ἐληλακότες	οὖν	ὡς	ʻ σταδίους	[a στάδια]
elēlakotes	*oun*	*hōs*	*stadious*	*stadia*
Having rowed	then	about	stadia	[idem]

1490.1 num card	1489.2 num card	3864.1 num card	2211.1 conj	4984.1 num card
ʻ εἰκοσιπέντε	[☆ εἴκοσι	πέντε]	ἢ	τριάκοντα
eikosipente	*eikosi*	*pente*	*ē*	*triakonta*
twenty-five	[idem]		or	thirty

2311.5 verb 3pl indic pres act	3450.6 art acc sing masc	2400.3 name acc masc	3906.11 verb acc part pres act	1894.3 prep
θεωροῦσιν	τὸν	Ἰησοῦν	περιπατοῦντα	ἐπὶ
theōrousin	*ton*	*Iēsoun*	*peripatounta*	*epi*
they see		Jesus	walking	on

3450.10 art gen sing fem	2258.2 noun gen sing fem	2504.1 conj	1445.1 adv	3450.2 art gen sing	4003.2 noun gen sing neu
τῆς	θαλάσσης,	καὶ	ἐγγὺς	τοῦ	πλοίου
tēs	*thalassēs*	*kai*	*engus*	*tou*	*ploiou*
the	sea,	and	near	the	boat

1090.20 verb sing part pres	2504.1 conj	5236.13 verb 3pl indic aor pass	3450.5 art sing masc	1156.2 conj
γινόμενον·	καὶ	ἐφοβήθησαν.	20. ὁ	δὲ
ginomenon	*kai*	*ephobēthēsan*	*ho*	*de*
coming,	and	they were frightened.	The	but

2978.5 verb 3sing indic pres act	840.2 prs-pron dat pl	1466.1 prs-pron nom 1sing	1498.2 verb 1sing indic pres act	3231.1 partic	5236.6 verb 2pl impr pres
λέγει	αὐτοῖς,	Ἐγώ	εἰμι·	μὴ	φοβεῖσθε.
legei	*autois*	*Egō*	*eimi*	*mē*	*phobeisthe*
says	to them,	I	am;	not	fear.

The reference to darkness (*skotia*) is important on both the historical and spiritual levels. "The disciples, left to themselves, are in 'darkness' (cf. 1:5), far from Jesus and exposed to the onslaughts of hostile forces" (Schnackenburg, *Gospel According to St. John*, 2:26). The Gospel of John frequently uses *skotia* (darkness) and *phōs* (light) to refer to both physical and spiritual realities. When Nicodemus came to Jesus "by night" (3:2) he was told that "men loved darkness rather than light, because their deeds were evil," that Jesus is the "light (who) is come into the world," and that "he that doeth truth cometh to the light" (3:19,21).

First John 1:5 states, "God is light, and in him is no darkness." In the Gospel of John, it is God's Son Jesus who comes as the Light of the World (John 8:12; 9:5), bringing life and light to men (John 1:4; 3:19) if they walk in the light (1 John 1:7). Ultimately, it is faith in Jesus which brings victory over darkness (1 John 5:4), and Jesus' sign of walking on the sea helped provide this kind of faith to the disciples.

Jesus had not given the disciples any indication as to when He would come to them. They were allowed to row in the darkness. They believed Jesus would come to them, but they did not know when. Jesus had gone to the mountain to pray during their brief separation from Him when their faith was sorely tested.

6:18. The sea began to be stirred up because a stormy wind was blowing. The Ghor (depression) of this area, almost 700 feet below sea level, provides a path for sudden and strong winds. Storms can be fierce on the Sea of Galilee. The disciples were experienced fishermen on the lake, but this storm was especially violent.

6:19. The distance would be equal to about halfway across the lake if they had gone on a straight course. The disciples had labored on the oars several hours.

"They see Jesus walking on the sea." Mark says the time was the fourth watch of the night (3–4 o'clock) when they saw Jesus coming toward them. They did not know it was Jesus, but thought it was a spirit (Mark 6:49). John says "they were afraid." The verb is an aorist tense matter-of-fact statement. John does not relate that Peter walked on the water to go to Jesus. The purpose of John's Gospel is to reveal Jesus as the Son of God through His mighty signs. Jesus walked on the sea as if His feet had solid support, yet the waves lashed high around Him and the wind blew with great force. Christ's calm majesty coupled with the miracle of walking on the water indicates His divine origin.

6:20. According to Mark 6:48, Jesus intended to pass by them. This may have been to give them opportunity to invite Him into

And it was now dark, and Jesus was not come to them: Darkness had overtaken them, *Berkeley* . . . By this time darkness, *TCNT* . . . By this time it had become dark, *Weymouth* . . . it was already dark, yet Jesus had not come back to them, *Norlie* . . . By this time it was already dark and Jesus had not yet arrived, *Barclay* . . . Jesus had not returned to them, *Phillips* . . . Jesus hadn't yet joined them, *Adams.*

18. And the sea arose by reason of a great wind that blew: . . . the Sea, too, was getting rough, *TCNT* . . . while the sea was mounting, *Berkeley* . . . the sea was boisterous against them, for a violent wind was blowing, *Murdock* . . . because a strong wind was blowing, *Phillips, Williams* . . . a tempestuous wind, *Campbell* . . . the lake became rough, *SEB* . . . it was blowing a gale, *ET* . . . by a great wind blowing, *Sawyer* . . . and stir up the lake, *Beck* . . . on account of the violent wind then blowing, *Fenton.*

19. So when they had rowed about five and twenty or thirty furlongs: After they had rowed three or four miles, *Montgomery.*

they see Jesus walking on the sea, and drawing nigh unto the ship: . . . getting close to the vessel, *Berkeley.*

and they were afraid: . . . and they were terrified, *Beck* . . . they were terror-stricken, *Williams* . . . fear gripped them, *Barclay* . . . they got frightened, *Norlie.*

20. But he saith unto them, It is I; be not afraid: But He told them, It is I; have no fear, *Berkeley* . . . stop being afraid, *Williams.*

John 6:21

2286.30 verb indic imperf act	3631.1 conj	2956.31 verb inf aor act	840.6 prs-pron acc sing masc	1519.1 prep	3450.16 art sing neu
21. Ἤθελον	οὖν	λαβεῖν	αὐτὸν	εἰς	τὸ
Ethelon	*oun*	*labein*	*auton*	*eis*	*to*
They were willing	then	to receive	him	into	the

4003.1 noun sing neu	2504.1 conj	2091.1 adv	3450.16 art sing neu	4003.1 noun sing neu	1090.33 verb 3sing indic aor mid
πλοῖον,	καὶ	εὐθέως	⸀ τὸ	πλοῖον	ἐγένετο
ploion	*kai*	*eutheōs*	*to*	*ploion*	*egeneto*
boat,	and	immediately	the	boat	was

1090.33 verb 3sing indic aor mid	3450.16 art sing neu	4003.1 noun sing neu	1894.3 prep	3450.10 art gen sing fem	1087.2 noun gen sing fem
[☆ ἐγένετο	τὸ	πλοῖον]	ἐπὶ	⸀ τῆς	γῆς
egeneto	*to*	*ploion*	*epi*	*tēs*	*gēs*
[was	the	boat]	at	the	land

21.a.**Var:** 01א-org,13,28, Tisc

3450.12 art acc sing fem	1087.4 noun acc sing fem	1519.1 prep	3614.12 rel-pron acc sing fem	5055.11 verb 3pl indic imperf act	3450.11 art dat sing fem
[a τὴν	γῆν]	εἰς	ἣν	ὑπῆγον.	**22.** Τῇ
tēn	*gēn*	*eis*	*hēn*	*hupēgon*	*Tē*
[the	land]	to	which	they were going.	On the

1872.1 adv	3450.5 art sing masc	3657.1 noun nom sing masc	3450.5 art sing masc	2449.27 verb nom sing masc part perf act
ἐπαύριον	ὁ	ὄχλος	ὁ	ἑστηκὼς
epaurion	*ho*	*ochlos*	*ho*	*hestēkōs*
next day	the	crowd	the	having stood

3871.1 adv	3450.10 art gen sing fem	2258.2 noun gen sing fem	1481.16 verb nom sing masc part aor act
πέραν	τῆς	θαλάσσης,	⸀ ἰδὼν
peran	*tēs*	*thalassēs*	*idōn*
the other side	of the	sea,	having seen

22.a.**Txt:** 017K,036,(037) ,1,13,byz.Gries,Word
Var: p75,02A,03B,(019), 032W,038,sa.bo.Lach, Treg,Alf,Tisc,We/Ho Weis,Sod,UBS/☆

1481.1 verb indic aor act	3617.1 conj	4002.1 noun nom sing neu	241.14 adj sing neu	3620.2 partic	1498.34 verb sing indic imperf act
[a☆ εἶδον]	ὅτι	πλοιάριον	ἄλλο	οὐκ	ἦν
eidon	*hoti*	*ploiarion*	*allo*	*ouk*	*ēn*
[saw]	that	small boat	other	no	was

22.b.**Txt:** (01-org),017K, 038,28,700,byz.
Var: p75,01א-corr,02A, 03B,019L,032W,1,565, 1079,it.bo.Gries,Lach, Treg,Alf,Tisc,We/Ho, Weis,Sod,UBS/☆

1550.1 adv	1479.1 conj	3231.1 partic	1518.9 num card neu	1552.16 dem-pron sing neu	1519.1 prep	3614.16 rel-pron sing neu
ἐκεῖ	εἰ	μὴ	ἓν	⸀b ἐκεῖνο	εἰς	ὃ
ekei	*ei*	*mē*	*hen*	*ekeino*	*eis*	*ho*
there	if	not	one	that	into	which

1671.2 verb 3pl indic aor act	3450.7 art pl masc	3073.5 noun nom pl masc	840.3 prs-pron gen sing	2504.1 conj	3617.1 conj	3620.3 partic
ἐνέβησαν	οἱ	μαθηταὶ	αὐτοῦ, ⸌	καὶ	ὅτι	οὐ
enebēsan	*hoi*	*mathētai*	*autou*	*kai*	*hoti*	*ou*
entered	the	disciples	his,	and	that	not

4747.1 verb 3sing indic aor act	3450.4 art dat pl	3073.7 noun dat pl masc	840.3 prs-pron gen sing	3450.5 art sing masc	2400.1 name nom masc
συνεισῆλθεν	τοῖς	μαθηταῖς	αὐτοῦ	ὁ	Ἰησοῦς
suneisēlthen	*tois*	*mathētais*	*autou*	*ho*	*Iēsous*
went with	the	disciples	his		Jesus

22.c.**Txt:** 036,037,038, byz.
Var: 01א,02A,03B,05D, 017K,019L,Gries,Lach, Treg,AlfTisc,We/Ho, Weis,Sod,UBS/☆

1519.1 prep	3450.16 art sing neu	4002.1 noun nom sing neu	4003.1 noun sing neu	233.2 conj	3304.5 adj nom pl masc
εἰς	τὸ	⸀ πλοιάριον,	[c☆ πλοῖον]	ἀλλὰ	μόνοι
eis	*to*	*ploiarion*	*ploion*	*alla*	*monoi*
into	the	small boat,	[idem]	but	alone

the boat. Because of His compassion for their fear, He spoke to them. "It is I; be not afraid." At this point Matthew 14:28 records Peter's desire to walk on the water as Jesus did. Fear dissipates when Jesus comes to us in our struggles. His words, "It is I," are most assuring. Jesus' words remove fear, and we become encouraged, like Peter, to undertake the impossible by relying on the Lord. Matthew records that Peter did walk (*peripatēsen,* aorist indicative verb) on the water. Usually some criticize Peter for sinking and forget that he did what no other man has done.

At first glance, the sign of walking on the sea may have little to do with Jesus' previous sign of feeding the multitude, or of the following discourse on the bread of life. There is a connection, however, and it is provided by Jesus' words, *egō eimi* ("I am"). These words are the divine revelation of who God (and therefore Jesus) is (cf. Exodus 3:6). This story, therefore, provides a corrective to the misunderstanding of the crowd who wanted to take Jesus by force and make Him king.

Throughout the ministry of Jesus, the crowds wanted to see spectacular deeds and have their physical needs met. The crowds, however, never understood that Jesus came not to entertain, nor to give physical water or bread; He wrought miracles so men might believe in Him as the Son of God (20:30,31). The crowds wanted to make Jesus a king; Jesus wanted to be known as the "I am." Four times in the remainder of this chapter Jesus refers to himself as the "I am." He is the Bread of Life (6:35,48); He is the Living Bread (6:51); He is the Bread which has come down from heaven (6:41).

6:21. "Then they willingly" means they desired greatly to take Him into the boat. No longer did they fear Him as a spirit, but they wanted Him to come aboard. "Immediately" indicates they had reached their destination. The last half of the trip was not accomplished by rowing, but by the divine action of Christ. John related the distance they had rowed (verse 19). But as soon as Jesus was on board, the boat glided swiftly to shore.

6:22. "The day following" means after the miracle occurred. The whole verse shows the astonishment of the multitude as to the whereabouts of Jesus. They had intended to make Him king. They thought He was still on the mountain. The multitude took note that the only boat in which Jesus could have crossed the lake was still there. They knew He had sent the disciples to the other side in the early part of the previous evening. Where could Jesus have gone? The multitude did not know that Jesus had walked across the lake.

21. Then they willingly received him into the ship: And after this they were glad to take him into the boat, *TCNT* . . . So they gladly took him aboard, *Phillips* . . . Then they wanted to take Him into, *Adams* . . . they agreed to take him on board, *Moffatt* . . . they willingly took him into the ship, *Sawyer.*

and immediately the ship was at the land whither they went: . . . and directly, *Murdock* . . . And in a moment the boat came to the shore, *Beck* . . . and immediately the boat reached the shore they were making for, *Montgomery* . . . at the point to which they were going, *Weymouth* . . . straight towards the land they steered for, *Fenton.*

22. The day following: On the morrow, *ASV* . . . Next morning, *Weymouth, Norlie.*

when the people which stood on the other side of the sea: The people who remained on the further side of the lake, *TCNT* . . . the people were still lingering, *Beck* . . . the crowd which was still on the other shore of the lake learned, *Norlie.*

saw that there was none other boat there: . . . that there was no other boat there, *HBIE* . . . that there had only been one boat there, *Barclay.*

save that one where into his disciples were entered: . . . had embarked, *Norlie.*

and that Jesus went not with his disciples into the boat: . . . and that Jesus had not gone aboard with his disciples, *Moffatt* . . . had not gone into the boat along with, *Norlie* . . . that Jesus had not embarked on it with his disciples, *Phillips* . . . Jesus had not got into the boat with his disciples, *Barclay.*

John 6:23

23.a.**Txt:** 02A,017K,032W,036,037,038,13,byz.Lach,Alf
Var: p75,03B,019L,1,bo.Treg,Tisc,We/Ho,Weis,Sod,UBS/☆

23.b.**Var:** 017K,019L,021M,036,1,33,Tisc,Sod

23.c.**Var:** p75,03B,Lach,We/Ho

3450.7 art pl masc	**3073.5** noun nom pl masc	**840.3** prs-pron gen sing	**562.1** verb indic aor act	**241.15** adj pl neu	**1156.2** conj
οἱ	μαθηταὶ	αὐτοῦ	ἀπῆλθον,	**23.** ἄλλα	⌜a δὲ ⌝
hoi	*mathētai*	*autou*	*apēlthon*	*alla*	*de*
the	disciples	his	went away,	other	but

2048.3 verb 3sing indic aor act	**2048.1** verb indic aor act	**4002.3** noun acc pl neu	**4003.4** noun pl neu	**1523.2** prep gen
⌜ ἦλθεν	[b ἦλθον]	⌜ πλοιάρια	[c πλοῖα]	ἐκ
ēlthen	*ēlthon*	*ploiaria*	*ploia*	*ek*
came	[idem]	small boats	[idem]	from

4933.1 name gen fem	**1445.1** adv	**3450.2** art gen sing	**4964.2** noun gen sing masc	**3562.1** adv	**2052.27** verb indic aor pass
Τιβεριάδος	ἐγγὺς	τοῦ	τόπου	ὅπου	ἔφαγον
Tiberiados	*engus*	*tou*	*topou*	*hopou*	*ephagon*
Tiberias	near	the	place	where	they ate

3450.6 art acc sing masc	**735.4** noun acc sing masc	**2149.12** verb gen sing masc part aor act	**3450.2** art gen sing	**2935.2** noun gen sing masc
τὸν	ἄρτον,	εὐχαριστήσαντος	τοῦ	κυρίου·
ton	*arton*	*eucharistēsantos*	*tou*	*kuriou*
the	bread,	having given thanks	the	Lord;

3616.1 conj	**3631.1** conj	**1481.3** verb 3sing indic aor act	**3450.5** art sing masc	**3657.1** noun nom sing masc	**3617.1** conj
24. ὅτε	οὖν	εἶδεν	ὁ	ὄχλος	ὅτι
hote	*oun*	*eiden*	*ho*	*ochlos*	*hoti*
when	therefore	saw	the	crowd	that

2400.1 name nom masc	**3620.2** partic	**1498.4** verb 3sing indic pres act	**1550.1** adv	**3624.1** adv	**3450.7** art pl masc
Ἰησοῦς	οὐκ	ἔστιν	ἐκεῖ	οὐδὲ	οἱ
Iēsous	*ouk*	*estin*	*ekei*	*oude*	*hoi*
Jesus	not	is	there	nor	the

24.a.**Txt:** 030U,036,Steph
Var: 01ℵ-corr,02A,03B,05D,017K,019L,037,038,byz.Gries,Lach,Treg,AlfTisc,We/Ho,Weis,Sod,UBS/☆

24.b.**Txt:** 02A,017K,036,037,038,1,byz.Gries,Word
Var: 01ℵ-corr,03B,05D,019L,33,Lach,Treg,Alf,Tisc,We/HoWeis,Sod,UBS/☆

3073.5 noun nom pl masc	**840.3** prs-pron gen sing	**1671.2** verb 3pl indic aor act	**2504.1** conj	**840.7** prs-pron nom pl masc	**1519.1** prep
μαθηταὶ	αὐτοῦ,	ἐνέβησαν	⌜a καὶ ⌝	αὐτοὶ	εἰς
mathētai	*autou*	*enebēsan*	*kai*	*autoi*	*eis*
disciples	his,	they entered	also	themselves	into

3450.17 art pl neu	**4003.4** noun pl neu	**4002.3** noun acc pl neu	**2504.1** conj	**2048.1** verb indic aor act	**1519.1** prep
τὰ	⌜ πλοῖα	[b☆ πλοιάρια]	καὶ	ἦλθον	εἰς
ta	*ploia*	*ploiaria*	*kai*	*ēlthon*	*eis*
the	boats	[idem]	and	came	to

2555.1 name fem	**2555.2** name fem	**2195.10** verb nom pl masc part pres act	**3450.6** art acc sing masc
⌜ Καπερναοὺμ,	[☆ Καφαρναοὺμ]	ζητοῦντες	τὸν
Kapernaoum	*Kapharnaoum*	*zētountes*	*ton*
Capernaum,	[idem]	seeking	

2400.3 name acc masc	**2504.1** conj	**2128.18** verb nom pl masc part aor act	**840.6** prs-pron acc sing masc	**3871.1** adv
Ἰησοῦν.	**25.** καὶ	εὑρόντες	αὐτὸν	πέραν
Iēsoun	*kai*	*heurontes*	*auton*	*peran*
Jesus.	And	having found	him	the other side

3450.10 art gen sing fem	**2258.2** noun gen sing fem	**1500.3** verb indic aor act	**840.4** prs-pron dat sing	**4318.1** noun sing masc	**4078.1** adv
τῆς	θαλάσσης,	εἶπον	αὐτῷ,	Ῥαββί,	πότε
tēs	*thalassēs*	*eipon*	*autō*	*Rhabbi*	*pote*
of the	sea,	they said	to him,	Rabbi,	when

6:23,24. John explains how the people came to meet Jesus at Capernaum. "Tiberias" was a Roman-built city on the western shore of the Sea of Galilee. This is the only mention of the city in the Bible. Tiberias was Herod Antipas' capital. It was considered a Gentile city; therefore, Jesus never ministered there (Matthew 15:24). Small boats came from Tiberias to the eastern shore, where Jesus fed the multitude.

"When the people therefore saw" explains why the people took passage in the little boats. They noted that Jesus was not on the eastern side of the lake; therefore He must have crossed the lake somehow. They reasoned that the Lord would not be separated from His disciples for long. They were correct.

The people seemed to know the most likely place to find Jesus would be Capernaum. (Capernaum had been Jesus' headquarters for quite some time [see 2:12].) Perhaps they reasoned (1) He had moved His residence there, (2) some of His disciples lived in the area, (3) His disciples had rowed their boats in that direction.

Capernaum ("village of Nahum") was a beautiful and flourishing area in the time of Jesus. The climate was thought ideal for Palestine. The site was situated near the Sea of Galilee which by elevation was nearly 600 feet below sea level. This provided a semitropical climate. The Lake of Galilee was fresh water with abundant fish. The size of the lake (6 to 7 miles wide by 12 to 13 miles long) provided fish and pleasure for multitudes. Capernaum occupied an ideal site.

The people came seeking for Jesus. However, Jesus knew their motive for seeking Him. Jesus' most important sermon deals basically with attitudes and motives (Matthew 5 to 7).

The people found Jesus at Capernaum, the site of many of the Saviour's outstanding miracles. In Mark 2:1-12 we read of Jesus healing and forgiving a paralytic. Jesus healed the paralyzed servant of the centurion (Matthew 8:5). Matthew also relates the miracle knowledge of Jesus in sending Peter to take money from the fish's mouth to pay their tax (Matthew 17:24-27). Another miracle performed by Jesus at Capernaum involved casting out an unclean demon from a man (Luke 4:33).

It was at Capernaum the nobleman's son lay sick, but Jesus sent the power to heal (4:46-54). It was the night before the people found Him that Jesus walked on the stormy waters of the Sea of Galilee. What a privileged people they were to have signs, wonders, and miracles occurring there. However, the most wonderful blessing of all was to have the presence of the Lord Jesus in their midst. His presence brought hope that once more God had come to deliver them. At last a prophet had come who could feed thousands with only five loaves and two fish!

6:25. The multitude sought Jesus. He was not difficult to find, for many people crowded around Him wherever He went. They asked, "Rabbi, when camest thou hither?" They had been watching

but that his disciples were gone away alone: . . . but that they had gone away without Him, *Beck* . . . gone away alone, *ET* . . . had set off by themselves, *JB* . . . but that they went away without Him, *Weymouth* . . . but the disciples had left by themselves, *Berkeley* . . . but that they had left by themselves, *Norlie* . . . who had left by themselves, *Moffatt.*

23. (Howbeit there came other boats from Tiberias nigh unto the place: By now some, *AmpB* . . . Some other small boats ...landed quite near the place, *Phillips* . . . However, crafts from Tiberias did land near the place, *Berkeley.*

where they did eat bread, after that the Lord had given thanks:): . . . after the Lord's thanksgiving, *Berkeley* . . . on the occasion when the Lord gave thanks, *ALBA.*

24. When the people therefore saw that Jesus was not there, neither his disciples: So, when the crowd realized, *SEB* . . . the throng perceived that, *Concordant* . . . So the people, finding that neither Jesus nor His disciples were there, *AmpB.*

they also took shipping: . . . they also got into boats, *Norlie* . . . they got on board these boats, *Norton.*

and came to Capernaum, seeking for Jesus: . . . searching for Jesus, *Fenton* . . . in search of Jesus, *Moffatt.*

25. And when they had found him on the other side of the sea, they said unto him: And finding Him across the lake, *Fenton* . . . having found him, on the opposite shore, *Campbell* . . . And upon finding Him across the sea, *Adams.*

John 6:26

5436.1 adv	1090.2 verb 2sing indic perf act	552.6 verb 3sing indic aor pass	840.2 prs-pron dat pl	3450.5 art sing masc
ὧδε	γέγονας;	26. Ἀπεκρίθη	αὐτοῖς	ὁ
hōde	*gegonas*	*Apekrithē*	*autois*	*ho*
here	have you come?	Answered	them	

2400.1 name nom masc	2504.1 conj	1500.5 verb 3sing indic aor act	279.1 partic	279.1 partic	2978.1 verb 1sing pres act	5050.3 prs-pron dat 2pl
Ἰησοῦς	καὶ	εἶπεν,	Ἀμὴν	ἀμὴν	λέγω	ὑμῖν,
Iēsous	*kai*	*eipen*	*Amēn*	*amēn*	*legō*	*humin*
Jesus	and	said,	Truly	truly	I say	to you,

2195.1 verb 2pl pres act	1466.6 prs-pron acc 1sing	3620.1 partic	3617.1 conj	1481.6 verb 2pl indic aor act	4447.2 noun pl neu
ζητεῖτέ	με	οὐχ	ὅτι	εἴδετε	σημεῖα,
zēteite	*me*	*ouch*	*hoti*	*eidete*	*sēmeia*
You seek	me,	not	because	you saw	signs,

233.1 conj	3617.1 conj	2052.30 verb 2pl indic aor pass	1523.2 prep gen	3450.1 art gen pl	735.6 noun gen pl masc	2504.1 conj
ἀλλ'	ὅτι	ἐφάγετε	ἐκ	τῶν	ἄρτων	καὶ
all'	*hoti*	*ephagete*	*ek*	*tōn*	*artōn*	*kai*
but	because	you ate	of	the	loaves	and

5361.4 verb 2pl indic aor pass	2021.1 verb 2pl pres	3231.1 partic	3450.12 art acc sing fem	1028.4 noun acc sing fem
ἐχορτάσθητε.	27. ἐργάζεσθε	μὴ	τὴν	βρῶσιν
echortasthēte	*ergazesthe*	*mē*	*tēn*	*brōsin*
were satisfied.	Work	not	the	food

3450.12 art acc sing fem	616.20 verb acc sing fem part pres mid	233.2 conj	3450.12 art acc sing fem	1028.4 noun acc sing fem	3450.12 art acc sing fem
τὴν	ἀπολλυμένην,	ἀλλὰ	τὴν	βρῶσιν	τὴν
tēn	*apollumenēn*	*alla*	*tēn*	*brōsin*	*tēn*
the	perishing,	but	the	food	the

3176.13 verb acc sing fem part pres act	1519.1 prep	2205.4 noun acc sing fem	164.1 adj sing	3614.12 rel-pron acc sing fem	3450.5 art sing masc
μένουσαν	εἰς	ζωὴν	αἰώνιον,	ἣν	ὁ
menousan	*eis*	*zōēn*	*aiōnion*	*hēn*	*ho*
remaining	unto	life	eternal,	which	the

27.a.**Var:** 01ℵ,05D,Tisc

5048.1 noun nom sing masc	3450.2 art gen sing	442.2 noun gen sing masc	5050.3 prs-pron dat 2pl	1319.38 verb 3sing indic fut act	1319.2 verb 3sing indic pres act
υἱὸς	τοῦ	ἀνθρώπου	ὑμῖν	δώσει·	[a δίδωσιν
huios	*tou*	*anthrōpou*	*humin*	*dōsei*	*didōsin*
Son		of man	to you	will give;	[gives

5050.3 prs-pron dat 2pl	3642.6 dem-pron acc sing masc	1056.1 conj	3450.5 art sing masc	3824.1 noun nom sing masc	4824.2 verb 3sing indic aor act
ὑμῖν·]	τοῦτον	γὰρ	ὁ	πατὴρ	ἐσφράγισεν
humin	*touton*	*gar*	*ho*	*patēr*	*esphragisen*
to you;]	this	for	the	Father	sealed,

3450.5 art sing masc	2296.1 noun nom sing masc	1500.3 verb indic aor act	3631.1 conj	4242.1 prep	840.6 prs-pron acc sing masc
ὁ	θεός.	28. Εἶπον	οὖν	πρὸς	αὐτόν,
ho	*theos*	*Eipon*	*oun*	*pros*	*auton*
	God.	They said	therefore	to	him,

28.a.**Txt:** Steph
Var: 01ℵ,02A,03B, 017K,019L,029T,036, 037,byz.Elzev,Gries, Lach,TregAlf,Tisc, We/Ho,Weis,Sod,UBS/☆

4949.9 intr-pron sing neu	4020.6 verb 1pl indic pres act	4020.73 verb 1pl subj pres act	2419.1 conj	2021.6 verb 1pl subj pres
Τί	ποιοῦμεν,	[a☆ ποιῶμεν]	ἵνα	ἐργαζώμεθα
Ti	*poioumen*	*poiōmen*	*hina*	*ergazōmetha*
What	do we,	[may we do]	that	we may work

the coast till late the preceding night and from early morning. "When?" This was important, but His secret was "how"! The "how" could have helped them to understand the "when." We can grasp *when* Jesus arrived in Capernaum better than *how* He came to Capernaum. The "how" of a miracle is incomprehensible.

Rabbi, when camest thou hither?: Teacher, when did you get here, *Williams.*

6:26. "Verily, verily" (*amēn, amēn*) can be rendered by "indeed, indeed" to impress the importance of the statement to follow.

"Ye seek me." It is a marvelous thing to seek the Lord, but Jesus pointed out rather abruptly that the motive for the search should be spiritual, not carnal. Their quest was in response to the desires of the flesh. Because of their natural desire for food, they wanted to make Him their king.

26. Jesus answered them and said, Verily, verily, I say unto you, Ye seek me not because ye saw the miracles: . . . you are looking for me, *Montgomery* . . . you are searching for me, *Weymouth.*

but because ye did eat of the loaves, and were filled: . . . and had plenty, *Williams* . . . and had your fill, *Moffatt* . . . had a hearty meal, *Weymouth* . . . and been well fed, *Beck* . . . and were satisfyingly filled, *Wuest.*

6:27. "Labor" (*ergazesthe*) is the word of emphasis and pivots two opposing efforts. The people had a natural hunger for food. If they could make Him their king, they could live in prosperity under His administration. However, Jesus pointed them to their most important need.

"That meat which endureth unto everlasting life" expresses the greatest need. The need for natural food is temporal. It is not as important as those things which endure (see Hebrews 12:27,28). In our Lord's Sermon on the Mount, He teaches His disciples to trust the Heavenly Father to care for His children by suppling their needs for food, drink, and clothing. He further commands that their search should be first of all for His kingdom and His righteousness (Matthew 6:31-33).

"The Son of man" (see 1:51) is significant here, because it is by virtue of the Incarnation that Jesus can provide the food "enduring unto everlasting life." It was necessary for the Son of God to become the Son of Man in order that He might fulfill His messianic office.

"For him hath God the Father sealed" gives the reason Jesus can give the enduring food. That is, that the Father "has set His seal" on Him (see 6:27, NASB). When a seal is placed on a thing, it marks it as a genuine product. The Father attested His Son at His birth, in His ministry, and at His resurrection. The miracle of feeding the five thousand was an impression of the seal of the Father. The bakers of Jesus' day sealed (impressed) a mark on their bread to insure its quality. The Lord will shortly tell them that He is their bread from heaven, bearing the Father's mark.

27. Labour not for the meat which perisheth: Work not for the food, *HBIE* . . . Stop toiling for the food that perishes, *Williams* . . . Strive not only for this perishable food, *Fenton* . . . that must decompose, *Berkeley* . . . food which spoils, *SEB.*

but for that meat which endureth unto everlasting life: . . . but rather for the food that lasts forever, *Norlie* . . . for enduring Life, *TCNT.*

which the Son of man shall give unto you:

for him hath God the Father sealed: . . . for the same the Father sealed, *Rotherham* . . . for God the Father has certified Him, *Berkeley* . . . has given his attestation, *Campbell* . . . put his mark, *BB* . . . set His seal on Him, *Norlie* . . . has sealed in Him the power to give it, *Beck* . . . the seal of his approval, *TCNT* . . . one who bears the stamp of God, *Phillips* . . . puts His stamp of approval on me, *SEB.*

6:28. Jesus told the people they must work for the food which endures. They replied by asking, "What shall we do, that we might work the works (*erga*) of God?"

28. Then said they unto him, What shall we do, that we might work the works of God?: What must we do to perform the works that God demands, *Williams*

John 6:29

29.a.**Txt:** 02A,03B,05D,017K,019L,029T,038,1,13,Steph,Lach,We/Ho,Sod
Var: p75,01ℵ,032W,036,037,byz.TiscWeis,UBS/☆

3450.17 art pl neu	**2024.4** noun pl neu	**3450.2** art gen sing	**2296.2** noun gen sing masc	**552.6** verb 3sing indic aor pass	**3450.5** art sing masc
τὰ	ἔργα	τοῦ	θεοῦ;	**29.** Ἀπεκρίθη	⸂[a] ὁ ⸃
ta	*erga*	*tou*	*theou*	*Apekrithē*	*ho*
the	works		of God?	Answered	

2400.1 name nom masc	**2504.1** conj	**1500.5** verb 3sing indic aor act	**840.2** prs-pron dat pl	**3642.17** dem-pron sing neu	**1498.4** verb 3sing indic pres act
Ἰησοῦς	καὶ	εἶπεν	αὐτοῖς,	Τοῦτό	ἐστιν
Iēsous	*kai*	*eipen*	*autois*	*Touto*	*estin*
Jesus	and	said	to them,	This	is

3450.16 art sing neu	**2024.1** noun sing neu	**3450.2** art gen sing	**2296.2** noun gen sing masc	**2419.1** conj	**3961.1** verb 2pl subj act
τὸ	ἔργον	τοῦ	θεοῦ,	ἵνα	⸂ πιστεύσητε
to	*ergon*	*tou*	*theou*	*hina*	*pisteusēte*
the	work		of God,	that	you should believe

29.b.**Txt:** 05D,017K,032W,036,037,13,byz.Gries,Lach
Var: 01ℵ,02A,03B,(019),029T,038,33,Treg,Alf,Tisc,We/Ho,Weis,Sod,UBS/☆

3961.8 verb 2pl subj pres act	**1519.1** prep	**3614.6** rel-pron acc sing masc	**643.8** verb 3sing indic aor act	**1552.3** dem-pron nom sing masc
[b☆ πιστεύητε]	εἰς	ὃν	ἀπέστειλεν	ἐκεῖνος.
pisteuēte	*eis*	*hon*	*apesteilen*	*ekeinos*
[idem]	on	whom	sent	that.

1500.3 verb indic aor act	**3631.1** conj	**840.4** prs-pron dat sing	**4949.9** intr-pron sing neu	**3631.1** conj
30. Εἶπον	οὖν	αὐτῷ,	Τί	οὖν
Eipon	*oun*	*autō*	*Ti*	*oun*
They said	therefore	to him,	What	then

4020.4 verb 2sing indic pres act	**4622.1** prs-pron nom 2sing	**4447.1** noun sing neu	**2419.1** conj	**1481.11** verb 1pl subj aor act	**2504.1** conj
ποιεῖς	σὺ	σημεῖον,	ἵνα	ἴδωμεν	καὶ
poieis	*su*	*sēmeion*	*hina*	*idōmen*	*kai*
do	you	sign,	that	we may see	and

3961.26 verb 1pl subj aor act	**4622.3** prs-pron dat 2sing	**4949.9** intr-pron sing neu	**2021.3** verb 2sing indic pres	**3450.7** art pl masc
πιστεύσωμέν	σοι;	τί	ἐργάζῃ;	**31.** οἱ
pisteusōmen	*soi*	*ti*	*ergazē*	*hoi*
may believe	you?	what	do you work?	The

3824.6 noun pl masc	**2231.2** prs-pron gen 1pl	**3450.16** art sing neu	**3103.1** noun sing neu	**2052.27** verb indic aor pass	**1706.1** prep	**3450.11** art dat sing fem
πατέρες	ἡμῶν	τὸ	μάννα	ἔφαγον	ἐν	τῇ
pateres	*hēmōn*	*to*	*manna*	*ephagon*	*en*	*tē*
fathers	our	the	manna	ate	in	the

2031.2 noun dat sing fem	**2503.1** conj	**1498.4** verb 3sing indic pres act	**1119.29** verb sing neu part perf pass	**735.4** noun acc sing masc
ἐρήμῳ,	καθώς	ἐστιν	γεγραμμένον,	Ἄρτον
erēmō	*kathōs*	*estin*	*gegrammenon*	*Arton*
wilderness,	as	it is	written,	Bread

1523.2 prep gen	**3450.2** art gen sing	**3636.2** noun gen sing masc	**1319.14** verb 3sing indic aor act	**840.2** prs-pron dat pl	**2052.25** verb inf aor act
ἐκ	τοῦ	οὐρανοῦ	ἔδωκεν	αὐτοῖς	φαγεῖν.
ek	*tou*	*ouranou*	*edōken*	*autois*	*phagein*
out of	the	heaven	he gave	them	to eat.

1500.5 verb 3sing indic aor act	**3631.1** conj	**840.2** prs-pron dat pl	**3450.5** art sing masc	**2400.1** name nom masc	**279.1** partic
32. Εἶπεν	οὖν	αὐτοῖς	ὁ	Ἰησοῦς,	Ἀμὴν
Eipen	*oun*	*autois*	*ho*	*Iēsous*	*Amēn*
Said	therefore	to them		Jesus,	Truly

6:29. "This is the work of God" (*ergon*). Jesus used the singular "work," not "works." They were thinking of "works" (verse 28). Their experience in religious things involved multitudes of requirements from the Law and the traditions of the elders. Jesus said there is but one work.

"That ye believe on him whom he hath sent" specifies the one work. Man is not saved by works of the Law, but by the work of believing. Jesus came as a revelation of the Father. To receive Him as that revelation and commit one's person to Jesus Christ is the sum and substance of eternal life. For notes on "believe" see 3:14-16.

In the last day, the Day of Judgment, one word will determine whether one's destiny will be heaven or hell. The one word is the one Jesus stresses here: believe! One will be accounted a Christian if he believes, but believing always brings forth results (see James 2:17-26). One always acts in accord with what he believes. This is not saying one is saved by his conduct. What he does will bring wages, but one is saved by receiving Christ as Saviour.

. . . What are the works God want us to do, *Beck* . . . to do habitually, *Montgomery* . . . to accomplish, *Berkeley* . . . to do as a habit of life, *Wuest* . . . must we do, in order that we may carry out the purposes of God? *Fenton.*

29. Jesus answered and said unto them, This is the work of God: The work that God would have you do, *TCNT* . . . This is the service God asks of you, *Knox* . . . this is the purpose of God, *Fenton.*

that ye believe on him whom he hath sent: . . . have faith in him whom God has sent, *BB* . . . rely on, *AmpB* . . . is to believe in him whom God sent as his messenger, *TCNT.*

6:30. It is an odd question that they ask Jesus in view of the grand sign they had witnessed only the day before. They cared nothing for the sign that He had given them. They wanted a more spectacular one. Signs (*sēmeion*) were meant to point in the direction of reality. For them the sign He had given did not encourage them toward faith in Christ.

He asked them to do a work (believe). They asked Him to perform a work (a sign).

30. They said therefore unto him, What sign shewest thou then: What sign then will you work, *Berkeley* . . . What sign can you give us to see, *NEB.*

that we may see, and believe thee?: . . . which we may see, and so believe you, *TCNT* . . . and confide in You? *Fenton.*

what dost thou work?: What works are you going to do, *Williams* . . . what will you perform? *Berkeley.*

6:31,32. "Our fathers did eat manna." The people tried to justify their demand for a sign. Moses' claim that he was sent by God was followed by signs. Psalm 78:24 tells us the manna was bread from heaven. The Jews asked for a like miracle to give proof of Jesus' claim. If the manna came from heaven, they thought, then Jesus should show some great sign from heaven.

Moses was credited by the people as the one who gave bread out of heaven. Jesus told them the Father had given the manna, not Moses. Furthermore, Jesus declared that the Father would give them the "true bread" from heaven. In the verses which follow, Jesus explained what the "true bread" is. The "bread of God" is that food which endures to eternal life (verse 27). In verse 32 it is called the "true bread," here the "bread of God." In verse 35 Jesus said He is the "bread of life," and in verse 51 He refers to himself as "the living bread." The manna was temporal and symbolic. The bread of God is eternal and fulfilling.

The comparison Jesus drew between manna as physical nourish-

31. Our fathers did eat manna in the desert: Our ancestors, *Berkeley* . . . Our forefathers ate manna, *Phillips* . . . in the deserted region, *Wuest.*

as it is written, He gave them bread from heaven to eat:

32. Then Jesus said unto them, Verily, verily, I say unto you, Moses gave you not that bread

John 6:33

279.1 partic	2978.1 verb 1sing pres act	5050.3 prs-pron dat 2pl	3620.3 partic	3337.1 name nom masc	3338.1 name nom masc
ἀμὴν	λέγω	ὑμῖν,	Οὐ	⸀ Μωσῆς	[☆ Μωϋσῆς]
amēn	legō	humin	Ou	Mōsēs	Mōusēs
truly	I say	to you,	Not	Moses	[idem]

32.a.**Var:** 03B,05D,019L, 032W,Lach,Treg,Alf, We/Ho

1319.33 verb 3sing indic perf act	1319.14 verb 3sing indic aor act	5050.3 prs-pron dat 2pl	3450.6 art acc sing masc	735.4 noun acc sing masc
⸀ δέδωκεν	[a ἔδωκεν]	ὑμῖν	τὸν	ἄρτον
dedōken	edōken	humin	ton	arton
has given	[gave]	you	the	bread

1523.2 prep gen	3450.2 art gen sing	3636.2 noun gen sing masc	233.1 conj	3450.5 art sing masc	3824.1 noun nom sing masc
ἐκ	τοῦ	οὐρανοῦ·	ἀλλ'	ὁ	πατήρ
ek	tou	ouranou	all'	ho	patēr
out of	the	heaven;	but		Father

1466.2 prs-pron gen 1sing	1319.2 verb 3sing indic pres act	5050.3 prs-pron dat 2pl	3450.6 art acc sing masc	735.4 noun acc sing masc	1523.2 prep gen
μου	δίδωσιν	ὑμῖν	τὸν	ἄρτον	ἐκ
mou	didōsin	humin	ton	arton	ek
my	gives	you	the	bread	out of

3450.2 art gen sing	3636.2 noun gen sing masc	3450.6 art acc sing masc	226.1 adj sing	3450.5 art sing masc	1056.1 conj
τοῦ	οὐρανοῦ	τὸν	ἀληθινόν.	33. ὁ	γὰρ
tou	ouranou	ton	alēthinon	ho	gar
the	heaven	the	true.	The	for

33.a.**Var:** 01ℵ,05D,038, Tisc

735.1 noun nom sing masc	3450.5 art sing masc	3450.2 art gen sing	2296.2 noun gen sing masc	1498.4 verb 3sing indic pres act	3450.5 art sing masc
ἄρτος	[a+ ὁ]	τοῦ	θεοῦ	ἐστιν	ὁ
artos	ho	tou	theou	estin	ho
bread	[the]		of God	is	the

2568.2 verb nom sing masc part pres act	1523.2 prep gen	3450.2 art gen sing	3636.2 noun gen sing masc	2504.1 conj	2205.4 noun acc sing fem
καταβαίνων	ἐκ	τοῦ	οὐρανοῦ,	καὶ	ζωὴν
katabainōn	ek	tou	ouranou	kai	zōēn
coming down	out of	the	heaven,	and	life

1319.5 verb nom sing masc part pres act	3450.3 art dat sing	2862.3 noun dat sing masc	1500.3 verb indic aor act	3631.1 conj
διδοὺς	τῷ	κόσμῳ.	34. Εἶπον	οὖν
didous	tō	kosmō	Eipon	oun
giving	to the	world.	They said	therefore

4242.1 prep	840.6 prs-pron acc sing masc	2935.5 noun voc sing masc	3704.1 adv	1319.25 verb 2sing impr aor act	2231.3 prs-pron dat 1pl
πρὸς	αὐτόν,	Κύριε,	πάντοτε	δὸς	ἡμῖν
pros	auton	Kurie	pantote	dos	hēmin
to	him,	Lord,	always	give	to us

35.a.**Txt:** 02A,017K,037, 1,byz.Lach
Var: p75,03B,019L, 029T,032W,syr.it.sa.bo. Treg,Alf,We/Ho,Weis, UBS/☆

3450.6 art acc sing masc	735.4 noun acc sing masc	3642.6 dem-pron acc sing masc	1500.5 verb 3sing indic aor act	1156.2 conj
τὸν	ἄρτον	τοῦτον.	35. εἶπεν	⸂a δὲ ⸃
ton	arton	touton	eipen	de
the	bread	this.	Said	and

840.2 prs-pron dat pl	3450.5 art sing masc	2400.1 name nom masc	1466.1 prs-pron nom 1sing	1498.2 verb 1sing indic pres act	3450.5 art sing masc
αὐτοῖς	ὁ	Ἰησοῦς,	Ἐγώ	εἰμι	ὁ
autois	ho	Iēsous	Egō	eimi	ho
to them		Jesus,	I	am	the

ment and true bread as spiritual nourishment is frequent in Scripture. In Deuteronomy 8:3, Moses told the people of Israel that God "humbled thee, and suffered thee to hunger, and fed thee with manna, which thou knewest not . . . that he might make thee know that man doth not live by bread only, but by every word that proceedeth out of the mouth of the Lord doth man live." Moses informed the people of Israel that the key to living is not found in "natural" things such as bread, but in the will of God. This is what Jesus meant when He rebuked Satan by telling him, "Man shall not live by bread alone, but by every word that proceedeth out of the mouth of God" (Matthew 4:4). When Satan tempted Jesus, Jesus was indeed hungry, but He told Satan that it was more important for Him to obey the will of God than to satisfy His physical needs. Nehemiah explained that God met both their spiritual and physical needs (Nehemiah 9:20).

6:33. This verse continues the teaching concerning the true bread. "Cometh down from heaven" indicates the source of the bread of God. "The Word was made flesh, and dwelt among us" (1:14).

"Giveth life unto the world" declares what the bread of God accomplishes. As the bread of God, Jesus feeds, nourishes, and sustains life. "The world" indicates the scope of the bread of God. It is not limited as the manna was.

6:34,35. "Lord" (*kurie*) is in this case a title of respect such as "mister" or "sir." The people did not see Jesus as deity.

What the water was for the Samaritan woman, the Bread of Life could be for these Jews. The Old Testament tabernacle type was called the bread of the Presence. The 12 cakes placed on the table of showbread spoke of the nourishment God gave to them. Jesus was thus teaching that He is their God who provides them with life.

Compare this with a different analogy Jesus used for the Samaritan woman (4:14). "Cometh to me" is synonymous with "believing" (verses 29,47) and "eat of this bread" (verses 51,53). "Come," "believe," and "eat" state the same fact.

"Shall never thirst" is added to reveal that Jesus was not talking about natural food and drink. What food and water are for the body, Jesus is to the life of man.

Verse 35 begins the first part of Jesus' Bread of Life discourse. This passage, reaching to verse 47, relates very strongly to verses in Psalm 78. Jesus had already quoted this psalm in verse 31, "He gave them bread from heaven to eat." Notice how Psalm 78:23-25 refers to the miracle of the manna: "He . . . opened the doors of heaven, and had rained down manna upon them to eat, and had

from heaven: Amen, Amen, *Confraternity* . . . Let Me assure you of this, *Adams* . . . Believe me, *TCNT* . . . Moses did not himself give, *Fenton.*

but my Father giveth you the true bread from heaven: . . . but what matters, *Phillips* . . . but my Father is giving you the bread—the true bread, *Weymouth* . . . but My Father gives you the real heavenly food, *Berkeley* . . . that which is genuine, *Wuest.*

33. For the bread of God is he which cometh down from heaven: God's food, *SEB* . . . the bread that God give, *TCNT* . . . is now descending, *Norton.*

and giveth life unto the world: . . . and gives life, *BB.*

34. Then said they unto him, Lord, evermore give us this bread: Ah, Lord, they said, give us that bread for ever! *BB* . . . always give us this bread, *Beck* . . . Sir, always give us this food, *SEB* . . . Give us, Sir, this bread always, *Fenton* . . . at all times, *ALBA* . . . all the time, *AmpB.*

35. And Jesus said unto them, I am the bread of life: And this was the answer, *BB* . . . I alone, in contradistinction to all others,

John 6:36

735.1 noun nom sing masc	3450.10 art gen sing fem	2205.2 noun gen sing fem	3450.5 art sing masc	2048.44 verb nom sing masc part pres	4242.1 prep
ἄρτος	τῆς	ζωῆς·	ὁ	ἐρχόμενος	πρός
artos	tēs	zōēs	ho	erchomenos	pros
bread	of the	life:	the	coming	to

35.b.**Txt:** 02A,05D,017K, 019L,032W,036,037, 038,1,13,etc.byz.Lach, Sod
Var: p75,01ℵ,03B,029T, Treg,Alf,Tisc,We/Ho, Weis,UBS/☆

1466.6 prs-pron acc 1sing	1466.7 prs-pron acc 1sing	3620.3 partic	3231.1 partic	3845.10 verb 3sing subj aor act	2504.1 conj	3450.5 art sing masc
⸀☆ με	[b ἐμὲ]	οὐ	μὴ	πεινάσῃ·	καὶ	ὁ
me	eme	ou	mē	peinasē	kai	ho
me	[idem]	not	not	may hunger,	and	the

3961.10 verb nom sing masc part pres act	1519.1 prep	1466.7 prs-pron acc 1sing	3620.3 partic	3231.1 partic	1366.9 verb 3sing subj aor act
πιστεύων	εἰς	ἐμὲ	οὐ	μὴ	⸀ διψήσῃ
pisteuōn	eis	eme	ou	mē	dipsēsē
believing	on	me	not	not	may thirst

35.c.**Txt:** 03B-corr,017K, 036,byz.Sod
Var: 01ℵ,02A,03B-org, 05D,019L,029T,037, 038,Lach,Treg,Alf,Tisc, We/HoWeis,UBS/☆

1366.10 verb 3sing indic fut act	4312.1 adv	233.1 conj	1500.3 verb indic aor act	5050.3 prs-pron dat 2pl
[c☆ διψήσει]	πώποτε.	36. ἀλλ'	εἶπον	ὑμῖν
dipsēsei	pōpote	all'	eipon	humin
[will thirst]	at any time.	But	I said	to you

36.a.**Txt:** p66,03B,05D, 017K,019L,032W,036, 037,038,1,13,etc.byz. Gries,Lach,TregWe/Ho, Weis,Sod,UBS/☆
Var: 01ℵ,02A,Tisc

3617.1 conj	2504.1 conj	3571.13 verb 2pl indic perf act	1466.6 prs-pron acc 1sing	2504.1 conj	3620.3 partic	3961.2 verb 2pl pres act
ὅτι	καὶ	ἑωράκατέ	⸂a με ⸃	καὶ	οὐ	πιστεύετε.
hoti	kai	heōrakate	me	kai	ou	pisteuete
that	also	you have seen	me	and	not	believe.

3820.17 adj sing neu	3614.16 rel-pron sing neu	1319.2 verb 3sing indic pres act	1466.4 prs-pron dat 1sing	3450.5 art sing masc	3824.1 noun nom sing masc
37. Πᾶν	ὃ	δίδωσίν	μοι	ὁ	πατὴρ
Pan	ho	didōsin	moi	ho	patēr
All	that	gives	me	the	Father

4242.1 prep	1466.7 prs-pron acc 1sing	2223.7 verb 3sing indic fut act	2504.1 conj	3450.6 art acc sing masc	2048.42 verb sing part pres
πρὸς	ἐμὲ	ἥξει·	καὶ	τὸν	ἐρχόμενον
pros	eme	hēxei	kai	ton	erchomenon
to	me	shall come,	and	the	coming

37.a.**Var:** p66,p75,01ℵ, 017K,029T,037,038,Tisc

4242.1 prep	1466.6 prs-pron acc 1sing	1466.7 prs-pron acc 1sing	3620.3 partic	3231.1 partic	1531.14 verb 1sing subj aor act	1838.1 prep gen
πρὸς	⸀ με	[a ἐμὲ]	οὐ	μὴ	ἐκβάλω	ἔξω·
pros	me	eme	ou	mē	ekbalō	exō
to	me	[idem]	not	not	will I cast	out.

38.a.**Txt:** 01ℵ,05D,017K, 036,037,1,byz.
Var: 02A,03B,019L, 029T,038,33,Lach,Treg Alf,Tisc,We/Ho,Weis, Sod,UBS/☆

3617.1 conj	2568.25 verb 1sing indic perf act	1523.2 prep gen	570.3 prep gen	3450.2 art gen sing
38. ὅτι	καταβέβηκα	⸀ ἐκ	[a☆ ἀπὸ]	τοῦ
hoti	katabebēka	ek	apo	tou
For	I have come down	out of	[from]	the

38.b.**Var:** 01ℵ,05D, 019L-org,037,Tisc

3636.2 noun gen sing masc	3620.1 partic	2419.1 conj	4020.1 verb 1sing pres act	4020.21 verb 1sing act	3450.16 art sing neu
οὐρανοῦ,	οὐχ	ἵνα	⸀ ποιῶ	[b ποιήσω]	τὸ
ouranou	ouch	hina	poiō	poiēsō	to
heaven,	not	that	I should do	[idem]	the

2284.1 noun sing neu	3450.16 art sing neu	1684.1 adj 1sing	233.2 conj	3450.16 art sing neu	2284.1 noun sing neu	3450.2 art gen sing
θέλημα	τὸ	ἐμὸν,	ἀλλὰ	τὸ	θέλημα	τοῦ
thelēma	to	emon	alla	to	thelēma	tou
will	the	my,	but	the	will	of the

given them of the corn of heaven. Man did eat angels' food." Men need to partake of the Bread of Life.

Wuest . . . I myself am the Life-giving Bread, *TCNT* . . . I am the food which gives life, *SEB.*

he that cometh to me shall never hunger: . . . will never be hungry, *Phillips, SEB* . . . shall positively not become hungry, *Wuest.*

and he that believeth on me shall never thirst: The one who commits himself to me, *SEB* . . . will never again be thirsty, *Moffatt* . . . will never be in need of a drink, *BB* . . . shall not suffer thirst any more, *Berkeley.*

6:36. "But" indicates a strong contrast. The Jews demanded a sign that they might believe. Jesus pointed out that He was the sign they asked for.

"Have seen" (*heōrakate*) is a perfect tense verb indicating their past knowledge by observing Him (that is, seeing Him in His work as Messiah), had no present result.

"And believe not" (*ou pisteuete*) is a present tense verb meaning they were not now believing what the sign was intended to indicate. As yet they were in His presence for their stomachs' sake and not for their souls' welfare (verse 26).

36. But I said unto you, That ye also have seen me, and believe not: . . . as I have said already, you have seen me, *TCNT* . . . you have actually seen me, *TCNT.*

6:37. "All that" (*pan ho*) is neuter singular, signifying the total group of believers and not individual members of the group. The character or nature of the group is stressed, not the identity.

Jesus expanded this statement in verse 45. The Father attracts, convicts, and convinces the individual by means of the Spirit's activity.

"The Father giveth" and the Son receives. It is the total company that the Father gives to the Son. But "him that cometh to me" speaks of the individual members of the group.

"I will in no wise cast out" expresses Jesus' promise to save the person who "comes," "believes," and "receives" Him. Jesus assures the one who comes that he will not be "cast out." To be "cast out" is to be separated from Him. One's relationship with Jesus depends on the action of his own will to come to Him.

37. All that the Father giveth me shall come to me: Listen; All whom the, *Norlie* . . . All that which the Father is giving me, *Rotherham* . . . Everything the Father gives Me will come to Me, *Beck.*

and him that cometh to me I will in no wise cast out: I will certainly not cast out, *Berkeley* . . . I will not reject, *Campbell* . . . I will never, no, never reject, *Williams* . . . never on any account drive away, *Weymouth* . . . never refuse anyone, *Phillips* . . . will I ever turn away, *TCNT* . . . I will positively not throw out into the outside, *Wuest.*

6:38. Jesus does the Father's will, and it is the Father's will that He makes known the Father to the world. Those who receive the revelation of the Father in Christ are accepted. Observe Jesus' claim of His preexistence in heaven before His incarnation.

"Not to do mine own will, but the will of him that sent me" are in perfect harmony. The Son receives the "comer" because the Father receives the believer.

38. For I came down from heaven, not to do mine own will: For I descended, *Campbell* . . . For I have left heaven and have come down to earth not to seek my own pleasure, *Weymouth* . . . not to carry out my own will, *Moffatt* . . . not to do what I want, *Phillips* . . . not in order that I might continually be doing my will, *Wuest* . . . My own intention, *Fenton.*

but the will of him that sent me: . . . what the One Who sent Me wants, *Adams* . . . and purpose of, *AmpB.*

6:39. "And this" (*touto de*) means "and this is the will of Him who sent me." Jesus then states the Father's will as (1) what the

3854.12 verb gen sing masc part aor act	1466.6 prs-pron acc 1sing	3642.17 dem-pron sing neu	1156.2 conj	1498.4 verb 3sing indic pres act
πέμψαντός	με.	39. τοῦτο	δέ	ἐστιν
pempsantos	me	touto	de	estin
having sent	me.	This	and	is

3450.16 art sing neu	2284.1 noun sing neu	3450.2 art gen sing	3854.12 verb gen sing masc part aor act	1466.6 prs-pron acc 1sing
τὸ	θέλημα	τοῦ	πέμψαντός	με,
to	thelēma	tou	pempsantos	me
the	will	of the	having sent	me

39.a.**Txt:** 017K,036,037, 038,13,byz.
Var: 01ℵ,02A,03B,04C, 05D,019L,029T,Gries, LachTreg,Alf,Tisc, We/Ho,Weis,Sod,UBS/☆

3824.2 noun gen sing masc	2419.1 conj	3820.17 adj sing neu	3614.16 rel-pron sing neu	1319.33 verb 3sing indic perf act	1466.4 prs-pron dat 1sing
⸂a πατρός ⸃	ἵνα	πᾶν	ὃ	δέδωκέν	μοι,
patros	hina	pan	ho	dedōken	moi
Father,	that	all	that	he has given	me,

3231.1 partic	616.4 verb 1sing subj aor act	1523.1 prep gen	840.3 prs-pron gen sing	233.2 conj	448.1 verb 1sing act
μὴ	ἀπολέσω	ἐξ	αὐτοῦ,	ἀλλὰ	ἀναστήσω
mē	apolesō	ex	autou	alla	anastēsō
not	I should lose	of	it,	but	should raise up

39.b.**Txt:** 01ℵ,02A,05D, 017K,041,13,33,sa.bo. Steph,Lach,TiscWeis, UBS/☆
Var: p66,p75,03B,04C, 019L,029T,032W,036, 037,038,1,byz.Treg,Alf, We/Ho,Sod

840.15 prs-pron sing neu	1706.1 prep	3450.11 art dat sing fem	2057.9 adj dat sing fem	2232.3 noun dat sing fem	3642.17 dem-pron sing neu
αὐτὸ	⸂b ἐν ⸃	τῇ	ἐσχάτῃ	ἡμέρᾳ.	40. τοῦτο
auto	en	tē	eschatē	hēmera	touto
it	in	the	last	day.	This

40.a.**Txt:** 07E,036,037, byz.
Var: 01ℵ,02A,03B,04C, 05D,017K,019L,030U, 038,041,Gries,Lach, Treg,AlfTisc,We/Ho, Weis,Sod,UBS/☆

1156.2 conj	1056.1 conj	1498.4 verb 3sing indic pres act	3450.16 art sing neu	2284.1 noun sing neu	3450.2 art gen sing
⸂ δέ	[a☆ γάρ]	ἐστιν	τὸ	θέλημα	⸂ τοῦ
de	gar	estin	to	thelēma	tou
and	[for]	is	the	will	of the

40.b.**Txt:** 02A,017K,036, 041,13,byz.
Var: 01ℵ,03B,04C,05D, 019L,029T,030U,038,sa. bo.Lach,Treg,AlfTisc, We/Ho,Weis,Sod,UBS/☆

3854.12 verb gen sing masc part aor act	1466.6 prs-pron acc 1sing	3450.2 art gen sing	3824.2 noun gen sing masc	1466.2 prs-pron gen 1sing
πέμψαντός	με,	[b☆ τοῦ	πατρός	μου,]
pempsantos	me	tou	patros	mou
having sent	me,	[of the	Father	my,]

2419.1 conj	3820.6 adj sing masc	3450.5 art sing masc	2311.9 verb nom sing masc part pres act	3450.6 art acc sing masc	5048.4 noun acc sing masc
ἵνα	πᾶς	ὁ	θεωρῶν	τὸν	υἱὸν
hina	pas	ho	theōrōn	ton	huion
that	everyone	the	seeing	the	Son

2504.1 conj	3961.10 verb nom sing masc part pres act	1519.1 prep	840.6 prs-pron acc sing masc	2174.7 verb 3sing subj pres act	2205.4 noun acc sing fem
καὶ	πιστεύων	εἰς	αὐτὸν,	ἔχῃ	ζωὴν
kai	pisteuōn	eis	auton	echē	zōēn
and	believing	on	him,	should have	life

164.1 adj sing	2504.1 conj	448.1 verb 1sing act	840.6 prs-pron acc sing masc	1466.1 prs-pron nom 1sing
αἰώνιον,	καὶ	ἀναστήσω	αὐτὸν	ἐγὼ
aiōnion	kai	anastēsō	auton	egō
eternal;	and	will raise up	him	I

40.c.**Var:** p66,01ℵ,02A, 05D,017K,019L,030U, 041,13,sa.bo.Lach,Tisc, Weis,UBS/☆

1706.1 prep	3450.11 art dat sing fem	2057.9 adj dat sing fem	2232.3 noun dat sing fem	1105.5 verb 3pl indic imperf act
[c☆+ ἐν]	τῇ	ἐσχάτῃ	ἡμέρᾳ.	41. Ἐγόγγυζον
en	tē	eschatē	hēmera	Egonguzon
[in]	at the	last	day.	Were grumbling

Father has given, (2) that "I . . . lose nothing," and (3) "but should raise it up again at the last day."

"Raise it up" refers to the dead as Jesus explained in 5:28,29. "It" (see *Interlinear, autou*) is a neuter singular pronoun referring to every part of that which the Father has given to the Son ("all that" of verse 37). "At the last day" is a phrase which is peculiar to John's Gospel. The assertion occurs 4 times (verses 39,40,44,54). "The last day" is the last day of the last days (see Acts 2:17). It is a day of resurrection for the bodies of those who believe in Jesus as the Christ. The believer is not cast outside, but is secure in the hands of Jesus who will lose nothing. This is the Father's will which will be accomplished.

39. And this is the Father's will which hath sent me: . . . and his will is this, *TCNT.*

that of all which he hath given me I shall lose nothing: . . . which He has entrusted to Me, *Fenton* . . . that I should lose none of all that He has given me, *Williams* . . . none of those who are his gift to me, *Moffatt* . . . I should not lose one of those whom He gave Me, *Norlie.*

but should raise it up again at the last day: . . . but should raise them to life on the last day, *Williams* . . . raise them from death, *TCNT* . . . should restore, *Fenton* . . . I must restore it to God on the last day, *SEB* . . . I should resurrect, *Adams.*

6:40. "And" (*de*) begins this verse. The word confirms and strengthens the last verse by further reasons. The prior statement stated the will of God from the divine perspective. This verse expresses the will of God from the human point of view.

"Every one which seeth the Son" suggests all those who receive the knowledge of Him. "Seeth" (*theōrōn*) refers to a continued gaze, not a casual glance.

"And believeth on him" means that one is believing as a result of the continuous gazing at the Son. "On him" (*eis auton*) refers to believing toward Christ as the object. This sort of faith is a growing belief in accord with the personal knowledge which one gains by means of the Word of God and communion with Jesus.

"May have everlasting life" again emphasizes the fact of man's greatest need. It is not the temporal life that man should be most concerned about, but rather his need for receiving eternal life. "May have" is a present possession. Believers often fail to realize their most valuable asset is not money, property, or talents, but the gift of eternal life in Jesus the Lord.

"I will" stresses the act of the Son. Jesus asserted His divine prerogative of the resurrection in 5:28,29. Here also Jesus states what He will do for the one who believes in Him. Only the Son of God can make the claim and perform the action. Jesus raised Lazarus from the grave (chapter 11) to give a foretaste of the resurrection of all the dead in the last day.

40. And this is the will of him that sent me: For this is the will of my Father, *ASV* . . . This is what my Father wants, *SEB.*

that every one which seeth the Son, and believeth on him: . . . whoever recognizes the Son, *Campbell* . . . behold the Son of God, *Weymouth* . . . who looks to the Son and believes in him, *NIV* . . . puts his faith in him, *NEB* . . . views the Son, *Rotherham* . . . who discerningly sees the Son, *Wuest.*

may have everlasting life: . . . should possess, *Moffatt* . . . should have eternal Life, *Weymouth.*

and I will raise him up at the last day: I should resurrect him, *Adams* . . . raise him to life, *Weymouth.*

6:41. "The Jews" are the subjects of Jesus' opposition. Again and again the term implies unbelief and hostility. It does not refer to the nationality, but to the Jewish religious leaders.

"Because he said" leads us to understand their reason for grumbling. Their understanding was sound. It was their judgment that was sick.

"I am the bread" implies that no other was the bread but He himself. The "I am" is emphatic, meaning "I myself am."

John 6:42

3631.1 conj	3450.7 art pl masc	2428.2 name-adj pl masc	3875.1 prep	840.3 prs-pron gen sing	3617.1 conj
οὖν	οἱ	Ἰουδαῖοι	περὶ	αὐτοῦ,	ὅτι
oun	*hoi*	*Ioudaioi*	*peri*	*autou*	*hoti*
therefore	the	Jews	about	him,	because

1500.5 verb 3sing indic aor act	1466.1 prs-pron nom 1sing	1498.2 verb 1sing indic pres act	3450.5 art sing masc	735.1 noun nom sing masc	3450.5 art sing masc
εἶπεν,	Ἐγώ	εἰμι	ὁ	ἄρτος	ὁ
eipen	*Egō*	*eimi*	*ho*	*artos*	*ho*
he said,	I	am	the	bread	the

2568.20 verb nom sing masc part aor act	1523.2 prep gen	3450.2 art gen sing	3636.2 noun gen sing masc	2504.1 conj
καταβὰς	ἐκ	τοῦ	οὐρανοῦ,	42. καὶ
katabas	*ek*	*tou*	*ouranou*	*kai*
having come down	out of	the	heaven.	And

42.a.**Txt:** p66,01ℵ,02A, 05D,017K,019L,036, 037,1,13,byz.it.Lach
Var: p75,03B,04C,029T, 032W,038,bo.Treg,Alf, Tisc,We/Ho,Weis,Sod, UBS/☆

2978.25 verb indic imperf act	3620.1 partic	3642.4 dem-pron nom sing masc	1498.4 verb 3sing indic pres act	2400.1 name nom masc	3450.5 art sing masc
ἔλεγον,	Οὐχ	οὗτός	ἐστιν	Ἰησοῦς	ὁ
elegon	*Ouch*	*houtos*	*estin*	*Iēsous*	*ho*
were saying,	Not	this	is	Jesus	the

5048.1 noun nom sing masc	2473.1 name masc	3614.2 rel-pron gen sing	2231.1 prs-pron nom 1pl	3471.5 verb 1pl indic perf act	3450.6 art acc sing masc
υἱὸς	Ἰωσήφ,	οὗ	ἡμεῖς	οἴδαμεν	τὸν
huios	*Iōsēph*	*hou*	*hēmeis*	*oidamen*	*ton*
Son	of Joseph,	of whom	we	know	the

42.b.**Txt:** 01ℵ,02A,017K, 036,037,13,byz.Lach, Tisc
Var: p66,p75,03B,04C, 05D,019L,029T,032W, 038,1,sa.bo.Treg,Alf, We/Ho,Weis,Sod,UBS/☆

3824.4 noun acc sing masc	2504.1 conj	3450.12 art acc sing fem	3251.4 noun acc sing fem	4316.1 adv	3631.1 conj	3431.1 adv
πατέρα	καὶ	τὴν	μητέρα;	πῶς	⸀ οὖν	[a☆ νῦν]
patera	*kai*	*tēn*	*mētera*	*pōs*	*oun*	*nun*
father	and	the	mother?	how	therefore	[now]

43.a.**Txt:** 01ℵ,02A,(05), 032W,037,038,byz.it. Lach
Var: p66,p75,03B,04C, 017K,019L,029T,13,sa. bo.Gries,Treg,Alf,Tisc We/Ho,Weis,Sod,UBS/☆

2978.5 verb 3sing indic pres act	3642.4 dem-pron nom sing masc	3617.1 conj	1523.2 prep gen	3450.2 art gen sing	3636.2 noun gen sing masc
λέγει	⸂b οὗτος, ⸃	Ὅτι	Ἐκ	τοῦ	οὐρανοῦ
legei	*houtos*	*Hoti*	*Ek*	*tou*	*ouranou*
says	this,		Out of	the	heaven

43.b.**Txt:** p66,02A,04C, 05D,017K,032W,036, 037,038,byz.Lach
Var: p75,01ℵ,03B,019L, 029T,sa.bo.TregTisc, We/Ho,Weis,Sod,UBS/☆

2568.25 verb 1sing indic perf act	552.6 verb 3sing indic aor pass	3631.1 conj	3450.5 art sing masc
καταβέβηκα;	43. Ἀπεκρίθη	⸂a οὖν ⸃	⸂b ὁ ⸃
katabebēka	*Apekrithē*	*oun*	*ho*
I have come down?	Answered	therefore	

2400.1 name nom masc	2504.1 conj	1500.5 verb 3sing indic aor act	840.2 prs-pron dat pl	3231.1 partic	1105.2 verb 2pl impr pres act
Ἰησοῦς	καὶ	εἶπεν	αὐτοῖς,	Μὴ	γογγύζετε
Iēsous	*kai*	*eipen*	*autois*	*Mē*	*gonguzete*
Jesus	and	said	to them,	Not	grumble

3196.2 prep	238.1 prs-pron gen pl	3625.2 num card nom masc	1404.4 verb 3sing indic pres	2048.23 verb inf aor act	4242.1 prep
μετ'	ἀλλήλων.	44. οὐδεὶς	δύναται	ἐλθεῖν	πρός
met'	*allēlōn*	*oudeis*	*dunatai*	*elthein*	*pros*
with	one another.	No one	is able	to come	to

44.a.**Var:** 03B,021M, 030U,037,038,TregAlf, Weis

1466.6 prs-pron acc 1sing	1466.7 prs-pron acc 1sing	1430.1 partic	3231.1 partic	3450.5 art sing masc	3824.1 noun nom sing masc	3450.5 art sing masc
⸀ με	[a ἐμὲ]	ἐὰν	μὴ	ὁ	πατὴρ	ὁ
me	*eme*	*ean*	*mē*	*ho*	*patēr*	*ho*
me	[idem]	if	not	the	Father	the

Furthermore, He said that He "came down from heaven." The Jews believed Jesus had a very lowly origin in the despised village of Nazareth. His statement as to His heavenly origin increased their antagonism. Each new comment was like a beacon light to lead the Jews to their secure harbor. Yet because of their obstinacy each new truth supplied fuel for their hatred.

41. The Jews then murmured at him: A buzz of critical comment rose from the Jews, *Barclay* . . . Judeans then muttered concerning Him, *Fenton* . . . began to murmur concerning him, *Rotherham* . . . began to find fault, *Montgomery* . . . began to protest, *ALBA* . . . grumbled about Him, *Berkeley* . . . the Jews complained, *Sawyer* . . . discontentedly complaining in a low, undertone, *Wuest.*

because he said, I am the bread which came down from heaven:

6:42. Their expectations for Messiah were based on a popular idea that when the Messiah came, he would (1) appear as a mature man, (2) have a spectacular arrival, and (3) be as a king. Jesus did not fit their expectations. They built their theology on the fact that the Messiah was to be the son of David. Thus he would conquer Israel's enemies as David did. For the Jews, political power and regal splendor were the supreme traits their Messiah would have.

42. And they said, Is not this Jesus, the son of Joseph, whose father and mother we know?: Is not this fellow, *Norlie.*

how is it then that he saith, I came down from heaven?: So how can He say, *Williams* . . . What does he mean by saying, *Norlie.*

6:43. "Murmur not" (*gonguzete*) literally means "stop (your) grumbling." The Greek negative *mē* with the imperative means "stop doing it." Jesus' statement is a strong command. The charge not to grumble is given first for their own welfare. They were in danger of the same judgment as Israel was in the wilderness. Secondly, the grumbling of the Jewish leaders would doubtless affect the spiritual condition of others who lacked the capacity to think for themselves. One's attitude is usually caught and reflected in the conduct of associates.

43. Jesus therefore answered and said unto them, Murmur not among yourselves: Stop grumbling to one another, *Phillips* . . . Stop your mutual mutterings! *Berkeley* . . . Stop your whispering campaign of complaint, *Barclay* . . . Do not find fault with me among yourselves, *TCNT, Montgomery.*

6:44. Men are by their nature sinners with no possibility of attaining salvation by themselves. "Except the Father which hath sent me draw him" indicates the only hope the sinner has of obtaining salvation. The word "draw" (*helkusē*) means "to draw or to lead, drag, or pull" (see Deuteronomy 21:3; John 12:32; 18:10; 21:6,11; Acts 16:19). The word is used as a metaphor here. The Father draws by sending the Son into the world with the revelation of himself. God draws the sinner by revealing His love displayed on Calvary. The drawing power of the Father takes place by the Holy Spirit's reproving, convincing, and convicting the sinner of sin, righteousness, and judgment to come (16:8-11).

The Old Testament likewise frequently speaks of people being "drawn" to God by His mercy. In Jeremiah 31:3 God says, "With loving-kindness have I drawn thee," and in Hosea 11:4 God says, "I drew them with cords of a man, with bands of love."

In John 12:32 Jesus assures His hearers that "I, if I be lifted up from the earth will draw all men unto me." The overriding theme

44. No man can come to me, except the Father which hath sent me draw him: . . . unless the Father, *RSV* . . . without being attracted to me by the Father, *Knox* . . . draws him to me, *TCNT.*

3854.11 verb nom sing masc part aor act	1466.6 prs-pron acc 1sing	1657.4 verb 3sing subj aor act	840.6 prs-pron acc sing masc	2504.1 conj
πέμψας	με	ἑλκύσῃ	αὐτόν,	‘ καὶ
pempsas	*me*	*helkusē*	*auton*	*kai*
having sent	me	draw	him,	and

44.b.**Var:** 02A,03B,04C,05D,017K,019L,029T,036,byz.it.sa.bo.Gries,Lach,Treg,Alf,WordTisc,We/Ho,Weis,Sod,UBS/☆

1466.1 prs-pron nom 1sing	2476.3 conj	448.1 verb 1sing act	840.6 prs-pron acc sing masc	1706.1 prep
ἐγὼ	[☆ κἀγὼ]	ἀναστήσω	αὐτὸν	[b☆+ ἐν]
egō	*kagō*	*anastēsō*	*auton*	*en*
I	[and I]	will raise up	him	[in]

3450.11 art dat sing fem	2057.9 adj dat sing fem	2232.3 noun dat sing fem	1498.4 verb 3sing indic pres act	1119.29 verb sing neu part perf pass
τῇ	ἐσχάτῃ	ἡμέρᾳ.	**45.** ἔστιν	γεγραμμένον
tē	*eschatē*	*hēmera*	*estin*	*gegrammenon*
at the	last	day.	It is	written

45.a.**Txt:** Steph
Var: 01ℵ,02A,03B,04C,05D,017K,019L,029T,036,037,038,byz.Gries,Lach,Treg,Alf,Word,Tisc,We/HoWeis,Sod,UBS/☆

1706.1 prep	3450.4 art dat pl	4254.6 noun dat pl masc	2504.1 conj	1498.43 verb 3pl indic fut mid	3820.7 adj pl masc
ἐν	τοῖς	προφήταις,	Καὶ	ἔσονται	πάντες
en	*tois*	*prophētais*	*Kai*	*esontai*	*pantes*
in	the	prophets,	And	they shall be	all

45.b.**Txt:** 02A,017K,036,037,038,1,byz.
Var: 01ℵ,03B,04C,05D,019L,029T,it.sa.bo.Gries,Lach,Treg,Alf,Tisc,We/Ho,Weis,Sod,UBS/☆

1312.1 adj nom pl masc	3450.2 art gen sing	2296.2 noun gen sing masc	3820.6 adj sing masc	3631.1 conj	3450.5 art sing masc
διδακτοὶ	‘a τοῦ ’	θεοῦ.	Πᾶς	‘b οὖν ’	ὁ
didaktoi	*tou*	*theou*	*Pas*	*oun*	*ho*
taught		of God.	Everyone	therefore	the

189.31 verb nom sing masc part aor act	3706.2 prep	3450.2 art gen sing	3824.2 noun gen sing masc	2504.1 conj	3101.12 verb nom sing masc part aor act
ἀκούσας	παρὰ	τοῦ	πατρὸς	καὶ	μαθὼν,
akousas	*para*	*tou*	*patros*	*kai*	*mathōn*
having heard	from	the	Father	and	having learned,

45.c.**Txt:** p66,02A,04C,05D,017K,019L,032W,036,037,1,13,byz.Lach,Sod
Var: p75,01ℵ,03B,029T,038,Treg,Tisc,We/Ho Weis,UBS/☆

2048.34 verb 3sing indic pres	4242.1 prep	1466.6 prs-pron acc 1sing	1466.7 prs-pron acc 1sing	3620.1 partic	3617.1 conj	3450.6 art acc sing masc
ἔρχεται	πρὸς	‘ με·	[c ἐμέ.]	**46.** οὐχ	ὅτι	τὸν
erchetai	*pros*	*me*	*eme*	*ouch*	*hoti*	*ton*
comes	to	me:	[idem]	not	that	the

3824.4 noun acc sing masc	4948.3 indef-pron nom sing	3571.11 verb 3sing indic perf act	3571.11 verb 3sing indic perf act	4948.3 indef-pron nom sing
πατέρα	‘ τις	ἑώρακέν,	[☆ ἑώρακέν	τις]
patera	*tis*	*heōraken*	*heōraken*	*tis*
Father	anyone	has seen,	[has seen	anyone]

1479.1 conj	3231.1 partic	3450.5 art sing masc	1498.21 verb sing masc part pres act	3706.2 prep	3450.2 art gen sing	2296.2 noun gen sing masc
εἰ	μὴ	ὁ	ὢν	παρὰ	τοῦ	θεοῦ,
ei	*mē*	*ho*	*ōn*	*para*	*tou*	*theou*
if	not	the	being	from		God,

46.a.**Var:** 01ℵ-org,05D,Tisc

3642.4 dem-pron nom sing masc	3571.11 verb 3sing indic perf act	3450.6 art acc sing masc	3824.4 noun acc sing masc	2296.4 noun acc sing masc
οὗτος	ἑώρακεν	τὸν	‘ πατέρα.	[a θεόν.]
houtos	*heōraken*	*ton*	*patera*	*theon*
this	has seen	the	Father.	[God.]

279.1 partic	279.1 partic	2978.1 verb 1sing pres act	5050.3 prs-pron dat 2pl	3450.5 art sing masc	3961.10 verb nom sing masc part pres act
47. ἀμὴν	ἀμὴν	λέγω	ὑμῖν,	ὁ	πιστεύων
amēn	*amēn*	*legō*	*humin*	*ho*	*pisteuōn*
Truly	truly	I say	to you,	The	believing

is on God's love which draws men to himself, so the emphasis should not be shifted to defend any certain view of election. John 6:44 does not teach particular election (i.e., the view that God determines who will be saved) because 6:45 opens salvation to "every man." Nor do 6:45 and 12:32 teach universalism, for 6:47 stresses that one must believe in order to get eternal life; it does not come unconditionally. Hebrews makes this clear when it says, "He that cometh to God must believe that he is" (Hebrews 11:6).

"I will raise him up at the last day." The refrain is repeated as in verses 39,40,44, and 54.

and I will raise him up at the last day: I will restore him at, *Fenton* . . . and I will resurrect him, *Adams* . . . from death, *TCNT* . . . to life, *Norlie.*

6:45. "The prophets" refers to the second division of the Old Testament, according to the Jewish system of dividing and describing the Scriptures. "And they shall be all taught of God" is a reference to Isaiah 54:13. The quotation is a free translation of the Septuagint, the standard Bible in Jesus' time. God draws by teaching as Isaiah predicted. "Drawing" is a prerequisite to "believing." Learning of Him brings rest from the burdens of life (Matthew 11:28-30).

45. It is written in the prophets, And they shall be all taught of God: It stands written in the Prophets, *Weymouth* . . . And they will all have teaching from God, *BB* . . . God will teach everyone, *Beck* . . . have Him in person for their teacher, *AmpB.*

Every man therefore that hath heard: If a man listens to the Father, *Barclay* . . . Every one who has listened to, *Fenton* . . . who has heard in the presence of and directly from the, *Wuest.*

and hath learned of the Father, cometh unto me: All who are instructed by the Father, *TCNT.*

6:46. The invisibility of God is taught in the Scriptures (1:18). This is the reason no image could be made of God (Exodus 20:4).

"Save he which is of God" (*ei mē ho ōn para tou theou*) is difficult to render literally because of the preposition "from" (*para*). It has the basic meaning of "beside." The same Greek word is used in 1:14 with reference to the Logos relationship with the Father. The "beside" relationship is much more expressive of a partnership and expresses the idea of a position. Therefore, because of the Son's position He is able to declare the Father.

"He hath seen." "He" (*houtos*, literally "this one") receives the emphasis of the statement. Since no human being has ever seen God to know Him that way, Jesus Christ is the only being who has perfect knowledge of the Father and, therefore, can accurately convey the revelation of God to man.

46. Not that any man hath seen the Father, save he which is of God: Which does not imply that anyone, *Berkeley* . . . That doesn't mean that anybody has seen the Father except, *Adams* . . . with the exception of the one who is from, *TCNT* . . . except He who is from God, *Norlie* . . . who has come from the presence of God, *Barclay* . . . from alongside of God, *Berkeley.*

he hath seen the Father: . . . he alone has seen, *ALBA* . . . is the one who was with God, *SEB.*

6:47. The manifestation of God through the Son is the subject of Jesus' discourse. The Person of the manifestation, therefore, must be believed in order that eternal life might be possessed. "He that believeth" (*ho pisteuōn*) denotes the one who is believing. The present condition of believing is followed by the present possession of "everlasting life." *Pisteuō* ("believe") is used more often than any other term to express one's experience in Christ. It is probably the

47. Verily, verily, I say unto you, He that believeth on me hath everlasting life: I say to you most solemnly, *Norlie* . . . In very truth

John 6:48

47.a.**Txt:** 02A,04C-corr, 05D,017K,036,037,1,13, byz.it.sa.bo.Gries,Lach, Treg,Alf
Var: p66,p75,01ℵ,03B, 04C-org,019L,029T, 032W,038,Tisc,We/Ho, WeisSod,UBS/☆

1519.1 prep	1466.7 prs-pron acc 1sing	2174.4 verb 3sing indic pres act	2205.4 noun acc sing fem	164.1 adj sing	1466.1 prs-pron nom 1sing
⸀[a] εἰς	ἐμὲ ⸌	ἔχει	ζωὴν	αἰώνιον.	**48.** ἐγώ
eis	*eme*	*echei*	*zōēn*	*aiōnion*	*egō*
on	me	has	life	eternal.	I

1498.2 verb 1sing indic pres act	3450.5 art sing masc	735.1 noun nom sing masc	3450.10 art gen sing fem	2205.2 noun gen sing fem	3450.7 art pl masc
εἰμι	ὁ	ἄρτος	τῆς	ζωῆς.	**49.** οἱ
eimi	*ho*	*artos*	*tēs*	*zōēs*	*hoi*
am	the	bread	of the	life.	The

3824.6 noun pl masc	5050.2 prs-pron gen 2pl	2052.27 verb indic aor pass	3450.16 art sing neu	3103.1 noun sing neu	1706.1 prep	3450.11 art dat sing fem
πατέρες	ὑμῶν	ἔφαγον	⸀ τὸ	μάννα	ἐν	τῇ
pateres	*humōn*	*ephagon*	*to*	*manna*	*en*	*tē*
fathers	your	ate	the	manna	in	the

2031.2 noun dat sing fem	1706.1 prep	3450.11 art dat sing fem	2031.2 noun dat sing fem	3450.16 art sing neu	3103.1 noun sing neu	2504.1 conj
ἐρήμῳ,	[☆ ἐν	τῇ	ἐρήμῳ	τὸ	μάννα]	καὶ
erēmō	*en*	*tē*	*erēmō*	*to*	*manna*	*kai*
desert,	[in	the	desert	the	manna]	and

594.9 verb indic aor act	3642.4 dem-pron nom sing masc	1498.4 verb 3sing indic pres act	3450.5 art sing masc	735.1 noun nom sing masc
ἀπέθανον·	**50.** οὗτός	ἐστιν	ὁ	ἄρτος
apethanon	*houtos*	*estin*	*ho*	*artos*
died.	This	is	the	bread

3450.5 art sing masc	1523.2 prep gen	3450.2 art gen sing	3636.2 noun gen sing masc	2568.2 verb nom sing masc part pres act	2419.1 conj
ὁ	ἐκ	τοῦ	οὐρανοῦ	καταβαίνων,	ἵνα
ho	*ek*	*tou*	*ouranou*	*katabainōn*	*hina*
the	out of	the	heaven	coming down,	that

4948.3 indef-pron nom sing	1523.1 prep gen	840.3 prs-pron gen sing	2052.17 verb 3sing subj aor act	2504.1 conj	3231.1 partic	594.13 verb 3sing subj aor act
τις	ἐξ	αὐτοῦ	φάγῃ	καὶ	μὴ	ἀποθάνῃ.
tis	*ex*	*autou*	*phagē*	*kai*	*mē*	*apothanē*
anyone	of	it	may eat	and	not	die.

1466.1 prs-pron nom 1sing	1498.2 verb 1sing indic pres act	3450.5 art sing masc	735.1 noun nom sing masc	3450.5 art sing masc	2180.10 verb sing part pres act
51. ἐγώ	εἰμι	ὁ	ἄρτος	ὁ	ζῶν,
egō	*eimi*	*ho*	*artos*	*ho*	*zōn*
I	am	the	bread	the	living,

3450.5 art sing masc	1523.2 prep gen	3450.2 art gen sing	3636.2 noun gen sing masc	2568.20 verb nom sing masc part aor act	1430.1 partic
ὁ	ἐκ	τοῦ	οὐρανοῦ	καταβάς·	ἐάν
ho	*ek*	*tou*	*ouranou*	*katabas*	*ean*
the	out of	the	heaven	having come down:	if

51.a.**Var:** 01ℵ,Tisc

51.b.**Txt:** p66,03B,04C, 017K,029T,036,037,1, 13,byz.LachWeis
Var: 01ℵ,05D,019L,038, 33,Tisc,We/Ho,Sod, UBS/☆

4948.3 indef-pron nom sing	2052.17 verb 3sing subj aor act	1523.2 prep gen	3642.1 dem-pron gen sing	3450.2 art gen sing
τις	φάγῃ	ἐκ	⸀ τούτου	τοῦ
tis	*phagē*	*ek*	*toutou*	*tou*
anyone	shall have eaten	of	this	the

3450.2 art gen sing	1684.11 adj gen 1sing neu	735.2 noun gen sing masc	2180.29 verb 3sing indic fut mid	2180.33 verb 3sing indic fut act
[[a] τοῦ	ἐμοῦ]	ἄρτου	⸀ ζήσεται	[[b]☆ ζήσει]
tou	*emou*	*artou*	*zēsetai*	*zēsei*
[the	my]	bread	he shall live	[idem]

most used term for Christians. Of all the terms for one's personal salvation, this is the most foundational and simple. The term is explained by "receiving Christ" (1:12), "coming to Jesus" (6:37), "born again" (3:3), and "drinking and eating of Christ" (6:54). In all these references the experience is the same, yet the vantage point differs.

"Hath everlasting life" is a present possession. By trusting in Jesus as the true and final revelation of the Father and by committing one's being to what He stands for, one has eternal life now. He did not say he who "believed" but *is* "believing." It is not sufficient to have trusted and committed at a time in the past. The experience must be a present practice.

I tell you, *Weymouth* . . . I tell you the truth, if you believe, you have everlasting life, *Beck* . . . I tell you most decisively that the believer possesses, *Fenton.*

6:48. "I am that bread of life." Jesus has just referred to eternal life (verse 47). Now He connects the "believeth" to himself as the nourishing, sustaining, and maintaining power of that present possession of everlasting life.

48. I am that bread of life: I am the Life-giving Bread, *TCNT* . . . I am the bread that gives life, *Williams.*

6:49. The Jews had wanted a sign like the manna in the wilderness. Jesus contrasted what the results were for their fathers with what could happen to them. The miracle manna was wonderful to sustain life, but it was temporary life. They died. The sign Jesus gives is greater than the manna because it provides everlasting life.

49. Your fathers did eat manna in the wilderness, and are dead: . . . forefathers, *ET* . . . in the desert, *Confraternity* . . . and they died, *ASV, Norlie* . . . nevertheless they died, *ALBA.*

6:50. "Which cometh down from heaven" has been stated by our Lord in verses 32,33,41,42,50,51, and 58. "That a man may eat thereof" further parallels Jesus as the Bread of Life with the manna. "Not die" expresses that eating of Him insures against spiritual death.

50. This is the bread which cometh down from heaven: There is a type of food which comes down from heaven, *SEB* . . . But here is the bread, *Williams* . . . The bread which comes down from heaven is such bread, *BB* . . . which out of heaven descends, *Wuest.*

that a man may eat thereof, and not die: . . . of which one may eat and never die, *Norlie* . . . so that anyone may eat, *Williams* . . . that any one may eat of it, and never die, *TCNT* . . . so that when people eat it they won't die, *Adams* . . . is such that one eats of it and never dies, *Moffatt* . . . is of such a kind that whoever eats it will not die, *TEV.*

6:51. "The living bread" corresponds to the term "bread of life" (John 6:35,48) in the same manner as "the living water" (John 4:10) corresponds to the term "water of life" (Revelation 21:6; 22:1,17). Jesus is living; therefore, the bread He gives is living bread. "The living bread" is subjective and the "bread of life" is objective. As the believer appropriates Jesus, He becomes the believer's life. Jesus can become life to the believer, because He is "the living bread." Up to this point the analogy was simple enough. The Old Testa-

51. I am the living bread which came down from heaven: . . . which descended from out of, *Fenton.*

if any man eat of this bread, he shall live for ever: Whoever eats of, *Norlie* . . . he schal lyve with outen ende, *Wycliffe* . . . he will have life for ever, *BB* . . . to the remotest age, *Rotherham* . . . in the future age, *Scarlett.*

1519.1 prep	**3450.6** art acc sing masc	**163.3** noun acc sing masc	**2504.1** conj	**3450.5** art sing masc	**735.1** noun nom sing masc	**1156.2** conj
εἰς	τὸν	αἰῶνα.	καὶ	ὁ	ἄρτος	δὲ
eis	*ton*	*aiōna*	*kai*	*ho*	*artos*	*de*
unto	the	age;	and	the	bread	also

3614.6 rel-pron acc sing masc	**1466.1** prs-pron nom 1sing	**1319.36** verb 1sing indic fut act	**3450.9** art nom sing fem	**4418.1** noun nom sing fem	**1466.2** prs-pron gen 1sing
ὃν	ἐγὼ	δώσω,	ἡ	σάρξ	μού
hon	*egō*	*dōsō*	*hē*	*sarx*	*mou*
which	I	will give,	the	flesh	my

51.c.**Txt:** 017K,036,037,038,1,13,byz.bo.
Var: 03B,04C,05D,019L,029T,33,sa.Lach,Treg,Alf,Tisc,We/Ho,Weis,Sod,UBS/⋆

1498.4 verb 3sing indic pres act	**3614.12** rel-pron acc sing fem	**1466.1** prs-pron nom 1sing	**1319.36** verb 1sing indic fut act	**5065.1** prep	**3450.10** art gen sing fem
ἐστιν,	⸀c ἣν	ἐγὼ	δώσω ⸃	ὑπὲρ	τῆς
estin	*hēn*	*egō*	*dōsō*	*huper*	*tēs*
is,	which	I	will give	for	the

3450.2 art gen sing	**2862.2** noun gen sing masc	**2205.2** noun gen sing fem	**3136.4** verb 3pl indic imperf	**3631.1** conj
τοῦ	κόσμου	ζωῆς.	**52.** Ἐμάχοντο	οὖν
tou	*kosmou*	*zōēs*	*Emachonto*	*oun*
of the	world	life.	Were contending	therefore

4242.1 prep	**238.3** prs-pron acc pl masc	**3450.7** art pl masc	**2428.2** name-adj pl masc	**2978.16** verb pl masc part pres act	**4316.1** adv
πρὸς	ἀλλήλους	οἱ	Ἰουδαῖοι,	λέγοντες,	Πῶς
pros	*allēlous*	*hoi*	*Ioudaioi*	*legontes*	*Pōs*
with	one another	the	Jews	saying,	How

1404.4 verb 3sing indic pres	**3642.4** dem-pron nom sing masc	**2231.3** prs-pron dat 1pl	**1319.31** verb inf aor act	**3450.12** art acc sing fem	**4418.4** noun acc sing fem
δύναται	οὗτος	ἡμῖν	δοῦναι	τὴν	σάρκα
dunatai	*houtos*	*hēmin*	*dounai*	*tēn*	*sarka*
is able	this	us	to give	the	flesh

52.a.**Var:** p66,03B,029T,892,1079,it.sa.bo.Lach,We/Ho

840.3 prs-pron gen sing	**2052.25** verb inf aor act	**1500.5** verb 3sing indic aor act	**3631.1** conj	**840.2** prs-pron dat pl
[a+ αὐτοῦ]	φαγεῖν;	**53.** Εἶπεν	οὖν	αὐτοῖς
autou	*phagein*	*Eipen*	*oun*	*autois*
[his]	to eat?	Said	therefore	to them

3450.5 art sing masc	**2400.1** name nom masc	**279.1** partic	**279.1** partic	**2978.1** verb 1sing pres act	**5050.3** prs-pron dat 2pl	**1430.1** partic
ὁ	Ἰησοῦς,	Ἀμὴν	ἀμὴν	λέγω	ὑμῖν,	ἐὰν
ho	*Iēsous*	*Amēn*	*amēn*	*legō*	*humin*	*ean*
	Jesus,	Truly	truly	I say	to you,	If

3231.1 partic	**2052.19** verb 2pl subj aor act	**3450.12** art acc sing fem	**4418.4** noun acc sing fem	**3450.2** art gen sing	**5048.2** noun gen sing masc
μὴ	φάγητε	τὴν	σάρκα	τοῦ	υἱοῦ
mē	*phagēte*	*tēn*	*sarka*	*tou*	*huiou*
not	you shall have eaten	the	flesh	of the	Son

3450.2 art gen sing	**442.2** noun gen sing masc	**2504.1** conj	**3956.17** verb 2pl subj aor act	**840.3** prs-pron gen sing	**3450.16** art sing neu
τοῦ	ἀνθρώπου	καὶ	πίητε	αὐτοῦ	τὸ
tou	*anthrōpou*	*kai*	*piēte*	*autou*	*to*
	of man	and	shall have drunk	his	the

129.1 noun sing neu	**3620.2** partic	**2174.2** verb 2pl pres act	**2205.4** noun acc sing fem	**1706.1** prep	**1431.7** prs-pron dat pl masc	**3450.5** art sing masc
αἷμα,	οὐκ	ἔχετε	ζωὴν	ἐν	ἑαυτοῖς.	**54.** ὁ
haima	*ouk*	*echete*	*zōēn*	*en*	*heautois*	*ho*
blood,	not	you have	life	in	yourselves.	The

ment miracle of manna gave life to the Israelites in the desert if they ate of it daily. Jesus proclaims himself as the Bread of Life in whom, if one believes, he has eternal life. The bread whose origin was heaven (not as the manna which formed on earth) stresses the source of the miracle as more important as a sign because (1) the heavenly origin is superior to the earthly, and (2) the result is eternal life as compared to temporal life.

Jesus pointed to himself as this bread. Unless bread is eaten, it cannot produce life. Manna would have done no Israelite any good had he refused to eat of it.

"He shall live for ever." This declaration is not essentially different from verse 50. Jesus said one who believes has everlasting life (verse 47). To "live forever" is to have everlasting life. The connective of eating of Jesus (as bread) and living forever was repugnant to the Jews.

"My flesh" indicates the tangible, physical part of Jesus' humanity. Flesh speaks of the frail, temporal, earthly being of the Lord. His "flesh" was the part of His humanity that could suffer and die for the benefit of the world.

"For the life of the world" (*huper tēs tou kosmou zōēs*) is literally "in behalf of or instead of the life of the world." Jesus took the place of anyone in the world who would believe in Him. In so doing He gave all that it was possible to give. He could not give up His deity, for He would not, nor could not, change His essential being. He could give that which was transitory and earthly, His flesh.

6:52. "To argue" (NASB; *emachonto*) is translated "strove" by the King James Version. The word literally means "to fight" (see James 4:2). Thus the word for "sword" (*machaira*) is derived from the same Greek word. The obvious use here is as a metaphor. The context indicates what their arguing was about.

"Flesh" (*sarka*) is not meant to be taken literally, though some of the Jews interpreted it that way. The arguing was over the literal versus the metaphorical meaning of the term.

6:53. "Except ye eat the flesh of the Son of man, and drink his blood." The Jews were not following His thought. The eating and drinking of Him meant believing and receiving Him as the revelation of the Father. He had explained that coming to Him, believing in Him, is to have eternal life (verse 47).

6:54. Jesus presented the negative aspect in verse 53. Now He states the same truth in the positive. "Whoso eateth (*ho trōgōn*) my

and the bread that I will give is my flesh: . . . moreover, the bread which, *Montgomery* . . . is my body, *Fenton, Norton.*

which I will give for the life of the world: . . . which I sacrifice, *ET* . . . given on behalf of, *Wuest* . . . for the world's life, *Rotherham* . . . I want the people of the world to live, *SEB.*

52. The Jews therefore strove among themselves, saying: At this, the Jews argued among, *Norlie* . . . The Jews therefore contended with one another, *HBIE* . . . Then the Jews began to dispute among themselves, *Montgomery* . . . This led to an angry debate among the Jews, *Weymouth* . . . This started an angry argument, *TEV* . . . led to a fierce argument, *Phillips* . . . wrangled with each other, *Berkeley* . . . disputed with each other, *Norton* . . . began wrangling with one another, *Wuest* . . . began disputing with one another, *TCNT* . . . had an angry discussion, *BB* . . . violently argued, *Adams.*

How can this man give us his flesh to eat?: How is it possible for, *TCNT.*

53. Then Jesus said unto them, Verily, verily, I say unto you: With all the earnestness I possess I tell you this, *LivB.*

Except ye eat the flesh of the Son of man, and drink his blood: . . . unless you appropriate His life, *AmpB..* . . and if you do not take his blood for drink, *BB* . . . Unless you do eat the body of the Son of Man and drink his blood, *Phillips.*

ye have no life in you: You cannot have any life in yourselves, *AmpB* . . . you have no inner life, *Berkeley* . . . you are not really living at all, *Phillips* . . . you are not having life in yourselves, *Wuest.*

John 6:55

5017.1 verb nom sing masc part pres act	**1466.2** prs-pron gen 1sing	**3450.12** art acc sing fem	**4418.4** noun acc sing fem	**2504.1** conj	**3956.8** verb nom sing masc part pres act
τρώγων	μου	τὴν	σάρκα,	καὶ	πίνων
trōgōn	*mou*	*tēn*	*sarka*	*kai*	*pinōn*
eating	my	the	flesh,	and	drinking

1466.2 prs-pron gen 1sing	**3450.16** art sing neu	**129.1** noun sing neu	**2174.4** verb 3sing indic pres act	**2205.4** noun acc sing fem	**164.1** adj sing
μου	τὸ	αἷμα,	ἔχει	ζωὴν	αἰώνιον,
mou	*to*	*haima*	*echei*	*zōēn*	*aiōnion*
my	the	blood,	has	life	eternal,

2504.1 conj	**1466.1** prs-pron nom 1sing	**2476.3** conj	**448.1** verb 1sing act	**840.6** prs-pron acc sing masc
ʼ καὶ	ἐγὼ	[☆ κἀγὼ]	ἀναστήσω	αὐτὸν
kai	*egō*	*kagō*	*anastēsō*	*auton*
and	I	[and I]	will raise up	him

54.a.**Var:** 04C,017K, 021M,029T,037,041,13, Lach,Weis,Sod

1706.1 prep	**3450.11** art dat sing fem	**2057.9** adj dat sing fem	**2232.3** noun dat sing fem	**3450.9** art nom sing fem	**1056.1** conj
[a+ ἐν]	τῇ	ἐσχάτῃ	ἡμέρᾳ·	**55.** ἡ	γὰρ
en	*tē*	*eschatē*	*hēmera*	*hē*	*gar*
[in]	in the	last	day;	the	for

55.a.**Txt:** p66-org,(05), 036,037,038,byz.it. **Var:** p66-corr,p75, 01ℵ-corr,03B,04C,017K, 019L,029T,032W,1,sa. bo.Lach,Treg,Alf,Tisc, We/HoWeis,Sod,UBS/☆

4418.1 noun nom sing fem	**1466.2** prs-pron gen 1sing	**228.1** adv	**225.2** adj nom sing	**1498.4** verb 3sing indic pres act
σάρξ	μου	ʼ ἀληθῶς	[a☆ ἀληθής]	ἐστιν
sarx	*mou*	*alēthōs*	*alēthēs*	*estin*
flesh	my	truly	[true]	is

1028.1 noun nom sing fem	**2504.1** conj	**3450.16** art sing neu	**129.1** noun sing neu	**1466.2** prs-pron gen 1sing	**228.1** adv
βρῶσις,	καὶ	τὸ	αἷμά	μου	ʼ ἀληθῶς
brōsis	*kai*	*to*	*haima*	*mou*	*alēthōs*
food,	and	the	blood	my	truly

55.b.**Txt:** p66-org,(05), 036,037,038,byz.it. **Var:** p66-corr,p75, 01ℵ-corr,03B,04C,017K, 019L,029T,032W,1,sa. bo.Lach,Treg,Alf,Tisc, We/HoWeis,Sod,UBS/☆

225.2 adj nom sing	**1498.4** verb 3sing indic pres act	**4072.1** noun nom sing fem	**3450.5** art sing masc	**5017.1** verb nom sing masc part pres act
[b☆ ἀληθής]	ἐστιν	πόσις.	**56.** ὁ	τρώγων
alēthēs	*estin*	*posis*	*ho*	*trōgōn*
[true]	is	drink.	The	eating

1466.2 prs-pron gen 1sing	**3450.12** art acc sing fem	**4418.4** noun acc sing fem	**2504.1** conj	**3956.8** verb nom sing masc part pres act	**1466.2** prs-pron gen 1sing
μου	τὴν	σάρκα	καὶ	πίνων	μου
mou	*tēn*	*sarka*	*kai*	*pinōn*	*mou*
my	the	flesh	and	drinking	my

3450.16 art sing neu	**129.1** noun sing neu	**1706.1** prep	**1466.5** prs-pron dat 1sing	**3176.1** verb 3sing indic act	**2476.3** conj	**1706.1** prep
τὸ	αἷμα,	ἐν	ἐμοὶ	μένει,	κἀγὼ	ἐν
to	*haima*	*en*	*emoi*	*menei*	*kagō*	*en*
the	blood,	in	me	remains,	and I	in

840.4 prs-pron dat sing	**2503.1** conj	**643.8** verb 3sing indic aor act	**1466.6** prs-pron acc 1sing	**3450.5** art sing masc
αὐτῷ.	**57.** καθὼς	ἀπέστειλέν	με	ὁ
autō	*kathōs*	*apesteilen*	*me*	*ho*
him.	As	sent	me	the

2180.10 verb sing part pres act	**3824.1** noun nom sing masc	**2476.3** conj	**2180.5** verb 1sing indic pres act	**1217.2** prep	**3450.6** art acc sing masc
ζῶν	πατὴρ,	κἀγὼ	ζῶ	διὰ	τὸν
zōn	*patēr*	*kagō*	*zō*	*dia*	*ton*
living	Father,	and I	live	because of	the

flesh" is a present participle meaning a habitual eating. The like present tense verb is used in verse 47 for "believeth." Therefore, the one believing is the one who is eating. The result is the same also, "hath eternal life."

"And I will raise him up at the last day." This is the fourth and final statement of the resurrection of the one who believes in Christ (see also verses 39,40). To eat and drink of Him is to appropriate the life of the One who is speaking. Observe that the statement is a promise to the believer and a prediction for all men. Take note that the time is mentioned "at the last day," meaning at the end of the last days.

54. Whoso eateth my flesh, and drinketh my blood: . . . whoever continues to eat...and drink, *Williams* . . . He who feeds on my flesh, *Moffatt, Montgomery* . . . is masticating My flesh, *Concordant.*

hath eternal life; and I will raise him up at the last day: Hath life age-abiding, *Rotherham* . . . already possesses, *Williams* . . . possesses now, *AmpB* . . . and I will restore him, *Fenton.*

6:55,56. "He that eateth . . . and drinketh" indicates a present tense habitual communion with Jesus. The meaning of verse 55 depends on whether one prefers the reading of *alēthōs* (an adverb meaning "truly" or "really") or *alēthēs* (an adjective meaning "true" or "real"). The adjectival reading (true or real) stresses the actual act of eating and drinking (i.e., one eats and drinks real flesh and real drink). This translation is unlikely because John regularly uses *alēthinos* to mean true or real (cf. 4:37; 8:16; 19:35). The adverbial reading stresses the reality (or better, reliability) of Jesus' bread and drink. They are the only valid way to attain life (cf. 14:6).

"Dwelleth in me" should have convinced the Jews and the disciples that Jesus was not speaking in literal terms. These words explain how the "I in him" relationship is by eating and drinking. This action binds the two parties as one. There is an interesting comparison in the Book of Revelation: "I will come in to him, and will dine with him, and he with me" (Revelation 3:20, NASB). This promise is made to the one who hears his voice and opens the door. Eating and drinking together is expressive of mutual participation and of fellowship in the highest sense.

55. For my flesh is meat indeed, and my blood is drink indeed: For my flesh is true food, and my blood is true drink, *Rotherham* . . . is real food and my blood is real drink, *Williams* . . . my flesh is truly meat, *Campbell* . . . genuine food, *Berkeley.*

56. He that eateth my flesh, and drinketh my blood, dwelleth in me, and I in him: Those who take my flesh for their food, *TCNT* . . . stay in me and I stay in him, *SEB* . . . abides in me, and I in him, *HBIE, Weymouth* . . . dwells continually in Me, *AmpB* . . . dwells continually in me and I dwell in him, *NEB* . . . continues to live in union, *Williams* . . . remains in me, *Adams, Berkeley* . . . shares my life and I share his, *Phillips* . . . in me is continually abiding, *Wuest.*

6:57. "The living Father" is a term that occurs only here, though the term "the living God" occurs 14 times in the New Testament (see 5:26). Jesus states three truths: (1) The Father lives, (2) because the Father lives the Son lives, and (3) because the Son lives the believer lives. It is the union with the living Father which makes eternal life possible and, furthermore, the continued communion with that life.

The preposition *dia* ("because of") used with the accusative can have two interpretations. It can express source (i.e., Jesus lives "through, by means of") which is the idea preferred here, or, as usual, finality (i.e., Jesus lives "for the sake of" the Father).

"Sent" (*apesteilen*) speaks of "sent with a commission." Christ came to bring life, but the life of God in the person is impossible without a vital relationship with Him.

57. As the living Father hath sent me, and I live by the Father: Just as the life-giving Father, *Berkeley* . . . on a mission, *Wuest* . . . and I live by reason of the Father, *Alford* . . . and I have life because of the Father, *BB* . . . I live through Him, *Norlie.*

3824.4 noun acc sing masc	2504.1 conj	3450.5 art sing masc	5017.1 verb nom sing masc part pres act	1466.6 prs-pron acc 1sing	2519.6 conj
πατέρα·	καὶ	ὁ	τρώγων	με,	κἀκεῖνος
patera	*kai*	*ho*	*trōgōn*	*me*	*kakeinos*
Father,	also	the	eating	me,	he also

57.a.**Txt:** p66,032W,036,037,1,byz.
Var: 01א,03B,04C-corr,017K,019L,029T,038,041,Lach,Treg,Alf,Tisc We/Ho,Weis,Sod,UBS/☆

2180.29 verb 3sing indic fut mid	2180.33 verb 3sing indic fut act	1217.1 prep	1466.7 prs-pron acc 1sing	3642.4 dem-pron nom sing masc
⸀ζήσεται	[a☆ ζήσει]	δι'	ἐμέ.	**58.** οὗτός
zēsetai	*zēsei*	*di'*	*eme*	*houtos*
shall live	[idem]	because of	me.	This

58.a.**Txt:** p66,01א,05D,017K,019L,032W,036,037,038,1,13,byz.Sod
Var: p75,03B,04C,029T,Lach,Treg,Alf,Tisc,We/HoWeis,UBS/☆

1498.4 verb 3sing indic pres act	3450.5 art sing masc	735.1 noun nom sing masc	3450.5 art sing masc	1523.2 prep gen	3450.2 art gen sing
ἐστιν	ὁ	ἄρτος	ὁ	⸀☆ ἐκ	τοῦ
estin	*ho*	*artos*	*ho*	*ek*	*tou*
is	the	bread	the	out of	the

58.b.**Txt:** 05D,017K,037,038,1,13,33,byz.it.sa.Sod
Var: p66,p75,01א,03B,04C,019L,029T,032W,bo.Lach,Treg,Alf,Tisc We/Ho,Weis,UBS/☆

1523.1 prep gen	3636.2 noun gen sing masc	2568.20 verb nom sing masc part aor act	3620.3 partic	2503.1 conj	2052.27 verb indic aor pass
[a ἐξ]	οὐρανοῦ	καταβάς·	οὐ	καθὼς	ἔφαγον
ex	*ouranou*	*katabas*	*ou*	*kathōs*	*ephagon*
[out of]	heaven	having come down.	Not	as	ate

58.c.**Txt:** 017K,036,037,038,1,13,565,byz.it.sa.Lach
Var: p66,p75,01א,03B,04C,05D,019L,029T,032W,33,bo.Gries,Treg,Alf,Tisc,We/Ho,Weis,Sod,UBS/☆

3450.7 art pl masc	3824.6 noun pl masc	5050.2 prs-pron gen 2pl	3450.16 art sing neu	3103.1 noun sing neu	2504.1 conj
οἱ	πατέρες	⸂b ὑμῶν ⸃	⸂c τὸ	μάννα, ⸃	καὶ
hoi	*pateres*	*humōn*	*to*	*manna*	*kai*
the	fathers	your	the	manna,	and

594.9 verb indic aor act	3450.5 art sing masc	5017.1 verb nom sing masc part pres act	3642.6 dem-pron acc sing masc	3450.6 art acc sing masc
ἀπέθανον·	ὁ	τρώγων	τοῦτον	τὸν
apethanon	*ho*	*trōgōn*	*touton*	*ton*
died:	the	eating	this	the

58.d.**Txt:** p66,05D,017K,021M,036,041,13,byz.Lach
Var: 01א,03B,04C,019L,029T,037,038,TregAlf,Tisc,We/Ho,Weis,Sod,UBS/☆

735.4 noun acc sing masc	2180.29 verb 3sing indic fut mid	2180.33 verb 3sing indic fut act	1519.1 prep	3450.6 art acc sing masc	163.3 noun acc sing masc
ἄρτον	⸀ζήσεται	[d☆ ζήσει]	εἰς	τὸν	αἰῶνα.
arton	*zēsetai*	*zēsei*	*eis*	*ton*	*aiōna*
bread	shall live	[idem]	unto	the	age.

3642.18 dem-pron pl neu	1500.5 verb 3sing indic aor act	1706.1 prep	4715.3 noun dat sing fem	1315.6 verb sing masc part pres act
59. Ταῦτα	εἶπεν	ἐν	συναγωγῇ	διδάσκων
Tauta	*eipen*	*en*	*sunagōgē*	*didaskōn*
These things	he said	in	synagogue	teaching

1706.1 prep	2555.1 name fem	2555.2 name fem	4044.7 adj nom pl masc
ἐν	⸀Καπερναούμ.	[☆ Καφαρναούμ.]	**60.** Πολλοὶ
en	*Kapernaoum*	*Kapharnaoum*	*Polloi*
in	Capernaum.	[idem]	Many

3631.1 conj	189.32 verb nom pl masc part aor act	1523.2 prep gen	3450.1 art gen pl	3073.6 noun gen pl masc	840.3 prs-pron gen sing
οὖν	ἀκούσαντες	ἐκ	τῶν	μαθητῶν	αὐτοῦ
oun	*akousantes*	*ek*	*tōn*	*mathētōn*	*autou*
therefore	having heard	of	the	disciples	his

60.a.**Txt:** 01א,02A,03B,04C,017K,019L,036,037,038,etc.byz.Lach,Tisc,Sod
Var: 05D,We/Ho,Weis,UBS/☆

1500.3 verb indic aor act	1500.28 verb 3pl indic aor act	4497.2 adj nom sing masc	1498.4 verb 3sing indic pres act	3642.4 dem-pron nom sing masc
⸀εἶπον,	[a☆ εἶπαν,]	Σκληρός	ἐστιν	⸀οὗτος
eipon	*eipan*	*Sklēros*	*estin*	*houtos*
said,	[idem]	Hard	is	this

"He that eateth me" indicates a partaking of the Son which results in the assimilation of life. The familiar act of eating is expressive of the life in union with Him.

so he that eateth me, even he shall live by me: . . . he also shall live because of me, *ASV* . . . so he who takes me for his food, *TCNT* . . . he who nourishes on Me, *Berkeley* . . . will have life because of me, *BB* . . . so also shall the one who feeds on Me live through Me, *Norlie.*

6:58. The figure of drinking His blood is dropped in verse 56. The metaphor of eating is sufficient to impress the truth of receiving life from the source of life.

This verse is a synopsis of the argument the Jews had with Jesus. They had asked for a sign similar to the manna in the desert wanderings (verses 31,32,49). The contrast is between their fathers who ate manna and died, and those who eat of Jesus and live forever. "Not as" shows the difference between the bread Jesus gives and the manna.

58. This is that bread which came down from heaven: Such is the bread, *Knox* . . . descending from, *Fenton.*

not as your fathers did eat manna, and are dead: . . . not such as your ancestors ate, and yet died, *TCNT* . . . it is unlike that which your forefathers ate—for they ate and yet died, *Weymouth.*

he that eateth of this bread: He that feedeth upon this bread, *Rotherham* . . . Whoever continues to eat this bread, *Williams.*

shall live for ever: . . . will have life for ever, *BB* . . . will live eternally, *Knox.*

6:59. Jesus' discourse on himself as the Bread of Life was given in the synagogue in Capernaum. Among the Jews the method of teaching was by questions and counterquestions, comments with opposing comments. The order of the synagogue service may be in part understood by a study of Luke 4:16-21.

59. These things said he in the synagogue, as he taught in Capernaum: This was the doctrine taught, *ALBA* . . . He uttered, *Berkeley* . . . He spoke thus while teaching in a synagogue at Capernaum, *TCNT.*

6:60. "His disciples" indicates the second of three groups of His hearers. The first group was the Jews; second, the disciples, followers; and third, the 12 apostles. A division of His disciples is affirmed by the word "many." This discourse in the synagogue of Capernaum divided even His followers.

"This is a hard saying." The word "hard" (*sklēros*) is found 6 times in the New Testament (Matthew 25:24; John 6:60; Acts 9:5; 26:14; James 3:4; Jude 15). The denotation of *sklēros* is "hard, rough, harsh, stern, severe, and violent." The word is sometimes used literally and often figuratively. Jesus' teaching was hard and offensive to many of His disciples (followers).

"Who can hear it?" expresses the idea of who is able to continue to hear this kind of teaching. Many were repelled, for they did not understand.

60. Many therefore of his disciples, when they had heard this, said: . . . this declaration, *Fenton.*

This is an hard saying; who can hear it?: . . . an extraordinary declaration! *Fenton* . . . This is hard to accept. Who can listen to such teaching, *Weymouth* . . . This is hard to take in! Who can listen to talk like this, *Moffatt*

6:61. "Knew in himself that his disciples murmured at it" indicates His divine knowledge of the spiritual condition of His followers (as in 2:25).

3450.5 art sing masc	3030.1 noun nom sing masc	3450.5 art sing masc	3030.1 noun nom sing masc	3642.4 dem-pron nom sing masc	4949.3 intr-pron nom sing
ὁ	λόγος˙	[☆ ὁ	λόγος	οὗτος˙]	τίς
ho	*logos*	*ho*	*logos*	*houtos*	*tis*
the	word;	[the	word	this;]	who

1404.4 verb 3sing indic pres	840.3 prs-pron gen sing	189.17 verb inf pres act	3471.18 verb nom sing masc part perf act	1156.2 conj	3450.5 art sing masc
δύναται	αὐτοῦ	ἀκούειν;	**61.** Εἰδὼς	δὲ	ὁ
dunatai	*autou*	*akouein*	*Eidōs*	*de*	*ho*
is able	it	to hear?	Knowing	but	

2400.1 name nom masc	1706.1 prep	1431.5 prs-pron dat 3sing masc	3617.1 conj	1105.1 verb 3pl indic pres act	3875.1 prep
Ἰησοῦς	ἐν	ἑαυτῷ	ὅτι	γογγύζουσιν	περὶ
Iēsous	*en*	*heautō*	*hoti*	*gonguzousin*	*peri*
Jesus	in	himself	that	grumble	concerning

3642.1 dem-pron gen sing	3450.7 art pl masc	3073.5 noun nom pl masc	840.3 prs-pron gen sing	1500.5 verb 3sing indic aor act	840.2 prs-pron dat pl
τούτου	οἱ	μαθηταὶ	αὐτοῦ	εἶπεν	αὐτοῖς,
toutou	*hoi*	*mathētai*	*autou*	*eipen*	*autois*
this	the	disciples	his	said	to them,

3642.17 dem-pron sing neu	5050.4 prs-pron acc 2pl	4479.1 verb 3sing indic pres act	1430.1 partic	3631.1 conj	2311.7 verb 2pl subj pres act
Τοῦτο	ὑμᾶς	σκανδαλίζει;	**62.** ἐὰν	οὖν	θεωρῆτε
Touto	*humas*	*skandalizei*	*ean*	*oun*	*theōrēte*
This	you	does offend?	If	then	you should see

3450.6 art acc sing masc	5048.4 noun acc sing masc	3450.2 art gen sing	442.2 noun gen sing masc	303.5 verb part pres act
τὸν	υἱὸν	τοῦ	ἀνθρώπου	ἀναβαίνοντα
ton	*huion*	*tou*	*anthrōpou*	*anabainonta*
the	Son		of man	ascending up

3562.1 adv	1498.34 verb sing indic imperf act	3450.16 art sing neu	4245.2 adj comp acc sing neu	3450.16 art sing neu	4011.1 noun sing neu
ὅπου	ἦν	τὸ	πρότερον;	**63.** τὸ	πνεῦμά
hopou	*ēn*	*to*	*proteron*	*to*	*pneuma*
where	he was	the	before?	The	Spirit

1498.4 verb 3sing indic pres act	3450.16 art sing neu	2210.3 verb sing neu part pres act	3450.9 art nom sing fem	4418.1 noun nom sing fem	3620.2 partic
ἐστιν	τὸ	ζῳοποιοῦν,	ἡ	σὰρξ	οὐκ
estin	*to*	*zōopoioun*	*hē*	*sarx*	*ouk*
it is	the	making alive,	the	flesh	not

5456.1 verb 3sing indic pres act	3625.6 num card neu	3450.17 art pl neu	4343.4 noun pl neu	3614.17 rel-pron pl neu	1466.1 prs-pron nom 1sing
ὠφελεῖ	οὐδέν˙	τὰ	ῥήματα	ἃ	ἐγὼ
ōphelei	*ouden*	*ta*	*rhēmata*	*ha*	*egō*
profits	nothing;	the	words	which	I

63.a.**Txt:** 036,037,byz. **Var:** 01ℵ,03B,04C,05D, 017K,019L,029T,030U, 038,it.bo.LachTreg,Alf, Tisc,We/Ho,Weis,Sod, UBS/☆

2953.1 verb 1sing pres act	2953.38 verb 1sing indic perf act	5050.3 prs-pron dat 2pl	4011.1 noun sing neu	1498.4 verb 3sing indic pres act
ʻ λαλῶ	[a☆ λελάληκα]	ὑμῖν,	πνεῦμά	ἐστιν
lalō	*lelalēka*	*humin*	*pneuma*	*estin*
speak	[have spoken]	to you,	spirit	are

2504.1 conj	2205.1 noun nom sing fem	1498.4 verb 3sing indic pres act	233.1 conj	1498.7 verb 3pl indic pres act	1523.1 prep gen	5050.2 prs-pron gen 2pl
καὶ	ζωή	ἐστιν.	**64.** ἀλλ'	εἰσὶν	ἐξ	ὑμῶν
kai	*zōē*	*estin*	*all'*	*eisin*	*ex*	*humōn*
and	life	are;	but	there are	of	you

Grumbling is thus equal to stumbling. To stumble sometimes means to fall. *Skandalizō* occurs 30 times in the New Testament of which 2 are found in John's Gospel. The verb is uniformly translated "offend" in the King James Version. The noun is rendered "offense," "stumble," "occasion of fall," and "stumbling block." This gives some idea of the term as gathered from its use.

"Murmured at it" points back to the preceding statements of the Lord and tells of the Jews' response to His teaching. John uses the verb for "murmuring" (*gonguzō*) which the Old Testament Septuagint employs for Israel's grumbling in the desert (see Exodus 16:7,8). Israel grumbled because of the manna (Numbers 11:6). The Jews grumbled at the Living Bread. As their fathers were, so were they! To have problems and suffering is human. To grumble and whine is to sin.

In our culture we may miss the import of bread. In the days of Jesus, bread was the important food: it was often the only food eaten at a meal. So when Jesus claimed to be their bread, He meant they could not live without Him.

6:62. Now He speaks of His ascension back to the Father (Acts 1:9). If they stumble at His descent from heaven, will they also stumble at His ascent back to heaven? This is Jesus' way of saying to His disciples, "Wait and I will prove to you all that I have taught by My resurrection and ascension." These events answered many of the disciples' questions.

6:63. "The Spirit" is contrasted with "the flesh." By expressing the two opposing ideas, the Lord asserts that His teaching is not offensive because He is not saying they are actually to eat His flesh. Eating the flesh would profit nothing.

"The words . . . are spirit, and . . . are life." God's desire and method is to impart eternal life through "the words." It is as though the breath of God breathes on man through Jesus' words, thus bringing life to the dead. God breathed on Adam's body, and he became a living being (Genesis 2:7).

6:64,65. "Jesus knew" speaks once again of His divine knowledge of all men. What He knew was that some of them did not believe. The difficulty was not in the truth of Jesus' discourse but in their unbelief.

Jesus recognized from the very beginning that apostasy would be a constant problem for the Church. His first indication of this

. . . This is more than we can stomach! *NEB* . . . This teaching is gruesome, *Norlie* . . . unbelievable! *Montgomery* . . . unreasonable, *ALBA* . . . able to take in such teaching? *BB.*

61. When Jesus knew in himself that his disciples murmured at it: But as Jesus naturally knew, *Williams* . . . Then Jesus, knowing intuitively, *Phillips* . . . that His disciples were complaining about this, *Beck* . . . were protesting about, *BB* . . . were finding fault with him about this teaching, *Montgomery.*

he said unto them, Doth this offend you?: Doth this cause you to stumble, *ASV* . . . Is this a stumbling block to you, *HBIE* . . . Is this snaring you? *Concordant* . . . Doth this stumble you? *Murdock* . . . This aggravates you? *Berkeley* . . . Does this displease you? *Montgomery* . . . Is this a hindrance to you, *TCNT.*

62. What and if ye shall see the Son of man ascend up where he was before?: What then if ye should behold the Son of man ascending up, *Alford* . . . where he was formerly? *Sawyer.*

63. It is the Spirit that quickeneth: It is the spirit that giveth life, *ASV* . . . The spirit is the life-giver, *BB* . . . It is the Spirit that gives Life, *TCNT* . . . What is spiritual gives life, *Norton* . . . which makes alive, *Sawyer.*

the flesh profiteth nothing: . . . not the flesh, *ALBA* . . . the flesh is of no value, *BB* . . . mere flesh is of no avail, *TCNT* . . . the body profiteth, *Murdock.*

the words that I speak unto you, they are spirit, and they are life: The words I have uttered to you are spirit and life, *Moffatt* . . . The messages I bring you are spirit and life, *Berkeley* . . . are spiritual, *Phillips.*

4948.7 indef-pron nom pl masc	3614.7 rel-pron nom pl masc	3620.3 partic	3961.3 verb 3pl pres act	3471.11 verb 3sing indic plperf act
τινες	οἵ	οὔ	πιστεύουσιν.	ᾔδει
tines	*hoi*	*ou*	*pisteuousin*	*ēdei*
some	who	not	believe.	Knew

1056.1 conj	1523.1 prep gen	741.2 noun gen sing fem	3450.5 art sing masc	2400.1 name nom masc	4949.6 intr-pron nom pl masc
γὰρ	ἐξ	ἀρχῆς	ὁ	Ἰησοῦς	τίνες
gar	*ex*	*archēs*	*ho*	*Iēsous*	*tines*
for	from	beginning		Jesus	who

1498.7 verb 3pl indic pres act	3450.7 art pl masc	3231.1 partic	3961.13 verb nom pl masc part pres act	2504.1 conj	4949.3 intr-pron nom sing
εἰσὶν	οἱ	μὴ	πιστεύοντες,	καὶ	τίς
eisin	*hoi*	*mē*	*pisteuontes*	*kai*	*tis*
they are	the	not	believing,	and	who

1498.4 verb 3sing indic pres act	3450.5 art sing masc	3722.25 verb nom sing masc part fut act	840.6 prs-pron acc sing masc	2504.1 conj
ἐστιν	ὁ	παραδώσων	αὐτόν.	**65.** καὶ
estin	*ho*	*paradōsōn*	*auton*	*kai*
is	the	shall be delivered up	him.	And

2978.26 verb 3sing indic imperf act	1217.2 prep	3642.17 dem-pron sing neu	2029.1 verb 1sing indic perf act	5050.3 prs-pron dat 2pl	3617.1 conj
ἔλεγεν,	Διὰ	τοῦτο	εἴρηκα	ὑμῖν,	ὅτι
elegen	*Dia*	*touto*	*eirēka*	*humin*	*hoti*
he said,	Because of	this	have I said	to you,	that

65.a.**Var:** 01א,04C,Tisc

3625.2 num card nom masc	1404.4 verb 3sing indic pres	2048.23 verb inf aor act	4242.1 prep	1466.6 prs-pron acc 1sing	1466.7 prs-pron acc 1sing
οὐδεὶς	δύναται	ἐλθεῖν	πρός	⸂ με	[a ἐμὲ]
oudeis	*dunatai*	*elthein*	*pros*	*me*	*eme*
no one	is able	to come	to	me	[idem]

65.b.**Txt:** 04C-corr,017K, 036,037,1,13,byz.
Var: 01א,03B,04C-org, 05D,019L,029T,038,28, Lach,Treg,Alf,Tisc, We/Ho,WeisSod,UBS/☆

1430.1 partic	3231.1 partic	1498.10 verb 3sing subj pres act	1319.56 verb nom sing neu part perf pass	840.4 prs-pron dat sing	1523.2 prep gen
ἐὰν	μὴ	ᾖ	δεδομένον	αὐτῷ	ἐκ
ean	*mē*	*ē*	*dedomenon*	*autō*	*ek*
if	not	it be	given	to him	from

66.a.**Var:** p66,01א,05D, 038,13,Tisc

3450.2 art gen sing	3824.2 noun gen sing masc	1466.2 prs-pron gen 1sing	1523.2 prep gen	3642.1 dem-pron gen sing	3631.1 conj
τοῦ	πατρός	⸂b μου. ⸃	**66.** Ἐκ	τούτου	[a+ οὖν]
tou	*patros*	*mou*	*Ek*	*toutou*	*oun*
the	Father	my.	From	this	[therefore]

66.b.**Var:** p66,03B,029T, 1,33,565,TregAlf,We/Ho

4044.7 adj nom pl masc	1523.2 prep gen	562.1 verb indic aor act	3450.1 art gen pl	3073.6 noun gen pl masc	840.3 prs-pron gen sing
πολλοὶ	[b+ ἐκ]	⸂ ἀπῆλθον	τῶν	μαθητῶν	αὐτοῦ
polloi	*ek*	*apēlthon*	*tōn*	*mathētōn*	*autou*
many	[from]	away went	of the	disciples	his

3450.1 art gen pl	3073.6 noun gen pl masc	840.3 prs-pron gen sing	562.1 verb indic aor act	1519.1 prep	3450.17 art pl neu
[☆ τῶν	μαθητῶν	αὐτοῦ	ἀπῆλθον]	εἰς	τὰ
tōn	*mathētōn*	*autou*	*apēlthon*	*eis*	*ta*
[of the	disciples	his	went away]	to	the

3557.1 adv	2504.1 conj	3629.1 adv	3196.2 prep	840.3 prs-pron gen sing	3906.29 verb 3pl indic imperf act
ὀπίσω,	καὶ	οὐκέτι	μετ'	αὐτοῦ	περιεπάτουν.
opisō	*kai*	*ouketi*	*met'*	*autou*	*periepatoun*
back,	and	no more	with	him	walked.

was when He spoke the Parable of the Wheat and the Tares (Matthew 13:24-30) in which "an enemy" (Matthew 13:28) sows weeds in the Church.

The Gospel of John also takes the destructive work of Satan seriously, especially in the case of Judas, who betrayed Christ (cf. 13:2,27). The First Epistle of John also shows an awareness that some will fall away (1 John 2:19) and attributes this to the work of false prophets (1 John 4:1) and the spirit of antichrist (1 John 4:3).

The sad words "many . . . walked no more with him" (John 6:66) recalls Paul's sadness over Demas who abandoned him (2 Timothy 4:10).

The Father has granted salvation by giving them His only begotten Son (3:16). The Father gives, but they must receive. No gift can benefit one until it is possessed.

"Of my Father" assures the hearer that the source of life is from (*ek*, "out of") the Father. Those who receive life from the Father, will be taking it through the Son, for His words (verse 63) bring eternal life to them.

6:66. "From that time" (*ek toutou*) literally rendered is "out of this," referring to the circumstances of His teaching in the synagogue.

"Went back" (*eis ta opisō*) means "toward the things behind." Its basic meaning is "back, behind, and after." The apostle Paul states that he forgot the things behind (*ta opisō*) (Philippians 3:13). Other uses of the word are interesting. See Matthew 24:18; Luke 9:62; 1 Timothy 5:15; 2 Peter 2:10; Revelation 13:3. Jesus used the Greek phrase *eis to opisō* in Luke 9:62, and the context of our passage fits perfectly. They were His disciples; thus they had put their hands to the plow. When the way became hard, they looked "to the things behind." Jesus said they were unfit for the kingdom of God.

Some of the saddest words recorded are here; they "walked no more with him." The words of emphasis are "no more." They come first in the Greek word order, but they are placed last in the English to stress their importance. "Walked no more" (*periepatoun*) is an imperfect tense verb to bring out the negative of habitual action. Some of the disciples began to follow Jesus when He multiplied the five loaves and two fish. He told them their discipleship was shallow because they followed for the natural food, not the spiritual (6:26,27). No matter how feeble the discipleship, the Great Shepherd must grieve over those who withdraw to seek the perishing food. Like those in the wilderness who ate the manna, they died.

6:67. This is the first mention of "the twelve" in John's Gospel. Three other references are made to the Twelve in this Gospel

64. But there are some of you that believe not: . . . who do not trust in me, *Williams* . . . who do not have faith, *ALBA* . . . who fail to believe, *Berkeley.*

For Jesus knew from the beginning who they were that believed not: For Jesus knew from the start who were the unbelievers, *Berkeley.*

and who should betray him: . . . and who would be His betrayer, *Berkeley.*

65. And he said, Therefore said I unto you, that no man can come unto me: He said, furthermore, *Norlie* . . . For this reason I forewarned you, *Fenton* . . . no one is able to come to me unless, *Moffatt* . . . This is why I told you that no one can come to me, *TCNT.*

except it were given unto him of my Father: . . . he is allowed by the Father, *Moffatt* . . . unless enabled by the Father, *TCNT* . . . only if the Father gives him the power, *Beck* . . . unless it is granted him, *Berkeley* . . . unless it is granted to him by, *Williams.*

66. From that time many of his disciples went back: . . . this speech, *Murdock* . . . As a consequence of this, *Phillips* . . . As a result many of His disciples went back to their old life, *Beck* . . . turned their backs, *Williams* . . . returned home, *Berkeley* . . . hereupon turned back, *Fenton* . . . of His pupils went away to the things they had left, *Wuest.*

and walked no more with him: . . . dropping behind, *Concordant* . . . and stopped accompanying Him, *Williams* . . . no longer associated, *Norlie* . . . no longer with him were they ordering their manner of life, *Wuest.*

1500.5 verb 3sing indic aor act	3631.1 conj	3450.5 art sing masc	2400.1 name nom masc	3450.4 art dat pl	1420.1 num card
67. εἶπεν	οὖν	ὁ	Ἰησοῦς	τοῖς	δώδεκα,
eipen	oun	ho	Iēsous	tois	dōdeka
Said	therefore		Jesus	to the	twelve,

3231.1 partic	2504.1 conj	5050.1 prs-pron nom 2pl	2286.5 verb 2pl indic pres act	5055.10 verb inf pres act	552.6 verb 3sing indic aor pass
Μὴ	καὶ	ὑμεῖς	θέλετε	ὑπάγειν;	68. Ἀπεκρίθη
Mē	kai	humeis	thelete	hupagein	Apekrithē
Not	also	you	are wishing	to go away?	Answered

68.a.**Txt:** 07E,021M,036, byz.
Var: 01ℵ,03B,04C, 017K,019L,030U,038, sa.bo.Gries,Lach,Treg Alf,Tisc,We/Ho,Weis, Sod,UBS/*

3631.1 conj	840.4 prs-pron dat sing	4468.1 name masc	3935.1 name nom masc	2935.5 noun voc sing masc	4242.1 prep	4949.1 intr-pron
[a οὖν]	αὐτῷ	Σίμων	Πέτρος,	Κύριε,	πρὸς	τίνα
oun	autō	Simōn	Petros	Kurie	pros	tina
therefore	him	Simon	Peter,	Lord,	to	whom

562.18 verb 1pl indic fut mid	4343.4 noun pl neu	2205.2 noun gen sing fem	164.2 adj gen sing	2174.3 verb 2sing indic pres act
ἀπελευσόμεθα;	ῥήματα	ζωῆς	αἰωνίου	ἔχεις·
apeleusometha	rhēmata	zōēs	aiōniou	echeis
shall we go?	words	of life	eternal	you have;

2504.1 conj	2231.1 prs-pron nom 1pl	3961.40 verb 1pl indic perf act	2504.1 conj	1091.33 verb 1pl indic perf act
69. καὶ	ἡμεῖς	πεπιστεύκαμεν	καὶ	ἐγνώκαμεν
kai	hēmeis	pepisteukamen	kai	egnōkamen
and	we	have believed	and	have known

69.a.**Txt:** 04C-corr,017K, 036,037,038,1,13,byz.
Var: p75,01ℵ,03B, 04C-org,05D,019L, 032W,Gries,Lach,Treg, Alf,Tisc,We/Ho,Weis, Sod,UBS/*

3617.1 conj	4622.1 prs-pron nom 2sing	1498.3 verb 2sing indic pres act	3450.5 art sing masc	5382.1 name nom masc	3450.5 art sing masc
ὅτι	σὺ	εἶ	[ὁ	χριστὸς	ὁ
hoti	su	ei	ho	christos	ho
that	you	are	the	Christ	the

69.b.**Txt:** 04C-corr,017K, 036,038-corr,13,byz.
Var: p75,01ℵ,03B, 04C-org,05D,019L, 032W,038-org,1,Gries, LachTreg,Alf,Tisc, We/Ho,Weis,Sod,UBS/*

5048.1 noun nom sing masc	3450.5 art sing masc	39.5 adj sing masc	3450.2 art gen sing	2296.2 noun gen sing masc	3450.2 art gen sing
υἱὸς	[a* ὁ	ἅγιος]	τοῦ	θεοῦ	[b τοῦ
huios	ho	hagios	tou	theou	tou
Son	[the	holy]		of God	the

2180.11 verb gen sing part pres act	552.6 verb 3sing indic aor pass	840.2 prs-pron dat pl	3450.5 art sing masc	2400.1 name nom masc
ζῶντος.]	70. Ἀπεκρίθη	αὐτοῖς	ὁ	Ἰησοῦς,
zōntos	Apekrithē	autois	ho	Iēsous
living.	Answered	them		Jesus,

3620.2 partic	1466.1 prs-pron nom 1sing	5050.4 prs-pron acc 2pl	3450.8 art acc pl masc	1420.1 num card	1573.1 verb 1sing indic aor mid
Οὐκ	ἐγὼ	ὑμᾶς	τοὺς	δώδεκα	ἐξελεξάμην,
Ouk	egō	humas	tous	dōdeka	exelexamēn
Not	I	you	the	twelve	did choose,

2504.1 conj	1523.1 prep gen	5050.2 prs-pron gen 2pl	1518.3 num card nom masc	1222.1 adj nom sing masc	1498.4 verb 3sing indic pres act
καὶ	ἐξ	ὑμῶν	εἷς	διάβολός	ἐστιν;
kai	ex	humōn	heis	diabolos	estin
and	of	you	one	a devil	is?

2978.26 verb 3sing indic imperf act	1156.2 conj	3450.6 art acc sing masc	2430.4 name acc masc	4468.2 name gen masc
71. Ἔλεγεν	δὲ	τὸν	Ἰούδαν	Σίμωνος
Elegen	de	ton	Ioudan	Simōnos
He spoke	but		of Judas	Simon's,

(6:70,71; 20:24). When the Twelve saw the withdrawal of so many disciples, they were shaken to the foundation of their faith. The Lord's question is put in a form that expects the negative answer, "No." "Will ye also" (*mē humeis thelete*) is spoken of with an emphasis on "ye" as compared to the disciples who withdrew from Jesus. "Will" is the Greek word usually rendered "wish." It expresses a decision based primarily on one's feelings. The Lord allowed those who wished to depart to do so; however His question reveals His desire that the Twelve stay with Him.

67. Then said Jesus unto the twelve, Will ye also go away?: Do ye also wish to go away, *Alford* . . . disposed to go away? *Murdock.*

6:68. "Simon Peter" usually speaks with great accuracy as here, but sometimes he blunders wildly (see Matthew 16:21-23). "Lord, to whom shall we go?" Peter expressed the feelings of every believer, for there is no other source of life. It is not a question of serving Christ or some other. There is no other (Acts 4:12).

"Thou hast the words of eternal life" (*rhēmata zōēs aiōniou echeis*). Peter echoed the statement Jesus made in verse 63. He added the word "eternal" to life because Jesus had made eternal life a theme of His discourse in the synagogue (verses 27,40,47,54). "The words of eternal life" are the reason to follow Jesus. The words of Christ are extensions of His being. They are parts of His nature, reaching out with life to share with His creation.

68. Then Simon Peter answered him, Lord, to whom shall we go?:

thou hast the words of eternal life: The words you have are words of, *Moffatt* . . . Your teachings tell us of eternal Life, *Weymouth* . . . You alone have the words that give eternal life, *LivB* . . . have the message that gives, *Williams* . . . hast declarations of, *Concordant* . . . have the promise, *Klingensmith* . . . the ideals of eternal life, *Fenton.*

69. And we believe and are sure that thou art that Christ, the Son of the living God: . . . and have grown certain, *Berkeley* . . . thou art the Holy One of God, *ASV.*

6:69. "We believe and are sure that thou art" (*pepisteukamen* and *egnōkamen*) are perfect tense verbs meaning the believing and the knowing began in the past and continue to the present, so that a result remained. Peter says then that we have believed and believe now; we have known and know now.

"Christ, the Son of the living God" is the same statement Peter made on another occasion (Matthew 16:16). Another textual source may be translated "the Holy One of God." This term indicates the messianic title of Jesus. The word *holy* has two basic ideas in it. First, *holy* means that which is separated to God for a special function. Second, the word *holy* means intrinsically pure as to the essence of Christ. The only being who is inherently holy is God himself.

70. Jesus answered them, Have not I chosen you twelve: Did I not choose you twelve, *Alford* . . . did I not select you, *Williams.*

and one of you is a devil?: . . . yet even of you one is an enemy, *Montgomery* . . . yet from among you one is an adversary, *Rotherham* . . . yet, even of you, one is playing the 'Devil's' part, *TCNT* . . . is a slanderer? *Concordant* . . . a Traitor? *Fenton* . . . a son of the Evil One? *BB.*

71. He spake of Judas Iscariot the son of Simon: But he was speaking of Judas, *HBIE* . . . He meant Judas...the man from Kerioth, *Beck* . . . He alluded to Judas, *Weymouth.*

6:70,71. Even though many of His followers had parted from Him, Jesus knew that the Twelve whom He had chosen were to be the foundation from which His words of eternal life would go forth.

John 7:1

71.a.**Txt:** 017K,036,037, 1,28,byz.bo.
Var: p66,p75,01ℵ corr, 03B,04C,019L,032W,sa. Lach,Treg,Alf,Tisc, We/Ho,WeisSod,UBS/☆

71.b.**Txt:** p66,05D,021M, 036,037,Steph
Var: 01ℵ,03B,04C, 017K,019L,030U,Lach, Treg,Alf,TiscWe/Ho, Weis,Sod,UBS/☆

71.c.**Txt:** p66,01ℵ, 04C-corr,017K,032W, 036,037,038,1,13,byz. Tisc,Sod
Var: p75,03B,04C-org, 05D,019L,Lach,Treg, Alf,We/HoWeis,UBS/☆

2442.4 name acc masc	**2442.2** name gen masc	**3642.4** dem-pron nom sing masc	**1056.1** conj
ʻ Ἰσκαριώτην·	[a☆ Ἰσκαριώτου·]	οὗτος	γὰρ
Iskariōtēn	*Iskariōtou*	*houtos*	*gar*
Iscariot,	[idem]	this	for

3165.21 verb 3sing indic imperf act	**3165.22** verb 3sing indic imperf act	**840.6** prs-pron acc sing masc	**3722.7** verb inf pres act
ʻ ἤμελλεν	[b☆ ἔμελλεν]	ʻ αὐτόν	παραδιδόναι,
ēmellen	*emellen*	*auton*	*paradidonai*
was about	[idem]	him	to deliver up,

3722.7 verb inf pres act	**840.6** prs-pron acc sing masc	**1518.3** num card nom masc	**1498.21** verb sing masc part pres act	**1523.2** prep gen
[☆ παραδιδόναι	αὐτόν,]	εἷς	ʻc ὢν ʼ	ἐκ
paradidonai	*auton*	*heis*	*ōn*	*ek*
[to betray	him,]	one	being	of

3450.1 art gen pl	**1420.1** num card	**2504.1** conj	**3906.28** verb 3sing indic imperf act	**3450.5** art sing masc	**2400.1** name nom masc
τῶν	δώδεκα.	7:1. Καὶ	ʻ περιεπάτει	ὁ	Ἰησοῦς
tōn	*dōdeka*	*Kai*	*periepatei*	*ho*	*Iēsous*
the	twelve.	And	was walking		Jesus

3196.3 prep	**3642.18** dem-pron pl neu	**3196.3** prep	**3642.18** dem-pron pl neu	**3906.28** verb 3sing indic imperf act
μετὰ	ταῦτα	[☆ μετὰ	ταῦτα	περιεπάτει
meta	*tauta*	*meta*	*tauta*	*periepatei*
after	these things	[after	these things	is walking

3450.5 art sing masc	**2400.1** name nom masc	**1706.1** prep	**3450.11** art dat sing fem	**1049.3** name dat sing fem	**3620.3** partic	**1056.1** conj
ὁ	Ἰησοῦς]	ἐν	τῇ	Γαλιλαίᾳ·	οὐ	γὰρ
ho	*Iēsous*	*en*	*tē*	*Galilaia*	*ou*	*gar*
	Jesus]	in		Galilee,	not	for

2286.32 verb 3sing indic imperf act	**1706.1** prep	**3450.11** art dat sing fem	**2424.3** name dat fem	**3906.17** verb inf pres act	**3617.1** conj
ἤθελεν	ἐν	τῇ	Ἰουδαίᾳ	περιπατεῖν,	ὅτι
ēthelen	*en*	*tē*	*Ioudaia*	*peripatein*	*hoti*
he did desire	in		Judea	to walk,	because

2195.26 verb 3pl indic imperf act	**840.6** prs-pron acc sing masc	**3450.7** art pl masc	**2428.2** name-adj pl masc	**609.12** verb inf aor act
ἐζήτουν	αὐτὸν	οἱ	Ἰουδαῖοι	ἀποκτεῖναι.
ezētoun	*auton*	*hoi*	*Ioudaioi*	*apokteinai*
were seeking	him	the	Jews	to kill.

1498.34 verb sing indic imperf act	**1156.2** conj	**1445.1** adv	**3450.9** art nom sing fem	**1844.1** noun nom sing fem	**3450.1** art gen pl
2. Ἦν	δὲ	ἐγγὺς	ἡ	ἑορτὴ	τῶν
En	*de*	*engus*	*hē*	*heortē*	*tōn*
Was	now	near	the	feast	of the

2428.3 name-adj gen pl masc	**3450.9** art nom sing fem	**4489.1** noun nom sing fem	**1500.3** verb indic aor act	**3631.1** conj
Ἰουδαίων	ἡ	σκηνοπηγία.	3. εἶπον	οὖν
Ioudaiōn	*hē*	*skēnopēgia*	*eipon*	*oun*
Jews,	the	tabernacles.	Said	therefore

4242.1 prep	**840.6** prs-pron acc sing masc	**3450.7** art pl masc	**79.6** noun pl masc	**840.3** prs-pron gen sing	**3197.4** verb 2sing impr aor act
πρὸς	αὐτὸν	οἱ	ἀδελφοὶ	αὐτοῦ,	Μετάβηθι
pros	*auton*	*hoi*	*adelphoi*	*autou*	*Metabēthi*
to	him	the	brothers	his,	Leave

The word "devil" (*diabolos*) means a slanderer and false accuser. Paul says that in the last days men shall be false accusers. Furthermore, Paul exhorts the aged women not to be false accusers (*diabolous*, Titus 2:3). This is sufficient to show that Judas was not the devil but a slanderer, a false accuser.

for he it was that should betray him, being one of the twelve: . . . for the same was about to deliver him up, *Rotherham* . . . for he ...was planning to betray Him, *Norlie* . . . was on the point of betraying Him, *Wuest* . . . would later betray him, *ALBA* . . . though he was one of the, *TCNT.*

7:1. "After these things" speaks of the feeding of the 5,000 and Jesus' subsequent discourse on himself as the Bread of Life. As a result of His teaching many professed disciples withdrew from Him, but the Twelve clung closer to Him as Peter's confession shows.

This verse indicates that Jesus' ministry for a prolonged period (perhaps 18 months) was confined to the northern part of the country. It is not clear if Jesus went to the Passover mentioned in 6:4. Perhaps He refrained from attending the Feast for the reason John states.

"He would not walk in Jewry" tells us He did not wish to walk there (*ēthelen*). The verb used is one that speaks of one's desire based on a particular reason. The reason was "because the Jews sought to kill him." The evidence for this is stated in 5:18, a year and a half before this time. The imperfect tense verb for "sought" to kill indicates that the Jews were in the process of seeking Him in order to kill Him. From this point in John's record the opposition to Jesus becomes prominent (see 7:19,30,32,44; 8:59; 10:39; 11:8,53).

1. After these things Jesus walked in Galilee: Following this, *Berkeley* . . . After this Jesus moved from place to place in Galilee, *Weymouth* . . . these events Jesus went about, *Norlie.*

for he would not walk in Jewry: . . . for he was not willing to walk in Judaea, *HBIE* . . . He did not wish to stay in Judea, *Norlie* . . . He didn't want to travel in Judea, *Beck.*

because the Jews sought to kill him: . . . were eager to put him to death, *TCNT* . . . were trying to kill Him, *Norlie, Berkeley* . . . were bent on killing him, *ALBA.*

7:2. The Feast of Tabernacles was a Jewish institution observed for 7 days (later an eighth day was added) (Leviticus 23:40-42; Nehemiah 8:14-16). The Feast was in the fall (October—7th month) and was also called the Feast of Ingathering and the Feast of Harvest. All Jews were to live in booths (brush arbors or tents) during the 8 days of the Feast to remind them that their forefathers had lived in tents during the 40 years of desert wandering. The Feast was a memorial to God for giving them the land on which they lived and for their food that came from the land. The occasion was one of gratitude to God for His provisions (Exodus 23:16; Deuteronomy 16:13-15). This feast was the greatest feast of joy of all the feasts of the Jews. The rabbis said, "The man who has not seen these festivities does not know what jubilee is." The Feast of Tabernacles (*hē heorte hē skēnopēgia*) occurs only here in the New Testament.

2. Now the Jews' feast of tabernacles was at hand: As the Jewish festival of booths was near, *Moffatt* . . . being near, *TCNT* . . . However, the Jewish Feast, *Berkeley* . . . of Dwelling in Tents, *Williams* . . . feast of tents, *BB* . . . of the Jewish camp meeting, *Klingensmith.*

7:3. "His brethren" are neither His cousins nor His stepbrothers, but His half brothers. They are the younger sons of Joseph and

3. His brethren therefore said unto him, Depart hence, and go

John 7:4

1766.1 adv	**2504.1** conj	**5055.6** verb 2sing impr pres act	**1519.1** prep	**3450.12** art acc sing fem	**2424.4** name acc fem
ἐντεῦθεν,	καὶ	ὕπαγε	εἰς	τὴν	Ἰουδαίαν,
enteuthen	*kai*	*hupage*	*eis*	*tēn*	*Ioudaian*
from here,	and	go	into		Judea,

2419.1 conj	**2504.1** conj	**3450.7** art pl masc	**3073.5** noun nom pl masc	**4622.2** prs-pron gen 2sing	**2311.18** verb 3pl subj aor act
ἵνα	καὶ	οἱ	μαθηταί	σου	⸂ θεωρήσωσιν
hina	*kai*	*hoi*	*mathētai*	*sou*	*theōrēsōsin*
that	also	the	disciples	your	may see

3.a.**Txt:** p66,03B-corr, 017K,036,038,1,byz. Lach,Sod
Var: p75,01ℵ-corr, 03B-org,05D,019L, 032W,037,Treg,Alf,Tisc, We/Ho,Weis,UBS/☆

2311.24 verb 3pl indic fut act	**3450.17** art pl neu	**2024.4** noun pl neu	**4622.2** prs-pron gen 2sing	**3614.17** rel-pron pl neu
[a☆ θεωρήσουσιν]	τὰ	ἔργα	σοῦ	ἃ
theōrēsousin	*ta*	*erga*	*sou*	*ha*
[will see]	the	works	your	which

4020.4 verb 2sing indic pres act	**3625.2** num card nom masc	**1056.1** conj	**1706.1** prep	**2899.3** adj dat sing neu	**4948.10** indef-pron sing neu
ποιεῖς·	4. οὐδεὶς	γάρ	⸂ ἐν	κρυπτῷ	τι
poieis	*oudeis*	*gar*	*en*	*kruptō*	*ti*
you do;	no one	for	in	secret	anything

4948.10 indef-pron sing neu	**1706.1** prep	**2899.3** adj dat sing neu	**4020.5** verb 3sing indic pres act	**2504.1** conj	**2195.5** verb 3sing indic pres act
[☆ τι	ἐν	κρυπτῷ]	ποιεῖ,	καὶ	ζητεῖ
ti	*en*	*kruptō*	*poiei*	*kai*	*zētei*
[anything	in	secret]	does,	and	seeks

4.a.**Var:** p66-org,03B, 032W,Lach

840.5 prs-pron nom sing masc	**840.15** prs-pron sing neu	**1706.1** prep	**3816.3** noun dat sing fem	**1498.32** verb inf pres act	**1479.1** conj
⸂ αὐτὸς	[a αὐτὸ]	ἐν	παρρησίᾳ	εἶναι.	εἰ
autos	*auto*	*en*	*parrhēsia*	*einai*	*ei*
himself	[it]	in	openness	to be.	If

3642.18 dem-pron pl neu	**4020.4** verb 2sing indic pres act	**5157.5** verb 2sing impr aor act	**4427.4** prs-pron acc 2sing masc	**3450.3** art dat sing
ταῦτα	ποιεῖς,	φανέρωσον	σεαυτὸν	τῷ
tauta	*poieis*	*phanerōson*	*seauton*	*tō*
these things	you do,	manifest	yourself	to the

2862.3 noun dat sing masc	**3624.1** adv	**1056.1** conj	**3450.7** art pl masc	**79.6** noun pl masc	**840.3** prs-pron gen sing
κόσμῳ.	5. Οὐδὲ	γὰρ	οἱ	ἀδελφοὶ	αὐτοῦ
kosmō	*Oude*	*gar*	*hoi*	*adelphoi*	*autou*
world.	Neither	for	the	brothers	his

3961.55 verb 3pl indic imperf act	**1519.1** prep	**840.6** prs-pron acc sing masc	**2978.5** verb 3sing indic pres act	**3631.1** conj	**840.2** prs-pron dat pl
ἐπίστευον	εἰς	αὐτόν.	6. Λέγει	οὖν	αὐτοῖς
episteuon	*eis*	*auton*	*Legei*	*oun*	*autois*
believed	on	him.	Says	therefore	to them

3450.5 art sing masc	**2400.1** name nom masc	**3450.5** art sing masc	**2511.1** noun nom sing masc	**3450.5** art sing masc	**1684.3** adj nom 1sing masc
ὁ	Ἰησοῦς,	Ὁ	καιρὸς	ὁ	ἐμὸς
ho	*Iēsous*	*Ho*	*kairos*	*ho*	*emos*
	Jesus,	The	time	the	my

3632.1 adv	**3780.2** verb 3sing indic pres act	**3450.5** art sing masc	**1156.2** conj	**2511.1** noun nom sing masc	**3450.5** art sing masc	**5052.3** adj nom 2sing masc
οὔπω	πάρεστιν·	ὁ	δὲ	καιρὸς	ὁ	ὑμέτερος
oupō	*parestin*	*ho*	*de*	*kairos*	*ho*	*humeteros*
not yet	is come,	the	but	time	the	your

Mary (see Matthew 13:55 and Mark 6:3). The names of His brothers are James, Joses, Simon, and Jude.

"Go into Judea." His brothers seemingly thought that the Jews' hostility had subsided; therefore, it would be safe for Jesus to minister in Judea. It had been about 18 months since He had ministered there.

"The works that thou doest" indicate miracles which John has not recorded. The time was about Passover (April) when Jesus multiplied the bread, and now the time was just prior to the Feast of Tabernacles (October).

"May behold" (NASB) states the possibility of a prolonged seeing of miracles.

into Judaea: You must leave here and go to Judea, *Williams* . . . leave this place, *Norlie.*

that thy disciples also may see the works that thou doest: . . . let Your disciples see the deeds You do, *Norlie.*

7:4. "There is no man that doeth any thing in secret." "Secret" (*kruptos*) is common in John. The word means "to hide or conceal something." Jesus knew that if He followed the suggestion of His brothers it would bring more active hostility from the Jews in Judea and accelerate the time of His crucifixion.

The brothers' words, "If thou do these things," seem to have been said in a sarcastic tone as a challenge for Jesus to take a risk. The brothers, though they did not personally believe on Him (verse 5), nevertheless wanted Him to go to Jerusalem and do His mighty works to enhance His reputation. Their sarcasm suggested that Jesus should capitalize on His miracles.

4. For there is no man that doeth any thing in secret: For no one does a thing privately, *TCNT.*

and he himself seeketh to be known openly: . . . whosoever courts renown, *Campbell* . . . desires to become famous himself, *Fenton* . . . seeks to be in the limelight, *Berkeley* . . . his aim is to be widely known, *TCNT* . . . if he wants to be in the public eye, *Norlie.*

If thou do these things: Since you are doing these deeds, *Weymouth* . . . Since you can do these deeds, *Moffatt* . . . these wonders, *Norlie.*

show thyself to the world: . . . display yourself to the world, *Moffatt* . . . exhibit Yourself, *Fenton* . . . publically, *Williams.*

7:5. "Neither did his brethren" presents a sad picture within the family of Jesus. Those who should have known Him best did not believe in Him. The imperfect tense verb *episteuon,* "were (not) believing," speaks of a habitual attitude of unbelief. "Neither" (*oude*) indicates "not even," meaning that in addition to the loss of so many disciples (6:66) and the Jews of Judea seeking to kill Him (verse 11), some of His own family members did not believe in Him.

This verse negates any positive advance toward spiritual life which may have been indicated by the prior verse. His brothers may have even spoken those words ironically.

5. For neither did his brethren believe in him: For even his brothers, *Murdock* . . . had any faith, *Norlie.*

7:6. "My time" (*ho kairos ho emos*) indicates His critical time. The word "time" means either the time of public manifestation in Jerusalem or the time of His passion. The first, naturally and brutally, would lead to the second. It makes little difference which we take it to mean. "My time" is contrasted to "your time." Nothing

6. Then Jesus said unto them, My time is not yet come: My time of going, *Scarlett* . . . My time has not yet arrived, *Berkeley* . . . It is not yet the right time for me, *Phillips* . . . It is not yet time for me to do so, *Williams* . . . My opportunity has not yet arrived, *Fenton* . . . is not as yet present, *Concordant* . . . My season not yet is here, *Rotherham.*

but your time is alway ready: . . . but any time is suitable for you, *Norlie* . . . is always opportune, *Berkeley* . . . Your time is any time, *Barclay* . . . is here always, *TCNT.*

3704.1 adv	**1498.4** verb 3sing indic pres act	**2071.2** adj nom sing masc	**3620.3** partic	**1404.4** verb 3sing indic pres	**3450.5** art sing masc
πάντοτέ	ἐστιν	ἕτοιμος.	**7.** οὐ	δύναται	ὁ
pantote	*estin*	*hetoimos*	*ou*	*dunatai*	*ho*
always	is	ready.	Not	is able	the

2862.1 noun nom sing masc	**3268.10** verb inf pres act	**5050.4** prs-pron acc 2pl	**1466.7** prs-pron acc 1sing	**1156.2** conj	**3268.3** verb 3sing indic pres act
κόσμος	μισεῖν	ὑμᾶς·	ἐμὲ	δὲ	μισεῖ,
kosmos	*misein*	*humas*	*eme*	*de*	*misei*
world	to hate	you,	me	but	it hates,

3617.1 conj	**1466.1** prs-pron nom 1sing	**3113.1** verb 1sing pres act	**3875.1** prep	**840.3** prs-pron gen sing	**3617.1** conj
ὅτι	ἐγὼ	μαρτυρῶ	περὶ	αὐτοῦ,	ὅτι
hoti	*egō*	*marturō*	*peri*	*autou*	*hoti*
because	I	bear witness	concerning	it,	that

3450.17 art pl neu	**2024.4** noun pl neu	**840.3** prs-pron gen sing	**4050.10** adj	**1498.4** verb 3sing indic pres act	**5050.1** prs-pron nom 2pl
τὰ	ἔργα	αὐτοῦ	πονηρά	ἐστιν.	**8.** ὑμεῖς
ta	*erga*	*autou*	*ponēra*	*estin*	*humeis*
the	works	of it	evil	are.	You,

8.a.**Txt:** 01ℵ-org,036, 037,byz.
Var: 01ℵ-corr,03B,05D, 017K,019L,029T,038,sa. bo.Lach,Treg,AlfTisc, We/Ho,Weis,Sod,UBS/☆

303.16 verb 2pl impr aor act	**1519.1** prep	**3450.12** art acc sing fem	**1844.4** noun acc sing fem	**3642.12** dem-pron acc sing fem	**1466.1** prs-pron nom 1sing
ἀνάβητε	εἰς	τὴν	ἑορτήν	⸂a ταύτην· ⸃	ἐγὼ
anabēte	*eis*	*tēn*	*heortēn*	*tautēn*	*egō*
go up	to	the	feast	this,	I

8.b.**Txt:** p66,p75,03B, 019L,029T,032W,036, 037,038,1,13,33,byz. Lach,We/Ho,Weis
Var: 01ℵ,05D,017K,041, 1079,1241,Gries,Treg, Alf,Tisc,Sod,UBS/☆

3632.1 adv	**3620.2** partic	**303.1** verb 1sing indic pres act	**1519.1** prep	**3450.12** art acc sing fem	**1844.4** noun acc sing fem
⸀ οὔπω	[b☆ οὐκ]	ἀναβαίνω	εἰς	τὴν	ἑορτὴν
oupō	*ouk*	*anabainō*	*eis*	*tēn*	*heortēn*
not yet	[not]	am going up	to	the	feast

8.c.**Txt:** 017K,036,037, byz.
Var: 01ℵ,03B,05D,019L, 029T,030U,038,Lach Treg,Alf,Tisc,We/Ho, Weis,Sod,UBS/☆

3642.12 dem-pron acc sing fem	**3617.1** conj	**3450.5** art sing masc	**2511.1** noun nom sing masc	**3450.5** art sing masc	**1684.3** adj nom 1sing masc
ταύτην,	ὅτι	ὁ	⸀ καιρὸς	ὁ	ἐμὸς
tautēn	*hoti*	*ho*	*kairos*	*ho*	*emos*
this,	for	the	time	the	my

9.a.**Txt:** 03B,019L,029T, 036,037,byz.sa.bo.Lach, We/Ho,WeisSod,UBS/☆
Var: 01ℵ,05D,017K,038, 041,1,33,GriesTreg,Tisc

1684.3 adj nom 1sing masc	**2511.1** noun nom sing masc	**3632.1** adv	**3997.29** verb 3sing indic perf pass	**3642.18** dem-pron pl neu
[c☆ ἐμὸς	καιρὸς]	οὔπω	πεπλήρωται.	**9.** Ταῦτα
emos	*kairos*	*oupō*	*peplērōtai*	*Tauta*
[my	time]	not yet	has been fulfilled.	These things

9.b.**Var:** p66,01ℵ, 05D-org,017K,019L, 032W,041,1,sa.bo.Tisc, Sod

1156.2 conj	**1500.15** verb nom sing masc part aor act	**840.2** prs-pron dat pl	**840.5** prs-pron nom sing masc	**3176.16** verb 3sing indic aor act
⸂a δὲ ⸃	εἰπὼν	⸀ αὐτοῖς	[b αὐτὸς]	ἔμεινεν
de	*eipōn*	*autois*	*autos*	*emeinen*
and	having said	to them	[he]	he stayed

1706.1 prep	**3450.11** art dat sing fem	**1049.3** name dat sing fem	**5453.1** conj	**1156.2** conj	**303.14** verb 3pl indic aor act	**3450.7** art pl masc
ἐν	τῇ	Γαλιλαίᾳ.	**10.** Ὡς	δὲ	ἀνέβησαν	οἱ
en	*tē*	*Galilaia*	*Hōs*	*de*	*anebēsan*	*hoi*
in		Galilee.	When	but	were gone up	the

79.6 noun pl masc	**840.3** prs-pron gen sing	**4966.1** adv	**2504.1** conj	**840.5** prs-pron nom sing masc	**303.13** verb 3sing indic aor act
ἀδελφοὶ	αὐτοῦ	⸀ τότε	καὶ	αὐτὸς	ἀνέβη,
adelphoi	*autou*	*tote*	*kai*	*autos*	*anebē*
brothers	his	then	also	he	went up

hindered His brothers from going to Jerusalem at any time, but His time to go was governed by the hour of His suffering in behalf of the world.

7. The world cannot hate you; but me it hateth: It is impossible for the world to hate you, *Williams* . . . but me it does hate, *Montgomery* . . . but I provoke hatred, *Phillips.*

because I testify of it, that the works thereof are evil: . . . for I testify against it, that its works are wicked, *Norlie* . . . its ways are wicked, *TCNT* . . . because I show the world how evil its deeds really are, *Phillips* . . . I disclose the wickedness of its actions, *Campbell* . . . I am bearing testimony against it, *Montgomery* . . . their lives are evil! *SEB* . . . I am a witness to the evil of its deeds, *Barclay.*

7:7. Jesus explained why they could go to Jerusalem at any time, but also why He could not go until the correct time. It was because of the world's hatred for Him and the lack of its hatred toward His brothers.

"I testify of it." "I" is emphatic. Jesus continued to speak of the contrast between Him and His brothers. "Testify" (*marturō*) is a present indicative verb signifying that Jesus was in the process of witnessing to the corrupt nature of the world (verse 4). This is the reason for the world's hatred of Him. "Evil" (*ponēra*) specifies an active form of evil.

8. Go ye up unto this feast: . . . to the Festival, *Weymouth.*

I go not up yet unto this feast: I am not going to this Festival yet, *TCNT* . . . I do not yet go up, *Berkeley.*

for my time is not yet full come: . . . because my time is not yet fulfilled, *ASV* . . . for it not quite time for me to go, *Williams* . . . My term, *Berkeley* . . . The time is not yet ripe for me, *SEB* . . . my appointed time has not yet been consummated, *Wuest* . . . not yet completed, *Murdock.*

7:8. "Go ye up unto this feast." "Ye" is the word of emphasis in contrast to "I." The "feast" is the Feast of Tabernacles. "This feast" places stress on "this" because He would not go up just yet. He would miss the festal caravan.

"My time" is again as in verse 6. "Time" (*kairos*) occurs but four times in John's Gospel (5:4; 7:6,8). Elsewhere John uses *hōra* ("time," "hour") and *chronos* ("time," "season").

9. When he had said these words unto them, he abode still in Galilee: Such was His answer, and He remained in, *Weymouth* . . . He stayed in Galilee, *NASB* . . . He remained there, *ET.*

7:9. The verb "abode" (*emeinen*) is an aorist tense word indicating a few days at the most. The festal caravan had departed, among whom were His family. By not going until later, Jesus avoided exciting the jealousy of the Jewish rulers. Among the crowds and His family He would be conspicuous. The people would have thronged Him.

Every move Jesus made was in accord with His Father's will. The Lord made no decisions which were not for the good of man and for the glory of God.

The sick sought Him for healing. The curious observers flocked to Him. Multitudes of His disciples gathered round Him wherever He went. Privacy was indeed difficult. It was easy for His enemies to discover where He was. The Jews sent spies to report on Jesus' whereabouts. The publicity of His miracles broadcasted His presence.

10. But when his brethren were gone up: But when his brothers had gone up, *HBIE.*

7:10. "But when his brethren were gone up" refers to verse 3. They urged Jesus to go to the Feast with them, but He refused for the very reason they suggested He should go (see verse 4).

1519.1 prep	3450.12 art acc sing fem	1844.4 noun acc sing fem	1519.1 prep	3450.12 art acc sing fem	1844.4 noun acc sing fem	4966.1 adv
εἰς	τὴν	ἑορτήν,	[☆ εἰς	τὴν	ἑορτήν,	τότε
eis	*tēn*	*heortēn*	*eis*	*tēn*	*heortēn*	*tote*
to	the	feast,	[to	the	feast,	then

2504.1 conj	840.5 prs-pron nom sing masc	303.13 verb 3sing indic aor act	3620.3 partic	5159.1 adv	233.1 conj
καὶ	αὐτὸς	ἀνέβη,]	οὐ	φανερῶς,	⸂☆ ἀλλ'
kai	*autos*	*anebē*	*ou*	*phanerōs*	*all'*
and	he	went up,]	not	openly,	but

10.a.**Txt:** p66,p75,03B,017K,019L,029T,032W,036,037,038,1,13,etc.byz.bo.Lach,We/Ho,Weis,Sod,UBS/☆
Var: 01א,05D,sa.Dia.Tisc

233.2 conj	5453.1 conj	1706.1 prep	2899.3 adj dat sing neu	3450.7 art pl masc	3631.1 conj
[ἀλλὰ]	⸂a ὡς ⸃	ἐν	κρυπτῷ.	**11.** Οἱ	οὖν
alla	*hōs*	*en*	*kruptō*	*Hoi*	*oun*
[idem]	as	in	secret.	The	therefore

2428.2 name-adj pl masc	2195.26 verb 3pl indic imperf act	840.6 prs-pron acc sing masc	1706.1 prep	3450.11 art dat sing fem	1844.3 noun dat sing fem
Ἰουδαῖοι	ἐζήτουν	αὐτὸν	ἐν	τῇ	ἑορτῇ,
Ioudaioi	*ezētoun*	*auton*	*en*	*tē*	*heortē*
Jews	were seeking	him	at	the	feast,

2504.1 conj	2978.25 verb indic imperf act	4085.1 adv	1498.4 verb 3sing indic pres act	1552.3 dem-pron nom sing masc	2504.1 conj
καὶ	ἔλεγον,	Ποῦ	ἐστιν	ἐκεῖνος;	**12.** Καὶ
kai	*elegon*	*Pou*	*estin*	*ekeinos*	*Kai*
and	said,	Where	is	that?	And

1106.1 noun nom sing masc	4044.5 adj nom sing masc	3875.1 prep	840.3 prs-pron gen sing	1498.34 verb sing indic imperf act
γογγυσμὸς	⸂ πολὺς	περὶ	αὐτοῦ	ἦν
gongusmos	*polus*	*peri*	*autou*	*ēn*
grumbling	much	concerning	him	there was

3875.1 prep	840.3 prs-pron gen sing	1498.34 verb sing indic imperf act	4044.5 adj nom sing masc	1706.1 prep	3450.4 art dat pl
[☆ περὶ	αὐτοῦ	ἦν	πολὺς]	ἐν	⸂ τοῖς
peri	*autou*	*ēn*	*polus*	*en*	*tois*
[concerning	him	there was	much]	among	the

12.a.**Var:** p66,01א,05D,33,it.bo.Dia.Tisc

3657.7 noun dat pl masc	3450.3 art dat sing	3657.3 noun dat sing masc	3450.7 art pl masc	3173.1 conj	2978.25 verb indic imperf act
ὄχλοις˙	[a τῷ	ὄχλῳ˙]	οἱ	μὲν	ἔλεγον,
ochlois	*tō*	*ochlō*	*hoi*	*men*	*elegon*
crowds.	[the	crowd.]	The	some	said,

12.b.**Txt:** p75,03B,017K,029T,032W,038,13,sa.Steph,Lach,We/HoWeis,Sod,UBS/☆
Var: p66,01א,05D,019L,036,037,byz.Gries,Tisc

3617.1 conj	18.6 adj nom sing masc	1498.4 verb 3sing indic pres act	241.6 adj nom pl masc	1156.2 conj	2978.25 verb indic imperf act
Ὅτι	Ἀγαθός	ἐστιν˙	ἄλλοι	⸂b δὲ ⸃	ἔλεγον,
Hoti	*Agathos*	*estin*	*alloi*	*de*	*elegon*
	Good	he is;	others	but	said,

3620.3 partic	233.2 conj	3966.1 verb 3sing indic pres act	3450.6 art acc sing masc	3657.4 noun acc sing masc	3625.2 num card nom masc
Οὔ˙	ἀλλὰ	πλανᾷ	τὸν	ὄχλον.	**13.** Οὐδεὶς
Ou	*alla*	*plana*	*ton*	*ochlon*	*Oudeis*
No;	but	he deceives	the	crowd.	No one

3175.1 conj	3816.3 noun dat sing fem	2953.45 verb 3sing indic imperf act	3875.1 prep	840.3 prs-pron gen sing
μέντοι	παρρησίᾳ	ἐλάλει	περὶ	αὐτοῦ,
mentoi	*parrhēsia*	*elalei*	*peri*	*autou*
however	in openness	spoke	concerning	him,

"Then went he also up unto the feast, not openly" reveals that He desired to go to Jerusalem, but in secret (verse 4). "Not openly" (*ouphanerōs*) means "not by way of manifestation." The word has to do with being openly seen and made evident to public view.

Frederic Godet, quoted in a footnote in Edersheim's *The Life and Times of Jesus the Messiah* (2:131), says: "The *qualified* expression, 'as it were in secret,' conveys to my mind only a contrast to the public pilgrim-bands, in which it was the custom to travel to the Feasts—a publicity, which His 'brethren' specially desired at this time. Besides, the 'in secret' of St. John might refer not so much to the journey as to the appearance of Christ at the Feast." Though Jesus had intended to go to the Feast all the time, He was conscious not only of "His time," but the need for a delay so He would not arrive with a large entourage that would attract attention.

then went he also up unto the feast: . . . to the feast, then he also went up, *HBIE.*

not openly, but as it were in secret: . . . not manifestly, *Rotherham* . . . not with a caravan, *Berkeley* . . . not publicly, but as it were in secret, *ASV* . . . not publicly, but in private, *RSV* . . . in hiding, *Concordant* . . . but as it were secretly, *Murdock* . . . but without being seen, *Beck* . . . quietly, *Fenton.*

7:11. "Then the Jews sought him at the feast." "The Jews" refers to the temple authorities, not to the people who came to the Feast. "Sought him" is a verb showing progress of action. As the caravans arrived, spies for the hostile Jews scanned all pilgrims in search of Jesus (see 5:18).

"Where is he?" The hostile Jews were adamant in their attitude and active in their search to destroy the One they detested so much.

11. Then the Jews sought him at the feast, and said, Where is he?: . . . persistently sought, *Wuest* . . . were looking for Him and inquired, *Berkeley* . . . Where can he be, *Knox* . . . Where is that man? *Panin.*

7:12. "Murmuring" (*gongusmos*) occurs in 6:41,43,61 and 7:32. The Greek word reproduces the sound of their voices. It is the same word used in the Septuagint for the grumbling of the Israelites in the wilderness, because of which they failed to enter the Promised Land. Grumbling is evidence of ingratitude and may be indicative of an immoral nature.

"The people" who came to the Feast were divided in their opinion. The religious leaders' influence can be noted among these people.

"He is a good man" indicates some believed Jesus was moral, honest, kind, and honorable. But they did not attribute to Him moral good in the absolute sense that God is good (see Mark 10:17,18).

"He deceiveth the people" is the other opinion stated concerning Jesus. "Deceiveth the people" (*plana*) means to cause them to wander from their correct path. The planets were thought to be wandering stars, and the same Greek word is used for their name "planet" (*plana*). The word also means "leads astray." This group from the multitude sided with the argument that Jesus was teaching the people to break the Sabbath law (5:16,18).

12. And there was much murmuring among the people concerning him: . . . and there were many whispers about him among the people, *TCNT* . . . and there was much disputing about him among the crowd, *Montgomery* . . . an undercurrent of discussion, *Phillips* . . . much altercation, *Murdock* . . . much heated discussion, *Norlie* . . . much complaining, *Sawyer* . . . considerable dispute about Him, *Berkeley* . . . among the crowd many different opinions were being whispered about him, *ALBA.*

for some said, He is a good man: others said, Nay; but he deceiveth the people: He is a benefactor, *Fenton* . . . Others said, Not so: he is imposing on the people, *Weymouth* . . . others that He was not, but was misleading the masses, *Williams* . . . he seduces the crowd, *Confraternity* . . . he is leading the people astray, *Norlie.*

7:13. "Spake openly" means literally speaking boldly for Jesus. The reason the people did not speak for Jesus was that they feared

13. Howbeit no man spake openly of him for fear of the Jews: . . . with plainness of speech,

1217.2 prep	3450.6 art acc sing masc	5238.4 noun acc sing masc	3450.1 art gen pl	2428.3 name-adj gen pl masc	2218.1 adv
διὰ	τὸν	φόβον	τῶν	Ἰουδαίων.	**14.** Ἤδη
dia	*ton*	*phobon*	*tōn*	*Ioudaiōn*	*Ēdē*
because of	the	fear	of the	Jews.	Now

14.a.**Txt:** 05D,017K,036,037,038,etc.byz.
Var: 01ℵ,03B,019L,029T,030U,Lach,Treg,Alf,TiscWe/Ho,Weis,Sod,UBS/☆

1156.2 conj	3450.10 art gen sing fem	1844.2 noun gen sing fem	3192.1 verb gen sing fem part pres act	303.13 verb 3sing indic aor act	3450.5 art sing masc
δὲ	τῆς	ἑορτῆς	μεσούσης	ἀνέβη	⸂a ὁ⸃
de	*tēs*	*heortēs*	*mesousēs*	*anebē*	*ho*
but	of the	feast	being the middle	went up	

2400.1 name nom masc	1519.1 prep	3450.16 art sing neu	2387.3 adj acc sing neu	2504.1 conj	1315.20 verb 3sing indic imperf act
Ἰησοῦς	εἰς	τὸ	ἱερὸν,	καὶ	ἐδίδασκεν.
Iēsous	*eis*	*to*	*hieron*	*kai*	*edidasken*
Jesus	into	the	temple,	and	was teaching:

15.a.Txt.017K,036,037,byz.
Var: 01ℵ,03B,05D,019L,029T,033X,038,33,sa.bo.Lach,Treg,Alf,Tisc,We/HoWeis,Sod,UBS/☆

2504.1 conj	2273.17 verb 3pl indic imperf act	2273.17 verb 3pl indic imperf act	3631.1 conj
15. ⸂ καὶ	ἐθαύμαζον	[a☆ ἐθαύμαζον	οὖν]
kai	*ethaumazon*	*ethaumazon*	*oun*
and	were marveling	[were marveling	therefore]

3450.7 art pl masc	2428.2 name-adj pl masc	2978.16 verb pl masc part pres act	4316.1 adv	3642.4 dem-pron nom sing masc
οἱ	Ἰουδαῖοι	λέγοντες,	Πῶς	οὗτος
hoi	*Ioudaioi*	*legontes*	*Pōs*	*houtos*
the	Jews	saying,	How	this one

16.a.**Var:** 01ℵ,03B,017K,029T,036,037,byz.Lach,Treg,Alf,Tisc We/Ho,Weis,Sod,UBS/☆

16.b.**Txt:** p66,05D,017K,019L,029T,032W,036,037,038,1,13,etc.byz.Gries,Lach,Alf,Weis,Sod
Var: p75,01ℵ,03B,33,Treg,Tisc,We/Ho,UBS/☆

1115.4 noun pl neu	3471.4 verb 3sing indic perf act	3231.1 partic	3101.14 verb nom sing masc part perf act	552.6 verb 3sing indic aor pass
γράμματα	οἶδεν,	μὴ	μεμαθηκώς;	**16.** Ἀπεκρίθη
grammata	*oiden*	*mē*	*memathēkōs*	*Apekrithē*
letters	knows,	not	having learned?	Answered

3631.1 conj	840.2 prs-pron dat pl	3450.5 art sing masc	2400.1 name nom masc	2504.1 conj	1500.5 verb 3sing indic aor act
[a☆+ οὖν]	αὐτοῖς	⸂b ὁ⸃	Ἰησοῦς	καὶ	εἶπεν,
oun	*autois*	*ho*	*Iēsous*	*kai*	*eipen*
[therefore]	them		Jesus	and	said,

3450.9 art nom sing fem	1684.6 adj nom 1sing fem	1316.1 noun nom sing fem	3620.2 partic	1498.4 verb 3sing indic pres act	1684.6 adj nom 1sing fem
Ἡ	ἐμὴ	διδαχὴ	οὐκ	ἔστιν	ἐμή,
Hē	*emē*	*didachē*	*ouk*	*estin*	*emē*
The	my	teaching	not	is	mine,

233.2 conj	3450.2 art gen sing	3854.12 verb gen sing masc part aor act	1466.6 prs-pron acc 1sing	1430.1 partic	4948.3 indef-pron nom sing
ἀλλὰ	τοῦ	πέμψαντός	με·	**17.** ἐάν	τις
alla	*tou*	*pempsantos*	*me*	*ean*	*tis*
but	the	having sent	me.	If	anyone

2286.8 verb 3sing subj pres act	3450.16 art sing neu	2284.1 noun sing neu	840.3 prs-pron gen sing	4020.20 verb inf pres act
θέλῃ	τὸ	θέλημα	αὐτοῦ	ποιεῖν,
thelē	*to*	*thelēma*	*autou*	*poiein*
desire	the	will	his	to practice,

1091.50 verb 3sing indic fut mid	3875.1 prep	3450.10 art gen sing fem	1316.2 noun gen sing fem	4079.1 intr-pron nom sing neu
γνώσεται	περὶ	τῆς	διδαχῆς	πότερον
gnōsetai	*peri*	*tēs*	*didachēs*	*poteron*
he shall know	concerning	the	teaching	whether

epercussions from the religious rulers. The people who were fa-
orable to Jesus did not wish to involve themselves or Jesus.

Rotherham . . . freely of him, *Campbell* . . . for the drede of Jewis, *Wycliffe.*

7:14. The Feast of Tabernacles lasted 8 days, but originally it as for 7 days (see verse 2). "The midst of the feast" indicates that days of the period had lapsed. The last day of the Feast was the th day (verse 37). "Jesus went up" is a literal statement since the emple was situated on the summit of Mount Moriah (2 Chronicles :1; Ezra 3:10-12; 5:11).

The Jews had relaxed the search for Jesus, since He did not ppear during the first half of the Feast. Suddenly and unexpect-dly He began to teach in the temple in the Court of the Gentiles. Vhat Jesus taught at this time is not stated.

14. Now about the midst of the feast Jesus went up into the temple, and taught: When the festival was half over, *Moffatt* . . . at its midway point, *Wuest* . . . Jesus went up to the Temple and began to teach, *Montgomery.*

15. And the Jews marvelled, saying: The Jews therefore wondered, *HBIE* . . . The Jews were amazed, *Phillips* . . . were dumbfounded, *Williams.*

How knoweth this man letters, having never learned?: How can this uneducated fellow manage to read, *Weymouth* . . . How can He know so much when He's never been to our schools, *LivB* . . . acquainted with letters, *Concordant* . . . this man literature, having not been educated? *Murdock* . . . this uneducated man know the Scriptures? *Williams* . . . know theology, having never studied? *Fenton* . . . got knowledge of books? *BB* . . . without a rabbinical education, *Adams* . . . a student of the law, *ALBA* . . . got his learning, when he has never studied? *TCNT.*

7:15. "The Jews" refers to the leading and learned men among ne priests and scribes.

"Marveled" (*ethaumazon*) speaks of a continuing condition of urprise and wonder.

Public teaching was done by those who were recognized as rabbis. he teacher usually quoted the elders on topics but did not state is own opinion. Jesus, however, never quoted men as authorities back His statements. He presented the Scriptures and gave their nterpretations which often clashed with the doctrines of the elders.

"Having never learned" is a correct statement because Jesus did ot attend the colleges of Hillel or Shammai in Jerusalem.

16. Jesus answered them, and said, My doctrine is not mine, but his that sent me: My teaching is not my own; it is his who sent me, *TCNT* . . . is not really Mine, *Adams.*

7:16. In the next three verses Jesus spoke of the divine authority f His teaching. "My doctrine is not mine." His teaching was de-gned to manifest God to man. He did not teach from a personal notive, but from the divine commission.

"But his that sent me" testified to the One who had given Him uthority. The rabbinical schools had not ordained Him nor granted Iim license to teach.

17. If any man will do his will, he shall know of the doctrine: If any man be willing to do his will, he shall know concerning the teaching, *Alford* . . . If any one wills to do God's will he shall know concerning my teaching, *Montgomery.*

7:17. "If any man will" (*ean tis thelē*) speaks of the desire one as to do God's will. The word *thelē* can even mean "wish." The ame verb occurs in 5:40. Man must have a wish, desire, or will "to o His will." The word for "will" in "do his will" is the same word

John 7:18

17.a.**Txt:** 03B,017K, 029T,036,037,038,etc. byz.Lach,We/HoWeis, Sod,UBS/⋆
Var: p66,01א,05D,Tisc

1523.2 prep gen	**3450.2** art gen sing	**2296.2** noun gen sing masc	**1498.4** verb 3sing indic pres act	**2211.1** conj	**1466.1** prs-pron nom 1sing
ἐκ	([a] τοῦ)	θεοῦ	ἐστιν,	ἢ	ἐγὼ
ek	*tou*	*theou*	*estin*	*ē*	*egō*
from		God	it is,	or	I

570.2 prep gen	**1670.1** prs-pron gen 1sing masc	**2953.1** verb 1sing pres act	**3450.5** art sing masc	**570.1** prep gen	**1431.4** prs-pron gen 3sing
ἀπ'	ἐμαυτοῦ	λαλῶ.	**18.** ὁ	ἀφ'	ἑαυτοῦ
ap'	*emautou*	*lalō*	*ho*	*aph'*	*heautou*
from	myself	speak.	The	from	himself

2953.12 verb nom sing masc part pres act	**3450.12** art acc sing fem	**1385.4** noun acc sing fem	**3450.12** art acc sing fem	**2375.11** adj acc sing fem
λαλῶν,	τὴν	δόξαν	τὴν	ἰδίαν
lalōn	*tēn*	*doxan*	*tēn*	*idian*
speaking,	the	glory	the	his own

2195.5 verb 3sing indic pres act	**3450.5** art sing masc	**1156.2** conj	**2195.8** verb nom sing masc part pres act	**3450.12** art acc sing fem	**1385.4** noun acc sing fem
ζητεῖ·	ὁ	δὲ	ζητῶν	τὴν	δόξαν
zētei	*ho*	*de*	*zētōn*	*tēn*	*doxan*
seeks;	the	but	seeking	the	glory

3450.2 art gen sing	**3854.12** verb gen sing masc part aor act	**840.6** prs-pron acc sing masc	**3642.4** dem-pron nom sing masc	**225.2** adj nom sing
τοῦ	πέμψαντος	αὐτόν,	οὗτος	ἀληθής
tou	*pempsantos*	*auton*	*houtos*	*alēthēs*
of the	having sent	him,	this	true

1498.4 verb 3sing indic pres act	**2504.1** conj	**92.1** noun nom sing fem	**1706.1** prep	**840.4** prs-pron dat sing	**3620.2** partic
ἐστιν,	καὶ	ἀδικία	ἐν	αὐτῷ	οὐκ
estin	*kai*	*adikia*	*en*	*autō*	*ouk*
is,	and	unrighteousness	in	him	not

1498.4 verb 3sing indic pres act	**3620.3** partic	**3337.1** name nom masc	**3338.1** name nom masc	**1319.33** verb 3sing indic perf act
ἔστιν.	**19.** οὐ	(Μωσῆς	[⋆ Μωϋσῆς]	(⋆ δέδωκεν
estin	*ou*	*Mōsēs*	*Mōusēs*	*dedōken*
is.	Not	Moses	[idem]	has given

19.a.**Txt:** p66,p75,01א, 017K,019L,029T,032W, 036,037,038,1,13,byz. Gries,TiscSod
Var: 03B,05D,Lach, Treg,Alf,We/HoWeis, UBS/⋆

1319.14 verb 3sing indic aor act	**5050.3** prs-pron dat 2pl	**3450.6** art acc sing masc	**3414.4** noun acc sing masc	**2504.1** conj	**3625.2** num card nom masc
[[a] ἔδωκεν]	ὑμῖν	τὸν	νόμον,	καὶ	οὐδεὶς
edōken	*humin*	*ton*	*nomon*	*kai*	*oudeis*
[gave]	you	the	law,	and	no one

1523.1 prep gen	**5050.2** prs-pron gen 2pl	**4020.5** verb 3sing indic pres act	**3450.6** art acc sing masc	**3414.4** noun acc sing masc	**4949.9** intr-pron sing neu
ἐξ	ὑμῶν	ποιεῖ	τὸν	νόμον·	τί
ex	*humōn*	*poiei*	*ton*	*nomon*	*ti*
of	you	practices	the	law?	Why

1466.6 prs-pron acc 1sing	**2195.1** verb 2pl pres act	**609.12** verb inf aor act	**552.6** verb 3sing indic aor pass	**3450.5** art sing masc
με	ζητεῖτε	ἀποκτεῖναι;	**20.** Ἀπεκρίθη	ὁ
me	*zēteite*	*apokteinai*	*Apekrithē*	*ho*
me	do you seek	to kill?	Answered	the

20.a.**Txt:** 05D,017K,036, 037,038,1,13,byz.Gries, Word
Var: 01א,03B,019L, 029T,033X,33,sa.bo. Lach,Treg,Alf,Tisc, We/Ho,WeisSod,UBS/⋆

3657.1 noun nom sing masc	**2504.1** conj	**1500.5** verb 3sing indic aor act	**1134.1** noun sing neu	**2174.3** verb 2sing indic pres act
ὄχλος	([a] καὶ	εἶπεν,)	Δαιμόνιον	ἔχεις·
ochlos	*kai*	*eipen*	*Daimonion*	*echeis*
crowd	and	said,	A demon	you have;

as the "will" man has. "Will" can be rendered "God's pleasure" (see Revelation 4:11; *Thelēma* is translated "pleasure" in the KJV and "will" in the NASB).

"He shall know" (*gnōsetai*) is a future tense thought of knowledge which comes by having a desire to do God's will (see also 5:46). Obedience to an individual's knowledge of God, in turn, brings about yet more knowledge. Man is granted enough sight to walk a step at a time. If the step is not taken, the light becomes darkness through disobedience.

"Or whether I speak of myself" is explained by our Lord in the next verse.

whether it be of God, or whether I speak of myself: . . . whether it originates from God, *Fenton* . . . whether it is from God or originates with me, *Weymouth* . . . proceeds from God, *Campbell* . . . whether my teaching is from God or whether I merely speak on my own authority, *Phillips* . . . or merely expresses my own ideas, *Williams.*

7:18. These three verses (16-18) form a close unit of thought. Verse 16 reveals that the authority of His teaching was from God. Verse 17 shows that the person who wished to know that His teaching was from God could know by simply making the first step toward believing by obedience. Verse 18 indicates the test that can be put to the source of the teaching by an examination of the motive which produced the teaching.

If a man seeks his own glory, he will teach and act from that motive. Jesus did not seek to glorify himself, but God who sent Him. God is the ultimate and only authority.

The one who is not self-seeking but teaches for the glory of God must be true. Jesus, therefore, is the true and righteous One (see Revelation 16:7 and 19:2). Jesus always stresses attitudes and motives rather than the overt acts (Matthew chapters 5 through 7). Deeds (works) are fruits which point to the nature of their origin. Thus Jesus said His origin could be discovered by an analysis of His works.

18. He that speaketh of himself seeketh his own glory: He who talks on his own authority aims at his own credit, *Moffatt* . . . studies his own reputation, *Fenton* . . . his own ideas, *Williams* . . . whose teaching originates with himself, *Weymouth* . . . has an eye for his own reputation, *Phillips.*

but he that seeketh his glory that sent him, the same it true: . . . but whoever seeks the honor of him who sent him is sincere, *Williams* . . . But He who wants to glorify the One who sent Him tells the truth, *Beck* . . . but he who seeks his sender's honor is sincere, *Berkeley* . . . is veracious, *Murdock.*

and no unrighteousness is in him: . . . there is no dishonesty in him, *Knox* . . . and in him there is no falsehood, *RSV* . . . a stranger to deceit, *Campbell.*

7:19. The Jews claimed to be disciples of Moses, their teacher, but Jesus pointed out that they did not observe his teachings (see 5:45,46).

"None of you keepeth the law." The Greek means "no one from among you does the Law."

To prove that they did not observe the Law, Jesus asked, "Why go ye about to kill me?" (see also 5:18). This made them guilty of plotting the murder of an innocent man. By denying Jesus' charge they added deception to their plans to murder Him.

19. Did not Moses give you the law: Was not it Moses who gave the Law? *TCNT.*

and yet none of you keepeth the law?: Yet not one of you obeys it! *TCNT.*

Why go ye about to kill me?: Else, why do you want to kill me, *Moffatt* . . . If so, why are you trying to kill me, *Williams* . . . Why have you a desire to put me to death, *BB* . . . aim at murdering Me? *Fenton.*

7:20. "Demon" (*daimonion*) is the literal and the English transliterated word rendered from the Greek. The word "demon" (NASB) is a better translation than "devil." The Jews slandered Jesus by

20. The people answered and said, Thou hast a devil: . . . the crowd shouted back at Him, *Norlie* . . . You have a demon! *Montgomery* . . . You are possessed! *NEB* . . . You must be mad! *Phillips.*

John 7:21

4949.3 intr-pron nom sing	4622.4 prs-pron acc 2sing	2195.5 verb 3sing indic pres act	609.12 verb inf aor act	552.6 verb 3sing indic aor pass
τίς	σε	ζητεῖ	ἀποκτεῖναι;	21. Ἀπεκρίθη
tis	*se*	*zētei*	*apokteinai*	*Apekrithē*
who	you	seeks	to kill?	Answered

21.a.**Txt:** 05D,017K, 019L,029T,030U,032W, (038),byz.Lach
Var: 01ℵ,03B,036,037, Treg,Alf,Tisc,We/Ho, WeisSod,UBS/☆

3450.5 art sing masc	2400.1 name nom masc	2504.1 conj	1500.5 verb 3sing indic aor act	840.2 prs-pron dat pl	1518.9 num card neu
⸂a ὁ ⸃	Ἰησοῦς	καὶ	εἶπεν	αὐτοῖς,	Ἓν
ho	*Iēsous*	*kai*	*eipen*	*autois*	*Hen*
	Jesus	and	said	to them,	One

2024.1 noun sing neu	4020.22 verb 1sing indic aor act	2504.1 conj	3820.7 adj pl masc	2273.1 verb 2pl pres act	1217.2 prep
ἔργον	ἐποίησα	καὶ	πάντες	θαυμάζετε.	22. διὰ
ergon	*epoiēsa*	*kai*	*pantes*	*thaumazete*	*dia*
work	I did,	and	all	you wonder.	Because of

3642.17 dem-pron sing neu	3337.1 name nom masc	3338.1 name nom masc	1319.33 verb 3sing indic perf act	5050.3 prs-pron dat 2pl
τοῦτο	⸀ Μωσῆς	[☆ Μωϋσῆς]	δέδωκεν	ὑμῖν
touto	*Mōsēs*	*Mōusēs*	*dedōken*	*humin*
this	Moses	[idem]	has given	you

3450.12 art acc sing fem	3921.4 noun acc sing fem	3620.1 partic	3617.1 conj	1523.2 prep gen	3450.2 art gen sing	3337.2 name gen masc
τὴν	περιτομήν,	οὐχ	ὅτι	ἐκ	τοῦ	Μωσέως
tēn	*peritomēn*	*ouch*	*hoti*	*ek*	*tou*	*Mōseōs*
the	circumcision,	not	that	of		Moses

1498.4 verb 3sing indic pres act	233.1 conj	1523.2 prep gen	3450.1 art gen pl	3824.7 noun gen pl masc	2504.1 conj	1706.1 prep
ἐστὶν,	ἀλλ'	ἐκ	τῶν	πατέρων·	καὶ	ἐν
estin	*all'*	*ek*	*tōn*	*paterōn*	*kai*	*en*
it is,	but	of	the	fathers,	and	on

4378.3 noun dat sing neu	3919.1 verb 2pl indic pres act	442.4 noun acc sing masc	1479.1 conj	3921.4 noun acc sing fem
σαββάτῳ	περιτέμνετε	ἄνθρωπον.	23. εἰ	περιτομὴν
sabbatō	*peritemnete*	*anthrōpon*	*ei*	*peritomēn*
sabbath	you circumcise	a man.	If	circumcision

23.a.**Var:** 03B,022N,038, 33,We/Ho,Weis,UBS/☆

2956.4 verb 3sing indic pres act	3450.5 art sing masc	442.1 noun nom sing masc	1706.1 prep	4378.3 noun dat sing neu	2419.1 conj
λαμβάνει	[a+ ὁ]	ἄνθρωπος	ἐν	σαββάτῳ	ἵνα
lambanei	*ho*	*anthrōpos*	*en*	*sabbatō*	*hina*
receives	[the]	a man	on	sabbath,	that

23.b.**Var:** p66,01ℵ,038, 041-corr,Tisc

3231.1 partic	3061.20 verb 3sing subj aor pass	3450.5 art sing masc	3414.1 noun nom sing masc	3450.5 art sing masc	3337.2 name gen masc
μὴ	λυθῇ	ὁ	νόμος	[b+ ὁ]	⸀ Μωσέως,
mē	*luthē*	*ho*	*nomos*	*ho*	*Mōseōs*
not	may be broken	the	law		of Moses,

3338.2 name gen masc	1466.5 prs-pron dat 1sing	5356.1 verb 2pl indic pres act	3617.1 conj	3513.1 adj sing
[☆ Μωϋσέως,]	ἐμοὶ	χολᾶτε	ὅτι	ὅλον
Mōuseōs	*emoi*	*cholate*	*hoti*	*holon*
[idem]	with me	are you angry	because	entirely

442.4 noun acc sing masc	5040.2 adj acc sing masc	4020.22 verb 1sing indic aor act	1706.1 prep	4378.3 noun dat sing neu	3231.1 partic
ἄνθρωπον	ὑγιῆ	ἐποίησα	ἐν	σαββάτῳ;	24. μὴ
anthrōpon	*hugiē*	*epoiēsa*	*en*	*sabbatō*	*mē*
a man	sound	I made	on	sabbath?	Not

this assertion four times in John alone (7:20; 8:48,52; 10:20).

"Who goeth about to kill thee?" This was a self-incriminating question. It may have been a half-truth, because many of the multitude may not have actively planned Jesus' death; but the Jewish leaders had.

who goeth about to kill thee? Who is trying to kill you, *Phillips* . . . Who is eager, *TCNT.*

21. Jesus answered and said unto them, I have done one work, and ye all marvel: I did one deed which made you wonder, *Norlie* . . . you all are staggered by it, *Torrey.*

7:21. The "one work" refers to the healing of the man at the Bethesda Pool. Jesus singled out this miracle because the Jews had opposed Him on the grounds that He worked on the Sabbath Day and taught others to do likewise (5:8,10,12,16).

Jesus defended His authority to heal on the Sabbath in chapter 5. Study the seven reasons Jesus gave in answer to their argument of His breaking the sabbatical law (see commentary on 5:10).

22. Moses therefore gave unto you circumcision: Well then, Moses gave you the rite of circumcision, *Weymouth.*

(not because it is of Moses, but of the fathers;): . . . not that its source, *HistNT* . . . (not that it came from Moses but from our ancestors), *Beck* . . . origin with Moses, *Williams* . . . not that Moses originated it, *Montgomery* . . . not...from Moses originally, *Phillips* . . . but from the patriarchs *Scarlett.*

and ye on the sabbath day circumcise a man: . . . and you will circumcise a man even on the Sabbath, *Phillips.*

7:22. The Jews had complained that Jesus healed on the Sabbath; therefore, He proceeded to point out that the rite of circumcision was performed on the Sabbath though it involved the work of cutting away the foreskin. If they condemned Him for healing on the Sabbath, then all those who performed the circumcision ritual stood condemned as well.

"Not because it is of Moses, but of the fathers," indicates that circumcision did not originate with Moses. The ceremony was commanded of Abraham, and it was practiced from Abraham to Moses (Genesis 17:10-14; Leviticus 12:3). Circumcision was a physical mark signifying a separation from the world, and it was indicative of ceremonial cleanliness.

23. If a man on the sabbath day receive circumcision, that the law of Moses should not be broken: When a man receives circumcision on a Sabbath to prevent the Law of Moses from being broken, *TCNT.*

are ye angry at me: . . . do you feel bitter toward Me, *Beck* . . . how can you be angry with me, *Montgomery* . . . do I raise your bile, *Concordant* . . . are you incensed against me, *Campbell* . . . are you enraged at Me, *Berkeley* . . . are ye wroth, *Panin* . . . are ye bitter as gall, *Clementson* . . . why are you bitter against Me, *Norlie.*

because I have made a man every whit whole on the sabbath day?: . . . perfectly well, *Williams* . . . I entirely healed, *Scarlett* . . . entirely whole, *HistNT* . . . for giving health, *ALBA* . . . for curing, not cutting, *Moffatt.*

7:23. "If a man on the sabbath day receive circumcision" shows that the practice of the ritual was considered more important than the Sabbath. If the Sabbath was the eighth day after the child's birth, the boy was circumcised on the Sabbath. Thus it was plain that the seal of the covenant was greater than the Sabbath law. Beyond this, Jesus implied that healing the whole man was superior even to circumcision, for circumcision attested only a part of the body and even that work was ceremonial. But He had made "an entire man well" (NASB). Jesus was and is concerned about the whole person, body, soul, and spirit.

The Saviour compared and contrasted the ceremonial law with the higher moral law. The Sabbath law had value, but the moral law was more important. The Sabbath was a shadow of good things to come. It taught the reality of rest in Christ, and it pointed to the truth Jesus came to reveal.

2892.3	2567.1	3663.2	233.2	3450.12	1337.12
verb 2pl pres act	prep	noun acc sing fem	conj	art acc sing fem	adj acc sing fem
κρίνετε	κατ'	ὄψιν,	ἀλλὰ	τὴν	δικαίαν
krinete	*kat'*	*opsin*	*alla*	*tēn*	*dikaian*
judge	according to	sight,	but	the	righteous

24.a.**Var:** p66,p75,03B, 05D,019L,029T,032W, 044,Lach,Treg,Alf, We/Ho

2893.4	2892.16	2892.3	2978.25	3631.1
noun acc sing fem	verb 2pl impr aor act	verb 2pl pres act	verb indic imperf act	conj
κρίσιν	⸀ κρίνατε.	[a κρίνετε.]	**25.** Ἔλεγον	οὖν
krisin	*krinate*	*krinete*	*Elegon*	*oun*
judgment	judge.	[idem]	Said	therefore

4948.7	1523.2	3450.1	2390.2	3620.1	3642.4
indef-pron nom pl masc	prep gen	art gen pl	name gen pl masc	partic	dem-pron nom sing masc
τινες	ἐκ	τῶν	Ἱεροσολυμιτῶν,	Οὐχ	οὗτός
tines	*ek*	*tōn*	*Hierosolumitōn*	*Ouch*	*houtos*
some	from		Jerusalem,	Not	this

1498.4	3614.6	2195.2	609.12	2504.1
verb 3sing indic pres act	rel-pron acc sing masc	verb 3pl pres act	verb inf aor act	conj
ἐστιν	ὃν	ζητοῦσιν	ἀποκτεῖναι;	**26.** καὶ
estin	*hon*	*zētousin*	*apokteinai*	*kai*
he is	whom	they seek	to kill?	and

1481.14	3816.3	2953.2	2504.1	3625.6	840.4
verb 2sing impr aor act	noun dat sing fem	verb sing indic pres act	conj	num card neu	prs-pron dat sing
ἴδε,	παῤῥησίᾳ	λαλεῖ,	καὶ	οὐδὲν	αὐτῷ
ide	*parrhēsia*	*lalei*	*kai*	*ouden*	*autō*
lo,	in frankness	he speaks,	and	nothing	to him

2978.3	3246.1	228.1	1091.18	3450.7
verb 3pl pres act	partic	adv	verb 3pl indic aor act	art pl masc
λέγουσιν.	μήποτε	ἀληθῶς	ἔγνωσαν	οἱ
legousin	*mēpote*	*alēthōs*	*egnōsan*	*hoi*
they say.	Perhaps	truly	have recognized	the

26.a.**Txt:** 036,037,byz. **Var:** 01ℵ,03B,05D, 017K,019L,029T,033X, 038,sa.bo.Gries,Lach, Treg,Alf,Tisc,We/Ho, Weis,Sod,UBS/⋆

752.5	3617.1	3642.4	1498.4	228.1
noun pl masc	conj	dem-pron nom sing masc	verb 3sing indic pres act	adv
ἄρχοντες,	ὅτι	οὗτός	ἐστιν	⸂a ἀληθῶς ⸃
archontes	*hoti*	*houtos*	*estin*	*alēthōs*
rulers,	that	this	is	truly

3450.5	5382.1	233.2	3642.6	3471.5
art sing masc	name nom masc	conj	dem-pron acc sing masc	verb 1pl indic perf act
ὁ	Χριστός;	**27.** ἀλλὰ	τοῦτον	οἴδαμεν
ho	*Christos*	*alla*	*touton*	*oidamen*
the	Christ?	But	this one	we know

4019.1	1498.4	3450.5	1156.2	5382.1	3615.1
adv	verb 3sing indic pres act	art sing masc	conj	name nom masc	conj
πόθεν	ἐστίν·	ὁ	δὲ	Χριστὸς	ὅταν
pothen	*estin*	*ho*	*de*	*Christos*	*hotan*
from where	he is.	The	but	Christ,	whenever

2048.38	3625.2	1091.3	4019.1	1498.4
verb 3sing subj pres	num card nom masc	verb 3sing indic pres act	adv	verb 3sing indic pres act
ἔρχηται,	οὐδεὶς	γινώσκει	πόθεν	ἐστίν.
erchētai	*oudeis*	*ginōskei*	*pothen*	*estin*
he may come,	no one	knows	from where	he is.

2869.11	3631.1	1706.1	3450.3	2387.2	1315.6
verb 3sing indic aor act	conj	prep	art dat sing	adj dat sing neu	verb sing masc part pres act
28. Ἔκραξεν	οὖν	ἐν	τῷ	ἱερῷ	διδάσκων
Ekraxen	*oun*	*en*	*tō*	*hierō*	*didaskōn*
Cried	therefore	in	the	temple	teaching

7:24. Decisions are often made on the basis of outward appear- nce. Jesus' statement was particularly appropriate because the Book f Ecclesiastes was read at the Feast of Tabernacles. The conclusion f the Book of Ecclesiastes stresses making sound judgments (Ec- lesiastes 12:11).

"Righteous judgment" is contrasted with judging according to ppearance. "Righteous" (*dikaian*) occurs only three times in this Gospel (5:30; 7:24; 17:25). The word means "righteous, just, and orrect." Some synonyms are "good," "beautiful," and "useful." In naking judgments, man comes very close to taking on himself the haracter of God. God does not judge by appearance. He looks on he inward part of the matter (Romans 8:27; 1 Thessalonians 2:4). The ceremonies were outward appearances, not inward realities. Life is more important than outward symbols of relationships. Thus o heal the entire man on the Sabbath was greater than the symbolic aw of the Sabbath.

7:25. "Then" (*oun*) refers to the situation just mentioned. "Some f them of Jerusalem" reveals that the plot to kill Jesus was known mong the people. The length of time they had sought for Jesus nd the widespread attitude of the rulers combined to make known heir murderous designs.

7:26. Some of the people of Jerusalem were surprised that (1) esus was speaking boldly in the temple, and (2) that the rulers vere doing nothing to hinder or persecute Him. "The rulers" were nembers of the Sanhedrin, the high council which had extensive olitical and civil powers. The council was composed of 71 leaders mong the priests, elders, and scribes.

The question the people asked each other implies a negative nswer. The people wondered why the rulers had not arrested esus since they were so hostile to Him and His message.

7:27. The people who asked the question of the last verse an- wered their question themselves. Their answer was founded on heir conception of the Christ who was to come. They rejected esus for two reasons combined in one.

First, "we know this man" and His origin. Jesus was from Naz- reth, a little, despised town in Galilee. His father was a mere arpenter, not a nobleman but a peasant. Therefore, they reasoned no Messiah could come from such a family or area of the country.

24. Judge not according to the appearance, but judge righteous judgment: . . . but make honest judgments, *Norlie* . . . Stop judging superficially; you must judge fairly, *Williams* . . . Do not decide at a glance, but think out the decision judicially, *Fenton* . . . be just—not superficial, *ALBA* . . . according to what is right, *JB* . . . but by the reality! *Phillips.*

25. Then said some of them of Jerusalem, Is not this he, whom they seek to kill?:

26. But, lo, he speaketh boldly, and they say nothing unto him: But here he is, speaking out boldly, *Weymouth* . . . they aren't saying a thing to him, *Norlie.*

Do the rulers know indeed that this is the very Christ?: Perhaps our elders have found out, *Lamsa* . . . actually have ascertained, *Weymouth* . . . haven't come to the conclusion, *Adams* . . . have really discovered that, *TCNT.*

27. Howbeit we know this man whence he is: . . . and where he comes from, *Phillips.*

but when Christ cometh, no man knoweth whence he is: But the Messiah—if He ever comes—no one will know from where He comes, *Norlie* . . . is completely unknown, *ALBA.*

28. Then cried Jesus in the temple as he taught, saying: So Jesus called out as He taught in the temple, *Berkeley* . . . Jesus

John 7:29

3450.5 art sing masc	**2400.1** name nom masc	**2504.1** conj	**2978.15** verb sing masc part pres act	**2476.2** conj	**3471.6** verb 2pl indic perf act	**2504.1** conj
ὁ	Ἰησοῦς	καὶ	λέγων,	Κἀμὲ	οἴδατε,	καὶ
ho	*lēsous*	*kai*	*legōn*	*Kame*	*oidate*	*kai*
	Jesus	and	saying,	Both me	you know,	and

3471.6 verb 2pl indic perf act	**4019.1** adv	**1498.2** verb 1sing indic pres act	**2504.1** conj	**570.2** prep gen	**1670.1** prs-pron gen 1sing masc
οἴδατε	πόθεν	εἰμί·	καὶ	ἀπ'	ἐμαυτοῦ
oidate	*pothen*	*eimi*	*kai*	*ap'*	*emautou*
you know	from where	I am;	and	of	myself

3620.2 partic	**2048.24** verb 1sing indic perf act	**233.1** conj	**1498.4** verb 3sing indic pres act	**226.2** adj sing masc	**3450.5** art sing masc
οὐκ	ἐλήλυθα,	ἀλλ'	ἔστιν	ἀληθινὸς	ὁ
ouk	*elēlutha*	*all'*	*estin*	*alēthinos*	*ho*
not	I have come,	but	is	true	the

3854.11 verb nom sing masc part aor act	**1466.6** prs-pron acc 1sing	**3614.6** rel-pron acc sing masc	**5050.1** prs-pron nom 2pl	**3620.2** partic	**3471.6** verb 2pl indic perf act
πέμψας	με,	ὃν	ὑμεῖς	οὐκ	οἴδατε·
pempsas	*me*	*hon*	*humeis*	*ouk*	*oidate*
having sent	me,	whom	you	not	know.

29.a.**Txt:** p66,01ℵ,05D, 033X,1,33,565,bo.Steph **Var:** 03B,017K,019L, 029T,036,037,038,byz. sa.Gries,Lach,TregAlf, Tisc,We/Ho,Weis,Sod, UBS/☆

1466.1 prs-pron nom 1sing	**1156.2** conj	**3471.2** verb 1sing indic perf act	**840.6** prs-pron acc sing masc	**3617.1** conj	**3706.1** prep
29. ἐγὼ	(a δὲ)	οἶδα	αὐτόν,	ὅτι	παρ'
egō	*de*	*oida*	*auton*	*hoti*	*par'*
I	but	know	him,	because	from

840.3 prs-pron gen sing	**1498.2** verb 1sing indic pres act	**2519.6** conj	**1466.6** prs-pron acc 1sing	**643.8** verb 3sing indic aor act
αὐτοῦ	εἰμι,	κἀκεῖνός	με	(ἀπέστειλεν.
autou	*eimi*	*kakeinos*	*me*	*apesteilen*
him	I am,	and that	me	sent.

29.b.**Var:** p66,01ℵ,05D, Tisc

643.17 verb 3sing indic perf act	**2195.26** verb 3pl indic imperf act	**3631.1** conj	**840.6** prs-pron acc sing masc
[b ἀπέσταλκεν.]	**30.** Ἐζήτουν	οὖν	αὐτὸν
apestalken	*Ezētoun*	*oun*	*auton*
[has sent.]	They were seeking	therefore	him

3945.6 verb inf aor act	**2504.1** conj	**3625.2** num card nom masc	**1896.3** verb 3sing indic aor act	**1894.2** prep	**840.6** prs-pron acc sing masc
πιάσαι·	καὶ	οὐδεὶς	ἐπέβαλεν	ἐπ'	αὐτὸν
piasai	*kai*	*oudeis*	*epebalen*	*ep'*	*auton*
to take,	but	no one	laid	upon	him

3450.12 art acc sing fem	**5331.4** noun acc sing fem	**3617.1** conj	**3632.1** adv	**2048.27** verb 3sing indic plperf act	**3450.9** art nom sing fem
τὴν	χεῖρα,	ὅτι	οὔπω	ἐληλύθει	ἡ
tēn	*cheira*	*hoti*	*oupō*	*elēluthei*	*hē*
the	hand,	because	not yet	had come	the

5443.2 noun nom sing fem	**840.3** prs-pron gen sing	**4044.7** adj nom pl masc	**1156.2** conj	**1523.2** prep gen	**3450.2** art gen sing
ὥρα	αὐτοῦ.	**31.** (Πολλοὶ	δὲ	ἐκ	τοῦ
hōra	*autou*	*Polloi*	*de*	*ek*	*tou*
hour	his.	Many	but	of	the

3657.2 noun gen sing masc	**3961.23** verb 3pl indic aor act	**1523.2** prep gen	**3450.2** art gen sing	**3657.2** noun gen sing masc	**1156.2** conj
ὄχλου	ἐπίστευσαν	[☆ Ἐκ	τοῦ	ὄχλου	δὲ
ochlou	*episteusan*	*Ek*	*tou*	*ochlou*	*de*
crowd	believed	[From	the	crowd	but

Second, when Christ comes "no one knows where He is from" (NASB). The theory may have been an interpretation of Malachi 3:1.

cried out loudly, *Norlie* . . . Jesus therefore raised his voice as he was teaching, *ALBA.*

Ye both know me, and ye know whence I am: Yes, you know me, and you know where I am from, *Weymouth* . . . do you know where I am from? *Berkeley.*

and I am not come of myself: But I have not come on my own initiative, *Moffatt* . . . of my own accord, *Murdock* . . . I have not come self-appointed, *Berkeley* . . . I didn't by Myself decide to come, *Beck* . . . And by my own volition I have not come, *Wuest.*

but he that sent me is true, whom ye know not: . . . but the One who has sent me exists as the Real One, *Williams* . . . but He who sent me is trustworthy, and him you do not know, *Montgomery.*

7:28. "Then" indicates that what Jesus did as recorded in this and the next verse was a consequence of the situation mentioned in the preceding verses. Jesus affirmed His divine origin in spite of His humble earthly rearing. While teaching He cried out that they knew Him from where He came, but they did not know His true origin nor His mission.

"Whom ye know not" refers to His Father who sent Him. Since they did not know His Father, they did not know Him or His origin.

29. But I know him; for I am from him, and he hath sent me: I am from His presence and He personally sent Me, *Berkeley* . . . for I came from, *Norlie* . . . am commissioned by him, *Campbell.*

7:29. "I" is the stressed word to contrast the words "whom you know not." The reason Jesus gave for knowing the Father was "for I am from Him." Thus Jesus asserted His knowledge and His origin. His knowledge was based on His origin. "And he hath sent me" finishes the triad. The word "sent" (*apesteilen*) means "commissioned." Notice the compactness of these three ideas Jesus asserted about himself. First, His knowledge was of God. Second, His origin was from God. And third, His commission (sent with God's authority) was from God.

30. Then they sought to take him: . . . had a desire, *BB* . . . Then they were anxious to arrest Him, *Berkeley* . . . to apprehend him, *Wuest* . . . Then they kept on trying to arrest Him, *Williams* . . . sought to arrest Him, *Fenton.*

but no man laid hands on him: . . . but no one touched him, *TCNT* . . . but actually no one laid a finger on him, *Phillips.*

because his hour was not yet come:

7:30. Some sought to seize Jesus while others believed on Him. "No man laid hands on him." This means they did not arrest Him even though they desired to do it.

"Because his hour was not yet come" gives the reason they did not arrest Him. God's plan was moving along the path of time. Whatever the surface reason was, whether because the leaders feared a riot in the temple or reluctance because of Christ's power, we do not know. The real reason behind it all, John's Gospel says, was that God did not allow it. "His hour" was still 6 months off. It was to be at the Passover the following April. The hour would come and Jesus knew the time (17:11).

31. And many of the people believed on him, and said: But among the crowd a large number

Until Jesus' hour came, His enemies had no power to arrest Him. God is sovereign. He sits on the throne of His power. No earthly might can stand before His plan and authority. The apostle Paul expressed his confidence in God's power in the most beautiful terms, "And we know that all things work together for good to them that love God, to them who are the called according to his purpose" (Romans 8:28). In other words, God allows only those forces to affect His children which are in accord with His will.

John 7:32

31.a.**Txt:** 017K,036,byz.
Var: 01ℵ,03B,05D,019L, 029T,030U,033X,037, 038,33,Lach,Treg,Alf, Tisc,We/Ho,Weis,Sod, UBS/☆

31.b.**Txt:** 021M,030U, 036,037,038,byz.
Var: 01ℵ,03B,05D, 017K,019L,029T,Lach, Treg,Alf,TiscWe/Ho, Weis,Sod,UBS/☆

31.c.**Txt:** 07E,030U,036, 037,byz.
Var: 01ℵ,03B,05D, 017K,019L,029T,033X, 038,it.Lach,TregAlf, Tisc,We/Ho,Weis,Sod, UBS/☆

31.d.**Var:** 01ℵ-org,05D, 038,13,Dia.Tisc

33.a.**Txt:** 029T,sa.Steph
Var: 01ℵ,03B,05D, 017K,019L,036,037,038, byz.bo.Gries,Lach,Treg, Alf,Tisc,We/Ho,Weis, Sod,UBS/☆

4044.7 adj nom pl masc πολλοὶ *polloi* many | **3961.23** verb 3pl indic aor act ἐπίστευσαν] *episteusan* believed] | **1519.1** prep εἰς *eis* on | **840.6** prs-pron acc sing masc αὐτόν, *auton* him, | **2504.1** conj καὶ *kai* and | **2978.25** verb indic imperf act ἔλεγον, *elegon* said,

3617.1 conj ⸀a Ὅτι ⸌ *Hoti* | **3450.5** art sing masc ὁ *ho* The | **5382.1** name nom masc Χριστὸς *Christos* Christ, | **3615.1** conj ὅταν *hotan* when | **2048.8** verb 3sing subj aor act ἔλθῃ *elthē* he comes, | **3252.1** partic ⸀ μήτι *mēti* not any

3231.1 partic [b☆ μὴ] *mē* [not] | **3979.1** adj comp acc πλείονα *pleiona* more | **4447.2** noun pl neu σημεῖα *sēmeia* signs | **3642.2** dem-pron gen pl ⸀c τουτων ⸌ *toutōn* than these | **4020.52** verb 3sing indic fut act ποιήσει *poiēsei* will he do

3614.1 rel-pron gen pl ὧν *hōn* which | **3642.4** dem-pron nom sing masc οὗτος *houtos* this | **4020.24** verb 3sing indic aor act ⸀ ἐποίησεν; *epoiēsen* did? | **4020.5** verb 3sing indic pres act [d ποιεῖ;] *poiei* [does?] | **189.24** verb 3pl indic aor act 32. Ἤκουσαν *Ēkousan* Heard

3450.7 art pl masc οἱ *hoi* the | **5168.4** name pl masc Φαρισαῖοι *Pharisaioi* Pharisees | **3450.2** art gen sing τοῦ *tou* of the | **3657.2** noun gen sing masc ὄχλου *ochlou* crowd | **1105.3** verb gen sing masc part pres act γογγύζοντος *gonguzontos* murmuring

3875.1 prep περὶ *peri* concerning | **840.3** prs-pron gen sing αὐτοῦ *autou* him | **3642.18** dem-pron pl neu ταῦτα· *tauta* these things, | **2504.1** conj καὶ *kai* and | **643.9** verb 3pl indic aor act ἀπέστειλαν *apesteilan* sent

3450.7 art pl masc ⸀ οἱ *hoi* the | **5168.4** name pl masc Φαρισαῖοι *Pharisaioi* Pharisees | **2504.1** conj καὶ *kai* and | **3450.7** art pl masc οἱ *hoi* the | **744.5** noun pl masc ἀρχιερεῖς *archiereis* chief priests | **3450.7** art pl masc [☆ οἱ *hoi* [the

744.5 noun pl masc ἀρχιερεῖς *archiereis* chief priests | **2504.1** conj καὶ *kai* and | **3450.7** art pl masc οἱ *hoi* the | **5168.4** name pl masc Φαρισαῖοι] *Pharisaioi* Pharisees] | **5095.6** noun acc pl masc ὑπηρέτας *hupēretas* officers, | **2419.1** conj ἵνα *hina* that

3945.4 verb 3pl subj aor act πιάσωσιν *piasōsin* they might take | **840.6** prs-pron acc sing masc αὐτόν. *auton* him. | **1500.5** verb 3sing indic aor act 33. εἶπεν *eipen* Said | **3631.1** conj οὖν *oun* therefore | **840.2** prs-pron dat pl ⸀a αὐτοῖς ⸌ *autois* to them

3450.5 art sing masc ὁ *ho* | **2400.1** name nom masc Ἰησοῦς, *Iēsous* Jesus, | **2068.1** adv Ἔτι *Eti* Yet | **3262.1** adj acc sing ⸀ μικρὸν *mikron* a little | **5385.4** noun acc sing masc χρόνον *chronon* time | **5385.4** noun acc sing masc [☆ χρόνον *chronon* [time

3262.1 adj acc sing μικρὸν] *mikron* a little] | **3196.1** prep μεθ᾽ *meth'* with | **5050.2** prs-pron gen 2pl ὑμῶν *humōn* you | **1498.2** verb 1sing indic pres act εἰμι, *eimi* I am, | **2504.1** conj καὶ *kai* and | **5055.1** verb 1sing indic pres act ὑπάγω *hupagō* I go

7:31. "And many of the people believed on him" testifies to the harvest Jesus gathered at the Feast of Tabernacles. Notice the word "people" is a neutral term meaning the mass of people. It was the common people who heard Jesus gladly (see Mark 12:37). Because of their unpretentiousness, they found it easy to believe in Him. Observe the groups of people as John divides them. There are the Jews, the multitudes, the disciples, and the Twelve (apostles). Each group has a definite connotation associated with the term. Those who "believed on him" from the multitude kept saying that if there were another who was the true Christ, he would not perform more miracles than this One did. Jesus' miracles were important credentials to His messianic character (Isaiah 35:5,6; 42:6,7; 61:1-3).

God made sure people would be able to recognize His Messiah when He came. The Law and the Prophets predicted the character and the work of God's Redeemer. Recall how Jesus answered John the Baptist when John sent some of his disciples to Jesus. In his imprisonment, John began to doubt the messiahship of Jesus. The baptizer asked, "Art thou he that should come? Or look we for another?" (Luke 7:20). Jesus did not rebuke John for his doubts. Rather, the Lord pointed to the miracles He was performing as evidence of who He was (Luke 7:21,22).

believed in, *Weymouth* . . . Nevertheless, there were many...who put faith in him, *ALBA*.

When Christ cometh will he do more miracles than these which this man hath done?: When the promised Savior comes, *Beck* . . . will he do more signs than, *RSV* . . . will He produce more proofs, *Fenton* . . . than this Teacher, *Weymouth* . . . will he achieve more signs, *Berkeley* . . . give more signs of his mission, *TCNT*.

7:32. The word "murmured" (*gonguzontos*) is the same as the one translated in 6:41,43, and 61. The word spread rapidly among the Pharisees in the temple as to how the people were reacting to Jesus' teaching. The twin sins of jealousy and envy stirred the Pharisees to conspire with the chief priests.

"And" (*kai*) links the hearing with the sending of officers to arrest Jesus.

"Chief priests" were the priests who were over the groups of priests who officiated at the temple.

They sent officers to seize Him. The officers were to stand ready and at a convenient moment arrest Jesus. The reason for their hesitation to arrest Him was because the people might be stirred to anger, perhaps resulting in a temple disturbance. The Jewish leaders were responsible to the Romans to keep peace. A riot in the temple could endanger Jewish authority granted by the Roman government.

32. The Pharisees heard that the people murmured such things concerning him: . . . under their breath, *Berkeley* . . . This discussion of the people came to the ears of the Pharisees, *BB* . . . thus expressing their various doubts about Him, *Weymouth* . . . overheard the crowd whispering these things about Him, *Norlie* . . . heard the crowd in an undertone conferring together with reference to these things concerning Him, *Wuest*.

and the Pharisees and the chief priests sent officers to take him: . . . despatched attendants to arrest him, *Moffatt* . . . sent constables to take him, *Murdock* . . . despatched officers, *Fenton* . . . sent agents, *ALBA* . . . to seize him, *HBIE* . . . charged with the responsibility of apprehending Him, *Wuest*.

7:33. These words spoken to the Jews correspond to those Jesus spoke to the disciples 6 months later (16:16-19). Jesus hereby predicted two aspects of His return to the One who sent Him. An urgency is expressed by "yet a little while." Jesus implied that they should take advantage of the time of their divine visitation. His "little while" at this point was a 6-month period. The officers had been sent to arrest Him. They were among the crowd when Jesus

33. Then said Jesus unto them, Yet a little while am I with you: Yett am I a lytell whyle with you, *Wycliffe* . . . Still for a short time, *Weymouth* . . . I shall be with you but a little longer, *TCNT* . . . only a little longer, *Norlie* . . . just a little longer, *Beck*.

4242.1 prep	3450.6 art acc sing masc	3854.14 verb acc sing masc part aor act	1466.6 prs-pron acc 1sing	2195.21 verb 2pl indic fut act
πρὸς	τὸν	πέμψαντά	με.	34. ζητήσετέ
pros	*ton*	*pempsanta*	*me*	*zētēsete*
to	the	having sent	me.	You will seek

34.a.**Var:** p75,03B,029T,033X,565,sa.bo.Lach,Alf,We/Ho

1466.6 prs-pron acc 1sing	2504.1 conj	3620.1 partic	2128.28 verb 2pl indic fut act	1466.6 prs-pron acc 1sing	2504.1 conj	3562.1 adv
με	καὶ	οὐχ	εὑρήσετέ·	[a+ με,]	καὶ	ὅπου
me	*kai*	*ouch*	*heurēsete*	*me*	*kai*	*hopou*
me	and	not	shall find,	[me,]	and	where

1498.2 verb 1sing indic pres act	1466.1 prs-pron nom 1sing	5050.1 prs-pron nom 2pl	3620.3 partic	1404.6 verb 2pl indic pres	2048.23 verb inf aor act
εἰμὶ	ἐγὼ	ὑμεῖς	οὐ	δύνασθε	ἐλθεῖν.
eimi	*egō*	*humeis*	*ou*	*dunasthe*	*elthein*
am	I	you	not	are able	to come.

1500.3 verb indic aor act	3631.1 conj	3450.7 art pl masc	2428.2 name-adj pl masc	4242.1 prep
35. Εἶπον	οὖν	οἱ	Ἰουδαῖοι	πρὸς
Eipon	*oun*	*hoi*	*Ioudaioi*	*pros*
Said	therefore	the	Jews	among

1431.8 prs-pron acc pl masc	4085.1 adv	3642.4 dem-pron nom sing masc	3165.3 verb 3sing indic pres act	4057.15 verb inf pres
ἑαυτούς,	Ποῦ	οὗτος	μέλλει	πορεύεσθαι
heautous	*Pou*	*houtos*	*mellei*	*poreuesthai*
themselves,	Where	this	is about	to go

35.a.**Txt:** 03B,017K,019L,029T,036,037,038,byz.sa.Lach,We/Ho,Weis,Sod,UBS/☆
Var: 01א,05D,bo.Tisc

3617.1 conj	2231.1 prs-pron nom 1pl	3620.1 partic	2128.27 verb 1pl indic fut act	840.6 prs-pron acc sing masc	3231.1 partic	1519.1 prep
ὅτι	(a ἡμεῖς)	οὐχ	εὑρήσομεν	αὐτόν;	μὴ	εἰς
hoti	*hēmeis*	*ouch*	*heurēsomen*	*auton*	*mē*	*eis*
that	we	not	shall find	him?	not	to

3450.12 art acc sing fem	1284.3 noun acc sing fem	3450.1 art gen pl	1659.5 name gen pl masc	3165.3 verb 3sing indic pres act
τὴν	διασπορὰν	τῶν	Ἑλλήνων	μέλλει
tēn	*diasporan*	*tōn*	*Hellēnōn*	*mellei*
the	dispersion	among the	Greeks	is he about

4057.15 verb inf pres	2504.1 conj	1315.10 verb inf pres act	3450.8 art acc pl masc	1659.7 name acc pl masc
πορεύεσθαι,	καὶ	διδάσκειν	τοὺς	Ἕλληνας;
poreuesthai	*kai*	*didaskein*	*tous*	*Hellēnas*
to go,	and	teach	the	Greeks?

4949.3 intr-pron nom sing	1498.4 verb 3sing indic pres act	3642.4 dem-pron nom sing masc	3450.5 art sing masc	3030.1 noun nom sing masc	3450.5 art sing masc
36. τίς	ἐστιν	(οὗτος	ὁ	λόγος	[☆ ὁ
tis	*estin*	*houtos*	*ho*	*logos*	*ho*
What	is	this	the	word	[the

3030.1 noun nom sing masc	3642.4 dem-pron nom sing masc	3614.6 rel-pron acc sing masc	1500.5 verb 3sing indic aor act	2195.21 verb 2pl indic fut act
λόγος	οὗτος]	ὃν	εἶπεν,	Ζητήσετέ
logos	*houtos*	*hon*	*eipen*	*Zētēsete*
word	this]	which	he said,	You will seek

1466.6 prs-pron acc 1sing	2504.1 conj	3620.1 partic	2128.28 verb 2pl indic fut act	2504.1 conj	3562.1 adv	1498.2 verb 1sing indic pres act
με,	καὶ	οὐχ	εὑρήσετέ·	καὶ	Ὅπου	εἰμὶ
me	*kai*	*ouch*	*heurēsete*	*kai*	*Hopou*	*eimi*
me,	and	not	shall find;	and	Where	am

made this statement. The Jews did not seem to understand what Jesus was saying (verse 35).

and then I go unto him that sent me: . . . and then I am going back to Him who has sent me, *Williams* . . . and then I go my way to Him who sent me, *Weymouth* . . . I withdraw to Him who, *Wuest.*

7:34. Notice the verbs of this verse: "shall seek," "shall not find," and "cannot come." The Jews were constant in their search for the Messiah, and behold, He stood before them. He indicated that when it was too late they would desire to have Him. They would not find their Messiah in any other person after Him. Furthermore, they would be unable to come to where He was going. They would be doomed if they did not come to realize their privilege of knowing Him during the "little while" He was with them.

34. Ye shall seek me, and shall not find me: You'll be looking for Me and won't find me, *Beck* . . . You will search for Me, *Norlie* . . . will not find me, *ALBA.*

and where I am, thither ye cannot come: . . . where I am you cannot come, *RSV* . . . you are unable to come, *Fenton.*

7:35. "The dispersed" indicates the Jews who were scattered among the nations.

"Teach the Gentiles" refers to those who were of the Greek nationality, not Jews who had adopted the Greek language and culture. "Gentiles" (*hellēn*) occurs 27 times in the New Testament. This word is properly used for those of Greek descent. The word *hellēnistes* means "hellenized Jews," Jews who took on the culture of Greeks; but it is not used here.

The Jews' sarcasm seems to mean first, the Jews (themselves) had rejected Him. Second, in consequence He would turn to the Jews scattered among the nations. But these also would reject Him. And third, as a last resort He would teach the Greeks. They thought they were belittling Him. Little did they realize that this "foolishness" was in the very plan of God. The apostle Paul took the message of Christ to the Jews first; but when they rejected Christ, he said, "Behold, we are turning to the Gentiles" (Acts 13:46, NASB).

Merrill Tenney gives a historical note and insight with these words: "At the time this Gospel was written, the message of Jesus had already been taken to the Gentiles by those who preached among the Jewish Diaspora and the Gentiles. An ironic touch is thus given to the speculation of the crowd, who had spoken of Jesus' going to the Gentiles as an improbability. The episode illustrates the exclusiveness of Judaism and implies the universality of the Gospel as the author saw it" (Tenney, *Expositor's Bible Commentary,* 9:85). We can be grateful the gospel was never intended as an exclusive message to a selected few.

35. Then said the Jews among themselves, Whither will he go, that we shall not find him?: Where's He intending to go, *Beck* . . . Where is he intending to go, *Berkeley* . . . Where can he be going that we shall not be able to find him? *ALBA* . . . so that we shall not find him, *Montgomery.*

will he go unto the dispersed among the Gentiles, and teach the Gentiles?: Is he off to the Dispersion among the Greeks, *Moffatt* . . . He is not going to our people scattered among the Greeks, *Williams* . . . some region of the Gentiles, and teach the profane? *Murdock* . . . To our countrymen scattered, *TCNT* . . . the non-Jews, *Beck* . . . to the dispersed Greeks, *Campbell* . . . teach the Hellenists, *Adams* . . . the exiles of the Greek world, *ALBA.*

36. What manner of saying is this that he said: What is this saying that he said, *Alford* . . . What does he mean by saying, *TCNT* . . . What is the Man's meaning, when He says, *Fenton.*

Ye shall seek me, and shall not find me: and where I am, thither ye cannot come?:

7:36. They seemed to understand the saying, yet it contained a dark, fearful mystery. Like Pilate, they allowed the matter to drop when they came to the end of their wits. Blessed are those who

1466.1 prs-pron nom 1sing	5050.1 prs-pron nom 2pl	3620.3 partic	1404.6 verb 2pl indic pres	2048.23 verb inf aor act	1706.1 prep
ἐγὼ	ὑμεῖς	οὐ	δύνασθε	ἐλθεῖν;	37. Ἐν
egō	humeis	ou	dunasthe	elthein	En
I	you	not	are able	to come?	In

1156.2 conj	3450.11 art dat sing fem	2057.9 adj dat sing fem	2232.3 noun dat sing fem	3450.11 art dat sing fem	3144.11 adj dat sing fem	3450.10 art gen sing fem
δὲ	τῇ	ἐσχάτῃ	ἡμέρᾳ	τῇ	μεγάλῃ	τῆς
de	tē	eschatē	hēmera	tē	megalē	tēs
and	the	last	day	the	great	of the

1844.2 noun gen sing fem	2449.22 verb 3sing indic plperf act	3450.5 art sing masc	2400.1 name nom masc	2504.1 conj	2869.11 verb 3sing indic aor act
ἑορτῆς	εἱστήκει	ὁ	Ἰησοῦς,	καὶ	ˊ ἔκραξεν
heortēs	heistēkei	ho	Iēsous	kai	ekraxen
feast	stood		Jesus,	and	cried,

37.a.**Var:** 01ℵ,05D,038, 1,sa.bo.Tisc

2869.17 verb 3sing indic imperf act	2978.15 verb sing masc part pres act	1430.1 partic	4948.3 indef-pron nom sing	1366.3 verb 3sing subj pres act
[a ἔκραζεν]	λέγων,	Ἐάν	τις	διψᾷ,
ekrazen	legōn	Ean	tis	dipsa
[cries]	saying,	If	anyone	thirst,

37.b.**Txt:** p66-corr,(p75), 01ℵ-corr,(03),017K, 019L,029T,032W,036, 037,038,1,13,565,700, etc.byz.it.sa.bo.Lach, We/Ho,Sod,UBS/☆
Var: p66-org,01ℵ-org, 05D,Tisc

2048.40 verb 3sing impr pres		4242.1 prep	1466.6 prs-pron acc 1sing	2504.1 conj	3956.7 verb 3sing impr pres act	3450.5 art sing masc
ἐρχέσθω	ˊb	πρός	με ˋ	καὶ	πινέτω·	38. ὁ
erchesthō		pros	me	kai	pinetō	ho
let him come		to	me	and	drink.	The

3961.10 verb nom sing masc part pres act	1519.1 prep	1466.7 prs-pron acc 1sing	2503.1 conj	1500.5 verb 3sing indic aor act
πιστεύων	εἰς	ἐμέ,	καθὼς	εἶπεν
pisteuōn	eis	eme	kathōs	eipen
believing	on	me,	as	said

3450.9 art nom sing fem	1118.1 noun nom sing fem	4074.5 noun nom pl masc	1523.2 prep gen	3450.10 art gen sing fem	2809.2 noun gen sing fem
ἡ	γραφή,	ποταμοὶ	ἐκ	τῆς	κοιλίας
hē	graphē	potamoi	ek	tēs	koilias
the	scripture,	rivers	out of	the	belly

840.3 prs-pron gen sing	4339.1 verb 3pl indic fut act	5045.2 noun gen sing neu	2180.11 verb gen sing part pres act	3642.17 dem-pron sing neu
αὐτοῦ	ῥεύσουσιν	ὕδατος	ζῶντος.	39. Τοῦτο
autou	rheusousin	hudatos	zōntos	Touto
his	shall flow	of water	living.	This

1156.2 conj	1500.5 verb 3sing indic aor act	3875.1 prep	3450.2 art gen sing	4011.2 noun gen sing neu
δὲ	εἶπεν	περὶ	τοῦ	πνεύματος
de	eipen	peri	tou	pneumatos
but	he said	concerning	the	Spirit

39.a.**Var:** 01ℵ,017K, 019L,036,037,038,Tisc, Sod

3614.2 rel-pron gen sing	3165.20 verb indic imperf act	3165.24 verb indic imperf act	2956.10 verb inf pres act	3450.7 art pl masc
οὗ	ˊ ἔμελλον	[a ἤμελλον]	λαμβάνειν	οἱ
hou	emellon	ēmellon	lambanein	hoi
which	were about	[idem]	to receive	the

39.b.**Txt:** 01ℵ,05D,017K, 036,037,038,1,13,700, byz.it.Tisc,Sod
Var: p66,03B,019L, 032W,Lach,Treg,Alf, We/Ho,Weis,UBS/☆

3961.13 verb nom pl masc part pres act	3961.31 verb nom pl masc part aor act	1519.1 prep	840.6 prs-pron acc sing masc	3632.1 adv
ˊ πιστεύοντες	[b☆ πιστεύσαντες]	εἰς	αὐτόν·	οὔπω
pisteuontes	pisteusantes	eis	auton	oupō
believing	[having believed]	on	him;	not yet

continue to meditate and search for meaning when the traces of knowledge become obscure.

7:37. This was the eighth day of the Feast of Tabernacles. It would seem that Jesus' days were spent teaching on the temple grounds. He spent His evenings in Bethany with His friends Lazarus, Martha, and Mary (see chapter 11).

The prerequisite for drinking is thirst. If the condition is right, the desire will follow. This is the same truth Jesus expressed to the Samaritan woman (4:14). Early in His ministry Jesus taught that those who hunger and thirst for righteousness would be satisfied (Matthew 5:6).

"Let him come unto me, and drink" is a beautiful invitation to partake of the free, gracious provision of God in Christ Jesus. The "him" refers to "any man" (*tis*) without distinction of sex, age, class, nationality, or race. Jesus did not say "any Jew" but "any one."

7:38. The "he that believeth" (*ho pisteuōn*) is a present tense participle signifying a continuing act of believing here and now. It is good to thirst and to seek; however, the satisfaction does not come in the thirsting or seeking, but in coming to Him, drinking of Him, believing in Him.

Jesus was not referring to a particular passage but rather to a composite of many references (Joel 3:18; Zechariah 14:8; Ezekiel 47:1-12).

The word "rivers" has the emphatic position in this verse. "Rivers" flow out of the innermost part of the individual. It is the secret place of one's life from which living waters gush forth. A person will give out what he is filled with. It is out of the abundance of the heart that a man speaks. Eternal things come out if the eternal blessings are stored in the recesses of the soul (Matthew 12:34, also compare Matthew 6:21).

7:39. This is one of the numerous references made to the Holy Spirit's person and activities in the Gospel of John. This verse is the explanation of what Jesus meant by the "rivers of living water." The coming of the Holy Spirit on the Day of Pentecost was like a stream flowing from Jerusalem, bringing life to the world. The flow of the Spirit brings personal enlightenment, joy, and power. It produces life for all who drink of its waters.

It was not that the Holy Spirit was inactive before that time, because the Spirit operated throughout the Old Testament period.

37. In the last day, that great day of the feast: On the final and most important day of the Feast, *Berkeley* . . . of the festivity, *Douay.*

Jesus stood and cried, saying: Jesus stood up and called out, *Norlie* . . . and proclaimed, *RSV.*

If any man thirst, let him come unto me, and drink: . . . Whoever is thirsty, *Berkeley.*

38. He that believeth on me, as the scripture hath said, out of his belly shall flow rivers of living water: Whoever trusts in Me, *Fenton* . . . continues to believe...continuously flowing, *Williams* . . . will be like the Scripture, *SEB* . . . shall be like a cistern, *Campbell* . . . from within him shall flow rivers of living water, *HBIE* . . . Out of the heart of the one who believes in Me there will flow, *Norlie* . . . Out from his innermost being springs and rivers of living water shall flow, *AmpB* . . . out of his body, *BB* . . . From his breast, *JB* . . . out of his inward being, *Klingensmith* . . . from his inmost heart, *Phillips* . . . shall gush rivers, *Concordant* . . . streams of water, *Berkeley.*

39. (But this spake he of the Spirit: And this he spoke concerning the Spirit, *HBIE* . . . He referred to the Spirit, *Weymouth.*

which they that believe on him should receive: . . . later to be received by, *ALBA* . . . were about to receive, *Alford* . . . which those who believed in Him were to receive, *Weymouth* . . . were afterwards to receive, *Fenton.*

John 7:40

39.c.**Txt:** p66-org,03B, 019L,032W,036,037,33, byz.Gries,WeisSod
Var: p66-org,p75,01ℵ, 017K,029T,038,bo.Lach, Tisc,We/Ho,UBS/☆

39.d.**Txt:** Steph
Var: 01ℵ,03B,05D, 017K,019L,029T,036, 037,038,byz.Lach,Treg, Alf,Tisc,We/Ho,WeisSod, UBS/☆

39.e.**Var:** 01ℵ,03B,05D, 038,Lach,Treg,Alf, We/Ho

40.a.**Txt:** 017K,036,037, 13,byz.
Var: p66-corr,p75,01ℵ, 03B,05D,019L,029T, 032W,033X,sa.bo.Lach Treg,Alf,Tisc,We/Ho, Weis,Sod,UBS/☆

40.b.**Txt:** 021M,033X, 036,byz.
Var: 01ℵ,03B,05D,019L, 029T,030U,Lach,Treg, Alf,TiscWe/Ho,Weis,Sod, UBS/☆

40.c.**Var:** 03B,05D,033X, Alf,We/Ho,Weis,UBS/☆

41.a.**Txt:** p66-org,01ℵ, 05D,017K,036,037,13, byz.bo.Tisc
Var: 03B,019L,029T, 033X,33,sa.Lach,Treg, AlfWe/Ho,Weis,Sod, UBS/☆

41.b.**Txt:** 03B,019L, 029T,033X,33,sa.bo. Steph,Lach,We/Ho,Weis, Sod,UBS/☆
Var: 01ℵ,05D,017K,036, 037,Tisc

42.a.**Txt:** 01ℵ,05D,017K, 032W,036,037,1,13,etc. byz.Gries,Tisc,Sod
Var: p66,p75,03B-corr, 019L,029T,038,Lach Treg,Alf,We/Ho,Weis, UBS/☆

1056.1 conj	**1498.34** verb sing indic imperf act	**4011.1** noun sing neu	**39.1** adj sing	**3617.1** conj	**3450.5** art sing masc
γὰρ	ἦν	πνεῦμα	⸂c ἅγιον, ⸃	ὅτι	⸂d ὁ ⸃
gar	*ēn*	*pneuma*	*hagion*	*hoti*	*ho*
for	was	Spirit	Holy,	because	

2400.1 name nom masc	**3627.1** adv	**3632.1** adv	**1386.22** verb 3sing indic aor pass	**4044.7** adj nom pl masc
Ἰησοῦς	⸂ οὐδέπω	[e οὔπω]	ἐδοξάσθη.	40. ⸂ πολλοὶ
Iēsous	*oudepō*	*oupō*	*edoxasthē*	*polloi*
Jesus	not yet	[idem]	was glorified.	Many

3631.1 conj	**1523.2** prep gen	**3450.2** art gen sing	**3657.2** noun gen sing masc	**1523.2** prep gen	**3450.2** art gen sing
οὖν	ἐκ	τοῦ	ὄχλου	[a☆ Ἐκ	τοῦ
oun	*ek*	*tou*	*ochlou*	*Ek*	*tou*
therefore	out of	the	crowd	[Out of	the

3657.2 noun gen sing masc	**3631.1** conj	**189.32** verb nom pl masc part aor act	**3450.6** art acc sing masc	**3030.4** noun acc sing masc
ὄχλου	οὖν]	ἀκούσαντες	⸂ τὸν	λόγον
ochlou	*oun*	*akousantes*	*ton*	*logon*
crowd	therefore]	having heard	the	word

3450.1 art gen pl	**3030.6** noun gen pl masc	**3642.2** dem-pron gen pl	**2978.25** verb indic imperf act	**3617.1** conj
[b☆ τῶν	λόγων	τούτων]	ἔλεγον,	[c+ ὅτι]
tōn	*logōn*	*toutōn*	*elegon*	*hoti*
[the	words	these]	said,	

3642.4 dem-pron nom sing masc	**1498.4** verb 3sing indic pres act	**228.1** adv	**3450.5** art sing masc	**4254.1** noun nom sing masc
Οὗτός	ἐστιν	ἀληθῶς	ὁ	προφήτης.
Houtos	*estin*	*alēthōs*	*ho*	*prophētēs*
This	is	truly	the	prophet.

241.6 adj nom pl masc	**2978.25** verb indic imperf act	**3642.4** dem-pron nom sing masc	**1498.4** verb 3sing indic pres act	**3450.5** art sing masc
41. Ἄλλοι	ἔλεγον,	Οὗτός	ἐστιν	ὁ
Alloi	*elegon*	*Houtos*	*estin*	*ho*
Others	said,	This	is	the

5382.1 name nom masc	**241.6** adj nom pl masc	**3450.7** art pl masc	**1156.2** conj	**2978.25** verb indic imperf act	**3231.1** partic
Χριστός.	⸂ Ἄλλοι	[a☆ οἱ]	⸂b δὲ ⸃	ἔλεγον,	Μὴ
Christos	*Alloi*	*hoi*	*de*	*elegon*	*Mē*
Christ.	Others	[the]	and	said,	Not

1056.1 conj	**1523.2** prep gen	**3450.10** art gen sing fem	**1049.2** name gen sing fem	**3450.5** art sing masc	**5382.1** name nom masc	**2048.34** verb 3sing indic pres
γὰρ	ἐκ	τῆς	Γαλιλαίας	ὁ	Χριστὸς	ἔρχεται;
gar	*ek*	*tēs*	*Galilaias*	*ho*	*Christos*	*erchetai*
then	out of		Galilee	the	Christ	comes?

3644.1 adv	**3620.1** partic	**3450.9** art nom sing fem	**1118.1** noun nom sing fem	**1500.5** verb 3sing indic aor act
42. ⸂ οὐχὶ	[a☆ οὐχ]	ἡ	γραφὴ	εἶπεν,
ouchi	*ouch*	*hē*	*graphē*	*eipen*
Not	[idem]	the	scripture	said,

3617.1 conj	**1523.2** prep gen	**3450.2** art gen sing	**4543.2** noun gen sing neu	**1132.1** name masc	**2504.1** conj	**570.3** prep gen
ὅτι	ἐκ	τοῦ	σπέρματος	Δαβίδ,	καὶ	ἀπὸ
hoti	*ek*	*tou*	*spermatos*	*Dabid*	*kai*	*apo*
that	out of	the	seed	of David,	and	from

Yet the fullness of the Spirit was not available for all until He was given as a gift to all believers (Acts 2:38). The word "given" is not in the Greek text. Thus "the Spirit was not yet" is the complete idea. He was "not yet" in the sense that He would be available to all believers from the birth of the Church on.

Jesus was "glorified" when His resurrection occurred. The Spirit can now point to Jesus with an intense, blazing spotlight and assert that Jesus Christ is the Lord.

for the Holy Ghost was not yet given: . . . for as yet there was no such thing as the Spirit, *Barclay* . . . for not yet was the Spirit sent, *Wuest* . . . for the Spirit had not yet come, *TCNT* . . . was not yet revealed, *Fenton* . . . there was no Spirit present, *HistNT.*

because that Jesus was not yet glorified.): . . . because Jesus had not yet been exalted, *TCNT* . . . the glory of Jesus was still to come, *BB* . . . not yet been raised to glory, *SEB.*

7:40. "Many of the people therefore" indicates that as the result of His teaching many were convinced of Jesus' messiahship. Multitudes of people attended the three annual feasts (Passover, Pentecost, and Tabernacles), Jews and proselytes from many areas of the world and Jews from Palestine.

Most Jews believed "the Prophet" predicted by Moses in Deuteronomy 18:15-18 was the Messiah. However, some seemed to think "the Prophet" was to be a forerunner of the Messiah (see Matthew 16:14; Malachi 4:5,6; John 1:21).

40. Many of the people therefore, when they heard this saying, said, Of a truth this is the Prophet: . . . among the crowd, *ALBA* . . . Listening to these teachings there were those in the crowd, *Berkeley* . . . On hearing His words, *Norlie* . . . This really is the prophet, *Berkeley* . . . Without doubt this man is the Prophet, *Montgomery* . . . This is certainly the prophet, *Campbell* . . . This is beyond doubt the Prophet, *Weymouth.*

7:41. Notice the progression of belief among the people. This assertion was more positive than the last one.

"Others said, This is the Christ." Another group within the multitude had grave doubts about Jesus being the Messiah. This group disagreed with the two previous groups by offering their objection based on the Scriptures. The question uses the Greek negative (*mē*) implying "certainly not." The widespread understanding of the prophecies indicated that the birthplace of Messiah was to be in Bethlehem (Micah 5:2; Matthew 2:4-6). These people were ignorant of the fact that Jesus was of the tribe of Judah, a descendant of King David, and born in Bethlehem. But they knew He grew up in Nazareth. If they had wanted to know the truth, they would have investigated. People who want only to hold to their selfish opinions do not make the effort of a full examination.

41. Others said, This is the Christ: . . . the Messiah, *Fenton* . . . This is the promised Savior, *Beck.*

But some said, Shall Christ come out of Galilee?: . . . No, the Christ was not to come out of, *Norlie* . . . What! does the Christ come from Galilee? *TCNT.*

42. Hath not the scripture said, That Christ cometh of the seed of David: Hasn't Scripture made it clear that, *ALBA* . . . that Christ will be descended from David, *Phillips* . . . Do not the Writings say, *BB* . . . come from the race of David, *Fenton* . . . from the descendants of David, *Beck.*

7:42. The argument of those who rejected Christ (in the prior verse) offered their understanding of the Scriptures. This should not surprise us, for even the devil quoted Scripture to Jesus during the temptation (Matthew 4:2-11). "Christ cometh of the seed of David, and out of the town of Bethlehem, where David was?" Many passages from the Old Testament indicated these facts about Christ's genealogy and nativity (see 2 Samuel 7:12,13; Psalms 89:19-29; 132:11; Isaiah 9:6,7; 11:1-5; Jeremiah 23:5,6; Micah 5:2).

958.1 name fem	3450.10 art gen sing fem	2941.1 noun gen sing fem	3562.1 adv	1498.34 verb sing indic imperf act	1132.1 name masc
Βηθλέεμ	τῆς	κώμης	ὅπου	ἦν	Δαβίδ,
Bēthleem	*tēs*	*kōmēs*	*hopou*	*ēn*	*Dabid*
Bethlehem	the	village	where	was	David,

3450.5 art sing masc	5382.1 name nom masc	2048.34 verb 3sing indic pres	2048.34 verb 3sing indic pres	3450.5 art sing masc	5382.1 name nom masc
‹☆ ὁ	Χριστὸς	ἔρχεται;	[ἔρχεται	ὁ	Χριστός;]
ho	*Christos*	*erchetai*	*erchetai*	*ho*	*Christos*
the	Christ	comes?	[comes	the	Christ?]

4830.1 noun nom sing neu	3631.1 conj	1706.1 prep	3450.3 art dat sing	3657.3 noun dat sing masc	1090.33 verb 3sing indic aor mid
43. Σχίσμα	οὖν	‹ ἐν	τῷ	ὄχλῳ	ἐγένετο
Schisma	*oun*	*en*	*tō*	*ochlō*	*egeneto*
A division	therefore	in	the	crowd	occurred

1090.33 verb 3sing indic aor mid	1706.1 prep	3450.3 art dat sing	3657.3 noun dat sing masc	1217.1 prep	840.6 prs-pron acc sing masc
[☆ ἐγένετο	ἐν	τῷ	ὄχλῳ]	δι'	αὐτόν.
egeneto	*en*	*tō*	*ochlō*	*di'*	*auton*
[occurred	in	the	crowd]	because of	him.

4948.7 indef-pron nom pl masc	1156.2 conj	2286.30 verb indic imperf act	1523.1 prep gen	840.1 prs-pron gen pl	3945.6 verb inf aor act
44. τινὲς	δὲ	ἤθελον	ἐξ	αὐτῶν	πιάσαι
tines	*de*	*ēthelon*	*ex*	*autōn*	*piasai*
Some	but	wanted	of	them	to take

44.a.**Var:** p75,03B,019L, 029T,Lach,Treg,Alf, Tisc,We/Ho

840.6 prs-pron acc sing masc	233.1 conj	3625.2 num card nom masc	1896.3 verb 3sing indic aor act	900.10 verb 3sing indic aor act	1894.2 prep
αὐτόν,	ἀλλ'	οὐδεὶς	‹ ἐπέβαλεν	[a ἔβαλεν]	ἐπ'
auton	*all'*	*oudeis*	*epebalen*	*ebalen*	*ep'*
him,	but	no one	laid	[idem]	on

840.6 prs-pron acc sing masc	3450.15 art acc pl fem	5331.8 noun acc pl fem	2048.1 verb indic aor act	3631.1 conj	3450.7 art pl masc
αὐτὸν	τὰς	χεῖρας.	45. Ἦλθον	οὖν	οἱ
auton	*tas*	*cheiras*	*Ēlthon*	*oun*	*hoi*
him	the	hands.	Came	therefore	the

5095.3 noun nom pl masc	4242.1 prep	3450.8 art acc pl masc	744.5 noun pl masc	2504.1 conj	5168.7 name acc pl masc
ὑπηρέται	πρὸς	τοὺς	ἀρχιερεῖς	καὶ	Φαρισαίους·
hupēretai	*pros*	*tous*	*archiereis*	*kai*	*Pharisaious*
officers	to	the	chief priests	and	Pharisees,

2504.1 conj	1500.3 verb indic aor act	840.2 prs-pron dat pl	1552.6 dem-pron nom pl masc	1296.1 adv	1217.2 prep
καὶ	εἶπον	αὐτοῖς	ἐκεῖνοι,	‹ Διατί	[☆ Διὰ
kai	*eipon*	*autois*	*ekeinoi*	*Diati*	*Dia*
and	said	to them	those,	Why	[Because of

4949.9 intr-pron sing neu	3620.2 partic	70.9 verb 2pl indic aor act	840.6 prs-pron acc sing masc	552.8 verb 3pl indic aor pass
τί]	οὐκ	ἠγάγετε	αὐτόν;	46. Ἀπεκρίθησαν
ti	*ouk*	*ēgagete*	*auton*	*Apekrithēsan*
what]	not	did you bring	him?	Answered

3450.7 art pl masc	5095.3 noun nom pl masc	3626.1 adv	3643.1 adv	2953.27 verb 3sing indic aor act
οἱ	ὑπηρέται,	Οὐδέποτε	‹ οὕτως	ἐλάλησεν
hoi	*hupēretai*	*Oudepote*	*houtōs*	*elalēsen*
the	officers,	Never	thus	spoke

7:43. "Division" (*schisma*) occurs eight times in the New Testament, three of which are in John. The word means "a rent, split, dissension." The people were sharply divided over whether Jesus was the Christ or not. At one point Jesus stated, "Think not that I am come to send peace on earth; I came not to send peace, but a sword" (Matthew 10:34). The sword severs and divides. This is what Jesus did by teaching in the temple at the Feast of Tabernacles. Those who received Him were given eternal life, but those who rejected Him became more deeply entrenched in darkness and death.

7:44. Some of the group who rejected Him on the grounds that He did not come from Bethlehem wanted to arrest Him. Doubtless a few were sent by the chief priests to stir up the people against Jesus. The hostile enemies of Jesus were hindered from taking Him because of their fear of His disciples and by their awe of His presence and the power by which He spoke and performed miracles. Not even the temple guards who were sent to arrest Jesus placed a hand on Him (verses 32,45).

7:45. "The officers" (*hupēretai*) is a term which appears 20 times in the New Testament. It is usually translated "officer" but sometimes "minister" and "servant." The officers were Levites who were appointed as temple police.

"Why have ye not brought him?" The question reveals the indignation of the chief priests and Pharisees who were the temple rulers.

The officers were taught by law and experience to be impartial. These men became typical of those observers who looked at and listened to the evidence concerning Jesus. On the one hand they found no reason to arrest Him and on the other hand they were impressed by the truth Jesus taught.

7:46. These words express their wonder and surprise. The officers had observed Jesus for a length of time, waiting for the opportune moment to arrest Him. The more they watched, the more astonished they became. They saw how He answered His enemies. His words had a ring of truth and a power of conviction that pierced the consciences and souls of His hearers (see Matthew 7:28,29). Jesus' words were so filled with light that they burned their message on the soul.

and out of the town of Bethlehem where David was?: . . . and from Bethlehem, *ASV* . . . the village...where David lived, *Williams, Norlie, Beck* . . . David's town, *Montgomery*.

43. So there was a division among the people because of him: So there was a dissension among the people on His account, *Weymouth* . . . So the people were in two minds about him, *Phillips* . . . The crowd were split in their attitude to him, *Barclay* . . . So, the people in the crowd were divided because of Jesus, *SEB* . . . a division or opinion, *TCNT* . . . among the masses, *Norlie* . . . among the multitude respecting him, *Murdock*.

44. And some of them would have taken him; but no man laid hands on him: . . . wanted to have Him arrested, *Norlie* . . . no one ventured to lay a hand upon Him, *Williams* . . . wished to apprehend him, *Montgomery* . . . yet no one touched him, *TCNT*.

45. Then came the officers to the chief priests and Pharisees; and they said unto them, Why have ye not brought him?: Meanwhile the attendants, *AmpB* . . . came back to the most important priests, *SEB* . . . they were met with the question, *TCNT* . . . Why didn't you bring him back with you, *Norlie*.

46. The officers answered, Never man spake like this man:

John 7:47

46.a.**Var:** p66-org, 01ℵ-org,(05),Tisc,Weis, UBS/⋆

47.a.**Txt:** 03B,017K, 019L,029T,036,037,038, etc.byz.Lach,We/Ho, Weis,Sod,UBS/⋆
Var: 01ℵ,05D,33,syr.it. sa.Alf,Tisc

47.b.**Txt:** 01ℵ,05D,019L, 029T,036,037,etc.byz. Lach,Tisc,We/HoWeis, Sod,UBS/⋆
Var: 03B,017K,038

2953.27 verb 3sing indic aor act	**3643.1** adv	**442.1** noun nom sing masc	**5453.1** conj	**3642.4** dem-pron nom sing masc
[⋆ ἐλάλησεν	οὕτως]	ἄνθρωπος	ὡς	οὗτος
elalēsen	*houtōs*	*anthrōpos*	*hōs*	*houtos*
[spoke	thus]	man	as	this

2953.2 verb sing indic pres act	**3450.5** art sing masc	**442.1** noun nom sing masc	**552.8** verb 3pl indic aor pass
[a+ λαλεῖ]	ὁ	ἄνθρωπος.	47. ᾿Απεκρίθησαν
lalei	*ho*	*anthrōpos*	*Apekrithēsan*
[speaks]	the	man.	Answered

3631.1 conj	**840.2** prs-pron dat pl	**3450.7** art pl masc	**5168.4** name pl masc	**3231.1** partic	**2504.1** conj
(a οὖν)	(b αὐτοῖς)	οἱ	Φαρισαῖοι,	Μὴ	καὶ
oun	*autois*	*hoi*	*Pharisaioi*	*Mē*	*kai*
therefore	them	the	Pharisees,	not	also

5050.1 prs-pron nom 2pl	**3966.21** verb 2pl indic perf pass	**3231.1** partic	**4948.3** indef-pron nom sing	**1523.2** prep gen	**3450.1** art gen pl
ὑμεῖς	πεπλάνησθε;	48. μή	τις	ἐκ	τῶν
humeis	*peplanēsthe*	*mē*	*tis*	*ek*	*tōn*
you	have been deceived?	Not	any one	of	the

752.6 noun gen pl masc	**3961.20** verb 3sing indic aor act	**1519.1** prep	**840.6** prs-pron acc sing masc	**2211.1** conj	**1523.2** prep gen	**3450.1** art gen pl
ἀρχόντων	ἐπίστευσεν	εἰς	αὐτὸν,	ἢ	ἐκ	τῶν
archontōn	*episteusen*	*eis*	*auton*	*ē*	*ek*	*tōn*
rulers	has believed	on	him,	or	of	the

5168.5 name gen pl masc	**233.1** conj	**233.2** conj	**3450.5** art sing masc	**3657.1** noun nom sing masc
Φαρισαίων;	49. (ἀλλ'	[⋆ ἀλλὰ]	ὁ	ὄχλος
Pharisaiōn	*all'*	*alla*	*ho*	*ochlos*
Pharisees?	But	[idem]	the	crowd

3642.4 dem-pron nom sing masc	**3450.5** art sing masc	**3231.1** partic	**1091.11** verb nom sing masc part pres act	**3450.6** art acc sing masc	**3414.4** noun acc sing masc
οὗτος	ὁ	μὴ	γινώσκων	τὸν	νόμον
houtos	*ho*	*mē*	*ginōskōn*	*ton*	*nomon*
this,	the	not	knowing	the	law,

49.a.**Txt:** 05D,017K, 019L,036,037,byz.
Var: 01ℵ,03B,029T,038, 33,Lach,Treg,Alf,Tisc, We/HoWeis,Sod,UBS/⋆

50.a.**Txt:** (05),(017), 021M,036,(037),038,1, 13,byz.
Var: p66,p75,01ℵ-corr, 03B,019L,029T,sa.Lach, Treg,Alf,We/Ho,Weis, Sod,UBS/⋆

50.b.**Var:** 075,01ℵ-corr, 03B,(019),029T,038,1, 13,sa.Lach,TregAlf, We/Ho,Weis,Sod,UBS/⋆

1929.2 adj nom pl masc	**1868.1** adj nom pl masc	**1498.7** verb 3pl indic pres act	**2978.5** verb 3sing indic pres act
(ἐπικατάρατοί	[a⋆ ἐπάρατοί]	εἰσιν.	50. Λέγει
epikataratoi	*eparatoi*	*eisin*	*Legei*
accursed	[idem]	are.	Says

3392.1 name nom masc	**4242.1** prep	**840.8** prs-pron acc pl masc	**3450.5** art sing masc	**2048.13** verb nom sing masc part aor act
Νικόδημος	πρὸς	αὐτούς,	ὁ	ἐλθὼν
Nikodēmos	*pros*	*autous*	*ho*	*elthōn*
Nicodemus	to	them,	the	having come

3433.2 noun gen sing fem	**4242.1** prep	**840.6** prs-pron acc sing masc	**4245.2** adj comp acc sing neu	**1518.3** num card nom masc
(a νυκτὸς)	πρὸς	αὐτὸν,	[b⋆+ πρότερον,]	εἷς
nuktos	*pros*	*auton*	*proteron*	*heis*
by night	to	him,	[firstly,]	one

1498.21 verb sing masc part pres act	**1523.1** prep gen	**840.1** prs-pron gen pl	**3231.1** partic	**3450.5** art sing masc	**3414.1** noun nom sing masc
ὢν	ἐξ	αὐτῶν,	51. Μὴ	ὁ	νόμος
ōn	*ex*	*autōn*	*Mē*	*ho*	*nomos*
being	of	themselves,	Not	the	law

No man ever spoke as this man speaks! *Berkeley.*

7:47. The question implies a negative answer, but the Pharisees certainly feared lest the officers become Jesus' disciples. The perfect tense verb "Are ye also deceived?" (*peplanēsthe*) means to have in the past gone after Jesus and now are of His persuasion. "Deceived" carries the idea of being led astray or wandering from the path.

47. Then answered them the Pharisees, Are ye also deceived?: The Pharisees exclaimed, *Norlie* . . . The Pharisees retorted, Are you misled as well, *Moffatt* . . . Has he pulled the wool over your eyes,too? *Phillips* . . . you too been taken in? *ALBA* . . . Are you deluded too? *Weymouth* . . . swept off your feet too, *Williams* . . . led astray? *Fenton* . . . been deceived? *Wilson* . . . been fooled, *SEB.*

7:48. Again the question expects a negative response. The Pharisees pointed out that no important or educated person had believed Jesus. This is not entirely true. Nicodemus was well on his way to becoming a disciple (see 3:1; 7:50-52; 19:38-40). The arrogance with which the Pharisees spoke and the ridicule heaped upon any who dared to follow Jesus were meant to dissuade the officers from inquiry into the truth.

48. Have any of the rulers or of the Pharisees believed on Him?: Have any of the authorities, *RSV* . . . the chiefs, *Murdock* . . . members of the Sanhedrin, *ET* . . . of our leading men, *TCNT.*

7:49. "But this people" refers to those of the common people. The Pharisees revealed their attitude toward the poor and the uneducated who had not been instructed in the schools where they would have been schooled in the Law. They were considered cursed of God. The Pharisees interpreted the blessing of God as prosperity, education, and social status. All those who lacked these were assumed to have no favor with God. The curses were pronounced on the disobedient in accord with Deuteronomy 28:15-35. For the Pharisees, wealth and education were proof of their acceptance with God.

The blessings and curses God pronounced were general and national, not specific and individual. To say that every disease or endowment is a direct result of personal sin or virtue was denied by the Lord Jesus (9:3).

49. But this people who knoweth not the law are cursed: As for this mob who do not understand the Law, *Montgomery* . . . But this crowd, which doesn't know the Bible, *Beck* . . . But this public that does not know the Law-accursed they are, *Berkeley* . . . is damned anyway! *Phillips* . . . As for this rabble...they are accursed, *Weymouth* . . . are contemptible, *Fenton* . . . they are blighted by their ignorance, *ALBA* . . . They should be condemned! *SEB* . . . is bound to be accursed! *Williams.*

7:50. "Nicodemus" is identified by John as "he that came to Jesus by night, being one of them" (see 3:1). Nicodemus was one of the Sanhedrin rulers and a member of the Pharisees. His name appears again in 19:39.

50. Nicodemus saith unto them, (he that came to Jesus by night, being one of them,): . . . ventured to say to them, *Norlie* . . . who had formerly had a meeting with Jesus, *ALBA.*

7:51. Nicodemus spoke up for justice and fairness. The Law did not condemn until the accused was heard and witnesses testified against him (Deuteronomy 17:8,9; 19:15-19). Nicodemus was saying that a man is innocent until he is proven guilty.

2231.2 prs-pron gen 1pl	2892.5 verb 3sing indic pres act	3450.6 art acc sing masc	442.4 noun acc sing masc	1430.1 partic	3231.1 partic
ἡμῶν	κρίνει	τὸν	ἄνθρωπον,	ἐὰν	μὴ
hēmōn	*krinei*	*ton*	*anthrōpon*	*ean*	*mē*
our	does judge	the	man,	if	not

51.a.**Txt:** 021M,030U, 036,037,byz.
Var: 01ℵ-corr,03B,05D, 019L,029T,038,33,Lach, Treg,Alf,Tisc,We/Ho, Weis,Sod,UBS/☆

189.18 verb sing act	3706.1 prep	840.3 prs-pron gen sing	4245.2 adj comp acc sing neu	4270.1 adv
ἀκούσῃ	ʻ παρ'	αὐτοῦ	πρότερον,	[a☆ πρῶτον
akousē	*par'*	*autou*	*proteron*	*prōton*
it have heard	from	himself	first,	[first

3706.1 prep	840.3 prs-pron gen sing	2504.1 conj	1091.22 verb 3sing subj aor act	4949.9 intr-pron sing neu	4020.5 verb 3sing indic pres act
παρ'	αὐτοῦ]	καὶ	γνῷ	τί	ποιεῖ;
par'	*autou*	*kai*	*gnō*	*ti*	*poiei*
from	him]	and	known	what	he does?

52.a.**Txt:** 01ℵ,019L,036, 037,byz.Sod
Var: 03B,05D,017K, 029T,038,33,Lach,Treg Alf,Tisc,We/Ho,Weis, UBS/☆

552.8 verb 3pl indic aor pass	2504.1 conj	1500.3 verb indic aor act	1500.28 verb 3pl indic aor act	840.4 prs-pron dat sing
52. Ἀπεκρίθησαν	καὶ	ʻ εἶπον	[a☆ εἶπαν]	αὐτῷ,
Apekrithēsan	*kai*	*eipon*	*eipan*	*autō*
They answered	and	said	[idem]	to him,

3231.1 partic	2504.1 conj	4622.1 prs-pron nom 2sing	1523.2 prep gen	3450.10 art gen sing fem	1049.2 name gen sing fem	1498.3 verb 2sing indic pres act
Μὴ	καὶ	σὺ	ἐκ	τῆς	Γαλιλαίας	εἶ;
Mē	*kai*	*su*	*ek*	*tēs*	*Galilaias*	*ei*
Not	also	you	of		Galilee	are?

52.b.**Var:** 01ℵ,03B-org, 029T,Treg,Alf,Tisc, We/Ho

2028.5 verb 2sing impr aor act	2020.5 verb 2sing impr aor act	2504.1 conj	1481.14 verb 2sing impr aor act	3617.1 conj
ʻ ἐρεύνησον	[b ἐραύνησον]	καὶ	ἴδε,	ὅτι
ereunēson	*eraunēson*	*kai*	*ide*	*hoti*
Search	[idem]	and	look,	that

4254.1 noun nom sing masc	1523.2 prep gen	3450.10 art gen sing fem	1049.2 name gen sing fem	1523.2 prep gen	3450.10 art gen sing fem
ʻ προφήτης	ἐκ	τῆς	Γαλιλαίας	[ἐκ	τῆς
prophētēs	*ek*	*tēs*	*Galilaias*	*ek*	*tēs*
a prophet	out of		Galilee	[from	

52.c.**Txt:** 07E,019L, 033X,Steph
Var: 01ℵ,03B,05D, 017K,029T,036,037,038, Lach,Treg,Alf,Tisc, We/Ho,WeisSod,UBS/☆

1049.2 name gen sing fem	4254.1 noun nom sing masc	3620.2 partic	1446.29 verb 3sing indic perf pass	1446.15 verb 3sing indic pres pass
Γαλιλαίας	προφήτης]	οὐκ	ʻ ἐγήγερται.	[c☆ ἐγείρεται.]
Galilaias	*prophētēs*	*ouk*	*egēgertai*	*egeiretai*
Galilee	a prophet]	not	has arisen.	[is arising.]

53.a."(7:53-8:11.deleted)"
Txt: 05D,017K,021M, 030U,036,28,700,byz. Gries,Word
Var: p66,p75,01ℵ,02A, 03B,04C,019L,029T, 032W,037,038,33,565, lect.sa.Lach,Treg,Alf, Tisc,We/Ho,Weis,Sod, UBS/☆

2504.1 conj	4057.16 verb 3sing indic aor pass	1524.3 adj nom sing masc	1519.1 prep	3450.6 art acc sing masc	3486.4 noun acc sing masc
53. ʻa Καὶ	ἐπορεύθη	ἕκαστος	εἰς	τὸν	οἶκον
Kai	*eporeuthē*	*hekastos*	*eis*	*ton*	*oikon*
And	went	each	to	the	house

840.3 prs-pron gen sing	2400.1 name nom masc	1156.2 conj	4057.16 verb 3sing indic aor pass	1519.1 prep	3450.16 art sing neu
αὐτοῦ,	**8:1.** Ἰησοῦς	δὲ	ἐπορεύθη	εἰς	τὸ
autou	*Iēsous*	*de*	*eporeuthē*	*eis*	*to*
his.	Jesus	but	went	to	the

3598.1 noun sing neu	3450.1 art gen pl	1623.4 noun gen pl fem	3585.1 noun gen sing masc	1156.2 conj	3687.1 adv
ὄρος	τῶν	ἐλαιῶν·	**2.** Ὄρθρου	δὲ	πάλιν
oros	*tōn*	*elaiōn*	*Orthrou*	*de*	*palin*
mount		of Olives.	At dawn	and	again

The Law gave the accused the opportunity to defend himself, but these rulers had condemned Jesus already (Deuteronomy 1:16,27). Nicodemus spoke for Jesus from a judicial viewpoint.

51. Doth our law judge any man, before it hear him: Does our Law pass judgment on a man without first giving him a hearing, *TCNT* . . . convict a man, *Fenton* . . . before hearing his defense, *Montgomery* . . . without first hearing what he has to say, *Beck.*

and know what he doeth?: . . . and finding out what he has been doing, *TCNT* . . . and ascertaining his behavior, *Berkeley* . . . and understanding his offence? *HistNT* . . . his offense, *Moffatt* . . . and without investigating his actions? *Barclay* . . . We must find out what he is doing, *SEB.*

7:52. The Jews promptly replied to Nicodemus with ridicule. They had no concern for justice. They used the same method on the officers (verses 47-49). Jesus resided in Galilee and chose His apostles from that region: thus to be called a Galilean was derogatory.

"Search, and look." They directed Nicodemus to the Scriptures. They asserted that no prophet had come from Galilee. They were certainly incorrect, for several prophets had risen from Galilee—Elijah (1 Kings 17:1), Elisha (1 Kings 19:16), Jonah (2 Kings 14:25), Nahum (Nahum 1:1), and Hosea (Hosea 7:1; 8:5,6). Isaiah predicted that from Galilee a great light would shine to bring deliverance (Isaiah 9:1,2). The verses that follow the prediction of the great light from Galilee certainly are messianic (Isaiah 9:3-7).

52. They answered and said unto him, Art thou also of Galilee?: They retorted, *Fenton* . . . You are not from Galilee, too, are you, *Williams.*

Search, and look: Search the record, *Williams* . . . Investigate and see, *Berkeley* . . . Search the Scriptures and see for yourself, *Norlie.*

for out of Galilee ariseth no prophet: . . . out of Galilee a prophet is not to arise, *Rotherham* . . . the Prophet doesn't come from Galilee, *Beck* . . . the Prophet doesn't come, *Beck* . . . is to arise in Galilee, *TCNT* . . . has ever sprung from, *Fenton* . . . no prophet emerges from Galilee, *Barclay.*

7:53. The Sanhedrin members could not arrive at a unanimous conclusion. They adjourned, not knowing what to do. The coals of hatred and frustration were left to smolder until the following Feast of Passover 6 months later.

53. And every man went unto his own house: Then everyone went home, *Norlie* . . . So they broke up their meeting, *Phillips* . . . They all went home, *Barclay.*

8:1. The passage 7:53 to 8:11 is not found in some early Greek texts. However, the incident could well have occurred and illustrates the antipathy of the Jewish leaders toward Jesus, His wisdom in dealing with His adversaries, and His compassion for the sinner.

Compare what Jesus did with what the council members did in the last verse of chapter 7. The Mount of Olives is located east of Jerusalem. Jesus often went there (see Mark 11:1,11; Luke 21:37; 22:39).

1. Jesus went unto the mount of Olives:

8:2. As soon as the people began coming to the temple, Jesus returned to resume His teaching ministry. The people of the East are accustomed to rising early and especially at the time of the annual feast. They needed to take advantage of every part of the temple worship since they had traveled far in order to be there.

The Law did not require the people to attend during the entire feast. Jesus was at this feast for half its time. The people who

John 8:3

3716.3 verb 3sing indic aor mid	1519.1 prep	3450.16 art sing neu	2387.3 adj acc sing neu	2504.1 conj	3820.6 adj sing masc
παρεγένετο	εἰς	τὸ	ἱερόν,	καὶ	πᾶς
paregeneto	*eis*	*to*	*hieron*	*kai*	*pas*
he came	into	the	temple,	and	all

3450.5 art sing masc	2967.1 noun sing masc	2048.59 verb 3sing indic imperf	4242.1 prep	840.6 prs-pron acc sing masc	2504.1 conj
ὁ	λαὸς	ἤρχετο	πρὸς	αὐτόν·	καὶ
ho	*laos*	*ērcheto*	*pros*	*auton*	*kai*
the	people	came	to	him;	and

2495.9 verb nom sing masc part aor act	1315.20 verb 3sing indic imperf act	840.8 prs-pron acc pl masc	70.3 verb 3pl indic pres act	1156.2 conj
καθίσας	ἐδίδασκεν	αὐτούς.	3. ἄγουσιν	δὲ
kathisas	*edidasken*	*autous*	*agousin*	*de*
having sat down	he was teaching	them.	Bring	and

3450.7 art pl masc	1116.2 noun pl masc	2504.1 conj	3450.7 art pl masc	5168.4 name pl masc	4242.1 prep
οἱ	γραμματεῖς	καὶ	οἱ	Φαρισαῖοι	πρὸς
hoi	*grammateis*	*kai*	*hoi*	*Pharisaioi*	*pros*
the	scribes	and	the	Pharisees	to

840.6 prs-pron acc sing masc	1129.4 noun acc sing fem	1706.1 prep	3293.2 noun dat sing fem	2608.12 verb acc sing fem part perf pass	2504.1 conj
αὐτὸν	γυναῖκα	ἐν	μοιχείᾳ	κατειλημμένην,	καὶ
auton	*gunaika*	*en*	*moicheia*	*kateilēmmenēn*	*kai*
him	a woman	in	adultery	having been taken,	and

2449.12 verb nom pl masc part aor act	840.12 prs-pron acc sing fem	1706.1 prep	3189.1 adj dat sing	2978.3 verb 3pl pres act	840.4 prs-pron dat sing
στήσαντες	αὐτὴν	ἐν	μέσῳ	4. λέγουσιν	αὐτῷ,
stēsantes	*autēn*	*en*	*mesō*	*legousin*	*autō*
having set	her	in	midst,	they say	to him,

1314.3 noun voc sing masc	3642.9 dem-pron nom sing fem	3450.9 art nom sing fem	1129.1 noun nom sing fem	2608.8 verb 3sing indic aor pass
Διδάσκαλε,	αὕτη	ἡ	γυνὴ	κατειλήφθη
Didaskale	*hautē*	*hē*	*gunē*	*kateilēphthē*
Teacher,	this	the	woman	was taken

1873.1 adv	1894.2 prep	841.1 adj dat sing masc	3294.8 verb nom sing fem part pres pass
ʻ ἐπαυτοφώρῳ	[ἐπ’	αὐτοφώρῳ]	μοιχευομένη.
epautophōrō	*ep’*	*autophōrō*	*moicheuomenē*
in the very act	[in	very act]	committing adultery.

1706.1 prep	1156.2 conj	3450.3 art dat sing	3414.3 noun dat sing masc	3337.1 name nom masc	3338.1 name nom masc
5. ἐν	δὲ	τῷ	νόμῳ	ʻ Μωσῆς	[Μωϋσῆς]
en	*de*	*tō*	*nomō*	*Mōsēs*	*Mōusēs*
In	now	the	law	Moses	[idem]

2231.3 prs-pron dat 1pl	1765.3 verb 3sing indic aor mid	3450.15 art acc pl fem	4955.13 dem-pron acc pl fem	3010.6 verb inf pres pass
ἡμῖν	ἐνετείλατο	τὰς	τοιαύτας	ʻ λιθοβολεῖσθαι·
hēmin	*eneteilato*	*tas*	*toiautas*	*lithoboleisthai*
us	commanded	the	such	to be stoned:

5.a.**Txt:** 07E,017K,byz.
Var: 05D,021M,030U,1,
13,Word

3008.9 verb inf pres act	4622.1 prs-pron nom 2sing	3631.1 conj	4949.9 intr-pron sing neu	2978.4 verb 2sing indic pres act
[a λιθάζειν·]	σὺ	οὖν	τί	λέγεις;
lithazein	*su*	*oun*	*ti*	*legeis*
[to stone:]	you	therefore	what	say you?

traveled 50 or 60 miles to attend underwent many traveling hardships and hazards. The poor of the land had financial burdens connected with attending the temple festivals. Doubtless the worshipers came to Jerusalem as vacationers. Happily the three feasts occurred at times of less demands on crop laborers. But for many, going to the temple meant no income for 2 weeks. The people walked in caravans from their homes to Jerusalem. This was a long and tedious trek for many. Those who attended the Feast this year were bountifully repaid by seeing their Lord and Saviour.

2. And early in the morning he came again into the temple, and all the people came unto him: But at daybreak, *Norlie* . . . the people flocked to him, *ALBA* . . . in a steady stream, *Wuest.*

and he sat down, and taught them: He seated Himself, and was teaching them, *Weymouth.*

8:3. While Jesus was engaged in His teaching ministry, "the scribes and Pharisees brought unto him a woman taken in adultery." It would seem that the action of the scribes and Pharisees was unwarranted since the Jews had courts to try such cases. Jesus was not a judge in such matters from the legal aspect. Why did the Jews not bring the man with the woman? The Law stipulated that both were to be tried in the court (Leviticus 20:10; Deuteronomy 22:22-24).

3. And the scribes and Pharisees brought unto him a woman taken in adultery: . . . when the doctors of the law, *ALBA* . . . a woman who had been caught in adultery, *TCNT*. . . the act of sinning against the married relation, *BB.*

and when they had set her in the midst: They made her stand in front, *Phillips* . . . led her out in front of everybody, *ALBA* . . . and, placing her in the center, *Berkeley* . . . in the centre of the court, *Weymouth* . . . in full view of everybody, *JB.*

8:4. The scribes and Pharisees called Jesus "teacher" (*didaskale*; "Master," KJV). A certain hypocrisy was involved, for they did not honestly attribute that high function to Him. The woman they brought was discovered in the very act of adultery. There was no doubt as to her guilt. Some have suggested that the reason they did not bring the man was that he was one of their number who contrived the plot to expose Jesus as a teacher who taught others to break the law of Moses.

4. They say unto him, Master, this woman was taken in adultery, in the very act: They said ...so they might trump up a charge, *Berkeley* . . . Teacher, this woman hath been caught in the very act of committing adultery, *Rotherham, ALBA* . . . has just now been caught, *Confraternity* . . . was surprised, *Campbell* . . . was caught openly, *Murdock.*

8:5. They were not zealous for the Law, but eager to find some way to trap Jesus so that they might condemn Him as a lawbreaker. Stoning was the legal means of execution among the Jews. If one was proven guilty by two or three witnesses, the witnesses and the people threw stones upon the person until he died. Several sins were punishable by this mode of justice; blasphemy, adultery, kidnapping, witchcraft, etc. (see Leviticus 20:10; Deuteronomy 22:22-24).

"What sayest thou?" "Thou" is the stressed word. They were putting Him on the spot. Either way He answered, they would have reason to accuse Him. If He said, "Stone her," they would accuse Him before the Romans, because they alone had authority to execute anyone in Palestine. If Jesus said, "Let her go free," He would be teaching against the law of Moses.

5. Now Moses in the law commanded us, that such should be stoned: . . . to stone such women to death, *TCNT* . . . In the Law, Moses ordered us, *Beck* . . . laid it down in the law, *ALBA* . . . to stone such like women, *Wilson.*

but what sayest thou?: But you, what do you say, *Montgomery.*

John 8:6

5.b.**Var:** 021M,030U,13, Word

3875.1 prep	**840.10** prs-pron gen sing fem	**3642.17** dem-pron sing neu	**1156.2** conj	**2978.25** verb indic imperf act
[b+ περὶ	αὐτῆς;]	**6.** Τοῦτο	δὲ	ἔλεγον
peri	*autēs*	*Touto*	*de*	*elegon*
[concerning	her?]	This	but	they said

3847.5 verb nom pl masc part pres act	**840.6** prs-pron acc sing masc	**2419.1** conj	**2174.10** verb 3pl subj pres act	**2693.8** verb inf pres act
πειράζοντες	αὐτόν	ἵνα	ἔχωσιν	κατηγορεῖν
peirazontes	*auton*	*hina*	*echōsin*	*katēgorein*
tempting	him	that	they might have	to accuse

840.3 prs-pron gen sing	**3450.5** art sing masc	**1156.2** conj	**2400.1** name nom masc	**2706.1** adv	**2928.1** verb nom sing masc part aor act
αὐτοῦ.	ὁ	δὲ	Ἰησοῦς	κάτω	κύψας,
autou	*ho*	*de*	*Iēsous*	*katō*	*kupsas*
him.		But	Jesus	after	having stooped down,

3450.3 art dat sing	**1142.2** noun dat sing masc	**1119.17** verb 3sing indic imperf act	**1519.1** prep	**3450.12** art acc sing fem	**1087.4** noun acc sing fem
τῷ	δακτύλῳ	ἔγραφεν	εἰς	τὴν	γῆν.
tō	*daktulō*	*egraphen*	*eis*	*tēn*	*gēn*
with	finger	wrote	on	the	ground.

5453.1 conj	**1156.2** conj	**1946.13** verb 3pl indic imperf act	**2049.5** verb nom pl masc part pres act	**840.6** prs-pron acc sing masc
7. ὡς	δὲ	ἐπέμενον	ἐρωτῶντες	αὐτόν,
hōs	*de*	*epemenon*	*erōtōntes*	*auton*
As	but	they continued	asking	him,

350.2 verb nom sing masc part aor act	**1500.5** verb 3sing indic aor act	**4242.1** prep	**840.8** prs-pron acc pl masc	**3450.5** art sing masc
ἀνακύψας	εἶπεν	πρὸς	αὐτούς,	Ὁ
anakupsas	*eipen*	*pros*	*autous*	*Ho*
having lifted up himself	he said	to	them,	The

359.1 adj nom sing masc	**5050.2** prs-pron gen 2pl	**4272.5** num ord nom sing masc	**3450.6** art acc sing masc	**3012.4** noun acc sing masc
ἀναμάρτητος	ὑμῶν	πρῶτος	τὸν	λίθον
anamartētos	*humōn*	*prōtos*	*ton*	*lithon*
sinless one	among you	first	the	stone

1894.2 prep	**840.11** prs-pron dat sing fem	**900.17** verb 3sing impr aor act	**2504.1** conj	**3687.1** adv	**2706.1** adv
ἐπ’	αὐτῇ	βαλέτω.	**8.** καὶ	πάλιν	κατω
ep'	*autē*	*baletō*	*kai*	*palin*	*katō*
at	her	let him cast.	And	again	after

2928.1 verb nom sing masc part aor act	**1119.17** verb 3sing indic imperf act	**1519.1** prep	**3450.12** art acc sing fem	**1087.4** noun acc sing fem	**3450.7** art pl masc
κύψας	ἔγραφεν	εἰς	τὴν	γῆν.	**9.** οἱ
kupsas	*egraphen*	*eis*	*tēn*	*gēn*	*hoi*
having stooped down	he wrote	on	the	ground.	The

1156.2 conj	**189.32** verb nom pl masc part aor act	**2504.1** conj	**5097.3** prep	**3450.10** art gen sing fem	**4743.2** noun gen sing fem
δὲ	ἀκούσαντες,	καὶ	ὑπὸ	τῆς	συνειδήσεως
de	*akousantes*	*kai*	*hupo*	*tēs*	*suneidēseōs*
but	having heard,	and	by	the	conscience

1638.10 verb nom pl masc part pres pass	**1814.39** verb 3pl indic imperf	**1518.3** num card nom masc	**2567.2** prep	**1518.3** num card nom masc
ἐλεγχόμενοι,	ἐξήρχοντο	εἷς	καθ’	εἷς,
elenchomenoi	*exērchonto*	*heis*	*kath'*	*heis*
being convicted,	went out	one	by	one,

8:6. "Tempting" (*peirazontes*) occurs twice in John and 39 times in the New Testament. The word is used in both the positive and negative sense. It often means "test," "prove," "tempt," "try," and "challenge."

People have used many mediums on which to write. This time it was His finger in the dust of the earth. Jesus seemed to ignore their harassment. He drew the attention of the people from the woman to focus on himself and prepared them for an important direction He was about to give. What He wrote (*egraphen*) in the dust is not stated, and it is futile to guess. It is better to concentrate one's study on what the Word of God reveals than to guess and speculate about areas the Lord has not made plain.

Three reasons may be offered as to why we should not conjecture. First, God's Word states that the secret things belong to the Lord. But these things which are revealed belong to us (Deuteronomy 29:29). Second, conclusions are often not rooted in fact and thus lead into error. Third, fruitless suppositions waste valuable time.

6. This they said, tempting him, that they might have to accuse him: They said this to test him, *Moffatt* . . . so they might trump up a charge against Him, *Berkeley* . . . They were trying to trap Him, so that they might find something against Him, *Norlie* . . . some good grounds for an accusation, *Phillips.*

But Jesus stooped down, and with his finger wrote on the ground, as though he heard them not: . . . and began to write on the ground with His finger, *Norlie* . . . on the floor, *BB* . . . with the fyngir in the erthe, *Wycliffe.*

8:7. "They continued asking him," thinking that they had Him at a disadvantage. But Jesus was thus drawing attention to the real issue. They thought they were the only righteous ones in the gathering, but with one short sentence Jesus silenced them.

Thus they ceased to be His judge or the woman's. They were told to examine themselves. It was an understood truth that there is no man who does not nor has not sinned (1 Kings 8:46). Besides, these men may have conspired together to trap the woman. Their real objective, however, was to ensnare Jesus.

7. So when they continued asking him: But as they persisted in their questioning, *Phillips* . . . as they kept pressing with their question, *ALBA.*

he lifted up himself, and said unto them: He got up and said, *Norlie.*

He that is without sin among you: Let the sinless man among you, *Weymouth* . . . him who is sinless, *Campbell* . . . is guiltless, *Scarlett* . . . the innocent among you, *Moffatt.*

let him first cast a stone at her: . . . be the first to throw a stone at her, *Weymouth.*

8:8. The reason He stooped down the second time was to give the Pharisees and scribes time to search their own hearts. Note that He made no decision, but asked them to judge themselves. He had not denied the law of Moses or acquitted the woman.

8. And again he stooped down, and wrote on the ground:

9. And they which heard it, being convicted by their own conscience, went out one by one: . . . his audience, *ALBA* . . . went away conscience-stricken one after the other, *Berkeley* . . . accused by their own conscience, *Norlie.*

8:9. The older ones were usually the ones to make judgments for the younger, since the experience of the older makes them wiser. (This concept was in the fabric of their culture.) Observe relevant passages on the wisdom associated with the elders (Matthew 15:2; 27:1,3,12,20).

Who was on trial that day? Was Jesus? Or the woman? No, certainly the Pharisees and scribes had their day in court as the accused. The disciples and the people were the observers, but the Pharisees

751.12 verb nom pl masc part aor mid	**570.3** prep gen	**3450.1** art gen pl	**4104.6** adj comp gen pl masc	**2175.1** conj	**3450.1** art gen pl
ἀρξάμενοι	ἀπὸ	τῶν	πρεσβυτέρων	ἕως	τῶν
arxamenoi	*apo*	*tōn*	*presbuterōn*	*heōs*	*tōn*
beginning	from	the	elder ones	until	the

2057.1 adj gen pl	**2504.1** conj	**2611.10** verb 3sing indic aor pass	**3304.2** adj nom sing masc	**3450.5** art sing masc	**2400.1** name nom masc
ἐσχάτων·	καὶ	κατελείφθη	μόνος	ὁ	Ἰησοῦς,
eschatōn	*kai*	*kateleiphthē*	*monos*	*ho*	*Iēsous*
last;	and	was left	alone		Jesus,

2504.1 conj	**3450.9** art nom sing fem	**1129.1** noun nom sing fem	**1706.1** prep	**3189.1** adj dat sing	**2449.34** verb nom sing fem part perf act
καὶ	ἡ	γυνὴ	ἐν	μέσῳ	⸂ ἑστῶσα.
kai	*hē*	*gunē*	*en*	*mesō*	*hestōsa*
and	the	woman	in	midst	standing.

9.a.**Var:** 05D,07E,021M, 030U,036,Word

1498.26 verb nom sing fem part pres act	**350.2** verb nom sing masc part aor act	**1156.2** conj	**3450.5** art sing masc	**2400.1** name nom masc
[a οὖσα.]	**10.** ἀνακύψας	δὲ	ὁ	Ἰησοῦς,
ousa	*anakupsas*	*de*	*ho*	*Iēsous*
[being.]	Having lifted up himself	and		Jesus,

2504.1 conj	**3235.4** num card acc masc	**2277.7** verb nom sing masc part aor mid	**3993.1** prep gen	**3450.10** art gen sing fem	**1129.2** noun gen sing fem
καὶ	μηδένα	θεασάμενος	πλὴν	τῆς	γυναικός,
kai	*mēdena*	*theasamenos*	*plēn*	*tēs*	*gunaikos*
and	no one	having seen	but	the	woman,

10.a.**Txt:** Steph **Var:** 05D,07E,017K, Word

1500.5 verb 3sing indic aor act	**840.11** prs-pron dat sing fem	**3450.9** art nom sing fem	**1129.1** noun nom sing fem	**4085.1** adv	**1498.7** verb 3pl indic pres act
εἶπεν	αὐτῇ,	⸂a Ἡ	γυνή, ⸃	ποῦ	εἰσιν
eipen	*autē*	*Hē*	*gunē*	*pou*	*eisin*
said	to her,	The	woman,	where	are

1552.6 dem-pron nom pl masc	**3450.7** art pl masc	**2695.2** noun nom pl masc	**4622.2** prs-pron gen 2sing	**3625.2** num card nom masc
ἐκεῖνοι	οἱ	κατήγοροί	σου,	οὐδείς
ekeinoi	*hoi*	*katēgoroi*	*sou*	*oudeis*
those	the	accusers	your,	no one

4622.4 prs-pron acc 2sing	**2602.4** verb 3sing indic aor act	**3450.9** art nom sing fem	**1156.2** conj	**1500.5** verb 3sing indic aor act	**3625.2** num card nom masc
σε	κατέκρινεν;	**11.** Ἡ	δὲ	εἶπεν,	Οὐδείς,
se	*katekrinen*	*Hē*	*de*	*eipen*	*Oudeis*
you	did condemn?	The	and	said,	No one,

2935.5 noun voc sing masc	**1500.5** verb 3sing indic aor act	**1156.2** conj	**840.11** prs-pron dat sing fem	**3450.5** art sing masc	**2400.1** name nom masc
κύριε.	Εἶπεν	δὲ	αὐτῇ	ὁ	Ἰησοῦς,
kurie	*Eipen*	*de*	*autē*	*ho*	*Iēsous*
Sir.	Said	and	to her		Jesus,

3624.1 adv	**1466.1** prs-pron nom 1sing	**4622.4** prs-pron acc 2sing	**2602.1** verb 1sing indic pres act	**4057.4** verb 2sing impr pres	**2504.1** conj
Οὐδὲ	ἐγώ	σε	κατακρίνω·	πορεύου	καὶ
Oude	*egō*	*se*	*katakrinō*	*poreuou*	*kai*
Neither	I	you	do condemn:	go,	and

3239.1 adv	**262.3** verb 2sing impr pres act	**3687.1** adv	**3631.1** conj	**3450.5** art sing masc	**2400.1** name nom masc
μηκέτι	ἁμάρτανε.	**12.** Πάλιν	οὖν	⸂ ὁ	Ἰησοῦς
mēketi	*hamartane*	*Palin*	*oun*	*ho*	*Iēsous*
no more	sin.	Again	therefore		Jesus

and scribes fled, weighted with guilty consciences. Alas, why did not their self-sentenced verdict produce in them godly sorrow and repentance?

beginning at the eldest, even unto the last: . . . beginning with the older men, *Moffatt* . . . with the older ones first, *TEV* . . . starting from the eldest, *ALBA* . . . from the oldest on down, *SEB* . . . till they all were gone, *Norlie* . . . till all were gone, *Weymouth* . . . until they had all gone, *Phillips.*

and Jesus was left alone, and the woman standing in the midst: . . . with the woman standing before him, *RSV* . . . who remained standing there, *JB* . . . until only Jesus was left, *NIV* . . . in the middle of the court, *Montgomery.*

8:10. The crafty schemers had disappeared by the time Jesus arose. They were willing for Jesus to deal with the woman they had accused.

If He had condemned her, the ones who caught her in adultery would have cast the first stones. But Jesus said the one without sin should cast the first stone.

10. When Jesus had lifted himself: Then, raising His head, *Weymouth* . . . So he straightened up once more, *ALBA.*

and saw none but the woman, he said unto her: . . . and, seeing no one there except the woman, *Norlie.*

Woman, where are those thine accusers? hath no man condemned thee?: Woman, where are your accusers? *Berkeley* . . . Woman, where are they? *Moffatt* . . . is there no one left to condemn you, *TEV* . . . passed sentence on you? *Campbell* . . . sentenced thee to death? *Scarlett.*

8:11. "No man, Lord" must have been expressed in humility and relief. "Neither do I condemn thee" means that Jesus did not act as a judge (Luke 12:13,14). "Go, and sin no more." This is the very command Jesus made to the infirm man in 5:14 (*mēketi hamartane*). These Greek words literally mean, "You are sinning; stop your practice of sin."

We hear no confession from her lips as we do from the Samaritan woman who was guilty of the identical sin. We can assume from her few words that she was humbled, submissive and perhaps repentant.

From this passage and the narrative of the Samaritan woman, we gather that God looks upon adultery as a terrible sin, but He is gentle in dealing with the sinner. All that Jesus said and did in these two accounts reflects God's forgiveness. "Sin no more" was not expressed in the Samaritan woman narrative, yet it was implied by the tenor of the conversation. Jesus does not look upon sin lightly, yet He who bore the sin of the world by His suffering forgives most graciously.

Jesus did not excuse the woman for her sin. He emphasized that the woman's life should give evidence of her repentance.

11. She said, No man, Lord. And Jesus said unto her, Neither do I condemn thee: go, and sin no more: . . . do I pass sentence on thee, *Scarlett* . . . go thy way, *ASV* . . . Go, and never sin again, *Montgomery* . . . and leave your life of sin, *NIV* . . . and from this time do not sin any more, *Weymouth* . . . Go and from now on stop sinning, *Barclay.*

8:12. As the *Logos* (the Word), Jesus was called "the true light" (1:9) and "the light" which is come into the world (3:19). In this verse Jesus claimed the distinction. Previously Jesus had said His disciples were "the light of the world" (Matthew 5:14). But the disciples were His reflected lights. "Light" (*phōs*) is the natural symbol for truth and the revelation of God. In his epistles John says that God is light (1 John 1:5). In the Old Testament, God was represented by the pillar of fire by night and the cloud by day. The light from the lampstand in the Holy Place also symbolized God to His people. Jesus is not a symbol of reality. He proclaimed,

John 8:13

840.2 prs-pron dat pl	2953.27 verb 3sing indic aor act		840.2 prs-pron dat pl	2953.27 verb 3sing indic aor act	3450.5 art sing masc
αὐτοῖς	ἐλάλησεν,	[☆	αὐτοῖς	ἐλάλησεν	ὁ
autois	elalēsen		autois	elalēsen	ho
to them	spoke,		[to them	spoke	

2400.1 name nom masc	2978.15 verb sing masc part pres act	1466.1 prs-pron nom 1sing	1498.2 verb 1sing indic pres act	3450.16 art sing neu
Ἰησοῦς]	λέγων,	Ἐγώ	εἰμι	τὸ
Iēsous	legōn	Egō	eimi	to
Jesus]	saying,	I	am	the

12.a.**Txt:** p66,01ℵ,05D,017K,019L,032W,036,037,038,etc.byz.Gries,Word,Tisc,Sod
Var: 03B,029T,Lach,Treg,We/HoWeis,UBS/☆

12.b.**Txt:** 05D,07E,021M,036,037,038,byz.
Var: 01ℵ,03B,017K,019L,029T,033X,Lach,TregAlf,Word,Tisc,We/Ho,Weis,Sod,UBS/☆

5295.1 noun sing neu	3450.2 art gen sing	2862.2 noun gen sing masc	3450.5 art sing masc	188.5 verb nom sing masc part pres act	1466.5 prs-pron dat 1sing
φῶς	τοῦ	κόσμου·	ὁ	ἀκολουθῶν	ʻ ἐμοὶ
phōs	tou	kosmou	ho	akolouthōn	emoi
light	of the	world;	the	following	me

1466.4 prs-pron dat 1sing	3620.3 partic	3231.1 partic	3906.25 verb 3sing indic fut act	3906.30 verb 3sing subj aor act
[a μοι]	οὐ	μὴ	ʻ περιπατήσει	[b☆ περιπατήσῃ]
moi	ou	mē	peripatēsei	peripatēsē
[idem]	not	not	shall walk	[idem]

1706.1 prep	3450.11 art dat sing fem	4508.3 noun dat sing fem	233.1 conj	2174.39 verb 3sing indic fut act	3450.16 art sing neu	5295.1 noun sing neu
ἐν	τῇ	σκοτίᾳ,	ἀλλ'	ἕξει	τὸ	φῶς
en	tē	skotia	all'	hexei	to	phōs
in	the	darkness,	but	shall have	the	light

3450.10 art gen sing fem	2205.2 noun gen sing fem	1500.3 verb indic aor act	3631.1 conj	840.4 prs-pron dat sing	3450.7 art pl masc
τῆς	ζωῆς.	13. Εἶπον	οὖν	αὐτῷ	οἱ
tēs	zōēs	Eipon	oun	autō	hoi
of the	life.	Said	therefore	to him	the

5168.4 name pl masc	4622.1 prs-pron nom 2sing	3875.1 prep	4427.1 prs-pron gen 2sing masc	3113.2 verb 2sing indic pres act
Φαρισαῖοι,	Σὺ	περὶ	σεαυτοῦ	μαρτυρεῖς·
Pharisaioi	Su	peri	seautou	martureis
Pharisees,	You	concerning	yourself	bear witness;

3450.9 art nom sing fem	3114.1 noun nom sing fem	4622.2 prs-pron gen 2sing	3620.2 partic	1498.4 verb 3sing indic pres act	225.2 adj nom sing
ἡ	μαρτυρία	σου	οὐκ	ἔστιν	ἀληθής.
hē	marturia	sou	ouk	estin	alēthēs
the	witness	your	not	is	true.

552.6 verb 3sing indic aor pass	2400.1 name nom masc	2504.1 conj	1500.5 verb 3sing indic aor act	840.2 prs-pron dat pl
14. Ἀπεκρίθη	Ἰησοῦς	καὶ	εἶπεν	αὐτοῖς,
Apekrithē	Iēsous	kai	eipen	autois
Answered	Jesus	and	said	to them,

2550.1 conj	1466.1 prs-pron nom 1sing	3113.1 verb 1sing pres act	3875.1 prep	1670.1 prs-pron gen 1sing masc
Κἂν	ἐγὼ	μαρτυρῶ	περὶ	ἐμαυτοῦ,
Kan	egō	marturō	peri	emautou
Even if	I	bear witness	concerning	myself,

225.2 adj nom sing	1498.4 verb 3sing indic pres act	3450.9 art nom sing fem	3114.1 noun nom sing fem	1466.2 prs-pron gen 1sing	3617.1 conj
ἀληθής	ἐστιν	ἡ	μαρτυρία	μου,	ὅτι
alēthēs	estin	hē	marturia	mou	hoti
true	is	the	witness	my,	because

"I am the light of the world." What God is, Jesus is. Notice the universal aspect of Jesus as "the light." He is for "the world," not merely Israel. Observe some Old Testament references which suggested that the Messiah was to be the people's light (Isaiah 42:6; 49:6; 60:1).

The only way to receive the benefits from His light is to follow Him (see 1 John 1:7, "if we walk in the light"). While one is close to the light, he is able to see. As one strays from the light, he is unable to see because of the darkness. Thus he falls, with injury or death as a result. The very nature of the world is darkness. Darkness is the absence of light. Those who sit in darkness are able by the aid of light to move about, manifesting signs of life (Isaiah 9:2; Matthew 4:16).

"But shall have the light of life." These words would be sheer blasphemy from the lips of any other being. The light of Jesus is the revelation of God himself. Only the knowledge of God can bring one to life. By following the light which He gives in His person, sayings, and ministry, one is brought to life. To believe on Him as the revelation of God is to have eternal life (1:4; 3:19; 5:24). John 8:12 is the only reference to "the light of life" in the New Testament.

12. Then spake Jesus again unto them, saying, I am the light of the world: Once more Jesus addressed them, *Montgomery* . . . again addressed them, *Williams, Fenton* . . . for the people of the world, *SEB.*

he that followeth me shall not walk in darkness: Whoever continues to follow me need never walk in darkness, *Williams* . . . He who habitually follows with me shall positively not order his behavior in the sphere of the darkness, *Wuest* . . . will in no wise walk, *Norlie* . . . will not be walking in the dark, *JB* . . . will never wander in the dark, *Beck.*

but shall have the light of life: . . . but to be in possession of the, *Barclay* . . . but will live his life in the light, *Phillips* . . . the light that means life, *Williams.*

8:13. The Pharisees challenged His statement, "I am the light of the world." They accused Him of being a self-witness, which, if unsupported, could not be admitted as evidence. The Law required two or three witnesses to validate the truth (Deuteronomy 17:6). Jesus had already given the Jews numerous witnesses to confirm His claim. See the seven witnesses to Jesus given in the commentary dealing with 5:32.

13. The Pharisees therefore said unto him, Thou bearest record of thyself; thy record is not true: You are testifying about yourself...Your testimony is therefore not sound, *Norlie* . . . the witness you give is about yourself, *BB* . . . You are giving evidence about Yourself; Your evidence is not reliable, *Fenton* . . . your testimony is not valid, *Berkeley* . . . is not trustworthy, *TCNT* . . . We can't depend on Your testimony, *Beck.*

8:14. In this verse and the next four verses Jesus revealed that His testimony was credible. He had an accurate knowledge of himself, His origin, and His destination. As opposed to His understanding, the Pharisees were ignorant of all three. Because they did not know, they were not qualified to be His judge. A court case is ideally settled according to the facts. The Pharisees were unaware of the facts; therefore their conclusion was false. Jesus had presented His messianic credentials, yet they refused to believe His mission (5:36; 3:2).

"While a person's testimony about himself may be biased by self-interest, it is equally true that no one knows more about his own nature and experience than the person himself. No individual can be sure of his own origin apart from external testimony, nor can he be sure of his future circumstances. Jesus, however, . . . knew 'that he had come from God and was returning to God' (13:3)"

14. Jesus answered and said unto them, Though I bear record of myself, yet my record is true: for I know whence I came, and whither I go: Granted that I am a witness in my own cause, *ALBA* . . . I am aware, *Concordant* . . . even if I am witnessing, *Panin* . . . nevertheless reliable, *Fenton* . . . "Even if I do so," *TCNT*

3471.2 verb 1sing indic perf act	4019.1 adv	2048.1 verb indic aor act	2504.1 conj	4085.1 adv	5055.1 verb 1sing indic pres act
οἶδα	πόθεν	ἦλθον	καὶ	ποῦ	ὑπάγω·
oida	*pothen*	*ēlthon*	*kai*	*pou*	*hupagō*
I know	from where	I came	and	where	I go:

5050.1 prs-pron nom 2pl	1156.2 conj	3620.2 partic	3471.6 verb 2pl indic perf act	4019.1 adv	2048.32 verb 1sing indic pres	2504.1 conj
ὑμεῖς	δὲ	οὐκ	οἴδατε	πόθεν	ἔρχομαι	ʻ καὶ
humeis	*de*	*ouk*	*oidate*	*pothen*	*erchomai*	*kai*
you	but	not	know	from where	I come	and

14.a.**Txt:** p75-org,01ℵ, 019L,032W,038,13,byz. it.Lach
Var: p39,p66,p75-corr, 03B,05D,017K,030U,1, sa.bo.Gries,Treg,Alf, Tisc,We/HoWeis,Sod, UBS/☆

2211.1 conj	4085.1 adv	5055.1 verb 1sing indic pres act	5050.1 prs-pron nom 2pl	2567.3 prep	3450.12 art acc sing fem
[a☆ ἢ]	ποῦ	ὑπάγω.	**15.** ὑμεῖς	κατὰ	τὴν
ē	*pou*	*hupagō*	*humeis*	*kata*	*tēn*
[or]	where	I go.	You	according to	the

4418.4 noun acc sing fem	2892.3 verb 2pl pres act	1466.1 prs-pron nom 1sing	3620.3 partic	2892.1 verb 1sing act	3625.3 num card acc masc
σάρκα	κρίνετε·	ἐγὼ	οὐ	κρίνω	οὐδένα.
sarka	*krinete*	*egō*	*ou*	*krinō*	*oudena*
flesh	judge,	I	not	judge	no one.

2504.1 conj	1430.1 partic	2892.1 verb 1sing act	1156.2 conj	1466.1 prs-pron nom 1sing	3450.9 art nom sing fem	2893.1 noun nom sing fem
16. καὶ	ἐὰν	κρίνω	δὲ	ἐγώ,	ἡ	κρίσις
kai	*ean*	*krinō*	*de*	*egō*	*hē*	*krisis*
And	if	judge	also	I,	the	judgment

16.a.**Txt:** p66,01ℵ,017K, 036,037,038,1,13,565, byz.Gries,Word
Var: p75,03B,05D,019L, 029T,032W,033X,33, Lach,Treg,Alf,Tisc, We/HoWeis,Sod,UBS/☆

3450.9 art nom sing fem	1684.6 adj nom 1sing fem	225.2 adj nom sing	226.5 adj nom sing fem	1498.4 verb 3sing indic pres act
ἡ	ἐμὴ	ʻ ἀληθής	[a☆ ἀληθινή]	ἐστιν·
hē	*emē*	*alēthēs*	*alēthinē*	*estin*
the	my	true	[idem]	is,

3617.1 conj	3304.2 adj nom sing masc	3620.2 partic	1498.2 verb 1sing indic pres act	233.1 conj	1466.1 prs-pron nom 1sing
ὅτι	μόνος	οὐκ	εἰμί,	ἀλλ'	ἐγὼ
hoti	*monos*	*ouk*	*eimi*	*all'*	*egō*
because	alone	not	I am,	but	I

16.b.**Txt:** p39,p66,p75, 01ℵ-corr,03B,017K, 019L,029T,032W,038,1, 13,565,700,etc.byz. Gries,Lach,Treg,Alf, We/Ho,Sod
Var: 01ℵ-org,05D,Tisc Weis,UBS/☆

2504.1 conj	3450.5 art sing masc	3854.11 verb nom sing masc part aor act	1466.6 prs-pron acc 1sing	3824.1 noun nom sing masc
καὶ	ὁ	πέμψας	με	ʻb πατήρ. ʼ
kai	*ho*	*pempsas*	*me*	*patēr*
and	the	having sent	me	Father.

2504.1 conj	1706.1 prep	3450.3 art dat sing	3414.3 noun dat sing masc	1156.2 conj	3450.3 art dat sing	5052.1 adj dat 2sing
17. καὶ	ἐν	τῷ	νόμῳ	δὲ	τῷ	ὑμετέρῳ
kai	*en*	*tō*	*nomō*	*de*	*tō*	*humeterō*
And	in	the	law	also	the	your

17.a.**Var:** 01ℵ,Tisc

1119.22 verb 3sing indic perf pass	1119.29 verb sing neu part perf pass	1498.4 verb 3sing indic pres act	3617.1 conj	1411.3 num card
ʻ γέγραπται,	[a γεγραμμένον	ἐστὶν]	ὅτι	δύο
gegraptai	*gegrammenon*	*estin*	*hoti*	*duo*
it has been written,	[having been written	is]	that	of two

442.7 noun gen pl masc	3450.9 art nom sing fem	3114.1 noun nom sing fem	225.2 adj nom sing	1498.4 verb 3sing indic pres act
ἀνθρώπων	ἡ	μαρτυρία	ἀληθής	ἐστιν.
anthrōpōn	*hē*	*marturia*	*alēthēs*	*estin*
men	the	witness	true	is.

(Tenney, *Expositor's Bible Commentary*, 9:92).

For a witness to be credible he must possess and render facts concerning that which he testifies. Jesus was a credible witness, for He possessed the facts and testified to the reality.

. . . my testimony is nonetheless valid, *ALBA* . . . because I know with an absolute knowledge, *Wuest.*

but ye cannot tell whence I come, and whither I go: But as for you, you have no idea where I come from or where I am going, *Phillips.*

8:15. Outward appearances are not valid as a standard from which to judge divine things. Judgments based on selfish motives and prejudiced viewpoints are fleshly and earthly standards. It is inevitable that they end in error. By using the term "flesh" (*sarx*), Jesus emphasized the weakness and wickedness of the Pharisees' judgment. It was superficial and based on externals only—what they could see and conclude in their myopic minds. The Jerusalem Bible translates this phrase, "by human standards" (see other translations in *Various Versions*).

"I judge no man" reminds us of the narrative just preceding. Jesus told the woman taken in adultery, "Neither do I condemn thee." And a short time earlier He had taught this principle: "Judge not according to the appearance, but judge righteous judgment" (7:24).

Jesus was not a civil judge nor did He come on a mission of condemnation. He came to seek and to save those who are condemned already (3:16-18).

15. Ye judge after the flesh; I judge no man: . . . you are in the habit of judging, *Wuest* . . . You condemn Me, *Norlie* . . . in accordance with external standards, *Williams* . . . judging by appearances, *TCNT* . . . from passion, *Campbell* . . . by human standards, *JB, Berkeley* . . . from a human standpoint, *Fenton* . . . You judge in a human way, a way in which I don't judge anybody, *Beck.*

8:16. "And yet if I judge, my judgment is true." The first statement is conditional. The conclusion is stated if the judgment is made. "My" is emphatic, stressing that the judgment He renders is in accord with the facts and proceeds from wisdom not tainted by selfish motives.

The word "judge" is used in a different sense. Here Jesus' judgment is by divine knowledge and according to truth. Donald Guthrie says: "The antithesis of judgment according to the flesh is judgment in harmony with the mind of the Father. *I and he who sent me* brings out the mission-consciousness of Jesus. His is not isolated judgment, but judgment within his whole life purpose, and it is therefore true" (Guthrie, *New Bible Commentary*, p.946).

The Father and the Son mutually think, speak, and work to accomplish their purposes for and within man. God is not prejudiced toward any man nor does He judge according to outward appearances (Hebrews 4:12).

16. And yet if I judge, my judgment is true: . . . if I should judge, *Phillips* . . . my judgment is trustworthy, *Montgomery* . . . my decision is right, *BB* . . . you can depend on My judgment, *Beck* . . . My decision would nevertheless be valid, *Fenton* . . . is genuine, *Rotherham* . . . is fair, *Williams.*

for I am not alone: . . . because I am not by myself, *Moffatt* . . . but there are two of us, *Williams.*

but I and the Father that sent me: . . . but the Father who sent me is with me, *TCNT* . . . there is myself and the Father who sent me, *Moffatt* . . . but concur with, *Campbell.*

8:17. "Your law" is literally "the Law" (*tō nomō*). To establish the truth of a matter, the Law required two or three witnesses who

17. It is also written in your law, that the testimony of two men it true: It is a maxim. . .the concurrent testimony of two is credible, *Campbell* . . . when two witnesses are in agreement their testimony is true, *ALBA* . . . of two persons, *Murdock* . . . is valid, *Berkeley, Norlie, Fenton.*

John 8:18

1466.1 prs-pron nom 1sing	1498.2 verb 1sing indic pres act	3450.5 art sing masc	3113.7 verb nom sing masc part pres act	3875.1 prep
18. ἐγώ	εἰμι	ὁ	μαρτυρῶν	περὶ
egō	*eimi*	*ho*	*marturōn*	*peri*
I	am	the	bearing witness	concerning

1670.1 prs-pron gen 1sing masc	2504.1 conj	3113.3 verb 3sing indic pres act	3875.1 prep	1466.3 prs-pron gen 1sing	3450.5 art sing masc
ἐμαυτοῦ	καὶ	μαρτυρεῖ	περὶ	ἐμοῦ	ὁ
emautou	*kai*	*marturei*	*peri*	*emou*	*ho*
myself,	and	bears witness	concerning	me	the

3854.11 verb nom sing masc part aor act	1466.6 prs-pron acc 1sing	3824.1 noun nom sing masc	2978.25 verb indic imperf act	3631.1 conj
πέμψας	με	πατήρ.	**19.** Ἔλεγον	οὖν
pempsas	*me*	*patēr*	*Elegon*	*oun*
having sent	me	Father.	They said	therefore

840.4 prs-pron dat sing	4085.1 adv	1498.4 verb 3sing indic pres act	3450.5 art sing masc	3824.1 noun nom sing masc	4622.2 prs-pron gen 2sing
αὐτῷ,	Ποῦ	ἐστιν	ὁ	πατήρ	σου;
autō	*Pou*	*estin*	*ho*	*patēr*	*sou*
to him,	Where	is	the	Father	your?

19.a.**Txt:** 01ℵ,032W,038, 13,33,Steph
Var: 03B,05D,017K, 019L,029T,036,037,byz. Gries,Lach,TregAlf,Tisc, We/Ho,Weis,Sod,UBS/☆

552.6 verb 3sing indic aor pass	3450.5 art sing masc	2400.1 name nom masc	3641.1 conj	1466.7 prs-pron acc 1sing	3471.6 verb 2pl indic perf act
Ἀπεκρίθη	⸂a ὁ ⸃	Ἰησοῦς,	Οὔτε	ἐμὲ	οἴδατε
Apekrithē	*ho*	*Iēsous*	*Oute*	*eme*	*oidate*
Answered		Jesus,	Neither	me	you know

3641.1 conj	3450.6 art acc sing masc	3824.4 noun acc sing masc	1466.2 prs-pron gen 1sing	1479.1 conj	1466.7 prs-pron acc 1sing	3471.12 verb 2pl indic plperf act
οὔτε	τὸν	πατέρα	μου·	εἰ	ἐμὲ	ᾔδειτε,
oute	*ton*	*patera*	*mou*	*ei*	*eme*	*ēdeite*
nor	the	Father	my.	If	me	you had known,

2504.1 conj	3450.6 art acc sing masc	3824.4 noun acc sing masc	1466.2 prs-pron gen 1sing	3471.12 verb 2pl indic plperf act
καὶ	τὸν	πατέρα	μου	⸀ ᾔδειτε
kai	*ton*	*patera*	*mou*	*ēdeite*
also	the	Father	my	you would have known.

300.1 partic	300.1 partic	3471.12 verb 2pl indic plperf act	3642.18 dem-pron pl neu	3450.17 art pl neu
ἂν.	[☆ ἂν	ᾔδειτε.]	**20.** Ταῦτα	τὰ
an	*an*	*ēdeite*	*Tauta*	*ta*
		[you would have known.]	These	the

20.a.**Txt:** 033X,036,037, byz.
Var: 01ℵ,03B,05D, 017K,019L,029T,038,sa. bo.Gries,Lach,TregAlf, Tisc,We/Ho,Weis,Sod, UBS/☆

4343.4 noun pl neu	2953.27 verb 3sing indic aor act	3450.5 art sing masc	2400.1 name nom masc	1706.1 prep	3450.3 art dat sing
ῥήματα	ἐλάλησεν	⸂a ὁ	Ἰησοῦς ⸃	ἐν	τῷ
rhēmata	*elalēsen*	*ho*	*Iēsous*	*en*	*tō*
words	spoke		Jesus	in	the

1042.2 noun dat sing neu	1042.4 noun dat sing neu	1315.6 verb sing masc part pres act	1706.1 prep
⸀ γαζοφυλακίῳ,	[☆ γαζοφυλακείῳ]	διδάσκων	ἐν
gazophulakiō	*gazophulakeiō*	*didaskōn*	*en*
treasury,	[idem]	teaching	in

3450.3 art dat sing	2387.2 adj dat sing neu	2504.1 conj	3625.2 num card nom masc	3945.1 verb 3sing indic aor act	840.6 prs-pron acc sing masc
τῷ	ἱερῷ·	καὶ	οὐδεὶς	ἐπίασεν	αὐτόν,
tō	*hierō*	*kai*	*oudeis*	*epiasen*	*auton*
the	temple;	and	no one	took	him,

were honest and of normal intelligence (Deuteronomy 17:6; 19:15). Jesus seized the opportunity to show the Pharisees that their ("your") law conflicted with their fleshly method of judgment.

18. I am one that bear witness of myself: I am a witness for Myself, *Berkeley* . . . So, I am testifying on my own behalf, *SEB* . . . It is I who make claims for myself, *Barclay* . . . I am testifying about Myself, *Adams* . . . I testify on my own behalf, *TEV* . . . in my own cause, *NEB*.

and the Father that sent me beareth witness of me: . . . and the second witness to me is the, *Phillips* . . . my other witness is, *NIV* . . . and the Father who sent me testifies concerning me, *HBIE* . . . is my witness too, *JB* . . . gives evidence about me, *Fenton*.

8:18. The two witnesses Jesus presented for the truth that He is the Light of the World are the Father and himself. These two are the only possible beings who know what reality is, therefore the only valid witnesses. Now if only two witnesses exist to attest to reality then two witnesses are valid to give testimony. No other witness could be accepted in a court of law. Jesus claimed the only valid witnesses are the members of the Godhead. Jesus was stating that the revelation of God's nature must come from God himself. It takes God to accurately reveal God to man. This truth is the very truth taught in the *Logos* teaching of 1:1-8. The same point of testimony to Jesus' identity came up in chapter 5 in regard to the healing of the impotent man. Study the Lord's statements in 5:31,32, and 37.

19. Then said they unto him, Where is thy Father? Jesus answered, Ye neither know me, nor my Father: You know my Father as little as you know me, *Weymouth* . . . You do not know my Father, returned Jesus, any more than you know me, *Phillips* . . . To know me is to know my Father too, *Barclay* . . . You are not acquainted with either Me or My Father, *Concordant*.

if ye had known me, ye should have known my Father also: If you knew Me, you would know My Father, *Beck*.

8:19. It is unclear as to the meaning of their question. Did they mean "father" in the sense Jesus meant "Father"? Or were they indicating a slur on His origin? (Some held that Jesus was a bastard.) They may have meant Joseph, who apparently was deceased. Whatever their implication, they would not receive an unseen or an absent witness. They asked "where" not "who."

Jesus' answer concerned "who" not "where." The Pharisees' ignorance of who He was, was equaled by their unenlightened condition concerning the Father. Jesus made the same assertion to Philip in 14:9. The Lord stated His argument more fully in 5:36-38. Further on in this chapter, Jesus again told the Jews they did not know His Father (verses 54,55). In the natural a father and his son are usually very much alike. When one sees either, one's mind reflects on the other. The qualities of Jesus' personality (attributes) should have suggested to the Jews the God they professed to know. Moreover, the works He did indicated His origin.

20. These words spake Jesus in the treasury, as he taught in the temple: These declarations, *Concordant* . . . These statements, *TCNT* . . . in the Temple precincts, *Barclay* . . . where the offering boxes were placed, *SEB*.

and no man laid hands on him; for his hour was not yet come: . . . none arrested Him, *Fenton*

8:20. The treasury (*tō gazophulakiō*) was a part of the temple. It was located in the Court of the Women. The offerings of money were deposited in large chests (13 of them, according to some scholars). The word "treasury" occurs five times in the New Testament (Mark 12:41,43; Luke 21:1; John 8:20).

This is the area in which Jesus taught. It may indicate that Jesus came for the Jewish nation, male and female. He often taught in

3617.1 conj	3632.1 adv	2048.27 verb 3sing indic plperf act	3450.9 art nom sing fem	5443.2 noun nom sing fem	840.3 prs-pron gen sing
ὅτι	οὔπω	ἐληλύθει	ἡ	ὥρα	αὐτοῦ.
hoti	*oupō*	*elēluthei*	*hē*	*hōra*	*autou*
for	not yet	had come	the	hour	his.

21.a.**Txt:** p66-corr,017K, 036,037,038,1,13,33, byz.it.sa.bo.
Var: p66-org,p75,01ℵ, 03B,05D,019L,029T, 033X,Lach,Treg,Alf,Tisc We/Ho,Weis,Sod,UBS/⋆

1500.5 verb 3sing indic aor act	3631.1 conj	3687.1 adv	840.2 prs-pron dat pl	3450.5 art sing masc	2400.1 name nom masc
21. Εἶπεν	οὖν	πάλιν	αὐτοῖς	⸂a ὁ	Ἰησοῦς, ⸃
Eipen	*oun*	*palin*	*autois*	*ho*	*Iēsous*
Said	therefore	again	to them		Jesus,

1466.1 prs-pron nom 1sing	5055.1 verb 1sing indic pres act	2504.1 conj	2195.21 verb 2pl indic fut act	1466.6 prs-pron acc 1sing	2504.1 conj
Ἐγὼ	ὑπάγω,	καὶ	ζητήσετέ	με,	καὶ
Egō	*hupagō*	*kai*	*zētēsete*	*me*	*kai*
I	go away,	and	you will seek	me,	and

1706.1 prep	3450.11 art dat sing fem	264.3 noun dat sing fem	5050.2 prs-pron gen 2pl	594.23 verb 2pl indic fut mid	3562.1 adv
ἐν	τῇ	ἁμαρτίᾳ	ὑμῶν	ἀποθανεῖσθε·	ὅπου
en	*tē*	*hamartia*	*humōn*	*apothaneisthe*	*hopou*
in	the	sin	your	you will die;	where

1466.1 prs-pron nom 1sing	5055.1 verb 1sing indic pres act	5050.1 prs-pron nom 2pl	3620.3 partic	1404.6 verb 2pl indic pres	2048.23 verb inf aor act
ἐγὼ	ὑπάγω	ὑμεῖς	οὐ	δύνασθε	ἐλθεῖν.
egō	*hupagō*	*humeis*	*ou*	*dunasthe*	*elthein*
I	go	you	not	are able	to come.

2978.25 verb indic imperf act	3631.1 conj	3450.7 art pl masc	2428.2 name-adj pl masc	3252.1 partic	609.14 verb 3sing indic fut act
22. Ἔλεγον	οὖν	οἱ	Ἰουδαῖοι,	Μήτι	ἀποκτενεῖ
Elegon	*oun*	*hoi*	*Ioudaioi*	*Mēti*	*apoktenei*
Said	therefore	the	Jews,	Not	will he kill

1431.6 prs-pron acc 3sing masc	3617.1 conj	2978.5 verb 3sing indic pres act	3562.1 adv	1466.1 prs-pron nom 1sing	5055.1 verb 1sing indic pres act
ἑαυτόν,	ὅτι	λέγει,	Ὅπου	ἐγὼ	ὑπάγω
heauton	*hoti*	*legei*	*Hopou*	*egō*	*hupagō*
himself,	that	he says,	Where	I	go

5050.1 prs-pron nom 2pl	3620.3 partic	1404.6 verb 2pl indic pres	2048.23 verb inf aor act	2504.1 conj	1500.5 verb 3sing indic aor act
ὑμεῖς	οὐ	δύνασθε	ἐλθεῖν;	**23.** Καὶ	⸀ εἶπεν
humeis	*ou*	*dunasthe*	*elthein*	*Kai*	*eipen*
you	not	are able	to come?	And	he said

23.a.**Txt:** 017K,036,037, byz.
Var: 01ℵ,03B,05D,019L, 029T,033X,038,Lach Treg,Alf,Tisc,We/Ho, Weis,Sod,UBS/⋆

2978.26 verb 3sing indic imperf act	840.2 prs-pron dat pl	5050.1 prs-pron nom 2pl	1523.2 prep gen	3450.1 art gen pl	2706.1 adv
[a⋆ ἔλεγεν]	αὐτοῖς,	Ὑμεῖς	ἐκ	τῶν	κάτω
elegen	*autois*	*Humeis*	*ek*	*tōn*	*katō*
[was saying]	to them,	You	from	the	below

1498.6 verb 2pl indic pres act	1466.1 prs-pron nom 1sing	1523.2 prep gen	3450.1 art gen pl	504.1 adv	1498.2 verb 1sing indic pres act
ἐστέ,	ἐγὼ	ἐκ	τῶν	ἄνω	εἰμί·
este	*egō*	*ek*	*tōn*	*anō*	*eimi*
are,	I	from	the	above	am;

5050.1 prs-pron nom 2pl	1523.2 prep gen	3450.2 art gen sing	2862.2 noun gen sing masc	3642.1 dem-pron gen sing	3642.1 dem-pron gen sing
ὑμεῖς	ἐκ	⸀ τοῦ	κόσμου	τούτου	[⋆ τούτου
humeis	*ek*	*tou*	*kosmou*	*toutou*	*toutou*
You	of	the	world	this	[this

the Court of the Gentiles, yet during this Feast of Tabernacles the teaching was for the Jews. Remember He had proclaimed to the Jews first that He is the "light of the world."

John mentions again that "no man laid hands on him; for his hour was not yet come." Jesus was invincible until His hour. Majesty and triumph are implied in the assertion. Whatever the immediate reason, they failed to arrest Him. John attributes the real reason to the plan of God. Jesus was to suffer and die at the next Passover, not during the Feast of Tabernacles. It was the Passover lamb that symbolized the Messiah's atonement. Moreover, the Day of Pentecost (50 days after Passover) had been designed as the Feast to typify the coming of the Holy Spirit into the Church.

. . . yet no one ventured to arrest Him, *Williams* . . . No one arrested Him, for His time, *Norlie*.

21. Then said Jesus again unto them, I go my way, and ye shall seek me, and shall die in your sins: He, therefore, further said, *Fenton* . . . I am going away, *Montgomery, ALBA* . . . where I withdraw, *Rotherham* . . . you will try to find me, *Barclay* . . . you are unable to follow, *Fenton* . . . you can never come, *Williams* . . . but death will overtake you in your sins, *BB* . . . under the curse of your sins, *Williams*.

whither I go, ye cannot come: . . . it is impossible for you to come, *Weymouth* . . . I withdraw, *Wuest* . . . you are not able to reach, *Berkeley* . . . you cannot come where I am going, *TCNT*.

8:21. "Again" marks another time He made a similar statement. Jesus had asserted the first two or three statements (see 7:34). The "I" or "I go away" (NASB) is emphatic.

"Sins" is a singular noun with the article (though translated plural in the KJV) indicating the collective sense and even the idea of sin in totality. The singular stresses "the sin" (*hamartia*) of unbelief from which the total accumulation of sins springs. The Jews persisted in their unbelief and rejection of Him; thus they "shall die" in their sin. Notice Jesus said "sins" in verse 24.

He had a positive knowledge of His departure. Compare the Lord's words to the Jews in 7:33,34 and His utterance to His disciples in 13:33. "Whither" ("where," NASB) indicates the Father's house (14:2,3).

22. Then said the Jews, Will he kill himself?: So the Jewish authorities said, *TEV* . . . Perhaps he will kill himself, *NEB* . . . he will not by any chance kill himself, *Wuest*.

because he saith, Whither I go, ye cannot come: . . . we cannot go where he is going? *TCNT*.

8:22. The Jews perverted Jesus' words and followed the perversion with sarcasm just as they had in 7:35, yet here they connected their mockery to His supposed eternal destiny (hell), not to His earthly ministry among the Gentiles. The Jews believed that the one who committed suicide was sent to the darkest place in Hades. The Jews turned Jesus' words concerning His earthly departure for heaven to the extreme contrast.

23. And he said unto them, Ye are from beneath; I am from above: The difference between us, *Phillips* . . . you are of this present world, *TCNT* . . . You belong to this present world, *Williams* . . . You are from below, *Norlie* . . . Your home is in this world. My home is not in this world, *Beck*.

ye are of this world; I am not of this world:

8:23. Jesus followed their mockery with patient and gentle teaching. What condescension and longsuffering!

"Ye are from beneath" means they had earthly views and their disposition was revealed by their insinuation. "I am from above" was the direct opposite. Next Jesus contrasted their origin and His. "This world" is their source (*ek*, "out of"). He used the negative concerning His origin, "not of this world." The Lord did not give

3450.2 art gen sing	2862.2 noun gen sing masc	1498.6 verb 2pl indic pres act	1466.1 prs-pron nom 1sing	3620.2 partic	1498.2 verb 1sing indic pres act
τοῦ	κόσμου]	ἐστέ,	ἐγὼ	οὐκ	εἰμὶ
tou	*kosmou*	*este*	*egō*	*ouk*	*eimi*
the	world]	are,	I	not	am

1523.2 prep gen	3450.2 art gen sing	2862.2 noun gen sing masc	3642.1 dem-pron gen sing	1500.3 verb indic aor act	3631.1 conj
ἐκ	τοῦ	κόσμου	τούτου.	**24.** εἶπον	οὖν
ek	*tou*	*kosmou*	*toutou*	*eipon*	*oun*
of	the	world	this.	I said	therefore

5050.3 prs-pron dat 2pl	3617.1 conj	594.23 verb 2pl indic fut mid	1706.1 prep	3450.14 art dat pl fem	264.7 noun dat pl fem
ὑμῖν	ὅτι	ἀποθανεῖσθε	ἐν	ταῖς	ἁμαρτίαις
humin	*hoti*	*apothaneisthe*	*en*	*tais*	*hamartiais*
to you	that	you will die	in	the	sins

5050.2 prs-pron gen 2pl	1430.1 partic	1056.1 conj	3231.1 partic	3961.1 verb 2pl subj act	3617.1 conj	1466.1 prs-pron nom 1sing
ὑμῶν·	ἐὰν	γὰρ	μὴ	πιστεύσητε	ὅτι	ἐγώ
humōn	*ean*	*gar*	*mē*	*pisteusēte*	*hoti*	*egō*
your;	if	for	not	you believe	that	I

1498.2 verb 1sing indic pres act	594.23 verb 2pl indic fut mid	1706.1 prep	3450.14 art dat pl fem	264.7 noun dat pl fem	5050.2 prs-pron gen 2pl
εἰμι,	ἀποθανεῖσθε	ἐν	ταῖς	ἁμαρτίαις	ὑμῶν.
eimi	*apothaneisthe*	*en*	*tais*	*hamartiais*	*humōn*
am,	you will die	in	the	sins	your.

2978.25 verb indic imperf act	3631.1 conj	840.4 prs-pron dat sing	4622.1 prs-pron nom 2sing	4949.3 intr-pron nom sing
25. Ἔλεγον	οὖν	αὐτῷ,	Σὺ	τίς
Elegon	*oun*	*autō*	*Su*	*tis*
They said	therefore	to him,	You	who

25.a.**Txt:** byz.
Var: 03B,019L,029T, 033X,038,33,Lach,Treg Alf,Word,Tisc,We/Ho, Weis,Sod,UBS/*

1498.3 verb 2sing indic pres act	2504.1 conj	1500.5 verb 3sing indic aor act	840.2 prs-pron dat pl	3450.5 art sing masc	2400.1 name nom masc
εἶ;	(a Καὶ)	εἶπεν	αὐτοῖς	ὁ	Ἰησοῦς,
ei	*Kai*	*eipen*	*autois*	*ho*	*Iēsous*
are?	And	said	to them		Jesus,

3450.12 art acc sing fem	741.4 noun acc sing fem	3614.16 rel-pron sing neu	4948.10 indef-pron sing neu	2504.1 conj	2953.1 verb 1sing pres act
Τὴν	ἀρχὴν	ὅ	τι	καὶ	λαλῶ
Tēn	*archēn*	*ho*	*ti*	*kai*	*lalō*
The	altogether	that	which	also	I say

5050.3 prs-pron dat 2pl	4044.17 adj pl neu	2174.1 verb 1sing pres act	3875.1 prep	5050.2 prs-pron gen 2pl	2953.24 verb inf pres act
ὑμῖν.	**26.** πολλὰ	ἔχω	περὶ	ὑμῶν	λαλεῖν
humin	*polla*	*echō*	*peri*	*humōn*	*lalein*
to you.	Many things	I have	concerning	you	to say

2504.1 conj	2892.12 verb inf pres act	233.1 conj	3450.5 art sing masc	3854.11 verb nom sing masc part aor act	1466.6 prs-pron acc 1sing
καὶ	κρίνειν·	ἀλλ'	ὁ	πέμψας	με
kai	*krinein*	*all'*	*ho*	*pempsas*	*me*
and	to judge;	but	the	having sent	me

225.2 adj nom sing	1498.4 verb 3sing indic pres act	2476.3 conj	3614.17 rel-pron pl neu	189.19 verb 1sing indic aor act	3706.1 prep
ἀληθής	ἐστιν,	κἀγὼ	ἃ	ἤκουσα	παρ'
alēthēs	*estin*	*kagō*	*ha*	*ēkousa*	*par'*
true	is,	and I	what	I heard	from

their sarcasm the respect of an answer, but proceeded to warn them of their horrible state of sin.

8:24. Because they were "from beneath," they thought and acted out of the state of darkness in which they lived.

"For if ye believe not that I am he" testifies to the one and only way of life. "I am he" (*egō eimi*) is the title for the Messiah and was applied by Jesus to himself (see Exodus 3:14). "I am" occurs 19 times in John and applies to Jesus Christ as to His deity. Jesus allowed the Jews to interpret the "I am he" for themselves on the basis of what He said about himself.

If they reject Him, He reiterated, "You shall die in your sins" (NASB). Thus they would be guilty of self-murder themselves, since they were responsible for their decisions of life or death.

8:25. The Jews asked Jesus, "Who art thou?" They wanted a definite answer on which they would be able to accuse Him of blasphemy. His response has three possibilities: (1) a direct answer, (2) an ambiguous response, (3) no answer at all. The translation is difficult; hence we find many varying renderings of His response. Notice some translations:

"Even what I have told you from the beginning" (RSV)
"Why should I speak to you at all?" (NEB)
"Altogether that which I say to you" (Darby)
"What should I tell you first?" (Beck)

Notice the Greek words and order. *Tēn archēn ho ti kai lalō humin* = "the beginning that which even I speak to you." These are the literal words in order of their occurrence.

"The beginning" is in the accusative case, meaning it is the object; but it is emphatic by its forward position in the statement, or it stands as a statement itself. No word for "from" occurs in the original. Jesus was saying that He himself is "the beginning." The Greek word for "beginning" (*tēn archēn*) is closely related to the word (*archēgos*) meaning "originator," "founder," "author," "ruler," and "source" (see Acts 3:15; 5:31; Hebrews 2:10; 12:2). Take note that this is the same word for "in the beginning" used in 1:1. The first word "the beginning" expressed His answer as to who He is, and the remaining part of the declaration should be taken as a separate statement: "What I have been telling you." If the Jews of this interview had as much difficulty understanding Jesus' assertion as scholars today have, it is no wonder they could not offer this statement as evidence of blasphemy.

8:26. Their mockery of Him may hinder them, but He will continue "to speak and to judge" (NASB). These two infinitives indicate

24. I said therefore unto you, that ye shall die in your sins:
for if ye believe not that I am he: . . . for unless you believe that I am the Christ, *Williams* . . . For unless you believe that I am who I am, *Phillips* . . . that I AM, *Fenton, Wuest.*
ye shall die in your sins: . . . you will die under the curse of your sins, *Williams* . . . you will die with your sins upon you, *Knox* . . . death will overtake you in your sins, *Norlie.*

25. Then said they unto him, Who art thou?: You—who are you? they asked, *Weymouth* . . . who are you anyway? *Williams* . . . Who do you think you are? *Norlie.*
And Jesus saith unto them, Even the same that I said unto you from the beginning: Why do I even talk to you at all? *Williams* . . . Even what I have told you from the beginning, *RSV* . . . Why ask exactly what I have been telling you? *TCNT* . . . I am essentially that which I also am telling you, *Wuest* . . . told you formerly, *Campbell.*

26. I have many things to say and to judge of you: I have much to say and to judge about you, *Berkeley* . . . much to condemn in you, *Williams* . . . judge concerning you, *Wuest.*
but he that sent me is true: But He who sent me is faithful, *Norlie* . . . but My Sender is reliable, *Berkeley.*
and I speak to the world those things which I have heard of him: I am only speaking to this world

John 8:27

26.a.**Txt:** 07E,021M,036, byz.
Var: 01ℵ,03B,05D, 017K,019L,029T,030U, 033X,037,038,it.Lach, Treg,Alf,Tisc,We/Ho, Weis,Sod,UBS/☆

840.3 prs-pron gen sing	3642.18 dem-pron pl neu	2978.1 verb 1sing pres act	2953.1 verb 1sing pres act	1519.1 prep	3450.6 art acc sing masc
αὐτοῦ,	ταῦτα	ʻ λέγω	[a☆ λαλῶ]	εἰς	τὸν
autou	*tauta*	*legō*	*lalō*	*eis*	*ton*
him,	these things	I say	[idem]	to	the

2862.4 noun acc sing masc	3620.2 partic	1091.18 verb 3pl indic aor act	3617.1 conj	3450.6 art acc sing masc	3824.4 noun acc sing masc
κόσμον.	27. Οὐκ	ἔγνωσαν	ὅτι	τὸν	πατέρα
kosmon	*Ouk*	*egnōsan*	*hoti*	*ton*	*patera*
world.	Not	they knew	that	the	Father

28.a.**Txt:** p66-corr,p75, 01ℵ,05D,017K,036,037, 038,13,etc.byz.Gries
Var: p66-org,03B,019L, 029T,032W,565,1241, Lach,Treg,AlfTisc, We/Ho,Weis,Sod,UBS/☆

840.2 prs-pron dat pl	2978.26 verb 3sing indic imperf act	1500.5 verb 3sing indic aor act	3631.1 conj	840.2 prs-pron dat pl
αὐτοῖς	ἔλεγεν.	28. Εἶπεν	οὖν	(a αὐτοῖς)
autois	*elegen*	*Eipen*	*oun*	*autois*
to them	he spoke of.	Said	therefore	to them

3450.5 art sing masc	2400.1 name nom masc	3615.1 conj	5150.4 verb 2pl subj aor act	3450.6 art acc sing masc
ὁ	Ἰησοῦς,	Ὅταν	ὑψώσητε	τὸν
ho	*Iēsous*	*Hotan*	*hupsōsēte*	*ton*
	Jesus,	When	you shall have lifted up	the

5048.4 noun acc sing masc	3450.2 art gen sing	442.2 noun gen sing masc	4966.1 adv	1091.51 verb 2pl indic fut mid	3617.1 conj
υἱὸν	τοῦ	ἀνθρώπου,	τότε	γνώσεσθε	ὅτι
huion	*tou*	*anthrōpou*	*tote*	*gnōsesthe*	*hoti*
Son		of man,	then	you shall know	that

1466.1 prs-pron nom 1sing	1498.2 verb 1sing indic pres act	2504.1 conj	570.2 prep gen	1670.1 prs-pron gen 1sing masc	4020.1 verb 1sing pres act
ἐγώ	εἰμι·	καὶ	ἀπ’	ἐμαυτοῦ	ποιῶ
egō	*eimi*	*kai*	*ap'*	*emautou*	*poiō*
I	am,	and	from	myself	I do

3625.6 num card neu	233.2 conj	2503.1 conj	1315.13 verb 3sing indic aor act	1466.6 prs-pron acc 1sing	3450.5 art sing masc
οὐδέν,	ἀλλὰ	καθὼς	ἐδίδαξέν	με	ὁ
ouden	*alla*	*kathōs*	*edidaxen*	*me*	*ho*
nothing,	but	as	taught	me	the

28.b.**Txt:** 03B,017K,036, 037,1,byz.sa.Gries,Weis
Var: 01ℵ,03B,019L, 029T,033X,038,Lach, TregAlf,Tisc,We/Ho,Sod, UBS/☆

3824.1 noun nom sing masc	1466.2 prs-pron gen 1sing	3642.18 dem-pron pl neu	2953.1 verb 1sing pres act	2504.1 conj	3450.5 art sing masc
πατήρ	(b μου,)	ταῦτα	λαλῶ.	29. καὶ	ὁ
patēr	*mou*	*tauta*	*lalō*	*kai*	*ho*
Father	my,	these things	I speak.	And	the

3854.11 verb nom sing masc part aor act	1466.6 prs-pron acc 1sing	3196.2 prep	1466.3 prs-pron gen 1sing	1498.4 verb 3sing indic pres act	3620.2 partic
πέμψας	με,	μετ’	ἐμοῦ	ἐστιν·	οὐκ
pempsas	*me*	*met'*	*emou*	*estin*	*ouk*
having sent	me,	with	me	is;	not

29.a.**Txt:** 07E,017K,036, 037,byz.
Var: 01ℵ,03B,05D,019L, 029T,033X,038,sa.bo. Lach,TregAlf,Tisc, We/Ho,Weis,Sod,UBS/☆

856.10 verb 3sing indic aor act	1466.6 prs-pron acc 1sing	3304.1 adj sing	3450.5 art sing masc	3824.1 noun nom sing masc	3617.1 conj
ἀφῆκέν	με	μόνον	(a ὁ	πατήρ,)	ὅτι
aphēken	*me*	*monon*	*ho*	*patēr*	*hoti*
left	me	alone	the	Father,	because

1466.1 prs-pron nom 1sing	3450.17 art pl neu	695.2 adj acc pl neu	840.4 prs-pron dat sing	4020.1 verb 1sing pres act	3704.1 adv
ἐγὼ	τὰ	ἀρεστὰ	αὐτῷ	ποιῶ	πάντοτε.
egō	*ta*	*aresta*	*autō*	*poiō*	*pantote*
I	the things	pleasing	to him	do	always.

that He will keep on telling them. But their rejection of His speaking turned His life-giving words into words of judgment.

Jesus was speaking as the voice of the Father. Their reaction to His speaking, therefore, was really their response to the Father who sent Him. He was the Father's ambassador.

what I myself have heard from him, *Phillips* . . . and I declare to the world what I have heard from him, *RSV* . . . which I have learned, *TCNT* . . . I tell forth to the world, *Weymouth.*

8:27. When they understood His meaning, they persistently ignored and ridiculed Him. The time came when they failed to follow His truth at all. Jesus brought them the words of eternal life, but because of their obstinate will His message was the seal of their doom.

27. They understood not that he spake to them of the Father: They did not realize, *Phillips* . . . However, they did not perceive, *Fenton* . . . They did not perceive that He was mentioning the Father, *Berkeley* . . . They did not realize that he was speaking to them, *Barclay* . . . of the heavenly Father, *SEB.*

8:28. Jesus continued to answer their question, "Who are you?" This verse is clearer for them to understand than verse 25, for He says, "I am he." The "I am" reminds us of God's self-disclosure to Moses in Exodus 3:14.

"When ye have lifted up the Son of man" is a parallel to the prophecy Jesus uttered to Nicodemus in 3:14. By "lift up" (*hupsōsēte*) Jesus meant His crucifixion. It is noteworthy that He said "the Son of man," not "the Son of God," for it was Jesus in His humiliation that yielded to the ordeal of suffering and death on a cross (Isaiah 53:10-12).

"Know" (*gnōsesthe*) is a knowledge gained by experience. Some of these very Jews became disciples after realizing they had crucified the Lord their Messiah (see Acts 2:36,37; 4:1-4). Jesus' assertion of "I am he" of verse 24 prompted the Jews to ask, "Who are you?" (*egō eimi*). In this verse (28) He restated the same claim. They did not understand what He was saying. This is the reason He said "then shall ye know" after His crucifixion, resurrection, and ascension.

The word "taught" is equivalent to what Jesus "saw" and "heard" of the Father (see 5:17; 8:38). The words "I speak" (*lalō*) indicate the method. *Lalō* occurs here and in verses 25 and 26. "These things" asserts the substance of His message.

28. Then said Jesus unto them, When ye have lifted up the Son of man: . . . so Jesus added, *TCNT* . . . when you raise me high, *SEB.*

then shall ye know that I am he: . . . you will realize, *AmpB* . . . you will understand that I am what I say, *TCNT* . . . you will know then who I am, *Moffatt* . . . that I AM, *Fenton, Wuest.*

and that I do nothing of myself: . . . do nothing on my own authority, *Williams* . . . that nothing I do has its source in myself, *Barclay.*

but as my Father hath taught me, I speak these things: . . . but speak simply, *Phillips* . . . I say exactly what my Father has instructed me to say, *Williams* . . . has directed me, *Norlie.*

8:29. "Me" is the emphatic word. The positive "with me" is followed by the negative "not left me alone" to stress the presence of the Father accompanying the Son.

They could not accuse Him of being disobedient to the Father. As the Son of Man, Jesus was humble and obedient to the Father's wishes. Either He is the most perfect being in the universe or He was the greatest imposter the world has yet produced. His teaching, ministry, and, beyond all, His resurrection proved He was and is who He claimed to be.

29. And he that sent me is with me; the Father hath not left me alone: My Sender, *Berkeley.*

for I do always those things that please him: . . . for I do invariably, *Berkeley* . . . because at all times I do the things which are pleasing to him, *BB* . . . because I always practice what pleases Him, *Williams.*

3642.18 dem-pron pl neu	**840.3** prs-pron gen sing	**2953.13** verb gen sing masc part pres act	**4044.7** adj nom pl masc	**3961.23** verb 3pl indic aor act
30. Ταῦτα	αὐτοῦ	λαλοῦντος	πολλοὶ	ἐπίστευσαν
Tauta	*autou*	*lalountos*	*polloi*	*episteusan*
These things	he	speaking	many	believed

1519.1 prep	**840.6** prs-pron acc sing masc	**2978.26** verb 3sing indic imperf act	**3631.1** conj	**3450.5** art sing masc	**2400.1** name nom masc
εἰς	αὐτόν.	**31.** Ἔλεγεν	οὖν	ὁ	Ἰησοῦς
eis	*auton*	*Elegen*	*oun*	*ho*	*Iēsous*
on	him.	Said	therefore		Jesus

4242.1 prep	**3450.8** art acc pl masc	**3961.47** verb acc pl masc part perf act	**840.4** prs-pron dat sing	**2428.5** name-adj acc pl masc
πρὸς	τοὺς	πεπιστευκότας	αὐτῷ	Ἰουδαίους,
pros	*tous*	*pepisteukotas*	*autō*	*Ioudaious*
to	the	had believed	on him	Jews,

1430.1 partic	**5050.1** prs-pron nom 2pl	**3176.20** verb 2pl subj aor act	**1706.1** prep	**3450.3** art dat sing	**3030.3** noun dat sing masc	**3450.3** art dat sing
Ἐὰν	ὑμεῖς	μείνητε	ἐν	τῷ	λόγῳ	τῷ
Ean	*humeis*	*meinēte*	*en*	*tō*	*logō*	*tō*
If	you	remain	in	the	word	the

1684.2 adj dat 1sing	**228.1** adv	**3073.5** noun nom pl masc	**1466.2** prs-pron gen 1sing	**1498.6** verb 2pl indic pres act	**2504.1** conj
ἐμῷ,	ἀληθῶς	μαθηταί	μού	ἐστε·	**32.** καὶ
emō	*alēthōs*	*mathētai*	*mou*	*este*	*kai*
my,	truly	disciples	my	you are.	And

1091.51 verb 2pl indic fut mid	**3450.12** art acc sing fem	**223.4** noun acc sing fem	**2504.1** conj	**3450.9** art nom sing fem	**223.1** noun nom sing fem
γνώσεσθε	τὴν	ἀλήθειαν,	καὶ	ἡ	ἀλήθεια
gnōsesthe	*tēn*	*alētheian*	*kai*	*hē*	*alētheia*
you shall know	the	truth,	and	the	truth

1646.3 verb 3sing indic fut act	**5050.4** prs-pron acc 2pl	**552.8** verb 3pl indic aor pass	**840.4** prs-pron dat sing
ἐλευθερώσει	ὑμᾶς.	**33.** Ἀπεκρίθησαν	(αὐτῷ,
eleutherōsei	*humas*	*Apekrithēsan*	*autō*
shall set free	you.	They answered	him,

33.a.**Txt:** 017K,036,037, byz.
Var: 01ℵ,03B,05D,019L, 033X,038,33,Lach,Treg Alf,Tisc,We/Ho,Weis, Sod,UBS/☆

4242.1 prep	**840.6** prs-pron acc sing masc	**4543.1** noun sing neu	**11.1** name masc	**1498.5** verb 1pl indic pres act	**2504.1** conj
[a☆ πρὸς	αὐτόν,]	Σπέρμα	Ἀβραάμ	ἐσμεν,	καὶ
pros	*auton*	*Sperma*	*Abraam*	*esmen*	*kai*
[to	him,]	Seed	Abraham's	we are,	and

3625.7 num card dat neu	**1392.12** verb 1pl indic perf act	**4312.1** adv	**4316.1** adv	**4622.1** prs-pron nom 2sing
οὐδενὶ	δεδουλεύκαμεν	πώποτε·	πῶς	σὺ
oudeni	*dedouleukamen*	*pōpote*	*pōs*	*su*
not to anyone	have been enslaved	never;	how	you

2978.4 verb 2sing indic pres act	**3617.1** conj	**1645.2** adj nom pl masc	**1090.70** verb 2pl indic fut mid	**552.6** verb 3sing indic aor pass
λέγεις,	Ὅτι	Ἐλεύθεροι	γενήσεσθε;	**34.** Ἀπεκρίθη
legeis	*Hoti*	*Eleutheroi*	*genēsesthe*	*Apekrithē*
say,		Free	you shall become?	Answered

34.a.**Txt:** 01ℵ,05D,017K, 019L,036,037,038,etc. byz.Treg,Alf,Tisc, We/Ho,Weis,Sod,UBS/☆
Var: p66,p75,03B,Lach

840.2 prs-pron dat pl	**3450.5** art sing masc	**2400.1** name nom masc	**279.1** partic	**279.1** partic	**2978.1** verb 1sing pres act	**5050.3** prs-pron dat 2pl
αὐτοῖς	(a ὁ)	Ἰησοῦς,	Ἀμὴν	ἀμὴν	λέγω	ὑμῖν,
autois	*ho*	*Iēsous*	*Amēn*	*amēn*	*legō*	*humin*
them		Jesus,	Truly	truly	I say	to you,

8:30. "These words" refers to the substance of His message, as "I speak these things" (*tauta lalō*) of verse 28 also indicates. It was His teaching that produced faith.

"Many believed on him." They had embarked on a journey of faith. The way might be hard at times; the light might become dim. Sweat might pour and tears might flow, but they had begun the heavenly trek. In the progress of their belief they would become more settled, and one day they would come to the gates of the City.

30. As he spake these words, many believed on him:

8:31. Jesus knew that some of the Jews had believed in Him; therefore He built on that faith. "My" in "my word" is emphasized to stress the message of Jesus' word as opposed to any other.

"Then are ye my disciples indeed." There is no Greek word for "then." The thought is that as they continued to cling to His Word, the doubts would dissipate and the assurance of the truth would become settled. They would understand reality by comprehending the evidence. True disciples are those who continue to follow Him, relying on His Word though sometimes not fully understanding it (6:63).

31. Then said Jesus to those Jews which believed on him:

If ye continue in my word: If ye abide in my word, *ASV* . . . If you live in My Word, *Beck* . . . If you arc faithful to what I have said, *Phillips* . . . if you hold fast to my teaching, *Weymouth* . . . If you adhere to, *Berkeley.*

then are ye my disciples indeed: . . . ye are truly my disciples, *HBIE* . . . you will in reality be My disciples, *Fenton* . . . you are truly my followers, *SEB.*

8:32. The result of abiding in His Word is that the Word will progressively become clear. This statement is similar to 7:17, "If any man will do his will, he shall know of the doctrine . . . ." The word "know" means "come to know" and connotes a knowledge that is learned through experience. The "truth" is Jesus Christ himself (14:6). It is so because He is the revelation of God to man (see 1:14). To be "free" is to be released from the bondage of sin, to have light instead of darkness. Verse 36 states that it is the Son who makes one free. The Scriptures teach that to live in sin, to practice sin, is to be in bondage to sin. Sin has power over the unbeliever. It must be broken by the power and authority of the Word of God. Yet a person must yield to the Lord so that He will work within the individual to bring deliverance (Philippians 2:13; Romans 6:17-20; 8:21; Hebrews 10:19; Ephesians 4:21).

32. And ye shall know the truth: . . . and you shall find out the Truth, *TCNT* . . . And you will have knowledge of what is true, *BB* . . . you will understand the truth, *Moffatt.*

and the truth shall make you free: . . . and the truth will set you free, *Williams.*

8:33. This statement reveals what they depended on for their salvation. They descended from Abraham, the founder of their religious heritage. We "have never yet been enslaved to anyone" (NASB). By this they meant in a religious sense. They were repeatedly dominated by foreign powers. Even then the Romans controlled Palestine politically.

33. They answered him, We be Abraham's seed: . . . the hecklers replied, *Norlie* . . . We are descendants of Abraham, *RSV.*

and were never in bondage to any man: . . . and have never yet been in slavery to any one, *TCNT* . . . have never been anybody's slaves, *Beck* . . . never bonde to eny man, *Tyndale* . . . in bondservice, *Rotherham.*

how sayest thou, Ye shall be made free?: . . . why do you say, You will become free, *BB* . . . be freemen? *Murdock.*

8:34. "Verily, verily" asserts an important statement is forthcoming. Jesus corrected their misconception that being the offspring

34. Jesus answered them, Verily, verily, I say unto you, Who-

3617.1 conj	3820.6 adj sing masc	3450.5 art sing masc	4020.15 verb sing masc part pres act	3450.12 art acc sing fem	264.4 noun acc sing fem
ὅτι	πᾶς	ὁ	ποιῶν	τὴν	ἁμαρτίαν
hoti	*pas*	*ho*	*poiōn*	*tēn*	*hamartian*
that	everyone	the	practicing	the	sin

1395.1 noun nom sing masc	1498.4 verb 3sing indic pres act	3450.10 art gen sing fem	264.1 noun fem	3450.5 art sing masc	1156.2 conj
δοῦλός	ἐστιν	τῆς	ἁμαρτίας.	**35.** ὁ	δὲ
doulos	*estin*	*tēs*	*hamartias*	*ho*	*de*
a slave	is	of the	sin.	The	now

1395.1 noun nom sing masc	3620.3 partic	3176.1 verb 3sing indic act	1706.1 prep	3450.11 art dat sing fem	3477.3 noun dat sing fem	1519.1 prep
δοῦλος	οὐ	μένει	ἐν	τῇ	οἰκίᾳ	εἰς
doulos	*ou*	*menei*	*en*	*tē*	*oikia*	*eis*
slave	not	remains	in	the	house	unto

3450.6 art acc sing masc	163.3 noun acc sing masc	3450.5 art sing masc	5048.1 noun nom sing masc	3176.1 verb 3sing indic act	1519.1 prep	3450.6 art acc sing masc
τὸν	αἰῶνα·	ὁ	υἱὸς	μένει	εἰς	τὸν
ton	*aiōna*	*ho*	*huios*	*menei*	*eis*	*ton*
the	age;	the	Son	remains	unto	the

163.3 noun acc sing masc	1430.1 partic	3631.1 conj	3450.5 art sing masc	5048.1 noun nom sing masc	5050.4 prs-pron acc 2pl
αἰῶνα.	**36.** ἐὰν	οὖν	ὁ	υἱὸς	ὑμᾶς
aiōna	*ean*	*oun*	*ho*	*huios*	*humas*
age.	If	therefore	the	Son	you

1646.2 verb 3sing subj aor act	3552.1 adv	1645.2 adj nom pl masc	1498.42 verb 2pl indic fut mid	3471.2 verb 1sing indic perf act
ἐλευθερώσῃ,	ὄντως	ἐλεύθεροι	ἔσεσθε.	**37.** οἶδα
eleutherōsē	*ontōs*	*eleutheroi*	*esesthe*	*oida*
shall set free,	really	free	you shall be.	I know

3617.1 conj	4543.1 noun sing neu	11.1 name masc	1498.6 verb 2pl indic pres act	233.2 conj	2195.1 verb 2pl pres act
ὅτι	σπέρμα	Ἀβραάμ	ἐστε·	ἀλλὰ	ζητεῖτέ
hoti	*sperma*	*Abraam*	*este*	*alla*	*zēteite*
that	seed	Abraham's	you are;	but	you seek

1466.6 prs-pron acc 1sing	609.12 verb inf aor act	3617.1 conj	3450.5 art sing masc	3030.1 noun nom sing masc	3450.5 art sing masc
με	ἀποκτεῖναι,	ὅτι	ὁ	λόγος	ὁ
me	*apokteinai*	*hoti*	*ho*	*logos*	*ho*
me	to kill,	because	the	word	the

1684.3 adj nom 1sing masc	3620.3 partic	5397.1 verb 3sing indic pres act	1706.1 prep	5050.3 prs-pron dat 2pl	1466.1 prs-pron nom 1sing
ἐμὸς	οὐ	χωρεῖ	ἐν	ὑμῖν.	**38.** ⸀ ἐγὼ
emos	*ou*	*chōrei*	*en*	*humin*	*egō*
my	no	has entrance	in	you.	I

3614.16 rel-pron sing neu	3614.17 rel-pron pl neu	1466.1 prs-pron nom 1sing	3571.9 verb 1sing indic perf act	3706.2 prep	3450.3 art dat sing
ὃ	[a☆ ἃ	ἐγὼ]	ἑώρακα	παρὰ	τῷ
ho	*ha*	*egō*	*heōraka*	*para*	*tō*
what	[what	I]	I have seen	with	the

3824.3 noun dat sing masc	1466.2 prs-pron gen 1sing	2953.1 verb 1sing pres act	2504.1 conj	5050.1 prs-pron nom 2pl	3631.1 conj
πατρὶ	⸂b μου ⸃	λαλῶ·	καὶ	ὑμεῖς	οὖν
patri	*mou*	*lalō*	*kai*	*humeis*	*oun*
Father	my	speak;	and	you	therefore

38.a.**Txt:** 017K,036,037, byz.
Var: 01ℵ,03B,04C,Lach, TregWe/Ho,Weis,Sod, UBS/☆

38.b.**Txt:** 01ℵ,017K,037, 038,1,13,28,565,700, byz.Gries
Var: p66,p75,03B,04C, 019L,Lach,Treg,Alf, Tisc,We/HoWeis,Sod, UBS/☆

of Abraham freed them from bondage. "Whosoever" includes old and young, Jews and Gentiles, rich and poor, male and female. The one who practices sin is under the authority and power of his master, because sin is the master who controls him. "Whosoever committeth" (*ho poiōn*) is literally "the one doing" as a matter of habit. Jesus did not come to bring political freedom, but freedom from the power and control of sin for the one who believes in Him.

soever committeth sin is the servant of sin: . . . everyone who lives in sin is a slave to sin, *Beck* . . . habitually commits sin, *Wuest.*

8:35. Jesus used the analogy of a slave in the household as opposed to the son who is heir of the household. A natural slave can be set free by the heir. Jesus is the Son and heir of all power and authority (Matthew 28:18) of the Father. If the Son frees the slave, then the slave is free.

35. And the servant abideth not in the house for ever: And a slave does not remain in the home always, *TCNT* . . . in his master's house, *Weymouth* . . . does not remain permanently in the household, *Mongomery* . . . abides not in the family perpetually, *Campbell* . . . is not assured, *JB.*

but the Son abideth ever: A son stays forever, *Beck* . . . the son of the house does, *Moffatt.*

8:36. Jesus was willing to free them from their slavery. They need not be slaves any longer. He is the Son and therefore heir. "Ye shall be free indeed." This beautiful analogy graphically illustrates His willingness and authority to release them from bondage.

Their bondage was the sin of unbelief. They did not believe His Word established by His miracles. They were in bondage to the traditions of the elders, the teachings of the scribes and Pharisees, plus culture and customs that were contrary to the teaching of the Scriptures. Jesus offered them freedom from their sin and freedom to serve God.

36. If the Son therefore shall make you free: So if the Son makes you free, *RSV* . . . So if the Son liberates you, *Berkeley.*

ye shall be free indeed: . . . you will be truly free, *BB* . . . then you are unquestionably free, *Berkeley.*

8:37. Jesus was aware of the Jews' descent from Abraham. This fact compounded their error. They should have been very godly people, since they had Abraham as their father. The sad fact was they did not follow the example of their father.

They sought to kill Him, Jesus said, "because my word hath no place in you." They were preoccupied with selfish desires and preconceived opinions concerning the Messiah. They were not interested in what the Word had to say to them. Their conception of truth was of their own hypocritical making.

37. I know that ye are Abraham's seed:

but ye seek to kill me, because my word hath no place in you: Yet you plot to murder Me, *Fenton* . . . because my word hath not free course in you, *ASV* . . . gaineth no ground in you, *Alford* . . . makes no headway among you! *Moffatt* . . . findeth no place in you, *Rotherham* . . . ye do not acquiesce, *Murdock* . . . there is no room in you for my teaching, *Williams* . . . takes no hold among you, *Confraternity.*

8:38. Jesus spoke of His doing the Father's will in natural, human terms. "I have seen with my Father" is equivalent to the Father's having taught the Son (verse 28). The "I" is stressed, and the verb "have seen" is the perfect tense indicating a past action with a present result or a part action with a continuous influence to the present.

38. I speak that which I have seen with my Father:

and ye do that which ye have seen with your father: . . . and you are practicing what you have

38.c.**Txt:** (p66),05D,037, byz.Gries
Var: 01א-corr,03B,04C, 019L,038,33,565,Lach, Treg,Alf,Tisc,We/Ho, Weis,Sod,UBS/☆

38.d.**Txt:** 05D,037,044, 28,700,byz.
Var: p66,(01),03B,(04), (017),019L,032W,(038), Lach,Treg,AlfTisc, We/Ho,Weis,UBS/☆

39.a.**Txt:** 017K,019L, 036,037,byz.Sod
Var: 01א,03B,04C,05D, 038,33,Lach,Treg,Alf, Tisc,We/HoWeis,UBS/☆

39.b.**Txt:** 04C,017K, 032W,036,037,038,1,13, byz.sa.bo.
Var: p66,p75,01א,03B, 05D,019L,029T,Gries Lach,Treg,Alf,Tisc, We/Ho,Weis,Sod,UBS/☆

39.c.**Txt:** p75,01א, 03B-corr,05D,019L, 029T,032W,036,037, 038,1,13,etc.byz.Lach, Tisc,Sod
Var: p66,03B-org,We/Ho Weis,UBS/☆

39.d.**Txt:** 01א-corr,04C, 017K,019L,037,byz. Lach,Sod
Var: 01א-org,03B,05D, 029T,036,038,Gries Treg,Alf,Tisc,We/Ho, Weis,UBS/☆

3614.16 rel-pron sing neu	**3571.13** verb 2pl indic perf act	**3614.17** rel-pron pl neu	**189.23** verb 2pl indic aor act	**3706.2** prep
⸀ὃ	ἑωράκατε	[c☆ ἃ	ἠκούσατε]	παρὰ
ho	*heōrakate*	*ha*	*ēkousate*	*para*
what	you have seen	[what	you heard]	with

3450.3 art dat sing	**3824.3** noun dat sing masc	**5050.2** prs-pron gen 2pl	**3450.2** art gen sing	**3824.2** noun gen sing masc	**4020.2** verb 2pl pres act
⸀τῷ	πατρὶ	ὑμῶν	[d☆ τοῦ	πατρὸς]	ποιεῖτε.
tō	*patri*	*humōn*	*tou*	*patros*	*poieite*
the	father	your	[the	father]	do.

552.8 verb 3pl indic aor pass	**2504.1** conj	**1500.3** verb indic aor act	**1500.28** verb 3pl indic aor act	**840.4** prs-pron dat sing
39. Ἀπεκρίθησαν	καὶ	⸀εἶπον	[a☆ εἶπαν]	αὐτῷ,
Apekrithēsan	*kai*	*eipon*	*eipan*	*autō*
They answered	and	said	[idem]	to him,

3450.5 art sing masc	**3824.1** noun nom sing masc	**2231.2** prs-pron gen 1pl	**11.1** name masc	**1498.4** verb 3sing indic pres act	**2978.5** verb 3sing indic pres act
Ὁ	πατὴρ	ἡμῶν	Ἀβραάμ	ἐστιν.	Λέγει
Ho	*patēr*	*hēmōn*	*Abraam*	*estin*	*Legei*
The	Father	our	Abraham	is.	Says

840.2 prs-pron dat pl	**3450.5** art sing masc	**2400.1** name nom masc	**1479.1** conj	**4891.4** noun pl neu	**3450.2** art gen sing	**11.1** name masc
αὐτοῖς	ὁ	Ἰησοῦς,	Εἰ	τέκνα	τοῦ	Ἀβραάμ
autois	*ho*	*Iēsous*	*Ei*	*tekna*	*tou*	*Abraam*
to them		Jesus,	If	children		of Abraham

1498.1 verb 2pl act	**1498.6** verb 2pl indic pres act	**3450.17** art pl neu	**2024.4** noun pl neu	**3450.2** art gen sing	**11.1** name masc
⸀ἦτε,	[b☆ ἐστε,]	τὰ	ἔργα	τοῦ	Ἀβραὰμ
ēte	*este*	*ta*	*erga*	*tou*	*Abraam*
you were,	[you are,]	the	works		of Abraham

4020.58 verb 2pl indic imperf act	**4020.2** verb 2pl pres act	**300.1** partic	**3431.1** adv	**1156.2** conj
⸀☆ ἐποιεῖτε	[c☆ ποιεῖτε]	⸂d ἂν˙ ⸃	40. νῦν	δὲ
epoieite	*poieite*	*an*	*nun*	*de*
you would do:	[you are doing]		now	but

2195.1 verb 2pl pres act	**1466.6** prs-pron acc 1sing	**609.12** verb inf aor act	**442.4** noun acc sing masc	**3614.5** rel-pron nom sing masc
ζητεῖτέ	με	ἀποκτεῖναι,	ἄνθρωπον	ὃς
zēteite	*me*	*apokteinai*	*anthrōpon*	*hos*
you seek	me	to kill,	a man	who

3450.12 art acc sing fem	**223.4** noun acc sing fem	**5050.3** prs-pron dat 2pl	**2953.38** verb 1sing indic perf act	**3614.12** rel-pron acc sing fem
τὴν	ἀλήθειαν	ὑμῖν	λελάληκα,	ἣν
tēn	*alētheian*	*humin*	*lelalēka*	*hēn*
the	truth	to you	has spoken,	which

189.19 verb 1sing indic aor act	**3706.2** prep	**3450.2** art gen sing	**2296.2** noun gen sing masc	**3642.17** dem-pron sing neu	**11.1** name masc
ἤκουσα	παρὰ	τοῦ	θεοῦ˙	τοῦτο	Ἀβραὰμ
ēkousa	*para*	*tou*	*theou*	*touto*	*Abraam*
I heard	from		God:	this	Abraham

3620.2 partic	**4020.24** verb 3sing indic aor act	**5050.1** prs-pron nom 2pl	**4020.2** verb 2pl pres act	**3450.17** art pl neu	**2024.4** noun pl neu
οὐκ	ἐποίησεν.	41. ὑμεῖς	ποιεῖτε	τὰ	ἔργα
ouk	*epoiēsen*	*humeis*	*poieite*	*ta*	*erga*
not	did.	You	do	the	works

The parallel is drawn between the things they had heard of their father and the things Jesus had seen of His Father. He did not say who He meant by their father. They assumed He meant Abraham (verse 44). They "do" the things they heard from their father. "Do" is the same word Jesus used in the next verse as the opposite of the "do" of Abraham.

learned from your father, *Williams* . . . your actions also reflect what, *AmpB* . . . the things which you heard in the presence of your father, *Wuest* . . . you behave as you have learned from, *Berkeley* . . . are acting as you have learned, *Montgomery* . . . in the presence of your, *Phillips* . . . what your father has told you, *TEV*.

8:39. "Abraham is our father" was their prior statement (verse 33). There Jesus acknowledged their natural lineage, yet here He denied they were truly Abraham's spiritual children. The strong attachment to Abraham declared here by the Pharisees reveals a misconception regarding spiritual heritage. It reflects the general belief that the promises and privileges of Abraham were brought to his heirs genetically. Jesus corrected this misconception by informing the Pharisees that Abraham's children "do" what Abraham "did." He believed God.

"If ye were Abraham's children, ye would do the works of Abraham." "Do" (*epoieite*) is either a statement (in the Greek indicative) or a command (Greek, imperative). The word order is "the works of Abraham do." The challenge Jesus put to these Jews was simple and forceful. Their conduct must indicate their spiritual genealogy; therefore, they should act like Abraham. That is, believe the Word of God and act on that faith.

39. They answered and said unto him, Abraham is our father: They retorted, *Fenton*.

Jesus saith unto them, If ye were Abraham's children, ye would do the works of Abraham: . . . to which Jesus replied, *Berkeley* . . . according to your assumption, *Wuest* . . . it is Abraham's deeds that you would be doing, *Weymouth* . . . you would act as Abraham acted, *Campbell* . . . follow the example, *ALBA* . . . you would continue the works, *Fenton* . . . you would do the sort of things, *Phillips* . . . you ought to act like, *Barclay* . . . you must be practicing what Abraham did, *Williams*.

8:40. This verse points to a solid proof that they were not children of Abraham, for it was revealed in their plot to murder Jesus. "But now ye seek to kill me." Jesus affirmed the fact stated in verse 37. It would be well to examine Jesus' teachings on motives in relation to others, as regarding the sixth commandment, "Thou shalt not kill" (Exodus 20:13; Matthew 5:21,22). Observe the steps in Jesus' statement: (1) a man you are seeking to kill, (2) the truth He told you, (3) from God the word came, (4) this Abraham did not do. Abraham did not do as they were doing. In verse 38 Jesus pointed out what He was doing and what they were doing. In verse 39 He challenged them to do the works of Abraham. In verse 40 He pointed out what Abraham did not do.

Thus the Jews' parentage was revealed by the works they did and the works they did not do. Jesus declared one's motives and actions reveal one's family relationship. If these religious Jews had worked in Abraham's ways they would have acted like Abraham.

40. But now ye seek to kill me: . . . but now you want to kill me, *Moffatt* . . . Instead you are trying to kill Me, *Norlie* . . . you plot to murder, *Fenton* . . . you are doing your best to kill me, *Barclay* . . . you are longing to kill me, *Weymouth*.

a man that hath told you the truth: All I have ever done is to tell you the truth, *TEV*.

which I have heard of God:

this did not Abraham: Abraham would never have done that, *Phillips* . . . Abraham did not do that, *BB* . . . did not act that way, *Berkeley*.

8:41. The Jews did not merely fail to follow Abraham. They did the works of their father (not Abraham). Jesus had pointed to their father in verse 38 and here; yet He had not identified their father. "Ye do" (*poieite*) is the same verb form Jesus used in verse 39.

41. Ye do the deeds of your father: You are practicing what your real father does, *Williams* . . . the works, *Fenton*.

John 8:42

41.a.**Txt:** 03B,04C,017K, 019L,036,037,etc.byz. Lach,Sod
Var: 01ℵ,05D,038,Tisc We/Ho,Weis,UBS/☆

41.b.**Txt:** p66,p75,04C, 05D,017K,036,037,038, 13,byz.sa.
Var: 01ℵ,03B,019L, 029T,032W,bo.Lach, TregAlf,Tisc,We/Ho, Weis,Sod,UBS/☆

41.c.**Txt:** p75,01ℵ-corr, 04C,05D-corr,017K,036, 037,038,1,byz.Tisc
Var: 03B,05D-org,Lach, Treg,AlfWe/Ho,Weis, UBS/☆

42.a.**Txt:** 01ℵ,05D, 021M,037,byz.sa.
Var: 03B,04C,017K, 019L,029T,036,038,bo. Gries,Lach,Treg,AlfTisc, We/Ho,Weis,Sod,UBS/☆

3450.2 art gen sing	**3824.2** noun gen sing masc	**5050.2** prs-pron gen 2pl	**1500.3** verb indic aor act	**1500.28** verb 3pl indic aor act	**3631.1** conj
τοῦ	πατρὸς	ὑμῶν.	⸂ Εἶπον	[a☆ εἶπαν]	⸂b οὖν ⸃
tou	*patros*	*humōn*	*Eipon*	*eipan*	*oun*
of the	father	your.	They said	[idem]	therefore

840.4 prs-pron dat sing	**2231.1** prs-pron nom 1pl	**1523.2** prep gen	**4061.1** noun fem	**3620.3** partic	**1074.24** verb 1pl indic perf pass
αὐτῷ,	Ἡμεῖς	ἐκ	πορνείας	⸂☆ οὐ	γεγεννήμεθα.
autō	*Hēmeis*	*ek*	*porneias*	*ou*	*gegennēmetha*
to him,	We	of	fornication	not	have been born;

3620.2 partic	**1074.14** verb 1pl indic aor pass	**1518.4** num card acc masc	**3824.4** noun acc sing masc	**2174.5** verb 1pl indic pres act
[c οὐκ	ἐγεννήθημεν,]	ἕνα	πατέρα	ἔχομεν,
ouk	*egennēthēmen*	*hena*	*patera*	*echomen*
[not	were born,]	one	Father	we have,

3450.6 art acc sing masc	**2296.4** noun acc sing masc	**1500.5** verb 3sing indic aor act	**3631.1** conj	**840.2** prs-pron dat pl	**3450.5** art sing masc
τὸν	θεόν.	42. Εἶπεν	⸂a οὖν ⸃	αὐτοῖς	ὁ
ton	*theon*	*Eipen*	*oun*	*autois*	*ho*
	God.	Said	therefore	to them	

2400.1 name nom masc	**1479.1** conj	**3450.5** art sing masc	**2296.1** noun nom sing masc	**3824.1** noun nom sing masc	**5050.2** prs-pron gen 2pl
Ἰησοῦς,	Εἰ	ὁ	θεὸς	πατὴρ	ὑμῶν
Iēsous	*Ei*	*ho*	*theos*	*patēr*	*humōn*
Jesus,	If		God	Father	your

1498.34 verb sing indic imperf act	**25.27** verb 2pl indic imperf act	**300.1** partic	**1466.7** prs-pron acc 1sing	**1466.1** prs-pron nom 1sing
ἦν,	ἠγαπᾶτε	ἂν	ἐμέ·	ἐγὼ
ēn	*ēgapate*	*an*	*eme*	*egō*
were,	you would have loved		me,	I

1056.1 conj	**1523.2** prep gen	**3450.2** art gen sing	**2296.2** noun gen sing masc	**1814.1** verb indic aor act	**2504.1** conj	**2223.1** verb 1sing indic pres act
γὰρ	ἐκ	τοῦ	θεοῦ	ἐξῆλθον	καὶ	ἥκω·
gar	*ek*	*tou*	*theou*	*exēlthon*	*kai*	*hēkō*
for	from		God	came forth	and	am come;

3624.1 adv	**1056.1** conj	**570.2** prep gen	**1670.1** prs-pron gen 1sing masc	**2048.24** verb 1sing indic perf act	**233.1** conj	**1552.3** dem-pron nom sing masc
οὐδὲ	γὰρ	ἀπ'	ἐμαυτοῦ	ἐλήλυθα,	ἀλλ'	ἐκεῖνός
oude	*gar*	*ap'*	*emautou*	*elēlutha*	*all'*	*ekeinos*
neither	for	of	myself	have I come,	but	that

1466.6 prs-pron acc 1sing	**643.8** verb 3sing indic aor act	**1296.1** adv	**1217.2** prep	**4949.9** intr-pron sing neu
με	ἀπέστειλεν.	43. ⸂ διατί	[☆ διὰ	τί]
me	*apesteilen*	*diati*	*dia*	*ti*
me	sent.	Why	[idem]	

3450.12 art acc sing fem	**2954.2** noun acc sing fem	**3450.12** art acc sing fem	**1684.9** adj acc 1sing fem	**3620.3** partic	**1091.5** verb 2pl indic pres act
τὴν	λαλιὰν	τὴν	ἐμὴν	οὐ	γινώσκετε;
tēn	*lalian*	*tēn*	*emēn*	*ou*	*ginōskete*
the	speech	the	my	not	do you know?

3617.1 conj	**3620.3** partic	**1404.6** verb 2pl indic pres	**189.17** verb inf pres act	**3450.6** art acc sing masc	**3030.4** noun acc sing masc
ὅτι	οὐ	δύνασθε	ἀκούειν	τὸν	λόγον
hoti	*ou*	*dunasthe*	*akouein*	*ton*	*logon*
Because	not	you are able	to hear	the	word

There it is a command and here a statement. The verb tense is one that expresses continuous action in the present.

They claimed to be genuine descendants of Abraham. They resisted Jesus' insinuation that they were bastards. According to Deuteronomy 23:2 all illegitimate persons were excluded from the assembly of the Lord. The Pharisees' exclamation, "We be not born of fornication" ("We are not illegitimate children," NIV, see other translations in *Various Versions*) may be more than a defense of their own birthright. It could imply that Jesus was himself illegitimate. Whether this was a slur by the Pharisees and whether it had any relationship to the Virgin Birth must be left to speculation. It is possible the mystery surrounding Christ's birth was known by these Pharisees.

But Donald Guthrie holds a different view. "The most natural interpretation of this statement is to understand *fornication* in a spiritual sense (as apostasy from God) as used in the OT (as, *e.g.*, in Hosea). This is more likely than to see here an indirect allusion to slanders regarding the birth of Jesus" (Guthrie, *New Bible Commentary*, p.948).

"We have one Father, even God." The Jews now changed their argument from their natural lineage to their spiritual genealogy. They claimed to be children of God.

Then said they to him, We be not born of fornication: . . . born fatherless, *Klingensmith* . . . We were not born illegitimately, *Norlie* . . . We are not bastards, *TCNT* . . . We weren't born outside of marriage, *Beck* . . . of prostitution! *Concordant* . . . of whoredom, *Murdock* . . . of infidelity, *ALBA*.

we have one Father, even God: . . . one Father—God himself, *TCNT*.

8:42. Within the family circle there is love. The Jews' treatment of God's Son proved they were not God's children. Jesus is of the same nature as God (Hebrews 1:3). To love God is revealed in loving Jesus.

Jesus spoke of His source ("proceedeth forth" [*exēlthon*]) and arrival on earth ("came" [*hēkō*] "from God" [*ek tou theou*]). "From God" has the emphatic position. This was Jesus' constant presentation and the reason they should accept Him. He compounded the point by saying, "Neither came I of myself, but he sent me." "Sent" (*apesteilen*) denotes sent with a commission and the authority of God His Father.

42. Jesus said unto them, If God were your Father: If God had been your father, *Rotherham* . . . If God were really your Father, *Phillips*.

ye would love me: . . . you would have love for me, *BB* . . . you would respect me, *Fenton*.

for I proceeded forth and came from God: . . . and am now come from God, *Montgomery* . . . for I proceeded and came forth, *RSV* . . . for I came out from God, and now am here, *TCNT* . . . for I came forth and am come, *Panin*.

neither came I of myself, but he sent me: I did not come of My own accord, *Norlie* . . . I have not come on my own authority, *Williams*.

8:43. Jesus pointed out the dullness of their understanding and their misinterpretation of His words. They were blind and did not realize their condition. They were deaf, unable to distinguish His words. What He said was like a foreign language to them. They could not comprehend His heavenly speech (see 3:11,12). These religious leaders had no desire to know the truth. They were unlike Nicodemus of chapter 3. It was difficult for Nicodemus to understand, but at least he desired to know the truth.

Was Jesus saying these Pharisees willfully closed their ears to the truth? Or were they unable to hear and understand because of their presuppositions regarding truth and their prejudice toward Him? His words show the Pharisees' inability to hear was a result

43. Why do ye not understand my speech?: . . . that you misunderstand, *Williams* . . . Why do you not understand My language, *Berkeley* . . . Why are my words not clear to you, *BB* . . . comprehend My language? *Fenton* . . . my discourse? *Scarlett*.

even because ye cannot hear my word: It is because you cannot bear to listen to my Message, *TCNT* . . . are unable to listen to what I am saying, *Moffatt*.

John 8:44

44.a.**Var:** 01ℵ,03B,04C, 05D,017K,019L,036, 037,038,byz.Gries,Lach Treg,Alf,Tisc,We/Ho, Weis,Sod,UBS/☆

3450.6 art acc sing masc	**1684.1** adj 1sing	**5050.1** prs-pron nom 2pl	**1523.2** prep gen	**3450.2** art gen sing	**3824.2** noun gen sing masc
τὸν	ἐμόν.	**44.** ὑμεῖς	ἐκ	[a☆+ τοῦ]	πατρὸς
ton	*emon*	*humeis*	*ek*	*tou*	*patros*
the	my.	You	of	[the]	father

3450.2 art gen sing	**1222.2** adj gen sing masc	**1498.6** verb 2pl indic pres act	**2504.1** conj	**3450.15** art acc pl fem	**1924.1** noun fem
τοῦ	διαβόλου	ἐστὲ,	καὶ	τὰς	ἐπιθυμίας
tou	*diabolou*	*este*	*kai*	*tas*	*epithumias*
the	devil	are,	and	the	lusts

3450.2 art gen sing	**3824.2** noun gen sing masc	**5050.2** prs-pron gen 2pl	**2286.5** verb 2pl indic pres act	**4020.20** verb inf pres act	**1552.3** dem-pron nom sing masc
τοῦ	πατρὸς	ὑμῶν	θέλετε	ποιεῖν.	ἐκεῖνος
tou	*patros*	*humōn*	*thelete*	*poiein*	*ekeinos*
of the	father	your	you desire	to do.	That

441.1 noun nom sing masc	**1498.34** verb sing indic imperf act	**570.2** prep gen	**741.2** noun gen sing fem	**2504.1** conj	**1706.1** prep
ἀνθρωποκτόνος	ἦν	ἀπ'	ἀρχῆς,	καὶ	ἐν
anthrōpoktonos	*ēn*	*ap'*	*archēs*	*kai*	*en*
a murderer	was	from	beginning,	and	in

44.b.**Txt:** p75,03B,017K, 041,1,565,700,byz.lect. Gries,Lach,Treg,Alf, Weis
Var: p66,01ℵ,03B,04C, 05D,019L,032W,037, 038,13,Tisc,We/Ho,Sod, UBS/☆

3450.11 art dat sing fem	**223.3** noun dat sing fem	**3620.1** partic	**3620.2** partic	**2449.18** verb 3sing indic perf act	**3617.1** conj
τῇ	ἀληθείᾳ	‹ οὐχ	[b☆ οὐκ]	ἕστηκεν,	ὅτι
tē	*alētheia*	*ouch*	*ouk*	*hestēken*	*hoti*
the	truth	not	[idem]	has stood,	because

3620.2 partic	**1498.4** verb 3sing indic pres act	**223.1** noun nom sing fem	**1706.1** prep	**840.4** prs-pron dat sing	**3615.1** conj
οὐκ	ἔστιν	ἀλήθεια	ἐν	αὐτῷ.	ὅταν
ouk	*estin*	*alētheia*	*en*	*autō*	*hotan*
not	there is	truth	in	him.	Whenever

2953.6 verb 3sing subj pres act	**3450.16** art sing neu	**5414.1** noun sing neu	**1523.2** prep gen	**3450.1** art gen pl	**2375.1** adj gen pl
λαλῇ	τὸ	ψεῦδος,	ἐκ	τῶν	ἰδίων
lalē	*to*	*pseudos*	*ek*	*tōn*	*idiōn*
he may speak	the	falsehood,	from	the	his own

2953.2 verb sing indic pres act	**3617.1** conj	**5418.1** noun nom sing masc	**1498.4** verb 3sing indic pres act	**2504.1** conj	**3450.5** art sing masc	**3824.1** noun nom sing masc
λαλεῖ·	ὅτι	ψεύστης	ἐστὶν	καὶ	ὁ	πατὴρ
lalei	*hoti*	*pseustēs*	*estin*	*kai*	*ho*	*patēr*
he speaks;	for	a liar	he is	and	the	father

840.3 prs-pron gen sing	**1466.1** prs-pron nom 1sing	**1156.2** conj	**3617.1** conj	**3450.12** art acc sing fem	**223.4** noun acc sing fem
αὐτοῦ.	**45.** ἐγὼ	δὲ	ὅτι	τὴν	ἀλήθειαν
autou	*egō*	*de*	*hoti*	*tēn*	*alētheian*
of it.	I	and	because	the	truth

2978.1 verb 1sing pres act	**3620.3** partic	**3961.2** verb 2pl pres act	**1466.4** prs-pron dat 1sing	**4949.3** intr-pron nom sing	**1523.1** prep gen
λέγω,	οὐ	πιστεύετέ	μοι.	**46.** τίς	ἐξ
legō	*ou*	*pisteuete*	*moi*	*tis*	*ex*
speak,	not	you do believe	me.	Which	of

5050.2 prs-pron gen 2pl	**1638.2** verb 3sing indic pres act	**1466.6** prs-pron acc 1sing	**3875.1** prep	**264.1** noun fem	**1479.1** conj
ὑμῶν	ἐλέγχει	με	περὶ	ἁμαρτίας;	εἰ
humōn	*elenchei*	*me*	*peri*	*hamartias*	*ei*
you	convinces	me	concerning	sin?	If

of their stubbornness and pride. They already knew the "truth"; why listen to this Nazarene? (cf. 7:14-17).

8:44. Jesus now identified their father as the devil. He had mentioned him in verses 38 and 41. It was not Abraham or God who was their father, but the devil. This verse makes it clear that the devil is as personal a being as Abraham or God. The point was that they desired to murder Jesus, thus revealing the source of their motive. By introducing death, the devil murdered Adam and Eve, and thus the whole human race. By satanic motivation Cain killed Abel and thus brought about physical murder. The Jews followed the same path. They revealed by their works that they were slaves of sin (verse 34). The devil is "a liar" and the Father of Lies. The devil is the originator of murder and lies (Genesis 3). The Jews were guilty of these two sins. They sought to murder Him and they denied it, thus making themselves liars.

In the Book of Revelation, the identification of the devil is clearly made as well as his murderous and deceitful deeds. He is identified as the great dragon, the old serpent, the devil and Satan. Six times the statement is made concerning how deceitful (from *planaō*) he is (Revelation 12:9). The dragon is depicted as waiting to devour the woman's child (Christ, Revelation 12:4). Satan through the Jews sought the Messiah's death.

8:45. Jesus contrasted their nature with His origin. The truth of this verse is opposite to the lie of the previous verse. They did not believe Him, because they were of a different nature. Like natures attract and opposite natures repel within this spiritual context. Jesus was not their kind of Messiah (see 5:43). They looked for a Messiah who conformed to their nature, but Jesus pointed out that their works (murderous intent and deception) were of the devil.

Truth and deception do not mix. Light and darkness have no relationship with one another. God and Satan have no fellowship. The Jews were bent on murder and lies. They would not listen to the truth. Jesus used the word "because" (*hoti*) indicating they would not hear the truth "because" they had a deceptive nature. Thus, they would not relate to the truth and believe.

8:46. Jesus asked if anyone could prove Him guilty of unfaithfulness to the Father, of hypocrisy, or of a single act of disobedience. Thus the sinlessness of His life was evidence of the truth of His message. The prophets of the Old Testament and the apos-

44. Ye are of your father the devil: . . . the adversary, *Rotherham* . . . Your father is the devil, *Beck.*

and the lusts of your father ye will do: . . . and you desire to do what gives him pleasure, *Weymouth* . . . and you are determined to do what your father loves to do, *TCNT* . . . longs to do, *Phillips* . . . and you want to do your father's lustful desires, *Norlie* . . . ye are disposed to do, *Murdock* . . . practise the lusts of your father, *Fenton* . . . the hankerings of your father, *Berkeley* . . . and you prefer to do, *JB* . . . the sinful things, *SEB* . . . ready to execute his evil purposes, *Norton.*

He was a murderer from the beginning: . . . from the very start, *Williams* . . . a manslayer, *Montgomery* . . . a man-killer, *Concordant* . . . a taker of life, *BB* . . . a destroyer of men, *ALBA.*

and abode not in the truth: . . . and he did not go in the true way, *BB* . . . swerved from the truth, *Campbell* . . . he could not stay in the truth, *Berkeley.*

because there is no truth in him: . . . the truth will have nothing to do with him, *Phillips* . . . no veracity in him, *Campbell.*

When he speaketh a lie:

he speaketh of his own: . . . he does what is natural to him, *TCNT* . . . speaks suitable to his character, *Campbell* . . . he makes them up himself, *Norlie* . . . he is expressing his own nature, *Moffatt.*

for he is a liar, and the father of it: . . . the father of what is false, *BB* . . . the liar's father, *HistNT.*

45. And because I tell you the truth, ye believe me not:

46. Which of you convinceth me of sin?: Who of you can prove me guilty of sin, *Williams* . . . can convict Me of wrong? *Fenton.*

John 8:47

46.a.**Txt:** 017K,036,037, byz.
Var: 01א,03B,04C,019L, 038,it.sa.bo.Gries,Lach, Treg,Alf,Tisc,We/Ho, Weis,Sod,UBS/☆

1156.2 conj	**223.4** noun acc sing fem	**2978.1** verb 1sing pres act	**1296.1** adv	**1217.2** prep	**4949.9** intr-pron sing neu
(a δὲ)	ἀλήθειαν	λέγω,	(διατί	[☆ διὰ	τί]
de	*alētheian*	*legō*	*diati*	*dia*	*ti*
but	truth	I speak,	why	[idem]	

5050.1 prs-pron nom 2pl	**3620.3** partic	**3961.2** verb 2pl pres act	**1466.4** prs-pron dat 1sing	**3450.5** art sing masc	**1498.21** verb sing masc part pres act
ὑμεῖς	οὐ	πιστεύετέ	μοι;	**47.** ὁ	ὢν
humeis	*ou*	*pisteuete*	*moi*	*ho*	*ōn*
you	not	do believe	me?	The	being

1523.2 prep gen	**3450.2** art gen sing	**2296.2** noun gen sing masc	**3450.17** art pl neu	**4343.4** noun pl neu	**3450.2** art gen sing	**2296.2** noun gen sing masc
ἐκ	τοῦ	θεοῦ	τὰ	ῥήματα	τοῦ	θεοῦ
ek	*tou*	*theou*	*ta*	*rhēmata*	*tou*	*theou*
of		God	the	words		of God

189.5 verb 3sing indic pres act	**1217.2** prep	**3642.17** dem-pron sing neu	**5050.1** prs-pron nom 2pl	**3620.2** partic	**189.2** verb 2pl pres act
ἀκούει·	διὰ	τοῦτο	ὑμεῖς	οὐκ	ἀκούετε,
akouei	*dia*	*touto*	*humeis*	*ouk*	*akouete*
hears:	because of	this	you	not	hear,

3617.1 conj	**1523.2** prep gen	**3450.2** art gen sing	**2296.2** noun gen sing masc	**3620.2** partic	**1498.6** verb 2pl indic pres act
ὅτι	ἐκ	τοῦ	θεοῦ	οὐκ	ἐστέ.
hoti	*ek*	*tou*	*theou*	*ouk*	*este*
because	of		God	not	you are.

48.a.**Txt:** 017K,036,037, byz.
Var: 01א,03B,04C,05D, 019L,038,sa.bo.Gries Lach,Treg,Alf,Tisc, We/Ho,Weis,Sod,UBS/☆

48.b.**Txt:** 017K,019L, 036,037,byz.Gries,Word, Sod
Var: 01א,03B,04C,05D, 038,33,Lach,Treg,Alf, Tisc,We/HoWeis,UBS/☆

552.8 verb 3pl indic aor pass	**3631.1** conj	**3450.7** art pl masc	**2428.2** name-adj pl masc	**2504.1** conj
48. Ἀπεκρίθησαν	(a οὖν)	οἱ	Ἰουδαῖοι	καὶ
Apekrithēsan	*oun*	*hoi*	*Ioudaioi*	*kai*
Answered	therefore	the	Jews	and

1500.3 verb indic aor act	**1500.28** verb 3pl indic aor act	**840.4** prs-pron dat sing	**3620.3** partic	**2544.1** adv	**2978.6** verb 1pl indic pres act
(εἶπον	[b☆ εἶπαν]	αὐτῷ,	Οὐ	καλῶς	λέγομεν
eipon	*eipan*	*autō*	*Ou*	*kalōs*	*legomen*
said	[idem]	to him,	Not	well	say

2231.1 prs-pron nom 1pl	**3617.1** conj	**4398.1** name nom sing masc	**4398.5** name nom sing masc	**1498.3** verb 2sing indic pres act
ἡμεῖς	ὅτι	(Σαμαρείτης	[☆ Σαμαρίτης]	εἶ
hēmeis	*hoti*	*Samareitēs*	*Samaritēs*	*ei*
we	that	a Samaritan	[idem]	are

4622.1 prs-pron nom 2sing	**2504.1** conj	**1134.1** noun sing neu	**2174.3** verb 2sing indic pres act	**552.6** verb 3sing indic aor pass
σὺ,	καὶ	δαιμόνιον	ἔχεις;	**49.** Ἀπεκρίθη
su	*kai*	*daimonion*	*echeis*	*Apekrithē*
you,	and	a demon	have?	Answered

2400.1 name nom masc	**1466.1** prs-pron nom 1sing	**1134.1** noun sing neu	**3620.2** partic	**2174.1** verb 1sing pres act	**233.2** conj
Ἰησοῦς,	Ἐγὼ	δαιμόνιον	οὐκ	ἔχω,	ἀλλὰ
Iēsous	*Egō*	*daimonion*	*ouk*	*echō*	*alla*
Jesus,	I	a demon	not	have;	but

4939.2 verb 1sing indic pres act	**3450.6** art acc sing masc	**3824.4** noun acc sing masc	**1466.2** prs-pron gen 1sing	**2504.1** conj	**5050.1** prs-pron nom 2pl
τιμῶ	τὸν	πατέρα	μου,	καὶ	ὑμεῖς
timō	*ton*	*patera*	*mou*	*kai*	*humeis*
I honor	the	Father	my,	and	you

tles (Acts 20:18-20) of the New Testament often validated their message by their righteous conduct. If a person's life is unrighteous, who will believe him? The truth is given credence by a godly life.

Furthermore, Jesus pointed out how that He was totally unlike them. He had shown them the positive and negative aspects of their parentage. Jesus asked them to find any flaw in His nature or prove any sin of His person. The fact that the Jews were unable to point to any sin in Jesus should have proved to them His true identity. Moreover, based on knowing a person's origin by his fruits, Jesus revealed His relationship with the Holy Father. Hereby, Jesus established the credibility of His testimony. They should have believed the evidence which pointed to His credentials.

8:47. The one who is "of God" (*tou theou*) lives from the Source of life. Peter said in 6:68, "Thou hast the words of eternal life." Using the figure of living water, Jesus made a parallel statement to the Samaritan woman by saying, "Whosoever drinketh of the water that I shall give him shall never thirst" (4:14). Life for the believer is in vital union with the Source of life through the means of life. The means of grace is "the words of God" (*ta rhēmata tou theou*). The Old Testament made it plain that man's life is dependent on the Word of God. Deuteronomy 8:3 assures man that "Man lives by everything that proceeds out of the mouth of the Lord" (NASB). These Jews were living on the carnal bread of this world. They had not discovered God's words as the source of life. Thus Jesus declared, "For this reason you do not hear them, because you are not of God" (NASB).

Children listen to their own parents like sheep hear and obey their shepherd. The Jews listened to their father who is a murderer and a liar. They did as their father does. If they were God's children they would listen and obey God.

8:48. The Jews retorted with the bitter lash of personal ridicule. Instead of staying on the subject, they resorted to degrading Jesus. They indicated that they had and were at that time calling Him a Samaritan, and furthermore, that He was possessed of a demon. For a Jew the worst name they could think of was "Samaritan." Samaritans were half Jew and half Gentile and thus considered illegitimate. To have a demon was to be possessed by a wicked spirit.

8:49. The Lord continued to assert His intimate relationship to His Father, and He continued to proclaim the life-producing power

And if I say the truth, why do ye not believe me?: Why then, if I am speaking the truth, *Montgomery* . . . If I say what is true, why have you no belief in me, *BB* . . . why do you refuse to believe? *ALBA.*

47. He that is of God heareth God's words: Every child of God, *Norlie* . . . He who comes from God listens to God's teaching, *TCNT* . . . Only he who is a child of God listens, *Weymouth* . . . Whoever is attracted by God, *Fenton.*

ye therefore hear them not: . . . you do not listen to them, *Moffatt* . . . You don't give ear to His Word, *Norlie* . . . On this account you are not hearing them, *Wuest.*

because ye are not of God: . . . because you do not belong to God, *Moffatt* . . . because you are not His children, *Norlie* . . . because you are not in harmony with, *Fenton.*

48. Then answered the Jews, and said unto him, Say we not well that thou art a Samaritan, and hast a devil?: Are we not right in saying...and are under the power of a demon? *Williams* . . . Were we not correct in saying, *Fenton* . . . that you are a foreign heretic, *ALBA* . . . and are possessed? *TCNT* . . . you have an evil spirit? *Norlie.*

49. Jesus answered, I have not a devil: I am not possessed by a demon, *Weymouth* . . . There's no devil in Me, *Beck* . . . I have not an evil spirit, *BB* . . . far from being possessed, *ALBA.*

but I honour my Father, and ye do dishonour me: . . . but I am showing reverence for, *TCNT* . . . and you are trying to dishonor me, *Phillips.*

812.2 verb 2pl indic pres act	**1466.6** prs-pron acc 1sing	**1466.1** prs-pron nom 1sing	**1156.2** conj	**3620.3** partic	**2195.3** verb 1sing indic pres act
ἀτιμάζετέ	με.	**50.** ἐγὼ	δὲ	οὐ	ζητῶ
atimazete	*me*	*egō*	*de*	*ou*	*zētō*
dishonor	me.	I	but	not	seek

3450.12 art acc sing fem	**1385.4** noun acc sing fem	**1466.2** prs-pron gen 1sing	**1498.4** verb 3sing indic pres act	**3450.5** art sing masc	**2195.8** verb nom sing masc part pres act
τὴν	δόξαν	μου·	ἔστιν	ὁ	ζητῶν
tēn	*doxan*	*mou*	*estin*	*ho*	*zētōn*
the	glory	my:	there is	the	seeking

2504.1 conj	**2892.8** verb sing masc part pres act	**279.1** partic	**279.1** partic	**2978.1** verb 1sing pres act	**5050.3** prs-pron dat 2pl	**1430.1** partic
καὶ	κρίνων.	**51.** ἀμὴν	ἀμὴν	λέγω	ὑμῖν,	ἐάν
kai	*krinōn*	*amēn*	*amēn*	*legō*	*humin*	*ean*
and	judging.	Truly	truly	I say	to you,	If

51.a.**Txt:** p66,017K,036,037,038,1,13,byz.it.Gries
Var: 01ℵ,03B,04C,05D,019L,033X,33,Lach,TregAlf,Tisc,We/Ho,Weis,Sod,UBS/☆

4948.3 indef-pron nom sing	**3450.6** art acc sing masc	**3030.4** noun acc sing masc	**3450.6** art acc sing masc	**1684.1** adj 1sing	**1684.1** adj 1sing
τις	τὸν	ʻ λόγον	τὸν	ἐμὸν	[a☆ ἐμὸν
tis	*ton*	*logon*	*ton*	*emon*	*emon*
anyone	the	word	the	my	[my

3030.4 noun acc sing masc	**4931.16** verb 3sing subj aor act	**2265.4** noun acc sing masc	**3620.3** partic	**3231.1** partic	**2311.17** verb 3sing subj aor act
λόγον]	τηρήσῃ,	θάνατον	οὐ	μὴ	θεωρήσῃ
logon	*tērēsē*	*thanaton*	*ou*	*mē*	*theōrēsē*
word]	keep,	death	not	not	shall he see

52.a.**Txt:** 03B,04C,017K,019L,036,037,byz.Lach,Sod
Var: 01ℵ,05D,038,Tisc,We/HoWeis,UBS/☆

1519.1 prep	**3450.6** art acc sing masc	**163.3** noun acc sing masc	**1500.3** verb indic aor act	**1500.28** verb 3pl indic aor act
εἰς	τὸν	αἰῶνα.	**52.** ʻ☆ Εἶπον	[a εἶπαν]
eis	*ton*	*aiōna*	*Eipon*	*eipan*
unto	the	age.	Said	[idem]

52.b.**Txt:** p75,05D,017K,019L,036,037,1,13,byz.
Var: 01ℵ,03B,04C,038,Lach,Treg,Alf,Tisc,We/HoWeis,Sod,UBS/☆

3631.1 conj	**840.4** prs-pron dat sing	**3450.7** art pl masc	**2428.2** name-adj pl masc	**3431.1** adv	**1091.33** verb 1pl indic perf act
ʻb οὖν ˋ	αὐτῷ	οἱ	Ἰουδαῖοι,	Νῦν	ἐγνώκαμεν
oun	*autō*	*hoi*	*Ioudaioi*	*Nun*	*egnōkamen*
therefore	to him	the	Jews,	Now	we know

3617.1 conj	**1134.1** noun sing neu	**2174.3** verb 2sing indic pres act	**11.1** name masc	**594.10** verb 3sing indic aor act	**2504.1** conj
ὅτι	δαιμόνιον	ἔχεις.	Ἀβραὰμ	ἀπέθανεν	καὶ
hoti	*daimonion*	*echeis*	*Abraam*	*apethanen*	*kai*
that	a demon	you have.	Abraham	died	and

3450.7 art pl masc	**4254.4** noun pl masc	**2504.1** conj	**4622.1** prs-pron nom 2sing	**2978.4** verb 2sing indic pres act	**1430.1** partic
οἱ	προφῆται,	καὶ	σὺ	λέγεις,	Ἐάν
hoi	*prophētai*	*kai*	*su*	*legeis*	*Ean*
the	prophets,	and	you	say,	If

4948.3 indef-pron nom sing	**3450.6** art acc sing masc	**3030.4** noun acc sing masc	**1466.2** prs-pron gen 1sing	**4931.16** verb 3sing subj aor act	**3620.3** partic
τις	τὸν	λόγον	μου	τηρήσῃ,	οὐ
tis	*ton*	*logon*	*mou*	*tērēsē*	*ou*
anyone	the	word	my	keep,	not

52.c.**Txt:** 07E,Steph
Var: 01ℵ,02A,04C,05D,017K,019L,036,037,038,byz.Gries,LachTreg,Alf,Tisc,We/Ho,Weis,Sod,UBS/☆

3231.1 partic	**1083.9** verb 3sing indic fut mid	**1083.4** verb 3sing subj aor mid	**2265.2** noun gen sing masc	**1519.1** prep	**3450.6** art acc sing masc
μὴ	ʻ γεύσεται	[c☆ γεύσηται]	θανάτου	εἰς	τὸν
mē	*geusetai*	*geusētai*	*thanatou*	*eis*	*ton*
not	shall he taste	[idem]	of death	unto	the

of His Father's word. Jesus did not reply to their attack of calling Him a Samaritan, but He denied having a demon. Jesus honored His Father by doing His Father's will and teaching His Father's word.

Jesus implied that to dishonor Him is to dishonor His Father (verse 28). Jesus had no man to speak for Him. He stood majestically alone in His arguments with the Jews. The Jews were disrespectful to His person and insulting toward His mission.

50. And I seek not mine own glory: I...am not in search of glory for myself, *BB* . . . I do not, however, strive for reputation for Myself, *Fenton* . . . I am not seeking honor for myself, *Williams* . . . I am not out for My glory, *Berkeley* . . . But I am not concerned with my own glory, *Phillips* . . . Not that I am eager for honour for myself, *TCNT* . . . am not aiming at glory for myself, *Weymouth.*

there is one that seeketh and judgeth: . . . there is one who is seeking my honour, *TCNT* . . . who cares for my credit, *Moffatt* . . . who wants Me to have it, and He's the Judge, *Beck* . . . Who investigates and judges, *Fenton* . . . One who takes care of that, *Berkeley.*

8:50. Certainly He received no glory from the Jews, only dishonor. This fact would not dissuade Him, because He came to glorify the Father, not himself. Jesus was willing to suffer reproach and death that He might honor His Father by carrying out His mission.

The "one" Jesus spoke of is the Father. Jesus was willing to leave His honor safely in the Father's care. In 4:23 Jesus stated that the Father seeks true worshipers. In this verse Jesus said the Father seeks true worshipers and "judges" false worshipers.

51. Verily, verily, I say unto you, If a man keep my saying: . . . if any one keeps my word, *HBIE* . . . anyone who observes My teaching, *Berkeley* . . . lays my Message to heart, *TCNT.*

he shall never see death: . . . he will never behold death, *HBIE* . . . never taste death, *Beck* . . . he will never experience death, *Williams.*

8:51. Death is the penalty for those who do not receive Christ as Saviour. The word of Jesus is that which brings eternal life (6:63). To "see" death is to experience death, just as to see the Kingdom is to experience the Kingdom (3:3). Jesus stated the truth to Martha at her brother's tomb (11:25). "Death" (*thanaton*) is that which happened to Adam when he sinned. God's statement as to the result of disobedience is "for in the day that you eat from it (the tree of the knowledge of good and evil) you shall surely die" (Genesis 2:17, NASB). All men live in a state of death until they believe in Christ and receive eternal life, or when they come to the realization of eternal death at the Great White Throne Judgment (Ephesians 2:15; Romans 5:12; 6:21,23; Revelation 20:11-15).

52. Then said the Jews unto him, Now we know that thou hast a devil: Now we know that you're mad, *Phillips* . . . Now we are sure that you are possessed, *TCNT* . . . that you are under the power of a demon, *Williams.*

Abraham is dead, and the prophets:

and thou sayest, If a man keep my saying, he shall never taste of death: If any one lays my Message to heart, *TCNT* . . . holds fast My message, *Fenton.*

8:52. The Jews were now assured that Jesus had a demon. They continued to explain their reasoning: Abraham and the prophets died (so who does He think He is?), and He says by keeping His word they "shall never taste of death." The Jews saw in this statement that Jesus claimed to be far superior to Abraham and the prophets. They died having and keeping the word of God. The Jews believed He was saying that His word was superior to God's word and that He was preeminently above the prophets and Abraham. The Jews substituted the word "taste" for His word "see." The two words are essentially the same. They took His statement on death to mean bodily death. (Physical death is only a part of

John 8:53

163.3 noun acc sing masc	53. 3231.1 partic	4622.1 prs-pron nom 2sing	3157.2 adj comp nom sing	1498.3 verb 2sing indic pres act	3450.2 art gen sing
αἰῶνα.	53. μὴ	σὺ	μείζων	εἶ	τοῦ
aiōna	*mē*	*su*	*meizōn*	*ei*	*tou*
age.	Not	you	greater	are	the

3824.2 noun gen sing masc	2231.2 prs-pron gen 1pl	11.1 name masc	3610.1 rel-pron nom sing masc	594.10 verb 3sing indic aor act	2504.1 conj
πατρὸς	ἡμῶν	Ἀβραάμ,	ὅστις	ἀπέθανεν;	καὶ
patros	*hēmōn*	*Abraam*	*hostis*	*apethanen*	*kai*
father	our	Abraham,	who	died?	and

53.a.**Txt:** 07E,021M, 030U,byz.
Var: 01ℵ,02A,03B,04C, 05D,017K,019L,036, 037,038,it.sa.bo.Gries, Lach,Treg,Alf,Tisc, We/Ho,Weis,Sod,UBS/⋆

3450.7 art pl masc	4254.4 noun pl masc	594.9 verb indic aor act	4949.1 intr-pron	4427.4 prs-pron acc 2sing masc	4622.1 prs-pron nom 2sing
οἱ	προφῆται	ἀπέθανον·	τίνα	σεαυτὸν	⸂a σὺ ⸃
hoi	*prophētai*	*apethanon*	*tina*	*seauton*	*su*
the	prophets	died!	whom	yourself	you

4020.4 verb 2sing indic pres act	54. 552.6 verb 3sing indic aor pass	2400.1 name nom masc	1430.1 partic	1466.1 prs-pron nom 1sing
ποιεῖς;	54. Ἀπεκρίθη	Ἰησοῦς,	Ἐὰν	ἐγὼ
poieis	*Apekrithē*	*Iēsous*	*Ean*	*egō*
make?	Answered	Jesus,	If	I

54.a.**Txt:** 01ℵ-corr, 04C-corr,017K,019L, 036,037,byz.
Var: 01ℵ-org,03B, 04C-org,05D,038,Lach, Treg,Alf,Tisc,We/HoSod, UBS/⋆

1386.1 verb 1sing indic pres act	1386.7 verb 1sing act	1670.3 prs-pron acc 1sing masc	3450.9 art nom sing fem	1385.1 noun nom sing fem
⸀ δοξάζω	[a⋆ δοξάσω]	ἐμαυτόν,	ἡ	δόξα
doxazō	*doxasō*	*emauton*	*hē*	*doxa*
glorify	[will glorify]	myself,	the	glory

1466.2 prs-pron gen 1sing	3625.6 num card neu	1498.4 verb 3sing indic pres act	1498.4 verb 3sing indic pres act	3450.5 art sing masc	3824.1 noun nom sing masc
μου	οὐδέν	ἐστιν·	ἔστιν	ὁ	πατήρ
mou	*ouden*	*estin*	*estin*	*ho*	*patēr*
my	nothing	is;	it is	the	Father

1466.2 prs-pron gen 1sing	3450.5 art sing masc	1386.4 verb nom sing masc part pres act	1466.6 prs-pron acc 1sing	3614.6 rel-pron acc sing masc	5050.1 prs-pron nom 2pl
μου	ὁ	δοξάζων	με,	ὃν	ὑμεῖς
mou	*ho*	*doxazōn*	*me*	*hon*	*humeis*
my	the	glorifying	me,	whom	you

54.b.**Txt:** p66-org,01ℵ, 03B-org,05D,700,lect.it. Steph,Lach,We/Ho,Sod
Var: p66-corr,p75,02A, 03B-corr,04C,017K, 019L,032W,036,037, 038,1,13,byz.sa.bo.Treg, Alf,Tisc,Weis,UBS/⋆

2978.2 verb 2pl pres act	3617.1 conj	2296.1 noun nom sing masc	5050.2 prs-pron gen 2pl	2231.2 prs-pron gen 1pl	1498.4 verb 3sing indic pres act
λέγετε,	ὅτι	θεὸς	⸀ ὑμῶν	[b⋆ ἡμῶν]	ἐστιν,
legete	*hoti*	*theos*	*humōn*	*hēmōn*	*estin*
say,	that	God	our	[your]	he is.

55. 2504.1 conj	3620.2 partic	1091.34 verb 2pl indic perf act	840.6 prs-pron acc sing masc	1466.1 prs-pron nom 1sing	1156.2 conj
55. καὶ	οὐκ	ἐγνώκατε	αὐτόν,	ἐγὼ	δὲ
kai	*ouk*	*egnōkate*	*auton*	*egō*	*de*
And	not	you have known	him,	I	but

55.a.**Txt:** p66,02A,04C, 017K,019L,036,037,038, byz.Sod
Var: p75,01ℵ,03B,05D, 032W,Lach,Treg,Tisc, We/Ho,Weis,UBS/⋆

3471.2 verb 1sing indic perf act	840.6 prs-pron acc sing masc	2504.1 conj	1430.1 partic	2550.1 conj	1500.6 verb 1sing subj aor act
οἶδα	αὐτόν·	⸀ καὶ	ἐὰν	[a⋆ κἂν]	εἴπω
oida	*auton*	*kai*	*ean*	*kan*	*eipō*
know	him;	and	if	[and if]	I say

3617.1 conj	3620.2 partic	3471.2 verb 1sing indic perf act	840.6 prs-pron acc sing masc	1498.38 verb 1sing indic fut mid	3527.2 adj nom sing masc
ὅτι	οὐκ	οἶδα	αὐτόν,	ἔσομαι	ὅμοιος
hoti	*ouk*	*oida*	*auton*	*esomai*	*homoios*
that	not	I know	him,	I shall be	like

the wide concept of death.) Their conclusion was that He had a demon (*daimonion*).

53. Art thou greater than our father Abraham, which is dead? and the prophets are dead: . . . our father Abraham? He died, and the prophets died, *Norlie.*

whom makest thou thyself?: Who are you making yourself out to be, *Montgomery* . . . Who do you think you are? *ALBA, Norlie.*

8:53. Abraham was the founder of their race. To be greater than Abraham was unthinkable. The prophets were the reformers who interpreted and preached the Law, thus preserving the nation. These all died, as great as they were. In chapter 4 the Samaritan woman asked Jesus if He was greater than Jacob. The Jews now asked if He thought He was greater than Abraham and the prophets. They meant to show contempt and to scorn Him for such a statement, little aware that their Creator and Sustainer stood before them. How dared they presume upon His longsuffering toward them! Had they only heard, but they were deaf. Had they merely seen, but they were blind. Had they but known; alas they were dull. They might have heard; they could have seen; they would have known. The sound of heaven's voice was speaking. The light of the eternal city was beaming. The truth from the celestial environment pervaded the scene. How could they stop their ears, close their eyes, and allow insane jealousy to block their reason!

54. Jesus answered, If I honoured myself, my honour is nothing: If I glorify myself, my glory is nothing, *Alford* . . . glorify Myself, My glory would count nothing, *Norlie* . . . If I commend myself, my commendation, *Campbell* . . . If I magnify myself, my credit is a mere nothing, *HistNT* . . . Yf I prayse my silfe, *Tyndale* . . . If self-glory were my ambition, *ALBA* . . . such glory amounts to nothing, *Williams* . . . would be worthless, *Berkeley.*

it is my Father that honoureth me: . . . it is my Father who gives me glory, *BB* . . . There is One who glorifies me—namely my Father, *Weymouth* . . . My Father Who is praising Me, *Fenton.*

of whom ye say, that he is your God: . . . the very one who you say is your God, *Phillips* . . . whom you call "our God," *Berkeley.*

8:54. In verse 53 we see the Jews reproaching Jesus for claiming to be superior to Abraham and the prophets. In this verse we see Jesus defending His statement by calling attention to the glory bestowed on Him by the Father. He denied He was glorifying Himself. The Father glorified Jesus by granting the miracles He performed (see 12:28).

The Jews had no evidence that they were the offspring of Abraham. They did not do the works of Abraham (see verses 37,39). Jesus implied here that if they were God's children, they would love Him (verse 42), and their works would indicate that the source of their life was from God. Unlike His claim which was proven by His works, their claim of being God's children had no evidence to substantiate it (James 2:17). What they said in words was not validated by their actions. They acted like children of Satan and professed to be children of the Heavenly Father. They did not honor God by the way they lived.

55. Yet ye have not known him; but I know him: And yet ye have not come to know him, *Rotherham* . . . You have never come to know Him, *Norlie.*

and if I should say, I know him not: Were I to say, I do not know him, *Montgomery.*

I shall be a liar like unto you: . . . I would be a liar like yourselves, *Moffatt* . . . a prevaricator like yourselves, *Berkeley.*

8:55. The Jews had not made God's acquaintance. God is a person, and nothing short of a personal knowledge of Him is sufficient. The enemies of Jesus knew about God, but they did not know Him.

"But I know him" testifies to a personal, intimate knowledge. The "I" means "I myself" which emphasizes "I" in contrast to them ("you").

"And if I should say, I know him not" asserts a possible statement, though He did not say such a thing. "If I say" parallels "I shall be"

John 8:56

55.b.**Txt:** (p66),01ℵ,04C,017K,019L,036,037,byz.Tisc,Sod
Var: p75,02A,03B,05D,032W,038,1,Lach,Treg,We/HoWeis,UBS/⋆

5050.2 prs-pron gen 2pl	**5050.3** prs-pron dat 2pl	**5418.1** noun nom sing masc	**233.1** conj	**233.2** conj
⸂ ὑμῶν,	[b⋆ ὑμῖν]	ψεύστης·	⸂ ἀλλ'	[⋆ ἀλλὰ]
humōn	*humin*	*pseustēs*	*all'*	*alla*
you,	[idem]	a liar.	But	[idem]

3471.2 verb 1sing indic perf act	**840.6** prs-pron acc sing masc	**2504.1** conj	**3450.6** art acc sing masc	**3030.4** noun acc sing masc	**840.3** prs-pron gen sing
οἶδα	αὐτὸν,	καὶ	τὸν	λόγον	αὐτοῦ
oida	*auton*	*kai*	*ton*	*logon*	*autou*
I know	him,	and	the	word	his

4931.1 verb 1sing indic pres act	**11.1** name masc	**3450.5** art sing masc	**3824.1** noun nom sing masc	**5050.2** prs-pron gen 2pl
τηρῶ.	**56.** Ἀβραὰμ	ὁ	πατὴρ	ὑμῶν
tērō	*Abraam*	*ho*	*patēr*	*humōn*
I keep.	Abraham	the	Father	your

56.a.**Var:** 01ℵ,02A,03B-org,05D-corr,032W,033X,Tisc

21.6 verb 3sing indic aor mid	**2419.1** conj	**1481.10** verb 3sing subj aor act	**3471.27** verb 3sing subj perf act	**3450.12** art acc sing fem
ἠγαλλιάσατο	ἵνα	⸂ ἴδῃ	[a εἴδῃ]	τὴν
ēgalliasato	*hina*	*idē*	*eidē*	*tēn*
rejoiced	in that	he should see	[idem]	the

2232.4 noun acc sing fem	**3450.12** art acc sing fem	**1684.9** adj acc 1sing fem	**2504.1** conj	**1481.3** verb 3sing indic aor act	**2504.1** conj
ἡμέραν	τὴν	ἐμήν·	καὶ	εἶδεν	καὶ
hēmeran	*tēn*	*emēn*	*kai*	*eiden*	*kai*
day	the	my,	and	he saw	and

57.a.**Txt:** 02A,03B,04C,017K,019L,036,037,byz.Lach,Sod
Var: 01ℵ,05D,038,Tisc,We/HoWeis,UBS/⋆

5299.16 verb 3sing indic aor pass	**1500.3** verb indic aor act	**1500.28** verb 3pl indic aor act	**3631.1** conj	**3450.7** art pl masc
ἐχάρη.	**57.** ⸂⋆ Εἶπον	[a εἶπαν]	οὖν	οἱ
echarē	*Eipon*	*eipan*	*oun*	*hoi*
rejoiced.	Said	[idem]	therefore	the

2428.2 name-adj pl masc	**4242.1** prep	**840.6** prs-pron acc sing masc	**3866.1** num card	**2073.3** noun pl neu	**3632.1** adv
Ἰουδαῖοι	πρὸς	αὐτόν,	Πεντήκοντα	ἔτη	οὔπω
Ioudaioi	*pros*	*auton*	*Pentēkonta*	*etē*	*oupō*
Jews	to	him,	Fifty	years	not yet

2174.3 verb 2sing indic pres act	**2504.1** conj	**11.1** name masc	**3571.10** verb 2sing indic perf act	**1500.5** verb 3sing indic aor act
ἔχεις,	καὶ	Ἀβραὰμ	ἑώρακας;	**58.** Εἶπεν
echeis	*kai*	*Abraam*	*heōrakas*	*Eipen*
are you,	and	Abraham	have you seen?	Said

58.a.**Txt:** p66,01ℵ,02A,05D,017K,019L,036,037,038,byz.Lach,Weis,Sod
Var: p75,03B,04C,Treg,Tisc,We/Ho,UBS/⋆

840.2 prs-pron dat pl	**3450.5** art sing masc	**2400.1** name nom masc	**279.1** partic	**279.1** partic	**2978.1** verb 1sing pres act
αὐτοῖς	⸂a ὁ ⸃	Ἰησοῦς,	Ἀμὴν	ἀμὴν	λέγω
autois	*ho*	*Iēsous*	*Amēn*	*amēn*	*legō*
to them		Jesus,	Truly	truly	I say

5050.3 prs-pron dat 2pl	**4109.1** adv	**11.1** name masc	**1090.63** verb inf aor mid	**1466.1** prs-pron nom 1sing	**1498.2** verb 1sing indic pres act
ὑμῖν,	πρὶν	Ἀβραὰμ	γενέσθαι	ἐγὼ	εἰμί.
humin	*prin*	*Abraam*	*genesthai*	*egō*	*eimi*
to you,	Before	Abraham	was	I	am.

142.10 verb 3pl indic aor act	**3631.1** conj	**3012.8** noun acc pl masc	**2419.1** conj	**900.15** verb 3pl subj aor act	**1894.2** prep
59. Ἦραν	οὖν	λίθους	ἵνα	βάλωσιν	ἐπ'
Eran	*oun*	*lithous*	*hina*	*balōsin*	*ep'*
They took up	therefore	stones	that	they might cast	at

of the next clause. "A liar" (*pseustēs*) occurs twice in this Gospel, 8:44 and here, and eight other times in the New Testament. The word denotes one who is false. Thus the word is close to the idea of a deceiver.

Jesus repeated, "But I know Him." In the first statement Jesus used the Greek (*de*) for "but"; this time He made the assertion stronger by using the Greek conjunction *alla* for "but." "And keep his saying" is proof that Jesus had an intimate and personal knowledge of the Father.

but I know him, and keep his saying: On the contrary, *Norlie* . . . but I have full knowledge of him, *BB* . . . and retain His message, *Fenton* . . . I do follow His teaching, *Williams.*

8:56. "Rejoiced" (*ēgalliasato*) appears 11 times in the New Testament. The same verb is used one other time in John (5:35). "Rejoice" is the usual rendering, yet the translation is sometimes "glad," or "exceeding joy." Jesus' words indicated that Abraham rejoiced even at the prospect of seeing Jesus' day. "My day" (*tēn hēmeran tēnemēn*) places the emphasis on "my." "My day" is the grand and glorious day of Messiah. This was the very time the Jews were witnessing but rebelling against. The phrase "He saw it" refers to the atoning work Jesus was to accomplish at Calvary.

Abraham saw Him by faith in God's word, and in a shadowy type. The Jews saw Him in the flesh. They mocked, but Abraham rejoiced.

56. Your father Abraham rejoiced to see my day: . . . exulted that he should see, *Rotherham* . . . exulted in the hope of seeing, *Williams* . . . was extremely happy in the prospect of seeing, *Berkeley* . . . ardently desired, *Wilson* . . . rejoiced at the thought, *Norlie* . . . was delighted to know of My day, *Beck.*

and he saw it, and was glad: . . . and was delighted, *Fenton.*

8:57. Why did they say 50 years when Jesus was only 33 years old? It is noteworthy that the ministers in the tabernacle ceased to minister at age 50 (Numbers 4:3; 8:25). Important matters were left to the elders; thus it might have been an implication that Jesus was not old enough to counsel them.

57. Then said the Jews unto him, Thou art not yet fifty years old: The Jews protested, *NEB* . . . you are not even fifty years old, *Norlie.*

and hast thou seen Abraham?:

8:58. "Verily, verily, I say unto you" (see comments on verse 51). "Was born" (NASB; *genesthai*) is an aorist verb marking a historical point in time. Jesus was saying that before Abraham's existence He himself was existing. However, "I am" means much more than that because He was less than 50 years old. He as a person exists in the ever present now no matter at what point on the time line one may identify. His statement about Abraham could be made about any man or being (1:1,30).

58. Jesus said unto them, Verily, verily, I say unto you, Before Abraham was, I am: Truly, I tell you, truly, *HistNT* . . . I most solemnly say to you, *Williams* . . . Before Abraham was born, I am, *ASV* . . . before there was an Abraham, I AM! *Phillips* . . . before Abraham existed, *Murdock* . . . came into existence, *Rotherham* . . . became, I am, *Panin* . . . I was alive before Abraham was born! *SEB.*

8:59. They regarded His words as blasphemy. The blasphemer was to be stoned until He died. The one who blasphemed was to be proven wrong. Their mistake was that they attempted to stone him without a trial.

59. Then took they up stones to cast at him: but Jesus hid himself, and went out of the temple: . . . to hurl at Him; but Jesus became invisible, *Fenton* . . . Jesus

John 9:1

840.6 prs-pron acc sing masc	2400.1 name nom masc	1156.2 conj	2900.5 verb 3sing indic aor pass	2504.1 conj	1814.3 verb 3sing indic aor act	1523.2 prep gen
αὐτόν·	Ἰησοῦς	δὲ	ἐκρύβη,	καὶ	ἐξῆλθεν	ἐκ
auton	*Iēsous*	*de*	*ekrubē*	*kai*	*exēlthen*	*ek*
him;	Jesus	but	hid himself,	and	went forth	out of

59.a.**Txt:** 02A,017K,037, 038-corr,1,13,28,565, 700,byz.lect.Lach
Var: p66,p75,01ℵ-org, 03B,05D,032W,038-org, it.sa.Gries,Treg,Alf,Tisc, We/Ho,WeisSod,UBS/☆

3450.2 art gen sing	2387.1 adj gen sing neu	1324.5 verb nom sing masc part aor act	1217.2 prep	3189.4 adj gen sing neu	840.1 prs-pron gen pl
τοῦ	ἱεροῦ,	⸂a διελθὼν	διὰ	μέσου	αὐτῶν·
tou	*hierou*	*dielthōn*	*dia*	*mesou*	*autōn*
the	temple,	going	through	the midst	of them,

2504.1 conj	3717.5 verb 3sing indic imperf act	3643.1 adv		2504.1 conj	3717.2 verb nom sing masc part pres act	1481.3 verb 3sing indic aor act
καὶ	παρῆγεν	οὕτως. ⸃	9:1.	Καὶ	παράγων	εἶδεν
kai	*parēgen*	*houtōs*		*Kai*	*paragōn*	*eiden*
and	passed on	thus.		And	passing on	he saw

442.4 noun acc sing masc	5026.4 adj acc sing masc	1523.2 prep gen	1072.1 noun gen sing fem		2504.1 conj	2049.10 verb 3pl indic aor act
ἄνθρωπον	τυφλὸν	ἐκ	γενετῆς.	2.	καὶ	ἠρώτησαν
anthrōpon	*tuphlon*	*ek*	*genetēs*		*kai*	*ērōtēsan*
a man	blind	from	birth.		And	asked

840.6 prs-pron acc sing masc	3450.7 art pl masc	3073.5 noun nom pl masc	840.3 prs-pron gen sing	2978.16 verb pl masc part pres act	4318.1 noun sing masc
αὐτὸν	οἱ	μαθηταὶ	αὐτοῦ	λέγοντες,	Ῥαββί,
auton	*hoi*	*mathētai*	*autou*	*legontes*	*Rhabbi*
him	the	disciples	his	saying,	Rabbi,

4949.3 intr-pron nom sing	262.13 verb 3sing indic aor act	3642.4 dem-pron nom sing masc	2211.1 conj	3450.7 art pl masc	1112.1 noun pl masc
τίς	ἥμαρτεν,	οὗτος	ἢ	οἱ	γονεῖς
tis	*hēmarten*	*houtos*	*ē*	*hoi*	*goneis*
who	sinned,	this	or	the	parents

840.3 prs-pron gen sing	2419.1 conj	5026.1 adj nom sing masc	1074.16 verb 3sing subj aor pass		552.6 verb 3sing indic aor pass
αὐτοῦ,	ἵνα	τυφλὸς	γεννηθῇ;	3.	Ἀπεκρίθη
autou	*hina*	*tuphlos*	*gennēthē*		*Apekrithē*
his,	that	blind	he should be born?		Answered

3.a.**Txt:** 05D,038, 041-corr,Steph
Var: 01ℵ,02A,03B,04C, 017K,019L,036,037, 041-org,etc.byz.Gries, Lach,Treg,Alf,Tisc, We/HoWeis,Sod,UBS/☆

3450.5 art sing masc	2400.1 name nom masc	3641.1 conj	3642.4 dem-pron nom sing masc	262.13 verb 3sing indic aor act	3641.1 conj
⸂a ὁ ⸃	Ἰησοῦς,	Οὔτε	οὗτος	ἥμαρτεν	οὔτε
ho	*Iēsous*	*Oute*	*houtos*	*hēmarten*	*oute*
	Jesus,	Neither	this	sinned	nor

3450.7 art pl masc	1112.1 noun pl masc	840.3 prs-pron gen sing	233.1 conj	2419.1 conj	5157.12 verb 3sing subj aor pass
οἱ	γονεῖς	αὐτοῦ	ἀλλ'	ἵνα	φανερωθῇ
hoi	*goneis*	*autou*	*all'*	*hina*	*phanerōthē*
the	parents	his;	but	that	should be manifested

3450.17 art pl neu	2024.4 noun pl neu	3450.2 art gen sing	2296.2 noun gen sing masc	1706.1 prep	840.4 prs-pron dat sing
τὰ	ἔργα	τοῦ	θεοῦ	ἐν	αὐτῷ.
ta	*erga*	*tou*	*theou*	*en*	*autō*
the	works		of God	in	him.

4.a.**Txt:** 01ℵ-corr,02A, 04C,017K,036,037,038, 1,13,33,byz.it.Gries, Lach
Var: p66,p75,01ℵ-org, 03B,05D,019L,032W,sa. Treg,Tisc,We/Ho,Weis, Sod,UBS/☆

	1466.7 prs-pron acc 1sing	2231.4 prs-pron acc 1pl	1158.1 verb 3sing indic pres act	2021.12 verb inf pres	3450.17 art pl neu
4.	⸂ ἐμὲ	[a☆ ἡμᾶς]	δεῖ	ἐργάζεσθαι	τὰ
	eme	*hēmas*	*dei*	*ergazesthai*	*ta*
	Me	[Us]	it is necessary	to work	the

"Hid" (*ekrubē*) is an aorist passive indicating He was hidden from the Jew's view. This meant He went along with the crowd, and the Jews could not see Him.

concealed himself, *Moffatt* . . . but Jesus disappeared, *Phillips* . . . got under cover, *Berkeley* . . . was concealed, *Rotherham*.

going through the midst of them, and so passed by: . . . unperceived, *Williams* . . . and left the temple grounds, *Adams* . . . and escaped from the temple, *Norlie*.

9:1. "And as Jesus passed by" may indicate that the healing of the blind man took place on the same Sabbath as the attempt to stone Jesus; however, the last verse of chapter 8 states that He "went out of the temple." The fact that the man had been blind "from his birth" is important to the narrative on two counts: (1) because of the doctrinal discussion prior to the man's healing, and (2) the man having been born blind makes the miracle more notable.

1. And as Jesus passed by: And when he went on his way, *BB* . . . was walking along the street, *Barclay* . . . As He was going along, *Fenton* . . . As He walked along, *Berkeley*.

he saw a man which was blind from his birth: He observed, *Fenton* . . . noticed a man, *TCNT* . . . whose blindness originated from his birth, *Wuest*.

9:2. The disciples' question assumed that some personal sin had caused the man's blindness. Had the blindness come to the man after birth the disciples would have no problem; but because he had been born blind, they had a theological dilemma. Personal sin often brings immediate consequences, but not always. The penalty for personal sin may not be forthcoming until the judgment day. The question the disciples asked was, Is sin by a fetus possible? and if not, did the parents' sin cause the man to be born blind?

2. And his disciples asked him, saying, Master, who did sin, this man, or his parents, that he was born blind?: Master, whose sin caused this man's blindness,...his own or his parents, *Phillips* . . . for whose sin was, *Williams* . . . in consequence of which he was born blind? *Fenton* . . . with the result that he was born blind? *Wuest*.

9:3. We must not take this to mean that neither the man nor his parents had sinned, but that their sin had not caused the man to be born blind. Obviously all men have sinned (Romans 3:23). Jesus denied that any particular sin had brought about this blindness. Many times specific sin does cause disease. As elders pray for the sick James said, "If he have committed sins, they shall be forgiven him. Confess your faults one to another, and pray one for another, that ye may be healed" (James 5:15,16).

However, some maladies come to man because sickness is common to all men, since all men inherit the consequences of man's original sin (Romans 5:12). We must not say that a great sufferer is a great sinner nor that his parents are responsible for his condition.

The Greek *phanerōthē* is usually translated "manifest." This verb is an aorist subjunctive suggesting a future result, not the reason for the man's blindness. The mercy and grace bestowed on the blind man is far more important than the cause of the disease.

3. Jesus answered, Neither hath this man sinned, nor his parents: . . . neither for his own sin, *Williams* . . . There was no sin, *ALBA*.

but that the works of God should be made manifest in him: . . . but to show what God could do in his case, *Williams* . . . It was to let God's work be shown plainly in him, *Norlie* . . . but to show the power of God at work in him, *Phillips* . . . what God is doing might be exhibited in his case, *TCNT* . . . in order that the workings of God may be displayed through him, *Fenton* . . . be displayed upon him, *Campbell* . . . might be seen openly in him, *BB*.

9:4. "We must work" is the reading of the better manuscripts (not "I must work" as the KJV has it). Jesus associated His work

4.b.**Var:** p66,p75, 01ℵ-org,019L,032W,Tisc

2024.4 noun pl neu	**3450.2** art gen sing	**3854.12** verb gen sing masc part aor act	**1466.6** prs-pron acc 1sing	**2231.4** prs-pron acc 1pl	**2175.1** conj
ἔργα	τοῦ	πέμψαντός	ʻ με	[b ἡμᾶς]	ἕως
erga	*tou*	*pempsantos*	*me*	*hēmas*	*heōs*
works	of the	having sent	me	[us]	while

2232.2 noun nom sing fem	**1498.4** verb 3sing indic pres act	**2048.34** verb 3sing indic pres	**3433.1** noun nom sing fem	**3616.1** conj	**3625.2** num card nom masc
ἡμέρα	ἐστίν·	ἔρχεται	νὺξ,	ὅτε	οὐδεὶς
hēmera	*estin*	*erchetai*	*nux*	*hote*	*oudeis*
day	it is;	comes	night,	when	no one

1404.4 verb 3sing indic pres	**2021.12** verb inf pres	**3615.1** conj	**1706.1** prep	**3450.3** art dat sing	**2862.3** noun dat sing masc
δύναται	ἐργάζεσθαι.	5. ὅταν	ἐν	τῷ	κόσμῳ
dunatai	*ergazesthai*	*hotan*	*en*	*tō*	*kosmō*
is able	to work.	While	in	the	world

1498.8 verb 1sing subj pres act	**5295.1** noun sing neu	**1498.2** verb 1sing indic pres act	**3450.2** art gen sing	**2862.2** noun gen sing masc
ὦ,	φῶς	εἰμι	τοῦ	κόσμου.
ō	*phōs*	*eimi*	*tou*	*kosmou*
I may be,	light	I am	of the	world.

3642.18 dem-pron pl neu	**1500.15** verb nom sing masc part aor act	**4287.1** verb 3sing indic aor act	**5312.1** adv	**2504.1** conj
6. Ταῦτα	εἰπὼν,	ἔπτυσεν	χαμαὶ,	καὶ
Tauta	*eipōn*	*eptusen*	*chamai*	*kai*
These things	having said,	he spat	on ground,	and

6.a.**Txt:** p66,p75,01ℵ, 02A,04C,05D,017K, 019L,032W,038,1,13, etc.byz.it.sa.bo.Lach,Sod **Var:** 03B,We/Ho,Weis, UBS/☆

4020.24 verb 3sing indic aor act	**3942.2** noun acc sing masc	**1523.2** prep gen	**3450.2** art gen sing	**4285.1** noun gen sing neu	**2504.1** conj
ἐποίησεν	πηλὸν	ἐκ	τοῦ	πτύσματος,	καὶ
epoiēsen	*pēlon*	*ek*	*tou*	*ptusmatos*	*kai*
made	clay	of	the	spittle,	and

6.b.**Var:** 01ℵ,02A,03B, 04C-corr,019L,038,33, Lach,Treg,Alf,Tisc, We/Ho,Weis,Sod,UBS/☆

2009.1 verb 3sing indic aor act	**1991.6** verb 3sing indic aor act	**840.3** prs-pron gen sing	**3450.6** art acc sing masc
ʻ☆ ἐπέχρισεν	[a ἐπέθηκεν]	[b☆+ αὐτοῦ]	τὸν
epechrisen	*epethēken*	*autou*	*ton*
applied	[put on]	[his]	the

6.c.**Txt:** 02A,04C,017K, 036,037,etc.byz.Lach **Var:** 01ℵ,03B,019L,038, 33,Treg,Alf,Tisc,We/Ho Weis,Sod,UBS/☆

3942.2 noun acc sing masc	**1894.3** prep	**3450.8** art acc pl masc	**3652.8** noun acc pl masc	**3450.2** art gen sing	**5026.2** adj gen sing masc
πηλὸν	ἐπὶ	τοὺς	ὀφθαλμοὺς	ʻc τοῦ	τυφλοῦ· ʼ
pēlon	*epi*	*tous*	*ophthalmous*	*tou*	*tuphlou*
clay	to	the	eyes	of the	blind.

2504.1 conj	**1500.5** verb 3sing indic aor act	**840.4** prs-pron dat sing	**5055.6** verb 2sing impr pres act	**3400.11** verb 2sing impr aor mid
7. καὶ	εἶπεν	αὐτῷ,	Ὕπαγε,	νίψαι
kai	*eipen*	*autō*	*Hupage*	*nipsai*
And	he said	to him,	Go,	wash

1519.1 prep	**3450.12** art acc sing fem	**2833.2** noun acc sing fem	**3450.2** art gen sing	**4466.1** name masc	**3614.16** rel-pron sing neu
εἰς	τὴν	κολυμβήθραν	τοῦ	Σιλωάμ,	ὃ
eis	*tēn*	*kolumbēthran*	*tou*	*Silōam*	*ho*
in	the	pool		of Siloam,	which

2043.1 verb 3sing indic pres pass	**643.29** verb nom sing masc part perf pass	**562.2** verb 3sing indic aor act	**3631.1** conj	**2504.1** conj
ἑρμηνεύεται,	Ἀπεσταλμένος.	ἀπῆλθεν	οὖν	καὶ
hermēneuetai	*Apestalmenos*	*apēlthen*	*oun*	*kai*
is interpreted,	Sent.	He went	therefore	and

with that of the disciples. What was true of Him in His work is true of all His disciples. "Must" is not a part of the curse of man; only the toil accompanying the work is a result of sin.

"While it is day" expresses two ideas. First, it indicates a given time in which work can be accomplished. Second, "while it is" suggests there is a limit to man's life and work. "We" work during our allotted time.

Cessation of labor will come. Opportunities to work will cease for all. Allotted gifts and the duration of their exercise will be withdrawn (Matthew 25:14-30).

4. I must work the works of him that sent me, while it is day: I must do the business of My Sender, *Fenton* . . . While daylight lasts, we must be busy with the work of him who sent me, *Moffatt* . . . so long as daytime lasts we must practice the works of My Sender, *Berkeley.*

the night cometh, when no man can work: There cometh a night, *Rotherham* . . . when no work may be done, *BB.*

9:5. Jesus had made this very statement in 8:12. See that reference for comments.

Jesus was about to give sight to the blind man as a sign that what He was to the blind man, He is to all men. If He can give sight to the blind, He can give truth to all men.

5. As long as I am in the world, I am the light of the world: While I am in the world, *Berkeley* . . . I am the world's light, *Phillips, Fenton.*

6. When he had thus spoken, he spat on the ground, and made clay of the spittle: . . . made clay with the saliva, *TCNT* . . . made some mud with the saliva, *Norlie* . . . made a paste, *ALBA.*

and he anointed the eyes of the blind man with the clay: . . . and smeared the clay on the man's eyes, *Montgomery* . . . daubed the mud on his eyes, *Berkeley* . . . applied it to, *Fenton.*

9:6. The connection between light and sight is clear. Jesus' claim, then, was evidenced by the healing of the blind man.

To accomplish some healings He merely spoke a few words; some persons received a touch; some were sent to the temple; others heard no word of healing, yet He cured them all. Not one on whom He placed His hand or pronounced His grace failed to become whole. The clay and the spittle were not a medical cure. Jesus was. Jesus applied His spittle in two other instances: (1) to heal another blind man, and (2) to heal a man's deafness and to loose his tongue (Mark 7:32,33; 8:23).

7. And said unto him, Go, wash in the pool of Siloam, (which is by interpretation, Sent.): . . . in the baptistery, *Murdock* . . . in the bathing-place, *Fenton* . . . being translated, "commissioned," *Concordant.*

He went his way therefore, and washed, and came seeing: So he went and washed and returned enjoying sight, *Berkeley* . . . washed his face, *TEV* . . . and returned seeing, *Weymouth* . . . came observing, *Concordant* . . . he came back with sight in his eyes, *Norlie* . . . with his sight restored, *ALBA* . . . and returned able to see, *TCNT.*

9:7. The pool is located to the south of the temple area of old Jerusalem. From the days of Hezekiah the pool's water came from Gihon Spring through an underground tunnel. The tunnel has an interesting history. Of its origin Mayfield wrote, "When the Assyrian armies marched into Palestine, Hezekiah abandoned the old waterworks outside the ramparts of Jerusalem. To supply the city with water in case of siege (2 Kings 20:20), he had a tunnel dug under the hill of Ophel, connecting the Gihon Spring to the Pool of Siloam within the city. The tunnel, 1,749 feet long and 6 feet high, was started from both ends by two teams of workers, moving toward each other until they met. In 1880, an inscription in ancient Hebrew characters was found carved in the rock, describing the course of the work on the tunnel. This inscription mentions the water flowed from its source to the pool. This was actually a fine engineering achievement for those early times" (Mayfield, *Beacon Bible Commentary,* 7:115).

John 9:8

3400.9 verb 3sing indic aor mid	2504.1 conj	2048.3 verb 3sing indic aor act	984.12 verb nom sing masc part pres act	3450.7 art pl masc	3631.1 conj
ἐνίψατο,	καὶ	ἦλθεν	βλέπων.	8. Οἱ	οὖν
enipsato	*kai*	*ēlthen*	*blepōn*	*Hoi*	*oun*
washed,	and	came	seeing.	The	therefore

1062.1 noun nom pl masc	2504.1 conj	3450.7 art pl masc	2311.11 verb nom pl masc part pres act	840.6 prs-pron acc sing masc	3450.16 art sing neu
γείτονες	καὶ	οἱ	θεωροῦντες	αὐτὸν	τὸ
geitones	*kai*	*hoi*	*theōrountes*	*auton*	*to*
neighbors	and	the	seeing	him	the

8.a.**Txt:** 04C-corr,036, 037,byz.
Var: 01ℵ,02A,03B, 04C-org,05D,017K, 019L,038,sa.bo.Gries, Lach,TregAlf,Tisc, We/Ho,Weis,Sod,UBS/☆

4245.2 adj comp acc sing neu	3617.1 conj	5026.1 adj nom sing masc	4177.1 noun nom sing masc	1498.34 verb sing indic imperf act
πρότερον	ὅτι	⸀ τυφλὸς	[a☆ προσαίτης]	ἦν,
proteron	*hoti*	*tuphlos*	*prosaitēs*	*ēn*
before	that	blind	[a beggar]	he was,

2978.25 verb indic imperf act	3620.1 partic	3642.4 dem-pron nom sing masc	1498.4 verb 3sing indic pres act	3450.5 art sing masc	2493.6 verb nom sing masc part pres
ἔλεγον,	Οὐχ	οὗτός	ἐστιν	ὁ	καθήμενος
elegon	*Ouch*	*houtos*	*estin*	*ho*	*kathēmenos*
said,	Not	this	is	the	was sitting

9.a.**Txt:** 02A,05D,017K, 036,037,038,1,byz.Lach, Sod
Var: 01ℵ,03B,04C,019L, 033X,33,bo.Treg,Alf, Tisc,We/Ho,Weis,UBS/☆

9.b.**Txt:** 02A,05D,017K, 036,037,13,byz.
Var: 01ℵ,03B,04C,019L, 033X,(038),33,Tisc, We/HoWeis,UBS/☆

9.c.**Var:** p66,01ℵ-org, 02A,04C-corr,017K,036, 041,13,33,Lach,Sod

2504.1 conj	4177.1 verb nom sing masc part pres act	241.6 adj nom pl masc	2978.25 verb indic imperf act	3617.1 conj	3642.4 dem-pron nom sing masc
καὶ	προσαιτῶν;	9. Ἄλλοι	ἔλεγον,	Ὅτι	Οὗτός
kai	*prosaitōn*	*Alloi*	*elegon*	*Hoti*	*Houtos*
and	begging?	Some	said,		This

1498.4 verb 3sing indic pres act	241.6 adj nom pl masc	1156.2 conj	3617.1 conj	2978.25 verb indic imperf act	3644.1 adv
ἐστιν·	ἄλλοι	⸂a δέ, ⸃	⸀ Ὅτι	[b☆ ἔλεγον,	Οὐχί,
estin	*alloi*	*de*	*Hoti*	*elegon*	*Ouchi*
it is,	others	but,		[were saying,	No,

10.a.**Var:** p66,01ℵ,04C, 05D,019L,033X,038, Lach,Alf,Tisc,We/Ho, Sod,UBS/☆

10.b.**Txt:** 02A,017K, 030U,038,041,(byz.), Steph
Var: 01ℵ,03B,04C,05D, 019L,036,037,(byz.), Lach,Treg,Alf,Tisc, We/HoWeis,Sod,UBS/☆

10.c.**Var:** it.Elzev

233.2 conj	3527.2 adj nom sing masc	840.4 prs-pron dat sing	1498.4 verb 3sing indic pres act	1552.3 dem-pron nom sing masc	1156.2 conj
ἀλλὰ]	ὅμοιος	αὐτῷ	ἐστιν.	Ἐκεῖνος	[c+ δὲ]
alla	*homoios*	*autō*	*estin*	*Ekeinos*	*de*
but]	Like	him	he is.	That	[but]

2978.26 verb 3sing indic imperf act	3617.1 conj	1466.1 prs-pron nom 1sing	1498.2 verb 1sing indic pres act	2978.25 verb indic imperf act
ἔλεγεν,	Ὅτι	Ἐγώ	εἰμι.	10. Ἔλεγον
elegen	*Hoti*	*Egō*	*eimi*	*Elegon*
said,		I	am.	They said

11.a.**Txt:** 02A,017K,036, 037,13,28,byz.it.bo.Lach
Var: p66,p75,01ℵ,03B, 04C,05D,019L,032W, 038,1,33,sa.Treg,Alf, Tisc,We/Ho,Weis,Sod, UBS/☆

11.b.**Var:** p66,01ℵ,03B, 019L,1,33,sa.Treg,Alf, Tisc,We/Ho,Weis,Sod, UBS/☆

3631.1 conj	840.4 prs-pron dat sing	4316.1 adv	3631.1 conj	453.20 verb 3pl indic aor pass
οὖν	αὐτῷ,	Πῶς	[a☆+ οὖν]	⸀ ἀνεῴχθησάν
oun	*autō*	*Pōs*	*oun*	*aneōchthēsan*
therefore	to him,	How	[therefore]	were opened

453.19 verb 3pl indic aor pass	4622.2 prs-pron gen 2sing	4622.3 prs-pron dat 2sing	3450.7 art pl masc	3652.5 noun nom pl masc
[b☆ ἠνεῴχθησάν]	⸀ σου	[c σοι]	οἱ	ὀφθαλμοί;
ēneōchthēsan	*sou*	*soi*	*hoi*	*ophthalmoi*
[idem]	your	[idem]	the	eyes?

552.6 verb 3sing indic aor pass	1552.3 dem-pron nom sing masc	2504.1 conj	1500.5 verb 3sing indic aor act	3450.5 art sing masc
11. Ἀπεκρίθη	ἐκεῖνος	⸂a καὶ	εἶπεν, ⸃	[b☆+ Ὁ]
Apekrithē	*ekeinos*	*kai*	*eipen*	*Ho*
Answered	that	and	said,	[The]

The pool seems to be referred to at least in three Old Testament passages (Nehemiah 3:15 and Isaiah 8:6). Second Kings 20:20 is surely a reference to this very pool. Jesus called upon the man for an act of obedience in connection with his healing: "Go wash." He simply commanded that he do it.

The Sent One (Jesus) sent the man born blind to the pool called Sent. The pool was symbolic of God's own gracious presence with His people. This is clear from Isaiah 8:6 where the gently flowing waters of Shiloah were rejected by the people. How appropriately the word *gently* sums up the characteristics of Jesus as the One who was sent by the Father.

The blind man did as He was commanded. "And came seeing" was plainly the result of his obedience. No mention is made concerning how he went or if his friends helped him. The simple facts are stated: The commands to "go" and "wash"; the obedience, "he went his way therefore, and washed"; and the miraculous result, "and came seeing."

8. The neighbours therefore, and they which before had seen him that he was blind: . . . the other people to whom he had been a familiar sight as a beggar, *Weymouth* . . . who had formerly observed him carefully, *Wuest* . . . who had known him formerly, *Norlie* . . . to whom he had been a familiar sight as a beggar, *Weymouth, Moffatt* . . . who used to know him by sight, *Montgomery* . . . was formerly blind, *Williams.*

said, Is not this he that sat and begged?: . . . began to wonder, *ALBA* . . . who customarily sat, *Wuest* . . . that sits and begs, *HBIE* . . . with his hand out for money, *BB.*

9:8. The man may not have returned to Jesus, for the mention of "the neighbors" seems to indicate that he went home. "Beg," *prosaiteō,* occurs but three times in the New Testament (Mark 10:46; Luke 18:35; and here). The word literally means "to ask with no promise to return what is given." Begging was the only means of support a blind man had. The man forsook that means of support as indicated by the word "before."

9. Some said, This is he: others said, He is like him: No, but he looks like him, *Beck* . . . No, but it surely does look like him, *Williams* . . . he only resembles him, *Confraternity.*

but he said, I am he: I am the man, *Moffatt* . . . I am the one, *Berkeley* . . . I'm the man, all right! *Phillips.*

9:9. The neighbors had three different opinions about the identity of the once blind man. First, as the last verse indicates, some of them questioned. Second, some said, "This is he," with no room for doubt. Third, others said, "He is like him." The contrast in the person before and after healing was remarkable. No wonder some had difficulty believing this was the same man. The blind man did not act like the same man after Jesus gave him sight. He came and went as he wished. How his world had changed! Jesus made the total difference.

"But he said" asserts repeated statements to the same effect. "I am he," that is, the one who was blind and you saw sitting and begging. One can faintly imagine the joy that filled the man's emotional outburst when he said those words, "I am he."

10. Therefore said they unto him, How were thine eyes opened?: . . . they demanded, *NIV* . . . Then how was your blindness cured? they asked, *Phillips* . . . How did you get your sight, *Beck, TCNT* . . . How in the world did you come to see? *Williams* . . . How is it that you can now see? *TEV.*

9:10. "Therefore" indicates what his neighbors said because of what he said: He kept saying, "I am he," and they kept saying, "How were thine eyes opened?" The answer to their question would assure them of his true identity. The healed man therefore began to narrate the facts.

John 9:12

11.c.**Var:** p66,01ℵ,03B,019L,1,33,sa.Treg,Alf,Tisc,We/Ho,Weis,Sod,UBS/☆

11.d.**Var:** 01ℵ,03B,019L,sa.bo.Treg,Tisc,We/Ho Weis,Sod,UBS/☆

11.e.**Txt:** 02A,017K,036,037,041,13,28,33,byz. **Var:** p66,p75,01ℵ,03B,05D,019L,032W,038,sa.bo.Gries,Lach,TregAlf,Tisc,We/Ho,Weis,Sod,UBS/☆

11.f.**Txt:** 02A,017K,036,037,13,byz.Gries **Var:** 01ℵ,03B,05D,019L,033X,038,33,sa.bo.Lach,Treg,Alf,Tisc,We/Ho,WeisSod,UBS/☆

12.a.**Var:** p75,01ℵ,03B,019L,032W,033X,1,33,Treg,We/HoWeis,Sod,UBS/☆

12.b.**Txt:** 02A,017K,019L,036,037,038,etc.byz.Sod **Var:** 01ℵ,03B,05D,Lach,TregAlf,Tisc,We/Ho,Weis,UBS/☆

12.c.**Txt:** p66,05D,017K,036,037,038,13,byz. **Var:** p75,01ℵ,02A,03B,019L,032W,033X,1,33,Lach,Treg,Alf,Tisc,We/HoWeis,Sod,UBS/☆

14.a.**Txt:** 02A,05D,017K,036,037,038,1,13,byz.sa.bo.Gries,Word,Sod **Var:** 01ℵ,03B,019L,033X,33,Lach,Treg,Alf,Tisc,We/HoWeis,UBS/☆

442.1 noun nom sing masc	**3450.5** art sing masc	**2978.30** verb nom sing masc part pres pass	**2400.1** name nom masc	**3942.2** noun acc sing masc
Ἄνθρωπος	[c☆+ ὁ]	λεγόμενος	Ἰησοῦς	πηλὸν
Anthrōpos	*ho*	*legomenos*	*Iēsous*	*pēlon*
A man	[the]	called	Jesus	clay

4020.24 verb 3sing indic aor act	**2504.1** conj	**2009.1** verb 3sing indic aor act	**1466.2** prs-pron gen 1sing	**3450.8** art acc pl masc	**3652.8** noun acc pl masc
ἐποίησεν	καὶ	ἐπέχρισέν	μου	τοὺς	ὀφθαλμοὺς,
epoiēsen	*kai*	*epechrisen*	*mou*	*tous*	*ophthalmous*
made	and	applied to	my	the	eyes,

2504.1 conj	**1500.5** verb 3sing indic aor act	**1466.4** prs-pron dat 1sing	**3617.1** conj	**5055.6** verb 2sing impr pres act	**1519.1** prep
καὶ	εἶπέν	μοι,	[d☆+ ὅτι]	Ὕπαγε	εἰς
kai	*eipen*	*moi*	*hoti*	*Hupage*	*eis*
and	said	to me,		Go	to

3450.12 art acc sing fem	**2833.2** noun acc sing fem	**3450.2** art gen sing	**3450.6** art acc sing masc	**4466.1** name masc
‛ τὴν	κολυμβήθραν	τοῦ	[e☆ τὸν]	Σιλωὰμ
tēn	*kolumbēthran*	*tou*	*ton*	*Silōam*
the	pool			of Siloam

2504.1 conj	**3400.11** verb 2sing impr aor mid	**562.6** verb nom sing masc part aor act	**1156.2** conj	**3631.1** conj	**2504.1** conj
καὶ	νίψαι.	ἀπελθὼν	‛ δὲ	[f☆ οὖν]	καὶ
kai	*nipsai*	*apelthōn*	*de*	*oun*	*kai*
and	wash:	having gone	and	[therefore]	and

3400.12 verb nom sing masc part aor mid	**306.2** verb 1sing indic aor act	**2504.1** conj	**1500.3** verb indic aor act
νιψάμενος	ἀνέβλεψα.	12. [a☆+ καὶ]	‛ Εἶπον
nipsamenos	*aneblepsa*	*kai*	*Eipon*
washed	I received sight.	[And]	They said

1500.28 verb 3pl indic aor act	**3631.1** conj	**840.4** prs-pron dat sing	**4085.1** adv	**1498.4** verb 3sing indic pres act
[b☆ εἶπαν]	‛c οὖν `	αὐτῷ,	Ποῦ	ἐστιν
eipan	*oun*	*autō*	*Pou*	*estin*
[idem]	therefore	to him,	Where	is

1552.3 dem-pron nom sing masc	**2978.5** verb 3sing indic pres act	**3620.2** partic	**3471.2** verb 1sing indic perf act	**70.3** verb 3pl indic pres act
ἐκεῖνος;	Λέγει,	Οὐκ	οἶδα.	13. Ἄγουσιν
ekeinos	*Legei*	*Ouk*	*oida*	*Agousin*
that?	He says,	Not	I know.	They bring

840.6 prs-pron acc sing masc	**4242.1** prep	**3450.8** art acc pl masc	**5168.7** name acc pl masc	**3450.6** art acc sing masc	**4077.1** adv
αὐτὸν	πρὸς	τοὺς	Φαρισαίους,	τόν	ποτε
auton	*pros*	*tous*	*Pharisaious*	*ton*	*pote*
him	to	the	Pharisees,	the	once

5026.4 adj acc sing masc	**1498.34** verb sing indic imperf act	**1156.2** conj	**4378.1** noun sing neu	**3616.1** conj	**1706.1** prep
τυφλόν.	14. ἦν	δὲ	σάββατον	‛ ὅτε	[a☆ ἐν
tuphlon	*ēn*	*de*	*sabbaton*	*hote*	*en*
blind.	It was	now	sabbath	when	[on

3614.11 rel-pron dat sing fem	**2232.3** noun dat sing fem	**3450.6** art acc sing masc	**3942.2** noun acc sing masc	**4020.24** verb 3sing indic aor act	**3450.5** art sing masc
ᾗ	ἡμέρᾳ]	τὸν	πηλὸν	ἐποίησεν	ὁ
hē	*hēmera*	*ton*	*pēlon*	*epoiēsen*	*ho*
which	day]	the	clay	made	

The neighbors asked "how?" The man knew to some extent the procedure of his healing. What he did not know was "how" Jesus could do such a wonderful act. When blind, the man stumbled and groped about. After the man was healed he groped for words to explain his benefactor's miracle.

11. He answered and said, A man that is called Jesus made clay, and anointed mine eyes: . . . is termed, Jesus, *Concordant* . . . He whose name is Jesus...made clay and smeared my eyes with it, *Weymouth* . . . made paste, *TCNT* . . . and daubed my eyes with it, *JB* . . . and rubbed it on, *Williams* . . . and spread it on my eyes, *Norlie.*

and said unto me, Go to the pool of Siloam, and wash: Go to Siloam and wash your eyes, *TCNT.*

and I went and washed, and I received sight: . . . and when I washed I could see, *JB* . . . So I went and washed and obtained sight, *Weymouth* . . . and gained my sight, *NEB* . . . and that's how I got my sight! *Phillips* . . . my sight was restored, *Murdock* . . . and now I can see, *ALBA* . . . gained my sight, *TCNT.*

9:11,12. He cautiously avoided expressing any opinion as to the character and mission of his healer. He wished merely to state the simple facts. The once blind man did not as yet possess a knowledge of who Jesus was (verse 36). The healed one was thoughtful, intelligent, slow in forming convictions; but once they were formed, he was steadfast.

"Where is he?" Their questions indicated they had no strong feelings against Jesus. The man's simple answer, "I do not know," is characteristic of all the answers he gave his friends. Unadorned facts are the only essentials for any man's testimony.

12. Then said they unto him, Where is he? He said, I know not: I am not aware, *Concordant.*

13. They brought to the Pharisees him that aforetime was blind: Then they conducted the man who had formerly, *AmpB* . . . They conducted the once-blind man, *Berkeley* . . . the man who had formerly been blind, *RSV* . . . this man who had once been blind, *Moffatt* . . . the one aforetime blind, *Panin.*

9:13. "They brought to the Pharisees" indicated the action the man's neighbors took next. The neighbors had examined him thoroughly (1) to determine he was indeed the previously blind man, (2) to find out how he was healed, and (3) to learn where the Healer was. The reference to "him that aforetime was blind" hints that the people were now convinced of the truth of the miracle. Having completed their investigation, they concluded it was time to bring him before the authorities.

Excitement ran high as the neighbors rushed the man to the seat of power. This was a miracle of a new kind! No person born blind had ever received his sight before (see verse 32). No Old Testament miracle was of that kind. They wanted to be first to tell their leaders what had happened. Perhaps they also desired credit for helping discipline the Teacher who had dared practice medicine on the Sabbath Day.

The Pharisees no doubt assembled daily at either the temple or in this case perhaps a neighborhood synagogue. They were the most numerous and powerful of the sects of the Jews. "Pharisees" here signified those who were leaders among the sect. Some may even have been members of the Sanhedrin. At any rate, they had the authority to exert appropriate discipline in this case. Having issued the threat of excommunication earlier, they would be anxious to act (verse 22).

14. And it was the sabbath day when Jesus made the clay, and opened his eyes: Jesus had made mud, *Norlie* . . . mixed the mud, *AmpB* . . . and had cured his

9:14. The man's healing mattered little to the Pharisees. They were more concerned that Jesus had worked on the Sabbath because He made the clay. Not that Jesus mixed clay only, but He

2400.1 name nom masc	2504.1 conj	453.5 verb 3sing indic aor act	840.3 prs-pron gen sing	3450.8 art acc pl masc	3652.8 noun acc pl masc
Ἰησοῦς	καὶ	ἀνέῳξεν	αὐτοῦ	τοὺς	ὀφθαλμούς.
Iēsous	*kai*	*aneōxen*	*autou*	*tous*	*ophthalmous*
Jesus	and	opened	his	the	eyes.

3687.1 adv	3631.1 conj	2049.17 verb 3pl indic imperf act	840.6 prs-pron acc sing masc	2504.1 conj	3450.7 art pl masc
15. πάλιν	οὖν	ἠρώτων	αὐτὸν	καὶ	οἱ
palin	*oun*	*ērōtōn*	*auton*	*kai*	*hoi*
Again	therefore	asked	him	also	the

5168.4 name pl masc	4316.1 adv	306.3 verb 3sing indic aor act	3450.5 art sing masc	1156.2 conj	1500.5 verb 3sing indic aor act
Φαρισαῖοι	πῶς	ἀνέβλεψεν.	ὁ	δὲ	εἶπεν
Pharisaioi	*pōs*	*aneblepsen*	*ho*	*de*	*eipen*
Pharisees	how	he received sight.	The	and	said

840.2 prs-pron dat pl	3942.2 noun acc sing masc	1991.6 verb 3sing indic aor act	1894.3 prep	3450.8 art acc pl masc	3652.8 noun acc pl masc
αὐτοῖς,	Πηλὸν	ἐπέθηκέν	⸀ἐπὶ	τοὺς	ὀφθαλμούς
autois	*Pēlon*	*epethēken*	*epi*	*tous*	*ophthalmous*
to them,	Clay	he put	on	the	eyes

1466.2 prs-pron gen 1sing	1466.2 prs-pron gen 1sing	1894.3 prep	3450.8 art acc pl masc	3652.8 noun acc pl masc	2504.1 conj
μου,	[☆ μου	ἐπὶ	τοὺς	ὀφθαλμούς,]	καὶ
mou	*mou*	*epi*	*tous*	*ophthalmous*	*kai*
my,	[my	on	the	eyes,]	and

3400.8 verb 1sing indic aor mid	2504.1 conj	984.2 verb 1sing indic pres act	2978.25 verb indic imperf act	3631.1 conj
ἐνιψάμην,	καὶ	βλέπω.	16. Ἔλεγον	οὖν
enipsamēn	*kai*	*blepō*	*Elegon*	*oun*
I washed,	and	I see.	Said	therefore

1523.2 prep gen	3450.1 art gen pl	5168.5 name gen pl masc	4948.7 indef-pron nom pl masc	3642.4 dem-pron nom sing masc	3450.5 art sing masc
ἐκ	τῶν	Φαρισαίων	τινές,	⸀Οὗτος	ὁ
ek	*tōn*	*Pharisaiōn*	*tines*	*Houtos*	*ho*
of	the	Pharisees	some,	This	the

442.1 noun nom sing masc	3620.2 partic	1498.4 verb 3sing indic pres act	3706.2 prep	3450.2 art gen sing	2296.2 noun gen sing masc
ἄνθρωπος	οὐκ	ἔστιν	παρὰ	τοῦ	θεοῦ,
anthrōpos	*ouk*	*estin*	*para*	*tou*	*theou*
man	not	is	from		God,

16.a.**Txt:** 02A,017K,036,037,byz.sa.bo. **Var:** 01ℵ,03B,05D,019L,033X,038,Lach,Treg,Alf,TiscWe/Ho,Weis,Sod,UBS/☆

3620.2 partic	1498.4 verb 3sing indic pres act	3642.4 dem-pron nom sing masc	3706.2 prep	2296.2 noun gen sing masc	3450.5 art sing masc
[a☆ Οὐκ	ἔστιν	οὗτος	παρὰ	θεοῦ	ὁ
Ouk	*estin*	*houtos*	*para*	*theou*	*ho*
[Not	is	this	from	God	the

442.1 noun nom sing masc	3617.1 conj	3450.16 art sing neu	4378.1 noun sing neu	3620.3 partic	4931.2 verb sing indic pres act
ἄνθρωπος,]	ὅτι	τὸ	σάββατον	οὐ	τηρεῖ.
anthrōpos	*hoti*	*to*	*sabbaton*	*ou*	*tērei*
man,]	for	the	sabbath	not	he does keep.

16.b.**Var:** 01ℵ,03B,05D,032W,1,13,We/HoWeis,Sod,UBS/☆

241.6 adj nom pl masc	1156.2 conj	2978.25 verb indic imperf act	4316.1 adv	1404.4 verb 3sing indic pres	442.1 noun nom sing masc
Ἄλλοι	[b☆+ δὲ]	ἔλεγον,	Πῶς	δύναται	ἄνθρωπος
Alloi	*de*	*elegon*	*Pōs*	*dunatai*	*anthrōpos*
Others	[but]	said,	How	can	a man

"opened his eyes" as well. Jesus had cured on the Sabbath before this man's healing (see John 5:16; Mark 3:4; Luke 13:14). The Saviour worked gracious and merciful miracles on the Sabbath, and He taught the Pharisees the true meaning of the Sabbath by what He did. Jesus seemed purposefully to challenge the Pharisees' interpretation of the laws concerning the Sabbath.

Clearly, Jesus' teachings conflicted not with the law of the sabbath but with Jewish traditions built around it. In another place as He was challenged by the distorted view of the religious leaders He asked, "Is it lawful to do good on the sabbath days, or to do evil? to save life, or to kill?" (Mark 3:4).

Answering His own questions He reasoned as with shepherds. If a sheep fell into a pit on the Sabbath, would they not rescue the trapped animal? Of course. Since men matter more than sheep, as to healing them He concluded, "Wherefore it is lawful to do well on the sabbath days" (Matthew 12:12).

blindness, *Barclay* . . . and gave him his sight, *Beck* . . . (It should be noted that Jesus made the clay and restored his sight on a Sabbath day.), *Phillips.*

15. Then again the Pharisees also asked him how he had received his sight. He said unto them, He put clay upon mine eyes, and I washed, and do see: So the man was again questioned, *TCNT* . . . went to questioning him, *Wuest* . . . He applied clay, *NASB* . . . and I washed them, and now I can see, *Moffatt.*

9:15. "Then again" indicates that the healed man had been questioned by his neighbors along the same line. The leaders wanted to know "how he had received his sight." They implied that a miracle had been performed.

Notice in verse 11 the man said, "Jesus made clay." To make clay implies work, while to apply clay may not. It depends on interpretation. The healed man said nothing about the spittle or the mixing of the clay and saliva. The man stated only what he himself knew by his feeling the clay being smeared on his eyes. He did not see what Jesus did prior to his healing.

"I washed, and do see" brings the man's testimony to a grand climax. "I washed" (*enipsamēn*) is an aorist middle verb stressing a historical fact that the washing of his eyes took place in behalf of himself. "I see" (*blepō*) is a present continuous act of seeing. What a miracle! The Light of the World had come to him. This one who sat in darkness saw a great light (Isaiah 9:2).

16. Therefore said some of the Pharisees, This man is not of God: This man is not from God, *Alford* . . . This man cannot be from God, *TCNT* . . . This is not a man of God, *Berkeley* . . . is not connected with God, *Fenton* . . . does not come from, *Williams.*

because he keepeth not the sabbath day: . . . since he does not observe the Sabbath, *Phillips.*

Others said, How can a man that is a sinner do such miracles?: How can a sinful man, *Rotherham* . . . How is it possible for a bad man to do such signs? *Weymouth* . . . How could such evidences be effected by a sinful man? *Fenton* . . . a bad man, *TCNT* . . . perform such wonder-works, *Williams* . . . to perform actions like this, *Barclay* . . . effect such signs? *Berkeley.*

9:16. The man's answers led to a heated discussion among the Pharisees. There was no dispute as to whether the man could see. The controversy centered on Christ's commission from God. "This man is not of God, because he keepeth not the sabbath day." This judgment was made because of their interpretation of how the Sabbath was to be kept. "This man" is a contemptuous designation for Jesus. Perhaps they wished to avoid the name of Jesus because it means "to save." The enemies of Christ often refrain from using His name. After Jesus' resurrection and the Church's witness in Jerusalem, the Jews did not make reference to His name. Sometimes they referred to Him as "this man" or "that one." Their lack of acknowledgment had little effect on the message of Christ. The

John 9:17

266.1 adj nom sing	**4955.14** dem-pron acc pl neu	**4447.2** noun pl neu	**4020.20** verb inf pres act	**2504.1** conj	**4830.1** noun nom sing neu
ἁμαρτωλὸς	τοιαῦτα	σημεῖα	ποιεῖν;	Καὶ	σχίσμα
hamartōlos	*toiauta*	*sēmeia*	*poiein*	*Kai*	*schisma*
a sinner	such	signs	do?	And	a division

17.a.**Var:** 01ℵ,02A,03B, 05D,019L,033X,038,sa. Lach,Treg,Alf,Word, Tisc,We/Ho,WeisSod, UBS/☆

1498.34 verb sing indic imperf act	**1706.1** prep	**840.2** prs-pron dat pl	**2978.3** verb 3pl pres act	**3631.1** conj
ἦν	ἐν	αὐτοῖς.	**17.** Λέγουσιν	[a☆+ οὖν]
ēn	*en*	*autois*	*Legousin*	*oun*
was	among	them.	They say	[therefore]

3450.3 art dat sing	**5026.3** adj dat sing masc	**3687.1** adv	**4622.1** prs-pron nom 2sing	**4949.9** intr-pron sing neu	**4949.9** intr-pron sing neu
τῷ	τυφλῷ	πάλιν,	ʼ Σὺ	Τί	[☆ Τί
tō	*tuphlō*	*palin*	*Su*	*Ti*	*Ti*
to the	blind	again,	You	what	[What

4622.1 prs-pron nom 2sing	**2978.4** verb 2sing indic pres act	**3875.1** prep	**840.3** prs-pron gen sing	**3617.1** conj	**453.4** verb 3sing indic aor act
σὺ]	λέγεις	περὶ	αὐτοῦ,	ὅτι	ʼ ἤνοιξέν
su	*legeis*	*peri*	*autou*	*hoti*	*ēnoixen*
you]	say	concerning	him,	for	he opened

17.b.**Txt:** 01ℵ,02A,036, byz.Lach,Tisc
Var: 03B,033X,037,Treg Alf,We/Ho,Weis

453.33 verb 3sing indic aor act	**4622.2** prs-pron gen 2sing	**3450.8** art acc pl masc	**3652.8** noun acc pl masc	**3450.5** art sing masc
[b☆ ἠνέῳξέν]	σου	τοὺς	ὀφθαλμούς;	Ὁ
ēneōxen	*sou*	*tous*	*ophthalmous*	*Ho*
[idem]	your	the	eyes?	The

1156.2 conj	**1500.5** verb 3sing indic aor act	**3617.1** conj	**4254.1** noun nom sing masc	**1498.4** verb 3sing indic pres act	**3620.2** partic
δὲ	εἶπεν	Ὅτι	Προφήτης	ἐστίν.	**18.** Οὐκ
de	*eipen*	*Hoti*	*Prophētēs*	*estin*	*Ouk*
and	said,		A prophet	he is.	Not

3961.23 verb 3pl indic aor act	**3631.1** conj	**3450.7** art pl masc	**2428.2** name-adj pl masc	**3875.1** prep
ἐπίστευσαν	οὖν	οἱ	Ἰουδαῖοι	περὶ
episteusan	*oun*	*hoi*	*Ioudaioi*	*peri*
did believe	therefore	the	Jews	concerning

840.3 prs-pron gen sing	**3617.1** conj	**5026.1** adj nom sing masc	**1498.34** verb sing indic imperf act	**1498.34** verb sing indic imperf act	**5026.1** adj nom sing masc
αὐτοῦ,	ὅτι	ʼ τυφλὸς	ἦν	[☆ ἦν	τυφλὸς]
autou	*hoti*	*tuphlos*	*ēn*	*ēn*	*tuphlos*
him,	that	blind	he was	[he was	blind]

2504.1 conj	**306.3** verb 3sing indic aor act	**2175.1** conj	**3618.1** rel-pron gen sing neu	**5291.7** verb 3pl indic aor act	**3450.8** art acc pl masc
καὶ	ἀνέβλεψεν,	ἕως	ὅτου	ἐφώνησαν	τοὺς
kai	*aneblepsen*	*heōs*	*hotou*	*ephōnēsan*	*tous*
and	received sight,	until	that	they called	the

1112.1 noun pl masc	**840.3** prs-pron gen sing	**3450.2** art gen sing	**306.10** verb gen sing masc part aor act	**2504.1** conj
γονεῖς	αὐτοῦ	τοῦ	ἀναβλέψαντος·	**19.** καὶ
goneis	*autou*	*tou*	*anablepsantos*	*kai*
parents	his	the	having received sight.	And

2049.10 verb 3pl indic aor act	**840.8** prs-pron acc pl masc	**2978.16** verb pl masc part pres act	**3642.4** dem-pron nom sing masc	**1498.4** verb 3sing indic pres act
ἠρώτησαν	αὐτοὺς	λέγοντες,	Οὗτός	ἐστιν
ērōtēsan	*autous*	*legontes*	*Houtos*	*estin*
they asked	them	saying,	This	is

name of Jesus was published everywhere. The name of Christ did not need enemies to spread it worldwide.

"Others" were more objective in their judgment. "How can a man that is a sinner do such miracles?" Those who asked this question were clearly in the minority. "And there was a division among them." This is yet another instance when the work of Jesus severed people from one another as if by a sword. Jesus said earlier, "I came not to send peace, but a sword" (Matthew 10:34).

The Pharisees could not agree whether miracles could be done by a man not sent from God. In other words, some of the Pharisees were inclined to accept the credentials of Jesus as indications of His messiahship. Other religious leaders would not grant His miracles as tokens of His office predicted in the Prophets of the Old Testament. Thus the Pharisees were divided concerning doctrinal issues which related to the miracles Jesus performed.

9:17. The Pharisees turned to the once "blind man." The conflict among members of the Pharisees was perhaps embarrassing; therefore, they turned to the man who was responsible for their agitation. "What sayest thou of him, that he hath opened thine eyes?" Notice their acknowledgment of the miracle.

The man's answer was "He is a prophet." A prophet was one who was sent from God with a message to the people. Prophets often performed mini-miracles (in comparison to Christ's miracles) as evidence of their divine commission.

The healed man was well on his way toward believing in Christ. Jesus was indeed a prophet like Moses. He was also a priest and king. These three offices of the Messiah were plainly taught in the prophecies concerning Him. The man's acknowlegment of Christ's prophetic office was a first step toward faith in Him. This acknowledgment was important. Jesus' miracles were the credentials of His person and office. If the Pharisees had acknowledged Jesus' signs and miracles as genuine, of logical necessity they would have recognized Him as a prophet of God. If they had believed He was a prophet, they must then have believed His word.

9:18. "The Jews" were the leaders who represented the people. Some of the leaders joined the Pharisees spoken of in the previous verses. The term "Jew" in this Gospel indicates those leaders who were hostile to Christ.

The Jews now made a feeble effort to discredit the miracle. They were partially successful until they were obliged to call the man's parents. How far the depraved will go seeking to justify the errors of his ways! If any possible proof could have been offered to discredit Jesus, these Jews would have found it! They poked into every nook and cranny that they might discredit the Lord who sought to

And there was a division among them: They were divided on this, *Moffatt* . . . So there was a disagreement among them, *Berkeley* . . . was a schism, *Concordant* . . . was a difference of opinion among them, *AmpB, Montgomery, Williams.*

17. They say unto the blind man again, What sayest thou of him, that he hath opened thine eyes?: What do you think, seeing that it was your eyes he opened? *ALBA* . . . it was your eyes that he opened, *Adams* . . . concerning him in view of the fact that he opened, *Wuest* . . . seeing that he hath opened, *Alford* . . . What have you to say about him for opening your eyes, *BB* . . . You're the one whose sight was restored, *Phillips.*

He said, He is a prophet: He must be, *AmpB* . . . I say he is a prophet, *Moffatt.*

18. But the Jews did not believe concerning him, that he had been blind, and received his sight: . . . did not believe about him that he was blind and had received his sight, *Montgomery* . . . didn't believe the man had been blind and got his sight, *Beck* . . . and had regained his sight, *Moffatt.*

until they called the parents of him that had received his sight: . . . until they had called his parents, *TCNT* . . . till they called in the parents of the man whose eyes had been opened, *Norlie* . . . until they summoned his parents, *ALBA* . . . who recovered sight, *Murdock.*

19. And they asked them, saying, Is this your son, who ye say was born blind?: . . . and questioned them, *Norton* . . . whom

John 9:20

3450.5 art sing masc	5048.1 noun nom sing masc	5050.2 prs-pron gen 2pl	3614.6 rel-pron acc sing masc	5050.1 prs-pron nom 2pl	2978.2 verb 2pl pres act
ὁ	υἱὸς	ὑμῶν,	ὃν	ὑμεῖς	λέγετε
ho	*huios*	*humōn*	*hon*	*humeis*	*legete*
the	son	your,	of whom	you	say

3617.1 conj	5026.1 adj nom sing masc	1074.13 verb 3sing indic aor pass	4316.1 adv	3631.1 conj	732.1 adv	984.4 verb 3sing indic pres act
ὅτι	τυφλὸς	ἐγεννήθη;	πῶς	οὖν	⸀ ἄρτι	βλέπει;
hoti	*tuphlos*	*egennēthē*	*pōs*	*oun*	*arti*	*blepei*
that	blind	he was born?	how	then	now	does he see?

20.a.**Var:** p66,p75,01ℵ, 03B,Lach,Tisc,We/Ho, Weis,UBS/☆

984.4 verb 3sing indic pres act	732.1 adv	552.8 verb 3pl indic aor pass	3631.1 conj
[☆ βλέπει	ἄρτι;]	**20.** Ἀπεκρίθησαν	[a☆+ οὖν]
blepei	*arti*	*Apekrithēsan*	*oun*
[does he see	now?]	Answered	[therefore]

20.b.**Txt:** 02A,05D,017K, 036,037,038,1,13,byz. Lach
Var: 01ℵ,03B,019L, 033X,Treg,Alf,Tisc, We/Ho,WeisSod,UBS/☆

840.2 prs-pron dat pl	3450.7 art pl masc	1112.1 noun pl masc	840.3 prs-pron gen sing	2504.1 conj	1500.3 verb indic aor act
⸂b αὐτοῖς ⸃	οἱ	γονεῖς	αὐτοῦ	καὶ	⸀ εἶπον,
autois	*hoi*	*goneis*	*autou*	*kai*	*eipon*
them	the	parents	his	and	said,

20.c.**Txt:** 02A,05D,017K, 036,037,038,etc.byz. Lach,Sod
Var: 01ℵ,03B,019L,33, Treg,Alf,Tisc,We/Ho, Weis,UBS/☆

1500.28 verb 3pl indic aor act	3471.5 verb 1pl indic perf act	3617.1 conj	3642.4 dem-pron nom sing masc	1498.4 verb 3sing indic pres act
[c☆ εἶπαν,]	Οἴδαμεν	ὅτι	οὗτός	ἐστιν
eipan	*Oidamen*	*hoti*	*houtos*	*estin*
[idem]	We know	that	this	is

3450.5 art sing masc	5048.1 noun nom sing masc	2231.2 prs-pron gen 1pl	2504.1 conj	3617.1 conj	5026.1 adj nom sing masc
ὁ	υἱὸς	ἡμῶν,	καὶ	ὅτι	τυφλὸς
ho	*huios*	*hēmōn*	*kai*	*hoti*	*tuphlos*
the	son	our,	and	that	blind

1074.13 verb 3sing indic aor pass	4316.1 adv	1156.2 conj	3431.1 adv	984.4 verb 3sing indic pres act	3620.2 partic	3471.5 verb 1pl indic perf act
ἐγεννήθη·	**21.** πῶς	δὲ	νῦν	βλέπει	οὐκ	οἴδαμεν,
egennēthē	*pōs*	*de*	*nun*	*blepei*	*ouk*	*oidamen*
he was born;	how	but	now	he sees	not	we know,

2211.1 conj	4949.3 intr-pron nom sing	453.4 verb 3sing indic aor act	840.3 prs-pron gen sing	3450.8 art acc pl masc	3652.8 noun acc pl masc
ἢ	τίς	ἤνοιξεν	αὐτοῦ	τοὺς	ὀφθαλμοὺς
ē	*tis*	*ēnoixen*	*autou*	*tous*	*ophthalmous*
or	who	opened	his	the	eyes

2231.1 prs-pron nom 1pl	3620.2 partic	3471.5 verb 1pl indic perf act	840.5 prs-pron nom sing masc	2227.3 noun acc sing fem	2174.4 verb 3sing indic pres act
ἡμεῖς	οὐκ	οἴδαμεν·	⸀ αὐτὸς	ἡλικίαν	ἔχει,
hēmeis	*ouk*	*oidamen*	*autos*	*hēlikian*	*echei*
we	not	know;	he	full age	has,

21.a.**Txt:** 02A,017K,036, 037,byz.
Var: 01ℵ-corr,03B,05D, 019L,033X,038,33,Treg, Alf,Tisc,We/Ho,Weis, Sod,UBS/☆

840.6 prs-pron acc sing masc	2049.13 verb 2pl impr aor act	840.6 prs-pron acc sing masc	2049.13 verb 2pl impr aor act	2227.3 noun acc sing fem
αὐτὸν	ἐρωτήσατε,	[a☆ αὐτὸν	ἐρωτήσατε,	ἡλικίαν
auton	*erōtēsate*	*auton*	*erōtēsate*	*hēlikian*
him	ask,	[him	ask,	full age

21.b.**Txt:** 05D,019L, 030U,037,Steph,Lach
Var: 01ℵ,02A,03B,07E, 017K,033X,036,038,byz. Treg,Tisc,We/HoWeis, Sod,UBS/☆

2174.4 verb 3sing indic pres act	840.5 prs-pron nom sing masc	3875.1 prep	1431.3 prs-pron gen sing	1431.4 prs-pron gen 3sing
ἔχει,]	αὐτὸς	περὶ	⸀ αὑτοῦ	[b☆ ἑαυτοῦ]
echei	*autos*	*peri*	*hautou*	*heautou*
he has,]	he	concerning	him	[himself]

save them. But, like Pilate, these Jews could discover no fault in Him. Yet they would not believe nor accept Him.

you report as having been born blind, *Berkeley*... and do you affirm that he was born blind, *Williams*... Do you claim, *SEB*.

how then doth he now see?: How does it happen he can see now, *Beck*... If so, how it is then that he now can see, *Williams*... How is it that now he can see? *Norlie*.

9:19. The Pharisees asked three questions of the parents of the onetime blind man. First, "Is this your son?" Second, "Who ye say was born blind?" Third, "How then doth he now see?" By their questions the leaders pressured the parents to deny the miracle performed on their son. The parents answered the first two questions, but they refused to become involved in the third.

20. His parents answered them and said, We know that this is our son, and that he was born blind: We know positively, *Wuest*.

9:20. The evidence was indisputable. The parents were honest and humble, and they gave direct and simple answers to some of the most wealthy and powerful leaders of their nation. Their son was a beggar; hence it is safe to assume they were very poor.

These parents were torn between their appreciation for the One who healed their son and their respect for their national leaders. The Scripture commands God's people to honor those who rule over them. This applies to civil and religious leaders. The parents respected the authorities and their honesty is commendable. Had they succumbed to the pressure of the Jews, they would have provided them with the deceptive testimony they sought against Jesus.

21. But by what means he now seeth, we know not: But we do not know how he now sees, *Norlie*... But as to how he can now see, *AmpB*... but we don't know how he now can see, *Adams*.

or who hath opened his eyes, we know not:

he is of age; ask him: he shall speak for himself:... he himself will give his own account of it, *Weymouth*... He has attained maturity, *Wuest*... He is a grown-up man; he can speak for himself, *Phillips*... He will tell his own story, *Norlie*... Ask him—He is old enough—he will tell you, *TCNT*... he is old enough to give an answer for himself, *BB*... lett hym answer for hym sylfe off thynges that pertayne to hym sylfe, *Tyndale*... he is of mature Age, *Wilson*.

9:21. "But by what means he now seeth, we know not." This was true for they had not been present at the healing. If they had given their son's testimony, their witness would not have been valid for it was secondhand. The "who hath opened his eyes" was equally unknown to the parents. They were wise not to give their opinion for, if they had, they knew the penalty would be excommunication from the synagogue (verse 22).

They went as far in their witness as was legally possible. The healed son was evidently a mature man. He was a credible and legal witness as to how he was healed and who healed him. One can detect a reticence on the part of the parents to become involved in this serious controversy. The authority of the leaders greatly influenced both the poor, as the man's parents were, and the wealthy and powerful, such as Nicodemus.

9:22. John gives an explanation as to why the parents conducted themselves with such reservation. The Jews had intimidated them and everyone else so that it was not wise to speak openly in favor of Jesus.

22.a.**Txt:** 02A,03B,05D, 017K,019L,036,037,038, etc.byz.Lach,Tisc,Sod
Var: 01ℵ,We/Ho,Weis, UBS/☆

2953.40 verb 3sing indic fut act	**3642.18** dem-pron pl neu	**1500.3** verb indic aor act	**1500.28** verb 3pl indic aor act	**3450.7** art pl masc
λαλήσει.	**22.** Ταῦτα	ʽ εἶπον	[a☆ εἶπαν]	οἱ
lalēsei	*Tauta*	*eipon*	*eipan*	*hoi*
shall speak.	These things	said	[idem]	the

1112.1 noun pl masc	**840.3** prs-pron gen sing	**3617.1** conj	**5236.25** verb 3pl indic imperf	**3450.8** art acc pl masc
γονεῖς	αὐτοῦ,	ὅτι	ἐφοβοῦντο	τοὺς
goneis	*autou*	*hoti*	*ephobounto*	*tous*
parents	his,	because	they feared	the

2428.5 name-adj acc pl masc	**2218.1** adv	**1056.1** conj	**4786.2** verb 3pl indic plperf mid	**3450.7** art pl masc
Ἰουδαίους·	ἤδη	γὰρ	συνετέθειντο	οἱ
Ioudaious	*ēdē*	*gar*	*sunetetheinto*	*hoi*
Jews;	already	for	had agreed together	the

2428.2 name-adj pl masc	**2419.1** conj	**1430.1** partic	**4948.3** indef-pron nom sing	**840.6** prs-pron acc sing masc	**3533.10** verb 3sing subj aor act
Ἰουδαῖοι,	ἵνα	ἐάν	τις	αὐτὸν	ὁμολογήσῃ
Ioudaioi	*hina*	*ean*	*tis*	*auton*	*homologēsē*
Jews,	that	if	anyone	him	should confess

5382.4 name acc masc	**650.1** adj nom sing masc	**1090.40** verb 3sing subj aor mid	**1217.2** prep
Χριστόν,	ἀποσυνάγωγος	γένηται.	**23.** διὰ
Christon	*aposunagōgos*	*genētai*	*dia*
Christ,	put out of the synagogue	he should be.	Because of

23.a.**Txt:** 02A,017K, 019L,036,037,038,etc. byz.Sod
Var: 01ℵ,03B,05D,Lach, TregAlf,Tisc,We/Ho, Weis,UBS/☆

3642.17 dem-pron sing neu	**3450.7** art pl masc	**1112.1** noun pl masc	**840.3** prs-pron gen sing	**1500.3** verb indic aor act	**1500.28** verb 3pl indic aor act
τοῦτο	οἱ	γονεῖς	αὐτοῦ	ʽ εἶπον,	[a☆ εἶπαν]
touto	*hoi*	*goneis*	*autou*	*eipon*	*eipan*
this	the	parents	his	said,	[idem]

3617.1 conj	**2227.3** noun acc sing fem	**2174.4** verb 3sing indic pres act	**840.6** prs-pron acc sing masc	**2049.13** verb 2pl impr aor act
Ὅτι	Ἡλικίαν	ἔχει,	αὐτὸν	ʽ ἐρωτήσατε.
Hoti	*Hēlikian*	*echei*	*auton*	*erōtēsate*
	Full age	he has,	him	ask.

23.b.**Txt:** 02A,017K, 019L,036,037,038,1,13, byz.Gries,Lach
Var: p66,p75,01ℵ,03B, 032W,Tisc,We/Ho,Weis, Sod,UBS/☆

1890.17 verb 2pl impr aor act	**5291.7** verb 3pl indic aor act	**3631.1** conj	**1523.2** prep gen
[b☆ ἐπερωτήσατε.]	**24.** Ἐφώνησαν	οὖν	ʽ ἐκ
eperōtēsate	*Ephōnēsan*	*oun*	*ek*
[idem]	They called	therefore	from

1202.1 num ord gen sing	**3450.6** art acc sing masc	**442.4** noun acc sing masc	**3450.6** art acc sing masc	**442.4** noun acc sing masc
δευτέρου	τὸν	ἄνθρωπον	[☆ τὸν	ἄνθρωπον
deuterou	*ton*	*anthrōpon*	*ton*	*anthrōpon*
second time	the	man	[the	man

1523.2 prep gen	**1202.1** num ord gen sing	**3614.5** rel-pron nom sing masc	**1498.34** verb sing indic imperf act	**5026.1** adj nom sing masc	**2504.1** conj
ἐκ	δευτέρου]	ὃς	ἦν	τυφλὸς,	καὶ
ek	*deuterou*	*hos*	*ēn*	*tuphlos*	*kai*
from	second time]	who	was	blind,	and

24.a.**Txt:** 02A,017K, 019L,036,037,etc.byz. Sod
Var: 01ℵ,03B,05D,038, Lach,Treg,Alf,Tisc, We/Ho,Weis,UBS/☆

1500.3 verb indic aor act	**1500.28** verb 3pl indic aor act	**840.4** prs-pron dat sing	**1319.25** verb 2sing impr aor act	**1385.4** noun acc sing fem	**3450.3** art dat sing
ʽ εἶπον	[a☆ εἶπαν]	αὐτῷ,	Δὸς	δόξαν	τῷ
eipon	*eipan*	*autō*	*Dos*	*doxan*	*tō*
said	[idem]	to him,	Give	glory	

"For the Jews had agreed already" indicates their private decisions made behind the scenes, not openly nor officially.

The fear of the Jews was that people would "confess Him to be Christ" (NASB).

The penalty for acknowledging Jesus as the Messiah was that "he should be put out of the synagogue." This was the Jewish leaders' most powerful weapon. Those who were excommunicated from the synagogues lived as social outcasts. Theirs was an isolated and dreary existence. Scholars agree that the first degree of expulsion was for a period of 30 days from the synagogue and temple, with a separation of at least 6 feet between the person and any friend, even one's wife and family. If the outcast persisted in his "rebellion," the time would be lengthened, and a curse was the second degree. The offender was prohibited from teaching or being taught, hiring or being hired. He could not buy or sell except for the bare necessities of life. The third stage was final separation from all future benefits whether religious or social. The threat indicated that the person who confessed Jesus as Christ was to be counted a spiritual leper. This was the cost of discipleship for many at the beginning of the Church.

22. These words spake his parents, because they feared the Jews: They said this because of their fear of the Jews, *BB* . . . they dreaded the Judeans, *Fenton.*

for the Jews had agreed already: . . . had already settled among themselves, *Weymouth* . . . had agreed among themselves, *Norlie.*

that if any man did confess that he was Christ: . . . that anyone who confessed him to be Christ, *Moffatt* . . . who admitted that Christ had done this thing, *Phillips* . . . every confessor of Christ, *Berkeley* . . . confess him as Christ, *Panin.*

he should be put out of the synagogue: . . . should be excommunicated, *Moffatt* . . . he should be expelled from the synagogue, *Norlie* . . . be debarred, *Berkeley* . . . shut out of the, *Williams* . . . become one who is excluded from, *Wuest.*

9:23. John relates, "Therefore said his parents, He is of age; ask him!" It is little wonder the parents did not wish to state anything but the simple facts: he is our son and he was born blind.

However, they could have shown more appreciation to Jesus. Why did they not speak highly of the One who had done such a marvelous miracle for their son? Is not Christ to be esteemed above all authorities, customs, and religions? But fear of the Jews kept them from showing honor to Jesus Christ. What a pity they were fearful of the Jews! They missed a beautiful opportunity to express their gratitude to the Lord.

23. Therefore said his parents, He is of age; ask him: He is an adult, *SEB* . . . Inquire of Him, *Concordant, Wuest* . . . He can speak for himself, *Phillips.*

24. Then again called they the man that was blind, and said unto him, Give God the praise: They accordingly recalled a second time, *Fenton* . . . a second time summoned, *Montgomery* . . . A second time therefore, *Weymouth* . . . Tell the truth before God! *ALBA* . . . Give the honour of your cure to God, *TCNT* . . . Speak in the fear of God, *Norton* . . . Promise before God that you will tell the truth! *TEV* . . . Give glory to God, *Wuest.*

9:24. "Then again" the Pharisees questioned the healed man. "Give God the praise." The essence of this idea is stated in a number of Scriptures (Joshua 7:19; 1 Samuel 6:5; Jeremiah 13:16; Luke 17:18). The meaning is somewhat ambiguous in the mouths of the Pharisees. It can mean "give the glory for your healing to God for it is from God," or it could mean "do not give any glory to this man Jesus, but give the glory to God."

Many who profess a belief in God deny the deity of Jesus. Sadly, some are of His own Jewish people now as then. John observed, "He came unto his own, and his own received him not" (1:11). Even with the Twelve He once urged, "Ye believe in God, believe also in me" (14:1).

The fact is God the Father rejects any supposed faith in himself apart from acceptance also of His Son. John boldly declared this

2296.3 noun dat sing masc	2231.1 prs-pron nom 1pl	3471.5 verb 1pl indic perf act	3617.1 conj	3450.5 art sing masc	442.1 noun nom sing masc
θεῷ˙	ἡμεῖς	οἴδαμεν	ὅτι	‘ ὁ	ἄνθρωπος
theō	*hēmeis*	*oidamen*	*hoti*	*ho*	*anthrōpos*
to God;	we	know	that	the	man

3642.4 dem-pron nom sing masc	3642.4 dem-pron nom sing masc	3450.5 art sing masc	442.1 noun nom sing masc	266.1 adj nom sing
οὗτος	[☆ οὗτος	ὁ	ἄνθρωπος]	ἁμαρτωλός
houtos	*houtos*	*ho*	*anthrōpos*	*hamartōlos*
this	[this	the	man]	a sinner

25.a.**Txt:** 017K,033X, 036,037,byz.bo.
Var: 01ℵ,02A,03B,05D, 019L,038,it.sa.LachTreg, Alf,Word,Tisc,We/Ho, Weis,Sod,UBS/☆

1498.4 verb 3sing indic pres act	552.6 verb 3sing indic aor pass	3631.1 conj	1552.3 dem-pron nom sing masc	2504.1 conj
ἐστιν.	25. ᾿Απεκρίθη	οὖν	ἐκεῖνος	(a καὶ
estin	*Apekrithē*	*oun*	*ekeinos*	*kai*
is.	Answered	therefore	he	and

1500.5 verb 3sing indic aor act	1479.1 conj	266.1 adj nom sing	1498.4 verb 3sing indic pres act	3620.2 partic
εἶπεν, `	Εἰ	ἁμαρτωλός	ἐστιν	οὐκ
eipen	*Ei*	*hamartōlos*	*estin*	*ouk*
said,	If	a sinner	he is	not

26.a.**Txt:** 01ℵ-corr,02A, 03B,05D,017K,019L, 038,etc.byz.Lach,Tisc, Sod
Var: 01ℵ-org,We/Ho, Weis,UBS/☆

3471.2 verb 1sing indic perf act	1518.9 num card neu	3471.2 verb 1sing indic perf act	3617.1 conj	5026.1 adj nom sing masc	1498.21 verb sing masc part pres act
οἶδα˙	ἓν	οἶδα,	ὅτι	τυφλὸς	ὢν
oida	*hen*	*oida*	*hoti*	*tuphlos*	*ōn*
I know.	One	I know,	that	blind	being

26.b.**Txt:** 02A,036,037, byz.
Var: 01ℵ-corr,03B,05D, 017K,019L,033X,038,sa. Lach,Treg,Alf,Tisc, We/HoWeis,Sod,UBS/☆

732.1 adv	984.2 verb 1sing indic pres act	1500.3 verb indic aor act	1500.28 verb 3pl indic aor act	1156.2 conj
ἄρτι	βλέπω.	26. (☆ Εἶπον	[a☆ εἶπαν]	‘ δὲ
arti	*blepō*	*Eipon*	*eipan*	*de*
now	I see.	They said	[idem]	and

26.c.**Txt:** p66,01ℵ-corr, 02A,017K,036,037,038, 1,13,byz.Gries,Word,Sod
Var: p75,01ℵ-org,03B, 05D,032W,sa.bo.Lach Treg,Alf,Tisc,We/Ho, Weis,UBS/☆

3631.1 conj	840.4 prs-pron dat sing	3687.1 adv	4949.9 intr-pron sing neu	4020.24 verb 3sing indic aor act
[b☆ οὖν]	αὐτῷ	(c πάλιν, `	Τί	ἐποίησέν
oun	*autō*	*palin*	*Ti*	*epoiēsen*
[therefore]	to him	again,	What	did he

4622.3 prs-pron dat 2sing	4316.1 adv	453.4 verb 3sing indic aor act	4622.2 prs-pron gen 2sing	3450.8 art acc pl masc	3652.8 noun acc pl masc
σοι;	πῶς	ἤνοιξέν	σου	τοὺς	ὀφθαλμούς;
soi	*pōs*	*ēnoixen*	*sou*	*tous*	*ophthalmous*
to you?	how	he opened	your	the	eyes?

552.6 verb 3sing indic aor pass	840.2 prs-pron dat pl	1500.3 verb indic aor act	5050.3 prs-pron dat 2pl	2218.1 adv	2504.1 conj
27. ᾿Απεκρίθη	αὐτοῖς,	Εἶπον	ὑμῖν	ἤδη,	καὶ
Apekrithē	*autois*	*Eipon*	*humin*	*ēdē*	*kai*
He answered	them,	I told	you	already,	and

3620.2 partic	189.23 verb 2pl indic aor act	4949.9 intr-pron sing neu	3687.1 adv	2286.5 verb 2pl indic pres act	189.17 verb inf pres act
οὐκ	ἠκούσατε˙	τί	πάλιν	θέλετε	ἀκούειν;
ouk	*ēkousate*	*ti*	*palin*	*thelete*	*akouein*
not	you did hear:	why	again	do you wish	to hear?

3231.1 partic	2504.1 conj	5050.1 prs-pron nom 2pl	2286.5 verb 2pl indic pres act	840.3 prs-pron gen sing	3073.5 noun nom pl masc	1090.63 verb inf aor mid
μὴ	καὶ	ὑμεῖς	θέλετε	αὐτοῦ	μαθηταὶ	γενέσθαι;
mē	*kai*	*humeis*	*thelete*	*autou*	*mathētai*	*genesthai*
not	also	do you	wish	his	disciples	to become?

in his first epistle. He wrote, "Whosoever denieth the Son, the same hath not the Father: but he that acknowledgeth the Son hath the Father also" (1 John 2:23).

To call Jesus a sinner as the Jewish leaders did here is a serious offense. To acknowledge He was a good man but not God helps none. Even to recognize Him as a prophet and yet deny His deity as in some religions, is totally unacceptable. Anyone who stops short of declaring the deity of Jesus joins himself with the "spirit of antichrist" (1 John 2:22; 4:3).

It is interesting that Jesus gave the Jews opportunity to prove Him a sinner. They could not! Yet, they declared, "We know that this man is a sinner." As we observe their lives, we note the statement came from the mouths of murderers and liars (8:44).

They accused Jesus of being a "sinner" (*hamartōlos*), i.e., one who misses the mark because he has broken their interpretation of the Law. The Pharisees were desperate men who would stop at nothing to guard their pride.

9:25. Notice how reluctant the man was to become involved in an argument pertaining to the Law. He would not attempt an apology for Jesus on the question as to whether or not He had broken the Sabbath.

His statement was a bold declaration to the healing power of Jesus. By what the man said, a certain impatience can be detected because of the dishonesty, hypocrisy, and jealousy of the Jews. The man gave the factual evidence, and the Jews willfully imposed fallacious conclusions.

9:26. The Pharisees further questioned the man by a general question, "What did he to thee?" and a more specific question, "How opened he thine eyes?" Both questions were attempts to make it appear that Jesus had worked on the Sabbath. Beyond the "what" and "how" they were hoping for some contradiction in the man's testimony and perhaps some bit that they could use against Jesus.

9:27. The indignation of the healed man was aroused by the Jews because of their stubborn refusal to believe the facts. Their obvious intent was to find flaws in his testimony to use in a malicious way against Jesus.

The beggar suggested that perhaps the Pharisees wanted to hear his story again that they might believe in Jesus. The little word "also" (*kai*) may indicate that the healed man was well on his way to becoming Jesus' disciple, or it may mean that perhaps the Phar-

we know that this man is a sinner: As for us, we know positively, *Wuest* . . . we are aware that, *Concordant* . . . this man, we know quite well, is only a sinner, *Moffatt* . . . who cured you is a sinner, *TEV* . . . a bad man, *TCNT* . . . that this fellow is wicked, *Fenton.*

25. He answered and said, Whether he be a sinner or no, I know not: I don't know if He's a sinner, *Beck.*

one thing I know, that: . . . all I know is this, *AmpB* . . . But one thing I am certain about, *BB* . . . I do know one thing, *Williams* . . . I am sure off, *Tyndale* . . . I know only one thing, *Adams.*

whereas I was blind, now I see: I was blind before, *AmpB* . . . that although I was blind, now I can see, *TCNT* . . . and lo, now I see, *Murdock.*

26. Then said they to him again, What did he to thee? how opened he thine eyes?: Once more they questioned him, *Norlie* . . . how did he give you the use of your eyes? *BB* . . . How is it that you can now see? *TEV* . . . How did he make you able to see? *Barclay.*

27. He answered them, I have told you already, and ye did not hear: Weren't you listening? *Phillips* . . . ye hearkened not, *Rotherham* . . . but you did not listen, *Norlie.*

wherefore would ye hear it again?: . . . why do ye wish to hear it again? *HBIE.*

will ye also be his disciples: Do you want to be disciples of his, *Moffatt* . . . is it your desire to become his disciples, *BB* . . . Do you really wish to become His disciples? *Fenton* . . . are you also willing, *Wilson.*

John 9:28

28.a.**Var:** p75,01ℵ-org, 03B,032W,We/Ho,Weis, UBS/*

28.b.**Txt:** 13,Steph
Var: p66,p75,01ℵ,02A, 03B,05D,017K,019L, 032W,036,037,038,byz. Gries,LachTreg,Alf, Word,Tisc,We/Ho,Weis, Sod,UBS/*

28.c.**Txt:** 02A,03B,017K, 019L,036,037,038,etc. byz.Lach,Sod
Var: 01ℵ,05D,Tisc, We/Ho,Weis,UBS/*

2504.1 conj	**3032.2** verb 3pl indic aor act	**3631.1** conj	**840.6** prs-pron acc sing masc	**2504.1** conj
28. [a*+ καὶ]	Ἐλοιδόρησαν	⌜b οὖν ⌝	αὐτὸν,	καὶ
kai	*Eloidorēsan*	*oun*	*auton*	*kai*
[And]	They ridiculed at	therefore	him,	and

1500.3 verb indic aor act	**1500.28** verb 3pl indic aor act	**4622.1** prs-pron nom 2sing	**1498.3** verb 2sing indic pres act	**3073.1** noun nom sing masc
⌜* εἶπον,	[c εἶπαν·]	Σὺ	⌜ εἶ	μαθητὴς
eipon	*eipan*	*Su*	*ei*	*mathētēs*
said,	[idem]	You	are	disciple

3073.1 noun nom sing masc	**1498.3** verb 2sing indic pres act	**1552.2** dem-pron gen sing	**2231.1** prs-pron nom 1pl	**1156.2** conj
[* μαθητὴς	εἶ]	ἐκείνου·	ἡμεῖς	δὲ
mathētēs	*ei*	*ekeinou*	*hēmeis*	*de*
[disciple	are]	of that,	we	but

3450.2 art gen sing	**3337.2** name gen masc	**3338.2** name gen masc	**1498.5** verb 1pl indic pres act	**3073.5** noun nom pl masc
τοῦ	⌜ Μωσέως	[* Μωϋσέως]	ἐσμὲν	μαθηταί.
tou	*Mōseōs*	*Mōuseōs*	*esmen*	*mathētai*
	Moses	[idem]	are	disciples.

2231.1 prs-pron nom 1pl	**3471.5** verb 1pl indic perf act	**3617.1** conj	**3337.4** name dat masc	**3338.3** name dat masc
29. ἡμεῖς	οἴδαμεν	ὅτι	⌜ Μωσῇ	[* Μωϋσεῖ]
hēmeis	*oidamen*	*hoti*	*Mōsē*	*Mōusei*
We	know	that	to Moses	[idem]

2953.39 verb 3sing indic perf act	**3450.5** art sing masc	**2296.1** noun nom sing masc	**3642.6** dem-pron acc sing masc	**1156.2** conj	**3620.2** partic
λελάληκεν	ὁ	θεός·	τοῦτον	δὲ	οὐκ
lelalēken	*ho*	*theos*	*touton*	*de*	*ouk*
has spoken		God;	this	but	not

3471.5 verb 1pl indic perf act	**4019.1** adv	**1498.4** verb 3sing indic pres act	**552.6** verb 3sing indic aor pass	**3450.5** art sing masc
οἴδαμεν	πόθεν	ἐστίν.	**30.** Ἀπεκρίθη	ὁ
oidamen	*pothen*	*estin*	*Apekrithē*	*ho*
we know	from where	he is.	Answered	the

442.1 noun nom sing masc	**2504.1** conj	**1500.5** verb 3sing indic aor act	**840.2** prs-pron dat pl	**1706.1** prep	**1056.1** conj
ἄνθρωπος	καὶ	εἶπεν	αὐτοῖς,	Ἐν	⌜ γὰρ
anthrōpos	*kai*	*eipen*	*autois*	*En*	*gar*
man	and	said	to them,	In	indeed

30.a.**Var:** 01ℵ,03B,019L, 33,Treg,Tisc,We/Ho, WeisSod,UBS/*

3642.5 dem-pron dat sing masc	**3642.5** dem-pron dat sing masc	**1056.1** conj	**3450.16** art sing neu	**2275.2** adj sing neu
τούτῳ	[* τούτῳ	γὰρ]	[a*+ τὸ]	θαυμαστόν
toutō	*toutō*	*gar*	*to*	*thaumaston*
this	[this	for]	[the]	a wonderful thing

1498.4 verb 3sing indic pres act	**3617.1** conj	**5050.1** prs-pron nom 2pl	**3620.2** partic	**3471.6** verb 2pl indic perf act	**4019.1** adv
ἐστιν,	ὅτι	ὑμεῖς	οὐκ	οἴδατε	πόθεν
estin	*hoti*	*humeis*	*ouk*	*oidate*	*pothen*
is,	that	you	not	know	from where

30.b.**Txt:** 02A,017K,036, 037,038,byz.
Var: 01ℵ,03B,05D,019L, Lach,Treg,Tisc,We/Ho, Weis,Sod,UBS/*

1498.4 verb 3sing indic pres act	**2504.1** conj	**453.5** verb 3sing indic aor act	**453.4** verb 3sing indic aor act	**1466.2** prs-pron gen 1sing	**3450.8** art acc pl masc
ἐστίν,	καὶ	⌜ ἀνέῳξέν	[b* ἤνοιξέν]	μου	τοὺς
estin	*kai*	*aneōxen*	*ēnoixen*	*mou*	*tous*
he is,	and	he opened	[idem]	my	the

isees were about to believe the evidence and follow Jesus. The man spoke in irony to taunt his hypocritical interrogators.

28. Then they reviled him, and said: Then they stormed at him, *Montgomery* . . . they retorted scornfully, *TCNT* . . . they turned on him furiously, *Phillips* . . . they abused him, *Norlie* . . . they jeered him, *Williams.*

Thou art his disciple; but we are Moses' disciples: You are that man's disciple, but we are disciples of Moses, *Weymouth.*

9:28. When argument failed to serve their ends, the Jews resorted to harsh abuse.

They belittled the man by calling him Jesus' disciple. They did not use Jesus' name, but the word "his" (*ekeinou*) meaning "that One." The Jews refused any attempt to connect them with the name of Jesus. To them Jesus, the Sabbath breaker, stood in stark contrast to Moses, the lawgiver. They were incurring the very curse which Moses pronounced on all who would not listen to and receive the teachings of Jesus Christ (Deuteronomy 18:15-19).

29. We know that God spake unto Moses: We do know that God spoke to Moses, *Williams.*

as for this fellow, we know not from whence he is: . . . we don't even know where he came from, *Phillips.*

9:29. They were correct in this statement, but what they failed to realize was that Jesus himself was the God who spoke to Moses (see 5:43-47; 6:30-32).

"As for this fellow" suggests that they were adding another insult and denying any knowledge of His origin.

If they knew where He was from, they would be obligated to acknowledge His commission. Thus they denied He was an ambassador sent from God with credentials made plain by miracles, signs, and wonders.

These Pharisees should have been as wise as Nicodemus who confessed to Jesus himself: "Rabbi, we know that thou art a teacher come from God: for no man can do these miracles that thou doest, except God be with him" (3:2).

It is amazing that they did not know where Jesus was from. They did not investigate where He was born. His lineage and birthplace would have connected Him with the prophecy of Micah 5:2. This fact would have led them to a knowledge of His heavenly origin.

30. The man answered and said unto them, Why herein is a marvellous thing: Well, there is something strange about this! *Williams* . . . This is surprising, *Campbell* . . . the marvel of it, *Berkeley* . . . This is truly astonishing, *Montgomery* . . . Well, that's strange! *Beck* . . . Well the wonder is that you should not know, *Fenton.*

that ye know not from whence he is: You have no knowledge where he comes from, *BB* . . . that you do not know where He is from, *Norlie* . . . where he hails from, *Berkeley.*

and yet he hath opened mine eyes: . . . though he gave me the use of my eyes, *BB* . . . and yet He gave me my sight, *Beck.*

9:30. The evidence was becoming clearer to the beggar the longer the Pharisees argued with him. Without realizing it the Pharisees were making the man a disciple of Jesus. The man stated all the proof that should have been needed for anyone, namely, that Jesus was "from God." They had scoffed "we do not know where He is from." The healed man implied that He was from God!

9:31. The Pharisees' theology was that Jesus was a sinner because He "worked" on the Sabbath. They said, "We know that God heareth not sinners." Therefore, they reasoned, God did not hear or answer Jesus' requests. They concluded that Jesus was not from

31.a.**Txt:** 02A,017K, 032W,036,037,byz.Gries **Var:** 01ℵ,03B,05D,019L, 038,33,sa.bo.Lach,Treg, Alf,Tisc,We/Ho,WeisSod, UBS/☆

3652.8 noun acc pl masc	3471.5 verb 1pl indic perf act	1156.2 conj	3617.1 conj	266.5 adj gen pl masc
ὀφθαλμούς.	**31.** οἴδαμεν	⸂a δὲ ⸃	ὅτι	⸂ ἁμαρτωλῶν
ophthalmous	*oidamen*	*de*	*hoti*	*hamartōlōn*
eyes.	We know	but	that	sinners

3450.5 art sing masc	2296.1 noun nom sing masc	3450.5 art sing masc	2296.1 noun nom sing masc	266.5 adj gen pl masc	3620.2 partic
ὁ	θεὸς	[ὁ	θεὸς	ἁμαρτωλῶν]	οὐκ
ho	*theos*	*ho*	*theos*	*hamartōlōn*	*ouk*
	God		[God	sinners]	not

189.5 verb 3sing indic pres act	233.1 conj	1430.1 partic	4948.3 indef-pron nom sing	2294.1 adj nom sing masc	1498.10 verb 3sing subj pres act
ἀκούει·	ἀλλ'	ἐάν	τις	θεοσεβὴς	ᾖ,
akouei	*all'*	*ean*	*tis*	*theosebēs*	*ē*
does hear;	but	if	anyone	God-fearing	be,

2504.1 conj	3450.16 art sing neu	2284.1 noun sing neu	840.3 prs-pron gen sing	4020.8 verb 3sing subj pres act	3642.1 dem-pron gen sing
καὶ	τὸ	θέλημα	αὐτοῦ	ποιῇ,	τούτου
kai	*to*	*thelēma*	*autou*	*poiē*	*toutou*
and	the	will	his	do,	this

189.5 verb 3sing indic pres act	1523.2 prep gen	3450.2 art gen sing	163.1 noun gen sing masc	3620.2 partic	189.48 verb 3sing indic aor pass
ἀκούει.	**32.** ἐκ	τοῦ	αἰῶνος	οὐκ	ἠκούσθη,
akouei	*ek*	*tou*	*aiōnos*	*ouk*	*ēkousthē*
he hears.	From	the	age	not	it was heard

32.a.**Txt:** 01ℵ,02A,05D, 017K,019L,036,byz. Lach,Tisc,Sod **Var:** 03B,033X,037, Treg,We/Ho,Weis, UBS/☆

3617.1 conj	453.4 verb 3sing indic aor act	453.33 verb 3sing indic aor act	4948.3 indef-pron nom sing	3652.8 noun acc pl masc
ὅτι	⸀☆ ἤνοιξέν	[a ἠνέῳξέν]	τις	ὀφθαλμοὺς
hoti	*ēnoixen*	*ēneōxen*	*tis*	*ophthalmous*
that	opened	[idem]	anyone	eyes

5026.2 adj gen sing masc	1074.27 verb gen sing masc part perf pass	1479.1 conj	3231.1 partic	1498.34 verb sing indic imperf act
τυφλοῦ	γεγεννημένου.	**33.** εἰ	μὴ	ἦν
tuphlou	*gegennēmenou*	*ei*	*mē*	*ēn*
of blind	having been born.	If	not	were

3642.4 dem-pron nom sing masc	3706.2 prep	2296.2 noun gen sing masc	3620.2 partic	1404.34 verb 3sing indic imperf	4020.20 verb inf pres act
οὗτος	παρὰ	θεοῦ	οὐκ	ἠδύνατο	ποιεῖν
houtos	*para*	*theou*	*ouk*	*ēdunato*	*poiein*
this	from	God	not	he could	do

34.a.**Txt:** 02A,017K, 019L,036,037,byz.Sod **Var:** 01ℵ,03B,05D,038, Lach,Treg,Alf,Tisc, We/Ho,Weis,UBS/☆

3625.6 num card neu	552.8 verb 3pl indic aor pass	2504.1 conj	1500.3 verb indic aor act	1500.28 verb 3pl indic aor act
οὐδέν.	**34.** Ἀπεκρίθησαν	καὶ	⸀☆ εἶπον	[a εἶπαν]
ouden	*Apekrithēsan*	*kai*	*eipon*	*eipan*
nothing.	They answered	and	said	[idem]

840.4 prs-pron dat sing	1706.1 prep	264.7 noun dat pl fem	4622.1 prs-pron nom 2sing	1074.12 verb 2sing indic aor pass	3513.4 adj nom sing masc
αὐτῷ,	Ἐν	ἁμαρτίαις	σὺ	ἐγεννήθης	ὅλος,
autō	*En*	*hamartiais*	*su*	*egennēthēs*	*holos*
to him,	In	sins	you	were born	wholly,

2504.1 conj	4622.1 prs-pron nom 2sing	1315.2 verb 2sing indic pres act	2231.4 prs-pron acc 1pl	2504.1 conj	1531.13 verb 3pl indic aor act
καὶ	σὺ	διδάσκεις	ἡμᾶς;	καὶ	ἐξέβαλον
kai	*su*	*didaskeis*	*hēmas*	*kai*	*exebalon*
and	you	teach	us?	And	they threw

God, nor did He work the works of God (compare Psalm 66:18 and Isaiah 1:15).

If God does not hear sinners' prayers, He will not bestow divine favors on them or grant their requests. This was the reasoning of the Pharisees in verse 16. Their reasoning was logical, but their premise was false.

The healed man reversed their argument of cause and effect. He began with the effect and reasoned to the cause, concluding that Jesus was from God because of the effect. The beggar's logic was something like this: Since He healed my eyes, it is evident that God heard Jesus. If God heard Him, He is not a sinner because God does not hear sinners. Therefore, the man concluded, Jesus was not a sinner. He had not broken the sabbatical law. God sent Him, God heard, and God answered Him. The man was yet to understand what John was asserting thus far in the Gospel. Beyond all, Jesus is God himself.

Some say the discussion here shows sinners should never pray. However, the question in this context does not relate to God's response to a prayer of repentance. On the basis of an Old Testament promise Paul declared, "For whosoever shall call upon the name of the Lord shall be saved" (Joel 2:32; Romans 10:13).

9:32. The healed man pointed to an outstanding fact. No man born blind had ever been healed. No prophet had performed such a miracle though they had worked miracles even to raising the dead. Giving sight to the blind was reserved for a credential of the Messiah (Isaiah 35:5; 42:7). Jesus made His claim to messiahship on this evidence (Luke 4:18). He reassured John the Baptist of His mission by pointing out that the "blind receive their sight, and the lame walk" (Matthew 11:5).

9:33. The beggar stated (verse 17) that he believed Jesus was a prophet. He affirmed the same idea; yet, the longer he was opposed, the stronger his conviction became. He saw through the mask of hypocrisy, and he boldly spoke his mind.

9:34. To the Jews the man's blindness was evidence of the curse of God upon him. They believed the curse was the result of his sins as had the disciples (according to their question in verse 2). The Jews argued that one who was so plagued with his own curse as a result of being born entirely in sins had no right to teach them about honesty and righteousness.

"Cast out" (*exebalon*) means literally "to throw out." (See verse 22 for comments on being put out of the synagogue.) The Pharisees barred the man from the synagogue so that he might not influence others to become disciples.

31. Now we know that God heareth not sinners: . . . know positively, *Wuest* . . . does not respond to, *Berkeley.*

but if any man be a worshipper of God, and doeth his will, him he heareth: . . . but He does hear one who reverences Him and does His will, *Berkeley* . . . is God-fearing, and does His will, *Fenton* . . . one who respects and obeys him, *ALBA* . . . who is devout, *Moffatt* . . . is religious and does God's will, *TCNT* . . . lives to do His will, *Williams.*

32. Since the world began was it not heard that any man opened the eyes of one that was born blind: It has never been heard of in this world, *Williams* . . . Through the ages this has never been heard of, *Berkeley* . . . From eternity past, *Adams* . . . Nobody has ever heard of anyone giving sight to a man born blind, *Beck* . . . it was unheard-of that, *Panin.*

33. If this man were not of God, he could do nothing: Assuming that this man was not from, *Wuest* . . . He couldn't do anything, *Beck* . . . could not have done anything like this, *Williams.*

34. They answered and said unto him, Thou wast altogether born in sins: They retorted, *Moffatt* . . . You were born in utter sin, *RSV* . . . They shouted back at him, "You are altogether depraved, *Norlie* . . . You were wholly begotten and born in sin, *Weymouth* . . . you, born in utter depravity! *Moffatt* . . . wholly born in sins, *Murdock* . . . in total depravity, *Williams* . . . from head to foot born in sins, *Fenton* . . . came to birth through sin, *BB* . . . were born totally depraved, *TCNT.*

and dost thou teach us?: . . . and So you would teach us, *Moffatt* . . . would you presume to teach us? *Fenton* . . . are you teaching us? *Wuest.*

And they cast him out: And so they turned him out of the synagogue, *Williams* . . . They accordingly kicked him out, *Fenton* . . . threw him clear outside, *Berkeley.*

John 9:35

35.a.**Txt:** p66,01ℵ-corr, 02A,05D,017K,019L, 032W,036,037,038,etc. byz.Lach,Sod
Var: p75,01ℵ-org,03B, Tisc,We/Ho,Weis,UBS/*

840.6 prs-pron acc sing masc	1838.1 prep gen	189.21 verb 3sing indic aor act	3450.5 art sing masc	2400.1 name nom masc	3617.1 conj
αὐτὸν	ἔξω.	35. Ἤκουσεν	(a ὁ \	Ἰησοῦς	ὅτι
auton	exō	Ekousen	ho	Iēsous	hoti
him	out.	Heard		Jesus	that

1531.13 verb 3pl indic aor act	840.6 prs-pron acc sing masc	1838.1 prep gen	2504.1 conj	2128.17 verb nom sing masc part aor act	840.6 prs-pron acc sing masc
ἐξέβαλον	αὐτὸν	ἔξω·	καὶ	εὑρὼν	αὐτὸν
exebalon	auton	exō	kai	heurōn	auton
they threw	him	out,	and	having found	him

35.b.**Txt:** p66,01ℵ-corr, 02A,017K,019L,036, 037,038,etc.byz.Lach, Sod
Var: p75,01ℵ-org,03B, 05D,032W,Tisc,We/Ho, Weis,UBS/*

1500.5 verb 3sing indic aor act	840.4 prs-pron dat sing	4622.1 prs-pron nom 2sing	3961.5 verb 2sing indic pres act	1519.1 prep
εἶπεν	(b αὐτῷ, \	Σὺ	πιστεύεις	εἰς
eipen	autō	Su	pisteueis	eis
said	to him,	You	believe	on

35.c.**Txt:** 02A,017K, 019L,036,037,038,1,13, 33,byz.it.Lach,Treg,Sod
Var: p66,p75,01ℵ,03B, 05D,032W,sa.Tisc, We/HoWeis,UBS/*

3450.6 art acc sing masc	5048.4 noun acc sing masc	3450.2 art gen sing	2296.2 noun gen sing masc	442.2 noun gen sing masc
τὸν	υἱὸν	τοῦ	(θεοῦ;	[c* ἀνθρώπου;]
ton	huion	tou	theou	anthrōpou
the	Son		of God?	[of man?]

36.a.**Var:** 01ℵ-corr,05D, 017K,036,037,byz.Gries, Treg,Alf,Tisc,We/Ho, Sod,UBS/*

552.6 verb 3sing indic aor pass	1552.3 dem-pron nom sing masc	2504.1 conj	1500.5 verb 3sing indic aor act	2504.1 conj
36. Ἀπεκρίθη	ἐκεῖνος	καὶ	εἶπεν,	[a*+ Καὶ]
Apekrithē	ekeinos	kai	eipen	Kai
Answered	that	and	said,	[And]

4949.3 intr-pron nom sing	1498.4 verb 3sing indic pres act	2935.5 noun voc sing masc	2419.1 conj	3961.17 verb 1sing act	1519.1 prep
Τίς	ἐστιν,	κύριε,	ἵνα	πιστεύσω	εἰς
Tis	estin	kurie	hina	pisteusō	eis
Who	is he,	Lord,	that	I may believe	on

37.a.**Txt:** 02A,017K, 019L,036,037,1,13,byz. Gries,Word,Sod
Var: 01ℵ,03B,05D, 033X,038,33,sa.bo.Lach, Treg,Alf,Tisc,We/Ho, Weis,UBS/*

840.6 prs-pron acc sing masc	1500.5 verb 3sing indic aor act	1156.2 conj	840.4 prs-pron dat sing	3450.5 art sing masc	2400.1 name nom masc
αὐτόν;	37. Εἶπεν	(a δὲ \	αὐτῷ	ὁ	Ἰησοῦς,
auton	Eipen	de	autō	ho	Iēsous
him?	Said	and	to him		Jesus,

2504.1 conj	3571.10 verb 2sing indic perf act	840.6 prs-pron acc sing masc	2504.1 conj	3450.5 art sing masc	2953.12 verb nom sing masc part pres act
Καὶ	ἑώρακας	αὐτὸν,	καὶ	ὁ	λαλῶν
Kai	heōrakas	auton	kai	ho	lalōn
Both	you have seen	him,	and	the	speaking

3196.3 prep	4622.2 prs-pron gen 2sing	1552.3 dem-pron nom sing masc	1498.4 verb 3sing indic pres act	3450.5 art sing masc	1156.2 conj
μετὰ	σοῦ	ἐκεῖνός	ἐστιν.	38. Ὁ	δὲ
meta	sou	ekeinos	estin	Ho	de
with	you	that	is.	The	and

5183.4 verb 3sing indic act	3961.4 verb 1sing indic pres act	2935.5 noun voc sing masc	2504.1 conj	4210.9 verb 3sing indic aor act
ἔφη,	Πιστεύω,	κύριε·	καὶ	προσεκύνησεν
ephē	Pisteuō	kurie	kai	prosekunēsen
said,	I believe,	Lord:	and	he worshiped

840.4 prs-pron dat sing	2504.1 conj	1500.5 verb 3sing indic aor act	3450.5 art sing masc	2400.1 name nom masc	1519.1 prep
αὐτῷ.	39. καὶ	εἶπεν	ὁ	Ἰησοῦς,	Εἰς
autō	kai	eipen	ho	Iēsous	Eis
him.	And	said		Jesus,	For

9:35. No mention is made of Jesus' supernatural knowledge, yet He certainly knew before He heard.

"When he had found him" implies the work of the Good Shepherd, which is the theme of the next chapter. The Jews were not shepherds, but hirelings for they did not care for the sheep. Jesus sought this sheep and found him. These words are characteristic of the Saviour.

"On" is the Greek preposition *eis* indicating the direction toward. Jesus identified himself as "the Son of Man" (NASB), a title of His humanity and messiahship. Some manuscripts, as in the King James, contain the words "the Son of God." "The Son of Man" was also a term applied to the coming Messiah. Prior to the interview the healed man had recognized Jesus as a prophet from God. Now Jesus questioned him that he might receive his Messiah.

9:36. This is the first time the man had actually seen Jesus. He had gone to the pool to wash off the clay and left seeing. He called Jesus "Lord" (*kurie*) not because he recognized Jesus as God here, but because he was aware that Jesus was his superior. "Might believe on him" means toward Him as to the identity of His person. The healed man was both intelligent and teachable. These two traits are foundational to producing a good disciple.

9:37. To the Samaritan woman Jesus plainly declared himself the Messiah; so also to this man Jesus unveiled His person. "Hast . . . seen him" pointed to far more than merely looking at Him. It reminded the man that his sight had been given that he might see his Saviour, and he was reminded that his Saviour was speaking to him. Sight and hearing are both ways to experience life; moreover, they are two of the greatest gifts from the grace of God.

9:38. The man made two responses to Jesus' declaration. First, he made his confession of faith, "Lord, I believe." This use of "Lord" (*kurie*) indicates Jesus' messiahship (and priestly deity). "Believe," *pisteuō*, is a present tense continuous action verb. His confession of faith was simple, yet it brought to him eternal life.

"And he worshipped him." By this second act the beggar attributed to Jesus that to which God alone is entitled. Jesus accepted the "worship." To worship God means to adore God, often on one's knees. What the grace of Christ did for this beggar, it does for all. He was once in poverty, but in Christ he was made wealthy. He was once blind, yet now he could see. He was once a beggar; nevertheless, now he was a sharer. Once he was lost, but Jesus found him.

35. Jesus heard that they had cast him out; and when he had found him: . . . encountering him, *Berkeley.*

he said unto him, Dost thou believe on the Son of God?: . . . into the Son of Mankind? *Concordant.*

36. He answered and said, Who is he, Lord, that I might believe on him?: . . . so that I may have faith in him, *BB.*

37. And Jesus said unto him, Thou hast both seen him: You have already seen him, *Montgomery.*

and it is he that talketh with thee: . . . in fact, He is talking with you now, *Berkeley* . . . you are talking to Him right now! *Williams.*

38. And he said, Lord, I believe. And he worshipped him: I believe, Master, *Weymouth* . . . then he kneeled before Him, *Norlie* . . . bending low, *TCNT* . . . he threw himself prostrate, *Wilson* . . . did him reverence, *Norton* . . . The man flung himself at his feet, and confessed, *ALBA* . . . and he bowed to Him, *Fenton.*

39. And Jesus said, For judgment I am come into this world: I came into the world to bring judgment, *Norlie* . . . to put men

2890.1 noun sing neu	1466.1 prs-pron nom 1sing	1519.1 prep	3450.6 art acc sing masc	2862.4 noun acc sing masc	3642.6 dem-pron acc sing masc
κρίμα	ἐγὼ	εἰς	τὸν	κόσμον	τοῦτον
krima	*egō*	*eis*	*ton*	*kosmon*	*touton*
judgment	I	into	the	world	this

2048.1 verb indic aor act	2419.1 conj	3450.7 art pl masc	3231.1 partic	984.14 verb nom pl masc part pres act	984.9 verb 3pl subj pres act	2504.1 conj
ἦλθον,	ἵνα	οἱ	μὴ	βλέποντες	βλέπωσιν,	καὶ
ēlthon	*hina*	*hoi*	*mē*	*blepontes*	*blepōsin*	*kai*
came,	that	the	not	seeing	might see,	and

40.a.**Txt:** 02A,017K,036,037,13,byz.Lach
Var: 01ℵ,03B,019L,033X,038,33,Treg,Alf Tisc,We/Ho,Weis,Sod,UBS/☆

3450.7 art pl masc	984.14 verb nom pl masc part pres act	5026.6 adj pl masc	1090.43 verb 3pl subj aor mid		2504.1 conj
οἱ	βλέποντες	τυφλοὶ	γένωνται.	**40.** ⌜a	Καὶ ⌝
hoi	*blepontes*	*tuphloi*	*genōntai*		*Kai*
the	seeing	blind	might become.		And

189.24 verb 3pl indic aor act	1523.2 prep gen	3450.1 art gen pl	5168.5 name gen pl masc	3642.18 dem-pron pl neu
ἤκουσαν	ἐκ	τῶν	Φαρισαίων	ταῦτα
ēkousan	*ek*	*tōn*	*Pharisaiōn*	*tauta*
heard	of	the	Pharisees	these things

3450.7 art pl masc	1498.23 verb nom pl masc part pres act	3196.2 prep	840.3 prs-pron gen sing	3196.2 prep	840.3 prs-pron gen sing
οἱ	⌜ ὄντες	μετ'	αὐτοῦ,	[☆ μετ'	αὐτοῦ
hoi	*ontes*	*met'*	*autou*	*met'*	*autou*
the	being	with	him,	[with	him

40.b.**Txt:** 03B,017K,019L,036,037,038,etc.byz.Lach,Sod
Var: 01ℵ,05D,Tisc,We/Ho,Weis,UBS/☆

1498.23 verb nom pl masc part pres act	2504.1 conj	1500.3 verb indic aor act	1500.28 verb 3pl indic aor act	840.4 prs-pron dat sing	3231.1 partic
ὄντες,]	καὶ	⌜☆ εἶπον	[b εἶπαν]	αὐτῷ,	Μὴ
ontes	*kai*	*eipon*	*eipan*	*autō*	*Mē*
being,]	and	they said	[idem]	to him,	Not

2504.1 conj	2231.1 prs-pron nom 1pl	5026.6 adj pl masc	1498.5 verb 1pl indic pres act	1500.5 verb 3sing indic aor act	840.2 prs-pron dat pl
καὶ	ἡμεῖς	τυφλοί	ἐσμεν;	**41.** Εἶπεν	αὐτοῖς
kai	*hēmeis*	*tuphloi*	*esmen*	*Eipen*	*autois*
also	we	blind	are?	Said	to them

3450.5 art sing masc	2400.1 name nom masc	1479.1 conj	5026.6 adj pl masc	1498.1 verb 2pl act	3620.2 partic	300.1 partic
ὁ	Ἰησοῦς,	Εἰ	τυφλοὶ	ἦτε,	οὐκ	ἂν
ho	*Iēsous*	*Ei*	*tuphloi*	*ēte*	*ouk*	*an*
	Jesus,	If	blind	you were,	not	

2174.47 verb 2pl indic imperf act	264.4 noun acc sing fem	3431.1 adv	1156.2 conj	2978.2 verb 2pl pres act	3617.1 conj
εἴχετε	ἁμαρτίαν·	νῦν	δὲ	λέγετε,	Ὅτι
eichete	*hamartian*	*nun*	*de*	*legete*	*Hoti*
you would have	sin;	now	but	you say	

41.a.**Txt:** 02A,036,037,byz.Gries,Lach
Var: 01ℵ,03B,05D,017K,019L,033X,038,33,sa.Treg,Alf,Tisc We/Ho,Weis,Sod,UBS/☆

984.5 verb 1pl indic pres act	3450.9 art nom sing fem	3631.1 conj	264.2 noun nom sing fem	5050.2 prs-pron gen 2pl
Βλέπομεν·	ἡ	⌜a οὖν ⌝	ἁμαρτία	ὑμῶν
Blepomen	*hē*	*oun*	*hamartia*	*humōn*
We see,	the	therefore	sin	your

3176.1 verb 3sing indic act	279.1 partic	279.1 partic	2978.1 verb 1sing pres act	5050.3 prs-pron dat 2pl	3450.5 art sing masc
μένει.	**10:1.** Ἀμὴν	ἀμὴν	λέγω	ὑμῖν,	ὁ
menei	*Amēn*	*amēn*	*legō*	*humin*	*ho*
remains.	Truly	truly	I say	to you,	The

9:39. Jesus did not come into the world to pass the final sentence of condemnation but to give salvation to those who, like the beggar, would believe in Him as their Saviour.

These are the ones who are aware of their blindness. They come to Christ to receive spiritual sight. This is vividly depicted in the blind man who received his physical sight. "They which see" only think they see. Darkness becomes more intense as they continue to reject the light (truth).

to the test, *TCNT* . . . My coming into this world is itself a judgment, *Phillips* . . . to be a Separator, *Fenton* . . . to carry out God's decisions, *TCNT*.

that they which see not might see: . . . to make the sightless see, *Moffatt* . . . those who cannot see have their eyes opened, *Phillips* . . . in order that those that cannot see may see, *TCNT*.

and that they which see might be made blind: . . . to make the seeing blind, *Moffatt* . . . and those who think they can see become blind, *Phillips*.

9:40. It is not clear who these Pharisees were. "Which were with him" may indicate disciples, but they may also be some of the Pharisees who were hostile to His teachings.

These men denied their blindness. They were not like the blind man who gladly received the grace extended from the Lord's hand. On the basis of their question and Jesus' answer, it appears they were not disciples, but hostile Pharisees.

40. And some of the Pharisees which were with him heard these words, and said unto him, Are we blind also?: . . . on hearing this remark, *Fenton* . . . near him overheard this and said, *Phillips* . . . We are not blind, are we? *Williams*.

9:41. If these Pharisees had become aware of their blindness, they would have acknowledged their need of sight. Since they did not realize they were blind sinners, they did not repent. If they had repented, they would have had no sin because God freely forgives.

These men said they were not blind. They persisted in their self-righteous hypocrisy. They were blind and did not realize it. They said in their hearts, "We have no need for Christ's spiritual help." The Pharisees lacked the initial step toward receiving anything from God. Jesus taught the fundamentals of entering the Kingdom in His Sermon on the Mount. "Blessed are the poor in spirit," He declared (Matthew 5:3). No one who is proud is able to enter the Kingdom.

41. Jesus said unto them, If ye were blind, ye should have no sin: . . . you would be blameless, *Berkeley* . . . you would not be guilty, *Williams* . . . you wouldn't be sinning, *Beck* . . . have had no sin to answer for, *TCNT*.

but now ye say, We see; therefore your sin remaineth: . . . but as a matter of fact you boast that you see, *Weymouth* . . . but since you claim to have sight, your sin remains, *Berkeley* . . . your sin is established, *Murdock*.

10:1. "Verily, verily" (*amēn*) occurs 25 times in John in this repeated form. It is always Jesus who says "verily, verily." The term introduces an important truth but not always a new subject (see 1:51). The teaching of the Good Shepherd was prompted by the way the religious leaders "put him (the beggar) out" or excommunicated him from the synagogue (9:22,34). Jesus brought to their attention the duty of spiritual guides. When the rulers put the man out, Jesus found him and received him (cf. Luke 15:3-7). John does not use the word "parable" (*parabolē*), but he does use the Greek word *paroimian* in verse 6 which may be translated "figure of speech." The same word is sometimes rendered "parable." Jesus related this allegory in verses 1-6 and amplified it in verses 7-18.

1. Verily, verily, I say unto you, He that entereth not by the door into the sheepfold: . . . he who

3231.1 partic	1511.31 verb nom sing masc part pres	1217.2 prep	3450.10 art gen sing fem	2351.1 noun fem	1519.1 prep	3450.12 art acc sing fem
μὴ	εἰσερχόμενος	διὰ	τῆς	θύρας	εἰς	τὴν
mē	*eiserchomenos*	*dia*	*tēs*	*thuras*	*eis*	*tēn*
not	entering in	by	the	door	to	the

827.3 noun acc sing fem	3450.1 art gen pl	4122.4 noun gen pl neu	233.2 conj	303.6 verb nom sing masc part pres act	235.1 adv
αὐλὴν	τῶν	προβάτων,	ἀλλὰ	ἀναβαίνων	ἀλλαχόθεν,
aulēn	*tōn*	*probatōn*	*alla*	*anabainōn*	*allachothen*
fold	of the	sheep,	but	mounts up	elsewhere,

1552.3 dem-pron nom sing masc	2785.1 noun nom sing masc	1498.4 verb 3sing indic pres act	2504.1 conj	3001.1 noun nom sing masc	3450.5 art sing masc
ἐκεῖνος	κλέπτης	ἐστὶν	καὶ	λῃστής·	2. ὁ
ekeinos	*kleptēs*	*estin*	*kai*	*lēstēs*	*ho*
that	a thief	is	and	a robber;	the

1156.2 conj	1511.31 verb nom sing masc part pres	1217.2 prep	3450.10 art gen sing fem	2351.1 noun fem	4026.1 noun nom sing masc
δὲ	εἰσερχόμενος	διὰ	τῆς	θύρας	ποιμήν
de	*eiserchomenos*	*dia*	*tēs*	*thuras*	*poimēn*
but	entering in	by	the	door	shepherd

1498.4 verb 3sing indic pres act	3450.1 art gen pl	4122.4 noun gen pl neu	3642.5 dem-pron dat sing masc	3450.5 art sing masc
ἐστιν	τῶν	προβάτων.	3. τούτῳ	ὁ
estin	*tōn*	*probatōn*	*toutō*	*ho*
is	of the	sheep.	This	the

2354.1 noun nom sing fem	453.1 verb 3sing indic pres act	2504.1 conj	3450.17 art pl neu	4122.3 noun pl neu	3450.10 art gen sing fem
θυρωρὸς	ἀνοίγει,	καὶ	τὰ	πρόβατα	τῆς
thurōros	*anoigei*	*kai*	*ta*	*probata*	*tēs*
doorkeeper	opens,	and	the	sheep	the

5292.2 noun gen sing fem	840.3 prs-pron gen sing	189.5 verb 3sing indic pres act	2504.1 conj	3450.17 art pl neu	2375.13 adj pl neu	4122.3 noun pl neu
φωνῆς	αὐτοῦ	ἀκούει,	καὶ	τὰ	ἴδια	πρόβατα
phōnēs	*autou*	*akouei*	*kai*	*ta*	*idia*	*probata*
voice	his	hear,	and	the	his own	sheep

2535.1 verb 3sing indic pres act	5291.1 verb 3sing indic pres act	2567.1 prep	3549.2 noun sing neu	2504.1 conj	1790.1 verb 3sing indic pres act
⸀ καλεῖ	[a☆ φωνεῖ]	κατ'	ὄνομα,	καὶ	ἐξάγει
kalei	*phōnei*	*kat'*	*onoma*	*kai*	*exagei*
he calls	[he summons]	by	name,	and	leads out

3.a.**Txt:** 017K,036,037,038,13,byz.Gries,Word
Var: 01ℵ,02A,03B,05D,019L,033X,33,Lach,TregAlf,Tisc,We/Ho,Weis,Sod,UBS/☆

840.16 prs-pron pl neu		2504.1 conj	3615.1 conj	3450.17 art pl neu	2375.13 adj pl neu	4122.3 noun pl neu
αὐτά.	4. ⸂a	καὶ ⸃	ὅταν	τὰ	ἴδια	⸀ πρόβατα
auta		*kai*	*hotan*	*ta*	*idia*	*probata*
them.		And	when	the	his own	sheep

4.a.**Txt:** 02A,05D,036,037,byz.Lach
Var: 01ℵ,03B,019L,038,33,sa.Treg,Alf,Tisc We/Ho,Weis,Sod,UBS/☆

3820.1 adj	1531.15 verb 3sing subj aor act	1699.1 prep gen	840.1 prs-pron gen pl	4057.2 verb 3sing indic pres
[b☆ πάντα]	ἐκβάλῃ	ἔμπροσθεν	αὐτῶν	πορεύεται·
panta	*ekbalē*	*emprosthen*	*autōn*	*poreuetai*
[all]	he puts forth	before	them	he goes;

4.b.**Txt:** 02A,017K,036,037,13,byz.Gries,Word
Var: 01ℵ-corr,03B,05D,019L,033X,038,33,sa.bo.Lach,Treg,Alf,Tisc,We/HoWeis,Sod,UBS/☆

2504.1 conj	3450.17 art pl neu	4122.3 noun pl neu	840.4 prs-pron dat sing	188.2 verb 3sing indic pres act	3617.1 conj
καὶ	τὰ	πρόβατα	αὐτῷ	ἀκολουθεῖ,	ὅτι
kai	*ta*	*probata*	*autō*	*akolouthei*	*hoti*
and	the	sheep	him	follow,	because

This verse teaches the difference between a true shepherd and "a thief and a robber." The "door" was the opening of the enclosure. Sometimes the shepherd stood in the entrance and literally became the door of the enclosure (verse 9). The "sheepfold" was the enclosure in which the sheep were kept for safety. The true shepherd protected his sheep by taking them into the fold at night. The thief and robber attempt to climb over the wall to exploit the sheep for greedy gain. "Thief" suggests one who gains by unethical means. "Robber" denotes how an immoral individual deprives his victim of a possession.

does not enter...by the gate, *Moffatt* . . . into the place where the sheep are kept, *BB* . . . into the walled-in enclosure, *Wuest.*

but climbeth up some other way: . . . climbs over the fence, *Campbell* . . . but climbs in elsewhere, *Fenton* . . . from some other quarter, *Wuest.*

the same is a thief and a robber: . . . is undoubtedly, *TCNT* . . . and an outlaw, *BB* . . . and a rogue, *Phillips* . . . is nigt thef and day thef, *Wycliffe.*

10:2. The shepherd has no fear of being recognized; he wishes to be seen. He uses the entrance without deceit. The contrast between the true shepherd and the thief is easily envisioned. The thief covers up his real intentions and sneaks in where he will least be detected. Guile and hypocrisy are the characteristics of his nature.

2. But he that entereth in by the door is the shepherd of the sheep: The shepherd of the sheep enters by the door, *Norlie* . . . he who enters by the gate, *Moffatt.*

10:3. "The porter" occurs four times in the New Testament. The NASB translates the Greek word by "doorkeeper." The King James translates the word twice as "porter" and twice as "that kept the door" (Mark 13:34 and John 10:3; John 18:16,17). Jesus was still relating the natural situation. He did not apply the allegory with verse 7.

The shepherd does three things. First, he allows the sheep to know he is near by the sound of his voice. Second, he calls the sheep by their names. The personal touch is made to specific sheep. Sheep need to know the shepherd is interested in them as individual beings. Third, the shepherd "leads them out" of the enclosure. The sheep become more vulnerable outside the sheepfold. The shepherd's presence and guidance become more necessary. They need the assurance of his care and protection.

3. To him the porter openeth: The doorkeeper opens the door to him, *Williams.*

and the sheep hear his voice: . . . and the sheep listen to his voice, *TCNT* . . . the sheep obey his voice, *Williams.*

and he calleth his own sheep by name, and leadeth them out: . . . one by one he calls, *JB* . . . his own sheep by their names, *Beck* . . . personally calls the sheep which are his private possessions, *Wuest.*

10:4. All are led out of the fold. The word "own" is significant, for it stresses the bond that exists between the shepherd and each of his sheep. The shepherd sees to it that all "his own sheep" become subject to the hazards of life. At the same time the shepherd's presence is assurance enough to guarantee their welfare (Matthew 28:20).

In the Middle East shepherds do not drive their sheep. They lead them; they go before them. The shepherd asks not that his sheep go anywhere that he himself has not gone. He is the path-

4. And when he putteth forth his own sheep: When he has brought his own sheep all out, *Weymouth* . . . when he has driven all his own flock outside, *Phillips* . . . when all his own sheep have run out, *Fenton* . . . So when he gets his sheep all out, *Williams.*

he goeth before them: . . . he walks at the head of them, *Weymouth.*

and the sheep follow him: for they know his voice: . . . they are acquainted, *Concordant* . . . because they recognize him, *Barclay.*

3471.8 verb 3pl indic perf act	**3450.12** art acc sing fem	**5292.4** noun acc sing fem	**840.3** prs-pron gen sing	**243.1** adj dat sing	**1156.2** conj
οἴδασιν	τὴν	φωνὴν	αὐτοῦ˙	5. ἀλλοτρίῳ	δὲ
oidasin	*tēn*	*phōnēn*	*autou*	*allotriō*	*de*
they know	the	voice	his.	A stranger	but

5.a.**Txt:** p6,p66,p75,01ℵ, 017K,019L,030U,032W, 036,038,1,13,byz.Sod
Var: 02A,03B,05D,037, Lach,Treg,Alf,Word, Tisc,We/Ho,Weis,UBS/☆

3620.3 partic	**3231.1** partic	**188.14** verb 3pl subj aor act	**188.25** verb 3pl indic fut act
οὐ	μὴ	˹ ἀκολουθήσωσιν,	[a☆ ἀκολουθήσουσιν]
ou	*mē*	*akolouthēsōsin*	*akolouthēsousin*
not	not	they should follow,	[they will follow]

233.2 conj	**5180.10** verb 3pl indic fut mid	**570.2** prep gen	**840.3** prs-pron gen sing	**3617.1** conj	**3620.2** partic	**3471.8** verb 3pl indic perf act
ἀλλὰ	φεύξονται	ἀπ᾽	αὐτοῦ˙	ὅτι	οὐκ	οἴδασιν
alla	*pheuxontai*	*ap'*	*autou*	*hoti*	*ouk*	*oidasin*
but	will flee	from	him,	because	not	they know

3450.1 art gen pl	**243.3** adj gen pl masc	**3450.12** art acc sing fem	**5292.4** noun acc sing fem	**3642.12** dem-pron acc sing fem
τῶν	ἀλλοτρίων	τὴν	φωνήν.	6. Ταύτην
tōn	*allotriōn*	*tēn*	*phōnēn*	*Tautēn*
of the	strangers	the	voice.	This

3450.12 art acc sing fem	**3804.2** noun acc sing fem	**1500.5** verb 3sing indic aor act	**840.2** prs-pron dat pl	**3450.5** art sing masc	**2400.1** name nom masc
τὴν	παροιμίαν	εἶπεν	αὐτοῖς	ὁ	Ἰησοῦς,
tēn	*paroimian*	*eipen*	*autois*	*ho*	*Iēsous*
the	allegory	spoke	to them		Jesus,

1552.6 dem-pron nom pl masc	**1156.2** conj	**3620.2** partic	**1091.18** verb 3pl indic aor act	**4949.1** intr-pron	**1498.34** verb sing indic imperf act
ἐκεῖνοι	δὲ	οὐκ	ἔγνωσαν	τίνα	˹ ἦν
ekeinoi	*de*	*ouk*	*egnōsan*	*tina*	*ēn*
those	but	not	knew	what	it was

6.a.**Var:** 07E,Treg

1498.10 verb 3sing subj pres act	**3614.17** rel-pron pl neu	**2953.45** verb 3sing indic imperf act	**840.2** prs-pron dat pl	**1500.5** verb 3sing indic aor act
[a ᾖ]	ἃ	ἐλάλει	αὐτοῖς.	7. Εἶπεν
ē	*ha*	*elalei*	*autois*	*Eipen*
[it may be]	which	he spoke	to them.	Said

7.a.**Txt:** 05D,019L,030U, 036,038,byz.Lach,Sod
Var: p75,03B,Alf,Tisc, We/HoWeis,UBS/☆

3631.1 conj	**3687.1** adv	**840.2** prs-pron dat pl	**3450.5** art sing masc	**2400.1** name nom masc	**279.1** partic
οὖν	πάλιν	˹a αὐτοῖς ˺	ὁ	Ἰησοῦς,	Ἀμὴν
oun	*palin*	*autois*	*ho*	*Iēsous*	*Amēn*
therefore	again	to them		Jesus,	Truly

7.b.**Txt:** 01ℵ,02A,05D, 021M,036,037,038, 041-corr,byz.LachTisc, Weis,UBS/☆
Var: p75,03B,017K, 019L,030U,033X, 041-org,33,Treg,We/Ho, Sod

279.1 partic	**2978.1** verb 1sing pres act	**5050.3** prs-pron dat 2pl	**3617.1** conj	**1466.1** prs-pron nom 1sing	**1498.2** verb 1sing indic pres act
ἀμὴν	λέγω	ὑμῖν,	˹b ὅτι ˺	ἐγώ	εἰμι
amēn	*legō*	*humin*	*hoti*	*egō*	*eimi*
truly	I say	to you,	that	I	am

3450.9 art nom sing fem	**2351.2** noun nom sing fem	**3450.1** art gen pl	**4122.4** noun gen pl neu	**3820.7** adj pl masc
ἡ	θύρα	τῶν	προβάτων.	8. πάντες
hē	*thura*	*tōn*	*probatōn*	*pantes*
the	door	of the	sheep.	All

3607.2 rel-pron nom pl masc	**4112.1** prep	**1466.3** prs-pron gen 1sing	**2048.1** verb indic aor act	**2048.1** verb indic aor act	**4112.1** prep
ὅσοι	˹ πρὸ	ἐμοῦ	ἦλθον	[☆ ἦλθον	πρὸ
hosoi	*pro*	*emou*	*ēlthon*	*ēlthon*	*pro*
whoever	before	me	came	[came	before

finder, the forerunner, and the guardian of the way.

It is natural for sheep to follow the shepherd. They have learned to know his voice and his watchfulness in their behalf. They trust him with their lives. It is "because they know his voice" (NASB) that they follow their shepherd. Notice the repetition of the word "voice" in verses 3,4,5,16, and 27. Disciples, like sheep, have learned to know the voice of the Good Shepherd.

5. And a stranger will they not follow, but will flee from him: But they will never come on behind a stranger, *Williams* . . . But one belonging to another flock they will positively not follow, *Wuest* . . . but will run away from him, *TCNT, ALBA* . . . on the contrary, they will run away, *Fenton* . . . they in no wise follow, *Clementson.*

for they know not the voice of strangers: . . . because they do not recognize the call of strangers, *Berkeley* . . . for they do not recognize strange voices, *Phillips.*

10:5. Sheep may pick up their ears when they hear a strange voice calling. After repeated calls they flee in fright. They follow only their own shepherd. Just as sheep have not proven the worthiness of the stranger's voice, the Christian is taught to prove all things. Many voices repeatedly call for attention, but the one who acts as a sheep is wise for he listens only to the voice of his shepherd.

6. This parable spake Jesus unto them: Jesus addressed this parable to them, *Barclay* . . . this similitude, *Rotherham* . . . Jesus spoke to them in this allegorical language, *Weymouth* . . . Jesus gave them this illustration, *Phillips* . . . This allegory, *Murdock, Williams.*

but they understood not what things they were which he spake unto them: . . . but they did not understand what He meant by it, *Williams* . . . but they did not catch the meaning of what He said to them, *Berkeley* . . . but they did not grasp the point of what he was saying to them, *Phillips.*

10:6. Our word "allegory" is close to the meaning of the word "parable." It could be thought of as an extended proverb (2 Peter 2:22).

Shepherds and sheep were common in Palestine. In Christ's time many people lived from the benefits of sheep. They should have known how to apply what Jesus was teaching, but failed to do so. The Jews often failed to grasp the truths of Jesus' sayings and particularly of His parables and figures of speech.

7. Then said Jesus unto them again, Verily, verily, I say unto you, I am the door of the sheep: I am the Door for the sheep, *Beck.*

10:7. The only door of the enclosure was an open entrance which was often occupied by the shepherd. The wall of the enclosure was piled high with field stones, and thorn bushes were fastened liberally around the top of the wall. Animals dared not climb the wall because of the thorns. The shepherd insured the safety of the flock by becoming the door. Jesus guarantees the well-being of His own. An enemy must attack Him before approaching His treasure. His sheep are His most prized possessions. The night may be black, the wind may howl, and the situation become hopeless. Yet no eternal hurt can pierce the entrance, for He stands guard during the storm.

8. All that ever came before me are thieves and robbers: . . . and false messiahs, *ET.*

10:8. The robbers and thieves attempt to use, misuse, and abuse the sheep. They try to come over the wall. They are false leaders.

1466.3 prs-pron gen 1sing	**2785.2** noun nom pl masc	**1498.7** verb 3pl indic pres act	**2504.1** conj	**3001.3** noun nom pl masc	**233.1** conj
ἐμοῦ]	κλέπται	εἰσὶν	καὶ	λῃσταί·	ἀλλ’
emou	*kleptai*	*eisin*	*kai*	*lēstai*	*all’*
me]	thieves	are	and	robbers;	but

3620.2 partic	**189.24** verb 3pl indic aor act	**840.1** prs-pron gen pl	**3450.17** art pl neu	**4122.3** noun pl neu	**1466.1** prs-pron nom 1sing
οὐκ	ἤκουσαν	αὐτῶν	τὰ	πρόβατα.	**9.** ἐγώ
ouk	*ēkousan*	*autōn*	*ta*	*probata*	*egō*
not	did hear	them	the	sheep.	I

1498.2 verb 1sing indic pres act	**3450.9** art nom sing fem	**2351.2** noun nom sing fem	**1217.1** prep	**1466.3** prs-pron gen 1sing	**1430.1** partic
εἰμι	ἡ	θύρα·	δι’	ἐμοῦ	ἐάν
eimi	*hē*	*thura*	*di’*	*emou*	*ean*
am	the	door:	by	me	if

4948.3 indef-pron nom sing	**1511.7** verb 3sing subj aor act	**4834.33** verb 3sing indic fut pass	**2504.1** conj	**1511.38** verb 3sing indic fut mid
τις	εἰσέλθῃ	σωθήσεται,	καὶ	εἰσελεύσεται
tis	*eiselthē*	*sōthēsetai*	*kai*	*eiseleusetai*
anyone	enter in	he shall be saved,	and	shall go in

2504.1 conj	**1814.36** verb 3sing indic fut mid	**2504.1** conj	**3405.1** noun acc sing fem	**2128.26** verb 3sing indic fut act	**3450.5** art sing masc
καὶ	ἐξελεύσεται,	καὶ	νομὴν	εὑρήσει.	**10.** ὁ
kai	*exeleusetai*	*kai*	*nomēn*	*heurēsei*	*ho*
and	shall go out,	and	pasture	shall find.	The

2785.1 noun nom sing masc	**3620.2** partic	**2048.34** verb 3sing indic pres	**1479.1** conj	**3231.1** partic	**2419.1** conj	**2786.8** verb 3sing subj aor act
κλέπτης	οὐκ	ἔρχεται	εἰ	μὴ	ἵνα	κλέψῃ
kleptēs	*ouk*	*erchetai*	*ei*	*mē*	*hina*	*klepsē*
thief	not	comes	if	not	that	he may steal

2504.1 conj	**2357.5** verb 3sing subj aor act	**2504.1** conj	**616.5** verb 3sing subj aor act	**1466.1** prs-pron nom 1sing	**2048.1** verb indic aor act
καὶ	θύσῃ	καὶ	ἀπολέσῃ·	ἐγὼ	ἦλθον
kai	*thusē*	*kai*	*apolesē*	*egō*	*ēlthon*
and	may kill	and	may destroy:	I	came

2419.1 conj	**2205.4** noun acc sing fem	**2174.10** verb 3pl subj pres act	**2504.1** conj	**3916.1** adj sing neu	**2174.10** verb 3pl subj pres act
ἵνα	ζωὴν	ἔχωσιν,	καὶ	περισσὸν	ἔχωσιν.
hina	*zōēn*	*echōsin*	*kai*	*perisson*	*echōsin*
that	life	they might have,	and	abundantly	might have.

1466.1 prs-pron nom 1sing	**1498.2** verb 1sing indic pres act	**3450.5** art sing masc	**4026.1** noun nom sing masc	**3450.5** art sing masc	**2541.3** adj nom sing masc
11. Ἐγώ	εἰμι	ὁ	ποιμὴν	ὁ	καλός·
Egō	*eimi*	*ho*	*poimēn*	*ho*	*kalos*
I	am	the	shepherd	the	good.

3450.5 art sing masc	**4026.1** noun nom sing masc	**3450.5** art sing masc	**2541.3** adj nom sing masc	**3450.12** art acc sing fem	**5425.4** noun acc sing fem
ὁ	ποιμὴν	ὁ	καλὸς	τὴν	ψυχὴν
ho	*poimēn*	*ho*	*kalos*	*tēn*	*psuchēn*
The	shepherd	the	good	the	life

840.3 prs-pron gen sing	**4935.2** verb 3sing indic pres act	**5065.1** prep	**3450.1** art gen pl	**4122.4** noun gen pl neu	**3450.5** art sing masc
αὐτοῦ	τίθησιν	ὑπὲρ	τῶν	προβάτων.	**12.** ὁ
autou	*tithēsin*	*huper*	*tōn*	*probatōn*	*ho*
his	lays down	for	the	sheep:	the

but the sheep did not hear them: . . . did not listen to them, *TCNT.*

10:9. "I am the door" is made emphatic by its repetition. In verse 7 the statement concerns the thieves and robbers who reject the door; here the emphasis is on the sheep who accept the door.

The condition, "if anyone enters" (NASB), is followed by four terms which express extensive blessings. First, "shall be saved" (*sō-thēstai*) asserts the general word for rescue and restoration from sin. All the grand truths of redemption are compressed in this verb: atonement, conversion, regeneration, grace, mercy, etc. This verb fits both sheep and souls.

Second, "shall go in" (*eiseleusetai*) expresses entering the enclosure. The sheep file into the fold, and believers enter the seclusion of worship. The world is closed out, and the Shepherd and His own are enclosed. The blessedness of worship in spirit and truth are known only to those who participate in its ecstasy (4:23).

Third, "shall go . . . out" points to the fact that as sheep must not live within the fold, believers are to go out into the world. As they do, they expose themselves to the hazards of the world, but the enclosure is not the place to carry out God's will.

Fourth, "find pasture" is appropriate to sheep, yet it graphically portrays the believer who is led by the Shepherd to lush pastures. The Shepherd leads the sheep into green pastures, but each sheep must browse for itself.

9. I am the door: I alone am the door, *Wuest.*

by me if any man enter in, he shall be saved: . . . if any one enter in through me, *HBIE* . . . Whoever comes in through Me, *Berkeley* . . . he will have salvation, *BB* . . . will be safe, *Norlie.*

and shall go in and out, and find pasture: . . . and will get food, *BB.*

10:10. The shepherd functions not only as the door but as the guide and provider. First, the Lord describes the thief. The description is given in three verbs, "to steal, and to kill, and to destroy." The purpose is stated both for the thief and "the good shepherd." The progression of the thief's design ends with everlasting doom. The word *perisson* ("abundantly") occurs 22 times in the New Testament, but only here in John. The word means "more than sufficient," "over and above," etc.

10. The thief cometh not, but for to steal, and to kill and to destroy: The thief never comes except to, *Montgomery* . . . The thief's purpose is, *LivB* . . . to butcher, *Berkeley.*

I am come that they might have life, and that they might have it more abundantly: . . . and have it overflowing in them, *Beck* . . . and have it to the full, *Moffatt* . . . My purpose is to give eternal life abundantly! *LivB* . . . having it superabundantly, *Concordant* . . . that they may enjoy life, *Fenton* . . . that which is excellent, *Murdock* . . . in greater measure, *BB* . . . in all its fulness, *ALBA* . . . and have it amply, *HistNT* . . . have it till it overflows, *Williams* . . . be possessing it in superabundance, *Wuest.*

10:11. The adjective "good" can be variously rendered "good," "excellent," "noble," "beautiful," "fair," and "ideal." The word is sometimes used to indicate outward appearance, but at other times it denotes inward quality.

Kings of the ancient Jews thought of themselves as shepherds of their people. The scepter the king held in his right hand emerged from the shepherd's staff. The shepherd-sheep motif comes from God who led His people in the desert as a shepherd leads his sheep. King David spoke of this analogy when he said, "The Lord is my shepherd" (Psalm 23:1). Jesus asserted this very office and function in this verse (10:11).

He is the ideal for every shepherd. Some shepherds died in he task of protecting their sheep. The shepherd possessed a love for

11. I am the good shepherd: the good shepherd giveth his life for the sheep: . . . the ideal Shepherd, *Concordant* . . . lays down his life, *HBIE* . . . will give his life for the sake of his sheep, *Phillips* . . . exposeth his life for, *Murdock* . . . on behalf of, *Fenton.*

12.a.**Txt:** 02A,017K,036, byz.sa.Lach
Var: 03B,019L,Tisc, We/HoWeis,Sod,UBS/☆

3275.1 adj nom sing masc	1156.2 conj	2504.1 conj	3620.2 partic	1498.21 verb sing masc part pres act	4026.1 noun nom sing masc
μισθωτὸς	(a δέ,)	καὶ	οὐκ	ὢν	ποιμήν,
misthōtos	*de*	*kai*	*ouk*	*ōn*	*poimēn*
hired servant	but,	and	not	being	shepherd,

12.b.**Txt:** 05D,017K,036, 037,byz.
Var: 01ℵ,02A,03B,019L, 033X,038,33,Lach,Treg Alf,Tisc,We/Ho,Weis, Sod,UBS/☆

3614.2 rel-pron gen sing	3620.2 partic	1498.7 verb 3pl indic pres act	1498.4 verb 3sing indic pres act	3450.17 art pl neu	4122.3 noun pl neu
οὗ	οὐκ	(εἰσὶν	[b☆ ἔστιν]	τὰ	πρόβατα
hou	*ouk*	*eisin*	*estin*	*ta*	*probata*
whose	not	are	[idem]	the	sheep

2375.13 adj pl neu	2311.4 verb 3sing indic pres act	3450.6 art acc sing masc	3046.2 noun acc sing masc	2048.42 verb sing part pres	2504.1 conj
ἴδια,	θεωρεῖ	τὸν	λύκον	ἐρχόμενον,	καὶ
idia	*theōrei*	*ton*	*lukon*	*erchomenon*	*kai*
own,	sees	the	wolf	coming,	and

856.4 verb 3sing indic pres act	3450.17 art pl neu	4122.3 noun pl neu	2504.1 conj	5180.1 verb 3sing indic pres act	2504.1 conj	3450.5 art sing masc
ἀφίησιν	τὰ	πρόβατα	καὶ	φεύγει·	καὶ	ὁ
aphiēsin	*ta*	*probata*	*kai*	*pheugei*	*kai*	*ho*
leaves	the	sheep,	and	flees;	and	the

12.c.**Txt:** 02A,017K,036, 037,13,byz.it.Lach
Var: 01ℵ,03B,04C,019L, 038,041,33,Treg,Tisc, We/Ho,Weis,Sod,UBS/☆

3046.1 noun nom sing masc	720.1 verb 3sing indic pres act	840.16 prs-pron acc pl neu	2504.1 conj	4505.1 verb 3sing indic pres act	3450.17 art pl neu
λύκος	ἁρπάζει	αὐτὰ	καὶ	σκορπίζει	(c τὰ
lukos	*harpazei*	*auta*	*kai*	*skorpizei*	*ta*
wolf	seizes	them	and	scatters	the

13.a.**Txt:** 02A-corr,017K, 036,037,13,byz.Lach
Var: 01ℵ,03B,05D,019L, 038,33,Treg,AlfTisc, We/Ho,Weis,Sod,UBS/☆

4122.3 noun pl neu	3450.5 art sing masc	1156.2 conj	3275.1 adj nom sing masc	5180.1 verb 3sing indic pres act
πρόβατα.)	**13.** (a ὁ	δὲ	μισθωτός	φεύγει)
probata	*ho*	*de*	*misthōtos*	*pheugei*
sheep.	The	now	hired servant	flees

3617.1 conj	3275.1 adj nom sing masc	1498.4 verb 3sing indic pres act	2504.1 conj	3620.3 partic	3169.1 verb 3sing indic pres act
ὅτι	μισθωτός	ἐστιν,	καὶ	οὐ	μέλει
hoti	*misthōtos*	*estin*	*kai*	*ou*	*melei*
because	a hired servant	he is,	and	not	is concerned

840.4 prs-pron dat sing	3875.1 prep	3450.1 art gen pl	4122.4 noun gen pl neu	1466.1 prs-pron nom 1sing	1498.2 verb 1sing indic pres act
αὐτῷ	περὶ	τῶν	προβάτων.	**14.** Ἐγώ	εἰμι
autō	*peri*	*tōn*	*probatōn*	*Egō*	*eimi*
himself	about	the	sheep.	I	am

3450.5 art sing masc	4026.1 noun nom sing masc	3450.5 art sing masc	2541.3 adj nom sing masc	2504.1 conj	1091.1 verb 1sing indic pres act
ὁ	ποιμὴν	ὁ	καλός·	καὶ	γινώσκω
ho	*poimēn*	*ho*	*kalos*	*kai*	*ginōskō*
the	shepherd	the	good;	and	I know

14.a.**Txt:** 02A,017K,036, 037,038,1,13,byz.Gries, Word,Sod
Var: p45-org,p66,p75, 01ℵ,03B,05D,019L, 032W,it.sa.bo.Lach,Treg, Alf,Tisc,We/Ho,Weis, UBS/☆

3450.17 art pl neu	1684.12 adj 1pl neu	2504.1 conj	1091.40 verb 1sing indic pres mid	5097.3 prep	3450.1 art gen pl	1684.13 adj gen 1pl neu
τὰ	ἐμὰ,	καὶ	(γινώσκομαι	ὑπὸ	τῶν	ἐμῶν.
ta	*ema*	*kai*	*ginōskomai*	*hupo*	*tōn*	*emōn*
the	mine,	and	am known	by	the	mine.

1091.53 verb 3pl indic pres act	1466.6 prs-pron acc 1sing	3450.17 art pl neu	1684.12 adj 1pl neu	2503.1 conj
[a☆ γινώσκουσί	με	τὰ	ἐμά,]	**15.** καθὼς
ginōskousi	*me*	*ta*	*ema*	*kathōs*
[know	me	the	mine,]	As

his sheep that motivated him even to die if need be.

"Lays down his life" (NASB) is expressed also in verses 15 and 17. "Lays down His life" is the shepherd's analogy for death on the cross. The prepositional phrase "for the sheep" is worthy of much study. "For" (*huper*) in this context signifies "in behalf of" and even "instead of." It was Jesus' death on the cross that brought salvation to believers (see 3:14,15). The thought is beautifully illustrated in 18:8: "If therefore ye seek me, let these go their way." He became our substitute. He became sin for us and died in our place (2 Corinthians 5:21).

10:12. "Whose own the sheep are not" explains why the hireling is not so interested in the sheep's welfare. Notice the three descriptive words that characterize the hireling during the critical time of danger. First, he "beholds" (NASB), meaning he stands in contemplation of what could happen to him if he defends the sheep from "the wolf" (*ton lukon*). Second, he "leaves" the sheep; that is, he departs to a place of temporary safety to observe. Third, he "flees," lest the wolf turn on him. The three verbs are in the present tense to show the action vividly.

The Lord next depicts the onslaught of the wolf. "Catcheth" is also rendered by "snatches" and "takes by force" (Matthew 11:12), but "pluck" in verses 28 and 29. "Scatters" describes the effect the wolf has on the flock.

10:13. "The hireling" serves for pay; therefore, it would not be to his gain to stay and fight the wolf. He will not risk his life nor suffer loss in behalf of the sheep for his loss may total more than his wages.

10:14. Jesus reiterated, "I am the good shepherd," that the nature of the hireling may be revealed (see verse 11).

The attachment between Jesus and His own is especially tender and endearing. His emphasis on "My own" (*ema*, see NASB) ties the two in an intimate union. The analogy of the shepherd's knowledge of each sheep, even to the name and character, faintly illustrates Jesus' understanding of His own. There is a mutual knowledge between Christ, the Good Shepherd, and His people, the sheep.

10:15. Jesus' knowledge of His sheep is revealed in the previous verse. Here He emphasized His and the Father's reciprocal knowledge of each other.

12. But he that is an hireling, and not the shepherd: The mere servant, *Fenton* . . . The hired servant, *Montgomery* . . . hired transient, *Klingensmith* . . . The hired man, *Williams.*

whose own the sheep are not: . . . doesn't own the sheep, *Beck.*

seeth the wolf coming, and leaveth the sheep, and fleeth: . . . leaves the sheep and runs away, *Beck* . . . deserts the sheep and runs when he sees, *Berkeley* . . . abandons the sheep, *Campbell* . . . deserts them, *Moffatt* . . . he takes to flight, *Fenton.*

and the wolf catcheth them, and scattereth the sheep: . . . and the wolf pounces down on the sheep, *Norlie* . . . and the wolf teareth them, *Alford* . . . carries off some...and scatters the flock, *Williams* . . . and disperses the flock, *Campbell.*

13. The hireling fleeth, because he is an hireling: . . . flees, *Berkeley* . . . just because he is a hired man, *Moffatt* . . . Since he only works for pay, *ALBA.*

and careth not for the sheep: . . . who has no interest in the sheep, *Moffatt* . . . is unconcerned, *Scarlett* . . . does not care a straw for, *Williams.*

14. I am the good shepherd, and know my sheep, and am known of mine: I know by experience, *Wuest* . . . and I know my own, and my own know me, *HBIE* . . . and I recognize My own. My own in turn recognize, *Berkeley* . . . my followers, *SEB* . . . those that are mine, *Phillips* . . . and my sheep know me, *Williams.*

1091.3 verb 3sing indic pres act	1466.6 prs-pron acc 1sing	3450.5 art sing masc	3824.1 noun nom sing masc	2476.3 conj	1091.1 verb 1sing indic pres act
γινώσκει	με	ὁ	πατήρ,	κἀγὼ	γινώσκω
ginōskei	*me*	*ho*	*patēr*	*kagō*	*ginōskō*
knows	me	the	Father,	I also	know

3450.6 art acc sing masc	3824.4 noun acc sing masc	2504.1 conj	3450.12 art acc sing fem	5425.4 noun acc sing fem	1466.2 prs-pron gen 1sing
τὸν	πατέρα·	καὶ	τὴν	ψυχήν	μου
ton	*patera*	*kai*	*tēn*	*psuchēn*	*mou*
the	Father;	and	the	life	my

4935.1 verb 1sing indic pres act	5065.1 prep	3450.1 art gen pl	4122.4 noun gen pl neu	2504.1 conj	241.15 adj pl neu
τίθημι	ὑπὲρ	τῶν	προβάτων.	16. καὶ	ἄλλα
tithēmi	*huper*	*tōn*	*probatōn*	*kai*	*alla*
I lay down	for	the	sheep.	And	other

4122.3 noun pl neu	2174.1 verb 1sing pres act	3614.17 rel-pron pl neu	3620.2 partic	1498.4 verb 3sing indic pres act	1523.2 prep gen	3450.10 art gen sing fem
πρόβατα	ἔχω,	ἃ	οὐκ	ἔστιν	ἐκ	τῆς
probata	*echō*	*ha*	*ouk*	*estin*	*ek*	*tēs*
sheep	I have,	which	not	are	of	the

827.1 noun gen sing fem	3642.10 dem-pron gen sing fem	2519.1 conj	1466.6 prs-pron acc 1sing	1158.1 verb 3sing indic pres act
αὐλῆς	ταύτης·	κἀκεῖνα	⸀ με	δεῖ
aulēs	*tautēs*	*kakeina*	*me*	*dei*
fold	this;	those also	me	it is necessary

1158.1 verb 3sing indic pres act	1466.6 prs-pron acc 1sing	70.15 verb inf aor act	2504.1 conj	3450.10 art gen sing fem	5292.2 noun gen sing fem
[☆ δεῖ	με]	ἀγαγεῖν,	καὶ	τῆς	φωνῆς
dei	*me*	*agagein*	*kai*	*tēs*	*phōnēs*
[it is necessary	me]	to bring,	and	the	voice

16.a.**Var:** p45,01ℵ-corr, 03B,05D,019L,032W, 038,33,565,sa.bo.Treg Alf,We/Ho,Sod

1466.2 prs-pron gen 1sing	189.44 verb 3pl indic fut act	2504.1 conj	1090.69 verb 3sing indic fut mid	1090.80 verb 3pl indic fut mid
μου	ἀκούσουσιν·	καὶ	⸀ γενήσεται	[a γενήσονται]
mou	*akousousin*	*kai*	*genēsetai*	*genēsontai*
my	they will hear;	and	there shall be	[idem]

1518.5 num card nom fem	4027.1 noun nom sing fem	1518.3 num card nom masc	4026.1 noun nom sing masc	1217.2 prep	3642.17 dem-pron sing neu
μία	ποίμνη,	εἷς	ποιμήν.	17. διὰ	τοῦτό
mia	*poimnē*	*heis*	*poimēn*	*dia*	*touto*
one	flock,	one	shepherd.	On account	this

3450.5 art sing masc	3824.1 noun nom sing masc	1466.6 prs-pron acc 1sing	1466.6 prs-pron acc 1sing	3450.5 art sing masc	3824.1 noun nom sing masc
⸀ ὁ	πατὴρ	με	[☆ με	ὁ	πατὴρ]
ho	*patēr*	*me*	*me*	*ho*	*patēr*
the	Father	me	[me	the	Father]

25.2 verb 3sing pres act	3617.1 conj	1466.1 prs-pron nom 1sing	4935.1 verb 1sing indic pres act	3450.12 art acc sing fem	5425.4 noun acc sing fem
ἀγαπᾷ,	ὅτι	ἐγὼ	τίθημι	τὴν	ψυχήν
agapa	*hoti*	*egō*	*tithēmi*	*tēn*	*psuchēn*
loves,	because	I	lay down	the	life

1466.2 prs-pron gen 1sing	2419.1 conj	3687.1 adv	2956.17 verb 1sing subj aor act	840.12 prs-pron acc sing fem	3625.2 num card nom masc
μου,	ἵνα	πάλιν	λάβω	αὐτήν.	18. οὐδεὶς
mou	*hina*	*palin*	*labō*	*autēn*	*oudeis*
my,	that	again	I may take	it.	No one

"And I lay down my life for the sheep" is repeated from verse 11, and He repeats the statement in verses 17 and 18. Jesus' knowledge of His own adequately enables Him to apply the best methods to attain the best ends. His knowledge of the Father guides His actions to fulfill the Father's will. "My life" refers to His person in its temporal existence. He saves His own by becoming their sacrifice. This verse implies the vicarious death of Christ (Isaiah 53:4).

15. As the Father knoweth me, even so know I the Father: . . . and as thoroughly as, *Fenton* . . . just as the Father knows me, *Barclay.*

and I lay down my life for the sheep: I am giving my own life, *Williams* . . . I am giving my life for the sake of, *Phillips* . . . and I lay down My life on behalf of the sheep, *Berkeley* . . . I lay down on behalf of and instead of, *Wuest* . . . My soul, *Worrell.*

10:16. The "other sheep . . . which are not of this fold" refers to believers among the Gentiles. The Jewish believers compose the first fold. "Other" sheep means other sheep of the same quality. Gentiles as well as Jews must come to God by believing in Jesus as God's revelation (the *logos* of 1:1).

"Must" is significant, for it means that Jesus brings this group due to moral necessity. His love and compassion urge Him to include all people of all lands and ages. He must lead these others along with the Jewish flock (3:15,16). It is doubtful that the Pharisees understood what He was saying.

Jesus said, "They shall hear my voice," meaning they recognize His voice and follow Him as sheep do their shepherd.

"Flock" is the better rendering. The fold is the enclosure where the sheep bed down for the night; the flock is composed of an aggregate of individual sheep (verse 1). The flock is the true, invisible Church which is made up of all those who rely on Jesus Christ as their personal Saviour. A full, definite description of the Church is given in Ephesians chapter 2.

16. And other sheep I have, which are not of this fold: I have other sheep too, that are not in this fold, *Beck* . . . other sheep besides, *TCNT* . . . which do not belong to this fold, *Montgomery.*

them also I must bring, and they shall hear my voice: I must gather, *Fenton* . . . I must lead those too, *Beck* . . . I must lead those also, *TCNT* . . . these too I must lead, *ALBA* . . . I must guide as well, *Berkeley* . . . and they will listen to my voice, *Weymouth.*

and there shall be one fold, and one shepherd: . . . become one flock, *Williams* . . . one flock, *JB* . . . under one Shepherd, *Weymouth* . . . having one shepherd, *PNT.*

10:17. Jesus here spoke of His death by crucifixion; yet He looked beyond His passion to His resurrection. His death was proven efficacious by His resurrection. As Paul later explained, the Father declared Jesus "to be the Son of God with power, according to the Spirit of holiness, by the resurrection from the dead" (Romans 1:4). Thus His words, "that I might take it again," were necessary complements to "I lay down my life."

17. Therefore doth my Father love me, because I lay down my life, that I might take it again: On account of this, *Wilson* . . . This is why the Father loves me, *TCNT, Williams* . . . I surrender my life, *Klingensmith.*

10:18. The Lord was master of His own life. "No man" took His life from Him. He on His own initiatives "lays it down." Jesus is active not passive in His deity. No one could make such an assertion but God himself. Compare the statements which godly men should make according to James 4:15.

Jesus demonstrated the reality of His words here the night He

18.a.**Txt:** p66,01ℵ-corr, 02A,05D,017K,019L, 032W,036,037,038,1,13, etc.byz.Lach,Tisc,Sod
Var: p45,01ℵ-org,03B, We/HoWeis,UBS/☆

142.2 verb 3sing indic pres act	142.8 verb 3sing indic aor act	840.12 prs-pron acc sing fem	570.2 prep gen	1466.3 prs-pron gen 1sing
⸀☆ αἴρει	[a ἦρεν]	αὐτὴν	ἀπ'	ἐμοῦ,
airei	ēren	autēn	ap'	emou
takes	[took]	it	from	me,

233.1 conj	1466.1 prs-pron nom 1sing	4935.1 verb 1sing indic pres act	840.12 prs-pron acc sing fem	570.2 prep gen	1670.1 prs-pron gen 1sing masc
ἀλλ'	ἐγὼ	τίθημι	αὐτὴν	ἀπ'	ἐμαυτοῦ.
all'	egō	tithēmi	autēn	ap'	emautou
but	I	lay down	it	of	myself.

1833.4 noun acc sing fem	2174.1 verb 1sing pres act	4935.17 verb inf aor act	840.12 prs-pron acc sing fem	2504.1 conj	1833.4 noun acc sing fem
ἐξουσίαν	ἔχω	θεῖναι	αὐτήν,	καὶ	ἐξουσίαν
exousian	echō	theinai	autēn	kai	exousian
Authority	I have	to lay down	it,	and	authority

2174.1 verb 1sing pres act	3687.1 adv	2956.31 verb inf aor act	840.12 prs-pron acc sing fem	3642.12 dem-pron acc sing fem	3450.12 art acc sing fem
ἔχω	πάλιν	λαβεῖν	αὐτήν·	ταύτην	τὴν
echō	palin	labein	autēn	tautēn	tēn
I have	again	to take	it.	This	the

1769.3 noun acc sing fem	2956.12 verb indic aor act	3706.2 prep	3450.2 art gen sing	3824.2 noun gen sing masc	1466.2 prs-pron gen 1sing
ἐντολὴν	ἔλαβον	παρὰ	τοῦ	πατρός	μου.
entolēn	elabon	para	tou	patros	mou
commandment	I received	from	the	Father	my.

19.a.**Txt:** p66,02A,05D, 017K,036,037,038,1,13, 565,1241,byz.bo.
Var: p75,01ℵ,03B,019L, 032W,033X,33,it.sa. Lach,Treg,Alf,Tisc, We/Ho,WeisSod,UBS/☆

4830.1 noun nom sing neu	3631.1 conj	3687.1 adv	1090.33 verb 3sing indic aor mid	1706.1 prep	3450.4 art dat pl
19. Σχίσμα	⸀a οὖν ⸌	πάλιν	ἐγένετο	ἐν	τοῖς
Schisma	oun	palin	egeneto	en	tois
A division	therefore	again	there was	among	the

2428.4 name-adj dat pl masc	1217.2 prep	3450.8 art acc pl masc	3030.8 noun acc pl masc	3642.8 dem-pron acc pl masc
Ἰουδαίοις	διὰ	τοὺς	λόγους	τούτους.
Ioudaiois	dia	tous	logous	toutous
Jews	on account of	the	words	these;

20.a.**Var:** 01ℵ-org,05D, 1,Tisc

2978.25 verb indic imperf act	1156.2 conj	3631.1 conj	4044.7 adj nom pl masc	1523.1 prep gen	840.1 prs-pron gen pl
20. ἔλεγον	⸀ δὲ	[a οὖν]	πολλοὶ	ἐξ	αὐτῶν,
elegon	de	oun	polloi	ex	autōn
said	but	[therefore]	many	of	them,

1134.1 noun sing neu	2174.4 verb 3sing indic pres act	2504.1 conj	3077.3 verb 3sing indic pres	4949.9 intr-pron sing neu	840.3 prs-pron gen sing
Δαιμόνιον	ἔχει	καὶ	μαίνεται·	τί	αὐτοῦ
Daimonion	echei	kai	mainetai	ti	autou
A demon	he has	and	is mad;	why	him

189.2 verb 2pl pres act	241.6 adj nom pl masc	2978.25 verb indic imperf act	3642.18 dem-pron pl neu	3450.17 art pl neu
ἀκούετε;	21. Ἄλλοι	ἔλεγον,	Ταῦτα	τὰ
akouete	Alloi	elegon	Tauta	ta
do you hear?	Others	said,	These	the

4343.4 noun pl neu	3620.2 partic	1498.4 verb 3sing indic pres act	1133.3 verb gen sing masc part pres	3231.1 partic
ῥήματα	οὐκ	ἔστιν	δαιμονιζομένου·	μὴ
rhēmata	ouk	estin	daimonizomenou	mē
sayings	not	are	of one possessed by a demon.	Not

was arrested. As the soldiers laid hands on Him Peter acted to make good his vow to defend his Master to the death (Mark 14:29-31). He drew his sword to "fight like a man," despite the futility of his efforts. Making a swing at one nearby, he removed an ear. Jesus rebuked his rashness with a command to return his sword to its place. He declared they who fight with the sword die by it. Then came the words, "Thinkest thou that I cannot now pray to my Father, and he shall presently give me more than twelve legions of angels?" (Matthew 26:53). With this He surrendered voluntarily to His captors.

In all Christ's mediatorial work the three members of the Godhead cooperate and perform in harmony with each other. The Son never works independently of the Father, nor the Father of the Son.

A commandment is usually an obligation carried out by an inferior, such as a soldier who receives a command from his officer. This is not the case here, for Jesus has just stated that on His own initiatives He surrenders to death on the cross. The commandment was mutually decided upon by both Father and Son. Therefore, the commandment was not an obligation imposed upon the Son by the Father, but it came as a result of their mutual agreement.

18. No man taketh it from me: No one snatches it from Me, *Berkeley* . . . No one can kill me without My consent, *LivB.*

but I lay it down of myself: . . . but I lay it down of my own free will, *Phillips* . . . but I am giving it as a free gift, *Williams* . . . I lay it down of my own accord, *RSV* . . . but I voluntarily lay it down, *Berkeley* . . . I lay down My life voluntarily, *LivB* . . . on the contrary, I resign it of My own free will, *Fenton.*

I have power to lay it down, and I have power to take it again: I have authority to lay it down...and to take it again, *HBIE* . . . I am authorized to lay it down, *Weymouth* . . . I am commissioned, *Norton* . . . and I have the right to take it back, *Williams* . . . to resume it, *Campbell.*

This commandment have I received of my Father: This precept, *Concordant* . . . This authority I received from My Father, *Norlie* . . . I received this injunction, *Berkeley* . . . This is an order that I have received, *Phillips* . . . These orders, *BB.*

10:19. The word "division" is stressed in this verse because of the order of the Greek words. It is placed in the forefront of the statement. Twice before a division has occurred because of His words (7:43 and 9:16). In each of these three verses John uses this Greek word. It is used five other times in the New Testament. Simeon made a prediction of it in Luke 2:34 (see Isaiah 8:14).

19. There was a division therefore again among the Jews for these sayings: These words again led to difference of opinion, *Williams* . . . a difference of opinion arose, *Norlie* . . . in consequence of these declarations, *Fenton.*

10:20. On other occasions some of the Jews had said Jesus had a demon (John 7:20; 8:48; Mark 3:22). Earlier some of the Jews had said Jesus had lost His senses (Mark 3:21). Here they said He was "insane" (NASB). It was their easy way to discredit the Messiah. One wonders just how insane these Jews were that they would stop their ears to their only salvation and drive their only hope from them. How could they refuse to listen to the sweetest news this earth has ever echoed through its ages.

20. And many of them said, He hath a devil, and is mad; why hear ye him?: He has an evil spirit and is out of his mind, *BB* . . . He has a devil, and is crazy, *Norlie* . . . is wholly beside himself, *Murdock* . . . raves, *Fenton* . . . and is raving mad, *Wuest* . . . Why listen to him? *Moffatt, ALBA.*

10:21. On one side of the "division" were the rejectors. This verse explains the effect His teaching had on "others" who were receptive. These "others" (*alloi*) were like those of the preceding

21. Others said, These are not the words of him that hath a devil: . . . not the sort of thing a devil-possessed man would say! *Phillips* . . . these are not the words of a madman, *Norlie* . . . of a demoniac, *HBIE* . . . a man havynge a fend, *Wycliffe* . . . of one demonized, *Rotherham* . . . of one who is possessed, *TCNT.*

John 10:22

21.a.**Txt:** 02A,05D,017K,036,037,byz.Gries,Lach **Var:** 01ℵ,03B,019L,033X,038,33,Treg,Alf Tisc,We/Ho,Weis,Sod,UBS/☆

22.a.**Txt:** p66-org,01ℵ,02A,05D,017K,036,037,038,13,byz.Lach,Tisc **Var:** p66-corr,p75,03B,019L,032W,33,We/Ho Weis,Sod,UBS/☆

22.b.**Var:** 01ℵ,03B-org,05D,019L,038,Tisc,We/HoWeis

22.c.**Txt:** 02A,03B,019L,038,33,Steph,Lach,Tisc We/Ho,Weis,Sod,UBS/☆ **Var:** p45,01ℵ,05D,017K,036,037,13,byz.

22.d.**Txt:** 02A,017K,021M,036,037,13,byz.Lach **Var:** 01ℵ,03B,05D,019L,033X,038,041,33,sa.bo. TregAlf,Tisc,We/Ho,Weis,Sod,UBS/☆

23.a.**Txt:** 01ℵ,02A,05D,019L,038,etc.byz.Lach,Tisc,We/Ho,Weis,Sod,UBS/☆ **Var:** 03B

24.a.**Txt:** p66,01ℵ-corr,02A,03B,05D,019L,038,etc.byz.Lach,WeisSod **Var:** 01ℵ-org,Tisc,We/Ho,UBS/☆

25.a.**Txt:** 01ℵ-corr,02A,03B,017K,019L,036,037,etc.byz.Lach,We/Ho Weis,Sod,UBS/☆ **Var:** p66,01ℵ-org,05D,038,Tisc

25.b.**Txt:** 01ℵ,02A,05D,017K,019L,036,037,038,etc.byz.Lach,Tisc,We/Ho,Weis,Sod,UBS/☆ **Var:** 03B

1134.1 noun	1404.4 verb	5026.7 adj	3652.8 noun	453.3 verb
sing neu	3sing indic pres	gen pl masc	acc pl masc	inf pres act
δαιμόνιον	δύναται	τυφλῶν	ὀφθαλμοὺς	⸂ ἀνοίγειν;
daimonion	dunatai	tuphlōn	ophthalmous	anoigein
a demon	is able	of blind	eyes	to open?

453.11 verb	1090.33 verb 3sing	1156.2	4966.1	3450.17
inf aor act	indic aor mid	conj	adv	art pl neu
[a☆ ἀνοῖξαι;]	22. Ἐγένετο	⸂ δὲ	[a☆ τότε]	τὰ
anoixai	Egeneto	de	tote	ta
[idem]	Took place	and	[then]	the

1449.1 noun	1449.2 noun	1706.1	3450.4	2389.3 name
nom pl neu	nom pl neu	prep	art dat pl	dat pl neu
⸂ ἐγκαίνια	[b ἐνκαίνια]	ἐν	⸂c τοῖς ⸃	Ἱεροσολύμοις,
enkainia	enkainia	en	tois	Hierosolumois
feast of dedication	[idem]	at		Jerusalem,

2504.1	5330.1 noun	1498.34 verb sing	2504.1	3906.28 verb 3sing
conj	nom sing masc	indic imperf act	conj	indic imperf act
⸂d καὶ ⸃	χειμὼν	ἦν·	23. καὶ	περιεπάτει
kai	cheimōn	ēn	kai	periepatei
and	winter	it was.	And	was walking

3450.5 art	2400.1 name	1706.1	3450.3 art	2387.2 adj	1706.1	3450.11 art
sing masc	nom masc	prep	dat sing	dat sing neu	prep	dat sing fem
⸂a ὁ ⸃	Ἰησοῦς	ἐν	τῷ	ἱερῷ	ἐν	τῇ
ho	Iēsous	en	tō	hierō	en	tē
	Jesus	in	the	temple	in	the

4596.1 noun	3450.2 art	4526.2 name	3450.2 art	4526.4 name
dat sing fem	gen sing	gen masc	gen sing	gen masc
στοᾷ	⸂ τοῦ	Σολομῶντος.	[☆ τοῦ	Σολομῶνος.]
stoa	tou	Solomōntos	tou	Solomōnos
porch		of Solomon.		[idem]

2917.1 verb 3pl	3631.1	840.6 prs-pron	3450.7 art	2428.2 name-
indic aor act	conj	acc sing masc	pl masc	adj pl masc
24. ἐκύκλωσαν	οὖν	αὐτὸν	οἱ	Ἰουδαῖοι,
ekuklōsan	oun	auton	hoi	Ioudaioi
Encircled	therefore	him	the	Jews,

2504.1	2978.25 verb	840.4 prs-	2175.1	4078.1	3450.12 art	5425.4 noun
conj	indic imperf act	pron dat sing	conj	adv	acc sing fem	acc sing fem
καὶ	ἔλεγον	αὐτῷ,	Ἕως	πότε	τὴν	ψυχὴν
kai	elegon	autō	Heōs	pote	tēn	psuchēn
and	said	to him,	Until	when	the	soul

2231.2 prs-	142.1 verb 2sing	1479.1	4622.1 prs-	1498.3 verb 2sing	3450.5 art
pron gen 1pl	indic pres act	conj	pron nom 2sing	indic pres act	sing masc
ἡμῶν	αἴρεις;	εἰ	σὺ	εἶ	ὁ
hēmōn	aireis	ei	su	ei	ho
our	hold you in suspense?	If	you	are	the

5382.1 name	1500.12 verb	1500.29 verb	2231.3 prs-	3816.3 noun
nom masc	2sing impr aor act	2sing impr aor act	pron dat 1pl	dat sing fem
Χριστός,	⸂☆ εἰπὲ	[a εἰπὸν]	ἡμῖν	παῤῥησίᾳ.
Christos	eipe	eipon	hēmin	parrhēsia
Christ,	tell	[idem]	us	plainly.

552.6 verb 3sing	840.2 prs-	3450.5 art	2400.1 name	1500.3 verb
indic aor pass	pron dat pl	sing masc	nom masc	indic aor act
25. Ἀπεκρίθη	⸂a αὐτοῖς ⸃	⸂b ὁ ⸃	Ἰησοῦς,	Εἶπον
Apekrithē	autois	ho	Iēsous	Eipon
Answered	them		Jesus,	I told

verse, yet they received and the others ("many of them") of verse 20 rejected.

"Hath a devil" occurs 13 times in the New Testament, but only here in John. It is interesting that John does not tell about Jesus expelling any demons. The times he mentions demons (six times), or as here, "hath a devil" (one time), are in relation to the Jews' charges. These are "not the words" of one demon possessed because a demon would not condemn his own evil activities. Jesus spoke the truth.

Can a devil open the eyes of the blind?: Can a devil give sight to the blind, *Beck* . . . Can a demoniac open the eyes of the blind, *Montgomery.*

22. And it was at Jerusalem the feast of the dedication, and it was winter: . . . the re-consecration of the temple, *Fenton* . . . the feast of the opening of the Temple, *BB.*

10:22. The Feast of Dedication commemorated the cleansing of the temple by Judas Maccabeus in 164 B.C. after it had been defiled by the wicked Syrian King, Antiochus Epiphanes. The celebration was held throughout Palestine, though the temple in Jerusalem was the focal locale. For further information see 1 Maccabees 4:52-59 and Josephus, *Antiquities of the Jews,* XII.VII.6,7.

This verse begins the narrative of events that took place about 3 months after verse 21. Chapter 7, verses 2 and 37, indicate that the events and teaching of 7:1 through 10:21 occurred during the Feast of Tabernacles in October. Jesus doubtless ministered in Judea during the 3 months' interval between the two feasts.

23. And Jesus walked in the temple in Solomon's porch: . . . walking back and forth in Solomon's cloister, *ALBA* . . . in the Colonnade of Solomon, *TCNT* . . . Solomon's vestibule, *Berkeley.*

10:23. "Winter," of verse 22, indicates not October but December weather. "Solomon's porch" gave some protection from the cold winds for it surrounded the east side of the temple enclosure. The action word "walked" has the position of emphasis in this verse. The Greek verb indicates continued action in the past. The word implies how difficult a moving person is to encircle; thus the Jews' determination to trap Jesus is revealed.

24. Then came the Jews round about him, and said unto him: There the Jews surrounded Him, *Beck* . . . So the Jews closed in on him, *Phillips* . . . So the Jews encircled Him and asked Him, *Berkeley* . . . kept asking him, *Montgomery, Williams.*

How long dost thou make us to doubt?: How much longer, *Williams* . . . dost thou hold us in suspense, *ASV* . . . will you keep us in suspense, *Campbell* . . . in doubt? *BB.*

If thou be the Christ, tell us plainly: If you really are Christ, tell us so straight out! *Phillips* . . . If You're the promised Savior, tell us frankly, *Beck* . . . Tell us definitely whether or not you are, *Barclay* . . . Tell us straight, if, *ALBA* . . . say so clearly, *BB* . . . tell us so openly, *Norlie.*

10:24. They surrounded Him as if to frighten or intimidate Him, repeatedly poking questions at Him.

They wanted Him to say "I am your Messiah" that they might have stronger language on which to charge Him with blasphemy. When Jesus spoke to them in parables and figures of speech (verses 1-19), they had difficulty understanding, and they would disagree among themselves as to what He said. Thus their testimonies would differ as they witnessed against Him.

Jesus surely declined to use the term *Messiah* because of the political connotation the Jews had attached to the title. If Jesus claimed the title openly, the Jews could charge Him with blasphemy against their religion and present Him to Pilate as guilty of treason

25. Jesus answered them, I told you, and ye believed not: I have said it and you have no belief, *BB.*

5050.3 prs-pron dat 2pl	2504.1 conj	3620.3 partic	3961.2 verb 2pl pres act	3450.17 art pl neu	2024.4 noun pl neu	3614.17 rel-pron pl neu
ὑμῖν,	καὶ	οὐ	πιστεύετε.	τὰ	ἔργα	ἃ
humin	*kai*	*ou*	*pisteuete*	*ta*	*erga*	*ha*
you,	and	not	you believe.	The	works	which

1466.1 prs-pron nom 1sing	4020.1 verb 1sing pres act	1706.1 prep	3450.3 art dat sing	3549.4 noun dat sing neu	3450.2 art gen sing
ἐγὼ	ποιῶ	ἐν	τῷ	ὀνόματι	τοῦ
egō	*poiō*	*en*	*tō*	*onomati*	*tou*
I	do	in	the	name	

3824.2 noun gen sing masc	1466.2 prs-pron gen 1sing	3642.18 dem-pron pl neu	3113.3 verb 3sing indic pres act	3875.1 prep	1466.3 prs-pron gen 1sing
πατρός	μου,	ταῦτα	μαρτυρεῖ	περὶ	ἐμοῦ·
patros	*mou*	*tauta*	*marturei*	*peri*	*emou*
of Father	my,	these	bear witness	concerning	me:

	233.1 conj	233.2 conj	5050.1 prs-pron nom 2pl	3620.3 partic	3961.2 verb 2pl pres act	3620.3 partic
26. ⸂	ἀλλ'	[☆ ἀλλὰ]	ὑμεῖς	οὐ	πιστεύετε,	⸂ οὐ
	all'	*alla*	*humeis*	*ou*	*pisteuete*	*ou*
	but	[idem]	you	not	believe,	not

26.a.**Txt:** 02A,017K,036, 037,byz.sa.bo.Gries, Lach,Alf
Var: 01ℵ,03B,05D,019L, 033X,038,28,33,Treg, Tisc,We/Ho,Weis,Sod, UBS/☆

1056.1 conj	3617.1 conj	3620.2 partic	1498.6 verb 2pl indic pres act	1523.2 prep gen	3450.1 art gen pl	4122.4 noun gen pl neu
γάρ	[a☆ ὅτι	οὐκ]	ἐστὲ	ἐκ	τῶν	προβάτων
gar	*hoti*	*ouk*	*este*	*ek*	*tōn*	*probatōn*
for	[because	not]	you are	of	the	sheep

26.b.**Txt:** 02A,05D,033X, 036,037,1,13,28,33,700, byz.it.Gries,Lach
Var: p66-corr,p75,01ℵ, 03B,017K,019L,032W, 038,sa.bo.Treg,Tisc, We/Ho,Weis,Sod,UBS/☆

3450.1 art gen pl	1684.13 adj gen 1pl neu	2503.1 conj	1500.3 verb indic aor act	5050.3 prs-pron dat 2pl	3450.17 art pl neu
τῶν	ἐμῶν,	⸂b καθὼς	εἶπον	ὑμῖν. ⸃	**27.** τὰ
tōn	*emōn*	*kathōs*	*eipon*	*humin*	*ta*
the	my,	as	I said	to you.	The

4122.3 noun pl neu	3450.17 art pl neu	1684.12 adj 1pl neu	3450.10 art gen sing fem	5292.2 noun gen sing fem	1466.2 prs-pron gen 1sing
πρόβατα	τὰ	ἐμὰ	τῆς	φωνῆς	μου
probata	*ta*	*ema*	*tēs*	*phōnēs*	*mou*
sheep	the	my	the	voice	my

27.a.**Txt:** p75,02A,05D, 017K,036,037,1,byz. Lach
Var: 01ℵ,03B,019L, 033X,038,13,33,Treg, Alf,Tisc,We/Ho,Weis, Sod,UBS/☆

189.5 verb 3sing indic pres act	189.3 verb 3pl pres act	2476.3 conj	1091.1 verb 1sing indic pres act	840.16 prs-pron pl neu
⸀ ἀκούει,	[a☆ ἀκούουσιν,]	κἀγὼ	γινώσκω	αὐτά·
akouei	*akouousin*	*kagō*	*ginōskō*	*auta*
hear,	[idem]	and I	know	them,

2504.1 conj	188.1 verb 3pl pres act	1466.4 prs-pron dat 1sing	2476.3 conj	2205.4 noun acc sing fem
καὶ	ἀκολουθοῦσίν	μοι,	**28.** κἀγὼ	⸂ ζωὴν
kai	*akolouthousin*	*moi*	*kagō*	*zōēn*
and	they follow	me;	and I	life

164.1 adj sing	1319.1 verb 1sing indic pres act	840.2 prs-pron dat pl	1319.1 verb 1sing indic pres act	840.2 prs-pron dat pl
αἰώνιον	δίδωμι	αὐτοῖς·	[☆ δίδωμι	αὐτοῖς
aiōnion	*didōmi*	*autois*	*didōmi*	*autois*
eternal	give	them;	[give	them

2205.4 noun acc sing fem	164.1 adj sing	2504.1 conj	3620.3 partic	3231.1 partic	616.30 verb 3pl subj aor mid
ζωὴν	αἰώνιον,]	καὶ	οὐ	μὴ	ἀπόλωνται
zōēn	*aiōnion*	*kai*	*ou*	*mē*	*apolōntai*
life	eternal,]	and	not	not	shall they perish

and rebellion against the Roman government (see Matthew 26:63; 27:11; John 19:12).

the works that I do in my Father's name, they bear witness of me: The works which I am doing on my Father's authority are my credentials, *Williams* . . . The works that I achieve, *Berkeley* . . . My actions as the representative of my, *Barclay* . . . which I am constantly doing in the Name, *Wuest* . . . they are evidence in support of Me, *Fenton* . . . these are my testimony, *ALBA* . . . is sufficient to prove my claim, *Phillips.*

10:25. The credentials of the Messiah were abundantly manifested by His ministry. Several times Jesus had pointed out that His works were the evidence of who He is (see 5:19; 7:31; 9:33). Jesus' works were done "in my Father's name" because the Father was made known by the miracles Jesus did. Jesus came to reveal God to man; miracles were attention-getters and finger-pointers to reality. Those who stopped, looked, and listened could see in Jesus the Father revealed to the world.

26. But ye believe not, because ye are not of my sheep, as I said unto you: But you do not believe me, because you are not of my flock, *TCNT* . . . but still you do not believe in me, *Williams* . . . because you do not belong to my sheep, *Moffatt.*

10:26. Several marks identify His sheep. The first mark is hearing His voice, and the second mark is following Him. Jesus picks up the allegory He had delivered 3 months previously (10:17). "Not of my sheep" stresses the word "my." Whose sheep they are (if sheep at all), He does not say. But they do not believe; therefore, they are not "of" (out of) His sheep (see 8:44). Elsewhere Jesus declared they could not simply claim Abraham as their father and belong to His flock. Said He, "God is able of these stones to raise up children unto Abraham" (Matthew 3:9).

27. My sheep hear my voice: My sheep listen to My voice, *Beck, Weymouth* . . . that are my very own, *Fenton* . . . are in the habit of listening to, *Wuest* . . . recognize My voice, *LivB* . . . to my call, *Berkeley.*

and I know them, and they follow me: . . . they take the same road that I take, *Wuest.*

10:27. Thus by "hear" Jesus implied "believe." The three verbs of this verse are in the present tense denoting continuous action: "hear," "know," and "follow" (see verses 3,4,14). "Hear" and "follow" are the actions of the sheep, and "know" is the progressive action of Jesus. Notice in this verse the three marks of His sheep. First, the sheep hear His voice as the one who speaks truth, life, and righteousness. Second, the sheep recognize and depend on His knowledge of them as individual sheep, both as to their call and personal guidance. Third, they follow, signifying they obey by submitting to His claims and will.

28. And I give unto them eternal life; and they shall never perish: . . . shall positively not perish, *Wuest* . . . at all forever, *Berkeley.*

10:28. Sheep are extremely vulnerable creatures. This vulnerability brings into focus the needs of His true disciples, for they are like sheep in this respect. Jesus supplies the three greatest needs of life. First, the gift of "eternal life" is given by Jesus to believing persons. Second, Jesus provides the assurance of complete security, "they shall never perish." Sheep are always in danger, but His disciples are not as sheep in this respect. The analogy falls far short of illustrating eternal realities. Third, the believer is promised protection from every external enemy. To "pluck" is from a Greek

John 10:29

1519.1 prep	3450.6 art acc sing masc	163.3 noun acc sing masc	2504.1 conj	3620.1 partic	720.7 verb 3sing indic fut act	4948.3 indef-pron nom sing
εἰς	τὸν	αἰῶνα,	καὶ	οὐχ	ἁρπάσει	τις
eis	*ton*	*aiōna*	*kai*	*ouch*	*harpasei*	*tis*
unto	the	age,	and	not	shall seize	anyone

29.a.**Txt:** 01ℵ-corr,02A,03B,05D,017K,019L,038,etc.byz.sa.bo.Gries,Lach,We/Ho,Weis,Sod,UBS/☆
Var: 01ℵ-org,it.Tisc

840.16 prs-pron pl neu	1523.2 prep gen	3450.10 art gen sing fem	5331.2 noun gen sing fem	1466.2 prs-pron gen 1sing	3450.5 art sing masc
αὐτὰ	ἐκ	τῆς	χειρός	μου.	**29.** ὁ
auta	*ek*	*tēs*	*cheiros*	*mou*	*ho*
them	out of	the	hand	my.	The

29.b.**Txt:** p66,02A,03B-corr,017K,036,037,038,byz.LachWeis
Var: 01ℵ,03B-org,05D,019L,032W,bo.TregAlf,Tisc,We/Ho,Sod,UBS/☆

3824.1 noun nom sing masc	1466.2 prs-pron gen 1sing	3614.5 rel-pron nom sing masc	3614.16 rel-pron sing neu	1319.33 verb 3sing indic perf act
πατήρ	⸂a μου ⸃	⸂ ὃς	[b☆ ὃ]	δέδωκέν
patēr	*mou*	*hos*	*ho*	*dedōken*
Father	my	who	[idem]	has given

29.c.**Txt:** p66,017K,036,037,041,1,33,byz.Lach
Var: 03B,Treg,Alf,Tisc,We/Ho,UBS/☆

1466.4 prs-pron dat 1sing	3157.7 adj comp sing neu	3820.4 adj gen pl	3820.4 adj gen pl	3157.7 adj comp sing neu
μοι	⸂ μεῖζόν	πάντων	[c☆ πάντων	μεῖζόν]
moi	*meizon*	*pantōn*	*pantōn*	*meizon*
to me	greater	of all	[of all	greater]

1498.4 verb 3sing indic pres act	2504.1 conj	3625.2 num card nom masc	1404.4 verb 3sing indic pres	720.4 verb inf pres act	1523.2 prep gen
ἐστιν·	καὶ	οὐδεὶς	δύναται	ἁρπάζειν	ἐκ
estin	*kai*	*oudeis*	*dunatai*	*harpazein*	*ek*
is,	and	no one	is able	to seize	out of

29.d.**Txt:** 02A,05D,017K,032W,033X,036,037,038,1,13,33,700,byz.it.sa.bo.Gries,Lach,Sod
Var: p66,p75,01ℵ,03B,019L,Alf,Tisc,We/Ho,Weis,UBS/☆

3450.10 art gen sing fem	5331.2 noun gen sing fem	3450.2 art gen sing	3824.2 noun gen sing masc	1466.2 prs-pron gen 1sing	1466.1 prs-pron nom 1sing
τῆς	χειρὸς	τοῦ	πατρός	⸂d μου. ⸃	**30.** ἐγὼ
tēs	*cheiros*	*tou*	*patros*	*mou*	*egō*
the	hand	of the	Father	my.	I

2504.1 conj	3450.5 art sing masc	3824.1 noun nom sing masc	1518.9 num card neu	1498.5 verb 1pl indic pres act	934.11 verb 3pl indic aor act
καὶ	ὁ	πατὴρ	ἕν	ἐσμεν.	**31.** Ἐβάστασαν
kai	*ho*	*patēr*	*hen*	*esmen*	*Ebastasan*
and	the	Father	one	are.	Took up

31.a.**Txt:** p66,02A,05D,017K,036,037,1,13,etc.byz.it.bo.Lach
Var: p75,01ℵ,03B,019L,032W,038,33,Tisc,We/Ho,Weis,Sod,UBS/☆

3631.1 conj	3687.1 adv	3012.8 noun acc pl masc	3450.7 art pl masc	2428.2 name-adj pl masc	2419.1 conj
⸂a οὖν ⸃	πάλιν	λίθους	οἱ	Ἰουδαῖοι	ἵνα
oun	*palin*	*lithous*	*hoi*	*Ioudaioi*	*hina*
therefore	again	stones	the	Jews	that

32.a.**Txt:** p66,05D,019L,036,037,13,byz.
Var: 01ℵ,02A,03B,017K,032W,041,33,Tisc,We/Ho,Weis,UBS/☆

3008.3 verb 3pl subj aor act	840.6 prs-pron acc sing masc	552.6 verb 3sing indic aor pass	840.2 prs-pron dat pl	3450.5 art sing masc
λιθάσωσιν	αὐτόν.	**32.** ἀπεκρίθη	αὐτοῖς	ὁ
lithasōsin	*auton*	*apekrithē*	*autois*	*ho*
they might stone	him.	Answered	them	

32.b.**Var:** 03B,We/Ho,Weis,UBS/☆

2400.1 name nom masc	4044.17 adj pl neu	2541.11 adj pl neu	2024.4 noun pl neu	1161.7 verb 1sing indic aor act	5050.3 prs-pron dat 2pl
Ἰησοῦς,	Πολλὰ	⸂a καλὰ ⸃	ἔργα	ἔδειξα	ὑμῖν
Iēsous	*Polla*	*kala*	*erga*	*edeixa*	*humin*
Jesus,	Many	good	works	I showed	you

32.c.**Txt:** p66,01ℵ-corr,02A,017K,019L,032W,036,037,1,13,33,byz.it.sa.bo.Lach
Var: 01ℵ-org,03B,05D,038,Alf,Tisc,We/Ho,Weis,Sod,UBS/☆

2541.11 adj pl neu	1523.2 prep gen	3450.2 art gen sing	3824.2 noun gen sing masc	1466.2 prs-pron gen 1sing	1217.2 prep
[b+ καλὰ]	ἐκ	τοῦ	πατρός	⸂c μου· ⸃	διὰ
kala	*ek*	*tou*	*patros*	*mou*	*dia*
[good]	from	the	Father	my;	because of

term also used in verse 12 of the wolf who snatches the sheep. The disciples need not fear that Satan will seize them, for they are in His Father's hand. They are safe, however, only as long as they stay in that place of security.

neither shall any man pluck them out of my hand: . . . no one shall snatch them, *ASV* . . . and none shall tear them out of, *Alford* . . . pluck them by force out, *Wuest* . . . nor shall any one wrest them from, *Weymouth* . . . they shall never at any time be lost, *Fenton* . . . and they shall never get lost, *Williams.*

10:29. This verse doubles the promise Jesus made in the previous verse. There it was "my (Jesus') hand" that securely protected the disciples. Here it is the "Father's hand" that secures the believer.

"Greater than all" refers to greater than any enemy and the combination of all enemies. Jesus uses the same Greek word for "pluck" in verses 28 and 29.

29. My Father, which gave them me, is greater than all: . . . as a permanent gift, *Wuest* . . . has entrusted to me is of more importance than all else, *TCNT* . . . What My Father has endowed Me with is mightier than all, *Fenton* . . . is stronger than all, *Montgomery, Williams* . . . is more precious, *Weymouth* . . . is mightier than all, *Berkeley* . . . stronger than anyone, *SEB.*

and no man is able to pluck them out of my Father's hand: . . . can snatch them out of my Father's hand, *Williams* . . . so no one can kidnap them from Me, *LivB* . . . can steal from the Father, *JB* . . . to wrest them, *Fenton, Berkeley.*

10:30. Jesus has just said that the sheep are equally safe in His hand and in His Father's hand. The power of the Son is equal to that of the Father, and while this is the contextual point of reference, much more is implied. Jesus asserted the essential unity of the Father and the Son in the word "one" (*hen*). It is a neuter number to indicate equality of essence, attributes, design, will, and work. "One" (meaning "one thing") is quite comprehensive, only excluding personal identity. Jesus distinguishes the "I" from the "Father" and uses the plural verb "are" denoting "we are." Thus these words separate the persons within the Godhead, but "one" asserts their unity of essence or nature as identical.

In verse 24 the Jews asked Jesus to tell them plainly who He was. This verse is plain. He does not say "I am Christ," but "I and my Father are one"—God!

30. I and my Father are one: . . . are united, *SEB* . . . in essence, *Wuest.*

10:31. The Jews understood Jesus correctly. There could be no mistake about His meaning. "Again" refers to 8:59 at which time the Jews also attempted to stone Him for blasphemy. Of course, both times they intended to kill Him. Stoning was the Jewish method of executing criminals (Leviticus 24:16).

31. Then the Jews took up stones again to stone him: . . . once more took up stones to throw at Him, *Norlie* . . . again armed themselves with stones, for the purpose of, *Fenton.*

10:32. "From my Father" indicated works which proceeded out of the Father, meaning the source of these works was the Father whom the Jews claimed as their Father. Illustrations of these works are made plain as signs in chapter 5 (the infirm man) and chapter 9 (the man born blind). Jesus called them "good" (*kala*) works, connecting the word "good" with "I am the 'good' shepherd." The word means "beautiful deeds" (see comments on "good" in verses 11 and 14). The Jews had stones in their hands, poised to fling them as Jesus spoke these words. Think of it! Stoning God, how could it be?

32. Jesus answered them, Many good works have I shewed you from my Father: Jesus remonstrated with them, *Weymouth* . . . I have shown you many of My Father's benevolent doings, *Berkeley* . . . You have seen me do many lovely things, things which had their source in, *Barclay* . . . My Father has enabled Me to do many...acts of mercy in your presence, *AmpB* . . . I have done in your presence many good actions, which were due to the Father, *TCNT* . . . the beneficent acts, *Fenton* . . . many a good deed of God, *Moffatt.*

32.d.**Txt:** p66,02A,05D,017K,032W,036,037,1,13,etc.byz.Lach
Var: 01ℵ,03B,019L,038,33,Treg,Alf,Tisc,We/Ho Weis,Sod,UBS/☆

4029.1 intr-pron sing	**840.1** prs-pron gen pl	**2024.1** noun sing neu	**3008.2** verb 2pl indic pres act	**1466.6** prs-pron acc 1sing	**1466.7** prs-pron acc 1sing
ποῖον	αὐτῶν	ἔργον	⸂ λιθάζετε	με;	[d☆ ἐμὲ
poion	*autōn*	*ergon*	*lithazete*	*me*	*eme*
which	of them	work	do you stone	me?	[me

3008.2 verb 2pl indic pres act	**552.8** verb 3pl indic aor pass	**840.4** prs-pron dat sing	**3450.7** art pl masc
λιθάζετε;]	33. Ἀπεκρίθησαν	αὐτῷ	οἱ
lithazete	*Apekrithēsan*	*autō*	*hoi*
do you stone?]	Answered	him	the

33.a.**Txt:** 05D,030U,036,037,byz.Gries
Var: 01ℵ,02A,03B,017K,019L,033X,038,it.sa.bo.Lach,TregAlf,Tisc,We/Ho,Weis,Sod,UBS/☆

2428.2 name-adj pl masc	**2978.16** verb pl masc part pres act	**3875.1** prep	**2541.9** adj gen sing neu	**2024.2** noun gen sing neu	**3620.3** partic
Ἰουδαῖοι	⸂a λεγοντες, ⸃	Περὶ	καλοῦ	ἔργου	οὐ
Ioudaioi	*legontes*	*Peri*	*kalou*	*ergou*	*ou*
Jews,	saying,	For	a good	work	not

3008.1 verb 1pl indic pres act	**4622.4** prs-pron acc 2sing	**233.2** conj	**3875.1** prep	**981.1** noun fem	**2504.1** conj
λιθάζομέν	σε,	ἀλλὰ	περὶ	βλασφημίας,	καὶ
lithazomen	*se*	*alla*	*peri*	*blasphēmias*	*kai*
we do stone	you,	but	for	blasphemy,	and

3617.1 conj	**4622.1** prs-pron nom 2sing	**442.1** noun nom sing masc	**1498.21** verb sing masc part pres act	**4020.4** verb 2sing indic pres act
ὅτι	σὺ	ἄνθρωπος	ὢν	ποιεῖς
hoti	*su*	*anthrōpos*	*ōn*	*poieis*
because	you	a man	being	make

34.a.**Txt:** 01ℵ,02A,05D,017K,019L,036,037,038,etc.byz.Lach,Tisc,We/Ho,Weis,Sod,UBS/☆
Var: p45,03B,032W

4427.4 prs-pron acc 2sing masc	**2296.4** noun acc sing masc	**552.6** verb 3sing indic aor pass	**840.2** prs-pron dat pl	**3450.5** art sing masc
σεαυτὸν	θεόν.	34. Ἀπεκρίθη	αὐτοῖς	⸂a ὁ ⸃
seauton	*theon*	*Apekrithē*	*autois*	*ho*
yourself	God.	Answered	them	

2400.1 name nom masc	**3620.2** partic	**1498.4** verb 3sing indic pres act	**1119.29** verb sing neu part perf pass	**1706.1** prep	**3450.3** art dat sing
Ἰησοῦς,	Οὐκ	ἔστιν	γεγραμμένον	ἐν	τῷ
Iēsous	*Ouk*	*estin*	*gegrammenon*	*en*	*tō*
Jesus,	Not	is it	written	in	the

34.b.**Var:** 01ℵ,03B,05D,019L,033X,038,33,Lach,Treg,Alf,Tisc,We/Ho,Weis,Sod,UBS/☆

3414.3 noun dat sing masc	**5050.2** prs-pron gen 2pl	**3617.1** conj	**1466.1** prs-pron nom 1sing	**1500.4** verb 1sing indic aor act
νόμῳ	ὑμῶν,	[b☆+ ὅτι]	Ἐγὼ	εἶπα,
nomō	*humōn*	*hoti*	*Egō*	*eipa*
law	your,		I	said,

2296.6 noun nom pl masc	**1498.6** verb 2pl indic pres act	**1479.1** conj	**1552.8** dem-pron acc pl masc	**1500.5** verb 3sing indic aor act	**2296.8** noun acc pl masc
Θεοί	ἐστε;	35. Εἰ	ἐκείνους	εἶπεν	θεοὺς,
Theoi	*este*	*Ei*	*ekeinous*	*eipen*	*theous*
gods	you are?	If	those	he called	gods,

4242.1 prep	**3614.8** rel-pron acc pl masc	**3450.5** art sing masc	**3030.1** noun nom sing masc	**3450.2** art gen sing	**2296.2** noun gen sing masc
πρὸς	οὓς	ὁ	λόγος	τοῦ	θεοῦ
pros	*hous*	*ho*	*logos*	*tou*	*theou*
to	whom	the	word		of God

1090.33 verb 3sing indic aor mid	**2504.1** conj	**3620.3** partic	**1404.4** verb 3sing indic pres	**3061.22** verb inf aor pass	**3450.9** art nom sing fem
ἐγένετο,	καὶ	οὐ	δύναται	λυθῆναι	ἡ
egeneto	*kai*	*ou*	*dunatai*	*luthēnai*	*hē*
came,	and	not	can	be broken	the

10:33. They did not deny His "good works." They even acknowledged that He performed them (3:22 and here).

"But for blasphemy" was their charge and the reason for their attempted stoning (see Leviticus 24:14-16 for the law concerning stoning for blasphemy). The death penalty was not within their authority. The Romans held that power as the Jews' conquerors and occupational government.

"Because that thou, being a man, makest thyself God." This was their charge of blasphemy against Him. Jesus did not correct their misunderstanding of His statement, because they accurately understood Him. There is no alternative interpretation of this passage; Jesus claimed all the essence and prerogatives of deity. For anyone to assign any other meaning is to be more erroneous than these blind, hypocritical Jews, for even they realized what He said (see 5:18 and 8:25,29).

Blaney declared the Pharisees by now had dropped the Sabbath-breaking charge against Jesus in healing the blind man. The facts of the case left them condemned by their conscience before the Master. He further wrote, "Earlier they had accused Jesus of being in a demented state of mind (8:48), but now they knew that they were not dealing with an irresponsible public menace, but with a sane, fully responsible adult who knew what He was talking about and was prepared to prove it. And so blasphemy was their only recourse for a charge against Him" (Blaney, *Wesleyan Bible Commentary*, 4:423).

10:34. "In your law" (not in *our* law) stresses the Law in which they said they trusted. The source they accepted was the one He pointed to, namely, the Old Testament, and especially Psalm 82:26. In this psalm the Jewish magistrates were called gods as bearing a commission from God. And Moses was also called "a god to Pharaoh" because God sent him (Exodus 7:1). Jesus' argument is that if those whom God sent were called gods to those in the Old Testament, how much less was Jesus guilty of blasphemy for God sent Him.

10:35. This reference is to the judges, magistrates, and princes who were commissioned by God to rule. Note the contrast between Jesus' mission directly from the Father and these judges' mission which came by the "word of God" as a lesser mode of communication of God's commission.

"And the Scripture cannot be broken" means that the Word of God cannot be explained away. The Jews should accept what the Scriptures teach. The charge of blasphemy could not stand.

for which of those works do ye stone me?: What is the character of that particular work...you are purposing to stone me? *Wuest.*

33. The Jews answered him, saying, For a good work we stone thee not; but for blasphemy: We are going to throw rocks at you, *SEB* . . . not for any good action, *TCNT* . . . For a noble work...for profane-speaking, *Rotherham* . . . but for evil words, *BB* . . . you slander, *Klingensmith.*

and because that thou, being a man, makest thyself God: . . . namely, because you, although a mere man, claim to be God, *Williams* . . . and because you, who are only a man, *Weymouth* . . . are making yourself out to be God, *Phillips* . . . because You, a man, claim to be God, *Beck* . . . you make yourself God, *BB* . . . a human being, make yourself God, *Berkeley* . . . are deifying yourself, *Wuest.*

34. Jesus answered them, Is it not written in your law, I said, Ye are gods?: Is there not a saying in your law, *BB* . . . Are there not...these words in your Law, *TCNT.*

35. If he called them gods, unto whom the word of God came: If those to whom God's word was addressed are called gods, *Weymouth.*

and the scripture cannot be broken: . . . (and the Scripture cannot be annulled), *Montgomery* . . . cannot be nullified, *Murdock* . . . cannot be set aside, *Fenton, Norlie* . . . be made null and void, *Williams* . . . is unexceptionable, *Campbell.*

1118.1 noun nom sing fem	3614.6 rel-pron acc sing masc	3450.5 art sing masc	3824.1 noun nom sing masc	37.5 verb 3sing indic aor act	2504.1 conj
γραφή·	36. ὃν	ὁ	πατὴρ	ἡγίασεν	καὶ
graphē	hon	ho	patēr	hēgiasen	kai
scripture,	whom	the	Father	sanctified	and

643.8 verb 3sing indic aor act	1519.1 prep	3450.6 art acc sing masc	2862.4 noun acc sing masc	5050.1 prs-pron nom 2pl	2978.2 verb 2pl pres act
ἀπέστειλεν	εἰς	τὸν	κόσμον,	ὑμεῖς	λέγετε,
apesteilen	eis	ton	kosmon	humeis	legete
sent	into	the	world,	you	do say,

36.a.**Txt:** 02A,03B,017K,019L,036,037,038,etc.byz.Lach,We/Ho,Weis,Sod,UBS/☆
Var: p66-org,01ℵ,05D,07E,032W,28,Tisc

3617.1 conj	980.1 verb 2sing indic pres act	3617.1 conj	1500.3 verb indic aor act	5048.1 noun nom sing masc	3450.2 art gen sing
ὅτι	Βλασφημεῖς,	ὅτι	εἶπον,	Υἱὸς	(a τοῦ)
hoti	Blasphēmeis	hoti	eipon	Huios	tou
	You blaspheme,	because	I said,	Son	

2296.2 noun gen sing masc	1498.2 verb 1sing indic pres act	1479.1 conj	3620.3 partic	4020.1 verb 1sing pres act	3450.17 art pl neu	2024.4 noun pl neu
θεοῦ	εἰμι;	37. εἰ	οὐ	ποιῶ	τὰ	ἔργα
theou	eimi	ei	ou	poiō	ta	erga
of God	I am?	If	not	I do	the	works

3450.2 art gen sing	3824.2 noun gen sing masc	1466.2 prs-pron gen 1sing	3231.1 partic	3961.2 verb 2pl pres act	1466.4 prs-pron dat 1sing
τοῦ	πατρός	μου,	μὴ	πιστεύετέ	μοι·
tou	patros	mou	mē	pisteuete	moi
of the	Father	my,	not	believe	me;

1479.1 conj	1156.2 conj	4020.1 verb 1sing pres act	2550.1 conj	1466.5 prs-pron dat 1sing	3231.1 partic	3961.8 verb 2pl subj pres act
38. εἰ	δὲ	ποιῶ,	κἂν	ἐμοὶ	μὴ	πιστεύητε,
ei	de	poiō	kan	emoi	mē	pisteuēte
if	but	I do,	even if	me	not	you believe,

38.a.**Txt:** p45,p66,02A,033X,036,13,byz.Gries,Alf,Sod
Var: 01ℵ,03B,05D,017K,019L,030U,038,041,33,Lach,Treg,Tisc,We/HoWeis,UBS/☆

3450.4 art dat pl	2024.6 noun dat pl neu	3961.29 verb 2pl impr aor act	3961.2 verb 2pl pres act	2419.1 conj
τοῖς	ἔργοις	(πιστεύσατε,	[a☆ πιστεύετε,]	ἵνα
tois	ergois	pisteusate	pisteuete	hina
the	works	believe,	[idem]	that

38.b.**Txt:** (01),02A,017K,036,037,13,28,byz.Gries,Word
Var: p45,p66,p75,03B,019L,(022),038,1,33,sa.bo.LachTreg,Alf,Tisc,We/Ho,Weis,Sod,UBS/☆

1091.19 verb 2pl aor act	2504.1 conj	3961.1 verb 2pl subj act	1091.54 verb 2pl subj pres act
γνῶτε	καὶ	(πιστεύσητε	[b☆ γινώσκητε]
gnōte	kai	pisteusēte	ginōskēte
you may perceive	and	may believe	[may know]

38.c.**Txt:** p45,02A,017K,036,037,038,1,13,byz.
Var: 01ℵ,03B,05D,019L,033X,33,sa.bo.LachTreg,Alf,Tisc,We/Ho,Weis,Sod,UBS/☆

3617.1 conj	1706.1 prep	1466.5 prs-pron dat 1sing	3450.5 art sing masc	3824.1 noun nom sing masc	2476.3 conj	1706.1 prep
ὅτι	ἐν	ἐμοὶ	ὁ	πατὴρ,	κἀγὼ	ἐν
hoti	en	emoi	ho	patēr	kagō	en
that	in	me	the	Father,	and I	in

840.4 prs-pron dat sing	3450.3 art dat sing	3824.3 noun dat sing masc	2195.26 verb 3pl indic imperf act	3631.1 conj
(αὐτῷ.	[c☆ τῷ	πατρί.]	39. Ἐζήτουν	(a οὖν)
autō	tō	patri	Ezētoun	oun
him.	[the	Father.]	They sought	therefore

39.a.**Txt:** 01ℵ,02A,017K,019L,033X,037,041,it.sa.Steph,LachTisc,We/Ho,Weis,Sod,UBS/☆
Var: 03B,07E,021M,030U,036,038,13,byz.bo.

3687.1 adv	840.6 prs-pron acc sing masc	840.6 prs-pron acc sing masc	3687.1 adv	3945.6 verb inf aor act	2504.1 conj
(☆ πάλιν	αὐτὸν	[αὐτὸν	πάλιν]	πιάσαι·	καὶ
palin	auton	auton	palin	piasai	kai
again	him	[him	again]	to take,	and

10:36. Both "sanctified" and "sent" referring to Jesus, form a contrast with "unto whom the word of God came," speaking of the judges. "Sanctified" here does not mean "cleansing," but "marked off for the purpose of manifesting the Father." "Sent" indicates a special commission (see 3:15,16).

"Say ye of him" is stressed and therefore rendered first in the verse, but in the original order it comes before the word *blaspheme*. The sole purpose in Jesus' argument was to clear himself of their charge of blasphemy. If the judges of the Old Testament were called gods, how could these Jews charge with blasphemy One who was appointed to manifest God to them?

36. Say ye of him, whom the Father hath sanctified, and sent into the world: Do you then accuse...Him whom the Father has consecrated, *Norlie* . . . to One whom the Father dedicated, *Berkeley* . . . to Me, whom the Father appointed for His holy purpose, *Beck* . . . has set apart to it, *Williams* . . . hallows and dispatches, *Concordant* . . . consecrated, *Wuest.*

Thou blasphemest; because I said, I am the Son of God?: Thou speakest profanely, *Rotherham* . . . because I said, I am God's Son, *Moffatt.*

10:37. Jesus continually pointed to "the works" as signs to them of who He is. The "works" revealed God's power through the Son whom He sent. Furthermore, many of the works revealed the Father's grace, love, mercy, goodness, and even forgiveness.

Jesus called upon the Jews to consider His works as an indication of who He is. He did not ask them to simply believe His word before they had examined His messianic credentials as demonstrated by His works. His works were tokens of divine power and convincing proofs that God was at work.

Jesus presented His case very clearly and with great logic. He asked the Jews to believe Him on the basis of the evidence. The evidence was of two kinds, His words and His works. Jesus as much as said He was not unreasonable. They should have accepted the words He spoke as proof enough.

The other kind of evidence was His works. They were credentials the Father had given him. Jesus did not take credit for the miracles He wrought. He called them "the works of my Father." Then He forthrightly declared that if the works He did were not valid, He did not expect His adversaries to accept Him. The miracles He had performed would satisfy the mind of any sincere and sensible inquirer.

37. If I do not the works of my Father, believe me not: . . . do not accomplish My Father's work, *Berkeley* . . . carry out the works, *Fenton* . . . don't trust Me, *Beck.*

38. But if I do, though ye believe me not, believe the works: . . . even if you don't trust Me, trust My works, *Beck* . . . give credit to the works, *Norton.*

that ye may know, and believe: . . . so that you may see clearly and be certain, *BB* . . . you may come to know and continue to know, *Williams* . . . and understand, *ASV.*

that the Father is in me, and I in him: . . . that the Father is in union with me, *Williams, TCNT* . . . the Father is one with Me, and I one, *Fenton.*

10:38. Now Jesus turned the tables on His accusers by putting *them* on trial. He was not asking them to believe Him, but He presents His works as proof of His relationship with the Father. "You do not want to believe me?" He says in essence. "All right, then what are you going to do about the works I have done and am doing?"

The works Jesus did were an evidence of His divine mission, that the Father had sent Him. Those works must have come from God, for only God could do such miracles. They were not only acts of power, they revealed God's love and mercy.

Jesus summed up His argument by driving home the point that if they could not believe Him on the basis of His words, His works

39. Therefore they sought again to take him; but he escaped out of their hand: Again they tried to arrest Him, *Beck* . . . They tried again to seize Him, *Norlie*

1814.3 verb 3sing indic aor act	1523.2 prep gen	3450.10 art gen sing fem	5331.2 noun gen sing fem	840.1 prs-pron gen pl	2504.1 conj
ἐξῆλθεν	ἐκ	τῆς	χειρὸς	αὐτῶν.	**40.** Καὶ
exēlthen	*ek*	*tēs*	*cheiros*	*autōn*	*Kai*
he went forth	out of	the	hand	their;	and

562.2 verb 3sing indic aor act	3687.1 adv	3871.1 adv	3450.2 art gen sing	2422.1 name gen masc	1519.1 prep
ἀπῆλθεν	πάλιν	πέραν	τοῦ	Ἰορδάνου,	εἰς
apēlthen	*palin*	*peran*	*tou*	*Iordanou*	*eis*
departed	again	beyond	the	Jordan,	to

3450.6 art acc sing masc	4964.4 noun acc sing masc	3562.1 adv	1498.34 verb sing indic imperf act	2464.1 name nom masc	3450.16 art sing neu
τὸν	τόπον	ὅπου	ἦν	Ἰωάννης	τὸ
ton	*topon*	*hopou*	*ēn*	*Iōannēs*	*to*
the	place	where	was	John	the

40.a.**Txt:** p45,p66,p75, 01ℵ,02A,05D,017K, 019L,032W,036,037, 038,1,13,etc.byz.Tisc, Sod
Var: 03B,Lach,We/Ho, Weis,UBS/☆

4270.1 adv	901.4 verb nom sing masc part pres act	2504.1 conj	3176.16 verb 3sing indic aor act	3176.29 verb 3sing indic imperf act
πρῶτον	βαπτίζων·	καὶ	⸀ἔμεινεν	[a☆ ἔμενεν]
prōton	*baptizōn*	*kai*	*emeinen*	*emenen*
first	baptizing;	and	he stayed	[idem]

1550.1 adv	2504.1 conj	4044.7 adj nom pl masc	2048.1 verb indic aor act	4242.1 prep	840.6 prs-pron acc sing masc	2504.1 conj
ἐκεῖ.	**41.** καὶ	πολλοὶ	ἦλθον	πρὸς	αὐτὸν,	καὶ
ekei	*kai*	*polloi*	*ēlthon*	*pros*	*auton*	*kai*
there.	And	many	came	to	him,	and

2978.25 verb indic imperf act	3617.1 conj	2464.1 name nom masc	3173.1 conj	4447.1 noun sing neu	4020.24 verb 3sing indic aor act
ἔλεγον,	Ὅτι	Ἰωάννης	μὲν	σημεῖον	ἐποίησεν
elegon	*Hoti*	*Iōannēs*	*men*	*sēmeion*	*epoiēsen*
said,		John	indeed	sign	did

3625.6 num card neu	3820.1 adj	1156.2 conj	3607.8 rel-pron pl neu	1500.5 verb 3sing indic aor act	2464.1 name nom masc
οὐδέν·	πάντα	δὲ	ὅσα	εἶπεν	Ἰωάννης
ouden	*panta*	*de*	*hosa*	*eipen*	*Iōannēs*
no;	all	but	whatsoever	said	John

3875.1 prep	3642.1 dem-pron gen sing	225.4 adj	1498.34 verb sing indic imperf act	2504.1 conj
περὶ	τούτου	ἀληθῆ	ἦν.	**42.** καὶ
peri	*toutou*	*alēthē*	*ēn*	*kai*
concerning	this,	true	were.	And

3961.23 verb 3pl indic aor act	4044.7 adj nom pl masc	1550.1 adv	1519.1 prep	840.6 prs-pron acc sing masc	4044.7 adj nom pl masc
⸀ἐπίστευσαν	πολλοὶ	ἐκεῖ	εἰς	αὐτόν.	[πολλοὶ
episteusan	*polloi*	*ekei*	*eis*	*auton*	*polloi*
believed	many	there	on	him.	[many

3961.23 verb 3pl indic aor act	1519.1 prep	840.6 prs-pron acc sing masc	1550.1 adv	1498.34 verb sing indic imperf act	1156.2 conj
ἐπίστευσαν	εἰς	αὐτὸν	ἐκεῖ.]	**11:1.** Ἦν	δέ
episteusan	*eis*	*auton*	*ekei*	*En*	*de*
believed	on	him	there.]	There was	now

4948.3 indef-pron nom sing	764.6 verb nom sing masc part pres act	2949.1 name nom masc	570.3 prep gen	956.2 name gen fem	1523.2 prep gen
τις	ἀσθενῶν	Λάζαρος	ἀπὸ	Βηθανίας,	ἐκ
tis	*asthenōn*	*Lazaros*	*apo*	*Bēthanias*	*ek*
a certain	sick,	Lazarus	of	Bethany,	of

were irrefutable evidence of His close relationship with God the Father.

. . . Once more they were trying to arrest, *Williams* . . . This made the Jews again eager to arrest him, *TCNT* . . . but he slipped through their hands, *Barclay* . . . moved out of their reach, *Phillips* . . . but He withdrew out of their power, *Weymouth.*

10:39. They sought "to seize" Him; that is, to arrest Him (see NASB). They refused to listen to His appeal to their reason.

They were powerless to carry out their purpose until His time had come. It is well to note that even when they did arrest Him, they could not have taken Him if He had not desired to yield to them (18:6).

40. And went away again beyond Jordan into the place where John at first baptized: and there he abode: He accordingly returned, *Fenton* . . . He again crossed the Jordan, *Williams* . . . and resorted once more, *Berkeley* . . . to the locality, *Fenton* . . . where John had formerly been baptizing, *ALBA* . . . to Transjordan and remained there, *Barclay* . . . and tarried there, *Murdock* . . . He stayed, *Norlie.*

10:40. Their rejection and hostility drove their Creator and Saviour from them. Jesus does not stay where He is not wanted. His presence permeates those who desire Him, and He departs from those who repel Him.

41. And many resorted unto him: Many came to Him there, *Norlie.*

and said, John did no miracle: Their report was, *Weymouth* . . . did nothing in which the action of God was visibly displayed, *Barclay.*

but all things that John spake of this man were true: . . . all that John said concerning this Man, *Fenton* . . . all that he said about this man was true, *Phillips.*

10:41. Those who came to Jesus beyond the Jordan River were from Jerusalem and Judea. The "many" seem to have come as a direct result of Jesus' ministry in Jerusalem during the Feast of Dedication.

The people who came remembered John the Baptist. Probably the place brought to their minds the multitudes who came there for water baptism about 2 years before. By hearing and obeying John the prophet, they believed on Jesus.

The people who came to Jesus reasoned that though John did no miracle, they believed what he said. How much more should they have confidence in Jesus who did many extraordinary signs. Besides, John identified Jesus as Christ.

42. And many believed on him there: And many came to the decision that He was the Messiah, *LivB.*

10:42. Success in Peraea was the climax of Jesus' ministry as recorded in chapters 7 through 10. We are not told who these believers were and how many. Yet John tells of a flourishing growth of disciples, though the Jewish leaders were hostile and even murderous toward Christ and His message.

1. Now a certain man was sick, named Lazarus, of Bethany: Now there was a man ill, Lazarus of Bethany, *Moffatt* . . . lay ill, *Norlie* . . . infirm man, *Concordant* . . . from Bethany, *Adams.*

11:1. The raising of Lazarus of Bethany from the dead is the most amazing miracle of all those Jesus performed on the human

John 11:2

1.a.Var: 01א,05D,Tisc

3450.10 art gen sing fem	**2941.1** noun gen sing fem	**3450.10** art gen sing fem	**3109.2** name gen fem	**2504.1** conj	**3108.2** name gen fem
τῆς	κώμης	[a+ τῆς]	Μαρίας	καὶ	Μάρθας
tēs	*kōmēs*	*tēs*	*Marias*	*kai*	*Marthas*
the	village		of Mary	and	Martha

3450.10 art gen sing fem	**78.2** noun gen sing fem	**840.10** prs-pron gen sing fem	**1498.34** verb sing indic imperf act	**1156.2** conj	**3109.1** name nom fem
τῆς	ἀδελφῆς	αὐτῆς.	2. ἦν	δὲ	‘ Μαρία
tēs	*adelphēs*	*autēs*	*ēn*	*de*	*Maria*
the	sister	her.	It was	and	Mary

3110.1 name fem	**3450.9** art nom sing fem	**216.5** verb nom sing fem part aor act	**3450.6** art acc sing masc	**2935.4** noun acc sing masc
[☆ Μαριὰμ]	ἡ	ἀλείψασα	τὸν	κύριον
Mariam	*hē*	*aleipsasa*	*ton*	*kurion*
[idem]	the	having anointed	the	Lord

3326.3 noun dat sing neu	**2504.1** conj	**1578.3** verb nom sing fem part aor act	**3450.8** art acc pl masc	**4087.7** noun acc pl masc
μύρῳ	καὶ	ἐκμάξασα	τοὺς	πόδας
murō	*kai*	*ekmaxasa*	*tous*	*podas*
with ointment	and	wiped	the	feet

840.3 prs-pron gen sing	**3450.14** art dat pl fem	**2336.5** noun dat pl fem	**840.10** prs-pron gen sing fem	**3614.10** rel-pron gen sing fem	**3450.5** art sing masc
αὐτοῦ	ταῖς	θριξὶν	αὐτῆς,	ἧς	ὁ
autou	*tais*	*thrixin*	*autēs*	*hēs*	*ho*
his	with the	hair	her,	whose	the

79.1 noun nom sing masc	**2949.1** name nom masc	**764.16** verb 3sing indic imperf act	**643.9** verb 3pl indic aor act	**3631.1** conj
ἀδελφὸς	Λάζαρος	ἠσθένει.	3. ἀπέστειλαν	οὖν
adelphos	*Lazaros*	*ēsthenei*	*apesteilan*	*oun*
brother	Lazarus	was sick.	Sent	therefore

3450.13 art pl fem	**78.5** noun nom pl fem	**4242.1** prep	**840.6** prs-pron acc sing masc	**2978.22** verb nom pl fem part pres act	**2935.5** noun voc sing masc
αἱ	ἀδελφαὶ	πρὸς	αὐτὸν	λέγουσαι,	Κύριε,
hai	*adelphai*	*pros*	*auton*	*legousai*	*Kurie*
the	sisters	to	him,	saying,	Lord,

1481.14 verb 2sing impr aor act	**3614.6** rel-pron acc sing masc	**5205.2** verb 2sing indic pres act	**764.2** verb 3sing indic pres act	**189.31** verb nom sing masc part aor act
ἴδε	ὃν	φιλεῖς	ἀσθενεῖ.	4. Ἀκούσας
ide	*hon*	*phileis*	*asthenei*	*Akousas*
lo,	he whom	you love	is sick.	Having heard

1156.2 conj	**3450.5** art sing masc	**2400.1** name nom masc	**1500.5** verb 3sing indic aor act	**3642.9** dem-pron nom sing fem	**3450.9** art nom sing fem
δὲ	ὁ	Ἰησοῦς	εἶπεν,	Αὕτη	ἡ
de	*ho*	*Iēsous*	*eipen*	*Hautē*	*hē*
but		Jesus	said,	This	the

763.2 noun nom sing fem	**3620.2** partic	**1498.4** verb 3sing indic pres act	**4242.1** prep	**2265.4** noun acc sing masc	**233.1** conj	**5065.1** prep
ἀσθένεια	οὐκ	ἔστιν	πρὸς	θάνατον,	ἀλλ'	ὑπὲρ
astheneia	*ouk*	*estin*	*pros*	*thanaton*	*all'*	*huper*
sickness	not	is	unto	death,	but	for

3450.10 art gen sing fem	**1385.2** noun gen sing fem	**3450.2** art gen sing	**2296.2** noun gen sing masc	**2419.1** conj	**1386.23** verb 3sing subj aor pass
τῆς	δόξης	τοῦ	θεοῦ,	ἵνα	δοξασθῇ
tēs	*doxēs*	*tou*	*theou*	*hina*	*doxasthē*
the	glory		of God,	that	may be glorified

body. He had raised two from the dead prior to this time—the widow's son at Nain (Luke 7:11-15) and the daughter of Jairus (Luke 8:41,42,49-56). These were raised the same day they died, but in the case of Lazarus, he had been dead 4 days. John alone records this mighty miracle of Christ. More is recorded concerning this wonderful sign than any other of our Lord's wonders.

The name Lazarus is the Greek form of the Hebrew name Eleazar, meaning "God is his help." John's Gospel is the only one that reveals Lazarus as the brother of Mary and Martha. Christ is, of course, the dominant person in this incident.

Bethany was a village about 2 miles east of Jerusalem and some 25 miles from the place beyond the Jordan River (10:40). Jesus probably stayed at the home in Bethany occasionally when He attended the festivals in Jerusalem. Both the home and the village provided a tranquil place to spend the evenings away from the busy and hostile Jews of Jerusalem (Mark 11:12; Luke 21:37).

"Mary" (*Marias*) and "Martha" (Greek, *Marthas*) are each named eight times in this chapter. No other Martha is recorded in the New Testament, but three other persons called "Mary" appear in the Gospels: Mary the mother of Jesus, the wife of Cleopas, and Mary Magdalene.

the town of Mary and her sister Martha: . . . the village of, *Norlie.*

2. (It was that Mary which anointed the Lord with ointment: Now, it was Mary, she who, *Wuest* . . . who rubbed the Lord Jesus' feet, *SEB* . . . with precious oil, *Norton* . . . it was that Mary who anointed the Lord with perfume, *Montgomery* . . . who poured the perfume, *Weymouth* . . . It was the Mary who poured the perfume upon the Lord, *Williams* . . . who bathed, *Fenton* . . . with attar, *Concordant* . . . with expensive perfume, *ALBA.*

and wiped his feet with her hair: . . . dried them, *SEB* . . . wiped his feet dry, *Confraternity.*

whose brother Lazarus was sick.):

11:2. "It was that Mary" indicates she was the one who anointed the Lord's feet (Matthew 26:6-13). Matthew did not identify her by name. He only called her a woman. It was Mary's brother Lazarus who was "sick" (*ēsthenei*) meaning "ailing, weak, feeble, and sick."

3. Therefore his sisters sent unto him, saying, Lord, behold, he whom thou lovest is sick: . . . dispatch to Him, *Concordant* . . . Alas, Lord, he whom You love is ill! *Norlie* . . . he whom you hold dear is ill, *Weymouth, Montgomery* . . . he of whom you are fond, *Wuest* . . . Your very dear friend, *Fenton* . . . the one you love so well, *Williams.*

11:3. As soon as Lazarus became ill, his sisters decided to send for Jesus. They knew His power to restore the sick to health.

Phileis ("love") is the word for friendship love. The message they sent implied, "Come soon to heal him"; yet the words did not call for Him to come to heal Lazarus. Even so, they expected that Jesus' fondness for His friend would prompt His speedy return.

4. When Jesus heard that, he said, This sickness is not unto death: This illness is not to end in death, *Weymouth* . . . will not prove fatal, *Campbell* . . . The purpose of this sickness, *Beck* . . . is not to culminate in death, *Berkeley* . . . is not with reference to death, *Wuest* . . . will end, not in death, *JB* . . . final result of this sickness will not be the death of Lazarus, *TEV.*

but for the glory of God: . . . but is to promote the glory of God, *Weymouth* . . . but is to honor God, *Williams.*

11:4. The Lord spoke to all who were in His presence at the time the messenger brought word from Lazarus' sisters. "Unto death" (*pros thanaton*) means that the final result would not be death. Jesus did not say Lazarus would not die. He did promise that his ailment would not bring Lazarus to death in its final state.

Those who heard must have thought He meant to return to Bethany shortly for the purpose of restoring Lazarus to health. "Glory" (*doxēs*) and "glorified" (*doxasthē*) both refer to God and

John 11:5

3450.5 art sing masc	5048.1 noun nom sing masc	3450.2 art gen sing	2296.2 noun gen sing masc	1217.1 prep	840.10 prs-pron gen sing fem
ὁ	υἱὸς	τοῦ	θεοῦ	δι'	αὐτῆς.
ho	*huios*	*tou*	*theou*	*di'*	*autēs*
the	Son		of God	by	it.

25.26 verb 3sing indic imperf act	1156.2 conj	3450.5 art sing masc	2400.1 name nom masc	3450.12 art acc sing fem	3108.3 name acc fem	2504.1 conj
5. Ἠγάπα	δὲ	ὁ	Ἰησοῦς	τὴν	Μάρθαν	καὶ
Egapa	*de*	*ho*	*Iēsous*	*tēn*	*Marthan*	*kai*
Loved	now		Jesus		Martha	and

3450.12 art acc sing fem	78.4 noun acc sing fem	840.10 prs-pron gen sing fem	2504.1 conj	3450.6 art acc sing masc	2949.2 name acc masc
τὴν	ἀδελφὴν	αὐτῆς	καὶ	τὸν	Λάζαρον.
tēn	*adelphēn*	*autēs*	*kai*	*ton*	*Lazaron*
the	sister	her	and		Lazarus.

5453.1 conj	3631.1 conj	189.21 verb 3sing indic aor act	3617.1 conj	764.2 verb 3sing indic pres act	4966.1 adv
6. ὡς	οὖν	ἤκουσεν	ὅτι	ἀσθενεῖ,	τότε
hōs	*oun*	*ēkousen*	*hoti*	*asthenei*	*tote*
When	therefore	he heard	that	he is sick,	then

3173.1 conj	3176.16 verb 3sing indic aor act	1706.1 prep	3614.3 rel-pron dat sing	1498.34 verb sing indic imperf act	4964.3 noun dat sing masc
μὲν	ἔμεινεν	ἐν	ᾧ	ἦν	τόπῳ
men	*emeinen*	*en*	*hō*	*ēn*	*topō*
indeed	he remained	in	which	he was	place

1411.3 num card	2232.1 noun fem	1884.1 adv	3196.3 prep	3642.17 dem-pron sing neu	2978.5 verb 3sing indic pres act
δύο	ἡμέρας.	7. Ἔπειτα	μετὰ	τοῦτο	λέγει
duo	*hēmeras*	*Epeita*	*meta*	*touto*	*legei*
two	days.	Then	after	this	he says

3450.4 art dat pl	3073.7 noun dat pl masc	70.4 verb 1pl subj pres act	1519.1 prep	3450.12 art acc sing fem	2424.4 name acc fem
τοῖς	μαθηταῖς,	Ἄγωμεν	εἰς	τὴν	Ἰουδαίαν
tois	*mathētais*	*Agōmen*	*eis*	*tēn*	*Ioudaian*
to the	disciples,	Let us go	into		Judea

3687.1 adv	2978.3 verb 3pl pres act	840.4 prs-pron dat sing	3450.7 art pl masc	3073.5 noun nom pl masc	4318.1 noun sing masc
πάλιν.	8. Λέγουσιν	αὐτῷ	οἱ	μαθηταί,	Ῥαββί,
palin	*Legousin*	*autō*	*hoi*	*mathētai*	*Rhabbi*
again.	Say	to him	the	disciples,	Rabbi,

3431.1 adv	2195.26 verb 3pl indic imperf act	4622.4 prs-pron acc 2sing	3008.5 verb inf aor act	3450.7 art pl masc	2428.2 name-adj pl masc
νῦν	ἐζήτουν	σε	λιθάσαι	οἱ	Ἰουδαῖοι,
nun	*ezētoun*	*se*	*lithasai*	*hoi*	*Ioudaioi*
just now	were seeking	you	to stone	the	Jews,

2504.1 conj	3687.1 adv	5055.2 verb 2sing indic pres act	1550.1 adv	552.6 verb 3sing indic aor pass	3450.5 art sing masc
καὶ	πάλιν	ὑπάγεις	ἐκεῖ;	9. Ἀπεκρίθη	⸀a ὁ ⸌
kai	*palin*	*hupageis*	*ekei*	*Apekrithē*	*ho*
and	again	you go	there?	Answered	

9.a.**Txt:** p45,030U,038,1, 565,Steph
Var: 01א,02A,03B,04C, 05D,017K,019L,036, 037,byz.Gries,Lach,Treg Alf,Tisc,We/Ho,Weis, Sod,UBS/☆

2400.1 name nom masc	3644.1 adv	1420.1 num card	1498.7 verb 3pl indic pres act	5443.5 noun nom pl fem	5443.5 noun nom pl fem
Ἰησοῦς,	Οὐχὶ	δώδεκα	⸀ εἰσιν	ὧραί	[☆ ὧραί
Iēsous	*Ouchi*	*dōdeka*	*eisin*	*hōrai*	*hōrai*
Jesus,	Not	twelve	there are	hours	[hours

Jesus here. Jesus said He and the Father would be glorified when He raised Lazarus from the grave.

that the Son of God might be glorified thereby: . . . be the means by which, *TEV* . . . the Son of God may be honoured through it, *TCNT* . . . it is to glorify God's Son, *Beck* . . . that the sonne off God myght be praysed by the reason of it, *Tyndale* . . . may win honour through it, *TCNT*.

11:5. "Now" is a connective word between the last thought concerning God's glory and the love Jesus had for the sisters and Lazarus. The word used here, *ēgapa*, means a deeper and more purposeful love than the word *phileis* which the sisters used in their message to Jesus (verse 3). The word John used shows that Jesus' delay in coming to Lazarus represented a higher love than friendship. Jesus loved, yet He tarried (verse 6). Often when the Lord does not answer our prayers as we want Him to, it is because He plans to do something even better for us. Jesus waited to come that their faith might grow toward perfection.

5. Now Jesus loved Martha, and her sister, and Lazarus: . . . was a dear friend to, *Berkeley* . . . held in loving esteem, *Williams* . . . had a friendship, *Fenton*.

11:6. Two reasons may account for the 2-day delay. First, perhaps His work in Peraea was not yet finished. He could have waited 10 or 20 days before He raised Lazarus from the grave. Doubtless He had been teaching and healing so that 2 days more were necessary for the manifestation of God's glory to be complete. Second, Jesus wanted the sisters to realize that His power was not limited to the sick and dying before the grave, but that He had authority over the living and the dead (see verse 25).

6. When he had heard therefore that he was sick: Yet, though He had heard that Lazarus was ill, *Norlie*.

he abode two days still in the same place where he was: . . . purposely stayed, *ET* . . . he still stayed, *TCNT* . . . He still remained two days in that same place, *Weymouth*.

7. Then after that saith he to his disciples, Let us go into Judaea again:

11:7. Jews buried their dead on the same day as they died partly for sanitary reasons and partly because the dead were sources of ceremonial defilement. According to the Law, anyone who touched a dead person was unclean for 7 days; thus the defiled lived in isolation during that time. Perhaps this practice taught that death was the direct result of sin (Genesis 3). It had been 3 months since the Feast of Dedication (December). It was now close to the Passover (March–April). Jesus did not say merely, "Let us go to Bethany where Lazarus was," but rather, "Let us go into Judea." This trip to Judea would be His last journey before Calvary. His words here implied all that He was to accomplish in Judea.

The lesson He had to teach by the raising of Lazarus would be more meaningful because of His personal demonstration and illustration of the truth He taught in 5:28,29.

8. His disciples say unto him, Master, the Jews of late sought to stone thee: . . . our Rabbi, *Murdock* . . . Jewish leaders, *SEB* . . . are now trying to stone you, *Klingensmith* . . . were just now attempting to stone, *Fenton* . . . it was but a short time ago, *ET* . . . recently the Jews wanted to, *ALBA* . . . eager to stone you, *TCNT* . . . as it is, the Jews want to stone you, *Berkeley*.

and goest thou thither again?: . . . and are you going there again, *RSV, Fenton* . . . are you planning to go back? *TEV* . . . and do you want to go there again? *Klingensmith* . . . Are you going back already? *ALBA*.

11:8. *Palin . . . ekei* ("again thither") refers to what had happened at the Feast of Dedication approximately 3 months before (10:31). The Greek word *nun* ("just now") stresses that the Jews were still in pursuit of Jesus' life. The word "again" is made emphatic in the disciples' statement. Literally, the original order of the words is "and again you are going there?"

9. Jesus answered, Are there not twelve hours in the day?: Does not the day have twelve hours, *Williams* . . . hours of daylight, aren't there? *Adams*.

1498.7 verb 3pl indic pres act	3450.10 art gen sing fem	2232.1 noun fem	1430.1 partic	4948.3 indef-pron nom sing	3906.6 verb 3sing subj pres act
εἰσιν]	τῆς	ἡμέρας;	ἐάν	τις	περιπατῇ
eisin	*tēs*	*hēmeras*	*ean*	*tis*	*peripatē*
there are]	in the	day?	If	anyone	walk

1706.1 prep	3450.11 art dat sing fem	2232.3 noun dat sing fem	3620.3 partic	4208.1 verb 3sing indic pres act	3617.1 conj
ἐν	τῇ	ἡμέρᾳ,	οὐ	προσκόπτει,	ὅτι
en	*tē*	*hēmera*	*ou*	*proskoptei*	*hoti*
in	the	day,	not	he stumbles,	because

3450.16 art sing neu	5295.1 noun sing neu	3450.2 art gen sing	2862.2 noun gen sing masc	3642.1 dem-pron gen sing	984.4 verb 3sing indic pres act
τὸ	φῶς	τοῦ	κόσμου	τούτου	βλέπει·
to	*phōs*	*tou*	*kosmou*	*toutou*	*blepei*
the	light	of the	world	this	he sees;

1430.1 partic	1156.2 conj	4948.3 indef-pron nom sing	3906.6 verb 3sing subj pres act	1706.1 prep	3450.11 art dat sing fem
10. ἐὰν	δέ	τις	περιπατῇ	ἐν	τῇ
ean	*de*	*tis*	*peripatē*	*en*	*tē*
if	but	anyone	walk	in	the

3433.3 noun dat sing fem	4208.1 verb 3sing indic pres act	3617.1 conj	3450.16 art sing neu	5295.1 noun sing neu	3620.2 partic
νυκτί,	προσκόπτει,	ὅτι	τὸ	φῶς	οὐκ
nukti	*proskoptei*	*hoti*	*to*	*phōs*	*ouk*
night,	he stumbles,	because	the	light	not

1498.4 verb 3sing indic pres act	1706.1 prep	840.4 prs-pron dat sing	3642.18 dem-pron pl neu	1500.5 verb 3sing indic aor act	2504.1 conj
ἔστιν	ἐν	αὐτῷ.	**11.** Ταῦτα	εἶπεν,	καὶ
estin	*en*	*autō*	*Tauta*	*eipen*	*kai*
is	in	him.	These things	he said;	and

3196.3 prep	3642.17 dem-pron sing neu	2978.5 verb 3sing indic pres act	840.2 prs-pron dat pl	2949.1 name nom masc	3450.5 art sing masc
μετὰ	τοῦτο	λέγει	αὐτοῖς,	Λάζαρος	ὁ
meta	*touto*	*legei*	*autois*	*Lazaros*	*ho*
after	this	he says	to them,	Lazarus	the

5224.1 adj nom sing masc	2231.2 prs-pron gen 1pl	2810.10 verb 3sing indic perf	233.2 conj	4057.1 verb 1sing indic pres
φίλος	ἡμῶν	κεκοίμηται·	ἀλλὰ	πορεύομαι
philos	*hēmōn*	*kekoimētai*	*alla*	*poreuomai*
friend	our	has fallen asleep;	but	I go

12.a.**Txt:** 02A,03B,04C, 05D,017K,019L,036, 037,etc.byz.Lach,Tisc, Sod
Var: 01ℵ,038,We/Ho, Weis,UBS/☆

12.b.**Var:** 01ℵ,05D, 017K,032W,041,sa. Lach,Tisc

12.c.**Txt:** 04C-corr,019L, 036,037,1,byz.
Var: p66,p75,03B, 04C-org,033X,038,bo. Treg,Alf,We/Ho,Weis, Sod,UBS/☆

2419.1 conj	1836.1 verb 1sing subj aor act	840.6 prs-pron acc sing masc	1500.3 verb indic aor act	1500.28 verb 3pl indic aor act
ἵνα	ἐξυπνίσω	αὐτόν.	**12.** ʻ Εἶπον	[a☆ εἶπαν]
hina	*exupnisō*	*auton*	*Eipon*	*eipan*
that	I may awake	him.	Said	[idem]

3631.1 conj	840.4 prs-pron dat sing	3450.7 art pl masc	3073.5 noun nom pl masc	840.3 prs-pron gen sing
οὖν	[b+ αὐτῷ]	οἱ	μαθηταὶ	ʻ αὐτοῦ,
oun	*autō*	*hoi*	*mathētai*	*autou*
therefore	[to him]	the	disciples	his,

840.4 prs-pron dat sing	2935.5 noun voc sing masc	1479.1 conj	2810.10 verb 3sing indic perf	4834.33 verb 3sing indic fut pass
[c☆ αὐτῷ,]	Κύριε,	εἰ	κεκοίμηται	σωθήσεται.
autō	*Kurie*	*ei*	*kekoimētai*	*sōthēsetai*
[to him,]	Lord,	if	he has fallen asleep	he will get well.

11:9. Jesus did not give a direct answer. Instead, He stated a principle drawn from everyday life. Jesus said, in effect, that just as man is allotted 12 hours during the day in which to accomplish his work, so He himself had a certain length of time to finish His mission (8:20). He walked in the light of the Father's will just as man walks in the light of day. A man does not stumble if he walks in the light. Jesus would not stumble by refusing to walk in the Father's will. Therefore He determined to go to Judea. It is clear from this verse that a person's walk is a metaphorical term for one's conduct. To walk in the light is to conduct oneself in the will of God according to the truth. The apostle John said later that the believer should walk in the light "as he (Jesus) is in the light" (see 1 John 1:5-7).

If any man walk in the day, he stumbleth not: Anyone can walk in day-time without stumbling, *NEB* . . . So whoever walks in broad daylight, *TEV* . . . during the day, *Norlie.*

because he seeth the light of this world: . . . the light of the universe, *Klingensmith* . . . for he has the daylight to see by, *Phillips* . . . because he can see the light of the sun, *TCNT.*

11:10. Darkness obscures the pitfalls and hazards which can easily be avoided in daylight. The "night" is the contrast to "the day" of verse 9. John's Gospel continues its contrasts of life with death and faith with doubt.

"Because there is no light in him" indicates that Jesus was not now using analogy. To have no light in him is to be dead. He walks in the night; thus he stumbles.

10. But if a man walk in the night, he stumbleth, because there is no light in him: . . . walks about in the night he will stumble, *Norlie* . . . for he lacks light, *Moffatt.*

11:11. The disciples had questioned the wisdom of going to Judea (verse 8). Now Jesus stated one reason for going to Bethany. In the Greek word order He said, "Lazarus, our friend." This places the emphasis on Lazarus. Notice the inclusion of the disciples in the word "our." "Sleepeth" (*kekoimētai*) is a perfect tense verb to denote a past event and the present state of Lazarus. Jesus spoke of Lazarus' death as sleep. Sleep is like death, and for the Christian it is a most comforting term. *Webster's Ninth New Collegiate Dictionary* points out that our English word *cemetery* comes from a form of the very word Jesus used, *koimētērion,* "sleeping chamber," or "burial place."

Jesus stated the purpose for which He was returning to Bethany. "That I may awake him" expresses what Jesus did (verse 43). His words there are like that used in calling someone to awake out of peaceful slumber. How calmly and naturally Jesus did His mighty miracles.

11. These things said he: and after that he saith unto them, Our friend Lazarus sleepeth: . . . our friend reposeth, *Murdock* . . . has gone to sleep, *Beck* . . . slumbers, *Fenton.*

but I go, that I may awake him out of sleep: . . . but I am setting out to wake him up, *Beck.*

11:12,13. The disciples did not understand Jesus. When a peaceful sleep comes to the sick it usually means the person is recovering. If this was so, then they believed Lazarus would recover without Jesus' endangering His life by returning to Judea.

12. Then said his disciples, Lord, if he sleep, he shall do well: . . . if he is fallen asleep, he will recover, *ASV* . . . if he has merely fallen asleep, *Williams* . . . he will get well, *TCNT* . . . will be restored, *Fenton.*

2029.7 verb 3sing indic plperf act	1156.2 conj	3450.5 art sing masc	2400.1 name nom masc	3875.1 prep	3450.2 art gen sing
13. Εἰρήκει	δὲ	ὁ	Ἰησοῦς	περὶ	τοῦ
Eirēkei	de	ho	Iēsous	peri	tou
Had spoken	but		Jesus	of	the

2265.2 noun gen sing masc	840.3 prs-pron gen sing	1552.6 dem-pron nom pl masc	1156.2 conj	1374.17 verb 3pl indic aor act	3617.1 conj
θανάτου	αὐτοῦ˙	ἐκεῖνοι	δὲ	ἔδοξαν	ὅτι
thanatou	autou	ekeinoi	de	edoxan	hoti
death	his,	those	but	thought	that

3875.1 prep	3450.10 art gen sing fem	2811.1 noun gen sing fem	3450.2 art gen sing	5096.1 noun gen sing masc	2978.5 verb 3sing indic pres act
περὶ	τῆς	κοιμήσεως	τοῦ	ὕπνου	λέγει.
peri	tēs	koimēseōs	tou	hupnou	legei
of	the	rest	of the	sleep	he speaks.

4966.1 adv	3631.1 conj	1500.5 verb 3sing indic aor act	840.2 prs-pron dat pl	3450.5 art sing masc	2400.1 name nom masc
14. τότε	οὖν	εἶπεν	αὐτοῖς	ὁ	Ἰησοῦς
tote	oun	eipen	autois	ho	Iēsous
Then	therefore	said	to them		Jesus

3816.3 noun dat sing fem	2949.1 name nom masc	594.10 verb 3sing indic aor act	2504.1 conj	5299.1 verb 1sing indic pres act
παῤῥησίᾳ,	Λάζαρος	ἀπέθανεν,	15. καὶ	χαίρω
parrhēsia	Lazaros	apethanen	kai	chairō
plainly,	Lazarus	died.	And	I rejoice

1217.1 prep	5050.4 prs-pron acc 2pl	2419.1 conj	3961.1 verb 2pl subj act	3617.1 conj	3620.2 partic
δι'	ὑμᾶς,	ἵνα	πιστεύσητε,	ὅτι	οὐκ
di'	humas	hina	pisteusēte	hoti	ouk
because of	you,	in order that	you may believe,	that	not

1498.46 verb 1sing indic imperf mid	1550.1 adv	233.1 conj	233.2 conj	70.4 verb 1pl subj pres act	4242.1 prep
ἤμην	ἐκεῖ˙	ʼ ἀλλ'	[☆ ἀλλὰ]	ἄγωμεν	πρὸς
ēmēn	ekei	all'	alla	agōmen	pros
I was	there.	But	[idem]	let us go	to

840.6 prs-pron acc sing masc	1500.5 verb 3sing indic aor act	3631.1 conj	2358.1 name nom masc	3450.5 art sing masc	2978.30 verb nom sing masc part pres pass
αὐτόν.	16. Εἶπεν	οὖν	Θωμᾶς,	ὁ	λεγόμενος
auton	Eipen	oun	Thōmas	ho	legomenos
him.	Said	therefore	Thomas,	the	being called

16.a.**Var:** 01ℵ,02A, 03B-org,04C,05D,019L, 037,038,Tisc,We/Ho, Weis

1318.1 name nom masc	3450.4 art dat pl	4678.1 noun dat pl masc	4678.2 noun dat pl masc
Δίδυμος,	τοῖς	ʼ συμμαθηταῖς,	[a συνμαθηταῖς˙]
Didumos	tois	summathētais	sunmathētais
Didymus,	to the	fellow disciples,	[idem]

70.4 verb 1pl subj pres act	2504.1 conj	2231.1 prs-pron nom 1pl	2419.1 conj	594.14 verb 1pl subj aor act	3196.2 prep
Ἄγωμεν	καὶ	ἡμεῖς,	ἵνα	ἀποθάνωμεν	μετ'
Agōmen	kai	hēmeis	hina	apothanōmen	met'
Let go	also	us,	that	we may die	with

17.a.**Var:** 04C-org,05D,it. Lach

840.3 prs-pron gen sing	2048.13 verb nom sing masc part aor act	2048.3 verb 3sing indic aor act	3631.1 conj	3450.5 art sing masc
αὐτοῦ.	17. ʼ Ἐλθὼν	[a Ἦλθεν]	οὖν	ὁ
autou	Elthōn	Elthen	oun	ho
him.	Having come	[came]	therefore	

Note the contrast between what Jesus spoke concerning Lazarus' "death" and what the disciples thought He meant (literal sleep).

13. Howbeit Jesus spake of his death: Yet Jesus had spoken about his death, *HBIE* . . . made a declaration, *Concordant* . . . meant that he was dead, *TCNT, Norlie* . . . referred to his death, *Fenton.*

but they thought that he had spoken of taking of rest in sleep: . . . referred to the rest, *Weymouth* . . . He meant he was only sleeping, *Beck* . . . they imagined he meant natural sleep, *Moffatt* . . . of the repose of sleep, *Campbell* . . . of refreshing sleep, *Fenton* . . . he meant ordinary sleep, *ALBA.*

11:14. When Jesus saw they were not understanding Him, He shocked them by the bold statement, "Lazarus is dead." He did not intend His figurative reference to sleep to be taken literally. Nor did others who use the word *koimaomai* ("sleep") other times in the New Testament to describe death. Among them Paul spoke of those who "sleep in Jesus" (1 Thessalonians 4:14). Death is not unconscious sleep, but conscious communion with the Lord (Revelation 7:13-17).

Jesus had not received a second message about Lazarus, but He knew because of His omniscience. Jesus was in touch with the situation, although neither the sisters nor the disciples were aware of His perception (Hebrews 4:12-15).

14. Then said Jesus unto them plainly, Lazarus is dead: . . . said to them explicitly, *Murdock* . . . told them outright, *Norlie* . . . said to them plainly, *TCNT.*

11:15. Jesus rejoiced not because of Lazarus' death, but because of His disciples. If He had been there, Lazarus would have been healed, thus preventing the greater sign of His glory.

"To the intent ye may believe" gives the reason for His rejoicing that He was not physically with Lazarus in time to heal him. Did they not already believe? Yes, they did believe Jesus was the Messiah. Yet there was so much about Jesus that they did not know. Believing is progressive. It is not a once-and-for-all act. Believing is a continuing quest. We cannot understand what eternal life is by saying it is life without an end. That would be merely to look at the distance of life's surface. Can we define "life"? No, we can speak of having self-awareness, existence, and mobility; yet these are feeble descriptions. We must know Jesus, be in total union with Him, and experience life from now through eternity. Salvation is ever growing and expanding. There will always be new vistas to explore, treasures to prize, and feasts to relish.

15. And I am glad for your sakes that I was not there, to the intent ye may believe: And I am rejoicing for you, *Wuest* . . . you may come to have real faith in me, *Williams.*

nevertheless let us go unto him: Come, let us go to him, *Montgomery* . . . And now, let us go to him, *Phillips.*

11:16. "Thomas" means "twin" in the Aramaic. The name occurs eight times in John's Gospel and four other times in the New Testament. When Thomas heard that Jesus was determined to go to Bethany, he spoke also with determination. Thomas is to be commended for his dedication to the Lord. Not many men would knowingly go where suffering and death might be the result. Thomas has been labeled "the doubter"; yet here his determination was to follow his Lord though his life would be in jeopardy. Thomas knew how close Jesus had been to death at the hands of the Jews 3 months before (10:39). He was willing to die rather than forsake his Lord. This apostle's brave resolution encouraged his fellows, and is a bright model for all believers. During this visit to Bethany and

16. Then said Thomas, which is called Didymus, unto his fellow-disciples: Whereupon, *Moffatt* . . . who was called 'The Twin,' *TCNT* . . . known as the twin, *Phillips.*

Let us also go, that we may die with him: Let's go too, *Adams* . . . Come on, then, *Phillips* . . . Let us go as well, *Fenton* . . . We might as well go back and die too, *ET* . . . We've got to go too, to die with him, *Barclay* . . . to mourn with him, *Torrey* . . . that we may be with him in death, *BB.*

John 11:18

17.b.**Var:** 04C-org,05D,it.
Lach

2400.1 name nom masc	2504.1 conj	2128.8 verb 3sing indic aor act	840.6 prs-pron acc sing masc	4913.3 num card acc pl
Ἰησοῦς	[b+ καὶ]	εὗρεν	αὐτὸν	τέσσαρας
Iēsous	*kai*	*heuren*	*auton*	*tessaras*
Jesus	[and]	found	him	four

2232.1 noun fem	2218.1 adv	2218.1 adv	2232.1 noun fem	2174.15 verb part pres act	1706.1 prep
⸉ ἡμέρας	ἤδη	[☆ ἤδη	ἡμέρας]	ἔχοντα	ἐν
hēmeras	*ēdē*	*ēdē*	*hēmeras*	*echonta*	*en*
days	already	[already	days]	having been	in

18.a.**Txt:** p66,01ℵ-corr,
02A,04C,05D,017K,
019L,036,037,038,etc.
byz.Lach,Sod
Var: 01ℵ-org,03B,Tisc,
We/HoWeis,UBS/☆

3450.3 art dat sing	3283.3 noun dat sing neu	1498.34 verb sing indic imperf act	1156.2 conj	3450.9 art nom sing fem	956.1 name nom fem
τῷ	μνημείῳ.	**18.** ἦν	δὲ	⸂a ἡ ⸃	Βηθανία
tō	*mnēmeiō*	*ēn*	*de*	*hē*	*Bēthania*
the	tomb.	Was	now		Bethany

1445.1 adv	3450.1 art gen pl	2389.2 name gen pl neu	5453.1 conj	570.3 prep gen	4563.2 noun gen pl
ἐγγὺς	τῶν	Ἱεροσολύμων,	ὡς	ἀπὸ	σταδίων
engus	*tōn*	*Hierosolumōn*	*hōs*	*apo*	*stadiōn*
near		to Jerusalem,	about	away	furlongs

19.a.**Txt:** 02A,017K,036,
037,byz.
Var: 01ℵ,03B,04C,05D,
019L,033X,038,33,sa.bo.
Lach,Treg,Alf,Tisc,
We/HoWeis,Sod,UBS/☆

1173.1 num card	2504.1 conj	4044.7 adj nom pl masc	4044.7 adj nom pl masc	1156.2 conj	1523.2 prep gen
δεκαπέντε	**19.** ⸉ καὶ	πολλοὶ	[a☆ πολλοὶ	δὲ]	ἐκ
dekapente	*kai*	*polloi*	*polloi*	*de*	*ek*
fifteen,	and	many	[many	and]	of

3450.1 art gen pl	2428.3 name-adj gen pl masc	2048.28 verb 3pl indic plperf act	4242.1 prep	3450.15 art acc pl fem	3875.1 prep
τῶν	Ἰουδαίων	ἐληλύθεισαν	πρὸς	⸉ τὰς	περὶ
tōn	*Ioudaiōn*	*elēlutheisan*	*pros*	*tas*	*peri*
the	Jews	had come	unto	the	around

19.b.**Txt:** 02A,04C-corr,
017K,036,037,038,1,13,
28,byz.Gries,Tisc,Sod
Var: p66,p75,01ℵ,03B,
04C-org,019L,032W,33,
Lach,Treg,Alf,We/Ho,
Weis,UBS/☆

3450.12 art acc sing fem	3108.3 name acc fem	2504.1 conj	3109.4 name acc fem	3110.1 name fem	2419.1 conj
[b☆ τὴν]	Μάρθαν	καὶ	⸉ Μαρίαν,	[☆ Μαριὰμ]	ἵνα
tēn	*Marthan*	*kai*	*Marian*	*Mariam*	*hina*
	Martha	and	Mary,	[idem]	that

3749.3 verb 3pl subj aor mid	840.13 prs-pron pl fem	3875.1 prep	3450.2 art gen sing	79.2 noun gen sing masc
παραμυθήσωνται	αὐτὰς	περὶ	τοῦ	ἀδελφοῦ
paramuthēsōntai	*autas*	*peri*	*tou*	*adelphou*
they might console	them	concerning	the	brother

19.c.**Txt:** 02A,04C,017K,
036,037,1,13,etc.byz.
Lach,Sod
Var: 01ℵ,03B,05D,019L,
038,Treg,Alf,Tisc,We/Ho
Weis,UBS/☆

840.1 prs-pron gen pl	3450.9 art nom sing fem	3631.1 conj	3108.1 name fem	5453.1 conj	189.21 verb 3sing indic aor act
⸂c αὐτῶν. ⸃	**20.** ἡ	οὖν	Μάρθα	ὡς	ἤκουσεν
autōn	*hē*	*oun*	*Martha*	*hōs*	*ēkousen*
their.		Therefore	Martha	when	she heard

20.a.**Txt:** 021M,038,
Steph
Var: 01ℵ,02A,03B,04C,
05D,017K,019L,036,
037,byz.Gries,Lach,
Treg,AlfTisc,We/Ho,
Weis,Sod,UBS/☆

3617.1 conj	3450.5 art sing masc	2400.1 name nom masc	2048.34 verb 3sing indic pres	5059.1 verb 3sing indic aor act	840.4 prs-pron dat sing
ὅτι	⸂a ὁ ⸃	Ἰησοῦς	ἔρχεται,	ὑπήντησεν	αὐτῷ·
hoti	*ho*	*Iēsous*	*erchetai*	*hupēntēsen*	*autō*
that		Jesus	is coming,	met	him;

3109.1 name nom fem	3110.1 name fem	1156.2 conj	1706.1 prep	3450.3 art dat sing	3486.3 noun dat sing masc
⸉ Μαρία	[☆ Μαριὰμ]	δὲ	ἐν	τῷ	οἴκῳ
Maria	*Mariam*	*de*	*en*	*tō*	*oikō*
Mary	[idem]	but	in	the	house

Jerusalem Jesus would indeed die, and the disciples would be scattered as sheep without their shepherd.

17. Then when Jesus came, he found that he had lain in the grave four days already: On His arrival Jesus found, *NEB* . . . When Jesus arrived...he had already been buried for four days, *Berkeley* . . . he made the discovery, *BB* . . . in the grave four days before, *SEB* . . . in the tomb, *Norlie.*

11:17. Lazarus died after the messengers were sent to Jesus. This would account for 1 day of the 4. Jesus remained in Peraea 2 more days (verse 6). The day of travel to Bethany accounts for the fourth day. The Jews reckoned a portion of a day as a whole day.

Jesus showed no anxiety over Lazarus' death and burial. He deliberately waited 4 days after the burial. Notice how calmly and majestically the Lord acted concerning this tragic circumstance. His compassion and affection for Lazarus, Mary, and Martha are obvious, and He was the master of the terrible situation. What a great blessing for this family—that they knew Jesus! Jesus arrived in time to bring light to the dark tomb and life to a dead believer.

18. Now Bethany was nigh unto Jerusalem, about fifteen furlongs off: . . . less than two miles, *Weymouth* . . . just under two miles from, *NEB* . . . was near Jerusalem, *RSV* . . . about two miles away, *BB.*

11:18. John's Gospel gives a bit of geography to those unacquainted with Palestine. The nearness of Bethany to Jerusalem reveals how dangerous it was for Jesus to go to Bethany. Any miracle in Bethany would be known in Jerusalem within an hour or two. The Jewish leaders were eager to hear where Jesus was that they might kill Him.

19. And many of the Jews came to Martha and Mary, to comfort them concerning their brother: . . . and a good many...had come...to offer them sympathy, *Phillips* . . . to speak to their hearts, *Murdock* . . . to console them, *ASV* . . . a considerable number...to express sympathy, *Weymouth* . . . to sympathize with them, *Williams, Montgomery* . . . in the loss of their brother, *NIV.*

11:19. The sisters and their brother must have been well-known in Jerusalem as well as in the village of Bethany. The term "Jews" is always used by John in the sense of those who were hostile toward Jesus. The miracle of the raising of Lazarus was to be an outstanding witness to Jesus' enemies. The Lord extended grace upon grace to convince the leaders in Jerusalem of His identity and mission. Perhaps Jesus tarried the extra days for the Jews' benefit as well as for the benefit of His disciples, and Martha and Mary.

20. Then Martha, as soon as she heard that Jesus was coming, went and met him: . . . as soon as she heard the tidings, 'Jesus is coming,' *Weymouth* . . . hearing of the arrival of, *Moffatt.*

but Mary sat still in the house: . . . but Mary remained sitting in the house, *Montgomery* . . . kept on sitting, *Wuest* . . . continued to sit, *SEB* . . . stayed in the house, *TEV* . . . sat quietly at home, *TCNT* . . . did not go from the house, *BB.*

11:20. This verse shows the difference in the natures of Martha and Mary. Martha was a woman of action and Mary a woman of contemplation: "Martha . . . went," "Mary sat." On a former occasion the same dispositions were exhibited (Luke 10:39,40). Mary was at Jesus' feet and Martha was distracted by her busy activities. Both sisters loved the Lord very much, but they revealed it in different ways.

2488.5 verb 3sing indic imperf	1500.5 verb 3sing indic aor act	3631.1 conj	3450.9 art nom sing fem	3108.1 name fem	4242.1 prep
ἐκαθέζετο.	21. εἶπεν	οὖν	ἡ	Μάρθα	πρὸς
ekathezeto	eipen	oun	hē	Martha	pros
was sitting.	Said	then		Martha	to

21.a.**Txt:** p45,p66,p75, 02A,04C-corr,05D,017K, 019L,032W,036,037, 038,1,13,etc.byz.Lach, WeisSod
Var: 01א,03B,04C-org, Tisc,We/Ho,UBS/☆

3450.6 art acc sing masc	2400.3 name acc masc	2935.5 noun voc sing masc	1479.1 conj	1498.35 verb 2sing indic imperf act	5436.1 adv
⸂[a] τὸν ⸃	Ἰησοῦν,	Κύριε,	εἰ	ἦς	ὧδε,
ton	Iēsoun	Kurie	ei	ēs	hōde
	Jesus,	Lord,	if	you had been	here,

3450.5 art sing masc	79.1 noun nom sing masc	1466.2 prs-pron gen 1sing	3620.2 partic	300.1 partic	2325.3 verb 3sing indic plperf act
⸀ ὁ	ἀδελφός	μου	οὐκ	ἂν	ἐτεθνήκει.
ho	adelphos	mou	ouk	an	etethnēkei
the	brother	my	not		had died;

21.b.**Txt:** 04C-corr,036, 037,(038),13,byz.Sod
Var: 01א,03B,04C-org, 019L,033X,33,Lach, TregTisc,We/Ho,Weis, UBS/☆

3620.2 partic	300.1 partic	594.10 verb 3sing indic aor act	3450.5 art sing masc	79.1 noun nom sing masc	1466.2 prs-pron gen 1sing
[b☆ οὐκ	ἂν	ἀπέθανεν	ὁ	ἀδελφός	μου·]
ouk	an	apethanen	ho	adelphos	mou
[not		would have died	the	brother	my.]

22.a.**Txt:** p45,p66, 01א-corr,02A,04C-corr, 05D,017K,019L,032W, 036,037,038,13,byz.Lach
Var: 01א-org,03B, 04C-org,033X,33,Treg, Alf,Tisc,We/HoWeis,Sod, UBS/☆

233.2 conj	2504.1 conj	3431.1 adv	3471.2 verb 1sing indic perf act	3617.1 conj	3607.8 rel-pron pl neu	300.1 partic
22. ⸂[a] ἀλλὰ ⸃	καὶ	νῦν	οἶδα	ὅτι	ὅσα	ἂν
alla	kai	nun	oida	hoti	hosa	an
but	even	now	I know	that	whatever	

153.1 verb sing subj aor	3450.6 art acc sing masc	2296.4 noun acc sing masc	1319.38 verb 3sing indic fut act	4622.3 prs-pron dat 2sing
αἰτήσῃ	τὸν	θεὸν,	δώσει	σοι
aitēsē	ton	theon	dōsei	soi
you may ask of		God,	will give	you

3450.5 art sing masc	2296.1 noun nom sing masc	2978.5 verb 3sing indic pres act	840.11 prs-pron dat sing fem	3450.5 art sing masc
ὁ	θεός.	23. Λέγει	αὐτῇ	ὁ
ho	theos	Legei	autē	ho
	God.	Says	to her	

2400.1 name nom masc	448.20 verb 3sing indic fut mid	3450.5 art sing masc	79.1 noun nom sing masc	4622.2 prs-pron gen 2sing
Ἰησοῦς,	Ἀναστήσεται	ὁ	ἀδελφός	σου.
Iēsous	Anastēsetai	ho	adelphos	sou
Jesus,	Will rise again	the	brother	your.

24.a.**Var:** 03B,04C-org, 05D,017K,019L,033X, 038,041,Lach,Treg,Alf, TiscWe/Ho,Weis,Sod, UBS/☆

2978.5 verb 3sing indic pres act	840.4 prs-pron dat sing	3450.9 art nom sing fem	3108.1 name fem	3471.2 verb 1sing indic perf act
24. Λέγει	αὐτῷ	[a☆+ ἡ]	Μάρθα,	Οἶδα
Legei	autō	hē	Martha	Oida
Says	to him		Martha,	I know

3617.1 conj	448.20 verb 3sing indic fut mid	1706.1 prep	3450.11 art dat sing fem	384.3 noun dat sing fem	1706.1 prep
ὅτι	ἀναστήσεται	ἐν	τῇ	ἀναστάσει	ἐν
hoti	anastēsetai	en	tē	anastasei	en
that	he will rise again	in	the	resurrection	in

3450.11 art dat sing fem	2057.9 adj dat sing fem	2232.3 noun dat sing fem	1500.5 verb 3sing indic aor act	840.11 prs-pron dat sing fem	3450.5 art sing masc
τῇ	ἐσχάτῃ	ἡμέρᾳ.	25. Εἶπεν	αὐτῇ	ὁ
tē	eschatē	hēmera	Eipen	autē	ho
the	last	day.	Said	to her	

11:21. Martha's remarks involved three things. First, she was disappointed that He was not there when they needed Him. Second, Martha showed she was a disciple of faith. She believed Jesus could heal. As deathly sick as Lazarus was, she had confidence that Jesus' power was sufficient to cure her brother. Third, her trust in Jesus was limited. Surely she had heard that He raised Jairus' daughter and the widow's son at Nain, yet they were raised before burial, not out of the grave after 4 days.

21. Then said Martha unto Jesus, Lord, if thou hadst been here, my brother had not died: . . . my brother would not have died, *Norlie.*

11:22. Martha's full statement revealed that she lacked complete confidence in Jesus' own power and authority. She thought of Him only as a mediator between God and man. Yet that within itself was a remarkable thing. Since Adam was expelled from fellowship with God in the Garden of Eden, no one—except perhaps Moses—has had direct access to Him apart from mediation (Genesis 3:22-24). The Lord provided the whole sacrificial system of the Old Testament to give sinful man a means of approach to a holy God. Job prayed for a "daysman," an arbiter, an umpire between God and man "that might lay his hand upon us both" (Job 9:33).

John reports Jesus announced himself to be such a Mediator. He declared whatever His followers would ask in His name the Father would grant it (16:23). Indeed, He made it clear that "no man cometh unto the Father, but by me" (14:6). Paul echoed this central truth of the gospel in 1 Timothy 2:5: "For there is one God, and one mediator between God and men, the man Christ Jesus."

So it is to Martha's credit she saw Jesus as the means of approach to the Father. However, the raising of Lazarus opened for her a more glorious vision of who Jesus really is.

22. But I know, that even now, whatsoever thou wilt ask of God, God will give it thee: And now I know positively, *Wuest* . . . I am aware, *Concordant* . . . But even now, nothing is impossible with God, *ET* . . . But, even as things are, *Barclay* . . . whatever request you make, *BB* . . . whatever you ask of God He will grant you, *Berkeley* . . . God will give you whatever you ask from him, *Phillips* . . . God will give You anything You ask Him, *Beck.*

11:23. Jesus spoke in an ambiguous way so that Martha might exercise faith. The future tense could mean either Lazarus' immediate restoration or the resurrection of the last day as she understood. It is rather amazing that she believed in a future resurrection since the Old Testament has only a few passages concerning the final resurrection.

23. Jesus saith unto her, Thy brother shall rise again: . . . will rise to life, *TEV* . . . Your brother shall rise to life, *TCNT* . . . Your brother will come to life again, *BB* . . . Your brother will be resurrected, *Adams.*

11:24. Martha's statement echoed Daniel 12:2 and doubtless was based on Jesus' teaching as He frequented their home.

24. Martha saith unto him, I know that he shall rise again in the resurrection at the last day: I know of a surety, *Wuest* . . . when all people are raised, *SEB* . . . in the consolation, *Murdock* . . . the again-rising, *Klingensmith.*

11:25. *Anastasis* ("resurrection") occurs 42 times in the New Testament and 4 times in John's Gospel (5:29; 11:24,25). The word

John 11:26

2400.1 name nom masc	**1466.1** prs-pron nom 1sing	**1498.2** verb 1sing indic pres act	**3450.9** art nom sing fem	**384.1** noun nom sing fem	**2504.1** conj
Ἰησοῦς,	Ἐγώ	εἰμι	ἡ	ἀνάστασις	καὶ
Iēsous	*Egō*	*eimi*	*hē*	*anastasis*	*kai*
Jesus,	I	am	thc	resurrection	and

3450.9 art nom sing fem	**2205.1** noun nom sing fem	**3450.5** art sing masc	**3961.10** verb nom sing masc part pres act	**1519.1** prep	**1466.7** prs-pron acc 1sing
ἡ	ζωή.	ὁ	πιστεύων	εἰς	ἐμὲ,
hē	*zōē*	*ho*	*pisteuōn*	*eis*	*eme*
the	life:	the	believing	on	me,

2550.1 conj	**594.13** verb 3sing subj aor act	**2180.29** verb 3sing indic fut mid	**2504.1** conj	**3820.6** adj sing masc	**3450.5** art sing masc
κἂν	ἀποθάνῃ	ζήσεται·	26. καὶ	πᾶς	ὁ
kan	*apothanē*	*zēsetai*	*kai*	*pas*	*ho*
though	he die	he shall live;	and	everyone	the

2180.10 verb sing part pres act	**2504.1** conj	**3961.10** verb nom sing masc part pres act	**1519.1** prep	**1466.7** prs-pron acc 1sing	**3620.3** partic
ζῶν	καὶ	πιστεύων	εἰς	ἐμὲ,	οὐ
zōn	*kai*	*pisteuōn*	*eis*	*eme*	*ou*
living	and	believing	on	me,	not

3231.1 partic	**594.13** verb 3sing subj aor act	**1519.1** prep	**3450.6** art acc sing masc	**163.3** noun acc sing masc	**3961.5** verb 2sing indic pres act
μὴ	ἀποθάνῃ	εἰς	τὸν	αἰῶνα.	πιστεύεις
mē	*apothanē*	*eis*	*ton*	*aiōna*	*pisteueis*
not	shall die	to	the	age.	Do you believe

3642.17 dem-pron sing neu	**2978.5** verb 3sing indic pres act	**840.4** prs-pron dat sing	**3346.1** partic	**2935.5** noun voc sing masc	**1466.1** prs-pron nom 1sing
τοῦτο;	27. Λέγει	αὐτῷ,	Ναί,	κύριε·	ἐγὼ
touto	*Legei*	*autō*	*Nai*	*kurie*	*egō*
this?	She says	to him,	Yes,	Lord;	I

3961.37 verb 1sing indic perf act	**3617.1** conj	**4622.1** prs-pron nom 2sing	**1498.3** verb 2sing indic pres act	**3450.5** art sing masc
πεπίστευκα	ὅτι	σὺ	εἶ	ὁ
pepisteuka	*hoti*	*su*	*ei*	*ho*
have believed	that	you	are	the

5382.1 name nom masc	**3450.5** art sing masc	**5048.1** noun nom sing masc	**3450.2** art gen sing	**2296.2** noun gen sing masc	**3450.5** art sing masc
Χριστὸς,	ὁ	υἱὸς	τοῦ	θεοῦ,	ὁ
Christos	*ho*	*huios*	*tou*	*theou*	*ho*
Christ,	the	Son		of God,	the

1519.1 prep	**3450.6** art acc sing masc	**2862.4** noun acc sing masc	**2048.44** verb nom sing masc part pres	**2504.1** conj	**3642.18** dem-pron pl neu
εἰς	τὸν	κόσμον	ἐρχόμενος.	28. Καὶ	⸀☆ ταῦτα
eis	*ton*	*kosmon*	*erchomenos*	*Kai*	*tauta*
into	the	world	coming.	And	these things

3642.17 dem-pron sing neu	**1500.20** verb nom sing fem part aor act	**562.2** verb 3sing indic aor act	**2504.1** conj	**5291.6** verb 3sing indic aor act
[a τοῦτο]	εἰποῦσα	ἀπῆλθεν,	καὶ	ἐφώνησεν
touto	*eipousa*	*apēlthen*	*kai*	*ephōnēsen*
[this]	having said	she went away,	and	called

3109.4 name acc fem	**3110.1** name fem	**3450.12** art acc sing fem	**78.4** noun acc sing fem	**840.10** prs-pron gen sing fem
⸀ Μαρίαν	[☆ Μαριὰμ]	τὴν	ἀδελφὴν	αὐτῆς
Marian	*Mariam*	*tēn*	*adelphēn*	*autēs*
Mary	[idem]	the	sister	her

28.a.**Txt:** p66,02A,05D, 017K,036,037,038,1,13, byz.it.sa.Gries,Lach **Var:** 01ℵ,03B,04C,019L, 033X,bo.Treg,Alf,Tisc, We/HoWeis,Sod,UBS/☆

literally means "to stand up." Its usage refers to the final resurrection or Christ's resurrection (Hebrews 11:35 may be an exception). This is the seventh of the great "I am" sayings of Jesus Christ. For a more complete list refer to the commentary on 4:26.

Jesus built upon what Martha already believed. She knew Lazarus would rise in the last day. Jesus stated that what He will be in the last day, He was right then. The "I am" is a present tense continuous action verb. Jesus, in effect, said, "What I was and what I shall be, I am now." He meant that His triumph over sin, Satan, and death did not need to wait to its final hour for the manifestation of its benefits. Every miracle He performed was another token of what He was, and shall be, manifested in the present. They were extensions of His deity as to His essence, omnipresence, and eternality.

Though his body perish, the one who believes in Jesus lives on as a person. Since God is the source and author of eternal life, death cannot bring the personality of the believer to a separation from life (God).

25. Jesus said unto her, I am the resurrection, and the life: I am myself resurrection and life, *Moffatt* . . . the Resurrection and the Life, *Norlie* . . . I am myself that day and that life, *BB* . . . and the life myself, *Williams.*

he that believeth in me, though he were dead, yet shall he live: He who has faith in me, *Norton* . . . even if he dies, *Norlie* . . . who commits himself to me will live, *SEB* . . . shall positively never die, *Wuest* . . . Even though he die shall live again! *Rotherham.*

26. And whosoever liveth and believeth in me shall never die: . . . and everybody who lives, *Adams* . . . shall never die in eternity, *Norlie* . . . will live even if he dies, *Beck* . . . lives again, *Rotherham* . . . And no one who is living and has faith in me will ever see death, *BB* . . . anywise die to the remotest age, *Rotherham.*

Believest thou this?: Do you believe this? *SEB* . . . Is this your faith, *BB.*

11:26. Verse 25 is parallel with this one, for "though he were dead" applied to Lazarus, while "whosoever liveth" refers to those like Martha. One article (*ho*) binds "liveth" and "believeth" together to connect with "in me" (*eis eme*), making one of the most dogmatic promises in Scripture, "shall never die." In physical death the one who lives and believes continues to live spiritually. He cannot enter eternity in the flesh; therefore he discards his temporary dwelling to await a body suited for his eternal habitation. Such a glorious exchange can hardly be called death.

It is not enough to give mental assent to the facts. "In me" means to grow in the relationship in Him based on the truth that He reveals.

27. She saith unto him, Yea, Lord: . . . thoroughly convinced, *Weymouth.*

I believe that thou art the Christ, the Son of God: . . . as for myself I have believed, *Wuest* . . . I still believe that you, *SEB* . . . You are the promised Savior, God's Son, *Beck.*

which should come into the world: . . . who was to come into the world, *Williams, Montgomery.*

11:27. The verb "believe" is a perfect tense verb form indicating a past action and its present fact. Martha therefore added to Jesus' present tense participle of verse 26 by stating that her present faith resulted from her past trust.

Martha defined her faith by her confession. She did not understand all there was to know about the resurrection, yet she affirmed her trust in Jesus.

Martha ascribes three titles in her confession. First, she called Jesus "the Christ" (*ho Christos*, "the anointed one").

Second, Martha called Jesus "the Son of God." The term refers to Jesus' relation to His Father and to His nature as God.

Third, Martha said that Jesus was "the Son of God, which should come into the world." The term has to do with the consummating

28. And when she had so said, she went her way, and called Mary her sister secretly, saying: . . . and summoned her sister, *Torrey* . . . she went away and quietly called, *Confraternity* . . . and secretly called Mary, *Wuest* . . . and quietly called for her, *Alba* . . . whispering, *Phillips* . . . privately whispering to her, *AmpB* . . . in a low voice, *JB*

John 11:29

28.b.**Var:** p66,03B, 04C-org,Treg,We/Ho

2950.1 adv	1500.20 verb nom sing fem part aor act	1500.32 verb nom sing fem part aor act	3450.5 art sing masc	1314.1 noun nom sing masc
λάθρα,	⸂ εἰποῦσα,	[b εἴπασα]	Ὁ	διδάσκαλος
lathra	*eipousa*	*eipasa*	*Ho*	*didaskalos*
secretly,	saying,	[idem]	The	teacher

29.a.**Var:** 01ℵ,03B, 04C-org,019L,033X,038, 33,sa.bo.TregWe/Ho, Weis,Sod,UBS/⋆

3780.2 verb 3sing indic pres act	2504.1 conj	5291.1 verb 3sing indic pres act	4622.4 prs-pron acc 2sing	1552.9 dem-pron nom sing fem
πάρεστιν	καὶ	φωνεῖ	σε.	**29.** Ἐκείνη
parestin	*kai*	*phōnei*	*se*	*Ekeinē*
is come	and	calls	you.	That

29.b.**Var:** p75,01ℵ,03B, 04C-org,05D,019L, 032W,033X,33,it.Lach, Treg,Alf,We/HoSod

1156.2 conj	5453.1 conj	189.21 verb 3sing indic aor act	1446.15 verb 3sing indic pres pass	1446.20 verb 3sing indic aor pass
[a⋆+ δὲ]	ὡς	ἤκουσεν	⸂ ἐγείρεται	[b ἠγέρθη]
de	*hōs*	*ēkousen*	*egeiretai*	*ēgerthē*
[and]	when	she heard	rises up	[arose]

29.c.**Txt:** p45,p66,02A, 04C-corr,05D,017K,036, 037,038,1,13,byz.Lach, Tisc
Var: p75,01ℵ,03B, 04C-org,019L,032W, 033X,33,it.Treg,Alf, We/HoWeis,Sod,UBS/⋆

4883.1 adj acc sing neu	2504.1 conj	2048.34 verb 3sing indic pres	2048.59 verb 3sing indic imperf	4242.1 prep	840.6 prs-pron acc sing masc
ταχὺ	καὶ	⸂ ἔρχεται	[c⋆ ἤρχετο]	πρὸς	αὐτόν.
tachu	*kai*	*erchetai*	*ērcheto*	*pros*	*auton*
quickly	and	comes	[was coming]	to	him.

3632.1 adv	1156.2 conj	2048.27 verb 3sing indic plperf act	3450.5 art sing masc	2400.1 name nom masc	1519.1 prep
30. οὔπω	δὲ	ἐληλύθει	ὁ	Ἰησοῦς	εἰς
oupō	*de*	*elēluthei*	*ho*	*Iēsous*	*eis*
Not yet	now	had come		Jesus	into

30.a.**Var:** 01ℵ,03B,04C, 032W,038,33,bo.Lach, Treg,Alf,We/Ho,Weis, Sod,UBS/⋆

3450.12 art acc sing fem	2941.3 noun acc sing fem	233.1 conj	1498.34 verb sing indic imperf act	2068.1 adv	1706.1 prep	3450.3 art dat sing
τὴν	κώμην,	ἀλλ'	ἦν	[a⋆+ ἔτι]	ἐν	τῷ
tēn	*kōmēn*	*all'*	*ēn*	*eti*	*en*	*tō*
the	village,	but	was	[still]	in	the

4964.3 noun dat sing masc	3562.1 adv	5059.1 verb 3sing indic aor act	840.4 prs-pron dat sing	3450.9 art nom sing fem	3108.1 name fem
τόπῳ	ὅπου	ὑπήντησεν	αὐτῷ	ἡ	Μάρθα.
topō	*hopou*	*hupēntēsen*	*autō*	*hē*	*Martha*
place	where	met	him		Martha.

3450.7 art pl masc	3631.1 conj	2428.2 name-adj pl masc	3450.7 art pl masc	1498.23 verb nom pl masc part pres act	3196.2 prep
31. οἱ	οὖν	Ἰουδαῖοι	οἱ	ὄντες	μετ'
hoi	*oun*	*Ioudaioi*	*hoi*	*ontes*	*met'*
The	therefore	Jews	the	being	with

840.10 prs-pron gen sing fem	1706.1 prep	3450.11 art dat sing fem	3477.3 noun dat sing fem	2504.1 conj	3749.2 verb nom pl masc part pres
αὐτῆς	ἐν	τῇ	οἰκίᾳ	καὶ	παραμυθούμενοι
autēs	*en*	*tē*	*oikia*	*kai*	*paramuthoumenoi*
her	in	the	house	and	consoling

840.12 prs-pron acc sing fem	1481.17 verb nom pl masc part aor act	3450.12 art acc sing fem	3109.4 name acc fem	3110.1 name fem
αὐτήν,	ἰδόντες	τὴν	⸂ Μαρίαν	[⋆ Μαριὰμ]
autēn	*idontes*	*tēn*	*Marian*	*Mariam*
her,	having seen		Mary	[idem]

3617.1 conj	4878.1 adv	448.2 verb 3sing indic aor act	2504.1 conj	1814.3 verb 3sing indic aor act	188.13 verb 3pl indic aor act
ὅτι	ταχέως	ἀνέστη	καὶ	ἐξῆλθεν,	ἠκολούθησαν
hoti	*tacheōs*	*anestē*	*kai*	*exēlthen*	*ēkolouthēsan*
that	quickly	she rose up	and	went out,	followed

power which He will demonstrate to bring about man's complete redemption.

Then Martha expressed her faith in Jesus as a Person regardless of what happened to Lazarus. She could not confess she believed the Lord would raise him from the dead immediately. Nor did Jesus demand she declare herself to that extent. Once she spoke her confidence in Him personally, He took the matter from there. Martha's faith followed the pattern of that of Daniel's three friends. They knew their God could deliver them from the furnace and trusted He would if He willed, but they stood firm in their faith in Him regardless (Daniel 3:16-18).

... and taking her aside, *NEB* ... without letting anyone else know, *Barclay* ... with the private message, *Berkeley* ... covertly, *Concordant.*

The master is come, and calleth for thee: The teacher is present, *Wuest* ... is asking for, *Montgomery* ... The Rabbi is here and is asking for you, *Weymouth* ... The Master is here and has sent for you, *BB* ... The Teacher is present, *Rotherham* ... and wants you to come, *Barclay.*

11:28. Martha was aware of the danger Jesus was in by coming to Bethany. Thus Martha told Mary "secretly."

Martha said, "The Master is come." He had arrived and all would be well. She continued, telling Mary that Jesus was asking for her. Jesus gave Mary a special invitation to come to Him for comfort in a great time of sorrow.

29. As soon as she heard that, she arose quickly, and came unto him: Hurriedly Mary arose, *Berkeley* ... she jumped up, *Williams* ... she sprang up quickly, *AmpB* ... went on her way to meet him, *Wuest.*

11:29. "As soon" shows Mary was ready to act on her confidence in the Lord. "And came" is an imperfect verb to show vividly the action taking place; the tense also indicates that more of the story is to follow. As Mary went she must have been filled with anticipation as to what might happen.

30. Now Jesus was not yet come into the town: ... had not yet entered the village, *Norlie* ... hadn't come into the village yet, *Adams* ... Jesus had not yet reached the village, *NEB.*

but was in that place where Martha met him: ... was still where Martha had met Him, *Beck* ... was still in the place, *Wuest.*

11:30. This verse explains why Mary went out to meet Jesus. Doubtless Jesus did not enter the village because of the Jews and because He might use this time to add His teaching to the miracle. By so doing Martha and Mary gained much faith.

31. The Jews then which were with her in the house, and comforted her: ... sympathizing with her, *Weymouth* ... trying to console her, *Montgomery.*

when they saw Mary, that she rose up hastily and went out, followed her: ... noticing the haste, *Fenton* ... saw how hastily Mary had arisen, *AmpB.*

11:31. The term "Jews" in John's Gospel always denotes leaders among the nation who were hostile to Jesus. These Jews thought Mary was going to the tomb to mourn, therefore they followed her. Weeping and mourning lasted many days. The greater the person was loved and the more important the deceased was, the longer the period of mourning.

John 11:32

31.a.**Txt:** p66,02A,04C-corr,017K,036,037,038,28,byz.it.sa.Gries,Lach
Var: 01ℵ,03B,04C-org,05D,019L,032W,1,13,bo.Treg,Alf,Tisc,We/Ho,Weis,Sod,UBS/☆

32.a.**Txt:** p45,01ℵ-corr,04C-corr,019L,032W,036,037,038,1,13,byz.
Var: 01ℵ-org,02A,03B,04C-org,05D,017K,033X,33,Lach,Treg,Alf,Tisc,We/Ho,WeisSod,UBS/☆

32.b.**Txt:** Steph,Lach
Var: 01ℵ,03B,04C-org,019L,033X,Treg,Alf,Tisc,We/HoWeis,UBS/☆

840.11 prs-pron dat sing fem	**2978.16** verb pl masc part pres act	**1374.21** verb nom pl masc part aor act	**3617.1** conj	**5055.3** verb 3sing indic pres act
αὐτῇ,	⸀ λέγοντες,	[a☆ δόξαντες]	"Οτι	ὑπάγει
autē	legontes	doxantes	Hoti	hupagei
her,	saying,	[thinking]		She is going

1519.1 prep	**3450.16** art sing neu	**3283.1** noun sing neu	**2419.1** conj	**2772.15** verb 3sing subj aor act	**1550.1** adv	**3450.9** art nom sing fem
εἰς	τὸ	μνημεῖον	ἵνα	κλαύσῃ	ἐκεῖ.	32. Ἡ
eis	to	mnēmeion	hina	klausē	ekei	Hē
to	the	grave	that	she may weep	there.	

3631.1 conj	**3109.1** name nom fem	**3110.1** name fem	**5453.1** conj	**2048.3** verb 3sing indic aor act
οὖν	⸀ Μαρία	[☆ Μαριὰμ]	ὡς	ἦλθεν
oun	Maria	Mariam	hōs	ēlthen
Therefore	Mary	[idem]	when	she came

3562.1 adv	**1498.34** verb sing indic imperf act	**3450.5** art sing masc	**2400.1** name nom masc	**1481.18** verb nom sing fem part aor act	**840.6** prs-pron acc sing masc
ὅπου	ἦν	⸂a ὁ ⸃	Ἰησοῦς,	ἰδοῦσα	αὐτὸν
hopou	ēn	ho	Iēsous	idousa	auton
where	was		Jesus,	seeing	him,

3959.5 verb 3sing indic aor act	**1519.1** prep	**3450.8** art acc pl masc	**4087.7** noun acc pl masc	**840.3** prs-pron gen sing	**840.3** prs-pron gen sing
ἔπεσεν	⸀ εἰς	τοὺς	πόδας	αὐτοῦ,	[b☆ αὐτοῦ
epesen	eis	tous	podas	autou	autou
fell	to	the	feet	his,	[his

4242.1 prep	**3450.8** art acc pl masc	**4087.7** noun acc pl masc	**2978.19** verb nom sing fem part pres act	**840.4** prs-pron dat sing	**2935.5** noun voc sing masc
πρὸς	τοὺς	πόδας,]	λέγουσα	αὐτῷ,	Κύριε,
pros	tous	podas	legousa	autō	Kurie
to	the	feet,]	saying	to him,	Lord,

1479.1 conj	**1498.35** verb 2sing indic imperf act	**5436.1** adv	**3620.2** partic	**300.1** partic	**594.10** verb 3sing indic aor act	**1466.2** prs-pron gen 1sing
εἰ	ἦς	ὧδε	οὐκ	ἂν	⸀ ἀπέθανεν	μου
ei	ēs	hōde	ouk	an	apethanen	mou
if	you had been	here	not		had died	my

1466.2 prs-pron gen 1sing	**594.10** verb 3sing indic aor act	**3450.5** art sing masc	**79.1** noun nom sing masc	**2400.1** name nom masc
[☆ μου	ἀπέθανεν]	ὁ	ἀδελφός.	33. Ἰησοῦς
mou	apethanen	ho	adelphos	Iēsous
[my	had died]	the	brother.	Jesus

3631.1 conj	**5453.1** conj	**1481.3** verb 3sing indic aor act	**840.12** prs-pron acc sing fem	**2772.10** verb acc sing fem part pres act	**2504.1** conj
οὖν	ὡς	εἶδεν	αὐτὴν	κλαίουσαν,	καὶ
oun	hōs	eiden	autēn	klaiousan	kai
therefore	when	he saw	her	weeping,	and

3450.8 art acc pl masc	**4755.8** verb acc pl masc part aor act	**840.11** prs-pron dat sing fem	**2428.5** name-adj acc pl masc	**2772.8** verb acc pl masc part pres act
τοὺς	συνελθόντας	αὐτῇ	Ἰουδαίους	κλαίοντας,
tous	sunelthontas	autē	Ioudaious	klaiontas
the	having come with	her	Jews	weeping,

1677.2 verb 3sing indic aor mid	**3450.3** art dat sing	**4011.3** noun dat sing neu	**2504.1** conj	**4866.3** verb 3sing indic aor act
ἐνεβριμήσατο	τῷ	πνεύματι,	καὶ	ἐτάραξεν
enebrimēsato	tō	pneumati	kai	etaraxen
he groaned	in the	spirit,	and	troubled

11:32. Commendably, Mary took her sorrow to Jesus rather than going back to the tomb to weep over the death of her brother still more. If she had returned to the burial site to mourn further in a depressed state, she would have sorrowed as those who have no hope (1 Thessalonians 4:13). The Epicurean philosophers of the time taught the soul simply dissolved at death. The Stoics said the soul is finally swallowed up in a fiery substance they identified with deity. They offered no hope, but Jesus did. Notice the progression of Mary's actions. She came, saw, fell, and said.

"Lord, if thou hadst been here, my brother had not died." These are the very words of Martha (verse 21). (See commentary on verse 21.) The two sisters surely made this remark to each other several times during the 4 days before Jesus' arrival.

saying, She goeth unto the grave to weep there: . . . under the impression, *TCNT* . . . they supposed, *NEB* . . . supposing that she was going unto the tomb, *ASV* . . . that she should be lamenting there, *Concordant* . . . imagining that she was going, *Phillips* . . . in the belief that, *BB* . . . thinking she was going, *Beck* . . . going to the tomb to wail there, *Weymouth* . . . she was withdrawing unto, *Rotherham* . . . to grieve there, *Fenton* . . . to mourn there, *ALBA* . . . to pour out her grief there, *AmpB, Williams.*

11:33. Our Lord's humanity is beautifully depicted here by His sympathy. He was moved to feel their grief even though He would soon relieve it. Death was the wage of sin, and it terrorized the human family. Even after being miraculously raised from the grave, Lazarus would still be held in death's power for he would die again.

"Was troubled" is paralleled in verse 38 by "again groaning in himself." Jesus is not a passive bystander in this death narrative of Lazarus or of the human race. He came to destroy the works of the devil. The worst result of Satan's work is death. This enemy (death) and Jesus stand face-to-face in this chapter. Jesus is certainly sympathetic with believers for He is human (as He also is deity). He is also indignant with the enemy of His own. Thus He is deeply moved by His feelings against the enemy, death, and behind death, Satan.

"And was troubled" is an aorist tense active voice verb from *tarassō* meaning "to stir up." *Heauton* indicates that it is not an outside force acting on Him, but that He "himself" is doing the stirring up. In other words, He stirs himself to battle Lazarus' enemy, death.

The long struggle between good and evil comes into focus here. The many years of Satan's assault on the human race troubled Jesus in His spirit. How He desired to put an end to the horrors which plague the human family. The conflict began in the Garden of Eden. The struggle involves every man, woman, and child from Adam on. No wonder the Lord groaned and was troubled! He feels the sorrows and pains of His own. Mary and Martha's troubles became His. Friends do sympathize with their fellows, but Jesus is more than a friend. He takes upon himself the sorrows of His own (Isaiah 53:4). Lazarus' enemy, Death, was also His enemy. Lazarus, Martha, and Mary could not stand before Satan, for they had no power to stand against the power of such a foe. Satan's opposition to Lazarus was another of his efforts to destroy God's creative purposes. Thus the enemy of man is in reality the opponent of God. Satan's onslaughts are by darkness, deception, and death. Jesus combats him by the power of the Resurrection.

32. Then when Mary was come where Jesus was, and saw him: But Mary went to the place where Jesus was, *Norlie.*

she fell down at his feet: . . . she bowed down at His feet, *Beck* . . . she dropped at his feet, *Moffatt* . . . she threw herself at his feet, *TCNT.*

saying unto him, Lord, if thou hadst been here, my brother had not died: . . . and exclaimed, *Weymouth* . . . accusing Him, *ET* . . . in that case my brother, *Wuest* . . . I should not have lost my brother! *TCNT.*

33. When Jesus therefore saw her weeping, and the Jews also weeping which came with her:

he groaned in the spirit, and was troubled: . . . was greatly moved in his spirit, *Alford* . . . he groaned deeply, and was greatly distressed, *TCNT* . . . He was moved with indignation, *LivB* . . . He sighed in sympathy, *Williams* . . . and was agitated, *Murdock* . . . curbing the strong emotion, *Weymouth* . . . he made noyse in spirit, *Wycliffe* . . . was deeply indignant in spirit and disquieted, *Berkeley* . . . visibly distressed, *Phillips.*

1431.6 prs-pron acc 3sing masc	2504.1 conj	1500.5 verb 3sing indic aor act	4085.1 adv	4935.19 verb 2pl indic perf act	840.6 prs-pron acc sing masc
ἑαυτόν,	34. καὶ	εἶπεν,	Ποῦ	τεθείκατε	αὐτόν;
heauton	*kai*	*eipen*	*Pou*	*tetheikate*	*auton*
himself,	and	said,	Where	have you laid	him;

2978.3 verb 3pl pres act	840.4 prs-pron dat sing	2935.5 noun voc sing masc	2048.39 verb 2sing impr pres	2504.1 conj	1481.14 verb 2sing impr aor act
Λέγουσιν	αὐτῷ,	Κύριε,	ἔρχου	καὶ	ἴδε.
Legousin	*autō*	*Kurie*	*erchou*	*kai*	*ide*
They say	to him,	Lord,	come	and	see.

1140.1 verb 3sing indic aor act	3450.5 art sing masc	2400.1 name nom masc	2978.25 verb indic imperf act	3631.1 conj
35. Ἐδάκρυσεν	ὁ	Ἰησοῦς.	36. ἔλεγον	οὖν
Edakrusen	*ho*	*Iēsous*	*elegon*	*oun*
Wept		Jesus.	Said	therefore

3450.7 art pl masc	2428.2 name-adj pl masc	1481.14 verb 2sing impr aor act	4316.1 adv	5205.11 verb 3sing indic imperf act	840.6 prs-pron acc sing masc
οἱ	Ἰουδαῖοι,	Ἴδε	πῶς	ἐφίλει	αὐτόν.
hoi	*Ioudaioi*	*Ide*	*pōs*	*ephilei*	*auton*
the	Jews,	Behold	how	he loved	him!

37.a.**Txt:** 01ℵ-corr,02A,03B,04C,017K,019L,036,037,038,etc.byz.Lach,Tisc,Sod
Var: 01ℵ-org,We/Ho,Weis,UBS/☆

37.b.**Txt:** 01ℵ,02A,03B-corr,019L,036,037,1,13,etc.byz.Gries,Word,Sod
Var: 03B-org,04C,05D,017K,038,041,Lach,Treg,Alf,Tisc,We/Ho,Weis,UBS/☆

4948.7 indef-pron nom pl masc	1156.2 conj	1523.1 prep gen	840.1 prs-pron gen pl	1500.3 verb indic aor act	1500.28 verb 3pl indic aor act
37. Τινὲς	δὲ	ἐξ	αὐτῶν	ˊ εἶπον,	[a☆ εἶπαν,]
Tines	*de*	*ex*	*autōn*	*eipon*	*eipan*
Some	but	of	them	said,	[idem]

3620.2 partic	1404.34 verb 3sing indic imperf	1404.35 verb 3sing indic imperf	3642.4 dem-pron nom sing masc	3450.5 art sing masc
Οὐκ	ˊ ἠδύνατο	[b☆ ἐδύνατο]	οὗτος	ὁ
Ouk	*ēdunato*	*edunato*	*houtos*	*ho*
Not	was able	[idem]	this	the

453.9 verb nom sing masc part aor act	3450.8 art acc pl masc	3652.8 noun acc pl masc	3450.2 art gen sing	5026.2 adj gen sing masc
ἀνοίξας	τοὺς	ὀφθαλμοὺς	τοῦ	τυφλοῦ,
anoixas	*tous*	*ophthalmous*	*tou*	*tuphlou*
having opened	the	eyes	of the	blind,

4020.41 verb inf aor act	2419.1 conj	2504.1 conj	3642.4 dem-pron nom sing masc	3231.1 partic	594.13 verb 3sing subj aor act
ποιῆσαι	ἵνα	καὶ	οὗτος	μὴ	ἀποθάνῃ;
poiēsai	*hina*	*kai*	*houtos*	*mē*	*apothanē*
to have caused	that	also	this one	not	should have died?

2400.1 name nom masc	3631.1 conj	3687.1 adv	1677.1 verb nom sing masc part pres	1706.1 prep
38. Ἰησοῦς	οὖν	πάλιν	ἐμβριμώμενος	ἐν
Iēsous	*oun*	*palin*	*embrimōmenos*	*en*
Jesus	therefore	again	groaning	in

1431.5 prs-pron dat 3sing masc	2048.34 verb 3sing indic pres	1519.1 prep	3450.16 art sing neu	3283.1 noun sing neu	1498.34 verb sing indic imperf act
ἑαυτῷ	ἔρχεται	εἰς	τὸ	μνημεῖον.	ἦν
heautō	*erchetai*	*eis*	*to*	*mnēmeion*	*ēn*
himself	comes	to	the	grave.	It was

1156.2 conj	4546.1 noun sing neu	2504.1 conj	3012.1 noun nom sing masc	1930.6 verb 3sing indic imperf	1894.2 prep
δὲ	σπήλαιον,	καὶ	λίθος	ἐπέκειτο	ἐπ’
de	*spēlaion*	*kai*	*lithos*	*epekeito*	*ep’*
now	a cave,	and	a stone	was lying	upon

11:34. The question may have been meant to stir some hope in heir sorrowing hearts.

Mary and Martha had left the entire situation in the hands of heir Lord. Jesus' question encouraged them to rely by faith on whatever He would or would not do. Faith always allows God to lo His own will and never imposes on Him limited human design and desire.

11:35. The New Testament speaks of three times Jesus shed tears John 11:35; Luke 19:41; Hebrews 5:7). It is interesting to note hat Jesus is never said to have laughed (*gelaō*) or to have engaged n laughter (*gelōs*). He did "rejoice" (*agalliaō*) according to Luke .0:21, and was "glad" (*chairō*) according to John 11:15.

The silent tears Jesus shed in this instance stand in contrast to he loud wailing expressed by the mourning Jews. His tears of ympathy speak to us of His tender, compassionate humanity. Jesus' ears disclosed how God feels toward suffering among us. When ve look upon our own departed, or draw near to our own separation, we can see Him with tears trickling down His face at the rave of Lazarus.

11:36. The hard, cruel, hostile Jews were temporarily disarmed nd revealed their admiration for Jesus. The Jews used the word loved" (*ephilei*) meaning the friendship association.

11:37. Some of the Jews acknowledged that Jesus healed the man orn blind (9:6,7). Their next assertion shows they had come to he same conclusion as Martha and Mary (verses 21,32).

11:38. When Jesus arrived at the tomb, He was "groaning" (*embrimōmenos*). The Greek word was also used in verse 33. It only ccurs in three other passages (Matthew 9:30; Mark 1:43; 14:5). In himself" is equivalent to "in the spirit" of verse 33. The passage n Mark 14:5 shows another connotation of this word, referring to ome who expressed their indignation at the waste of money when ne woman poured out the alabaster box of ointment. Thus it ppears the Greek word rendered "groaning" could be rendered indignant." Jesus was indignant toward the enemy death and Satan ho caused it, not at the sisters or the Jews. He placed himself in attle array against this enemy of the human family.

34. And said, Where have ye laid him?:

They say unto him, Lord, come and see:

35. Jesus wept: Jesus burst into tears, *Moffatt, Williams* . . . And Jesus himself was weeping, *BB* . . . Tears came to Jesus' eyes, *LivB* . . . the tears of Jesus came, *Murdock.*

36. Then said the Jews, Behold how he loved him!: See! how tenderly he loved him! *Rotherham* . . . How he must have loved him! *TCNT* . . . See how dear he was to him! *BB.*

37. And some of them said, Could not this man, which opened the eyes of the blind, have caused that even this man should not have died?: Could not he...have prevented his death, *Berkeley* . . . have kept this man from dying, *Norlie* . . . also have arranged, *Fenton.*

38. Jesus therefore again groaning in himself cometh to the grave: . . . sighing in Himself, *Fenton* . . . again showing great distress, *Norlie* . . . Groaning deeply again, *Beck* . . . deeply vexed inwardly, *Berkeley* . . . moved with indignation in himself, *Wuest* . . . again felt anger, *ALBA* . . . groaning angrily within, *Adams.*

It was a cave, and a stone lay upon it: . . . closed up at the entrance, *Fenton* . . . a stone lay against the mouth of it, *TCNT.*

840.4 prs-pron dat sing	**2978.5** verb 3sing indic pres act	**3450.5** art sing masc	**2400.1** name nom masc	**142.15** verb 2pl impr aor act	**3450.6** art acc sing masc
αὐτῷ.	**39.** λέγει	ὁ	Ἰησοῦς,	Ἄρατε	τὸν
autō	*legei*	*ho*	*Iēsous*	*Arate*	*ton*
it.	Says		Jesus,	Take away	the

3012.4 noun acc sing masc	**2978.5** verb 3sing indic pres act	**840.4** prs-pron dat sing	**3450.9** art nom sing fem	**78.1** noun nom sing fem	**3450.2** art gen sing
λίθον.	Λέγει	αὐτῷ	ἡ	ἀδελφὴ	τοῦ
lithon	*Legei*	*autō*	*hē*	*adelphē*	*tou*
stone.	Says	to him	the	sister	of the

39.a.**Txt:** 04C-corr,036,037,byz.
Var: 01א,02A,03B,04C-org,05D,017K,019L,041,33,Lach,Treg,Alf,Tisc,We/Ho,WeisSod,UBS/☆

2325.5 verb gen sing masc part perf act	**4901.7** verb gen sing part perf act	**3108.1** name fem	**2935.5** noun voc sing masc
⸂ τεθνηκότος	[a☆ τετελευτηκότος]	Μάρθα,	Κύριε,
tethnēkotos	*teteleutēkotos*	*Martha*	*Kurie*
having died,	[idem]	Martha,	Lord,

2218.1 adv	**3467.1** verb 3sing indic pres act	**4914.1** adj nom sing masc	**1056.1** conj	**1498.4** verb 3sing indic pres act	**2978.5** verb 3sing indic pres act
ἤδη	ὄζει·	τεταρταῖος	γάρ	ἐστιν.	**40.** Λέγει
ēdē	*ozei*	*tetartaios*	*gar*	*estin*	*Legei*
already	he stinks,	four days	for	it is.	Says

840.11 prs-pron dat sing fem	**3450.5** art sing masc	**2400.1** name nom masc	**3620.2** partic	**1500.3** verb indic aor act	**4622.3** prs-pron dat 2sing	**3617.1** conj
αὐτῇ	ὁ	Ἰησοῦς,	Οὐκ	εἶπόν	σοι,	ὅτι
autē	*ho*	*Iēsous*	*Ouk*	*eipon*	*soi*	*hoti*
to her		Jesus,	Not	said I	to you,	that

40.a.**Txt:** 017K,030U,036,Steph,Gries
Var: 01א,02A,03B,04C,05D,019L,037,038,byz.Lach,Treg,Alf,Tisc,We/Ho,WeisSod,UBS/☆

1430.1 partic	**3961.24** verb 2sing subj aor act	**3571.29** verb 2sing indic fut mid	**3571.39** verb 2sing indic fut mid	**3450.12** art acc sing fem
ἐὰν	πιστεύσῃς	⸂ ὄψει	[a☆ ὄψῃ]	τὴν
ean	*pisteusēs*	*opsei*	*opsē*	*tēn*
if	you should believe,	you shall see	[idem]	the

1385.4 noun acc sing fem	**3450.2** art gen sing	**2296.2** noun gen sing masc	**142.10** verb 3pl indic aor act	**3631.1** conj	**3450.6** art acc sing masc
δόξαν	τοῦ	θεοῦ;	**41.** Ἦραν	οὖν	τὸν
doxan	*tou*	*theou*	*Eran*	*oun*	*ton*
glory		of God?	They took away	therefore	the

41.a.**Txt:** 04C-corr,07E,030U,036,037,13,byz.
Var: 01א,03B,04C-org,05D,019L,033X,038,33,sa.Gries,Lach,TregAlf,Tisc,We/Ho,Weis,Sod,UBS/☆

3012.4 noun acc sing masc	**3619.1** adv	**1498.34** verb sing indic imperf act	**3450.5** art sing masc	**2325.4** verb nom sing masc part perf act
λίθον	⸂a οὗ	ἦν	ὁ	τεθνηκὼς
lithon	*hou*	*ēn*	*ho*	*tethnēkōs*
stone	where	was	the	having died

2719.5 verb nom sing masc part pres	**3450.5** art sing masc	**1156.2** conj	**2400.1** name nom masc	**142.8** verb 3sing indic aor act	**3450.8** art acc pl masc
κείμενος. ⸃	Ὁ	δὲ	Ἰησοῦς	ἦρεν	τοὺς
keimenos	*Ho*	*de*	*Iēsous*	*ēren*	*tous*
having laid.		And	Jesus	lifted	the

3652.8 noun acc pl masc	**504.1** adv	**2504.1** conj	**1500.5** verb 3sing indic aor act	**3824.5** noun voc sing masc	**2149.1** verb 1sing indic pres act
ὀφθαλμοὺς	ἄνω,	καὶ	εἶπεν,	Πάτερ,	εὐχαριστῶ
ophthalmous	*anō*	*kai*	*eipen*	*Pater*	*eucharistō*
eyes	upwards,	and	said,	Father,	I thank

4622.3 prs-pron dat 2sing	**3617.1** conj	**189.20** verb 2sing indic aor act	**1466.2** prs-pron gen 1sing	**1466.1** prs-pron nom 1sing	**1156.2** conj
σοι	ὅτι	ἤκουσάς	μου.	**42.** ἐγὼ	δὲ
soi	*hoti*	*ēkousas*	*mou*	*egō*	*de*
you	that	you heard	me;	I	and

Tombs were located outside the village because contact with the bodies brought defilement for 7 days. Sometimes artificial caves were dug out of hillsides to form tombs. A large stone was lying against the opening so that animals could not disturb the remains of Lazarus. Ordinarily the stones which blocked a tomb's entrance were kept whitewashed to mark them as graves.

11:39. With little or no hesitation upon arriving at the tomb, Jesus gave the first of three commands which brought about this great miracle. He allowed the attendants to assist in a natural, normal way so that they might participate in this grand wonder. The stone was very heavy so that robbers, vandals, or animals would have difficulty entering the tomb.

Martha was a realistic woman and probably the older sister; thus she was the guardian of Lazarus' remains. Doubtless she ministered to her brother in his sickness and had seen him die 4 days before. Now she reminded her Lord that Lazarus was stinking from his decaying flesh. She hesitated to believe in what Jesus was about to do.

11:40. Jesus reminded Martha of what He had said to her upon His arrival, because He wished to confirm her faith (verses 20-27): "If thou wouldest believe, thou shouldest see."

"The glory of God" refers to God's person and presence becoming known by some miracle. Anytime God is manifested, it is a display of His glory.

11:41. Martha did not object to the removal of the stone after Jesus' reminder.

The attendants lifted up the stone, and Jesus lifted up His eyes. The physical effort and spiritual prayer combined to bring about the miracle. Jesus also lifted up His eyes at the beginning of His high priestly prayer (chapter 17).

The Lord prayed a simple prayer containing 26 words in the original. The prayer began with "Father" as a recognition of their relationship. Next, Jesus offered thanks to the Father who hears prayer. He was certain of His relationship to the Father, and He gave thanks for their mutual communion.

11:42. The Father and Son always have perfect communion and unity of purpose. Jesus was absolutely conscious of this, and yet

39. Jesus said, Take ye away the stone: Slip the stone aside, *Williams* . . . at once, *Wuest.*

Martha, the sister of him that was dead, saith unto him, Lord, by this time he stinketh: . . . sister of the deceased, *Berkeley* . . . There will be a bad smell, *TEV* . . . by this time he is offensive, *HBIE* . . . Lord, there is already an odor, *Norlie* . . . he is putrid, *Murdock* . . . the smell is offensive, *Campbell* . . . there is a foul smell, *Weymouth* . . . he will be decaying, *Phillips.*

for he hath been dead four days: . . . for he has been four days in the tomb, *Montgomery* . . . three days, *Weymouth.*

40. Jesus saith unto her, Said I not unto thee, that, if thou wouldest believe: . . . if you had faith, *BB* . . . if you will only believe, *Moffatt.*

thou shouldest see the glory of God?: . . . see the majesty of God, *Fenton* . . . you would see the wonder of what God can do, *Phillips.*

41. Then they took away the stone from the place where the dead was laid: They then removed the stone, *Norlie.*

And Jesus lifted up his eyes, and said: . . . eyes heavenward, *Norlie* . . . looking upward, *Fenton* . . . His eyes on high, *Berkeley.*

Father, I thank thee that thou hast heard me: I thank you for listening to me, *Williams* . . . for having heard Me, *Berkeley.*

3471.9 verb 1sing indic plperf act	3617.1 conj	3704.1 adv	1466.2 prs-pron gen 1sing	189.4 verb 2sing indic pres act	233.2 conj
ᾔδειν	ὅτι	πάντοτέ	μου	ἀκούεις·	ἀλλὰ
ēdein	hoti	pantote	mou	akoueis	alla
knew	that	always	me	you hear;	but

1217.2 prep	3450.6 art acc sing masc	3657.4 noun acc sing masc	3450.6 art acc sing masc	3889.2 verb acc sing masc part perf act
διὰ	τὸν	ὄχλον	τὸν	περιεστῶτα
dia	ton	ochlon	ton	periestōta
because of	the	crowd	the	having stood around

1500.3 verb indic aor act	2419.1 conj	3961.27 verb 3pl subj aor act	3617.1 conj	4622.1 prs-pron nom 2sing	1466.6 prs-pron acc 1sing
εἶπον	ἵνα	πιστεύσωσιν	ὅτι	σύ	με
eipon	hina	pisteusōsin	hoti	su	me
I said,	that	they might believe	that	you	me

643.7 verb 2sing indic aor act		2504.1 conj	3642.18 dem-pron pl neu	1500.15 verb nom sing masc part aor act	5292.3 noun dat sing fem
ἀπέστειλας.	**43.**	καὶ	ταῦτα	εἰπὼν	φωνῇ
apesteilas		kai	tauta	eipōn	phōnē
sent.		And	these things	having said,	with a voice

44.a.**Txt:** 01א,02A, 04C-corr,017K,032W, 036,037,038,1,13,byz. Lach,Sod
Var: p45,p66,p75,03B, 04C-org,019L,044,sa. Gries,TregAlf,Tisc, We/Ho,Weis,UBS/☆

3144.11 adj dat sing fem	2878.2 verb 3sing indic aor act	2949.3 name voc masc	1198.1 adv	1838.1 prep gen		2504.1 conj
μεγάλῃ	ἐκραύγασεν,	Λάζαρε,	δεῦρο	ἔξω.	**44.**	⸂a Καὶ ⸃
megalē	ekraugasen	Lazare	deuro	exō		Kai
loud	he cried,	Lazarus,	come	outside.		And

1814.3 verb 3sing indic aor act	3450.5 art sing masc	2325.4 verb nom sing masc part perf act	1204.17 verb nom sing masc part perf pass	3450.8 art acc pl masc
ἐξῆλθεν	ὁ	τεθνηκώς,	δεδεμένος	τοὺς
exēlthen	ho	tethnēkōs	dedemenos	tous
came forth	the	having died,	having been bound	the

4087.7 noun acc pl masc	2504.1 conj	3450.15 art acc pl fem	5331.8 noun acc pl fem	2720.1 noun dat pl fem	2504.1 conj
πόδας	καὶ	τὰς	χεῖρας	κειρίαις,	καὶ
podas	kai	tas	cheiras	keiriais	kai
feet	and	the	hands	with grave clothes,	and

3450.9 art nom sing fem	3663.1 noun nom sing fem	840.3 prs-pron gen sing	4529.1 noun dat sing neu	3882.1 verb 3sing indic plperf pass
ἡ	ὄψις	αὐτοῦ	σουδαρίῳ	περιεδέδετο.
hē	opsis	autou	soudariō	periededeto
the	face	his	with a handkerchief	bound about.

2978.5 verb 3sing indic pres act	840.2 prs-pron dat pl	3450.5 art sing masc	2400.1 name nom masc	3061.12 verb 2pl impr aor act	840.6 prs-pron acc sing masc
λέγει	αὐτοῖς	ὁ	Ἰησοῦς,	Λύσατε	αὐτὸν
legei	autois	ho	Iēsous	Lusate	auton
Says	to them		Jesus,	Loose	him

44.b.**Var:** p45,p66,p75, 03B,04C-org,019L,038, 33,bo.Treg,Alf,Tisc We/Ho,Weis,Sod,UBS/☆

2504.1 conj	856.18 verb 2pl impr aor act	840.6 prs-pron acc sing masc	5055.10 verb inf pres act		4044.7 adj nom pl masc
καὶ	ἄφετε	[b☆+ αὐτὸν]	ὑπάγειν.	**45.**	Πολλοὶ
kai	aphete	auton	hupagein		Polloi
and	let	[him]	go.		Many

3631.1 conj	1523.2 prep gen	3450.1 art gen pl	2428.3 name-adj gen pl masc	3450.7 art pl masc	2048.16 verb nom pl masc part aor act
οὖν	ἐκ	τῶν	Ἰουδαίων	οἱ	ἐλθόντες
oun	ek	tōn	Ioudaiōn	hoi	elthontes
therefore	of	the	Jews	the	having come

He prayed. The Jews who stood by had accused Him of working miracles by the power of Beelzebub. Satan does not restore the sick to health or raise the dead to the glory of God. Jesus demonstrated the power of the resurrection and ascribed all the glory to God.

"That they may believe that thou hast sent me" shows the relationship of God the Father to Jesus Christ the Son, and the purpose is "that they may believe." When God is glorified, He is known for who He is. This was revealed by the work of Jesus Christ in the performance of the miracle. The sign in turn testified to the truth that the Father had sent Him. This knowledge would lead believers to receive eternal life through Him.

42. And I knew that thou hearest me always: Moreover, I knew positively, *Wuest* . . . I know that you always hear me, *Phillips.*

but because of the people which stand by I said it: . . . but I said it because of these who are here, *BB* . . . who surround me, *Campbell.*

that they may believe that thou hast sent me: . . . that they may come to believe, *Williams* . . . you sent me on a mission, *Wuest* . . . Thou didst send me, *Weymouth.*

11:43. This crying "with a loud voice" was not done that Lazarus might hear, but that the witnesses might focus their attention on Him and the miracle. Jesus uttered no mutterings or magical formulas. His voice will stir and raise all believers in the resurrection, for so the Scriptures declare (John 5:28,29; 1 Corinthians 15:51-55; 1 Thessalonians 4:16,17).

The Lord called to His friend by name. With majestic authority Jesus called, "Lazarus, come forth." This was the second command (see verse 39 for the first command). At the raising of the other two dead ones, Jesus had said, "Arise" (Mark 5:41; Luke 7:14; 8:54), but here He said, "Come forth." Literally, the Greek words mean "come out." Jesus called to Lazarus, "Depart from the grave and come to Me."

We can but vaguely imagine how Jesus' voice impregnated the stiff and decaying corpse and sent a thrill through the place of departed spirits that the man and his body came together to obey the command of the Resurrection and Life (verse 25). What a moment for the petrified Jewish mourners.

43. And when he thus had spoken, he cried with a loud voice, Lazarus, come forth: Jesus called in a loud voice, *TCNT* . . . After He had said this, He called out loud, *Beck* . . . shouted with a great, *Wuest* . . . He shouted aloud, *Williams* . . . He called out strongly, *Berkeley* . . . come thou out, *Wycliffe* . . . come here, *TCNT.*

44. And he that was dead came forth: The dead man came out, *RSV* . . . Out came the one who had died, *Berkeley* . . . walked out, *TCNT.*

bound hand and foot with graveclothes: . . . swathed hand and foot, *Fenton* . . . with swathing-bands, *Wuest* . . . his hands and feet bound with bandages, *RSV.*

and his face was bound about with a napkin: . . . and his countenance had been bound about, *Concordant* . . . with a handkerchief, *Wuest* . . . and a cloth about his face, *BB.*

Jesus saith unto them, Loose him, and let him go: Unwrap him, *Beck, Adams* . . . Untie him, and let him go, *SEB, Montgomery* . . . Unbind him, *RSV* . . . Make him free, *BB* . . . and let him walk, *Fenton* . . . give him a chance to move, *Berkeley* . . . and let him go home, *Phillips, ALBA.*

11:44,45. The response was identical to the command. The grave clothes hindered Lazarus' movement, but he obeyed nevertheless. Clarke wrote of procedures in wrapping the dead. People used "long slips of linen a few inches in breadth, with which the body and limbs of the dead were swathed, and especially those who were embalmed, that the aromatics might be kept in contact with the flesh. But as it is evident that Lazarus had not been embalmed, it is probable that his limbs were not swathed *together,* as is the constant case with those who are embalmed, but *separately,* so that he could come out of the tomb at the command of Christ, though he could not walk *freely* till the rollers (cloth) were taken away" (Clarke, *Clarke's Commentary,* 5:603).

"Loose him, and let him go." This is the third command (see verses 39 and 43). Notice the witnesses participated in obeying the

45. Then many of the Jews which came to Mary, and had seen the things which Jesus did: . . . and who saw what Jesus had

45.a.**Txt:** p6,p45,p66-org, 01ℵ,02A-org,017K, 019L,032W,036,037, 038,13,byz.it.bo.Gries, Lach,Tisc
Var: 02A-corr,03B, 04C-org,05D,sa.Treg, Alf,We/Ho,WeisSod, UBS/☆

45.b.**Txt:** (01),04C-corr, 05D,017K,036,037,byz.
Var: 02A,03B,04C-org, 019L,038,sa.bo.Gries, Lach,Treg,Alf,Word, Tisc,We/Ho,WeisSod, UBS/☆

46.a.**Txt:** 02A,03B,04C, 017K,019L,036,037,038, etc.byz.Lach,Sod
Var: 01ℵ,05D,Tisc, We/Ho,Weis,UBS/☆

46.b.**Txt:** 01ℵ,02A,017K, 036,037,038,etc.byz.Sod
Var: 03B,04C,05D,019L, Lach,Treg,Alf,Tisc, We/HoWeis,UBS/☆

4242.1 prep	**3450.12** art acc sing fem	**3109.4** name acc fem	**3110.1** name fem	**2504.1** conj	**2277.8** verb nom pl masc part aor mid
πρὸς	τὴν	⸀ Μαρίαν	[☆ Μαριὰμ]	καὶ	θεασάμενοι
pros	*tēn*	*Marian*	*Mariam*	*kai*	*theasamenoi*
to		Mary	[idem]	and	having seen

3614.17 rel-pron pl neu	**3614.16** rel-pron sing neu	**4020.24** verb 3sing indic aor act	**3450.5** art sing masc	**2400.1** name nom masc
⸂☆ ἃ	[a ὃ]	ἐποίησεν	⸂b ὁ	Ἰησοῦς, ⸃
ha	*ho*	*epoiēsen*	*ho*	*Iēsous*
what	[idem]	did		Jesus,

3961.23 verb 3pl indic aor act	**1519.1** prep	**840.6** prs-pron acc sing masc	**4948.7** indef-pron nom pl masc	**1156.2** conj	**1523.1** prep gen
ἐπίστευσαν	εἰς	αὐτόν.	**46.** τινὲς	δὲ	ἐξ
episteusan	*eis*	*auton*	*tines*	*de*	*ex*
believed	on	him;	some	but	of

840.1 prs-pron gen pl	**562.1** verb indic aor act	**4242.1** prep	**3450.8** art acc pl masc	**5168.7** name acc pl masc	**2504.1** conj
αὐτῶν	ἀπῆλθον	πρὸς	τοὺς	Φαρισαίους	καὶ
autōn	*apēlthon*	*pros*	*tous*	*Pharisaious*	*kai*
them	went	to	the	Pharisees	and

1500.3 verb indic aor act	**1500.28** verb 3pl indic aor act	**840.2** prs-pron dat pl	**3614.17** rel-pron pl neu	**4020.24** verb 3sing indic aor act
⸀ εἶπον	[a☆ εἶπαν]	αὐτοῖς	ἃ	ἐποίησεν
eipon	*eipan*	*autois*	*ha*	*epoiēsen*
told	[idem]	them	what	did

3450.5 art sing masc	**2400.1** name nom masc	**4714.8** verb 3pl indic aor act	**3631.1** conj	**3450.7** art pl masc
⸂b ὁ ⸃	Ἰησοῦς.	**47.** συνήγαγον	οὖν	οἱ
ho	*Iēsous*	*sunēgagon*	*oun*	*hoi*
	Jesus.	Gathered	therefore	the

744.5 noun pl masc	**2504.1** conj	**3450.7** art pl masc	**5168.4** name pl masc	**4742.1** noun sing neu	**2504.1** conj
ἀρχιερεῖς	καὶ	οἱ	Φαρισαῖοι	συνέδριον,	καὶ
archiereis	*kai*	*hoi*	*Pharisaioi*	*sunedrion*	*kai*
chief priests	and	the	Pharisees	a council,	and

2978.25 verb indic imperf act	**4949.9** intr-pron sing neu	**4020.6** verb 1pl indic pres act	**3617.1** conj	**3642.4** dem-pron nom sing masc	**3450.5** art sing masc
ἔλεγον,	Τί	ποιοῦμεν·	ὅτι	οὗτος	ὁ
elegon	*Ti*	*poioumen*	*hoti*	*houtos*	*ho*
said,	What	do we?	for	this	the

442.1 noun nom sing masc	**4044.17** adj pl neu	**4447.2** noun pl neu	**4020.5** verb 3sing indic pres act	**4020.5** verb 3sing indic pres act
ἄνθρωπος	πολλὰ	⸀ σημεῖα	ποιεῖ.	[☆ ποιεῖ
anthrōpos	*polla*	*sēmeia*	*poiei*	*poiei*
man	many	signs	does.	[does

4447.2 noun pl neu	**1430.1** partic	**856.15** verb 1pl subj aor act	**840.6** prs-pron acc sing masc	**3643.1** adv	**3820.7** adj pl masc
σημεῖα;]	**48.** ἐὰν	ἀφῶμεν	αὐτὸν	οὕτως,	πάντες
sēmeia	*ean*	*aphōmen*	*auton*	*houtōs*	*pantes*
signs?]	If	we let alone	him	thus,	all

3961.51 verb 3pl indic fut act	**1519.1** prep	**840.6** prs-pron acc sing masc	**2504.1** conj	**2048.57** verb 3pl indic fut mid	**3450.7** art pl masc
πιστεύσουσιν	εἰς	αὐτόν·	καὶ	ἐλεύσονται	οἱ
pisteusousin	*eis*	*auton*	*kai*	*eleusontai*	*hoi*
will believe	on	him,	and	will come	the

first and last command. Lazarus obeyed the second order. Those who shared the activities connected with the miracle could hardly deny its reality (see verses 46,47). We read of Lazarus in one further instance (12:2).

The mourners departed, having nothing more to weep over. The miracle had made God known. Jesus had performed the outstanding sign of His ministry.

done, *Williams* . . . had viewed attentively, *Wuest* . . . had witnessed His deeds, *Weymouth* . . . who had come with Mary, and had seen what he did, *Montgomery.*

believed on him: . . . became believers in Him, *Weymouth* . . . accepted His Messiahship, *ET.*

11:46. "But some of them" means out of those who believed of verse 45. These went to the Pharisees and told them. The reason for their going is not stated, yet their intention may have been to present evidence of the great miracle in an effort to convince the Pharisees that Jesus was indeed the Messiah.

They may have singled out the Pharisees in the hope they would accept the truth about Lazarus, since a belief in the resurrection was a part of their theology (Acts 23:8-10). In fact, they were willing to fight for their position on the issue. However, it was in their case as Jesus said. If people will not accept the facts of Scripture, "neither will they be persuaded, though one rose from the dead" (Luke 16:31). Then what followed is of little surprise.

46. But some of them went their ways to the Pharisees, and told them what things Jesus had done: . . . reported his action, *ALBA* . . . to the Orthodox, *Klingensmith.*

11:47. The "some" who shared what Jesus had done with their Pharisaic friends did not win them over to a belief that Jesus was their Messiah. The Pharisees counseled together with the chief priests and convened a council. This was the Sanhedrin composed of about 71 members of the chief priests, scribes, and elders of the nation. The purpose of the emergency meeting was to decide what could be done because a number of the Pharisees had become believers due to the raising of Lazarus.

"What do we?" means "What are we going to do about the situation?" "For" (*hoti*) gives their reason. They must act because Jesus was "performing many signs" (NASB).

47. Then gathered the chief priests and the Pharisees a council: The most important priests, *SEB* . . . accordingly convened a meeting of the Senate, *Fenton* . . . convoked a council, *Wuest* . . . called a meeting of the council, *Beck* . . . a meeting of the Sanhedrin, *Moffatt* . . . Therefore, the Sanhedrin, or Great Council, was called together, *Norlie* . . . the bischops, *Wycliffe* . . . convened the Sanhedrin, *Wilson.*

and said, What do we?: What are we to do, *Rotherham* . . . What shall we do? *Norlie.*

for this man doeth many miracles: For this fellow is doing many miracles, *Norlie* . . . performs numerous signs, *Berkeley* . . . is doing many signs, *HBIE* . . . many marvels, *Norton.*

11:48. This verse gives the reason for the fear of the Sanhedrin. They were probably referring to the nation as a whole and not to every individual. "All" (*pantes*) is sometimes used in the general sense. It is evident that the leaders had no intention of believing in Jesus as their Messiah. They reasoned that if all men believed in Him then the leaders would be forced to give up their "place" (*topon*) and "nation." "Place" may refer to the temple or their place of leadership. They said it was their place and their nation. The

48. If we let him thus alone: If we let him go on this way, *Berkeley* . . . If we let Him keep on this way, *Norlie* . . . If we disregard him in this manner, *Wuest* . . . If we let him thus alone, *Panin.*

all men will believe on him: . . . we shall have everybody believing in him, *Phillips.*

John 11:49

4371.3 name-adj nom pl masc	2504.1 conj	142.21 verb 3pl indic fut act	2231.2 prs-pron gen 1pl	2504.1 conj	3450.6 art acc sing masc
Ῥωμαῖοι	καὶ	ἀροῦσιν	ἡμῶν	καὶ	τὸν
Rhōmaioi	*kai*	*arousin*	*hēmōn*	*kai*	*ton*
Romans	and	will takc away	our	both	the

4964.4 noun acc sing masc	2504.1 conj	3450.16 art sing neu	1477.1 noun sing neu	1518.3 num card nom masc	1156.2 conj	4948.3 indef-pron nom sing
τόπον	καὶ	τὸ	ἔθνος.	**49.** εἷς	δέ	τις
topon	*kai*	*to*	*ethnos*	*heis*	*de*	*tis*
place	and	the	nation.	One	but	a certain

1523.1 prep gen	840.1 prs-pron gen pl	2505.1 name nom masc	744.1 noun nom sing masc	1498.21 verb sing masc part pres act
ἐξ	αὐτῶν,	Καϊάφας,	ἀρχιερεὺς	ὢν
ex	*autōn*	*Kaiaphas*	*archiereus*	*ōn*
of	them,	Caiaphas,	high priest	being

3450.2 art gen sing	1747.1 noun gen sing masc	1552.2 dem-pron gen sing	1500.5 verb 3sing indic aor act	840.2 prs-pron dat pl	5050.1 prs-pron nom 2pl
τοῦ	ἐνιαυτοῦ	ἐκείνου,	εἶπεν	αὐτοῖς,	Ὑμεῖς
tou	*eniautou*	*ekeinou*	*eipen*	*autois*	*Humeis*
of the	year	that,	said	to them,	You

50.a.**Txt:** 017K,036,037, byz.
Var: 01ℵ,02A,03B,05D, 019L,038,Lach,Treg,Alf, TiscWe/Ho,Weis,Sod, UBS/☆

3620.2 partic	3471.6 verb 2pl indic perf act	3625.6 num card neu	3624.1 adv	1254.1 verb 2pl indic pres
οὐκ	οἴδατε	οὐδέν,	**50.** οὐδὲ	⸀ διαλογίζεσθε
ouk	*oidate*	*ouden*	*oude*	*dialogizesthe*
not	know	nothing,	nor	consider

50.b.**Txt:** 02A,017K, 032W,037,038,1,13,33, byz.sa.Gries,Lach
Var: p45,p66,03B,05D, 019L,036,1241,bo.Treg, Alf,Tisc,We/HoWeis,Sod, UBS/☆

3023.1 verb 2pl pres	3617.1 conj	4702.1 verb 3sing indic pres act	2231.3 prs-pron dat 1pl	5050.3 prs-pron dat 2pl
[a☆ λογίζεσθε]	ὅτι	συμφέρει	⸀ ἡμῖν	[b☆ ὑμῖν]
logizesthe	*hoti*	*sumpherei*	*hēmin*	*humin*
[idem]	that	it is profitable	for us	[for you]

2419.1 conj	1518.3 num card nom masc	442.1 noun nom sing masc	594.13 verb 3sing subj aor act	5065.1 prep	3450.2 art gen sing
ἵνα	εἷς	ἄνθρωπος	ἀποθάνῃ	ὑπὲρ	τοῦ
hina	*heis*	*anthrōpos*	*apothanē*	*huper*	*tou*
that	one	man	should die	for	the

2967.2 noun gen sing masc	2504.1 conj	3231.1 partic	3513.1 adj sing	3450.16 art sing neu	1477.1 noun sing neu	616.24 verb 3sing subj aor mid
λαοῦ,	καὶ	μὴ	ὅλον	τὸ	ἔθνος	ἀπόληται.
laou	*kai*	*mē*	*holon*	*to*	*ethnos*	*apolētai*
people,	and	not	whole	the	nation	should perish.

3642.17 dem-pron sing neu	1156.2 conj	570.1 prep gen	1431.4 prs-pron gen 3sing	3620.2 partic	1500.5 verb 3sing indic aor act
51. Τοῦτο	δὲ	ἀφ᾽	ἑαυτοῦ	οὐκ	εἶπεν,
Touto	*de*	*aph'*	*heautou*	*ouk*	*eipen*
This	but	from	himself	not	he said,

233.2 conj	744.1 noun nom sing masc	1498.21 verb sing masc part pres act	3450.2 art gen sing	1747.1 noun gen sing masc	1552.2 dem-pron gen sing
ἀλλὰ	ἀρχιερεὺς	ὢν	τοῦ	ἐνιαυτοῦ	ἐκείνου,
alla	*archiereus*	*ōn*	*tou*	*eniautou*	*ekeinou*
but	high priest	being	of the	year	that,

51.a.**Txt:** 02A,017K,036, 037,byz.
Var: 01ℵ,03B,05D,019L, 033X,038,33,Lach,Treg Alf,Tisc,We/Ho,Weis, Sod,UBS/☆

4253.8 verb 3sing indic aor act	4253.16 verb 3sing indic aor act	3617.1 conj	3165.22 verb 3sing indic imperf act
⸀ προεφήτευσεν	[a☆ ἐπροφήτευσεν]	ὅτι	⸀ ἔμελλεν
proephēteusen	*eprophēteusen*	*hoti*	*emellen*
prophesied	[idem]	that	was about

leaders had placed themselves in God's stead because He is the possessor of the place and nation. They feared that the nation would receive Jesus as the Messiah. Jesus would then sit on the throne and drive the Romans from their borders. However, they believed Rome's power was greater than that of Jesus and His followers. Therefore, the Romans would overthrow all authority, destroy the temple, and kill the people.

and the Romans shall come and take away both our place and nation: . . . and blot out both our city and nation, *Williams* . . . and take away from us both land and people, *Norlie* . . . and rob us of both our sacred place and of our people, *Montgomery* . . . our temple, *ET* . . . take away our positions, *Adams* . . . our very existence as a nation! *Phillips.*

11:49. Caiaphas is identified as the high priest. His words carried the authority of the highest office in the council and represented the religious voice for the whole nation. Caiaphas is named five times in John's Gospel, and in chapter 18 he is the chief mover of Jesus' crucifixion (verses 13,14,24,28).

This one statement unveiled the very soul of Caiaphas. He was an overbearing tyrant who was impatient, discourteous, and insulting. By his dictatorial method Caiaphas forced a decision to be made regarding Jesus' death. Those who were present were controlled by the high priest out of a motive of gain of wealth and power. They feared Jesus would cause the loss of their easy and affluent lives. Caiaphas had willing associates in his heinous deed against the world's Saviour.

49. And one of them, named Caiaphas, being the high priest that same year:

said unto them, Ye know nothing at all: You know nothing about it, *Weymouth* . . . You are utterly mistaken, *TCNT* . . . You plainly don't understand what is involved here, *Phillips* . . . You're ignorant! *Adams* . . . You don't seem to have grasped the situation at all, *JB.*

50. Nor consider that it is expedient for us: . . . nor do ye take account that, *ASV* . . . you do not understand that, *RSV.*

that one man should die for the people:

and that the whole nation perish not: . . . instead of the whole nation being destroyed, *Moffatt* . . . rather than have the whole nation ruined, *Berkeley.*

11:50. "Expedient" (*sumpherei*) means that it is to one's advantage. Jesus used the same word in 16:7. He told the disciples it was to their advantage that He should go away so that the Spirit might come in His fullness. Caiaphas spoke of the expediency of politics. He disregarded principles and justice. If Jesus was out of the way, the nation and their positions would be spared. What he said sounded good for the people, yet he really wanted to keep the people under the control of the leaders; he cared little about their welfare.

51. And this spake he not of himself: Now he did not say this of his own accord, *Montgomery* . . . It was not of his own impulse that he thus spoke, *Weymouth* . . . he did not say this on his own authority, *Williams* . . . on his own initiative, *Phillips* . . . from his own initiative, *Berkeley.*

but being high priest that year:

he prophesied that Jesus should die for that nation: . . . and his words were a prophecy, *Moffatt* . . . he uttered this prophecy

11:51. As the high priest, Caiaphas represented the people to their God. His words were spoken with his own meaning. However, God sometimes uses wicked men through whom He receives glory. Caiaphas was not speaking of the plan of God, nor did he realize the import of Christ's substitutionary sacrifice (implied by the phrase "for the people," verse 50). But God used Caiaphas' ambiguity to speak of Christ's vicarious death as expedient for the people's salvation.

Pilate's words also were significant far beyond what he intended: "Jesus of Nazareth the King of the Jews" (19:19). The Spirit used

John 11:52

51.b.**Var:** p45,p66,02A, 03B-corr,05D,019L, 030U,032W,037,038,33, Lach,Treg,Alf,Tisc,Sod

51.c.**Txt:** 038,041-corr, Steph
Var: 01ℵ,02A,03B,05D, 017K,019L,036,037, 041-org,byz.GriesLach, Treg,Alf,Tisc,We/Ho, Weis,Sod,UBS/☆

3165.21 verb 3sing indic imperf act	**3450.5** art sing masc	**2400.1** name nom masc	**594.8** verb inf pres act	**5065.1** prep
[b ἤμελλεν]	⸂c ὁ ⸃	Ἰησοῦς	ἀποθνῄσκειν	ὑπὲρ
ēmellen	*ho*	*Iēsous*	*apothnēskein*	*huper*
[idem]		Jesus	to die	for

3450.2 art gen sing	**1477.2** noun gen sing neu		**2504.1** conj	**3620.1** partic	**5065.1** prep	**3450.2** art gen sing	**1477.2** noun gen sing neu
τοῦ	ἔθνους,	52.	καὶ	οὐχ	ὑπὲρ	τοῦ	ἔθνους
tou	*ethnous*		*kai*	*ouch*	*huper*	*tou*	*ethnous*
the	nation;		and	not	for	the	nation

3303.1 adv	**233.1** conj	**2419.1** conj	**2504.1** conj	**3450.17** art pl neu	**4891.4** noun pl neu	**3450.2** art gen sing	**2296.2** noun gen sing masc
μόνον,	ἀλλ'	ἵνα	καὶ	τὰ	τέκνα	τοῦ	θεοῦ
monon	*all'*	*hina*	*kai*	*ta*	*tekna*	*tou*	*theou*
only,	but	that	also	the	children		of God

3450.17 art pl neu	**1281.6** verb acc pl neu part perf pass	**4714.9** verb 3sing subj aor act	**1519.1** prep
τὰ	διεσκορπισμένα	συναγάγῃ	εἰς
ta	*dieskorpismena*	*sunagagē*	*eis*
the	having been scattered abroad	he might gather together	into

53.a.**Txt:** 02A,017K, 019L,036,037,1,byz.Sod
Var: p45,p66,p75,01ℵ, 03B,05D,032W,038,13, Lach,Treg,Tisc,We/Ho Weis,UBS/☆

54.a.**Txt:** 02A,05D,017K, 036,037,13,byz.Gries, Lach,Tisc
Var: 01ℵ,03B,019L, 021M,033X,(038),Treg, Alf,We/Ho,Weis,Sod, UBS/☆

1518.9 num card neu		**570.2** prep gen	**1552.10** dem-pron gen sing fem	**3631.1** conj	**3450.10** art gen sing fem
ἕν.	53.	ἀπ'	ἐκείνης	οὖν	τῆς
hen		*ap'*	*ekeinēs*	*oun*	*tēs*
one.		From	that	therefore	the

2232.1 noun fem	**4674.3** verb 3pl indic aor mid	**1003.5** verb 3pl indic aor mid	**2419.1** conj
ἡμέρας	⸀ συνεβουλεύσαντο	[a☆ ἐβουλεύσαντο]	ἵνα
hēmeras	*sunebouleusanto*	*ebouleusanto*	*hina*
day	they took counsel together	[they took counsel]	that

609.9 verb 3pl subj aor act	**840.6** prs-pron acc sing masc		**2400.1** name nom masc	**3631.1** conj	**3450.5** art sing masc
ἀποκτείνωσιν	αὐτόν.	54.	⸀ Ἰησοῦς	οὖν	[a☆ Ὁ
apokteinōsin	*auton*		*Iēsous*	*oun*	*Ho*
they might kill	him.		Jesus	therefore	

3631.1 conj	**2400.1** name nom masc	**3620.2** partic	**2068.1** adv	**3629.1** adv	**3816.3** noun dat sing fem
οὖν	Ἰησοῦς]	⸀ οὐκ	ἔτι	[☆ οὐκέτι]	παῤῥησίᾳ
oun	*Iēsous*	*ouk*	*eti*	*ouketi*	*parrhēsia*
[therefore	Jesus]	no	longer	[no longer]	publicly

3906.28 verb 3sing indic imperf act	**1706.1** prep	**3450.4** art dat pl	**2428.4** name-adj dat pl masc	**233.2** conj	**562.2** verb 3sing indic aor act
περιεπάτει	ἐν	τοῖς	Ἰουδαίοις,	ἀλλὰ	ἀπῆλθεν
periepatei	*en*	*tois*	*Ioudaiois*	*alla*	*apēlthen*
walked	among	the	Jews,	but	went away

1551.1 adv	**1519.1** prep	**3450.12** art acc sing fem	**5396.4** noun acc sing fem	**1445.1** adv	**3450.10** art gen sing fem
ἐκεῖθεν	εἰς	τὴν	χώραν	ἐγγὺς	τῆς
ekeithen	*eis*	*tēn*	*chōran*	*engus*	*tēs*
from there	into	the	country	near	the

2031.1 noun gen sing fem	**1519.1** prep	**2169.1** name masc	**2978.35** verb acc sing fem part pres pass	**4032.4** noun acc sing fem	**2517.1** conj
ἐρήμου,	εἰς	Ἐφραὶμ	λεγομένην	πόλιν,	κἀκεῖ
erēmou	*eis*	*Ephraim*	*legomenēn*	*polin*	*kakei*
desert,	to	Ephraim	called	a city,	and there

Caiaphas' words as the last prophecy of the old institutional economy (see Isaiah 53:8).

from God, *Williams* . . . It was a prediction that Jesus' death, *LivB* . . . spoke as a prophet, *Norlie* . . . he was in fact inspired to say, *Phillips* . . . under a divine impulse, his words signifying, *Norton.*

11:52. "And not for that nation only" indicates that the benefits of Christ's atonement would not be limited to the nation of Israel. "For that nation" has the same preposition "for" (*huper*) as that used also in verses 51 and 50, meaning "instead of" or "in behalf of." This is the substitutionary atonement truth which Paul explains in Galatians 3:13.

This verse contains a far-reaching prophecy. The statement is founded on Isaiah 49:6-23, which indicates that Gentiles are to receive salvation through the merits of Israel's Messiah. The gathering together "into one" depicts the purpose for which Jesus came and the mediatorial work which He would accomplish. The term "gather together" is similar to gathering together into one flock of sheep as Jesus illustrated in His statement, "And they shall become one flock with one shepherd" (NASB, John 10:16; see also Ephesians 1:19; 2:13; 1 John 2:2). Even the term "scattered abroad" portrays sheep in need of a shepherd. The Good Shepherd had begun His mission of gathering His stray sheep. Soon the nations of the world would hear His voice. Those who would hear and obey would be gathered into His fold (10:4,16). For them security is assured, provisions are abundant, and personal benefits are eternal.

52. And not for that nation only, but that also he should gather together in one: . . . would not be for Israel only, *LivB* . . . but for the gathering together in one body, *Norlie* . . . but in order to unite into one body, *Weymouth.*

the children of God that were scattered abroad: . . . the widely scattered children of God, *Montgomery* . . . all the children of God scattered around the world, *LivB* . . . that were dispersed, *Murdock.*

11:53. Caiaphas had spoken. None dared nor desired to oppose him. His key argument, "it is expedient for us," was most persuasive. The leaders cared little for justice so long as their greed was gratified. They could not legally carry out their decision to kill Jesus. They must work their madness through the Roman governor who alone had authority to administer the death sentence.

The council had met to make their final decision to receive Jesus as their Messiah or to reject Him. They chose to reject Him. The term "took counsel" is a historical, factual statement. "From that day forth" brands their decision as decisive.

53. Then from that day forth they took counsel together for to put him to death: . . . they schemed to put Jesus to death, *Weymouth* . . . they were resolved, *ALBA.*

11:54. Until the Passover Jesus avoided the city and crowds of Jerusalem. He knew when His hour was to be. Earlier Jesus' brothers urged Him to go to Jerusalem so men might see His works. He replied, "My time is not yet come" (7:6,8). He, not His enemies, controlled His destiny. John tells us He stayed at the city called Ephraim. The exact location has been in dispute. The village was "near to the wilderness" between Judea and the Jordan River. The place was a fitting situation in which to stay "with his disciples."

54. Jesus therefore walked no more openly among the Jews: In consequence of this, *TCNT* . . . was not moving around among, *SEB* . . . no longer appeared in public, *Moffatt* . . . no more appeared, *Williams* . . . No longer publicly, *Fenton* . . . walked boldly, *Concordant.*

but went thence unto a country near to the wilderness: . . . the uninhabited region, *Wuest* . . . the edge of the desert, *ALBA* . . . but left that neighbourhood and went into the country bordering on the desert, *TCNT.*

John 11:55

54.b.**Txt:** p45,p66-corr, 02A,05D,017K,036,037, 038,1,13,33,byz.it.Gries, Lach,Tisc,Sod
Var: p66-org,p75,01ℵ, 03B,019L,032W,Treg Alf,We/Ho,Weis,UBS/☆

54.c.**Txt:** 02A,017K, 033X,038,041,1,13,byz. it.Lach
Var: 01ℵ,03B,05D,019L, 036,037,33,Treg,Alf, Tisc,We/Ho,Weis,Sod, UBS/☆

56.a.**Var:** 01ℵ,05D,Tisc

57.a.**Txt:** 05D,07E,036, byz.Gries
Var: 01ℵ,02A,03B, 017K,019L,037,038,it. bo.Lach,TregAlf,Tisc, We/Ho,Weis,Sod,UBS/☆

57.b.**Txt:** p66,02A,05D, 017K,019L,036,037,038, 13,33,byz.it.sa.bo.Gries, Lach
Var: 01ℵ,03B,021M, TregAlf,Tisc,We/Ho, Weis,Sod,UBS/☆

1298.5 verb 3sing indic imperf act	**3176.16** verb 3sing indic aor act	**3196.3** prep	**3450.1** art gen pl	**3073.6** noun gen pl masc
⸂☆ διέτριβεν	[ᵇ ἔμεινεν]	μετὰ	τῶν	μαθητῶν
dietriben	*emeinen*	*meta*	*tōn*	*mathētōn*
he stayed	[he remained]	with	the	disciples

840.3 prs-pron gen sing	**1498.34** verb sing indic imperf act	**1156.2** conj	**1445.1** adv	**3450.16** art sing neu	**3818.1** noun sing neu
⸂ᶜ αὐτοῦ. ⸃	**55.** ᾿Ην	δὲ	ἐγγὺς	τὸ	πάσχα
autou	*En*	*de*	*engus*	*to*	*pascha*
his.	Was	now	near	the	passover

3450.1 art gen pl	**2428.3** name-adj gen pl masc	**2504.1** conj	**303.14** verb 3pl indic aor act	**4044.7** adj nom pl masc	**1519.1** prep
τῶν	Ἰουδαίων,	καὶ	ἀνέβησαν	πολλοὶ	εἰς
tōn	*Ioudaiōn*	*kai*	*anebēsan*	*polloi*	*eis*
of the	Jews,	and	went up	many	to

2389.1 name	**1523.2** prep gen	**3450.10** art gen sing fem	**5396.1** noun fem	**4112.1** prep	**3450.2** art gen sing
Ἱεροσόλυμα	ἐκ	τῆς	χώρας	πρὸ	τοῦ
Hierosoluma	*ek*	*tēs*	*chōras*	*pro*	*tou*
Jerusalem	out of	the	country	before	the

3818.1 noun sing neu	**2419.1** conj	**47.2** verb 3pl subj aor act	**1431.8** prs-pron acc pl masc	**2195.26** verb 3pl indic imperf act
πάσχα,	ἵνα	ἁγνίσωσιν	ἑαυτούς.	**56.** ἐζήτουν
pascha	*hina*	*hagnisōsin*	*heautous*	*ezētoun*
passover,	that	they might purify	themselves.	They were seeking

3631.1 conj	**3450.6** art acc sing masc	**2400.3** name acc masc	**2504.1** conj	**2978.25** verb indic imperf act	**2978.40** verb indic act
οὖν	τὸν	Ἰησοῦν,	καὶ	⸀ ἔλεγον	[ᵃ ἔλεγαν]
oun	*ton*	*Iēsoun*	*kai*	*elegon*	*elegan*
therefore		Jesus,	and	were saying	[idem]

3196.2 prep	**238.1** prs-pron gen pl	**1706.1** prep	**3450.3** art dat sing	**2387.2** adj dat sing neu	**2449.29** verb nom pl masc part perf act
μετ'	ἀλλήλων	ἐν	τῷ	ἱερῷ	ἑστηκότες,
met'	*allēlōn*	*en*	*tō*	*hierō*	*hestēkotes*
among	one another	in	the	temple	standing,

4949.9 intr-pron sing neu	**1374.5** verb 3sing indic pres act	**5050.3** prs-pron dat 2pl	**3617.1** conj	**3620.3** partic	**3231.1** partic	**2048.8** verb 3sing subj aor act
Τί	δοκεῖ	ὑμῖν,	ὅτι	οὐ	μὴ	ἔλθῃ
Ti	*dokei*	*humin*	*hoti*	*ou*	*mē*	*elthē*
What	does it seem	to you,	that	not	not	he will come

1519.1 prep	**3450.12** art acc sing fem	**1844.4** noun acc sing fem	**1319.35** verb 3pl indic plperf act	**1156.2** conj	**2504.1** conj
εἰς	τὴν	ἑορτήν;	**57.** Δεδώκεισαν	δὲ	⸂ᵃ καὶ ⸃
eis	*tēn*	*heortēn*	*Dedōkeisan*	*de*	*kai*
to	the	feast?	Had given	now	both

3450.7 art pl masc	**744.5** noun pl masc	**2504.1** conj	**3450.7** art pl masc	**5168.4** name pl masc	**1769.3** noun acc sing fem
οἱ	ἀρχιερεῖς	καὶ	οἱ	Φαρισαῖοι	⸂☆ ἐντολὴν,
hoi	*archiereis*	*kai*	*hoi*	*Pharisaioi*	*entolēn*
the	chief priests	and	the	Pharisees	a command,

1769.7 noun acc pl fem	**2419.1** conj	**1430.1** partic	**4948.3** indef-pron nom sing	**1091.22** verb 3sing subj aor act	**4085.1** adv
[ᵇ ἐντολὰς]	ἵνα	ἐάν	τις	γνῷ	ποῦ
entolas	*hina*	*ean*	*tis*	*gnō*	*pou*
[commands]	that	if	anyone	should know	where

The special mention of the disciples doubtless means that Jesus spent this time teaching them.

into a city called Ephraim, and there continued with his disciples: . . . where he was for some time, *BB.*

11:55. The Greek word *pascha* ("passover") occurs 29 times in the New Testament and 10 times in John's Gospel. This may be the fourth Passover Feast mentioned in this Gospel (see 5:1). The connotation of the Passover's designation being "of the Jews" is as if the term indicates an estranged people.

In the Old Testament, when the nation continued in sin, God would not claim them as His people. For example, at the Exodus, the people demanded that Aaron make a golden calf to worship. God spoke of them as "thy people" and "this people." Also, in the Book of Daniel this detached relationship is indicated by the term "the God of heaven" instead of God's covenant name, LORD (*Yahweh*). Thus God no longer claimed the Passover as His. It had become merely a part of Jewish culture. The tradition of its observance no longer had God's glory as its motivation. The sacred celebration was now "the Jews' passover."

"To purify" implies that the people spoken of ("many") would not be eligible as worshipers at this feast unless they ceremonially had cleansed themselves. One could not eat the Passover lamb if he was defiled. There were many causes of ceremonial defilement, such as touching a dead animal or person, the menstrual flow, the birth of a child, etc. (See Numbers 9:10; 19:11,12.) The nature of the defilement dictated the length of time and the sacrifices necessary to become ceremonially clean.

55. And the Jews' passover was nigh at hand: The Jews' Passover was approaching, *Berkeley.*

and many went out of the country up to Jerusalem before the passover: . . . and many came from the country to Jerusalem, *Beck* . . . and many people from the countryside, *Norlie* . . . prior to the, *Fenton.*

to purify themselves: They wanted to make themselves pure, *SEB* . . . might ceremonially purify, *Wuest* . . . to make themselves clean, *BB* . . . to go through ceremonial cleansing, *Phillips* . . . in time to purify themselves, *ALBA.*

11:56. The word "they" signifies the people who came to the Feast to purify themselves. Jesus was the topic of their conversation. The people questioned each other as they looked for Him. "What think ye?" This was their inquiry. Then some answered their own question: "He will not come to the feast." The word "not" (*ou mē*) is a strong negative indicating "by no means" will He come. The people knew about the Jewish leaders' decision to kill Christ. Thus the people did not think Jesus would come to the Feast, not even for one day.

This was a normal conclusion. However, Jesus was walking according to the will of His Father, though in so doing suffering and death would be the result. The Father's will was not arbitrary, but designed to manifest His love.

56. Then sought they for Jesus: Naturally, they looked around, *Norlie* . . . They therefore searched for, *Fenton* . . . So they kept looking for Jesus, *Williams.*

and spake among themselves, as they stood in the temple: . . . and asking one another as they stood, *Beck* . . . while they stood around in the Temple, *Klingensmith* . . . as they stood in the Temple Courts, *TCNT.*

What think ye: What is your opinion? *BB* . . . What do you suppose? *Concordant* . . . What do you think? *Fenton.*

that he will not come to the feast?: He certainly will not come to the feast, will he? *Wuest* . . . Will he not come to the feast, *BB* . . . to the festival, *Norlie.*

11:57. "The chief priests and the Pharisees" were the determined murderers. They were the most religious and the most numerous. The Sadducees were as resolute in their purpose; but they, because of their doctrines, would not be expected to entertain the Christ who came. The rulers gave "commandment, that, if any man knew

57. Now both the chief priests and the Pharisees had given a commandment: . . . a Command, *Wilson* . . . had given commands, *Rotherham* . . . had given orders, *HBIE* . . . had given directions, *Concordant* . . . issued instructions, *Fenton* . . . had given commands to the effect, *Wuest.*

that, if any man knew where he were: . . . was acquainted with His whereabouts, *Fenton* . . . that if anyone should learn where He was, *Williams.*

John 12:1

1498.4 verb 3sing indic pres act	3245.2 verb 3sing subj aor act	3567.1 conj	3945.4 verb 3pl subj aor act
ἐστιν	μηνύσῃ,	ὅπως	πιάσωσιν
estin	*mēnusē*	*hopōs*	*piasōsin*
he is	he should make known,	that	they might take

840.6 prs-pron acc sing masc	3450.5 art sing masc	3631.1 conj	2400.1 name nom masc	4112.1 prep	1787.1 num card
αὐτόν.	**12:1.** Ὁ	οὖν	Ἰησοῦς	πρὸ	ἓξ
auton	*Ho*	*oun*	*Iēsous*	*pro*	*hex*
him.		Therefore	Jesus	before	six

2232.6 noun gen pl fem	3450.2 art gen sing	3818.1 noun sing neu	2048.3 verb 3sing indic aor act	1519.1 prep	956.4 name acc fem	3562.1 adv
ἡμερῶν	τοῦ	πάσχα	ἦλθεν	εἰς	Βηθανίαν,	ὅπου
hēmerōn	*tou*	*pascha*	*ēlthen*	*eis*	*Bēthanian*	*hopou*
days	the	passover	came	to	Bethany,	where

1.a.**Txt:** p66,02A,05D, 017K,036,037,038,1,33, byz.bo.Gries,Lach,Sod **Var:** 01ℵ,03B,019L, 032W,sa.Tisc,We/Ho, Weis,UBS/☆

1498.34 verb sing indic imperf act	2949.1 name nom masc	3450.5 art sing masc	2325.4 verb nom sing masc part perf act	3614.6 rel-pron acc sing masc
ἦν	Λάζαρος	⸀a ὁ	τεθνηκώς, ⸌	ὃν
ēn	*Lazaros*	*ho*	*tethnēkōs*	*hon*
was	Lazarus	the	having died,	whom

1.b.**Var:** p66,01ℵ,02A, 03B,05D,019L,041,sa. bo.Lach,Treg,Alf,Tisc, We/HoWeis,Sod,UBS/☆

1446.5 verb 3sing indic aor act	1523.2 prep gen	3361.2 adj gen pl	3450.5 art sing masc	2400.1 name nom masc
ἤγειρεν	ἐκ	νεκρῶν.	[b+ ὁ	Ἰησοῦς.]
ēgeiren	*ek*	*nekrōn*	*ho*	*Iēsous*
he raised	from among	dead.		[Jesus.]

4020.27 verb 3pl indic aor act	3631.1 conj	840.4 prs-pron dat sing	1168.1 noun sing neu	1550.1 adv	2504.1 conj
2. ἐποίησαν	οὖν	αὐτῷ	δεῖπνον	ἐκεῖ,	καὶ
epoiēsan	*oun*	*autō*	*deipnon*	*ekei*	*kai*
They made	therefore	him	a supper	there,	and

3450.9 art nom sing fem	3108.1 name fem	1241.15 verb 3sing indic imperf act	3450.5 art sing masc	1156.2 conj	2949.1 name nom masc
ἡ	Μάρθα	διηκόνει·	ὁ	δὲ	Λάζαρος
hē	*Martha*	*diēkonei*	*ho*	*de*	*Lazaros*
	Martha	served,		but	Lazarus

2.a.**Var:** 01ℵ,03B,019L, Alf,Tisc,We/Ho,Weis, UBS/☆

1518.3 num card nom masc	1498.34 verb sing indic imperf act	1523.2 prep gen	3450.1 art gen pl	4724.2 verb gen pl masc part pres
εἷς	ἦν	[a☆+ ἐκ]	τῶν	⸀ συνανακειμένων
heis	*ēn*	*ek*	*tōn*	*sunanakeimenōn*
one	was	[of]	of the	reclining with

2.b.**Txt:** 28,Steph **Var:** 01ℵ,02A,03B,05D, 017K,019L,036,037,038, byz.Gries,LachTreg,Alf, Tisc,We/Ho,Weis,Sod, UBS/☆

343.4 verb gen pl masc part pres	4713.1 prep dat	840.4 prs-pron dat sing	3450.9 art nom sing fem	3631.1 conj
[b☆ ἀνακειμένων	σὺν]	αὐτῷ.	**3.** Ἡ	οὖν
anakeimenōn	*sun*	*autō*	*Hē*	*oun*
[idem]		him.		Therefore

3109.1 name nom fem	3110.1 name fem	2956.29 verb nom sing fem part aor act	3020.1 noun acc sing fem	3326.2 noun gen sing neu
⸀ Μαρία	[☆ Μαριὰμ]	λαβοῦσα	λίτραν	μύρου
Maria	*Mariam*	*labousa*	*litran*	*murou*
Mary	[idem]	having taken	a pound	of ointment

3350.1 noun gen sing fem	3962.1 adj gen sing fem	4046.2 adj gen sing fem	216.2 verb 3sing indic aor act	3450.8 art acc pl masc	4087.7 noun acc pl masc
νάρδου	πιστικῆς	πολυτίμου,	ἤλειψεν	τοὺς	πόδας
nardou	*pistikēs*	*polutimou*	*ēleipsen*	*tous*	*podas*
of nard	pure	of great price,	anointed	the	feet

where he were, he should show it." This is the reason the pilgrims at the temple did not think Jesus would come to the Passover. The leaders were seeking to kill Jesus by "legal" means, not by assassination as was carried out by Jewish Zealots so often. It is amazing that their Messiah would ride triumphantly into Jerusalem as their promised Messiah, providing them with evidence from prophecy that He was indeed their Messiah.

he should shew it: . . . he should be divulging it, *Concordant* . . . he should give information, *TCNT* . . . he should report it, *Fenton* . . . he must tell us, *SEB* . . . should let them know, *RSV.*

that they might take him: . . . that they might seize him, *HBIE* . . . so that they might get hold of Him, *Berkeley* . . . so that they could arrest him, *Phillips.*

12:1. Just 6 days before the Passover the Master left the seclusion of Ephraim to go to Jerusalem (see 11:54). Blaney observed, "How He had needed those days of quiet and prayer! How important they were in preparation for the ordeal of the succeeding week! Not as one walking to his death, neither as one who might be surprised by some unexpected turn of events, but with the certainty of one who has considered all the possibilities and risks and who moves ahead in the knowledge of a task to be done and a destiny to be fulfilled" (Blaney, *Wesleyan Bible Commentary,* 4:430).

This Passover was the Lord's fourth and last of His ministry. It was also the last Passover recognized by God under the Old Testament economy. At this point Jesus was within a few days of the Cross. John supplements Matthew's account (Matthew 26:6-13) and Mark's account (Mark 14:3-9) of the events at Bethany. Most probably Jesus and His disciples arrived at Bethany on Friday afternoon before the regular Jewish Sabbath on Saturday. The date was early spring, April A.D. 30. The connection of Lazarus with Bethany identifies this Bethany as the one in which Jesus performed the miracle only a short time before.

1. Then Jesus six days before the passover came to Bethany: Jesus, however, six days prior to, *Fenton.*

where Lazarus was which had been dead, whom he raised from the dead: . . . where Lazarus...was living, *TCNT* . . . the man who had died, *Norlie.*

12:2. According to Matthew, the place was the house of Simon the leper (Matthew 26:6).

John reports that Martha served. The sisters and Lazarus may have been relatives of Simon. Martha took her characteristic way of showing her love for God as did Mary. Lazarus was a guest of honor, perhaps in celebration of having been raised from the dead.

In Bethany Jesus' friends defied the command that "if any man knew where he were, he should show it, that they might take him" (11:57). At great risk to themselves "they made him a supper." With tension running so high, it was a bold thing to schedule a banquet where Jesus was the chief guest of honor, but true love wins over fear in doing what pleases the Lord.

2. There they made him a supper: . . . in honor of Jesus, *Williams* . . . So they gave a dinner for him there, *Montgomery* . . . a meal at eventide, *Wuest.*

and Martha served: but Lazarus was one of them that sat at the table with him: . . . and Martha waited tables, *Berkeley* . . . Martha superintended, *Fenton* . . . waited on the party, *Phillips* . . . Lazarus reclined with him, *ET* . . . and Lazarus was one of the guests, *Murdock.*

12:3. Mary's gratitude was so great that she spared no expense to express it. The King James Version indicates the substance Mary used to anoint Jesus was "ointment of spikenard, very costly." It was not a mixture of an adulterated preparation. John states that

3. Then took Mary a pound of ointment of spikenard, very costly: . . . took a whole pint, *TEV* . . . taking a full pound of genuine and very costly perfume, *ALBA* . . . pure nard, very precious, *ASV* . . . choice spikenard perfume of great value, *TCNT* . . . a pound of perfumed oil, *BB* . . . perfecte and precious, *Tyndale* . . . a Pound of Balsam, *Wilson* . . . of pure oil of spikenard, *Norton* . . . or veritable nard attar, *Concordant* . . . of the balsam of spikenard, *Campbell* . . . that was very expensive, *AmpB* . . . which was very valuable, *Fenton.*

3450.2 art gen sing	2400.2 name masc	2504.1 conj	1578.2 verb 3sing indic aor act	3450.14 art dat pl fem	2336.5 noun dat pl fem
τοῦ	Ἰησοῦ,	καὶ	ἐξέμαξεν	ταῖς	θριξὶν
tou	*Iēsou*	*kai*	*exemaxen*	*tais*	*thrixin*
	of Jesus,	and	wiped	with the	hair

840.10 prs-pron gen sing fem	3450.8 art acc pl masc	4087.7 noun acc pl masc	840.3 prs-pron gen sing	3450.9 art nom sing fem	1156.2 conj	3477.2 noun nom sing fem
αὐτῆς	τοὺς	πόδας	αὐτοῦ·	ἡ	δὲ	οἰκία
autēs	*tous*	*podas*	*autou*	*hē*	*de*	*oikia*
her	the	feet	his;	the	and	house

3997.20 verb 3sing indic aor pass	1523.2 prep gen	3450.10 art gen sing fem	3606.2 noun gen sing fem	3450.2 art gen sing	3326.2 noun gen sing neu
ἐπληρώθη	ἐκ	τῆς	ὀσμῆς	τοῦ	μύρου.
eplērōthē	*ek*	*tēs*	*osmēs*	*tou*	*murou*
was filled	with	the	odor	of the	ointment.

4.a.**Txt:** 02A,05D,017K,026Q,036,037,038,1,13,byz.Lach,Sod
Var: p66,01ℵ,03B,032W,bo.Tisc,We/Ho,Weis,UBS/☆

2978.5 verb 3sing indic pres act	3631.1 conj	1156.2 conj	1518.3 num card nom masc	1523.2 prep gen	3450.1 art gen pl
4. λέγει	ʼ οὖν	[a☆ δὲ]	ʼ εἷς	ἐκ	τῶν
legei	*oun*	*de*	*heis*	*ek*	*tōn*
Says	therefore	[and]	one	of	the

3073.6 noun gen pl masc	840.3 prs-pron gen sing	2430.1 name nom masc	4468.2 name gen masc	2442.1 name nom masc
μαθητῶν	αὐτοῦ,	Ἰούδας,	Σίμωνος	Ἰσκαριώτης,
mathētōn	*autou*	*Ioudas*	*Simōnos*	*Iskariōtēs*
disciples	his,	Judas,	Simon's	Iscariot,

4.b.**Txt:** 02A,(017),026Q,036,037,038,13,byz.Lach
Var: p66,p75,03B,019L,032W,33,Treg,We/Ho Weis,UBS/☆

2430.1 name nom masc	3450.5 art sing masc	2442.1 name nom masc	1518.3 num card nom masc	3450.1 art gen pl
[b☆ Ἰούδας	ὁ	Ἰσκαριώτης	εἷς	τῶν
Ioudas	*ho*	*Iskariōtēs*	*heis*	*tōn*
[Judas		Iscariot	one	of the

3073.6 noun gen pl masc	840.3 prs-pron gen sing	3450.5 art sing masc	3165.12 verb nom sing masc part pres act	840.6 prs-pron acc sing masc
μαθητῶν	αὐτοῦ,]	ὁ	μέλλων	αὐτὸν
mathētōn	*autou*	*ho*	*mellōn*	*auton*
disciples	his,]	the	being about	him

3722.7 verb inf pres act	1296.1 adv	1217.2 prep	4949.9 intr-pron sing neu	3642.17 dem-pron sing neu	3450.16 art sing neu
παραδιδόναι,	5. ʼ Διατί	[☆ Διὰ	τί]	τοῦτο	τὸ
paradidonai	*Diati*	*Dia*	*ti*	*touto*	*to*
to deliver up,	Why	[idem]		this	the

3326.1 noun sing neu	3620.2 partic	3958.4 verb 3sing indic aor pass	4986.1 num card gen	1214.3 noun gen pl neu
μύρον	οὐκ	ἐπράθη	τριακοσίων	δηναρίων,
muron	*ouk*	*eprathē*	*triakosiōn*	*dēnariōn*
ointment	not	was sold	for three hundred	denarii,

2504.1 conj	1319.44 verb 3sing indic aor pass	4292.6 adj dat pl masc	1500.5 verb 3sing indic aor act	1156.2 conj	3642.17 dem-pron sing neu
καὶ	ἐδόθη	πτωχοῖς;	6. Εἶπεν	δὲ	τοῦτο,
kai	*edothē*	*ptōchois*	*Eipen*	*de*	*touto*
and	given	to poor?	He said	but	this,

3620.1 partic	3617.1 conj	3875.1 prep	3450.1 art gen pl	4292.5 adj gen pl masc	3169.3 verb 3sing indic imperf act	840.4 prs-pron dat sing
οὐχ	ὅτι	περὶ	τῶν	πτωχῶν	ἔμελεν	αὐτῷ,
ouch	*hoti*	*peri*	*tōn*	*ptōchōn*	*emelen*	*autō*
not	that	for	the	poor	was caring	he,

the quantity was "a pound." Whether Mary had heard of a previous anointing of Jesus by a woman of Capernaum (Luke 7:37), we have no way of knowing. Mary's appreciation before her brother's resurrection was great, but now she felt she must express her overflowing love to Christ.

She anointed His feet. Matthew and Mark say she anointed Jesus' head. John's Gospel takes for granted the reader knows the other two Gospels and thus supplements them by including the anointing of Jesus' feet. When guests entered a banquet, servants customarily washed the guest's feet and dried them with towels. Thus Mary's act went far beyond the service of a slave. The deed was done in humility and with great personal loss. Mary's use of her hair as a towel emphasized her extreme submissiveness; plus, it was His feet that she dried with the hair of her head. A woman's hair was a sign of her glory as the apostle Paul states in 1 Corinthians 11:15. By her act she abandoned her glory to Him who would soon die for her. To be at His feet was an act of submission, but Mary also exhibited humility in her devotion to Jesus.

"The house was filled with the odor of the ointment" is mentioned only by John, but the other two Gospels give us Jesus' words that the deed would be told as "a memorial of her" wherever the gospel was preached. As the fragrance of the ointment filled the house, so her devotion to Christ inspires all Christians to a life of humble service.

12:4. John alone records the name of the one who criticized Mary for her deed. No matter how good one's motive or the blessed results of one's actions, criticism and opposition may come. Censure did not proceed solely from people like Judas Iscariot. "His disciples" were indignant (Matthew 26:8); "some" were angry (Mark 14:4). John indicates it was Judas who stirred the others to criticize Mary.

12:5. Judas asked, "Why?" and Jesus answered the "Why?" in verses 7 and 8. The monetary value of the ointment was equal to 11 months' wages. One pence was the amount paid for an ordinary laborer for 1 day's work. This was a considerable sum. "And given to the poor" expresses Judas' chief argument against the monetary loss. According to John, Judas was the treasurer for the disciples (13:26,29), and he may have had the authority to distribute to the poor.

12:6. What Judas said would have made good sense under usual circumstances; however, this was not an ordinary situation. John relates the real motive behind Judas' criticism. The negative com-

and anointed the feet of Jesus, and wiped his feet with her hair: . . . and bathed the feet, *Fenton* . . . spread it on the feet of Jesus, rubbed it in, *Wuest.*

and the house was filled with the odour of the ointment: . . . the fragrance of the perfume, *Montgomery, Weymouth* . . . the perfume of the essence, *Fenton* . . . with the scent of, *ALBA* . . . The sweet smell, *TEV* . . . with the aroma, *Wuest.*

4. Then saith one of his disciples, Judas Iscariot, Simon's son, which should betray him: Judas the Traitor, *Torrey* . . . the one who would betray Him, *LivB* . . . One of Jesus' followers was ready to turn against Jesus, *SEB* . . . who was about to betray Him, *Adams, Montgomery* . . . burst out, *Phillips* . . . then demanded, *ET.*

5. Why was not this ointment sold for three hundred pence, and given to the poor?: Why wasn't this perfume sold, *Beck* . . . and the proceeds, *Montgomery* . . . given to the destitute? *Rotherham.*

6. This he said, not that he cared for the poor: . . . not that for the destitute, *Rotherham.*

233.1 conj	3617.1 conj	2785.1 noun nom sing masc	1498.34 verb sing indic imperf act	2504.1 conj	3450.16 art sing neu
ἀλλ'	ὅτι	κλέπτης	ἦν,	καὶ	τὸ
all'	*hoti*	*kleptēs*	*ēn*	*kai*	*to*
but	because	a thief	he was,	and	the

6.a.**Txt:** 02A,017K,036, 037,byz.Gries,Lach **Var:** 01ℵ,03B,05D,019L, 026Q,038,33,sa.bo.Treg, Alf,Tisc,We/Ho,Weis, Sod,UBS/⋆

1095.1 noun acc sing neu	2174.44 verb 3sing indic imperf act	2504.1 conj	2174.17 verb nom sing masc part pres act	3450.17 art pl neu
γλωσσόκομον	ʼ εἶχεν,	καὶ	[a⋆ ἔχων]	τὰ
glōssokomon	*eichen*	*kai*	*echōn*	*ta*
money box	had,	and	[having]	what

900.29 verb acc pl neu part pres pass	934.16 verb 3sing indic imperf act	1500.5 verb 3sing indic aor act	3631.1 conj	3450.5 art sing masc
βαλλόμενα	ἐβάσταζεν.	7. εἶπεν	οὖν	ὁ
ballomena	*ebastazen*	*eipen*	*oun*	*ho*
was put into	carried.	Said	therefore	

7.a.**Var:** 01ℵ,03B,05D, 017K,019L,026Q,033X, 038,33,it.sa.bo.Lach, Treg,Alf,Word,Tisc, We/Ho,WeisSod,UBS/⋆

2400.1 name nom masc	856.17 verb 2sing impr aor act	840.12 prs-pron acc sing fem	2419.1 conj	1519.1 prep	3450.12 art acc sing fem
Ἰησοῦς,	Ἄφες	αὐτήν·	[a⋆+ ἵνα]	εἰς	τὴν
Iēsous	*Aphes*	*autēn*	*hina*	*eis*	*tēn*
Jesus,	Let alone	her:	[that]	for	the

2232.4 noun acc sing fem	3450.2 art gen sing	1764.1 noun gen sing masc	1466.2 prs-pron gen 1sing	4931.24 verb 3sing indic perf act
ἡμέραν	τοῦ	ἐνταφιασμοῦ	μου	ʼ τετήρηκεν
hēmeran	*tou*	*entaphiasmou*	*mou*	*tetērēken*
day	of the	burial	my	has she kept

7.b.**Txt:** 02A,036,037,1, 13,byz. **Var:** 01ℵ,03B,05D, 017K,019L,026Q,033X, 038,33,it.sa.bo.Lach Treg,Alf,Word,Tisc, We/Ho,Weis,Sod,UBS/⋆

4931.16 verb 3sing subj aor act	840.15 prs-pron sing neu	3450.8 art acc pl masc	4292.7 adj acc pl masc	1056.1 conj
[b⋆ τηρήσῃ]	αὐτό·	8. τοὺς	πτωχοὺς	γὰρ
tērēsē	*auto*	*tous*	*ptōchous*	*gar*
[she may keep]	it:	the	poor	for

3704.1 adv	2174.2 verb 2pl pres act	3196.1 prep	1431.2 prs-pron gen pl	1466.7 prs-pron acc 1sing	1156.2 conj	3620.3 partic
πάντοτε	ἔχετε	μεθ'	ἑαυτῶν,	ἐμὲ	δὲ	οὐ
pantote	*echete*	*meth'*	*heautōn*	*eme*	*de*	*ou*
always	you have	with	yourselves,	me	but	not

9.a.**Var:** 01ℵ-org, 03B-org,019L,Tisc, We/Ho,Sod,UBS/⋆

3704.1 adv	2174.2 verb 2pl pres act	1091.17 verb 3sing indic aor act	3631.1 conj	3450.5 art sing masc
πάντοτε	ἔχετε.	9. Ἔγνω	οὖν	[a⋆+ ὁ]
pantote	*echete*	*Egnō*	*oun*	*ho*
always	you have.	Knew	therefore	[the]

3657.1 noun nom sing masc	4044.5 adj nom sing masc	1523.2 prep gen	3450.1 art gen pl	2428.3 name-adj gen pl masc	3617.1 conj	1550.1 adv
ὄχλος	πολὺς	ἐκ	τῶν	Ἰουδαίων	ὅτι	ἐκεῖ
ochlos	*polus*	*ek*	*tōn*	*Ioudaiōn*	*hoti*	*ekei*
crowd	great	of	the	Jews	that	there

1498.4 verb 3sing indic pres act	2504.1 conj	2048.1 verb indic aor act	3620.3 partic	1217.2 prep	3450.6 art acc sing masc
ἐστιν,	καὶ	ἦλθον,	οὐ	διὰ	τὸν
estin	*kai*	*ēlthon*	*ou*	*dia*	*ton*
he is;	and	they came,	not	because of	

2400.3 name acc masc	3303.1 adv	233.1 conj	2419.1 conj	2504.1 conj	3450.6 art acc sing masc	2949.2 name acc masc
Ἰησοῦν	μόνον,	ἀλλ'	ἵνα	καὶ	τὸν	Λάζαρον
Iēsoun	*monon*	*all'*	*hina*	*kai*	*ton*	*Lazaron*
Jesus	only,	but	that	also		Lazarus

ment is given first: "Not that he cared for the poor." Second, John relates the positive aspect of his censure: "but because he was a thief." The word "thief" (*kleptēs*) signifies one who steals in secret, as opposed to one who robs in a bold and violent manner.

In whatever manner, stealing is repulsive. The eighth commandment prohibits it (Exodus 20:15). Paul wrote, "Let him that stole steal no more" (Ephesians 4:28). However, to steal from a church group as Judas did seems worse than from others.

"And had the bag." Jesus and His disciples had a common treasury from which their needs were met and distribution was made to the poor. The word *glōssokomon* indicates a case used in holding pieces for musical instruments; thus it could mean either a box or a bag.

but because he was a thief, and had the bag: . . . a pilferer, *Wuest* . . . he had charge of the money-bag, *Berkeley* . . . having charge of the money-box, *Norlie* . . . being in charge of the purse, *TCNT* . . . had the treasure-chest, *Sawyer.*

and bare what was put therein: . . . used to help himself from the contents, *Phillips* . . . took for himself what was put into it, *BB* . . . pilfered the collections, *Berkeley* . . . what things were deposited in it, *Wilson* . . . take what was put into it, *Norlie* . . . he was in the habit of taking what was put into it, *Williams.*

12:7. Judas' rebuke was spoken to Mary, but Jesus defended her by saying, "Let her alone: against the day of my burying hath she kept this." It was not for Judas or the disciples (Matthew 26:8-10) to reproach Mary. Jesus was the recipient of the honor. It was His right to approve or disapprove of her devotion. Too often a critical spirit works through the conduct of disciples. Mary's labor of love and personal sacrifice brought harsh, pain-inflicting treatment from the disciples, but Jesus brought comfort to her devoted soul. Jesus saw her innermost motive. "My burying" indicates that Mary sensed Jesus would soon give His life, and she poured out this treasured ointment as a tribute to His honor.

7. Then said Jesus, Let her alone: Jesus replied to this outburst, *Phillips.*

against the day of my burying hath she kept this: Let her do it for the day of My burial, *Beck* . . . She did it in preparation for My burial, *LivB* . . . my funeral, *Williams* . . . for the day of my embalming, *Young.*

8. For the poor always ye have with you; but me ye have not always: . . . but you will not always have Me, *Norlie.*

12:8. There is always opportunity to help the poor. To share with others is an unending task on this side of heaven. "Not always" points to a peculiar opportunity which but a few had to honor Him in such a manner while He was in the flesh. Mary's devoted soul seized the occasion just in time.

9. Much people of the Jews therefore knew that he was there: The masses of the Judeans, *Fenton* . . . Then the common people among, *Wuest.*

and they came not for Jesus' sake only: . . . flocked to the place, *Fenton* . . . not merely to see Jesus, *Norlie.*

12:9. This narrative (verses 2-8) helps to prepare the reader for Judas' betrayal. The passage also reveals that the raising of Lazarus produced gratitude in the hearts of many, but also further hostility from Jesus' enemies. A great multitude of "the Jews" were eager to see Jesus and Lazarus because of his resurrection. Jesus, by His bold appearances and messianic miracles, convinced many of His enemies.

That they came to "see Lazarus" indicates the natural curiosity of people. They surely had many questions to ask Lazarus about his 4-day experience of death, but John's Gospel does not satisfy our inquisitive minds. Rather, it continues with the theme of the

John 12:10

1481.13 verb 3pl subj aor act	3614.6 rel-pron acc sing masc	1446.5 verb 3sing indic aor act	1523.2 prep gen	3361.2 adj gen pl
ἴδωσιν	ὃν	ἤγειρεν	ἐκ	νεκρῶν.
idōsin	*hon*	*ēgeiren*	*ek*	*nekrōn*
they might see	whom	he raised	from among	dead.

10. 1003.5 verb 3pl indic aor mid	1156.2 conj	3450.7 art pl masc	744.5 noun pl masc	2419.1 conj	2504.1 conj
10. ἐβουλεύσαντο	δὲ	οἱ	ἀρχιερεῖς	ἵνα	καὶ
ebouleusanto	*de*	*hoi*	*archiereis*	*hina*	*kai*
Took counsel	but	the	chief priests	that	also

3450.6 art acc sing masc	2949.2 name acc masc	609.9 verb 3pl subj aor act	11. 3617.1 conj	4044.7 adj nom pl masc
τὸν	Λάζαρον	ἀποκτείνωσιν,	11. ὅτι	πολλοὶ
ton	*Lazaron*	*apokteinōsin*	*hoti*	*polloi*
	Lazarus	they might kill,	because	many

1217.1 prep	840.6 prs-pron acc sing masc	5055.11 verb 3pl indic imperf act	3450.1 art gen pl	2428.3 name-adj gen pl masc
δι'	αὐτὸν	ὑπῆγον	τῶν	Ἰουδαίων
di'	*auton*	*hupēgon*	*tōn*	*Ioudaiōn*
by reason of	him	were going away	of the	Jews

2504.1 conj	3961.55 verb 3pl indic imperf act	1519.1 prep	3450.6 art acc sing masc	2400.3 name acc masc	12. 3450.11 art dat sing fem
καὶ	ἐπίστευον	εἰς	τὸν	Ἰησοῦν.	12. Τῇ
kai	*episteuon*	*eis*	*ton*	*Iēsoun*	*Tē*
and	were believing	on		Jesus.	On the

12.a.**Var:** p66,03B,019L, 038,13,We/HoWeis, UBS/☆

1872.1 adv	3450.5 art sing masc	3657.1 noun nom sing masc	4044.5 adj nom sing masc	3450.5 art sing masc
ἐπαύριον	[a☆+ ὁ]	ὄχλος	πολὺς	ὁ
epaurion	*ho*	*ochlos*	*polus*	*ho*
morrow	[the]	crowd	great	the

2048.13 verb nom sing masc part aor act	1519.1 prep	3450.12 art acc sing fem	1844.4 noun acc sing fem	189.32 verb nom pl masc part aor act
ἐλθὼν	εἰς	τὴν	ἑορτήν,	ἀκούσαντες
elthōn	*eis*	*tēn*	*heortēn*	*akousantes*
having come	to	the	feast,	having heard

12.b.**Txt:** p66,p75,03B, 036,038,13,Steph,Sod
Var: 01א,02A,05D, 017K,019L,026Q,037, byz.Gries,Lach,Treg,Alf Word,Tisc,We/Ho,Weis, UBS/☆

3617.1 conj	2048.34 verb 3sing indic pres	3450.5 art sing masc	2400.1 name nom masc	1519.1 prep	2389.1 name
ὅτι	ἔρχεται	⌜b ὁ ⌝	Ἰησοῦς	εἰς	Ἱεροσόλυμα,
hoti	*erchetai*	*ho*	*Iēsous*	*eis*	*Hierosoluma*
that	is coming		Jesus	into	Jerusalem,

13. 2956.12 verb indic aor act	3450.17 art pl neu	896.1 noun acc pl neu	3450.1 art gen pl	5241.2 noun gen pl masc	2504.1 conj
13. ἔλαβον	τὰ	βαΐα	τῶν	φοινίκων	καὶ
elabon	*ta*	*baia*	*tōn*	*phoinikōn*	*kai*
took	the	branches	of the	palms	and

1814.1 verb indic aor act	1519.1 prep	5060.1 noun acc sing fem	840.4 prs-pron dat sing	2504.1 conj	2869.18 verb 3pl indic imperf act
ἐξῆλθον	εἰς	ὑπάντησιν	αὐτῷ,	καὶ	⌜ ἔκραζον,
exēlthon	*eis*	*hupantēsin*	*autō*	*kai*	*ekrazon*
went out	to	meet	him,	and	were crying,

13.a.**Txt:** 02A,017K,036, 037,038,1,13,byz.Gries, Word
Var: p75,01א,03B-corr, 05D,019L,026Q,032W, Lach,Treg,Alf,Tisc, We/Ho,Weis,Sod,UBS/☆

2878.6 verb 3pl indic imperf act	5446.1 partic	2108.15 verb nom sing masc part perf pass	3450.5 art sing masc
[a☆ ἐκραύγαζον,]	Ὡσαννά,	εὐλογημένος	ὁ
ekraugazon	*Hōsanna*	*eulogēmenos*	*ho*
[idem]	Hosanna,	blessed	the

Book's message, namely, the Son of God who came to bring eternal life to all who would believe.

but that they might see Lazarus also, whom he had raised from the dead: . . . whom He had brought back to life, *Weymouth.*

12:10. "The chief priests" who took counsel together were probably priests appointed over the 24 orders of priests and were members of the Sanhedrin. They did not form the entire Council but would have had a powerful voice in Council matters. Some scholars think they were Sadducees, and if so, they would have reason to destroy Lazarus. The Sadducees did not believe in miracles or in the resurrection of the dead. Lazarus was living evidence of both.

10. But the chief priests consulted that they might put Lazarus also to death: . . . made plans to kill Lazarus, too, *Berkeley* . . . took counsel to kill, *Wuest* . . . consulted together, *Weymouth* . . . plotted to murder, *Fenton* . . . plotted to kill Lazarus too, *Montgomery* . . . about killing even Lazarus, *Murdock* . . . to destroy Lazarus as well, *ALBA.*

12:11. "Because that by reason of him," makes the reason emphatic for the chief priests' desire to kill Lazarus as well as Christ.

"Many of the Jews went away" describes the continued process of the action. "Went away" and "believing" are, in the Greek, imperfect tense verbs. The latter verb is dependent on the former. Therefore, Jesus was winning some of His enemies, and the enemies were losing their fellow supporters.

How interesting to speculate! Had the chief priests succeeded in putting Lazarus to death, would Jesus have raised him a second time? The foolish Jews did not stop to consider He could do it again. They did think of putting both Jesus and Lazarus to death, yet did not consider His promise of 2:19.

11. Because that by reason of him many of the Jews went away, and believed on Jesus: . . . he was the reason many Jews were going over to Jesus, *Beck* . . . on his account many Jews were rejecting them and believing in, *TEV* . . . were being converted, *ALBA* . . . on his account, *Murdock* . . . because it was owing to him, *TCNT.*

12:12. The triumphant entry of Jesus into Jerusalem was an important public presentation of Jesus as the nation's Messiah. It was an unexpected manifestation that drew attention to the greatest multitudes during Jesus' ministry. John presents the event only briefly, and Luke gives the narrative at greatest length (Luke 19:29-44). Matthew 21:1-11 and Mark 11:1-11 describe the details vividly.

This great multitude should be distinguished from the group in verse 9. In this verse the multitude is the same group of pilgrims of 11:56 who asked, "What think ye, that he will not come to the feast?" But He did come and with the most notable manifestation of His glory.

12. On the next day much people that were come to the feast: On the following day, *Fenton* . . . a great multitude that had come, *HBIE* . . . a great crowd of those who were there for the festival, *Norlie* . . . an immense body of people, *Berkeley* . . . the big crowd who had come up for the Passover, *Montgomery.*

when they heard that Jesus was coming to Jerusalem: Next day it came to the ears of the multitude, *ALBA* . . . that Jesus was coming into Jerusalem, *Phillips.*

12:13. They "took branches of palm trees." This gives the name of Palm Sunday to the Sunday before Easter. It was only a few days before the Crucifixion and a week before His resurrection. The palm branches were symbolic of rejoicing and triumph (Leviticus 23:40; Revelation 7:9). The people honored and worshiped Jesus because of the miracles they had seen and especially for the raising of Lazarus.

13. Took branches of palm trees, and went forth to meet him: . . . plucked palm branches, *ET.*

and cried, Hosanna: . . . shouting all the while, *Berkeley* . . . shouting, God save him! *Phillips* . . . and kept on shouting: Blessings on Him! *Williams* . . . Send help! *Klingensmith* . . . Our Savior! *Beck* . . . Praise to God! *ALBA.*

John 12:14

13.b.**Var:** 01ℵ,03B,019L, 026Q,032W,bo.Treg,Alf, Tisc,We/Ho,Weis,Sod, UBS/☆

2048.44 verb nom sing masc part pres	**1706.1** prep	**3549.4** noun dat sing neu	**2935.2** noun gen sing masc		**2504.1** conj	**3450.5** art sing masc
ἐρχόμενος	ἐν	ὀνόματι	κυρίου,	[b☆+	καὶ]	ὁ
erchomenos	*en*	*onomati*	*kuriou*		*kai*	*ho*
coming	in	name	of Lord,		[and]	the

928.1 noun nom sing masc	**3450.2** art gen sing	**2447.1** name masc	**2128.17** verb nom sing masc part aor act	**1156.2** conj	**3450.5** art sing masc
βασιλεὺς	τοῦ	Ἰσραήλ.	**14.** Εὑρὼν	δὲ	ὁ
basileus	*tou*	*Israēl*	*Heurōn*	*de*	*ho*
king		of Israel.	Having found	and	

2400.1 name nom masc	**3541.1** noun acc sing neu	**2495.3** verb 3sing indic aor act	**1894.2** prep	**840.15** prs-pron sing neu	**2503.1** conj
Ἰησοῦς	ὀνάριον	ἐκάθισεν	ἐπ’	αὐτό,	καθώς
Iēsous	*onarion*	*ekathisen*	*ep'*	*auto*	*kathōs*
Jesus	a young ass	sat	upon	it,	as

1498.4 verb 3sing indic pres act	**1119.29** verb sing neu part perf pass	**3231.1** partic	**5236.5** verb 2sing impr pres	**2341.1** noun nom sing fem
ἐστιν	γεγραμμένον,	**15.** Μὴ	φοβοῦ,	⸂ θυγάτηρ
estin	*gegrammenon*	*Mē*	*phobou*	*thugatēr*
it is	written,	Not	fear,	daughter

15.a.**Txt:** 01ℵ,07E,021M, 030U,036,038,1,13,33, byz.Gries,Sod
Var: p66,02A,03B-org, 05D,017K,019L,026Q, 032W,037,021M8,Lach Treg,Alf,Word,Tisc, We/Ho,Weis,UBS/☆

2341.1 noun nom sing fem	**4477.1** name fem	**1481.20** verb 2sing impr aor mid	**3450.5** art sing masc	**928.1** noun nom sing masc
[a☆ θυγάτηρ]	Σιών·	ἰδοὺ,	ὁ	βασιλεύς
thugatēr	*Siōn*	*idou*	*ho*	*basileus*
[idem]	of Zion:	behold,	the	king

4622.2 prs-pron gen 2sing	**2048.34** verb 3sing indic pres	**2493.6** verb nom sing masc part pres	**1894.3** prep	**4311.1** noun acc sing masc	**3551.2** noun gen sing
σου	ἔρχεται,	καθήμενος	ἐπὶ	πῶλον	ὄνου.
sou	*erchetai*	*kathēmenos*	*epi*	*pōlon*	*onou*
your	comes,	sitting	on	a colt	of an ass.

16.a.**Txt:** 02A,05D,017K, 036,037,1,13,byz.bo. Lach
Var: 01ℵ,03B,019L, 026Q,038,sa.Treg,Alf Tisc,We/Ho,Weis,Sod, UBS/☆

3642.18 dem-pron pl neu	**1156.2** conj	**3620.2** partic	**1091.18** verb 3pl indic aor act	**3450.7** art pl masc	**3073.5** noun nom pl masc
16. ταῦτα	⸂a δὲ ⸃	οὐκ	ἔγνωσαν	⸂ οἱ	μαθηταὶ
tauta	*de*	*ouk*	*egnōsan*	*hoi*	*mathētai*
These things	now	not	knew	the	disciples

840.3 prs-pron gen sing	**840.3** prs-pron gen sing	**3450.7** art pl masc	**3073.5** noun nom pl masc	**3450.16** art sing neu
αὐτοῦ	[☆ αὐτοῦ	οἱ	μαθηταὶ]	τὸ
autou	*autou*	*hoi*	*mathētai*	*to*
his	[his	the	disciples]	the

16.b.**Txt:** p66-corr,05D, 032W,038,13,33,1241, Steph,Lach
Var: 01ℵ,02A,03B, 017K,019L,026Q,036, 037,byz.TregAlf,Word, Tisc,We/Ho,Weis,Sod, UBS/☆

4270.1 adv	**233.1** conj	**3616.1** conj	**1386.22** verb 3sing indic aor pass	**3450.5** art sing masc	**2400.1** name nom masc
πρῶτον,	ἀλλ’	ὅτε	ἐδοξάσθη	⸂b ὁ ⸃	Ἰησοῦς
prōton	*all'*	*hote*	*edoxasthē*	*ho*	*Iēsous*
first,	but	when	was glorified		Jesus

4966.1 adv	**3279.4** verb 3pl indic aor pass	**3617.1** conj	**3642.18** dem-pron pl neu	**1498.34** verb sing indic imperf act	**1894.2** prep
τότε	ἐμνήσθησαν	ὅτι	ταῦτα	ἦν	ἐπ’
tote	*emnēsthēsan*	*hoti*	*tauta*	*ēn*	*ep'*
then	they remembered	that	these things	were	of

840.4 prs-pron dat sing	**1119.31** verb acc pl neu part perf	**2504.1** conj	**3642.18** dem-pron pl neu	**4020.27** verb 3pl indic aor act
αὐτῷ	γεγραμμένα,	καὶ	ταῦτα	ἐποίησαν
autō	*gegrammena*	*kai*	*tauta*	*epoiēsan*
him	having been written,	and	these things	they did

"Hosanna!" This is the Greek abbreviation (*hōsanna*) of two Hebrew words meaning "save now." This and the following words are taken from Psalm 118:25,26. "Blessed is He who comes in the name of the Lord, even the King of Israel" (NASB). After Jesus had miraculously fed the five thousand, the people were attempting to force Him to be their king. Many were convinced that the time had come (Zechariah 9:9).

Blessed is the King of Israel that cometh in the name of the Lord: Blessings on him, *ALBA* . . . who in times past has been eulogized, be regarded, *Wuest* . . . Israel's King, *Campbell.*

12:14. John does not give the particulars as the other Gospels do. The donkey was used by persons of highest rank according to Judges 5:10 and 10:4. The use of a donkey in this instance was appropriate because of Zechariah's prophecy (Zechariah 9:9). At Jesus' second coming He will ride a white horse (Revelation 19:11), for the horse is symbolic of war and victory in battle. It was not then His time to ride the horse of victory and sit on the throne of David. He had presented His credentials as Messiah. It was their opportunity to welcome their messianic King.

14. And Jesus, when he had found a young ass, sat thereon; as it is written: . . . found a young donkey and mounted it, *Williams* . . . a young burro, *Klingensmith* . . . agreeably to what is written, *Campbell.*

15. Fear not, daughter of Sion: Have no fear, daughter of Zion! *Berkeley.*

behold, thy King cometh, sitting on an ass's colt: See, your King comes, *Norlie* . . . sitting on a donkey's colt! *AmpB* . . . the foal of an ass, *Fenton.*

12:15. This verse is a free translation of Zechariah 9:9. The sense of "rejoice greatly" is reproduced in "fear not." It is wonderful that the message of Christ is so often prefaced by "fear not." The term "daughter of Zion" is an elevated title of honor. The title occurs in the New Testament only here and in Matthew 21:5.

"Behold, thy King" speaks of the Saviour's role as the ideal king of Israel. Most of the kings through Israel's long history were corrupt and unrighteous. Jesus was symbolized by some good kings such as David to whom many kings of the southern kingdom were compared. The Messiah was to be an ideal king whom David, His ancestor, prefigured.

"Thy King cometh, sitting on an ass's colt." Luke relates that the colt was an untamed one, "whereon yet never man sat" (Luke 19:30). This bit of information indicates how remarkable it was that Jesus could ride such an unbroken animal. Compare the account of Solomon's proclamation as king to sit on David's throne (1 Kings 1:33).

16. These things understood not his disciples at the first: . . . the significance, *Phillips* . . . What this meant was not at all clear, *Norlie* . . . did not comprehend this at the time, *Fenton.*

but when Jesus was glorified: . . . but, when Jesus had been exalted, *ET* . . . had been exalted to glory, *ALBA* . . . was raised to life in glory, *SEB* . . . had entered on his glory, *TCNT.*

then remembered they that these things were written of him: . . . this was recorded, *Fenton* . . . concerning Him, *Norton, Campbell* . . . then they recalled that, *ALBA.*

12:16. The disciples were unaware of the significance of many events and their relationship to prophecies concerning Jesus. This statement is evidence of the disciples' simplicity and their truthfulness in setting down an accurate record.

Two things kept Jesus' students from understanding concerning His resurrection. First, grasping concepts may come slowly in the learning process. Indeed, the disciples had pondered His proph-

840.4 prs-pron dat sing	3113.29 verb 3sing indic imperf act	3631.1 conj	3450.5 art sing masc	3657.1 noun nom sing masc	3450.5 art sing masc
αὐτῷ.	17. ἐμαρτύρει	οὖν	ὁ	ὄχλος	ὁ
autō	*emarturei*	*oun*	*ho*	*ochlos*	*ho*
to him.	Bore witness	therefore	the	crowd	the

17.a.**Var:** p66,05D,017K, 019L,041,sa.bo.Elzev, Gries,Lach,Tisc

1498.21 verb sing masc part pres act	3196.2 prep	840.3 prs-pron gen sing	3616.1 conj	3617.1 conj	3450.6 art acc sing masc
ὢν	μετ'	αὐτοῦ,	⸀ ὅτε	[a ὅτι]	τὸν
ōn	*met'*	*autou*	*hote*	*hoti*	*ton*
being	with	him,	when	[that]	

2949.2 name acc masc	5291.6 verb 3sing indic aor act	1523.2 prep gen	3450.2 art gen sing	3283.2 noun gen sing neu	2504.1 conj
Λάζαρον	ἐφώνησεν	ἐκ	τοῦ	μνημείου,	καὶ
Lazaron	*ephōnēsen*	*ek*	*tou*	*mnēmeiou*	*kai*
Lazarus	he called	out of	the	tomb,	and

1446.5 verb 3sing indic aor act	840.6 prs-pron acc sing masc	1523.2 prep gen	3361.2 adj gen pl	1217.2 prep
ἤγειρεν	αὐτὸν	ἐκ	νεκρῶν.	18. διὰ
ēgeiren	*auton*	*ek*	*nekrōn*	*dia*
raised	him	from among	dead.	Because of

3642.17 dem-pron sing neu	2504.1 conj	5059.1 verb 3sing indic aor act	840.4 prs-pron dat sing	3450.5 art sing masc	3657.1 noun nom sing masc
τοῦτο	καὶ	ὑπήντησεν	αὐτῷ	ὁ	ὄχλος,
touto	*kai*	*hupēntēsen*	*autō*	*ho*	*ochlos*
this	also	met	him	the	crowd,

18.a.**Txt:** 07E,030U,036, 037,byz.
Var: 01ℵ,02A,03B,05D, 017K,019L,021M,026Q, 038,it.sa.bo.Gries,Lach, Treg,Alf,Word,Tisc, We/HoWeis,Sod,UBS/*

3617.1 conj	189.21 verb 3sing indic aor act	189.24 verb 3pl indic aor act	3642.17 dem-pron sing neu	840.6 prs-pron acc sing masc
ὅτι	⸀ ἤκουσεν	[a☆ ἤκουσαν]	τοῦτο	αὐτὸν
hoti	*ēkousen*	*ēkousan*	*touto*	*auton*
because	it heard	[they heard]	this	of his

4020.45 verb indic perf act	3450.16 art sing neu	4447.1 noun sing neu	3450.7 art pl masc	3631.1 conj
πεποιηκέναι	τὸ	σημεῖον.	19. οἱ	οὖν
pepoiēkenai	*to*	*sēmeion*	*hoi*	*oun*
having done	the	sign.	The	therefore

19.a.**Txt:** 02A,05D,017K, 019L,026Q,036,037,038, etc.byz.Lach,Sod
Var: 01ℵ,03B,Treg,Tisc, We/HoWeis,UBS/*

5168.4 name pl masc	1500.3 verb indic aor act	1500.28 verb 3pl indic aor act	4242.1 prep	1431.8 prs-pron acc pl masc
Φαρισαῖοι	⸀ εἶπον	[a☆ εἶπαν]	πρὸς	ἑαυτούς,
Pharisaioi	*eipon*	*eipan*	*pros*	*heautous*
Pharisees	said	[idem]	among	themselves,

2311.1 verb 2pl pres act	3617.1 conj	3620.2 partic	5456.2 verb 2pl indic pres act	3625.6 num card neu	1481.14 verb 2sing impr aor act
Θεωρεῖτε	ὅτι	οὐκ	ὠφελεῖτε	οὐδέν,	ἴδε
Theōreite	*hoti*	*ouk*	*ōpheleite*	*ouden*	*ide*
Do you see	that	not	you gain	nothing?	lo,

3450.5 art sing masc	2862.1 noun nom sing masc	3557.1 adv	840.3 prs-pron gen sing	562.2 verb 3sing indic aor act
ὁ	κόσμος	ὀπίσω	αὐτοῦ	ἀπῆλθεν.
ho	*kosmos*	*opisō*	*autou*	*apēlthen*
the	world	after	him	is gone.

1498.37 verb 3pl indic imperf act	1156.2 conj	4948.7 indef-pron nom pl masc	1659.4 name nom pl masc	1659.4 name nom pl masc
20. ⸂Ἦσαν	δὲ	⸀ τινες	Ἕλληνές	[☆ Ἕλληνές
Esan	*de*	*tines*	*Hellēnes*	*Hellēnes*
There were	and	certain	Greeks	[Greeks

ecies on resurrection in an effort to comprehend. Once Mark recorded they were "questioning one with another what the rising from the dead should mean" (Mark 9:10). Again, when Jesus told them He would rise the third day, Mark wrote, "They understood not that saying, and were afraid to ask him" (Mark 9:32). Second, some prophecies are often understood best near the time of or even after they have been fulfilled. When Daniel sought to know the full meaning of what he wrote, he learned "the words are closed up and sealed till the time of the end" (Daniel 12:9).

It was only after the Resurrection that they remembered what had been "written of him." That which they recorded was objective and without exaggeration or error. The writers of the Scriptures took no glory to themselves. The Spirit illuminated the Old Testament Scriptures and made Jesus' words real to them (14:26; 16:13,14). Jesus was glorified after His resurrection, and shortly after, the Spirit descended on the Day of Pentecost. Until Jesus was crucified and the disciples could see the power and wisdom of God in it, they did not associate His atonement with the Old Testament predictions and types. Furthermore, the Spirit illuminated what Jesus had accomplished in His redemptive activities.

12:17. "The people therefore that was with him," having seen the raising of Lazarus, "bare record." Note the passage in 11:42,43. Their hosannas were initiated by the resurrection of Lazarus. The people testified to the truth of the miracle. The eyewitnesses stirred the multitude to join their loud acclamation.

12:18. This was the second multitude group. The first was the multitude of Bethany who saw Jesus raise Lazarus and then witnessed to the larger multitude who were pilgrims to the Passover. The second group went out of Jerusalem to meet Jesus. The raising of Lazarus was the reason for their coming out to welcome Him.

12:19. The Pharisees formed the opposition group. Thus John tells of four groups in relationship to Jesus in this passage: (1) Jesus' disciples who remained with Him; (2) the multitude who were in Bethany when He raised Lazarus from the grave; (3) the multitude of pilgrims who were told by the prior company about the resurrection of Lazarus; (4) the Pharisees whose language in this verse implies their anger and despair. "The world is gone after him" is an exaggerated statement of Jesus' great popularity. It seemed to the Pharisees that nearly everyone had joined Him.

and that they had done these things unto him: . . . and what they had done to him, *Montgomery* . . . and that they had fulfilled it in His case, *Williams.*

17. The people therefore that was with him when he called Lazarus out of his grave, and raised him from the dead, bare record: . . . and resurrected him from the dead testified to the fact, *Adams* . . . were telling of it, *ALBA* . . . attested that, *Campbell* . . . related what they had witnessed, *Weymouth* . . . were continually talking about him, *Phillips* . . . were also giving testimony, *Norlie* . . . kept on bearing testimony, *Wuest* . . . were telling every one about it, *TCNT.*

18. For this cause the people also met him: This reason, *Murdock* . . . This, indeed, was why the crowd met him, *TCNT* . . . Therefore, also, the vast throng meets Him, *Concordant.*

for that they heard that he had done this miracle: . . . that He had performed this wonder-work, *Williams* . . . they had learned of this great miracle which He had worked, *ALBA* . . . this sign, *Rotherham.*

19. The Pharisees therefore said among themselves, Perceive ye how ye prevail nothing?: Be considering that you are not doing even one thing that would be of help to us, *Wuest* . . . You see! There is nothing you can do! *ALBA* . . . See how futile your efforts are! *Weymouth* . . . Nothing we do does any good, *SEB* . . . Do you realize that we are not getting anywhere? *Norlie* . . . that you are benefiting nothing, *Concordant* . . . ye are effecting nothing, *HBIE* . . . You see, you're not getting anywhere, *Beck* . . . You see? There's nothing one can do! *Phillips* . . . are gaining nothing, *Fenton.*

behold, the world is gone after him: Just look, *Adams* . . . Why, the whole world is running after him, *Norlie* . . . all the world, *Fenton* . . . Everyone is following Jesus! *SEB* . . . See the universe going after him, *Klingensmith.*

John 12:21

4948.7 indef-pron nom pl masc	1523.2 prep gen	3450.1 art gen pl	303.8 verb gen pl masc part pres act	2419.1 conj
τινες]	ἐκ	τῶν	ἀναβαινόντων	ἵνα
tines	*ek*	*tōn*	*anabainontōn*	*hina*
certain]	among	the	having come up	that

20.a.**Var:** 05D,019L,037, Lach,Treg,Alf

4210.13 verb 3pl subj aor act	4210.22 verb 3pl indic fut act	1706.1 prep	3450.11 art dat sing fem
⸀ προσκυνήσωσιν	[a προσκυνήσουσιν]	ἐν	τῇ
proskunēsōsin	*proskunēsousin*	*en*	*tē*
they might worship	[they will worship]	in	the

1844.3 noun dat sing fem	3642.7 dem-pron nom pl masc	3631.1 conj	4193.2 verb 3pl indic aor act	5213.3 name dat masc
ἑορτῇ·	21. οὗτοι	οὖν	προσῆλθον	Φιλίππῳ,
heortē	*houtoi*	*oun*	*prosēlthon*	*Philippō*
feast;	these	therefore	came	to Philip,

3450.3 art dat sing	570.3 prep gen	959.2 name fem	3450.10 art gen sing fem	1049.2 name gen sing fem	2504.1 conj
τῷ	ἀπὸ	Βηθσαϊδὰ	τῆς	Γαλιλαίας,	καὶ
tō	*apo*	*Bēthsaida*	*tēs*	*Galilaias*	*kai*
to the	from	Bethsaida		of Galilee,	and

2049.17 verb 3pl indic imperf act	840.6 prs-pron acc sing masc	2978.16 verb pl masc part pres act	2935.5 noun voc sing masc	2286.4 verb 1pl indic pres act
ἠρώτων	αὐτὸν	λέγοντες,	Κύριε,	θέλομεν
ērōtōn	*auton*	*legontes*	*Kurie*	*thelomen*
they asked	him	saying,	Sir,	we want

22.a.**Var:** p66,p75,03B, 019L,033X,041-corr,33, Treg,Alf,We/HoWeis, UBS/☆

3450.6 art acc sing masc	2400.3 name acc masc	1481.19 verb inf aor act	2048.34 verb 3sing indic pres	3450.5 art sing masc
τὸν	Ἰησοῦν	ἰδεῖν.	22. Ἔρχεται	[a☆+ ὁ]
ton	*Iēsoun*	*idein*	*Erchetai*	*ho*
	Jesus	to see.	Comes	

22.b.**Txt:** p66-org,(05), 017K,(032),036,037,1, 13,byz.
Var: p75,02A,03B,019L, Lach,Treg,Alf,Tisc, We/HoWeis,UBS/☆

5213.1 name nom masc	2504.1 conj	2978.5 verb 3sing indic pres act	3450.3 art dat sing	404.3 name dat masc	2504.1 conj	3687.1 adv
Φίλιππος	καὶ	λέγει	τῷ	Ἀνδρέᾳ·	⸀ καὶ	πάλιν
Philippos	*kai*	*legei*	*tō*	*Andrea*	*kai*	*palin*
Philip	and	tells		Andrew,	and	again

22.c.**Var:** p75,01ℵ,02A, 03B,019L,Lach,Treg,Alf Tisc,We/Ho,Weis,Sod, UBS/☆

2048.34 verb 3sing indic pres	404.1 name nom masc	2504.1 conj	5213.1 name nom masc	2504.1 conj
[b☆ ἔρχεται]	Ἀνδρέας	καὶ	Φίλιππος	[c☆+ καὶ]
erchetai	*Andreas*	*kai*	*Philippos*	*kai*
[comes]	Andrew	and	Philip	[and]

2978.3 verb 3pl pres act	3450.3 art dat sing	2400.2 name masc	3450.5 art sing masc	1156.2 conj	2400.1 name nom masc
λέγουσιν	τῷ	Ἰησοῦ.	23. ὁ	δὲ	Ἰησοῦς
legousin	*tō*	*Iēsou*	*ho*	*de*	*Iēsous*
tell		Jesus.		But	Jesus

23.a.**Txt:** 02A,05D,017K, 036,037,1,byz.Lach, Weis,Sod
Var: p66,p75,01ℵ,03B, 019L,032W,033X,33, Treg,Tisc,We/Ho,UBS/☆

552.7 verb 3sing indic aor mid	552.2 verb 3sing indic pres	840.2 prs-pron dat pl	2978.15 verb sing masc part pres act
⸀ ἀπεκρίνατο	[a☆ ἀποκρίνεται]	αὐτοῖς	λέγων,
apekrinato	*apokrinetai*	*autois*	*legōn*
answered	[answers]	them	saying,

2048.26 verb 3sing indic perf act	3450.9 art nom sing fem	5443.2 noun nom sing fem	2419.1 conj	1386.23 verb 3sing subj aor pass
Ἐλήλυθεν	ἡ	ὥρα	ἵνα	δοξασθῇ
Elēluthen	*hē*	*hōra*	*hina*	*doxasthē*
Has come	the	hour	that	should be glorified

12:20. The "certain Greeks" were "proselytes of the gate" who were uncircumcised but who observed the moral laws of Moses. Gentile proselytes were of two kinds: proselytes of the gates and proselytes of righteousness. The last were considered religious Jews. These Greek proselytes "came up to worship at the feast." Many Gentiles saw the immorality of their own religions as compared with the Jewish code of ethics. Thus the Jews carried on a successful missionary effort among the Gentiles.

12:21. The Greek proselytes approached Philip to secure an interview with Jesus. Philip is a Greek name; therefore, the Greeks may have felt a kinship with him. Philip's name occurs in 1:43,44. Why John identifies Philip as being from Bethsaida is uncertain. It could be merely the simple identification of Philip, or it is possible the references point to Philip's Gentile associations.

The Greeks had heard of Christ because of His triumphal entrance into Jerusalem and the news that Jesus had raised Lazarus from the dead. It is interesting that the Magi were from the east, and these Greeks were from the west. The first, at His birth, and the second, near to His death. The Greeks surely shared the messianic hope. They wished to discover for themselves whether Jesus was the predicted Christ.

12:22. There was logic in their approach to Jesus. First, the Greeks came to Philip. Second, Philip contacted Andrew. Third, both Andrew and Philip approached Jesus. Philip spoke to Andrew before going to Jesus perhaps because Andrew was also of the town of Bethsaida, or perhaps he was a close friend of Philip (1:44). And they "tell Jesus." They took the Greek's request to Jesus himself. Three things are evident. First, Philip did not trust his own judgment but sought another disciple's. Second, Philip and Andrew consulted together. Third, the two came in reverence to Jesus with the Greek's request.

12:23. To whom did Jesus speak? The natural sense of the context indicates that Jesus spoke to His disciples who came to Him with the Greeks. Thus, the next several verses were directed to His disciples with an indirect teaching for the Greeks.

Several times the statement is made in this Gospel that "his hour was not yet come" (see 7:30; 8:20). Christ's passion, resurrection and ascension were necessary prerequisites to the fulfillment of God's plan of redemption and the outpouring of the Spirit. The

20. And there were certain Greeks among them that came up to worship at the feast: Some non-Jewish people, *SEB.*

21. The same came therefore to Philip, which was of Bethsaida of Galilee, and desired him, saying: . . . and appealed to him, saying, *Moffatt* . . . and asked him, *Berkeley* . . . applied to Philip, *Fenton* . . . They kept saying to him, *SEB* . . . and made a request of him, *Norton.*

Sir, we would see Jesus: Sir, we wish to see Jesus, *HBIE* . . . we are desiring to see Jesus, *Wuest* . . . we want to become acquainted with, *Concordant.*

22. Philip cometh and telleth Andrew:

and again Andrew and Philip tell Jesus: Philip went and told Andrew, *Norlie* . . . then together they went and told Jesus, *TCNT.*

23. And Jesus answered them, saying, The hour is come: . . . addressing them in reply, *Fenton* . . . The time is at hand, *Norlie.*

that the Son of man should be glorified: . . . will be honored, *Fenton* . . . to receive great glory, *TEV* . . . for me to receive glory, *SEB.*

3450.5 art sing masc	5048.1 noun nom sing masc	3450.2 art gen sing	442.2 noun gen sing masc	279.1 partic	279.1 partic
ὁ	υἱὸς	τοῦ	ἀνθρώπου.	**24.** ἀμὴν	ἀμὴν
ho	*huios*	*tou*	*anthrōpou*	*amēn*	*amēn*
the	Son		of man.	Truly	truly

2978.1 verb 1sing pres act	5050.3 prs-pron dat 2pl	1430.1 partic	3231.1 partic	3450.5 art sing masc	2821.1 noun nom sing masc	3450.2 art gen sing
λέγω	ὑμῖν,	ἐὰν	μὴ	ὁ	κόκκος	τοῦ
legō	*humin*	*ean*	*mē*	*ho*	*kokkos*	*tou*
I say	to you,	If	not	the	grain	of the

4476.1 noun gen sing neu	3959.11 verb nom sing masc part aor act	1519.1 prep	3450.12 art acc sing fem	1087.4 noun acc sing fem	594.13 verb 3sing subj aor act
σίτου	πεσὼν	εἰς	τὴν	γῆν	ἀποθάνῃ,
sitou	*pesōn*	*eis*	*tēn*	*gēn*	*apothanē*
wheat	falling	into	the	ground	should die,

840.5 prs-pron nom sing masc	3304.2 adj nom sing masc	3176.1 verb 3sing indic act	1430.1 partic	1156.2 conj	594.13 verb 3sing subj aor act
αὐτὸς	μόνος	μένει·	ἐὰν	δὲ	ἀποθάνῃ,
autos	*monos*	*menei*	*ean*	*de*	*apothanē*
it	alone	remains;	if	but	it should die,

4044.6 adj acc sing masc	2561.3 noun acc sing masc	5179.2 verb 3sing indic pres act	3450.5 art sing masc	5205.5 verb nom sing masc part pres act
πολὺν	καρπὸν	φέρει.	**25.** ὁ	φιλῶν
polun	*karpon*	*pherei*	*ho*	*philōn*
much	fruit	it bears.	The	loving

25.a.**Txt:** 02A,05D,017K, 036,037,038,1,13,etc. byz.Gries,Lach,Alf **Var:** p66,p75,01ℵ,03B, 019L,032W,33,Treg, Tisc,We/Ho,Weis,Sod, UBS/⋆

3450.12 art acc sing fem	5425.4 noun acc sing fem	840.3 prs-pron gen sing	616.13 verb 3sing indic fut act	616.31 verb 3sing indic pres act
τὴν	ψυχὴν	αὐτοῦ	ʻ ἀπολέσει	[a⋆ ἀπολλύει]
tēn	*psuchēn*	*autou*	*apolesei*	*apolluei*
the	life	his	shall lose	[loses]

840.12 prs-pron acc sing fem	2504.1 conj	3450.5 art sing masc	3268.5 verb nom sing masc part pres act	3450.12 art acc sing fem	5425.4 noun acc sing fem
αὐτήν,	καὶ	ὁ	μισῶν	τὴν	ψυχὴν
autēn	*kai*	*ho*	*misōn*	*tēn*	*psuchēn*
it,	and	the	hating	the	life

840.3 prs-pron gen sing	1706.1 prep	3450.3 art dat sing	2862.3 noun dat sing masc	3642.5 dem-pron dat sing masc	1519.1 prep	2205.4 noun acc sing fem
αὐτοῦ	ἐν	τῷ	κόσμῳ	τούτῳ	εἰς	ζωὴν
autou	*en*	*tō*	*kosmō*	*toutō*	*eis*	*zōēn*
his	in	the	world	this	to	life

164.1 adj sing	5278.14 verb 3sing indic fut act	840.12 prs-pron acc sing fem	1430.1 partic	1466.5 prs-pron dat 1sing
αἰώνιον	φυλάξει	αὐτήν.	**26.** ἐὰν	ἐμοί
aiōnion	*phulaxei*	*autēn*	*ean*	*emoi*
eternal	shall keep	it.	If	me

1241.2 verb 3sing subj pres act	4948.3 indef-pron nom sing	4948.3 indef-pron nom sing	1241.2 verb 3sing subj pres act	1466.5 prs-pron dat 1sing
ʻ διακονῇ	τις,	[⋆ τις	διακονῇ,]	ἐμοὶ
diakonē	*tis*	*tis*	*diakonē*	*emoi*
serve	anyone,	[anyone	serves,]	me

188.4 verb 3sing impr pres act	2504.1 conj	3562.1 adv	1498.2 verb 1sing indic pres act	1466.1 prs-pron nom 1sing	1550.1 adv
ἀκολουθείτω·	καὶ	ὅπου	εἰμὶ	ἐγὼ	ἐκεῖ
akoloutheitō	*kai*	*hopou*	*eimi*	*egō*	*ekei*
let him follow;	and	where	am	I	there

Gentiles were to be included within His redemptive work (Acts chapters 2,10,13). Jesus' glorification was the point from which Gentiles were given access into God's presence without becoming proselytes to Judaism. Probably for this reason Jesus did not answer the Greeks directly. Another reason Jesus mentioned His "hour" is indicated by the verse which follows. His glorification was a fruit of His death just as the grain of wheat that dies bears much fruit (verse 24).

24. Verily, verily, I say unto you, Except a corn of wheat fall into the ground and die: Let Me assure you that unless, *Adams* . . . most solemnly I tell you, *AmpB* . . . a grain of wheat, *ASV* . . . if a kernel of wheat doesn't fall, *Beck* . . . thrown into the ground, does not arise from its bed, *Fenton.*

it abideth alone: . . . it remains a single grain, *Williams* . . . it remains a single kernel, *Montgomery* . . . it remains solitary, *TCNT* . . . it remains what it was—a single, *Weymouth.*

but if it die, it bringeth forth much fruit: . . . but, if it dies, it becomes very fruitful, *TCNT* . . . but through its death, *BB* . . . it makes a rich yield, *Weymouth* . . . it brings a good harvest, *Phillips* . . . it produces much grain, *Beck* . . . bears a great crop, *Montgomery* . . . it bears plentiful fruit, *HistNT* . . . numerous fruits, *Murdock* . . . it produces many others, *AmpB* . . . it will produce a large cluster, *SEB* . . . it produces a big crop, *Klingensmith* . . . it will bear much fruit, *Adams.*

12:24. "A corn of wheat" dies that it might bear much fruit. Is it strange that the Messiah must also die that He might produce a plenteous harvest? Nature abounds with illustrations that life originates from the womb of death. Higher forms of life are made possible because of the death of lower forms. The grain of wheat contains a germ of life which can only be released by the death of the grain. Jesus died in behalf of others that they might be the fruit of His death. Life comes forth from His death: the resurrection of all believers will come as a result of Christ's resurrection. Just as the grain of wheat sprouts in the earth, Jesus came from the grave as the firstborn (*prōtotokos*) from the dead (Colossians 1:18). He is the first in a new order of beings. This is the "much fruit" Jesus speaks about.

25. He that loveth his life shall lose it; and he that hateth his life in this world: . . . loves his lower life, *Williams* . . . The lover of his life, *Fenton, Berkeley* . . . He who is fond of his soul-life, is losing it, *Wuest* . . . Love your life and lose it, *Beck* . . . destroys it, *Rotherham* . . . will destroy it, *Phillips* . . . who does not value, *SEB.*

shall keep it unto life eternal: . . . shall keep it forever and ever, *Norlie* . . . will preserve it for eternal life, *Moffatt* . . . preserve it eternally, *Campbell.*

12:25. In verses 23 and 24 Jesus speaks of the life-out-of-death principle as it applied to Him. In verses 25 and 26 He applied the same principle to His disciples. The life the disciple loves or hates is his soul (*psuchēn*). The life he loves (*philōn*) he loses because he protects it from falling to the earth and dying. It is a life lived in selfishness, greed, and pleasure. To hate his life (soul) is a comparative view meaning he is willing to hazard his life (Acts 15:26). The use of "hate" here is as in Luke 14:26 regarding a Christian's relationship to his unbelieving relatives. In Matthew 10:37 we learn the word means simply to "love less." Those who follow Jesus, willing to give up wealth and pleasure, are the ones who hate their lives. These are those who "shall keep it unto life eternal."

On the concept in this verse Tenney observed, "Parallels to this statement appear in the Synoptic Gospels (Matthew 10:39; Mark 8:36; Luke 14:26). These were not all spoken on the same occasion. The statement in Matthew was part of a charge given to the disciples when Jesus sent them on a mission; that in Mark was given to them and a crowd that joined them (Mark 8:34); and the Lukan pronouncement was spoken to a mixed audience at an undefined point in Jesus' career, at some time within the last year of his life. Since this seems to have been a major principle of his teaching, its repetition at different times and under different circumstances is not at all unlikely" (Tenney, *Expositor's Bible Commentary*, 9:129).

26. If any man serve me, let him follow me: Let one who serves Me follow Me, *Berkeley* . . . If any one is ready to serve me, *Montgomery* . . . and my servant also must go wherever I go, *Williams* . . . minister to me, *Douay.*

2504.1 conj	3450.5 art sing masc	1243.1 noun nom sing masc	3450.5 art sing masc	1684.3 adj nom 1sing masc	1498.40 verb 3sing indic fut mid
καὶ	ὁ	διάκονος	ὁ	ἐμὸς	ἔσται·
kai	*ho*	*diakonos*	*ho*	*emos*	*estai*
also	the	servant	the	my	shall be.

26.a.**Txt:** 02A,017K,036, 037,byz.bo.
Var: 01ℵ,03B,05D,019L, 033X,038,sa.Gries,Lach, Treg,Alf,Tisc,We/Ho, Weis,Sod,UBS/⋆

2504.1 conj	1430.1 partic	4948.3 indef-pron nom sing	1466.5 prs-pron dat 1sing	1241.2 verb 3sing subj pres act	4939.10 verb 3sing indic fut act
⸂[a] καὶ ⸃	ἐάν	τις	ἐμοί	διακονῇ,	τιμήσει
kai	*ean*	*tis*	*emoi*	*diakonē*	*timēsei*
And	if	anyone	me	serve,	will honor

840.6 prs-pron acc sing masc	3450.5 art sing masc	3824.1 noun nom sing masc	3431.1 adv	3450.9 art nom sing fem	5425.1 noun sing fem
αὐτὸν	ὁ	πατήρ.	27. Νῦν	ἡ	ψυχή
auton	*ho*	*patēr*	*Nun*	*hē*	*psuchē*
him	the	Father.	Now	the	soul

1466.2 prs-pron gen 1sing	4866.11 verb 3sing indic perf pass	2504.1 conj	4949.9 intr-pron sing neu	1500.6 verb 1sing subj aor act
μου	τετάρακται,	καὶ	τί	εἴπω;
mou	*tetaraktai*	*kai*	*ti*	*eipō*
my	has been troubled,	and	what	shall I say?

3824.5 noun voc sing masc	4834.6 verb 2sing impr aor act	1466.6 prs-pron acc 1sing	1523.2 prep gen	3450.10 art gen sing fem	5443.1 noun fem
Πάτερ,	σῶσόν	με	ἐκ	τῆς	ὥρας
Pater	*sōson*	*me*	*ek*	*tēs*	*hōras*
Father,	save	me	from	the	hour

3642.10 dem-pron gen sing fem	233.2 conj	1217.2 prep	3642.17 dem-pron sing neu	2048.1 verb indic aor act	1519.1 prep
ταύτης.	ἀλλὰ	διὰ	τοῦτο	ἦλθον	εἰς
tautēs	*alla*	*dia*	*touto*	*ēlthon*	*eis*
this.	But	because of	this	I came	to

3450.12 art acc sing fem	5443.4 noun acc sing fem	3642.12 dem-pron acc sing fem	3824.5 noun voc sing masc	1386.13 verb 2sing impr aor act
τὴν	ὥραν	ταύτην.	28. Πάτερ,	δόξασόν
tēn	*hōran*	*tautēn*	*Pater*	*doxason*
the	hour	this.	Father,	glorify

4622.2 prs-pron gen 2sing	3450.16 art sing neu	3549.2 noun sing neu	2048.3 verb 3sing indic aor act	3631.1 conj	5292.1 noun nom sing fem
σου	τὸ	ὄνομα.	Ἦλθεν	οὖν	φωνὴ
sou	*to*	*onoma*	*Ēlthen*	*oun*	*phōnē*
your	the	name.	Therefore	came	a voice

1523.2 prep gen	3450.2 art gen sing	3636.2 noun gen sing masc	2504.1 conj	1386.8 verb 1sing indic aor act	2504.1 conj
ἐκ	τοῦ	οὐρανοῦ,	Καὶ	ἐδόξασα	καὶ
ek	*tou*	*ouranou*	*Kai*	*edoxasa*	*kai*
out of	the	heaven,	Both	I glorified	and

3687.1 adv	1386.7 verb 1sing act	3450.5 art sing masc	3631.1 conj	3657.1 noun nom sing masc	3450.5 art sing masc
πάλιν	δοξάσω.	29. Ὁ	οὖν	ὄχλος	ὁ
palin	*doxasō*	*Ho*	*oun*	*ochlos*	*ho*
again	will glorify.	The	therefore	crowd	the

29.a.**Var:** 02A,05D, 017K,021M,032W,033X, 038,041,Lach

2449.26 verb sing part perf act	2449.27 verb nom sing masc part perf act	2504.1 conj	189.31 verb nom sing masc part aor act	2978.26 verb 3sing indic imperf act
⸂ ἑστὼς	[[a] ἑστηκὼς]	καὶ	ἀκούσας	ἔλεγεν
hestōs	*hestēkōs*	*kai*	*akousas*	*elegen*
having stood	[idem]	and	having heard	said,

12:26. "Serve" and "follow" are the two words of action for the one who wishes to keep his soul to life eternal. Those who serve Him are those who practice the same principles of life that He followed. To "follow" Him is to walk in His footsteps. The pronoun "me" is emphatic and in opposition to man's self. Worldly people serve their own souls; thus they lose them.

Jesus promises that those who serve and follow Him will go where He goes; that is, to heaven.

Jesus indicated that three benefits are secure for those who follow Him. First, they keep their souls unto eternal life (verse 25). Second, they have His fellowship both here and hereafter (verse 26). And third, they shall have honor of the Father (verse 26).

and where I am, there shall also my servant be: . . . because wherever I am My servant must be, *Norlie* . . . and my servant also must go wherever I go, *Williams.*

if any man serve me, him will my Father honour: If a man is ready to serve me, my Father will honour him, *TCNT* . . . becomes My servant, My Father will give him honor, *Norlie.*

12:27. "Now" relates to the hour of verse 23. This statement was not a part of Jesus' answer to His disciples, but proceeded as a consequence of His teaching concerning His death and glorification. The word for His "soul" is the same as the word for "life" (*psuchē*) in verse 25. The word "troubled" is a perfect tense verb of the Greek verb *tarassō* which is also used in 11:33 and 13:21. Everywhere in his Gospel John asserts the deity of Christ and assumes His humanity. Even in Christ's darkest hours He was perfectly aware of His relationship to His Father. Jesus did not really ask the Father to save Him "from this hour" (Greek, *ek*, meaning "out of") for He was conscious that this was the purpose for which He came. This verse is a prelude to His Gethsemane struggle which John's Gospel does not record.

27. Now is my soul troubled; and what shall I say?: . . . is now very distressed, *ET.*

Father, save me from this hour: Father, bring me safe through this hour, *TCNT* . . . save Me from what is going to happen? *Beck* . . . deliver Me, *Fenton.*

but for this cause came I unto this hour: No! It was for this purpose that I came, *Norlie* . . . No! I came to suffer this now, *Beck* . . . On the contrary, *Fenton.*

12:28. Jesus asked the Father to "glorify" His (the Father's) name. To glorify the Father's name is to make His name known. Jesus' hour of suffering reveals how much God loves the lost (3:16). The resurrection of Jesus shows who He is by the display of His power. The Father is glorified by Jesus' being revealed.

"I . . . will glorify it again" is indicative of the greatest miracle of power ever displayed. This was the resurrection of Jesus Christ himself.

How God spoke from heaven is not revealed. Three times the Father spoke from heaven: here, at Jesus' baptism, and at His transfiguration. Each time the Father spoke it was for the benefit of the disciples, not for Jesus' sake.

28. Father, glorify thy name: Father, honor your own name! *Phillips* . . . bring glory to Your name! *SEB.*

Then came there a voice from heaven, saying, I have both glorified it: At that a voice echoed from heaven, *ALBA* . . . I have given it glory, *BB.*

and will glorify it again: . . . and I will give it glory again, *BB.*

12:29. The multitude heard the sound of the Father's voice. Some perceived nothing more than a loud noise like thunder. Thunder is associated with the divine voice in several Scriptures (see Revelation 6:1; 14:2; 16:17,18).

29. The people therefore that stood by, and heard it, said that it thundered: The crowd of bystanders on hearing it said, *Williams.*

John 12:30

1020.2 noun acc sing fem	**1090.13** verb inf perf act	**241.6** adj nom pl masc	**2978.25** verb indic imperf act	**32.1** noun nom sing masc
βροντὴν	γεγονέναι.	ἄλλοι	ἔλεγον,	Ἄγγελος
brontēn	*gegonenai*	*alloi*	*elegon*	*Angelos*
Thunder	to have been:	others	said,	An angel

30.a.**Txt:** 02A,019L, 030U,037,038,1,13,byz. Lach
Var: p66,p75,01ℵ,03B, 05D,017K,032W,033X, 036,041,TregAlf,Tisc, We/Ho,Weis,Sod,UBS/☆

840.4 prs-pron dat sing	**2953.39** verb 3sing indic perf act	**552.6** verb 3sing indic aor pass	**3450.5** art sing masc	**2400.1** name nom masc
αὐτῷ	λελάληκεν.	**30.** Ἀπεκρίθη	(a ὁ)	Ἰησοῦς
autō	*lelalēken*	*Apekrithē*	*ho*	*Iēsous*
to him	has spoken.	Answered		Jesus

2504.1 conj	**1500.5** verb 3sing indic aor act	**3620.3** partic	**1217.1** prep	**1466.7** prs-pron acc 1sing	**3642.9** dem-pron nom sing fem
καὶ	εἶπεν,	Οὐ	δι’	ἐμὲ	‘ αὕτη
kai	*eipen*	*Ou*	*di’*	*eme*	*hautē*
and	said,	Not	because of	me	this

3450.9 art nom sing fem	**5292.1** noun nom sing fem	**3450.9** art nom sing fem	**5292.1** noun nom sing fem	**3642.9** dem-pron nom sing fem
ἡ	φωνὴ	[☆ ἡ	φωνὴ	αὕτη]
hē	*phōnē*	*hē*	*phōnē*	*hautē*
the	voice	[the	voice	this]

1090.3 verb 3sing indic perf act	**233.2** conj	**1217.1** prep	**5050.4** prs-pron acc 2pl	**3431.1** adv	**2893.1** noun nom sing fem
γέγονεν,	ἀλλὰ	δι’	ὑμᾶς.	**31.** νῦν	κρίσις
gegonen	*alla*	*di’*	*humas*	*nun*	*krisis*
has come,	but	because of	you.	Now	judgment

1498.4 verb 3sing indic pres act	**3450.2** art gen sing	**2862.2** noun gen sing masc	**3642.1** dem-pron gen sing	**3431.1** adv	**3450.5** art sing masc
ἐστὶν	τοῦ	κόσμου	τούτου·	νῦν	ὁ
estin	*tou*	*kosmou*	*toutou*	*nun*	*ho*
is	of the	world	this;	now	the

752.1 noun nom sing masc	**3450.2** art gen sing	**2862.2** noun gen sing masc	**3642.1** dem-pron gen sing	**1531.31** verb 3sing indic fut pass	**1838.1** prep gen
ἄρχων	τοῦ	κόσμου	τούτου	ἐκβληθήσεται	ἔξω·
archōn	*tou*	*kosmou*	*toutou*	*ekblēthēsetai*	*exō*
ruler	of the	world	this	shall be cast	out:

2476.3 conj	**1430.1** partic	**5150.6** verb 1sing subj aor pass	**1523.2** prep gen	**3450.10** art gen sing fem	**1087.2** noun gen sing fem
32. κἀγὼ	ἐὰν	ὑψωθῶ	ἐκ	τῆς	γῆς,
kagō	*ean*	*hupsōthō*	*ek*	*tēs*	*gēs*
and I	if	I be lifted up	from	the	earth,

3820.8 adj acc pl masc	**1657.6** verb 1sing indic fut act	**4242.1** prep	**1670.3** prs-pron acc 1sing masc	**3642.17** dem-pron sing neu	**1156.2** conj
πάντας	ἑλκύσω	πρὸς	ἐμαυτόν.	**33.** Τοῦτο	δὲ
pantas	*helkusō*	*pros*	*emauton*	*Touto*	*de*
all	will draw	to	myself.	This	but

2978.26 verb 3sing indic imperf act	**4446.1** verb nom sing masc part pres act	**4029.2** intr-pron dat sing	**2265.3** noun dat sing masc	**3165.21** verb 3sing indic imperf act
ἔλεγεν,	σημαίνων	ποίῳ	θανάτῳ	ἤμελλεν
elegen	*sēmainōn*	*poiō*	*thanatō*	*ēmellen*
he said,	signifying	by what	death	he was about

34.a.**Var:** 01ℵ,03B,019L, 033X,sa.Alf,Tisc,We/Ho, WeisSod,UBS/☆

594.8 verb inf pres act	**552.6** verb 3sing indic aor pass	**3631.1** conj	**840.4** prs-pron dat sing	**3450.5** art sing masc
ἀποθνῄσκειν.	**34.** ἀπεκρίθη	[a☆+ οὖν]	αὐτῷ	ὁ
apothnēskein	*apekrithē*	*oun*	*autō*	*ho*
to die.	Answered	[therefore]	him	the

"Others said, An angel spake to him." These "others" had a greater degree of understanding of the nature of the communication. In the Old Testament it is recorded that many times God spoke through angels (see Galatians 3:19; Hebrews 2:2). This same reaction occurred when Jesus himself spoke to Saul on the Damascus Road (Acts 9:7; 22:9).

12:30. The voice did not need to be audible for Jesus to know of His Father's support. However, the multitude and the disciples needed this confirmation of their faith in Him as the Messiah. John and the other disciples probably understood the words. How the communication was perceived indicated the level of their spiritual growth. God seems to reveal himself according to one's faith, spiritual maturity, and need.

12:31. "Judgment" (*krisis*) means the act of judgment is to take place on the world through the death of Christ. It was the Cross that revealed the world's hostility toward God, but the Cross also demonstrates God's love for the world (3:16,17).

"Now" is repeated, emphasizing that the judgment occurred at the Cross. "The prince of this world" refers to Satan. There are five times when it is recorded that Satan is cast out. First, Satan was cast out of heaven before the creation. Second, at the Cross he was cast out of his seat of power over all who believe. Third, he is cast out on the earth (Revelation 12:9). Fourth, Satan will be cast into a pit of the abyss (Revelation 20:3). Fifth, the old serpent, Satan, will be cast into the lake of fire (Revelation 20:10).

12:32. Jesus spoke here of the way He was to suffer death. He did not express doubt as to His crucifixion, for He had indicated it would take place "now" as verse 31 states. Prior to this He made His knowledge of the Cross clear to Nicodemus (3:14) and later to others (8:28). Thus to be "lifted up from the earth" was a vivid way to express crucifixion.

"Will draw all men unto me" does not mean the totality of the human race, but "all" refers to all men generally in the universal sense. As Jesus explained to Nicodemus, those who looked to the serpent on the pole were granted life (3:14), so Jesus' cross was to be the focus of man's attention. As many as look to Him receive eternal life. "Will draw" is used six times in the New Testament, five of which are in John (6:44; 12:32; 18:10; 21:6,11). It is the same drawing mentioned as being done by the Father (6:44). No

others said, An angel spake to him:

30. Jesus answered and said, This voice came not because of me, but for your sakes: Not on my account has this voice come, *Wuest.*

31. Now is the judgment of this world: Now this world is on its trial, *TCNT* . . . Now is this world to be judged, *Moffatt* . . . is judgment passing upon the world, *Norton* . . . This world is now in process of judgment, *Williams* . . . Now has come the judgement, *ALBA* . . . This world is now on its trial, *TCNT.*

now shall the prince of this world be cast out: . . . now will the Prince of this world be driven out, *Weymouth* . . . now shall the ruler of this world be expelled, *Berkeley* . . . the ruler of this world will be thrown out, clean out, *Wuest* . . . to be thrown out, *SEB* . . . will be thrown out, *Beck* . . . be cast [out] outside, *Panin* . . . will be overthrown, *TEV* . . . The Spirit that rules it will now be driven out, *TCNT* . . . Now shall the Chief of this world, *Concordant.*

32. And I, if I be lifted up from the earth: As for me, when I shall be lifted, *Campbell* . . . when I am lifted up, *Moffatt* . . . And once I have been lifted up, *Beck* . . . if I should be exalted out of the earth, *Concordant* . . . lifted up out from underneath the earth, *Wuest.*

will draw all men unto me: I will attract, *SEB* . . . shall draw everyone to Myself, *Berkeley* . . . all sorts of people, *Adams* . . . draw all things to myself, *Confraternity* . . . And I...will make all men come to me, *BB.*

33. This he said, signifying what death he should die: . . . pointing to the sort of death he would have, *BB* . . . alluding to the death, *Campbell* . . . indicating the sort of death, *Norlie* . . . however, illustrative of the death He was about to die, *Fenton* . . . in prediction of how he was going to die, *ALBA.*

John 12:35

3657.1 noun nom sing masc	2231.1 prs-pron nom 1pl	189.22 verb 1pl indic aor act	1523.2 prep gen	3450.2 art gen sing	3414.2 noun gen sing masc
ὄχλος,	Ἡμεῖς	ἠκούσαμεν	ἐκ	τοῦ	νόμου
ochlos	*Hēmeis*	*ēkousamen*	*ek*	*tou*	*nomou*
crowd,	We	heard	out of	the	law

3617.1 conj	3450.5 art sing masc	5382.1 name nom masc	3176.1 verb 3sing indic act	1519.1 prep	3450.6 art acc sing masc	163.3 noun acc sing masc
ὅτι	ὁ	Χριστὸς	μένει	εἰς	τὸν	αἰῶνα,
hoti	*ho*	*Christos*	*menei*	*eis*	*ton*	*aiōna*
that	the	Christ	remains	to	the	age,

2504.1 conj	4316.1 adv	4622.1 prs-pron nom 2sing	2978.4 verb 2sing indic pres act	2978.4 verb 2sing indic pres act	4622.1 prs-pron nom 2sing
καὶ	πῶς	⸀☆ σὺ	λέγεις,	[λέγεις	σύ]
kai	*pōs*	*su*	*legeis*	*legeis*	*su*
and	how	you	say,	[say	you]

3617.1 conj	1158.1 verb 3sing indic pres act	5150.10 verb inf aor pass	3450.6 art acc sing masc	5048.4 noun acc sing masc	3450.2 art gen sing
Ὅτι	δεῖ	ὑψωθῆναι	τὸν	υἱὸν	τοῦ
Hoti	*dei*	*hupsōthēnai*	*ton*	*huion*	*tou*
that	must	be lifted up	the	Son	

442.2 noun gen sing masc	4949.3 intr-pron nom sing	1498.4 verb 3sing indic pres act	3642.4 dem-pron nom sing masc	3450.5 art sing masc
ἀνθρώπου;	τίς	ἐστιν	οὗτος	ὁ
anthrōpou	*tis*	*estin*	*houtos*	*ho*
of man?	Who	is	this	the

5048.1 noun nom sing masc	3450.2 art gen sing	442.2 noun gen sing masc	1500.5 verb 3sing indic aor act	3631.1 conj
υἱὸς	τοῦ	ἀνθρώπου;	35. Εἶπεν	οὖν
huios	*tou*	*anthrōpou*	*Eipen*	*oun*
Son		of man?	Said	therefore

840.2 prs-pron dat pl	3450.5 art sing masc	2400.1 name nom masc	2068.1 adv	3262.1 adj acc sing	5385.4 noun acc sing masc	3450.16 art sing neu
αὐτοῖς	ὁ	Ἰησοῦς,	Ἔτι	μικρὸν	χρόνον	τὸ
autois	*ho*	*Iēsous*	*Eti*	*mikron*	*chronon*	*to*
to them		Jesus,	Yet	a little	time	the

35.a.**Txt:** 02A,030U,036,037,byz.sa.
Var: 01ℵ,03B,05D,017K,019L,021M,033X,038,041,it.bo.GriesLach,Treg,Alf,Tisc,We/Ho,Weis,Sod,UBS/☆

35.b.**Txt:** p66,01ℵ,036,037,038,1,13,byz.Gries,Word
Var: 02A,03B,05D,017K,019L,033X,041,33,Lach,Treg,Alf,Tisc,We/Ho,Weis,Sod,UBS/☆

5295.1 noun sing neu	3196.1 prep	5050.2 prs-pron gen 2pl	1706.1 prep	5050.3 prs-pron dat 2pl	1498.4 verb 3sing indic pres act
φῶς	⸀ μεθ'	ὑμῶν	[a☆ ἐν	ὑμῖν]	ἐστιν.
phōs	*meth'*	*humōn*	*en*	*humin*	*estin*
light	with	you	[among	you]	is.

3906.1 verb 2pl pres act	2175.1 conj	5453.1 conj	3450.16 art sing neu	5295.1 noun sing neu	2174.2 verb 2pl pres act
περιπατεῖτε	⸀ ἕως	[b☆ ὡς]	τὸ	φῶς	ἔχετε,
peripateite	*heōs*	*hōs*	*to*	*phōs*	*echete*
Walk	while	[idem]	the	light	you have,

2419.1 conj	3231.1 partic	4508.1 noun nom sing fem	5050.4 prs-pron acc 2pl	2608.3 verb 3sing subj aor act	2504.1 conj	3450.5 art sing masc
ἵνα	μὴ	σκοτία	ὑμᾶς	καταλάβῃ·	καὶ	ὁ
hina	*mē*	*skotia*	*humas*	*katalabē*	*kai*	*ho*
that	not	darkness	you	may overtake.	And	the

3906.12 verb nom sing masc part pres act	1706.1 prep	3450.11 art dat sing fem	4508.3 noun dat sing fem	3620.2 partic	3471.4 verb 3sing indic perf act
περιπατῶν	ἐν	τῇ	σκοτίᾳ	οὐκ	οἶδεν
peripatōn	*en*	*tē*	*skotia*	*ouk*	*oiden*
walking	in	the	darkness	not	knows

violence or force compels man to come to Jesus. Man's will is free. He may look and live. If he refuses to look to the Cross, he remains in darkness and death.

12:33. John saw in Jesus' statement of verse 32 both the fact of His death and the mode by which He was to die. The cross is the most significant symbol of Christianity.

12:34. The multitude reasoned that Jesus could not be the Messiah if He was to die by being lifted up on a cross, because the Old Testament ("the Law") said that "Christ abideth for ever." They based their opinion on several passages of Scripture (see Psalm 89:29,36; Isaiah 9:7; Ezekiel 37:25; Daniel 7:13,14).

If Christ was to abide forever, how then could the Christ die? The multitude certainly understood that the "lifting up" meant death. It did not occur to them that their interpretations of the Scriptures were faulty. They were inclined to believe because of His miracles, but His teachings were hard for them to accept. Each time they were prone to believe, a new impediment arose to hinder their progress. The word "this" is emphasized because they saw a different Son of Man in His statements than what they understood was meant by the Son of Man in their Law.

12:35. Jesus did not directly answer their question. His indirect answer asserted that they should take advantage of the light they had with them. Their opportunities would soon be gone. He is the embodiment of truth. As the Son of Man He is the light to all mankind, and furthermore, "the Son of Man" is His messianic title. Jesus had revealed himself as the Light of the World and illustrated this truth by opening the eyes of the man born blind. This sign was common knowledge among them, and the raising of Lazarus was still fresh in their minds. Thus Jesus was speaking of His credentials as the starting point for their trust in Him as Messiah (see 8:12; 9:4,5).

12:36. Jesus indicated by the word "while" that the time would come when the light would not be available. Either the light would be withdrawn, or because of blindness they would be unable to see it. The admonition is to believe to the same degree to which you

34. The people answered him, We have heard out of the law that Christ abideth for ever: The crowd responded, *Adams* . . . We have learned from the law...is to remain here forever, *Williams* . . . people hurled back at Him, *Berkeley* . . . the Christ lives forever, *Wuest* . . . the Messiah continues, *NEB* . . . will live forever, *Campbell.*

and how sayest thou: . . . what do you mean by saying, *Moffatt.*

The Son of man must be lifted up?: . . . must go away? *Torrey* . . . must be nailed to a cross? *SEB.*

who is this Son of man?: What Messiah are You talking about, *LivB* . . . What Son of Man is this? *Torrey.*

35. Then Jesus said unto them, Yet a little while is the light with you: . . . the Light shines among you, *Berkeley* . . . for a little longer yet, *Moffatt.*

Walk while ye have the light, lest darkness come upon you: . . . walk while you possess the Light, *Fenton* . . . Be ordering your behavior according as you are having the light, *Wuest* . . . or darkness will overtake you, *Beck* . . . that darkness apprehend you not, *Panin.*

for he that walketh in darkness knoweth not whither he goeth: . . . within the sphere of the darkness...does not know where he is departing, *Wuest* . . . has no idea where he is going, *Phillips* . . . where he is drifting, *Rotherham.*

John 12:36

36.a.**Txt:** p66,017K, 033X,036,037,1,13,byz. GriesWord
Var: 01ℵ,02A,03B,05D, 019L,038,041-org,33, Lach,Treg,Alf,Tisc, We/Ho,WeisSod,UBS/☆

36.b.**Txt:** p75,01ℵ-corr, 02A,017K,036,037,038, etc.byz.Gries,Sod
Var: p66,01ℵ-org,03B, 05D,019L,044,Lach, TregAlf,Tisc,We/Ho, Weis,UBS/☆

4085.1 adv	**5055.3** verb 3sing indic pres act		**2175.1** conj	**5453.1** conj	**3450.16** art sing neu	**5295.1** noun sing neu
ποῦ	ὑπάγει.	**36.** ⸀	ἕως	[a☆ ὡς]	τὸ	φῶς
pou	*hupagei*		*heōs*	*hōs*	*to*	*phōs*
where	he goes.		While	[idem]	the	light

2174.2 verb 2pl pres act	**3961.2** verb 2pl pres act	**1519.1** prep	**3450.16** art sing neu	**5295.1** noun sing neu	**2419.1** conj	**5048.6** noun pl masc
ἔχετε,	πιστεύετε	εἰς	τὸ	φῶς,	ἵνα	υἱοὶ
echete	*pisteuete*	*eis*	*to*	*phōs*	*hina*	*huioi*
you have,	believe	in	the	light,	that	sons

5295.2 noun gen sing neu	**1090.42** verb 2pl subj aor mid	**3642.18** dem-pron pl neu	**2953.27** verb 3sing indic aor act	**3450.5** art sing masc
φωτὸς	γένησθε.	Ταῦτα	ἐλάλησεν	⸂b ὁ ⸃
phōtos	*genēsthe*	*Tauta*	*elalēsen*	*ho*
of light	you may become.	These things	spoke	

2400.1 name nom masc	**2504.1** conj	**562.6** verb nom sing masc part aor act	**2900.5** verb 3sing indic aor pass	**570.2** prep gen	**840.1** prs-pron gen pl
Ἰησοῦς,	καὶ	ἀπελθὼν	ἐκρύβη	ἀπ'	αὐτῶν.
Iēsous	*kai*	*apelthōn*	*ekrubē*	*ap'*	*autōn*
Jesus,	and	going away	was hid	from	them.

4965.9 dem-pron pl neu	**1156.2** conj	**840.3** prs-pron gen sing	**4447.2** noun pl neu	**4020.48** verb gen sing masc part perf act
37. Τοσαῦτα	δὲ	αὐτοῦ	σημεῖα	πεποιηκότος
Tosauta	*de*	*autou*	*sēmeia*	*pepoiēkotos*
So many	but	he	signs	having done

1699.1 prep gen	**840.1** prs-pron gen pl	**3620.2** partic	**3961.55** verb 3pl indic imperf act	**1519.1** prep	**840.6** prs-pron acc sing masc
ἔμπροσθεν	αὐτῶν	οὐκ	ἐπίστευον	εἰς	αὐτόν,
emprosthen	*autōn*	*ouk*	*episteuon*	*eis*	*auton*
before	them	not	they believed	on	him,

2419.1 conj	**3450.5** art sing masc	**3030.1** noun nom sing masc	**2246.6** name gen masc	**3450.2** art gen sing	**4254.2** noun gen sing masc
38. ἵνα	ὁ	λόγος	Ἠσαΐου	τοῦ	προφήτου
hina	*ho*	*logos*	*Esaiou*	*tou*	*prophētou*
that	the	word	of Isaiah	the	prophet

3997.22 verb 3sing subj aor pass	**3614.6** rel-pron acc sing masc	**1500.5** verb 3sing indic aor act	**2935.5** noun voc sing masc	**4949.3** intr-pron nom sing
πληρωθῇ,	ὃν	εἶπεν,	Κύριε,	τίς
plērōthē	*hon*	*eipen*	*Kurie*	*tis*
might be fulfilled,	which	he said,	Lord,	who

3961.20 verb 3sing indic aor act	**3450.11** art dat sing fem	**187.3** noun dat sing fem	**2231.2** prs-pron gen 1pl	**2504.1** conj	**3450.5** art sing masc
ἐπίστευσεν	τῇ	ἀκοῇ	ἡμῶν;	καὶ	ὁ
episteusen	*tē*	*akoē*	*hēmōn*	*kai*	*ho*
believed	the	report	our?	and	the

1016.1 noun nom sing masc	**2935.2** noun gen sing masc	**4949.2** intr-pron dat sing	**596.7** verb 3sing indic aor pass	**1217.2** prep
βραχίων	κυρίου	τίνι	ἀπεκαλύφθη;	**39.** Διὰ
brachiōn	*kuriou*	*tini*	*apekaluphthē*	*Dia*
arm	of Lord	to whom	was it revealed?	Because of

3642.17 dem-pron sing neu	**3620.2** partic	**1404.36** verb 3pl indic imperf	**3961.16** verb inf pres act	**3617.1** conj	**3687.1** adv
τοῦτο	οὐκ	ἠδύναντο	πιστεύειν,	ὅτι	πάλιν
touto	*ouk*	*ēdunanto*	*pisteuein*	*hoti*	*palin*
this	not	they could	believe,	because	again

have the light (truth of God's revelation in Christ). If the light is dim, your faith is small; yet, as you believe, the light will become brighter and faith will increase. In *Pilgrim's Progress,* the Evangelist asked Pilgrim if he saw the yonder light. Pilgrim said, "I think I do." The Evangelist answered, "Keep that light in your eye, and go up directly thereto; so shall you see the gate."

"*Children* of light" has no article; therefore their nature is indicated, rather than their age. The word used is *huioi* ("sons" rather than "children"). To be born of the light is to become a child of light. But a "son" (*huios*) is more mature than a child. Jesus desired them to grow in the truth so that they "become" (*genēsthe*) sons of light.

The literal verb for "did hide" is passive, meaning "was hidden." Thus He did not actively hide himself. He probably retired to Bethany to spend some days before the Passover. His withdrawal from them foreshadowed that which unbelief and hostility bring about. The light withdrew and the Jews sat in darkness.

36. While ye have light, believe in the light: . . . put faith in the Light, *Berkeley.*

that ye may be the children of light: . . . so that you may become sons of Light, *Norlie, Williams* . . . in order to become enlightened people, *Beck.*

These things spake Jesus, and departed, and did hide himself from them: Having made these remarks, Jesus took His departure, withdrawing from them privately, *Fenton* . . . After saying this, Jesus...hid from them, *Berkeley* . . . went away and hid Himself, *Williams.*

12:37,38. The "many miracles" refers to the light Jesus spoke of in the previous verse. The "miracles" were visible tokens of His personal identity as their Lord. The perfect participle "had done" indicates past actions with lasting results. The Jews did not deny the miracles, but they refused to connect His miracles with the source of His power. They were adamant in their resistance to the light. They were habitual in their refusal to believe Him. The logical consequence of acknowledging that God was the power source of Jesus' miracles was to confess Jesus as their Messiah. Because the Jews could not disprove the genuineness of His miracles, they stopped at this point. They were forced by logical necessity to attribute His wonders to Satan. Since the miracles Jesus did were clearly superhuman and because only two powers exist beyond the human, the Jews rejected the divine power as Jesus' source and claimed He worked by the power of the devil. Even their rejection of Him as their Messiah pointed to who He was. The result of the Messiah's ministry was foreknown by God, and God inspired the prophet to foretell the refusal.

37. But though he had done so many miracles before them: . . . produced so many evidences, *Fenton.*

yet they believed not on him: . . . they still had no belief in him, *BB.*

38. That the saying of Esaias the prophet might be fulfilled, which he spake: . . . so that the prophecy of Isaiah was fulfilled, when he said, *Phillips* . . . be verified, *Fenton.*

Lord, who hath believed our report?: . . . who gave credence, *Young* . . . what they heard from us, *Williams* . . . our statement, *Fenton* . . . our preaching? *Weymouth, Wuest.*

and to whom hath the arm of the Lord been revealed?: . . . the might of the Lord, *TCNT* . . . the mighty arm...been shown? *Williams* . . . been unveiled? *Weymouth* . . . off the Lorde declared? *Tyndale* . . . And the Lord's power, *Wuest* . . . show His power? *SEB* . . . made manifest? *Norton* . . . been disclosed? *HistNT* . . . been uncovered, *Beck.*

12:39. John is not eliminating the responsibility for their actions. He is stating that due to God's foreknowledge of the situation, what God had caused to be written would of necessity take place.

39. Therefore they could not believe, because that Esaias said again: For this reason, *Fenton*

12:40. The quotation of Isaiah 6:10 is a free one. The blinding and hardening takes place because the revelator is presented. God

1500.5 verb 3sing indic aor act	2246.5 name nom masc	40. 5027.2 verb 3sing indic perf act	840.1 prs-pron gen pl	3450.8 art acc pl masc
εἶπεν	Ἠσαΐας,	Τετύφλωκεν	αὐτῶν	τοὺς
eipen	Esaias	Tetuphlōken	autōn	tous
said	Isaiah,	He has blinded	their	the

3652.8 noun acc pl masc	2504.1 conj	‹ 4313.1 verb 3sing indic perf act	[a☆ 4313.6 verb 3sing indic aor act	840.1 prs-pron gen pl
ὀφθαλμοὺς	καὶ	πεπώρωκεν	ἐπώρωσεν]	αὐτῶν
ophthalmous	kai	pepōrōken	epōrōsen	autōn
eyes	and	has hardened	[hardened]	their

3450.12 art acc sing fem	2559.4 noun acc sing fem	2419.1 conj	3231.1 partic	1481.13 verb 3pl subj aor act	3450.4 art dat pl
τὴν	καρδίαν·	ἵνα	μὴ	ἴδωσιν	τοῖς
tēn	kardian	hina	mē	idōsin	tois
the	heart,	that	not	they should see	with the

3652.7 noun dat pl masc	2504.1 conj	3401.6 verb 3pl subj aor act	3450.11 art dat sing fem	2559.3 noun dat sing fem	2504.1 conj
ὀφθαλμοῖς	καὶ	νοήσωσιν	τῇ	καρδίᾳ	καὶ
ophthalmois	kai	noēsōsin	tē	kardia	kai
eyes	and	understand	with the	heart	and

‹ 1978.18 verb 3pl subj aor pass	[b☆ 4613.11 verb 3pl subj aor pass	2504.1 conj	‹ 2367.7 verb 1sing subj aor mid
ἐπιστραφῶσιν,	στραφῶσιν,]	καὶ	ἰάσωμαι
epistraphōsin	straphōsin	kai	iasōmai
be converted,	[idem]	and	I should heal

[c☆ 2367.19 verb 1sing indic fut mid	840.8 prs-pron acc pl masc	41. 3642.18 dem-pron pl neu	1500.5 verb 3sing indic aor act
ἰάσομαι]	αὐτούς.	Ταῦτα	εἶπεν
iasomai	autous	Tauta	eipen
[I will heal]	them.	These things	said

2246.5 name nom masc	‹ 3616.1 conj	[a☆ 3617.1 conj	1481.3 verb 3sing indic aor act	3450.12 art acc sing fem
Ἠσαΐας,	ὅτε	ὅτι]	εἶδεν	τὴν
Esaias	hote	hoti	eiden	tēn
Isaiah,	when	[because]	he saw	the

1385.4 noun acc sing fem	840.3 prs-pron gen sing	2504.1 conj	2953.27 verb 3sing indic aor act	3875.1 prep	840.3 prs-pron gen sing
δόξαν	αὐτοῦ,	καὶ	ἐλάλησεν	περὶ	αὐτοῦ.
doxan	autou	kai	elalēsen	peri	autou
glory	his,	and	spoke	concerning	him.

42. 3539.1 adv	3175.1 conj	2504.1 conj	1523.2 prep gen	3450.1 art gen pl	752.6 noun gen pl masc
ὅμως	μέντοι	καὶ	ἐκ	τῶν	ἀρχόντων
homōs	mentoi	kai	ek	tōn	archontōn
Although	indeed	even	from among	the	rulers

4044.7 adj nom pl masc	3961.23 verb 3pl indic aor act	1519.1 prep	840.6 prs-pron acc sing masc	233.2 conj	1217.2 prep
πολλοὶ	ἐπίστευσαν	εἰς	αὐτόν·	ἀλλὰ	διὰ
polloi	episteusan	eis	auton	alla	dia
many	believed	on	him,	but	because of

3450.8 art acc pl masc	5168.7 name acc pl masc	3620.1 partic	3533.14 verb 3pl indic imperf act	2419.1 conj	3231.1 partic
τοὺς	Φαρισαίους	οὐχ	ὡμολόγουν,	ἵνα	μὴ
tous	Pharisaious	ouch	hōmologoun	hina	mē
the	Pharisees	not	they confessed,	that	not

40.a.**Txt:** 03B-corr,036,037,1,565,700,892,byz. Gries,Lach
Var: 02A,03B-org,019L,033X,038,33,Treg,Alf Tisc,We/Ho,Weis,Sod,UBS/☆

40.b.**Txt:** 02A,05D-corr,030U,036,037,1,byz.
Var: 01ℵ,03B,05D-org,33,Lach,Treg,Alf,Tisc,We/Ho,Weis,Sod,UBS/☆

40.c.**Txt:** 019L,030U-corr,036,038,1,(byz.),Steph
Var: 01ℵ,02A,03B,05D,017K,030U-org,037,(byz.),Lach,Treg,Alf,Tisc,We/HoWeis,Sod,UBS/☆

41.a.**Txt:** 05D,017K,036,037,041,13,565,700,byz. it.
Var: p66,p75,01ℵ,02A,03B,019L,033X,038,33,sa.bo.Gries,LachTreg,Alf,Tisc,We/Ho,Weis,Sod,UBS/☆

turned their willful blindness into penal blindness. God provided the occasion for them to close their eyes and harden their hearts; therefore, by granting the Jews the opportunity He brought about the rejection of Christ. What God indirectly causes or even allows is viewed as from God.

. . . The reason why they could not believe is stated again by Isaiah, *Norlie* . . . the reason why they could not believe was also given by Isaia, *ALBA* . . . they were not able to be believing, *Wuest.*

12:41. This verse ties Isaiah chapters 6 and 53 together as one. However, the statement reaches far beyond that.

In Isaiah chapter 6, the prophet saw God sitting upon the throne. In chapter 53 the seer viewed Christ upon the Cross. Isaiah and John connect these two beings together as one. The One upon the throne and the One upon the cross are one and the same—God himself! Isaiah saw His glory in chapters 6 and 53. It was most difficult for the Jews to associate their Messiah with suffering and death. This was their stone of stumbling. Yet Isaiah connected the glory and the suffering together, and John pointed to Jesus as the God whom Isaiah spoke of in both chapters.

The natural mind often associates suffering with weakness. The Jews reasoned their Messiah would be like King David, a conqueror, not a weak, yielding sufferer. But the Old Testament also pictured their Messiah as a suffering substitute for sin (Isaiah 53). Many of the Jews completely overlooked or disregarded the teaching of this mission of the Saviour. They interpreted God's salvation with respect to their own desires. They wanted a deliverer but one who would bring them political freedom. They desired to continue in their unethical and hypocritical behavior. How easy it was for them to rationalize their conduct as legally correct. At the same time they condemned Jesus as being a lawbreaker. What more excuse did they need that they might continue in their sins.

40. He hath blinded their eyes, and hardened their heart: . . . has calloused their hearts, *Berkeley* . . . and made their hearts insensible, *Moffatt* . . . blunted their understanding, *Campbell* . . . benumbed their hearts, *Williams* . . . made their minds callous, *Weymouth* . . . their heart degenerated, *Fenton* . . . closed their minds, *ALBA.*

that they should not see with their eyes, nor understand with their heart: . . . so they may neither see...nor understand, *Berkeley* . . . perceive with the heart, *Wuest* . . . comprehend, *Campbell.*

and be converted, and I should heal them: . . . and lest they should repent, *Norlie* . . . and change their mind, *Wuest* . . . And turn to me to cure them, *Williams.*

41. These things said Esaias, when he saw his glory, and spake of him: . . . when he made this prediction, *LivB* . . . saw His rectifying power, *Fenton.*

12:42. "Nevertheless" turns to the other side of the Jewish response, for not all the multitude nor all the Pharisees rejected the light they saw. Many even of the rulers believed in Him. Two of them were Joseph of Arimathea and Nicodemus. They previewed that wonderful day when Luke wrote, "And a great company of the priests were obedient to the faith" (Acts 6:7).

"Because of the Pharisees" gives the reason Jesus had few who spoke in His behalf. "They did not confess him" is an action in the imperfect tense meaning it was not their habitual practice to speak favorably about Him. In 7:13 we read that some only whispered to one another of Jesus out of fear of the Jews. The power the leaders had in casting believers from the synagogue was an effective weapon against the Messiah. As this verse indicates many of the chief rulers did believe on Him. The test of their trust in Him came in their confession of Him before their social and religious peers.

42. Nevertheless among the chief rulers also many believed on him: . . . a number even of the authorities, *Moffatt* . . . of the chiefs, *Murdock.*

but because of the Pharisees they did not confess him: . . . but wouldn't say so publicly, *Beck* . . . confess openly, *ET* . . . they did not profess their belief, *Norton* . . . they did not own it, *Williams* . . . failed to confess it so, *Berkeley.*

650.2 adj nom pl masc	1090.43 verb 3pl subj aor mid	25.16 verb 3pl indic aor act	1056.1 conj
ἀποσυνάγωγοι	γένωνται.	43. ἠγάπησαν	γὰρ
aposunagōgoi	genōntai	ēgapēsan	gar
put out of the synagogue	they might be;	they loved	for

3450.12 art acc sing fem	1385.4 noun acc sing fem	3450.1 art gen pl	442.7 noun gen pl masc	3095.1 adv comp	2238.1 conj
τὴν	δόξαν	τῶν	ἀνθρώπων	μᾶλλον	ἤπερ
tēn	doxan	tōn	anthrōpōn	mallon	ēper
the	glory	of the	men	more	than

3450.12 art acc sing fem	1385.4 noun acc sing fem	3450.2 art gen sing	2296.2 noun gen sing masc	2400.1 name nom masc	1156.2 conj
τὴν	δόξαν	τοῦ	θεοῦ.	44. Ἰησοῦς	δὲ
tēn	doxan	tou	theou	Iēsous	de
the	glory		of God.	Jesus	but

2869.11 verb 3sing indic aor act	2504.1 conj	1500.5 verb 3sing indic aor act	3450.5 art sing masc	3961.10 verb nom sing masc part pres act	1519.1 prep
ἔκραξεν	καὶ	εἶπεν,	Ὁ	πιστεύων	εἰς
ekraxen	kai	eipen	Ho	pisteuōn	eis
cried	and	said,	The	believing	on

1466.7 prs-pron acc 1sing	3620.3 partic	3961.6 verb 3sing indic pres act	1519.1 prep	1466.7 prs-pron acc 1sing	233.1 conj	233.2 conj
ἐμὲ	οὐ	πιστεύει	εἰς	ἐμὲ,	ʼ ἀλλʼ	[☆ ἀλλὰ]
eme	ou	pisteuei	eis	eme	all'	alla
me,	not	believes	on	me,	but	[idem]

1519.1 prep	3450.6 art acc sing masc	3854.14 verb acc sing masc part aor act	1466.6 prs-pron acc 1sing	2504.1 conj	3450.5 art sing masc
εἰς	τὸν	πέμψαντά	με·	45. καὶ	ὁ
eis	ton	pempsanta	me	kai	ho
on	the	having sent	me;	and	he that

2311.9 verb nom sing masc part pres act	1466.7 prs-pron acc 1sing	2311.4 verb 3sing indic pres act	3450.6 art acc sing masc	3854.14 verb acc sing masc part aor act
θεωρῶν	ἐμὲ,	θεωρεῖ	τὸν	πέμψαντά
theōrōn	eme	theōrei	ton	pempsanta
beholds	me,	beholds	the	having sent

1466.6 prs-pron acc 1sing	1466.1 prs-pron nom 1sing	5295.1 noun sing neu	1519.1 prep	3450.6 art acc sing masc	2862.4 noun acc sing masc
με.	46. ἐγὼ	φῶς	εἰς	τὸν	κόσμον
me	egō	phōs	eis	ton	kosmon
me.	I	a light	into	the	world

2048.24 verb 1sing indic perf act	2419.1 conj	3820.6 adj sing masc	3450.5 art sing masc	3961.10 verb nom sing masc part pres act	1519.1 prep
ἐλήλυθα,	ἵνα	πᾶς	ὁ	πιστεύων	εἰς
elēlutha	hina	pas	ho	pisteuōn	eis
have come,	that	everyone	the	believing	on

1466.7 prs-pron acc 1sing	1706.1 prep	3450.11 art dat sing fem	4508.3 noun dat sing fem	3231.1 partic	3176.19 verb 3sing subj aor act	2504.1 conj
ἐμὲ	ἐν	τῇ	σκοτίᾳ	μὴ	μείνῃ.	47. καὶ
eme	en	tē	skotia	mē	meinē	kai
me	in	the	darkness	not	may abide.	And

1430.1 partic	4949.3 intr-pron nom sing	1466.2 prs-pron gen 1sing	189.18 verb sing act	3450.1 art gen pl	4343.5 noun gen pl neu
ἐάν	τίς	μου	ἀκούσῃ	τῶν	ῥημάτων
ean	tis	mou	akousē	tōn	rhēmatōn
if	anyone	my	hear	the	words

lest they should be put out of the synagogue:

12:43. Many Jews weighed the temporal benefits of Christ and the fleeting social benefits of their religion and chose their religion over their Messiah. "Of men" is compared to "of God." The word "praise" in both "of men" and "of God" is the Greek word *doxa* meaning "glory." What men thought about them was more important to them than what God thought about them. How tragic when social pressure dictates the faith and practice of God's creatures.

43. For they loved the praise of men more than the praise of God: . . . the approbation of men, *Campbell* . . . valued honour from men more than honour from God, *TCNT* . . . their reputation among men...the approval of God, *Norlie* . . . the approbation of God, *Fenton* . . . they preferred men's esteem to divine approval, *Berkeley.*

12:44. The first part of this verse indicates a loud public declaration used in public teaching. The word "cried," from *krazō*, is used several places in John's Gospel (1:15; 7:28,37; 12:13,44; 19:12).

Jesus is the manifestation of the Father on earth so that believing "on" (*eis*) or toward Him as the Messiah is actually placing one's confidence in the God who sent Him. The first two words for "me" are emphatic and therefore are to be emphasized in the thought. By believing in Jesus one's faith reaches to the One He came to reveal. The Lord told the disciples the same truth in these words, "He that hath seen me hath seen the Father" (14:9).

44. Jesus cried and said, He that believeth on me: He who has faith in me, *BB.*

believeth not on me, but on him that sent me: . . . has faith not in me, *BB* . . . believes not only on Me, *Norlie* . . . does not believe in Me but in My Sender, *Berkeley.*

12:45. The word for "seeth" is the same for both uses of the word in this verse. It refers to a continued gaze and contemplation of Jesus. The same word is employed 23 times in John's Gospel. This verse states the very heart of the Gospel. What is recorded in 1:18, Jesus declares here.

45. And he that seeth me seeth him that sent me: . . . is seeing the one who sent me, *Phillips.*

12:46. We should review 1:4,5,7,9, and 14 as a commentary on this verse. The beginning of this verse is "I am come a light" to stress what Jesus is to the dark world. The word *elēlutha* ("have come") is a perfect tense verb to assert a past action with a present result. Jesus' coming was to give sight to spiritually blinded eyes. That light was His revelation of the total reality of God. All we know of God, we know by the revelation of Jesus Christ the light.

Men of the world are in darkness, and unless they accept the light, they remain in darkness. To be in darkness is to be ignorant of God, in a state of alienation and separation from God. This condition is known as being dead in trespasses and sin. (For a description of those in darkness, turn to Ephesians 2:1.)

46. I am come a light into the world: I, in contradistinction to all others, *Wuest.*

that whosoever believeth on me should not abide in darkness: . . . so that no one who continues to believe in me can remain in darkness, *Williams* . . . everyone who places his trust in me may not remain in the sphere of the darkness, *Beck* . . . may not continue in the darkness, *Fenton.*

12:47. Jesus came to bring light to the world in darkness. His "words" refer to His teachings which the multitude have had dif-

47. And if any man hear my words, and believe not: . . . and keep them not, *ASV* . . . fails to observe them, *Berkeley* . . . fail to observe them, *Fenton.*

John 12:48

47.a.**Txt:** 07E,021M,030U,036,037,byz.
Var: 01ℵ,02A,03B,05D,017K,019L,033X,038,041,1,13,33,sa.bo.Lach,Treg,Alf,Word,Tisc,We/HoWeis,Sod,UBS/☆

2504.1 conj	**3231.1** partic	**3961.25** verb 3sing subj aor act	**5278.20** verb 3sing subj aor act	**1466.1** prs-pron nom 1sing	**3620.3** partic
καὶ	μὴ	ʻ πιστεύσῃ,	[a☆ φυλάξῃ,]	ἐγὼ	οὐ
kai	*mē*	*pisteusē*	*phulaxē*	*egō*	*ou*
and	not	believe,	[keep,]	I	not

2892.1 verb 1sing act	**840.6** prs-pron acc sing masc	**3620.3** partic	**1056.1** conj	**2048.1** verb indic aor act	**2419.1** conj
κρίνω	αὐτόν·	οὐ	γὰρ	ἦλθον	ἵνα
krinō	*auton*	*ou*	*gar*	*ēlthon*	*hina*
do judge	him,	not	for	I came	that

2892.1 verb 1sing act	**3450.6** art acc sing masc	**2862.4** noun acc sing masc	**233.1** conj	**2419.1** conj	**4834.4** verb 1sing act
κρίνω	τὸν	κόσμον,	ἀλλ'	ἵνα	σώσω
krinō	*ton*	*kosmon*	*all'*	*hina*	*sōsō*
I might judge	the	world,	but	that	I might save

3450.6 art acc sing masc	**2862.4** noun acc sing masc	**3450.5** art sing masc	**114.5** verb nom sing masc part pres act	**1466.7** prs-pron acc 1sing	**2504.1** conj
τὸν	κόσμον.	**48.** ὁ	ἀθετῶν	ἐμὲ	καὶ
ton	*kosmon*	*ho*	*athetōn*	*eme*	*kai*
the	world.	The	rejecting	me	and

3231.1 partic	**2956.8** verb nom sing masc part pres act	**3450.17** art pl neu	**4343.4** noun pl neu	**1466.2** prs-pron gen 1sing	**2174.4** verb 3sing indic pres act
μὴ	λαμβάνων	τὰ	ῥήματά	μου,	ἔχει
mē	*lambanōn*	*ta*	*rhēmata*	*mou*	*echei*
not	does receive	the	words	my,	has

3450.6 art acc sing masc	**2892.10** verb acc sing masc part pres act	**840.6** prs-pron acc sing masc	**3450.5** art sing masc	**3030.1** noun nom sing masc
τὸν	κρίνοντα	αὐτόν·	ὁ	λόγος
ton	*krinonta*	*auton*	*ho*	*logos*
the	judging	him:	the	word

3614.6 rel-pron acc sing masc	**2953.26** verb 1sing indic aor act	**1552.3** dem-pron nom sing masc	**2892.25** verb 3sing indic fut act	**840.6** prs-pron acc sing masc
ὃν	ἐλάλησα,	ἐκεῖνος	κρινεῖ	αὐτὸν
hon	*elalēsa*	*ekeinos*	*krinei*	*auton*
which	I spoke,	that	shall judge	him

1706.1 prep	**3450.11** art dat sing fem	**2057.9** adj dat sing fem	**2232.3** noun dat sing fem	**3617.1** conj	**1466.1** prs-pron nom 1sing	**1523.1** prep gen
ἐν	τῇ	ἐσχάτῃ	ἡμέρᾳ.	**49.** ὅτι	ἐγὼ	ἐξ
en	*tē*	*eschatē*	*hēmera*	*hoti*	*egō*	*ex*
in	the	last	day;	for	I	from

1670.1 prs-pron gen 1sing masc	**3620.2** partic	**2953.26** verb 1sing indic aor act	**233.1** conj	**3450.5** art sing masc	**3854.11** verb nom sing masc part aor act
ἐμαυτοῦ	οὐκ	ἐλάλησα·	ἀλλ'	ὁ	πέμψας
emautou	*ouk*	*elalēsa*	*all'*	*ho*	*pempsas*
myself	not	spoke,	but	the	having sent

1466.6 prs-pron acc 1sing	**3824.1** noun nom sing masc	**840.5** prs-pron nom sing masc	**1466.4** prs-pron dat 1sing	**1769.3** noun acc sing fem
με	πατὴρ,	αὐτός	μοι	ἐντολὴν
me	*patēr*	*autos*	*moi*	*entolēn*
me	Father,	himself	me	commandment

49.a.**Txt:** 05D,017K,019L,036,037,038,byz.Gries
Var: 01ℵ,02A,03B,021M,033X,Lach,Treg,Alf,Word,Tisc,We/HoWeis,Sod,UBS/☆

1319.14 verb 3sing indic aor act	**1319.33** verb 3sing indic perf act	**4949.9** intr-pron sing neu	**1500.6** verb 1sing subj aor act	**2504.1** conj
ʻ ἔδωκεν	[a☆ δέδωκεν]	τί	εἴπω	καὶ
edōken	*dedōken*	*ti*	*eipō*	*kai*
gave	[has given]	what	I should say	and

ficulty accepting. The particular saying was that He must be lifted up (verses 32,33).

The one who "hears" and "believes not" His teaching was not to be judged at His first coming. This does not contradict the fact that He shall judge the world in the last day (see John 5:22,27; Acts 17:31).

The mission of Christ was to save, not condemn (see 3:17). "Judge" and "save" are in direct contrast to each other. The Old Testament and Jesus' sayings will be the criteria from which the world will be judged, but Jesus did not come to judge men while He dwelt among them in the flesh.

I judge him not: I don't condemn him, *Beck.*

for I came not to judge the world, but to save the world: ... because I didn't come to condemn...but to save, *Beck.*

12:48. Believing Him as a person promotes faith in His teaching ("sayings," NASB). His words brought life to those who were spiritually dead (6:63). The very same word (*rhēma*) is used in 6:63 and here. If one rejected Him, it was evident that he would not receive His sayings. The steps toward spiritual life depend upon, first, being aware that His miracles were from God; second, accepting Him as sent from His Father; and third, receiving His sayings. Except the multitude followed these three steps, they could not be saved.

The Word (*logos*) of God will also judge. Some make a distinction between *rhēma* and *logos,* both rendered "word" in the New Testament. For them *logos* speaks of truth as it is recorded in the written Word of God, while *rhēma* connotes "revelational" truth. In their view "revelational" truth comes by an operation of the Spirit and makes possible a spoken word by which a believer confesses something into being. However, Jesus used the two words here as synonyms. Peter did the same in his first letter. He declared Christians are born of the Word (*logos*) (1 Peter 1:23), the word (*rhēma*) preached unto them (1 Peter 1:25). In both cases he referred to the written Word.

48. He that rejecteth me, and receiveth not my words: Whoever persistently rejects me and refuses to accept, *Williams* ... who is repudiating Me, *Concordant* ... and does not accept My teachings, *Norlie.*

hath one that judgeth him: ... has a judge already, *TCNT* ... will not accept My declarations, is self-condemned, *Fenton* ... he has one that is condemning him, *Beck.*

the word that I have spoken, the same shall judge him in the last day: The word that I spoke, that will judge him, *HBIE* ... the very message I have spoken, *Williams* ... it shall sentence him, *Berkeley.*

12:49. "For" (*hoti*) is often translated "because." The reason for judgment on the criterion of His "word" is that He does not speak as a mere man, but He comes from His Father, the Almighty God. Jesus stressed His commission as an ambassador. Rejecting Him and His message is a repudiation of the authority of God. Jesus' commandment was His commission to reveal God (as stated in 1:18).

49. For I have not spoken of myself: ... of my own accord, *Berkeley* ... on My own initiative, *NASB.*

but the Father which sent me, he gave me a commandment: ... on the contrary, *Norlie* ... gave me orders, *BB.*

what I should say, and what I should speak: ... told Me what to say and what to preach, *Norlie* ... how to say it, *ALBA* ... and I had to speak, *JB* ... and what I should declare, *Confraternity* ... I should publish, *Fenton.*

12:50. The Father's commandment is the same as Jesus' sayings. The choice is either "eternal life" contained in His sayings or judg-

4949.9 intr-pron sing neu	2953.25 verb 1sing act		2504.1 conj	3471.2 verb 1sing indic perf act	3617.1 conj	3450.9 art nom sing fem
τί	λαλήσω·	50.	καὶ	οἶδα	ὅτι	ἡ
ti	lalēsō		kai	oida	hoti	hē
what	I should speak;		and	I know	that	the

1769.1 noun nom sing fem	840.3 prs-pron gen sing	2205.1 noun nom sing fem	164.3 adj nom sing	1498.4 verb 3sing indic pres act
ἐντολὴ	αὐτοῦ	ζωὴ	αἰώνιός	ἐστιν·
entolē	autou	zōē	aiōnios	estin
commandment	his	life	eternal	is.

3614.17 rel-pron pl neu	3631.1 conj	2953.1 verb 1sing pres act	1466.1 prs-pron nom 1sing	1466.1 prs-pron nom 1sing
ἃ	οὖν	' λαλῶ	ἐγὼ,	[☆ ἐγὼ
ha	oun	lalō	egō	egō
What	therefore	speak	I,	[I

2953.1 verb 1sing pres act	2503.1 conj	2029.3 verb 3sing indic perf act	1466.4 prs-pron dat 1sing	3450.5 art sing masc	3824.1 noun nom sing masc
λαλῶ,]	καθὼς	εἴρηκέν	μοι	ὁ	πατήρ,
lalō	kathōs	eirēken	moi	ho	patēr
speak,]	as	has said	to me	the	Father,

3643.1 adv	2953.1 verb 1sing pres act		4112.1 prep	1156.2 conj	3450.10 art gen sing fem	1844.2 noun gen sing fem
οὕτως	λαλῶ.	13:1.	Πρὸ	δὲ	τῆς	ἑορτῆς
houtōs	lalō		Pro	de	tēs	heortēs
so	I speak.		Before	now	the	feast

3450.2 art gen sing	3818.1 noun sing neu	3471.18 verb nom sing masc part perf act	3450.5 art sing masc	2400.1 name nom masc	3617.1 conj
τοῦ	πάσχα,	εἰδὼς	ὁ	Ἰησοῦς	ὅτι
tou	pascha	eidōs	ho	Iēsous	hoti
of the	passover,	knowing		Jesus	that

1.a.**Txt:** 07E,030U,036, 037,byz.
Var: 01ℵ,02A,03B, 017K,019L,021M,033X, 038,041,Lach,Treg,Alf, TiscWe/Ho,Weis,Sod, UBS/☆

2048.26 verb 3sing indic perf act	2048.3 verb 3sing indic aor act	840.3 prs-pron gen sing	3450.9 art nom sing fem	5443.2 noun nom sing fem
' ἐλήλυθεν	[a☆ ἦλθεν]	αὐτοῦ	ἡ	ὥρα
elēluthen	ēlthen	autou	hē	hōra
has come	[came]	his	the	hour

2419.1 conj	3197.3 verb 3sing subj aor act	1523.2 prep gen	3450.2 art gen sing	2862.2 noun gen sing masc	3642.1 dem-pron gen sing
ἵνα	μεταβῇ	ἐκ	τοῦ	κόσμου	τούτου
hina	metabē	ek	tou	kosmou	toutou
that	he should depart	out	of the	world	this

4242.1 prep	3450.6 art acc sing masc	3824.4 noun acc sing masc	25.20 verb nom sing masc part aor act	3450.8 art acc pl masc	2375.8 adj acc pl masc
πρὸς	τὸν	πατέρα,	ἀγαπήσας	τοὺς	ἰδίους
pros	ton	patera	agapēsas	tous	idious
to	the	Father,	having loved	the	his own

3450.8 art acc pl masc	1706.1 prep	3450.3 art dat sing	2862.3 noun dat sing masc	1519.1 prep	4904.1 noun sing neu	25.14 verb 3sing indic aor act
τοὺς	ἐν	τῷ	κόσμῳ	εἰς	τέλος	ἠγάπησεν
tous	en	tō	kosmō	eis	telos	ēgapēsen
the	in	the	world	to	end	he loved

2.a.**Txt:** 01ℵ-corr,02A, 05D,017K,036,037,038, 1,13,33,byz.it.Lach,Alf
Var: 01ℵ-org,03B,019L, 032W,033X,1241,Treg Tisc,We/Ho,Weis,Sod, UBS/☆

840.8 prs-pron acc pl masc		2504.1 conj	1168.2 noun gen sing neu	1090.50 verb gen sing part aor mid	1090.77 verb gen sing neu part pres
αὐτούς.	2.	καὶ	δείπνου	' γενομένου	[a☆ γινομένου,]
autous		kai	deipnou	genomenou	ginomenou
them.		And	supper	taking place,	[idem]

ment in the last day for rejecting Him and His word (verse 48). The knowledge of God in His words brought life. Later Jesus said: "And this is life eternal, that they might know thee the only true God, and Jesus Christ, whom thou has sent" (17:3).

"I speak" refers to the revelation which the Son of God brought. The Father and the Son speak with one voice. Their unity of objective and their communication guarantee eternal life to those who accept Him.

13:1. Old Testament passages assert that the Feast of Passover was to be celebrated beginning at sundown the 14th day of the first month, followed on the 15th by the Feast of Unleavened Bread (Exodus 12:6-11; Leviticus 23:5,6; Deuteronomy 16:1).

This verse gives us another indication of our Lord's omniscience. His enemies could not seize Him until His hour had come, and even then He yielded himself into their hands. They could not take Him by force.

The term "depart" means "to pass from one place to another." It is a beautiful expression for death. Death is not a cessation of activity but a change of its sphere. Jesus left this world to continue His life with the Father.

He must have been torn between leaving His infant church and His return to His celestial home. In the Father's presence He had perfect harmony and communion, but in the world He was confronted by misunderstanding, criticism, and hostility.

"Having loved his own which were in the world" expresses His love not merely for the 11 faithful apostles, but for all those who heard and followed Him as sheep hear and follow their shepherd (see 10:16; 17:20,21). The Great Shepherd was willing and able to lay down His life for His flock.

"He loved them unto the end." The word for "love" (*agapaō*) refers to the deep, compassionate love of God for the world (3:16). "Unto the end" is usually interpreted as meaning to the end of His earthly life. But the meaning may go beyond that idea, because the word "end" (*telos*) bears the idea of completeness; without the article, the quality of His love is indicated. Thus, He loves perfectly.

13:2. The events connected with the supper are linked to His love for His own in the preceding verse by the word "and." The supper was in progress. The reason for this statement "supper being ended" is noted by reading verse 4. Jesus allowed ample time for the customary courtesy of washing the feet to have taken place. But not one of the disciples was willing to humble himself to perform a servant's duties.

What had been in the heart of the devil was put into the heart of Judas. Judas had already bargained with the Jewish leaders to betray his Lord (Matthew 26:14; Mark 14:10; Luke 22:3-6). Judas

50. And I know that his commandment is life everlasting: I know with a positive knowledge that, *Wuest* . . . And I am aware that His precept is eonian life, *Concordant* . . . I know what He orders is everlasting life, *Beck* . . . what he commands means eternal life, *Phillips* . . . his command leads to, *NIV* . . . that His order is life eternal, *Fenton* . . . stands for eternal life, *ALBA* . . . life eternal, *Murdock.*

whatsoever I speak therefore even as the Father said unto me, so I speak: Therefore, whatever I say, I say only what the Father has taught me, *TCNT* . . . I speak only in accordance, *Phillips* . . . I am saying exactly, *SEB* . . . I am saying...what My Father has told Me to say and in accordance with His instructions, *AmpB* . . . as the Father has bidden me, *Confraternity* . . . in accordance with the Father's instruction to Me, *Fenton* . . . has told me to say, *ALBA* . . . has directed me, *Norton* . . . as the Father has told me, *Montgomery* . . . has bidden me, *Weymouth* . . . what the Father has told me is what I speak, *JB.*

1. Now before the feast of the passover: Before the festival of the Passover began, *Phillips.*

When Jesus knew that his hour was come: Jesus realized, *Phillips* . . . that his time had finally arrived, *ET* . . . aware that for Him the time had come, *Berkeley* . . . that His hour to leave this world and go to the Father had come, *Adams.*

that he should depart out of this world unto the Father: . . . for Him to leave this world, *Weymouth* . . . for him to pass from this world to the Father, *Williams* . . . to remove our of this world, *Campbell* . . . the time for departure from this world, *Fenton.*

having loved his own which were in the world: . . . and as He had loved His own in the world, *Williams.*

he loved them unto the end: . . . showed forth his love to the end, *Montgomery* . . . to the highest degree, *AmpB* . . . to the consummation, *Concordant* . . . He loved them to the uttermost, *Wuest.*

3450.2 art gen sing	1222.2 adj gen sing masc	2218.1 adv	900.23 verb gen sing masc part perf act	1519.1 prep	3450.12 art acc sing fem
τοῦ	διαβόλου	ἤδη	βεβληκότος	εἰς	τὴν
tou	*diabolou*	*ēdē*	*beblēkotos*	*eis*	*tēn*
the	devil	already	having put	into	the

2559.4 noun acc sing fem	2430.2 name masc	4468.2 name gen masc	2442.2 name gen masc	2419.1 conj	840.6 prs-pron acc sing masc
καρδίαν	⸀ Ἰούδα	Σίμωνος	Ἰσκαριώτου,	ἵνα	αὐτὸν
kardian	*Iouda*	*Simōnos*	*Iskariōtou*	*hina*	*auton*
heart	of Judas,	of Simon	Iscariot,	that	him

3722.16 verb 3sing subj aor act	2419.1 conj	3722.45 verb 3sing subj aor act	840.6 prs-pron acc sing masc
παραδῷ,	[b☆ ἵνα	παραδοῖ	αὐτὸν
paradō	*hina*	*paradoi*	*auton*
he should deliver up,	[that	should deliver up	him

2430.1 name nom masc	4468.2 name gen masc	2442.2 name gen masc	3471.18 verb nom sing masc part perf act	3450.5 art sing masc
Ἰούδας	Σίμωνος	Ἰσκαριώτου,]	3. εἰδὼς	⸀a ὁ
Ioudas	*Simōnos*	*Iskariōtou*	*eidōs*	*ho*
Judas	of Simon	Iscariot,]	knowing	

2400.1 name nom masc	3617.1 conj	3820.1 adj	1319.33 verb 3sing indic perf act	1319.14 verb 3sing indic aor act
Ἰησοῦς ⸁	ὅτι	πάντα	⸀ δέδωκεν	[b☆ ἔδωκεν]
Iēsous	*hoti*	*panta*	*dedōken*	*edōken*
Jesus	that	all things	has given	[gave]

840.4 prs-pron dat sing	3450.5 art sing masc	3824.1 noun nom sing masc	1519.1 prep	3450.15 art acc pl fem	5331.8 noun acc pl fem	2504.1 conj
αὐτῷ	ὁ	πατὴρ	εἰς	τὰς	χεῖρας,	καὶ
autō	*ho*	*patēr*	*eis*	*tas*	*cheiras*	*kai*
him	the	Father	into	the	hands,	and

3617.1 conj	570.3 prep gen	2296.2 noun gen sing masc	1814.3 verb 3sing indic aor act	2504.1 conj	4242.1 prep	3450.6 art acc sing masc
ὅτι	ἀπὸ	θεοῦ	ἐξῆλθεν	καὶ	πρὸς	τὸν
hoti	*apo*	*theou*	*exēlthen*	*kai*	*pros*	*ton*
that	from	God	he came out	and	to	

2296.4 noun acc sing masc	5055.3 verb 3sing indic pres act	1446.15 verb 3sing indic pres pass	1523.2 prep gen	3450.2 art gen sing	1168.2 noun gen sing neu
θεὸν	ὑπάγει,	4. ἐγείρεται	ἐκ	τοῦ	δείπνου
theon	*hupagei*	*egeiretai*	*ek*	*tou*	*deipnou*
God	goes,	he rises	from	the	supper

2504.1 conj	4935.2 verb 3sing indic pres act	3450.17 art pl neu	2416.4 noun pl neu	2504.1 conj	2956.25 verb nom sing masc part aor act
καὶ	τίθησιν	τὰ	ἱμάτια,	καὶ	λαβὼν
kai	*tithēsin*	*ta*	*himatia*	*kai*	*labōn*
and	lays aside	the	garments	and	having taken

2986.2 noun acc sing neu	1235.1 verb 3sing indic aor act	1431.6 prs-pron acc 3sing masc	1520.1 adv	900.2 verb 3sing indic pres act	5045.1 noun sing neu
λέντιον	διέζωσεν	ἑαυτόν·	5. εἶτα	βάλλει	ὕδωρ
lention	*diezōsen*	*heauton*	*eita*	*ballei*	*hudōr*
a towel	he girded	himself:	afterwards	he pours	water

1519.1 prep	3450.6 art acc sing masc	3399.1 noun acc sing masc	2504.1 conj	751.5 verb 3sing indic aor mid	3400.2 verb inf pres act
εἰς	τὸν	νιπτῆρα,	καὶ	ἤρξατο	νίπτειν
eis	*ton*	*niptēra*	*kai*	*ērxato*	*niptein*
into	the	washing basin,	and	began	to wash

2.b.**Txt:** 02A,05D-corr, 017K,036,037,038,1, byz.it.sa.
Var: 01ℵ-org,03B,(019), Treg,Alf,Tisc,We/Ho, Weis,UBS/☆

3.a.**Txt:** 02A,017K,036, 037,038,1,byz.bo.Gries, Lach
Var: 01ℵ,03B,05D,019L, 033X,Treg,Alf,Tisc, We/HoWeis,Sod,UBS/☆

3.b.**Txt:** p66,02A,05D, 036,037,038,13,33, 1241,byz.Gries,Lach,Alf
Var: 01ℵ,03B,017K, 019L,Treg,Tisc,We/Ho, Weis,Sod,UBS/☆

became a willing instrument of the devil. Notice "the devil" has the article to identify the person of the devil.

Judas' backsliding is pathetic. Though the Bible at once identifies him as the betrayer of Jesus (Mark 3:19) and the "traitor" (Luke 6:16), at first he was far from that. Jesus chose him as one of the Twelve because of potential for leadership. The group selected him treasurer, though one might think they would have chosen Matthew. But greed grabbed his heart. He embezzled church funds (12:6). He allowed Satan to move him to betray the Master (Luke 22:3,4). He rejected the Lord's final attempt to restore him (13:26,27). Realizing his tragic mistake, he committed suicide (Matthew 27:3-5).

2. And supper being ended: And supper being in progress, *Rotherham* . . . so at supper, *Moffatt.*

the devil having now put into the heart of Judas Iscariot, Simon's son, to betray him: The Devil having already put, *HBIE* . . . been injected by Satan, *Murdock* . . . the devil had suggested to Judas, *Williams* . . . having thrust into the heart, *Rotherham* . . . when the devil had already poured the purpose into the heart, *Berkeley* . . . had already put the idea of betraying Jesus into the mind, *Beck* . . . the idea of betraying Jesus, *Beck* . . . having already hurled into the heart, *Wuest* . . . that he should deliver him up, *Rotherham* . . . had already put the thought of betraying Jesus, *Phillips.*

13:3. "Knowing" is repeated from verse 1. Jesus was conscious of His authority ("had given all things"), His origin ("was come from God"), and His destination ("was going back to God," NASB). "Knowing" is mentioned to show that the act He was about to perform was consistent with His deity and the effect His example would have on His own. If He the Lord of the universe stooped to wash the disciples' feet, no believer should think himself above serving his fellowman. "Had given all things into his hands" speaks of His authority as deity, for no creature could have the capacity of such a trust. His eternal origin "was come from God," was a consciousness He possessed even as a boy of 12 (Luke 2:49). His awareness of His divine deity, "was going back to God" (NASB), completes the cycle of His cognizance.

3. Jesus knowing that the Father had given all things into his hands: Him complete power, *TEV.*

and that he was come from God, and went to God: . . . had come from God and was going back to God, *Beck* . . . and was to return to God, *TCNT* . . . and to God He was departing, *Wuest.*

13:4. No servant had washed their feet as was the custom in those days. Luke tells us there was a dispute among the disciples as to who among them was regarded as the greatest (Luke 22:24). The bickering may have risen as to their place at the table.

"Laid aside his garments" refers to those worn on the upper part of His person. One could not work with outer flowing garments for they would become wet and soiled in washing feet. "And took a towel, and girded himself" states His final preparation for the task which none were willing to perform. The towel was the emblem of a servant and served as an apron and a drying cloth.

This verse favorably compares with the teaching of the apostle Paul in Philippians 2:5-7. Jesus did not cease to be what He was because He took upon himself the duties and functions of a slave; but God, while remaining what He is and "knowing" (verse 3) who He was, condescended to perform the task of a slave.

4. He riseth from supper, and laid aside his garments: . . . got up from table, *ALBA* . . . got up from the evening meal, *SEB* . . . rising from dinner, *Concordant* . . . took off His outer clothes, *Williams* . . . rose from the table, put away His robe, *Berkeley* . . . and put off his cloak, *Norton.*

and took a towel, and girded himself: . . . and tied a towel around him, *Moffatt* . . . took a cloth, *Norlie* . . . bound it around himself, *Wuest* . . . wrapped a towel round him, *ALBA* . . . wrapped it around his waist, *SEB.*

5. After that he poureth water into a bason: . . . draining water, *Concordant* . . . into a washbasin, *Norlie.*

13:5. John's Gospel describes vividly the details of the washing of the disciples' feet. The events of that evening remained indelibly

3450.8 art acc pl masc	4087.7 noun acc pl masc	3450.1 art gen pl	3073.6 noun gen pl masc	2504.1 conj	1578.1 verb inf pres act
τοὺς	πόδας	τῶν	μαθητῶν,	καὶ	ἐκμάσσειν
tous	*podas*	*tōn*	*mathētōn*	*kai*	*ekmassein*
the	feet	of the	disciples,	and	to wipe

3450.3 art dat sing	2986.1 noun dat sing neu	3614.3 rel-pron dat sing	1498.34 verb sing indic imperf act	1235.3 verb nom sing masc part perf mid
τῷ	λεντίῳ	ᾧ	ἦν	διεζωσμένος.
tō	*lentiō*	*hō*	*ēn*	*diezōsmenos*
with the	towel	with which	he was	girded.

6.a.**Txt:** 01ℵ,02A,017K, 032W,036,037,038,1,13, byz.Lach,Sod
Var: p66,03B,05D,019L, it.sa.bo.TregAlf,Tisc, We/Ho,Weis,UBS/☆

6.b.**Txt:** 01ℵ-corr,02A, 05D,017K,019L,032W, 036,037,038,1,13,byz. Sod
Var: p66,01ℵ-org,03B, Lach,Alf,Tisc,We/Ho, Weis,UBS/☆

2048.34 verb 3sing indic pres	3631.1 conj	4242.1 prep	4468.4 name acc masc	3935.4 name acc masc	2504.1 conj
6. ἔρχεται	οὖν	πρὸς	Σίμωνα	Πέτρον·	⸂a καὶ ⸃
erchetai	*oun*	*pros*	*Simōna*	*Petron*	*kai*
He comes	therefore	to	Simon	Peter,	and

2978.5 verb 3sing indic pres act	840.4 prs-pron dat sing	1552.3 dem-pron nom sing masc	2935.5 noun voc sing masc	4622.1 prs-pron nom 2sing
λέγει	αὐτῷ	⸂b ἐκεῖνος, ⸃	Κύριε,	σύ
legei	*autō*	*ekeinos*	*Kurie*	*su*
says	to him	that,	Lord,	you

1466.2 prs-pron gen 1sing	3400.1 verb 2sing indic pres act	3450.8 art acc pl masc	4087.7 noun acc pl masc	552.6 verb 3sing indic aor pass
μου	νίπτεις	τοὺς	πόδας;	**7.** Ἀπεκρίθη
mou	*nipteis*	*tous*	*podas*	*Apekrithē*
my	washes	the	feet?	Answered

2400.1 name nom masc	2504.1 conj	1500.5 verb 3sing indic aor act	840.4 prs-pron dat sing	3614.16 rel-pron sing neu	1466.1 prs-pron nom 1sing
Ἰησοῦς	καὶ	εἶπεν	αὐτῷ,	Ὃ	ἐγὼ
Iēsous	*kai*	*eipen*	*autō*	*Ho*	*egō*
Jesus	and	said	to him,	What	I

4020.1 verb 1sing pres act	4622.1 prs-pron nom 2sing	3620.2 partic	3471.3 verb 2sing indic perf act	732.1 adv	1091.48 verb 2sing indic fut mid
ποιῶ	σὺ	οὐκ	οἶδας	ἄρτι,	γνώσῃ
poiō	*su*	*ouk*	*oidas*	*arti*	*gnōsē*
do	you	not	know	now,	you shall know

1156.2 conj	3196.3 prep	3642.18 dem-pron pl neu	2978.5 verb 3sing indic pres act	840.4 prs-pron dat sing	3935.1 name nom masc	3620.3 partic
δὲ	μετὰ	ταῦτα.	**8.** Λέγει	αὐτῷ	Πέτρος,	Οὐ
de	*meta*	*tauta*	*Legei*	*autō*	*Petros*	*Ou*
but	after	these things.	Says	to him	Peter,	Not

3231.1 partic	3400.6 verb 2sing subj aor act	3450.8 art acc pl masc	4087.7 noun acc pl masc	1466.2 prs-pron gen 1sing	1466.2 prs-pron gen 1sing
μὴ	νίψῃς	⸀ τοὺς	πόδας	μου	[☆ μου
mē	*nipsēs*	*tous*	*podas*	*mou*	*mou*
not	you may wash	the	feet	my	[my

3450.8 art acc pl masc	4087.7 noun acc pl masc	1519.1 prep	3450.6 art acc sing masc	163.3 noun acc sing masc	552.6 verb 3sing indic aor pass
τοὺς	πόδας]	εἰς	τὸν	αἰῶνα.	Ἀπεκρίθη
tous	*podas*	*eis*	*ton*	*aiōna*	*Apekrithē*
the	feet]	to	the	age.	Answered

8.a.**Txt:** (p66),01ℵ,(032), 036,037,(038),1,13,byz. Gries,Word
Var: 02A,03B,04C-org, 019L,Lach,Treg,Alf, Tisc,We/HoWeis,Sod, UBS/☆

840.4 prs-pron dat sing	3450.5 art sing masc	2400.1 name nom masc	2400.1 name nom masc	840.4 prs-pron dat sing	1430.1 partic
⸀ αὐτῷ	ὁ	Ἰησοῦς,	[a☆ Ἰησοῦς	αὐτῷ,]	Ἐὰν
autō	*ho*	*Iēsous*	*Iēsous*	*autō*	*Ean*
him		Jesus,	[Jesus	him,]	If

recorded on John's memory.

People did not wear socks and shoes that enclosed the feet. Sandals were the sole protection from sharp stones and the dusty road. The feet became the most unclean part of the body. Washing the feet of guests was common courtesy, and the deed brought refreshing satisfaction to the recipient. According to the custom the guests reclined on low couches with heads toward the central table. The sandals had been left at the entrance, and the bare feet were extended so that the washing could be easily done. Thus Jesus functioned as a slave.

and began to wash the disciples' feet, and to wipe them:
with the towel wherewith he was girded: . . . tied around His waist, *ET.*

6. Then cometh he to Simon Peter: So He approached Simon Peter, *Berkeley.*
and Peter saith unto him, Lord, dost thou wash my feet?: You, Master! Are you going to wash my feet, *TCNT.*

13:6. Jesus was interrupted in His work by Peter's protest. We are not told who Jesus washed first, but Peter does not seem to be the first. Peter connected the two pronouns in close relationship. Both "thou" and "my" are emphatic. He felt shame for allowing his Lord to wash their feet. Peter indicated that the two roles were reversed. His objection was well-founded for the creature should serve the Creator.

7. Jesus answered and said unto him, What I do thou knowest not now: What I do is not clear to you now, *BB* . . . You do not realize now what I am doing, *Phillips* . . . you do not comprehend, *Campbell* . . . You may not understand what I am doing now, *SEB* . . . What I am doing is not clear to you now, *ALBA.*
but thou shalt know hereafter: . . . but thou shalt understand afterwards, *Alford* . . . but by-and-by you will learn, *Williams* . . . But later you will understand, *Beck* . . . shall learn by experience after these things, *Wuest.*

13:7. But Jesus had more than one reason for washing their feet. His first lesson had made its mark upon Peter's soul. Jesus used the same pronouns that Peter had, but His emphasis was reversed. What "I" am doing "thou" knowest not. Peter knew the earthly concept that the inferior served the superior, and he recognized his Lord as his superior. But Peter did not know that in God's economy the servant is greater than the one who is served. When would Peter understand what Jesus was doing? Jesus told Peter he would know "hereafter." The two words for "knowest" and "shalt know" are synonyms with a broad range of interpretations which sometimes overlap. Jesus perhaps was implying that what Peter did not know now intellectually, he would learn by experience later. Moreover, Peter was to learn by experience what Jesus was teaching by example. In Peter's second epistle he calls himself a bond-servant (*doulos,* a slave). When a believer realizes he is a servant to all, he has begun to understand the meaning Jesus attached to His washing of the disciples' feet.

If Jesus had not shocked the Twelve out of their wrong view of greatness, it would have wrecked the Church early after the Cross. Often they "had disputed among themselves, who should be the greatest" (Mark 9:34). For this reason He told them, "The princes of the Gentiles exercise dominion over them" (Matthew 20:25). He also declared, "Whosoever will be chief among you, let him be your servant" (Matthew 20:27). Then He said, "Even as the Son of man came not to be ministered unto, but to minister, and to give his life a ransom for many" (Matthew 20:28).

8. Peter saith unto him, Thou shalt never wash my feet: No!...You'll never wash my feet, *Beck* . . . You shall never, never wash my feet! *Berkeley* . . . never at any time, *Fenton* . . . Never while the world lasts, *Weymouth* . . . whill the worlde stondeth, *Tyndale.*
Jesus answered him, If I wash thee not, thou hast no part with me: Unless you let me wash you, Peter, *Phillips* . . . you have

3231.1 partic	**3400.5** verb 1sing subj aor act	**4622.4** prs-pron acc 2sing	**3620.2** partic	**2174.3** verb 2sing indic pres act	**3183.1** noun sing neu	**3196.2** prep
μὴ	νίψω	σε,	οὐκ	ἔχεις	μέρος	μετ'
mē	*nipsō*	*se*	*ouk*	*echeis*	*meros*	*met'*
not	I wash	you,	not	you have	part	with

1466.3 prs-pron gen 1sing	**2978.5** verb 3sing indic pres act	**840.4** prs-pron dat sing	**4468.1** name masc	**3935.1** name nom masc	**2935.5** noun voc sing masc
ἐμοῦ.	**9.** Λέγει	αὐτῷ	Σίμων	Πέτρος,	Κύριε,
emou	*Legei*	*autō*	*Simōn*	*Petros*	*Kurie*
me.	Says	to him	Simon	Peter,	Lord,

3231.1 partic	**3450.8** art acc pl masc	**4087.7** noun acc pl masc	**1466.2** prs-pron gen 1sing	**3303.1** adv	**233.2** conj	**2504.1** conj
μὴ	τοὺς	πόδας	μου	μόνον,	ἀλλὰ	καὶ
mē	*tous*	*podas*	*mou*	*monon*	*alla*	*kai*
not	the	feet	my	only,	but	also

10.a.**Txt:** p66,01ℵ,02A, 04C,05D,017K,019L, 036,037,038,etc.byz. LachWeis,Sod
Var: 03B,Tisc,We/Ho, UBS/☆

3450.15 art acc pl fem	**5331.8** noun acc pl fem	**2504.1** conj	**3450.12** art acc sing fem	**2747.4** noun acc sing fem	**2978.5** verb 3sing indic pres act
τὰς	χεῖρας	καὶ	τὴν	κεφαλήν.	**10.** Λέγει
tas	*cheiras*	*kai*	*tēn*	*kephalēn*	*Legei*
the	hands	and	the	head.	Says

10.b.**Txt:** 04C-corr,05D, 017K,019L,036,037,038, 1,13,byz.
Var: p66,01ℵ,02A,03B, 04C-org,032W,Lach, Treg,Alf,WordTisc, We/Ho,Weis,Sod,UBS/☆

840.4 prs-pron dat sing	**3450.5** art sing masc	**2400.1** name nom masc	**3450.5** art sing masc	**3040.5** verb nom sing masc part perf	**3620.3** partic
αὐτῷ	⌜a ὁ ⌝	Ἰησοῦς,	Ὁ	λελουμένος	⌜ οὐ
autō	*ho*	*Iēsous*	*Ho*	*leloumenos*	*ou*
to him		Jesus,	The	having been washed	not

10.c.**Txt:** 04C-corr,036, 037,byz.
Var: p66,03B,04C-org, 019L,032W,038,13,it.sa. bo.Lach,TregAlf,We/Ho, Weis,Sod,UBS/☆

5367.3 noun acc sing fem	**2174.4** verb 3sing indic pres act	**3620.2** partic	**2174.4** verb 3sing indic pres act	**5367.3** noun acc sing fem	**2211.1** conj
χρείαν	ἔχει	[b☆ οὐκ	ἔχει	χρείαν]	⌜ ἢ
chreian	*echei*	*ouk*	*echei*	*chreian*	*ē*
need	has	[not	has	need]	than

10.d.**Txt:** p66,03B,04C, 019L,032W,036,037, 038,13,byz.it.sa.bo.Lach, We/Ho,Weis,Sod,UBS/☆
Var: 01ℵ,Tisc

1479.1 conj	**3231.1** partic	**3450.8** art acc pl masc	**4087.7** noun acc pl masc	**3400.13** verb inf aor mid	**233.1** conj
[c☆ εἰ	μὴ]	⌜d τοὺς	πόδας ⌝	νίψασθαι,	ἀλλ'
ei	*mē*	*tous*	*podas*	*nipsasthai*	*all'*
[if	not]	the	feet	to wash,	but

1498.4 verb 3sing indic pres act	**2485.3** adj nom sing masc	**3513.4** adj nom sing masc	**2504.1** conj	**5050.1** prs-pron nom 2pl	**2485.4** adj nom pl masc
ἔστιν	καθαρὸς	ὅλος·	καὶ	ὑμεῖς	καθαροί
estin	*katharos*	*holos*	*kai*	*humeis*	*katharoi*
is	clean	wholly;	and	you	clean

1498.6 verb 2pl indic pres act	**233.1** conj	**3644.1** adv	**3820.7** adj pl masc	**3471.11** verb 3sing indic plperf act	**1056.1** conj	**3450.6** art acc sing masc
ἐστε,	ἀλλ'	οὐχὶ	πάντες.	**11.** ᾔδει	γὰρ	τὸν
este	*all'*	*ouchi*	*pantes*	*ēdei*	*gar*	*ton*
are,	but	not	all.	He knew	for	the

3722.5 verb acc sing masc part pres act	**840.6** prs-pron acc sing masc	**1217.2** prep	**3642.17** dem-pron sing neu	**1500.5** verb 3sing indic aor act
παραδιδόντα	αὐτόν·	διὰ	τοῦτο	εἶπεν,
paradidonta	*auton*	*dia*	*touto*	*eipen*
delivering up	him:	because of	this	he said,

11.a.**Var:** 03B,04C,019L, 33,Lach,Treg,Alf,Tisc, We/Ho,WeisSod,UBS/☆

3617.1 conj	**3644.1** adv	**3820.7** adj pl masc	**2485.4** adj nom pl masc	**1498.6** verb 2pl indic pres act	**3616.1** conj
[a☆+ ὅτι]	Οὐχὶ	πάντες	καθαροί	ἐστε.	**12.** Ὅτε
hoti	*Ouchi*	*pantes*	*katharoi*	*este*	*Hote*
	Not	all	clean	you are.	When

13:8. Peter thought Jesus had degraded himself by stooping to a servant's duties. Peter spoke in humility and modesty but with determination. His motive was good, but his understanding was faulty.

Two ideas are evident in Jesus' stern response. First, persistent disobedience to the Master will exclude a disciple from the benefits Christ came to bestow. Second, a disciple who wishes to continue his walk with the Saviour is in need of, and indeed must have, continuous cleansing by His hands (1 John 1:7-9).

no share with me, *Weymouth* . . . you will not share my lot, *Moffatt* . . . you will have no fellowship with Me, *Norlie* . . . you can have nothing in common with me, *JB* . . . you are not sharing with me, *SEB, Berkeley* . . . your place is not with me, *ALBA* . . . nothing in common with me, *TCNT* . . . you will no longer be my disciple, *TEV*.

13:9. The impetuous disciple submitted to Christ's cleansing. He was willing for his hands and his head to be bathed also. Peter wanted all the benefits and blessings his Master wished to bestow.

9. Simon Peter saith unto him, Lord, not my feet only, but also my hands and my head: In that case, Lord, *ALBA* . . . Lord, do not stop with my feet, *Williams*.

13:10. "Washed" indicates one who has had the whole body bathed. This is the figure of one who by faith has entered into a saving relationship with the Saviour. "But is clean" means that because he has had a bath, there is no need to wash the entire body again.

The disciples remained in the saving relationship with Jesus except for Judas who was already stealing from the treasury of the apostles (6:70; 12:6).

10. Jesus saith to him, He that is washed needeth not save to wash his feet: When one has fully bathed one needs no further washing, *ALBA* . . . who had just taken a bath, *Williams* . . . had lately bathed, *Weymouth* . . . only needs to have his feet washed, *Moffatt* . . . He who has been bathing, *Campbell* . . . only requires to have, *Fenton* . . . does not need to be washed further, *Berkeley* . . . to be completely clean, *Norlie* . . . unless it be their feet, *TCNT*.

but is clean every whit: and ye are clean, but not all: . . . but is wholly pure, *Sawyer* . . . but is entirely pure, *Klingensmith* . . . And you are clean—though not all of you, *Phillips* . . . And you my disciples are clean, and yet this is not true of all of you, *Weymouth* . . . but not every one of you, *Norlie* . . . but is altogether clean, *ALBA*.

13:11. Judas had engaged in a contract to betray Jesus (Mark 14:1,10,11). Judas needed a bath; the other disciples merely needed their feet washed. Washing of the feet indicated the disciples' continuous need for cleansing as the laver in the Old Testament tabernacle taught the need for cleansing before entering the presence of God. Jesus taught the same truth when He said, "Blessed are the pure in heart: for they shall see God" (Matthew 5:8).

11. For he know who should betray him: . . . who was false to him, *BB* . . . (he knew the traitor), *Moffatt* . . . For he knew his betrayer, *HBIE, Fenton* . . . who was turning against him, *SEB*.

therefore said he, Ye are not all clean: . . . on this account, *Wuest* . . . he said to the disciples, *TCNT*.

13:12. Jesus continued the task of a slave until He had washed the feet of the 12 apostles. Then He laid the towel aside, took up His garments, and reclined at the table again. Reclining at the meal seems odd to Westerners, but in Biblical culture the custom was deeply rooted.

His question, "Know ye what I have done to you?" was not meant to be answered. It was introductory to His teaching. By asking the question He focused their attention on His explanation.

3631.1 conj	3400.4 verb 3sing indic aor act	3450.8 art acc pl masc	4087.7 noun acc pl masc	840.1 prs-pron gen pl	2504.1 conj
οὖν	ἔνιψεν	τοὺς	πόδας	αὐτῶν,	καὶ
oun	*enipsen*	*tous*	*podas*	*autōn*	*kai*
therefore	he had washed	the	feet	their,	and

12.a.**Var:** p66,01א, 02A-corr,03B,04C-org, 019L,032W,33,bo.Lach, TregAlf,Tisc,We/Ho, Weis,Sod,UBS/☆

2956.14 verb 3sing indic aor act	3450.17 art pl neu	2416.4 noun pl neu	840.3 prs-pron gen sing	2504.1 conj
ἔλαβεν	τὰ	ἱμάτια	αὐτοῦ,	[a☆+ καὶ]
elaben	*ta*	*himatia*	*autou*	*kai*
taken	the	garments	his,	[and]

12.b.**Txt:** p66,01א-corr, 02A,04C-corr,05D,017K, 019L,036,037,038,33, byz.Lach
Var: 01א-org,03B, 04C-org,032W,Treg,Alf, Tisc,We/Ho,WeisSod, UBS/☆

375.4 verb nom sing masc part aor act	375.1 verb 3sing indic aor act	3687.1 adv	1500.5 verb 3sing indic aor act	840.2 prs-pron dat pl
ʻ ἀναπεσὼν	[b☆ ἀνέπεσεν]	πάλιν,	εἶπεν	αὐτοῖς,
anapesōn	*anepesen*	*palin*	*eipen*	*autois*
having reclined	[reclined]	again,	he said	to them,

1091.5 verb 2pl indic pres act	4949.9 intr-pron sing neu	4020.42 verb 1sing indic perf act	5050.3 prs-pron dat 2pl	5050.1 prs-pron nom 2pl
Γινώσκετε	τί	πεποίηκα	ὑμῖν;	**13.** ὑμεῖς
Ginōskete	*ti*	*pepoiēka*	*humin*	*humeis*
Do you know	what	I have done	to you?	You

5291.2 verb 2pl indic pres act	1466.6 prs-pron acc 1sing	3450.5 art sing masc	1314.1 noun nom sing masc	2504.1 conj	3450.5 art sing masc
φωνεῖτέ	με	Ὁ	διδάσκαλος	καὶ	Ὁ
phōneite	*me*	*Ho*	*didaskalos*	*kai*	*Ho*
call	me	the	Teacher	and	the

2935.1 noun nom sing masc	2504.1 conj	2544.1 adv	2978.2 verb 2pl pres act	1498.2 verb 1sing indic pres act	1056.1 conj
κύριος,	καὶ	καλῶς	λέγετε,	εἰμὶ	γάρ.
kurios	*kai*	*kalōs*	*legete*	*eimi*	*gar*
Lord,	and	well	you say,	I am	for.

1479.1 conj	3631.1 conj	1466.1 prs-pron nom 1sing	3400.3 verb 1sing indic aor act	5050.2 prs-pron gen 2pl	3450.8 art acc pl masc
14. εἰ	οὖν	ἐγὼ	ἔνιψα	ὑμῶν	τοὺς
ei	*oun*	*egō*	*enipsa*	*humōn*	*tous*
If	therefore	I	washed	your	the

4087.7 noun acc pl masc	3450.5 art sing masc	2935.1 noun nom sing masc	2504.1 conj	3450.5 art sing masc	1314.1 noun nom sing masc
πόδας,	ὁ	κύριος	καὶ	ὁ	διδάσκαλος,
podas	*ho*	*kurios*	*kai*	*ho*	*didaskalos*
feet,	the	Lord	and	the	Teacher,

2504.1 conj	5050.1 prs-pron nom 2pl	3648.1 verb 2pl pres act	238.1 prs-pron gen pl	3400.2 verb inf pres act	3450.8 art acc pl masc
καὶ	ὑμεῖς	ὀφείλετε	ἀλλήλων	νίπτειν	τοὺς
kai	*humeis*	*opheilete*	*allēlōn*	*niptein*	*tous*
also	you	ought	of one another	to wash	the

15.a.**Var:** p66,01א,02A, 017K,021M,041,1,13, 28,33,700,1241,Tisc

4087.7 noun acc pl masc	5100.2 noun acc sing neu	1056.1 conj	1319.12 verb 1sing indic aor act	1319.32 verb 1sing indic perf act
πόδας.	**15.** ὑπόδειγμα	γὰρ	ʻ ἔδωκα	[a δέδωκα]
podas	*hupodeigma*	*gar*	*edōka*	*dedōka*
feet;	an example	for	I gave	[I have given]

5050.3 prs-pron dat 2pl	2419.1 conj	2503.1 conj	1466.1 prs-pron nom 1sing	4020.22 verb 1sing indic aor act	5050.3 prs-pron dat 2pl
ὑμῖν,	ἵνα	καθὼς	ἐγὼ	ἐποίησα	ὑμῖν,
humin	*hina*	*kathōs*	*egō*	*epoiēsa*	*humin*
you,	that	as	I	did	to you,

13:13. "Master" (Teacher) and "Lord" were titles often given to rabbis by their students. But here the definite article is used with both "the teacher" and "the Lord." The word "Lord" in the Septuagint is rendered from the Hebrew word *Yahweh*, the name of their covenant-keeping God. There is no doubt that when *ho kurios* ("the Lord") is applied to Jesus it means a title of deity. Jesus himself accepted both titles by saying (literally), "You have said it well; for I am."

The lesson Jesus taught was a very practical one. He did not institute a mere ceremony. If He as their Teacher and Lord condescended to do for them the work of a servant, they should be willing to serve one another. Jesus said that He had given them an example: "If I then, your Lord and Master, have washed your feet . . . ." He expected them to emulate His example. His relationship to them called for no such service, but their relationship to Him and to each other required them to serve one another in humility.

The concept of serving one another is widely taught in the New Testament. The Lord Jesus emphasized it here, and the apostle Paul stressed it in his epistles. For example, in Galatians 6:2 he says believers are to bear one another's burdens.

13:14. The word "ought" means "to owe," "to be in debt," and "to be due." The word is used twice in John (here and in 19:7) and 36 times in the New Testament. The synonym for "ought" (*dei*) means a duty or necessity as existing in the thing itself, and "ought" (as here used: Greek, *opheilō*) refers to the obligation as actually imposed. The only New Testament reference to believers washing one another's feet occurs in 1 Timothy 5:10 and refers to the widows in good standing with the church. One of the widows' labors of love was that they "washed the saints' feet." If Jesus had been instituting an ordinance there would have been more than one reference.

13:15. Jesus had just washed the disciples' feet, including those of Judas the betrayer. *Hupodeigma* ("example") occurs six times in the New Testament and only here in John. The word means "a figure which teaches by making known a truth."

Jesus did not say "*what* I did to you," but "*as* (*kathōs*) I have done to you." The disciples were to act from the same self-sacrificing humility which the Saviour exemplified.

The world has influenced believers by its spirit of competition, its love of authority, power, and wealth. The Lord will accept no ritual of foot washing as a substitute for the believers' conduct as love-slaves to one another. Believers are debtors to all men (Romans

12. So after he had washed their feet, and had taken his garments: . . . and redressing, *Berkeley.*

and was set down again: . . . and reclined again at table, *HBIE* . . . and resumed his place, *RSV, ALBA.*

he said unto them, Know ye what I have done to you?: Do you understand, *Weymouth* . . . what I have been doing to you, *Montgomery* . . . Do you realize what I have just done to you, *Phillips* . . . do you see what it means? *ALBA.*

13. Ye call me Master and Lord: You are shouting to Me, *Concordant* . . . Teacher and Lord, *ASV* . . . Our Rabbi, *Murdock.*

and ye say well; for so I am: . . . and you speak correctly, *Fenton* . . . and rightly so, because I am, *Berkeley* . . . You are right, for I am all of that, *Norlie.*

14. If I then, your Lord and Master, have washed your feet: . . . your Master and Rabbi, *Weymouth.*

ye also ought to wash one another's feet: . . . it is also your duty, *Weymouth* . . . you also have a moral obligation, *Wuest* . . . you surely ought to wash, *Berkeley* . . . you must be ready to wash one another's feet, *Phillips.*

15. For I have given you an example:

that ye should do as I have done to you: . . . you too may practice what I have done, *Williams.*

2504.1 conj	5050.1 prs-pron nom 2pl	4020.9 verb 2pl subj pres act	279.1 partic	279.1 partic	2978.1 verb 1sing pres act
καὶ	ὑμεῖς	ποιῆτε.	16. ἀμὴν	ἀμὴν	λέγω
kai	*humeis*	*poiēte*	*amēn*	*amēn*	*legō*
also	you	should do.	Truly	truly	I say

5050.3 prs-pron dat 2pl	3620.2 partic	1498.4 verb 3sing indic pres act	1395.1 noun nom sing masc	3157.2 adj comp nom sing	3450.2 art gen sing
ὑμῖν,	οὐκ	ἔστιν	δοῦλος	μείζων	τοῦ
humin	*ouk*	*estin*	*doulos*	*meizōn*	*tou*
to you,	Not	is	a slave	greater	the

2935.2 noun gen sing masc	840.3 prs-pron gen sing	3624.1 adv	646.1 noun nom sing masc	3157.2 adj comp nom sing	3450.2 art gen sing
κυρίου	αὐτοῦ,	οὐδὲ	ἀπόστολος	μείζων	τοῦ
kuriou	*autou*	*oude*	*apostolos*	*meizōn*	*tou*
master	his,	nor	a messenger	greater	the

3854.12 verb gen sing masc part aor act	840.6 prs-pron acc sing masc	1479.1 conj	3642.18 dem-pron pl neu	3471.6 verb 2pl indic perf act
πέμψαντος	αὐτόν.	17. εἰ	ταῦτα	οἴδατε,
pempsantos	*auton*	*ei*	*tauta*	*oidate*
having sent	him.	If	these things	you know,

3079.4 adj nom pl masc	1498.6 verb 2pl indic pres act	1430.1 partic	4020.9 verb 2pl subj pres act	840.16 prs-pron pl neu	3620.3 partic	3875.1 prep
μακάριοί	ἐστε	ἐὰν	ποιῆτε	αὐτά.	18. οὐ	περὶ
makarioi	*este*	*ean*	*poiēte*	*auta*	*ou*	*peri*
blessed	are you	if	you do	them.	Not	of

3820.4 adj gen pl	5050.2 prs-pron gen 2pl	2978.1 verb 1sing pres act	1466.1 prs-pron nom 1sing	3471.2 verb 1sing indic perf act	3614.8 rel-pron acc pl masc
πάντων	ὑμῶν	λέγω˙	ἐγὼ	οἶδα	⸀ οὓς
pantōn	*humōn*	*legō*	*egō*	*oida*	*hous*
all	you	I speak.	I	know	whom

18.a.**Txt:** p66,02A,05D,017K,032W,036,037,038,1,13,byz.Lach
Var: 01ℵ,03B,04C,019L,021M,33,Treg,Alf,Tisc,We/HoWeis,Sod,UBS/☆

4949.8 intr-pron acc pl fem	1573.1 verb 1sing indic aor mid	233.1 conj	2419.1 conj	3450.9 art nom sing fem	1118.1 noun nom sing fem
[a☆ τίνας]	ἐξελεξάμην˙	ἀλλ'	ἵνα	ἡ	γραφὴ
tinas	*exelexamēn*	*all'*	*hina*	*hē*	*graphē*
[idem]	I chose,	but	that	the	scripture

18.b.**Txt:** p66,01ℵ,02A,05D,017K,032W,036,037,038,1,13,etc.byz.it.Gries,Lach,Tisc
Var: 03B,04C,019L,sa.Treg,Alf,We/Ho,Weis,UBS/☆

3997.22 verb 3sing subj aor pass	3450.5 art sing masc	5017.1 verb nom sing masc part pres act	3196.2 prep	1466.3 prs-pron gen 1sing
πληρωθῇ,	Ὁ	τρώγων	⸀ μετ'	ἐμοῦ
plērōthē	*Ho*	*trōgōn*	*met'*	*emou*
might be fulfilled,	The	eating	with	me

18.c.**Var:** 01ℵ,02A,030U,032W,038,041,Tisc

1466.2 prs-pron gen 1sing	3450.6 art acc sing masc	735.4 noun acc sing masc	1854.2 verb 3sing indic aor act	1854.12 verb 3sing indic perf act
[b☆ μου]	τὸν	ἄρτον	⸀ ἐπῆρεν	[c ἐπῆρκεν]
mou	*ton*	*arton*	*epēren*	*epērken*
[idem]	the	bread	lifted up	[has lifted up]

1894.2 prep	1466.7 prs-pron acc 1sing	3450.12 art acc sing fem	4276.1 noun acc sing fem	840.3 prs-pron gen sing	570.2 prep gen
ἐπ'	ἐμὲ	τὴν	πτέρναν	αὐτοῦ.	19. ἀπ'
ep'	*eme*	*tēn*	*pternan*	*autou*	*ap'*
against	me	the	heel	his.	From

732.1 adv	2978.1 verb 1sing pres act	5050.3 prs-pron dat 2pl	4112.1 prep	3450.2 art gen sing	1090.63 verb inf aor mid
ἄρτι	λέγω	ὑμῖν	πρὸ	τοῦ	γενέσθαι,
arti	*legō*	*humin*	*pro*	*tou*	*genesthai*
this time	I tell	you,	before	the	to come to pass,

:14). If we have the attitude of debtors, we will serve others out of humility because of the debt we owe them.

16. Verily, verily, I say unto you, The servant is not greater than his lord: . . . a slave is not greater than his master, *Montgomery* . . . A servant is not superior, *Berkeley* . . . than his boss, *Klingensmith.*

neither he that is sent greater than he that sent him: . . . not is a messenger greater than He who sent him, *Norlie* . . . the apostle greater than, *Campbell.*

13:16. "Verily, verily" is again stated to emphasize the forthcoming statement (see 1:51 for comments). Jesus' words as recorded n this verse occur four times in the Gospels. The connection is lifferent in each (Matthew 10:24; Luke 6:40; here, and 15:20). We may infer from this that that saying was one of our Lord's most repeated statements.

17. If ye know these things, happy are ye if ye do them: If you grasp these teachings, *Berkeley* . . . you will be happy if you practice them, *SEB* . . . spiritually prosperous ones you are if, *Wuest* . . . this you will be blessed, if you do it, *Norlie* . . . if you act accordingly, *Weymouth* . . . If you understand the lesson, act on it and you are blessed, *ALBA.*

13:17. Jesus had given them the example and explained it to them; it remained for them to practice His teaching. "Happy are e if ye do them." *Makarios* ("happy, blessed") occurs 50 times in the New Testament, but only twice in John's Gospel (here and 20:29). This is the same word used in the Beatitudes (Matthew 5:3-1). The blessing Jesus pronounced produces happiness in this life nd the reward of the Lord at the judgment seat of Christ (Romans 4:10; 2 Corinthians 5:10).

18. I speak not of you all: I do not mean all of you, *Williams.*

I know whom I have chosen: I know the men of my choice, *Moffatt* . . . I selected, *Wuest.*

but that the scripture may be fulfilled: . . . but I know that the Scriptures must be fulfilled, *Williams* . . . the writings might be completed, *Klingensmith* . . . must come true, *SEB.*

He that eateth bread with me hath lifted up his heel against me: He who eats my bread kicks me, *Beck* . . . He who is masticating bread with Me, *Concordant* . . . One who shared meals with me has turned against me, *ALBA* . . . rebels against me, *JB* . . . has plotted my overthrow, *Norton.*

13:18. Strong social custom forbade betraying one with whom a meal had been eaten. This social prohibition of New Testament imes prevailed as far back as the early Old Testament. Because of : Lot offered his daughters for sexual exploitation rather than urrender his two guests to the homosexuals of Sodom (Genesis 19:8). His sole reason for such an act (unthinkable in our modern world) was simply, "For therefore came they under the shadow of my roof." He must protect them even with his life if necessary. Yet Judas broke this obligation to his friend and Lord.

19. Now I tell you before it come: From this time I tell you, before it comes to pass, *HBIE* . . . From now on I'm telling you these things before they happen, *Beck* . . . I am telling you now, before it happens, *SEB* . . . before they happen, *Weymouth.*

13:19. Jesus spoke of the betrayal and the coming crucifixion. Thus He pointed back to Psalm 41:9 as a prophecy concerning Himself. His betrayal, seizure, and crucifixion could shatter their faith in Him as their Messiah. Yet, because He had known and foretold this was to happen, they would be encouraged to believe.

Jesus meant His prophetic teachings to serve a practical purpose. He never intended His discussion of the future to appeal to curiosity as in the case of the fortune-teller. Indeed the Bible prohibits people from consulting such persons (Deuteronomy 18:10-12). Instead, God promised to raise up a Prophet whose guidance for tomorrow is sufficient (Deuteronomy 18:15). That Prophet, of

19.a.**Txt:** 02A,05D, 032W,036,037,038,1,13, byz.Lach
Var: 03B,Treg,We/Ho, Weis,UBS/☆

2419.1 conj	**3615.1** conj	**1090.40** verb 3sing subj aor mid	**3961.1** verb 2pl subj act	**3961.1** verb 2pl subj act
ἵνα	⸂ ὅταν	γένηται,	πιστεύσητε	[a☆ πιστεύσητε
hina	*hotan*	*genētai*	*pisteusēte*	*pisteusēte*
that	when	it come to pass,	you may believe	[you may believe

3615.1 conj	**1090.40** verb 3sing subj aor mid	**3617.1** conj	**1466.1** prs-pron nom 1sing	**1498.2** verb 1sing indic pres act	**279.1** partic
ὅταν	γένηται]	ὅτι	ἐγώ	εἰμι.	**20.** ἀμὴν
hotan	*genētai*	*hoti*	*egō*	*eimi*	*amēn*
when	it happens]	that	I	am.	Truly

279.1 partic	**2978.1** verb 1sing pres act	**5050.3** prs-pron dat 2pl	**3450.5** art sing masc	**2956.8** verb nom sing masc part pres act	**1430.1** partic
ἀμὴν	λέγω	ὑμῖν,	Ὁ	λαμβάνων	⸂ ἐάν
amēn	*legō*	*humin*	*Ho*	*lambanōn*	*ean*
truly	I say	to you,	The	receiving	

20.a.**Txt:** p66-corr,05D, 030U,036,037,038,1,13, byz.
Var: 01ℵ,03B,04C, 017K,019L,021M,033X, 041,33,Lach,Treg,Alf, TiscWe/Ho,Weis,Sod, UBS/☆

300.1 partic	**4948.5** indef-pron	**3854.4** verb 1sing act	**1466.7** prs-pron acc 1sing	**2956.4** verb 3sing indic pres act
[a☆ ἄν]	τινα	πέμψω,	ἐμὲ	λαμβάνει·
an	*tina*	*pempsō*	*eme*	*lambanei*
	whomever	I shall send,	me	receives;

3450.5 art sing masc	**1156.2** conj	**1466.7** prs-pron acc 1sing	**2956.8** verb nom sing masc part pres act	**2956.4** verb 3sing indic pres act	**3450.6** art acc sing masc
ὁ	δὲ	ἐμὲ	λαμβάνων,	λαμβάνει	τὸν
ho	*de*	*eme*	*lambanōn*	*lambanei*	*ton*
the	and	me	receiving,	receives	the

3854.14 verb acc sing masc part aor act	**1466.6** prs-pron acc 1sing	**3642.18** dem-pron pl neu	**1500.15** verb nom sing masc part aor act
πέμψαντά	με.	**21.** Ταῦτα	εἰπὼν
pempsanta	*me*	*Tauta*	*eipōn*
having sent	me.	These things	having said

21.a.**Txt:** p66-corr,02A, 04C,05D,017K,032W, 036,037,038,1,13,etc. byz.Gries,Lach,Sod
Var: p66-org,01ℵ,03B, 019L,Treg,Alf,Tisc, We/Ho,Weis,UBS/☆

3450.5 art sing masc	**2400.1** name nom masc	**4866.7** verb 3sing indic aor pass	**3450.3** art dat sing	**4011.3** noun dat sing neu	**2504.1** conj
⸂a ὁ ⸃	Ἰησοῦς	ἐταράχθη	τῷ	πνεύματι,	καὶ
ho	*Iēsous*	*etarachthē*	*tō*	*pneumati*	*kai*
	Jesus	was troubled	in the	spirit,	and

3113.16 verb 3sing indic aor act	**2504.1** conj	**1500.5** verb 3sing indic aor act	**279.1** partic	**279.1** partic	**2978.1** verb 1sing pres act
ἐμαρτύρησεν	καὶ	εἶπεν,	Ἀμὴν	ἀμὴν	λέγω
emarturēsen	*kai*	*eipen*	*Amēn*	*amēn*	*legō*
testified	and	said,	Truly	truly	I say

5050.3 prs-pron dat 2pl	**3617.1** conj	**1518.3** num card nom masc	**1523.1** prep gen	**5050.2** prs-pron gen 2pl	**3722.23** verb 3sing indic fut act
ὑμῖν,	ὅτι	εἷς	ἐξ	ὑμῶν	παραδώσει
humin	*hoti*	*heis*	*ex*	*humōn*	*paradōsei*
to you,	that	one	of	you	will deliver up

22.a.**Txt:** p66,01ℵ-org, 02A,05D,017K,019L, 032W,036,037,038,1,13, etc.byz.Lach,Weis,Sod
Var: 01ℵ-corr,03B,04C, 044,Alf,Tisc,We/Ho, UBS/☆

1466.6 prs-pron acc 1sing	**984.23** verb 3pl indic imperf act	**3631.1** conj	**1519.1** prep	**238.3** prs-pron acc pl masc
με.	**22.** Ἔβλεπον	⸂a οὖν ⸃	εἰς	ἀλλήλους
me	*Eblepon*	*oun*	*eis*	*allēlous*
me.	Looked	therefore	upon	one another

3450.7 art pl masc	**3073.5** noun nom pl masc	**633.3** verb nom pl masc part pres mid	**3875.1** prep	**4949.4** intr-pron gen sing
οἱ	μαθηταὶ,	ἀπορούμενοι	περὶ	τίνος
hoi	*mathētai*	*aporoumenoi*	*peri*	*tinos*
the	disciples,	doubting	of	whom

course, was Jesus. What He foretold strengthens faith. Prophecies of the Bible also have a sanctifying effect on the lives of believers, such as those about the second coming of Christ (1 John 3:3).

Jesus' concern was that the disciples believe—but believe what? He emphasized the title He so often used in the Book of John: "I am He." Literally the original is "I myself am" or "I am who I am." These are the very words God used when speaking to Moses from the burning bush (Exodus 3:14). The present tense verb "am" with the intensive pronoun "I" are stressed in His statement by their position at the end of the verse. The disciples were to believe that Jesus is the One who lives in the present tense regardless of where one locates a point on the time line continuum. But for the present they were to believe He was the Messiah God had sent.

that, when it is come to pass: . . . so that when it does occur, *Berkeley* . . . in order that when they do happen, *Weymouth.*

ye may believe that I am he: . . . you may believe who I am, *Moffatt* . . . you may believe that I am He, *Weymouth* . . . that I AM, *Fenton* . . . the Messiah, *SEB.*

13:20. "Verily, verily" indicates that another important declaration is forthcoming (see 1:51 for comments).

Jesus had been speaking of His rejection by the Jews. The Jews had not received Him nor His Father; therefore, His death at their hands would be the consequence. The leaders would not receive the Father because they did not receive Him. But those who did receive Him, would also receive the Father. In addition, they would receive the apostles as His ambassadors.

20. Verily, verily, I say unto you, He that receiveth whomsoever I send receiveth me: With twofold assurance I tell you, *Berkeley* . . . Let Me assure you, whoever receives anybody, *Adams* . . . if you receive anyone I send, you receive Me, *Beck.*

and he that receiveth me receiveth him that sent me: . . . is taking Him who, *Concordant* . . . and he who welcomes Me, welcomes My Sender, *Berkeley.*

13:21. The Lord foretold His betrayal by Judas in this section. John's Gospel is more thorough than the Synoptic Gospels in giving details about Judas (see Matthew 26:20-24; Mark 14:17-21; Luke 22:14-30).

All that Jesus did for Judas failed to bring him to repentance. "He was troubled in spirit" refers to Jesus' reaction to Judas' hardened persistence to sin. "Troubled" is an aorist active verb of *tarassō* meaning "to be troubled, disturbed, and stirred up." For the use of this Greek word check its meaning in 5:4,7; 11:33; and 12:27. It is used in 14:1 and 27 with reference to the disciples.

Notice Jesus prefaced the cause of His agitation by "verily, verily" (see 1:51). "One of you shall betray me." Betrayal by a friend was highly unusual. Of all social sins this was counted most grave and solemn. When the betrayal is viewed in the light of the most intimate and ultimate fellowship possible, one can begin to see what a horrible sin Judas committed.

21. When Jesus had thus said, he was troubled in spirit: On saying this, Jesus, *Moffatt* . . . was disturbed in spirit, *Norlie* . . . was inwardly disturbed, *Berkeley* . . . was distressed in spirit, *Fenton, Wuest* . . . clearly in anguish of soul, *Phillips* . . . in deep anguish of spirit, *ALBA* . . . was deeply moved in spirit, *Williams.*

and testified, and said: . . . and said with deep earnestness, *Weymouth.*

Verily, verily, I say unto you, that one of you shall betray me: One from among you will deliver me up, *Rotherham.*

13:22. The disciples' reaction revealed three things. First, they knew they had not consciously betrayed Him, though at times they failed to understand what He meant. Second, the disciples had not distinctly realized His earlier intimations about His betrayal. Third,

22. Then the disciples looked one on another: The disciples kept looking at one another, *Williams* . . . completely mystified, *Phillips.*

John 13:23

23.a.**Txt:** p66,01ℵ,02A, 04C-corr,05D,017K, 032W,036,037,038,1,13, etc.byz.sa.bo.Gries,Lach, Sod
Var: 03B,04C-org,019L, 044,Treg,Alf,Tisc, We/Ho,Weis,UBS/*

23.b.**Var:** 01ℵ,02A,03B, 04C,05D,017K,019L, 032W,037,041,it.bo. Gries,Lach,TregAlf, Word,Tisc,We/Ho,Weis, Sod,UBS/*

24.a.**Txt:** p66-corr,02A, 017K,032W,036,037, (038),1,28,byz.sa.Gries
Var: 03B,04C,019L, 033X,068,33,Lach,Treg Alf,Tisc,We/Ho,Weis, Sod,UBS/*

25.a.**Txt:** p66-corr, 01ℵ-org,02A,04C-corr, 05D,032W,036,037,038, 1,13,byz.Tisc,Sod
Var: 01ℵ-corr,03B, 04C-org,017K,019L, 033X,LachTreg,Alf, We/Ho,Weis,UBS/*

25.b.**Txt:** 02A,07E,017K, 030U,036,038,byz.Lach, Sod
Var: 03B,04C,Treg,Alf, We/HoWeis,UBS/*

25.c.**Var:** 03B,04C,019L, 021M,033X,037,28,33, Treg,Alf,TiscWe/Ho, Weis,Sod,UBS/*

26.a.**Var:** 01ℵ-corr,03B, 04C-org,019L,033X, Lach,AlfWe/Ho,Weis, Sod,UBS/*

2978.5 verb 3sing indic pres act — λέγει. — *legei* — he speaks.

23. **1498.34** verb sing indic imperf act — ἦν — *ēn* — There was
1156.2 conj — ⸂a δὲ ⸃ — *de* — but
343.2 verb nom sing masc part pres — ἀνακείμενος — *anakeimenos* — reclining
1518.3 num card nom masc — εἷς — *heis* — one
1523.2 prep gen — [b☆+ ἐκ] — *ek* — [of]
3450.1 art gen pl — τῶν — *tōn* — of the
3073.6 noun gen pl masc — μαθητῶν — *mathētōn* — disciples
840.3 prs-pron gen sing — αὐτοῦ — *autou* — his
1706.1 prep — ἐν — *en* — in
3450.3 art dat sing — τῷ — *tō* — the
2831.1 noun dat sing masc — κόλπῳ — *kolpō* — bosom
3450.2 art gen sing — τοῦ — *tou*
2400.2 name masc — Ἰησοῦ, — *Iēsou* — of Jesus,
3614.6 rel-pron acc sing masc — ὃν — *hon* — whom
25.26 verb 3sing indic imperf act — ἠγάπα — *ēgapa* — loved
3450.5 art sing masc — ὁ — *ho*
2400.1 name nom masc — Ἰησοῦς· — *Iēsous* — Jesus.

24. **3368.1** verb 3sing indic pres act — νεύει — *neuei* — Makes a sign
3631.1 conj — οὖν — *oun* — therefore
3642.5 dem-pron dat sing masc — τούτῳ — *toutō* — to him
4468.1 name masc — Σίμων — *Simōn* — Simon
3935.1 name nom masc — Πέτρος — *Petros* — Peter
4299.5 verb inf aor mid — ⸂ πυθέσθαι — *puthesthai* — to ask
4949.3 intr-pron nom sing — τίς — *tis* — who
300.1 partic — ἂν — *an*
1498.14 verb 3sing opt pres act — εἴη — *eiē* — might be
2504.1 conj — [a καὶ — *kai* — [and
2978.5 verb 3sing indic pres act — λέγει — *legei* — says
840.4 prs-pron dat sing — αὐτῷ· — *autō* — to him,
1500.12 verb 2sing impr aor act — εἰπὲ — *eipe* — say
4949.3 intr-pron nom sing — τίς — *tis* — who
1498.4 verb 3sing indic pres act — ἐστιν] — *estin* — it is]
3875.1 prep — περὶ — *peri* — of
3614.2 rel-pron gen sing — οὗ — *hou* — whom
2978.5 verb 3sing indic pres act — λέγει. — *legei* — he speaks.

25. **1953.4** verb nom sing masc part aor act — ⸂ ἐπιπεσὼν — *epipesōn* — Having leaned
375.4 verb nom sing masc part aor act — [a☆ ἀναπεσὼν] — *anapesōn* — [having leaned back]
1156.2 conj — ⸂b δὲ ⸃ — *de* — and
1552.3 dem-pron nom sing masc — ἐκεῖνος — *ekeinos* — that
3643.1 adv — [c☆+ οὕτως] — *houtōs* — [thus]
1894.3 prep — ἐπὶ — *epi* — on
3450.16 art sing neu — τὸ — *to* — the
4589.1 noun acc sing neu — στῆθος — *stēthos* — breast
3450.2 art gen sing — τοῦ — *tou*
2400.2 name masc — Ἰησοῦ, — *Iēsou* — of Jesus,
2978.5 verb 3sing indic pres act — λέγει — *legei* — says
840.4 prs-pron dat sing — αὐτῷ, — *autō* — to him,
2935.5 noun voc sing masc — Κύριε, — *Kurie* — Lord,
4949.3 intr-pron nom sing — τίς — *tis* — who
1498.4 verb 3sing indic pres act — ἐστιν; — *estin* — is it?

26. **552.2** verb 3sing indic pres — Ἀποκρίνεται — *Apokrinetai* — Answers
3631.1 conj — [a+ οὖν] — *oun* — [therefore]
3450.5 art sing masc — ὁ — *ho*
2400.1 name nom masc — Ἰησοῦς, — *Iēsous* — Jesus,
1552.3 dem-pron nom sing masc — Ἐκεῖνός — *Ekeinos* — That
1498.4 verb 3sing indic pres act — ἐστιν — *estin* — it is
3614.3 rel-pron dat sing — ᾧ — *hō* — to whom
1466.1 prs-pron nom 1sing — ἐγὼ — *egō* — I,
905.2 verb nom sing masc part aor act — ⸂ βάψας — *bapsas* — having dipped

not until they received the fullness of the Holy Spirit would they know that the Old Testament prophecies referred to Jesus their Lord.

13:23. John's position at the table is given with reference to Jesus. The Jews, Persians, Greeks, and Romans reclined around the table while they ate their meals. They leaned on the left arm and ate with the right. This posture indicates that John was reclining at Jesus' right so that by leaning backward John's position was "on Jesus' bosom."

"Whom Jesus loved" could be said of any of the Lord's disciples because He loved all equally. However, this was John's favorite designation of himself in his Gospel. Four times John used this beautiful appellation (13:23; 19:26; 21:7; 21:20).

13:24. Where Simon Peter reclined at the table is not stated, but it was near enough that he could "gesture" (see NASB) to John that he might learn the identity of the traitor. John was on Jesus' right, and Judas as treasurer was on Jesus' left. John occupied a favored position at the table and one which gave him easy access to Jesus.

13:25. This verse indicates a nearness to Jesus that would provide secrecy for conversation. The preposition "on" (*epi*) bears the meaning of "upon" in this verse while in verse 23 "on" (*en*) means "in the area of," or "the momentary position."

John asked bluntly, "Lord, who is it?" He meant, "Who of your disciples would betray you?"

13:26. Jesus did not answer by giving Judas' name. His answer came in gesture form. Tenney explains that the bread used "in this context does not mean the modern spongy loaf used in most Western nations. It was probably a piece of flat bread, somewhat leathery in consistency, which could be used to scoop bits of meat taken from the pot in which they were cooked" (Tenney, *Expositor's Bible Commentary*, 9:140). To give the dipped morsel on such an occasion was equivalent to serving the choicest piece of steak at a banquet. Judas knew the significance of Jesus' action. But Judas received the morsel in formal courtesy with an unrepentant soul.

doubting of whom he spake: . . . wondering whom he meant, *TCNT* . . . undecided to whom He referred, *Berkeley* . . . being perplexed about whom he spoke, *PNT* . . . being at a loss concerning whom, *Wuest* . . . wondering which of them he could have in mind, *ALBA*.

23. Now there was leaning on Jesus' bosom one of his disciples: . . . was leaning upon the lap, *Fenton*.

whom Jesus loved: . . . whom Jesus specially loved, *Williams* . . . he was the favourite of Jesus, *Moffatt*.

24. Simon Peter therefore beckoned to him: . . . maketh a sign to him, *Alford* . . . motioned to him, *Beck*.

that he should ask who it should be of whom he spake: . . . to ask Him to tell of whom it was He had spoken, *Norlie*.

25. He then lying on Jesus' breast: So that disciple just leaned back against Jesus' breast, *Montgomery* . . . resting his head on, *BB* . . . Leaning back against Jesus, *Adams* . . . So, that follower moved very close to Jesus, *SEB* . . . He simply leaned forward, *Phillips* . . . falling back thus upon the breast of, *Rotherham* . . . leaned back close to, *NEB* . . . fell upon, *Murdock*.

saith unto him, Lord, who is it?: . . . and whispered to him, *SEB*.

26. Jesus answered, He it is, to whom I shall give a sop: It is the one to whom I give this piece of bread, *Norlie* . . . I will give it to that person, *SEB* . . . to give this morsel of food, *AmpB* . . . a little piece, *Wilson*.

26.b.**Txt:** p66,01ℵ,036, 037,038,byz.
Var1: .02A,05D,017K, 041,1,13,Lach
Var2: .03B,04C,019L,sa. bo.Treg,Alf,Tisc,We/Ho, Weis,Sod,UBS/*

26.c.**Txt:** p66,01ℵ,02A, 05D,017K,036,037,038, 1,13,byz.it.Lach
Var: 03B,04C,sa.bo.Treg Alf,Tisc,We/Ho,Weis, UBS/*

26.d.**Txt:** p66-corr,02A, 017K,032W,036,037, 038,1,13,byz.it.sa.bo. Lach
Var: 01ℵ,03B,04C,019L, 033X,33,Treg,Alf,Tisc, We/HoWeis,Sod,UBS/*

26.e.**Var:** 01ℵ-corr,03B, 04C,019L,033X,33,Treg, Alf,Tisc,We/Ho,Weis, Sod,UBS/*

26.f.**Txt:** p66,02A,017K, 032W,036,037,1,13,byz. Lach
Var: 01ℵ,03B,04C,019L, 033X,038,33,sa.TregAlf, Tisc,We/Ho,Weis,Sod, UBS/*

27.a.**Txt:** p66,01ℵ,02A, 04C,05D,017K,032W, 036,037,038,byz.Lach, Weis,Sod
Var: 03B,019L,Treg,Alf Tisc,We/Ho,UBS/*

29.a.**Txt:** p66,04C,05D, 017K,036,037,038,byz.
Var: 01ℵ,02A,03B,019L, 021M,030U,033X,33, Lach,Treg,Alf,Tisc, We/HoWeis,Sod,UBS/*

1673.1 verb nom sing masc part aor act	**905.4** verb 1sing indic fut act	**3450.16** art sing neu	**5431.1** noun acc sing neu	**1914.3** verb 1sing indic fut act
[1b ἐμβάψας	2* βάψω]	τὸ	ψωμίον	‹ ἐπιδώσω.
embapsas	bapsō	to	psōmion	epidōsō
[idem	shall dip]	the	morsel,	shall give.

2504.1 conj	**1319.36** verb 1sing indic fut act	**840.4** prs-pron dat sing	**2504.1** conj	**1673.1** verb nom sing masc part aor act
[c* καὶ	δώσω	αὐτῷ.]	‹ Καὶ	ἐμβάψας
kai	dōsō	autō	Kai	embapsas
[and	I shall give	him.]	And	having dipped

905.2 verb nom sing masc part aor act	**3631.1** conj	**3450.16** art sing neu	**5431.1** noun acc sing neu	**2956.4** verb 3sing indic pres act
[d* βάψας	οὖν]	τὸ	ψωμίον	[e*+ λαμβάνει
bapsas	oun	to	psōmion	lambanei
[having dipped	therefore]	the	morsel	[he takes

2504.1 conj	**1319.2** verb 3sing indic pres act	**2430.3** name dat masc	**4468.2** name gen masc	**2442.3** name dat masc
καὶ]	δίδωσιν	Ἰούδᾳ	Σίμωνος	‹ Ἰσκαριώτῃ.
kai	didōsin	Iouda	Simōnos	Iskariōtē
and]	he gives	to Judas,	Simon's	Iscariot.

2442.2 name gen masc	**2504.1** conj	**3196.3** prep	**3450.16** art sing neu	**5431.1** noun acc sing neu
[f* Ἰσκαριώτου.]	27. καὶ	μετὰ	τὸ	ψωμίον,
Iskariōtou	kai	meta	to	psōmion
[idem]	And	after	the	morsel,

4966.1 adv	**1511.3** verb 3sing indic aor act	**1519.1** prep	**1552.5** dem-pron acc sing masc	**3450.5** art sing masc	**4423.1** noun nom sing masc
τότε	εἰσῆλθεν	εἰς	ἐκεῖνον	ὁ	σατανᾶς.
tote	eisēlthen	eis	ekeinon	ho	satanas
then	entered	into	that		Satan.

2978.5 verb 3sing indic pres act	**3631.1** conj	**840.4** prs-pron dat sing	**3450.5** art sing masc	**2400.1** name nom masc	**3614.16** rel-pron sing neu
λέγει	οὖν	αὐτῷ	(a ὁ)	Ἰησοῦς,	Ὃ
legei	oun	autō	ho	Iēsous	Ho
Says	therefore	to him		Jesus,	What

4020.4 verb 2sing indic pres act	**4020.34** verb 2sing impr aor act	**4880.1** adv comp	**3642.17** dem-pron sing neu	**1156.2** conj
ποιεῖς,	ποίησον	τάχιον.	28. Τοῦτο	δὲ
poieis	poiēson	tachion	Touto	de
you do,	do	quickly.	This	but

3625.2 num card nom masc	**1091.17** verb 3sing indic aor act	**3450.1** art gen pl	**343.4** verb gen pl masc part pres	**4242.1** prep	**4949.9** intr-pron sing neu
οὐδεὶς	ἔγνω	τῶν	ἀνακειμένων	πρὸς	τί
oudeis	egnō	tōn	anakeimenōn	pros	ti
no one	knew	of the	reclining	about	what

1500.5 verb 3sing indic aor act	**840.4** prs-pron dat sing	**4948.7** indef-pron nom pl masc	**1056.1** conj	**1374.23** verb 3pl indic imperf act	**1878.1** conj
εἶπεν	αὐτῷ.	29. τινὲς	γὰρ	ἐδόκουν,	ἐπεὶ
eipen	autō	tines	gar	edokoun	epei
he spoke	to him;	some	for	thought,	since

3450.16 art sing neu	**1095.1** noun acc sing neu	**2174.44** verb 3sing indic imperf act	**3450.5** art sing masc	**2430.1** name nom masc
τὸ	γλωσσόκομον	εἶχεν	(a ὁ)	Ἰούδας,
to	glōssokomon	eichen	ho	Ioudas
the	money box	had		Judas,

Blaney notes that Judas had previously rejected Jesus' efforts to turn him from the sin ahead in the footwashing episode. He pictured the Master symbolically saying, "Let me wash this evil from your mind and heart. You have been one of my disciples, and I love you in spite of your plans. I know about them, and I understand—for I too know what it is like to be tempted. Our fellowship has been good. This need not be the end. Will you not begin to resist the thought of betrayal before it becomes too strong for you?" (Blaney, *Wesleyan Bible Commentary*, 4:437). Now the traitor rejects even this final act of love from the Master.

when I have dipped it: . . . after I have put it in the vessel, *BB* . . . dipped the morsel, *Fenton* . . . when I have dipte it: and he wet a soppe, *Geneva* . . . dipped it in the dish, *NIV*.

And when he had dipped the sop, he gave it to Judas Iscariot, the son of Simon: . . . dipping the mouthful, *Sawyer*.

13:27. Indeed, instead of responding to the gesture of compassion in the sop repentantly, Judas was hardened by it. The tenderness of Jesus failed to achieve its intended effect. "As soon as Judas took the bread, Satan entered into him" (NIV). Defiantly he permanently settled the decision to betray Jesus. Knowing this the Lord said, "That thou doest, do quickly." Judas needed now to be separated from the group at once.

"And after the sop" speaks a solemn message. What a difference in Judas before and after the morsel. *Before,* Judas was an apostle; *after*, he was an apostate. Now he became determined. He fully acted according to the desire of Satan. Satan had found an effective tool for his use. The Greek word *Satanas* ("Satan") occurs 36 times in the New Testament, yet only here in John's Gospel. The Greek article *ho* is used to point out Satan's identity. The meaning of the word *satan* is "adversary." *Devil* means "slanderer, accuser" (see John 8:44; Revelation 2:10; 12:9,12; 20:2,10).

Jesus allowed Judas to do what he had determined to do. How deplorable was his decision and regrettable his destiny.

27. And after the sop Satan entered into him: And after the mouthful, Satan entered into him, *Berkeley* . . . After the incident of the bread, *ALBA* . . . Right after taking the piece of bread, *Adams* . . . the Adversary, *Young* . . . Satan entered his heart, *Phillips* . . . Satan took possession of him, *Torrey, TCNT* . . . took possession of, *AmpB*.

Then said Jesus unto him, That thou doest, do quickly: So at once what you are going to do, *TCNT* . . . Do quickly what you are about to do, *Norlie* . . . Make quick work of what, *Williams* . . . What you have to do, *Fenton* . . . do at once, *Wuest* . . . do it at once, *PNT* . . . do it soon, *ALBA* . . . what you are doing! *Berkeley*.

13:28. Judas acted alone in his treacherous deed. Not even John could bring himself to think Judas capable of such a traitorous act, nor did Judas approach any of the others in his plans to betray his Lord.

28. Now no man at the table know for what intent he spake this unto him: None of those at table understood why, *Moffatt* . . . Now it was not clear to anyone...why he said this to him, *BB* . . . none of the others at table knew exactly why he said this, *ALBA* . . . why he gave this order, *Campbell*.

13:29. This verse is John's statement to indicate the group had a treasurer, and at least during some extended period Judas kept the money (see 12:6). Judas made purchases for the group's food and disbursed help to the poor. Probably sacrifices, offerings, and taxes were paid from the box. "The bag" was a box, case, or bag in which money was kept. In the New Testament it occurs only here and in 12:6. The Feast would last 8 days so that provisions would need to be arranged for, to ensure their supplies. The disciples thought Jesus had spoken of their supplies or that Judas should arrange something for the poor.

29. For some of them thought, because Judas had the bag: Some imagined, *HistNT* . . . some supposed that, as Judas was treasurer, *Fenton* . . . because Judas had the money-bag, *HBIE* . . . had charge of the money-box, *Norlie*.

John 13:30

29.b.**Txt:** p66,02A,04C,05D,017K,019L,032W,036,037,038,13,byz.Lach,Sod
Var: 01ℵ,03B,Alf,Tisc,We/HoWeis,UBS/☆

30.a.**Txt:** 02A,017K,036,037,038,1,33,byz.
Var: 01ℵ,03B,04C,05D,019L,033X,Lach,Treg,Alf,TiscWe/Ho,Weis,Sod,UBS/☆

31.a.**Var:** 01ℵ,03B,04C,05D,019L,033X,038,33,Elzev,Lach,Treg,Alf,Tisc,We/Ho,WeisSod,UBS/☆

31.b.**Txt:** 02A,04C,05D,017K,032W,036,038,1,13,etc.byz.Lach,Sod
Var: p66,01ℵ,03B,019L,037,Treg,Alf,Tisc,We/Ho Weis,UBS/☆

32.a.**Txt:** 01ℵ-corr,02A,04C-corr,017K,036,037,038,13,byz.sa.Gries,Lach,Tisc,Weis,Sod,UBS/☆
Var: p66,01ℵ-org,03B,04C-org,05D,019L,032W,033X,1,it.We/Ho

32.b.**Txt:** 01ℵ-corr,02A,05D,017K,019L,032W,036,037,038,1,13,byz.it.Gries,Lach,Sod
Var: p66,01ℵ-org,03B,sa.bo.Treg,Tisc,We/Ho,Weis,UBS/☆

3617.1 conj	**2978.5** verb 3sing indic pres act	**840.4** prs-pron dat sing	**3450.5** art sing masc	**2400.1** name nom masc	**58.10** verb 2sing impr aor act
ὅτι	λέγει	αὐτῷ	(b ὁ \	Ἰησοῦς,	Ἀγόρασον
hoti	*legei*	*autō*	*ho*	*Iēsous*	*Agorason*
that	is saying	to him		Jesus,	Buy

3614.1 rel-pron gen pl	**5367.3** noun acc sing fem	**2174.5** verb 1pl indic pres act	**1519.1** prep	**3450.12** art acc sing fem	**1844.4** noun acc sing fem	**2211.1** conj
ὧν	χρείαν	ἔχομεν	εἰς	τὴν	ἑορτήν,	ἢ
hōn	*chreian*	*echomen*	*eis*	*tēn*	*heortēn*	*ē*
what things	need	we have	for	the	feast;	or

3450.4 art dat pl	**4292.6** adj dat pl masc	**2419.1** conj	**4948.10** indef-pron sing neu	**1319.19** verb 3sing subj aor act	**2956.25** verb nom sing masc part aor act
τοῖς	πτωχοῖς	ἵνα	τι	δῷ.	**30.** λαβὼν
tois	*ptōchois*	*hina*	*ti*	*dō*	*labōn*
to the	poor	that	something	he should give.	Having received

3631.1 conj	**3450.16** art sing neu	**5431.1** noun acc sing neu	**1552.3** dem-pron nom sing masc	**2091.1** adv	**1814.3** verb 3sing indic aor act
οὖν	τὸ	ψωμίον	ἐκεῖνος	(εὐθέως	ἐξῆλθεν·
oun	*to*	*psōmion*	*ekeinos*	*eutheōs*	*exēlthen*
therefore	the	morsel	that	immediately	went out;

1814.3 verb 3sing indic aor act	**2098.1** adv	**1498.34** verb sing indic imperf act	**1156.2** conj	**3433.1** noun nom sing fem
[a☆ ἐξῆλθεν	εὐθύς·]	ἦν	δὲ	νύξ.
exēlthen	*euthus*	*ēn*	*de*	*nux*
[went out	immediately]	it was	and	night.

3616.1 conj	**3631.1** conj	**1814.3** verb 3sing indic aor act	**2978.5** verb 3sing indic pres act	**3450.5** art sing masc
31. Ὅτε	[a☆+ οὖν]	ἐξῆλθεν	λέγει	(b ὁ \
Hote	*oun*	*exēlthen*	*legei*	*ho*
When	[therefore]	he was gone out	says	

2400.1 name nom masc	**3431.1** adv	**1386.22** verb 3sing indic aor pass	**3450.5** art sing masc	**5048.1** noun nom sing masc	**3450.2** art gen sing
Ἰησοῦς,	Νῦν	ἐδοξάσθη	ὁ	υἱὸς	τοῦ
Iēsous	*Nun*	*edoxasthē*	*ho*	*huios*	*tou*
Jesus,	Now	has been glorified	the	Son	

442.2 noun gen sing masc	**2504.1** conj	**3450.5** art sing masc	**2296.1** noun nom sing masc	**1386.22** verb 3sing indic aor pass	**1706.1** prep
ἀνθρώπου,	καὶ	ὁ	θεὸς	ἐδοξάσθη	ἐν
anthrōpou	*kai*	*ho*	*theos*	*edoxasthē*	*en*
of man,	and		God	has been glorified	in

840.4 prs-pron dat sing		**1479.1** conj	**3450.5** art sing masc	**2296.1** noun nom sing masc	**1386.22** verb 3sing indic aor pass	**1706.1** prep
αὐτῷ.	**32.** (a☆	εἰ	ὁ	θεὸς	ἐδοξάσθη	ἐν
autō		*ei*	*ho*	*theos*	*edoxasthē*	*en*
him.		If		God	has been glorified	in

840.4 prs-pron dat sing	**2504.1** conj	**3450.5** art sing masc	**2296.1** noun nom sing masc	**1386.16** verb 3sing indic fut act	**840.6** prs-pron acc sing masc
αὐτῷ, \	καὶ	ὁ	θεὸς	δοξάσει	αὐτὸν
autō	*kai*	*ho*	*theos*	*doxasei*	*auton*
him,	also		God	shall glorify	him

1706.1 prep	**1431.5** prs-pron dat 3sing masc	**840.4** prs-pron dat sing	**2504.1** conj	**2098.1** adv	**1386.16** verb 3sing indic fut act
ἐν	(ἑαυτῷ,	[b☆ αὐτῷ,]	καὶ	εὐθὺς	δοξάσει
en	*heautō*	*autō*	*kai*	*euthus*	*doxasei*
in	himself,	[him,]	and	immediately	shall glorify

That they thought the Lord had instructed Judas to buy something for the poor suggests He often gave such direction. Judas tried to hypocritically capitalize on this fact in his earlier protest that the expensive perfume Mary poured on Jesus should have been sold and the money given to the poor (12:5). Some take the Master's response about us having the poor with us always as showing a lack of concern for them (12:8). What happened here speaks loudly to the contrary. Indeed, the Lord taught part of the basis for judgment will be the way people have treated the destitute (Matthew 25:35-40).

that Jesus had said unto him, Buy those things that we have need of against the feast: . . . expressly charged him to buy, *Murdock* . . . Buy what we require for the Festival, *Weymouth* . . . Buy the necessaries, *Fenton* . . . Purchase in the market, *Wuest.*

or, that he should give something to the poor:

13:30. Judas knew the significance of the morsel. He understood that the Master knew what his plans were. Instead of repenting, Judas hastened out into the darkness so he might gain 30 pieces of silver.

The betrayer rushed down the road of sin. "As soon as Judas had taken the bread, he went out" (NIV). The seed of sin germinated quickly to produce a deadly fruit. James describes what happened. Judas was "drawn away of his own lust, and enticed" (James 1:14). His lust conceived and brought forth sin. When it was finished, it brought forth death (James 1:15).

The sun had set, beginning a night of infamy. Judas' soul was as black as the night. He was in the darkness and the darkness in him. How great was his darkness! In John's Gospel, darkness and night often signify moral darkness (1:5; 8:12; 12:35,46).

30. He then, having received the sop, went immediately out: and it was night: Then at once, after taking the bite of bread, he went out, *Berkeley* . . . he left the room, *Williams.*

31. Therefore, when he was gone out, Jesus said, Now is the Son of man glorified: Now at last the Son of man is glorified, *Moffatt* . . . Now is glory given to the Son of man, *BB* . . . Now the Son of Man has been exalted, *TCNT* . . . Now I am given glory, *SEB* . . . shall be exalted, *Fenton.*

and God is glorified in him: . . . in me, God is given glory, *SEB* . . . and in Him God is glorified, *Beck* . . . has been exalted, *TCNT.*

13:31,32. It was after Judas left that Jesus disclosed His most intimate feelings. It was to His faithful followers that He desired to unfold the burden of His soul. From this point on the most holy ground of the Gospel is unveiled.

Jesus often taught the Twelve special truths. He taught the crowds only "as they were able to hear it," but "when they were alone, he expounded all things to his disciples" (Mark 4:33,34). In His last trip through Galilee on His way to Jerusalem "he would not that any man should know it. For he taught his disciples" plainly of His coming death (Mark 9:30,31).

The departure of Judas made possible, first, a more intimate disclosure of Jesus' feelings, and second, the betrayal and sacrifice of the Lamb of God. Jesus marked His hour from "now." He called himself "the Son of man" for it is the title that designated Him as man's substitute in His redemptive work. "Glorified" means to be made known for who He is in reality. The verb *doxazō* occurs five times in verses 31 and 32. It was very important that at this crisis hour the reality of both the Son and the Father should be manifest.

32. If God be glorified in him, God shall also glorify him in himself: And God shall give Me His own glory, *LivB.*

and shall straightway glorify him: . . . at once, *Confraternity* . . . and will glorify Him without delay, *Weymouth* . . . and that immediately, *TCNT* . . . and glorify him at once, *Moffatt* . . . will glorify him speedily, *Murdock* . . . and that without delay, *Campbell.*

840.6 prs-pron acc sing masc	4888.1 noun voc pl neu	2068.1 adv	3261.1 adv	3196.1 prep	5050.2 prs-pron gen 2pl
αὐτόν.	33. Τεκνία,	ἔτι	μικρὸν	μεθ'	ὑμῶν
auton	*Teknia*	*eti*	*mikron*	*meth'*	*humōn*
him.	Little children,	yet	a little while	with	you

1498.2 verb 1sing indic pres act	2195.21 verb 2pl indic fut act	1466.6 prs-pron acc 1sing	2504.1 conj	2503.1 conj	1500.3 verb indic aor act
εἰμι.	ζητήσετέ	με,	καὶ	καθὼς	εἶπον
eimi	*zētēsete*	*me*	*kai*	*kathōs*	*eipon*
I am.	You will seek	me;	and,	as	I said

3450.4 art dat pl	2428.4 name-adj dat pl masc	3617.1 conj	3562.1 adv	5055.1 verb 1sing indic pres act	1466.1 prs-pron nom 1sing
τοῖς	Ἰουδαίοις,	Ὅτι	ὅπου	⸀ ὑπάγω	ἐγώ,
tois	*Ioudaiois*	*Hoti*	*hopou*	*hupagō*	*egō*
to the	Jews,	That	where	go	I,

1466.1 prs-pron nom 1sing	5055.1 verb 1sing indic pres act	5050.1 prs-pron nom 2pl	3620.3 partic	1404.6 verb 2pl indic pres	2048.23 verb inf aor act
[☆ ἐγὼ	ὑπάγω]	ὑμεῖς	οὐ	δύνασθε	ἐλθεῖν,
egō	*hupagō*	*humeis*	*ou*	*dunasthe*	*elthein*
[I	go]	you	not	are able	to come,

2504.1 conj	5050.3 prs-pron dat 2pl	2978.1 verb 1sing pres act	732.1 adv	1769.3 noun acc sing fem	2508.5 adj acc sing fem
καὶ	ὑμῖν	λέγω	ἄρτι.	34. ἐντολὴν	καινὴν
kai	*humin*	*legō*	*arti*	*entolēn*	*kainēn*
also	to you	I say	now.	A commandment	new

1319.1 verb 1sing indic pres act	5050.3 prs-pron dat 2pl	2419.1 conj	25.1 verb 2pl pres act	238.3 prs-pron acc pl masc
δίδωμι	ὑμῖν,	ἵνα	ἀγαπᾶτε	ἀλλήλους·
didōmi	*humin*	*hina*	*agapate*	*allēlous*
I give	to you,	that	you should love	one another;

2503.1 conj	25.12 verb 1sing indic aor act	5050.4 prs-pron acc 2pl	2419.1 conj	2504.1 conj	5050.1 prs-pron nom 2pl	25.1 verb 2pl pres act
καθὼς	ἠγάπησα	ὑμᾶς,	ἵνα	καὶ	ὑμεῖς	ἀγαπᾶτε
kathōs	*ēgapēsa*	*humas*	*hina*	*kai*	*humeis*	*agapate*
according as	I loved	you,	that	also	you	should love

238.3 prs-pron acc pl masc	1706.1 prep	3642.5 dem-pron dat sing masc	1091.52 verb 3pl indic fut mid	3820.7 adj pl masc	3617.1 conj
ἀλλήλους.	35. ἐν	τούτῳ	γνώσονται	πάντες	ὅτι
allēlous	*en*	*toutō*	*gnōsontai*	*pantes*	*hoti*
one another.	By	this	shall know	all	that

1684.4 adj nom 1pl masc	3073.5 noun nom pl masc	1498.6 verb 2pl indic pres act	1430.1 partic	26.4 noun acc sing fem	2174.9 verb 2pl subj pres act
ἐμοὶ	μαθηταί	ἐστε,	ἐὰν	ἀγάπην	ἔχητε
emoi	*mathētai*	*este*	*ean*	*agapēn*	*echēte*
to me	disciples	you are,	if	love	you have

1706.1 prep	238.2 prs-pron dat pl	2978.5 verb 3sing indic pres act	840.4 prs-pron dat sing	4468.1 name masc	3935.1 name nom masc
ἐν	ἀλλήλοις.	36. Λέγει	αὐτῷ	Σίμων	Πέτρος,
en	*allēlois*	*Legei*	*autō*	*Simōn*	*Petros*
among	one another.	Says	to him	Simon	Peter,

36.a.**Txt:** 01ℵ,04C-corr, 05D,017K,032W,036, 037,(038),1,13,byz.Sod **Var:** 03B,04C-org,019L, Lach,Treg,Alf,Tisc, We/Ho,Weis,UBS/☆

2935.5 noun voc sing masc	4085.1 adv	5055.2 verb 2sing indic pres act	552.6 verb 3sing indic aor pass	840.4 prs-pron dat sing
Κύριε,	ποῦ	ὑπάγεις;	ἀπεκρίθη	⸀a αὐτῷ
Kurie	*pou*	*hupageis*	*apekrithē*	*autō*
Lord,	where	are you going?	Answered	him

The purpose for which the Son came into the world was to make God known by the Son's becoming known. This was the reason Jesus had so much to say about the Father. The glorification of which Jesus spoke was not merely a future manifestation when God will be fully known. It was "now" that God desired to be glorified that the world might believe. Men cannot believe unless they see God in Christ and Christ in His disciples.

God revealed His love by sending Jesus into the world to give His life on the cross. But God is a God of holiness and justice as well. The judgment for man's sin fell upon Christ. Thus on the one hand God is glorified as the God of love and mercy in Christ. But on the other hand God is known (glorified) as the God of holiness and justice.

13:33. "Little children" is used in the Gospel only here. It is a term of tender affection. The term made a deep impression on John, for he used it seven times in his first epistle.

"A little while" should be compared with 7:33,34 and 8:21. Jesus reminded His disciples that He had spoken these words to the Jews (8:21,22), but the difference is remarkable. The word "now" is emphatic because it is placed last in the sentence, and for this reason follows "I say to you" (see *Interlinear*). But it would be a redundancy to state "I say to you now," therefore it appears likely the "now" should go with "you cannot come." Compare a similar construction in Luke 23:43 where it would be redundant to say, "I say unto you today." Thus the Jews could not come (7:34). Jesus' disciples could not come "just now," but they would come later. (See verse 36 for the use of "thou canst not follow me now.")

13:34. The word "new" means new in quality. "As I have loved you" stresses the quality of love with which believers are to "love one another." The demonstration of Jesus' love in the past is not all that is indicated. Jesus did not merely command the disciples to love one another, but He exemplified it and enabled the disciples to love by an endowment of His grace. The disciples were to be learners of the same principles of life Jesus demonstrated. Thus by following His principles and examples and being endued by His power, the disciples were able not only to love one another but also their enemies.

13:35. Jesus depended upon all His disciples to make Him known. The apostle Paul stressed the same idea when he stated, "Ye are

33. Little children, yet a little while I am with you: I shall be with you only a little while, *Norlie* . . . I am with you but a little longer, *Berkeley* . . . I have now but a little time to be with you, *Campbell* . . . I still have a short while with you, *ALBA* . . . I will be with you only a little while longer, *Adams.*

Ye shall seek me: Then you will be looking for me, *BB* . . . You will search for Me, *Fenton.*

and as I said unto the Jews, Whither I go, ye cannot come; so now say I to you: . . . and, as I told the Jews I tell you now, *Moffatt* . . . you are unable to follow, *Fenton* . . . so I now say to you, *Murdock.*

34. A new commandment I give unto you, That ye love one another: I give you a new law, *BB* . . . A new precept, *Concordant* . . . I'm giving you a new order, *Beck* . . . Now I am giving you a new command—Love one another, *Phillips* . . . should be constantly loving one another with a divine and self-sacrificial love, *Wuest* . . . be affectionate, *Murdock.*

as I have loved you, that ye also love one another: . . . in the same way you ought to, *Fenton.*

35. By this shall all men know that ye are my disciples: . . . by this everyone will recognize that, *Moffatt* . . . By this it will be clear to all men, *BB* . . . By this token will, *Norlie.*

if ye have love one to another: . . . if you keep showing love for one another, *Williams* . . . if you keep on showing love among yourselves, *AmpB* . . . You must have love for, *SEB.*

36. Simon Peter said unto him, Lord, whither goest thou?: Lord, where are you going, *RSV, Montgomery* . . . where are you departing? *Wuest.*

36.b.**Var:** 01ℵ,05D,030U,033X,044,13,33,Tisc,Sod

36.c.**Txt:** 04C-corr,05D,017K,036,037,13,byz.
Var: 01ℵ,03B,04C-org,019L,033X,33,it,Lach Treg,Alf,Tisc,We/Ho,Weis,Sod,UBS/☆

37.a.**Txt:** p66,03B,019L-org,021M,032W,33,Steph,We/Ho,Weis,Sod,UBS/☆
Var: 01ℵ,02A,04C,017K,019L-corr,036,037,038,byz.Gries,Lach Treg,Alf,Word,Tisc

37.b.**Var:** 03B,(04-org),Treg,We/Ho

38.a.**Txt:** 04C-corr,036,037,byz.
Var: 01ℵ,02A,03B,04C-org,019L,033X,038,LachTreg,Alf,Word,Tisc,We/Ho,Weis,Sod,UBS/☆

38.b.**Txt:** 04C,05D,019L,021M,038,13,Steph,Gries
Var: 01ℵ,02A,03B,017K,036,037,Lach,Treg,Alf,TiscWe/Ho,Weis,Sod,UBS/☆

38.c.**Txt:** 01ℵ,02A,04C,017K,021M,032W,036,037,038,13,byz.
Var: 03B,05D,019L,033X,Lach,Treg,Alf,Tisc,We/Ho,WeisSod,UBS/☆

3450.5 art sing masc	**2400.1** name nom masc	**3562.1** adv	**1466.1** prs-pron nom 1sing	**5055.1** verb 1sing indic pres act	**3620.3** partic
ὁ	Ἰησοῦς,	Ὅπου	[b+ ἐγὼ]	ὑπάγω	οὐ
ho	*Iēsous*	*Hopou*	*egō*	*hupagō*	*ou*
	Jesus,	Where	[I]	I go	not

1404.3 verb 2sing indic pres	**1466.4** prs-pron dat 1sing	**3431.1** adv	**188.18** verb inf aor act	**5142.1** adv comp
δύνασαί	μοι	νῦν	ἀκολουθῆσαι·	‹ ὕστερον
dunasai	*moi*	*nun*	*akolouthēsai*	*husteron*
you are able	me	now	to follow,	afterwards

1156.2 conj	**188.20** verb 2sing indic fut act	**1466.4** prs-pron dat 1sing	**188.20** verb 2sing indic fut act	**1156.2** conj
δὲ	ἀκολουθήσεις	μοι.	[c☆ ἀκολουθήσεις	δὲ
de	*akolouthēseis*	*moi*	*akolouthēseis*	*de*
but	you shall follow	me.	[you shall follow	but

5142.1 adv comp	**2978.5** verb 3sing indic pres act	**840.4** prs-pron dat sing	**3450.5** art sing masc	**3935.1** name nom masc
ὕστερον.]	37. Λέγει	αὐτῷ	‹a ὁ ›	Πέτρος,
husteron	*Legei*	*autō*	*ho*	*Petros*
afterwards.]	Says	to him		Peter,

2935.5 noun voc sing masc	**1296.1** adv	**1217.2** prep	**4949.9** intr-pron sing neu	**3620.3** partic	**1404.1** verb 1sing indic pres	**4622.3** prs-pron dat 2sing
Κύριε,	‹ διατί	[☆ διὰ	τί]	οὐ	δύναμαί	σοι
Kurie	*diati*	*dia*	*ti*	*ou*	*dunamai*	*soi*
Lord,	why	[idem]		not	am I able	you

188.18 verb inf aor act	**188.23** verb inf pres act	**732.1** adv	**3450.12** art acc sing fem	**5425.4** noun acc sing fem
‹ ἀκολουθῆσαι	[b ἀκολουθεῖν]	ἄρτι;	τὴν	ψυχήν
akolouthēsai	*akolouthein*	*arti*	*tēn*	*psuchēn*
to follow	[idem]	now?	the	life

1466.2 prs-pron gen 1sing	**5065.1** prep	**4622.2** prs-pron gen 2sing	**4935.21** verb 1sing indic fut act	**552.6** verb 3sing indic aor pass
μου	ὑπὲρ	σοῦ	θήσω.	38. ‹ Ἀπεκρίθη
mou	*huper*	*sou*	*thēsō*	*Apekrithē*
my	for	you	I will lay down.	Answered

840.4 prs-pron dat sing	**3450.5** art sing masc	**552.2** verb 3sing indic pres	**2400.1** name nom masc	**3450.12** art acc sing fem
αὐτῷ	ὁ	[a☆ ἀποκρίνεται]	Ἰησοῦς,	Τὴν
autō	*ho*	*apokrinetai*	*Iēsous*	*Tēn*
him		[answers]	Jesus,	The

5425.4 noun acc sing fem	**4622.2** prs-pron gen 2sing	**5065.1** prep	**1466.3** prs-pron gen 1sing	**4935.22** verb 2sing indic fut act	**279.1** partic
ψυχήν	σου	ὑπὲρ	ἐμοῦ	θήσεις;	ἀμὴν
psuchēn	*sou*	*huper*	*emou*	*thēseis*	*amēn*
life	your	for	me	you will lay down!	Truly

279.1 partic	**2978.1** verb 1sing pres act	**4622.3** prs-pron dat 2sing	**3620.3** partic	**3231.1** partic	**218.1** noun nom sing masc	**5291.12** verb 3sing indic fut act
ἀμὴν	λέγω	σοι,	οὐ	μὴ	ἀλέκτωρ	‹ φωνήσει
amēn	*legō*	*soi*	*ou*	*mē*	*alektōr*	*phōnēsei*
truly	I say	to you,	not	not	cock	will crow

5291.15 verb 3sing subj aor act	**2175.1** conj	**3619.1** adv	**529.1** verb 2sing mid	**714.21** verb 2sing indic fut mid
[b☆ φωνήσῃ]	ἕως	οὗ	‹ ἀπαρνήσῃ	[c☆ ἀρνήσῃ]
phōnēsē	*heōs*	*hou*	*aparnēsē*	*arnēsē*
[idem]	until	which	you will deny	[idem]

manifestly declared to be the epistle of Christ . . . written not with ink, but with the Spirit of the living God" (2 Corinthians 3:3). John says in his first epistle, "We know that we have passed from death unto life, because we love the brethren" (1 John 3:14). How will the world distinguish Jesus' disciples? The answer Jesus gave is both simple and practical, "By this shall all men know . . . if ye have love one to another." The primary mark of a family relationship is not similar physical features, but love. John's first epistle asserts how ridiculous it is to say we love God whom we have not seen and hate our brother whom we have seen (1 John 4:20).

Jesus answered him, Whither I go, thou canst not follow me now: I am going where you cannot follow me at present, *Moffatt* . . . Where I am going you may not come with me now, *BB.*

but thou shalt follow me afterwards: . . . but later you will follow Me, *Norlie* . . . yet you shall be following subsequently, *Concordant* . . . but thou wilt at last come, *Murdock* . . . but one day you will, *NEB.*

13:36. Peter's question was self-incriminating. Peter should have known at this point that Jesus was returning to the Father.

See the word "now" in verse 33. The "now" (Greek, *nun*) is essentially the same as "now" (Greek, *arti*) of verse 33. It was not Peter's time to follow. He must live a life of love in order to manifest Christ's grace and power to the world. Jesus' prayer revealed the reason (17:15,18), "I pray not that thou shouldest take them out of the world, but that thou shouldest keep them from the evil. . . . As thou hast sent me into the world, even so have I also sent them into the world." Jesus' mission of love was to become the disciples' mission of love. The disciples could not follow until that mission was accomplished.

37. Peter said unto him, Lord, why cannot I follow thee now?:

I will lay down my life for thy sake: I'll give my life for you, *Beck* . . . on your behalf, *Wuest.*

38. Jesus answered him, Wilt thou lay down thy life for my sake?: Will you lay down your life for me, *TCNT.*

Verily, verily, I say unto thee, The cock shall not crow, till thou hast denied me thrice: With twofold affirmation, *Berkeley* . . . the bugle will not sound, *Fenton* . . . before the cock crows, you will three times disown me! *Williams* . . . The rooster shall not crow until you have thrice disclaimed Me, *Berkeley* . . . you will be renouncing Me, *Concordant* . . . three different times, *SEB.*

13:37. Peter wanted to follow Jesus "now" (Greek, *arti*). He displayed his usual impulsiveness, but without an adequate understanding. Peter's mission was not finished. He seemed to understand that following Jesus at that time would mean his death along with his Saviour's, but he did not realize that would abort his ministry.

13:38. Jesus' response to Peter was meant to warn him about his impulsive assertions. The apostle would indeed be a martyr, but not without the process of refining his dedication, for soon Peter would deny his Lord repeatedly.

The assertion concerning the cock's crowing revealed four items of interest. First, the statement assumed that Jesus knew His own identity. Second, the Lord knew the Old Testament prophecies that the Shepherd would be smitten and the sheep would be scattered (Zechariah 13:7; Matthew 26:31). Third, Jesus knew the character of Peter and that under stress Peter would sin by betraying Him. Fourth, the Lord could see the events of the future.

John 14:1

1466.6 prs-pron acc 1sing	4994.1 adv	3231.1 partic	4866.6 verb 3sing impr pres pass	5050.2 prs-pron gen 2pl
με	τρίς.	14:1. Μὴ	ταρασσέσθω	ὑμῶν
me	*tris*	*Mē*	*tarassesthō*	*humōn*
me	three times.	Not	let be troubled	your

3450.9 art nom sing fem	2559.2 noun nom sing fem	3961.2 verb 2pl pres act	1519.1 prep	3450.6 art acc sing masc	2296.4 noun acc sing masc
ἡ	καρδία·	πιστεύετε	εἰς	τὸν	θεόν,
hē	*kardia*	*pisteuete*	*eis*	*ton*	*theon*
the	heart;	you believe	on		God,

2504.1 conj	1519.1 prep	1466.7 prs-pron acc 1sing	3961.2 verb 2pl pres act	1706.1 prep	3450.11 art dat sing fem
καὶ	εἰς	ἐμὲ	πιστεύετε.	2. ἐν	τῇ
kai	*eis*	*eme*	*pisteuete*	*en*	*tē*
also	on	me	believe.	In	the

3477.3 noun dat sing fem	3450.2 art gen sing	3824.2 noun gen sing masc	1466.2 prs-pron gen 1sing	3301.2 noun nom pl fem	4044.13 adj nom pl fem
οἰκίᾳ	τοῦ	πατρός	μου	μοναὶ	πολλαί
oikia	*tou*	*patros*	*mou*	*monai*	*pollai*
house	of the	Father	my	rooms	many

1498.7 verb 3pl indic pres act	1479.1 conj	1156.2 conj	3231.1 partic	1500.3 verb indic aor act	300.1 partic	5050.3 prs-pron dat 2pl
εἰσιν·	εἰ	δὲ	μή,	εἶπον	ἂν	ὑμῖν
eisin	*ei*	*de*	*mē*	*eipon*	*an*	*humin*
there are;	if	but	not	I would have told		you;

2.a.**Var:** p66-corr,01א, 02A,03B,04C-org,05D, 017K,019L,032W,1,33, 565,sa.bo.Lach,Treg,Alf Word,Tisc,We/Ho,Weis, Sod,UBS/☆

3617.1 conj	4057.1 verb 1sing indic pres	2069.11 verb inf aor act	4964.4 noun acc sing masc	5050.3 prs-pron dat 2pl
[a☆+ ὅτι]	πορεύομαι	ἑτοιμάσαι	τόπον	ὑμῖν;
hoti	*poreuomai*	*hetoimasai*	*topon*	*humin*
[because]	I go	to prepare	a place	for you;

3.a.**Txt:** 01א,03B,04C, 019L,022N,030U,041, 33,byz.it.TiscWe/Ho, Weis,Sod,UBS/☆
Var: 02A,05D,017K, 021M,036,037,038,Lach

2504.1 conj	1430.1 partic	4057.18 verb 1sing subj aor pass	2504.1 conj	2069.6 verb 1sing subj aor act	5050.3 prs-pron dat 2pl
3. καὶ	ἐὰν	πορευθῶ	⸂a καὶ ⸃	ἑτοιμάσω	⸂ ὑμῖν
kai	*ean*	*poreuthō*	*kai*	*hetoimasō*	*humin*
and	if	I go	and	prepare	for you

4964.4 noun acc sing masc	4964.4 noun acc sing masc	5050.3 prs-pron dat 2pl	3687.1 adv	2048.32 verb 1sing indic pres	2504.1 conj
τόπον,	[☆ τόπον	ὑμῖν,]	πάλιν	ἔρχομαι	καὶ
topon	*topon*	*humin*	*palin*	*erchomai*	*kai*
a place,	[a place	for you,]	again	I am coming	and

3.b.**Txt:** 03B-corr,04C, 017K,019L,036,037,038, byz.Sod
Var: 01א,02A,03B-org, 05D,022N,033X,Lach, Treg,Alf,TiscWe/Ho, Weis,UBS/☆

3741.14 verb 1sing indic fut mid	3741.17 verb 1sing indic fut mid	5050.4 prs-pron acc 2pl	4242.1 prep
⸂ παραλήψομαι	[b☆ παραλήμψομαι]	ὑμᾶς	πρὸς
paralēpsomai	*paralēmpsomai*	*humas*	*pros*
will receive	[idem]	you	to

1670.3 prs-pron acc 1sing masc	2419.1 conj	3562.1 adv	1498.2 verb 1sing indic pres act	1466.1 prs-pron nom 1sing	2504.1 conj	5050.1 prs-pron nom 2pl
ἐμαυτόν·	ἵνα	ὅπου	εἰμὶ	ἐγώ,	καὶ	ὑμεῖς
emauton	*hina*	*hopou*	*eimi*	*egō*	*kai*	*humeis*
myself,	that	where	am	I	also	you

4.a.**Txt:** 01א,02A,03B, 04C,017K,022N,026Q, 036,037,etc.byz.bo.Lach, Tisc,We/Ho,WeisSod, UBS/☆
Var: p66,05D,019L, 032W,033X,038,13

1498.1 verb 2pl act	2504.1 conj	3562.1 adv	1466.1 prs-pron nom 1sing	5055.1 verb 1sing indic pres act	3471.6 verb 2pl indic perf act
ἦτε.	4. καὶ	ὅπου	⸂a ἐγὼ ⸃	ὑπάγω	οἴδατε
ēte	*kai*	*hopou*	*egō*	*hupagō*	*oidate*
may be.	And	where	I	go	you know

14:1. The disciples were troubled because of several depressing occurrences. First, Jesus had told them He was departing from them (13:33). Second, He implied that He would suffer death by crucifixion (12:32,33). Third, He said all would forsake Him and Peter would deny Him (13:38). Fourth, He pointed out that one of their number was resolute in his decision to betray Him (13:21). Fifth, they had noted that the betrayal had troubled Jesus though they were unable to interpret it correctly (13:21). And sixth, He had told them they could not follow Him until later (13:36). The 11 apostles were in need of the encouraging discourse of the next 3 chapters (14-16).

Jesus used the word "heart" in the singular, indicating the collective sense and making the admonition appropriate to each member of the group. "Heart" is used as the deepest recesses of the soul. It usually signifies the emotions, which reflect the attitude and will of the entire person. To be troubled is a human reaction to adverse circumstances. It is not a sin to be troubled or else our Lord would not have been troubled (13:21). Furthermore, His troublings were due to His imminent betrayal and the burden of sin which He, our holy Sacrifice, was about to assume.

1. Let not your heart be troubled: Do not allow, *Fenton* . . . Don't feel troubled, *Beck* . . . Stop letting, *Williams* . . . be disquieted, *Moffatt* . . . You must not let yourselves be distressed, *Phillips* . . . Don't be upset, *LivB* . . . continue to be agitated, *Wuest* . . . worried and upset, *TEV* . . . disheartened, *TCNT.*

ye believe in God, believe also in me: You trust in God, *Montgomery* . . . have faith in God, and have faith in me, *BB* . . . keep on believing in God, *Williams* . . . Be putting your trust, *Wuest.*

14:2. The verses that follow give substance to the believing commanded in verse 1. Faith is never without a basis of evidence. God asks no man to trust without evidence (Hebrews 11:1).

The Father's house is what we call "heaven." It is where Jesus came from and where He was going (13:33). It is impossible to locate the position of heaven in space, but Jesus assured us that the Father's house exists. "Mansions" indicates permanent places. The Greek word is derived from the word for "remain." Three phrases have been given here of heaven's realities: "my Father's house," "many mansions," and "a place for you." The first two narrow down into the third—the individual and personal designation.

2. In my Father's house are many mansions: . . . are rooms enough, *BB* . . . abiding places, *HBIE* . . . are many dwelling places, *Williams* . . . dwellings, *TCNT* . . . many abodes, *Concordant, Fenton.*

if it were not so, I would have told you: Otherwise, *Norlie.*

I go to prepare a place for you: I am going to make ready a place, *Concordant* . . . I am taking a trip to prepare a place, *SEB.*

14:3. There was no uncertainty about His departure. "A place for you" is the complementary reason for going and preparing.

Jesus promised to go and He did! He promised to prepare a place for each believer and He is! He promised to come again and He will! His coming cannot be fully realized until the Second Advent at the end of the age. It is then that His people will enjoy the benefits of His complete redemptive work.

First, He spoke of "my Father's house." Second, He pointed out that there were "many mansions" (dwelling places). Third, He assured the disciples of "a place for you." Fourth, and with rapturous

3. And if I go and prepare a place for you: . . . for I am going away to make ready a place for you, *Williams* . . . Since I am leaving to prepare, *SEB* . . . after I have gone and prepared a place, *Fenton.*

I will come again, and receive you unto myself: I am coming again, and will take you to myself, *HBIE* . . . I shall return, *TCNT* . . . I will return and will take you to be with me, *Montgomery* . . . take you to be face to face with me, *Williams* . . . and take you home with Me, *Beck* . . . take you to be with me, *Weymouth.*

that where I am, there ye may be also: . . . so that you may be where I am, *Norlie* . . . may always be right where I am, *Williams.*

4.b.**Txt:** p66-org,02A, 04C-corr,05D,017K, 022N,036,037,1,13,565, 700,byz.it.sa.Gries,Lach **Var:** p66-corr,01ℵ,03B, 04C-org,019L,026Q, 032W,033X,33,bo.Treg, Alf,Tisc,We/Ho,Weis, Sod,UBS/☆

4.c.**Txt:** p66-org,02A, 04C-corr,05D,017K, 022N,036,037,1,13,565, 700,byz.it.sa.Gries,Lach **Var:** p66-corr,01ℵ,03B, 04C-org,019L,026Q, 032W,033X,33,bo.Treg, Alf,Tisc,We/Ho,Weis, Sod,UBS/☆

5.a.**Txt:** 01ℵ,02A, 04C-corr,017K,022N, 026Q,036,037,038,1,13, etc.byz.Tisc,Sod **Var:** p66,03B,04C-org, 019L,032W,Lach,Treg, We/HoWeis,UBS/☆

5.b.**Txt:** p66,(01),02A, 04C-corr,(017),019L, 022N,026Q,032W,036, 037,038,1,13,etc.byz.Sod **Var:** 03B,04C-org,(05), Lach,Treg,Alf,Tisc, We/Ho,Weis,UBS/☆

6.a.**Txt:** 02A,03B, 04C-corr,05D,017K, 022N,026Q,032W,036, 037,038,1,13,etc.byz. Lach,Weis,Sod **Var:** p66,01ℵ,04C-org, 019L,Tisc,We/Ho,UBS/☆

7.a.**Var:** 01ℵ,05D-org,it. bo.Tisc

7.b.**Txt:** 02A,04C-corr, 017K,022N,036,037, (038),13,28,byz.Lach, Sod **Var:** 03B,04C-org,(019), 026Q,033X,1,33,Treg Alf,We/Ho,Weis,UBS/☆

7.c.**Txt:** p66,01ℵ,02A, 04C-corr,05D,017K, 022N,032W,036,037, 038,13,byz.Lach,Tisc **Var:** 03B,04C-org,019L, 026Q,33,Treg,Alf, We/Ho,WeisSod,UBS/☆

7.d.**Txt:** p66,01ℵ,02A, 04C-corr,05D,017K, 019L,022N,026Q,032W, 036,037,038,1,13,etc. byz.it.sa.bo.Lach,Tisc, Sod **Var:** 03B,04C-org,We/Ho Weis,UBS/☆

2504.1 conj	**3450.12** art acc sing fem	**3461.4** noun acc sing fem	**3471.6** verb 2pl indic perf act	**2978.5** verb 3sing indic pres act	**840.4** prs-pron dat sing
(b καὶ)	τὴν	ὁδόν	(c οἴδατε.)	5. Λέγει	αὐτῷ
kai	*tēn*	*hodon*	*oidate*	*Legei*	*autō*
and	the	way	you know.	Says	to him

2358.1 name nom masc	**2935.5** noun voc sing masc	**3620.2** partic	**3471.5** verb 1pl indic perf act	**4085.1** adv	**5055.2** verb 2sing indic pres act
Θωμᾶς,	Κύριε,	οὐκ	οἴδαμεν	ποῦ	ὑπάγεις,
Thōmas	*Kurie*	*ouk*	*oidamen*	*pou*	*hupageis*
Thomas,	Lord,	not	we know	where	you are going,

2504.1 conj	**4316.1** adv	**1404.5** verb 1pl indic pres	**3450.12** art acc sing fem	**3461.4** noun acc sing fem	**3471.25** verb inf perf act
(a καὶ)	πῶς	(☆ δυνάμεθα	τὴν	ὁδὸν	εἰδέναι;
kai	*pōs*	*dunametha*	*tēn*	*hodon*	*eidenai*
and	how	can we	the	way	know?

3471.5 verb 1pl indic perf act	**3450.12** art acc sing fem	**3461.4** noun acc sing fem	**2978.5** verb 3sing indic pres act	**840.4** prs-pron dat sing	**3450.5** art sing masc
[b οἴδαμεν	τὴν	ὁδόν;]	6. Λέγει	αὐτῷ	(a ὁ)
oidamen	*tēn*	*hodon*	*Legei*	*autō*	*ho*
[do we know	the	way?]	Says	to him	

2400.1 name nom masc	**1466.1** prs-pron nom 1sing	**1498.2** verb 1sing indic pres act	**3450.9** art nom sing fem	**3461.1** noun nom sing fem	**2504.1** conj
Ἰησοῦς,	Ἐγώ	εἰμι	ἡ	ὁδὸς	καὶ
Iēsous	*Egō*	*eimi*	*hē*	*hodos*	*kai*
Jesus,	I	am	the	way	and

3450.9 art nom sing fem	**223.1** noun nom sing fem	**2504.1** conj	**3450.9** art nom sing fem	**2205.1** noun nom sing fem	**3625.2** num card nom masc
ἡ	ἀλήθεια	καὶ	ἡ	ζωή·	οὐδεὶς
hē	*alētheia*	*kai*	*hē*	*zōē*	*oudeis*
the	truth	and	the	life.	No one

2048.34 verb 3sing indic pres	**4242.1** prep	**3450.6** art acc sing masc	**3824.4** noun acc sing masc	**1479.1** conj	**3231.1** partic	**1217.1** prep
ἔρχεται	πρὸς	τὸν	πατέρα	εἰ	μὴ	δι'
erchetai	*pros*	*ton*	*patera*	*ei*	*mē*	*di'*
comes	to	the	Father	if	not	by

1466.3 prs-pron gen 1sing	**1479.1** conj	**1091.34** verb 2pl indic perf act	**1466.6** prs-pron acc 1sing	**1091.34** verb 2pl indic perf act
ἐμοῦ.	7. εἰ	(ἐγνώκατέ	με,	[a☆ ἐγνώκατε
emou	*ei*	*egnōkate*	*me*	*egnōkate*
me.	If	you have known	me,	[you have known

1466.6 prs-pron acc 1sing	**2504.1** conj	**3450.6** art acc sing masc	**3824.4** noun acc sing masc	**1466.2** prs-pron gen 1sing	**1091.36** verb 2pl indic plperf act
μέ,]	καὶ	τὸν	πατέρα	μου	(ἐγνώκειτε
me	*kai*	*ton*	*patera*	*mou*	*egnōkeite*
me,]	also	the	Father	my	you had known;

300.1 partic	**300.1** partic	**3471.12** verb 2pl indic plperf act	**2504.1** conj	**570.2** prep gen	**732.1** adv
ἄν·	[b ἄν	ᾔδειτε.]	(c καὶ)	ἀπ'	ἄρτι
an	*an*	*ēdeite*	*kai*	*ap'*	*arti*
		[you would have known.]	and	from	now on

1091.5 verb 2pl indic pres act	**840.6** prs-pron acc sing masc	**2504.1** conj	**3571.13** verb 2pl indic perf act	**840.6** prs-pron acc sing masc
γινώσκετε	αὐτὸν,	καὶ	ἑωράκατε	(d αὐτόν.)
ginōskete	*auton*	*kai*	*heōrakate*	*auton*
you know	him,	and	have seen	him.

finality, He promised He himself would receive them that "where I am, there ye may be also."

4. And whither I go ye know, and the way ye know: And you know the way to the place where I am going, *Williams* . . . you know the road, *Klingensmith, Wuest.*

14:4. Jesus had spoken both in public and in private concerning His departure (6:62; 7:36; 13:33,36). The disciples knew where He was going; He had just told them the Father's house was His destination.

The word "know" shows the close relationship of both these sentences. He was going to the Father's house, and they would follow after. Jesus was their way to the Father's house because He was the revelation of the Father (1:4,12; 10:7,9; 11:25).

5. Thomas saith unto him, Lord, we know not whither thou goest: . . . we have no knowledge of, *BB* . . . we do not know where you are going, *Wuest* . . . we don't know where you are going, *Adams.*

and how can we know the way?: . . . how is it possible for us, *Wuest* . . . and how can we know what road you're going to take, *Phillips* . . . so how can we know the way? *Adams* . . . How know we the road? *Klingensmith.*

14:5. Thomas is noted for his skepticism and his questions, yet he should be remembered also for his amazing confession of faith (20:28). The question he asked was doubtless in the minds of all the disciples.

Thomas was not far from scholars' critical inquiries. Today we still do not know where heaven is. Thomas was not alone in his question. The other disciples also wished for more definite knowledge about heaven and the way to get there.

6. Jesus saith unto him, I am the way, the truth, and the life: I alone, *Wuest* . . . I am the real and living way, *Moffatt* . . . and Eternal Life, *Norton.*

no man cometh unto the Father, but by me: . . . but through me, *Alford* . . . except by means of me, *Moffatt* . . . except through me, *Williams, Fenton, Wuest.*

14:6. Had it not been for Thomas' question, we might not have this precious statement from our Lord. This is a triple "I am" of Jesus (see 1:51). "The way" means the road on which one travels to the Father's house. Jesus is like a bridge-road spanning the gulf between earth to heaven. "The truth" and "the life" are eternal aspects of Christ's nature. Christ stated the temporary aspect before the eternal. Thomas and the disciples had hoped to satisfy their curious minds, but Jesus wished to promote their safe arrival in heaven. "The way" is the road the disciples were to travel. "The truth" guaranteed the light for their safe journey. "The life" would provide the necessary energy to assure their reaching their destination.

7. If ye had known me: If you had recognized me, *TCNT* . . . If you had known who I am, *Phillips* . . . If you have learned to know Me, *Beck* . . . you had learned to know me through experience, *Wuest.*

ye should have known my Father also: . . . you would have known my Father also, *TCNT* . . . you'll know My Father too, *Beck.*

and from henceforth ye know him, and have seen him: From now on, you have known and have seen him, *Klingensmith* . . . as from now, *ALBA* . . . see Him with discernment, *Wuest.*

14:7. "Had known" is a perfect verb for a knowledge that often comes from personal experience. It was by seeing Jesus that the Father was known, for Jesus was the brightness of His glory and the express image of His person (Hebrews 1:3; Colossians 1:15; 1 Timothy 6:16).

John 14:8

2978.5 verb 3sing indic pres act	840.4 prs-pron dat sing	5213.1 name nom masc	2935.5 noun voc sing masc	1161.9 verb 2sing impr aor act
8. Λέγει	αὐτῷ	Φίλιππος,	Κύριε,	δεῖξον
Legei	*autō*	*Philippos*	*Kurie*	*deixon*
Says	to him	Philip,	Lord,	show

2231.3 prs-pron dat 1pl	3450.6 art acc sing masc	3824.4 noun acc sing masc	2504.1 conj	708.1 verb 3sing indic pres act	2231.3 prs-pron dat 1pl
ἡμῖν	τὸν	πατέρα,	καὶ	ἀρκεῖ	ἡμῖν.
hēmin	*ton*	*patera*	*kai*	*arkei*	*hēmin*
us	the	Father,	and	it is enough	for us.

2978.5 verb 3sing indic pres act	840.4 prs-pron dat sing	3450.5 art sing masc	2400.1 name nom masc	4965.1 dem-pron acc sing
9. Λέγει	αὐτῷ	ὁ	Ἰησοῦς,	⸀ Τοσοῦτον
Legei	*autō*	*ho*	*Iēsous*	*Tosouton*
Says	to him		Jesus,	So long

9.a.**Var:** 01א-org,05D, 019L,026Q,032W,Lach, Tisc

5385.4 noun acc sing masc	4965.8 dem-pron dat sing neu	5385.3 noun dat sing masc	3196.1 prep	5050.2 prs-pron gen 2pl	1498.2 verb 1sing indic pres act
χρόνον	[a τοσούτῳ	χρόνῳ]	μεθ'	ὑμῶν	εἰμι,
chronon	*tosoutō*	*chronō*	*meth'*	*humōn*	*eimi*
a time	[so long	a time]	with	you	am I,

2504.1 conj	3620.2 partic	1091.31 verb 2sing indic perf act	1466.6 prs-pron acc 1sing	5213.5 name voc masc	3450.5 art sing masc
καὶ	οὐκ	ἔγνωκάς	με,	Φίλιππε;	ὁ
kai	*ouk*	*egnōkas*	*me*	*Philippe*	*ho*
and	not	you have known	me,	Philip?	The

3571.16 verb nom sing masc part perf act	1466.7 prs-pron acc 1sing	3571.11 verb 3sing indic perf act	3450.6 art acc sing masc	3824.4 noun acc sing masc
ἑωρακὼς	ἐμὲ,	ἑώρακεν	τὸν	πατέρα·
heōrakōs	*eme*	*heōraken*	*ton*	*patera*
having seen	me,	has seen	the	Father;

9.b.**Txt:** 02A,05D,017K, 019L,022N,036,037,038, 1,13,byz.Treg,Sod
Var: p66,01א,03B,026Q, 032W,Lach,Tisc,We/Ho Weis,UBS/⋆

2504.1 conj	4316.1 adv	4622.1 prs-pron nom 2sing	2978.4 verb 2sing indic pres act	1161.9 verb 2sing impr aor act	2231.3 prs-pron dat 1pl
⸂b καὶ ⸃	πῶς	σὺ	λέγεις,	Δεῖξον	ἡμῖν
kai	*pōs*	*su*	*legeis*	*Deixon*	*hēmin*
and	how	you	say,	Show	us

3450.6 art acc sing masc	3824.4 noun acc sing masc	3620.3 partic	3961.5 verb 2sing indic pres act	3617.1 conj	1466.1 prs-pron nom 1sing
τὸν	πατέρα;	10. οὐ	πιστεύεις	ὅτι	ἐγὼ
ton	*patera*	*ou*	*pisteueis*	*hoti*	*egō*
the	Father?	Not	you believe	that	I

1706.1 prep	3450.3 art dat sing	3824.3 noun dat sing masc	2504.1 conj	3450.5 art sing masc	3824.1 noun nom sing masc	1706.1 prep
ἐν	τῷ	πατρὶ,	καὶ	ὁ	πατὴρ	ἐν
en	*tō*	*patri*	*kai*	*ho*	*patēr*	*en*
in	the	Father,	and	the	Father	in

1466.5 prs-pron dat 1sing	1498.4 verb 3sing indic pres act	3450.17 art pl neu	4343.4 noun pl neu	3614.17 rel-pron pl neu	1466.1 prs-pron nom 1sing
ἐμοί	ἐστιν;	τὰ	ῥήματα	ἃ	ἐγὼ
emoi	*estin*	*ta*	*rhēmata*	*ha*	*egō*
me	is?	The	words	which	I

10.a.**Txt:** p66,01א,02A, 017K,026Q,032W,036, 037,038,1,13,etc.byz. Gries,Lach,Sod
Var: p75,03B-corr,019L, 022N,033X,Treg,Alf, Tisc,We/HoWeis,UBS/⋆

2953.1 verb 1sing pres act	2978.1 verb 1sing pres act	5050.3 prs-pron dat 2pl	570.2 prep gen	1670.1 prs-pron gen 1sing masc	3620.3 partic
⸀⋆ λαλῶ	[a λέγω]	ὑμῖν,	ἀπ'	ἐμαυτοῦ	οὐ
lalō	*legō*	*humin*	*ap'*	*emautou*	*ou*
speak	[say]	to you,	from	myself	not

14:8. Philip, like Thomas, did not understand. His request has been in the heart of man from creation. Adam communed with God in the Garden. Abraham saw a theophany of God. Moses was granted a view of God's afterglow. Usually man had believed that if he saw God, he would die. Jesus had told them that the pure in heart would see God (Matthew 5:8). Now that Jesus had spoken of seeing the Father (verse 7), Philip thought it could be possible at that time.

Philip thought that a spectacular display of the Father's presence would suffice to dispel their doubts and fears. Man has longed for the sensational phenomenon to produce trust and allegiance, but this is not God's method. Though the disciples had difficulty perceiving it, God was in Christ reconciling the world unto himself (2 Corinthians 5:19).

The believer should be aware that God does manifest himself in spectacular ways; however, His usual method is not detectable by the natural man. Philip had been looking for sensational manifestations as evidence of the Father. Yet, Jesus had been God's very presence among them. How easily Philip overlooked the revelation of God by looking for the extraordinary phenomena!

8. Philip saith unto him, Lord, shew us the Father, and it sufficeth us: . . . point out to us, *Rotherham* . . . and it is enough for us, *Berkeley* . . . that will satisfy us, *Fenton* . . . the Father at once, *Wuest* . . . and we are content, *Klingensmith* . . . that is all we need, *Weymouth.*

14:9. Philip was converted in the early ministry of Jesus (1:43). This accounts for about 3½ years of companionship. During this time Philip had looked upon the incarnate God, and yet he desired to be granted a vision of God! Most disciples are very poor observers.

The Father has no separate manifestation from the Son. The Son is the only manifestation and revelation of the Father. What is known of the Father is revealed through the Son. To see the Son is to see the essence of the Father (John 1:1,18; 10:30; 12:45; Colossians 1:15; Hebrews 1:3).

Jesus was somewhat saddened by Philip's dullness, and His words imply it. Yet Jesus only mildly rebuked Philip in compassion. The Lord always shows longsuffering, patience, and love toward the ignorant or immature but sincere disciple. Disciples often reveal how immature, insensitive, and stupid they are by the questions they ask. But how kind and considerate the Good Shepherd is!

9. Jesus saith unto him, Have I been so long time with you: . . . have I been with you all this time, *BB.*

and yet hast thou not known me, Philip?: . . . without your recognizing Me, Philip! *Berkeley* . . . and yet you do not understand me, *Moffatt.*

he that hath seen me hath seen the Father: He who has looked on Me, has looked on the Father, *Berkeley.*

and how sayest thou then, Shew us the Father?: Why do you say, Let us see the Father, *BB* . . . Cause us to see, *Montgomery.*

14:10. Philip's question implied that he did not believe this truth. Jesus had taught publicly and surely privately to His disciples (10:38) the mutual indwelling of the Father and the Son. The disciples seemed not to make the connection between His teaching and this truth. It is not easy to disregard the natural and worldly view of God's kingdom. The natural man must be born again, and he must also tune himself to the things of the Spirit (1 Corinthians 2:14).

10. Believest thou not that I am in the Father: Don't you believe, *Beck* . . . that I am in union, *Williams.*

and the Father in me?: . . . and that the Father is in union with me, *Williams* . . . who is in me all the time, *BB* . . . Father dwelling in me, *ALBA.*

the words that I speak unto you I speak not of myself: The things that I tell you all, *Weymouth* . . . The declarations which I am speaking, *Concordant* . . . I am not myself the source of the words I speak to you, *NEB* . . . are not words I use on my own, *SEB* . . . proceed not from myself, *Campbell* . . . I do not speak of my own accord, *Moffatt* . . . of my own authority, *Williams* . . . of My own accord, *AmpB.*

John 14:11

10.b.**Txt:** 01א,02A,05D, 017K,022N,026Q,032W, 036,037,038,byz.Lach, Tisc,Sod
Var: p66,p75,03B,019L, We/Ho,Weis,UBS/☆

2953.1 verb 1sing pres act	**3450.5** art sing masc	**1156.2** conj	**3824.1** noun nom sing masc	**3450.5** art sing masc	**1706.1** prep	**1466.5** prs-pron dat 1sing
λαλῶ·	ὁ	δὲ	πατὴρ	(b ὁ)	ἐν	ἐμοὶ
lalō	*ho*	*de*	*patēr*	*ho*	*en*	*emoi*
I speak;	the	but	Father	the	in	me

3176.10 verb nom sing masc part pres act	**840.5** prs-pron nom sing masc	**4020.5** verb 3sing indic pres act	**3450.17** art pl neu	**2024.4** noun pl neu
μένων	(αὐτὸς	ποιεῖ	τὰ	ἔργα·
menōn	*autos*	*poiei*	*ta*	*erga*
residing	he	does	the	works.

10.c.**Txt:** 02A,017K, 026Q,036,037,038,1,13, byz.
Var: p66,01א,03B,05D, Lach,Treg,Alf,Tisc, We/Ho,Weis,UBS/☆

4020.5 verb 3sing indic pres act	**3450.17** art pl neu	**2024.4** noun pl neu	**840.3** prs-pron gen sing	**3961.2** verb 2pl pres act
[c☆ ποιεῖ	τὰ	ἔργα	αὐτοῦ.]	**11.** πιστεύετέ
poiei	*ta*	*erga*	*autou*	*pisteuete*
[does	the	works	his.]	Believe

1466.4 prs-pron dat 1sing	**3617.1** conj	**1466.1** prs-pron nom 1sing	**1706.1** prep	**3450.3** art dat sing	**3824.3** noun dat sing masc	**2504.1** conj
μοι	ὅτι	ἐγὼ	ἐν	τῷ	πατρὶ,	καὶ
moi	*hoti*	*egō*	*en*	*tō*	*patri*	*kai*
me	that	I	in	the	Father,	and

3450.5 art sing masc	**3824.1** noun nom sing masc	**1706.1** prep	**1466.5** prs-pron dat 1sing	**1479.1** conj	**1156.2** conj	**3231.1** partic
ὁ	πατὴρ	ἐν	ἐμοί·	εἰ	δὲ	μή,
ho	*patēr*	*en*	*emoi*	*ei*	*de*	*mē*
the	Father	in	me;	if	but	not,

11.a.**Txt:** 02A,03B,017K, 026Q,036,037,038,1,13, 28,byz.Lach,Treg
Var: p66,p75,01א,05D, 019L,032W,33,Tisc, We/Ho,Weis,Sod,UBS/☆

1217.2 prep	**3450.17** art pl neu	**2024.4** noun pl neu	**840.16** prs-pron pl neu	**3961.2** verb 2pl pres act	**1466.4** prs-pron dat 1sing
διὰ	τὰ	ἔργα	αὐτὰ	πιστεύετε	(a μοι.)
dia	*ta*	*erga*	*auta*	*pisteuete*	*moi*
because of	the	works	themselves	believe	me.

279.1 partic	**279.1** partic	**2978.1** verb 1sing pres act	**5050.3** prs-pron dat 2pl	**3450.5** art sing masc	**3961.10** verb nom sing masc part pres act
12. Ἀμὴν	ἀμὴν	λέγω	ὑμῖν,	ὁ	πιστεύων
Amēn	*amēn*	*legō*	*humin*	*ho*	*pisteuōn*
Truly	truly	I say	to you,	The	believing

1519.1 prep	**1466.7** prs-pron acc 1sing	**3450.17** art pl neu	**2024.4** noun pl neu	**3614.17** rel-pron pl neu	**1466.1** prs-pron nom 1sing	**4020.1** verb 1sing pres act
εἰς	ἐμὲ,	τὰ	ἔργα	ἃ	ἐγὼ	ποιῶ,
eis	*eme*	*ta*	*erga*	*ha*	*egō*	*poiō*
on	me,	the	works	which	I	do,

2519.6 conj	**4020.52** verb 3sing indic fut act	**2504.1** conj	**3157.1** adj comp acc	**3642.2** dem-pron gen pl	**4020.52** verb 3sing indic fut act
κἀκεῖνος	ποιήσει,	καὶ	μείζονα	τούτων	ποιήσει,
kakeinos	*poiēsei*	*kai*	*meizona*	*toutōn*	*poiēsei*
also he	shall do,	and	greater	than these	he shall do,

12.a.**Txt:** 017K,036,037, byz.
Var: 01א,02A,03B,05D, 019L,026Q,033X,038, 33,Lach,Treg,Alf,Tisc, We/HoWeis,Sod,UBS/☆

3617.1 conj	**1466.1** prs-pron nom 1sing	**4242.1** prep	**3450.6** art acc sing masc	**3824.4** noun acc sing masc	**1466.2** prs-pron gen 1sing
ὅτι	ἐγὼ	πρὸς	τὸν	πατέρα	(a μου)
hoti	*egō*	*pros*	*ton*	*patera*	*mou*
because	I	to	the	Father	my

4057.1 verb 1sing indic pres	**2504.1** conj	**3614.16** rel-pron sing neu	**4948.10** indef-pron sing neu	**300.1** partic	**153.15** verb 2pl subj aor act
πορεύομαι·	**13.** καὶ	ὃ	τι	ἂν	αἰτήσητε
poreuomai	*kai*	*ho*	*ti*	*an*	*aitēsēte*
go.	And	what	ever		you may ask

R.V.G. Tasker says of Philip: "To see God with his physical eyes, to know Him by what men tend to regard as the sure evidence of the senses, that will indeed satisfy Philip and remove his doubts, and he asks for nothing more. But the very fact that he makes such a request after having been so long with Jesus reveals a pathetic misunderstanding both of the Person and the work of his Lord. Because Jesus lives in perpetual union of purpose and will with His Father, His words and actions are God's words and actions" (Tasker, *Tyndale New Testament Commentaries*, 20:165).

Jesus did the Father's work. Both the teachings and works of Christ were manifestations of the Father. How could they ask to be shown the Father when for 3 years they had been listening to the Father's voice and observing the Father's signs, wonders, and miracles. Jesus did nothing independent of His Father.

but the Father that dwelleth in me, he doeth the works: . . . but the Father, who ever dwells in me, *Montgomery* . . . Father dwelling within me carries on His own work, *Weymouth* . . . Who lives continually in Me, *AmpB* . . . the Father Who remains in, *Adams* . . . carries on His activities, *Berkeley* . . . The Father performs His miracles; He stays in me, *SEB* . . . who always remains in union with me is doing these things Himself, *Williams.*

14:11. The emphasis in verse 10 is on "the words" (sayings or teachings) and "the works" (miracles). This verse continues the emphasis on "the works."

"Believe (in) me" is an imperative concerning His teaching. The teaching is that "I am in the Father, and the Father in me" (see also 10:30). There is often difficulty in understanding, trusting, and appropriating the teaching. "The words" (teaching) are made credible by "the works."

"The works" were to point toward His words which produce life in the souls of those who receive them (1:12; 6:63). His teachings bring life because they make God known (17:3).

11. Believe me that I am in the Father, and the Father in me: You must believe me, *Williams* . . . that I am in union with the Father, *TCNT* . . . Have faith, *BB.*

or else believe me for the very works' sake: Or else believe Me on account of My works, *Beck* . . . But if not, because of the works themselves, *Wuest* . . . on the evidence of these works, *Norton.*

14:12. "He that believeth on me" (as verse 11 states) should have what verse 12 promises. "Me" is emphatic. It must be one who is believing in a continuing sense. Furthermore, the believing must be in accord with the manifestation of the Father as revealed by Jesus Christ the Son. All Jesus did, He did from the initiative of the Father, not from His own initiative (verse 10). The promise of verse 12 will be fulfilled in accord with the Father's initiative, not from the believer's initiative.

Jesus referred to His miracles as "works" (7:21; 10:32), but He also spoke of believing as a work in 6:29 and 8:39. What Abraham did is called "works." These "works" (*erga*) refer to less spectacular acts of faith rather than miracles. The word "works" refers to miracles primarily, but to the conduct of faith secondarily.

The Book of Acts gives us accounts of a great number of miracles, but none surpassed those of Jesus himself. Therefore, we conclude that Jesus meant greater in quantity. What was performed by Jesus could be multiplied in and through His disciples. If we conclude that the works of faith are secondary references, then the quantity of works produced by the believing one is astounding. "He" indicates a collective singular. The Church is viewed as performing "greater works" through individual believers.

12. Verily, verily, I say unto you, He that believeth on me: He who puts his faith in me, *BB* . . . whoever perseveres in believing in me, *Williams* . . . he who trusts in me, *Montgomery.*

the works that I do shall he do also: . . . will do the very deeds I do, *Moffatt* . . . will do the very things I am doing, *Norlie* . . . which I am constantly doing, *Wuest.*

and greater works than these shall he do: . . . and he shall do greater deeds than these, *Weymouth.*

because I go unto my Father: I am proceeding to, *Wuest.*

John 14:14

1706.1 prep	3450.3 art dat sing	3549.4 noun dat sing neu	1466.2 prs-pron gen 1sing	3642.17 dem-pron sing neu	4020.21 verb 1sing act	2419.1 conj
ἐν	τῷ	ὀνόματί	μου,	τοῦτο	ποιήσω,	ἵνα
en	*tō*	*onomati*	*mou*	*touto*	*poiēsō*	*hina*
in	thc	name	my,	this	will I do,	that

1386.23 verb 3sing subj aor pass	3450.5 art sing masc	3824.1 noun nom sing masc	1706.1 prep	3450.3 art dat sing	5048.3 noun dat sing masc
δοξασθῇ	ὁ	πατὴρ	ἐν	τῷ	υἱῷ˙
doxasthē	*ho*	*patēr*	*en*	*tō*	*huiō*
may be glorified	the	Father	in	the	Son.

14.a.**Var:** p66,01א,03B, 032W,036,037,038,13, 33,Lach,Tisc,We/Ho Weis,Sod,UBS/☆

1430.1 partic	4948.10 indef-pron sing neu	153.15 verb 2pl subj aor act	1466.6 prs-pron acc 1sing	1706.1 prep	3450.3 art dat sing
14. ἐάν	τι	αἰτήσητέ	[a☆+ με]	ἐν	τῷ
ean	*ti*	*aitēsēte*	*me*	*en*	*tō*
If	anything	you ask	[me]	in	the

3549.4 noun dat sing neu	1466.2 prs-pron gen 1sing	1466.1 prs-pron nom 1sing	4020.21 verb 1sing act	1430.1 partic
ὀνόματί	μου,	ἐγὼ	ποιήσω.	**15.** Ἐὰν
onomati	*mou*	*egō*	*poiēsō*	*Ean*
name	my,	I	will do.	If

25.1 verb 2pl pres act	1466.6 prs-pron acc 1sing	3450.15 art acc pl fem	1769.7 noun acc pl fem	3450.15 art acc pl fem
ἀγαπᾶτέ	με,	τὰς	ἐντολὰς	τὰς
agapate	*me*	*tas*	*entolas*	*tas*
you love	me,	the	commandments	the

15.a.**Txt:** 02A,05D,017K, 026Q,032W,036,037, 038,1,13,byz.it.Lach,Sod
Var: 03B,019L,044,sa. bo.Treg,Tisc,We/Ho, Weis,UBS/☆

1684.10 adj acc 1pl fem	4931.19 verb 2pl impr aor act	4931.40 verb 2pl indic fut act	2504.1 conj	1466.1 prs-pron nom 1sing
ἐμὰς	ʽ τηρήσατε˙	[a☆ τηρήσετε˙]	**16.** ʽ καὶ	ἐγὼ
emas	*tērēsate*	*tērēsete*	*kai*	*egō*
my	keep.	[you will keep.]	And	I

2476.3 conj	2049.8 verb 1sing act	3450.6 art acc sing masc	3824.4 noun acc sing masc	2504.1 conj	241.5 adj acc sing masc
[☆ κἀγὼ]	ἐρωτήσω	τὸν	πατέρα,	καὶ	ἄλλον
kagō	*erōtēsō*	*ton*	*patera*	*kai*	*allon*
[and I]	will ask	the	Father,	and	another

3736.2 noun acc sing masc	1319.38 verb 3sing indic fut act	5050.3 prs-pron dat 2pl	2419.1 conj	3176.7 verb 3sing subj pres act
παράκλητον	δώσει	ὑμῖν,	ἵνα	ʽ μένῃ
paraklēton	*dōsei*	*humin*	*hina*	*menē*
Paraclete	he will give	you,	that	he may remain

16.a.**Txt:** p66,02A,05D, 017K,032W,036,037, 038,1,13,byz.
Var1: .p75,03B,044, Lach,Weis
Var2: .01א,Tisc
Var3: .019L,026Q,033X, 33,bo.Treg,Alf,We/Ho, Sod,UBS/☆

3196.1 prep	5050.2 prs-pron gen 2pl	1519.1 prep	3450.6 art acc sing masc	163.3 noun acc sing masc	3196.1 prep	5050.2 prs-pron gen 2pl
μεθ᾽	ὑμῶν	εἰς	τὸν	αἰῶνα,	[1a☆ μεθ᾽	ὑμῶν
meth'	*humōn*	*eis*	*ton*	*aiōna*	*meth'*	*humōn*
with	you	in	the	age,	[with	you

1519.1 prep	3450.6 art acc sing masc	163.3 noun acc sing masc	1498.10 verb 3sing subj pres act	3196.1 prep	5050.2 prs-pron gen 2pl
εἰς	τὸν	αἰῶνα	ᾖ	2 μεθ᾽	ὑμῶν
eis	*ton*	*aiōna*	*ē*	*meth'*	*humōn*
in	the	age	he may be	with	you

1498.10 verb 3sing subj pres act	1519.1 prep	3450.6 art acc sing masc	163.3 noun acc sing masc	1498.10 verb 3sing subj pres act	3196.1 prep
ᾖ	εἰς	τὸν	αἰῶνα	3 ᾖ	μεθ᾽
ē	*eis*	*ton*	*aiōna*	*ē*	*meth'*
he may be	in	the	age	he may be	with

It was on the condition of His going away that the Holy Spirit would come to endue each believer with power for service (see Acts 1:5,8; 2:4). All the works which believers do are done on the basis of Jesus' redemptive work and His return to the Father. The Book of Acts is a commentary on this verse.

13. And whatsoever ye shall ask in my name, that will I do: And anything you ask for as bearers of my name I will do for you, *Williams* . . . And whatever request you make, *BB* . . . and I will do whatever you ask, *Moffatt* . . . I will do anything, *Beck.*

that the Father may be glorified in the Son: . . . may be honoured, *TCNT* . . . may have glory, *Norlie.*

14:13,14. The reiteration of the promise serves to impress it. It is Jesus who does the work, not the believers. The works are accomplished because of His merits and believers working as His ambassadors. "In my name" means asking for His will to be done on earth as it is in heaven. The glory of God is the reason He answers believers' prayers. Jesus came to glorify the Father; believers have the same mission.

14. If ye shall ask any thing in my name I will do it: If you make any request of me, *Weymouth* . . . Yes, I repeat it, anything you ask for as bearers of my name, *Williams* . . . as my followers, *TCNT* . . . I will grant it, *Phillips.*

14:15,16. The natural outgrowth of love is a desire to conduct one's life in obedience to the Lord's wishes. The teachings of Christ become commandments for the believers.

The Holy Spirit is called "another Comforter" (Helper). "Another" means another of the same kind that Jesus was. The disciples did not need to be concerned that some circumstances such as Jesus' crucifixion would separate the "other Comforter" from them.

This verse supports the doctrine of the Trinity. Just as at the account of Jesus' baptism by John, so the three members of the Godhead are evident here. Jesus said "I"—here is the Son. He would ask the "Father" to send "another Comforter" (the Holy Spirit). "Comforter" here is the Paraclete, one called alongside as a helper, adviser, counselor, or an advocate (cf. 1 John 2:1). The concept of "intercessor" is also found in *paraklētos.*

This Comforter would do for the disciples in the future what Jesus had done for them while He was with them. The Holy Spirit would "abide" ("be, stay, remain, continue") with them. He would not leave them alone. Merrill Tenney writes: "The ministry of the Spirit, however, would be directed primarily to the disciples. He would direct their decisions, counsel them continually, and remain with them forever. He would be invisible to all and unapprehended by the world at large since the world would not recognize him. To use a modern metaphor, he would not operate on the world's wavelength. His presence was already *with* the disciples insofar as they were under his influence. Later, he would indwell them, when Jesus himself had departed. This distinction marks the difference between the Old Testament experience of the Holy Spirit and the post-Pentecostal experience of the church. The individual indwelling of the Spirit is the specific privilege of the Christian believer (see John 7:39)" (Tenney, *Expositor's Bible Commentary,* 9:146,147).

15. If ye love me, keep my commandments: . . . you will do what I order, *Beck.*

16. And I will pray the Father: And I will ask the Father, *NASB* . . . And I will request the Father, *Rotherham.*

and he shall give you another Comforter: . . . to give you another Helper, *Moffatt* . . . another Advocate, *HBIE* . . . Counselor, *RSV* . . . some one else to stand by you, *Phillips* . . . another consoler, *Concordant* . . . another teacher, *Norton.*

that he may abide with you for ever: . . . to stay with you forever, *Berkeley* . . . to remain with you to the end of the age, *Williams* . . . to continue with you forever, *Campbell, Fenton.*

5050.2 prs-pron gen 2pl	1519.1 prep	3450.6 art acc sing masc	163.3 noun acc sing masc	3450.16 art sing neu	4011.1 noun sing neu
ὑμῶν	εἰς	τὸν	αἰῶνα,]	**17.** τὸ	πνεῦμα
humōn	*eis*	*ton*	*aiōna*	*to*	*pneuma*
you	in	the	age,]	the	Spirit

3450.10 art gen sing fem	223.2 noun gen sing fem	3614.16 rel-pron sing neu	3450.5 art sing masc	2862.1 noun nom sing masc	3620.3 partic
τῆς	ἀληθείας,	ὃ	ὁ	κόσμος	οὐ
tēs	*alētheias*	*ho*	*ho*	*kosmos*	*ou*
of the	truth,	whom	the	world	not

17.a.**Txt:** p66-corr,02A, 017K,033X,036,037, 038,1,13,etc.byz.Lach, Tisc,Sod
Var: p66-org,p75,01ℵ, 03B,032W,We/Ho,Weis, UBS/☆

1404.4 verb 3sing indic pres	2956.31 verb inf aor act	3617.1 conj	3620.3 partic	2311.4 verb 3sing indic pres act	840.15 prs-pron sing neu
δύναται	λαβεῖν,	ὅτι	οὐ	θεωρεῖ	αὐτὸ,
dunatai	*labein*	*hoti*	*ou*	*theōrei*	*auto*
can	receive,	because	not	it does see	him,

17.b.**Txt:** 02A,05D,017K, 036,037,038,1,13,etc. byz.Lach
Var: p66,p75,01ℵ,03B, 026Q,032W,Alf,Tisc, We/HoWeis,Sod,UBS/☆

3624.1 adv	1091.3 verb 3sing indic pres act	840.15 prs-pron sing neu	5050.1 prs-pron nom 2pl	1156.2 conj	1091.5 verb 2pl indic pres act
οὐδὲ	γινώσκει	(a αὐτό· \	ὑμεῖς	(b δὲ \	γινώσκετε
oude	*ginōskei*	*auto*	*humeis*	*de*	*ginōskete*
nor	know	him;	you	but	know

840.15 prs-pron sing neu	3617.1 conj	3706.1 prep	5050.3 prs-pron dat 2pl	3176.1 verb 3sing indic act	2504.1 conj	1706.1 prep
αὐτό,	ὅτι	παρ'	ὑμῖν	μένει,	καὶ	ἐν
auto	*hoti*	*par'*	*humin*	*menei*	*kai*	*en*
him,	for	with	you	he resides,	and	in

17.c.**Var:** p66-org,03B, 05D-org,032W,1,565, Lach,Treg,Alf,We/Ho,it.

5050.3 prs-pron dat 2pl	1498.40 verb 3sing indic fut mid	1498.4 verb 3sing indic pres act	3620.2 partic	856.20 verb 1sing indic fut act
ὑμῖν	(ἔσται.	[c ἐστίν.]	**18.** Οὐκ	ἀφήσω
humin	*estai*	*estin*	*Ouk*	*aphēsō*
you	shall be.	[are.]	Not	I will leave

5050.4 prs-pron acc 2pl	3600.1 adj acc pl masc	2048.32 verb 1sing indic pres	4242.1 prep	5050.4 prs-pron acc 2pl	2068.1 adv
ὑμᾶς	ὀρφανούς·	ἔρχομαι	πρὸς	ὑμᾶς.	**19.** ἔτι
humas	*orphanous*	*erchomai*	*pros*	*humas*	*eti*
you	orphans,	I am coming	to	you.	Yet

3261.1 adv	2504.1 conj	3450.5 art sing masc	2862.1 noun nom sing masc	1466.6 prs-pron acc 1sing	3620.2 partic
μικρὸν	καὶ	ὁ	κόσμος	με	(οὐκ
mikron	*kai*	*ho*	*kosmos*	*me*	*ouk*
a little while	and	the	world	me	no

2068.1 adv	3629.1 adv	2311.4 verb 3sing indic pres act	5050.1 prs-pron nom 2pl	1156.2 conj	2311.1 verb 2pl pres act
ἔτι	[☆ οὐκέτι]	θεωρεῖ,	ὑμεῖς	δὲ	θεωρεῖτέ
eti	*ouketi*	*theōrei*	*humeis*	*de*	*theōreite*
longer	[no longer]	sees,	you	but	see

1466.6 prs-pron acc 1sing	3617.1 conj	1466.1 prs-pron nom 1sing	2180.5 verb 1sing indic pres act	2504.1 conj	5050.1 prs-pron nom 2pl
με·	ὅτι	ἐγὼ	ζῶ,	καὶ	ὑμεῖς
me	*hoti*	*egō*	*zō*	*kai*	*humeis*
me:	because	I	live,	also	you

19.a.**Txt:** p66,01ℵ,02A, 05D,017K,026Q,032W, 036,037,038,1,13,etc. byz.Lach,Sod
Var: p75,03B,019L, 033X,Treg,Alf,Tisc, We/Ho,Weis,UBS/☆

2180.31 verb 2pl indic fut mid	2180.34 verb 2pl indic fut act	1706.1 prep	1552.11 dem-pron dat sing fem	3450.11 art dat sing fem
(ζήσεσθε.	[a☆ ζήσετε.]	**20.** ἐν	ἐκείνῃ	τῇ
zēsesthe	*zēsete*	*en*	*ekeinē*	*tē*
shall live.	[idem]	In	that	the

14:17. We should recall what Jesus meant by saying He is truth and apply these to the Spirit. The Spirit brings light, illumination, revelation, and the reality of Jesus to bear upon the soul.

The word "know" here can imply experiential knowledge. The disciples of Jesus Christ had a vital relationship with the Spirit. When Jesus indicated "another Comforter" was coming (verse 16), He meant a Helper with whom they were acquainted.

When they believed, the Holy Spirit came into their lives. The Spirit was with them in the person of Christ and "in" them in His regenerating life-giving power.

Three prepositions were used by Jesus to reveal the Spirit's relationship to believers. First, Jesus stated that the Helper would abide "with" the believer as a companion for the journey (verse 16). Second, in verse 17 the Spirit of Truth would abide "with" believers as a defender of their spiritual welfare (verse 17). Third, the Spirit would be "in" believers as the energizer of power from on high. Three excellent reasons our hearts should not be troubled (verse 1)!

14:18. Jesus assured His disciples that His returning to the Father would in no way leave them in a defenseless condition. They should have no fears of being alone as fatherless children. Orphans were often mistreated and sometimes sold as slaves because they had no protector. Jesus had no intention of abandoning His own.

Jesus indicated that He would come to them in the person of the Holy Spirit whom He was sending (see verse 23). The verse which follows shows that He was not speaking of His bodily presence.

14:19. "A little while" refers to the few hours until His burial and resurrection. "But ye (will) see (behold) me" refers to either the 40-day post-Resurrection period or that they would behold Him in the presence and activity of the Helper He would send.

His continued living ensures life for all believers. It is because He lives, and has power over death that all believers are comforted by the reality of eternal life.

14:20. "At that day" signifies the time beginning with the Day of Pentecost until His second coming. The term occurs in 16:23 and 26 in which the phrase refers to answers to prayer. Here the phrase relates to the union of the believer with the Father and the Son that is made possible by the indwelling of the Holy Spirit.

"Ye shall know" here means that the believer attains a knowledge by experience. What the disciples would gain by experience was

17. Even the Spirit of truth: Even the Spirit of true knowledge, *BB.*

whom the world cannot receive: That Spirit the world cannot receive, *Weymouth* . . . the world cannot receive him, *Moffatt* . . . cannot accept, *Fenton, Williams* . . . the world is not able to take to its heart, *BB.*

because it seeth him not, neither knoweth him: . . . because it doesn't see or know Him, *Beck* . . . neither observes nor understands Him, *Berkeley* . . . it beholdeth, *Panin* . . . or recognize Him, *Williams* . . . nor perceives it, *Rotherham.*

but ye know him; for he dwelleth with you, and shall be in you: . . . because he abides with you, *HBIE* . . . He remains by your side, *Weymouth* . . . He lives with you, *Beck* . . . he is with you now and will be in your hearts, *Phillips* . . . is remaining, *Concordant* . . . He is going to remain with you, *Williams* . . . he is ever with you, *BB, Norlie* . . . because by your side He dwells, *Wuest* . . . he stays with you, *SEB.*

18. I will not leave you comfortless: I will not leave you desolate, *ASV* . . . I will not abandon you, *SEB* . . . bereft, *Rotherham* . . . orphans, *Alford* . . . fatherless, *Norlie, Fenton* . . . bereaved, *Concordant, Weymouth* . . . helpless, *Williams* . . . leave you behind, helpless, *Wuest* . . . without a friend, *BB* . . . forlorn, *Moffatt.*

I will come to you:

19. Yet a little while, and the world seeth me no more: In a short time, *Adams* . . . the world shall see me no more, *Montgomery* . . . will not see me anymore, *SEB.*

but ye see me: . . . but you will still see me, *TCNT* . . . but as for you, *Wuest.*

because I live, ye shall live also: I am always living and you will be living also, *TCNT* . . . Because I am to live on, you too will live on, *Williams* . . . because I am living, *Fenton.*

John 14:21

2232.3 noun dat sing fem	1091.51 verb 2pl indic fut mid	5050.1 prs-pron nom 2pl	3617.1 conj	1466.1 prs-pron nom 1sing	1706.1 prep	3450.3 art dat sing
ἡμέρᾳ	γνώσεσθε	ὑμεῖς	ὅτι	ἐγὼ	ἐν	τῷ
hēmera	*gnōsesthe*	*humeis*	*hoti*	*egō*	*en*	*tō*
day	shall know	you	that	I	in	the

3824.3 noun dat sing masc	1466.2 prs-pron gen 1sing	2504.1 conj	5050.1 prs-pron nom 2pl	1706.1 prep	1466.5 prs-pron dat 1sing	2476.3 conj
πατρί	μου,	καὶ	ὑμεῖς	ἐν	ἐμοὶ,	κἀγὼ
patri	*mou*	*kai*	*humeis*	*en*	*emoi*	*kagō*
Father	my,	and	you	in	me,	and I

1706.1 prep	5050.3 prs-pron dat 2pl	3450.5 art sing masc	2174.17 verb nom sing masc part pres act	3450.15 art acc pl fem	1769.7 noun acc pl fem
ἐν	ὑμῖν·	**21.** ὁ	ἔχων	τὰς	ἐντολάς
en	*humin*	*ho*	*echōn*	*tas*	*entolas*
in	you.	The	having	the	commandments

1466.2 prs-pron gen 1sing	2504.1 conj	4931.8 verb nom sing masc part pres act	840.13 prs-pron pl fem	1552.3 dem-pron nom sing masc	1498.4 verb 3sing indic pres act
μου	καὶ	τηρῶν	αὐτὰς,	ἐκεῖνός	ἐστιν
mou	*kai*	*tērōn*	*autas*	*ekeinos*	*estin*
my	and	keeping	them,	that	is

3450.5 art sing masc	25.8 verb nom sing masc part pres act	1466.6 prs-pron acc 1sing	3450.5 art sing masc	1156.2 conj	25.8 verb nom sing masc part pres act
ὁ	ἀγαπῶν	με·	ὁ	δὲ	ἀγαπῶν
ho	*agapōn*	*me*	*ho*	*de*	*agapōn*
the	loving	me;	the	but	loving

1466.6 prs-pron acc 1sing	25.32 verb 3sing indic fut pass	5097.3 prep	3450.2 art gen sing	3824.2 noun gen sing masc	1466.2 prs-pron gen 1sing
με,	ἀγαπηθήσεται	ὑπὸ	τοῦ	πατρός	μου·
me	*agapēthēsetai*	*hupo*	*tou*	*patros*	*mou*
me,	shall be loved	by	the	Father	my;

2504.1 conj	1466.1 prs-pron nom 1sing	2476.3 conj	25.23 verb 1sing indic fut act	840.6 prs-pron acc sing masc	2504.1 conj
ʻ καὶ	ἐγὼ	[☆ κἀγὼ]	ἀγαπήσω	αὐτὸν,	καὶ
kai	*egō*	*kagō*	*agapēsō*	*auton*	*kai*
and	I	[and I]	will love	him,	and

1702.6 verb 1sing indic fut act	840.4 prs-pron dat sing	1670.3 prs-pron acc 1sing masc	2978.5 verb 3sing indic pres act	840.4 prs-pron dat sing
ἐμφανίσω	αὐτῷ	ἐμαυτόν.	**22.** Λέγει	αὐτῷ
emphanisō	*autō*	*emauton*	*Legei*	*autō*
will manifest	to him	myself.	Says	to him

22.a.**Var:** p66-corr,01א,017K,021M,026Q,032W,036,037,1,13,28,byz.Alf,Word,TiscWeis,Sod,UBS/☆

2430.1 name nom masc	3620.1 partic	3450.5 art sing masc	2442.1 name nom masc	2935.5 noun voc sing masc	2504.1 conj
Ἰούδας	οὐχ	ὁ	Ἰσκαριώτης,	Κύριε,	[a☆+ καὶ]
Ioudas	*ouch*	*ho*	*Iskariōtēs*	*Kurie*	*kai*
Judas,	not		Iscariot,	Lord,	[and]

4949.9 intr-pron sing neu	1090.3 verb 3sing indic perf act	3617.1 conj	2231.3 prs-pron dat 1pl	3165.2 verb 2sing indic pres act	1702.2 verb inf pres act
τί	γέγονεν	ὅτι	ἡμῖν	μέλλεις	ἐμφανίζειν
ti	*gegonen*	*hoti*	*hēmin*	*melleis*	*emphanizein*
what	has occurred	that	to us	you are about	to manifest

4427.4 prs-pron acc 2sing masc	2504.1 conj	3644.1 adv	3450.3 art dat sing	2862.3 noun dat sing masc	552.6 verb 3sing indic aor pass
σεαυτὸν,	καὶ	οὐχὶ	τῷ	κόσμῳ;	**23.** Ἀπεκρίθη
seauton	*kai*	*ouchi*	*tō*	*kosmō*	*Apekrithē*
yourself,	and	not	to the	world?	Answered

what they did not then understand. "And I in you" signifies the mystic and esoteric element in Christianity. The apostle Paul states that the indwelling presence of Christ guarantees the believer his hope of glory (Colossians 1:27). The same preposition "in" (*en*) is used in all the relationships expressed in this verse. As the believer dwells in Christ and Christ in God, so Jesus dwells in him. Numerous times in the Book of Ephesians we read of being "in Christ," "in Him," and "in whom." It is a key phrase which permeates the Epistle.

20. At that day ye shall know that I am in my Father, and ye in me, and I in you: At that time it will be clear to you, *BB* . . . On that day, *ALBA* . . . that you are in me, and I am in you, *Phillips.*

14:21. Jesus' commandments are not only His imperative commands but His words, sayings, and teachings. The believer keeps them by conforming his conduct to their admonitions. The natural response of love is to please the loved.

The word "loved" is a passive verb indicating that the natural consequence of our loving Christ brings the Father's love to us.

There is no substitute for knowing the Lord's teachings and obeying them. In so doing we are promised the love of the Father and the Son, plus the personal, intimate communion with Christ. Jesus asked for obedience out of love for Him, not out of fear.

21. He that hath my commandments, and keepeth them: He who has My orders and observes them, *Berkeley*. . . lay them to heart, *TCNT* . . . and habitually keeps them, *Wuest* . . . who accepts my commands, *SEB.*

he it is that loveth me: and he that loveth me shall be loved of my Father: . . . and regards then, *Fenton.*

and I will love him, and will manifest myself to him: . . . and make myself real to him, *Williams* . . . show Myself to him, *Norlie* . . . reveal myself to him, *Weymouth, ALBA* . . . make myself known to him, *SEB, Fenton* . . . shall be disclosing Myself, *Concordant*. . . shall disclose myself to him, *Wuest.*

14:22. "Judas" is an apostle distinct from Judas Iscariot. This Judas is also known as Thaddeus (see Matthew 10:3). This is the only remark attributed to this Judas in the whole Bible.

The disciples had expected Jesus to establish His messianic kingdom on earth at that time. Judas wanted to know why Jesus would confine His manifestation to them. If Jesus disclosed himself only to them, how could He defeat their enemies as the Messiah was to do?

22. Judas saith unto him, Not Iscariot:

Lord, how it is: Why is it, Lord, *Williams* . . . Explain how, *ET* . . . what has occurred, *Wilson* . . . what has come to pass, *Wuest* . . . what has happened, *SEB* . . . What has happened, Master, *TCNT.*

that thou wilt manifest thyself unto us, and not unto the world?: . . . you are about to be disclosing yourself, *Wuest* . . . that you are ready to reveal yourself to us, but not to the people, *SEB.*

14:23. The Lord did not answer Judas' question directly, but replied by repeating and further explaining His own statement that had elicited the question. Judas' problem involved his expectation of a material manifestation of the Messiah while Jesus was referring to a spiritual manifestation.

Jesus repeated the truth that the condition of receiving the revelation of Him depended upon the disciples' "love" and obedience to His "words."

The "we" of "we will come unto him" refers to the Father, the Son and the Holy Spirit. This took place for the disciples at Pentecost. "Unto him" indicates a personal, intimate, face-to-face experience.

John 14:24

23.a.**Txt:** 021M,033X, Steph
Var: 01ℵ,02A,03B,05D, 017K,019L,036,037,038, etc.byz.Gries,Lach,Treg, Alf,Word,Tisc,We/Ho Weis,Sod,UBS/☆

3450.5 art sing masc	**2400.1** name nom masc	**2504.1** conj	**1500.5** verb 3sing indic aor act	**840.4** prs-pron dat sing	**1430.1** partic	**4948.3** indef-pron nom sing
(a ὁ)	Ἰησοῦς	καὶ	εἶπεν	αὐτῷ,	Ἐάν	τις
ho	*Iēsous*	*kai*	*eipen*	*autō*	*Ean*	*tis*
	Jesus	and	said	to him,	If	anyone

25.2 verb 3sing pres act	**1466.6** prs-pron acc 1sing	**3450.6** art acc sing masc	**3030.4** noun acc sing masc	**1466.2** prs-pron gen 1sing	**4931.27** verb 3sing indic fut act
ἀγαπᾷ	με,	τὸν	λόγον	μου	τηρήσει,
agapa	*me*	*ton*	*logon*	*mou*	*tērēsei*
love	me,	the	word	my	he will keep,

2504.1 conj	**3450.5** art sing masc	**3824.1** noun nom sing masc	**1466.2** prs-pron gen 1sing	**25.25** verb 3sing indic fut act	**840.6** prs-pron acc sing masc	**2504.1** conj
καὶ	ὁ	πατήρ	μου	ἀγαπήσει	αὐτόν,	καὶ
kai	*ho*	*patēr*	*mou*	*agapēsei*	*auton*	*kai*
and	the	Father	my	will love	him,	and

4242.1 prep	**840.6** prs-pron acc sing masc	**2048.56** verb 1pl indic fut mid	**2504.1** conj	**3301.1** noun acc sing fem	**3706.1** prep
πρὸς	αὐτὸν	ἐλευσόμεθα,	καὶ	μονὴν	παρ'
pros	*auton*	*eleusometha*	*kai*	*monēn*	*par'*
to	him	we will come,	and	dwelling place	with

23.b.**Txt:** 02A,017K,036, 037,038,byz.Gries,Weis
Var: p66,p75,01ℵ,03B, 019L,032W,033X,33, Lach,Treg,Alf,Tisc, We/Ho,Sod,UBS/☆

840.4 prs-pron dat sing	**4020.53** verb 1pl indic fut act	**4020.78** verb 1pl indic fut mid	**3450.5** art sing masc	**3231.1** partic
αὐτῷ	(ποιησόμεν.	[b☆ ποιησόμεθα.]	**24.** ὁ	μὴ
autō	*poiēsomen*	*poiēsometha*	*ho*	*mē*
him	will make.	[idem]	The	not

25.8 verb nom sing masc part pres act	**1466.6** prs-pron acc 1sing	**3450.8** art acc pl masc	**3030.8** noun acc pl masc	**1466.2** prs-pron gen 1sing	**3620.3** partic
ἀγαπῶν	με,	τοὺς	λόγους	μου	οὐ
agapōn	*me*	*tous*	*logous*	*mou*	*ou*
loving	me,	the	words	my	not

4931.2 verb sing indic pres act	**2504.1** conj	**3450.5** art sing masc	**3030.1** noun nom sing masc	**3614.6** rel-pron acc sing masc	**189.2** verb 2pl pres act
τηρεῖ·	καὶ	ὁ	λόγος	ὃν	ἀκούετε
tērei	*kai*	*ho*	*logos*	*hon*	*akouete*
does keep;	and	the	word	which	you hear

3620.2 partic	**1498.4** verb 3sing indic pres act	**1684.3** adj nom 1sing masc	**233.2** conj	**3450.2** art gen sing	**3854.12** verb gen sing masc part aor act
οὐκ	ἔστιν	ἐμὸς,	ἀλλὰ	τοῦ	πέμψαντός
ouk	*estin*	*emos*	*alla*	*tou*	*pempsantos*
not	is	mine,	but	the	having sent

1466.6 prs-pron acc 1sing	**3824.2** noun gen sing masc	**3642.18** dem-pron pl neu	**2953.38** verb 1sing indic perf act	**5050.3** prs-pron dat 2pl
με	πατρός.	**25.** Ταῦτα	λελάληκα	ὑμῖν
me	*patros*	*Tauta*	*lelalēka*	*humin*
me	Father.	These things	I have said	to you,

3706.1 prep	**5050.3** prs-pron dat 2pl	**3176.10** verb nom sing masc part pres act	**3450.5** art sing masc	**1156.2** conj
παρ'	ὑμῖν	μένων·	**26.** ὁ	δὲ
par'	*humin*	*menōn*	*ho*	*de*
with	you	while abiding;	the	but

3736.1 noun nom sing masc	**3450.16** art sing neu	**4011.1** noun sing neu	**3450.16** art sing neu	**39.1** adj sing	**3614.16** rel-pron sing neu
παράκλητος,	τὸ	πνεῦμα	τὸ	ἅγιον,	ὃ
paraklētos	*to*	*pneuma*	*to*	*hagion*	*ho*
Paraclete,	the	Spirit	the	Holy,	whom

This promise refers to the indwelling presence of the Triune God in the personality of the believer. The disciple becomes the residence of God. The term "abode" is the same as that used in verse 2 which the KJV renders "mansions." Those who love Jesus and treasure His Word become temples for His presence. Christ "dwelt" (tented) among us in the flesh (1:14), but when He dwells in the believer the word "abode" is used. A tent is a temporary structure, but an abode is a lasting habitation. The apostle Paul elaborates on this wonderful truth when he says, "Know ye not that ye are the temple of God, and that the Spirit of God dwelleth in you?" (1 Corinthians 3:16). (See also 1 Corinthians 6:19.) The apostle implies it is possible for believers to be ignorant of their greatest possession.

The disciples sometimes had difficulty understanding their Lord. Awareness of spiritual truth and Christian maturity must be cultivated; but the Spirit is faithful to illuminate teachable disciples.

23. Jesus answered and said unto him, If a man love me, he will keep my words: If any one loves me, *HBIE* . . . he will obey my word, *Moffatt* . . . will be faithful to my word, *ALBA* . . . he will obey my teaching, *Weymouth* . . . observeth my instruction, *Murdock* . . . He will retain My message, *Fenton.*

and my Father will love him, and we will come unto him, and make our abode with him: . . . and both of us will come in face-to-face fellowship with him...we will make our special dwelling place with him, *Williams* . . . we shall come, and an abiding place with him we shall make for ourselves, *Wuest* . . . and will stay with him, *ALBA* . . . our living-place, *BB* . . . our home, *TCNT* . . . and live with him, *SEB.*

14:24. "My sayings" and "the word" signify Jesus' teachings (plural, words) and His message (singular, the Word). The believer who stores up the Lord's teachings and observes their truths makes known his love for the Son and the Father.

24. He that loveth me not keepeth not my sayings: . . . who has no love for me, *Weymouth* . . . will not obey my teachings, *SEB* . . . is not faithful to my words, *ALBA.*

and the word which ye hear is not mine, but the Father's which sent me: . . . but belongs to Him who sent me, *Wuest.*

14:25. "These things" seems to indicate that Jesus had taught them only things which He desired to say. He could not teach all because of their inability to understand.

25. These things have I spoken unto you being yet present with you: . . . while abiding with you, *Wuest.*

14:26. This verse states Jesus' second promise of the Spirit's coming. It also explains in more detail what the Spirit will do when He comes. As the Holy Spirit He is the believer's "Helper" to foster growth in holiness in character and conduct. The one who is holy is set apart as God's own possession and is progressively cleansed to maintain the proper relationship with the Lord.

"In my name" means He will come in behalf of Christ and accomplish the same work as Christ.

Two activities of the Holy Spirit are mentioned by Jesus. First, "He shall teach you all things." This is a parallel to 16:13, "He will guide you into all truth." The Spirit progressively taught the disciples things they were unable to comprehend when Jesus was with them in the flesh (16:12). Illumination and prophecy are included within this activity of the Spirit. A second aspect of the Spirit's teaching concerns "things to come" (16:13). This second aspect includes prediction and inspiration. The first aspect of the Spirit's

26. But the Comforter, which is the Holy Ghost: . . . the Helper, *BB* . . . the Advocate, the Holy Spirit, *ALBA* . . . to stand by you, *Phillips.*

3854.18 verb 3sing indic fut act	3450.5 art sing masc	3824.1 noun nom sing masc	1706.1 prep	3450.3 art dat sing	3549.4 noun dat sing neu
πέμψει	ὁ	πατὴρ	ἐν	τῷ	ὀνόματί
pempsei	*ho*	*patēr*	*en*	*tō*	*onomati*
will send	the	Father	in	the	name

1466.2 prs-pron gen 1sing	1552.3 dem-pron nom sing masc	5050.4 prs-pron acc 2pl	1315.19 verb 3sing indic fut act	3820.1 adj	2504.1 conj
μου,	ἐκεῖνος	ὑμᾶς	διδάξει	πάντα,	καὶ
mou	*ekeinos*	*humas*	*didaxei*	*panta*	*kai*
my,	that	you	will teach	all things,	and

5117.5 verb 3sing indic fut act	5050.4 prs-pron acc 2pl	3820.1 adj	3614.17 rel-pron pl neu	1500.3 verb indic aor act
ὑπομνήσει	ὑμᾶς	πάντα	ἃ	εἶπον
hupomnēsei	*humas*	*panta*	*ha*	*eipon*
will bring to remembrance	your	all things	which	I said

26.a.**Var:** 03B,019L, We/HoWeis,UBS/☆

5050.3 prs-pron dat 2pl	1466.1 prs-pron nom 1sing	1503.4 noun acc sing fem	856.3 verb 1sing indic pres act	5050.3 prs-pron dat 2pl
ὑμῖν.	[a☆+ ἐγώ.]	**27.** Εἰρήνην	ἀφίημι	ὑμῖν,
humin	*egō*	*Eirēnēn*	*aphiēmi*	*humin*
to you.	[I.]	Peace	I leave	with you;

1503.4 noun acc sing fem	3450.12 art acc sing fem	1684.9 adj acc 1sing fem	1319.1 verb 1sing indic pres act	5050.3 prs-pron dat 2pl	3620.3 partic
εἰρήνην	τὴν	ἐμὴν	δίδωμι	ὑμῖν·	οὐ
eirēnēn	*tēn*	*emēn*	*didōmi*	*humin*	*ou*
peace	the	my	I give	to you;	not

2503.1 conj	3450.5 art sing masc	2862.1 noun nom sing masc	1319.2 verb 3sing indic pres act	1466.1 prs-pron nom 1sing	1319.1 verb 1sing indic pres act
καθὼς	ὁ	κόσμος	δίδωσιν,	ἐγὼ	δίδωμι
kathōs	*ho*	*kosmos*	*didōsin*	*egō*	*didōmi*
as	the	world	gives,	I	give

5050.3 prs-pron dat 2pl	3231.1 partic	4866.6 verb 3sing impr pres pass	5050.2 prs-pron gen 2pl	3450.9 art nom sing fem	2559.2 noun nom sing fem
ὑμῖν·	μὴ	ταρασσέσθω	ὑμῶν	ἡ	καρδία,
humin	*mē*	*tarassesthō*	*humōn*	*hē*	*kardia*
to you.	Not	let be troubled	your	the	heart,

3234.1 adv	1163.1 verb 3sing impr pres act	189.23 verb 2pl indic aor act	3617.1 conj	1466.1 prs-pron nom 1sing	1500.3 verb indic aor act
μηδὲ	δειλιάτω.	**28.** ἠκούσατε	ὅτι	ἐγὼ	εἶπον
mēde	*deiliatō*	*ēkousate*	*hoti*	*egō*	*eipon*
nor	let it fear.	You heard	that	I	said

5050.3 prs-pron dat 2pl	5055.1 verb 1sing indic pres act	2504.1 conj	2048.32 verb 1sing indic pres	4242.1 prep	5050.4 prs-pron acc 2pl
ὑμῖν,	Ὑπάγω	καὶ	ἔρχομαι	πρὸς	ὑμᾶς.
humin	*Hupagō*	*kai*	*erchomai*	*pros*	*humas*
to you,	I am going away	and	I am coming	to	you.

1479.1 conj	25.27 verb 2pl indic imperf act	1466.6 prs-pron acc 1sing	5299.18 verb 2pl indic aor pass	300.1 partic	3617.1 conj
εἰ	ἠγαπᾶτέ	με,	ἐχάρητε	ἂν	ὅτι
ei	*ēgapate*	*me*	*echarēte*	*an*	*hoti*
If	you loved	me,	you would have rejoiced		that

28.a.**Txt:** 07E,017K-corr, 021M,036,037,byz. **Var:** 01ℵ,02A,03B,05D, 017K-org,019L,033X, 038,it.bo.Gries,Lach, Treg,AlfTisc,We/Ho, Weis,Sod,UBS/☆

1500.3 verb indic aor act	4057.1 verb 1sing indic pres	4242.1 prep	3450.6 art acc sing masc	3824.4 noun acc sing masc	3617.1 conj
(a εἶπον,)	Πορεύομαι	πρὸς	τὸν	πατέρα·	ὅτι
eipon	*Poreuomai*	*pros*	*ton*	*patera*	*hoti*
I said,	I am going	to	the	Father,	for

teaching produced for the disciples personal knowledge and understanding. By this they were enabled to conform their conduct to the will of God. Under the second aspect the disciples were enabled to preach and write the Word of God.

The second activity of the "Comforter" was to "bring all things to your remembrance, whatsoever I have said unto you." "Remembrance" means "to cause one to remember," "to remind one," "to put into one's mind." The Gospel of John is an excellent example of how the Spirit brought back to John's mind the wonderful ministry of Christ even after nearly 60 years.

The Spirit's activity is to illuminate the Scriptures to believers' hearts and to remind them of those Scriptures.

whom the Father will send in my name: . . . to represent me, *Williams* . . . with My power, *Fenton* . . . sent at my request, *Weymouth* . . . with my authority, *SEB* . . . for my sake, *Norton.*

he shall teach you all things: . . . will put you in mind, *Rotherham* . . . will instruct you, *Norton* . . . everything, *Murdock, Fenton* . . . recall to your mind all things, *Wuest* . . . cause you to remember, *SEB* . . . to your memories, *Weymouth* . . . will bring to your minds all that I have told you, *ALBA.*

and bring all things to your remembrance, whatsoever I have said unto you: . . . will remind you of all that I have told you, *Berkeley.*

14:27. Jesus desired to comfort the hearts of the disciples during the dark days of His betrayal and crucifixion. Therefore, He began by assuring them of the Father's house for the future and the promise of the Holy Spirit's coming and help.

"Peace" is the first word in the statement, yet it is the object of the sentence. Therefore, the emphasis is placed on peace. "Peace" is one of the most beautiful and meaningful words in the Christian's vocabulary. The word was used as the usual Hebrew greeting (*shalom*) as English-speaking people say "hello." It is often used in the Epistles with "grace" as a greeting. Peace has both a negative and positive aspect. It means an absence of disorder and a beautiful harmonious relationship with God and men. Man's peace with God is purchased by Jesus as the propitiation for his sin. The peace between man and man was secured by Christ's work in bringing all believers into the family of God and thus in harmony with each other.

27. Peace I leave with you, my peace I give unto you: . . . now I leave you a blessing; it is my own blessing, *TCNT* . . . Peace I bequeath to you, *Berkeley* . . . peace, mine own, *Rotherham* . . . I leave you peace, *Panin* . . . I now leave you the blessing of peace, *Williams* . . . I am leaving behind for you, *Wuest.*

not as the world giveth, give I unto you: It is not the world's 'Peace' I give you, *Montgomery* . . . as the world gives gifts, *Adams.*

Let not your heart be troubled, neither let it be afraid: Let not your hearts be disquieted, *Moffatt* . . . Do not allow your hearts to be unsettled or intimidated, *Berkeley* . . . be troubled, or dismayed, *TCNT* . . . continue to be agitated, *Wuest* . . . Be not disheartened, *Campbell* . . . Don't feel troubled or afraid, *Beck* . . . it be timid, *Concordant* . . . nor yet be discouraged, *Fenton* . . . let it be without fear, *BB* . . . must not be daunted, *Phillips.*

14:28. The disciples did love Him, but their love was based on an imperfect knowledge of His person and the nature of His work. For example, they expected a materialistic messianic kingdom to be set up with Israel at the head of the nations of the world (see Acts 1:6). Their rejoicing should have been for spiritual blessing such as proceeded from His redemptive atonement. Their interest centered on carnal wealth and political position.

The phrase "my Father is greater than I" raises a question. Does it mean the Son is inferior to the Father? No, for Philippians 2:6 points out that in His preincarnate existence Jesus "thought it not robbery to be equal with God." What does the statement mean then? Simply this. In the Incarnation Jesus deliberately subordinated himself. He who had been "in the form of God" took upon himself the "form of a servant" and the "likeness of men" (Philippians 2:6,7). This voluntary humbling did not affect His essential deity.

28. Ye have heard how I said unto you, I go away, and come again unto you: You heard me say that I was going away and would return to you, *TCNT* . . . and yet I am coming to you, *Montgomery.*

If ye loved me, ye would rejoice: . . . you should be glad, *Norlie* . . . you would have been delighted, *Adams.*

John 14:29

28.b.**Txt:** 01ℵ-org, 05D-corr,017K,036,037, 038,13,byz.bo.Gries, Lach
Var: 01ℵ-corr,02A,03B, 05D-org,019L,033X,33, Treg,Alf,Tisc,We/Ho, Weis,Sod,UBS/*

3450.5 art sing masc	3824.1 noun nom sing masc	1466.2 prs-pron gen 1sing	3157.2 adj comp nom sing	1466.2 prs-pron gen 1sing	1498.4 verb 3sing indic pres act
ὁ	πατήρ	(b μου)	μείζων	μού	ἐστιν.
ho	patēr	mou	meizōn	mou	estin
the	Father	my	greater	me	is.

	2504.1 conj	3431.1 adv	2029.1 verb 1sing indic perf act	5050.3 prs-pron dat 2pl	4109.1 adv	1090.63 verb inf aor mid
29.	καὶ	νῦν	εἴρηκα	ὑμῖν	πρὶν	γενέσθαι,
	kai	nun	eirēka	humin	prin	genesthai
	And	now	I have told	you	before	to come to pass,

2419.1 conj	3615.1 conj	1090.40 verb 3sing subj aor mid	3961.1 verb 2pl subj act		3620.2 partic
ἵνα	ὅταν	γένηται	πιστεύσητε.	30.	(οὐκ
hina	hotan	genētai	pisteusēte		ouk
that	when	it shall have come to pass	you may believe.		No

2068.1 adv	3629.1 adv	4044.17 adj pl neu	2953.25 verb 1sing act	3196.1 prep	5050.2 prs-pron gen 2pl
ἔτι	[* οὐκέτι]	πολλὰ	λαλήσω	μεθ'	ὑμῶν·
eti	ouketi	polla	lalēsō	meth'	humōn
longer	[no longer]	much	I will speak	with	you,

30.a.**Txt:** it.bo.Steph
Var: 01ℵ,02A,03B,05D, 017K,019L,033X,036, 037,038,byz.Gries,Lach, Treg,Alf,Word,Tisc, We/HoWeis,Sod,UBS/*

2048.34 verb 3sing indic pres	1056.1 conj	3450.5 art sing masc	3450.2 art gen sing	2862.2 noun gen sing masc	3642.1 dem-pron gen sing
ἔρχεται	γὰρ	ὁ	τοῦ	κόσμου	(a τούτου)
erchetai	gar	ho	tou	kosmou	toutou
comes	for	the	of the	world	this

752.1 noun nom sing masc	2504.1 conj	1706.1 prep	1466.5 prs-pron dat 1sing	3620.2 partic	2174.4 verb 3sing indic pres act	3625.6 num card neu
ἄρχων,	καὶ	ἐν	ἐμοὶ	οὐκ	ἔχει	οὐδέν·
archōn	kai	en	emoi	ouk	echei	ouden
ruler,	and	in	me	not	he has	nothing;

	233.1 conj	2419.1 conj	1091.22 verb 3sing subj aor act	3450.5 art sing masc	2862.1 noun nom sing masc	3617.1 conj
31.	ἀλλ'	ἵνα	γνῷ	ὁ	κόσμος	ὅτι
	all'	hina	gnō	ho	kosmos	hoti
	but	that	may know	the	world	that

25.5 verb 1sing indic pres act	3450.6 art acc sing masc	3824.4 noun acc sing masc	2504.1 conj	2503.1 conj	1765.3 verb 3sing indic aor mid
ἀγαπῶ	τὸν	πατέρα,	καὶ	καθὼς	(ἐνετείλατο
agapō	ton	patera	kai	kathōs	eneteilato
I love	the	Father,	and	as	commanded

31.a.**Var:** 03B,019L,it. LachTreg,We/Ho

1769.3 noun acc sing fem	1319.14 verb 3sing indic aor act	1466.4 prs-pron dat 1sing	3450.5 art sing masc	3824.1 noun nom sing masc	3643.1 adv
[a ἐντολὴν	ἔδωκέν]	μοι	ὁ	πατήρ,	οὕτως
entolēn	edōken	moi	ho	patēr	houtōs
[a command	he has given]	me	the	Father,	thus

4020.1 verb 1sing pres act	1446.18 verb 2pl impr pres pass	70.4 verb 1pl subj pres act	1766.1 adv		1466.1 prs-pron nom 1sing
ποιῶ.	Ἐγείρεσθε,	ἄγωμεν	ἐντεῦθεν.	15:1.	Ἐγώ
poiō	Egeiresthe	agōmen	enteuthen		Egō
I do.	Rise up,	let us go	from here.		I

1498.2 verb 1sing indic pres act	3450.9 art nom sing fem	286.1 noun nom sing fem	3450.9 art nom sing fem	226.5 adj nom sing fem	2504.1 conj
εἰμι	ἡ	ἄμπελος	ἡ	ἀληθινή,	καὶ
eimi	hē	ampelos	hē	alēthinē	kai
am	the	vine	the	true,	and

14:29. Jesus had spoken of His sufferings, His ascension and the coming of the Holy Spirit. Thus, when they happened, the disciples would recall what Jesus had said (verse 26).

When they recalled what He said, they would consider the Lord's knowledge of things to come. Only God can know events that are in the future (compare Isaiah 41:21-24).

because I said, I go unto the Father:

for my Father is greater than I: I am traveling to the Father, *SEB.*

29. And not I have told you before it come to pass: . . . before it takes place, *RSV.*

that, when it is come to pass, ye might believe:

14:30. The Lord was soon to be seized, judged, and led to the Cross. He had but little time to speak to them.

Satan was the one Jesus referred to here. The political powers were dominated by Satan, and he controlled the hearts of the majority of men. Satan's attack on Jesus was through the religious leaders of the Jews and the political power of the Romans.

There was nothing in Jesus which Satan could control, and there was no common ground between them. Satan could find no weakness or sin in Jesus by which he could get advantage of the Lord. Satan's attempt at Jesus' defeat was thwarted.

30. Hereafter I will not talk much with you: I will no longer talk much with you, *HBIE* . . . After this, *Norlie.*

for the prince of this world cometh: . . . for the world's ruler comes, *Berkeley* . . . the chefe ruelar, *Tyndale* . . . for the evil ruler of this world, *Williams* . . . of this world approaches, *Fenton.*

and hath nothing in me: He has no hold on me, *Moffatt* . . . nothing in common with me, *TCNT, Fenton* . . . no power over me, *RSV* . . . Now he doesn't have any authority over Me, *Adams* . . . any power against me, *ALBA.*

14:31. Jesus endured the conflict with Satan and the sufferings of the Cross that He might show the world His love for the Father. His love for His Father prompted Him to carry out the Father's commandment. He is the believers' example to show their love for Him by obedience to His words (see 14:23).

Jesus and the disciples may have left the Upper Room at this point. If so, the content of chapters 15 and 16 would have been given on the way to the Garden of Gethsemane, perhaps near the temple or the wall of Jerusalem. However, Jesus may have given the discourses of chapters 15 and 16 while still in the room (see 18:1).

The statement assuredly reveals the determination of our Lord to do the Father's will by moving toward Gethsemane where He knew the Jews would arrest Him (see Luke 9:51).

31. But that the world may know that I love the Father: But I want the world to know that, *Beck* . . . but this is necessary in order that the world may learn, *Fenton.*

and as the Father gave me commandment, even so I do: . . . and am doing what the Father has ordered me to do, *Williams* . . . I do as He has commanded Me, *Norlie.*

Arise, let us go hence: Rise! Let us go away from here! *Berkeley* . . . Get up now! Let us leave this place, *Phillips* . . . Come, let us be going, *Norlie.*

15:1. The "I am" should be reviewed from 6:51. What Jesus said about being "the true bread" (6:32) and John's record of Jesus as "the true Light" (1:9) are related to Jesus' statement here. Earthly bread and light are mere symbols of the true bread and light. The Greek word for "the true" indicates Jesus as being the original vine from which the branches grow. He is the origin and source of the believer's life. In His early beginnings, He appeared as a dry root out of the parched ground (Isaiah 53:2). However, that root became the vine from which branches grew.

"Husbandman" means the farmer who owns the land and cares for the vineyard. The "husbandman" works the earth as a farmer

1. I am the true vine: . . . the real Vine, *Moffatt.*

3450.5 art sing masc	**3824.1** noun nom sing masc	**1466.2** prs-pron gen 1sing	**3450.5** art sing masc	**1086.1** noun nom sing masc	**1498.4** verb 3sing indic pres act
ὁ	πατήρ	μου	ὁ	γεωργός	ἐστιν.
ho	*patēr*	*mou*	*ho*	*geōrgos*	*estin*
the	Father	my	the	farmer	is.

3820.17 adj sing neu	**2787.1** noun sing neu	**1706.1** prep	**1466.5** prs-pron dat 1sing	**3231.1** partic	**5179.11** verb acc sing neu part pres act
2. πᾶν	κλῆμα	ἐν	ἐμοὶ	μὴ	φέρον
pan	*klēma*	*en*	*emoi*	*mē*	*pheron*
Every	branch	in	me	not	bearing

2561.3 noun acc sing masc	**142.2** verb 3sing indic pres act	**840.15** prs-pron sing neu	**2504.1** conj	**3820.17** adj sing neu	**3450.16** art sing neu
καρπόν,	αἴρει	αὐτό·	καὶ	πᾶν	τὸ
karpon	*airei*	*auto*	*kai*	*pan*	*to*
fruit,	he takes away	it;	and	everyone	the

2561.3 noun acc sing masc	**5179.11** verb acc sing neu part pres act	**2480.1** verb 3sing indic pres act	**840.15** prs-pron sing neu	**2419.1** conj
καρπὸν	φέρον,	καθαίρει	αὐτὸ	ἵνα
karpon	*pheron*	*kathairei*	*auto*	*hina*
fruit	bearing,	he cleanses	it	that

3979.1 adj comp acc	**2561.3** noun acc sing masc	**2561.3** noun acc sing masc	**3979.1** adj comp acc	**5179.4** verb 3sing subj pres act
ʻ πλείονα	καρπὸν	[☆ καρπὸν	πλείονα]	φέρῃ.
pleiona	*karpon*	*karpon*	*pleiona*	*pherē*
more	fruit	[fruit	more]	it may bear.

2218.1 adv	**5050.1** prs-pron nom 2pl	**2485.4** adj nom pl masc	**1498.6** verb 2pl indic pres act	**1217.2** prep	**3450.6** art acc sing masc
3. ἤδη	ὑμεῖς	καθαροί	ἐστε	διὰ	τὸν
ēdē	*humeis*	*katharoi*	*este*	*dia*	*ton*
Already	you	clean	are	because of	the

3030.4 noun acc sing masc	**3614.6** rel-pron acc sing masc	**2953.38** verb 1sing indic perf act	**5050.3** prs-pron dat 2pl	**3176.23** verb 2pl impr aor act	**1706.1** prep
λόγον	ὃν	λελάληκα	ὑμῖν.	4. μείνατε	ἐν
logon	*hon*	*lelalēka*	*humin*	*meinate*	*en*
word	which	I have spoken	to you.	Remain	in

1466.5 prs-pron dat 1sing	**2476.3** conj	**1706.1** prep	**5050.3** prs-pron dat 2pl	**2503.1** conj	**3450.16** art sing neu	**2787.1** noun sing neu
ἐμοί,	κἀγὼ	ἐν	ὑμῖν.	καθὼς	τὸ	κλῆμα
emoi	*kagō*	*en*	*humin*	*kathōs*	*to*	*klēma*
me,	and I	in	you.	As	the	branch

3620.3 partic	**1404.4** verb 3sing indic pres	**2561.3** noun acc sing masc	**5179.12** verb inf pres act	**570.1** prep gen	**1431.4** prs-pron gen 3sing	**1430.1** partic
οὐ	δύναται	καρπὸν	φέρειν	ἀφ'	ἑαυτοῦ	ἐὰν
ou	*dunatai*	*karpon*	*pherein*	*aph'*	*heautou*	*ean*
not	is able	fruit	to bear	of	itself	if

4.a.**Txt:** p66,02A,05D,017K,033X,036,037,038,1,13,byz.it.Lach,Treg
Var: 01ℵ,03B,019L,Tisc,We/HoWeis,Sod,UBS/☆

3231.1 partic	**3176.19** verb 3sing subj aor act	**3176.7** verb 3sing subj pres act	**1706.1** prep	**3450.11** art dat sing fem	**286.3** noun dat sing fem	**3643.1** adv
μὴ	ʻ μείνῃ	[a☆ μένῃ]	ἐν	τῇ	ἀμπέλῳ,	οὕτως
mē	*meinē*	*menē*	*en*	*tē*	*ampelō*	*houtōs*
not	it remain	[idem]	in	the	vine,	so

3624.1 adv	**5050.1** prs-pron nom 2pl	**1430.1** partic	**3231.1** partic	**1706.1** prep	**1466.5** prs-pron dat 1sing	**3176.20** verb 2pl subj aor act
οὐδὲ	ὑμεῖς	ἐὰν	μὴ	ἐν	ἐμοὶ	ʻ μείνητε.
oude	*humeis*	*ean*	*mē*	*en*	*emoi*	*meinēte*
neither	you	if	not	in	me	you abide.

tills his land to produce crops. The Father owns the land and tends the vineyard. He is vitally interested and cares for it.

and my Father is the husbandman: . . . and my Father is the vinedresser, *RSV, Norlie* . . . the gardener, *NEB* . . . the cultivator, *Williams* . . . the Tiller, *Berkeley.*

15:2. "Branch" refers to a shoot which comes forth from the central vine. Its life and growth depend on the trunk of the grapevine. The branch "in me" signifies the believers in vital union and communion with their life source and fruit-producing supply. The branch grows and produces grapes. The nonproductive branch hinders the growth of fruit on other branches. Therefore, the vinedresser prunes it so the nourishment that feeds it may produce fruit in other branches.

"Fruit" is a combined effort of the source of life-giving substance from the vine and root. The branch collects the necessities of earth and heaven to support the fruit. Spiritually, "fruit" is a work of the Spirit produced in and through the believer in vital union with Jesus (Galatians 5:22-23). The vinedresser notes the fruit which the branches bear and desires more and larger grapes; therefore, he prunes (KJV, "purgeth") it. "Prunes" (NASB) means "to cleanse or purify a thing or person."

Notice the vinedresser's close examination of every branch. He knows the branches that produce no fruit and those that produce some fruit. He knows what to prune and what to leave. Three kinds of branches are indicated. First, some branches produce no fruit and are cut off. Second, others bear some fruit and are left on the vine. Third, the ones which are pruned bear more fruit as the result of pruning. In verse 5 the Lord speaks of a fourth kind of branch. This one bears "much fruit."

2. Every branch in me that beareth not fruit he taketh away: Every shoot, *Rotherham* . . . Any unfruitful branch, *TCNT* . . . He prunes away, *Berkeley* . . . he lops off, *Campbell* . . . cuts away, *Williams.*

and every branch that beareth fruit, he purgeth it: . . . he cleanseth, *Alford* . . . he prunes, *RSV* . . . he cleans by pruning, *Campbell* . . . repeatedly prunes, *Williams* . . . every fertile branch, *Fenton* . . . trims each branch, *SEB.*

that it may bring forth more fruit: . . . to increase its yield, *Phillips* . . . to make it bear more fruit, *Beck* . . . to render it more fruitful, *Campbell* . . . become still more productive, *Fenton.*

15:3. "Clean" is the same word as the word for "purgeth" or "prune" (NASB) of verse 2. "The ancients spoke of pruning as a 'cleansing' of the branches, just as we speak of 'cleansing' the land" (Tasker, *Tyndale New Testament Commentaries,* 20:175). The Saviour says that the disciples are already spiritually pruned. "Ye" is emphatic. By "the word" Jesus was referring to the whole of His teaching. Spiritual cleansing is a process. Jesus' disciples were exposed to His words over a period of time. As they heard and received His teaching, the sin in their lives was exposed and pruned. This pruning prepared them for the growth of Jesus' life (the Vine) in them. It is the same with believers today. "Clean" does not mean perfection. God's Word exposes sin, and the life of Christ in believers brings growth and holiness.

3. Now are ye clean through the word which I have spoken unto you: You are already cleansed by means of the Word, *Norlie* . . . already pruned, *Fenton* . . . are now pure, *Klingensmith* . . . because of the teaching that, *TCNT* . . . through the instructions, *Campbell* . . . I have talked over with you, *Berkeley.*

15:4. "Abide" implies that the believer is already in Christ. The ideas of "stay, remain continuously" are expressed in "abide." To

4. Abide in me, and I in you: Remain in me, as I remain in you, *Moffatt* . . . Remain united to me, *TCNT* . . . as I am with you, *ALBA* . . . Maintain a living communion with me, *Wuest.*

As the branch cannot bear fruit of itself, except it abide in the vine: . . . unless it remains in a living union, *Wuest* . . . unless it is united with the vine, *ALBA* . . . without staying on the vine, *Berkeley* . . . unless it shares the life of the vine, *Phillips* . . . it if does not continue in the vine, *Weymouth* . . . if it is not still on the vine, *BB.*

no more can ye, except ye abide in me: . . . so neither can ye, *HBIE* . . . nor more can you unless you stay in me, *Klingensmith.*

John 15:5

4.b.**Txt:** 05D,017K,033X, 036,037,038-corr,1,13, etc.byz.
Var: 01ℵ,02A,03B,019L, 038-org,Lach,Treg,Alf, Tisc,We/HoWeis,Sod, UBS/☆

3176.31 verb 2pl subj pres act	**1466.1** prs-pron nom 1sing	**1498.2** verb 1sing indic pres act	**3450.9** art nom sing fem	**286.1** noun nom sing fem
[b☆ μένητε.]	5. ἐγώ	εἰμι	ἡ	ἄμπελος,
menēte	*egō*	*eimi*	*hē*	*ampelos*
[idem]	I	am	the	vine,

5050.1 prs-pron nom 2pl	**3450.17** art pl neu	**2787.2** noun nom pl neu	**3450.5** art sing masc	**3176.10** verb nom sing masc part pres act	**1706.1** prep
ὑμεῖς	τὰ	κλήματα.	ὁ	μένων	ἐν
humeis	*ta*	*klēmata*	*ho*	*menōn*	*en*
you	the	branches.	The	remaining	in

1466.5 prs-pron dat 1sing	**2476.3** conj	**1706.1** prep	**840.4** prs-pron dat sing	**3642.4** dem-pron nom sing masc	**5179.2** verb 3sing indic pres act
ἐμοὶ,	κἀγὼ	ἐν	αὐτῷ,	οὗτος	φέρει
emoi	*kagō*	*en*	*autō*	*houtos*	*pherei*
me,	and I	in	him,	this	bears

2561.3 noun acc sing masc	**4044.6** adj acc sing masc	**3617.1** conj	**5400.1** prep gen	**1466.3** prs-pron gen 1sing	**3620.3** partic
καρπὸν	πολύν·	ὅτι	χωρὶς	ἐμοῦ	οὐ
karpon	*polun*	*hoti*	*chōris*	*emou*	*ou*
fruit	much;	for	apart from	me	not

1404.6 verb 2pl indic pres	**4020.20** verb inf pres act	**3625.6** num card neu	**1430.1** partic	**3231.1** partic	**4948.3** indef-pron nom sing
δύνασθε	ποιεῖν	οὐδέν.	6. ἐὰν	μή	τις
dunasthe	*poiein*	*ouden*	*ean*	*mē*	*tis*
you are able	to do	nothing.	If	not	anyone

6.a.**Txt:** 01ℵ-corr,017K, 019L,036,037,1,13,byz. Gries
Var: p66,01ℵ-org,02A, 03B,05D,038,Lach,Treg, TiscWe/Ho,Weis,Sod, UBS/☆

3176.19 verb 3sing subj aor act	**3176.7** verb 3sing subj pres act	**1706.1** prep	**1466.5** prs-pron dat 1sing	**900.30** verb 3sing indic aor pass
ᵃ μείνῃ	[a☆ μένῃ]	ἐν	ἐμοί,	ἐβλήθη
meinē	*menē*	*en*	*emoi*	*eblēthē*
remain	[idem]	in	me,	he is cast

1838.1 prep gen	**5453.1** conj	**3450.16** art sing neu	**2787.1** noun sing neu	**2504.1** conj	**3445.3** verb 3sing indic aor pass	**2504.1** conj
ἔξω	ὡς	τὸ	κλῆμα,	καὶ	ἐξηράνθη,	καὶ
exō	*hōs*	*to*	*klēma*	*kai*	*exēranthē*	*kai*
out	as	the	branch,	and	is dried up,	and

6.b.**Var:** 01ℵ,05D,019L, 033X,037,1,13,33,Tisc, Sod

6.c.**Var:** 01ℵ,02A,03B, 07E,017K,019L,021M, 030U,036,037,038,Treg, Alf,Word,Tisc,We/Ho Sod,UBS/☆

4714.3 verb 3pl indic pres act	**840.16** prs-pron pl neu	**840.15** prs-pron sing neu	**2504.1** conj	**1519.1** prep	**3450.16** art sing neu
συνάγουσιν	ᵇ αὐτὰ	[b αὐτὸ]	καὶ	εἰς	[c☆+ τὸ]
sunagousin	*auta*	*auto*	*kai*	*eis*	*to*
they gather	them	[it]	and	into	[the]

4300.1 noun sing neu	**900.4** verb 3pl indic pres act	**2504.1** conj	**2516.2** verb 3sing indic pres pass	**1430.1** partic	**3176.20** verb 2pl subj aor act
πῦρ	βάλλουσιν,	καὶ	καίεται.	7. ἐὰν	μείνητε
pur	*ballousin*	*kai*	*kaietai*	*ean*	*meinēte*
a fire	cast,	and	it is burned.	If	you remain

1706.1 prep	**1466.5** prs-pron dat 1sing	**2504.1** conj	**3450.17** art pl neu	**4343.4** noun pl neu	**1466.2** prs-pron gen 1sing	**1706.1** prep
ἐν	ἐμοὶ,	καὶ	τὰ	ῥήματά	μου	ἐν
en	*emoi*	*kai*	*ta*	*rhēmata*	*mou*	*en*
in	me,	and	the	words	my	in

5050.3 prs-pron dat 2pl	**3176.19** verb 3sing subj aor act	**3614.16** rel-pron sing neu	**1430.1** partic	**2286.9** verb 2pl subj pres act	**153.34** verb 2pl indic fut mid
ὑμῖν	μείνῃ,	ὃ	ἐὰν	θέλητε	ᶜ αἰτήσεσθε,
humin	*meinē*	*ho*	*ean*	*thelēte*	*aitēsesthe*
you	remain,	what	ever	you will	you shall ask,

"abide in" Christ is to experience an unbroken fellowship and personal communion with Him. He desires to abide in the believer, yet His abiding is contingent upon the believer's welcome and continuing cultivation of His personal presence.

5. I am the vine, ye are the branches:

He that abideth in me, and I in him: Whoever remains in union with me and I in union with him, *Williams* . . . that remain united to me, *TCNT.*

the same bringeth forth much fruit: . . . will bear abundant fruit, *Williams* . . . produces plenty of fruit, *Fenton* . . . who bear fruit plentifully, *TCNT.*

for without me ye can do nothing: . . . for apart from me, *ASV* . . . but, severed from Me, *Fenton* . . . you are useless, *ET.*

15:5. The truth has been implied in the preceding verses. Now it is distinctly stated (verse 1). "Much fruit" is borne by the reciprocal abiding. The way to "much fruit" is by unrestricted love and fellowship.

All fruit produced by the believer is Christ's own fruit. The Lord himself receives the glory for the gifts, graces, and deeds of righteousness produced by the believer.

6. If any man abide not in me: The man who does not share my life, *Phillips* . . . Yff a man byde nott in me, *Tyndale* . . . schal not dwelle in me, *Wycliffe.*

he is cast forth as a branch, and is withered: . . . he's thrown away like a branch and dries up, *Beck* . . . he is trimmed off like a dry branch, *Norlie* . . . he is thrown away as a mere branch and is dried up, *Williams* . . . he becomes dead, *BB* . . . like the unfruitful branch, *Weymouth.*

and men gather them:

and cast them into the fire, and they are burned: Such branches they gather up, *Weymouth.*

15:6. The possibility of being "cast forth" or "thrown away" (NASB) for not abiding is clear. His abiding in the believer is assured. The only question is if the believer will abide in Him. As the branch which is severed from the vine dies, so the believer who severs his relationship with Jesus dies.

Branches which have been severed from the vine are quite worthless. They are not even good for firewood. The one detached from Christ is destined for destruction. The one in Christ is productive and secure.

7. If ye abide in me, and my words abide in you: Remain within the sphere of the love which is mine, *Wuest* . . . If you remain in union with me and my words remain in you, *Williams* . . . continue in me, *Weymouth* . . . and my instructions, *Murdock* . . . what I say stays in you, *Beck* . . . remains in your hearts, *TCNT.*

ye shall ask what ye will, and it shall be done unto you: . . . you may ask whatever you please and you shall have it, *Williams*

15:7. The believer must will to remain in Jesus and to store His sayings in his soul. Jesus dwells in the soul by the "words." These two simple acts of one's will bring divine security: first, a commitment to remain in Him and, second, a reception of His teachings ("words").

The limitation to positive answers to prayer is stated in "if ye." The first words of this verse indicate the comprehensiveness of praying. When believers "abide in" Him, they feel what He feels, His wishes and will become theirs, so that they desire to further His cause and glorify Him. Selfish praying will cease. Efforts to impose their wills on Him will end. For His glory, to make Him known, for His will to be done on earth as it is in heaven will be the passion of their souls. His "words" (teachings) will guide attitude and actions in the way of righteous conduct. Believers become His love slaves to follow His instructions. The slave is an arm of his master. He speaks at the suggestion of his lord. He moves or refrains from action by the wishes of his chief. The mind of the Lord on any given thing is the mind of the one abiding in Him.

John 15:8

7.a.**Txt:** 01ℵ,07E,017K, 030U,037,038,byz. **Var:** 02A,03B,05D,019L, 021M,033X,036,1,Lach, Treg,Alf,Word,Tisc, We/Ho,Weis,Sod,UBS/☆

153.37 verb 2pl impr aor mid	**2504.1** conj	**1090.69** verb 3sing indic fut mid	**5050.3** prs-pron dat 2pl	**1706.1** prep
[a☆ αἰτήσασθε,]	καὶ	γενήσεται	ὑμῖν.	**8.** ἐν
aitēsasthe	*kai*	*genēsetai*	*humin*	*en*
[idem]	and	it shall come to pass	to you.	In

3642.5 dem-pron dat sing masc	**1386.22** verb 3sing indic aor pass	**3450.5** art sing masc	**3824.1** noun nom sing masc	**1466.2** prs-pron gen 1sing	**2419.1** conj
τούτῳ	ἐδοξάσθη	ὁ	πατήρ	μου,	ἵνα
toutō	*edoxasthē*	*ho*	*patēr*	*mou*	*hina*
this	is glorified	the	Father	my,	that

2561.3 noun acc sing masc	**4044.6** adj acc sing masc	**5179.5** verb 2pl subj pres act	**2504.1** conj	**1090.70** verb 2pl indic fut mid
καρπὸν	πολὺν	φέρητε,	καὶ	ʼ γένησεσθε
karpon	*polun*	*pherēte*	*kai*	*genēsesthe*
fruit	much	you should bear,	and	you shall become

8.a.**Var:** p66,03B,05D, 019L,021M,033X,038, 565,it.sa.bo.Lach,Treg, Alf,We/Ho

1090.42 verb 2pl subj aor mid	**1684.4** adj nom 1pl masc	**3073.5** noun nom pl masc	**2503.1** conj	**25.14** verb 3sing indic aor act
[a γένησθε]	ἐμοὶ	μαθηταί.	**9.** καθὼς	ἠγάπησέν
genēsthe	*emoi*	*mathētai*	*kathōs*	*ēgapēsen*
[idem]	to me	disciples.	As	loved

1466.6 prs-pron acc 1sing	**3450.5** art sing masc	**3824.1** noun nom sing masc	**2476.3** conj	**25.12** verb 1sing indic aor act	**5050.4** prs-pron acc 2pl
με	ὁ	πατήρ,	κἀγὼ	ʼ ἠγάπησα	ὑμᾶς˙
me	*ho*	*patēr*	*kagō*	*ēgapēsa*	*humas*
me	the	Father,	I also	loved	you:

5050.4 prs-pron acc 2pl	**25.12** verb 1sing indic aor act	**3176.23** verb 2pl impr aor act	**1706.1** prep	**3450.11** art dat sing fem	**26.3** noun dat sing fem
[☆ ὑμᾶς	ἠγάπησα˙]	μείνατε	ἐν	τῇ	ἀγάπῃ
humas	*ēgapēsa*	*meinate*	*en*	*tē*	*agapē*
[you	loved.]	remain	in	the	love

3450.11 art dat sing fem	**1684.8** adj dat 1sing fem	**1430.1** partic	**3450.15** art acc pl fem	**1769.7** noun acc pl fem	**1466.2** prs-pron gen 1sing
τῇ	ἐμῇ.	**10.** ἐὰν	τὰς	ἐντολάς	μου
tē	*emē*	*ean*	*tas*	*entolas*	*mou*
the	my.	If	the	commandments	my

4931.17 verb 2pl subj aor act	**3176.28** verb 2pl indic fut act	**1706.1** prep	**3450.11** art dat sing fem	**26.3** noun dat sing fem
τηρήσητε,	μενεῖτε	ἐν	τῇ	ἀγάπῃ
tērēsēte	*meneite*	*en*	*tē*	*agapē*
you keep,	you shall remain	in	the	love

1466.2 prs-pron gen 1sing	**2503.1** conj	**1466.1** prs-pron nom 1sing	**3450.15** art acc pl fem	**1769.7** noun acc pl fem	**3450.2** art gen sing
μου˙	καθὼς	ἐγὼ	ʼ τὰς	ἐντολὰς	τοῦ
mou	*kathōs*	*egō*	*tas*	*entolas*	*tou*
my,	as	I	the	commandments	of the

3824.2 noun gen sing masc	**1466.2** prs-pron gen 1sing	**3450.2** art gen sing	**3824.2** noun gen sing masc	**1466.2** prs-pron gen 1sing	**3450.15** art acc pl fem
πατρός	μου	[τοῦ	πατρός	μου	τὰς
patros	*mou*	*tou*	*patros*	*mou*	*tas*
Father	my	[the	Father	my	the

1769.7 noun acc pl fem	**4931.22** verb 1sing indic perf act	**2504.1** conj	**3176.3** verb 1sing indic pres act	**840.3** prs-pron gen sing
ἐντολὰς]	τετήρηκα,	καὶ	μένω	αὐτοῦ
entolas	*tetērēka*	*kai*	*menō*	*autou*
commandments]	have kept,	and	remain	his

15:8. "Much fruit" is evidence to all men of the reality of the Father. Christians should bear fruit that the Father might be known. When the Father is revealed, the world sees and some believe unto salvation. This is God's great evangelistic program. A disciple is one who glorifies the Father by producing fruit. He abides in Christ, and Christ's words abide in him.

15:9. Jesus encouraged the disciples to love by holding up the Father's love for Him as their example. The disciples had witnessed Jesus' love for them; therefore, His love was more readily understood and hence more easily followed.

"My" is emphasized because His love is the model for the believer's love. The Father's love is absolutely perfect. To abide in His love is to place the soul in His care, to continually allow His love to penetrate the inner being, to rest under the constant sense of it, and to let the exercise of His love flow through us to others (Romans 5:5,8).

15:10. The thought is if we want to sense His love, we must keep His commandments. The Saviour's perfect obedience to the Father's will reveals His sense of the Father's love. Love produces obedience. Likewise, keeping the Lord's words fosters love. The degree of the disciple's love is measured by his obedience to Jesus' teachings. Some may disassociate their salvation from habitual obedience to His commandments, but Jesus connects them inseparably. Holy living is the result of keeping Jesus' teachings. And keeping His teachings reveals the disciple's love for His person. This is the essence of abiding in Him and having His words abide in us (14:15,24).

15:11. Jesus here gives the conclusion to His teaching on the allegory of the vine and the branches as it concerned their mutual fellowship.

Christ experienced joy in the consciousness of His union with the Father, and believers may experience this same joy that supported Him in His sufferings. Jesus prayed for them to that end (17:13).

Jesus revealed that His joy came from keeping the Father's commandments and abiding in His love. The fullness of the disciple's

. . . anything for which you make a request, *BB* . . . it shall be granted you, *Campbell.*

8. Herein is my Father glorified: My Father is honored in this, *Berkeley* . . . This is how my Father will be glorified, *Phillips.*

that ye bear much fruit: . . . produce rich fruit, *Berkeley* . . . by your bearing fruit plentifully, *TCNT.*

so shall ye be my disciples: . . . and so prove to be my disciples, *RSV.*

9. As the Father hath loved me, so have I loved you: I have loved you just as the Father has loved e, *Williams.*

continue ye in my love: You must remain in my love, *Williams* . . . go on living in my love, *Phillips* . . . abide in my love, *Confraternity* . . . Stay in my love, *SEB.*

10. If ye keep my commandments, ye shall abide in my love: If you obey my commands, *Montgomery* . . . If you continue to keep my commands, *Williams* . . . you shall stay, *Adams.*

even as I have kept my Father's commandments, and abide in his love: . . . just as I have kept, *Williams* . . . and I stay in his love, *SEB.*

1706.1 prep	3450.11 art dat sing fem	26.3 noun dat sing fem	3642.18 dem-pron pl neu	2953.38 verb 1sing indic perf act	5050.3 prs-pron dat 2pl
ἐν	τῇ	ἀγάπῃ.	11. Ταῦτα	λελάληκα	ὑμῖν,
en	tē	agapē	Tauta	lelalēka	humin
in	the	love.	These things	I have spoken	to you,

2419.1 conj	3450.9 art nom sing fem	5315.1 noun sing fem	3450.9 art nom sing fem	1684.6 adj nom 1sing fem	1706.1 prep	5050.3 prs-pron dat 2pl
ἵνα	ἡ	χαρὰ	ἡ	ἐμὴ	ἐν	ὑμῖν
hina	hē	chara	hē	emē	en	humin
that	the	joy	the	my	in	you

11.a.**Txt:** 01ℵ,017K,019L,036,037,13,byz. **Var:** 02A,03B,05D,038,33,Lach,Treg,Alf,Tisc,We/Ho,WeisSod,UBS/☆

3176.19 verb 3sing subj aor act	1498.10 verb 3sing subj pres act	2504.1 conj	3450.9 art nom sing fem	5315.1 noun sing fem	5050.2 prs-pron gen 2pl
⸀ μείνῃ,	[a☆+ ᾖ]	καὶ	ἡ	χαρὰ	ὑμῶν
meinē	ē	kai	hē	chara	humōn
may remain,	[may be]	and	the	joy	your

3997.22 verb 3sing subj aor pass	3642.9 dem-pron nom sing fem	1498.4 verb 3sing indic pres act	3450.9 art nom sing fem	1769.1 noun nom sing fem
πληρωθῇ.	12. αὕτη	ἐστὶν	ἡ	ἐντολὴ
plērōthē	hautē	estin	hē	entolē
may be full.	This	is	the	commandment

3450.9 art nom sing fem	1684.6 adj nom 1sing fem	2419.1 conj	25.1 verb 2pl pres act	238.3 prs-pron acc pl masc	2503.1 conj
ἡ	ἐμή,	ἵνα	ἀγαπᾶτε	ἀλλήλους,	καθὼς
hē	emē	hina	agapate	allēlous	kathōs
the	my,	that	you love	one another,	as

25.12 verb 1sing indic aor act	5050.4 prs-pron acc 2pl	3157.1 adj comp acc	3642.10 dem-pron gen sing fem	26.4 noun acc sing fem
ἠγάπησα	ὑμᾶς.	13. μείζονα	ταύτης	ἀγάπην
ēgapēsa	humas	meizona	tautēs	agapēn
I loved	you.	Greater than	this	love

3625.2 num card nom masc	2174.4 verb 3sing indic pres act	2419.1 conj	4948.3 indef-pron nom sing	3450.12 art acc sing fem	5425.4 noun acc sing fem
οὐδεὶς	ἔχει,	ἵνα	τις	τὴν	ψυχὴν
oudeis	echei	hina	tis	tēn	psuchēn
no one	has,	that	one	the	life

840.3 prs-pron gen sing	4935.13 verb 3sing subj aor act	5065.1 prep	3450.1 art gen pl	5224.5 adj gen pl masc	840.3 prs-pron gen sing
αὐτοῦ	θῇ	ὑπὲρ	τῶν	φίλων	αὐτοῦ.
autou	thē	huper	tōn	philōn	autou
his	should lay down	for	the	friends	his.

5050.1 prs-pron nom 2pl	5224.4 adj nom pl masc	1466.2 prs-pron gen 1sing	1498.6 verb 2pl indic pres act	1430.1 partic	4020.9 verb 2pl subj pres act
14. ὑμεῖς	φίλοι	μού	ἐστε	ἐὰν	ποιῆτε
humeis	philoi	mou	este	ean	poiēte
You	friends	my	are	if	you practice

14.a.**Txt:** 02A,017K,036,037,038,byz. **Var1:** .p66,01ℵ,05D,019L,033X,13,it.Lach Treg,Alf,Tisc,Sod **Var2:** .03B,We/Ho,Weis,UBS/☆

3607.8 rel-pron pl neu	3614.17 rel-pron pl neu	3614.16 rel-pron sing neu	1466.1 prs-pron nom 1sing	1765.1 verb 1sing indic pres
⸀ ὅσα	[1a☆ ἃ	2 ὃ]	ἐγὼ	ἐντέλλομαι
hosa	ha	ho	egō	entellomai
whatever	[what	idem]	I	command

5050.3 prs-pron dat 2pl	3629.1 adv	5050.4 prs-pron acc 2pl	2978.1 verb 1sing pres act	2978.1 verb 1sing pres act	5050.4 prs-pron acc 2pl
ὑμῖν.	15. οὐκέτι	⸀ ὑμᾶς	λέγω	[☆ λέγω	ὑμᾶς]
humin	ouketi	humas	legō	legō	humas
you.	No longer	you	I call	[I call	you]

joy also comes as a result of perfect obedience to His teachings and abiding in Him (verse 10).

11. These things have I spoken unto you: . . . these admonitions, *Campbell.*

that my joy might remain in you: . . . so that my own joy may be yours, *TCNT* . . . so that you can share my joy, *Phillips* . . . that My delight may be in you, *Fenton* . . . my joy may be felt by you, *Norton* . . . that my joy may be yours, *ALBA* . . . that I may continue to have joy in you, *Campbell* . . . and you will be very happy, *Beck* . . . your happiness may be complete, *TCNT.*

and that your joy might be full: . . . and that your joy may become perfect, *Weymouth* . . . your joy made perfect, *Norton* . . . be filled full, *Wuest.*

15:12. In this verse Jesus stated one of His commandments. Obedience to this commandment will produce joy in any disciple. Jesus called this His commandment, for He gave it, demonstrated it, and taught how it works. A few days before this He taught that all the Law and the Prophets could be summed up by the two great commandments, "Love . . . God with all thy heart" and "Love thy neighbor as thyself" (Matthew 22:37-40). Love is the sum of both commandments. To love one's neighbor presupposes one's love for God.

We love one another because we love Him. We love others because they bear His likeness. Our love for each other cannot go to the extreme that His love did in His redemptive work. But our love can be the same quality as His. We share His love; therefore, we can be patient, kind, without envy, without arrogance, rejoicing in goodness, forbearing, trusting, hopeful and Christlike (1 Corinthians 13:4-8).

12. This is my commandment: This is My instruction, *Berkeley.*

That ye love one another, as I have loved you: Love one another, *Beck* . . . This is the law I give you, *BB* . . . to keep on loving one another, *Williams.*

15:13. Jesus here stated the measure and degree of love He has for believers. It is also the stimulus for the disciple's love. No love is greater.

This verse relates to the Good Shepherd teaching. The Good Shepherd gave His life for the sheep (see 10:11,15,17). Here Jesus spoke not of sheep but of His "friends." One may sacrifice much for the sake of a friend, but to give one's life for a friend is rare indeed. Jesus surpassed one who might rarely die for his friends—He died in behalf of and for His enemies. The Lord mentioned only friends here because He was speaking to His friends. He knew in a few hours His sufferings and crucifixion would occur.

13. Greater love hath no man than this: Stronger love, *Fenton* . . . no one can give greater proof of love, *TCNT.*

that a man lay down his life for his friends: . . . that any one may be laying down his soul for the sake of his friends, *Concordant* . . . than by laying down his life for his friends, *TCNT* . . . than he who gives his life, *Beck* . . . in behalf of, *Wilson, Wuest.*

15:14. "Ye" is emphatic. Only those who keep Jesus' sayings are His friends. He was still stressing what He taught in verses 10 and 14.

14. Ye are my friends, if ye do whatsoever I command you: . . . if you habitually do that which I am enjoining upon you, *Wuest* . . . so long as you, *ALBA* . . . if you keep on doing, *Williams* . . . whatever I am directing you, *Concordant* . . . give you orders to do, *BB.*

15:15. The Lord elevated His disciples to a higher position than that of servants. The level of friends is one of equals in some

15. Henceforth I call you not servants: No longer do I call, *ASV* . . . I no longer call you slaves, *Montgomery, Williams* . . . I have never called you slaves, *Klingensmith* . . . terming you slaves, *Concordant.*

1395.9 noun acc pl masc	3617.1 conj	3450.5 art sing masc	1395.1 noun nom sing masc	3620.2 partic	3471.4 verb 3sing indic perf act	4949.9 intr-pron sing neu
δούλους,	ὅτι	ὁ	δοῦλος	οὐκ	οἶδεν	τί
doulous	*hoti*	*ho*	*doulos*	*ouk*	*oiden*	*ti*
slaves,	for	the	slave	not	knows	what

4020.5 verb 3sing indic pres act	840.3 prs-pron gen sing	3450.5 art sing masc	2935.1 noun nom sing masc	5050.4 prs-pron acc 2pl	1156.2 conj
ποιεῖ	αὐτοῦ	ὁ	κύριος·	ὑμᾶς	δὲ
poiei	*autou*	*ho*	*kurios*	*humas*	*de*
is doing	his	the	master.	You	but

2029.1 verb 1sing indic perf act	5224.7 adj acc pl masc	3617.1 conj	3820.1 adj	3614.17 rel-pron pl neu	189.19 verb 1sing indic aor act
εἴρηκα	φίλους,	ὅτι	πάντα	ἃ	ἤκουσα
eirēka	*philous*	*hoti*	*panta*	*ha*	*ēkousa*
I have called	friends,	for	all things	which	I heard

3706.2 prep	3450.2 art gen sing	3824.2 noun gen sing masc	1466.2 prs-pron gen 1sing	1101.3 verb 1sing indic aor act	5050.3 prs-pron dat 2pl
παρὰ	τοῦ	πατρός	μου	ἐγνώρισα	ὑμῖν.
para	*tou*	*patros*	*mou*	*egnōrisa*	*humin*
of	the	Father	my	I made known	to you.

3620.1 partic	5050.1 prs-pron nom 2pl	1466.6 prs-pron acc 1sing	1573.4 verb 2pl indic aor mid	233.1 conj	1466.1 prs-pron nom 1sing
16. οὐχ	ὑμεῖς	με	ἐξελέξασθε,	ἀλλ'	ἐγὼ
ouch	*humeis*	*me*	*exelexasthe*	*all'*	*egō*
Not	you	me	chose,	but	I

1573.1 verb 1sing indic aor mid	5050.4 prs-pron acc 2pl	2504.1 conj	4935.8 verb 1sing indic aor act	5050.4 prs-pron acc 2pl	2419.1 conj
ἐξελεξάμην	ὑμᾶς,	καὶ	ἔθηκα	ὑμᾶς	ἵνα
exelexamēn	*humas*	*kai*	*ethēka*	*humas*	*hina*
chose	you,	and	appointed	you	that

5050.1 prs-pron nom 2pl	5055.5 verb 2pl subj pres act	2504.1 conj	2561.3 noun acc sing masc	5179.5 verb 2pl subj pres act	2504.1 conj
ὑμεῖς	ὑπάγητε	καὶ	καρπὸν	φέρητε,	καὶ
humeis	*hupagēte*	*kai*	*karpon*	*pherēte*	*kai*
you	should go	and	fruit	you should bear,	and

3450.5 art sing masc	2561.1 noun nom sing masc	5050.2 prs-pron gen 2pl	3176.7 verb 3sing subj pres act	2419.1 conj	3614.16 rel-pron sing neu
ὁ	καρπὸς	ὑμῶν	μένῃ·	ἵνα	ὅ
ho	*karpos*	*humōn*	*menē*	*hina*	*ho*
the	fruit	your	should remain;	that	what

4948.10 indef-pron sing neu	300.1 partic	153.15 verb 2pl subj aor act	3450.6 art acc sing masc	3824.4 noun acc sing masc	1706.1 prep	3450.3 art dat sing
τι	ἂν	αἰτήσητε	τὸν	πατέρα	ἐν	τῷ
ti	*an*	*aitēsēte*	*ton*	*patera*	*en*	*tō*
ever		you may ask	the	Father	in	the

3549.4 noun dat sing neu	1466.2 prs-pron gen 1sing	1319.19 verb 3sing subj aor act	5050.3 prs-pron dat 2pl	3642.18 dem-pron pl neu
ὀνόματί	μου	δῷ	ὑμῖν.	**17.** ταῦτα
onomati	*mou*	*dō*	*humin*	*tauta*
name	my	he may give	you.	These things

1765.1 verb 1sing indic pres	5050.3 prs-pron dat 2pl	2419.1 conj	25.1 verb 2pl pres act	238.3 prs-pron acc pl masc	1479.1 conj
ἐντέλλομαι	ὑμῖν,	ἵνα	ἀγαπᾶτε	ἀλλήλους.	**18.** Εἰ
entellomai	*humin*	*hina*	*agapate*	*allēlous*	*Ei*
I command	you,	that	you love	one another.	If

respects. A servant is not told his master's mind, purpose, or plans. The slave is told and expected to execute the master's commands while often remaining ignorant of his reasons.

Friends inform each other and trust each other. Jesus had been teaching His disciples, and in these verses He introduced the friendship relationship with them. Those who treasure His words and abide in His love are His friends. By His grace, those who grasp hold of His sayings are enlightened as His friends. Christians will always be the Lord's servants, but when they love as He commanded He shares with them as friends.

for the servant knoweth not what his lord doeth: . . . does not know what his master is working out, *Berkeley* . . . does not share his master's confidence, *Phillips.*

but I have called you friends: for all things that I have heard of my Father I have made known unto you: I have learned, *Montgomery, Fenton* . . . I have acquainted you with everything, *Berkeley* . . . I've told you everything I heard from My Father, *Beck* . . . I have imparted, *Moffatt* . . . because I have revealed to you everything, *SEB.*

15:16. Students sometimes choose their own teachers, but Christ reversed this order. His association with the disciples went far beyond that of the pupil-teacher relationship. His disciples were handpicked to become the foundation of His Church.

"Ye" is emphatic as used with "have not chosen." The special emphasis is paralleled by the emphatic "I" with "have chosen" (see Matthew 4:18-22; Mark 2:14). Jesus selected the Twelve and endued them with power for a special mission (Matthew 10:1; Mark 3:13-15; Luke 6:13-16). His selection was by His grace, not because of their merit. The word "chose" implies that His choice was in behalf of himself and His plans. He was calling them to ministry here, not to salvation.

The allegory of the branches now became reality in their lives as they carried out the Lord's instructions. They were to go into all the world, manifesting the reality of the Father. They were to win souls, found churches, establish believers (Matthew 28:19,20).

The word "remain" (*menē*) is from the Greek word *menō*, and is also translated "abide," or "continue in" 10 previous times in this chapter. We understand from this verse that Jesus was speaking of two areas in which "your fruit should remain." First, He implied the subjective area. Each disciple should bear the fruit of the Spirit in accord with Galatians 5:22,23. Jesus' desire for His own is that they be mature Christians. Second, Jesus referred to the objective area. The believer is to produce fruit by his life's ministry of sharing with others. The disciple's testimony and good deeds bring men to Jesus. Both aspects of the disciple's fruit come as the result of abiding in Christ.

The last part of this verse indicates that acting and receiving are related to the disciple's ministry to the cause of Christ (see comments on verse 7).

16. Ye have not chosen me: but I have chosen you, and ordained you: . . . but I chose you and appointed you, *Montgomery* . . . I planted you, *Fenton.*

that ye should go and bring forth fruit, and that your fruit should remain: . . . will prove permanent, *Campbell* . . . that you might take root, *Fenton* . . . go out and produce fruit, *Berkeley* . . . that your fruit abide, *Panin* . . . will be lasting, *Phillips, Norlie* . . . that doesn't pass away, *Beck* . . . fruit as may be lasting, *Norton.*

that whatsoever ye shall ask of the Father in my name, he may give it you: . . . so that the Father, *Moffatt* . . . He may grant it, *Fenton* . . . may grant you, as bearers of my name, whatever you ask Him for, *Williams* . . . may give you everything that you may ask for in, *Norlie.*

15:17. By "these things," Jesus referred to the previously mentioned commandment to "love one another" (verse 12) as well as the command in this verse. The Lord has spoken of this command to love one another in 13:34,35 and 15:12 and here (see these references for comments). John had so much to say about love that

17. These things I command you: . . . am ordering you, *SEB* . . . These are My injunctions to you, *Berkeley* . . . So this is My command to you, *Norlie.*

that ye love one another: . . . ye love to gedder, *Tyndale.*

3450.5 art sing masc	**2862.1** noun nom sing masc	**5050.4** prs-pron acc 2pl	**3268.3** verb 3sing indic pres act	**1091.5** verb 2pl indic pres act	**3617.1** conj
ὁ	κόσμος	ὑμᾶς	μισεῖ,	γινώσκετε	ὅτι
ho	*kosmos*	*humas*	*misei*	*ginōskete*	*hoti*
thc	world	you	hates,	you know	that

1466.7 prs-pron acc 1sing	**4270.1** adv	**5050.2** prs-pron gen 2pl	**3268.16** verb 3sing indic perf act	**1479.1** conj	**1523.2** prep gen
ἐμὲ	πρῶτον	ὑμῶν	μεμίσηκεν.	**19.** εἰ	ἐκ
eme	*prōton*	*humōn*	*memisēken*	*ei*	*ek*
me	before	you	it has hated.	If	of

3450.2 art gen sing	**2862.2** noun gen sing masc	**1498.1** verb 2pl act	**3450.5** art sing masc	**2862.1** noun nom sing masc	**300.1** partic
τοῦ	κόσμου	ἦτε,	ὁ	κόσμος	ἂν
tou	*kosmou*	*ēte*	*ho*	*kosmos*	*an*
the	world	you were,	the	world	would

3450.16 art sing neu	**2375.4** adj acc sing	**5205.11** verb 3sing indic imperf act	**3617.1** conj	**1156.2** conj	**1523.2** prep gen	**3450.2** art gen sing
τὸ	ἴδιον	ἐφίλει·	ὅτι	δὲ	ἐκ	τοῦ
to	*idion*	*ephilei*	*hoti*	*de*	*ek*	*tou*
the	its own	love;	because	but	of	the

2862.2 noun gen sing masc	**3620.2** partic	**1498.6** verb 2pl indic pres act	**233.1** conj	**1466.1** prs-pron nom 1sing	**1573.1** verb 1sing indic aor mid
κόσμου	οὐκ	ἐστέ,	ἀλλ'	ἐγὼ	ἐξελεξάμην
kosmou	*ouk*	*este*	*all'*	*egō*	*exelexamēn*
world	not	you are,	but	I	chose

5050.4 prs-pron acc 2pl	**1523.2** prep gen	**3450.2** art gen sing	**2862.2** noun gen sing masc	**1217.2** prep	**3642.17** dem-pron sing neu
ὑμᾶς	ἐκ	τοῦ	κόσμου,	διὰ	τοῦτο
humas	*ek*	*tou*	*kosmou*	*dia*	*touto*
you	out of	the	world,	because of	this

3268.3 verb 3sing indic pres act	**5050.4** prs-pron acc 2pl	**3450.5** art sing masc	**2862.1** noun nom sing masc	**3285.1** verb 2pl pres act
μισεῖ	ὑμᾶς	ὁ	κόσμος.	**20.** μνημονεύετε
misei	*humas*	*ho*	*kosmos*	*mnēmoneuete*
hates	you	the	world.	Remember

3450.2 art gen sing	**3030.2** noun gen sing masc	**3614.2** rel-pron gen sing	**1466.1** prs-pron nom 1sing	**1500.3** verb indic aor act	**5050.3** prs-pron dat 2pl
τοῦ	λόγου	οὗ	ἐγὼ	εἶπον	ὑμῖν,
tou	*logou*	*hou*	*egō*	*eipon*	*humin*
the	word	which	I	said	to you,

3620.2 partic	**1498.4** verb 3sing indic pres act	**1395.1** noun nom sing masc	**3157.2** adj comp nom sing	**3450.2** art gen sing	**2935.2** noun gen sing masc
Οὐκ	ἔστιν	δοῦλος	μείζων	τοῦ	κυρίου
Ouk	*estin*	*doulos*	*meizōn*	*tou*	*kuriou*
Not	is	a slave	greater than	the	master

840.3 prs-pron gen sing	**1479.1** conj	**1466.7** prs-pron acc 1sing	**1371.14** verb 3pl indic aor act	**2504.1** conj	**5050.4** prs-pron acc 2pl
αὐτοῦ.	εἰ	ἐμὲ	ἐδίωξαν,	καὶ	ὑμᾶς
autou	*ei*	*eme*	*ediōxan*	*kai*	*humas*
his.	If	me	they persecuted,	also	you

1371.19 verb 3pl indic fut act	**1479.1** conj	**3450.6** art acc sing masc	**3030.4** noun acc sing masc	**1466.2** prs-pron gen 1sing
διώξουσιν·	εἰ	τὸν	λόγον	μου
diōxousin	*ei*	*ton*	*logon*	*mou*
they will persecute;	if	the	word	my

he has been called the apostle of love. It is because his master was the Lord of love (see 14:15,21,23).

18. If the world hate you, ye know that it hated me before it hated you: . . . continues to hate you, remember, *Williams* . . . remember that, *Norlie* . . . that it has first hated me as the fixed object of its hatred, *Weymouth.*

15:18. Jesus prepared the disciples for their hostile reception by the world. It is the nature of man to want sympathy and understanding. It can be very discouraging to be hated when one acts from the purest motives and performs righteous deeds. Thc Lord Jesus comforted His disciples by preparing them for the sufferings they would undergo because of His name. The apostle Peter passed on the same truth in 1 Peter 4:12,13 because it had been a comfort to him.

The word "world" is the most common Greek word used for the world. It embodies the contrast to God's orderly economy. God is revealed by His love, and the world is noted for its hatred. The disciples were assured that the world would hate and persecute them because it hated and murdered Him.

19. If ye were of the world, the world would love his own: If you belonged to the world, *Berkeley* . . . would love you as its own, *Norlie.*

but because ye are not of the world:

but I have chosen you out of the world: . . . and I have selected you from the world, *Berkeley* . . . having selected you, *Campbell.*

therefore the world hateth you: . . . on this account, *Wuest* . . . for this cause, *Murdock* . . . That is why the people of the world hate you, *SEB* . . . for that reason the world hates you, *Weymouth.*

15:19. In John 7:5,7 Jesus told His earthly family who did not believe on Him that the world would not hate them. It was because they were as the world. The world claims unbelievers as its own. Disciples have a different master from that of the world. The believer's desires are not the sinful lusts of the world. The believer's conduct does not conform to the pleasures of the world. The believer's hopes are based on that which is incomprehensible to the world. The world does not share the aims and destiny of the disciples of Christ.

The emphasis Jesus placed on the sinful nature of the world is reflected in all of John's writings. For John, as with his Lord, one is either a believer or a member of the hostile world. One either lives in the light or in darkness. He is either headed for the Father's house or for destruction. Christ is his master or he is of his father, the devil.

20. Remember the word that I said unto you: Bear in mind, *Weymouth* . . . Do you remember what I told you? *LivB* . . . Remember what I said to you, *Campell* . . . Remember My suggestion to you, *Berkeley* . . . the lesson I taught you, *SEB.*

The servant is not greater than his lord: A slave isn't greater than his master! *LivB* . . . is not superior, *Fenton.*

If they have persecuted me, they will also persecute you: If they were cruel to me, *BB* . . . Since me they persecuted, *Wuest.*

if they have kept my saying, they will keep yours also: . . . regarded my teaching, *Norton*

15:20. The Jews had already shown hostility to Jesus, as the disciples were aware. The disciples surely knew that they would have trials.

Jesus warned that just as the world had rejected Him and His teachings, so it would reject the teaching of the disciples. Beginning with the Jews at the temple, hostility continued toward the disciples. The Book of Acts is a commentary of evidence revealing the fulfillment of this prediction. The Jews failed to believe the message of Jesus even though they knew of His glorious resurrection.

4931.14 verb 3pl indic aor act	**2504.1** conj	**3450.6** art acc sing masc	**5052.2** adj acc 2sing	**4931.28** verb 3pl indic fut act	**233.2** conj
ἐτήρησαν,	καὶ	τὸν	ὑμέτερον	τηρήσουσιν.	**21.** ἀλλὰ
etērēsan	*kai*	*ton*	*humeteron*	*tērēsousin*	*alla*
they kept,	also	the	yours	they will keep.	But

21.a.**Txt:** 02A,05D-corr, 017K,022N,036,037,13, byz.Gries,Word
Var: p66,01ℵ-corr,03B, 05D-org,019L,038,33, Lach,Treg,Alf,Tisc, We/Ho,Weis,Sod,UBS/☆

3642.18 dem-pron pl neu	**3820.1** adj	**4020.55** verb 3pl indic fut act	**5050.3** prs-pron dat 2pl	**1519.1** prep	**5050.4** prs-pron acc 2pl
ταῦτα	πάντα	ποιήσουσιν	ʻ ὑμῖν	[a☆ εἰς	ὑμᾶς]
tauta	*panta*	*poiēsousin*	*humin*	*eis*	*humas*
these things	all	they will do	to you	[idem]	

1217.2 prep	**3450.16** art sing neu	**3549.2** noun sing neu	**1466.2** prs-pron gen 1sing	**3617.1** conj	**3620.2** partic
διὰ	τὸ	ὄνομά	μου,	ὅτι	οὐκ
dia	*to*	*onoma*	*mou*	*hoti*	*ouk*
because of	the	name	my,	because	not

3471.8 verb 3pl indic perf act	**3450.6** art acc sing masc	**3854.14** verb acc sing masc part aor act	**1466.6** prs-pron acc 1sing	**1479.1** conj	**3231.1** partic
οἴδασιν	τὸν	πέμψαντά	με.	**22.** εἰ	μὴ
oidasin	*ton*	*pempsanta*	*me*	*ei*	*mē*
they know	the	having sent	me.	If	not

2048.1 verb indic aor act	**2504.1** conj	**2953.26** verb 1sing indic aor act	**840.2** prs-pron dat pl	**264.4** noun acc sing fem	**3620.2** partic
ἦλθον	καὶ	ἐλάλησα	αὐτοῖς,	ἁμαρτίαν	οὐκ
ēlthon	*kai*	*elalēsa*	*autois*	*hamartian*	*ouk*
I had come	and	spoken	to them,	sin	not

22.a.**Txt:** 02A,05D-corr, 017K,022N-corr,036, 037,038,13,Gries,Word
Var: 01ℵ,03B,019L, 022N-org,33,Lach,Treg, Alf,TiscWe/Ho,Weis,Sod, UBS/☆

2174.42 verb indic imperf act	**2174.55** verb 3pl indic imperf act	**3431.1** adv	**1156.2** conj	**4250.2** noun acc sing fem	**3620.2** partic
ʻ εἴχον˙	[a☆ εἴχοσαν˙]	νῦν	δὲ	πρόφασιν	οὐκ
eichon	*eichosan*	*nun*	*de*	*prophasin*	*ouk*
they had had;	[idem]	now	but	a pretext	not

2174.6 verb 3pl indic pres act	**3875.1** prep	**3450.10** art gen sing fem	**264.1** noun fem	**840.1** prs-pron gen pl	**3450.5** art sing masc
ἔχουσιν	περὶ	τῆς	ἁμαρτίας	αὐτῶν.	**23.** ὁ
echousin	*peri*	*tēs*	*hamartias*	*autōn*	*ho*
they have	for	the	sin	their.	The

1466.7 prs-pron acc 1sing	**3268.5** verb nom sing masc part pres act	**2504.1** conj	**3450.6** art acc sing masc	**3824.4** noun acc sing masc	**1466.2** prs-pron gen 1sing
ἐμὲ	μισῶν,	καὶ	τὸν	πατέρα	μου
eme	*misōn*	*kai*	*ton*	*patera*	*mou*
me	hating,	also	the	Father	my

3268.3 verb 3sing indic pres act	**1479.1** conj	**3450.17** art pl neu	**2024.4** noun pl neu	**3231.1** partic	**4020.22** verb 1sing indic aor act
μισεῖ.	**24.** εἰ	τὰ	ἔργα	μὴ	ἐποίησα
misei	*ei*	*ta*	*erga*	*mē*	*epoiēsa*
hates.	If	the	works	not	I had done

1706.1 prep	**840.2** prs-pron dat pl	**3614.17** rel-pron pl neu	**3625.2** num card nom masc	**241.4** adj nom sing masc	**4020.43** verb 3sing indic perf act
ἐν	αὐτοῖς	ἃ	οὐδεὶς	ἄλλος	ʻ πεποίηκεν,
en	*autois*	*ha*	*oudeis*	*allos*	*pepoiēken*
among	them	which	no	other one	has done,

24.a.**Txt:** 017K,021M, 030U,036,037,byz.
Var: 01ℵ,02A,03B,05D, 017K,019L,033X,038, 33,Lach,Treg,Alf,Tisc, We/HoWeis,Sod,UBS/☆

4020.24 verb 3sing indic aor act	**264.4** noun acc sing fem	**3620.2** partic	**2174.42** verb indic imperf act
[a☆ ἐποίησεν,]	ἁμαρτίαν	οὐκ	ʻ εἴχον˙
epoiēsen	*hamartian*	*ouk*	*eichon*
[did,]	sin	not	they had had,

"The Lord who was personally persecuted on earth continued to be persecuted, even in his exaltation, in the person of his persecuted followers. Their being persecuted for his sake was a sign that they belonged to him, as it was a token of coming judgment on their persecutors" (Bruce, p.313).

. . . have given heed, *Weymouth* . . . they obeyed my teaching, *SEB* . . . If they had obeyed My message, they would obey, *Fenton* . . . Assuming that they kept my word, *Wuest.*

15:21. "All these things" embraces all the persecutions of believers from the Day of Pentecost until the present time, even until His great appearance. The disciples' persecutions and martyrdoms came as the result of their relationship with Him. "For my name's sake" means literally "because of My name." All that His blessed name stands for, the world opposes. His very name condemns their thoughts, plans, and deeds.

This verse reveals the importance of knowing and how terrible is ignorance. The knowledge of God invites believing in Christ. To "know" leads to eternal life. How sad that the world is ignorant of God and of Jesus Christ.

21. But all these things will they do unto you for my name's sake: . . . they will inflict all this suffering upon you on account of your bearing my name, *Weymouth* . . . on account of my name, *Moffatt* . . . because of my name, *Fenton* . . . on account of all that I am in my Person, *Wuest* . . . give you on my account, *Campbell.*

because they know not him that sent me: . . . for they do not know My Sender, *Berkeley* . . . seeing that they are not acquainted with Him, *Concordant.*

15:22. The world lives in darkness and commits the works of darkness (3:18,19). From the infancy of the world's creation men have covered themselves with fig leaves of excuses. But whatever form the excuses take, they give evidence that the light has been shining. There is no reason or even excuse for sin. Jesus has come and His presence is light. It is impossible to hide sin behind transparent aprons (Genesis 3:7-11).

22. If I had not come and spoken unto them, they had not had sin: . . . they would not have been guilty, *Norlie* . . . they would have had no sin to answer for, *TCNT.*

but now they have no cloke for their sin: . . . but as the case stands, *Weymouth* . . . no excuse, *ASV, Norlie, Fenton, Wuest, ALBA* . . . for their guilt, *Scarlett.*

15:23. Jesus is the revelation of the Father. If a person does not like what he sees when he views Christ, he will have no love for the Son or the Father. The Son's nature is the Father's nature. To love the nature of one is to love the nature of the other.

23. He that hateth me hateth my Father also: Whoever hates Me also hates, *Norlie* . . . Whoever continues to hate me, *Williams.*

15:24. Jesus pointed to "the works" as evidence of His identity. The works He did were predicted of the Messiah in the Law and the Prophets. His messianic credentials were presented, but the Jews rejected their validity. Study the passages in which Jesus stressed His works as a beginning for belief in Him and His message (see 5:36; 10:38; 14:10,11).

"They had not had sin" is rendered "they would not be guilty of sin" in the NIV. (See other translations in the *Various*

24. If I had not done among them the works which none other man did: . . . such work as no one else ever did, *TCNT* . . . things that no other man has ever done, *Phillips* . . . If I hadn't done works among them that were unlike works that anybody else had done, *Adams* . . . as no one else ever did, *Weymouth* . . . the works no one else has done, *Beck.*

they had not had sin: . . . they would be blameless, *Berkeley* . . . they wouldn't be guilty of sin, *Adams.*

24.b.**Txt:** 02A,05D-corr,017K,019L-corr,036,037,038,041-org,13,byz.
Var: 01ℵ,03B,019L-org,041-corr,33,Lach,Treg,Alf,TiscWe/Ho,Weis,Sod,UBS/☆

2174.55 verb 3pl indic imperf act	**3431.1** adv	**1156.2** conj	**2504.1** conj	**3571.14** verb 3pl indic perf act	**2504.1** conj
[b☆ εἴχοσαν·]	νῦν	δὲ	καὶ	ἑωράκασιν	καὶ
eichosan	*nun*	*de*	*kai*	*heōrakasin*	*kai*
[idem]	now	but	both	they have seen	and

3268.17 verb 3pl indic perf act	**2504.1** conj	**1466.7** prs-pron acc 1sing	**2504.1** conj	**3450.6** art acc sing masc	**3824.4** noun acc sing masc
μεμισήκασιν	καὶ	ἐμὲ	καὶ	τὸν	πατέρα
memisēkasin	*kai*	*eme*	*kai*	*ton*	*patera*
have hated	both	me	and	the	Father

1466.2 prs-pron gen 1sing		**233.1** conj	**2419.1** conj	**3997.22** verb 3sing subj aor pass	**3450.5** art sing masc	**3030.1** noun nom sing masc
μου·	25.	ἀλλ'	ἵνα	πληρωθῇ	ὁ	λόγος
mou		*all'*	*hina*	*plērōthē*	*ho*	*logos*
my.		But	that	might be fulfilled	the	word

3450.5 art sing masc	**1119.24** verb nom sing masc part perf pass	**1706.1** prep	**3450.3** art dat sing	**3414.3** noun dat sing masc	**840.1** prs-pron gen pl
ὁ	⸀γεγραμμένος	ἐν	τῷ	νόμῳ	αὐτῶν
ho	*gegrammenos*	*en*	*tō*	*nomō*	*autōn*
the	having been written	in	the	law	their,

1706.1 prep	**3450.3** art dat sing	**3414.3** noun dat sing masc	**840.1** prs-pron gen pl	**1119.24** verb nom sing masc part perf pass	**3617.1** conj
[☆ ἐν	τῷ	νόμῳ	αὐτῶν	γεγραμμένος]	Ὅτι
en	*tō*	*nomō*	*autōn*	*gegrammenos*	*Hoti*
[in	the	law	their	having been written]	

26.a.**Txt:** 02A,05D,017K,019L,036,038,1,13,byz.Lach,Sod
Var: p22,01ℵ,03B,037,Tisc,We/Ho,Weis,UBS/☆

3268.14 verb 3pl indic aor act	**1466.6** prs-pron acc 1sing	**1425.1** adv		**3615.1** conj	**1156.2** conj
Ἐμίσησάν	με	δωρεάν.	26.	Ὅταν	⸂a δὲ⸃
Emisēsan	*me*	*dōrean*		*Hotan*	*de*
They hated	me	without cause.		When	but

2048.8 verb 3sing subj aor act	**3450.5** art sing masc	**3736.1** noun nom sing masc	**3614.6** rel-pron acc sing masc	**1466.1** prs-pron nom 1sing
ἔλθῃ	ὁ	παράκλητος,	ὃν	ἐγὼ
elthē	*ho*	*paraklētos*	*hon*	*egō*
is come	the	Paraclete,	whom	I

3854.4 verb 1sing act	**5050.3** prs-pron dat 2pl	**3706.2** prep	**3450.2** art gen sing	**3824.2** noun gen sing masc	**3450.16** art sing neu
πέμψω	ὑμῖν	παρὰ	τοῦ	πατρός,	τὸ
pempsō	*humin*	*para*	*tou*	*patros*	*to*
will send	to you	from	the	Father,	the

4011.1 noun sing neu	**3450.10** art gen sing fem	**223.2** noun gen sing fem	**3614.16** rel-pron sing neu	**3706.2** prep	**3450.2** art gen sing
πνεῦμα	τῆς	ἀληθείας,	ὃ	παρὰ	τοῦ
pneuma	*tēs*	*alētheias*	*ho*	*para*	*tou*
Spirit	of the	truth,	who	from	the

3824.2 noun gen sing masc	**1594.1** verb 3sing indic pres	**1552.3** dem-pron nom sing masc	**3113.28** verb 3sing indic fut act	**3875.1** prep
πατρὸς	ἐκπορεύεται,	ἐκεῖνος	μαρτυρήσει	περὶ
patros	*ekporeuetai*	*ekeinos*	*marturēsei*	*peri*
Father	goes forth,	that	will bear witness	concerning

1466.3 prs-pron gen 1sing		**2504.1** conj	**5050.1** prs-pron nom 2pl	**1156.2** conj	**3113.5** verb 2pl indic pres act	**3617.1** conj
ἐμοῦ·	27.	καὶ	ὑμεῖς	δὲ	μαρτυρεῖτε,	ὅτι
emou		*kai*	*humeis*	*de*	*martureite*	*hoti*
me;		also	you	and	bear witness,	because

Versions column on the right.) This is understood to be the sin of rejecting Jesus. Merrill Tenney gives us insight with these words: "The sin of Jesus' enemies was both deliberate and inexcusable. Accredited by the miracles that he performed, he brought condemnation on them (cf. John 9:30-33, 39-41). His foes had heard his words and had witnessed his supporting miracles. Consequently, their reaction against him could not have been attributed to ignorance of his words or to lack of evidence substantiating them" (Tenney, *Expositor's Bible Commentary*, 9:154).

but now have they both seen and hated both me and my Father: But now the fact is, they have seen and even hated both my Father and me, *Williams* . . . have seen and also hated, *Weymouth* . . . and they still maintain that attitude of hate, *Wuest.*

15:25. "Their law" is the broad designation for the whole of the Old Testament, not merely the Torah. The Jews divided their Scriptures into three parts: the Law, the Prophets, and the Writings. Sometimes the writings were titled Psalms, the first book of the group (Luke 24:44). In this statement "law" refers to the Psalms (see Psalm 69:4). Jesus referred to the Scriptures as "your law" and here as "their law" (8:17). The Saviour never included himself with the people by saying "our law." He is the author of the Law and not a fellow subject of it. This is not to say that He failed to keep it.

"Without a cause" is hard to render in English. *Dōrean* is usually translated "gift" because it refers to something freely given. The idea is the Jews hated so "freely" that their hatred was a gift prompted without merit to warrant it. Thus "without a cause" expresses the idea.

25. But this cometh to pass, that the word might be fulfilled that is written in their law: This, however, was bound to happen, *TEV* . . . But so it had to be, *ALBA* . . . Thus they verify that passage, *Campbell* . . . Thus the saying in their law...had to be fulfilled, *Norlie* . . . But thus is accomplished the statement recorded, *Fenton.*

They hated me without a cause: . . . without any reason, *Beck* . . . for no reason at all, *TEV.*

15:26. "Comforter" has been referred to twice before this (14:16,26). John 16:7 mentions the name once more. Some translations render the Greek "Advocate," "Counselor," "Standby," etc. All these add to the idea involved in the person and function of the Spirit; however, they all are short of the mark. We must study the Scriptures for an understanding of who the "Comforter" is and what He does.

"Whom I will send" asserts what Jesus will do for them after the Resurrection and Ascension. This statement is a declaration of His equality with the Father. What stronger evidence of His claim to deity do we need!

26. But when the Comforter is come, whom I will send unto you from the Father: . . . the Paraclete comes, *ET* . . . the Counselor comes, *Adams* . . . Consoler, *Concordant* . . . I Myself will send, *Fenton* . . . from the presence of the Father, *Wuest.*

even the Spirit of truth: I mean the Spirit of Truth, *TCNT.*

which proceedeth from the Father: . . . who issues from the Father, *Moffatt* . . . which goes out from the Father, *Berkeley* . . . who goes forth from the Father, *Norlie, Adams* . . . who is coming out from, *SEB.*

he shall testify of me: He Himself, *Fenton* . . . He will testify regarding Me, *Berkeley* . . . bear witness concerning Me, *Norlie* . . . he will speak plainly about me, *Phillips* . . . give witness about me, *BB* . . . He will be my witness, *ALBA* . . . he will tell the truth about me, *SEB* . . . he shall witness about, *Klingensmith.*

15:27. "Ye" is the emphatic word. The testimony of the disciples was partly because of what they were as believers. But their active witness depended upon the power of the Spirit. It is the Spirit who makes real the things of Christ, illuminates the Scriptures, and anoints the message with power to convince the world concerning Christ.

27. And ye also shall bear witness: . . . and you too are witnesses, *Moffatt* . . . you also can corroborate, *Fenton* . . . but you also must testify, *NIV.*

because ye have been with me from the beginning: . . . from the start, *Williams* . . . from the first, *Montgomery* . . . from the outset, *JB* . . . from the very beginning, *Moffatt.*

570.2 prep gen	741.2 noun gen sing fem	3196.2 prep	1466.3 prs-pron gen 1sing	1498.6 verb 2pl indic pres act	3642.18 dem-pron pl neu
ἀπ'	ἀρχῆς	μετ'	ἐμοῦ	ἐστε.	**16:1.** Ταῦτα
ap'	*archēs*	*met'*	*emou*	*este*	*Tauta*
from	beginning	with	me	you are.	These things

2953.38 verb 1sing indic perf act	5050.3 prs-pron dat 2pl	2419.1 conj	3231.1 partic	4479.10 verb 2pl subj aor pass
λελάληκα	ὑμῖν	ἵνα	μὴ	σκανδαλισθῆτε.
lelalēka	*humin*	*hina*	*mē*	*skandalisthēte*
I have spoken	to you	that	not	you may be offended.

650.3 adj acc pl masc	4020.55 verb 3pl indic fut act	5050.4 prs-pron acc 2pl	233.1 conj	2048.34 verb 3sing indic pres
2. ἀποσυναγώγους	ποιήσουσιν	ὑμᾶς·	ἀλλ'	ἔρχεται
aposunagōgous	*poiēsousin*	*humas*	*all'*	*erchetai*
Out of the synagogues	they will put	you;	but	is coming

5443.2 noun nom sing fem	2419.1 conj	3820.6 adj sing masc	3450.5 art sing masc	609.10 verb nom sing masc part aor act	5050.4 prs-pron acc 2pl
ὥρα	ἵνα	πᾶς	ὁ	ἀποκτείνας	ὑμᾶς
hōra	*hina*	*pas*	*ho*	*apokteinas*	*humas*
an hour	that	everyone	the	having killed	you

1374.19 verb 3sing subj aor act	2972.3 noun acc sing fem	4232.10 verb inf pres act	3450.3 art dat sing	2296.3 noun dat sing masc
δόξῃ	λατρείαν	προσφέρειν	τῷ	θεῷ.
doxē	*latreian*	*prospherein*	*tō*	*theō*
will think	service	to render		to God;

3.a.**Txt:** 01ℵ,05D,019L, 044,1,13,565,sa.bo. Steph,Sod
Var: 02A,03B,017K,036, 037,038,700,892,byz. Gries,LachTreg,Alf,Tisc, We/Ho,Weis,UBS/*

2504.1 conj	3642.18 dem-pron pl neu	4020.55 verb 3pl indic fut act	5050.3 prs-pron dat 2pl	3617.1 conj	3620.2 partic
3. καὶ	ταῦτα	ποιήσουσιν	⸂[a] ὑμῖν ⸃	ὅτι	οὐκ
kai	*tauta*	*poiēsousin*	*humin*	*hoti*	*ouk*
and	these things	they will do	to you	because	not

1091.18 verb 3pl indic aor act	3450.6 art acc sing masc	3824.4 noun acc sing masc	3624.1 adv	1466.7 prs-pron acc 1sing	233.2 conj
ἔγνωσαν	τὸν	πατέρα	οὐδὲ	ἐμέ.	**4.** ἀλλὰ
egnōsan	*ton*	*patera*	*oude*	*eme*	*alla*
they knew	the	Father	nor	me.	But

3642.18 dem-pron pl neu	2953.38 verb 1sing indic perf act	5050.3 prs-pron dat 2pl	2419.1 conj	3615.1 conj	2048.8 verb 3sing subj aor act
ταῦτα	λελάληκα	ὑμῖν	ἵνα	ὅταν	ἔλθῃ
tauta	*lelalēka*	*humin*	*hina*	*hotan*	*elthē*
these things	I have said	to you,	that	when	may have come

4.a.**Var:** p66,02A,03B, 038,041-org,33,Lach, TregAlf,We/Ho,Weis, Sod,UBS/*

3450.9 art nom sing fem	5443.2 noun nom sing fem	840.1 prs-pron gen pl	3285.4 verb 2pl subj pres act	840.1 prs-pron gen pl
ἡ	ὥρα	[[a]+ αὐτῶν]	μνημονεύητε	αὐτῶν
hē	*hōra*	*autōn*	*mnēmoneuēte*	*autōn*
the	hour	[their]	you may remember	them

3617.1 conj	1466.1 prs-pron nom 1sing	1500.3 verb indic aor act	5050.3 prs-pron dat 2pl	3642.18 dem-pron pl neu	1156.2 conj
ὅτι	ἐγὼ	εἶπον	ὑμῖν·	Ταῦτα	δὲ
hoti	*egō*	*eipon*	*humin*	*Tauta*	*de*
that	I	said	to you.	These things	but

5050.3 prs-pron dat 2pl	1523.1 prep gen	741.2 noun gen sing fem	3620.2 partic	1500.3 verb indic aor act	3617.1 conj	3196.1 prep
ὑμῖν	ἐξ	ἀρχῆς	οὐκ	εἶπον	ὅτι	μεθ'
humin	*ex*	*archēs*	*ouk*	*eipon*	*hoti*	*meth'*
to you	from	beginning	not	I did say	because	with

The words "ye have been with me from the beginning" are best seen in the light of Peter's comment before the Day of Pentecost. The believers present selected a witness to stand with the Eleven in the place of Judas. One qualification was that he be a person who had been with them "all the time that the Lord Jesus went in and out among us" (Acts 1:21).

16:1. Jesus took time for His intimate discourses recorded in chapters 13 to 16. If He had not made the disciples ready for the onslaught of the powers of darkness, His death might have completely crushed their confidence in Him. The Greek word for "offended" is the one from which we get our English word *scandal.* One who causes a scandal is one who has stumbled (i.e., sinned). The word refers to being caught in a trap or a snare, or to stumble over a block in one's path. The noun is used for the bait or trigger-stick of a trap.

16:2. The synagogue was the center of social and religious activities among the Jews. To deprive the Jews of these privileges was an extreme punishment indeed. This snare was an effort by the leaders to force Jews to have nothing to do with Christ.

The prophecy is best illustrated by Saul the persecutor who became Paul the Apostle (Acts 26:8-22). The Greek word *latreia* ("service") occurs five times in the New Testament. The verb *latruō* is often rendered "worship" even though it comes from *latris* meaning "hired servant."

16:3. See comments on 15:21, where Jesus indicated that these persecutions would come out of the world's ignorance and hatred. "They" here refers to unbelieving Jews, the ones who would put believers out of synagogues. John's Gospel speaks often of the relationship between obedient faith and knowing God. It was "his own," the Jews, who are spoken of as "the world" that knew not Jesus because they "received him not" (1:10,11).

Jesus explained to Nicodemus why those who did not believe on Him were condemned. Their rejection of Him placed them under God's condemnation. They rejected Him because He was the Light; they loved darkness because the Light revealed their evil deeds (3:18,19).

Logically, all Jews should have recognized Jesus and believed on Him since they knew the prophecies. We see here the principle that it is not intellectual knowledge that brings the knowledge of God. Knowing God is the result of faith—an attitude of humble obedience to His Word.

Jesus told them that they would not have had sin if He had not done the works no other had done (15:24). They were not neces-

1. These things have I spoken unto you: I have told you these things, *Norlie* . . . I have said all this, *RSV.*

that ye should not be offended: . . . to guard against your losing faith, *ALBA* . . . will upset your faith, *Beck* . . . from falling over stumbling blocks, *Williams* . . . not be made to stumble, *Wuest* . . . to clear stumbling blocks out of your path, *Weymouth* . . . not falter, *Fenton* . . . not be trapped, *Berkeley* . . . lest ye be ensnared, *Rotherham* . . . not be snared, *Concordant* . . . not be scandalized, *Confraternity* . . . not be taken unawares, *Norlie.*

2. They shall put you out of the synagogues: They will expel you from their Synagogues, *TCNT* . . . excommunicate you, *Montgomery* . . . blacklist you, *Klingensmith* . . . make you outcast, *Wuest* . . . shut you out from, *Berkeley* . . . be excluded, *Weymouth* . . . eject you, *Murdock.*

yea, the time cometh, that whosoever killeth you will think that he doeth God service: . . . who murders you will think he's serving God, *Beck* . . . rendering a religious service to God, *Williams* . . . who kills you will be of the opinion that he is offering a sacred service to God, *Wuest* . . . indeed, the hour is coming, *RSV* . . . is offering sacrifice to God, *HBIE* . . . is rendering service to God, *Berkeley* . . . is doing God's pleasure, *BB* . . . offering divine service, *Concordant* . . . offering worship to God, *ALBA* . . . presenteth an offering, *Murdock.*

3. And these things will they do unto you:

because they have not known the Father, nor me: . . . had any true knowledge, *Phillips* . . . have never come to know God nor me, *Williams* . . . they neither recognised, *Fenton.*

4. But these things have I told you, that when the time shall come: . . . when the time for it arrives, *Moffatt.*

ye may remember that I told you of them: . . . you may be reminded that I told you, *Fenton* . . . you may recollect that, *Weymouth* . . . I forewarned you, *Norlie.*

And these things I said not unto you at the beginning: Yet I avoided telling you, *Fenton* . . . I did not tell you these things at the start, *Williams.*

5050.2 prs-pron gen 2pl	1498.46 verb 1sing indic imperf mid	3431.1 adv	1156.2 conj	5055.1 verb 1sing indic pres act	4242.1 prep
ὑμῶν	ἤμην.	5. νῦν	δὲ	ὑπάγω	πρὸς
humōn	*ēmēn*	*nun*	*de*	*hupagō*	*pros*
you	I was.	Now	but	I go	to

3450.6 art acc sing masc	3854.14 verb acc sing masc part aor act	1466.6 prs-pron acc 1sing	2504.1 conj	3625.2 num card nom masc	1523.1 prep gen
τὸν	πέμψαντά	με,	καὶ	οὐδεὶς	ἐξ
ton	*pempsanta*	*me*	*kai*	*oudeis*	*ex*
the	having sent	me,	and	none	of

5050.2 prs-pron gen 2pl	2049.1 verb 3sing pres act	1466.6 prs-pron acc 1sing	4085.1 adv	5055.2 verb 2sing indic pres act	233.1 conj
ὑμῶν	ἐρωτᾷ	με,	Ποῦ	ὑπάγεις;	6. ἀλλ'
humōn	*erōta*	*me*	*Pou*	*hupageis*	*all'*
you	asks	me,	Where	are you going?	But

3617.1 conj	3642.18 dem-pron pl neu	2953.38 verb 1sing indic perf act	5050.3 prs-pron dat 2pl	3450.9 art nom sing fem
ὅτι	ταῦτα	λελάληκα	ὑμῖν	ἡ
hoti	*tauta*	*lelalēka*	*humin*	*hē*
because	these things	I have said	to you	the

3049.1 noun nom sing fem	3997.10 verb 3sing indic perf act	5050.2 prs-pron gen 2pl	3450.12 art acc sing fem	2559.4 noun acc sing fem
λύπη	πεπλήρωκεν	ὑμῶν	τὴν	καρδίαν.
lupē	*peplērōken*	*humōn*	*tēn*	*kardian*
grief	has filled	your	the	heart.

233.1 conj	1466.1 prs-pron nom 1sing	3450.12 art acc sing fem	223.4 noun acc sing fem	2978.1 verb 1sing pres act	5050.3 prs-pron dat 2pl
7. ἀλλ'	ἐγὼ	τὴν	ἀλήθειαν	λέγω	ὑμῖν,
all'	*egō*	*tēn*	*alētheian*	*legō*	*humin*
But	I	the	truth	say	to you,

4702.1 verb 3sing indic pres act	5050.3 prs-pron dat 2pl	2419.1 conj	1466.1 prs-pron nom 1sing	562.3 verb 1sing subj aor act	1430.1 partic
συμφέρει	ὑμῖν	ἵνα	ἐγὼ	ἀπέλθω·	ἐὰν
sumpherei	*humin*	*hina*	*egō*	*apelthō*	*ean*
It is profitable	for you	that	I	should go away;	if

7.a.**Var:** 02A,017K,036,037,13,33,byz.it.Lach,Alf,Word

1056.1 conj	1466.1 prs-pron nom 1sing	3231.1 partic	562.3 verb 1sing subj aor act	3450.5 art sing masc	3736.1 noun nom sing masc
γὰρ	[a+ ἐγὼ]	μὴ	ἀπέλθω	ὁ	παράκλητος
gar	*egō*	*mē*	*apelthō*	*ho*	*paraklētos*
for	[I]	not	I go away	the	Paraclete

7.b.**Txt:** 01ℵ,02A,05D,017K,036,037,038,1,13,etc.byz.Lach,Tisc,Sod
Var: 03B,019L,044,33,Treg,We/Ho,Weis,UBS/☆

3620.2 partic	2048.55 verb 3sing indic fut mid	3620.3 partic	3231.1 partic	2048.8 verb 3sing subj aor act	4242.1 prep
☆ οὐκ	ἐλεύσεται	[b οὐ	μὴ	ἔλθῃ]	πρὸς
ouk	*eleusetai*	*ou*	*mē*	*elthē*	*pros*
not	will come	[not	not	comes]	to

5050.4 prs-pron acc 2pl	1430.1 partic	1156.2 conj	4057.18 verb 1sing subj aor pass	3854.4 verb 1sing act	840.6 prs-pron acc sing masc	4242.1 prep
ὑμᾶς·	ἐὰν	δὲ	πορευθῶ,	πέμψω	αὐτὸν	πρὸς
humas	*ean*	*de*	*poreuthō*	*pempsō*	*auton*	*pros*
you;	if	but	I go,	I will send	him	to

5050.4 prs-pron acc 2pl	2504.1 conj	2048.13 verb nom sing masc part aor act	1552.3 dem-pron nom sing masc	1638.7 verb 3sing indic fut act
ὑμᾶς·	8. καὶ	ἐλθὼν	ἐκεῖνος	ἐλέγξει
humas	*kai*	*elthōn*	*ekeinos*	*elenxei*
you.	And	having come	that	will convict

sarily ignorant nor passively ignorant. They voluntarily, actively, and freely chose to *ignore* the righteousness of God (Romans 10:2,3). In rejecting Jesus they proved that they did not *know* the God they spoke about with such zeal.

because I was with you: . . . still with, *Norlie* . . . continually with you, *Wuest.*

16:4. Jesus repeated the objective He had in view by forewarning the disciples of the coming trials (verse 1).

This was to be a source of encouragement. Jesus knew these things were to happen, but He also knew how to help the disciples through the persecutions in victory. Jesus told them the things that would help them to make progress in their walk with Him. Jesus had forewarned them of coming persecution earlier (Matthew 5:10; 10:16; Luke 6:22f.), but not in the same context as here. He was at this time showing the coming trials in relation to (1) their ongoing faith and ministry, and (2) His going away and the coming of the Holy Spirit.

5. But now I go my way to him that sent me:

and none of you asketh me, Whither goest thou?: Where are you going, *TCNT* . . . and nonc of you is interested in the purpose of My going, *LivB* . . . where I am going, *Norlie.*

6. But because I have said these things unto you, sorrow hath filled your heart: . . . you are so distressed, *Phillips* . . . full of sadness, *Fenton* . . . grief has filled your hearts, *Weymouth* . . . and is now controlling it, *Wuest* . . . you are overwhelmed, *Campbell* . . . sorrow has taken complete possession, *Williams.*

16:5,6. Jesus had repeatedly spoken about His coming and the Father's sending Him. It was also necessary for Him to explain to them the coming persecutions and the coming of the Spirit.

But now that the disciples had begun to understand the reality of His death, they were mute in asking about His departure.

"Sorrow" was the reason they had not asked the question, "Where are you going?" But their sorrow was to be replaced by confidence and power.

7. Nevertheless I tell you the truth: Yet I am only telling you the truth, *TCNT* . . . I have, however, told you nothing but the truth, *Fenton.*

It is expedient for you that I go away: It is profitable for you that I depart, *Rotherham* . . . it is better, *Fenton* . . . it is to your advantage, *Weymouth* . . . it is for your good, *Campbell, Norlie* . . . My going is for your benefit, *Berkeley.*

for if I go not away, the Comforter will not come unto you: . . . will not come into close fellowship with you, *Williams* . . . your Advocate, *NEB* . . . the Helper, *NASB* . . . the divine helper, *Phillips* . . . the Counselor will not come to you, *RSV* . . . positively not come, *Wuest.*

but if I depart, I will send him unto you: . . . but if I go, *ASV* . . . but, if I leave you, *TCNT.*

16:7. Jesus placed special emphasis on "I" because He wished to assure them that He knew what He was speaking of, and He had never misled them.

It was to the disciples' advantage that Jesus should leave them. His returning to the Father made it possible for Him to prepare a place for them (14:3). Furthermore, by His going (death), He would make the exhaustless resources of heaven available to all believers.

Jesus emphasized that His going would make possible the advent of "the Comforter." "The Comforter" is the same word used also in 14:26 and 15:26. The root meaning of "the Comforter" is "to call to one's aid." The Spirit is in the believer not merely to give first aid, but continuing and final aid. The Helper is our defense and offense. He comes to offer His aid in our approach to God. He stands as a defense against the stratagem of the believer's enemy, Satan.

Jesus clearly stated that until He ascended back to the Father the Helper would not come.

3450.6 art	**2862.4** noun	**3875.1**	**264.1**	**2504.1**	**3875.1**
acc sing masc	acc sing masc	prep	noun fem	conj	prep
τὸν	κόσμον	περὶ	ἁμαρτίας	καὶ	περὶ
ton	*kosmon*	*peri*	*hamartias*	*kai*	*peri*
the	world	concerning	sin	and	concerning

1336.2 noun	**2504.1**	**3875.1**	**2893.2** noun	**3875.1**
gen sing fem	conj	prep	gen sing fem	prep
δικαιοσύνης	καὶ	περὶ	κρίσεως·	**9.** περὶ
dikaiosunēs	*kai*	*peri*	*kriseōs*	*peri*
righteousness	and	concerning	judgment.	Concerning

264.1	**3173.1**	**3617.1**	**3620.3**	**3961.3** verb	**1519.1**
noun fem	conj	conj	partic	3pl pres act	prep
ἁμαρτίας	μέν,	ὅτι	οὐ	πιστεύουσιν	εἰς
hamartias	*men*	*hoti*	*ou*	*pisteuousin*	*eis*
sin,		because	not	they believe	on

1466.7 prs-pron acc 1sing	**3875.1**	**1336.2** noun	**1156.2**	**3617.1**	**4242.1**
	prep	gen sing fem	conj	conj	prep
ἐμέ·	**10.** περὶ	δικαιοσύνης	δέ,	ὅτι	πρὸς
eme	*peri*	*dikaiosunēs*	*de*	*hoti*	*pros*
me;	concerning	righteousness		because	to

10.a.**Txt:** 02A,017K,036,037,038,13,byz.Gries,Lach,Sod
Var: 01ℵ,03B,05D,019L,032W,33,bo.Treg,Tisc,We/Ho,Weis,UBS/☆

3450.6 art	**3824.4** noun	**1466.2** prs-pron gen 1sing	**5055.1** verb 1sing	**2504.1**	**3620.2**
acc sing masc	acc sing masc		indic pres act	conj	partic
τὸν	πατέρα	⸂a μου⸃	ὑπάγω,	καὶ	⸀ οὐκ
ton	*patera*	*mou*	*hupagō*	*kai*	*ouk*
the	Father	my	I go away,	and	no

2068.1	**3629.1**	**2311.1** verb	**1466.6** prs-pron acc 1sing	**3875.1**
adv	adv	2pl pres act		prep
ἔτι	[☆ οὐκέτι]	θεωρεῖτέ	με·	**11.** περὶ
eti	*ouketi*	*theōreite*	*me*	*peri*
longer	[no longer]	you behold	me;	concerning

1156.2	**2893.2** noun	**3617.1**	**3450.5** art	**752.1** noun	**3450.2** art
conj	gen sing fem	conj	sing masc	nom sing masc	gen sing
δὲ	κρίσεως,	ὅτι	ὁ	ἄρχων	τοῦ
de	*kriseōs*	*hoti*	*ho*	*archōn*	*tou*
but	judgment,	because	the	ruler	of the

2862.2 noun	**3642.1** dem-pron gen sing	**2892.38** verb 3sing	**2068.1**	**4044.17**
gen sing masc		indic perf pass	adv	adj pl neu
κόσμου	τούτου	κέκριται.	**12.** Ἔτι	πολλὰ
kosmou	*toutou*	*kekritai*	*Eti*	*polla*
world	this	has been judged.	Yet	many things

2174.1 verb	**2978.24** verb	**5050.3** prs-pron	**5050.3** prs-pron	**2978.24** verb	**233.1**
1sing pres act	inf pres act	dat 2pl	dat 2pl	inf pres act	conj
ἔχω	⸀ λέγειν	ὑμῖν,	[☆ ὑμῖν	λέγειν,]	ἀλλ'
echō	*legein*	*humin*	*humin*	*legein*	*all'*
I have	to say	to you,	[to you	to say,]	but

3620.3	**1404.6** verb	**934.8** verb	**732.1**	**3615.1**	**1156.2**
partic	2pl indic pres	inf pres act	adv	conj	conj
οὐ	δύνασθε	βαστάζειν	ἄρτι·	**13.** ὅταν	δὲ
ou	*dunasthe*	*bastazein*	*arti*	*hotan*	*de*
not	you are able	to bear them	now.	When	but

2048.8 verb 3sing	**1552.3** dem-pron	**3450.16** art	**4011.1** noun	**3450.10** art
subj aor act	nom sing masc	sing neu	sing neu	gen sing fem
ἔλθῃ	ἐκεῖνος,	τὸ	πνεῦμα	τῆς
elthē	*ekeinos*	*to*	*pneuma*	*tēs*
may have come	that,	the	Spirit	of the

The work of the Spirit proceeds in two areas. First, He is active toward those who are in darkness (verses 7-11). Second, He is the Spirit of Truth to believers (verses 12-15).

16:8. This verse begins an explanation of the Spirit's threefold office as the Pleader and Advocate toward the world. Those who are in the world cannot be brought to Christ except through the work of the Spirit. "Convict" is the action word that applies to the three areas of the Spirit's activities. It is clear by the way the word is used that its meaning is "convince" as in John 8:46, "tell his fault" (Matthew 18:15), "reprove" and "expose" (Ephesians 5:11,13), and "rebuke" (1 Timothy 5:20; Titus 1:13; 2:15; Revelation 3:19). The best two renderings are "convict" and "convince." First, "convict" is a good rendering because the Spirit impresses the standard of the Law upon the sinner and brings him to feel guilt. Second, "convince" is a good rendering because the Spirit brings the truth before the soul of and displays the evidence so that the lost may be persuaded of the reality of Christ.

16:9. Unbelief is the source from which all sin originates. The pronoun "me" is emphatic. By rejecting Christ, man severs himself from all that God is and God's redemptive benefits for man. The true nature of sin is revealed as unbelief in God and God's ambassador (12:48,49).

16:10. Jesus was the only righteous man, the only One to lead a perfectly righteous life. He is the standard of righteousness. To the sinner He is the one standard which shows them "weighed and wanting." Man realizes his unrighteousness as the Holy Spirit reveals Christ's righteousness. Jesus' departure to the Father and acceptance by the Father made possible the believer's righteousness.

16:11. The works of Satan were destroyed by Christ's righteous life and His death on the cross. The Spirit convicts the world because Satan has been judged. Our Lord's matchless life and efficacious death judged Satan and destroyed his power over man (1 John 3:8). The Spirit shows us that Satan is defeated because of Calvary. The world is convicted as to their sure judgment because their ruler, Satan, stands judged.

16:12. Jesus left many of His directives to the ministry of the Spirit (Luke 24:32; Acts 1:3,8). He told the disciples the Spirit

8. And when he is come, he will reprove the world: . . . will make the world conscious, *BB* . . . he will convince the world, *RSV, Norlie* . . . conscious of sin, *BB*.

of sin, and of righteousness, and of judgment: . . . respecting sin, *Worrell* . . . about a Rectification, *Fenton* . . . of justice, *Confraternity* . . . of the meaning of sin, of true goodness, *Phillips* . . . uprightness, and of condemnation, *HistNT*.

9. Of sin, because they believe not on me: . . . they have not faith, *BB* . . . as proved by, *TCNT* . . . by their refusal to believe in me, *NEB*.

10. Of righteousness, because I go to my Father:

and ye see me no more:

11. Of judgment, because the prince of this world is judged: . . . has been convicted, *Norlie* . . . the judgment passed upon the Spirit, *TCNT* . . . when the Leader of this Conspiracy is convicted, *Fenton* . . . is under sentence, *Weymouth* . . . and is now under judgment, *Wuest*.

12. I have yet many things to say unto you:

but ye cannot bear them now: . . . but you are not strong enough for it now, *BB* . . . but it would be too much for you now, *Beck* . . . ye cannot comprehend now, *Murdock*.

13. Howbeit when he, the Spirit of truth, is come:

223.2 noun gen sing fem	3457.4 verb 3sing indic fut act	5050.4 prs-pron acc 2pl	1519.1 prep	3820.12 adj acc sing fem	3450.12 art acc sing fem
ἀληθείας,	ὁδηγήσει	ὑμᾶς	ʻ εἰς	πᾶσαν	τὴν
alētheias	hodēgēsei	humas	eis	pasan	tēn
truth,	he will guide	you	into	all	the

223.4 noun acc sing fem	1706.1 prep	3450.11 art dat sing fem	223.3 noun dat sing fem	3820.11 adj dat sing fem	3620.3 partic
ἀλήθειαν·	[☆ ἐν	τῇ	ἀληθείᾳ	πάσῃ·]	οὐ
alētheian	en	tē	alētheia	pasē	ou
truth;	[into	the	truth	all.]	not

13.a.**Txt:** 02A,05D-corr, 07E,017K,021M,036, 037,038,13,byz.
Var: 01ℵ,03B,05D-org, 019L,032W,33,Lach, TregAlf,Tisc,We/Ho, Weis,Sod,UBS/☆

1056.1 conj	2953.40 verb 3sing indic fut act	570.1 prep gen	1431.4 prs-pron gen 3sing	233.1 conj	3607.8 rel-pron pl neu	300.1 partic
γὰρ	λαλήσει	ἀφ'	ἑαυτοῦ,	ἀλλ'	ὅσα	ʻ[a] ἂν ˎ
gar	lalēsei	aph'	heautou	all'	hosa	an
for	he will speak	from	himself,	but	whatever	

13.b.**Txt:** 02A,07E-corr, 017K,021M,036,037,13, byz.Lach
Var1: .03B,05D,07E-org, 032W,038,044,TregAlf, Sod
Var2: .01ℵ,019L,33, Tisc,We/HoWeis,UBS/☆

189.18 verb sing act	189.42 verb 3sing indic fut act	189.5 verb 3sing indic pres act	2953.40 verb 3sing indic fut act	2504.1 conj
ʻ ἀκούσῃ	[[1b]☆ ἀκούσει	[2] ἀκούει]	λαλήσει,	καὶ
akousē	akousei	akouei	lalēsei	kai
he may hear	[he will hear	he hears]	he will speak;	and

3450.17 art pl neu	2048.52 verb acc pl neu part pres	310.9 verb 3sing indic fut act	5050.3 prs-pron dat 2pl	1552.3 dem-pron nom sing masc
τὰ	ἐρχόμενα	ἀναγγελεῖ	ὑμῖν.	**14.** ἐκεῖνος
ta	erchomena	anangelei	humin	ekeinos
the things	coming	he will announce	to you.	That

1466.7 prs-pron acc 1sing	1386.16 verb 3sing indic fut act	3617.1 conj	1523.2 prep gen	3450.2 art gen sing	1684.11 adj gen 1sing neu
ἐμὲ	δοξάσει,	ὅτι	ἐκ	τοῦ	ἐμοῦ
eme	doxasei	hoti	ek	tou	emou
me	will glorify,	for	of	the	mine

14.a.**Txt:** 03B-corr,017K, 019L,036,037,038,byz. Sod
Var: 01ℵ,02A,03B-org, 05D,Lach,Treg,Alf,Tisc, We/Ho,Weis,UBS/☆

2956.39 verb 3sing indic fut mid	2956.45 verb 3sing indic fut mid	2504.1 conj	310.9 verb 3sing indic fut act	5050.3 prs-pron dat 2pl
ʻ λήψεται,	[[a]☆ λήμψεται]	καὶ	ἀναγγελεῖ	ὑμῖν.
lēpsetai	lēmpsetai	kai	anangelei	humin
he will receive,	[idem]	and	will announce	to you.

3820.1 adj	3607.8 rel-pron pl neu	2174.4 verb 3sing indic pres act	3450.5 art sing masc	3824.1 noun nom sing masc
15. πάντα	ὅσα	ἔχει	ὁ	πατὴρ
panta	hosa	echei	ho	patēr
All things	whatever	has	the	Father

1684.12 adj 1pl neu	1498.4 verb 3sing indic pres act	1217.2 prep	3642.17 dem-pron sing neu	1500.3 verb indic aor act	3617.1 conj
ἐμά	ἐστιν·	διὰ	τοῦτο	εἶπον,	ὅτι
ema	estin	dia	touto	eipon	hoti
mine	are;	because of	this	I said,	that

15.a.**Txt:** (01-corr),(02), 017K,041,bo.Steph
Var: 03B,05D,019L,037, 038,byz.Gries,LachTreg, Alf,Word,Tisc,We/Ho, Weis,Sod,UBS/☆

1523.2 prep gen	3450.2 art gen sing	1684.11 adj gen 1sing neu	2956.39 verb 3sing indic fut mid	2956.4 verb 3sing indic pres act
ἐκ	τοῦ	ἐμοῦ	ʻ λήψεται,	[[a]☆ λαμβάνει]
ek	tou	emou	lēpsetai	lambanei
of	the	mine	he will receive,	[he receives]

2504.1 conj	310.9 verb 3sing indic fut act	5050.3 prs-pron dat 2pl	3261.1 adv	2504.1 conj	3620.3 partic
καὶ	ἀναγγελεῖ	ὑμῖν.	**16.** Μικρὸν	καὶ	ʻ οὐ
kai	anangelei	humin	Mikron	kai	ou
and	will announce	to you.	A little	and	not

would guide them "into all truth" (verse 13). Their capacity to receive further revelations would increase when the Spirit of Truth had come.

he will guide you into all truth: . . . will conduct you, *Campbell* . . . into everything that is true, *Phillips* . . . into every truth, *Berkeley* . . . into the whole truth, *Montgomery.*

for he shall not speak of himself: . . . of his own accord, *Moffatt* . . . from his own mind, *Murdock* . . . His utterances do not proceed from Himself, *Fenton.*

but whatsoever he shall hear, that shall he speak: . . . he will say whatever he is told, *Moffatt.*

and he will shew you things to come: . . . and he will declare to you, *HBIE* . . . the events that are coming, *Fenton* . . . make known the future to you, *Weymouth* . . . will he rehearse to you, *Rotherham.*

16:13. Verses 13 and 14 reveal three functions of the Spirit in relation to the believer: first, the Spirit as a guide; second, the Spirit as a discloser of coming things; and third, the Spirit as the One who glorifies Christ.

The important word in verse 13 is *hodēgēsei* ("will guide"). It is rendered by "lead" and "guide." In the Greek Septuagint (the Old Testament), the word is also translated "instruct," "teach," and "conduct." The Holy Spirit points out the way to go through the maze of worldly roads. He guides through the dangers that lurk along the path. By His teachings and counseling, many pits of destruction are avoided. The Greek preposition *eis* indicates a relationship movement toward all the truth.

The word "show" is the verb which indicates the second function of the Spirit in relation to the believer. The Spirit does not limit himself to inspiration, for He illuminates what He has inspired. He discloses to all believers the hope of their destiny. The believer's future is more important than his past, and both are buckled together by the present.

14. He shall glorify me: He will bring glory to me, *Phillips* . . . He shall exalt me, *HistNT.*

for he shall receive of mine: . . . shall take out from that which pertains to me, *Wuest* . . . will take of what is Mine, *Norlie* . . . He will take what I am saying, *SEB* . . . draw on my truth, *Phillips* . . . by taking My things, *Adams.*

and shall shew it unto you: . . . declare, *ASV* . . . announce, *Rotherham, ALBA* . . . and disclose it to you, *Moffatt* . . . and will tell it to you, *SEB* . . . He will transmit to you, *Fenton* . . . and reveal it to you, *Norlie* . . . and make it known to you, *Wuest* . . . make it clear to you, *BB.*

16:14. This is the third great function of the Spirit in relation to the believer. As the Son glorifies the Father in giving himself as a ransom for the lost, so the Holy Spirit glorifies the Son so that the Son can glorify the Father (1:18; 17:4). The Son makes the Father known, and the Spirit makes the Son known.

By taking the things of Christ and displaying them to the believers, the Spirit is glorifying Christ. The Holy Spirit takes "out of" Christ (Greek, *ek tou emou*) the necessary truths to help the believer in his time of need. The Spirit operates through His gifts and graces to glorify Jesus (1 Corinthians 12 to 14).

15. All things that the Father hath are mine: All that the Father possesses is mine, *Fenton* . . . Everything that belongs to my, *SEB* . . . Whatever the Father has is Mine, *Norlie.*

therefore said I, that he shall take of mine: On this account, *Wuest.*

and shall shew it unto you: . . . and tell them to you, *Williams* . . . to communicate to you, *Campbell.*

16:15. When the Spirit shows to the believer the things of Christ, He is also disclosing the things of the Father. Such perfect harmony exists between the Holy Three that what is said of one can be said of the other two.

The Spirit was operative from creation through the whole of the Old Testament millenia. However, His exposure of truth was limited to prophecies which He inspired. He often revealed reality through types and shadows by the use of people, events, and things.

John 16:17

16.a.**Txt:** 02A,017K,036,037,13,byz.bo.
Var: 01ℵ,03B,05D,019L,038,33,Lach,Alf,Tisc,We/HoWeis,Sod,UBS/☆

16.b.**Txt:** 02A,017K,036,037,038,1,13,33,byz.bo.Lach
Var: p5,p66,01ℵ,03B,05D,019L,032W,it.Treg,Alf,Tisc,We/Ho,Weis,Sod,UBS/☆

16.c.**Txt:** 33,bo.Steph
Var: p5,p66,01ℵ,02A,03B,05D,019L,032W,038,etc.byz.Lach,Treg,Alf,Tisc,We/Ho,WeisSod,UBS/☆

16.d.**Txt:** 02A,017K,036,037,038,1,13,33,byz.bo.Lach
Var: p5,p66,01ℵ,03B,05D,019L,032W,it.Treg,Alf,Tisc,We/Ho,Weis,Sod,UBS/☆

17.a.**Txt:** 01ℵ,02A,05D,019L,038,etc.byz.Lach,Tisc,Sod
Var: 03B,We/Ho,Weis,UBS/☆

17.b.**Txt:** 05D,017K,032W,036,037,038,byz.
Var: 01ℵ,02A,03B,019L,021M,041,Lach,TregAlf,Word,Tisc,We/Ho,Weis,Sod,UBS/☆

18.a.**Txt:** 01ℵ-org,02A,05D,017K,032W,036,037,038,1,13,etc.byz.Lach,Tisc,Weis,Sod,UBS/☆
Var: 01ℵ-corr,03B,019L,044,Treg,Alf,We/Ho

3629.1 adv	2311.1 verb 2pl pres act	1466.6 prs-pron acc 1sing	2504.1 conj	3687.1 adv
[[a]☆ οὐκέτι]	θεωρεῖτέ	με,	καὶ	πάλιν
ouketi	*theōreite*	*me*	*kai*	*palin*
[no longer]	you do see	me;	and	again

3261.1 adv	2504.1 conj	3571.33 verb 2pl indic fut mid	1466.6 prs-pron acc 1sing	3617.1 conj	1466.1 prs-pron nom 1sing
μικρὸν	καὶ	ὄψεσθέ	με,	⸂[b] ὅτι ⸃	⸂[c] ἐγὼ ⸃
mikron	*kai*	*opsesthe*	*me*	*hoti*	*egō*
a little	and	you shall see	me,	because	I

5055.1 verb 1sing indic pres act	4242.1 prep	3450.6 art acc sing masc	3824.4 noun acc sing masc	1500.3 verb indic aor act
⸂[d] ὑπάγω	πρὸς	τὸν	πατέρα. ⸃	**17.** ⸂ Εἶπον
hupagō	*pros*	*ton*	*patera*	*Eipon*
go away	to	the	Father.	Said

1500.28 verb 3pl indic aor act	3631.1 conj	1523.2 prep gen	3450.1 art gen pl	3073.6 noun gen pl masc	840.3 prs-pron gen sing
[[a]☆ εἶπαν]	οὖν	ἐκ	τῶν	μαθητῶν	αὐτοῦ
eipan	*oun*	*ek*	*tōn*	*mathētōn*	*autou*
[idem]	therefore	of	the	disciples	his

4242.1 prep	238.3 prs-pron acc pl masc	4949.9 intr-pron sing neu	1498.4 verb 3sing indic pres act	3642.17 dem-pron sing neu	3614.16 rel-pron sing neu
πρὸς	ἀλλήλους,	Τί	ἐστιν	τοῦτο	ὃ
pros	*allēlous*	*Ti*	*estin*	*touto*	*ho*
to	one another,	What	is	this	which

2978.5 verb 3sing indic pres act	2231.3 prs-pron dat 1pl	3261.1 adv	2504.1 conj	3620.3 partic	2311.1 verb 2pl pres act	1466.6 prs-pron acc 1sing
λέγει	ἡμῖν,	Μικρὸν	καὶ	οὐ	θεωρεῖτέ	με,
legei	*hēmin*	*Mikron*	*kai*	*ou*	*theōreite*	*me*
he says	to us,	A little	and	not	you do see	me;

2504.1 conj	3687.1 adv	3261.1 adv	2504.1 conj	3571.33 verb 2pl indic fut mid	1466.6 prs-pron acc 1sing	2504.1 conj
καὶ	πάλιν	μικρὸν	καὶ	ὄψεσθέ	με;	καί
kai	*palin*	*mikron*	*kai*	*opsesthe*	*me*	*kai*
and	again	a little	and	you shall see	me?	and

3617.1 conj	1466.1 prs-pron nom 1sing	5055.1 verb 1sing indic pres act	4242.1 prep	3450.6 art acc sing masc	3824.4 noun acc sing masc
⸀Ὅτι	⸂[b] ἐγὼ ⸃	ὑπάγω	πρὸς	τὸν	πατέρα;
Hoti	*egō*	*hupagō*	*pros*	*ton*	*patera*
Because	I	go away	to	the	Father?

2978.25 verb indic imperf act	3631.1 conj	3642.17 dem-pron sing neu	4949.9 intr-pron sing neu	1498.4 verb 3sing indic pres act
18. Ἔλεγον	οὖν,	⸂ Τοῦτο	τί	ἐστιν
Elegon	*oun*	*Touto*	*ti*	*estin*
They said	therefore,	This	what	is

4949.9 intr-pron sing neu	1498.4 verb 3sing indic pres act	3642.17 dem-pron sing neu	3614.16 rel-pron sing neu	2978.5 verb 3sing indic pres act
[Τί	ἐστιν	τοῦτο]	ὃ	λέγει,
Ti	*estin*	*touto*	*ho*	*legei*
[What	is	this]	which	he says,

3450.16 art sing neu	3261.1 adv	3620.2 partic	3471.5 verb 1pl indic perf act	4949.9 intr-pron sing neu	2953.2 verb sing indic pres act
⸂[a] τὸ ⸃	μικρόν;	οὐκ	οἴδαμεν	τί	λαλεῖ.
to	*mikron*	*ouk*	*oidamen*	*ti*	*lalei*
the	little?	Not	we do know	what	he speaks.

The shadows of the good things gave way to reality. Now the Spirit of Truth need no longer point to Him through the dim mirror of types.

Jesus made it plain that the Spirit enlightens the believer in three areas. First, the Spirit of Truth leads the believers toward a fullness of the truth.

Second, the enlightenment is in the sphere of the future. This aspect is a validation of the truth. It serves the same function which Jesus' miracles did in pointing out who He was by acting as credentials for His person.

Third, the Spirit enlightens the believer in the person and the work of Jesus as Lord.

After His resurrection and a little while before His ascension, Jesus related more about the Spirit's function through the believer. In Acts 1:8 the Lord impressed them with the next phase of His revelation. The Spirit empowers the believer. The empowerment is revealed in three closely connected ways.

First, the Spirit empowers the believer to be a witness with emphasis on "shall be" (Acts 1:8). A witness must be credible. The believer is credible by his character and reputation. The Spirit endeavors to conform the believer to the image of Jesus Christ his Lord (Romans 8:29). The best witness is one who exhibits the virtues and graces of Christ.

Second, the Spirit empowers the believer to conduct his life in such a way that his good works glorify the Father.

Third, the Spirit empowers the believer to function to his full capacity as a witness by anointing his testimony.

16:16,17. "A little while" refers to the stressful time before His death. "Again" refers to the period between His burial and resurrection.

But sorrow had blurred the disciple's vision. They could not understand what He meant.

16:18. They continued to admit their ignorance to each other. He had told them He was going to the Father's house and that He would prepare a place for them so that they might be with Him. Yet, now He spoke as if they would not see Him, but afterward they would see Him. They were perplexed.

16:19. They seemed fearful to expose their ignorance to Him though they freely confessed it to each other. Part of their embar-

16. A little while, and ye shall not see me: Soon you will see me no more, *ALBA* . . . Before long you won't see me, *Adams.*

and again, a little while, and ye shall see me, because I go to the Father: . . . you will see me indeed, *TCNT.*

17. Then said some of his disciples among themselves: Some of Jesus' followers, *SEB* . . . then remarked one to another, *Fenton.*

What is this that he saith unto us: What can He mean, *Norlie* . . . What does He mean by telling us, *Williams.*

A little while, and ye shall not see me:

and again, a little while, and ye shall see me:

and, Because I go to the Father?:

18. They said therefore, What is this that he saith, A little while?: What is the meaning of 'In a little,' *Moffatt* . . . What can He mean by this 'soon'? *ALBA* . . . What does he mean by a little while, *Berkeley.*

we cannot tell what he saith: We have no idea what he is talking about, *Berkeley* . . . We do not understand, *Norlie* . . . we do not know what he is talking about, *TCNT* . . . We do not comprehend it, *Campbell.*

John 16:19

19.a.**Txt:** 02A,017K,036,037,13,byz.Lach
Var: p5,p66,03B,019L,032W,Treg,Alf,Tisc,We/HoSod,UBS/⋆

1091.17 verb 3sing indic aor act	**3631.1** conj	**3450.5** art sing masc	**2400.1** name nom masc	**3617.1** conj	**2286.30** verb indic imperf act
19. Ἔγνω	⸂a οὖν	ὁ ⸃	Ἰησοῦς	ὅτι	ἤθελον
Egnō	*oun*	*ho*	*Iēsous*	*hoti*	*ēthelon*
Knew	therefore		Jesus	that	they desired

840.6 prs-pron acc sing masc	**2049.7** verb inf pres act	**2504.1** conj	**1500.5** verb 3sing indic aor act	**840.2** prs-pron dat pl	**3875.1** prep
αὐτὸν	ἐρωτᾶν,	καὶ	εἶπεν	αὐτοῖς,	Περὶ
auton	*erōtan*	*kai*	*eipen*	*autois*	*Peri*
him	to ask,	and	said	to them,	Concerning

3642.1 dem-pron gen sing	**2195.1** verb 2pl pres act	**3196.2** prep	**238.1** prs-pron gen pl	**3617.1** conj	**1500.3** verb indic aor act
τούτου	ζητεῖτε	μετ'	ἀλλήλων,	ὅτι	εἶπον,
toutou	*zēteite*	*met'*	*allēlōn*	*hoti*	*eipon*
this	do you inquire	among	one another,	that	I said,

3261.1 adv	**2504.1** conj	**3620.3** partic	**2311.1** verb 2pl pres act	**1466.6** prs-pron acc 1sing	**2504.1** conj	**3687.1** adv
Μικρὸν	καὶ	οὐ	θεωρεῖτέ	με,	καὶ	πάλιν
Mikron	*kai*	*ou*	*theōreite*	*me*	*kai*	*palin*
A little	and	not	you do see	me;	and	again

3261.1 adv	**2504.1** conj	**3571.33** verb 2pl indic fut mid	**1466.6** prs-pron acc 1sing	**279.1** partic	**279.1** partic
μικρὸν	καὶ	ὄψεσθέ	με;	**20.** ἀμὴν	ἀμὴν
mikron	*kai*	*opsesthe*	*me*	*amēn*	*amēn*
a little	and	you shall see	me?	Truly	truly

2978.1 verb 1sing pres act	**5050.3** prs-pron dat 2pl	**3617.1** conj	**2772.17** verb 2pl indic fut act	**2504.1** conj	**2331.2** verb 2pl indic fut act
λέγω	ὑμῖν,	ὅτι	κλαύσετε	καὶ	θρηνήσετε
legō	*humin*	*hoti*	*klausete*	*kai*	*thrēnēsete*
I say	to you,	that	will weep	and	will lament

5050.1 prs-pron nom 2pl	**3450.5** art sing masc	**1156.2** conj	**2862.1** noun nom sing masc	**5299.23** verb 3sing indic fut pass	**5050.1** prs-pron nom 2pl
ὑμεῖς,	ὁ	δὲ	κόσμος	χαρήσεται·	ὑμεῖς
humeis	*ho*	*de*	*kosmos*	*charēsetai*	*humeis*
you,	the	but	world	will rejoice;	you

20.a.**Txt:** 02A,017K,019L,032W,036,037,038,13,byz.Gries,Word,Sod
Var: p5,01ℵ-org,03B,05D,it.bo.Lach,Treg,Alf,TiscWe/Ho,Weis,UBS/⋆

1156.2 conj	**3048.17** verb 2pl indic fut pass	**233.1** conj	**3450.9** art nom sing fem	**3049.1** noun nom sing fem	**5050.2** prs-pron gen 2pl
⸂a δὲ ⸃	λυπηθήσεσθε,	ἀλλ'	ἡ	λύπη	ὑμῶν
de	*lupēthēsesthe*	*all'*	*hē*	*lupē*	*humōn*
but	will be grieved,	but	the	grief	your

1519.1 prep	**5315.4** noun acc sing fem	**1090.69** verb 3sing indic fut mid	**3450.9** art nom sing fem	**1129.1** noun nom sing fem	**3615.1** conj
εἰς	χαρὰν	γενήσεται.	**21.** ἡ	γυνὴ	ὅταν
eis	*charan*	*genēsetai*	*hē*	*gunē*	*hotan*
to	joy	shall become.	The	woman	when

4936.2 verb 3sing subj pres act	**3049.4** noun acc sing fem	**2174.4** verb 3sing indic pres act	**3617.1** conj	**2048.3** verb 3sing indic aor act
τίκτῃ,	λύπην	ἔχει,	ὅτι	ἦλθεν
tiktē	*lupēn*	*echei*	*hoti*	*ēlthen*
she gives birth,	grief	has,	because	came

3450.9 art nom sing fem	**5443.2** noun nom sing fem	**840.10** prs-pron gen sing fem	**3615.1** conj	**1156.2** conj	**1074.6** verb 3sing subj aor act
ἡ	ὥρα	αὐτῆς·	ὅταν	δὲ	γεννήσῃ
hē	*hōra*	*autēs*	*hotan*	*de*	*gennēsē*
the	hour	her;	when	but	she brings forth

rassment involved the prior question asked by Peter, Thomas, Philip, and Judas. Yet they failed to understand, so Jesus took the matter to them. The word "knew" implies that He knew from His divine insight the hearts of the disciples. He read their thoughts.

In this verse we note the Lord's concerns about the disciples' lack of understanding. Furthermore, it is characteristic of Jesus to explain what they needed to know. Christ's compassion extends not merely to those suffering physical handicaps, but to those who suffer intellectual and spiritual darkness. The disciples were sincere in their desire to know what Jesus meant. Therefore, in love and compassion Jesus made clear what He meant by "a little while."

19. Now Jesus knew that they were desirous to ask him: Jesus perceived that, *ASV* . . . Jesus took note that, *Rotherham* . . . they were anxious, *Fenton* . . . they wanted to ask Him, *Norlie.*

and said unto them, Do ye enquire among yourselves of that I said: Are you discussing among yourselves why I said, *Norlie* . . . Is it about this remark of Mine that you are questioning one another, *Fenton* . . . Were you arguing with one another, *SEB* . . . seeking each other's opinions, *Adams.*

A little while, and ye shall not see me: and again, a little while, and ye shall see me?:

16:20. Jesus began to explain what was to transpire in a short time. "Verily, verily" should be studied from 1:51 and several other occurrences of the words. "You" and "the world" are in opposition to each other. Both verbs "weep and lament" express outward forms of grief which were fulfilled (Luke 23:27; John 20:11). The disciples were already sorrowful because of His disclosure about His death. Their sorrow was to increase. The world would rejoice because they would believe they had been triumphant over the Saviour.

The death and burial of Jesus seemed to bring to an end all the hopes of the disciples. The Lord had predicted His resurrection, but that was not seen through their tearful eyes. The days of His burial were sorrowful, but the Resurrection was like a burst of light in the darkest night. Their joy was so great that they felt they dare not believe it. Their sorrow was brief, but their joy was lasting. It was rooted in Jesus who died for our sins, was buried, but who came forth in a glorified body with superlative power. All that Jesus had taught was vindicated by His resurrection. The sufferings of Christ, symbolized by the Cross, are to be remembered in the light of His triumphant resurrection from the dead. The disciples' joy was a result of His victory over sin and death in the believer's behalf (Romans 4:25; Galatians 6:14; 1 Peter 1:3).

20. Verily, verily, I say unto you, That ye shall weep and lament: . . . you will be weeping and wailing, *Montgomery* . . . will be pained, *Adams* . . . weeping and moaning, *Berkeley* . . . You shall weep audibly, and you shall audibly lament, *Wuest* . . . you will mourn, *Weymouth* . . . you will cry and mourn, *Beck* . . . will be pained, *Adams.*

but the world shall rejoice: . . . will make merry, *Norlie* . . . but the world will be glad, *Weymouth* . . . while the world feels glad, *Berkeley.*

and ye shall be sorrowful: But though you will be plunged in grief, *NEB* . . . made to grieve, *Wuest* . . . be grief-stricken, *Montgomery.*

but your sorrow shall be turned into joy: . . . your grief will be turned into gladness, *Williams* . . . your grief will be transformed to gladness, *Fenton.*

16:21. Jesus used an experience of life to illustrate both joy and sorrow. Many analogies express joy or grief, but not both. The choice of the comparison is an excellent one for the intensity of both sorrow and joy is particularly appropriate. The primary truth in this very brief parable is that oftentimes suffering is a necessary prelude to lasting joy. Paul stated this principle forcefully: "The sufferings of this present time are not worthy to be compared with the glory which shall be revealed in us" (Romans 8:18).

Jesus illustrated the joy which the disciples would have after the pangs of sorrow. Childbirth is a trying ordeal, yet the sufferings

21. A woman when she is in travail hath sorrow: The mother in childbirth has anguish, *Berkeley* . . . A woman in labour is in pain, *TCNT* . . . is in agony, *Fenton.*

because her hour is come:

3450.16 art sing neu	3676.1 noun sing masc	3620.2 partic	2068.1 adv	3629.1 adv	3285.2 verb 3sing indic pres act
τὸ	παιδίον,	⸀οὐκ	ἔτι	[☆ οὐκέτι]	μνημονεύει
to	*paidion*	*ouk*	*eti*	*ouketi*	*mnēmoneuei*
the	child,	no	longer	[no longer]	she remembers

3450.10 art gen sing fem	2324.2 noun gen sing fem	1217.2 prep	3450.12 art acc sing fem	5315.4 noun acc sing fem	3617.1 conj
τῆς	θλίψεως,	διὰ	τὴν	χαρὰν	ὅτι
tēs	*thlipseōs*	*dia*	*tēn*	*charan*	*hoti*
the	tribulation,	because of	the	joy	that

1074.13 verb 3sing indic aor pass	442.1 noun nom sing masc	1519.1 prep	3450.6 art acc sing masc	2862.4 noun acc sing masc	2504.1 conj
ἐγεννήθη	ἄνθρωπος	εἰς	τὸν	κόσμον.	**22.** καὶ
egennēthē	*anthrōpos*	*eis*	*ton*	*kosmon*	*kai*
has been born	a man	into	the	world.	And

5050.1 prs-pron nom 2pl	3631.1 conj	3049.4 noun acc sing fem	3173.1 conj	3431.1 adv	3431.1 adv	3173.1 conj
ὑμεῖς	οὖν	⸀λύπην	μὲν	νῦν	[☆ νῦν	μὲν
humeis	*oun*	*lupēn*	*men*	*nun*	*nun*	*men*
you	therefore	grief	indeed	now	[now	indeed

22.a.**Var:** p66,01ℵ-corr, 02A,05D,(019), 032W-org,038,33,Lach, Sod

3049.4 noun acc sing fem	2174.2 verb 2pl pres act	2174.40 verb 2pl indic fut act	3687.1 adv	1156.2 conj	3571.28 verb 1sing indic fut mid
λύπην]	⸀ἔχετε·	[a ἕξετε·]	πάλιν	δὲ	ὄψομαι
lupēn	*echete*	*hexete*	*palin*	*de*	*opsomai*
grief]	have;	[will have;]	again	but	I will see

5050.4 prs-pron acc 2pl	2504.1 conj	5299.23 verb 3sing indic fut pass	5050.2 prs-pron gen 2pl	3450.9 art nom sing fem	2559.2 noun nom sing fem
ὑμᾶς,	καὶ	χαρήσεται	ὑμῶν	ἡ	καρδία,
humas	*kai*	*charēsetai*	*humōn*	*hē*	*kardia*
you,	and	shall rejoice	your	the	heart,

2504.1 conj	3450.12 art acc sing fem	5315.4 noun acc sing fem	5050.2 prs-pron gen 2pl	3625.2 num card nom masc	142.2 verb 3sing indic pres act
καὶ	τὴν	χαρὰν	ὑμῶν	οὐδεὶς	⸀αἴρει
kai	*tēn*	*charan*	*humōn*	*oudeis*	*airei*
and	the	joy	your	no one	takes

22.b.**Var:** p5,03B, 05D-org,036,sa.bo.Lach, Treg,AlfWe/Ho

142.31 verb 3sing indic fut act	570.1 prep gen	5050.2 prs-pron gen 2pl	2504.1 conj	1706.1 prep	1552.11 dem-pron dat sing fem
[b ἀρεῖ]	ἀφ'	ὑμῶν.	**23.** καὶ	ἐν	ἐκείνῃ
arei	*aph'*	*humōn*	*kai*	*en*	*ekeinē*
[idem]	from	you.	And	in	that

3450.11 art dat sing fem	2232.3 noun dat sing fem	1466.7 prs-pron acc 1sing	3620.2 partic	2049.15 verb 2pl indic fut act	3625.6 num card neu
τῇ	ἡμέρᾳ	ἐμὲ	οὐκ	ἐρωτήσετε	οὐδέν.
tē	*hēmera*	*eme*	*ouk*	*erōtēsete*	*ouden*
the	day	my	not	you shall ask	nothing.

23.a.**Txt:** p22,01ℵ, 05D-corr,017K,032W, 036,037,038,1,13,byz. Lach
Var: p5,03B,04C, 05D-org,019L,Treg,Alf, Tisc,We/HoWeis,Sod, UBS/☆

279.1 partic	279.1 partic	2978.1 verb 1sing pres act	5050.3 prs-pron dat 2pl	3617.1 conj	3607.8 rel-pron pl neu
Ἀμὴν	ἀμὴν	λέγω	ὑμῖν,	⸂a ὅτι ⸃	⸀ὅσα
Amēn	*amēn*	*legō*	*humin*	*hoti*	*hosa*
Truly	truly	I say	to you,	That	whatever

23.b.**Txt:** 036,037,byz.
Var: p5,03B,04C,019L, it.Lach,Treg,Alf,Tisc, We/Ho,Weis,Sod,UBS/☆

300.1 partic	300.1 partic	4948.10 indef-pron sing neu	153.15 verb 2pl subj aor act	3450.6 art acc sing masc	3824.4 noun acc sing masc
ἂν	[b☆ ἂν	τι]	αἰτήσητε	τὸν	πατέρα
an	*an*	*ti*	*aitēsēte*	*ton*	*patera*
		[whatever]	you may ask	the	Father

are quickly forgotten after the child has been born. The prophets spoke of the analogy of childbirth frequently (Isaiah 21:3; 37:3; 66:7; Hosea 13:13; Micah 4:9). The reality always exceeds the illustration, and here the sorrow and the joy are extremely intensified.

Just as a woman in childbirth experiences suffering, so the disciples would have sorrow. Some commentators have pressed the analogy to refer to a specific woman or persons. Some see the woman as Eve, whose seed would bruise the head of the serpent (Genesis 3:15). Others think Jesus drew the figure from His own birth. Another theory is that the woman is the Church in travail until the glorified Christ appears. Some even go so far as to say that the woman is the one who brings forth a man-child (Revelation 12:1-5).

It is not necessary to see in the analogy anything more than a most vivid and apt comparison. The illustration is taken from the universal experience of women: the joy of a child exceeding the sorrow of labor.

but as soon as she is delivered of the child, she remembereth no more the anguish: . . . but when the baby is born, she forgets her pain, *Williams* . . . her agony, *Phillips* . . . the affliction, *Concordant, Berkeley* . . . the tribulation, *Rotherham* . . . the distress, *Sawyer* . . . is put out of her mind, *BB*.

for joy that a man is born into the world: . . . she's so happy a child was brought into the world, *Beck* . . . but when the baby is born, *Williams* . . . a human being, *Murdock*.

16:22. Jesus carefully explained to them what He meant by "a little while" (verse 18). He told them three times that they would see Him again (verses 16,17,19). "See" (Greek, *opsomai*) is the same Greek verb in the four occurrences.

Notice that Jesus used the singular noun for "heart" (Greek, *hē kardia*) to indicate the unity of the group of believers concerning the joy they would all share. Their sorrow would continue for a little while, but their joy would be everlasting. Their joy would not depend upon the circumstances. It would be as eternal as His completed victory.

His terrible death by crucifixion would bring them sorrow, but their joy would come from His resurrection. When He said, "I will see you again," He assured them of His future life and theirs, and He promised that their rejoicing would endure.

22. And ye now therefore have sorrow: And so for the present you are also in distress, *Fenton* . . . have grief, *Rotherham*.

but I will see you again:

and your heart shall rejoice: . . . and then your hearts will be glad, *Norlie* . . . will thrill with joy, *Phillips*.

and your joy no man taketh away from you: . . . no one can rob you of your happiness, *Williams* . . . and no one shall be able to deprive you of that joy, *Berkeley* . . . and your joy shall no man snatch away from you, *Montgomery* . . . will rob you of your joy, *TCNT*.

16:23. The "day" Jesus spoke of was ushered in on the Day of Pentecost. The Spirit descended to become to them their guide "into all truth" (verse 13). They would not need to ask the questions they were now asking. The questions that perplexed them were: "What is this 'little while'? How can we know the way? Where are You going? How is it that You will manifest yourself to us and not to the world?"

One of the most interesting and practical phrases occurs in this verse: "In my name." The term is used in this chapter three times (verses 23,24,26). In chapter 14 Jesus used it three times (verses 13,14,26). Chapter 15 has the phrase once (verse 16). It is obvious by this repetition that great advantage accrues to the one who uses

23. And in that day ye shall ask me nothing: . . . will request nothing from me, *Fenton*.

Verily, verily, I say unto you:

Whatsoever ye shall ask the Father in my name, he will give it you: . . . he will give it you in my name, *HBIE* . . . he will grant

John 16:24

1706.1 prep	3450.3 art dat sing	3549.4 noun dat sing neu	1466.2 prs-pron gen 1sing	1319.38 verb 3sing indic fut act	5050.3 prs-pron dat 2pl
☆ ἐν	τῷ	ὀνόματί	μου	δώσει	ὑμῖν.
en	tō	onomati	mou	dōsei	humin
in	the	name	my	he will give	you.

23.c.**Txt:** 02A,04C-corr, 05D,017K,032W,036, 038,1,13,byz.it.bo.Lach **Var:** 01ℵ,03B,04C-org, 019L,037,sa.Treg,Alf, TiscWe/Ho,Weis,Sod, UBS/☆

1319.38 verb 3sing indic fut act	5050.3 prs-pron dat 2pl	1706.1 prep	3450.3 art dat sing	3549.4 noun dat sing neu	1466.2 prs-pron gen 1sing
[c δώσει	ὑμῖν	ἐν	τῷ	ὀνόματί	μου.]
dōsei	humin	en	tō	onomati	mou
[he will give	you	in	the	name	my.]

2175.1 conj	732.1 adv	3620.2 partic	153.12 verb 2pl indic aor act	3625.6 num card neu	1706.1 prep	3450.3 art dat sing
24. ἕως	ἄρτι	οὐκ	ᾐτήσατε	οὐδὲν	ἐν	τῷ
heōs	arti	ouk	ētēsate	ouden	en	tō
Until	now	not	you asked	nothing	in	the

3549.4 noun dat sing neu	1466.2 prs-pron gen 1sing	153.2 verb 2pl pres act	2504.1 conj	2956.41 verb 2pl indic fut mid
ὀνόματί	μου·	αἰτεῖτε,	καὶ	λήψεσθε,
onomati	mou	aiteite	kai	lēpsesthe
name	my:	ask,	and	you shall receive,

24.a.**Txt:** 03B-corr,04C, 017K,033X,036,037, 038,byz.Sod **Var:** 01ℵ,02A,03B-org, 05D,019L,037,Lach,Tisc rAlf,TiscWe/Ho,Weis, UBS/☆

2956.47 verb 2pl indic fut mid	2419.1 conj	3450.9 art nom sing fem	5315.1 noun sing fem	5050.2 prs-pron gen 2pl
[a☆ λήμψεσθε,]	ἵνα	ἡ	χαρὰ	ὑμῶν
lēmpsesthe	hina	hē	chara	humōn
[idem]	that	the	joy	your

1498.10 verb 3sing subj pres act	3997.32 verb nom sing fem part perf pass	3642.18 dem-pron pl neu	1706.1 prep	3804.3 noun dat pl fem
ᾖ	πεπληρωμένη.	25. Ταῦτα	ἐν	παροιμίαις
ē	peplērōmenē	Tauta	en	paroimiais
may be	having been full.	These things	in	allegories

25.a.**Txt:** 02A,04C-corr, 05D-corr,017K,036,037, (038),byz.Lach **Var:** 01ℵ,03B,04C-org, 05D-org,019L,032W, 033X,33,sa.bo.Gries Treg,Alf,Tisc,We/Ho, Weis,Sod,UBS/☆

2953.38 verb 1sing indic perf act	5050.3 prs-pron dat 2pl	233.1 conj	2048.34 verb 3sing indic pres	5443.2 noun nom sing fem
λελάληκα	ὑμῖν·	(a ἀλλ')	ἔρχεται	ὥρα
lelalēka	humin	all'	erchetai	hōra
I have spoken	to you;	but	is coming	an hour

3616.1 conj	3620.2 partic	2068.1 adv	3629.1 adv	1706.1 prep	3804.3 noun dat pl fem
ὅτε	(οὐκ	ἔτι	[☆ οὐκέτι]	ἐν	παροιμίαις
hote	ouk	eti	ouketi	en	paroimiais
when	no	longer	[no longer]	in	allegories

2953.25 verb 1sing act	5050.3 prs-pron dat 2pl	233.2 conj	3816.3 noun dat sing fem	3875.1 prep	3450.2 art gen sing
λαλήσω	ὑμῖν,	ἀλλὰ	παῤῥησίᾳ	περὶ	τοῦ
lalēsō	humin	alla	parrhēsia	peri	tou
I will speak	to you,	but	plainly	concerning	the

25.b.**Txt:** 04C-corr,07E, 036,037,1,13,byz.Gries **Var:** (01),02A,03B, 04C-org,05D,017K, 019L,033X,038,Lach, Treg,Alf,TiscWe/Ho, Weis,Sod,UBS/☆

3824.2 noun gen sing masc	310.8 verb 1sing indic fut act	514.11 verb 1sing indic fut act	5050.3 prs-pron dat 2pl	1706.1 prep
πατρὸς	(ἀναγγελῶ	[b☆ ἀπαγγελῶ]	ὑμῖν.	26. ἐν
patros	anangelō	apangelō	humin	en
Father	I will announce	[idem]	to you.	In

1552.11 dem-pron dat sing fem	3450.11 art dat sing fem	2232.3 noun dat sing fem	1706.1 prep	3450.3 art dat sing	3549.4 noun dat sing neu
ἐκείνῃ	τῇ	ἡμέρᾳ	ἐν	τῷ	ὀνόματί
ekeinē	tē	hēmera	en	tō	onomati
that	the	day	in	the	name

the term. (However, the phrase was never meant to be an incantation to produce magic effects.) Advantages are promised under certain conditions. Furthermore, blessings bestowed may not always be personal to the one who uses "in Jesus' name." Sometimes the request is in behalf of another. Beyond these the use of His name is intended to glorify the Father.

Before one can use the name of Jesus effectively he must have an intimate relationship with Him. By virtue of the relationship that person will know the desires of his Lord by the Spirit and His Word. The relationship with Jesus and the knowledge of His will are followed by a commission and anointing to function as Jesus would if He were on earth himself. The disciple can then make his request in the name of Jesus with confidence that God will accomplish that which he asks.

it to you in my Name, *TCNT* . . . because you use My name, *LivB.*

16:24. The disciples had asked nothing in His name because He was with them. He had not been fully known for who He was, because He was to be revealed by the Resurrection and by the Holy Spirit's work of glorifying Him as the Son of God.

Notice their asking was to be done in His name as if He were the One making the request to the Father. Again, see the prior verse and reference stated there.

24. Hitherto have ye asked nothing in my name: And yet you have not asked for anything, *Weymouth* . . . So far you haven't asked for anything in My name, *Beck.*

ask, and ye shall receive: . . . you must keep on asking, *Williams* . . . shall request, *Wuest* . . . you shall obtain, *Concordant* . . . do so, and it will be answered, *BB.*

that your joy may be full: . . . so that your joy may be complete, *Norlie* . . . in order that your enjoyment may be complete, *Fenton* . . . may be overflowing, *Phillips* . . . may be full to the brim, *Williams.*

16:25. "These things" refers to Jesus' sayings in this discourse. "In proverbs" is in contrast to "plainly." The thought is that Jesus could not say things He wished because at this time they had little capacity to understand. "The time" He referred to is the one of 16:23. The "hour" (*hōra*) was the period from His resurrection until the Holy Spirit's outpouring at Pentecost (Acts 2). The clearer revelation of Him was only possible by these two great events. The Resurrection sealed Him forever as the Lord from heaven and validated His manifestation of the Father. The outpouring of the Spirit caused every believer to know that Jesus lives.

25. These things have I spoken unto you in proverbs: . . . in illustrations, *Berkeley* . . . in figurative speech, *Norlie* . . . in dark sayings, *ASV* . . . in similitudes, *HBIE* . . . veiled speech, *Beck* . . . in figures of speech, *Fenton* . . . symbolic examples, *SEB.*

but the time cometh, when I shall no more speak unto you in proverbs: . . . use examples like that, *SEB* . . . when no longer in similes and comparisons, *Wuest.*

but I shall shew you plainly of the Father: . . . but shall be reporting to you boldly concerning, *Concordant* . . . about the Father Whom I announce to you, *Fenton* . . . I will tell you concerning the Father, *Wuest* . . . shall talk about My Father in plain words, *Norlie, Beck.*

16:26. Jesus began to unfold to the disciples their full state of communion with the Father and himself. He stated the relationship in the strongest terms. Note He used the word "day" (Greek, *hēmera*) to indicate the long period, not "hour" of the last verse. By the use of "day," the implication is that all believers are included. Jesus used the term "in my name" three times in four verses (16:23-26). The relationship between the believer and the Son is so close that when any request is made to the Father, the Father sees Christ's

26. At that day ye shall ask in my name: . . . you will pray in my name, *ALBA* . . . in view of all that I am in His estimation, *Wuest* . . . you will be requesting, *Concordant* . . . you will use my name to ask for things, *SEB* . . . you shall pray in my name, *Montgomery.*

1466.2 prs-pron gen 1sing	153.34 verb 2pl indic fut mid	2504.1 conj	3620.3 partic	2978.1 verb 1sing pres act	5050.3 prs-pron dat 2pl
μου	αἰτήσεσθε,	καὶ	οὐ	λέγω	ὑμῖν
mou	aitēsesthe	kai	ou	legō	humin
my	you shall ask;	and	not	I say	to you

3617.1 conj	1466.1 prs-pron nom 1sing	2049.8 verb 1sing act	3450.6 art acc sing masc	3824.4 noun acc sing masc	3875.1 prep
ὅτι	ἐγὼ	ἐρωτήσω	τὸν	πατέρα	περὶ
hoti	egō	erōtēsō	ton	patera	peri
that	I	will ask	the	Father	for

5050.2 prs-pron gen 2pl	840.5 prs-pron nom sing masc	1056.1 conj	3450.5 art sing masc	3824.1 noun nom sing masc	5205.3 verb 3sing indic pres act
ὑμῶν·	27. αὐτὸς	γὰρ	ὁ	πατὴρ	φιλεῖ
humōn	autos	gar	ho	patēr	philei
you,	him	for	the	Father	loves

27.a.**Txt:** 03B,04C,05D, 019L,032W,1,13,etc.byz. Treg,Alf,Tisc,We/HoSod, UBS/☆
Var: p5,01א,02A,038, 33,Lach,Weis

27.b.**Var:** 01א-corr,03B, 04C-org,05D,019L, 033X,sa.bo.Treg,Alf, We/Ho

28.a.**Txt:** p5,p22,01א, 02A,04C-corr,017K,036, 037,038,1,13,byz.Gries
Var: 03B,04C-org,019L, 033X,33,Lach,Treg,Alf, Tisc,We/HoWeis,Sod, UBS/☆

5050.4 prs-pron acc 2pl	3617.1 conj	5050.1 prs-pron nom 2pl	1466.7 prs-pron acc 1sing	5205.10 verb 2pl indic perf act	2504.1 conj
ὑμᾶς,	ὅτι	ὑμεῖς	ἐμὲ	πεφιλήκατε,	καὶ
humas	hoti	humeis	eme	pephilēkate	kai
you,	because	you	me	have loved,	and

3961.41 verb 2pl indic perf act	3617.1 conj	1466.1 prs-pron nom 1sing	3706.2 prep	3450.2 art gen sing	2296.2 noun gen sing masc
πεπιστεύκατε	ὅτι	ἐγὼ	παρὰ	⸂a τοῦ ⸃	⸀ θεοῦ
pepisteukate	hoti	egō	para	tou	theou
have believed	that	I	from		God

3824.2 noun gen sing masc	1814.1 verb indic aor act	1814.1 verb indic aor act	3706.2 prep	1523.2 prep gen
[b πατρός]	ἐξῆλθον.	28. ἐξῆλθον	⸀☆ παρὰ	[a ἐκ]
patros	exēlthon	exēlthon	para	ek
[Father]	came out.	I came out	from	[out of]

3450.2 art gen sing	3824.2 noun gen sing masc	2504.1 conj	2048.24 verb 1sing indic perf act	1519.1 prep	3450.6 art acc sing masc	2862.4 noun acc sing masc
τοῦ	πατρὸς	καὶ	ἐλήλυθα	εἰς	τὸν	κόσμον·
tou	patros	kai	elēlutha	eis	ton	kosmon
the	Father	and	have come	into	the	world;

3687.1 adv	856.3 verb 1sing indic pres act	3450.6 art acc sing masc	2862.4 noun acc sing masc	2504.1 conj	4057.1 verb 1sing indic pres
πάλιν	ἀφίημι	τὸν	κόσμον	καὶ	πορεύομαι
palin	aphiēmi	ton	kosmon	kai	poreuomai
again	I leave	the	world	and	go

29.a.**Txt:** p5-corr,02A, 04C-corr,05D-corr,017K, 019L,032W,036,037,13, byz.Lach
Var: 01א,03B,04C-org, 05D-org,038,041,Treg Alf,Tisc,We/Ho,Weis, Sod,UBS/☆

29.b.**Var:** 01א,03B,04C, 05D,Lach,Treg,Alf,Tisc, We/Ho,WeisSod,UBS/☆

4242.1 prep	3450.6 art acc sing masc	3824.4 noun acc sing masc	2978.3 verb 3pl pres act	840.4 prs-pron dat sing
πρὸς	τὸν	πατέρα.	29. Λέγουσιν	⸂a αὐτῷ ⸃
pros	ton	patera	Legousin	autō
to	the	Father.	Say	to him

3450.7 art pl masc	3073.5 noun nom pl masc	840.3 prs-pron gen sing	1481.14 verb 2sing impr aor act	3431.1 adv	1706.1 prep
οἱ	μαθηταὶ	αὐτοῦ,	Ἴδε,	νῦν	[b☆+ ἐν]
hoi	mathētai	autou	Ide	nun	en
the	disciples	his,	Lo,	now	[in]

3816.3 noun dat sing fem	2953.3 verb 2sing indic pres act	2504.1 conj	3804.2 noun acc sing fem	3625.5 num card acc fem
παῤῥησίᾳ	λαλεῖς,	καὶ	παροιμίαν	οὐδεμίαν
parrhēsia	laleis	kai	paroimian	oudemian
plainly	you speak,	and	allegory	no

own desire and merit as prompting the request. The believer never asks in his own merits, but those of Jesus.

and I say not unto you, that I will pray the Father for you: I will intercede with the Father for you, *TCNT* . . . and I shall not have to ask the Father in your behalf, *Norlie* . . . but I don't promise to ask, *Adams* . . . I will entreat, *Campbell.*

16:27. The work of Jesus is so thorough and effective that believers gain a like personal relationship with the Father as Christ has. "Himself" is emphatic and emphasizes that the Father's love for the believer is equal to Christ's love for the disciples. The Greek word for "love" indicates a fondness or friendship love. It is the word for a fellowship type of love. In 5:20 Jesus stated that the Father loves (Greek, *philei*) the Son.

"Because" states the reason the Father loves the believer. Two reasons are given. First, "ye have loved me." "Me" is stressed. The love began at a time in the past and continues to the present. This word for love is the same as the "love" by which God loves the believer (*philei*). Jesus has called the disciples "friends" (Greek, *philous*) (15:15). The words for "friend" and "friendship love" are clearly related. By acting as a friend one shows friendly love. The believer who loves Jesus is loved by the Father. Observe the mutual love of the believers, the Son, and the Father.

The second reason the Father loves the believer is that the believer has "believed," believed in the past and continues to believe.

27. For the Father himself loveth you: . . . dearly loveth you, *Rotherham* . . . is fond of you, *Wuest* . . . tenderly loves you Himself, *Williams* . . . holds you dear, *Weymouth.*

because ye have loved me: Because ye have dearly loved me, *Rotherham* . . . you now tenderly love me, *Williams.*

and have believed that I came out from God: . . . that I from the presence of God came, *Wuest.*

16:28. The stressed idea is that the Son came out of the Father. The emphasis on the Son's proceeding from the same eternal substance as the Father is very strong. The church fathers called it the eternal generation of the Son. The truth of His origin is stressed so often by the Lord that to pass over it lightly would be a terrible mistake. (Review chapters 1:1; 3:13,31; 6:62; 8:42.)

This verse is a concise, Biblical creed as given by Jesus himself. The Lord came out of the Father to seek and to save some out of the world. He left the world to go to the Father as an intercessor in behalf of those whom He redeemed.

28. I came forth from the Father, and am come into the world: From the Father I came and I entered the world, *Moffatt* . . . the universe, *Wuest* . . . I left the Father, *Beck.*

again, I leave the world, and go to the Father: . . . and going back to the Father, *Williams* . . . the universe behind and proceed on my way, *Wuest* . . . and return to the Father, *Phillips.*

16:29. The Lord seems to speak as He had before, yet the disciples seem to understand better than they had (verses 16-19). They are the same words "plainly" and "no proverb" which He used in verse 25.

29. His disciples said unto him, Lo, now speakest thou plainly, and speakest no proverb: . . . thou spekist opynli, *Wycliffe* . . . no figure of speech, *Weymouth.*

16:30. Sometimes we think that we know. Rarely do we know that we know. But here the disciples did not know that they did

2978.4 verb 2sing indic pres act	3431.1 adv	3471.5 verb 1pl indic perf act	3617.1 conj	3471.3 verb 2sing indic perf act
λέγεις.	30. νῦν	οἴδαμεν	ὅτι	οἶδας
legeis	*nun*	*oidamen*	*hoti*	*oidas*
speak.	Now	we know	that	you have known

3820.1 adj	2504.1 conj	3620.3 partic	5367.3 noun acc sing fem	2174.3 verb 2sing indic pres act	2419.1 conj	4949.3 intr-pron nom sing
πάντα,	καὶ	οὐ	χρείαν	ἔχεις	ἵνα	τίς
panta	*kai*	*ou*	*chreian*	*echeis*	*hina*	*tis*
all things,	and	not	need	has	that	anyone

4622.4 prs-pron acc 2sing	2049.1 verb 3sing pres act	1706.1 prep	3642.5 dem-pron dat sing masc	3961.7 verb 1pl indic pres act	3617.1 conj
σε	ἐρωτᾷ.	ἐν	τούτῳ	πιστεύομεν	ὅτι
se	*erōta*	*en*	*toutō*	*pisteuomen*	*hoti*
you	should ask.	By	this	we believe	that

570.3 prep gen	2296.2 noun gen sing masc	1814.2 verb 2sing indic aor act	552.6 verb 3sing indic aor pass	840.2 prs-pron dat pl
ἀπὸ	θεοῦ	ἐξῆλθες.	31. Ἀπεκρίθη	αὐτοῖς
apo	*theou*	*exēlthes*	*Apekrithē*	*autois*
from	God	you came forth.	Answered	them

3450.5 art sing masc	2400.1 name nom masc	732.1 adv	3961.2 verb 2pl pres act	1481.20 verb 2sing impr aor mid
(a ὁ)	Ἰησοῦς,	Ἄρτι	πιστεύετε;	32. ἰδοὺ,
ho	*Iēsous*	*Arti*	*pisteuete*	*idou*
	Jesus,	Now	do you believe?	Lo,

2048.34 verb 3sing indic pres	5443.2 noun nom sing fem	2504.1 conj	3431.1 adv	2048.26 verb 3sing indic perf act	2419.1 conj
ἔρχεται	ὥρα	καὶ	(a νῦν)	ἐλήλυθεν,	ἵνα
erchetai	*hōra*	*kai*	*nun*	*elēluthen*	*hina*
is coming	an hour	and	now	has come,	that

4505.3 verb 2pl subj aor pass	1524.3 adj nom sing masc	1519.1 prep	3450.17 art pl neu	2375.13 adj pl neu	2504.1 conj
σκορπισθῆτε	ἕκαστος	εἰς	τὰ	ἴδια,	(καὶ
skorpisthēte	*hekastos*	*eis*	*ta*	*idia*	*kai*
you will be scattered	each	to	the	his own,	and

1466.7 prs-pron acc 1sing	2476.2 conj	3304.1 adj sing	856.16 verb 2pl subj aor act	2504.1 conj	3620.2 partic
ἐμὲ	[☆ κἀμὲ]	μόνον	ἀφῆτε·	καὶ	οὐκ
eme	*kame*	*monon*	*aphēte*	*kai*	*ouk*
me	[and me]	alone	you will leave;	and	not

1498.2 verb 1sing indic pres act	3304.2 adj nom sing masc	3617.1 conj	3450.5 art sing masc	3824.1 noun nom sing masc	3196.2 prep
εἰμὶ	μόνος,	ὅτι	ὁ	πατὴρ	μετ'
eimi	*monos*	*hoti*	*ho*	*patēr*	*met'*
I am	alone,	for	the	Father	with

1466.3 prs-pron gen 1sing	1498.4 verb 3sing indic pres act	3642.18 dem-pron pl neu	2953.38 verb 1sing indic perf act	5050.3 prs-pron dat 2pl
ἐμοῦ	ἐστιν.	33. ταῦτα	λελάληκα	ὑμῖν
emou	*estin*	*tauta*	*lelalēka*	*humin*
me	is.	These things	I have spoken	to you

2419.1 conj	1706.1 prep	1466.5 prs-pron dat 1sing	1503.4 noun acc sing fem	2174.9 verb 2pl subj pres act	1706.1 prep
ἵνα	ἐν	ἐμοὶ	εἰρήνην	ἔχητε.	ἐν
hina	*en*	*emoi*	*eirēnēn*	*echēte*	*en*
that	in	me	peace	you may have.	In

31.a.**Txt:** 01ℵ,02A,05D, 017K,019L,036,037,1, 13,byz.Gries,LachWeis, Sod
Var: p22,p66,03B,04C, 032W,038,Treg,AlfTisc, We/Ho,UBS/☆

32.a.**Txt:** 04C-corr, 05D-corr,017K,036,037, 038,1,13,byz.it.
Var: 01ℵ,02A,03B, 04C-org,05D-org,019L, 033X,33,bo.Lach,Treg, AlfTisc,We/Ho,Weis,Sod, UBS/☆

not know. They thought they knew, yet they did not. They would all forsake Him before the night was over. He had revealed to them the thoughts of their hearts (verse 19). This is convincing proof of His knowledge. For the first time they seemed impressed with His knowledge even though on numerous occasions He had manifested divine knowledge (1:48).

Because of His perfect knowledge, they believed. God is all-knowing and Jesus revealed the attribute; therefore they believed that He "came from God." What they realized, however, was sufficient to build toward the complete revelation of His person and work.

16:31. The disciples supposed that their knowledge was complete. Jesus did not stop to correct their half-knowledge. The Lord reserved that ministry for the Spirit. Jesus did point out that their confidence in Him was shallow. His question cautioned them about their immature assurance. His tone perhaps expressed a touch of disappointment and a bit of warning. The text reveals how much was lacking in their knowledge of Him and commitment to Him.

16:32. The statement refers to verse 25. Note the meaning of "hour" as compared with "day" in verse 26. The hour was at hand. In a few hours He was to be crucified, and in 3 days the Resurrection would occur. Between these two events they were to experience unparalleled sorrow.

"Scattered" is descriptive of sheep left without a shepherd (10:11,12). The same Greek word for "scattered" is used here as in John 10:12 (see Zechariah 13:7). "Each to his own" is fulfilled in this very Gospel (20:10).

The disciples were told that they would "leave" Him, but that He was not alone "because the Father is with me." But Christ was truly man as He was truly God. As a man He had the need of sympathy in the hour of trial as any man would. Surely He felt deeply the pain of being forsaken by those He loved.

16:33. In this verse Jesus closed His wonderful discourse. He had spoken to encourage the disciples in their hour of sorrow and to comfort them by His promise of the Spirit and His own presence in the near future. In the distant future they were promised a place with Him. Peace (Greek, *eirēnēn*) sums up His message of comfort. The two aspects of peace are the absence of all confusion, disorder, and conflict, but also a beautiful harmonious relationship.

Jesus faithfully alerted His disciples to the fact that the world has no harmony or unity with believers. The world will cause "trib-

30. Now are we sure that thou knowest all things: Now we are certain, *ALBA* . . . that you are acquainted with, *Berkeley* . . . that You have the knowledge of everything, *Norlie.*

and needest not that any man should ask thee: . . . requirest no one to, *HistNT* . . . need to be pressed with, *Weymouth* . . . and need no one to put questions to you, *Moffatt* . . . and don't need anyone to tell You anything, *LivB.*

by this we believe that thou camest forth from God:

31. Jesus answered them, Do ye now believe?: . . . believe me now, *Weymouth* . . . Do you believe that already, *TCNT.*

32. Behold, the hour cometh, yea, is now come, that ye shall be scattered: . . . but mark, *Weymouth* . . . it's already here, *SEB* . . . it's here now, *Beck* . . . The hour is coming—in fact, it is already here—when you will be scattered to the winds, *Norlie* . . . you shall disperse, *Campbell* . . . hither and thither, *Fenton* . . . each going his own way, leaving me alone, *TCNT.*

every man to his own, and shall leave me alone: . . . each to his place, *Berkeley* . . . to the things he possesses, *Wuest* . . . every man for himself, and I shall be left alone, *Norlie* . . . You will abandon me, *SEB.*

and yet I am not alone, because the Father is with me: Yet I am not really alone, *Phillips.*

33. These things I have spoken unto you: I have told you this, *Norlie.*

that in me ye might have peace: . . . so that through me you may find peace, *Montgomery* . . . united with me, *ALBA* . . . you might enjoy perfect confidence in Me, *Fenton* . . . that you through union with me may have peace, *Williams.*

John 17:1

33.a.**Var:** 05D,1,13, Elzev,Lach

3450.3 art dat sing	2862.3 noun dat sing masc	2324.4 noun acc sing fem	2174.2 verb 2pl pres act	2174.40 verb 2pl indic fut act
τῷ	κόσμῳ	θλῖψιν	⸀ἔχετε˙	[a ἕξετε˙]
tō	*kosmō*	*thlipsin*	*echete*	*hexete*
the	world	tribulation	you have;	[you will have.]

233.2 conj	2270.2 verb 2pl impr pres act	1466.1 prs-pron nom 1sing	3390.13 verb 1sing indic perf act	3450.6 art acc sing masc
ἀλλὰ	θαρσεῖτε,	ἐγὼ	νενίκηκα	τὸν
alla	*tharseite*	*egō*	*nenikēka*	*ton*
but	be of good courage,	I	have overcome	the

1.a.**Txt:** p60,02A,04C, 05D,019L,032W,1,13, etc.byz.Lach,Sod **Var:** 01א,03B,038,Tisc We/Ho,Weis,UBS/☆

2862.4 noun acc sing masc	3642.18 dem-pron pl neu	2953.27 verb 3sing indic aor act	3450.5 art sing masc	2400.1 name nom masc
κόσμον.	17:1. Ταῦτα	ἐλάλησεν	⸂a ὁ ⸃	Ἰησοῦς,
kosmon	*Tauta*	*elalēsen*	*ho*	*Iēsous*
world.	These things	spoke		Jesus,

1.b.**Txt:** 02A,04C-corr, 017K,036,037,byz.it. **Var:** 01א,03B,04C-org, 05D,019L,033X,038,33, bo.Lach,Treg,Alf,Tisc, We/Ho,WeisSod,UBS/☆

1.c.**Txt:** 02A,04C-corr, 017K,036,037,byz.it. **Var:** 01א,03B,04C-org, 05D,019L,033X,038,33, bo.Lach,Treg,Alf,Tisc, We/HoWeis,Sod,UBS/☆

2504.1 conj	1854.2 verb 3sing indic aor act	1854.5 verb nom sing masc part aor act	3450.8 art acc pl masc	3652.8 noun acc pl masc
καὶ	⸀ἐπῆρεν	[b☆ ἐπάρας]	τοὺς	ὀφθαλμοὺς
kai	*epēren*	*eparas*	*tous*	*ophthalmous*
and	lifted up	[having lifted up]	the	eyes

840.3 prs-pron gen sing	1519.1 prep	3450.6 art acc sing masc	3636.4 noun acc sing masc	2504.1 conj	1500.5 verb 3sing indic aor act
αὐτοῦ	εἰς	τὸν	οὐρανὸν	⸂c καὶ ⸃	εἶπεν,
autou	*eis*	*ton*	*ouranon*	*kai*	*eipen*
his	to	the	heaven	and	said,

3824.5 noun voc sing masc	2048.26 verb 3sing indic perf act	3450.9 art nom sing fem	5443.2 noun nom sing fem	1386.13 verb 2sing impr aor act
Πάτερ,	ἐλήλυθεν	ἡ	ὥρα˙	δόξασόν
Pater	*elēluthen*	*hē*	*hōra*	*doxason*
Father,	has come	the	hour;	glorify

1.d.**Txt:** 04C-corr,017K, 019L,036,037,13,byz. **Var:** 01א,02A,03B, 04C-org,05D,038,bo. LachTreg,Alf,Word,Tisc, We/Ho,Weis,Sod,UBS/☆

1.e.**Txt:** 02A,04C-corr, 05D,017K,019L,036, 037,038,1,13,byz.it.sa. bo.Gries,Lach,Sod **Var:** 01א,03B,04C-org, 032W,Treg,Tisc,We/Ho, Weis,UBS/☆

4622.2 prs-pron gen 2sing	3450.6 art acc sing masc	5048.4 noun acc sing masc	2419.1 conj	2504.1 conj	3450.5 art sing masc
σου	τὸν	υἱόν,	ἵνα	⸂d καὶ ⸃	ὁ
sou	*ton*	*huion*	*hina*	*kai*	*ho*
your	the	Son,	that	also	the

5048.1 noun nom sing masc	4622.2 prs-pron gen 2sing	1386.11 verb 3sing subj aor act	4622.4 prs-pron acc 2sing	2503.1 conj
υἱὸς	⸂e σου ⸃	δοξάσῃ	⸆σέ˙	2. καθὼς
huios	*sou*	*doxasē*	*se*	*kathōs*
Son	your	may glorify	you;	as

1319.13 verb 2sing indic aor act	840.4 prs-pron dat sing	1833.4 noun acc sing fem	3820.10 adj gen sing fem	4418.2 noun gen sing fem	2419.1 conj
ἔδωκας	αὐτῷ	ἐξουσίαν	πάσης	σαρκός,	ἵνα
edōkas	*autō*	*exousian*	*pasēs*	*sarkos*	*hina*
you gave	him	authority	over all	flesh,	that

3820.17 adj sing neu	3614.16 rel-pron sing neu	1319.11 verb 2sing indic act	840.4 prs-pron dat sing	1319.20 verb 3sing subj aor act
πᾶν	ὃ	δέδωκας	αὐτῷ,	⸀δώσῃ
pan	*ho*	*dedōkas*	*autō*	*dōsē*
all	which	you have given	him,	he should give

2.a.**Var:** 03B,07E,030U, 036,037,13,Alf,We/Ho, Sod

1319.38 verb 3sing indic fut act	840.2 prs-pron dat pl	2205.4 noun acc sing fem	164.1 adj sing	3642.9 dem-pron nom sing fem	1156.2 conj
[a δώσει]	αὐτοῖς	ζωὴν	αἰώνιον.	3. αὕτη	δέ
dōsei	*autois*	*zōēn*	*aiōnion*	*hautē*	*de*
[he will give]	to them	life	eternal.	This	and

ulation" or distress for those who are not in agreement with them.

"Overcome" is a perfect tense verb meaning He has gained the victory over the world, and He possesses the triumph. The word means "to conquer," "to prevail," and "to be victorious." Jesus overcame the world by His sinless life and His substitutionary death.

In the world ye shall have tribulations: . . . you are under pressure, *Berkeley* . . . you have affliction, *Weymouth* . . . you will find trouble, *TCNT* . . . you have suffering, *ALBA*.

but be of good cheer: . . . but be courageous, *Montgomery* . . . But be brave! *TEV* . . . But keep up your courage, *Weymouth* . . . but be confident! *Berkeley* . . . But take heart, *Norlie* . . . but, never lose heart, *Phillips* . . . but cheer up! *LivB*.

I have overcome the world: I have conquered the world, *Williams, Fenton, ALBA* . . . I have defeated, *TEV* . . . I have won the victory over the world, *Weymouth* . . . I have vanquished, *Murdock* . . . I have come off victorious over the world with a permanent victory, *Wuest*.

17:1. How wonderful that the Gospel of John records our Lord's intercessory prayer. The most intimate feelings, intentions, and thoughts are spoken prior to death. In this prayer He bared His heart. The focus is on Jesus alone. The prayer was prayed somewhere between the Upper Room and the Garden of Gethsemane. His upward look is symbolic of His confident victory.

His sonship is the foundation for His prayer. Jesus said "the Father," or "My Father," but never "our Father" except when He taught His disciples to pray. He stressed His relationship to the Father as being unique. "The hour" was the term for His sufferings and crucifixion in which His atoning work would be completed.

By His suffering as an innocent sacrifice and His resurrection from the dead, He would be known for who He is. The only request He made in behalf of himself was that He be made known by and through the horrible ordeal of the Cross. As we know the Son, we know the Father. It is not possible to know the Father if the Son is excluded (see 14:9).

1. These words spake Jesus, and lifted up his eyes to heaven: Jesus said this, then raised His eyes toward heaven, *Berkeley* . . . his eyes heavenward, *TCNT* . . . When Jesus had thus spoken, He lifted His face, *Norlie*.

and said, Father, the hour is come:

glorify thy Son, that thy Son also may glorify thee: . . . honour thy Son, that thy Son may honour thee, *TCNT* . . . give glory to your Son, *BB* . . . perfect Your Son...may magnify You, *Fenton*.

17:2,3. Through His redemptive work, Christ obtained the right to exercise His power to give eternal life. The Father bestows on the Son the power to save those who believe on Him.

In this chapter, five references are made to what has been "given": (1) the Father had given Jesus authority (*exousia*) over all flesh (verse 2); (2) Jesus is the Giver of eternal life (verse 2); (3) Jesus had given His followers the Word of God (verses 8,14); (4) the Father had given Jesus glory which He gave to His disciples (verse 22); (5) the Father had given the disciples to Jesus (verses 6,24). Matchless Grace!

Those who know God possess eternal life. The verb "know" is a present active subjunctive indicating a continuous action. Eternal life is a personal relationship with God gained by experiential knowledge of Him. It is not the *cause* of eternal life nor the *prelude* to eternal life; this experiential knowing is the very eternal life itself.

This is one of the few instances in the Gospels where the compound title "Jesus Christ" is used. It is found often in the Epistles. As "Jesus Christ," He is the Revealer of the Father: Saviour-Messiah, the Anointed King.

2. As thou hast given him power over all flesh: . . . invested Him with, *Fenton* . . . authority, *Murdock* . . . over all mankind, *Norlie, Williams, Berkeley*.

that he should give eternal life to as many as thou hast given him:

John 17:4

1498.4 verb 3sing indic pres act	**3450.9** art nom sing fem	**164.3** adj nom sing	**2205.1** noun nom sing fem	**2419.1** conj	**1091.8** verb 3pl subj pres act
ἐστιν	ἡ	αἰώνιος	ζωή,	ἵνα	‘ γινώσκωσιν
estin	*hē*	*aiōnios*	*zōē*	*hina*	*ginōskōsin*
is	the	eternal	life,	that	they should know

3.a.**Var:** 02A,05D,019L, 032W,037,33,Treg,Tisc

1091.13 verb pl pres act	**4622.4** prs-pron acc 2sing	**3450.6** art acc sing masc	**3304.1** adj sing	**226.1** adj sing
[a γινώσκουσιν]	σὲ	τὸν	μόνον	ἀληθινὸν
ginōskousin	*se*	*ton*	*monon*	*alēthinon*
[they know]	you	the	only	true

2296.4 noun acc sing masc	**2504.1** conj	**3614.6** rel-pron acc sing masc	**643.7** verb 2sing indic aor act	**2400.3** name acc masc
θεὸν,	καὶ	ὃν	ἀπέστειλας	Ἰησοῦν
theon	*kai*	*hon*	*apesteilas*	*Iēsoun*
God,	and	whom	you sent	Jesus

5382.4 name acc masc	**1466.1** prs-pron nom 1sing	**4622.4** prs-pron acc 2sing	**1386.8** verb 1sing indic aor act	**1894.3** prep	**3450.10** art gen sing fem
Χριστόν.	**4.** ἐγώ	σε	ἐδόξασα	ἐπὶ	τῆς
Christon	*egō*	*se*	*edoxasa*	*epi*	*tēs*
Christ.	I	you	glorified	on	the

4.a.**Txt:** 05D,033X,036, 038,13,byz.Gries,Word **Var:** 01ℵ,02A,03B,04C, 019L,041,33,bo.Lach, Treg,Alf,Tisc,We/Ho, Weis,Sod,UBS/☆

1087.2 noun gen sing fem	**3450.16** art sing neu	**2024.1** noun sing neu	**4896.1** verb 1sing indic aor act	**4896.19** verb nom sing masc part aor act
γῆς·	τὸ	ἔργον	‘ ἐτελείωσα	[a☆ τελειώσας]
gēs	*to*	*ergon*	*eteleiōsa*	*teleiōsas*
earth;	the	work	I completed,	[having finished]

3614.16 rel-pron sing neu	**1319.11** verb 2sing indic act	**1466.4** prs-pron dat 1sing	**2419.1** conj	**4020.21** verb 1sing act	**2504.1** conj
ὃ	δέδωκάς	μοι	ἵνα	ποιήσω·	**5.** καὶ
ho	*dedōkas*	*moi*	*hina*	*poiēsō*	*kai*
which	you have given	me	that	I should do;	and

3431.1 adv	**1386.13** verb 2sing impr aor act	**1466.6** prs-pron acc 1sing	**4622.1** prs-pron nom 2sing	**3824.5** noun voc sing masc	**3706.2** prep
νῦν	δόξασόν	με	σύ·	πάτερ,	παρὰ
nun	*doxason*	*me*	*su*	*pater*	*para*
now	glorify	me	you,	Father,	with

4427.2 prs-pron dat 2sing masc	**3450.11** art dat sing fem	**1385.3** noun dat sing fem	**3614.11** rel-pron dat sing fem	**2174.42** verb indic imperf act	**4112.1** prep
σεαυτῷ,	τῇ	δόξῃ	ᾗ	εἶχον	πρὸ
seautō	*tē*	*doxē*	*hē*	*eichon*	*pro*
yourself,	with the	glory	which	I had	before

3450.2 art gen sing	**3450.6** art acc sing masc	**2862.4** noun acc sing masc	**1498.32** verb inf pres act	**3706.2** prep	**4622.3** prs-pron dat 2sing
τοῦ	τὸν	κόσμον	εἶναι	παρὰ	σοί.
tou	*ton*	*kosmon*	*einai*	*para*	*soi*
the	the	world	to be	with	you.

5157.2 verb 1sing indic aor act	**4622.2** prs-pron gen 2sing	**3450.16** art sing neu	**3549.2** noun sing neu	**3450.4** art dat pl	**442.8** noun dat pl masc
6. Ἐφανέρωσά	σου	τὸ	ὄνομα	τοῖς	ἀνθρώποις
Ephanerōsa	*sou*	*to*	*onoma*	*tois*	*anthrōpois*
I manifested	your	the	name	to the	men

6.a.**Txt:** p60,04C,019L, 033X,036,037,1,13,byz. GriesWord,Sod **Var:** 01ℵ,02A,03B,05D, 017K,032W,038,041, Lach,Treg,Tisc,We/Ho, Weis,UBS/☆

3614.8 rel-pron acc pl masc	**1319.11** verb 2sing indic act	**1319.13** verb 2sing indic aor act	**1466.4** prs-pron dat 1sing	**1523.2** prep gen
οὓς	‘ δέδωκάς	[a☆ ἔδωκάς]	μοι	ἐκ
hous	*dedōkas*	*edōkas*	*moi*	*ek*
whom	you have given,	[you gave]	me	out of

Nowhere is Jesus' deity stated more clearly than here. No created person could use such terminology when speaking to God.

In the prayer Jesus made six references to being sent by the Father (verses 3,8,18,21,23,25). In each reference the word "sent" means "to be commissioned." The Son's requests are the result of His commission to make the Father known and to bring eternal life. That knowledge is revealed by the Son of God alone. It is the One "sent" of God who brings the knowledge of God. The One "sent" is no mere creature. Only deity could reveal deity.

3. And this is life eternal, that they might know thee the only true God: . . . that they get to know thee, the only real God, *Rotherham.*

and Jesus Christ, whom thou hast sent: . . . and Jesus the Christ whom You have sent, *Norlie* . . . and knowing Jesus your messenger as Christ, *Williams.*

4. I have glorified thee on the earth: I have given you glory, *BB* . . . I have brought you honor upon the earth, *Phillips* . . . down here upon the earth, *Williams.*

I have finished the work which thou gavest me to do: . . . having done perfectly the work, *Weymouth* . . . by completing the work, *TCNT* . . . I have completed the task, *Berkeley* . . . You entrusted to Me, *Fenton.*

17:4. "I" is emphatic to stress the personal fulfillment of His commission as the Christ. Jesus "glorified" the Father by revealing Him in His life and ministry. The aorist verb draws a circle about His manifestation and blankets it in its totality.

Christ's "work" was making God known to the world. His miracles, teachings, and life exposed God to human gaze. Those who bathe in the light of His revelation are robed in His righteousness and receive His gift of life.

5. And now, O Father, glorify thou me with thine own self: . . . let me have glory with you, *BB* . . . honor me in your own presence, *Phillips* . . . glorify Me at Your side, *Beck* . . . glorify me up there in your presence, *Williams.*

with the glory which I had with thee before the world was: . . . which I enjoyed in thy presence before the world began, *Moffatt* . . . before the world existed, *Williams, Fenton.*

17:5. Jesus' request in verse 1 was that He be made known on earth that He might make God known to mankind. Here His request went beyond the earthly scene to heaven itself. His request involved nothing that was not His right. He had not renounced His deity. He had assumed humanity in behalf of God and for the sake of the world. He asked now for the return of His eternal manifestation, having completed His earthly revelation.

In His incarnation, Jesus had temporarily laid aside some of the glory of His eternal state (Philippians 2:5-8). The degree of glory He had while on earth was veiled by human flesh. Along with Peter and James, John had seen a revelation of His majesty at His transfiguration (Mark 9:2-8; 2 Peter 1:16-18), and a degree of glory hitherto unknown to them.

Jesus was praying for the full restoration of His essential glory. He knew that this restoration was in the eternal plan of God; it was part of the joy set before Him as He faced the agony and shame of Gethsemane and Calvary (Hebrews 12:2).

6. I have manifested thy name unto the men which thou gavest me out of the world: I have revealed Thy name, *Weymouth* . . . made known, *Montgomery* . . . made Your power known, *Fenton* . . . made your very self known, *Williams* . . . I have shown your self to the men whom you gave me, *Phillips* . . . schewid thi name, *Wycliffe.*

17:6. In the first five verses we have His prayer for His own glorification that the world might know the Father. In verses 6-19 we have Jesus' prayer for His first-century disciples. First, He prayed that they might be kept, guarded, and unified (verses 11,15). Sec-

3450.2 art gen sing	**2862.2** noun gen sing masc	**4622.3** prs-pron dat 2sing	**1498.37** verb 3pl indic imperf act	**2504.1** conj	**1466.5** prs-pron dat 1sing
τοῦ	κόσμου·	σοὶ	ἦσαν,	ʻ καὶ	ἐμοὶ
tou	*kosmou*	*soi*	*ēsan*	*kai*	*emoi*
the	world.	Yours	they were,	and	to me

6.b.**Txt:** 04C,033X,036,037,byz.
Var: 01ℵ,02A,03B,05D,017K,019L,038,041,Lach,Treg,Tisc,We/Ho,Weis,Sod,UBS/☆

2476.1 conj	**840.8** prs-pron acc pl masc	**1319.11** verb 2sing indic act	**1319.13** verb 2sing indic aor act
[☆ κἀμοὶ]	αὐτοὺς	ʻ δέδωκας·	[b☆ ἔδωκας,]
kamoi	*autous*	*dedōkas*	*edōkas*
[and to me]	them	you have given	[you gave,]

2504.1 conj	**3450.6** art acc sing masc	**3030.4** noun acc sing masc	**4622.2** prs-pron gen 2sing	**4931.25** verb 3pl indic perf act
καὶ	τὸν	λόγον	σου	ʻ τετηρήκασιν.
kai	*ton*	*logon*	*sou*	*tetērēkasin*
and	the	word	your	they have kept.

6.c.**Txt:** 02A,04C,017K,036,037,038,1,13,byz.Sod
Var: 03B,05D,019L,032W,Lach,Treg,Alf,Tisc,We/HoWeis,UBS/☆

7.a.**Var:** 02A,(03),Lach,We/Ho

4931.39 verb 3pl indic perf act	**3431.1** adv	**1091.35** verb 3pl indic perf act	**3617.1** conj	**3820.1** adj
[c☆ τετήρηκαν.]	7. νῦν	ἔγνωκαν	ὅτι	πάντα
tetērēkan	*nun*	*egnōkan*	*hoti*	*panta*
[idem]	Now	they have known	that	all things

3607.8 rel-pron pl neu	**1319.11** verb 2sing indic act	**1319.13** verb 2sing indic aor act	**1466.4** prs-pron dat 1sing	**3706.2** prep
ὅσα	ʻ δέδωκάς	[a ἔδωκάς]	μοι,	παρὰ
hosa	*dedōkas*	*edōkas*	*moi*	*para*
whatever	you have given	[you gave]	me,	of

7.b.**Txt:** 02A,05D,017K,036,037,038,1,13,byz.Gries,Lach
Var: 01ℵ,03B,04C,019L,033X,33,Treg,Alf,Tisc,We/HoWeis,Sod,UBS/☆

4622.2 prs-pron gen 2sing	**1498.4** verb 3sing indic pres act	**1498.7** verb 3pl indic pres act	**3617.1** conj	**3450.17** art pl neu	**4343.4** noun pl neu
σοῦ	ʻ ἐστιν·	[b☆ εἰσίν·]	8. ὅτι	τὰ	ῥήματα
sou	*estin*	*eisin*	*hoti*	*ta*	*rhēmata*
you	are;	[idem]	the	for	words

8.a.**Txt:** 01ℵ,017K,019L,033X,036,037,038,041-corr,1,13,byz.Sod
Var: 02A,(03),04C,05D,032W,041-org,Lach,Treg,AlfTisc,We/Ho,Weis,UBS/☆

3614.17 rel-pron pl neu	**1319.11** verb 2sing indic act	**1319.13** verb 2sing indic aor act	**1466.4** prs-pron dat 1sing	**1319.32** verb 1sing indic perf act
ἃ	ʻ δέδωκάς	[a☆ ἔδωκάς]	μοι	δέδωκα
ha	*dedōkas*	*edōkas*	*moi*	*dedōka*
which	you have given	[you gave]	me	I have given

840.2 prs-pron dat pl	**2504.1** conj	**840.7** prs-pron nom pl masc	**2956.12** verb indic aor act	**2504.1** conj	**1091.18** verb 3pl indic aor act	**228.1** adv
αὐτοῖς·	καὶ	αὐτοὶ	ἔλαβον,	καὶ	ἔγνωσαν	ἀληθῶς
autois	*kai*	*autoi*	*elabon*	*kai*	*egnōsan*	*alēthōs*
them,	and	they	received,	and	knew	truly

3617.1 conj	**3706.2** prep	**4622.2** prs-pron gen 2sing	**1814.1** verb indic aor act	**2504.1** conj	**3961.23** verb 3pl indic aor act	**3617.1** conj
ὅτι	παρὰ	σοῦ	ἐξῆλθον,	καὶ	ἐπίστευσαν	ὅτι
hoti	*para*	*sou*	*exēlthon*	*kai*	*episteusan*	*hoti*
that	from	you	I came out,	and	they believed	that

4622.1 prs-pron nom 2sing	**1466.6** prs-pron acc 1sing	**643.7** verb 2sing indic aor act	**1466.1** prs-pron nom 1sing	**3875.1** prep
σύ	με	ἀπέστειλας.	9. ἐγὼ	περὶ
su	*me*	*apesteilas*	*egō*	*peri*
you	me	sent.	I	concerning

840.1 prs-pron gen pl	**2049.2** verb 1sing indic pres act	**3620.3** partic	**3875.1** prep	**3450.2** art gen sing	**2862.2** noun gen sing masc
αὐτῶν	ἐρωτῶ·	οὐ	περὶ	τοῦ	κόσμου
autōn	*erōtō*	*ou*	*peri*	*tou*	*kosmou*
them	make request;	not	concerning	the	world

ond, He desired that the disciples might have His joy (verse 13). Third, He requested their sanctification (verses 17,19).

Ephanerōsa ("manifested") is an active voice verb indicating the whole of what Jesus did. The word means "to make visible, clear, or known." The word indicates that Jesus made known the reality of God's nature and character.

A threefold relationship is described: (1) Jesus was the One who revealed God's name (His essential nature and being) to men; (2) the Father was the One who drew them to Christ (6:44,65); (3) "the men" are the ones who have kept God's Word. God draws all men (12:32), but only those who *keep* His Word will be saved.

The Father gave the disciples to the Son for special care under the provisions of His redemptive work. All creation is the property of God, but only those from the world who receive the revelation of the Father through the Son can be included in the Father's gift to the Son. "Thy word" refers to the revelation of the Father. The disciples received Christ as God's manifestation and kept it, meaning they treasured and guarded what they received.

thine they were: . . . they were thy own, *TCNT* . . . They were your men, *Phillips* . . . At first they were yours, *Williams.*

and thou gavest them me: . . . but now you have given them to me, *Williams.*

and they have kept thy word: . . . have held to thy word, *Moffatt* . . . and they have obeyed Thy teaching, *Weymouth* . . . carefully observed, *Fenton.*

7. Now they have known that all things whatsoever thou hast given me are of thee: They recognize now, *TCNT* . . . Now they have realized, *Berkeley* . . . You have entrusted to me proceeds from Yourself, *Fenton* . . . They now understand, *Norlie* . . . that whatever thou hast given me was from thee, *Montgomery.*

17:7,8. "Now" indicates the progress the disciples had attained up to that moment.

"The words" refers to His teachings as God's message to them. "The words" (plural) refer to His separate sayings. The Word (singular) denotes the totality of His sayings and His manifestation of the Father.

Jesus asserted what the disciples confessed in 16:30. The disciples realized that Jesus' mission was from the Father. They accepted Jesus for the One He claimed to be, as far as they were able to understand. The disciples' faith depended upon the fact that He came forth from the Father. Jesus pointed to this fact repeatedly as the beginning point for faith.

8. For I have given unto them the words which thou gavest me: . . . for I have imparted, *Norton* . . . the declarations which thou gavest me, *Rotherham* . . . the truths which You have imparted to Me, *Fenton* . . . truths which Thou didst teach me, *Weymouth.*

and they have received them: . . . and they have accepted them, *Berkeley* . . . and they have come to know in reality, *Williams* . . . clearly understood, *TCNT.*

and have known surely that I came out from thee: . . . knowing for certain, *Campbell* . . . it was from beside thee that I came, *TCNT* . . . from your presence, *Wuest* . . . have certain knowledge that I came from you, *BB.*

and they have believed that thou didst send me: . . . and they have faith, *BB* . . . are convinced that you did send me, *Williams* . . . known for certain, *Weymouth* . . . am commissioned by thee, *Campbell.*

17:9. The disciples were the ones through whom the world would hear the gospel. Therefore, Jesus focused His request on His disciples. (Verses 21 and 23 assure us of the Lord's interest in the world.) He asked that His own be kept, be full of joy, be sanctified, etc. But when He prayed for the world, He prayed that they might believe and know His mission.

Jesus' exclusion of the world from this particular prayer is no evidence of lack of love for the unconverted. This prayer was specifically one for preservation, sanctification, and glorification. Those who are in the world can also become the object of His priestly intercession only after they are converted.

9. I pray for them: I intercede for them, *TCNT* . . . I entreat, *Wilson* . . . making petition, *Weymouth* . . . I make request concerning them, *Wuest.*

2049.2 verb 1sing indic pres act	233.2 conj	3875.1 prep	3614.1 rel-pron gen pl	1319.11 verb 2sing indic act
ἐρωτῶ,	ἀλλὰ	περὶ	ὧν	δέδωκάς
erōtō	*alla*	*peri*	*hōn*	*dedōkas*
make I request,	but	concerning	whom	you have given

1466.4 prs-pron dat 1sing	3617.1 conj	4622.3 prs-pron dat 2sing	1498.7 verb 3pl indic pres act	2504.1 conj	3450.17 art pl neu
μοι,	ὅτι	σοί	εἰσιν,	**10.** καὶ	τὰ
moi	*hoti*	*soi*	*eisin*	*kai*	*ta*
me,	for	yours	they are:	and	the things

1684.12 adj 1pl neu	3820.1 adj	4528.9 adj 2pl neu	1498.4 verb 3sing indic pres act	2504.1 conj	3450.17 art pl neu
ἐμὰ	πάντα	σά	ἐστιν,	καὶ	τὰ
ema	*panta*	*sa*	*estin*	*kai*	*ta*
my	all	yours	are,	and	the things

4528.9 adj 2pl neu	1684.12 adj 1pl neu	2504.1 conj	1386.25 verb 1sing indic perf pass	1706.1 prep	840.2 prs-pron dat pl
σὰ	ἐμά,	καὶ	δεδόξασμαι	ἐν	αὐτοῖς.
sa	*ema*	*kai*	*dedoxasmai*	*en*	*autois*
yours	mine:	and	I have been glorified	in	them.

2504.1 conj	3620.2 partic	2068.1 adv	3629.1 adv	1498.2 verb 1sing indic pres act	1706.1 prep
11. καὶ	ʻ οὐκ	ἔτι	[☆ οὐκέτι]	εἰμὶ	ἐν
kai	*ouk*	*eti*	*ouketi*	*eimi*	*en*
And	no	longer	[no longer]	I am	in

11.a.**Txt:** 04C,05D,017K, 019L,032W,036,037, 038,1,13,byz.Lach,Weis, Sod
Var: 01ℵ,03B,Tisc, We/Ho,UBS/☆

3450.3 art dat sing	2862.3 noun dat sing masc	2504.1 conj	3642.7 dem-pron nom pl masc	840.7 prs-pron nom pl masc	1706.1 prep
τῷ	κόσμῳ,	καὶ	ʻ οὗτοι	[a☆ αὐτοὶ]	ἐν
tō	*kosmō*	*kai*	*houtoi*	*autoi*	*en*
the	world,	and	these	[they]	in

3450.3 art dat sing	2862.3 noun dat sing masc	1498.7 verb 3pl indic pres act	2504.1 conj	1466.1 prs-pron nom 1sing	2476.3 conj
τῷ	κόσμῳ	εἰσίν,	ʻ καὶ	ἐγω	[☆ κἀγὼ]
tō	*kosmō*	*eisin*	*kai*	*egō*	*kagō*
the	world	are,	and	I	[and I]

4242.1 prep	4622.4 prs-pron acc 2sing	2048.32 verb 1sing indic pres	3824.5 noun voc sing masc	39.6 adj voc sing masc	4931.18 verb 2sing impr aor act
πρὸς	σὲ	ἔρχομαι.	Πάτερ	ἅγιε,	τήρησον
pros	*se*	*erchomai*	*Pater*	*hagie*	*tērēson*
to	you	come.	Father	Holy,	keep

840.8 prs-pron acc pl masc	1706.1 prep	3450.3 art dat sing	3549.4 noun dat sing neu	4622.2 prs-pron gen 2sing	3614.8 rel-pron acc pl masc
αὐτοὺς	ἐν	τῷ	ὀνόματί	σου	ʻ οὓς
autous	*en*	*tō*	*onomati*	*sou*	*hous*
them	in	the	name	your	whom

11.b.**Txt:** 05D-corr, 022N-corr,Steph
Var: p60,p66,01ℵ,02A, 03B,04C,017K,019L, 032W,036,037,038,1,13, byz.Gries,Lach,Treg,Alf, Tisc,We/HoWeis,Sod, UBS/☆

3614.3 rel-pron dat sing	1319.11 verb 2sing indic act	1466.4 prs-pron dat 1sing	2419.1 conj	1498.12 verb 3pl subj pres act	1518.9 num card neu
[b☆ ᾧ]	δέδωκάς	μοι,	ἵνα	ὦσιν	ἓν,
hō	*dedōkas*	*moi*	*hina*	*ōsin*	*hen*
[which]	you have given	me,	that	they may be	one,

2503.1 conj	2231.1 prs-pron nom 1pl	3616.1 conj	1498.46 verb 1sing indic imperf mid	3196.2 prep	840.1 prs-pron gen pl
καθὼς	ἡμεῖς.	**12.** ὅτε	ἤμην	μετ'	αὐτῶν
kathōs	*hēmeis*	*hote*	*ēmēn*	*met'*	*autōn*
as	we.	When	I was	with	them

When Philip told Him of certain Greeks who desired to "see Jesus" (12:21,22), He did not respond as expected. He knew that "his hour was come" (12:23; 13:1), that He was entering a new sphere of mediatorial work as He approached His death.

The disciples belonged to both the Father and the Son, though the Father granted the Son all who believe on Him (verse 6). The relationship of the disciples to the Son and the Father is clear proof of the deity of the Son (verse 8).

I pray not for the world: I am not interceding, *TCNT* . . . any request, *Norlie* . . . I am not praying for the world now, *Williams.*

but for them which thou hast given me; for they are thine:

17:10. Jesus was made known (glorified) through those who believed. "In them" refers to the fact that they believed His revelation and witnessed to the truth before the world. As they possessed the life of Christ in their hearts, they became His light to others. To glorify the Lord is a believer's highest function in behalf of His Saviour and the greatest service he can render to his fellowman.

10. And all mine are thine, and thine are mine: And all my possessions are thine, *Rotherham* . . . Yes, all who are Mine, are Thine, *Berkeley.*

and I am glorified in them: I am crowned with glory, *Weymouth* . . . I am honoured among them, *Fenton.*

17:11. Jesus spoke of His separation from His disciples as though it were already a fact.

His first request in behalf of His disciples was that they be kept. The disciples knew the Father through the Son. It is as believers maintain their knowledge of the one true God that they are kept in the covenant relationship with Him.

In the opening of His prayer, Jesus said simply "Father" (17:1). Now as He prayed for their sanctification, He addressed Him as "*Holy* Father." When He later mentioned the world, ripe for judgment, He prayed "*righteous* Father."

Unity is an important aspect of being kept. Christ prayed that the entire group of disciples might maintain the unity of belief in the Father's revelation as He manifested it.

11. And now I am no more in the world: I am to be in the world no longer, *Moffatt* . . . My presence in the world is over, *Berkeley.*

but these are in the world, and I come to thee: . . . but they remain in the world, *ALBA.*

Holy Father, keep through thine own name those whom thou hast given me: . . . preserve in Thy name those whom, *Berkeley* . . . keep them true to Thy name, *Weymouth* . . . preserve them as thy ministers, *Norton* . . . maintain a watchful care over them, *Wuest* . . . preserve by Your power, *Fenton* . . . which you have entrusted to me, *ALBA* . . . in the knowledge of thyself, *TCNT.*

that they may be one, as we are:

17:12. Our Lord contemplated His earthly work as completed. "In thy name" refers to the manifestation of God to the disciples. The Father had given the Son the authority to be the revelation of all that God is. Jesus was zealous to keep His disciples from any error that would hinder the manifestation of God's revelation. If Jesus had not guarded them, the doctrines of the Pharisees and Sadducees would have contaminated the truth of His manifestation.

Jesus both "kept" and "guarded" the disciples. The first word means "to have watchful care." The second implies custody and protection. The words "none of them is lost, *but* the son of per-

12. While I was with them in the world:

John 17:13

12.a.**Txt:** 02A,04C-corr,017K,036,037,038,13,byz.Gries,Word
Var: 01ℵ,03B,04C-org,05D,019L,sa.bo.Lach,TregAlf,Tisc,We/Ho,Weis,Sod,UBS/☆

12.b.**Txt:** 02A,04C-corr,05D,017K,033X,036,037,038,1,13,byz.it.Lach,Sod
Var: p66-corr,03B,04C-org,019L,032W,33,Treg,AlfTisc,We/Ho,Weis,UBS/☆

12.c.**Var:** p66,01ℵ,03B,04C-org,019L,032W,33,sa.bo.Lach,Treg,Alf,Tisc We/Ho,Weis,Sod,UBS/☆

1706.1 prep	**3450.3** art dat sing	**2862.3** noun dat sing masc	**1466.1** prs-pron nom 1sing	**4931.29** verb indic imperf act	**840.8** prs-pron acc pl masc
⸂a ἐν	τῷ	κόσμῳ, ⸃	ἐγὼ	ἐτήρουν	αὐτοὺς
en	*tō*	*kosmō*	*egō*	*etēroun*	*autous*
in	the	world	I	was keeping	them

1706.1 prep	**3450.3** art dat sing	**3549.4** noun dat sing neu	**4622.2** prs-pron gen 2sing	**3614.8** rel-pron acc pl masc	**3614.3** rel-pron dat sing
ἐν	τῷ	ὀνόματί	σου	⸂ οὓς	[b☆ ᾧ]
en	*tō*	*onomati*	*sou*	*hous*	*hō*
in	the	name	your:	whom	[which]

1319.11 verb 2sing indic act	**1466.4** prs-pron dat 1sing	**2504.1** conj	**5278.7** verb 1sing indic aor act	**2504.1** conj
δέδωκάς	μοι	[c☆+ καὶ]	ἐφύλαξα,	καὶ
dedōkas	*moi*	*kai*	*ephulaxa*	*kai*
you have given	me	[and]	I guarded,	and

3625.2 num card nom masc	**1523.1** prep gen	**840.1** prs-pron gen pl	**616.22** verb 3sing indic aor mid	**1479.1** conj	**3231.1** partic	**3450.5** art sing masc
οὐδεὶς	ἐξ	αὐτῶν	ἀπώλετο,	εἰ	μὴ	ὁ
oudeis	*ex*	*autōn*	*apōleto*	*ei*	*mē*	*ho*
no one	of	them	perished,	if	not	the

5048.1 noun nom sing masc	**3450.10** art gen sing fem	**677.2** noun gen sing fem	**2419.1** conj	**3450.9** art nom sing fem	**1118.1** noun nom sing fem
υἱὸς	τῆς	ἀπωλείας,	ἵνα	ἡ	γραφὴ
huios	*tēs*	*apōleias*	*hina*	*hē*	*graphē*
son	of the	destruction,	that	the	scripture

3997.22 verb 3sing subj aor pass	**3431.1** adv	**1156.2** conj	**4242.1** prep	**4622.4** prs-pron acc 2sing	**2048.32** verb 1sing indic pres
πληρωθῇ.	**13.** νῦν	δὲ	πρὸς	σὲ	ἔρχομαι,
plērōthē	*nun*	*de*	*pros*	*se*	*erchomai*
might be fulfilled.	Now	and	to	you	I come;

2504.1 conj	**3642.18** dem-pron pl neu	**2953.1** verb 1sing pres act	**1706.1** prep	**3450.3** art dat sing	**2862.3** noun dat sing masc	**2419.1** conj
καὶ	ταῦτα	λαλῶ	ἐν	τῷ	κόσμῳ	ἵνα
kai	*tauta*	*lalō*	*en*	*tō*	*kosmō*	*hina*
and	these things	I speak	in	the	world	that

2174.10 verb 3pl subj pres act	**3450.12** art acc sing fem	**5315.4** noun acc sing fem	**3450.12** art acc sing fem	**1684.9** adj acc 1sing fem
ἔχωσιν	τὴν	χαρὰν	τὴν	ἐμὴν
echōsin	*tēn*	*charan*	*tēn*	*emēn*
they may have	the	joy	the	my

13.a.**Txt:** p66,01ℵ-org,04C-corr,05D,017K,019L,036,037,038,1,13,byz.Lach,Sod
Var: 01ℵ-corr,02A,03B,032W,033X,041,Treg Alf,Tisc,We/Ho,Weis,UBS/☆

3997.33 verb acc sing fem part perf pass	**1706.1** prep	**840.2** prs-pron dat pl	**1431.7** prs-pron dat pl masc	**1466.1** prs-pron nom 1sing
πεπληρωμένην	ἐν	⸂☆ αὐτοῖς.	[a ἑαυτοῖς.]	**14.** ἐγὼ
peplērōmenēn	*en*	*autois*	*heautois*	*egō*
having been fulfilled	in	them.	[themselves.]	I

1319.32 verb 1sing indic perf act	**840.2** prs-pron dat pl	**3450.6** art acc sing masc	**3030.4** noun acc sing masc	**4622.2** prs-pron gen 2sing	**2504.1** conj
δέδωκα	αὐτοῖς	τὸν	λόγον	σου,	καὶ
dedōka	*autois*	*ton*	*logon*	*sou*	*kai*
have given	them	the	word	your,	and

3450.5 art sing masc	**2862.1** noun nom sing masc	**3268.13** verb 3sing indic aor act	**840.8** prs-pron acc pl masc	**3617.1** conj	**3620.2** partic
ὁ	κόσμος	ἐμίσησεν	αὐτούς,	ὅτι	οὐκ
ho	*kosmos*	*emisēsen*	*autous*	*hoti*	*ouk*
the	world	hated	them,	because	not

dition" show that Judas was one of those whom Jesus had guarded. *Ei mē* can be translated "but," "if not," "only," or "except." God had given Judas to Jesus, and Jesus had guarded him with the others. Even God himself cannot save a willful reprobate from voluntarily leaving His care (Acts 1:17-25; Romans 8:13).

Judas is called "the son of perdition" because he became the product of that which brings ruin. The Greek words translated "lost" and "perdition" have the same basic meaning except the first is a verb and the second is a noun. The word means "to suffer utter loss."

The prediction of Judas' sin did not cause the event. The betrayer made his own choice and suffered the consequence of it.

I kept them in thy name: I kept them safe, *Norlie* . . . I kept them by the power that you gave me, *Phillips.*

those that thou gavest me I have kept: . . . and I kept watch, *Rotherham* . . . protected them, *ALBA, Williams* . . . I guarded them, *Phillips, Fenton.*

and none of them is lost: . . . and not one of them has come to destruction, *BB* . . . destroyed himself, *Rotherham.*

but the son of perdition: . . . only the son of perdition, *Moffatt* . . . except that lost one, *Beck* . . . who was bound to be lost, *TEV* . . . the son of destruction, *Rotherham* . . . that lost chylde, *Tyndale* . . . who is now doomed to be lost, *Williams.*

that the scripture might be fulfilled: . . . might come true, *TEV* . . . as the scripture foretold, *Campbell* . . . the Bible says had to come true, *Beck* . . . might be verified, *Fenton.*

17:13. "And now" marks a contrast of His place with the disciples and the change of His position to heaven. He has been watching and guarding them, "and now" He will no longer be with them in the flesh.

One can feel the pathos of Jesus in regard to leaving His disciples. They were weak, vulnerable, and ignorant about so much of His mission and theirs. Yet Jesus knew they would be filled with the Spirit to carry on His mission in the world. Jesus had two great desires: first, the desire to be in the immediate presence and fellowship with the Father; second, the fellowship and training of His disciples. The Lord yielded to the will of His Father. He knew it was time to go home.

He spoke "these things" so that His joy might be made full in His disciples. He expressed a like idea in 15:11. The joy which Jesus experienced was His constant fellowship with the Father. His desire for His disciples was that they would be secure in their relationship by following the will of the Father as He himself did. He had given them the secret of His joy.

His second request for His disciples was for His joy to be their joy. Observe what the kingdom of God is according to Paul's epistle to the Romans: "the kingdom of God is . . . joy in the Holy Spirit" (Romans 14:17, NASB).

13. And now come I to thee; and these things I speak in the world: . . . declare these facts to the world, *Fenton* . . . and I am speaking thus, while still in the world, *TCNT.*

that they might have my joy fulfilled in themselves: . . . in order that they may be constantly having, *Wuest* . . . that they may have my own joy, in all its fulness in their hearts, *TCNT* . . . so that these men may have my complete joy in them, *SEB* . . . My joy completed in their hearts, *Berkeley* . . . my gladness within them filling their hearts, *Weymouth* . . . my own joy perfected in themselves, *Fenton* . . . may be completely felt by them, *Norton.*

17:14. "I" is the emphatic position and "the world" is in opposition to "I." "Thy word" (Greek, *ton logon sou*) is the revelation which He came to manifest to the world in darkness (see verses 6 and 8).

"Hath hated" should be viewed as a complete and total act. The reason for the world's hatred is that Jesus was not of the same origin or family relationship as they. The disciples were like Him,

14. I have given them thy word: I have delivered to them, *Norton* . . . I have delivered Your message to them, *Fenton* . . . I have given them Your commands, *LivB.*

and the world hath hated them:

1498.7 verb 3pl	**1523.2**	**3450.2** art	**2862.2** noun	**2503.1**	**1466.1** prs-
indic pres act	prep gen	gen sing	gen sing masc	conj	pron nom 1sing
εἰσὶν	ἐκ	τοῦ	κόσμου,	καθὼς	ἐγὼ
eisin	*ek*	*tou*	*kosmou*	*kathōs*	*egō*
they are	of	the	world,	as	I

3620.2	**1498.2** verb 1sing	**1523.2**	**3450.2** art	**2862.2** noun	**3620.2**
partic	indic pres act	prep gen	gen sing	gen sing masc	partic
οὐκ	εἰμὶ	ἐκ	τοῦ	κόσμου.	**15.** οὐκ
ouk	*eimi*	*ek*	*tou*	*kosmou*	*ouk*
not	am	of	the	world.	Not

2049.2 verb 1sing	**2419.1**	**142.11** verb 2sing	**840.8** prs-pron	**1523.2**
indic pres act	conj	subj aor act	acc pl masc	prep gen
ἐρωτῶ	ἵνα	ἄρῃς	αὐτοὺς	ἐκ
erōtō	*hina*	*arēs*	*autous*	*ek*
I do make request	that	you should take	them	out of

3450.2 art	**2862.2** noun	**233.1**	**2419.1**	**4931.15** verb	**840.8** prs-pron
gen sing	gen sing masc	conj	conj	2sing subj aor act	acc pl masc
τοῦ	κόσμου,	ἀλλ'	ἵνα	τηρήσῃς	αὐτοὺς
tou	*kosmou*	*all'*	*hina*	*tērēsēs*	*autous*
the	world,	but	that	you should keep	them

1523.2	**3450.2** art	**4050.2** adj	**1523.2**	**3450.2** art	**2862.2** noun
prep gen	gen sing	gen sing	prep gen	gen sing	gen sing masc
ἐκ	τοῦ	πονηροῦ.	**16.** ἐκ	τοῦ	κόσμου
ek	*tou*	*ponērou*	*ek*	*tou*	*kosmou*
from	the	evil one.	Of	the	world

3620.2	**1498.7** verb 3pl	**2503.1**	**1466.1** prs-	**1523.2**	**3450.2** art
partic	indic pres act	conj	pron nom 1sing	prep gen	gen sing
οὐκ	εἰσὶν,	καθὼς	ἐγὼ	ʻ ἐκ	τοῦ
ouk	*eisin*	*kathōs*	*egō*	*ek*	*tou*
not	they are,	as	I	of	the

2862.2 noun	**3620.2**	**1498.2** verb 1sing	**3620.2**	**1498.2** verb 1sing	**1523.2**
gen sing masc	partic	indic pres act	partic	indic pres act	prep gen
κόσμου	οὐκ	εἰμί.	[☆ οὐκ	εἰμὶ	ἐκ
kosmou	*ouk*	*eimi*	*ouk*	*eimi*	*ek*
world	not	am.	[not	am	of

3450.2 art	**2862.2** noun	**37.8** verb 2sing	**840.8** prs-pron	**1706.1**	**3450.11** art
gen sing	gen sing masc	impr aor act	acc pl masc	prep	dat sing fem
τοῦ	κόσμου.]	**17.** ἁγίασον	αὐτοὺς	ἐν	τῇ
tou	*kosmou*	*hagiason*	*autous*	*en*	*tē*
the	world.]	Sanctify	them	by	the

17.a.**Txt:** 01ℵ-corr, 04C-corr,017K,033X, 036,037,041-org,13,byz. bo.Sod
Var: 01ℵ-org,02A,03B, 04C-org,05D,019L,038, 041-corr,sa.Lach,Treg Alf,Tisc,We/Ho,Weis, UBS/☆

223.3 noun	**4622.2** prs-	**3450.5** art	**3030.1** noun	**3450.5** art	**4528.2** adj
dat sing fem	pron gen 2sing	sing masc	nom sing masc	sing masc	nom 2sing masc
ἀληθείᾳ	⸂a σου· ⸃	ὁ	λόγος	ὁ	σὸς
alētheia	*sou*	*ho*	*logos*	*ho*	*sos*
truth	your;	the	word	the	your

223.1 noun	**1498.4** verb 3sing	**2503.1**	**1466.7** prs-	**643.7** verb 2sing
nom sing fem	indic pres act	conj	pron acc 1sing	indic aor act
ἀλήθειά	ἐστιν.	**18.** καθὼς	ἐμὲ	ἀπέστειλας
alētheia	*estin*	*kathōs*	*eme*	*apesteilas*
truth	is.	As	me	you sent

1519.1	**3450.6** art	**2862.4** noun	**2476.3**	**643.6** verb 1sing	**840.8** prs-pron
prep	acc sing masc	acc sing masc	conj	indic aor act	acc pl masc
εἰς	τὸν	κόσμον,	κἀγὼ	ἀπέστειλα	αὐτοὺς
eis	*ton*	*kosmon*	*kagō*	*apesteila*	*autous*
into	the	world,	I also	sent	them

for they did not depend upon the world for their life support. The world hated the disciples as they did Him.

because they are not of the world, even as I am not of the world: . . . for they are not worldly, *Berkeley.*

17:15. Jesus made clear the nature of the protection for which He prayed. The disciples knew they would remain on earth when He departed (also see 13:33).

It should be noted that Jesus prayed in the will of the Father. Jesus did not pray for the departure of the disciples. Instead, He prayed that the disciples would continue as His living witnesses. It was the Father's will and Jesus' prayer that the disciples themselves should remain in the world. The "evil one" fears the powerful witness of believers. Thus Jesus prayed that the disciples would be kept "from the evil."

This is the second mention of "keep them" (see verse 11 of the *Interlinear*). In verse 11 the idea was "keep" and in verse 12 "guard." Here the word "keep" is used again. "From the evil" can mean the "evil one" or the evil thing since the ending can be either masculine or neuter. The use of the definite "the" (*tou*) points to a specific evil. If the "evil one" is meant then the meaning is "the devil" or "the world." The word "from" (*ek*) means "out of." The evil is an evil in an active sense. The disciples would be endangered by the evil, therefore Jesus prayed that they be kept out of the evil.

15. I pray not that thou shouldest take them out of the world: I'm not asking You to take them out, *Beck* . . . remove them out of the world, *Weymouth.*

but that thou shouldest keep them from evil: . . . but rather, *Adams* . . . you should guard them safely from the reach of Pernicious One, *Wuest* . . . from the evil one, *Norlie* . . . from what is evil, *Norton* . . . out of the wickedness, *Concordant.*

16. They are not of the world, even as I am not of the world: They are no more sons of the world than I am, *Phillips* . . . any more than I belong to the world, *Moffatt.*

17:16,17. Their source of life was the same as His (see verse 14). A father takes care of his own. If the disciples were of the world, the world would take care of them.

Verse 17 states our Lord's third request in behalf of His disciples. The verb "sanctify" means first, "to mark off, to separate and to set apart for God's glory"; second, "to cleanse and to make holy."

"Thy word" refers to the total revelation of truth Jesus came to manifest. It includes the written Word but is the whole of what Jesus is and does. The revelation of God is the means of consecrating and cleansing believers.

17. Sancitify them through thy truth: Consecrate them in the sphere of truth, *Wuest* . . . Hallow them, *Concordant* . . . dedicate them to yourself, *TEV* . . . make them holy by the truth, *Phillips, Fenton* . . . holy in the truth, *Klingensmith* . . . Consecrate them, *Torrey, Berkeley* . . . Make them devoted to the Truth, *TCNT.*

thy word is truth: . . . thy Message is Truth, *TCNT* . . . the truth make them holy! *SEB.*

18. As thou hast sent me into the world: Just as you sent Me, *Norlie.*

17:18,19. The word for "sent" means "to send with a commission." The disciples were to carry the revelation of Christ to the world, a further reason for the disciples to be "kept" and "sanctified" (verses 11,15,17,19).

As applied to Christ, the word "sanctify" means He separated himself and devoted himself to the work of redemption. It was through His action that the disciples were sanctified.

19.a.**Txt:** p60,03B,04C, 05D,019L,038,1,13,etc. byz.Lach,We/HoWeis, Sod,UBS/☆
Var: 01ℵ,02A,032W,it. sa.Tisc

1519.1 prep	3450.6 art acc sing masc	2862.4 noun acc sing masc	2504.1 conj	5065.1 prep	840.1 prs-pron gen pl	1466.1 prs-pron nom 1sing
εἰς	τὸν	κόσμον·	19. καὶ	ὑπὲρ	αὐτῶν	⸂a ἐγὼ ⸃
eis	*ton*	*kosmon*	*kai*	*huper*	*autōn*	*egō*
into	the	world;	and	for	them	I

37.1 verb 1sing indic pres act	1670.3 prs-pron acc 1sing masc	2419.1 conj	2504.1 conj	840.7 prs-pron nom pl masc	1498.12 verb 3pl subj pres act
ἁγιάζω	ἐμαυτόν,	ἵνα	⸀ καὶ	αὐτοὶ	ὦσιν
hagiazō	*emauton*	*hina*	*kai*	*autoi*	*ōsin*
sanctify	myself,	that	also	they	may be

1498.12 verb 3pl subj pres act	2504.1 conj	840.7 prs-pron nom pl masc	37.17 verb nom pl masc part perf pass	1706.1 prep
[☆ ὦσιν	καὶ	αὐτοὶ]	ἡγιασμένοι	ἐν
ōsin	*kai*	*autoi*	*hēgiasmenoi*	*en*
[may be	and	they]	having been sanctified	in

20.a.**Txt:** 05D-corr,it.sa. Steph
Var: 01ℵ,02A,03B,04C, 05D-org,017K,019L,036, 037,038,byz.Gries,Lach, Treg,Alf,Word,Tisc, We/HoWeis,Sod,UBS/☆

223.3 noun dat sing fem	3620.3 partic	3875.1 prep	3642.2 dem-pron gen pl	1156.2 conj	2049.2 verb 1sing indic pres act
ἀληθείᾳ.	20. Οὐ	περὶ	τούτων	δὲ	ἐρωτῶ
alētheia	*Ou*	*peri*	*toutōn*	*de*	*erōtō*
truth.	Not	for	these	and	make I request

3303.1 adv	233.2 conj	2504.1 conj	3875.1 prep	3450.1 art gen pl	3961.52 verb gen pl masc part fut act
μόνον,	ἀλλὰ	καὶ	περὶ	τῶν	⸀ πιστευσόντων
monon	*alla*	*kai*	*peri*	*tōn*	*pisteusontōn*
only,	but	also	for	the	shall be believing

3961.14 verb gen pl masc part pres act	1217.2 prep	3450.2 art gen sing	3030.2 noun gen sing masc	840.1 prs-pron gen pl	1519.1 prep
[a☆ πιστευόντων]	διὰ	τοῦ	λόγου	αὐτῶν	εἰς
pisteuontōn	*dia*	*tou*	*logou*	*autōn*	*eis*
[believing]	through	the	word	their	on

21.a.**Txt:** 01ℵ,02A,04C, 017K,019L,036,037,038, 1,13,byz.Lach,Sod
Var: 03B,05D,032W, TregAlf,Tisc,We/Ho, Weis,UBS/☆

1466.7 prs-pron acc 1sing	2419.1 conj	3820.7 adj pl masc	1518.9 num card neu	1498.12 verb 3pl subj pres act	2503.1 conj
ἐμέ·	21. ἵνα	πάντες	ἓν	ὦσιν,	καθὼς
eme	*hina*	*pantes*	*hen*	*ōsin*	*kathōs*
me;	that	all	one	may be,	as

4622.1 prs-pron nom 2sing	3824.5 noun voc sing masc	3824.1 noun nom sing masc	1706.1 prep	1466.5 prs-pron dat 1sing	2476.3 conj
σύ,	⸀☆ πάτερ,	[a πατήρ,]	ἐν	ἐμοὶ	κἀγὼ
su	*pater*	*patēr*	*en*	*emoi*	*kagō*
you,	Father,	[idem]	in	me,	and I

21.b.**Txt:** 01ℵ,02A, 04C-corr,017K,019L, 036,037,038,1,13,byz. Gries,Lach,Sod
Var: p66,03B,04C-org, 05D,032W,it.sa.Treg,Alf Tisc,We/Ho,Weis,UBS/☆

1706.1 prep	4622.3 prs-pron dat 2sing	2419.1 conj	2504.1 conj	840.7 prs-pron nom pl masc	1706.1 prep	2231.3 prs-pron dat 1pl
ἐν	σοί,	ἵνα	καὶ	αὐτοὶ	ἐν	ἡμῖν
en	*soi*	*hina*	*kai*	*autoi*	*en*	*hēmin*
in	you,	that	also	they	in	us

21.c.**Txt:** p60,01ℵ-corr, 02A,04C-corr,05D,017K, 019L,036,037,038,1,13, byz.Lach,Weis,Sod
Var: p66,01ℵ-org,03B, 04C-org,032W,Treg, Tisc,We/Ho,UBS/☆

1518.9 num card neu	1498.12 verb 3pl subj pres act	2419.1 conj	3450.5 art sing masc	2862.1 noun nom sing masc	3961.25 verb 3sing subj aor act
⸂b ἓν ⸃	ὦσιν·	ἵνα	ὁ	κόσμος	⸀ πιστεύσῃ
hen	*ōsin*	*hina*	*ho*	*kosmos*	*pisteusē*
one	may be,	that	the	world	may believe

3961.62 verb 3sing subj pres act	3617.1 conj	4622.1 prs-pron nom 2sing	1466.6 prs-pron acc 1sing	643.7 verb 2sing indic aor act
[c☆ πιστεύῃ]	ὅτι	σύ	με	ἀπέστειλας.
pisteuē	*hoti*	*su*	*me*	*apesteilas*
[idem]	that	you	me	sent.

17:20. The third division of Jesus' prayer begins here. Thus far He had prayed for himself (verses 1-5) and for His early disciples (verses 6-19); here He prayed for all believers (verses 20-26).

He had previously made reference to "other sheep" that were not of the Jewish fold (10:16). These "other sheep," who would believe on Him through the word of the disciples, were as yet a part of the world.

Jesus came from the Father to reveal God to men. The disciples received and believed. Afterward the disciples took the message to others who believed when they heard the gospel. Jesus now made request for those who would believe on Him through the witnessing of the disciples. "Their word" refers to this witnessing. "On me" (Greek, *eis eme*) is an emphatic pronoun, placing emphasis on Him as God's final revelation to man. Eternal life is impossible without believing in Him as God's manifestation.

17:21. Jesus' prayer now focused on the unity of His disciples which the indwelling Spirit would make possible.

The Godhead is the ideal and perfect unity. Jesus asked for His disciples to experience a unity beyond the unity of purpose and disposition. His desire was that His own would have the unity whereby each member shared the life source of God himself.

By having the same Spirit the Saviour has, and bearing the same character, believers are one in the Father and in the Son ("one in us").

Jesus asserted for the first time that the world had a place in His priestly prayer. He had stated (verse 9) that He was not asking on behalf of the world. But this verse makes it clear that the world was in His loving concern. Jesus now prayed that the world "may believe" when they see the oneness of believers. Christian unity is strong evidence of truth. Notice that Jesus repeatedly mentioned the importance of believing that "thou hast sent me." Those who begin at this point of believing will experience all the reality of Christ's revelation.

17:22. What is the glory He speaks of? It is the revelation of God. He makes God real to all disciples. By the knowledge of God, the believer has eternal life. We know what glory is by knowing what God is. John said in 1:14 that they beheld His glory. To see the glory of the Father one should look upon the revelation of Him in the Son (17:3).

This is the third time He presented to the Father His desire for believers' unity (17:11,21,22). He mentioned it again in the next verse. The glory He gives to believers prepares them for the unity for which He prayed. By unity He meant the vital relationship

even so have I also sent them into the world: . . . so I sent off them on a mission into the world, *Wuest.*

19. And for their sakes I sanctify myself: I dedicate myself, *Montgomery* . . . I am consecrating myself, *Williams* . . . And for them I make myself holy, *BB.*

that they also might be sanctified through the truth: . . . that they may be made holy by the truth, *Phillips* . . . may be thoroughly dedicated in the truth, *Montgomery.*

20. Neither pray I for these alone: But it is not only for them that I am interceding, *TCNT* . . . do I make request, *Rotherham.*

but for them also which shall believe on me through their word: . . . but for all who will have faith in me, *BB* . . . through their message, *Williams* . . . their discourse, *Murdock* . . . thorowe their preachynge, *Tyndale* . . . by their spoken word, *Moffatt.*

21. That they all may be one: May they all be one, *Norlie.*

as thou, Father, art in me, and I in thee: Just as you, Father, live in me and I live in you, *Phillips.*

that they also may be one in us: . . . let them be united in us, *ALBA.*

that the world may believe that thou hast sent me: . . . so that the world may be convinced, *Williams* . . . that the world may believe, *Norlie* . . . that Thou didst commission me, *Concordant.*

22. ʼ καὶ ἐγὼ [☆ κἀγὼ] τὴν δόξαν
2504.1 conj kai And | 1466.1 prs-pron nom 1sing egō I | 2476.3 conj kagō [and I] | 3450.12 art acc sing fem tēn the | 1385.4 noun acc sing fem doxan glory

ἣν δέδωκάς μοι δέδωκα αὐτοῖς,
3614.12 rel-pron acc sing fem hēn which | 1319.11 verb 2sing indic act dedōkas you have given | 1466.4 prs-pron dat 1sing moi me | 1319.32 verb 1sing indic perf act dedōka have given | 840.2 prs-pron dat pl autois them,

ἵνα ὦσιν ἓν, καθὼς ἡμεῖς ἕν
2419.1 conj hina that | 1498.12 verb 3pl subj pres act ōsin they may be | 1518.9 num card neu hen one, | 2503.1 conj kathōs as | 2231.1 prs-pron nom 1pl hēmeis we | 1518.9 num card neu hen one

22.a.**Txt:** 01ℵ-corr,02A, 04C-corr,017K,036,037, 038,13,byz.it.sa.bo. Gries,Lach
Var: 01ℵ-org,03B, 04C-org,05D,019L,33, Treg,Alf,TiscWe/Ho, Weis,Sod,UBS/☆

ʼa ἐσμεν· ˋ 23. ἐγὼ ἐν αὐτοῖς, καὶ σὺ
1498.5 verb 1pl indic pres act esmen are: | 1466.1 prs-pron nom 1sing egō I | 1706.1 prep en in | 840.2 prs-pron dat pl autois them, | 2504.1 conj kai and | 4622.1 prs-pron nom 2sing su you

ἐν ἐμοί, ἵνα ὦσιν τετελειωμένοι εἰς
1706.1 prep en in | 1466.5 prs-pron dat 1sing emoi me, | 2419.1 conj hina that | 1498.12 verb 3pl subj pres act ōsin they may be | 4896.16 verb nom pl masc part perf pass teteleiōmenoi having been perfected | 1519.1 prep eis into

23.a.**Txt:** 02A,017K,036, 037,038,byz.
Var: 03B,04C,05D,019L, 033X,33,bo.LachTreg, Alf,Tisc,We/Ho,Weis, Sod,UBS/☆

ἕν, ʼa καὶ ˋ ἵνα γινώσκῃ ὁ κόσμος
1518.9 num card neu hen one, | 2504.1 conj kai and | 2419.1 conj hina that | 1091.6 verb 3sing subj pres act ginōskē may know | 3450.5 art sing masc ho the | 2862.1 noun nom sing masc kosmos world

ὅτι σύ με ἀπέστειλας, καὶ ἠγάπησας
3617.1 conj hoti that | 4622.1 prs-pron nom 2sing su you | 1466.6 prs-pron acc 1sing me me | 643.7 verb 2sing indic aor act apesteilas sent, | 2504.1 conj kai and | 25.13 verb 2sing indic aor act ēgapēsas loved

24.a.**Txt:** 01ℵ,04C,05D, 019L,032W,038,1,13, etc.byz.Sod
Var: 02A,03B,Lach, Treg,Alf,TiscWe/Ho, Weis,UBS/☆

αὐτοὺς καθὼς ἐμὲ ἠγάπησας. 24. ʼ☆ Πάτερ,
840.8 prs-pron acc pl masc autous them | 2503.1 conj kathōs as | 1466.7 prs-pron acc 1sing eme me | 25.13 verb 2sing indic aor act ēgapēsas you loved. | 3824.5 noun voc sing masc Pater Father,

24.b.**Txt:** 02A,04C,017K, 019L,036,037,1,13,byz. it.sa.Lach
Var: p60,01ℵ,03B,05D, 032W,bo.Treg,Alf,Tisc, We/HoWeis,Sod,UBS/☆

[a Πατήρ,] ʼ οὓς [b☆ ὃ] δέδωκάς μοι
3824.1 noun nom sing masc Patēr [idem] | 3614.8 rel-pron acc pl masc hous whom | 3614.16 rel-pron sing neu ho [which] | 1319.11 verb 2sing indic act dedōkas you have given | 1466.4 prs-pron dat 1sing moi me

θέλω ἵνα ὅπου εἰμὶ ἐγὼ κἀκεῖνοι
2286.1 verb 1sing pres act thelō I desire | 2419.1 conj hina that | 3562.1 adv hopou where | 1498.2 verb 1sing indic pres act eimi am | 1466.1 prs-pron nom 1sing egō I | 2519.4 conj kakeinoi those also

ὦσιν μετ' ἐμοῦ, ἵνα θεωρῶσιν τὴν δόξαν
1498.12 verb 3pl subj pres act ōsin may be | 3196.2 prep met' with | 1466.3 prs-pron gen 1sing emou me, | 2419.1 conj hina that | 2311.8 verb 3pl subj pres act theōrōsin they may see | 3450.12 art acc sing fem tēn the | 1385.4 noun acc sing fem doxan glory

which He expressed in the analogy of the vine and the branches (John 15). The glory of Christ's manifestation of the Father unifies all believers into a brotherhood which should be as inseparable as the Godhead itself. Jesus pointed to the unity of the triune God as the pattern for His Church.

22. And the glory which thou gavest me I have given them: . . . the glorious office, *Norton* . . . the honor, *AmpB* . . . I have imparted, *Fenton.*

that they may be one, even as we are one: May be completely united, *SEB.*

17:23. Unity is a result of completeness. The word "perfect" is a perfect participle indicating a process which brings believers to a completeness. The process continues until completeness is attained in quantity and quality. Unity is not possible until all parts have been assembled and the quality of the parts fit and function harmoniously. The preposition "in" furthers the thought of progress "toward." It is the believer's duty as a disciple to work toward the example of the Godhead unity. Jesus related unity to some extremely significant truths. Notice the associations: (1) in verse 11 of the disciples' unity maintained through the Father's name; (2) in verse 21 of being a disciple connected to believing the revelation of God in Christ; (3) in verse 22 of being disciples together joined to the glory Jesus came to impart; (4) in verse 23 of the presence of the Son and the Father preparing for the unity which brings a knowledge of God to the world.

The Father's love for us is measured by the Father's love for His Son. Ordinarily, believers contemplate and meditate on the Son's devotion to the Father. Perhaps contemplation of the Father's love and care for the Son could encourage believers to realize the extent to which the Father loves them.

23. I in them, and thou in me: I in union with them and thou with me, *TCNT.*

that they may be made perfect in one: May they be completely united, *SEB* . . . that they are completey one with Us, *Adams* . . . they may be completed in one, *Klingensmith* . . . they may stand in perfect union, *Weymouth* . . . so they may be perfectly one, *TCNT* . . . so that they may be perfectly united, *Williams* . . . may be perfected into one, *Murdock* . . . may persist in that state of completeness, *Wuest* . . . may be made completely one, *Norlie* . . . may grow complete into one, *Phillips* . . . may be perfect in unity, *Fenton.*

and that the world may know that thou hast sent me: . . . that the world may recognize, *Berkeley, Montgomery* . . . may realize, *Phillips* . . . and the world may be sure that you sent me, *Williams* . . . may know You sent Me, *Beck* . . . to the end that the world might be understanding, *Wuest.*

and hast loved them, as thou hast loved me: . . . and loved them as You loved me, *Beck.*

17:24. Thus far, Jesus had prayed for the Church's unity. In this verse His plea concerned two further requests.

In saying "where I am" He referred to himself as being already in heaven. His request, therefore, concerned the disciples' destiny. He looked beyond the years, trials, and joy, to their safe arrival to be with Him. "With me" expressed His desire for the believers' eternal fellowship with Him.

"My glory" refers to the glory of Jesus as the full and complete Redeemer (see verse 5). On earth believers know only a fraction of what their redemption means, but in heaven they will understand and behold the fullness of His revelation.

24. Father, I will that they also, whom thou hast given me: Father, I desire that, *ASV, Norlie* . . . Father, I want those, *Phillips* . . . I purpose that those, *Klingensmith* . . . all whom you have given me, *ALBA* . . . entrusted to me, *Fenton* . . . these, thy gift to me, *Moffatt* . . . as a permanent gift, *Wuest.*

be with me where I am: . . . to be with me where I am, *Phillips.*

17:25. The world does not know God. Christ knows God, so then Christ is the only possible mediator between the Father and the world. The disciples knew that the Father had sent Him. Everyone

24.c.**Txt:** 03B,07E,017K,036,038,byz.Weis
Var: 01ℵ,02A,04C,05D,019L,021M,032W,033X,037,13,Lach,TregAlf,Word,Tisc,We/Ho,Sod,UBS/☆

3450.12 art acc sing fem	**1684.9** adj acc 1sing fem	**3614.12** rel-pron acc sing fem	**1319.13** verb 2sing indic aor act	**1319.11** verb 2sing indic act
τὴν	ἐμὴν	ἣν	⸂ ἔδωκάς	[c☆ δέδωκάς]
tēn	*emēn*	*hēn*	*edōkas*	*dedōkas*
the	my	which	you gave	[you have given]

1466.4 prs-pron dat 1sing	**3617.1** conj	**25.13** verb 2sing indic aor act	**1466.6** prs-pron acc 1sing	**4112.1** prep	**2573.1** noun gen sing fem
μοι,	ὅτι	ἠγάπησάς	με	πρὸ	καταβολῆς
moi	*hoti*	*ēgapēsas*	*me*	*pro*	*katabolēs*
me,	for	you loved	me	before	foundation

25.a.**Txt:** p59,01ℵ,04C,05D,019L,032W,038,1,13,byz.Sod
Var: 02A,03B,Lach,Treg,Alf,TiscWe/Ho,Weis,UBS/☆

2862.2 noun gen sing masc		**3824.5** noun voc sing masc	**3824.1** noun nom sing masc	**1337.5** adj voc sing masc	**2504.1** conj
κόσμου.	**25.** ⸂☆	Πάτερ	[a πατὴρ]	δίκαιε,	καὶ
kosmou		*Pater*	*patēr*	*dikaie*	*kai*
of world.		Father	[idem]	righteous,	and

3450.5 art sing masc	**2862.1** noun nom sing masc	**4622.4** prs-pron acc 2sing	**3620.2** partic	**1091.17** verb 3sing indic aor act	**1466.1** prs-pron nom 1sing
ὁ	κόσμος	σε	οὐκ	ἔγνω,	ἐγὼ
ho	*kosmos*	*se*	*ouk*	*egnō*	*egō*
the	world	you	not	knew,	I

1156.2 conj	**4622.4** prs-pron acc 2sing	**1091.15** verb 1sing indic aor act	**2504.1** conj	**3642.7** dem-pron nom pl masc	**1091.18** verb 3pl indic aor act	**3617.1** conj
δέ	σε	ἔγνων,	καὶ	οὗτοι	ἔγνωσαν	ὅτι
de	*se*	*egnōn*	*kai*	*houtoi*	*egnōsan*	*hoti*
but	you	knew,	and	these	knew	that

4622.1 prs-pron nom 2sing	**1466.6** prs-pron acc 1sing	**643.7** verb 2sing indic aor act	**2504.1** conj	**1101.3** verb 1sing indic aor act
σύ	με	ἀπέστειλας·	**26.** καὶ	ἐγνώρισα
su	*me*	*apesteilas*	*kai*	*egnōrisa*
you	me	sent.	And	I made known

840.2 prs-pron dat pl	**3450.16** art sing neu	**3549.2** noun sing neu	**4622.2** prs-pron gen 2sing	**2504.1** conj	**1101.10** verb 1sing indic fut act
αὐτοῖς	τὸ	ὄνομά	σου,	καὶ	γνωρίσω·
autois	*to*	*onoma*	*sou*	*kai*	*gnōrisō*
to them	the	name	your,	and	will make known;

2419.1 conj	**3450.9** art nom sing fem	**26.1** noun nom sing fem	**3614.12** rel-pron acc sing fem	**25.13** verb 2sing indic aor act	**1466.6** prs-pron acc 1sing
ἵνα	ἡ	ἀγάπη	ἣν	ἠγάπησάς	με
hina	*hē*	*agapē*	*hēn*	*ēgapēsas*	*me*
that	the	love	with which	you loved	me

1706.1 prep	**840.2** prs-pron dat pl	**1498.10** verb 3sing subj pres act	**2476.3** conj	**1706.1** prep	**840.2** prs-pron dat pl	**3642.18** dem-pron pl neu
ἐν	αὐτοῖς	ᾖ,	κἀγὼ	ἐν	αὐτοῖς.	**18:1.** Ταῦτα
en	*autois*	*ē*	*kagō*	*en*	*autois*	*Tauta*
in	them	may be;	and I	in	them.	These things

1.a.**Txt:** p60,02A,04C,05D,017K,019L-corr,032W,036,037,038,byz.Lach,Sod
Var: 01ℵ,03B,019L-org,Treg,Alf,Tisc,We/Ho,Weis,UBS/☆

1500.15 verb nom sing masc part aor act	**3450.5** art sing masc	**2400.1** name nom masc	**1814.3** verb 3sing indic aor act	**4713.1** prep dat	**3450.4** art dat pl
εἰπὼν	⸂a ὁ ⸃	Ἰησοῦς	ἐξῆλθεν	σὺν	τοῖς
eipōn	*ho*	*Iēsous*	*exēlthen*	*sun*	*tois*
having said		Jesus	went out	with	the

3073.7 noun dat pl masc	**840.3** prs-pron gen sing	**3871.1** adv	**3450.2** art gen sing	**5329.1** noun gen sing masc	**3450.1** art gen pl
μαθηταῖς	αὐτοῦ	πέραν	τοῦ	χειμάρρου	⸂ τῶν
mathētais	*autou*	*peran*	*tou*	*cheimarrhou*	*tōn*
disciples	his	beyond	the	winter stream	of the

could receive the same revelation, believe in Christ, and become part of God's family.

17:26. The past tense verb "have declared" and the future tense verb "will declare" refer to His earthly and heavenly work. His future work would be done by His intercessions for them and the Holy Spirit's ministry among them. "Thy name" refers to the revelation of God which He began to unfold when He became flesh (1:14). The process of making God known is an ever-increasing manifestation.

This verse expresses Christ's fourth request (see verse 24). Jesus prayed that the same love which exists within the Godhead would be extended from the Father to the disciples. How a holy God's love can be "in them" is the work of His redemption. It goes beyond His purchase to a realization of the believer's holiness. It is the love of God in believers which makes possible all future sanctification. The believer's holiness brings about constant fellowship with the holy God (1 John 1:3,7). Thus, Jesus interceded as the High Priest to bring God and the believer into perfect unity. That becomes possible when the same love shared by the Father and the Son is shared by the believer. The believer is not forced by law to become holy, nor would it be possible. The believer is compelled by love toward holiness. By sharing God's love, the believer is empowered toward reaching his standing already credited to his account through the merits of Christ.

"And I in them" is also expressed in verse 23. This was Jesus' fifth and last request in behalf of all believers (verse 20). Jesus was inseparable from the love He had just asked to dwell in them. Whatever happens to believers happens to Him. He cannot be separated from them (Romans 8:37-39). The Father's love for Him will be the same as His love for believers because He dwells "in them." The Father's love, union, and fellowship is complete "in them" because it is perfect in Him.

18:1. At this point John's Gospel proceeds to record our Lord's sacrificial work. Chapters 18 to 20 have much in common with the Synoptics. However, John's Gospel does not include some of the incidents related by Matthew, Mark, and Luke, but contains other important details not recorded in them.

When Jesus "went forth" here, we have the first indication of a change of place since He and His disciples came to the room for the Last Supper (13:1). We conclude that the events connected with the supper and His entire discourse were located in the same room. It was probably about midnight when Jesus and the Eleven left the room for the Garden.

that they may behold my glory, which thou hast given me: . . . might be continually beholding, *Wuest* . . . let them have a vision of my glory, *ALBA*.

for thou lovedst me before the foundation of the world: . . . the beginning of the world, *TCNT* . . . before the world was made, *Beck* . . . before the disruption of the world, *Concordant* . . . before the world began, *ALBA* . . . before the foundation of the universe, *Wuest* . . . before the formation, *Campbell* . . . before the world was created, *SEB* . . . the founding of the world, *Berkeley* . . . the creation, *Williams, Confraternity*.

25. O righteous Father, the world hath not known thee: Just Father, *Concordant* . . . indeed knew you not, *Fenton* . . . has failed to recognize Thee, *Weymouth*.

but I have known thee, and these have known that thou hast sent me: . . . that I have thy commission, *Campbell*.

26. And I have declared unto them thy name, and will declare it: I have made known, *Confraternity* . . . I revealed Your name, *SEB* . . . I made known to them your very self, *Williams* . . . revealed to them Your power, and will continue to reveal it, *Fenton* . . . I have made your self known to them and I will continue to do so, *Phillips*.

that the love wherewith thou hast loved me: . . . the same love that You have for me, *SEB* . . . so that the love, *Williams* . . . they may share in the love, *Campbell* . . . You have bestowed upon me, *AmpB*.

may be in them, and I in them: . . . may be felt in them, *Williams* . . . may be in their hearts, *Phillips*.

1. When Jesus had spoken these words: After offering this prayer, *Weymouth* . . . Having thus spoken, *Norton* . . . These things spake Jesus, *Murdock*.

he went forth with his disciples over the brook Cedron: . . . across the Kidron valley, *RSV* . . . and crossed the gorge, *ALBA* . . . to a place across the Ravine of Cedars, *Montgomery* . . . Brook of the Cedars, *Panin* . . . the Kedron winter brook, *Concordant*

John 18:2

1.b.**Txt:** 01א-corr,03B,04C,019L,022N,036,038,1,13,byz.We/Ho
Var1: .02A,037,Gries,LachWeis,Sod,UBS/☆
Var2: .01א-org,05D,032W,sa.Tisc

2718.1 name gen pl fem	[1b☆ **3450.2** art gen sing	**2718.1** name masc	2 **3450.2** art gen sing	**2718.2** name gen sing masc	**3562.1** adv
Κέδρων,	τοῦ	Κεδρὼν,	τοῦ	κέδρου,]	ὅπου
Kedrōn	*tou*	*Kedrōn*	*tou*	*kedrou*	*hopou*
Cedron,	[of the	Cedron,	of the	Cedron,]	where

1498.34 verb sing indic imperf act	**2752.1** noun nom sing masc	**1519.1** prep	**3614.6** rel-pron acc sing masc	**1511.3** verb 3sing indic aor act	**840.5** prs-pron nom sing masc
ἦν	κῆπος,	εἰς	ὃν	εἰσῆλθεν	αὐτὸς
ēn	*kēpos*	*eis*	*hon*	*eisēlthen*	*autos*
was	a garden,	into	which	entered	he

2504.1 conj	**3450.7** art pl masc	**3073.5** noun nom pl masc	**840.3** prs-pron gen sing	**3471.11** verb 3sing indic plperf act	**1156.2** conj	**2504.1** conj
καὶ	οἱ	μαθηταὶ	αὐτοῦ.	2. ᾔδει	δὲ	καὶ
kai	*hoi*	*mathētai*	*autou*	*ēdei*	*de*	*kai*
and	the	disciples	his.	Had known	and	also

2430.1 name nom masc	**3450.5** art sing masc	**3722.3** verb nom sing masc part pres act	**840.6** prs-pron acc sing masc	**3450.6** art acc sing masc	**4964.4** noun acc sing masc
Ἰούδας	ὁ	παραδιδοὺς	αὐτὸν	τὸν	τόπον·
Ioudas	*ho*	*paradidous*	*auton*	*ton*	*topon*
Judas	the	delivering up	him	the	place,

2.a.**Txt:** 02A,04C,05D,017K,032W,036,037,038,1,13,byz.Gries,Lach,Sod
Var: 01א,03B,019L,033X,Treg,Alf,Tisc,We/Ho,Weis,UBS/☆

3617.1 conj	**4038.1** adv	**4714.19** verb 3sing indic aor pass	**3450.5** art sing masc	**2400.1** name nom masc	**1550.1** adv
ὅτι	πολλάκις	συνήχθη	(a ὁ)	Ἰησοῦς	ἐκεῖ
hoti	*pollakis*	*sunēchthē*	*ho*	*Iēsous*	*ekei*
because	often	was gathered		Jesus	there

3196.3 prep	**3450.1** art gen pl	**3073.6** noun gen pl masc	**840.3** prs-pron gen sing	**3450.5** art sing masc	**3631.1** conj
μετὰ	τῶν	μαθητῶν	αὐτοῦ.	3. ὁ	οὖν
meta	*tōn*	*mathētōn*	*autou*	*ho*	*oun*
with	the	disciples	his.		Therefore

2430.1 name nom masc	**2956.25** verb nom sing masc part aor act	**3450.12** art acc sing fem	**4539.3** noun acc sing fem	**2504.1** conj	**1523.2** prep gen
Ἰούδας	λαβὼν	τὴν	σπεῖραν,	καὶ	ἐκ
Ioudas	*labōn*	*tēn*	*speiran*	*kai*	*ek*
Judas	having received	the	band,	and	from

3.a.**Var:** 01א-org,05D,019L,Tisc,We/Ho,Sod,UBS/☆

3450.1 art gen pl	**744.6** noun gen pl masc	**2504.1** conj	**1523.2** prep gen	**3450.1** art gen pl
τῶν	ἀρχιερέων	καὶ	[a☆+ ἐκ	τῶν]
tōn	*archiereōn*	*kai*	*ek*	*tōn*
the	chief priests	and	[from	the]

5168.5 name gen pl masc	**5095.6** noun acc pl masc	**2048.34** verb 3sing indic pres	**1550.1** adv	**3196.3** prep	**5160.1** noun gen pl masc
Φαρισαίων	ὑπηρέτας,	ἔρχεται	ἐκεῖ	μετὰ	φανῶν
Pharisaiōn	*hupēretas*	*erchetai*	*ekei*	*meta*	*phanōn*
Pharisees	officers,	comes	there	with	torches

2504.1 conj	**2958.3** noun gen pl fem	**2504.1** conj	**3559.2** noun gen pl neu	**2400.1** name nom masc	**3631.1** conj
καὶ	λαμπάδων	καὶ	ὅπλων.	4. Ἰησοῦς	οὖν
kai	*lampadōn*	*kai*	*hoplōn*	*Iēsous*	*oun*
and	lamps	and	weapons.	Jesus	therefore

3471.18 verb nom sing masc part perf act	**3820.1** adj	**3450.17** art pl neu	**2048.52** verb acc pl neu part pres	**1894.2** prep	**840.6** prs-pron acc sing masc
εἰδὼς	πάντα	τὰ	ἐρχόμενα	ἐπ'	αὐτὸν,
eidōs	*panta*	*ta*	*erchomena*	*ep'*	*auton*
having known	all things	the	coming	upon	him,

It may be coincidental, but it is surely interesting to note that man's original home was a garden (Genesis 2:8), he fell in that garden (Genesis 3:8), Jesus drank the cup of man's fall in a garden (Matthew 26:36), and the healing of nations will come from the tree of life in a gardenlike place (Revelation 22:2).

This verse shows that Jesus' high priestly prayer was made before His Garden of Gethsemane prayers, which are reported by the Synoptics (Matthew 26:39-46; Mark 14:35-41; Luke 22:41-46).

The "garden" is identified by Matthew and Mark as the Garden of Gethsemane (Matthew 26:36; Mark 14:32). It was likely owned by a friend, and its location was on the western slope of the Mount of Olives.

18:2. Probably the events of the evening were prearranged. John says that Judas knew "the place." Jesus and His disciples often resorted to the Garden while in Jerusalem.

Evidently the shadowing olive trees made a comfortable place where Jesus could teach His disciples. Perhaps they also slept there often when in the vicinity (Luke 21:37). It may be that Judas expected to find them all asleep. We are not told why they would leave the shelter of the home where they had eaten to go into the Garden at that hour. Jesus, knowing what was coming, may have felt the Garden was a safer place for the disciples.

18:3. A Roman cohort was a force of 600 men when at full strength. The cohort was stationed in the Tower of Antonia, the castle fortress at the northwest corner of the temple area, and its chief duty was to maintain peace in Jerusalem. Some of the cohort were doubtless left in the tower, and a strong contingent followed Judas to seize Jesus.

"Officers from the chief priests" were Levitical temple guards. According to Luke 22:52 some of the chief priests and elders were present to arrest Jesus. "And Pharisees" indicates the sect who were foremost in their opposition to Jesus.

The "lanterns" (*phanōn*) and "torches" (*lampadōn*) are very similar in meaning, both having been translated "torch" on occasion. It appears that *phanōn* referred to torches made up of strips of resin-treated wood tied together. *Lampadōn* were containers with space for oil and a wick. The word is used in Matthew 25 to describe the lamps of the 10 virgins. The mob came to make a thorough search of the Garden.

18:4. "Knowing" (Greek, *eidōs*) is used of Jesus' divine knowledge at least eight times in John's Gospel (6:6,61,64; 13:1,3,11; 18:4;

. . . the winter-torrent, *Rotherham* . . . the winter-stream, *PNT.*

where was a garden, into the which he entered, and his disciples: . . . to an orchard, *Moffatt* . . . There was a garden there, *Norlie.*

2. And Judas also, which betrayed him, knew the place: Judas the Traitor also knew this place, *Montgomery, ALBA* . . . was well known to, *TCNT* . . . who was false to him, *BB* . . . the one who turned against Jesus, *SEB* . . . the betrayer, *Murdock* . . . is acquainted with the place, *Concordant* . . . knew the spot, *Norlie.*

for Jesus ofttimes resorted thither with his disciples: . . . had often met there, *Montgomery, TCNT* . . . because frequently Jesus met there, *Wuest* . . . had often met in it, *ALBA* . . . assembled there, *Concordant.*

3. Judas then, having received a band of men and officers from the chief priests and Pharisees: So after procuring troops and some attendants, *Moffatt* . . . taking charge of, *AmpB* . . . So Judas fetched, *Phillips* . . . a squad and deputies, *Concordant* . . . So after getting troops and some Temple police, *Montgomery* . . . the Roman garrison, *Williams* . . . take a company, *Norlie* . . . a regiment, *Murdock* . . . a Roman cohort, *Adams.*

cometh thither with lanterns and torches and weapons: . . . and arms, *Fenton, Campbell* . . . they were armed, *TEV* . . . Judas came there with, *Montgomery.*

4. Jesus therefore, knowing all things that should come upon him: Jesus, fully realizing all that was going to happen to him, *Phillips* . . . fully aware, *Concordant* . . . knowing exactly what was going to happen to Him, *Beck* . . . He knew everything that was going to befall, *Williams* . . . knowing all the events that were coming upon Him, *Fenton*

John 18:5

4.a.**Txt:** 01ℵ,02A, 04C-corr,017K,019L, 032W,036,037,038,13, byz.Gries,Word
Var: 03B,04C-org,05D,1, LachTreg,Alf,Tisc, We/Ho,Weis,Sod,UBS/☆

1814.13 verb nom sing masc part aor act	**1500.5** verb 3sing indic aor act	**1814.3** verb 3sing indic aor act	**2504.1** conj	**2978.5** verb 3sing indic pres act
⸀ ἐξελθὼν	εἶπεν	[a☆ ἐξῆλθεν	καὶ	λέγει]
exelthōn	*eipen*	*exēlthen*	*kai*	*legei*
having gone forth	said	[went forth	and	says]

840.2 prs-pron dat pl	**4949.1** intr-pron	**2195.1** verb 2pl pres act	**552.8** verb 3pl indic aor pass	**840.4** prs-pron dat sing
αὐτοῖς,	Τίνα	ζητεῖτε;	5. Ἀπεκρίθησαν	αὐτῷ,
autois	*Tina*	*zēteite*	*Apekrithēsan*	*autō*
to them,	Whom	seek you?	They answered	him,

2400.3 name acc masc	**3450.6** art acc sing masc	**3343.3** name acc sing masc	**2978.5** verb 3sing indic pres act	**840.2** prs-pron dat pl
Ἰησοῦν	τὸν	Ναζωραῖον.	Λέγει	αὐτοῖς
Iēsoun	*ton*	*Nazōraion*	*Legei*	*autois*
Jesus	the	Nazarene.	Says	to them

5.a.**Txt:** 02A,04C,017K, 019L,032W,036,037, 038,1,13,etc.byz.sa.bo. Lach,Sod
Var: p60,03B,05D,it. Treg,Alf,We/Ho,Weis, UBS/☆

3450.5 art sing masc	**2400.1** name nom masc	**1466.1** prs-pron nom 1sing	**1498.2** verb 1sing indic pres act	**2449.22** verb 3sing indic plperf act
⸂a ὁ	Ἰησοῦς, ⸃	Ἐγώ	εἰμι.	Εἱστήκει
ho	*Iēsous*	*Egō*	*eimi*	*Heistēkei*
	Jesus,	I	am.	Had stood

1156.2 conj	**2504.1** conj	**2430.1** name nom masc	**3450.5** art sing masc	**3722.3** verb nom sing masc part pres act	**840.6** prs-pron acc sing masc
δὲ	καὶ	Ἰούδας	ὁ	παραδιδοὺς	αὐτὸν
de	*kai*	*Ioudas*	*ho*	*paradidous*	*auton*
and	also	Judas	the	delivering up	him

6.a.**Txt:** 04C,07E,017K, 036,037,13,byz.Gries, Word
Var: 01ℵ,02A,03B,05D, 019L,033X,33,Lach, TregTisc,We/Ho,Weis, Sod,UBS/☆

3196.2 prep	**840.1** prs-pron gen pl	**5453.1** conj	**3631.1** conj	**1500.5** verb 3sing indic aor act	**840.2** prs-pron dat pl
μετ'	αὐτῶν.	6. Ὡς	οὖν	εἶπεν	αὐτοῖς,
met'	*autōn*	*Hōs*	*oun*	*eipen*	*autois*
with	them.	When	therefore	he said	to them,

6.b.**Txt:** 02A,04C,017K, 019L,038,etc.byz.Weis, Sod
Var: 01ℵ,03B,05D,Lach, TregAlf,Tisc,We/Ho, UBS/☆

3617.1 conj	**1466.1** prs-pron nom 1sing	**1498.2** verb 1sing indic pres act	**562.1** verb indic aor act	**562.21** verb 3pl indic aor act
⸂a Ὅτι ⸃	Ἐγώ	εἰμι,	⸀☆ ἀπῆλθον	[b ἀπῆλθαν]
Hoti	*Egō*	*eimi*	*apēlthon*	*apēlthan*
	I	am,	they went	[idem]

6.c.**Txt:** 02A,017K,021M, 036,037,038,byz.
Var: 01ℵ,03B,04C,05D, 019L,033X,33,Lach, TregAlf,Tisc,We/Ho, Weis,Sod,UBS/☆

1519.1 prep	**3450.17** art pl neu	**3557.1** adv	**2504.1** conj	**3959.3** verb indic aor act	**3959.6** verb 3pl indic aor act
εἰς	τὰ	ὀπίσω	καὶ	⸀ ἔπεσον	[c☆ ἔπεσαν]
eis	*ta*	*opisō*	*kai*	*epeson*	*epesan*
into	the	behind	and	fell	[idem]

5312.1 adv	**3687.1** adv	**3631.1** conj	**840.8** prs-pron acc pl masc	**1890.6** verb 3sing indic aor act
χαμαί.	7. πάλιν	οὖν	⸀ αὐτους	ἐπηρώτησεν,
chamai	*palin*	*oun*	*autous*	*epērōtēsen*
to ground.	Again	therefore	them	he questioned,

1890.6 verb 3sing indic aor act	**840.8** prs-pron acc pl masc	**4949.1** intr-pron	**2195.1** verb 2pl pres act	**3450.7** art pl masc	**1156.2** conj
[☆ ἐπηρώτησεν	αὐτούς,]	Τίνα	ζητεῖτε;	Οἱ	δὲ
epērōtēsen	*autous*	*Tina*	*zēteite*	*Hoi*	*de*
[he questioned	them,]	Whom	seek you?	The	and

7.a.**Txt:** 01ℵ,02A,03B, 04C,019L,038,etc.byz. Lach,Tisc,Sod
Var: 05D,033X,We/Ho, Weis,UBS/☆

1500.3 verb indic aor act	**1500.28** verb 3pl indic aor act	**2400.3** name acc masc	**3450.6** art acc sing masc	**3343.3** name acc sing masc
⸀ εἶπον,	[a☆ εἶπαν,]	Ἰησοῦν	τὸν	Ναζωραῖον.
eipon	*eipan*	*Iēsoun*	*ton*	*Nazōraion*
said,	[idem]	Jesus	the	Nazarene.

19:28). His divine knowledge prompted Him to go forth to meet His enemies. Their lanterns, torches, and weapons were unnecessary baggage. He did not hide but "went forth," not as a guilty criminal but as a judge who takes charge of the trial.

He yielded himself as a voluntary offering. In asking the question, "Whom seek ye?" He diverted attention from His disciples and focused the Jews' attention on their dreadful intent.

. . . was about to befall him, *AmpB* . . . knew all that was going to happen to him, *ALBA* . . . all that was to come upon him, *Confraternity.*

went forth, and said unto them, Whom seek ye?: . . . advanced and asked, *Fenton* . . . Who is it that you are looking for? *Montgomery* . . . Who is it you want? *ALBA* . . . For whom are you looking, *Norlie.*

18:5. "Jesus of Nazareth" was a contemptuous expression in their thinking (see 19:19). He was called a Nazarene because He resided in Nazareth. There is no connection between Jesus and the idea of a Nazarite vow. Jesus was not a Nazarite. If He were at any time a Nazarite, the New Testament writers have not recorded it.

"I am he" is the tone of deity, for the Jews would remember that these Greek words were the very expression of the Greek Septuagint of Exodus 3:14, in which it is the title of God himself.

5. They answered him, Jesus of Nazareth. Jesus saith unto them, I am he: . . . the Nazarene, *Murdock.*

And Judas also, which betrayed him, stood with them: Now Judas also...was standing with them, *Rotherham* . . . stood among them, *ALBA* . . . the one who turned against Jesus, *SEB.*

18:6. "Fell to the ground" cannot be accounted for by the unexpected appearance of the Lord Jesus in the light of their torches. The words He spoke conveyed such power of His deity that His enemies "fell to the ground." It is a foreshadowing of the time when all shall prostrate themselves before Him! Did He not say, "Lazarus, come forth," and a burst of resurrection energy quickened the man? Could He who spoke the world into existence not call 12 legions of angels to His aid, or slay the wicked by His mouth (Isaiah 11:4)? Could He not prostrate a few hundred? The question is not could He do it. Rather, how could He filter such power so that it would not slay them before their Day of Judgment?

Jesus came to seek and to save, not to condemn and judge. His grace and mercy hold His wrath fast until His enemies have sufficient time to consider their rebellion against God.

6. As soon then as he had said unto them, I am he, they went backward, and fell to the ground: . . . they backed away, *Adams* . . . they stepped backward, *Norlie* . . . they drew back, *SEB, TCNT* . . . they moved back, *TEV* . . . they took a lurch backward, *Williams.*

7. Then asked he them again, Whom seek ye?: Whom are you looking for? *Adams.*

And they said, Jesus of Nazareth:

18:7. This verse refers to the second assertion of the same question because the first had confused them. When they were sufficiently recovered, they answered His restatement of the question.

18:8. For a second time Jesus said, "I am he." The "he" is not in the Greek; therefore the title of deity is more evident (see verse

8.a.**Txt:** 05D,033X,Steph
Var: 01ℵ,02A,03B,04C,017K,019L,036,037,038,byz.Gries,LachTreg,Alf,Tisc,We/Ho,Weis,Sod,UBS/☆

552.6 verb 3sing indic aor pass	**3450.5** art sing masc	**2400.1** name nom masc	**1500.3** verb indic aor act	**5050.3** prs-pron dat 2pl	**3617.1** conj
8. Ἀπεκρίθη	(a ὁ)	Ἰησοῦς,	Εἶπον	ὑμῖν	ὅτι
Apekrithē	*ho*	*Iēsous*	*Eipon*	*humin*	*hoti*
Answered		Jesus,	I told	you	that

1466.1 prs-pron nom 1sing	**1498.2** verb 1sing indic pres act	**1479.1** conj	**3631.1** conj	**1466.7** prs-pron acc 1sing	**2195.1** verb 2pl pres act
ἐγώ	εἰμι.	εἰ	οὖν	ἐμὲ	ζητεῖτε,
egō	*eimi*	*ei*	*oun*	*eme*	*zēteite*
I	am.	If	therefore	me	you seek,

856.18 verb 2pl impr aor act	**3642.8** dem-pron acc pl masc	**5055.10** verb inf pres act	**2419.1** conj	**3997.22** verb 3sing subj aor pass
ἄφετε	τούτους	ὑπάγειν·	**9.** ἵνα	πληρωθῇ
aphete	*toutous*	*hupagein*	*hina*	*plērōthē*
allow	these	to go away;	that	might be fulfilled

3450.5 art sing masc	**3030.1** noun nom sing masc	**3614.6** rel-pron acc sing masc	**1500.5** verb 3sing indic aor act	**3617.1** conj	**3614.8** rel-pron acc pl masc
ὁ	λόγος	ὃν	εἶπεν.	Ὅτι	Οὓς
ho	*logos*	*hon*	*eipen*	*Hoti*	*Hous*
the	word	which	he said,		Whom

1319.11 verb 2sing indic act	**1466.4** prs-pron dat 1sing	**3620.2** partic	**616.2** verb 1sing indic aor act	**1523.1** prep gen	**840.1** prs-pron gen pl
δέδωκάς	μοι	οὐκ	ἀπώλεσα	ἐξ	αὐτῶν
dedōkas	*moi*	*ouk*	*apōlesa*	*ex*	*autōn*
you have given	me	not	I lost	of	them

3625.3 num card acc masc	**4468.1** name masc	**3631.1** conj	**3935.1** name nom masc	**2174.17** verb nom sing masc part pres act
οὐδένα.	**10.** Σίμων	οὖν	Πέτρος	ἔχων
oudena	*Simōn*	*oun*	*Petros*	*echōn*
not one.	Simon	therefore	Peter	having

3134.4 noun acc sing fem	**1657.2** verb 3sing indic aor act	**840.12** prs-pron acc sing fem	**2504.1** conj	**3680.1** verb 3sing indic aor act	**3450.6** art acc sing masc
μάχαιραν	εἵλκυσεν	αὐτὴν,	καὶ	ἔπαισεν	τὸν
machairan	*heilkusen*	*autēn*	*kai*	*epaisen*	*ton*
a sword,	drew	it,	and	struck	the

3450.2 art gen sing	**744.2** noun gen sing masc	**1395.4** noun acc sing masc	**2504.1** conj	**604.1** verb 3sing indic aor act	**840.3** prs-pron gen sing
τοῦ	ἀρχιερέως	δοῦλον,	καὶ	ἀπέκοψεν	αὐτοῦ
tou	*archiereōs*	*doulon*	*kai*	*apekopsen*	*autou*
of the	high priest	servant,	and	cut off	his

10.a.**Txt:** p66,02A,04C-corr,05D,017K,036,037,038,1,13,byz.Gries,Lach
Var: p60,01ℵ,03B,04C-org,019L,032W,033X,Treg,Alf,Tisc,We/Ho,WeisSod,UBS/☆

3450.16 art sing neu	**5454.2** noun acc sing neu	**5453.1** noun acc sing neu	**3450.16** art sing neu	**1182.1** adj acc sing
τὸ	(ὠτίον	[a☆ ὠτάριον]	τὸ	δεξιόν.
to	*ōtion*	*ōtarion*	*to*	*dexion*
the	ear	[idem]	the	right.

1498.34 verb sing indic imperf act	**1156.2** conj	**3549.2** noun sing neu	**3450.3** art dat sing	**1395.3** noun dat sing masc	**3096.1** name nom masc
ἦν	δὲ	ὄνομα	τῷ	δούλῳ	Μάλχος.
ēn	*de*	*onoma*	*tō*	*doulō*	*Malchos*
Was	and	name	the	servant's	Malchus.

1500.5 verb 3sing indic aor act	**3631.1** conj	**3450.5** art sing masc	**2400.1** name nom masc	**3450.3** art dat sing	**3935.3** name dat masc
11. εἶπεν	οὖν	ὁ	Ἰησοῦς	τῷ	Πέτρῳ,
eipen	*oun*	*ho*	*Iēsous*	*tō*	*Petrō*
Said	therefore		Jesus		to Peter,

6). He stated from His own lips His identity. There was no need for Judas to come with them to identify Him with a kiss.

In His greatest peril, He thought of His disciples' welfare. As the Good Shepherd He placed himself in the position of danger; His disciples would be safe.

The disciples surely remembered how thoughtful Jesus was of their safety. Furthermore, the words "let these go" served as a signal for His friends to depart from Him that they might not share His arrest. He had forbidden the disciples to use force in protecting His personal well-being. Now He excused them from the bitter trial into which He was entering in their behalf. After more than 60 years, John still recalled the blessed care Jesus demonstrated in their behalf that night.

For a second time Jesus protected His flock when Annas questioned Him concerning His disciples and His teaching (verse 19). He ignored the question about His disciples and focused their attention on himself and His teaching.

8. Jesus answered, I have told you that I am he:

if therefore ye seek me: If, then, you are looking for me, *Montgomery.*

let these go their way: . . . let these escape, *Berkeley* . . . permit these to go, *Wilson* . . . suffer these to withdraw, *Rotherham* . . . allow these men to go, *TCNT* . . . my disciples go, *Weymouth* . . . let these men go free, *SEB* . . . these men get away, *Moffatt.*

18:9. This verse refers to 17:12. The statement shows that Jesus' prayer to the Father concerning the protection of His disciples was still being answered.

It is characteristic of Jesus to lose or waste nothing. When He multiplied the bread, the fragments were gathered up. As to His time, Jesus never wasted it. When a disciple turned his back on Jesus, His sensitive heart felt it deeply. But this verse expresses the confidence Jesus has in making secure every disciple who wishes to follow Him.

9. That the saying might be fulfilled, which he spake: He did this to carry out the prophecy, *LivB* . . . that which he had spoken verified, *Campbell.*

Of them which thou gavest me have I lost none: . . . me as a permanent gift, I lost not even one of them, *Wuest* . . . I have not lost a single one, *Fenton* . . . let go to destruction, *Berkeley*

18:10. His faithful followers were confused because He was yielding to the arrest. If Jesus had encouraged them, the disciples would have fought the Roman cohort.

The apostles were indeed brave men, yet not so fearless without the sword. According to Luke 22:49, Peter asked if he should smite with the sword but did not wait for a reply.

Peter struck the high priest's servant and cut off his right ear. The servant's name was Malchus. Malchus was probably near Jesus and may have stretched out his hand to seize Jesus. John states particulars of this incident: Peter is identified as the defender of his Lord; Malchus is pointed to as the one who nearly lost his head. Mentioning the right ear is indicative of an eyewitness account.

One cannot help wondering what effect the healing of the ear had upon Malchus. When he had time to consider how swiftly the loss of his ear might have been his head, would he have been inclined to believe in Christ? One cannot help but wonder if Malchus' life was influenced by that night's experience.

10. Then Simon Peter having a sword drew it, and smote the high priest's servant: . . . drew it and wounded, *JB* . . . and aiming it at, *Weymouth* . . . and aimed a blow at, *TCNT* . . . and slashed at, *Phillips* . . . and hits the chief priest's slave, *Concordant.*

and cut off his right ear: . . . and sliced his right ear off, *Adams* . . . and strikes off his right ear, *Concordant* . . . and cut off the tip of, *Fenton.*

The servant's name was Malchus: . . . the slave's name, *ET.*

11. Then said Jesus unto Peter, Put up thy sword into the sheath: Jesus commanded Peter, *NIV*

11.a.**Txt:** Steph
Var: 01ℵ,02A,03B,04C, 05D,017K,019L,036, 037,038,byz.Gries,Lach Treg,Alf,Word,Tisc, We/Ho,Weis,Sod,UBS/☆

900.16 verb 2sing impr aor act	**3450.12** art acc sing fem	**3134.4** noun acc sing fem	**4622.2** prs-pron gen 2sing	**1519.1** prep	**3450.12** art acc sing fem
Βάλε	τὴν	μάχαιραν	(a σου)	εἰς	τὴν
Bale	*tēn*	*machairan*	*sou*	*eis*	*tēn*
Put	the	sword	your	into	the

2313.1 noun acc sing fem	**3450.16** art sing neu	**4080.1** noun sing neu	**3614.16** rel-pron sing neu	**1319.33** verb 3sing indic perf act	**1466.4** prs-pron dat 1sing
θήκην.	τὸ	ποτήριον	ὃ	δέδωκέν	μοι
thēkēn	*to*	*potērion*	*ho*	*dedōken*	*moi*
sheath;	the	cup	which	has given	me

3450.5 art sing masc	**3824.1** noun nom sing masc	**3620.3** partic	**3231.1** partic	**3956.14** verb 1sing subj aor act	**840.15** prs-pron sing neu
ὁ	πατὴρ	οὐ	μὴ	πίω	αὐτό;
ho	*patēr*	*ou*	*mē*	*piō*	*auto*
the	Father	not	not	I drink	it?

3450.9 art nom sing fem	**3631.1** conj	**4539.1** noun nom sing fem	**2504.1** conj	**3450.5** art sing masc	**5341.1** noun nom sing masc
12. Ἡ	οὖν	σπεῖρα	καὶ	ὁ	χιλίαρχος
Hē	*oun*	*speira*	*kai*	*ho*	*chiliarchos*
The	therefore	band	and	the	chief captain

2504.1 conj	**3450.7** art pl masc	**5095.3** noun nom pl masc	**3450.1** art gen pl	**2428.3** name-adj gen pl masc	**4666.1** verb act
καὶ	οἱ	ὑπηρέται	τῶν	Ἰουδαίων	συνέλαβον
kai	*hoi*	*hupēretai*	*tōn*	*Ioudaiōn*	*sunelabon*
and	the	officers	of the	Jews	took hold of

3450.6 art acc sing masc	**2400.3** name acc masc	**2504.1** conj	**1204.2** verb 3pl indic aor act	**840.6** prs-pron acc sing masc	**2504.1** conj
τὸν	Ἰησοῦν,	καὶ	ἔδησαν	αὐτὸν,	**13.** καὶ
ton	*Iēsoun*	*kai*	*edēsan*	*auton*	*kai*
	Jesus,	and	bound	him;	and

13.a.**Txt:** 01ℵ-corr,02A, 04C,017K,019L,036, 037,038,1,byz.
Var: 01ℵ-org,03B,05D, 032W,Treg,Tisc,We/Ho, Weis,Sod,UBS/☆

516.3 verb 3pl indic aor act	**840.6** prs-pron acc sing masc	**70.10** verb 3pl indic aor act	**4242.1** prep	**450.3** name acc masc
(ἀπήγαγον	αὐτὸν	[a☆ ἤγαγον]	πρὸς	Ἄνναν
apēgagon	*auton*	*ēgagon*	*pros*	*Annan*
they led away	him	[led]	to	Annas

4270.1 adv	**1498.34** verb sing indic imperf act	**1056.1** conj	**3857.1** noun nom sing masc	**3450.2** art gen sing	**2505.2** name gen masc
πρῶτον·	ἦν	γὰρ	πενθερὸς	τοῦ	Καϊάφα,
prōton	*ēn*	*gar*	*pentheros*	*tou*	*Kaiapha*
first;	he was	for	father-in-law		of Caiaphas,

3614.5 rel-pron nom sing masc	**1498.34** verb sing indic imperf act	**744.1** noun nom sing masc	**3450.2** art gen sing	**1747.1** noun gen sing masc	**1552.2** dem-pron gen sing
ὃς	ἦν	ἀρχιερεὺς	τοῦ	ἐνιαυτοῦ	ἐκείνου·
hos	*ēn*	*archiereus*	*tou*	*eniautou*	*ekeinou*
who	was	high priest	of the	year	that.

1498.34 verb sing indic imperf act	**1156.2** conj	**2505.1** name nom masc	**3450.5** art sing masc	**4674.2** verb nom sing masc part aor act	**3450.4** art dat pl
14. ἦν	δὲ	Καϊάφας	ὁ	συμβουλεύσας	τοῖς
ēn	*de*	*Kaiaphas*	*ho*	*sumbouleusas*	*tois*
It was	and	Caiaphas	the	having given counsel	to the

2428.4 name-adj dat pl masc	**3617.1** conj	**4702.1** verb 3sing indic pres act	**1518.4** num card acc masc	**442.4** noun acc sing masc
Ἰουδαίοις,	ὅτι	συμφέρει	ἕνα	ἄνθρωπον
Ioudaiois	*hoti*	*sumpherei*	*hena*	*anthrōpon*
Jews,	that	it is profitable	for one	man

18:11. Jesus did two things to correct Peter's actions. First, He said to Peter, "Put up thy sword into the sheath." This taught Peter not to use violence to promote the kingdom of God. Second, Jesus touched Malchus' ear and healed him (Luke 22:51). Verse 26 states that a relative of Malchus identified Peter as one of Jesus' disciples.

"The cup" refers to Jesus' sufferings and crucifixion (compare Mark 10:38; Luke 22:42). The Saviour saw this hour as the time in the divine plan for His work of redemption. He yielded himself to the desires of His enemies. He did not allow man to force Him to the Cross. His own words were: "I lay down My life that I may take it again. No one has taken it away from Me" (10:17,18, NASB).

. . . Sheathe your sword, *Moffatt* . . . Put your sword into its scabbard, *Beck* . . . back into its place! *SEB.*

the cup which my Father hath given me, shall I not drink it?: The chalice which, *Douay* . . . Must I not drink the cup which the Father has handed me, *Williams* . . . Shall I refuse to drink the cup, *Weymouth* . . . Shall I not willingly accept whatever the Father sends me, however bitter it may be? *Barclay* . . . the cup of sorrow, *Weymouth.*

18:12. Peter's attempt to fight prompted the "captain and officers of the Jews" to make Jesus secure by binding His arms. The other Gospels record Jesus' protest of the manner in which the Jews and Romans came to take Him (Matthew 26:55; Mark 14:48; Luke 22:52). This He did to emphasize that He was a willing sufferer. What He did was in behalf of others and not because of any wrong that He had done.

The officers made sure of their prisoner by binding Him, thus identifying Him as the prisoner. Binding was a confining condition, part of the humiliation of Jesus. Jesus, the God-man, voluntarily yielded to the shame of being confined by His ignorant and unjust creatures.

12. Then the band and the captain and the officers of the Jews took Jesus, and bound him: So the troops, *AmpB* . . . So the troops and their commandant and the Jewish police, *Montgomery* . . . Then the company of soldiers, with their captain and Jewish underlings, *Norlie* . . . The squad apprehended Jesus, *Concordant* . . . Jewish constables ...put him in chains, *TCNT* . . . headed by their colonel, *Fenton* . . . seized Jesus and bound him, *ASV* . . . seized Jesus, *Confraternity* . . . arrested Jesus and put handcuffs on him, *Williams* . . . put cords round him, *BB* . . . tied him up, *SEB* . . . and tied his hands together, *Phillips.*

18:13. This verse explains why the mob took Jesus first to Annas. Annas had been high priest and still held the power as head of the family of which Caiaphas, his son-in-law, was a part. Both men were wealthy and possessed the influence and dignity of the highest office in the Jewish nation. "Annas" occurs four times in the New Testament (Luke 3:2; John 18:13,24; Acts 4:6). "Caiaphas" occurs nine times in the New Testament and five times in John's Gospel (11:49; 18:13,14,24,28).

13. And led him away to Annas first; for he was father in law to Caiaphas, which was the high priest that same year: . . . in the first instance to Annas, *Fenton.*

14. Now Caiaphas was he, which gave counsel to the Jews: He had advised the Jewish leaders, *SEB.*

18:14. This verse refers to the facts stated in 11:49f. The high priest was the head of the priesthood and all religious functions. The first high priest was Aaron, and the high priest's office was passed on to his family. The mention of Caiaphas here indicates that the trial of Jesus would be a mockery for its outcome was predetermined by the high priest and the Sanhedrin. Therefore, a fair trial was not to be expected (see comments on 11:49).

Caiaphas occupied the seat of highest religious authority among the Jews. He presided over the Sanhedrin, the nation's highest

John 18:15

14.a.**Txt:** 02A,04C-corr,017K,021M,036,037,byz.Gries,Word,Sod
Var: 01א,03B,04C-org,05D,019L,038,33,it.bo.Lach,Treg,Alf,Tisc,We/HoWeis,UBS/☆

616.26 verb inf aor mid	**594.20** verb inf aor act	**5065.1** prep	**3450.2** art gen sing	**2967.2** noun gen sing masc
ʼ ἀπολέσθαι	[a☆ ἀποθανεῖν]	ὑπὲρ	τοῦ	λαοῦ.
apolesthai	*apothanein*	*huper*	*tou*	*laou*
to perish	[to die]	for	the	people.

188.21 verb 3sing indic imperf act	**1156.2** conj	**3450.3** art dat sing	**2400.2** name masc	**4468.1** name masc	**3935.1** name nom masc
15. Ἠκολούθει	δὲ	τῷ	Ἰησοῦ	Σίμων	Πέτρος
Ekolouthei	*de*	*tō*	*Iēsou*	*Simōn*	*Petros*
There followed	now		Jesus	Simon	Peter

15.a.**Txt:** 01א-corr,04C,017K,019L,036,037,038,1,13,byz.Gries
Var: p66,01א-org,02A,03B,05D,032W,sa.bo.Lach,Tisc,We/Ho,Weis,Sod,UBS/☆

2504.1 conj	**3450.5** art sing masc	**241.4** adj nom sing masc	**3073.1** noun nom sing masc	**3450.5** art sing masc	**1156.2** conj	**3073.1** noun nom sing masc
καὶ	ʼa ὁ ʽ	ἄλλος	μαθητής.	ὁ	δὲ	μαθητὴς
kai	*ho*	*allos*	*mathētēs*	*ho*	*de*	*mathētēs*
and	the	other	disciple.	The	and	disciple

1552.3 dem-pron nom sing masc	**1498.34** verb sing indic imperf act	**1104.1** adj nom sing masc	**3450.3** art dat sing	**744.3** noun dat sing masc	**2504.1** conj
ἐκεῖνος	ἦν	γνωστὸς	τῷ	ἀρχιερεῖ,	καὶ
ekeinos	*ēn*	*gnōstos*	*tō*	*archierei*	*kai*
that	was	known	to the	high priest,	and

4747.1 verb 3sing indic aor act	**3450.3** art dat sing	**2400.2** name masc	**1519.1** prep	**3450.12** art acc sing fem	**827.3** noun acc sing fem
συνεισῆλθεν	τῷ	Ἰησοῦ	εἰς	τὴν	αὐλὴν
suneisēlthen	*tō*	*Iēsou*	*eis*	*tēn*	*aulēn*
entered with		Jesus	into	the	court

3450.2 art gen sing	**744.2** noun gen sing masc	**3450.5** art sing masc	**1156.2** conj	**3935.1** name nom masc	**2449.22** verb 3sing indic plperf act
τοῦ	ἀρχιερέως·	**16.** ὁ	δὲ	Πέτρος	εἱστήκει
tou	*archiereōs*	*ho*	*de*	*Petros*	*heistēkei*
of the	high priest,		but	Peter	had stood

4242.1 prep	**3450.11** art dat sing fem	**2351.3** noun dat sing fem	**1838.1** prep gen	**1814.3** verb 3sing indic aor act	**3631.1** conj	**3450.5** art sing masc
πρὸς	τῇ	θύρᾳ	ἔξω.	ἐξῆλθεν	οὖν	ὁ
pros	*tē*	*thura*	*exō*	*exēlthen*	*oun*	*ho*
at	the	door	outside.	Went out	therefore	the

16.a.**Txt:** 01א,02A,04C-corr,05D,017K,032W,033X,036,037,038,1,13,byz.it.Lach
Var: 03B,04C-org,019L,TregAlf,Tisc,We/Ho,Weis,Sod,UBS/☆

3073.1 noun nom sing masc	**3450.5** art sing masc	**241.4** adj nom sing masc	**3614.5** rel-pron nom sing masc	**1498.34** verb sing indic imperf act	**3450.5** art sing masc
μαθητὴς	ὁ	ἄλλος	ʼ ὃς	ἦν	[a☆ ὁ]
mathētēs	*ho*	*allos*	*hos*	*ēn*	*ho*
disciple	the	other	who	was	[the]

16.b.**Txt:** 01א,02A,04C-corr,05D,017K,032W,036,037,038,1,13,byz.Lach
Var: 03B,04C-org,019L,033X,Treg,Alf,Tisc,We/Ho,WeisSod,UBS/☆

1104.1 adj nom sing masc	**3450.3** art dat sing	**744.3** noun dat sing masc	**3450.2** art gen sing	**744.2** noun gen sing masc
γνωστὸς	ʼ τῷ	ἀρχιερεῖ,	[b☆ τοῦ	ἀρχιερέως]
gnōstos	*tō*	*archierei*	*tou*	*archiereōs*
known	to the	high priest,	[of the	high priest]

2504.1 conj	**1500.5** verb 3sing indic aor act	**3450.11** art dat sing fem	**2354.2** noun dat sing fem	**2504.1** conj	**1507.1** verb 3sing indic aor act
καὶ	εἶπεν	τῇ	θυρωρῷ	καὶ	εἰσήγαγεν
kai	*eipen*	*tē*	*thurōrō*	*kai*	*eisēgagen*
and	spoke	to the	doorkeeper	and	brought in

3450.6 art acc sing masc	**3935.4** name acc masc	**2978.5** verb 3sing indic pres act	**3631.1** conj	**3450.9** art nom sing fem
τὸν	Πέτρον.	**17.** λέγει	οὖν	ʼ ἡ
ton	*Petron*	*legei*	*oun*	*hē*
Peter.	Peter.	Says	therefore	the

court. But his thoughts were selfish, his words were malicious, and his conduct was wicked.

18:15. All the disciples except "Simon Peter" and "another disciple" fled when Jesus was arrested. John was the other disciple who followed Jesus to Annas' court.

It is not certain how John was acquainted with the high priest. It is likely that John's family was wealthy and had some influence.

Some of the homes of the Jewish well-to-do at this time were built in a horseshoe shape enclosing an open court. A gate gave access to the court through which entry into the house was made. Jesus was likely led to an entrance to one of the chambers opening into the court. John "went in with Jesus into the palace of the high priest." The court was doubtless large since public examinations occurred there at times. This may have been the official residence of the high priest and his family. Perhaps Annas and Caiaphas dwelt in adjoining homes.

18:16. Peter stood outside the gate of the court because he had not followed the mob closely enough (Luke 22:54) to gain access with them. John, as the other disciple, either followed closely enough to the mob to gain entrance or the maid opened the gate for him because she knew him. John's influence obtained Peter's entry.

Once inside the court Peter and John could observe the proceedings. These two disciples were together during many remarkable experiences. It is interesting to note that these two disciples went through nearly identical trials, yet John was spared the onslaught of Satan's testings. Peter, however, was severely tested. John was not questioned about his relationship with Jesus, but Peter was confronted three times.

We have no way of knowing for sure what John would have done if he had been questioned in the same way Peter was. It seems significant that God allowed Peter to be so tried. Jesus warned him and also assured him that He had prayed that his faith would not fail (Luke 22:31,32).

We recognize that Peter was even then being prepared for his future ministry. God did not, of course, want Peter to fail, but He did want Peter to learn something he evidently could learn no other way. He wanted Peter to see how frail human self-determination is. That Peter did indeed learn the lesson is a matter of church history.

18:17. It is customary in the East, even to the present day, for doors of the wealthy to be superintended by a porter or portress

that it was expedient that one man should die for the people: . . . that it was for their welfare, *Williams* . . . it was for their advantage, *TCNT* . . . that in their own interest, *ALBA* . . . would benefit the people, *Berkeley* . . . It is better that one man dies instead of the people, *Beck* . . . it would be best if, *Norlie* . . . on behalf, *Fenton, Wuest.*

15. And Simon Peter followed Jesus, and so did another disciples: And Simon Peter and another disciple followed Jesus, *HBIE.*

that disciples was known unto the high priest: . . . being well-known to the High Priest, *TCNT* . . . was known personally to the High Priest, *Phillips* . . . was an acquaintance, *Norton* . . . chief priest, *Wuest.*

and went in with Jesus into the palace of the high priest: . . . uncovered courtyard of, *Wuest* . . . the court of the high priest's palace, *Montgomery* . . . into the high priest's courtyard, *Beck.*

16. But Peter stood at the door without: . . . whereas Peter remained standing at the door outside, *Rotherham* . . . was left standing at, *ALBA* . . . but Peter was standing near the outer door, *Fenton.*

Then went out that other disciple, which was known unto the high priest: . . . until the other disciple...came out, *ALBA* . . . who was acquainted, *Weymouth* . . . who was known personally, *Phillips.*

and spake unto her that kept the door, and brought in Peter: . . . and had a word with, *BB* . . . and talked to the girl watching the door, *Beck* . . . the doormaid, *Norlie* . . . spoke to the doorkeeper and brought Peter in, *Montgomery* . . . spoke to the portress, *Campbell, Fenton* . . . to the gatekeeper, *Klingensmith* . . . was in charge of the door, *Barclay* . . . and induced the portress to, *Weymouth* . . . and told the woman at the door to admit Peter, *Moffatt* . . . and led Peter in, *Concordant.*

3677.1 noun nom sing fem	3450.9 art nom sing fem	2354.1 noun nom sing fem	3450.3 art dat sing	3935.3 name dat masc	3450.3 art dat sing
παιδίσκη	ἡ	θυρωρὸς	τῷ	Πέτρῳ,	[☆ τῷ
paidiskē	*hē*	*thurōros*	*tō*	*Petrō*	*tō*
maid	the	doorkeeper		to Peter,	

3935.3 name dat masc	3450.9 art nom sing fem	3677.1 noun nom sing fem	3450.9 art nom sing fem	2354.1 noun nom sing fem	3231.1 partic
Πέτρῳ	ἡ	παιδίσκη	ἡ	θυρωρός,]	Μὴ
Petrō	*hē*	*paidiskē*	*hē*	*thurōros*	*Mē*
[to Peter	the	maid	the	doorkeeper,]	not

2504.1 conj	4622.1 prs-pron nom 2sing	1523.2 prep gen	3450.1 art gen pl	3073.6 noun gen pl masc	1498.3 verb 2sing indic pres act
καὶ	σὺ	ἐκ	τῶν	μαθητῶν	εἶ
kai	*su*	*ek*	*tōn*	*mathētōn*	*ei*
also	you	of	the	disciples	are

3450.2 art gen sing	442.2 noun gen sing masc	3642.1 dem-pron gen sing	2978.5 verb 3sing indic pres act	1552.3 dem-pron nom sing masc	3620.2 partic
τοῦ	ἀνθρώπου	τούτου;	Λέγει	ἐκεῖνος,	Οὐκ
tou	*anthrōpou*	*toutou*	*Legei*	*ekeinos*	*Ouk*
of the	man	this?	Says	that,	Not

1498.2 verb 1sing indic pres act	2449.24 verb 3pl indic plperf act	1156.2 conj	3450.7 art pl masc	1395.6 noun pl masc	2504.1 conj
εἰμί.	**18.** Εἱστήκεισαν	δὲ	οἱ	δοῦλοι	καὶ
eimi	*Heistēkeisan*	*de*	*hoi*	*douloi*	*kai*
I am.	Were standing	but	the	slaves	and

3450.7 art pl masc	5095.3 noun nom pl masc	437.1 noun acc sing fem	4020.49 verb nom pl masc part perf act	3617.1 conj	5427.1 noun sing neu
οἱ	ὑπηρέται	ἀνθρακιὰν	πεποιηκότες,	ὅτι	ψῦχος
hoi	*hupēretai*	*anthrakian*	*pepoiēkotes*	*hoti*	*psuchos*
the	officers,	a fire of coals	having made,	for	cold

1498.34 verb sing indic imperf act	2504.1 conj	2305.4 verb 3pl indic imperf	1498.34 verb sing indic imperf act	1156.2 conj
ἦν,	καὶ	ἐθερμαίνοντο·	ἦν	δὲ
ēn	*kai*	*ethermainonto*	*ēn*	*de*
it was,	and	were warming themselves;	was	and

18.a.**Txt:** 02A,05D,017K, 036,037,038,1,13,byz. **Var:** 01ℵ,03B,04C,019L, 033X,33,Lach,Treg,Alf, Tisc,We/HoWeis,Sod, UBS/☆

3196.2 prep	840.1 prs-pron gen pl	3450.5 art sing masc	3935.1 name nom masc	2504.1 conj	3450.5 art sing masc	3935.1 name nom masc
‘ μετ’	αὐτῶν	ὁ	Πέτρος	[a☆ καὶ	ὁ	Πέτρος
met'	*autōn*	*ho*	*Petros*	*kai*	*ho*	*Petros*
with	them		Peter	[and		Peter

3196.2 prep	840.1 prs-pron gen pl	2449.26 verb sing part perf act	2504.1 conj	2305.2 verb nom sing masc part pres
μετ’	αὐτῶν]	ἑστὼς	καὶ	θερμαινόμενος.
met'	*autōn*	*hestōs*	*kai*	*thermainomenos*
with	them]	having stood	and	having warmed himself.

3450.5 art sing masc	3631.1 conj	744.1 noun nom sing masc	2049.9 verb 3sing indic aor act	3450.6 art acc sing masc
19. Ὁ	οὖν	ἀρχιερεὺς	ἠρώτησεν	τὸν
Ho	*oun*	*archiereus*	*ērōtēsen*	*ton*
The	therefore	high priest	questioned	

2400.3 name acc masc	3875.1 prep	3450.1 art gen pl	3073.6 noun gen pl masc	840.3 prs-pron gen sing	2504.1 conj
Ἰησοῦν	περὶ	τῶν	μαθητῶν	αὐτοῦ,	καὶ
Iēsoun	*peri*	*tōn*	*mathētōn*	*autou*	*kai*
Jesus	concerning	the	disciples	his,	and

(10:3). The servant usually received a fee from visitors, a practice much like our custom of tipping. The slave-girl's question made it easier for Peter to make his first denial of his Lord. She probably observed Peter when she let him in and felt responsible for her action. Thus she approached him with her question. Her question expects a negative answer. She hoped Peter was not Jesus' disciple though she believed that he was. "This man" was used in a contemptuous sense as she pointed to Jesus.

Peter knew that he was in great danger on two accounts. First, he was associated with Jesus whom they were determined to kill. Second, Peter had attempted to slay Malchus, the servant of the high priest. Peter's denial came quickly: "I am not." The other Gospels go further with Peter's denials by indicating he claimed to be a stranger and bystander in the events (Matthew 26:69-75; Mark 14:66-72; Luke 22:55-62). The Gospels of Matthew and Mark state that Peter cursed and swore. It was because Peter had denied his Lord repeatedly even with oaths that he was later reluctant to think Jesus would forgive him. This fact accounts for Jesus' repeatedly questioning Peter as to Peter's love for Him (21:15-17). How thoroughly Jesus reinstated the fallen disciple.

17. Then saith the damsel that kept the door unto Peter: . . . the female slave, *Wuest* . . . the doormaid, *Norlie* . . . The maid on duty at the door, *JB* . . . The girl in charge of the door then said to Peter, *Berkeley.*

Art not thou also one of this man's disciples?: Are not you also, *Montgomery* . . . Art thou also from among the disciples of this man? *Rotherham* . . . Are you another of this man's disciples? *NEB.*

He saith, I am not: In answer he said, *BB* . . . Not I, *Klingensmith.*

18:18. Some of the slaves and officers who had arrested Jesus had made a fire to warm themselves because the weather was cold. This was April A.D. 30 early in the morning. The court was an open yard and the night air was chilly. Peter stood with the soldiers, warming himself, pretending to be indifferent to the trial of Jesus. Luke says Peter "sat by the fire" (Luke 22:56), which likely means he tried to ignore the trial by keeping his face toward the fire.

18. And the servants and officers stood there, who had made a fire of coals: . . . the slaves, *Adams* . . . and attendants, *Confraternity* . . . and guards, *AmpB* . . . those who had been sent to apprehend Jesus, *Norton* . . . by a pile of, *Berkeley* . . . a charcoal fire, *Concordant, Norlie* . . . which they had lit, *Moffatt.*

for it was cold:

and they warmed themselves: . . . sharing the warmth, *NEB.*

and Peter stood with them, and warmed himself:

18:19. At this point Annas was referred to as the high priest. The questioning was a preliminary hearing to determine grounds for a formal trial. This gave the impression that Jesus was a leader of revolt against Rome and a false prophet among the Jews. Thus the crafty, old interrogator impressed the Roman commander with the serious nature of the case.

The question concerning the disciples would imply that the followers of Jesus might be used as soldiers. When local leaders gained enough supporters, there was danger of uprisings against Rome. This seems to be the high priest's insinuation. Furthermore, the questions concerning Jesus' "doctrine" might have had political overtones. Annas was searching for every possible bit of falsehood to use against Jesus. The Jewish leaders had sent spies to entrap Jesus during His teaching on hills and plains. They had dogged His steps in local synagogues. They confronted Him in the temple.

19. The high priest then asked Jesus of his disciples, and of his doctrine: . . . interrogated Jesus, *Phillips, ALBA* . . . questioned Jesus about, *Montgomery* . . . questioned Jesus concerning his, *Confraternity* . . . respecting his doctrine, *Murdock* . . . relative to His disciples, and His teaching, *Fenton.*

John 18:20

3875.1 prep	**3450.10** art gen sing fem	**1316.2** noun gen sing fem	**840.3** prs-pron gen sing	**552.6** verb 3sing indic aor pass
περὶ	τῆς	διδαχῆς	αὐτοῦ.	**20.** ἀπεκρίθη
peri	*tēs*	*didachēs*	*autou*	*apekrithē*
concerning	the	teaching	his.	Answered

20.a.**Txt:** 02A,04C,017K, 032W,036,037,1,13,byz. GriesLach,Weis,Sod
Var: p66,01ℵ,03B,05D, 019L,038,Treg,Tisc We/Ho,UBS/☆

840.4 prs-pron dat sing	**3450.5** art sing masc	**2400.1** name nom masc	**1466.1** prs-pron nom 1sing	**3816.3** noun dat sing fem
αὐτῷ	([a] ὁ)	Ἰησοῦς,	Ἐγὼ	παῤῥησίᾳ
autō	*ho*	*Iēsous*	*Egō*	*parrhēsia*
him		Jesus,	I	openly

20.b.**Txt:** 04C-corr,05D, 017K,032W,036,038,13, byz.Gries
Var: 01ℵ,02A,03B, 04C-org,019L,033X,037, Lach,TregAlf,Word,Tisc, We/Ho,Weis,Sod,UBS/☆

2953.26 verb 1sing indic aor act	**2953.38** verb 1sing indic perf act	**3450.3** art dat sing	**2862.3** noun dat sing masc	**1466.1** prs-pron nom 1sing
(ἐλάλησα	[[b]☆ λελάληκα]	τῷ	κόσμῳ˙	ἐγὼ
elalēsa	*lelalēka*	*tō*	*kosmō*	*egō*
spoke	[have spoken]	to the	world;	I

20.c.**Txt:** Steph
Var: 01ℵ,02A,03B,04C, 05D,019L,038,etc.byz. Gries,Lach,Treg,Alf, Word,Tisc,We/HoWeis, Sod,UBS/☆

3704.1 adv	**1315.11** verb 1sing indic aor act	**1706.1** prep	**3450.11** art dat sing fem	**4715.3** noun dat sing fem	**2504.1** conj	**1706.1** prep
πάντοτε	ἐδίδαξα	ἐν	([c] τῇ)	συναγωγῇ	καὶ	ἐν
pantote	*edidaxa*	*en*	*tē*	*sunagōgē*	*kai*	*en*
always	taught	in	the	synagogue	and	in

20.d.**Txt:** 04C-corr,05D, 017K,036,037,byz.
Var: 01ℵ,02A,03B, 04C-org,019L,032W, 033X,038,041,1,13,it.sa. bo.Gries,Lach,Treg,Alf, WordTisc,We/Ho,Weis, Sod,UBS/☆

3450.3 art dat sing	**2387.2** adj dat sing neu	**3562.1** adv	**3704.1** adv	**3820.7** adj pl masc	**3450.7** art pl masc
τῷ	ἱερῷ,	ὅπου	(πάντοτε	[[d]☆ πάντες]	οἱ
tō	*hierō*	*hopou*	*pantote*	*pantes*	*hoi*
the	temple,	where	always	[all]	the

2428.2 name-adj pl masc	**4755.16** verb 3pl indic pres	**2504.1** conj	**1706.1** prep	**2899.3** adj dat sing neu	**2953.26** verb 1sing indic aor act
Ἰουδαῖοι	συνέρχονται,	καὶ	ἐν	κρυπτῷ	ἐλάλησα
Ioudaioi	*sunerchontai*	*kai*	*en*	*kruptō*	*elalēsa*
Jews	come together,	and	in	secret	I spoke

3625.6 num card neu	**4949.9** intr-pron sing neu	**1466.6** prs-pron acc 1sing	**1890.2** verb 2sing indic pres act	**1890.8** verb 2sing impr aor act
οὐδέν.	**21.** τί	με	(ἐπερωτᾷς;	ἐπερώτησον
ouden	*ti*	*me*	*eperōtas*	*eperōtēson*
nothing.	Why	me	do you question?	question

21.a.**Txt:** 04C-corr,05D, 017K,036,037,byz.
Var: 01ℵ,03B,04C-org, 019L,033X,Lach,Treg, Alf,TiscWe/Ho,Weis,Sod, UBS/☆

2049.18 verb 2sing indic pres act	**2049.19** verb 2sing impr aor act	**3450.8** art acc pl masc	**189.41** verb acc pl masc part perf act	**4949.9** intr-pron sing neu
[[a]☆ ἐρωτᾷς;	ἐρώτησον]	τοὺς	ἀκηκοότας	τί
erōtas	*erōtēson*	*tous*	*akēkootas*	*ti*
[do you question?	question]	the	having heard	what

2953.26 verb 1sing indic aor act	**840.2** prs-pron dat pl	**1481.14** verb 2sing impr aor act	**3642.7** dem-pron nom pl masc	**3471.8** verb 3pl indic perf act
ἐλάλησα	αὐτοῖς˙	ἴδε	οὗτοι	οἴδασιν
elalēsa	*autois*	*ide*	*houtoi*	*oidasin*
I spoke	to them;	lo,	these	have known

3614.17 rel-pron pl neu	**1500.3** verb indic aor act	**1466.1** prs-pron nom 1sing	**3642.18** dem-pron pl neu	**1156.2** conj	**840.3** prs-pron gen sing
ἃ	εἶπον	ἐγώ.	**22.** Ταῦτα	δὲ	αὐτοῦ
ha	*eipon*	*egō*	*Tauta*	*de*	*autou*
what	said	I.	These things	but	on his

1500.16 verb gen sing masc part aor act	**1518.3** num card nom masc	**3450.1** art gen pl	**5095.4** noun gen pl masc	**3798.15** verb nom sing masc part perf act
εἰπόντος	εἷς	(τῶν	ὑπηρετῶν	παρεστηκὼς
eipontos	*heis*	*tōn*	*hupēretōn*	*parestēkōs*
having said	one	of the	officers	having stood by

To the last they were determined to misconstrue His teaching, disgrace His person, and crush His very life.

18:20. Jesus ignored any references to His disciples so that they might not be implicated in any charges. Jesus focused the attention on himself. The emphatic use of the pronoun "I" (*egō*) introduces each clause. His "I have spoken openly" (NASB) is in sharp contrast to the shady treachery of His enemies. "Openly" (*parrhēsia*) implies "without reserve" as well as "publicly." He said His teaching had been given in three public areas: synagogues, the temple, and wherever the Jews came together. His teaching was public knowledge, and as such, anyone who heard Him could freely witness to His teaching.

As a teacher Jesus taught nothing which He did not openly proclaim. He held no secret meetings in which He conspired against the government of Rome or His nation. Annas did not question Him to ascertain the truth, but to ensnare Him through a manipulation of His words.

18:21. How calm, patient, and dignified the Lord was before His accusers. He was aware of their false intent, yet He spoke simply, candidly, and without fear. An accused person has the right to counter the charges brought against him. He is not under obligation to witness against himself. Jesus pointed out that if witnesses had brought a charge against Him, He would answer, but there was no reason to interrogate Him without a charge. He challenged them to a fair investigation. The tense of the verb *akēkootas* ("having heard") and the pronoun *houtoi* ("these") seem to refer to persons present or nearby who were able to speak with full knowledge regarding His teaching. According to the rules established by the Sanhedrin, the first order of a trial was to be the calling of witnesses for the defense.

Jesus set an example for His disciples who were to be brought before judges in the future (see Acts 5:17-32; 7:1-60; 16:19-37; chapters 22 to 26). Like Jesus who witnessed a good confession "before" (Greek, *epi,* meaning "upon") Pontius Pilate (1 Timothy 6:13), His followers are also to proclaim His salvation.

18:22. "One of the officers" was a Levitical guard of the temple. He struck the first blow of the many that followed that morning.

20. Jesus answered him, I spake openly to the world: I have spoken publicly to the world, *Beck* . . . For my part...I have spoken to all the world openly, *TCNT* . . . I have spoken boldly, *Concordant* . . . with plainness of speech, *Rotherham* . . . spoken plainly, *SEB* . . . openly for all the world to hear, *JB* . . . to the world perfectly openly, *Barclay.*

I ever taught in the synagogue, and in the temple: I have always, *Norlie* . . . I have continually taught in some synagogue or in the Temple, *Weymouth* . . . I have taught constantly, *Torrey* . . . I constantly taught, *Fenton* . . . I at all times taught, *Wuest* . . . in the temple precincts, *ET.*

whither the Jews always resort: . . . where all the Jews habitually come together, *Wuest* . . . where all Jews meet together, *Phillips* . . . to which places the Jews go at all times, *Norlie* . . . the Jews assemble, *Murdock* . . . are in the habit of meeting, *Williams* . . . are accustomed to assemble, *Fenton* . . . congregate, *AmpB.*

and in secret have I said nothing: I have uttered nothing, *Torrey* . . . I speak nothing in hiding, *Concordant.*

21. Why askest thou me?: Why are you questioning me, *BB, Norlie* . . . Why do you examine me? *Campbell.*

ask them which heard me, what I have said to them: . . . question them who have heard what I spake, *Rotherham* . . . Ask my hearers what I have said to them, *Moffatt* . . . Examine those who heard what, *Berkeley.*

behold, they know what I said: Of course, they know, *Williams* . . . these witnesses here know what I said, *Montgomery* . . . Obviously they are the ones who know what I actually said, *Phillips.*

22. And when he had thus spoken, one of the officers which stood by struck Jesus with the

3798.15 verb nom sing masc part perf act	3450.1 art gen pl	5095.4 noun gen pl masc	1319.14 verb 3sing indic aor act	4332.1 noun acc sing neu
[☆ παρεστηκὼς	τῶν	ὑπηρετῶν]	ἔδωκεν	ῥάπισμα
parestēkōs	*tōn*	*hupēretōn*	*edōken*	*rhapisma*
[having stood up	of the	officers]	gave	a slap

3450.3 art dat sing	2400.2 name masc	1500.15 verb nom sing masc part aor act	3643.1 adv	552.1 verb 2sing indic pres	3450.3 art dat sing
τῷ	Ἰησοῦ,	εἰπών,	Οὕτως	ἀποκρίνῃ	τῷ
tō	*Iēsou*	*eipōn*	*Houtōs*	*apokrinē*	*tō*
	to Jesus,	saying,	Thus	you answer	the

23.a.**Txt:** 02A,04C-corr, 05D,017K,036,037,1, byz.Gries,Weis,Sod **Var:** 03B,04C-org,019L, 038,Lach,Treg,Alf,Tisc, We/Ho,UBS/☆

744.3 noun dat sing masc	552.6 verb 3sing indic aor pass	840.4 prs-pron dat sing	3450.5 art sing masc	2400.1 name nom masc
ἀρχιερεῖ;	23. Ἀπεκρίθη	αὐτῷ	(a ὁ)	Ἰησοῦς,
archierei	*Apekrithē*	*autō*	*ho*	*Iēsous*
high priest?	Answered	him		Jesus,

1479.1 conj	2532.1 adv	2953.26 verb 1sing indic aor act	3113.21 verb 2sing impr aor act	3875.1 prep
Εἰ	κακῶς	ἐλάλησα,	μαρτύρησον	περὶ
Ei	*kakōs*	*elalēsa*	*marturēson*	*peri*
If	evil	I spoke,	bear witness	concerning

3450.2 art gen sing	2527.8 adj gen sing neu	1479.1 conj	1156.2 conj	2544.1 adv	4949.9 intr-pron sing neu	1466.6 prs-pron acc 1sing
τοῦ	κακοῦ·	εἰ	δὲ	καλῶς,	τί	με
tou	*kakou*	*ei*	*de*	*kalōs*	*ti*	*me*
the	evil;	if	but	well,	why	me

24.a.**Var:** 03B,04C-org, 019L,033X,037,038, Elzev,Lach,Treg,Alf, Tisc,We/HoWeis,Sod, UBS/☆

1188.1 verb 2sing indic pres act	643.8 verb 3sing indic aor act	3631.1 conj	840.6 prs-pron acc sing masc
δέρεις;	24. Ἀπέστειλεν	[a☆+ οὖν]	αὐτὸν
dereis	*Apesteilen*	*oun*	*auton*
do you strike?	Sent	[therefore]	him

3450.5 art sing masc	450.1 name nom masc	1204.16 verb sing part perf	4242.1 prep	2505.3 name acc masc
ὁ	Ἄννας	δεδεμένον	πρὸς	Καϊάφαν
ho	*Annas*	*dedemenon*	*pros*	*Kaiaphan*
	Annas	having been bound	to	Caiaphas

3450.6 art acc sing masc	744.4 noun acc sing masc	1498.34 verb sing indic imperf act	1156.2 conj	4468.1 name masc	3935.1 name nom masc
τὸν	ἀρχιερέα.	25. Ἦν	δὲ	Σίμων	Πέτρος
ton	*archierea*	*En*	*de*	*Simōn*	*Petros*
the	high priest.	Was	now	Simon	Peter

2449.26 verb sing part perf act	2504.1 conj	2305.2 verb nom sing masc part pres	1500.3 verb indic aor act	3631.1 conj
ἑστὼς	καὶ	θερμαινόμενος.	εἶπον	οὖν
hestōs	*kai*	*thermainomenos*	*eipon*	*oun*
having stood	and	having warmed himself.	They said	therefore

840.4 prs-pron dat sing	3231.1 partic	2504.1 conj	4622.1 prs-pron nom 2sing	1523.2 prep gen	3450.1 art gen pl	3073.6 noun gen pl masc
αὐτῷ,	Μὴ	καὶ	σὺ	ἐκ	τῶν	μαθητῶν
autō	*Mē*	*kai*	*su*	*ek*	*tōn*	*mathētōn*
to him,	Not	also	you	of	the	disciples

840.3 prs-pron gen sing	1498.3 verb 2sing indic pres act	714.7 verb 3sing indic aor mid	1552.3 dem-pron nom sing masc	2504.1 conj	1500.5 verb 3sing indic aor act
αὐτοῦ	εἶ;	Ἠρνήσατο	ἐκεῖνος,	καὶ	εἶπεν,
autou	*ei*	*Ērnēsato*	*ekeinos*	*kai*	*eipen*
his	are?	He denied	that one,	and	said,

The Greek word *rhapisma* occurs three times in the New Testament (Mark 14:65; John 18:22; 19:3). The word means a blow in the mouth to indicate that Jesus had spoken disrespectfully to the high priest and that the accused should keep silent. When the apostle Paul stood before Ananias the high priest, a like blow was struck. Notice the reactions of Christ and Paul (Acts 23:2-5).

palm of his hand: . . . gave Him a slap, *Norlie* . . . gave him a blow with his hand, *TCNT* . . . a smart-blow to, *Rotherham* . . . with his open hand, *BB* . . . with a rod, *Worrell.*

saying, Answerest thou the high priest so?: Is that how you answer the high priest, *RSV* . . . How dare you talk like, *TEV* . . . Is this the way to answer the high priest, *Berkeley* . . . in that fashion? *Fenton.*

18:23. Jesus' answers showed His clear presence of mind. He had a sense of the indignity He had received, and yet He displayed majestic serenity. He appealed to the unworthy officer's sense of justice. The guard was zealous for the high priest, but totally ignorant of his God and disrespectful of justice.

Jesus knew the outcome of the so-called trial. He was patiently awaiting His hour. His mouth was doubtless bleeding from the blow, yet He serenely stood in a majestic attitude before His judges. He used no force, either by persuasion of words nor physical power to free himself from the circumstances He was in at the time. Jesus knew He was walking in the will of His Father. This awareness was His strength.

23. Jesus answered him, If I have spoken evil: If I have said anything wrong, *Montgomery, Norlie* . . . If abusively I spake, *Rotherham* . . . Assuming that I spoke evil, *Wuest.*

bear witness of the evil: . . . on oath tell what it is, *Williams* . . . bring proof of the wrong, *Fenton* . . . give evidence of the wrong, *Berkeley* . . . then prove it, *Norlie* . . . in what the wrong consists, *Campbell.*

but if well, why smitest thou me?: . . . but if, respectfully, *Rotherham* . . . but if what I have said is true, *Williams* . . . If it was good, *SEB* . . . then why do you strike Me, *Norlie* . . . are you lashing Me? *Concordant.*

18:24. Thus far in the narrative "Annas" has been referred to as the high priest though he was the deposed high priest (verses 19,22). Annas sent Jesus bound to Caiaphas the high priest. It is unlikely that Jesus was untied during His appearance before Annas, indicating the shameful treatment Annas heaped upon the nation's Messiah. The irony is how the leaders treated their long awaited Saviour. For hundreds of years the nation had prayed for His coming. Now that He had come they treated Him with every shameful indecency.

24. Now Annas had sent him bound unto Caiaphas the high priest: Annas, then dispatches Him, *Concordant* . . . sent him in chains, *Montgomery* . . . sent him chained to, *BB* . . . sent Him, still bound, to Caiaphas, *Beck* . . . with his hands still tied, *Phillips* . . . sente hym bounden to caifas the bischop, *Wycliffe.*

18:25. The time was somewhere about 1 or 2 o'clock in the morning. Peter had denied the Lord once. To his shame this was the second time. He was standing with his face to the fire and someone said, "Art not thou also one of his disciples?" It may be that Peter's reaction to the blow Jesus received was detected by the attendants. At any rate they hounded Peter with their questions, and he denied any acquaintance with Jesus.

John's Gospel uses the plural pronoun "they" of those who asked Peter questions. Mark 14:69 says a maid; Matthew 26:71 states another maid asked Peter; Luke 22:58 indicates it was a man who

25. And Simon Peter stood and warmed himself:

They said therefore unto him, Art thou also one of his disciples?: Surely you are not another of his, *NIV.*

John 18:26

27.a.**Txt:** p60,01ℵ, 04C-corr,021M,033X, 038,13,Steph,Weis,Sod **Var:** 02A,03B,04C-org, 05D,017K,019L,032W, 036,037,byz.Lach,Treg Alf,Tisc,We/Ho,UBS/⋆

28.a.**Txt:** 07E,017K,036, 038,Steph **Var:** 01ℵ,02A,03B,04C, 05D,019L,021M,033X, 037,Gries,Lach,Treg, Alf,Tisc,We/HoWeis,Sod, UBS/⋆

28.b.**Txt:** 04C-corr,017K, 019L,036,13,33,byz. Gries,Word **Var:** 01ℵ,02A,03B, 04C-org,05D,037,038, Lach,TregAlf,Tisc, We/Ho,Weis,Sod,UBS/⋆

3620.2 partic Οὐκ *Ouk* Not	**1498.2** verb 1sing indic pres act εἰμί. *eimi* I am.	**2978.5** verb 3sing indic pres act **26.** Λέγει *Legei* Says	**1518.3** num card nom masc εἷς *heis* one	**1523.2** prep gen ἐκ *ek* of	**3450.1** art gen pl τῶν *tōn* the
1395.7 noun gen pl masc δούλων *doulōn* servants	**3450.2** art gen sing τοῦ *tou* of the	**744.2** noun gen sing masc ἀρχιερέως, *archiereōs* high priest,	**4624.1** adj nom sing συγγενὴς *sungenēs* relative	**1498.21** verb sing masc part pres act ὢν *ōn* being	
3614.2 rel-pron gen sing οὗ *hou* of whom	**604.1** verb 3sing indic aor act ἀπέκοψεν *apekopsen* cut off	**3935.1** name nom masc Πέτρος *Petros* Peter	**3450.16** art sing neu τὸ *to* the	**5454.2** noun acc sing neu ὠτίον, *ōtion* ear,	**3620.2** partic Οὐκ *Ouk* Not
1466.1 prs-pron nom 1sing ἐγώ *egō* I	**4622.4** prs-pron acc 2sing σε *se* you	**1481.1** verb indic aor act εἶδον *eidon* saw	**1706.1** prep ἐν *en* in	**3450.3** art dat sing τῷ *tō* the	**2752.2** noun dat sing masc κήπῳ *kēpō* garden
3196.2 prep μετ' *met'* with	**840.3** prs-pron gen sing αὐτοῦ; *autou* him?	**3687.1** adv **27.** Πάλιν *Palin* Again	**3631.1** conj οὖν *oun* therefore	**714.7** verb 3sing indic aor mid ἠρνήσατο *ērnēsato* denied	**3450.5** art sing masc ⸂a ὁ ⸃ *ho*
3935.1 name nom masc Πέτρος, *Petros* Peter,	**2504.1** conj καὶ *kai* and	**2091.1** adv εὐθέως *eutheōs* immediately	**218.1** noun nom sing masc ἀλέκτωρ *alektōr* a cock	**5291.6** verb 3sing indic aor act ἐφώνησεν. *ephōnēsen* crew.	
70.3 verb 3pl indic pres act **28.** Ἄγουσιν *Agousin* They lead	**3631.1** conj οὖν *oun* therefore	**3450.6** art acc sing masc τὸν *ton*	**2400.3** name acc masc Ἰησοῦν *Iēsoun* Jesus	**570.3** prep gen ἀπὸ *apo* from	**3450.2** art gen sing τοῦ *tou*
2505.2 name gen masc Καϊάφα *Kaiapha* Caiaphas	**1519.1** prep εἰς *eis* into	**3450.16** art sing neu τὸ *to* the	**4091.1** noun sing neu πραιτώριον· *praitōrion* praetorium,	**1498.34** verb sing indic imperf act ἦν *ēn* it was	**1156.2** conj δὲ *de* and
4263.1 noun nom sing fem ⸀ πρωΐα· *prōia* early.	**4262.1** adv [a⋆ πρωΐ·] *prōi* [idem]	**2504.1** conj καὶ *kai* And	**840.7** prs-pron nom pl masc αὐτοὶ *autoi* they	**3620.2** partic οὐκ *ouk* not	**1511.1** verb indic aor act εἰσῆλθον *eisēlthon* entered
1519.1 prep εἰς *eis* into	**3450.16** art sing neu τὸ *to* the	**4091.1** noun sing neu πραιτώριον, *praitōrion* praetorium,	**2419.1** conj ἵνα *hina* that	**3231.1** partic μὴ *mē* not	**3256.2** verb 3pl subj aor pass μιανθῶσιν *mianthōsin* they might be defiled,
233.1 conj ⸀ ἀλλ' *all'* but	**233.2** conj [b⋆ ἀλλὰ] *alla* [idem]	**2419.1** conj ἵνα *hina* that	**2052.20** verb 3pl subj aor act φάγωσιν *phagōsin* they might eat	**3450.16** art sing neu τὸ *to* the	**3818.1** noun sing neu πάσχα. *pascha* passover.

asked Peter. Doubtless Peter was harassed by several people. Thus, John says "they" indicating all those who asked.

He denied it, and said, I am not: . . . denied it flatly, *ALBA.*

18:26. This is the third and strongest onslaught against Peter. We have noted the first weak question of the maid who actually expected a negative answer. The second time a number of voices accused Peter of being a follower of Jesus. But now it was a relative of the one Peter had nearly beheaded who asked concerning Peter's presence in the Garden with Jesus. This servant was one of the arresting party. He had recognized Peter as one who had resisted Jesus' arrest. Peter was terrified, for his very life was in jeopardy if the relative of Malchus pressed his accusation.

26. One of the servants of the high priest, being his kinsman whose ear Peter cut off: . . . being a relative of him whose ear, *Wuest* . . . his cosyn, *Tyndale* . . . oon of the bischopis scruauntis cosyn of hym whos eere petir citte of, *Wycliffe* . . . hys cosyn whose eare Peter spote of, *Cranmer.*

saith, Did not I see thee in the garden with him?: I saw you with Jesus in the, *SEB* . . . with him in the orchard, *Moffatt* . . . with him in the olive grove? *NIV.*

18:27. John records Peter's simple but emphatic statement of denial. Matthew 26:74 and Mark 14:71 state that Peter began to curse and swear that he might enforce his denial of Jesus.

When the cock crew Peter began to realize the weakness of his will and the shallowness of his dedication to Jesus. The sound of the crowing rooster registered deeply on his mind. The pressure of the test revealed the difference between Peter's earlier assertions and his later conduct.

27. Peter then denied again; and immediately the cock crew: Once more Peter made denial, *Norlie* . . . Then once more Peter denied it, *Adams* . . . Peter denyed it agayne, *Tyndale* . . . He disowns, *Concordant* . . . and at that very moment, *Montgomery* . . . Instantly the rooster crowed, *Berkeley* . . . at once the bugle sounded, *Fenton* . . . and thereupon, *Torrey* . . . And straight away a cock gave its cry, *BB.*

18:28. "The hall of judgment" (Greek, *to praitōrion,* "praetorium") was the governor's official residence while he was in Jerusalem. Jesus was led from the high priest Caiaphas to the Roman governor Pilate.

"It was early." A condemnation at night was technically illegal. An early meeting of the Sanhedrin seems to have been held to confirm the decision already made. A Roman court could be held anytime after sunrise. This one was probably as early as possible.

The Jews would not enter a Gentile's home because it was unclean and would make them ceremonially unclean. They would be unclean until evening and therefore unfit to eat the Passover meal. They had eaten the Paschal lamb the night before. The Passover Feast lasted 7 days (2 Chronicles 30:22). There was to be on each day a burnt offering. Unleavened bread was to be eaten throughout the week. The Jews would not enter a Gentile dwelling for fear of becoming defiled, yet they committed the murder of their Creator!

28. Then led they Jesus from Caiaphas unto the hall of judgment: Next, they marched Jesus to the governor's palace, *Norlie* . . . to the Praetorium, *Weymouth* . . . to the Government House, *TCNT.*

and it was early: It was now early morning, *Phillips.*

and they themselves went not into the judgment hall: They did not enter the palace, *Norlie.*

lest they should be defiled: . . . in case of being, *Moffatt* . . . should defile themselves, *Murdock* . . . for fear that they would be contaminated, *Phillips* . . . so not in a condition, *Campbell* . . . that they might not be ceremonially defiled, *Montgomery* . . . lest they should be polluted, *Fenton* . . . from getting unclean, *Beck* . . . to keep themselves ritually clean, *TEV* . . . to avoid becoming 'defiled,' *TCNT.*

but that they might eat the passover: . . . (they wanted to celebrate the Passover), *Beck.*

18:29. "Pilate" was the Roman governor of Judea and Samaria from A.D. 25 until about A.D. 35. He was noted for his cruelty

John 18:29

29.a.**Var:** p66,01ℵ,03B,04C-org,019L,032W,033X,038,33,Lach,Treg Alf,Tisc,We/Ho,Weis,Sod,UBS/⭑

29.b.**Txt:** 02A,04C-corr,05D,017K,036,037,038,13,byz.Lach
Var: 01ℵ,03B,04C-org,019L,033X,33,Treg,Alf Tisc,We/Ho,Weis,Sod,UBS/⭑

29.c.**Txt:** p66,01ℵ-corr,02A,04C,05D,019L,032W,038,1,13,byz.Lach,Sod
Var: 01ℵ-org,03B,Tisc,We/HoWeis,UBS/⭑

30.a.**Txt:** 02A,05D,017K,019L,036,037,038,byz.Sod
Var: 01ℵ,03B,04C,Lach,TregAlf,Tisc,We/Ho,Weis,UBS/⭑

30.b.**Txt:** 02A,04C-corr,05D,017K,036,037,038,1,13,565,byz.Gries,Lach
Var: 01ℵ-corr,03B,019L,032W,Treg,Alf,Tisc,We/Ho,WeisSod,UBS/⭑

31.a.**Txt:** 01ℵ,02A,04C-corr,05D,017K,019L,038,etc.byz.Lach,TiscWeis,Sod,UBS/⭑
Var: 03B,04C-org,Treg,AlfWe/Ho

31.b.**Txt:** p60,01ℵ,019L,032W,036,037,13,byz.Tisc,Sod
Var: p66,03B,04C,sa.bo.Lach,Treg,Alf,We/Ho,Weis,UBS/⭑

1814.3 verb 3sing indic aor act	**3631.1** conj	**3450.5** art sing masc	**3952.1** name nom masc	**1838.1** prep gen
29. ἐξῆλθεν	οὖν	ὁ	Πιλᾶτος	[a☆+ ἔξω]
exēlthen	*oun*	*ho*	*Pilatos*	*exō*
Went forth	therefore		Pilate	[outside]

4242.1 prep	**840.8** prs-pron acc pl masc	**2504.1** conj	**1500.5** verb 3sing indic aor act	**5183.2** verb 3sing indic pres act	**4949.1** intr-pron
πρὸς	αὐτοὺς,	καὶ	ʼ εἶπεν,	[b☆ φησίν,]	Τίνα
pros	*autous*	*kai*	*eipen*	*phēsin*	*Tina*
to	them,	and	said,	[says,]	What

2694.2 noun acc sing fem	**5179.1** verb 2pl pres act	**2567.3** prep	**3450.2** art gen sing	**442.2** noun gen sing masc
κατηγορίαν	φέρετε	ʼc κατὰ ˎ	τοῦ	ἀνθρώπου
katēgorian	*pherete*	*kata*	*tou*	*anthrōpou*
accusation	bring you	against	the	man

3642.1 dem-pron gen sing	**552.8** verb 3pl indic aor pass	**2504.1** conj	**1500.3** verb indic aor act	**1500.28** verb 3pl indic aor act
τούτου;	**30.** Ἀπεκρίθησαν	καὶ	ʼ εἶπον	[a☆ εἶπαν]
toutou	*Apekrithēsan*	*kai*	*eipon*	*eipan*
this?	They answered	and	said	[idem]

840.4 prs-pron dat sing	**1479.1** conj	**3231.1** partic	**1498.34** verb sing indic imperf act	**3642.4** dem-pron nom sing masc	**2526.1** adj nom sing masc
αὐτῷ,	Εἰ	μὴ	ἦν	οὗτος	ʼ κακοποιός,
autō	*Ei*	*mē*	*ēn*	*houtos*	*kakopoios*
to him,	If	not	were	that	an evildoer,

2527.7 adj sing neu	**4020.15** verb sing masc part pres act	**3620.2** partic	**300.1** partic	**4622.3** prs-pron dat 2sing
[b☆ κακὸν	ποιῶν,]	οὐκ	ἄν	σοι
kakon	*poiōn*	*ouk*	*an*	*soi*
[evil	doing,]	not		to you

3722.11 verb 1pl indic aor act	**840.6** prs-pron acc sing masc	**1500.5** verb 3sing indic aor act	**3631.1** conj
παρεδώκαμεν	αὐτόν.	**31.** Εἶπεν	οὖν
paredōkamen	*auton*	*Eipen*	*oun*
we would have delivered up	him.	Said	therefore

840.2 prs-pron dat pl	**3450.5** art sing masc	**3952.1** name nom masc	**2956.24** verb 2pl impr aor act	**840.6** prs-pron acc sing masc	**5050.1** prs-pron nom 2pl
αὐτοῖς	ʼa ὁ ˎ	Πιλᾶτος,	Λάβετε	αὐτὸν	ὑμεῖς,
autois	*ho*	*Pilatos*	*Labete*	*auton*	*humeis*
to them		Pilate,	Take	him	you,

2504.1 conj	**2567.3** prep	**3450.6** art acc sing masc	**3414.4** noun acc sing masc	**5050.2** prs-pron gen 2pl	**2892.16** verb 2pl impr aor act
καὶ	κατὰ	τὸν	νόμον	ὑμῶν	κρίνατε
kai	*kata*	*ton*	*nomon*	*humōn*	*krinate*
and	according to	the	law	your	judge

840.6 prs-pron acc sing masc	**1500.3** verb indic aor act	**3631.1** conj	**840.4** prs-pron dat sing	**3450.7** art pl masc	**2428.2** name-adj pl masc
αὐτόν.	Εἶπον	ʼb οὖν ˎ	αὐτῷ	οἱ	Ἰουδαῖοι,
auton	*Eipon*	*oun*	*autō*	*hoi*	*Ioudaioi*
him.	Said	therefore	to him	the	Jews,

2231.3 prs-pron dat 1pl	**3620.2** partic	**1815.1** verb 3sing indic pres act	**609.12** verb inf aor act	**3625.3** num card acc masc	**2419.1** conj
Ἡμῖν	οὐκ	ἔξεστιν	ἀποκτεῖναι	οὐδένα·	**32.** ἵνα
Hēmin	*ouk*	*exestin*	*apokteinai*	*oudena*	*hina*
To us	not	it is permitted	to put to death	no one;	that

and for several massacres to which Luke refers (Luke 13:1). The governor went "out unto them" so that the Jews would not become defiled by entering his residence.

Pilate would not pass judgment until he knew the charge. At this time Pontius Pilate did not know they desired to kill Jesus. This is revealed by the next verse. In this instance, Pilate's use of the term "this man" was a neutral way of identifying the accused. Pilate had heard of Jesus prior to this time, yet it seems he had never seen Him.

The governor may have been eager to see Jesus. King Herod wished very much to see the One many had spoken about with love or malice. This was Pilate's day of visitation. He may have thought he was the judge, but actually it was Pilate's time of visitation. The opportunities of God come in times and ways little understood or expected by men like Pilate. Doubtless Pilate marched out before the Jews befitting a governor of the Roman occupation. With an air of contempt for the Jews he asked about the accusation.

29. Pilate then went out unto them, and said, What accusation bring ye against this man?: Accordingly Pilate, *Weymouth* . . . What have you to say against this man, *Norlie* . . . What is the charge you bring against this man, *Williams* . . . What do you accuse this man of? *TEV.*

30. They answered and said unto him, If he were not a malefactor: If he had not been a criminal, *Moffatt, Fenton* . . . were not an habitual evildoer, *Wuest* . . . He's a wrongdoer, *ALBA* . . . an evil-doer, *Norlie.*

we would not have delivered him up unto thee: . . . we would not have committed him to you, *Berkeley* . . . we would never have brought him to you, *Norlie.*

18:30. The Jews ignored Pilate's question by pretending to be insulted because he wanted to know the accusation. They were pressing Pilate to approve of their verdict. "Malefactor" means one who does bad things. This was a general charge and could not be backed by specific information. They said nothing of the charge of blasphemy by which they had judged Him guilty. They evaded the charge, knowing Pilate might dismiss the accusation.

31. Then said Pilate unto them, Take ye him, and judge him according to your law: . . . and try him by your own Law, *TCNT* . . . sentence him, *Berkeley.*

The Jews therefore said unto him, It is not lawful for us to put any man to death: Under Roman law, it is not legal for us to execute anyone, *SEB* . . . It is not legal, *Wuest* . . . We have no power, *Weymouth* . . . We are not allowed, *Montgomery* . . . to kill, *Concordant* . . . not allowed to kill anyone, *Beck, Klingensmith* . . . to execute the death penalty, *Williams* . . . to slay any one, *Rotherham* . . . to execute capital punishment, *ALBA* . . . to execute anyone, *Berkeley.*

18:31. The Roman governors allowed the Jews certain authority to govern their internal matters. However, in extreme cases, such as those which demanded the death penalty, the Romans reserved the right to decide. Furthermore, Pilate attempted to avoid making any decision concerning Jesus. This may have been due to his wife's influence because of her dream (Matthew 27:19).

"Ye" is the emphatic word. Pilate did not wish to deal with Jesus' case. First, he pressed the Jews to judge the case themselves. Second, he sent Jesus to Herod. Third, he contrasted Barabbas with Jesus, thinking perhaps he was pointing out the innocence of Christ. Fourth, he had Jesus scourged to emphasize that He had suffered enough. This did not appeal to the Jews' pity or justice. They merely increased their efforts to murder Christ.

There seems ample evidence that the Jews could not put a man to death. First, they stated the fact. Second, the Jewish historian Josephus says the high priest could not call for a judicial trial by the Sanhedrin without the governor's permission. Third, the Tal-

3450.5 art sing masc	3030.1 noun nom sing masc	3450.2 art gen sing	2400.2 name masc	3997.22 verb 3sing subj aor pass	3614.6 rel-pron acc sing masc
ὁ	λόγος	τοῦ	Ἰησοῦ	πληρωθῇ	ὃν
ho	*logos*	*tou*	*Iēsou*	*plērōthē*	*hon*
the	word		of Jesus	might be fulfilled	which

1500.5 verb 3sing indic aor act	4446.1 verb nom sing masc part pres act	4029.2 intr-pron dat sing	2265.3 noun dat sing masc	3165.21 verb 3sing indic imperf act
εἶπεν	σημαίνων	ποίῳ	θανάτῳ	ἤμελλεν
eipen	*sēmainōn*	*poiō*	*thanatō*	*ēmellen*
he spoke	signifying	by what	death	he was about

594.8 verb inf pres act	1511.3 verb 3sing indic aor act	3631.1 conj	1519.1 prep	3450.16 art sing neu
ἀποθνῄσκειν.	33. Εἰσῆλθεν	οὖν	⸂ εἰς	τὸ
apothnēskein	*Eisēlthen*	*oun*	*eis*	*to*
to die.	Entered	therefore	into	the

4091.1 noun sing neu	3687.1 adv	3687.1 adv	1519.1 prep	3450.16 art sing neu	4091.1 noun sing neu
πραιτώριον	πάλιν	[☆ πάλιν	εἰς	τὸ	πραιτώριον]
praitōrion	*palin*	*palin*	*eis*	*to*	*praitōrion*
praetorium	again	[again	into	the	praetorium]

3450.5 art sing masc	3952.1 name nom masc	2504.1 conj	5291.6 verb 3sing indic aor act	3450.6 art acc sing masc	2400.3 name acc masc
ὁ	Πιλᾶτος,	καὶ	ἐφώνησεν	τὸν	Ἰησοῦν,
ho	*Pilatos*	*kai*	*ephōnēsen*	*ton*	*Iēsoun*
	Pilate,	and	called		Jesus,

34.a.**Txt:** 01ℵ,04C-corr, 017K,036,037,13,byz. **Var:** p60,p66,02A,03B, 04C-org,05D,019L, 033X,33,it.sa.bo.Lach Treg,Alf,Word,Tisc, We/Ho,Weis,Sod,UBS/☆

34.b.**Txt:** p60,01ℵ,02A, 04C,05D,017K,032W, 036,037,038,13,byz.Sod **Var:** p66,03B,019L, 033X,Lach,Treg,Alf, Tisc,We/HoWeis,UBS/☆

34.c.**Var:** p66,01ℵ,03B, 04C-org,019L,022N, LachTreg,Alf,We/Ho,Sod

2504.1 conj	1500.5 verb 3sing indic aor act	840.4 prs-pron dat sing	4622.1 prs-pron nom 2sing	1498.3 verb 2sing indic pres act	3450.5 art sing masc
καὶ	εἶπεν	αὐτῷ,	Σὺ	εἶ	ὁ
kai	*eipen*	*autō*	*Su*	*ei*	*ho*
and	said	to him,	You	are	the

928.1 noun nom sing masc	3450.1 art gen pl	2428.3 name-adj gen pl masc	552.6 verb 3sing indic aor pass	840.4 prs-pron dat sing
βασιλεὺς	τῶν	Ἰουδαίων;	34. Ἀπεκρίθη	⸀a αὐτῷ ⸁
basileus	*tōn*	*Ioudaiōn*	*Apekrithē*	*autō*
king	of the	Jews?	Answered	him

3450.5 art sing masc	2400.1 name nom masc	570.1 prep gen	1431.4 prs-pron gen 3sing	570.3 prep gen	4427.1 prs-pron gen 2sing masc
⸀b ὁ ⸁	Ἰησοῦς,	⸂ Ἀφ'	ἑαυτοῦ	[c ἀπὸ	σεαυτοῦ]
ho	*Iēsous*	*Aph'*	*heautou*	*apo*	*seautou*
	Jesus,	From	yourself	[from	yourself]

4622.1 prs-pron nom 2sing	3642.17 dem-pron sing neu	2978.4 verb 2sing indic pres act	2211.1 conj	241.6 adj nom pl masc	4622.3 prs-pron dat 2sing
σὺ	τοῦτο	λέγεις,	ἢ	ἄλλοι	⸂ σοι
su	*touto*	*legeis*	*ē*	*alloi*	*soi*
you	this	say,	or	others	to you

1500.3 verb indic aor act	1500.3 verb indic aor act	4622.3 prs-pron dat 2sing	3875.1 prep	1466.3 prs-pron gen 1sing
εἶπόν	[☆ εἶπόν	σοι]	περὶ	ἐμοῦ;
eipon	*eipon*	*soi*	*peri*	*emou*
did say	[did say	to you]	concerning	me?

552.6 verb 3sing indic aor pass	3450.5 art sing masc	3952.1 name nom masc	3252.1 partic	1466.1 prs-pron nom 1sing
35. Ἀπεκρίθη	ὁ	Πιλᾶτος,	Μήτι	ἐγὼ
Apekrithē	*ho*	*Pilatos*	*Mēti*	*egō*
Answered		Pilate,	Perhaps	I

mud states that the Jews lost authority to execute the penalty 40 years before the destruction of the temple. This would have been prior to Christ's crucifixion. Another account implies that about A.D. 6 the Jews, when Archelaus was disposed, were not permitted capital punishment.

32. That the saying of Jesus might be fulfilled: . . . so the prediction of Jesus, *ALBA* . . . thus fulfilling Jesus' prophecy, *Phillips* . . . In saying this, they showed the truth of the words Jesus had used in foretelling, *Norlie* . . . in fulfilment of what Jesus had said, *TCNT* . . . This made it possible for the word of Jesus to be fulfilled, *Williams* . . . the word ...might be verified, *Wilson* . . . were completed, *Klingensmith.*

which he spake, signifying what death he should die: . . . said when alluding to, *TCNT* . . . indicating the nature of His impending death, *Berkeley* . . . foretelling the nature of the death, *Fenton* . . . the sort of death, *Norlie.*

18:32. Jesus was not stoned to death in the Jewish mode of capital punishment. His crucifixion was hardly possible unless the Romans had power to execute in their fashion. Jesus had said He would be lifted up on a cross (John 3:14; 8:28; 12:32; Matthew 20:19; Mark 10:32,33; Luke 18:32,33).

How ironic that the Jews should force an issue that would fulfill the very words of Jesus. Had the Jews killed Jesus by their method of execution (stoning till dead), Jesus' prophecy would have proven false. But in their ignorance the Jews helped to verify who Jesus was by fulfilling His prediction.

33. Then Pilate entered into the judgment hall again, and called Jesus, and said unto him: . . . therefore again entered his residence and summoned Jesus, *ALBA.*

Art thou the King of the Jews?:

18:33. The judgment hall was the proper place for administering justice (see verse 28). Pilate desired to examine Jesus without the presence of the Jews, for the Jews would not enter for fear of defilement (verse 29).

Jesus did not look like a king for He was dressed as a poor peasant. To the Romans a king was proud and displayed pomp and splendor. There must have been some sarcasm in Pilate's question. Jesus did claim to be a spiritual king (1:49; 12:13), but the Jews led Pilate to believe Jesus was making a claim to kingship in the political sense, and was, therefore, a rival of Caesar.

34. Jesus answered him, Sayest thou this thing of thyself, or did others tell it thee of me?: Do you ask me this on your own initiative, or have others suggested it to you about me? *Williams* . . . Did you think of that yourself, *Beck* . . . Does this question come from you, *TEV* . . . this of your own accord, *Montgomery* . . . Is that your own idea, or have others suggested it to you? *NEB* . . . are others talking to you about me? *Klingensmith* . . . or did others tell you concerning Me? *Concordant* . . . or did others say it about me, *BB* . . . or have other people said that to you, *TCNT* . . . did others say this to you concerning me? *Wuest.*

18:34. Jesus' answer implied that Pilate should make it plain whether he had heard of any rebellion against the Roman government. If a witness had brought him such information, it should be made clear in the accusation. Jesus' claim as the Jews' Messiah did not interfere with submission to the Roman rule.

18:35. Pilate's reply shows indignation. He was a proud Roman, and he despised the Jews and their ways. He had little patience with them and no love for them. Pilate's only reply was that Jesus'

2428.6 name-adj nom masc	1498.2 verb 1sing indic pres act	3450.16 art sing neu	1477.1 noun sing neu	3450.16 art sing neu	4528.8 adj 2sing neu
Ἰουδαῖός	εἰμι;	τὸ	ἔθνος	τὸ	σὸν
Ioudaios	*eimi*	*to*	*ethnos*	*to*	*son*
a Jew	am?	The	nation	the	your

2504.1 conj	3450.7 art pl masc	744.5 noun pl masc	3722.14 verb 3pl indic aor act	4622.4 prs-pron acc 2sing	1466.5 prs-pron dat 1sing
καὶ	οἱ	ἀρχιερεῖς	παρέδωκάν	σε	ἐμοί·
kai	*hoi*	*archiereis*	*paredōkan*	*se*	*emoi*
and	the	chief priests	delivered up	you	to me:

36.a.**Txt:** 037,041-corr, Steph
Var: 01ℵ,02A,03B,04C, 05D,017K,019L,036, 038,byz.Lach,Treg,Alf, TiscWe/Ho,Weis,Sod, UBS/⋆

4949.9 intr-pron sing neu	4020.23 verb 2sing indic aor act	552.6 verb 3sing indic aor pass	3450.5 art sing masc	2400.1 name nom masc
τί	ἐποίησας;	36. Ἀπεκρίθη	⸂a ὁ⸃	Ἰησοῦς,
ti	*epoiēsas*	*Apekrithē*	*ho*	*Iēsous*
what	did you do?	Answered		Jesus,

3450.9 art nom sing fem	926.2 noun nom sing fem	3450.9 art nom sing fem	1684.6 adj nom 1sing fem	3620.2 partic	1498.4 verb 3sing indic pres act
Ἡ	βασιλεία	ἡ	ἐμὴ	οὐκ	ἔστιν
Hē	*basileia*	*hē*	*emē*	*ouk*	*estin*
The	kingdom	the	my	not	is

1523.2 prep gen	3450.2 art gen sing	2862.2 noun gen sing masc	3642.1 dem-pron gen sing	1479.1 conj	1523.2 prep gen	3450.2 art gen sing
ἐκ	τοῦ	κόσμου	τούτου·	εἰ	ἐκ	τοῦ
ek	*tou*	*kosmou*	*toutou*	*ei*	*ek*	*tou*
of	the	world	this;	if	of	the

2862.2 noun gen sing masc	3642.1 dem-pron gen sing	1498.34 verb sing indic imperf act	3450.9 art nom sing fem	926.2 noun nom sing fem	3450.9 art nom sing fem
κόσμου	τούτου	ἦν	ἡ	βασιλεία	ἡ
kosmou	*toutou*	*ēn*	*hē*	*basileia*	*hē*
world	this	were	the	kingdom	the

1684.6 adj nom 1sing fem	3450.7 art pl masc	5095.3 noun nom pl masc	300.1 partic	3450.7 art pl masc	1684.4 adj nom 1pl masc
ἐμή,	οἱ	ὑπηρέται	⸀ ἂν	οἱ	ἐμοὶ
emē	*hoi*	*hupēretai*	*an*	*hoi*	*emoi*
my,	the	attendants		the	my

74.5 verb 3pl indic imperf mid	3450.7 art pl masc	1684.4 adj nom 1pl masc	74.5 verb 3pl indic imperf mid	300.1 partic	2419.1 conj
ἠγωνίζοντο	[οἱ	ἐμοὶ	ἠγωνίζοντο	ἄν,]	ἵνα
ēgōnizonto	*hoi*	*emoi*	*ēgōnizonto*	*an*	*hina*
would fight	[the	my	would fight,]		that

3231.1 partic	3722.34 verb 1sing subj aor pass	3450.4 art dat pl	2428.4 name-adj dat pl masc	3431.1 adv	1156.2 conj
μὴ	παραδοθῶ	τοῖς	Ἰουδαίοις·	νῦν	δὲ
mē	*paradothō*	*tois*	*Ioudaiois*	*nun*	*de*
not	I might be delivered up	to the	Jews;	now	but

3450.9 art nom sing fem	926.2 noun nom sing fem	3450.9 art nom sing fem	1684.6 adj nom 1sing fem	3620.2 partic	1498.4 verb 3sing indic pres act
ἡ	βασιλεία	ἡ	ἐμὴ	οὐκ	ἔστιν
hē	*basileia*	*hē*	*emē*	*ouk*	*estin*
the	kingdom	the	my	not	is

1766.1 adv	1500.5 verb 3sing indic aor act	3631.1 conj	840.4 prs-pron dat sing	3450.5 art sing masc
ἐντεῦθεν.	37. Εἶπεν	οὖν	αὐτῷ	ὁ
enteuthen	*Eipen*	*oun*	*autō*	*ho*
from here.	Said	therefore	to him	

own nation and chief priests had delivered Him to be judged. The governor had no information which would link Jesus with political affairs or insurrection against Rome. The term *king* could have political connections, yet not as used in the religious sense. The Jews were implying that Jesus had presented himself as their political king. It is true that many people had wanted Jesus to be their deliverer-king in a political sense, but Jesus had refused. It is indeed odd that what they wanted Him to be, they accused Him before Pilate of being. They would not accept Him as their deliverer from sin. But they accused Him of wanting to be a political deliverer. Man has usually been more eager for physical and material freedom than liberty of the spiritual man. The natural man is not aware of sin as bondage. Jesus said a man in sin is a slave of sin. How tragic that the religious leaders did not recognize their true enemy. Jesus was not their enemy. Not even the Romans were their greatest enemies. Their sinful natures and wicked conduct were their tyrants and enemies. They were filled with self-centeredness, greed, hypocrisy, pride, and rebellion against their God. Pilate wanted to know what Jesus had done to justify such hatred. Pilate's interest in Jesus was perhaps similar to Herod's (Luke 23:6-12).

18:36. Jesus disclaimed any political or civil kingdom. The Jews expected the Messiah to be a political ruler at His first coming, but Jesus persisted in His insistence that His kingdom was a spiritual one. The conduct of the Jews and His disciples gave evidence to the truth of His statement. Those who wish to maintain political power rely on force. Jesus had forbidden His disciples to defend Him in the Garden, for His kingdom was not worldly but spiritual.

All of this was strange and puzzling to Pilate, but being with Jesus made an impact on him. Pilate was ignorant of spiritual things, but he was well aware of justice. His failure, however, was in both areas.

The reason for Pilate's failure in the area of justice parallels his nation's failure to carry out justice. The substance of justice is righteousness. Righteousness devoid of God becomes centered in the character of the judge. Not only this, but even the rules of the game are composed and arranged for the benefits of the composers. God is an impartial lawgiver, therefore, His laws are just and right. Pilate was governed by the rules drawn up by his own nation for the benefit of his nation. Besides this, Pilate interpreted the law for his own selfish ends. Therefore Pilate failed in the area of justice though he professed to be a just judge.

18:37. Pilate's question, "Art thou a king then?" may have a mixture of significance. Perhaps some awe, curiosity, and scorn

35. Pilate answered, Am I a Jew?:

Thine own nation and the chief priests have delivered thee unto me: Thy countrymen, *Murdock* . . . No, your own people...have given you into my hands, *Norlie.*

what hast thou done?: What did you do? *Wuest.*

36. Jesus answered, My kingdom is not of this world: My realm does not belong to this world, *Moffatt* . . . My kingdom is not founded in this world, *Phillips* . . . belongs not to this world, *AmpB.*

if my kingdom were of this world, then would my servants fight: . . . my followers would, *Norlie* . . . my subjects would have fought, *Weymouth* . . . my adherents, *Campbell* . . . my retainers, *Torrey* . . . my officers, *Wilson* . . . my attendants would have struggled to prevent, *Berkeley* . . . would have contended, *Concordant* . . . have struggled, *Clementson.*

that I should not be delivered to the Jews: . . . to prevent my being given up to the Jews, *TCNT* . . . to prevent my being surrendered to the Jews, *JB* . . . to prevent my falling into, *Campbell* . . . to prevent my arrest, *NIV* . . . not be turned once to, *Norlie.*

but now is my kingdom not from hence: But really the source of My kingdom is not here, *Berkeley* . . . in fact my kingdom is not founded on all this! *Phillips* . . . My kingly authority comes from elsewhere, *NEB* . . . my Kingdom has not this origin, *Weymouth* . . . does not come from such a source, *Williams* . . . is not of such origin, *Montgomery* . . . is not derived hence, *Norton* . . . is not of this kind, *JB* . . . is not from this place, *Wuest* . . . does not belong here, *TEV* . . . is nothing of that kind, *TCNT.*

37.a.**Txt:** 01ℵ,02A,03B, 05D,017K,037,038,1,13, byz.LachTisc,We/Ho,Sod, UBS/⋆
Var: p60,019L,032W, 033X,036,33,Weis

37.b.**Txt:** 02A,017K, 033X,036,037,038,byz. sa.bo.LachWeis
Var: p60,01ℵ,03B,05D, 019L,032W,1,13,33, Treg,Tisc,We/Ho,Sod, UBS/⋆

3952.1 name nom masc	**3630.1** conj	**928.1** noun nom sing masc	**1498.3** verb 2sing indic pres act	**4622.1** prs-pron nom 2sing
Πιλᾶτος,	Οὐκοῦν	βασιλεὺς	εἶ	σύ;
Pilatos	*Oukoun*	*basileus*	*ei*	*su*
Pilate,	Then	a king	are	you?

552.6 verb 3sing indic aor pass	**3450.5** art sing masc	**2400.1** name nom masc	**4622.1** prs-pron nom 2sing	**2978.4** verb 2sing indic pres act
Ἀπεκρίθη	⸂a ὁ⸃	Ἰησοῦς,	Σὺ	λέγεις,
Apekrithē	*ho*	*Iēsous*	*Su*	*legeis*
Answered		Jesus,	You	say,

3617.1 conj	**928.1** noun nom sing masc	**1498.2** verb 1sing indic pres act	**1466.1** prs-pron nom 1sing	**1466.1** prs-pron nom 1sing	**1519.1** prep
ὅτι	βασιλεύς	εἰμι	⸂b ἐγώ·⸃	ἐγὼ	εἰς
hoti	*basileus*	*eimi*	*egō*	*egō*	*eis*
that	a king	am	I.	I	for

3642.17 dem-pron sing neu	**1074.22** verb 1sing indic perf pass	**2504.1** conj	**1519.1** prep	**3642.17** dem-pron sing neu	**2048.24** verb 1sing indic perf act
τοῦτο	γεγέννημαι	καὶ	εἰς	τοῦτο	ἐλήλυθα
touto	*gegennēmai*	*kai*	*eis*	*touto*	*elēlutha*
this	have been born,	and	for	this	I have come

1519.1 prep	**3450.6** art acc sing masc	**2862.4** noun acc sing masc	**2419.1** conj	**3113.19** verb 1sing subj aor act	**3450.11** art dat sing fem
εἰς	τὸν	κόσμον,	ἵνα	μαρτυρήσω	τῇ
eis	*ton*	*kosmon*	*hina*	*marturēsō*	*tē*
into	the	world,	that	I may bear witness	to the

223.3 noun dat sing fem	**3820.6** adj sing masc	**3450.5** art sing masc	**1498.21** verb sing masc part pres act	**1523.2** prep gen	**3450.10** art gen sing fem
ἀληθείᾳ.	πᾶς	ὁ	ὢν	ἐκ	τῆς
alētheia	*pas*	*ho*	*ōn*	*ek*	*tēs*
truth.	Everyone	the	being	of	the

223.2 noun gen sing fem	**189.5** verb 3sing indic pres act	**1466.2** prs-pron gen 1sing	**3450.10** art gen sing fem	**5292.2** noun gen sing fem
ἀληθείας	ἀκούει	μου	τῆς	φωνῆς.
alētheias	*akouei*	*mou*	*tēs*	*phōnēs*
truth	hears	my	the	voice.

2978.5 verb 3sing indic pres act	**840.4** prs-pron dat sing	**3450.5** art sing masc	**3952.1** name nom masc	**4949.9** intr-pron sing neu
38. Λέγει	αὐτῷ	ὁ	Πιλᾶτος,	Τί
Legei	*autō*	*ho*	*Pilatos*	*Ti*
Says	to him		Pilate,	What

1498.4 verb 3sing indic pres act	**223.1** noun nom sing fem	**2504.1** conj	**3642.17** dem-pron sing neu	**1500.15** verb nom sing masc part aor act
ἐστιν	ἀλήθεια;	Καὶ	τοῦτο	εἰπὼν,
estin	*alētheia*	*Kai*	*touto*	*eipōn*
is	truth?	And	this	having said,

3687.1 adv	**1814.3** verb 3sing indic aor act	**4242.1** prep	**3450.8** art acc pl masc	**2428.5** name-adj acc pl masc	**2504.1** conj
πάλιν	ἐξῆλθεν	πρὸς	τοὺς	Ἰουδαίους,	καὶ
palin	*exēlthen*	*pros*	*tous*	*Ioudaious*	*kai*
again	he went out	to	the	Jews,	and

2978.5 verb 3sing indic pres act	**840.2** prs-pron dat pl	**1466.1** prs-pron nom 1sing	**3625.5** num card acc fem	**155.3** noun acc sing fem
λέγει	αὐτοῖς,	Ἐγὼ	οὐδεμίαν	⸂ αἰτίαν
legei	*autois*	*Egō*	*oudemian*	*aitian*
says	to them,	I	not any	fault

may have been the motivation for the cruel man's words.

Jesus said that it was as Pilate stated. Though not political, He was nevertheless a king. He indicated that He by His very nature is King. He was of the Davidic family and could trace His legal genealogy through the kings of Judea to King David (see Matthew 1:6-16). However, Jesus did not claim at this time the political kingdom, but He asserted His messiahship.

Pilate understood little of this statement or the one to follow. The apostle Paul made reference to this witness of Jesus to Pilate (1 Timothy 6:13). Paul called this statement of Jesus a "good" confession.

The Lord did not come to teach human philosophy or to reason with people about truth. He came to actively proclaim and demonstrate truth. Truth is no mere statement of fact; it is the reality itself. A fact is fragmental; truth is total and complete in itself (himself).

Exposure to Jesus is the acid test of being "of the truth." The person who is so foolish as to reject reality, choosing to believe lies, will inevitably reject Jesus, the Truth and Life.

To hear His voice implies that He is the shepherd and the one who hears is His own sheep (10:27). Jesus' testimony to Pilate concerned truth, which all men profess to search for. Jesus appealed to the Roman governor's conscience. To the Jewish high priest, Jesus witnessed to the prophecies of Psalm 110:1 and Daniel 7:13 (see Matthew 26:64). The witness He offers is relevant to the needs of the one He confronts. Pilate could have found his way if he had inquired. But when Pilate inquired, he turned without desiring to hear what truth is. Perhaps he feared he would hear more than he wished to hear. Pilate was a judge who professed to stand for justice, but instead he was swept by events over the brink of disaster. The Lord offered to rescue him, but he refused to grasp hold of the line.

18:38. If Pilate had waited for an answer, he might have heard Jesus say something similar to 1:9,14,17,18; 14:6; and 16:3. "Truth" is Jesus Christ who came as a revelation of God. To state it another way, "truth" is all that God made known in Jesus Christ. By knowing Him, the Truth, man has eternal life (17:3). "Truth" makes Christian conduct possible. Those who are "of the truth" will follow the will of God as revealed in Jesus Christ, the complete and final revelation of the Father.

Pilate obviously thought he had accomplished a coup d'état. All the philosophy of his age had reached the conclusion that nothing could be known with absolute truth. Political and military leaders accepted what the philosophers taught. They therefore were concerned only with material, tangible things.

37. Pilate therefore said unto him, Art thou a king then?: You are a king, then? *Montgomery* . . . Nevertheless, you are a king? *ALBA* . . . So then, you are a king! *SEB.*

Jesus answered, Thou sayest that I am a king: I am, as you say, a King, *Norlie* . . . Indeed I am a King, *Phillips* . . . "King" is your word, *NEB* . . . You are right in saying I am a king, *NIV.*

To this end was I born, and for this cause came I into the world, that I should bear witness unto the truth: I was born and came into the world to testify to the truth, *Beck* . . . The reason I was born, *SEB* . . . For this I was born, *Campbell.*

Every one that is of the truth heareth my voice: Every one who is on the side of truth listens to my voice, *TCNT* . . . Everyone who stands for the truth, *ALBA* . . . Every one who loves the Truth, *Norton* . . . all who are not deaf to truth listen, *NEB* . . . who is a friend of the truth, *Weymouth* . . . who loves truth recognizes my voice, *Phillips* . . . Every one who lives on truth listens to My voice, *Berkeley.*

38. Pilate saith unto him, What is truth?:

And when he had said this, he went out again unto the Jews, and saith unto them: . . . and with this remark, *Norlie.*

I find in him no fault at all: As far as I can see, *Williams* . . . I find no crime in this man, *Montgomery* . . . I don't find this Man guilty of anything, *Beck* . . . I can find no ground for a charge against Him, *Williams* . . . not any

2128.2 verb 1sing indic pres act	1706.1 prep	840.4 prs-pron dat sing	2128.2 verb 1sing indic pres act	1706.1 prep	840.4 prs-pron dat sing
εὑρίσκω	ἐν	αὐτῷ.	[☆ εὑρίσκω	ἐν	αὐτῷ
heuriskō	*en*	*autō*	*heuriskō*	*en*	*autō*
find	in	him.	[find	in	him

155.3 noun acc sing fem	1498.4 verb 3sing indic pres act	1156.2 conj	4764.1 noun nom sing fem	5050.3 prs-pron dat 2pl	2419.1 conj
αἰτίαν.]	39. ἔστιν	δὲ	συνήθεια	ὑμῖν	ἵνα
aitian	*estin*	*de*	*sunētheia*	*humin*	*hina*
fault.]	It is	but	a custom	with you	that

1518.4 num card acc masc	5050.3 prs-pron dat 2pl	624.5 verb 1sing act	624.5 verb 1sing act	5050.3 prs-pron dat 2pl
ἕνα	⸂ ὑμῖν	ἀπολύσω	[☆ ἀπολύσω	ὑμῖν]
hena	*humin*	*apolusō*	*apolusō*	*humin*
one	to you	I should release	[I should release	to you]

1706.1 prep	3450.3 art dat sing	3818.1 noun sing neu	1007.5 verb 2pl indic pres	3631.1 conj	5050.3 prs-pron dat 2pl
ἐν	τῷ	πάσχα·	βούλεσθε	οὖν	⸂ ὑμῖν
en	*tō*	*pascha*	*boulesthe*	*oun*	*humin*
at	the	passover;	will you	therefore	to you

624.5 verb 1sing act	624.5 verb 1sing act	5050.3 prs-pron dat 2pl	3450.6 art acc sing masc	928.4 noun acc sing masc
ἀπολύσω	[☆ ἀπολύσω	ὑμῖν]	τὸν	βασιλέα
apolusō	*apolusō*	*humin*	*ton*	*basilea*
I should release	[I should release	to you]	the	king

3450.1 art gen pl	2428.3 name-adj gen pl masc	2878.3 verb 3pl indic aor act	3631.1 conj	3687.1 adv
τῶν	Ἰουδαίων;	40. Ἐκραύγασαν	οὖν	πάλιν
tōn	*Ioudaiōn*	*Ekraugasan*	*oun*	*palin*
of the	Jews?	They cried out	therefore	again

40.a.**Txt:** p66,02A,017K, 036,037,038,byz.Lach
Var: p60,01ℵ,03B,019L, 032W,033X,28,Tisc, We/Ho,Weis,Sod,UBS/☆

3820.7 adj pl masc	2978.16 verb pl masc part pres act	3231.1 partic	3642.6 dem-pron acc sing masc	233.2 conj	3450.6 art acc sing masc
⸂a πάντες, ⸃	λέγοντες,	Μὴ	τοῦτον,	ἀλλὰ	τὸν
pantes	*legontes*	*Mē*	*touton*	*alla*	*ton*
all,	saying,	Not	this one,	but	

907.2 name acc masc	1498.34 verb sing indic imperf act	1156.2 conj	3450.5 art sing masc	907.1 name nom masc	3001.1 noun nom sing masc
Βαραββᾶν·	ἦν	δὲ	ὁ	Βαραββᾶς	λῃστής.
Barabban	*ēn*	*de*	*ho*	*Barabbas*	*lēstēs*
Barabbas.	Was	now		Barabbas	a robber.

4966.1 adv	3631.1 conj	2956.14 verb 3sing indic aor act	3450.5 art sing masc	3952.1 name nom masc
19:1. Τότε	οὖν	ἔλαβεν	ὁ	Πιλᾶτος
Tote	*oun*	*elaben*	*ho*	*Pilatos*
Then	therefore	took		Pilate

3450.6 art acc sing masc	2400.3 name acc masc	2504.1 conj	3118.2 verb 3sing indic aor act	2504.1 conj	3450.7 art pl masc
τὸν	Ἰησοῦν	καὶ	ἐμαστίγωσεν.	2. καὶ	οἱ
ton	*Iēsoun*	*kai*	*emastigōsen*	*kai*	*hoi*
	Jesus	and	whipped.	And	the

4608.4 noun nom pl masc	3980.1 verb nom pl masc part aor act	4586.2 noun acc sing masc	1523.1 prep gen	171.2 noun gen pl fem
στρατιῶται	πλέξαντες	στέφανον	ἐξ	ἀκανθῶν
stratiōtai	*plexantes*	*stephanon*	*ex*	*akanthōn*
soldiers	having plaited	a crown	of	thorns

Humanistic pragmatism pervades prevailing philosophies. Its assumption is that truth is "whatever works for you" and that it is always changing. Having rejected the Word of God, pragmatism has no objective standard by which to evaluate what is true.

Like Pilate, *every* human being will give account to God for what he did with truth. God's *judgment* is according to truth (Romans 2:2). Even the pagan who has not the gospel does have a revelation of truth sufficient to cause him to seek after more knowledge of God. Creation reveals God's deity and power (Romans 1:18-32), and conscience reveals one's accountability to his Creator (Romans 2:15).

When Pilate walked away from Jesus he was rejecting truth that alone could bring eternal life.

crime, *Murdock* . . . I find nothing culpable, *Campbell* . . . I find no guilt, *Norlie* . . . I do not find a cause for accusation in him, not one bit, *Wuest* . . . an accusation against him, *Adams* . . . in him not a single fault! *Rotherham.*

18:39. Pilate wanted to keep peace in Jerusalem, and he could not afford to have the Jews complain to Caesar. His intent seemed to be that he would compare the gentle and innocent Jesus to the hardened, condemned murderer so that the Jews would realize their mistake in seeking Jesus' death. The "custom" of releasing condemned prisoners is not known beyond the Gospels. The governor perhaps supposed that the popularity of Jesus, indicated by the Triumphal Entry a few days before, would carry over so that many of the crowd would call for Jesus' release. Pilate miscalculated the attitude of the crowd.

39. But ye have a custom, that I should release unto you one at the passover: But I have an arrangement with you, *Phillips* . . . that I set someone free for you at the Passover, *Beck* . . . that I should release one prisoner, *Weymouth* . . . that I should liberate, *Fenton.*

will ye therefore that I release unto you the King of the Jews?: Do you wish, therefore, *Confraternity* . . . Is it your wish, *Norlie* . . . is it your reasoned desire, *Wuest* . . . so, do you want me to liberate for you, *Berkeley* . . . would you like me to set the King, *Beck.*

18:40. Their loud cries remind one of the barks of dogs on the trail of their victim. The closer they came to their prey, the louder they yelped.

They chose Barabbas instead of their Teacher, Healer, Messiah, and God. John says Barabbas was a robber, and Luke says he was thrown in prison for insurrection and murder (Luke 23:19).

40. Then cried they all again, saying: Then they yelled, *Beck.*

Not this man, but Barabbas: No, not him! Bar-Abbas! *Moffatt* . . . Not this fellow, *Norlie.*

Now Barabbas was a robber: . . . a bandit, *Phillips* . . . Now Barabbas was an outlaw, *BB* . . . a revolutionary, *ALBA.*

19:1. The Greek word *oun* is often translated "therefore." Pilate's attempt to release Jesus by comparing Him to Barabbas failed. "Therefore," he tried to appease the Jews by the severe and degrading torture of scourging Jesus. According to some authorities, the person was stripped to the waist and tied to a pillar in a stooping position. The back was lacerated by a whip made of leather thongs, into which were tied bits of bone and metal and weighted with lumps of lead at the tip of each thong. The lash often tore the skin

1. Then Pilate therefore took Jesus, and scourged him: . . . had him flogged, *Phillips, Norlie* . . . and let Him be lashed, *Berkeley* . . . and had him whipped with cords, *BB.*

2. And the soldiers platted a crown of thorns: . . . knygtis foldinge a crowne, *Wycliffe* . . . braiding a wreath, *Concordant* . . . twisted thorn twigs into a crown, *Phillips* . . . twisted some thorns into a crown, *Beck.*

John 19:3

1991.7 verb 3pl indic aor act	840.3 prs-pron gen sing	3450.11 art dat sing fem	2747.3 noun dat sing fem	2504.1 conj	2416.1 noun sing neu
ἐπέθηκαν	αὐτοῦ	τῇ	κεφαλῇ,	καὶ	ἱμάτιον
epethēkan	*autou*	*tē*	*kephalē*	*kai*	*himation*
put on	his	the	head,	and	a cloak

3.a.**Var:** 01ℵ,03B,019L, 030U,033X,038,33,it.sa. bo.Lach,Treg,Alf,Tisc, We/HoWeis,Sod,UBS/☆

4069.1 adj acc sing neu	3879.3 verb 3pl indic aor act	840.6 prs-pron acc sing masc		2504.1 conj
πορφυροῦν	περιέβαλον	αὐτόν,	3. [a☆+	καὶ
porphuroun	*periebalon*	*auton*		*kai*
purple	cast around	him,		[and

2048.60 verb 3pl indic imperf	4242.1 prep	840.6 prs-pron acc sing masc	2504.1 conj	2978.25 verb indic imperf act	5299.6 verb 2sing impr pres act
ἤρχοντο	πρὸς	αὐτὸν]	καὶ	ἔλεγον,	Χαῖρε,
ērchonto	*pros*	*auton*	*kai*	*elegon*	*Chaire*
came	to	him]	and	said,	Hail,

3.b.**Txt:** 02A,05D,017K, 036,037,038,13,byz. Gries
Var: p66,01ℵ,03B,019L, 032W,033X,LachTreg, Alf,Tisc,We/Ho,Weis, Sod,UBS/☆

3450.5 art sing masc	928.1 noun nom sing masc	3450.1 art gen pl	2428.3 name-adj gen pl masc	2504.1 conj	1319.41 verb 3pl indic imperf act
ὁ	βασιλεὺς	τῶν	Ἰουδαίων·	καὶ	⸀ἐδίδουν
ho	*basileus*	*tōn*	*Ioudaiōn*	*kai*	*edidoun*
the	king	of the	Jews!	and	they gave

4.a.**Var:** p66-org,02A, 03B,017K,019L,033X, 041,Lach,Treg,Alf, We/Ho,Weis,UBS/☆

1319.67 verb 3pl indic imperf act	840.4 prs-pron dat sing	4332.3 noun acc pl neu		2504.1 conj
[b☆ ἐδίδοσαν]	αὐτῷ	ῥαπίσματα.	4. [a☆+	Καὶ]
edidosan	*autō*	*rhapismata*		*Kai*
[idem]	him	slaps.		[And]

4.b.**Txt:** p66-corr,021M, 030U,032W,037,038,13, byz.Sod
Var: p66-org,01ℵ,02A, 03B,05D,017K,019L, 036,Gries,Lach,Treg, Alf,Tisc,We/HoWeis, UBS/☆

1814.3 verb 3sing indic aor act	3631.1 conj	3687.1 adv	1838.1 prep gen	3450.5 art sing masc	3952.1 name nom masc
Ἐξῆλθεν	⸂b οὖν ⸃	πάλιν	ἔξω	ὁ	Πιλᾶτος
Exēlthen	*oun*	*palin*	*exō*	*ho*	*Pilatos*
Went	therefore	again	outside		Pilate,

2504.1 conj	2978.5 verb 3sing indic pres act	840.2 prs-pron dat pl	1481.14 verb 2sing impr aor act	70.1 verb 1sing indic pres act	5050.3 prs-pron dat 2pl
καὶ	λέγει	αὐτοῖς,	Ἴδε	ἄγω	ὑμῖν
kai	*legei*	*autois*	*Ide*	*agō*	*humin*
and	says	to them,	Behold,	I bring	to you

840.6 prs-pron acc sing masc	1838.1 prep gen	2419.1 conj	1091.19 verb 2pl aor act	3617.1 conj	1706.1 prep	840.4 prs-pron dat sing
αὐτὸν	ἔξω,	ἵνα	γνῶτε	ὅτι	⸀ἐν	αὐτῷ
auton	*exō*	*hina*	*gnōte*	*hoti*	*en*	*autō*
him	out,	that	you may know	that	in	him

3625.5 num card acc fem	155.3 noun acc sing fem	2128.2 verb 1sing indic pres act	3625.5 num card acc fem	155.3 noun acc sing fem
οὐδεμίαν	αἰτίαν	εὑρίσκω.	[☆ οὐδεμίαν	αἰτίαν
oudemian	*aitian*	*heuriskō*	*oudemian*	*aitian*
not any	fault	I find.	[not any	fault

2128.2 verb 1sing indic pres act	1706.1 prep	840.4 prs-pron dat sing	1814.3 verb 3sing indic aor act	3631.1 conj	3450.5 art sing masc
εὑρίσκω	ἐν	αὐτῷ.]	5. Ἐξῆλθεν	οὖν	ὁ
heuriskō	*en*	*autō*	*Exēlthen*	*oun*	*ho*
I find	in	him.]	Went	therefore	

2400.1 name nom masc	1838.1 prep gen	5246.2 verb nom sing masc part pres act	3450.6 art acc sing masc	172.1 adj acc sing masc
Ἰησοῦς	ἔξω,	φορῶν	τὸν	ἀκάνθινον
Iēsous	*exō*	*phorōn*	*ton*	*akanthinon*
Jesus	out,	wearing	the	thorny

and muscle and exposed the bones of the back. Some accounts state that the internal organs of the body were often exposed. Doubtless the lead-weighted ends of the thongs were buried in the flesh on the sides and underside of the body. When the whip was dragged back, it tore the flesh wherever the whip was embedded.

The Psalmist depicts the agony of Christ's terrible lashing by stating, "The plowers plowed upon my back: they made long their furrows" (Psalm 129:3).

19:2. The scourging led to the soldier's mocking. A deep-seated enmity existed between Romans and Jews. This mocking was aimed at the Jews. Jesus took the scorn, ridicule, and humiliation meant for others. The "crown of thorns" they placed upon His head was made of a common thornbush which grows abundantly in Palestine.

The robe was purple, the color worn by Roman emperors and military officers of high rank. This particular "robe" may have been an old garment good for nothing. Matthew 27:29 states the soldiers put a reed in His right hand as a mock scepter.

19:3. The soldiers formed a line as if invited to present themselves before their monarch. Each saluted Jesus in a mocking allusion to His claim as Messiah. Their words were meant to humiliate the Jews in the person of Jesus.

19:4. The word "again" is significant. Jesus had been tried six times: first, before Annas; second, before Caiaphas; third, before the Sanhedrin in formal session; fourth, before Pilate; fifth, before Herod Antipas; and sixth, before Pilate the second time.

Pilate brought Jesus out of the judgment hall where He had been scourged and mocked. Pilate assumed that by the scourging of Jesus the Jews would be appeased and willing to release the humiliated man. Pilate therefore declared that he found "no fault in him."

Pilate knew Jesus was innocent, but his desire for personal advantage was stronger than his desire for justice. Why did he not release Jesus? First, Pilate's duty was to keep the peace in Jerusalem. Mob violence, riots, and disorders could cause his removal as governor. Second, Pilate needed to be known as a popular governor. If the Jews complained to the emperor, he could lose favor with that ruler. Caesar did not appoint governors who were a constant source of problems. Thus Pilate desired to pacify his subjects.

and put it on his head, and they put on him a purple robe: . . . threw a purple cloak about him, *Montgomery* . . . robed Him in royal purple, *LivB* . . . having thrown a purple mantle, *Campbell.*

3. And said, Hail, King of the Jews!: . . . and they came unto him, and said, *ASV* . . . They kept coming up to him and saying, *TCNT* . . . Good health to the King of the Judeans! *Fenton* . . . Long life to the King of the Jews! *BB* . . . and kept marching up to Him, *Williams* . . . Joy to thee! O King of the Jews! *Rotherham.*

and they smote him with their hands: . . . struck Him blows with their hands, *Norlie* . . . gave him blow after blow, *TCNT* . . . They hit him many times, *SEB.*

4. Pilate therefore went forth again, and saith unto them, Behold, I bring him forth to you: I am going to bring Him out to you, *Williams.*

that ye may know: . . . to let you know, *Beck* . . . to let you clearly understand, *Weymouth.*

that I find no fault in him: . . . nothing with which he can be charged, *TCNT* . . . I find him not guilty, *Berkeley* . . . I do not find a cause for accusation in him, not one bit, *Wuest* . . . that I find nothing wrong with him, *SEB* . . . I can't find any ground for an accusation against him, *Adams.*

5. Then came Jesus forth, wearing the crown of thorns, and the purple robe. And Pilate saith unto them, Behold the man!: Then Jesus came out, *SEB*

John 19:6

4586.2 noun acc sing masc	2504.1 conj	3450.16 art sing neu	4069.1 adj acc sing neu	2416.1 noun sing neu	2504.1 conj
στέφανον	καὶ	τὸ	πορφυροῦν	ἱμάτιον.	καὶ
stephanon	*kai*	*to*	*porphuroun*	*himation*	*kai*
crown	and	the	purple	cloak;	and

5.a.**Txt:** 02A,05D,017K, 036,037,038,13,byz.Lach
Var: 01ℵ,03B,019L, 033X,33,Treg,Alf,Tisc, We/HoWeis,Sod,UBS/☆

2978.5 verb 3sing indic pres act	840.2 prs-pron dat pl	1481.14 verb 2sing impr aor act	1481.20 verb 2sing impr aor mid	3450.5 art sing masc
λέγει	αὐτοῖς,	⌜ Ἴδε	[a☆ Ἰδοὺ]	ὁ
legei	*autois*	*Ide*	*Idou*	*ho*
he says	to them,	Behold	[idem]	the

6.a.**Var:** 01ℵ,02A,05D, 017K,019L,021M,033X, 041,Tisc

442.1 noun nom sing masc	3616.1 conj	3631.1 conj	1481.1 verb indic aor act	1481.21 verb indic aor act
ἄνθρωπος.	6. Ὅτε	οὖν	⌜ εἶδον	[a ἴδον]
anthrōpos	*Hote*	*oun*	*eidon*	*idon*
man!	When	therefore	saw	[idem]

840.6 prs-pron acc sing masc	3450.7 art pl masc	744.5 noun pl masc	2504.1 conj	3450.7 art pl masc	5095.3 noun nom pl masc
αὐτὸν	οἱ	ἀρχιερεῖς	καὶ	οἱ	ὑπηρέται
auton	*hoi*	*archiereis*	*kai*	*hoi*	*hupēretai*
him	the	chief priests	and	the	officers

6.b.**Txt:** 02A,03B,05D, 019L,038,etc.byz.Lach, We/Ho,Weis,Sod,UBS/☆
Var: 01ℵ,Tisc

2878.3 verb 3pl indic aor act	2978.16 verb pl masc part pres act	4568.6 verb 2sing impr aor act	4568.6 verb 2sing impr aor act
ἐκραύγασαν	⌜b λέγοντες, ⌝	Σταύρωσον,	σταύρωσον.
ekraugasan	*legontes*	*Staurōson*	*staurōson*
they cried out	saying,	Crucify,	crucify.

2978.5 verb 3sing indic pres act	840.2 prs-pron dat pl	3450.5 art sing masc	3952.1 name nom masc	2956.24 verb 2pl impr aor act
Λέγει	αὐτοῖς	ὁ	Πιλᾶτος,	Λάβετε
Legei	*autois*	*ho*	*Pilatos*	*Labete*
Says	to them		Pilate,	Take

840.6 prs-pron acc sing masc	5050.1 prs-pron nom 2pl	2504.1 conj	4568.7 verb 2pl impr aor act	1466.1 prs-pron nom 1sing	1056.1 conj
αὐτὸν	ὑμεῖς	καὶ	σταυρώσατε·	ἐγὼ	γὰρ
auton	*humeis*	*kai*	*staurōsate*	*egō*	*gar*
him	you	and	crucify,	I	for

3620.1 partic	2128.2 verb 1sing indic pres act	1706.1 prep	840.4 prs-pron dat sing	155.3 noun acc sing fem	552.8 verb 3pl indic aor pass
οὐχ	εὑρίσκω	ἐν	αὐτῷ	αἰτίαν.	7. Ἀπεκρίθησαν
ouch	*heuriskō*	*en*	*autō*	*aitian*	*Apekrithēsan*
not	find	in	him	a fault.	Answered

840.4 prs-pron dat sing	3450.7 art pl masc	2428.2 name-adj pl masc	2231.1 prs-pron nom 1pl	3414.4 noun acc sing masc	2174.5 verb 1pl indic pres act
αὐτῷ	οἱ	Ἰουδαῖοι,	Ἡμεῖς	νόμον	ἔχομεν,
autō	*hoi*	*Ioudaioi*	*Hēmeis*	*nomon*	*echomen*
him	the	Jews,	We	a law	have,

7.a.**Txt:** p60,02A,017K, 033X,036,038,1,13,byz. sa.bo.Gries,Word,Sod
Var: p66,01ℵ,03B,05D, 019L,032W,037,it.Lach, Treg,Alf,Tisc,We/Ho, Weis,UBS/☆

2504.1 conj	2567.3 prep	3450.6 art acc sing masc	3414.4 noun acc sing masc	2231.2 prs-pron gen 1pl	3648.3 verb 3sing indic pres act
καὶ	κατὰ	τὸν	νόμον	⌜a ἡμῶν ⌝	ὀφείλει
kai	*kata*	*ton*	*nomon*	*hēmōn*	*opheilei*
and	according to	the	law	our	he ought

594.20 verb inf aor act	3617.1 conj	1431.6 prs-pron acc 3sing masc	5048.4 noun acc sing masc	2296.2 noun gen sing masc
ἀποθανεῖν,	ὅτι	⌜ ἑαυτὸν	υἱὸν	θεοῦ
apothanein	*hoti*	*heauton*	*huion*	*theou*
to die,	because	himself	Son	of God

19:5. Jesus was bleeding from the scourging and abuse to which He had been subjected. He came "wearing" the crown and the robe as if it were His normal attire. Pilate supposed that the crowd surely would feel compassion or at least placating contempt. In spite of the indignities He had suffered, Jesus displayed a dignity.

This time Pilate did not say "the King of the Jews." Now, he said in effect, "Look upon this person who has suffered patiently and for what, for He is innocent. Take Him from me and release Him for I find no fault in Him."

Pilate said, "Behold the man!" Jesus was truly man, yet a man unlike other men in that He had not been born in sin, nor had He committed any act of sin. Though He was tempted as we are, He was pure and sinless. He knew no sin until He carried our sins upon himself in His atonement.

19:6. The chief priests and the officers are especially mentioned as preventing any release of Jesus. The chief priests were heads over the 24 courses into which the priesthood was divided. The officers were Levitical temple guards who acted under the influence of the chief priests.

"Crucify, crucify" is a double aorist imperative verb indicating a demanding action. The leaders would not be persuaded by the sight of the mangled form of Jesus. They knew Pilate was yielding to their murderous plans.

For the third time Pilate announced Jesus' innocence (18:38; 19:4), yet he surrendered Him to the madness of His enemies. What Pilate said was spoken in outrage and weakness. Pilate did not want to be responsible for the death of Jesus. He had no love for the Jews but he feared their united influence at Rome. He felt he must yield to them to keep peace in Jerusalem and remain as the governor.

19:7. The Jews answered Pilate by referring to their law. A blasphemer was to be put to death by stoning (Leviticus 24:13-16). The Sanhedrin had indeed condemned Jesus on this charge. Had the Roman restraint not been in force they would have executed their sentence. The Jewish leaders were correct as to what the Law stated, but false because their trial of Jesus was a sham.

19:8. Pilate's actions were the result of several factors. First, Pilate had observed Jesus in His time of stress. Jesus' entire demeanor

... wearing the thorny wreath, *Concordant* ... the wreath of thorns, *Weymouth* ... the thorny crown, *Berkeley* ... the thorny victor's crown, *Wuest* ... the scarlet robe, *ALBA* ... Lo! the Man! *Rotherham* ... See, there is the man, *Weymouth.*

6. When the chief priests therefore and officers saw him, they cried out, saying: ... most important priests, *SEB* ... their underlings, *Norlie* ... they gave a loud cry, *BB* ... raised the cry, *Norlie* ... and their attendants, *Moffatt.*

Crucify him, crucify him: To the cross! to the cross! *BB, Weymouth* ... Hang him, *Murdock* ... Nail him to a cross! *SEB* ... crucify him, at once, *Wuest.*

Pilate saith unto them, Take ye him, and crucify him: Take him yourselves and put him on the cross, *BB.*

for I find no fault in him: I, at any rate, find no, *Weymouth* ... for I find no crime in him, *HBIE* ... no guilt, *Confraternity* ... For my part, I find nothing with which he can be charged, *TCNT* ... him not guilty, *Norlie.*

7. The Jews answered him, We have a law, and by our law he ought to die: The Jews insisted, *NIV* ... he should be put to death, *Norlie* ... he is under moral obligation to die, *Wuest* ... by our Law he is bound to die, *Moffatt* ... in accordance, *Weymouth* ... he is guilty of death, *Torrey.*

because he made himself the Son of God: ... for he claims, *Norlie* ... claimed to be the Son

5048.4 noun acc sing masc	**2296.2** noun gen sing masc	**1431.6** prs-pron acc 3sing masc	**4020.24** verb 3sing indic aor act	**3616.1** conj
[☆ υἱὸν	θεοῦ	ἑαυτὸν]	ἐποίησεν.	**8.** Ὅτε
huion	*theou*	*heauton*	*epoiēsen*	*Hote*
[Son	of God	himself]	he made.	When

3631.1 conj	**189.21** verb 3sing indic aor act	**3450.5** art sing masc	**3952.1** name nom masc	**3642.6** dem-pron acc sing masc	**3450.6** art acc sing masc
οὖν	ἤκουσεν	ὁ	Πιλᾶτος	τοῦτον	τὸν
oun	*ēkousen*	*ho*	*Pilatos*	*touton*	*ton*
therefore	heard		Pilate	this	the

3030.4 noun acc sing masc	**3095.1** adv comp	**5236.12** verb 3sing indic aor pass	**2504.1** conj	**1511.3** verb 3sing indic aor act	**1519.1** prep
λόγον	μᾶλλον	ἐφοβήθη,	**9.** καὶ	εἰσῆλθεν	εἰς
logon	*mallon*	*ephobēthē*	*kai*	*eisēlthen*	*eis*
word	more	he was afraid,	and	went	into

3450.16 art sing neu	**4091.1** noun sing neu	**3687.1** adv	**2504.1** conj	**2978.5** verb 3sing indic pres act	**3450.3** art dat sing
τὸ	πραιτώριον	πάλιν,	καὶ	λέγει	τῷ
to	*praitōrion*	*palin*	*kai*	*legei*	*tō*
the	praetorium	again,	and	says	

2400.2 name masc	**4019.1** adv	**1498.3** verb 2sing indic pres act	**4622.1** prs-pron nom 2sing	**3450.5** art sing masc
Ἰησοῦ,	Πόθεν	εἶ	σύ;	Ὁ
Iēsou	*Pothen*	*ei*	*su*	*Ho*
to Jesus,	From where	are	you?	

1156.2 conj	**2400.1** name nom masc	**606.2** noun acc sing fem	**3620.2** partic	**1319.14** verb 3sing indic aor act	**840.4** prs-pron dat sing
δὲ	Ἰησοῦς	ἀπόκρισιν	οὐκ	ἔδωκεν	αὐτῷ.
de	*Iēsous*	*apokrisin*	*ouk*	*edōken*	*autō*
But	Jesus	an answer	not	did give	him.

10.a.**Txt:** 01ℵ-corr,03B,05D,017K,019L,038,1,etc.byz.Gries,Lach,We/HoWeis,Sod,UBS/☆ **Var:** 01ℵ-org,02A,13,28,bo.Tisc

2978.5 verb 3sing indic pres act	**3631.1** conj	**840.4** prs-pron dat sing	**3450.5** art sing masc	**3952.1** name nom masc
10. λέγει	(a οὖν)	αὐτῷ	ὁ	Πιλᾶτος,
legei	*oun*	*autō*	*ho*	*Pilatos*
Says	therefore	to him		Pilate,

1466.5 prs-pron dat 1sing	**3620.3** partic	**2953.3** verb 2sing indic pres act	**3620.2** partic	**3471.3** verb 2sing indic perf act	**3617.1** conj
Ἐμοὶ	οὐ	λαλεῖς;	οὐκ	οἶδας	ὅτι
Emoi	*ou*	*laleis*	*ouk*	*oidas*	*hoti*
To me	not	speak you?	Not	you have known	that

1833.4 noun acc sing fem	**2174.1** verb 1sing pres act	**4568.9** verb inf aor act	**4622.4** prs-pron acc 2sing	**2504.1** conj
ἐξουσίαν	ἔχω	(σταυρῶσαί	σε,	καὶ
exousian	*echō*	*staurōsai*	*se*	*kai*
authority	I have	to crucify	you,	and

1833.4 noun acc sing fem	**2174.1** verb 1sing pres act	**624.13** verb inf aor act	**4622.4** prs-pron acc 2sing	**624.13** verb inf aor act
ἐξουσίαν	ἔχω	ἀπολῦσαί	σε;	[☆ ἀπολῦσαί
exousian	*echō*	*apolusai*	*se*	*apolusai*
authority	I have	to release	you?	[to release

4622.4 prs-pron acc 2sing	**2504.1** conj	**1833.4** noun acc sing fem	**2174.1** verb 1sing pres act	**4568.9** verb inf aor act	**4622.4** prs-pron acc 2sing
σε	καὶ	ἐξουσίαν	ἔχω	σταυρῶσαί	σε;]
se	*kai*	*exousian*	*echō*	*staurōsai*	*se*
you	and	authority	I have	to crucify	you?]

indicated an extraordinary being. Pilate had only a vague idea of what "the Son of God" meant, yet he had observed enough to cause him fear. After all, had he not abused Christ? Had his wife not sent word to warn him concerning Christ?

Second, Pilate feared the consequences of going against the Jews' demands. The fear of being removed from his position was strong in Pilate.

Third, Pilate was keenly aware that as the Roman governor his first priority was to Roman justice. If he condemned Jesus, he would be guilty of abuse of power.

Fourth, Pilate's administration must keep the Roman peace in Palestine. A religious revolt could cost numerous Roman soldiers' lives, and the destruction of Jewish property might reduce the Roman tax revenue.

19:9. The governor pursued Jesus' claim that He was "the Son of God." He expected some statement concerning the place of His divine origin. Pilate knew Jesus was a Nazarene as to His earthly residence.

Pilate would not have understood if Jesus had told him, so He "gave him no answer." Jesus knew the events which were to transpire before they happened. He had told His disciples that He on His own initiative would lay down His life, that no man was able to take it (10:17,28). He could have called 12 legions of angels to deliver Him (Matthew 26:53). A Roman legion was as many as 6,000 soldiers; thus 12 legions would be approximately 72,000 angels. No, Jesus would not call even one legion to remove Him from His hour of agony. His sacrifice for us was voluntary. He said later that it was "necessary for the Christ to suffer these things" (Luke 24:26, NASB).

19:10. Pilate was worried and tormented by his fears. The pressure of the Jews and his troubled sense of justice brought him into a dilemma for which he was an unwilling judge. He boasted of his authority, but he was reluctant to exercise it in the cause of justice. Pilate emphasized the pronoun "I," and he paralleled "to release" with "to crucify." Pilate had said to the Jews that they should take to themselves the responsibility (verse 6), yet here he admitted that he had the authority. He wanted the authority without having to be accountable for its use.

Pilate tried to threaten Jesus and make Him talk by this declaration of authority. Jesus' silence unnerved Pilate. "Speakest thou not unto me" (the "unto me" is emphatic) from the lips of Pilate

of God, *Weymouth* . . . he assumed the title of the Son of God, *Campbell* . . . and that by nature, *Wuest.*

8. When Pilate therefore heard that saying, he was the more afraid: When Pilate heard mention of this, *ALBA* . . . heard that declaration, he feared the more, *Murdock* . . . he was much disturbed, *Torrey* . . . he became much more uneasy, *Phillips* . . . his fears increased, *JB* . . . he was frightened more than ever, *Beck* . . . he was more afraid than ever, *Phillips* . . . he became still more alarmed, *TCNT* . . . more awestricken, *Williams* . . . still more terrified, *Fenton* . . . his fear became greater, *BB* . . . he dredde more, *Wycliffe* . . . than before, *ET.*

9. And went again into the judgment hall, and saith unto Jesus, Whence art thou?: . . . went back into the fortress, *SEB* . . . Where do you come from, *Moffatt* . . . What is your origin, *Weymouth.*

But Jesus gave him no answer: . . . no reply, *Norlie.*

10. Then saith Pilate unto him, Speakest thou not unto me?: Do you refuse to speak to me, *Williams* . . . Will you not speak to me? *Campbell* . . . Why don't you speak to me? *Norlie.*

knowest thou not that I have power to crucify thee, and I have power to release thee?: Are you ignorant that, *Norton* . . . Don't you realize, *Phillips* . . . that I have it in my power either to release you or to crucify you, *Weymouth* . . . to nail you to a cross! *SEB* . . . set you free, *Norlie* . . . to liberate you, *Berkeley* . . . to discharge you, *Fenton.*

11.a.**Var:** p60,01ℵ,03B,05D,019L,032W,1,33,sa.Lach,Treg,Alf,We/Ho,Sod

11.b.**Txt:** p60,01ℵ,02A,019L,033X,037,038,1,13,Steph,Sod **Var:** 03B,05D,017K,036,byz.Gries,Lach,Treg,Alf Word,Tisc,We/Ho,Weis,UBS/☆

11.c.**Txt:** 02A,05D,017K,019L,032W,036,1,13,byz.GriesTreg,Sod **Var:** 01ℵ,03B,07E,037,038,Lach,Tisc,We/Ho,Weis,UBS/☆

12.a.**Txt:** 01ℵ-corr,07E,017K,036,037,byz. **Var1:** .(02),(019),032W,038,041,1,13,Lach,Tisc,Sod **Var2:** .03B,05D,33,Treg,We/HoWeis,UBS/☆

552.6 verb 3sing indic aor pass **11.** ᾿Απεκρίθη *Apekrithē* Answered	**840.4** prs-pron dat sing [a+ αὐτῷ] *autō* [him]	**3450.5** art sing masc (b ὁ) *ho*	**2400.1** name nom masc ᾿Ιησοῦς, *Iēsous* Jesus,	**3620.2** partic Οὐκ *Ouk* Not
2174.43 verb 2sing indic imperf act εἶχες *eiches* you have	**1833.4** noun acc sing fem ἐξουσίαν *exousian* authority	**3625.5** num card acc fem (οὐδεμίαν *oudemian* not any	**2567.1** prep κατ᾿ *kat'* against	**1466.3** prs-pron gen 1sing ἐμοῦ *emou* me
2567.1 prep [☆ κατ᾿ *kat'* [against	**1466.3** prs-pron gen 1sing ἐμοῦ *emou* me	**3625.5** num card acc fem οὐδεμίαν] *oudemian* not any]	**1479.1** conj εἰ *ei* if	**3231.1** partic μὴ *mē* not
1498.34 verb sing indic imperf act ἦν *ēn* it were	**4622.3** prs-pron dat 2sing (σοι *soi* to you	**1319.56** verb nom sing neu part perf pass δεδομένον *dedomenon* having been given	**1319.56** verb nom sing neu part perf pass [☆ δεδομένον *dedomenon* [having been given	**4622.3** prs-pron dat 2sing σοι] *soi* to you]
505.1 adv ἄνωθεν· *anōthen* from above.	**1217.2** prep διὰ *dia* Because of	**3642.17** dem-pron sing neu τοῦτο *touto* this	**3450.5** art sing masc ὁ *ho* the	**3722.3** verb nom sing masc part pres act (παραδιδούς *paradidous* delivering up
3722.17 verb nom sing masc part aor act [c☆ παραδούς] *paradous* [having delivered]	**1466.6** prs-pron acc 1sing μέ *me* me	**4622.3** prs-pron dat 2sing σοι *soi* to you	**3157.1** adj comp acc μείζονα *meizona* greater	**264.4** noun acc sing fem ἁμαρτίαν *hamartian* sin
2174.4 verb 3sing indic pres act ἔχει. *echei* has.	**1523.2** prep gen **12.** ᾿Εκ *Ek* From	**3642.1** dem-pron gen sing τούτου *toutou* this	**2195.23** verb 3sing indic imperf act (ἐζήτει *ezētei* sought	**3450.5** art sing masc ὁ *ho*
3952.1 name nom masc Πιλᾶτος *Pilatos* Pilate	**3450.5** art sing masc [☆ ὁ *ho*	**3952.1** name nom masc Πιλᾶτος *Pilatos* [Pilate	**2195.23** verb 3sing indic imperf act ἐζήτει] *ezētei* sought]	**624.13** verb inf aor act ἀπολῦσαι *apolusai* to release
840.6 prs-pron acc sing masc αὐτόν. *auton* him;	**3450.7** art pl masc οἱ *hoi* the	**1156.2** conj δὲ *de* but	**2428.2** name-adj pl masc ᾿Ιουδαῖοι *Ioudaioi* Jews	**2869.18** verb 3pl indic imperf act (ἐκραζον, *ekrazon* cried out,
2878.6 verb 3pl indic imperf act [1a☆ ἐκραύγαζον *ekraugazon* [idem	**2878.3** verb 3pl indic aor act 2 ἐκραύγασαν] *ekraugasan* idem]	**2978.16** verb pl masc part pres act λέγοντες, *legontes* saying,	**1430.1** partic ᾿Εὰν *Ean* If	**3642.6** dem-pron acc sing masc τοῦτον *touton* this
624.8 verb 2sing subj aor act ἀπολύσῃς *apolusēs* you release	**3620.2** partic οὐκ *ouk* not	**1498.3** verb 2sing indic pres act εἶ *ei* you are	**5224.1** adj nom sing masc φίλος *philos* a friend	**3450.2** art gen sing τοῦ *tou*
2512.1 name gen masc Καίσαρος. *Kaisaros* of Caesar.	**3820.6** adj sing masc πᾶς *pas* Everyone			

suggest Jesus' silence was contempt of court. Pilate therefore sought to make Jesus talk by this self-centered statement regarding authority.

11. Jesus answered, Thou couldest have no power at all against me: Jesus replied to him, *ET*... You have not power whatever of your own, *Berkeley* ... against Me in a single thing except, *Concordant.*

except it were given thee from above: ... had it not been granted you from above, *Weymouth*... if it was not given to you by God, *BB.*

therefore he that delivered me unto thee hath the greater sin: That is why the man who handed Me over to you is guilty of a greater sin, *Beck*... the one who betrayed me, *Norlie* ... is more guilty than you are, *Weymouth* ... greater sin to answer for, *TCNT* ... has even more guilt, *SEB.*

19:11. These are Christ's last words to Pilate. Jesus did not say "from My Father." He used the general term "from above." Jesus also used the pronoun "me" (Greek, *emou*) in the emphatic sense. Jesus pointed out that the authority Pilate had was delegated from God, not merely from Pilate's emperor.

Merrill Tenney comments: "Jesus looked on Pilate as checked by the hand of God. Pilate was simply an instrument in the divine purpose. The real guilt lay with those who had delivered Jesus to Pilate in the first place. The reference is to Caiaphas and the Jewish hierarchy who had initiated the trial" (Tenney, *Expositor's Bible Commentary,* 9:177). This last comment enlarges our understanding and shifts the focus from Judas to the Jewish leaders.

12. And from thenceforth Pilate sought to release him: This made Pilate anxious to release him, *TCNT*... And for this reason, *Murdock* ... Out of this Pilate looked for a way to free Him, *Adams* ... Because of this Pilate kept on trying to set Him free, *Williams* ... Because of this Pilate made repeated efforts to release Him, *Wuest*... was earnest to release him, *Norton* ... was disposed, *Murdock* ... was looking for a way to, *Confraternity* ... was anxious, *Berkeley*... tried hard to set him free, *Phillips* ... tried hard to set Jesus free, *SEB.*

but the Jews cried out, saying, If thou let this man go, thou art not Caesar's friend: ... yet the Jews clamored, *Concordant* ... the Judeans were shrieking out, *Fenton* ... kept clamouring, *HistNT*... continued to yell, *SEB* ... If you liberate him, you are no friend of Caesar's, *Berkeley* ... If you release this fellow, *Wuest*... the Emperor's! *TCNT.*

19:12. Pilate seemed to redouble his efforts to release Jesus, but the Jews had reserved their most powerful weapon until now. It was a personal threat to the position of Pilate as governor. The title "a friend of Caesar" was bestowed upon those who acted for the emperor. The Jews' words conveyed the idea that Pilate would not be loyal to Caesar if he released Jesus.

The Caesars were jealous of their power. The Jews could plant just enough seeds of doubt in the emperor's mind to cause the governor's recall. If Pilate was to retain his position of governor he must be Caesar's friend. Any doubt cast upon that relationship could have adverse consequences. Pilate would not risk his seat of power and prestige. Thus the Jewish leaders had calculated in their unrighteous councils. They knew the strategy that would cause Pilate to yield to their scheming. After all, the Jewish leaders themselves were demanding the murder of Christ to insure their own position of power.

Though Jesus had shown that He did not aspire to an earthly throne, Caesar would not understand. The Jews implied that they would see that Caesar heard about the rival king in Palestine. Treason was dealt with most ruthlessly by the Romans. Fear pressed its darkness into Pilate's soul, and justice failed to occupy the seat of decision. Pilate reasoned to this effect: If Caesar heard the word *king,* he would not consider the context. Thus Tiberias Caesar could very well have suspicions as to whether Pontius Pilate had the emperor's best interests at heart. How cunning and deceitful

John 19:13

12.b.**Txt:** Steph
Var: 01ℵ,02A,03B,05D,017K,019L,036,037,038,byz.Gries,LachTreg,Alf,Tisc,We/Ho,Weis,Sod,UBS/☆

3450.5 art sing masc	**928.4** noun acc sing masc	**840.6** prs-pron acc sing masc	**1431.6** prs-pron acc 3sing masc	**4020.15** verb sing masc part pres act
ὁ	βασιλέα	ʿ αὐτὸν	[ᵇ☆ ἑαυτὸν]	ποιῶν
ho	*basilea*	*auton*	*heauton*	*poiōn*
the	king	himself	[idem]	making

480.1 verb 3sing indic pres act	**3450.3** art dat sing	**2512.2** name dat masc	**3450.5** art sing masc	**3631.1** conj
ἀντιλέγει	τῷ	Καίσαρι.	**13.** ʿΟ	οὖν
antilegei	*tō*	*Kaisari*	*Ho*	*oun*
speaks against		Caesar.		Therefore

3952.1 name nom masc	**189.31** verb nom sing masc part aor act	**3642.6** dem-pron acc sing masc	**3450.6** art acc sing masc	**3030.4** noun acc sing masc
Πιλᾶτος	ἀκούσας	ʿ τοῦτον	τὸν	λόγον,
Pilatos	*akousas*	*touton*	*ton*	*logon*
Pilate	having heard	this	the	word,

13.a.**Txt:** 017K,022N,030U,byz.

3450.1 art gen pl	**3030.6** noun gen pl masc	**3642.2** dem-pron gen pl	**70.8** verb 3sing indic aor act	**1838.1** prep gen	**3450.6** art acc sing masc
[ᵃ☆ τῶν	λόγων	τούτων]	ἤγαγεν	ἔξω	τὸν
tōn	*logōn*	*toutōn*	*ēgagen*	*exō*	*ton*
[the	words	these]	led	out	

13.b.**Txt:** 07E,017K,021M,032W,036,037,038,13,byz.
Var: 01ℵ,02A,03B,05D,019L,033X,Lach,Treg,Alf,WordTisc,We/Ho,Weis,Sod,UBS/☆

2400.3 name acc masc	**2504.1** conj	**2495.3** verb 3sing indic aor act	**1894.3** prep	**3450.2** art gen sing	**961.1** noun gen sing neu
Ἰησοῦν,	καὶ	ἐκάθισεν	ἐπὶ	ʿᵇ τοῦ ˎ	βήματος,
Iēsoun	*kai*	*ekathisen*	*epi*	*tou*	*bēmatos*
Jesus,	and	sat down	upon	the	judgment seat,

1519.1 prep	**4964.4** noun acc sing masc	**2978.29** verb acc sing part pres pass	**3011.1** name acc masc	**1440.1** name-adv
εἰς	τόπον	λεγόμενον	Λιθόστρωτον,	Ἑβραϊστὶ
eis	*topon*	*legomenon*	*Lithostrōton*	*Hebraisti*
at	a place	called	Pavement,	in Hebrew

14.a.**Txt:** 07E,036,038,byz.
Var: 01ℵ,02A,03B,05D,019L,021M,037,Lach Treg,Alf,Word,Tisc,We/Ho,Weis,Sod,UBS/☆

1156.2 conj	**1035.1** name neu	**1498.34** verb sing indic imperf act	**1156.2** conj	**3765.1** noun nom sing fem	**3450.2** art gen sing
δὲ	Γαββαθα·	**14.** ἦν	δὲ	παρασκευὴ	τοῦ
de	*Gabbatha*	*ēn*	*de*	*paraskeuē*	*tou*
but	Gabbatha:	it was	and	preparation	of the

14.b.**Txt:** 05D,021M,037,1,Steph
Var: 01ℵ,02A,03B,017K,019L,036,038,byz.Lach,Treg,Alf,Tisc,We/Ho,WeisSod,UBS/☆

3818.1 noun sing neu	**5443.2** noun nom sing fem	**1156.2** conj	**1498.34** verb sing indic imperf act	**5448.1** adv	**5453.1** conj
πάσχα,	ὥρα	ʿ δὲ	[ᵃ☆ ἦν]	ʿ ὡσεὶ	[ᵇ☆ ὡς]
pascha	*hōra*	*de*	*ēn*	*hōsei*	*hōs*
passover,	hour	and	[it was]	about	[idem]

14.c.**Var:** 01ℵ-corr,05D,019L,033X,037,044

1608.3 num ord nom sing fem	**4995.4** num ord nom sing fem	**2504.1** conj	**2978.5** verb 3sing indic pres act	**3450.4** art dat pl	**2428.4** name-adj dat pl masc
ʿ ἕκτη·	[ᶜ τρίτη·]	καὶ	λέγει	τοῖς	Ἰουδαίοις,
hektē	*tritē*	*kai*	*legei*	*tois*	*Ioudaiois*
the sixth;	[third.]	and	he says	to the	Jews,

1481.14 verb 2sing impr aor act	**3450.5** art sing masc	**928.1** noun nom sing masc	**5050.2** prs-pron gen 2pl	**3450.7** art pl masc	**1156.2** conj
Ἴδε	ὁ	βασιλεὺς	ὑμῶν.	**15.** ʿ Οἱ	δὲ
Ide	*ho*	*basileus*	*humōn*	*Hoi*	*de*
Behold	the	king	your!	The	but

15.a.**Txt:** 02A,07E,021M,036,037,1,13,byz.Gries,Lach
Var: 01ℵ-corr,03B,019L,033X,Treg,Alf,Tisc,We/Ho,WeisSod,UBS/☆

2878.3 verb 3pl indic aor act	**2878.3** verb 3pl indic aor act	**3631.1** conj	**1552.6** dem-pron nom pl masc
ἐκραύγασαν,	[ᵃ☆ ἐκραύγασαν	οὖν	ἐκεῖνοι,]
ekraugasan	*ekraugasan*	*oun*	*ekeinoi*
cried out,	[cried out	therefore	those,]

the Jews made their plans. They would use Pilate's selfish nature to carry out their wicked plans.

19:13. Pilate yielded to the mob's pressure. Jesus was brought out to the full view of the mob, still bleeding and mangled by His scourging and harsh treatment.

The verdict was given formally from "the judgment seat" (Greek, *bēmatos*). The seat was a movable, chairlike throne on which final decisions were made. "The Pavement" or "Gabbatha" was an elevated platform of stone on which the *bema* (judgment seat) rested. Pilate now "sat down in the judgment seat," indicating that he was about to make his final decision.

"It must be accounted a curiosity of translation and exegesis that in a number of versions (e.g., those of Moffatt, Goodspeed and C. B. Williams), Pilate is said to have made *Jesus* sit on the tribunal." Though *ekathisen* may be transitive as well as intransitive, having Jesus sit on the judgment seat is not something Pilate would allow (Bruce, p.364).

Pilate had been forced into the corner of his own selfishness—a small space it was! As a Roman governor, he took pride in executing justice. Now, however, he was caught within the vise of his own self-interest. The pressure on his soul crushed him like an eggshell. From this point on he would rationalize his vile and corrupt decision.

19:14. The hurried trials, execution, and removal from the cross must have taken place on the day of "preparation" (Friday of Passover week). Mark 15:25ff. states that Jesus was on the cross 6 hours, from 9 o'clock in the morning until 3 o'clock in the afternoon. The last 3 hours were in terrible darkness.

Pilate had yielded to the pressures of the people he feared and hated. His statement, "Behold your King!" was one of weakness in him and scorn for them. Pilate hated them for their superior force and hated himself for his cowardly weakness. His words were half of fear and half an unwitting prophecy. The religious head of the nation had proclaimed that it was expedient that "one man should die for the people" (11:50). He spoke more than he knew. The political authority now also declared that Jesus was their King and Messiah. Thus from the mouth of a tyrant, Jesus was proclaimed for who He is! Even in man's wrath God receives glory. Pilate asserted Jesus' deity by saying, "Behold your King!"

19:15. The mob joined with their leaders when they demanded, "Away with him, . . . crucify him." They wanted nothing to do with such a pitiful king.

whosoever maketh himself a king speaketh against Caesar: Whoever sets himself up as a king is a rebel against, *Norlie* . . . is a rebel against the Emperor, *Montgomery* . . . is contradicting Caesar! *Concordant* . . . is the adversary, *Murdock* . . . is uttering treason, *Williams* . . . is a traitor against the Emperor, *Fenton* . . . challenges Caesar! *Adams* . . . is anti-Caesar! *Phillips* . . . is against Caesar, *Beck* . . . declares himself a rebel, *Weymouth* . . . declares himself against, *Wuest* . . . does so in defiance of, *ALBA.*

13. When Pilate therefore heard that saying, he brought Jesus forth, and sat down in the judgment seat: On hearing what they said...took his seat upon the Bench, *TCNT* . . . on hearing this cry, *Norlie* . . . the Tribunal, *Wilson* . . . an elevated-bench, *Rotherham* . . . on a raised platform provided for a judge, *Wuest.*

in a place that is called the Pavement, but in the Hebrew, Gabbatha: In the Aramaic language, *SEB* . . . mosaic pavement, *Wuest.*

14. And it was the preparation of the passover: . . . the preparation day, *Norlie.*

and about the sixth hour: . . . and about the noon hour, *Norlie* . . . about twelve o'clock, *Berkeley* . . . about midday, *ALBA.*

and he saith unto the Jews, Behold your King!: Look, here's your king! *Phillips* . . . Here is your king, *NIV.*

15. But they cried out, Away with him, away with him, crucify him: This caused a storm of outcries, *Weymouth* . . . At that the

142.13 verb 2sing impr aor act	142.13 verb 2sing impr aor act	4568.6 verb 2sing impr aor act	840.6 prs-pron acc sing masc	2978.5 verb 3sing indic pres act
Ἆρον	ἆρον,	σταύρωσον	αὐτόν.	Λέγει
Aron	*aron*	*staurōson*	*auton*	*Legei*
Away,	away,	crucify	him.	Says

840.2 prs-pron dat pl	3450.5 art sing masc	3952.1 name nom masc	3450.6 art acc sing masc	928.4 noun acc sing masc	5050.2 prs-pron gen 2pl
αὐτοῖς	ὁ	Πιλᾶτος,	Τὸν	βασιλέα	ὑμῶν
autois	*ho*	*Pilatos*	*Ton*	*basilea*	*humōn*
to them		Pilate,	The	king	your

4568.4 verb 1sing subj aor act	552.8 verb 3pl indic aor pass	3450.7 art pl masc	744.5 noun pl masc	3620.2 partic
σταυρώσω;	Ἀπεκρίθησαν	οἱ	ἀρχιερεῖς,	Οὐκ
staurōsō	*Apekrithēsan*	*hoi*	*archiereis*	*Ouk*
shall I crucify?	Answered	the	chief priests,	Not

2174.5 verb 1pl indic pres act	928.4 noun acc sing masc	1479.1 conj	3231.1 partic	2512.3 name acc masc	4966.1 adv	3631.1 conj
ἔχομεν	βασιλέα	εἰ	μὴ	Καίσαρα.	**16.** Τότε	οὖν
echomen	*basilea*	*ei*	*mē*	*Kaisara*	*Tote*	*oun*
we have	a king	if	not	Caesar.	Then	therefore

16.a.**Txt:** 02A,07E,017K, 036,037,038,byz.
Var: 03B,05D,019L, 033X,33,bo.Lach,Treg Alf,Tisc,We/Ho,Weis, Sod,UBS/☆

3722.10 verb 3sing indic aor act	840.6 prs-pron acc sing masc	840.2 prs-pron dat pl	2419.1 conj	4568.13 verb 3sing subj aor pass
παρέδωκεν	αὐτὸν	αὐτοῖς	ἵνα	σταυρωθῇ.
paredōken	*auton*	*autois*	*hina*	*staurōthē*
he delivered up	him	to them	that	he might be crucified.

16.b.**Txt:** 02A,Steph
Var: 03B,019L,033X,33, bo.Lach,Treg,Alf,Tisc, We/HoWeis,Sod,UBS/☆

3741.4 verb indic aor act	1156.2 conj	3631.1 conj	3450.6 art acc sing masc	2400.3 name acc masc	2504.1 conj
Παρέλαβον	⸀ δὲ	[a☆ οὖν]	τὸν	Ἰησοῦν	⸂b καὶ
Parelabon	*de*	*oun*	*ton*	*Iēsoun*	*kai*
They took	and	[therefore]		Jesus	and

516.3 verb 3pl indic aor act	2504.1 conj	934.5 verb nom sing masc part pres act	3450.6 art acc sing masc	4567.4 noun acc sing masc
ἀπήγαγον· ⸃	**17.** καὶ	βαστάζων	⸂ τὸν	σταυρὸν
apēgagon	*kai*	*bastazōn*	*ton*	*stauron*
led away.	And	bearing	the	cross

17.a.**Txt:** 017K,036,byz.
Var: p60,p66-corr,01א, 019L,032W,041,Tisc Weis,Sod,UBS/☆

840.3 prs-pron gen sing	840.4 prs-pron dat sing	3450.6 art acc sing masc	4567.4 noun acc sing masc	1814.3 verb 3sing indic aor act
αὐτοῦ	[a☆ αὐτῷ	τὸν	σταυρὸν]	ἐξῆλθεν
autou	*autō*	*ton*	*stauron*	*exēlthen*
his	[to him	the	cross]	he went out

1519.1 prep	3450.6 art acc sing masc	2978.29 verb acc sing part pres pass	2871.1 noun gen sing neu	4964.4 noun acc sing masc	3614.5 rel-pron nom sing masc
εἰς	τὸν	λεγόμενον	κρανίου	τόπον,	⸂ ὃς
eis	*ton*	*legomenon*	*kraniou*	*topon*	*hos*
to	the	called	of a skull	place,	which

17.b.**Txt:** 05D,07E,021M, 036,038,1,13,byz.Gries, Lach,Sod
Var: p66,01א,02A,03B, 017K,032W,Treg,Alf, Tisc,We/HoWeis,UBS/☆

3614.16 rel-pron sing neu	2978.28 verb 3sing indic pres pass	1440.1 name-adv	1109.2 name	3562.1 adv
[b☆ ὃ]	λέγεται	Ἑβραϊστὶ	Γολγοθα,	**18.** ὅπου
ho	*legetai*	*Hebraisti*	*Golgotha*	*hopou*
[idem]	is called	in Hebrew	Golgotha:	where

840.6 prs-pron acc sing masc	4568.3 verb 3pl indic aor act	2504.1 conj	3196.2 prep	840.3 prs-pron gen sing	241.8 adj acc pl masc
αὐτὸν	ἐσταύρωσαν,	καὶ	μετ'	αὐτοῦ	ἄλλους
auton	*estaurōsan*	*kai*	*met'*	*autou*	*allous*
him	they crucified,	and	with	him	others

The chief priests are singled out as the spokesmen for they had renounced their messianic hopes and abandoned their godly heritage. "The reply of the chief priests is astonishing: 'We have no king but Caesar.' The official heads of the nation, who would gladly have welcomed independence, put themselves on record as subjects of the pagan emperor. Even allowing for the fact that the Sadducean priesthood was willing to compromise with the Romans for the sake of political advantage, nothing revealed their lack of spiritual principles so vividly as this act of betrayal. It was the final step in the process initially described in the Prologue . . . (John 1:11)" (Tenney, *Expositor's Bible Commentary*, 9:178).

There was no repentance when John the Baptist preached, nor when Jesus proclaimed the Kingdom was near. The Jews continued their opposition to Jesus, and the ax was applied to the roots of their national tree. Their covenant with Yahweh was doomed.

19:16. Pilate merely delivered Jesus to them. Perhaps Pilate purposely avoided a formal statement of the guilty verdict. Crucifixion was the most harsh, cruel, and ignominious punishment known among the ancient peoples. Crosses were of differing sizes and the pieces crossed in various ways. A simple stake made a cross to impale a man. The T form was used, as well as an X, but the common form of a cross was the T. It is likely that the last form of the cross was the one used for Jesus. The upright piece probably remained on the site of executions and the heavy crosspiece was carried by Jesus to Golgotha.

19:17. The Lord was stripped of His purple robe and given His own garments (Matthew 27:31). It was usual for the criminal to carry his own cross except when scourging had weakened him so that he was unable to do so. John's Gospel says nothing about the help Simon the Cyrenian gave. Jesus had been without sleep, and the loss of so much blood had weakened Him.

The "place" was called Golgotha, "the place of a skull." The Gospels do not say the site was a hill, yet an elevated area would be the logical place for executing malefactors, because their executions were meant to be deterrents to crime.

19:18. Jesus was fastened to the cross by nails through His hands and feet. The feet could have been separated or united and were

people shouted, *TCNT* . . . They yelled, Take him away! *SEB* . . . hang him, hang him, *Murdock* . . . Off with him! Off with him! Crucify him! *Moffatt.*

Pilate saith unto them, Shall I crucify your King?: Must I crucify your king, *Williams* . . . Should I nail your King to a cross, *SEB.*

The chief priests answered, We have no king but Caesar: We have no king but the emperor! *Williams* . . . and no one else, *Phillips.*

16. Then delivered he him therefore unto them to be crucified: Then at that point, *Adams* . . . So in the end, *JB* . . . Finally Pilate handed him over, *NIV* . . . Then at last, to satisfy them, he handed Jesus over, *NEB.*

And they took Jesus, and led him away: The soldiers took him in charge, *ALBA* . . . So they took hold of Jesus, *SEB.*

17. And he bearing his cross went forth into a place called the place of a skull: Carrying his own cross, *NIV* . . . bearing His own cross, to the spot called...Skull, *AmpB* . . . Carrying His cross, He came to a spot named the Place of the Skull, *Norlie* . . . Skull Hill, *Phillips* . . . "Skull-field," *Fenton* . . . the place off deed menns sculles, *Tyndale* . . . place of a cranium, *Sawyer* . . . named Dead Man's Head, *BB.*

which is called in the Hebrew Golgotha: . . . which the Jews called Golgotha, *Beck.*

18. Where they crucified him, and two other with him: There they crucified him, and two others, *Phillips* . . . Here they crucified him, and with him two others, *NIV.*

1411.3 num card	**1766.1** adv	**2504.1** conj	**1766.1** adv	**3189.5** adj acc sing neu	**1156.2** conj
δύο	ἐντεῦθεν	καὶ	ἐντεῦθεν,	μέσον	δὲ
duo	*enteuthen*	*kai*	*enteuthen*	*meson*	*de*
two	on this side	and	on that side,	in the middle	and

3450.6 art acc sing masc	**2400.3** name acc masc	**1119.8** verb 3sing indic aor act	**1156.2** conj	**2504.1** conj	**4950.1** noun acc sing masc
τὸν	Ἰησοῦν.	**19.** Ἔγραψεν	δὲ	καὶ	τίτλον
ton	*Iēsoun*	*Egrapsen*	*de*	*kai*	*titlon*
	Jesus.	Wrote	and	also	a title

3450.5 art sing masc	**3952.1** name nom masc	**2504.1** conj	**4935.10** verb 3sing indic aor act	**1894.3** prep	**3450.2** art gen sing
ὁ	Πιλᾶτος	καὶ	ἔθηκεν	ἐπὶ	τοῦ
ho	*Pilatos*	*kai*	*ethēken*	*epi*	*tou*
	Pilate	and	put	on	the

4567.2 noun gen sing masc	**1498.34** verb sing indic imperf act	**1156.2** conj	**1119.29** verb sing neu part perf pass	**2400.1** name nom masc
σταυροῦ·	ἦν	δὲ	γεγραμμένον,	Ἰησοῦς
staurou	*ēn*	*de*	*gegrammenon*	*Iēsous*
cross.	It was	and	having been written,	Jesus

3450.5 art sing masc	**3343.1** name nom sing masc	**3450.5** art sing masc	**928.1** noun nom sing masc	**3450.1** art gen pl
ὁ	Ναζωραῖος,	ὁ	βασιλεὺς	τῶν
ho	*Nazōraios*	*ho*	*basileus*	*tōn*
the	Nazarene,	the	king	of the

2428.3 name-adj gen pl masc	**3642.6** dem-pron acc sing masc	**3631.1** conj	**3450.6** art acc sing masc	**4950.1** noun acc sing masc
Ἰουδαίων.	**20.** Τοῦτον	οὖν	τὸν	τίτλον
Ioudaiōn	*Touton*	*oun*	*ton*	*titlon*
Jews.	This	therefore	the	title

4044.7 adj nom pl masc	**312.7** verb 3pl indic aor act	**3450.1** art gen pl	**2428.3** name-adj gen pl masc	**3617.1** conj	**1445.1** adv
πολλοὶ	ἀνέγνωσαν	τῶν	Ἰουδαίων,	ὅτι	ἐγγὺς
polloi	*anegnōsan*	*tōn*	*Ioudaiōn*	*hoti*	*engus*
many	read	of the	Jews,	for	near

1498.34 verb sing indic imperf act	**3450.10** art gen sing fem	**4032.2** noun gen sing fem	**3450.5** art sing masc	**4964.1** noun nom sing masc	**3450.5** art sing masc
ἦν	ʽ τῆς	πόλεως	ὁ	τόπος,	[☆ ὁ
ēn	*tēs*	*poleōs*	*ho*	*topos*	*ho*
was	the	city	the	place,	[the

4964.1 noun nom sing masc	**3450.10** art gen sing fem	**4032.2** noun gen sing fem	**3562.1** adv	**4568.12** verb 3sing indic aor pass	**3450.5** art sing masc
τόπος	τῆς	πόλεως]	ὅπου	ἐσταυρώθη	ὁ
topos	*tēs*	*poleōs*	*hopou*	*estaurōthē*	*ho*
place	the	city]	where	was crucified	

2400.1 name nom masc	**2504.1** conj	**1498.34** verb sing indic imperf act	**1119.29** verb sing neu part perf pass	**1440.1** name-adv
Ἰησοῦς	καὶ	ἦν	γεγραμμένον	Ἑβραϊστί,
Iēsous	*kai*	*ēn*	*gegrammenon*	*Hebraisti*
Jesus;	and	it was	having been written	in Hebrew,

1662.1 name-adv	**4372.1** name-adv	**4372.1** name-adv	**1662.1** name-adv
ʽ Ἑλληνιστί,	Ῥωμαϊστί.	[☆ Ῥωμαϊστί,	Ἑλληνιστί.]
Hellēnisti	*Rhōmaisti*	*Rhōmaisti*	*Hellēnisti*
in Greek,	in Latin.	[in Latin,	in Greek.]

but a couple of feet from the ground. Nails were driven through the hands in the palms or between the bones in the wrist. To prevent the hands from tearing away from the nails, a large wooden pin was inserted in the upright timber on which the groin rested. By pressing upward on the pin, pain could be alleviated somewhat, and breathing could take its natural course. Life on a cross followed a cycle of conscious and unconscious moments. Those who fainted easily because of the excruciating pain were blessed indeed. Men often lingered near death for days before their welcomed end came. Some records say that 7 to 9 days on a cross was common. Among the Jews, however, bodies were removed before the Sabbath. Thus 6 days was the greatest length of time. Jesus' short 6 hours on the cross was not due entirely to His terrible scourging and maltreatment; rather, He released His spirit when He had fully paid our debt of sin.

The two men crucified with Jesus were possibly companions of Barabbas. John's Gospel recorded the details of this horrible day. The apostle's tender conscience retained a vivid image of the scene even after many years. It may be that Jesus' cross was slightly elevated above the other two so Pilate might emphasize his hatred of the Jews.

19:19. The inscription signified to the public the crime of the crucified. Perhaps the sign hung about the neck of the criminal as he was led to the execution site and was fixed to his cross at crucifixion for all to view. John's Gospel says they put it "on (Greek, *epi*) the cross," and Luke 23:38 says they put it "over (Greek, *ep*) him." Since *epi* can be translated in a variety of ways, the Greek can mean "on" Him or on the cross above Him. If it means above Him, then the form of the cross was the usual form of a cross which we commonly visualize.

"Jesus of Nazareth the King of the Jews" was written on the inscription. This was the crime for which He was found guilty.

19:20. The site was not far from the northern wall of Jerusalem. Great crowds gathered and gazed at the crucifixions. Many people experience a sadistic pleasure in watching the effect pain has on others. Fallen man seems to be drawn to such events as executions, gladiator conflicts, and tortures. Many of the people and leaders came to heap their insults upon the patient Sufferer (Matthew 27:39-44; Mark 15:29-32; Luke 23:35-39).

The inscription of guilt was written in the three languages so that whoever looked upon the condemned and crucified could fear

on either side one, and Jesus in the midst: . . . one on each side, *Douay* . . . oon on this side, oon on that side, and ihesus in the myddil, *Wycliffe* . . . and Jesus in between, *Norlie* . . . in the middle, *Murdock* . . . in the center, *Confraternity, Berkeley.*

19. And Pilate wrote a title, and put it on the cross: Moreover, Pilate also wrote a notice on a placard, *Wuest* . . . Pilate made a sign, *SEB* . . . wrote a caption, *Norlie* . . . an inscription to be put on the cross, *Moffatt* . . . an inscription on a placard, *AmpB* . . . wrote a notice, *Beck* . . . also wrote a tablet, and affixed it to his cross, *Murdock* . . . and had it fastened to the top of the cross, *Weymouth* . . . put on the cross a statement in writing, *BB.*

and the writing was, JESUS OF NAZARETH THE KING OF THE JEWS: It ran thus, *Weymouth* . . . OF THE JUDEANS, *Fenton.*

20. This title then read many of the Jews: for the place where Jesus was crucified was nigh to the city: . . . read this label, *Murdock* . . . this placard, *Williams, Wuest* . . . was quite near Jerusalem, *Phillips.*

and it was written in Hebrew, and Greek, and Latin: . . . in Aramaic, *SEB.*

2978.25 verb indic imperf act	3631.1 conj	3450.3 art dat sing	3952.3 name dat masc	3450.7 art pl masc	744.5 noun pl masc
21. ἔλεγον	οὖν	τῷ	Πιλάτῳ	οἱ	ἀρχιερεῖς
elegon	*oun*	*tō*	*Pilatō*	*hoi*	*archiereis*
Said	therefore		to Pilate	the	chief priests

3450.1 art gen pl	2428.3 name-adj gen pl masc	3231.1 partic	1119.4 verb 2sing impr pres act	3450.5 art sing masc	928.1 noun nom sing masc
τῶν	Ἰουδαίων,	Μὴ	γράφε,	Ὁ	βασιλεὺς
tōn	*Ioudaiōn*	*Mē*	*graphe*	*Ho*	*basileus*
of the	Jews,	Not	write,	The	king

3450.1 art gen pl	2428.3 name-adj gen pl masc	233.1 conj	3617.1 conj	1552.3 dem-pron nom sing masc	1500.5 verb 3sing indic aor act
τῶν	Ἰουδαίων·	ἀλλ'	ὅτι	ἐκεῖνος	εἶπεν,
tōn	*Ioudaiōn*	*all'*	*hoti*	*ekeinos*	*eipen*
of the	Jews,	but	that	that	said,

928.1 noun nom sing masc	1498.2 verb 1sing indic pres act	3450.1 art gen pl	2428.3 name-adj gen pl masc	552.6 verb 3sing indic aor pass
Βασιλεύς	εἰμι	τῶν	Ἰουδαίων.	22. Ἀπεκρίθη
Basileus	*eimi*	*tōn*	*Ioudaiōn*	*Apekrithē*
King	I am	of the	Jews.	Answered

3450.5 art sing masc	3952.1 name nom masc	3614.16 rel-pron sing neu	1119.16 verb 1sing indic perf act	1119.16 verb 1sing indic perf act
ὁ	Πιλᾶτος,	Ὃ	γέγραφα,	γέγραφα.
ho	*Pilatos*	*Ho*	*gegrapha*	*gegrapha*
	Pilate,	What	I have written	I have written.

3450.7 art pl masc	3631.1 conj	4608.4 noun nom pl masc	3616.1 conj	4568.3 verb 3pl indic aor act
23. Οἱ	οὖν	στρατιῶται,	ὅτε	ἐσταύρωσαν
Hoi	*oun*	*stratiōtai*	*hote*	*estaurōsan*
The	therefore	soldiers,	when	they crucified

3450.6 art acc sing masc	2400.3 name acc masc	2956.12 verb indic aor act	3450.17 art pl neu	2416.4 noun pl neu	840.3 prs-pron gen sing	2504.1 conj
τὸν	Ἰησοῦν	ἔλαβον	τὰ	ἱμάτια	αὐτοῦ,	καὶ
ton	*Iēsoun*	*elabon*	*ta*	*himatia*	*autou*	*kai*
	Jesus	took	the	garments	his,	and

4020.27 verb 3pl indic aor act	4913.5 num card pl neu	4913.6 num card pl neu	3183.4 noun acc pl neu	1524.4 adj dat sing masc
ἐποίησαν	ʻ☆ τέσσαρα	[τέσσερα]	μέρη,	ἑκάστῳ
epoiēsan	*tessara*	*tessera*	*merē*	*hekastō*
made	four	[idem]	parts,	to each

4608.2 noun dat sing masc	3183.1 noun sing neu	2504.1 conj	3450.6 art acc sing masc	5345.2 noun acc sing masc	1498.34 verb sing indic imperf act
στρατιώτῃ	μέρος,	καὶ	τὸν	χιτῶνα.	ἦν
stratiōtē	*meros*	*kai*	*ton*	*chitōna*	*ēn*
soldier	a part,	and	the	tunic;	was

23.a.**Var:** 01ℵ,02A,05D,017K,019L,021M,030U,033X,036,038,byz.Treg,Alf,Tisc,We/HoSod

1156.2 conj	3450.5 art sing masc	5345.1 noun nom sing masc	723.1 adj nom sing	683.1 adj nom sing masc	1523.2 prep gen
δὲ	ὁ	χιτὼν	ʻ ἄρραφος,	[a ἄραφος,]	ἐκ
de	*ho*	*chitōn*	*arrhaphos*	*araphos*	*ek*
but	the	tunic	seamless,	[idem]	from

3450.1 art gen pl	505.1 adv	5145.1 adj nom sing masc	1217.1 prep	3513.2 adj gen sing	1500.3 verb indic aor act
τῶν	ἄνωθεν	ὑφαντὸς	δι'	ὅλου.	24. ʻ εἶπον
tōn	*anōthen*	*huphantos*	*di'*	*holou*	*eipon*
the	top	woven	through	whole.	They said

lest they commit the same crime. Beyond this practical reason for the three languages of the inscription, Jesus' true identity was communicated to all mankind. Jesus was not merely the King of the Jews but the Saviour and Sovereign of the whole world (John 4:42; Revelation 19:16).

21. Then said the chief priests of the Jews to Pilate, Write not, The King of the Jews; but that he said, I am King of the Jews: The chief priests of the Jews protested to Pilate, *NIV* . . . therefore remonstrated with Pilate, *Weymouth* . . . You should not write, *NEB* . . . Do not allow it to remain written, *Wuest* . . . Do not put, The King of the Jews, *BB* . . . but merely that, *Fenton* . . . this man claimed to be, *ALBA* . . . This man said, *SEB*.

19:21. The chief priests understood the implication of the title, and it vexed them. They demanded that Pilate change what he had written. Pilate's words indicated that Jesus was their king. This association was unbearable to them.

22. Pilate answered, What I have written I have written: To which Pilate retorted, *Phillips* . . . will not be changed, *BB* . . . stands written, *Wuest* . . . stays, *SEB* . . . stay written, *TEV*.

19:22. The two verbs for "have written" are in the perfect tense, signifying the permanence of his inscription. Pilate had written Jesus' title to avenge himself on the Jews. He had vented his anger toward his detestable subjects who had pressured him into violating his sense of justice. The Jews' demands had been met, but to this request he remained adamant. Pilate's own interests were not now at stake, and he had nothing to lose. Perhaps he felt he would have the last laugh. The Jews must be content with the way he allowed their demands to be carried out. He would not yield to further intimidation.

23. Then the soldiers, when they had crucified Jesus, took his garments: . . . had nailed Jesus to the cross, they took his mantle, *Campbell* . . . the men of the army took, *BB* . . . took possession of his clothes, *NEB* . . . took his clothes, *TCNT* . . . outer garments, *Norlie, Wuest*.

and made four parts, to every soldier a part: . . . and made four parcels of them, a parcel for each of the soldiers, *Murdock* . . . and divided them into four shares—a share for each soldier, *TCNT* . . . divided them into four parts, one for each soldier, *Moffatt* . . . one share for each soldier, *AmpB* . . . one part for each soldier, *Weymouth*.

and also his coat: now the coat was without seam, woven from the top throughout: The tunic was without seam, woven in one piece from top to bottom, *Beck*.

19:23. According to Luke 23:26-33 a great multitude followed the procession of soldiers with their prisoners to Golgotha. The soldiers proceeded to crucify their prisoners. After the cruel task was completed, they remained close by to prevent any rescue, while they drank, gambled, and passed their time until the victims were dead. Soon they "took his garments, and made four parts, to every soldier a part." The garments of the crucified were given to the soldiers who carried out the bloody work. The only clothing the Saviour wore on the cross was a linen cloth bound about His loins. The Romans had long before acquiesced to the Jews' sense of modesty by allowing loincloths for the victims of crucifixion. Removal of bodies from the crosses before the Sabbath also was granted the Jews.

The "coat" was like a shirt or inner garment which covered the body from the neck to below the knees. It had no seams. If the coat had been torn in four pieces, it would have been worthless. A tunic worn next to the skin could be an important item in the wardrobe, especially if it were soft material and of exquisite work-

John 19:25

24.a.**Txt:** 02A,03B,05D,017K,036,038,byz.Lach,Sod
Var: 01ℵ,019L,033X,TiscWe/Ho,Weis,UBS/☆

24.b.**Txt:** 02A,05D,017K,032W,033X,036,038,1,13,byz.Sod
Var: 01ℵ,03B,it.sa.Lach,Tisc,We/Ho,Weis,UBS/☆

1500.28 verb 3pl indic aor act	**3631.1** conj	**4242.1** prep	**238.3** prs-pron acc pl masc	**3231.1** partic	**4829.2** verb 1pl subj aor act
[a☆ εἶπαν]	οὖν	πρὸς	ἀλλήλους,	Μὴ	σχίσωμεν
eipan	*oun*	*pros*	*allēlous*	*Mē*	*schisōmen*
[idem]	therefore	to	one another,	Not	let us rend

840.6 prs-pron acc sing masc	**233.2** conj	**2948.2** verb 1pl subj aor act	**3875.1** prep	**840.3** prs-pron gen sing	**4949.4** intr-pron gen sing
αὐτόν,	ἀλλὰ	λάχωμεν	περὶ	αὐτοῦ	τίνος
auton	*alla*	*lachōmen*	*peri*	*autou*	*tinos*
it,	but	let us cast lots	for	it	whose

1498.40 verb 3sing indic fut mid	**2419.1** conj	**3450.9** art nom sing fem	**1118.1** noun nom sing fem	**3997.22** verb 3sing subj aor pass
ἔσται·	ἵνα	ἡ	γραφὴ	πληρωθῇ
estai	*hina*	*hē*	*graphē*	*plērōthē*
it shall be;	that	the	scripture	might be fulfilled

3450.9 art nom sing fem	**2978.19** verb nom sing fem part pres act	**1260.6** verb 3pl indic aor mid	**3450.17** art pl neu	**2416.4** noun pl neu
⸂b ἡ	λέγουσα, ⸃	Διεμερίσαντο	τὰ	ἱμάτιά
hē	*legousa*	*Diemerisanto*	*ta*	*himatia*
which	says,	They divided	the	garments

1466.2 prs-pron gen 1sing	**1431.7** prs-pron dat pl masc	**2504.1** conj	**1894.3** prep	**3450.6** art acc sing masc	**2417.4** noun acc sing masc
μου	ἑαυτοῖς·	καὶ	ἐπὶ	τὸν	ἱματισμόν
mou	*heautois*	*kai*	*epi*	*ton*	*himatismon*
my	among themselves,	and	for	the	clothing

1466.2 prs-pron gen 1sing	**900.11** verb 3pl indic aor act	**2792.3** noun acc sing masc	**3450.7** art pl masc	**3173.1** conj	**3631.1** conj
μου	ἔβαλον	κλῆρον.	Οἱ	μὲν	οὖν
mou	*ebalon*	*klēron*	*Hoi*	*men*	*oun*
my	they cast	a lot.	The		therefore

4608.4 noun nom pl masc	**3642.18** dem-pron pl neu	**4020.27** verb 3pl indic aor act	**2449.24** verb 3pl indic plperf act
στρατιῶται	ταῦτα	ἐποίησαν.	**25.** Εἱστήκεισαν
stratiōtai	*tauta*	*epoiēsan*	*Heistēkeisan*
soldiers	these things	did.	Had stood

1156.2 conj	**3706.2** prep	**3450.3** art dat sing	**4567.3** noun dat sing masc	**3450.2** art gen sing	**2400.2** name masc	**3450.9** art nom sing fem
δὲ	παρὰ	τῷ	σταυρῷ	τοῦ	Ἰησοῦ	ἡ
de	*para*	*tō*	*staurō*	*tou*	*Iēsou*	*hē*
and	by	the	cross		of Jesus	the

3251.1 noun nom sing fem	**840.3** prs-pron gen sing	**2504.1** conj	**3450.9** art nom sing fem	**78.1** noun nom sing fem	**3450.10** art gen sing fem	**3251.2** noun gen sing fem
μήτηρ	αὐτοῦ,	καὶ	ἡ	ἀδελφὴ	τῆς	μητρὸς
mētēr	*autou*	*kai*	*hē*	*adelphē*	*tēs*	*mētros*
mother	his,	and	the	sister	of the	mother

840.3 prs-pron gen sing	**3109.1** name nom fem	**3450.9** art nom sing fem	**3450.2** art gen sing	**2805.1** name gen masc	**2504.1** conj
αὐτοῦ,	Μαρία	ἡ	τοῦ	Κλωπᾶ,	καὶ
autou	*Maria*	*hē*	*tou*	*Klōpa*	*kai*
his,	Mary	the		of Cleophas,	and

3109.1 name nom fem	**3450.9** art nom sing fem	**3066.1** name nom fem	**2400.1** name nom masc	**3631.1** conj
Μαρία	ἡ	Μαγδαληνή.	**26.** Ἰησοῦς	οὖν
Maria	*hē*	*Magdalēnē*	*Iēsous*	*oun*
Mary	the	Magdalene.	Jesus	therefore

manship. The tunic may have been a love gift from someone with special skills.

24. They said therefore among themselves, Let us not rend it, but cast lots for it, whose it shall be: Let us not tear it, *RSV* . . . Let's draw lots, *Phillips* . . . let us draw for it to see who gets it, *Williams* . . . let us throw for, *Fenton* . . . gamble for it, *Klingensmith.*

that the scripture might be fulfilled which saith: . . . by this verifying the scripture, *Campbell.*

They parted my raiment among them, and for my vesture they did cast lots: THEY THREW DICE, *Fenton.*

These things therefore the soldiers did: This was what the soldiers did, *TCNT* . . . This is exactly what the soldiers did, *JB.*

19:24. The soldiers decided that to tear the tunic would destroy its value so they "cast lots for it." The Psalmist stated, "They part my garments among them, and cast lots upon my vesture" (Psalm 22:18). The apostle John quotes the Septuagint precisely as we have it today. God inspired the Psalmist to write about the very events at the foot of the cross. Psalm 22 begins with the words Christ uttered from the cross: "My God, my God, why hast thou forsaken me?" (cf. Matthew 27:46; Mark 15:34). Many of the verses in Psalm 22 describe the suffering and feelings of Christ during the Crucifixion. The soldiers unwittingly fulfilled what the omniscient God foretold through the Psalmist. What was prophesied was consistent with the free choice of the soldiers. The prophecy was quite specific: the outer garments were to be divided, but at least one piece of clothing was to be gambled away by the soldiers. The garments were not to be given to members of the family. The custom of the soldiers dividing clothing of the crucified men was taken into account by the Lord's foreknowledge. This prophecy came forth from the pen of David nearly 1,000 years before the event. Who but God would know the specific details of customs a thousand years in the future?

25. Now there stood by the cross of Jesus his mother, and his mother's sister, Mary the wife of Cleophas, and Mary Magdalene: Meanwhile near the cross, *TCNT.*

26. When Jesus therefore saw his mother, and the disciple standing by, whom he loved: So when Jesus saw, *Moffatt.*

19:25. John's Gospel allows us to view some of those who were close to Jesus at the cross. The soldiers were first spoken of for they were there to the bitter end. John alone relates the touching scene described in verses 25-27. Those who were close to the cross were women. Perhaps the disciples were fearful for their lives. John, of course, was close by.

Regarding the number of women at the cross, F.F. Bruce says: "If we take John's language by itself, it is uncertain whether he mentions three women or four; Mary the wife of Clopas might be the sister of Jesus' mother or might be a separate person. If, however, we correlate John's information with that about the women who were 'looking on from afar' in Mark 15:40f. and Matthew 27:55f., we might conclude that the sister was Salome (mother of the sons of Zebedee), while Mary the wife of Clopas was Mary the mother of James the younger and of Joses (Joseph). John nowhere refers to the mother of Jesus by name, possibly to avoid confusion with other women named Mary. . . . Mary of Magdala (a town on the west shore of the lake of Galilee, two or three miles north of Tiberias) figures in the passion narratives of all four gospels" (Bruce, p.371). Mary, Jesus' mother, was present. What her mental anguish

1481.16 verb nom sing masc part aor act	3450.12 art acc sing fem	3251.4 noun acc sing fem	2504.1 conj	3450.6 art acc sing masc	3073.4 noun acc sing masc
ἰδὼν	τὴν	μητέρα,	καὶ	τὸν	μαθητὴν
idōn	*tēn*	*mētera*	*kai*	*ton*	*mathētēn*
having seen	the	mother,	and	the	disciple

26.a.**Txt:** 02A,05D,017K,036,038,13,byz.Lach **Var:** 01ℵ,03B,019L,033X,Treg,Tisc,We/Ho,Weis,Sod,UBS/☆

3798.16 verb acc sing masc part perf act	3614.6 rel-pron acc sing masc	25.26 verb 3sing indic imperf act	2978.5 verb 3sing indic pres act	3450.11 art dat sing fem
παρεστῶτα	ὃν	ἠγάπα.	λέγει	τῇ
parestōta	*hon*	*ēgapa*	*legei*	*tē*
having stood by	whom	he loved,	says	to the

26.b.**Txt:** 01ℵ,02A,017K,019L,032W,036,038,13,byz.Sod **Var:** 03B,05D,021M,033X,Gries,Lach,Treg,Alf,Tisc,We/HoWeis,UBS/☆

3251.3 noun dat sing fem	840.3 prs-pron gen sing	1129.5 noun voc sing fem	1481.20 verb 2sing impr aor mid	1481.14 verb 2sing impr aor act
μητρί	⌈a αὐτοῦ, ⌉	Γύναι,	⌈ ἰδοὺ	[b☆ ἴδε]
mētri	*autou*	*Gunai*	*idou*	*ide*
mother	his,	Woman,	behold	[idem]

3450.5 art sing masc	5048.1 noun nom sing masc	4622.2 prs-pron gen 2sing	1520.1 adv	2978.5 verb 3sing indic pres act	3450.3 art dat sing
ὁ	υἱός	σου.	27. Εἶτα	λέγει	τῷ
ho	*huios*	*sou*	*Eita*	*legei*	*tō*
the	son	your.	Then	he says	to the

27.a.**Txt:** 02A,05D,017K,021M,033X,036,1,byz. **Var:** 01ℵ,03B,019L,038,Gries,Lach,Treg,Alf,Tisc,We/HoWeis,Sod,UBS/☆

3073.3 noun dat sing masc	1481.20 verb 2sing impr aor mid	1481.14 verb 2sing impr aor act	3450.9 art nom sing fem	3251.1 noun nom sing fem
μαθητῇ,	⌈ Ἰδοὺ	[a☆ Ἴδε]	ἡ	μήτηρ
mathētē	*Idou*	*Ide*	*hē*	*mētēr*
disciple,	Behold	[idem]	the	mother

4622.2 prs-pron gen 2sing	2504.1 conj	570.2 prep gen	1552.10 dem-pron gen sing fem	3450.10 art gen sing fem	5443.1 noun fem	2956.14 verb 3sing indic aor act
σου.	Καὶ	ἀπ'	ἐκείνης	τῆς	ὥρας	ἔλαβεν
sou	*Kai*	*ap'*	*ekeinēs*	*tēs*	*hōras*	*elaben*
your.	And	from	that	the	hour	took

840.12 prs-pron acc sing fem	3450.5 art sing masc	3073.1 noun nom sing masc	3450.5 art sing masc	3073.1 noun nom sing masc	840.12 prs-pron acc sing fem
⌈☆ αὐτὴν	ὁ	μαθητὴς	[ὁ	μαθητὴς	αὐτὴν]
autēn	*ho*	*mathētēs*	*ho*	*mathētēs*	*autēn*
her	the	disciple	[the	disciple	her]

1519.1 prep	3450.17 art pl neu	2375.13 adj pl neu	3196.3 prep	3642.17 dem-pron sing neu	3471.18 verb nom sing masc part perf act
εἰς	τὰ	ἴδια.	28. Μετὰ	τοῦτο	εἰδὼς
eis	*ta*	*idia*	*Meta*	*touto*	*eidōs*
to	the	his own.	After	this,	having known

3450.5 art sing masc	2400.1 name nom masc	3617.1 conj	3820.1 adj	2218.1 adv	2218.1 adv	3820.1 adj
ὁ	Ἰησοῦς	ὅτι	⌈ πάντα	ἤδη	[☆ ἤδη	πάντα]
ho	*Iēsous*	*hoti*	*panta*	*ēdē*	*ēdē*	*panta*
	Jesus	that	all things	now	[now	all things]

4903.13 verb 3sing indic perf pass	2419.1 conj	4896.10 verb 3sing subj aor pass	3450.9 art nom sing fem	1118.1 noun nom sing fem
τετέλεσται,	ἵνα	τελειωθῇ	ἡ	γραφή
tetelestai	*hina*	*teleiōthē*	*hē*	*graphē*
have been finished,	that	might be fulfilled	the	scripture

29.a.**Txt:** 05D,017K,036,038,1,13,byz.Sod **Var:** 02A,03B,019L,032W,033X,it.Lach,Treg Alf,Word,Tisc,We/Ho,Weis,UBS/☆

2978.5 verb 3sing indic pres act	1366.1 verb 1sing pres act	4487.1 noun sing neu	3631.1 conj	2719.10 verb 3sing indic imperf
λέγει,	Διψῶ.	29. Σκεῦος	⌈a οὖν ⌉	ἔκειτο
legei	*Dipsō*	*Skeuos*	*oun*	*ekeito*
he says,	I thirst.	A vessel	therefore	was set

must have been, one can only imagine. The prophecy made in Luke 2:35 now had reality for her.

he saith unto his mother, Woman, behold thy son!: Mother, there is your son! *BB.*

19:26. Jesus had spoken two of His seven sayings from the cross. First, He said, "Father, forgive them; for they know not what they do" (Luke 23:34). Second, Jesus assured the thief on the next cross by saying, "Verily I say unto thee, Today shalt thou be with me in paradise" (Luke 23:43). Jesus was now about to utter His third saying from the awful place of torture.

Our Lord's physical condition may have hindered His vision, for His eyes may have been caked by blood from His brow, and His pain had weakened His body to an almost unconsciouslike condition. Furthermore, Mary and John may have moved closer as the crucifixion time progressed. Two hours had transpired by this time.

Jesus now commended His mother to the care of John the apostle. Perhaps a glance at John indicated to Mary whom Jesus meant. "Woman" was an honorable title. He used the same form of address in 2:4. Our Lord remembered others during His most terrible sufferings. He will not forget us in His hour of triumph.

27. Then saith he to the disciple, Behold thy mother!: There is your mother! *Beck.*

And from that hour that disciple took her unto his own home: And from that moment...into his keeping, *Berkeley* . . . to his house, *BB* . . . took charge of her, *Norton.*

28. After this, Jesus knowing that all things were now accomplished, that the scripture might be fulfilled: . . . that everything had been done to fulfill the Scriptures, *Norlie* . . . so that the Writings might come true, *BB* . . . was already completed to the fulfillment, *Berkeley* . . . may be perfected, *Concordant.*

saith, I thirst:

29. Now there was set a vessel full of vinegar: . . . sour wine, *Phillips* . . . a bowl standing there full of common wine, *TCNT.*

19:27. Jesus next turned His suffering head toward John and said, "Behold thy mother!" John understood what Jesus wanted him to do. He records that "from that hour that disciple took her unto his own home." John was well-to-do for he had servants and a fishing business (see Mark 1:19,20).

Jesus wished to leave His earthly mother to someone who could and would care for and protect her. One can but faintly sense John's joy as he realized the confidence Jesus had in him. John had gained a mother, and Mary had a son to care for her. John used the phrase "from that hour" as an equivalent of immediately. "Unto his own home" indicates the privileges and security John's home provided. Doubtless, Mary was supported and protected by John for the rest of her life.

19:28. The third saying of Christ from the cross was related in verses 26 and 27. Both Matthew 27:46 and Mark 15:34 record the fourth saying, "My God, my God, why hast thou forsaken me?" John alone records the fifth saying, "I thirst." This was a natural result of the physical and mental stress accompanied by the intense fever associated with His sufferings. It revealed His condition as prophesied in Psalm 22:15, "My strength is dried up like a potsherd;

John 19:30

3553.1 noun gen sing neu	3194.1 adj sing	3450.7 art pl masc	1156.2 conj	3990.3 verb nom pl masc part aor act	4552.1 noun acc sing masc
ὄξους	μεστόν·	⸂ οἱ	δὲ	πλησαντες	σπόγγον
oxous	meston	hoi	de	plēsantes	spongon
of vinegar	full,	the	and	having filled	a sponge

29.b.**Txt:** 02A,05D,017K, 036,(038),(13),byz. **Var:** p66,01א-corr,03B, 019L,032W,33,Lach Treg,Alf,We/Ho,Weis, Sod,UBS/☆

3553.1 noun gen sing neu	2504.1 conj	4552.1 noun acc sing masc	3631.1 conj	3194.1 adj sing	3450.2 art gen sing
ὄξους,	καὶ	[b☆ σπόγγον	οὖν	μεστὸν	τοῦ
oxous	kai	spongon	oun	meston	tou
with vinegar,	and	[a sponge	therefore	full	of the

3553.1 noun gen sing neu	5138.2 noun dat sing masc	3920.6 verb nom pl masc part aor act	4232.14 verb 3pl indic aor act	840.3 prs-pron gen sing
ὄξους]	ὑσσώπῳ	περιθέντες	προσήνεγκαν	αὐτοῦ
oxous	hussōpō	perithentes	prosēnenkan	autou
vinegar]	hyssop	having put on	they brought	it

3450.3 art dat sing	4601.3 noun dat sing neu	3616.1 conj	3631.1 conj	2956.14 verb 3sing indic aor act	3450.16 art sing neu
τῷ	στόματι.	30. ὅτε	οὖν	ἔλαβεν	τὸ
tō	stomati	hote	oun	elaben	to
to the	mouth.	When	therefore	took	the

3553.2 noun acc sing neu	3450.5 art sing masc	2400.1 name nom masc	1500.5 verb 3sing indic aor act	4903.13 verb 3sing indic perf pass
ὄξος	ὁ	Ἰησοῦς	εἶπεν,	Τετέλεσται·
oxos	ho	Iēsous	eipen	Tetelestai
vinegar		Jesus	said,	It has been finished;

2504.1 conj	2800.5 verb nom sing masc part aor act	3450.12 art acc sing fem	2747.4 noun acc sing fem	3722.10 verb 3sing indic aor act	3450.16 art sing neu
καὶ	κλίνας	τὴν	κεφαλὴν	παρέδωκεν	τὸ
kai	klinas	tēn	kephalēn	paredōken	to
and	having bowed	the	head	he yielded up	the

31.a.**Var:** p66,01א,03B, 019L,032W,033X,1,13, 33,sa.bo.Treg,Alf,Tisc, We/Ho,WeisSod,UBS/☆

4011.1 noun sing neu	3450.7 art pl masc	3631.1 conj	2428.2 name-adj pl masc	1878.1 conj
πνεῦμα.	31. Οἱ	οὖν	Ἰουδαῖοι,	[a☆+ ἐπεὶ
pneuma	Hoi	oun	Ioudaioi	epei
spirit.	The	therefore	Jews,	[since

3765.1 noun nom sing fem	1498.34 verb sing indic imperf act	2419.1 conj	3231.1 partic	3176.19 verb 3sing subj aor act	1894.3 prep
παρασκευὴ	ἦν,]	ἵνα	μὴ	μείνῃ	ἐπὶ
paraskeuē	ēn	hina	mē	meinē	epi
preparation	it was,]	that	not	might remain	on

3450.2 art gen sing	4567.2 noun gen sing masc	3450.17 art pl neu	4835.4 noun pl neu	1706.1 prep	3450.3 art dat sing
τοῦ	σταυροῦ	τὰ	σώματα	ἐν	τῷ
tou	staurou	ta	sōmata	en	tō
the	cross	the	bodies	on	the

31.b.**Txt:** 02A,(05),017K, 021M,036,038,byz.Lach **Var:** p66,01א,03B,019L, 032W,033X,1,13,33,sa. bo.TregAlf,Tisc,We/Ho, Weis,Sod,UBS/☆

4378.3 noun dat sing neu	1878.1 conj	3765.1 noun nom sing fem	1498.34 verb sing indic imperf act	1498.34 verb sing indic imperf act
σαββάτῳ,	⸂b ἐπεὶ	παρασκευὴ	ἦν, ⸃	ἦν
sabbatō	epei	paraskeuē	ēn	ēn
sabbath,	because	preparation	it was,	was

1056.1 conj	3144.9 adj sing fem	3450.9 art nom sing fem	2232.2 noun nom sing fem	1552.2 dem-pron gen sing	3450.2 art gen sing
γὰρ	μεγάλη	ἡ	ἡμέρα	ἐκείνου	τοῦ
gar	megalē	hē	hēmera	ekeinou	tou
for	great	the	day	that	the

and my tongue cleaveth to my jaws." Such a statement unveils the humanity of our Lord. He possessed the same capacity for need as does any man.

The fifth saying was spoken because Jesus knew "that all things were now accomplished." Many times the Gospel of John says Jesus knew. To know the future is somewhat like living in the future. To live in the future is a trait of the eternality which belongs to God only (Exodus 3:14; John 14:6).

and they filled a sponge with vinegar: So they soaked a sponge in the wine, *Phillips.*

and put it upon hyssop, and put it to his mouth: . . . and put it upon a stalk of hyssop, *Montgomery.*

19:29. The "vinegar" was probably an inferior common wine drunk by soldiers and laborers. Whether the jar of sour wine was for the soldiers or the sufferers or both, we do not know.

30. When Jesus therefore had received the vinegar, he said, It is finished: All is finished! *TCNT* . . . It has been accomplished! *Concordant* . . . Lo; Done, *Murdock* . . . It is consummated! *Confraternity.*

and he bowed his head, and gave up the ghost: And inclining his head, *Wilson* . . . His head fell forward, *Phillips* . . . yielded up his spirit, *Campbell* . . . and expired, *Norton.*

19:30. Jesus had refused to take the drugged wine (Mark 15:23), yet now He received the "vinegar." A few sips from the sponge was all the creature could offer his Creator. Perhaps Jesus accepted the barbarians' courtesy as an indication of His approval of the alleviation of all suffering, not merely His own.

Only John's Gospel records the sixth saying from the cross: "It is finished." The verb is in the perfect tense and means "it stands completed." Jesus was speaking of His redemptive work. All that He came to accomplish had been done. He had followed the Father's will, revealed the Father's nature, and fulfilled the Old Testament prophecies. He lived sinlessly, taught perfectly, and died efficaciously. His earthly work was completed. Who but God our Saviour would dare say, "It is finished." Jesus said, "I thirst." Man would say this. God would have no need, yet the God-Man said both, "I am thirsty" and "It is finished."

All men die when they are forced to do so, yet Jesus' death was under His own will and power. Luke 23:46 states the seventh saying from the cross: "Father, into thy hands I commend my spirit." The word means to place His spirit beside the Father. No man took His life from Him. He laid His life down and placed His spirit beside the Father (10:17,18).

31. The Jews therefore, because it was the preparation:

that the bodies should not remain upon the cross on the sabbath day: . . . wanted to avoid the bodies being left on the crosses, *Phillips* . . . to prevent the bodies' hanging on the cross during the Sabbath, *Montgomery* . . . must not remain all night, *Murdock.*

(for that sabbath day was an high day,): . . . a particularly important Sabbath, *Phillips* . . . a great day, *Norlie* . . . was a very important one, *Williams* . . . of special solemnity, *Weymouth, ALBA* . . . because the sabbath was dawning, *Murdock* . . . was especially holy, *TEV.*

19:31. "The preparation" was the day before the Passover season, during which all leaven was to be disposed of and all ceremonial cleansing was to be finished.

"High day" means that the regular Sabbath and the Passover were the same day, making the one day especially important.

4378.2 noun gen sing neu	**2049.10** verb 3pl indic aor act	**3450.6** art acc sing masc	**3952.4** name acc masc	**2419.1** conj
σαββάτου,	ἠρώτησαν	τὸν	Πιλᾶτον	ἵνα
sabbatou	*ērōtēsan*	*ton*	*Pilaton*	*hina*
sabbath,	requested		Pilate	that

2579.3 verb 3pl subj aor pass	**840.1** prs-pron gen pl	**3450.17** art pl neu	**4483.1** noun acc pl neu	**2504.1** conj	**142.25** verb 3pl subj aor pass
κατεαγῶσιν	αὐτῶν	τὰ	σκέλη,	καὶ	ἀρθῶσιν.
kateagōsin	*autōn*	*ta*	*skelē*	*kai*	*arthōsin*
might be broken	their	the	legs,	and	taken away.

2048.1 verb indic aor act	**3631.1** conj	**3450.7** art pl masc	**4608.4** noun nom pl masc	**2504.1** conj	**3450.2** art gen sing
32. ἦλθον	οὖν	οἱ	στρατιῶται,	καὶ	τοῦ
ēlthon	*oun*	*hoi*	*stratiōtai*	*kai*	*tou*
Came	therefore	the	soldiers,	and	of the

3173.1 conj	**4272.3** num ord gen sing	**2579.1** verb 3pl indic aor act	**3450.17** art pl neu	**4483.1** noun acc pl neu	**2504.1** conj	**3450.2** art gen sing
μὲν	πρώτου	κατέαξαν	τὰ	σκέλη	καὶ	τοῦ
men	*prōtou*	*kateaxan*	*ta*	*skelē*	*kai*	*tou*
	first	broke	the	legs	and	of the

32.a.**Var:** 01ℵ,02A,03B, 05D,019L,Lach,Treg,Alf Tisc,We/Ho,Weis

241.2 adj gen sing	**3450.2** art gen sing	**4809.2** verb gen sing masc part aor pass	**4809.6** verb gen sing masc part aor pass
ἄλλου	τοῦ	ʼ συσταυρωθέντος	[a συνσταυρωθέντος]
allou	*tou*	*sustaurōthentos*	*sunstaurōthentos*
other	of the	was crucified with	[idem]

840.4 prs-pron dat sing	**1894.3** prep	**1156.2** conj	**3450.6** art acc sing masc	**2400.3** name acc masc	**2048.16** verb nom pl masc part aor act
αὐτῷ·	**33.** ἐπὶ	δὲ	τὸν	Ἰησοῦν	ἐλθόντες,
autō	*epi*	*de*	*ton*	*Iēsoun*	*elthontes*
him;	to	but		Jesus	having come,

5453.1 conj	**1481.1** verb indic aor act	**840.6** prs-pron acc sing masc	**2218.1** adv	**2218.1** adv	**840.6** prs-pron acc sing masc
ὡς	εἶδον	ʼ αὐτὸν	ἤδη	[☆ ἤδη	αὐτὸν]
hōs	*eidon*	*auton*	*ēdē*	*ēdē*	*auton*
when	they saw	he	already	[already	he]

2325.6 verb acc sing masc part perf act	**3620.3** partic	**2579.1** verb 3pl indic aor act	**840.3** prs-pron gen sing	**3450.17** art pl neu	**4483.1** noun acc pl neu
τεθνηκότα,	οὐ	κατέαξαν	αὐτοῦ	τὰ	σκέλη·
tethnēkota	*ou*	*kateaxan*	*autou*	*ta*	*skelē*
having died,	not	they did break	his	the	legs,

233.1 conj	**1518.3** num card nom masc	**3450.1** art gen pl	**4608.5** noun gen pl masc	**3031.1** noun dat sing fem
34. ἀλλ'	εἷς	τῶν	στρατιωτῶν	λόγχῃ
all'	*heis*	*tōn*	*stratiōtōn*	*lonchē*
but	one	of the	soldiers	with a spear

840.3 prs-pron gen sing	**3450.12** art acc sing fem	**3985.1** noun acc sing fem	**3434.1** verb 3sing indic aor act	**2504.1** conj	**2098.1** adv
αὐτοῦ	τὴν	πλευρὰν	ἔνυξεν,	καὶ	ʼ εὐθὺς
autou	*tēn*	*pleuran*	*enuxen*	*kai*	*euthus*
his	the	side	pierced,	and	immediately

1814.3 verb 3sing indic aor act	**1814.3** verb 3sing indic aor act	**2098.1** adv	**129.1** noun sing neu	**2504.1** conj
ἐξῆλθεν	[☆ ἐξῆλθεν	εὐθὺς]	αἷμα	καὶ
exēlthen	*exēlthen*	*euthus*	*haima*	*kai*
came out	[there came out	immediately]	blood	and

The added shock of the breaking of the legs hastened death. However, the breaking of the legs made it impossible for the crucified to push up with his legs so that he could breathe. A small peg was located near the feet on which the feet pressed to relieve pain on the hands and to allow the lungs to obtain air. If the feet could not press the body upward, death was swift.

besought Pilate that their legs might be broken: . . . the Jews requested Pilate, *ALBA* . . . requested, *Murdock* . . . they asked Pilate to have the legs of the men broken, *Beck* . . . to hurry their death by breaking their legs, *SEB* . . . to have the legs of the dying men broken, *Weymouth* . . . might be fracturing, *Concordant.*

and that they might be taken away: . . . and the bodies taken away, *Beck, Norlie* . . . and the victims removed, *ALBA* . . . and take them down, *Murdock* . . . and remove them, *Adams.*

19:32. Pilate permitted the Jews to remove the corpse from the cross. Roman policy usually respected the religious customs of their subject nations. The Romans often left the bodies on the crosses as food for the birds of prey. These corpses were also a warning to potential offenders; this would be their fate if they broke Roman law. But here the Roman custom was set aside in preference to the Jewish custom. The soldiers were glad to be relieved from their duty by the quick death of the accused. The soldiers broke the legs of the two robbers, thus bringing on their death speedily. The penitent robber was released from his tortured body to enter paradise (Luke 23:43). The other robber was left to his own fate. What a difference of destiny an act of the will makes!

32. Then came the soldiers, and brake the legs of the first, and of the other which was crucified with him: . . . first of the one and then of the other, *Norlie.*

33. But when they came to Jesus, and saw that he was dead already, they brake not his legs: . . . they refrained from breaking his legs, *Weymouth.*

19:33. The breaking of the legs to hasten death was done so that the three might be buried before sundown, because this was the preparation day. At sunset the Passover commenced. At such time no work was allowed. The Romans had granted the Jews this concession. When the soldiers examined Jesus they discovered that He was already dead. There was no reason to break His legs. He had been the Master of His own death.

34. But one of the soldiers with a spear pierced his side: Instead therefore, *ALBA* . . . Instead, *Adams* . . . ran his spear into his side, *Norton* . . . however, made a thrust at His side, *Weymouth* . . . plunged his spear, *TEV* . . . did plunge his spear into Jesus' side, *SEB* . . . stabbed his side with a spear, *ALBA* . . . one of the soldiers punctures His side, *Concordant* . . . opened his side with a lance, *Confraternity, HistNT.*

and forthwith came there out blood and water: . . . and instantly blood and water came out, *Berkeley* . . . and at once there was an outrush of, *Phillips* . . . issued out, *Murdock* . . . immediately issued, *Campbell* . . . at once issued from it, *Fenton.*

19:34. The soldiers were bound to fulfill their task or they would endanger their own lives. This is the reason the soldier pierced Jesus' "side." This spear was a lance of sharp-pointed iron. It was used by soldiers as a bayonet.

The piercing of Jesus' side was an important proof of Jesus' death. No one could claim that He revived in the cool tomb. John's is the only Gospel that tells us a soldier pierced Jesus' side.

Some scholars believe that the lance entered the left side of Jesus at the heart and that Jesus died of a broken heart. This is the reason a mixture of blood and water flowed forth. To these scholars the blood and water flow was only possible if Jesus died of a ruptured heart. The shedding of Jesus' blood speaks of the price He paid for the sin of the world (John 1:29; Colossians 1:20). The

John 19:35

5045.1 noun sing neu	2504.1 conj	3450.5 art sing masc	3571.16 verb nom sing masc part perf act	3113.27 verb 3sing indic perf act
ὕδωρ.	35. καὶ	ὁ	ἑωρακὼς	μεμαρτύρηκεν,
hudōr	kai	ho	heōrakōs	memarturēken
water.	And	the	having seen	has borne witness,

2504.1 conj	226.5 adj nom sing fem	840.3 prs-pron gen sing	1498.4 verb 3sing indic pres act	3450.9 art nom sing fem	3114.1 noun nom sing fem
καὶ	ἀληθινὴ	αὐτοῦ	ἐστιν	ἡ	μαρτυρία,
kai	alēthinē	autou	estin	hē	marturia
and	true	his	is	the	witness,

2519.6 conj	2504.1 conj	1552.3 dem-pron nom sing masc	3471.4 verb 3sing indic perf act	3617.1 conj	225.4 adj
⸂ κἀκεῖνος	[☆ καὶ	ἐκεῖνος]	οἶδεν	ὅτι	ἀληθῆ
kakeinos	kai	ekeinos	oiden	hoti	alēthē
and that one	[idem]		has known	that	true

35.a.**Var:** 01ℵ,02A,03B, 05D,017K,019L,033X, 038,it.sa.GriesLach, Treg,Alf,Tisc,We/Ho, Weis,Sod,UBS/☆

2978.5 verb 3sing indic pres act	2419.1 conj	2504.1 conj	5050.1 prs-pron nom 2pl	3961.1 verb 2pl subj act
λέγει,	ἵνα	[a☆+ καὶ]	ὑμεῖς	⸂☆ πιστεύσητε.
legei	hina	kai	humeis	pisteusēte
he says,	that	[also]	you	may believe.

35.b.**Txt:** 01ℵ-corr,02A, 05D,017K,019L,033X, 036,038,1,13,etc.byz. Gries,Lach,Treg,Weis Sod
Var: 01ℵ-org,03B,044, TiscWe/Ho,UBS/☆

3961.8 verb 2pl subj pres act	1090.33 verb 3sing indic aor mid	1056.1 conj	3642.18 dem-pron pl neu	2419.1 conj	3450.9 art nom sing fem
[b πιστεύητε.]	36. ἐγένετο	γὰρ	ταῦτα	ἵνα	ἡ
pisteuēte	egeneto	gar	tauta	hina	hē
[idem]	Took place	for	these things	that	the

1118.1 noun nom sing fem	3997.22 verb 3sing subj aor pass	3609.1 noun nom sing neu	3620.3 partic	4789.8 verb 3sing indic fut pass
γραφὴ	πληρωθῇ,	Ὀστοῦν	οὐ	συντριβήσεται
graphē	plērōthē	Ostoun	ou	suntribēsetai
scripture	might be fulfilled,	A bone	not	shall be broken

840.3 prs-pron gen sing	2504.1 conj	3687.1 adv	2066.9 adj	1118.1 noun nom sing fem	2978.5 verb 3sing indic pres act
αὐτοῦ.	37. καὶ	πάλιν	ἑτέρα	γραφὴ	λέγει,
autou	kai	palin	hetera	graphē	legei
of him.	And	again	another	scripture	says,

3571.34 verb 3pl indic fut mid	1519.1 prep	3614.6 rel-pron acc sing masc	1561.1 verb 3pl indic aor act	3196.3 prep
Ὄψονται	εἰς	ὃν	ἐξεκέντησαν.	38. Μετὰ
Opsontai	eis	hon	exekentēsan	Meta
They shall look	on	him whom	they pierced.	After

38.a.**Txt:** 02A,036,037, 038,Steph
Var: 01ℵ,03B,05D, 017K,019L,021M,033X, 33,Lach,Treg,Alf,Word, TiscWe/Ho,Weis,Sod, UBS/☆

1156.2 conj	3642.18 dem-pron pl neu	2049.9 verb 3sing indic aor act	3450.6 art acc sing masc	3952.4 name acc masc	3450.5 art sing masc
δὲ	ταῦτα	ἠρώτησεν	τὸν	Πιλάτον	⸂a ὁ ⸃
de	tauta	ērōtēsen	ton	Pilaton	ho
and	these things	asked		Pilate	

38.b.**Txt:** 01ℵ,017K, 032W,036,037,038,1,13, byz.Tisc,Sod
Var: 02A,03B,05D,019L, 044,Lach,Treg,Alf, We/HoWeis,UBS/☆

2473.1 name masc	3450.5 art sing masc	570.3 prep gen	701.2 name gen fem	1498.21 verb sing masc part pres act
Ἰωσὴφ	⸂b ὁ ⸃	ἀπὸ	Ἀριμαθαίας,	ὢν
Iōsēph	ho	apo	Harimathaias	ōn
Joseph		from	Arimathea,	being

3073.1 noun nom sing masc	3450.2 art gen sing	2400.2 name masc	2900.8 verb nom sing masc part perf pass	1156.2 conj
μαθητὴς	τοῦ	Ἰησοῦ,	κεκρυμμένος	δὲ
mathētēs	tou	Iēsou	kekrummenos	de
a disciple		of Jesus,	having been concealed	but

"water" signifies the power of His sacrifice which cleanses us from our filthiness (John 3:5; 1 John 5:6; Titus 3:5,6).

35. And he that saw it bare record, and his record it true: The one who has recorded this was an eyewitness, *Norlie* . . . The one who saw it has testified, *Adams* . . . And the eye-witness gives this evidence, *Fenton* . . . and he knows that he is telling the truth, *Montgomery* . . . an eye-witness, who attests this, and his testimony deserves credit, *Campbell* . . . This is vouched for by an eyewitness, *NEB* . . . gives this evidence, *AmpB* . . . and his testimony is at present on record, *Wuest* . . . and his testimony is trustworthy, *Montgomery*.

and he knoweth that he saith true, that ye might believe: You must believe, too, *SEB*.

19:35. John affirmed the truthfulness of his testimony because he was an eyewitness and could give details of what happened, based on his own personal knowledge of the events. John's Gospel indicates that Jesus fulfilled the Old Testament prophecies concerning the Messiah.

36. For these things were done, that the scripture should be fulfilled, A bone of him shall not be broken: These things happened to fulfil the Scripture, *Adams* . . . For this happened, *Phillips* . . . things occurred, *Murdock* . . . which declares, *Weymouth* . . . shall not be crushed, *Rotherham, Concordant* . . . shall you break, *Confraternity*.

37. And again another scripture saith, They shall look on him whom they pierced: And another text says, *NEB* . . . they shall gaze, *Norlie* . . . see Him Whom they stab, *Concordant* . . . who was wounded by their spears, *BB* . . . the one they wounded, *SEB* . . . whom they impaled, *HistNT*.

19:36,37. The events just related concerning the Lord's crucifixion are what John's Gospel refers to as "these things." The sequence is this: God by His omniscience knew the events which were to occur; He moved on the prophets to record the details of the Messiah's person and ministry; and finally, the events happened as He foreknew and inspired the prophets to write.

The Passover was celebrated by eating the Passover lamb. According to Exodus 12:46 and Numbers 9:12, not a bone of the lamb was to be broken. This law indicated by type that Jesus' bones were not to be broken, in spite of the extremely cruel treatment He was prophesied to receive. The type of the lamb which God would provide became a plain prophecy in Psalm 34:20. It came to pass just as the type and prophecy had indicated; they did not break His legs for He was already dead (verse 33).

"The Jews looked upon *him whom they pierced*, but their look was not prompted by the godly sorrow that leads to repentance (see 2 Cor. vii. 10). It was left for the new Israel, converted Jews and converted Gentiles, to turn in penitence to the pierced side of Jesus and receive from Him the gift of forgiveness and eternal life" (Tasker, *Tyndale New Testament Commentaries*, 4:214).

38. And after this Joseph of Arimathea, being a disciple of Jesus, but secretly for fear of the Jews: . . . of Ramah, *TCNT* . . . After these events, *Norlie* . . . but a concealed disciple, *Campbell* . . . but having kept it secret through, *Rotherham*

19:38. "Joseph of Arimathea" was a man of high rank among the Jews and a member of the Sanhedrin. He is described by Luke as a man who was waiting for the kingdom of God (Luke 23:50,51).

The word *secret* means "to hide," "to conceal," and "to keep safe." Joseph did not publicly proclaim that Jesus was the Messiah. The Sanhedrin had made acknowledgment of Jesus as Messiah hazardous, for one could lose his social and religious status.

It required courage to ask for the body of a crucified man. Yet Mark states that Joseph went boldly at a time of extreme danger to his person.

1217.2 prep	3450.6 art acc sing masc	5238.4 noun acc sing masc	3450.1 art gen pl	2428.3 name-adj gen pl masc	2419.1 conj
διὰ	τὸν	φόβον	τῶν	Ἰουδαίων,	ἵνα
dia	*ton*	*phobon*	*tōn*	*Ioudaiōn*	*hina*
through	the	fear	of the	Jews,	that

142.12 verb 3sing subj aor act	3450.16 art sing neu	4835.1 noun sing neu	3450.2 art gen sing	2400.2 name masc	2504.1 conj
ἄρῃ	τὸ	σῶμα	τοῦ	Ἰησοῦ·	καὶ
arē	*to*	*sōma*	*tou*	*Iēsou*	*kai*
he might take away	the	body		of Jesus:	and

38.c.**Var:** 01ℵ-org,022N, 032W,it.Tisc

38.d.**Var:** 01ℵ-org,022N, 032W,it.Tisc

1994.3 verb 3sing indic aor act	3450.5 art sing masc	3952.1 name nom masc	2048.3 verb 3sing indic aor act	2048.1 verb indic aor act
ἐπέτρεψεν	ὁ	Πιλᾶτος.	⸀ ἦλθεν	[c ἦλθον]
epetrepsen	*ho*	*Pilatos*	*ēlthen*	*ēlthon*
gave leave		Pilate.	He came	[idem]

38.e.**Txt:** p66,01ℵ-corr, 03B,017K,019L,033X, 036,037,038,1,13,etc. byz.sa.bo.Lach,We/Ho, WeisSod,UBS/☆
Var: 01ℵ-org,032W,it. Tisc

3631.1 conj	2504.1 conj	142.8 verb 3sing indic aor act	142.10 verb 3pl indic aor act	3450.16 art sing neu	4835.1 noun sing neu
οὖν	καὶ	⸀ ἦρεν	[d ἦραν]	⸀e τὸ	σῶμα ⸌
oun	*kai*	*ēren*	*ēran*	*to*	*sōma*
therefore	and	took away	[idem]	the	body

38.f.**Txt:** 05D,017K,036, 037,038,1,13,byz.bo.
Var1: .p66,01ℵ-corr, 03B,019L,033X,sa.Lach, Treg,AlfWe/Ho,Weis, Sod,UBS/☆
Var2: .01ℵ-org,032W,it. Tisc

3450.2 art gen sing	2400.2 name masc	840.3 prs-pron gen sing	840.6 prs-pron acc sing masc	2048.3 verb 3sing indic aor act
⸀ τοῦ	Ἰησοῦ.	[1f☆ αὐτοῦ.	2 αὐτόν.]	39. ἦλθεν
tou	*Iēsou*	*autou*	*auton*	*ēlthen*
	of Jesus.	[his.	him.]	Came

1156.2 conj	2504.1 conj	3392.1 name nom masc	3450.5 art sing masc	2048.13 verb nom sing masc part aor act	4242.1 prep
δὲ	καὶ	Νικόδημος,	ὁ	ἐλθὼν	πρὸς
de	*kai*	*Nikodēmos*	*ho*	*elthōn*	*pros*
and	also	Nicodemus,	the	having come	to

39.a.**Txt:** 01ℵ,05D,017K, 032W,036,037,038,1, byz.Sod
Var: p66-corr,02A,03B, 019L,030U,033X,Lach, TregAlf,Tisc,We/Ho, Weis,UBS/☆

3450.6 art acc sing masc	2400.3 name acc masc	840.6 prs-pron acc sing masc	3433.2 noun gen sing fem	3450.16 art sing neu	4270.1 adv
⸀ τον	Ἰησουν	[a☆ αὐτὸν]	νυκτὸς	τὸ	πρῶτον,
ton	*Iēsoun*	*auton*	*nuktos*	*to*	*prōton*
	Jesus	[him]	by night	the	first,

5179.7 verb nom sing masc part pres act	3259.1 noun acc sing neu	4521.1 noun gen sing fem	2504.1 conj	248.1 noun gen sing fem	5448.1 adv
φέρων	μίγμα	σμύρνης	καὶ	ἀλόης	⸀ ὡσεὶ
pherōn	*migma*	*smurnēs*	*kai*	*aloēs*	*hōsei*
bearing	a mixture	of myrrh	and	aloes	about

39.b.**Txt:** p66,02A,030U, 032W,033X,1,13,33, Steph
Var: 01ℵ,03B,05D, 017K,019L,036,037,038, Gries,Lach,Treg,Alf, Word,Tisc,We/HoWeis, Sod,UBS/☆

5453.1 conj	3020.2 noun acc pl fem	1526.1 num card	2956.12 verb indic aor act	3631.1 conj	3450.16 art sing neu
[b☆ ὡς]	λίτρας	ἑκατόν.	40. ἔλαβον	οὖν	τὸ
hōs	*litras*	*hekaton*	*elabon*	*oun*	*to*
[idem]	pounds	a hundred.	They took	therefore	the

4835.1 noun sing neu	3450.2 art gen sing	2400.2 name masc	2504.1 conj	1204.2 verb 3pl indic aor act	840.15 prs-pron sing neu	3470.2 noun dat pl neu
σῶμα	τοῦ	Ἰησοῦ,	καὶ	ἔδησαν	αὐτὸ	ὀθονίοις
sōma	*tou*	*Iēsou*	*kai*	*edēsan*	*auto*	*othoniois*
body		of Jesus,	and	bound	it	in linen cloths

3196.3 prep	3450.1 art gen pl	753.1 noun gen pl neu	2503.1 conj	1478.1 noun sing neu	1498.4 verb 3sing indic pres act
μετὰ	τῶν	ἀρωμάτων,	καθὼς	ἔθος	ἐστὶν
meta	*tōn*	*arōmatōn*	*kathōs*	*ethos*	*estin*
with	the	aromatics,	as	a custom	is

All four Gospels narrate Joseph's part in taking down the body of Jesus and the burial. The responsibility of a proper funeral was usually assumed by relatives or friends.

. . . but did not openly profess himself to be, *Norton* . . . and kept concealed, *Murdock* . . . out of fear, *ALBA* . . . owing to his dread of the Judeans, *Fenton.*

besought Pilate that he might take away the body of Jesus: . . . was approached by Joseph, *NEB* . . . requested Pilate, *Rotherham* . . . asked for permission to take the body of Jesus, *Montgomery* . . . to remove the body of Jesus, *Williams, Norlie.*

and Pilate gave him leave. He came therefore, and took the body of Jesus: Pilate gave permission, *Confraternity* . . . Pilate allowed Joseph to do this, *SEB* . . . and Pilate allowed it, *ALBA* . . . having granted, *Campbell* . . . gave approval, *Norlie* . . . So he went and removed the body, *Moffatt.*

19:39. "Nicodemus" is referred to twice before in this Gospel. Nicodemus was a ruler and a Pharisee (3:1). Nicodemus spoke in behalf of the Lord at a gathering of the Council (7:50). Joseph asked for the body, took Jesus down from the cross, brought the linen wrappings (Mark 15:46), and gave his new-hewn tomb for Jesus' burial (Matthew 27:60). Nicodemus brought approximately 100 pounds of spices to put within the folds of the linen wrappings. Burial could not have been carried out without the two men bringing together the necessary linen wrappings and spices for the preparation of the body. Joseph and Nicodemus planned for Jesus' burial during the 6 hours Jesus hung on the cross. Perhaps they were standing at a distance considering arrangements, for they knew the body must be interred before sunset. Notice the dedication of the two men. Their part in the burial of Jesus would bring them 7 days of ceremonial pollution. During the entire Passover season they would be unclean. They could not participate in any Passover worship or activity (Numbers 19:11). Their love for Jesus was stronger than their love for their Law, customs, and personal safety.

"Myrrh" is mentioned only at the birth and death of the Saviour. Myrrh was an aromatic gum used for perfume and for embalming. "Aloes" occurs only here. "Aloes are derived from the pulp in the leaves of a plant that belongs to the lily family. The spice is fragrant and bitter to the taste. Used with myrrh, it acts as a drying agent; and the fragrance would counteract the odor of decaying flesh" (Tenney, *Expositor's Bible Commentary*, 9:186). Aloes and myrrh were mixed together as a powder and poured between the folds of the linen wrappings as the strips were wound around the legs, arms, and trunk of Jesus' body.

39. And there came also Nicodemus, which at the first came to Jesus by night, and brought a mixture of myrrh and aloes, about an hundred pound weight: . . . he was joined by, *ALBA* . . . who previously came to Jesus, *Murdock* . . . who in the first instance came to Him by night, *Fenton.*

40. Then took they the body of Jesus, and wound it in linen clothes with the spices: . . . and wound it in the linens, *Murdock* . . . wrapped it in linen sheets, *Norlie* . . . and wrapped it in bandages with the spices, *Williams* . . . and wrapped it up in a winding-sheet, *Fenton* . . . with the sweet-smelling spices, *SEB* . . . with those confeccions, *Tyndale.*

19:40. "They" refers to Joseph and Nicodemus; however, others may have been in attendance. We know of the growth of Nicodemus' faith in Christ from his interview with Jesus recorded in chapter 3, his plea for justice and fairness for Jesus (7:50,51), and here his open declaration of love for the Lord.

Jesus' body was prepared for burial "as the manner of the Jews is to bury." "Linen" indicates more than one strip of cloth with which Jesus' body was bound. Each of His limbs was bound separately, and the spices were applied within the wrappings. The internal organs were not removed as was the manner of the Egyptians in embalming. It is possible that the entire body except the head

3450.4 art dat pl	2428.4 name-adj dat pl masc	1763.1 verb inf pres act	1498.34 verb sing indic imperf act	1156.2 conj
τοῖς	Ἰουδαίοις	ἐνταφιάζειν.	41. ἦν	δὲ
tois	*Ioudaiois*	*entaphiazein*	*ēn*	*de*
among the	Jews	to prepare for burial.	There was	now

1706.1 prep	3450.3 art dat sing	4964.3 noun dat sing masc	3562.1 adv	4568.12 verb 3sing indic aor pass	2752.1 noun nom sing masc
ἐν	τῷ	τόπῳ	ὅπου	ἐσταυρώθη	κῆπος,
en	*tō*	*topō*	*hopou*	*estaurōthē*	*kēpos*
in	the	place	where	he was crucified	a garden,

2504.1 conj	1706.1 prep	3450.3 art dat sing	2752.2 noun dat sing masc	3283.1 noun sing neu	2508.1 adj sing	1706.1 prep
καὶ	ἐν	τῷ	κήπῳ	μνημεῖον	καινὸν,	ἐν
kai	*en*	*tō*	*kēpō*	*mnēmeion*	*kainon*	*en*
and	in	the	garden	a tomb	new,	in

41.a.**Txt:** 02A,05D,017K, 019L,036,037,038,1,13, etc.byz.Lach,Tisc
Var: 01ℵ,03B,032W, We/HoWeis,Sod,UBS/☆

3614.3 rel-pron dat sing	3627.1 adv	3625.2 num card nom masc	4935.29 verb 3sing indic aor pass	1498.34 verb sing indic imperf act
ᾧ	οὐδέπω	οὐδεὶς	‘ ἐτέθη.	[a☆ ἦν
hō	*oudepō*	*oudeis*	*etethē*	*ēn*
which	no one	not ever	was laid.	[was

4935.43 verb nom sing masc part perf pass	1550.1 adv	3631.1 conj	1217.2 prep	3450.12 art acc sing fem
τεθειμένος·]	42. ἐκεῖ	οὖν	διὰ	τὴν
tetheimenos	*ekei*	*oun*	*dia*	*tēn*
having been placed.]	There	therefore	because of	the

3765.2 noun acc sing fem	3450.1 art gen pl	2428.3 name-adj gen pl masc	3617.1 conj	1445.1 adv	1498.34 verb sing indic imperf act
παρασκευὴν	τῶν	Ἰουδαίων,	ὅτι	ἐγγὺς	ἦν
paraskeuēn	*tōn*	*Ioudaiōn*	*hoti*	*engus*	*ēn*
preparation	of the	Jews,	because	near	was

3450.16 art sing neu	3283.1 noun sing neu	4935.11 verb 3pl indic aor act	3450.6 art acc sing masc	2400.3 name acc masc
τὸ	μνημεῖον,	ἔθηκαν	τὸν	Ἰησοῦν.
to	*mnēmeion*	*ethēkan*	*ton*	*Iēsoun*
the	tomb,	they laid		Jesus.

3450.11 art dat sing fem	1156.2 conj	1518.7 num card dat fem	3450.1 art gen pl	4378.4 noun gen pl neu	3109.1 name nom fem
20:1. Τῇ	δὲ	μιᾷ	τῶν	σαββάτων	Μαρία
Tē	*de*	*mia*	*tōn*	*sabbatōn*	*Maria*
On the	but	first	of the	week	Mary

3450.9 art nom sing fem	3066.1 name nom fem	2048.34 verb 3sing indic pres	4262.1 adv	4508.2 noun gen sing fem	2068.1 adv
ἡ	Μαγδαληνὴ	ἔρχεται	πρωῒ	σκοτίας	ἔτι
hē	*Magdalēnē*	*erchetai*	*prōi*	*skotias*	*eti*
the	Magdalene	comes	early	dark	still

1498.27 verb gen sing fem part pres act	1519.1 prep	3450.16 art sing neu	3283.1 noun sing neu	2504.1 conj	984.4 verb 3sing indic pres act
οὔσης	εἰς	τὸ	μνημεῖον,	καὶ	βλέπει
ousēs	*eis*	*to*	*mnēmeion*	*kai*	*blepei*
it being	to	the	tomb,	and	sees

3450.6 art acc sing masc	3012.4 noun acc sing masc	142.28 verb acc sing masc part perf pass	1523.2 prep gen	3450.2 art gen sing	3283.2 noun gen sing neu
τὸν	λίθον	ἠρμένον	ἐκ	τοῦ	μνημείου.
ton	*lithon*	*ērmenon*	*ek*	*tou*	*mnēmeiou*
the	stone	taken away	from	the	tomb.

was wrapped laterally many times with strips of bandagelike linen with the spices within. After this the long 14- by 3-foot pieces of linen cloth covered the body from head to feet and covered both back and front.

as the manner of the Jews is to bury: . . . as the custom of the Jews is, *ASV* . . . as is the Jews' customary way to prepare for burial, *AmpB* . . . manner of preparing for burial, *Confraternity* . . . Jewish mode of preparing for burial, *Weymouth* . . . in preparing for burial, *Norlie* . . . according to the Jews' mode of interment, *Norton* . . . manner of embalming, *Campbell* . . . way of burial, *TCNT.*

19:41. Only John's Gospel tells us of the garden in the place "where he was crucified." Matthew says the garden tomb belonged to Joseph (Matthew 27:60). Natural caves were used as tombs, but often hillsides were ideal to form man-dug cave tombs. The tomb seems to be in preparation for Joseph's death. When members of a family died, dirt and stones were excavated to provide room for another body. The "new sepulchre" had not been used. Jesus' burial in Joseph's tomb fulfilled Isaiah's prediction. Thus He died with criminals, but He was interred in a rich man's tomb.

41. Now in the place where he was crucified there was a garden: There was a garden near the place, *Montgomery, Norlie* . . . at the place, *Weymouth* . . . in proximity to the spot, *Fenton* . . . an orchard, *Moffatt.*

and in the garden a new sepulchre, wherein was never man yet laid: . . . a new tomb, *ASV, Norlie, Wuest* . . . in the yerd a newe grave, *Wycliffe* . . . a newly-made tomb, *TCNT.*

19:42. Only a short time remained before sunset on the day of preparation; therefore, of necessity the garden tomb was selected as Jesus' grave. The implication is that a more prominent site would have been chosen had they had time for its preparation. They desired that Jesus might have the greatest honor paid to Him. None of the disciples expected the Resurrection, so the tomb seemed quite important. They little expected that within 3 days He would not have need of a tomb.

The other evangelists tell us that the women watched the burial of Christ. They took note where He was buried so that they could express their devotion to Him by bringing spices and perfumes to the tomb after the Passover (Matthew 27:61; Mark 15:47; Luke 23:55,56). Matthew also relates how the chief priests and Pharisees requested soldiers of Pilate, to guard the tomb and to secure it by sealing the entrance with a stone (Matthew 27:62-66).

42. There laid they Jesus therefore because of the Jews' preparation day; for the sepulchre was nigh at hand: In that place therefore, *Wuest* . . . they deposited Jesus, *Campbell, Fenton* . . . because the sabbath had commenced, *Murdock* . . . because it was the eve of the Jewish sabbath, *ALBA* . . . and the tomb was near by, *Norlie* . . . the tomb was conveniently near, *Phillips.*

20:1. Jesus was buried before sundown on Friday (the day of preparation). No work or travel was done on the Sabbath, and Sunday morning Jesus arose. By Jewish reckoning, 3 days had transpired since the burial. Any part of a day was counted as a day.

All four Gospels relate that the stone over the entrance had been removed. Matthew notes that an angel of the Lord rolled away the stone. Mark reveals the stone was extremely large. Matthew also tells us the stone was sealed to insure that no one tampered with the tomb (Matthew 27:66). But all the Roman guards and the sealing did was to assure a greater witness to the Lord's resurrection.

1. The first day of the week cometh Mary Magdalene early, when it was yet dark, unto the sepulchre: Early on the Sunday morning, *ALBA* . . . the first day of the sabbaths, *Worrell* . . . Mary of Magdala went early to the tomb, *Moffatt* . . . in fact, still dusk, *Fenton.*

and seeth the stone taken away from the sepulchre: . . . and discovered that the stone, *Montgomery* . . . and noticed that, *Phillips* . . . and sees the stone taken away out of the tomb, *HBIE* . . . saw that the stone had been removed, *TCNT, Murdock, ALBA* . . . the stone had been removed from its entrance, *Fenton* . . . been removed from the entrance, *Campbell* . . . moved away from the entrance, *NEB.*

4983.2 verb 3sing indic pres act	3631.1 conj	2504.1 conj	2048.34 verb 3sing indic pres	4242.1 prep	4468.4 name acc masc
2. τρέχει	οὖν	καὶ	ἔρχεται	πρὸς	Σίμωνα
trechei	*oun*	*kai*	*erchetai*	*pros*	*Simōna*
She runs	therefore	and	comes	to	Simon

3935.4 name acc masc	2504.1 conj	4242.1 prep	3450.6 art acc sing masc	241.5 adj acc sing masc	3073.4 noun acc sing masc
Πέτρον	καὶ	πρὸς	τὸν	ἄλλον	μαθητὴν
Petron	*kai*	*pros*	*ton*	*allon*	*mathētēn*
Peter	and	to	the	other	disciple

3614.6 rel-pron acc sing masc	5205.11 verb 3sing indic imperf act	3450.5 art sing masc	2400.1 name nom masc	2504.1 conj	2978.5 verb 3sing indic pres act
ὃν	ἐφίλει	ὁ	Ἰησοῦς,	καὶ	λέγει
hon	*ephilei*	*ho*	*Iēsous*	*kai*	*legei*
whom	loved		Jesus,	and	says

840.2 prs-pron dat pl	142.10 verb 3pl indic aor act	3450.6 art acc sing masc	2935.4 noun acc sing masc	1523.2 prep gen	3450.2 art gen sing
αὐτοῖς,	Ἦραν	τὸν	κύριον	ἐκ	τοῦ
autois	*Eran*	*ton*	*kurion*	*ek*	*tou*
to them,	They took away	the	Lord	out of	the

3283.2 noun gen sing neu	2504.1 conj	3620.2 partic	3471.5 verb 1pl indic perf act	4085.1 adv	4935.11 verb 3pl indic aor act
μνημείου,	καὶ	οὐκ	οἴδαμεν	ποῦ	ἔθηκαν
mnēmeiou	*kai*	*ouk*	*oidamen*	*pou*	*ethēkan*
tomb,	and	not	we know	where	they laid

840.6 prs-pron acc sing masc	1814.3 verb 3sing indic aor act	3631.1 conj	3450.5 art sing masc	3935.1 name nom masc	2504.1 conj
αὐτόν.	3. Ἐξῆλθεν	οὖν	ὁ	Πέτρος	καὶ
auton	*Exēlthen*	*oun*	*ho*	*Petros*	*kai*
him.	Went forth	therefore		Peter	and

3450.5 art sing masc	241.4 adj nom sing masc	3073.1 noun nom sing masc	2504.1 conj	2048.60 verb 3pl indic imperf	1519.1 prep	3450.16 art sing neu
ὁ	ἄλλος	μαθητής,	καὶ	ἤρχοντο	εἰς	τὸ
ho	*allos*	*mathētēs*	*kai*	*ērchonto*	*eis*	*to*
the	other	disciple,	and	came	to	the

3283.1 noun sing neu	4983.14 verb 3pl indic imperf act	1156.2 conj	3450.7 art pl masc	1411.3 num card	3537.1 adv
μνημεῖον.	4. ἔτρεχον	δὲ	οἱ	δύο	ὁμοῦ·
mnēmeion	*etrechon*	*de*	*hoi*	*duo*	*homou*
tomb.	Ran	and	the	two	together,

2504.1 conj	3450.5 art sing masc	241.4 adj nom sing masc	3073.1 noun nom sing masc	4248.1 verb 3sing indic aor act	4880.1 adv comp
καὶ	ὁ	ἄλλος	μαθητὴς	προέδραμεν	τάχιον
kai	*ho*	*allos*	*mathētēs*	*proedramen*	*tachion*
and	the	other	disciple	ran forward	faster

3450.2 art gen sing	3935.2 name gen masc	2504.1 conj	2048.3 verb 3sing indic aor act	4272.5 num ord nom sing masc	1519.1 prep
τοῦ	Πέτρου,	καὶ	ἦλθεν	πρῶτος	εἰς
tou	*Petrou*	*kai*	*ēlthen*	*prōtos*	*eis*
	Peter,	and	came	first	to

3450.16 art sing neu	3283.1 noun sing neu	2504.1 conj	3740.2 verb nom sing masc part aor act	984.4 verb 3sing indic pres act
τὸ	μνημεῖον,	5. καὶ	παρακύψας	βλέπει
to	*mnēmeion*	*kai*	*parakupsas*	*blepei*
the	tomb,	and	having stooped down	he sees

20:2. As we begin to read chapter 20 we feel we enter an entirely new world. The landscape is calm, the shouts of "Crucify, crucify" are gone. No sound is heard of nails being driven through quivering flesh or weeping and groans from compassionate friends. The storm is over, and a strange new peace permeates the atmosphere. The Victor over the old curse is ready to make His triumphal appearance.

The Gospel of John does not relate the resurrection of Christ itself, and neither do the other evangelists. No one knows exactly when Jesus came out of the tomb. Matthew says, "There was a great earthquake: for the angel of the Lord descended from heaven, and came and rolled back the stone from the door, and sat upon it" (Matthew 28:2). Yet the angel did not roll back the stone to allow Jesus out. He was already out. He was already risen. The angel merely revealed that Jesus was gone. Now the women could go in.

John's Gospel does not relate the angel's appearance to Mary, but the other evangelists do. Mark 16:7 states that the angel told Mary to tell Peter. Mary found Peter, and later John, and related her strange experience. John does not mention himself by name. He used the often related reference, "the other disciple, whom Jesus loved," although the word for "loved" (Greek, *ephilei*) is not the same as in 19:26. The former word indicates an emphasis on friendship and the latter means a godly, compassionate love.

Mary is definite as to who "they" are. To Mary the only explanation for Jesus' disappearance from the tomb was that either friends (Joseph and Nicodemus) or foes (Romans or Jews) had removed His body. Mary says "we"; therefore, the other women are clearly implied (see Luke 24:10).

20:3. No statement is made as to where Peter and John had been. The important thing was that they both were eager to go to the grave. *Mnēmeion* (translated "sepulchre" here) occurs 16 times in John's Gospel. It is sometimes translated "grave" or "tomb." Luke 24:12 mentions only Peter going to the tomb, but John says that he also went after hearing Mary's message.

20:4. Note their haste, for the two "ran both together." John says "the other disciple (meaning himself) did outrun Peter, and came first to the sepulchre." Perhaps John was younger than Peter and more active physically.

How often Peter and John were together. Many of their most wonderful experiences were shared. Their relationship to Jesus was the focal point of their relationship. Peter was quick, impulsive, and prone to error. John was slow, meditative, and prone to reflection. Yet, different as they were, they were fellow sharers of the grace of Jesus Christ.

2. Then she runneth, and cometh to Simon Peter, and to the other disciple, whom Jesus loved: So she came running, *Montgomery, Norlie* . . . whom Jesus tenderly loved, *Williams* . . . who was dear to, *Weymouth.*

and saith unto them, They have taken away the Lord out of the sepulchre, and we know not where they have laid him: . . . they have placed Him, *Fenton* . . . They have taken the Lord out of his tomb, *NEB* . . . out of the grave, *Beck* . . . we are not aware where they place Him! *Concordant.*

3. Peter therefore went forth, and that other disciple, and came to the sepulchre: Now the two raced alike, and the other disciple runs more swiftly, *Concordant* . . . Both set off together, running, but the other disciple outran Peter and arrived at it first, *ALBA* . . . Then Peter and the other disciple set out on their way to the tomb, *Norlie* . . . left the city and started for the tomb, *Williams* . . . running side by side, *Beck, NEB.*

4. So they ran both together: and the other disciple did outrun Peter, and came first to the sepulchre: . . . and was first to arrive at the tomb, *Phillips* . . . ran faster than Peter, and reached the tomb first, *TCNT* . . . arrived first, *Norlie.*

6.a.**Var:** p66,01ℵ-corr, 03B,019L,032W,033X, 33,Treg,Alf,We/Ho, Weis,Sod,UBS/☆

2719.9 verb acc pl neu part pres	**3450.17** art pl neu	**3470.3** noun acc pl neu	**3620.3** partic	**3175.1** conj	**1511.3** verb 3sing indic aor act
κείμενα	τὰ	ὀθόνια,	οὐ	μέντοι	εἰσῆλθεν.
keimena	*ta*	*othonia*	*ou*	*mentoi*	*eisēlthen*
lying	the	linen cloths;	not	however	he entered.

2048.34 verb 3sing indic pres	**3631.1** conj	**2504.1** conj	**4468.1** name masc	**3935.1** name nom masc
6. ἔρχεται	οὖν	[a☆+ καὶ]	Σίμων	Πέτρος
erchetai	*oun*	*kai*	*Simōn*	*Petros*
Comes	then	[also]	Simon	Peter

188.5 verb nom sing masc part pres act	**840.4** prs-pron dat sing	**2504.1** conj	**1511.3** verb 3sing indic aor act	**1519.1** prep	**3450.16** art sing neu
ἀκολουθῶν	αὐτῷ,	καὶ	εἰσῆλθεν	εἰς	τὸ
akolouthōn	*autō*	*kai*	*eisēlthen*	*eis*	*to*
following	him,	and	entered	into	the

3283.1 noun sing neu	**2504.1** conj	**2311.4** verb 3sing indic pres act	**3450.17** art pl neu	**3470.3** noun acc pl neu	**2719.9** verb acc pl neu part pres
μνημεῖον,	καὶ	θεωρεῖ	τὰ	ὀθόνια	κείμενα,
mnēmeion	*kai*	*theōrei*	*ta*	*othonia*	*keimena*
tomb,	and	sees	the	linen cloths	lying,

2504.1 conj	**3450.16** art sing neu	**4529.2** noun acc sing neu	**3614.16** rel-pron sing neu	**1498.34** verb sing indic imperf act	**1894.3** prep
7. καὶ	τὸ	σουδάριον	ὃ	ἦν	ἐπὶ
kai	*to*	*soudarion*	*ho*	*ēn*	*epi*
and	the	handkerchief	which	was	upon

3450.10 art gen sing fem	**2747.2** noun gen sing fem	**840.3** prs-pron gen sing	**3620.3** partic	**3196.3** prep	**3450.1** art gen pl	**3470.1** noun gen pl neu
τῆς	κεφαλῆς	αὐτοῦ,	οὐ	μετὰ	τῶν	ὀθονίων
tēs	*kephalēs*	*autou*	*ou*	*meta*	*tōn*	*othoniōn*
the	head	his,	not	with	the	linen cloths

2719.4 verb acc sing part pres	**233.2** conj	**5400.1** prep gen	**1778.2** verb acc sing neu part perf pass	**1519.1** prep	**1518.4** num card acc masc
κείμενον,	ἀλλὰ	χωρὶς	ἐντετυλιγμένον	εἰς	ἕνα
keimenon	*alla*	*chōris*	*entetuligmenon*	*eis*	*hena*
lying,	but	by itself	having been folded up	in	one

4964.4 noun acc sing masc	**4966.1** adv	**3631.1** conj	**1511.3** verb 3sing indic aor act	**2504.1** conj	**3450.5** art sing masc
τόπον.	**8.** τότε	οὖν	εἰσῆλθεν	καὶ	ὁ
topon	*tote*	*oun*	*eisēlthen*	*kai*	*ho*
place.	Then	therefore	entered	also	the

241.4 adj nom sing masc	**3073.1** noun nom sing masc	**3450.5** art sing masc	**2048.13** verb nom sing masc part aor act	**4272.5** num ord nom sing masc	**1519.1** prep
ἄλλος	μαθητὴς	ὁ	ἐλθὼν	πρῶτος	εἰς
allos	*mathētēs*	*ho*	*elthōn*	*prōtos*	*eis*
other	disciple	the	having come	first	to

3450.16 art sing neu	**3283.1** noun sing neu	**2504.1** conj	**1481.3** verb 3sing indic aor act	**2504.1** conj	**3961.20** verb 3sing indic aor act
τὸ	μνημεῖον,	καὶ	εἶδεν	καὶ	ἐπίστευσεν·
to	*mnēmeion*	*kai*	*eiden*	*kai*	*episteusen*
the	tomb,	and	saw	and	believed;

3627.1 adv	**1056.1** conj	**3471.13** verb 3pl indic plperf act	**3450.12** art acc sing fem	**1118.4** noun acc sing fem	**3617.1** conj
9. οὐδέπω	γὰρ	ᾔδεισαν	τὴν	γραφὴν,	ὅτι
oudepō	*gar*	*ēdeisan*	*tēn*	*graphēn*	*hoti*
not yet	for	they had known	the	scripture,	that

20:5. John arrived at the tomb before Peter, but he did not enter. It was typical of John to think things through. By entering a tomb one became defiled for 7 days. Perhaps John hesitated because of the possibility of defilement.

"Stooping" and "looking in" implies a low opening. John could see the linen wrappings lying there. John must have thought, "If someone has stolen the body, would they have left the graveclothes behind?" "Stooping" is an interesting word. It occurs five times in the New Testament (Luke 24:12; John 20:5,11; James 1:25; 1 Peter 1:12). The first three references concern stooping over Jesus' graveclothes, and the last two have to do with a careful search for truth. By diligent study of the Resurrection one finds ultimate truth.

5. And he stooping down, and looking in, saw the linen clothes lying: As he stooped, *Berkeley* . . . Bending forward, *ALBA* . . . stooping to look in, he saw the linen wrappings lying there, *Norlie* . . . There on the floor he saw the wrappings, *Weymouth* . . . he sees at a glance the strips of linen cloth lying, *Wuest.*

yet went he not in: Nevertheless, *Clementson* . . . he did not, however, enter, *Fenton.*

20:6. Peter entered the tomb without fear or thought. "Seeth" indicates an intense survey of the graveclothes. Peter was not going to make a hasty entrance and exit, but he examined more closely than John who "saw" (Greek, *blepei,* verse 5) the linen wrappings from outside the tomb.

6. Then cometh Simon Peter following him, and went into the sepulchre, and seeth the linen clothes lie: . . . coming up behind him, *Norlie* . . . and he gazed at the linen wrappings as they lay, *Montgomery.*

20:7. The orderly arrangement of the graveclothes indicated no hurried removal of the body. Disorder of the tomb and its contents would have been signs of Roman soldiers or thieves, yet in the tomb of Jesus there was no evidence of this. Though Jesus had repeatedly spoken of His resurrection, neither Peter nor John seemed to understand at first.

7. And the napkin, that was about his head, not lying with the linen clothes, but wrapped together in a place by itself: . . . the handkerchief, *Norlie* . . . but rolled up in a place by itself, *BB* . . . but apart, folded up into one place, *Rotherham* . . . Instead, it was all alone, folded in one place, *SEB* . . . but rolled up on one side separately, *TCNT* . . . rolled up in its own place, *Adams* . . . in a corner, *ALBA.*

20:8. Next, John entered the tomb. John believed what he saw, but how he interpreted what he saw is not clear. He saw the bandagelike linen wrappings. Were they intact as though the body came through them like light passing through a window glass? It appears so, for the Saviour's glorified body was not subject to material limitations. Later He appeared through a closed door (20:19). This verse speaks of John's faith as the first apostle to perceive what had actually happened to Jesus. John had not seen his Lord as yet, but he believed.

8. Then went in also that other disciple which came first to the sepulchre: . . . who had reached the tomb first, *Williams.*

and he saw, and believed: . . . saw what had happened and believed, *Phillips* . . . and saw and was convinced, *Weymouth* . . . the report, *Campbell.*

20:9. This verse limits the extent of faith expressed in the last verse. It is wonderful to believe, but faith must find its sure ground

9. For as yet they knew not the scripture: . . . for they had hitherto not understood from the, *ALBA* . . . they did not understand from the scriptures, *Campbell* . . . had not previously understood, *Williams* . . . not yet learned, *Murdock* . . . not even then familiar, *TCNT* . . . the statement, *AmpB* . . . what the Bible meant when, *Beck.*

John 20:10

1158.1 verb 3sing indic pres act	840.6 prs-pron acc sing masc	1523.2 prep gen	3361.2 adj gen pl	448.14 verb inf aor act
δεῖ	αὐτὸν	ἐκ	νεκρῶν	ἀναστῆναι.
dei	*auton*	*ek*	*nekrōn*	*anastēnai*
it is necessary	him	from among	dead	to rise.

562.1 verb indic aor act	3631.1 conj	3687.1 adv	4242.1 prep	1431.8 prs-pron acc pl masc
10. ἀπῆλθον	οὖν	πάλιν	πρὸς	‹ ἑαυτοὺς
apēlthon	*oun*	*palin*	*pros*	*heautous*
Went away	therefore	again	to	themselves

1431.16 prs-pron acc pl masc	3450.7 art pl masc	3073.5 noun nom pl masc	3109.1 name nom fem	1156.2 conj
[a☆ αὐτοὺς]	οἱ	μαθηταί.	**11.** Μαρία	δὲ
hautous	*hoi*	*mathētai*	*Maria*	*de*
[them]	the	disciples.	Mary	but

10.a.**Txt:** 01ℵ-corr,02A,05D,017K,032W,033X,036,037,038,1,13,etc.byz.Lach,Weis,Sod
Var: 01ℵ-org,03B,019L,TregTisc,We/Ho,UBS/☆

11.a.**Txt:** 017K,033X,036,byz.
Var: 02A,03B,05D,019L,037,(038),Gries,Lach,TregAlf,Word,Tisc,We/Ho,Weis,Sod,UBS/☆

2449.22 verb 3sing indic plperf act	4242.1 prep	3450.16 art sing neu	3283.1 noun sing neu	3450.3 art dat sing
εἱστήκει	πρὸς	‹ τὸ	μνημεῖον	[a☆ τῷ
heistēkei	*pros*	*to*	*mnēmeion*	*tō*
had stood	at	the	tomb	[the

3283.3 noun dat sing neu	2772.9 verb nom sing fem part pres act	1838.1 prep gen	1838.1 prep gen	2772.9 verb nom sing fem part pres act
μνημείῳ]	‹ κλαίουσα	ἔξω.	[☆ ἔξω	κλαίουσα.]
mnēmeiō	*klaiousa*	*exō*	*exō*	*klaiousa*
tomb]	weeping	outside.	[outside	weeping.]

5453.1 conj	3631.1 conj	2772.19 verb 3sing indic imperf act	3740.1 verb 3sing indic aor act	1519.1 prep	3450.16 art sing neu
ὡς	οὖν	ἔκλαιεν,	παρέκυψεν	εἰς	τὸ
hōs	*oun*	*eklaien*	*parekupsen*	*eis*	*to*
As	therefore	she wept,	she stooped down	into	the

3283.1 noun sing neu	2504.1 conj	2311.4 verb 3sing indic pres act	1411.3 num card	32.8 noun acc pl masc	1706.1 prep
μνημεῖον,	**12.** καὶ	θεωρεῖ	δύο	ἀγγέλους	ἐν
mnēmeion	*kai*	*theōrei*	*duo*	*angelous*	*en*
tomb,	and	beholds	two	angels	in

2996.2 adj dat pl	2488.3 verb acc pl masc part pres	1518.4 num card acc masc	4242.1 prep	3450.11 art dat sing fem
λευκοῖς	καθεζομένους,	ἕνα	πρὸς	τῇ
leukois	*kathezomenous*	*hena*	*pros*	*tē*
white	sitting,	one	at	the

2747.3 noun dat sing fem	2504.1 conj	1518.4 num card acc masc	4242.1 prep	3450.4 art dat pl	4087.6 noun dat pl masc	3562.1 adv
κεφαλῇ	καὶ	ἕνα	πρὸς	τοῖς	ποσίν,	ὅπου
kephalē	*kai*	*hena*	*pros*	*tois*	*posin*	*hopou*
head	and	one	at	the	feet,	where

2719.10 verb 3sing indic imperf	3450.16 art sing neu	4835.1 noun sing neu	3450.2 art gen sing	2400.2 name masc	2504.1 conj
ἔκειτο	τὸ	σῶμα	τοῦ	Ἰησοῦ.	**13.** καὶ
ekeito	*to*	*sōma*	*tou*	*Iēsou*	*kai*
was laid	the	body		of Jesus.	And

2978.3 verb 3pl pres act	840.11 prs-pron dat sing fem	1552.6 dem-pron nom pl masc	1129.5 noun voc sing fem	4949.9 intr-pron sing neu
λέγουσιν	αὐτῇ	ἐκεῖνοι,	Γύναι,	τί
legousin	*autē*	*ekeinoi*	*Gunai*	*ti*
say	to her	they,	Woman,	why

in the Scripture. John believed that the graveclothes supplied evidence of Christ's resurrection, yet the Old Testament prophecies concerning Christ's resurrection had not been made real to him. "For" states a reason, and "must" (Greek, *dei*) indicates the necessity stated by Scriptures. A number of passages in the Old Testament refer to His rising from the dead: Psalm 16:9,10; Isaiah 26:19; 53:10-12. The coming of the Holy Spirit on the Day of Pentecost (Acts 2) enabled the disciples to understand fully the reality of the Resurrection.

that he must rise again from the dead:

10. Then the disciples went away again unto their own home: . . . then returned to their companions, *TCNT.*

20:10. "Unto their own home" is literally "to themselves." It would serve no purpose to remain at the tomb. In fact, if they were caught there, they could be accused of stealing the body of Jesus. The disciples did not have permanent residence in Jerusalem. When they came to the temple for worship, they had no place to lodge except with friends.

11. But Mary stood without at the sepulchre weeping: Meanwhile, *ALBA* . . . But Mary remained standing without, *Norton* . . . remained standing at, *Murdock* . . . continued standing, facing the tomb, outside, weeping audibly, *Wuest* . . . stood sobbing outside, *Moffatt* . . . lamenting, *Concordant* . . . crying while she was praying, *SEB.*

and as she wept, she stooped down, and looked into the sepulchre: . . . she stooped to look into the tomb, *HBIE.*

20:11. This passage begins the post-Resurrection appearances of our Lord. John records 4 of the 12 appearances (20:11-18; 20:19-25; 20:26-31; 21:1-25). First, Jesus appeared to Mary Magdalene at the tomb (20:11-18). Second, He appeared to the 10 assembled disciples (20:19-25). Third, He manifested himself to the Eleven in Jerusalem (20:26-29). And fourth, He was present in visible form with seven disciples at the Sea of Galilee (21:1-25).

Mary had returned to the tomb after bearing the message to Peter and John (verse 2). Mary was "weeping" because her Lord had died and His body was missing. She "stooped" because the top entrance was low, and she could not otherwise get a view of the inside of the tomb.

12. And seeth two angels in white sitting: . . . two angels in white raiment, *Weymouth* . . . two messengers, *Rotherham* . . . clothed in white, *TCNT* . . . in glistening white, *Montgomery.*

the one at the head, and the other at the feet, where the body of Jesus had lain: . . . one facing the head and one facing the feet, *Wuest* . . . They were seated where Jesus' body had been lying, *SEB.*

20:12. Mary "seeth" something beyond what Peter and John had seen (verses 5 and 6). She saw two angels. Their garments were "white." The word "white" in the Greek is plural perhaps indicating the clothing of both angels. An angel basically means a messenger.

13. And they say unto her, Woman, why weepest thou?: . . . why are you weeping? *Norlie*

20:13. "They" is an emphatic pronoun in the sentence. The angels asked the same concerned question that Jesus asked (verse 15). Even the angels are compassionate toward God's sorrowing believ-

John 20:14

2772.3 verb 2sing indic pres act	2978.5 verb 3sing indic pres act	840.2 prs-pron dat pl	3617.1 conj	142.10 verb 3pl indic aor act
κλαίεις;	Λέγει	αὐτοῖς,	Ὅτι	Ἦραν
klaieis	*Legei*	*autois*	*Hoti*	*Eran*
do you weep?	She says	to them,	Because	they took away

3450.6 art acc sing masc	2935.4 noun acc sing masc	1466.2 prs-pron gen 1sing	2504.1 conj	3620.2 partic	3471.2 verb 1sing indic perf act	4085.1 adv
τὸν	κύριόν	μου,	καὶ	οὐκ	οἶδα	ποῦ
ton	*kurion*	*mou*	*kai*	*ouk*	*oida*	*pou*
the	Lord	my,	and	not	I know	where

14.a.**Txt:** 07E,017K,036,037,13,byz. **Var:** 01ℵ,02A,03B,05D,033X,038,33,it.sa.bo. Gries,Lach,Treg,Alf,Tisc,We/Ho,WeisSod,UBS/*

4935.11 verb 3pl indic aor act	840.6 prs-pron acc sing masc		2504.1 conj	3642.18 dem-pron pl neu	1500.20 verb nom sing fem part aor act
ἔθηκαν	αὐτόν.	**14.**	⸂a Καὶ ⸃	ταῦτα	εἰποῦσα
ethēkan	*auton*		*Kai*	*tauta*	*eipousa*
they laid	him.		And	these things	having said

4613.5 verb 3sing indic aor pass	1519.1 prep	3450.17 art pl neu	3557.1 adv	2504.1 conj	2311.4 verb 3sing indic pres act
ἐστράφη	εἰς	τὰ	ὀπίσω,	καὶ	θεωρεῖ
estraphē	*eis*	*ta*	*opisō*	*kai*	*theōrei*
she turned	into	the	behind,	and	beholds

3450.6 art acc sing masc	2400.3 name acc masc	2449.25 verb acc part perf act	2504.1 conj	3620.2 partic	3471.11 verb 3sing indic plperf act
τὸν	Ἰησοῦν	ἑστῶτα·	καὶ	οὐκ	ᾔδει
ton	*Iēsoun*	*hestōta*	*kai*	*ouk*	*ēdei*
	Jesus	having stood,	and	not	had known

14.b.**Txt:** Steph **Var:** 01ℵ,02A,03B,05D,017K,019L,036,037,038,byz.Gries,LachTreg,Alf,Tisc,We/Ho,Weis,Sod,UBS/*

3617.1 conj	3450.5 art sing masc	2400.1 name nom masc	1498.4 verb 3sing indic pres act	2978.5 verb 3sing indic pres act	840.11 prs-pron dat sing fem
ὅτι	⸂b ὁ ⸃	Ἰησοῦς	ἐστιν.	**15.** λέγει	αὐτῇ
hoti	*ho*	*Iēsous*	*estin*	*legei*	*autē*
that		Jesus	it is.	Says	to her

15.a.**Txt:** 02A,05D,017K,036,037,038,1,13,byz.GriesWeis,Sod **Var:** p66,01ℵ,03B,019L,032W,Lach,Treg,Alf,TiscWe/Ho,UBS/*

3450.5 art sing masc	2400.1 name nom masc	1129.5 noun voc sing fem	4949.9 intr-pron sing neu	2772.3 verb 2sing indic pres act	4949.1 intr-pron
⸂a ὁ ⸃	Ἰησοῦς,	Γύναι,	τί	κλαίεις;	τίνα
ho	*Iēsous*	*Gunai*	*ti*	*klaieis*	*tina*
	Jesus,	Woman,	why	do you weep?	Whom

2195.4 verb 2sing indic pres act	1552.9 dem-pron nom sing fem	1374.11 verb nom sing fem part pres act	3617.1 conj	3450.5 art sing masc
ζητεῖς;	Ἐκείνη	δοκοῦσα	ὅτι	ὁ
zēteis	*Ekeinē*	*dokousa*	*hoti*	*ho*
do you seek?	That	thinking	that	the

2753.1 noun nom sing masc	1498.4 verb 3sing indic pres act	2978.5 verb 3sing indic pres act	840.4 prs-pron dat sing	2935.5 noun voc sing masc	1479.1 conj
κηπουρός	ἐστιν,	λέγει	αὐτῷ,	Κύριε,	εἰ
kēpouros	*estin*	*legei*	*autō*	*Kurie*	*ei*
gardener	it is,	says	to him,	Sir,	if

4622.1 prs-pron nom 2sing	934.9 verb 2sing indic aor act	840.6 prs-pron acc sing masc	1500.12 verb 2sing impr aor act	1466.4 prs-pron dat 1sing
σὺ	ἐβάστασας	αὐτόν,	εἰπέ	μοι
su	*ebastasas*	*auton*	*eipe*	*moi*
you	did carry off	him,	tell	me

4085.1 adv	840.6 prs-pron acc sing masc	4935.9 verb 2sing indic aor act	4935.9 verb 2sing indic aor act	840.6 prs-pron acc sing masc	2476.3 conj
ποῦ	⸂ αὐτὸν	ἔθηκας·	[★ ἔθηκας	αὐτόν,]	κἀγὼ
pou	*auton*	*ethēkas*	*ethēkas*	*auton*	*kagō*
where	him	did you lay,	[did you lay	him,]	and I

ers. Their question was meant to help Mary realize there was more hope than she suspected. Her answer was a normal reaction under the circumstances. She wanted to know where her Lord had been taken. She thought of what others had done to Jesus, not what Jesus had done for others. It had not yet entered her mind that by His own power He had risen from the dead.

Did Mary recognize these two personages as angels? The text does not indicate she did. Later, she did not recognize Jesus at first, but thought He was the gardener. Mary's grief clouded her sense of reality and kept her from realizing the identities of God's messengers and God's Son. Grief as an emotion can often alter our perception of reality. It magnifies the past, distorts the present, and hides the future. The sorrowing person, often absorbed and almost submerged in grief, is preoccupied with thoughts of and duties toward the departed one.

20:14. Mary did not wait for the angels' answer. No hint is given as to why Mary "turned." Did she feel someone's presence behind her? Perhaps she heard a slight sound. The fact is stated, not the reason for it. Mark 16:9 also records this first appearance of Jesus to Mary Magdalene. Mary "saw" Jesus, but she failed to recognize Him. "Standing" is a perfect active verb meaning He had been standing there for some time. We can only guess how compassionately our Lord stood there sympathizing with His weeping disciple. The last sight Mary had of Jesus' mangled, bloody, matted body contrasted sharply with the form of the man she saw before her. Her eyes were blurred by tears, her mind was filled with fear; therefore it is not strange that in seeking the dead she did not see the living.

20:15. Mary did not recognize the sound of Jesus' voice nor His appearance. She did not comprehend that this One before her was Jesus. All she could think of was her concern for the body of the One who had died the most brutal death a man ever suffered?

Gardeners did attend their work in the orchards early in the morning. If this man was the gardener, he would likely know of the activities which took place at the garden tomb before she arrived.

Mary asked the supposed gardener where he had taken Jesus' body. Her only concern was for the suffering, dead, and buried Christ. In her devotion to Him she overlooked her weakness and lamented, "I will take him away." She did not consider the impossibility of this task; somehow she would move His dear corpse to an honorable tomb.

. . . Why are you crying? *Phillips* . . . Why are you sobbing? *TCNT* . . . why do you mourn? *Klingensmith.*

She saith unto them, Because they have taken away my Lord, and I know not where they have laid him: . . . she replied, *JB* . . . my master, *Moffatt* . . . and I have no knowledge where, *BB* . . . have placed Him, *Berkeley.*

14. And when she had thus said, she turned herself back: . . . she turned around, *Norlie* . . . And then looking round, *BB.*

and saw Jesus standing, and knew not that it was Jesus: . . . and noticed Jesus, *ET* . . . and saw Jesus standing there, *Montgomery* . . . but had no idea that it was Jesus, *BB* . . . but did not recognize Him, *Weymouth* . . . but didn't realize that it, *Adams* . . . without realizing that it was, *Phillips.*

15. Jesus saith unto her, Woman, why weepest thou? whom seekest thou?: . . . why are you crying? *NIV* . . . For whom are you looking? *Norlie* . . . Who is it you are looking for? *NEB.*

She supposing him to be the gardener, saith unto him:

Sir, if thou have borne him hence: Mister, if you, *SEB* . . . Sir, if you have carried him off, *Berkeley* . . . if you have removed him, *Torrey* . . . taken Him away from here, *Norlie* . . . if you have conveyed him hence, *Campbell.*

tell me where thou hast laid him, and I will take him away: I will remove him, *Weymouth* . . . and I will get him, *NIV.*

John 20:16

16.a.**Txt:** 01ℵ,02A,017K, 032W,036,037,1,13,etc. byz.Gries,Weis,Sod
Var: 03B,05D,019L,038, Lach,Treg,Alf,Tisc, We/Ho,UBS/☆

840.6 prs-pron acc sing masc αὐτὸν *auton* him	**142.20** verb 1sing indic fut act ἀρῶ. *arō* will take away.	**2978.5** verb 3sing indic pres act **16.** Λέγει *Legei* Says	**840.11** prs-pron dat sing fem αὐτῇ *autē* to her	**3450.5** art sing masc ⸀a ὁ ⸌ *ho*

2400.1 name nom masc Ἰησοῦς, *Iēsous* Jesus,	**3109.1** name nom fem ⸀☆ Μαρία. *Maria* Mary.	**3110.1** name fem [Μαριάμ.] *Mariam* [idem]	**4613.10** verb nom sing fem part aor pass Στραφεῖσα *Strapheisa* Having turned around

16.b.**Var:** 01ℵ,03B,05D, 019L,033X,037,(038), 33,sa.bo.LachTreg,Alf, Tisc,We/Ho,Weis,Sod, UBS/☆

1552.9 dem-pron nom sing fem ἐκείνη *ekeinē* that	**2978.5** verb 3sing indic pres act λέγει *legei* says	**840.4** prs- pron dat sing αὐτῷ *autō* to him,	**1440.1** name-adv [b☆+ Ἑβραϊστί,] *Hebraisti* [in Hebrew,]

4319.3 noun voc sing masc Ῥαββουνί· *Rhabbouni* Rabboni,	**3614.16** rel- pron sing neu ὃ *ho* that	**2978.28** verb 3sing indic pres pass λέγεται, *legetai* is to say,	**1314.3** noun voc sing masc Διδάσκαλε. *Didaskale* Teacher.	**2978.5** verb 3sing indic pres act **17.** λέγει *legei* Says

17.a.**Txt:** 01ℵ,02A,017K, 021M-corr,032W,036, 037,038,1,13,byz.Sod
Var: 03B,05D,019L, 021M-org,044,Lach, Treg,AlfTisc,We/Ho, Weis,UBS/☆

840.11 prs-pron dat sing fem αὐτῇ *autē* to her	**3450.5** art sing masc ⸀a ὁ ⸌ *ho*	**2400.1** name nom masc Ἰησοῦς, *Iēsous* Jesus,	**3231.1** partic Μή *Mē* Not	**1466.2** prs- pron gen 1sing μου *mou* me	**674.6** verb 2sing impr pres mid ἅπτου, *haptou* touch,

3632.1 adv οὔπω *oupō* not yet	**1056.1** conj γὰρ *gar* for	**303.21** verb 1sing indic perf act ἀναβέβηκα *anabebēka* have I ascended	**4242.1** prep πρὸς *pros* to	**3450.6** art acc sing masc τὸν *ton* the	**3824.4** noun acc sing masc πατέρα *patera* Father

17.b.**Txt:** p66,02A,017K, 019L,033X,036,037,038, 1,13,565,700,byz.it.sa. bo.Gries,Lach
Var: 01ℵ,03B,05D, 032W,Treg,Alf,Tisc, We/Ho,WeisSod,UBS/☆

1466.2 prs- pron gen 1sing ⸀b μου· ⸌ *mou* my;	**4057.4** verb 2sing impr pres πορεύου *poreuou* go	**1156.2** conj δὲ *de* but	**4242.1** prep πρὸς *pros* to	**3450.8** art acc pl masc τοὺς *tous* the	**79.9** noun acc pl masc ἀδελφούς *adelphous* brothers

1466.2 prs- pron gen 1sing μου, *mou* my,	**2504.1** conj καὶ *kai* and	**1500.12** verb 2sing impr aor act εἰπὲ *eipe* say	**840.2** prs- pron dat pl αὐτοῖς, *autois* to them,	**303.1** verb 1sing indic pres act Ἀναβαίνω *Anabainō* I ascend	**4242.1** prep πρὸς *pros* to

3450.6 art acc sing masc τὸν *ton* the	**3824.4** noun acc sing masc πατέρα *patera* Father	**1466.2** prs- pron gen 1sing μου *mou* my	**2504.1** conj καὶ *kai* and	**3824.4** noun acc sing masc πατέρα *patera* Father	**5050.2** prs- pron gen 2pl ὑμῶν *humōn* your,	**2504.1** conj καὶ *kai* and

2296.4 noun acc sing masc θεόν *theon* God	**1466.2** prs- pron gen 1sing μου *mou* my	**2504.1** conj καὶ *kai* and	**2296.4** noun acc sing masc θεὸν *theon* God	**5050.2** prs- pron gen 2pl ὑμῶν. *humōn* your.	**2048.34** verb 3sing indic pres **18.** Ἔρχεται *Erchetai* Comes

3109.1 name nom fem ⸀☆ Μαρία *Maria* Mary	**3110.1** name fem [Μαριὰμ] *Mariam* [idem]	**3450.9** art nom sing fem ἡ *hē* the	**3066.1** name nom fem Μαγδαληνὴ *Magdalēnē* Magdalene

20:16. "Mary." This was the awakening word. Her weeping, sorrows, and fears fled when He spoke her name. She knew then He was alive. No matter how impossible, He was alive! When He spoke her name, He brought to her the assurance of His love, care, and understanding. When Jesus uttered the general title, "Woman," she had felt no personal message; but when He called her name, "Mary," she knew joy beyond believing.

The impact Jesus' presence made on Mary is best noted in her first outburst of devotion. She called Him by the title that meant most to her. *Rhabboni* occurs only here and in Mark 10:51 where it is translated "Lord." "Rabboni" is from the word *rabbi.* Jesus had delivered Mary from seven demons, but she did not call Him "healer." To her the fact that He had taught her the way of life was most important. He was her teacher and she was His disciple. To each disciple Jesus is so intimately personal that all others seem excluded from the relationship.

16. Jesus saith unto her, Mary. She turned herself, and saith unto him, Rabboni: She turned round, and exclaimed in Hebrew, *TCNT* . . . Turning completely round, *Berkeley.*

which is to say, Master: . . . which is interpreted, *Murdock* . . . My teacher! *SEB.*

20:17. The present imperative verb "touch" used with the Greek negative *mē* means "stop doing what you are doing." The thought is "stop clinging." Mary's desire was that she would never allow Him to leave her. Jesus prohibited this for the same reason He told the apostles it was expedient for them that He return to the Father (16:7). When He returned to the Father He would send the other Helper. If Mary's wish had been granted for all the disciples, the outpouring of the Spirit would not have happened.

Mary was sent as the first evangelist of the resurrected Christ. The disciples surely felt that by forsaking Him they had forfeited their association with Him. But Mary brought them the comforting assurances of His continued love and fellowship. She was sent to His disciples with a message of comfort.

"My Father" is His eternal relationship with the One whose commission He has carried out. "Your Father" is the disciples' relationship with His Father by virtue of His redemptive work.

"My God" refers to Jesus' relation to God in His humanity. It was in His manhood as well as in His deity that He restored the loss which came through Adam's sin. "Your God" implies they had need of a mediator that God might become their Father.

17. Jesus saith unto her, Touch me not: Be not detaining me, *Rotherham* . . . Do not hold me, *TCNT* . . . Do not cling to Me, *Berkeley* . . . Cease clinging to me, *Moffatt, Montgomery* . . . Stop clinging, *Wuest* . . . No! said Jesus, do not hold me now, *Phillips* . . . Do not hold on to me, *TEV* . . . Don't hold onto Me, *Adams* . . . Do not put your hand on me, *BB.*

for I am not yet ascended to my Father: . . . for I have not gone up, *BB* . . . but before I ascend, *Torrey* . . . I have not yet returned, *NIV* . . . I didn't go up to the Father yet, *Beck.*

but go to my brethren, and say unto them, I ascend unto my Father, and your Father; and to my God, and your God: . . . to my Brothers, and tell them, *TCNT.*

20:18. It was a dramatic moment as Mary reported to the disciples what had happened. The first words were that "she had seen the Lord." Mark 16:10,11 says Mary reported to the disciples "as they mourned and wept." Mark adds that the disciples did not believe Mary.

18. Mary Magdalene came and told the disciples that she had seen the Lord: Away went Mary Magdalene to the disciples with the tidings, *Montgomery* . . . goes,

18.a.**Txt:** p66-corr, 01ℵ-corr,05D,017K, 019L,036,038,1,13,byz. **Var:** p66-org,01ℵ-org, 02A,03B,033X,Lach, Treg,Alf,Tisc,We/Ho Weis,Sod,UBS/⋆

18.b.**Txt:** 02A,05D,019L, 038,1,13,byz.it.Lach, Weis,Sod **Var:** p66,01ℵ,03B,022N, 032W,033X,sa.bo.Treg, Alf,Tisc,We/Ho,UBS/⋆

514.6 verb nom sing fem part pres act	**31.1** verb nom sing fem part pres act	**3450.4** art dat pl	**3073.7** noun dat pl masc
⸀ ἀπαγγέλλουσα	[a⋆ ἀγγέλλουσα]	τοῖς	μαθηταῖς
apangellousa	*angellousa*	*tois*	*mathētais*
bringing word	[idem]	to the	disciples

3617.1 conj	**3571.11** verb 3sing indic perf act	**3571.9** verb 1sing indic perf act	**3450.6** art acc sing masc	**2935.4** noun acc sing masc	**2504.1** conj
ὅτι	⸀ ἑώρακεν	[b⋆ Ἑώρακα]	τὸν	κύριον,	καὶ
hoti	*heōraken*	*Heōraka*	*ton*	*kurion*	*kai*
	she has seen	[I have seen]	the	Lord,	and

3642.18 dem-pron pl neu	**1500.5** verb 3sing indic aor act	**840.11** prs-pron dat sing fem	**1498.27** verb gen sing fem part pres act	**3631.1** conj
ταῦτα	εἶπεν	αὐτῇ.	**19.** Οὔσης	οὖν
tauta	*eipen*	*autē*	*Ousēs*	*oun*
these things	he said	to her.	It being	therefore

3662.2 adj gen sing fem	**3450.11** art dat sing fem	**2232.3** noun dat sing fem	**1552.11** dem-pron dat sing fem	**3450.11** art dat sing fem	**1518.7** num card dat fem
ὀψίας	τῇ	ἡμέρᾳ	ἐκείνῃ,	τῇ	μιᾷ
opsias	*tē*	*hēmera*	*ekeinē*	*tē*	*mia*
evening	on the	day	that,	the	first

19.a.**Txt:** 05D,017K,036, 037,038,1,13,byz. **Var:** p66,01ℵ,02A,03B, 019L,032W,33,Lach, Treg,Alf,Tisc,We/Ho, Weis,Sod,UBS/⋆

19.b.**Txt:** 07E,017K, 019L,033X,036,037,038, 1,13,byz.sa.bo.Sod **Var:** 01ℵ,02A,03B,05D, Lach,Treg,Alf,Tisc, We/Ho,Weis,UBS/⋆

3450.1 art gen pl	**4378.4** noun gen pl neu	**2504.1** conj	**3450.1** art gen pl	**2351.6** noun gen pl fem	**2781.11** verb gen pl fem part perf pass
⸂a τῶν ⸃	σαββάτων,	καὶ	τῶν	θυρῶν	κεκλεισμένων
tōn	*sabbatōn*	*kai*	*tōn*	*thurōn*	*kekleismenōn*
of the	week,	and	the	doors	having been shut

3562.1 adv	**1498.37** verb 3pl indic imperf act	**3450.7** art pl masc	**3073.5** noun nom pl masc	**4714.24** verb nom pl masc part perf pass
ὅπου	ἦσαν	οἱ	μαθηταὶ	⸂b συνηγμένοι, ⸃
hopou	*ēsan*	*hoi*	*mathētai*	*sunēgmenoi*
where	were	the	disciples	having been assembled,

1217.2 prep	**3450.6** art acc sing masc	**5238.4** noun acc sing masc	**3450.1** art gen pl	**2428.3** name-adj gen pl masc	**2048.3** verb 3sing indic aor act
διὰ	τὸν	φόβον	τῶν	Ἰουδαίων,	ἦλθεν
dia	*ton*	*phobon*	*tōn*	*Ioudaiōn*	*ēlthen*
through	the	fear	of the	Jews,	came

3450.5 art sing masc	**2400.1** name nom masc	**2504.1** conj	**2449.3** verb 3sing indic aor act	**1519.1** prep	**3450.16** art sing neu	**3189.5** adj acc sing neu
ὁ	Ἰησοῦς	καὶ	ἔστη	εἰς	τὸ	μέσον,
ho	*Iēsous*	*kai*	*estē*	*eis*	*to*	*meson*
	Jesus	and	stood	in	the	midst,

2504.1 conj	**2978.5** verb 3sing indic pres act	**840.2** prs-pron dat pl	**1503.1** noun nom sing fem	**5050.3** prs-pron dat 2pl	**2504.1** conj
καὶ	λέγει	αὐτοῖς,	Εἰρήνη	ὑμῖν.	**20.** Καὶ
kai	*legei*	*autois*	*Eirēnē*	*humin*	*Kai*
and	says	to them,	Peace	to you.	And

3642.17 dem-pron sing neu	**1500.15** verb nom sing masc part aor act	**1161.8** verb 3sing indic aor act	**840.2** prs-pron dat pl	**3450.15** art acc pl fem
τοῦτο	εἰπὼν	ἔδειξεν	⸀ αὐτοῖς	τὰς
touto	*eipōn*	*edeixen*	*autois*	*tas*
this	having said	he showed	to them	the

20.a.**Txt:** 017K,019L, 033X,036,037,038,13, byz. **Var:** (01),02A,03B,(05), Lach,Treg,Alf,We/Ho, Weis,UBS/⋆

5331.8 noun acc pl fem	**2504.1** conj	**3450.12** art acc sing fem	**3985.1** noun acc sing fem	**840.3** prs-pron gen sing	**3450.15** art acc pl fem
χεῖρας	καὶ	τὴν	πλευρὰν	αὐτοῦ.	[a⋆ τὰς
cheiras	*kai*	*tēn*	*pleuran*	*autou*	*tas*
hands	and	the	side	of himself.	[the

After the first appearance of Jesus, He appeared the second time to the other women in Jerusalem as reported by Matthew 28:9,10. Third, the Lord walked with two disciples traveling to Emmaus as reported in Mark 16:12-23 and Luke 24:13-32. Fourth, Jesus appeared to Simon, recorded in Luke 24:34 and 1 Corinthians 15:5.

20:19. This passage is our Lord's fifth appearance; it is also reported in Mark 16:4 and Luke 24:36-43. It is the Gospel of John's second recorded appearance of Jesus. John states that the disciples were present except Thomas (verse 24). This means that the Ten were there.

John's Gospel does not attempt to elaborate on all the appearances of Jesus. It gives only four but adds details that were not expressed by the other evangelists. It was early evening of that first day, and He had appeared four times before this. It was His first appearance to the apostles as a group. "When the doors were shut" shows that Jesus entered the house in some miraculous way (see also verse 26).

Perhaps the place was the Upper Room in which He had eaten the Last Supper with them. If so, it is interesting that upon departing the Upper Room He had desired His peace to be theirs (16:33). When He returned after the Resurrection, His bestowal to them was, "Peace be unto you." His disciples had deserted Him in His hour of trial, yet now He spoke comforting words of peace. It is not easy to understand what Jesus meant by "peace." It is like trying to enclose the moon in one's arms. Peace is all that Jesus is, and what He is He gives to us! In His redemptive work He brought perfect harmony between the sinner and the holy God. The guilty sinner stands acquitted before the bar of justice because of Jesus' merits. Not only that, but all the holiness of Christ is imputed to the forgiven sinner. There is even more, for fellowship with the Father is a part of the peace bestowed by Jesus. "Peace" speaks of the continual, harmonious relationship with the Father and the Son purchased for the believer by Jesus our Lord.

20:20. As Luke 24:38,39 also points out, Jesus calmed the fearful and doubting hearts of His disciples by showing them His hands and feet. The wounds were completely healed, but the scars remained to demonstrate the reality of His resurrection.

Jesus' resurrection body possessed certain characteristics. First, He consumed food as a living, physical, mortal body. Second, He was able to transport himself behind locked doors into the presence of His disciples (20:19). Third, His wounds were visible and material, for they could be touched (John 20:20; Luke 24:39). Fourth,

announcing to the disciples, *Wuest* . . . and informed the, *Campbell* . . . reporting to the disciples, *Fenton, Concordant* . . . bringing the disciples news...that she, *AmpB* . . . went to the disciples with the news, *NIV* . . . reported to the disciples, *ET.*

and that he had spoken these things unto her: . . . and that He said this to her, *Beck.*

19. Then the same day at evening, being the first day of the week: That Sunday evening, *Beck* . . . When it was late that same day, *Confraternity.*

when the doors were shut where the disciples were assembled for fear of the Jews: . . . when the assembled disciples had, *ALBA* . . . the doors having been shut and at that time tightly closed, *Wuest* . . . the doors were locked where the disciples were, *Beck* . . . having been locked, *Concordant* . . . within closed doors, *Moffatt* . . . the doors of the room bolted, *Williams* . . . were convened, *Campbell* . . . were gathered, *Norlie* . . . the disciples were gathered, *TEV* . . . owing to dread of the Judeans, *Fenton.*

came Jesus and stood in the midst: Jesus came among them, *BB* . . . and stood in the middle of them, *SEB.*

and saith unto them, Peace be unto you: . . . and gave them his blessing, *TCNT* . . . God's blessing be on you! *Barclay.*

20. And when he had so said, he shewed unto them his hands and his side: Having said this, *Murdock* . . . he let them see his hands, *BB.*

5331.8 noun acc pl fem	2504.1 conj	3450.12 art acc sing fem	3985.1 noun acc sing fem	840.2 prs-pron dat pl	5299.19 verb 3pl indic aor pass
χεῖρας	καὶ	τὴν	πλευρὰν	αὐτοῖς.]	ἐχάρησαν
cheiras	*kai*	*tēn*	*pleuran*	*autois*	*echarēsan*
hands	and	the	side	to them.]	Rejoiced

3631.1 conj	3450.7 art pl masc	3073.5 noun nom pl masc	1481.17 verb nom pl masc part aor act	3450.6 art acc sing masc	2935.4 noun acc sing masc
οὖν	οἱ	μαθηταὶ	ἰδόντες	τὸν	κύριον.
oun	*hoi*	*mathētai*	*idontes*	*ton*	*kurion*
therefore	the	disciples	having seen	the	Lord.

21.a.**Txt:** 02A,03B,017K,036,037,038,byz.Gries,Lach,We/HoWeis,UBS/☆
Var: 01ℵ,05D,019L,032W,033X,sa.bo.Treg Tisc,Sod

1500.5 verb 3sing indic aor act	3631.1 conj	840.2 prs-pron dat pl	3450.5 art sing masc	2400.1 name nom masc	3687.1 adv
21. εἶπεν	οὖν	αὐτοῖς	⸂a ὁ	Ἰησοῦς ⸃	πάλιν,
eipen	*oun*	*autois*	*ho*	*Iēsous*	*palin*
Said	therefore	to them		Jesus	again,

1503.1 noun nom sing fem	5050.3 prs-pron dat 2pl	2503.1 conj	643.17 verb 3sing indic perf act	1466.6 prs-pron acc 1sing	3450.5 art sing masc
Εἰρήνη	ὑμῖν·	καθὼς	ἀπέσταλκέν	με	ὁ
Eirēnē	*humin*	*kathōs*	*apestalken*	*me*	*ho*
Peace	to you:	as	has sent forth	me	the

3824.1 noun nom sing masc	2476.3 conj	3854.1 verb 1sing indic pres act	5050.4 prs-pron acc 2pl	2504.1 conj	3642.17 dem-pron sing neu
πατήρ,	κἀγὼ	πέμπω	ὑμᾶς.	22. Καὶ	τοῦτο
patēr	*kagō*	*pempō*	*humas*	*Kai*	*touto*
Father,	I also	send	you.	And	this

1500.15 verb nom sing masc part aor act	1704.1 verb 3sing indic aor act	2504.1 conj	2978.5 verb 3sing indic pres act	840.2 prs-pron dat pl
εἰπὼν	ἐνεφύσησεν	καὶ	λέγει	αὐτοῖς,
eipōn	*enephusēsen*	*kai*	*legei*	*autois*
having said	he breathed into,	and	says	to them,

2956.24 verb 2pl impr aor act	4011.1 noun sing neu	39.1 adj sing	300.1 partic	4948.4 indef-pron gen pl	856.16 verb 2pl subj aor act
Λάβετε	πνεῦμα	ἅγιον.	23. ἄν	τινων	ἀφῆτε
Labete	*pneuma*	*hagion*	*an*	*tinōn*	*aphēte*
Receive	Spirit	Holy:		of whomever	you may remit

23.a.**Txt:** 03B-corr,017K,032W,036,037,038,byz.bo.
Var: 01ℵ-corr,02A,05D,019L,033X,1,13,Lach Treg,Alf,Tisc,We/Ho,Sod,UBS/☆

3450.15 art acc pl fem	264.1 noun fem	856.26 verb 3pl indic pres pass	856.29 verb 3pl indic perf pass
τὰς	ἁμαρτίας,	⸀ ἀφίενται	[a☆ ἀφέωνται]
tas	*hamartias*	*aphientai*	*apheōntai*
the	sins,	they are remitted	[they have been forgiven]

840.2 prs-pron dat pl	300.1 partic	4948.4 indef-pron gen pl	2875.5 verb 2pl subj pres act	2875.24 verb 3pl indic perf pass
αὐτοῖς·	ἄν	τινων	κρατῆτε,	κεκράτηνται.
autois	*an*	*tinōn*	*kratēte*	*kekratēntai*
to them;		of whomever	you may retain,	they have been retained.

2358.1 name nom masc	1156.2 conj	1518.3 num card nom masc	1523.2 prep gen	3450.1 art gen pl	1420.1 num card
24. Θωμᾶς	δὲ,	εἷς	ἐκ	τῶν	δώδεκα
Thōmas	*de*	*heis*	*ek*	*tōn*	*dōdeka*
Thomas	but,	one	of	the	twelve

3450.5 art sing masc	2978.30 verb nom sing masc part pres pass	1318.1 name nom masc	3620.2 partic	1498.34 verb sing indic imperf act	3196.2 prep
ὁ	λεγόμενος	Δίδυμος,	οὐκ	ἦν	μετ'
ho	*legomenos*	*Didumos*	*ouk*	*ēn*	*met'*
the	being called	Didymus,	not	was	with

His body consisted of flesh and bone, though it was no longer subject to decay and humiliation.

Then were the disciples glad, when they saw the Lord: Then the disciples rejoiced, *HBIE, Murdock* . . . were filled with joy at seeing the Lord, *Weymouth* . . . were thrilled with joy over seeing their Lord, *Williams* . . . were accordingly delighted, *Fenton* . . . the Master, *Norton.*

20:21. Jesus did not censure the disciples for their past failures. Instead, He repeated His salutation of peace. No possession is as meaningful to the believer as the assurance that all is well with his soul. Jesus' "Peace" is more than a greeting; it is a bestowment of all that the word means.

Jesus' earthly mission was finished, but His heavenly work would continue. He remains the Head of the Church. He directs the functions of His Body and the activities of each member in particular. In chapter 17 Jesus said He was sending His disciples into the world with the same revelation He himself bore to the world. It is the believer's commission to be His witness (Acts 1:8). He now restates it, emphasizing the shared source and driving force of their mission.

21. Then said Jesus to them again, Peace be unto you: As the Father has sent me as his Messenger, *TCNT.*

as my Father hath sent me, even so send I you: . . . sent me forth, *HistNT* . . . so in the same way, *Fenton* . . . I am sending you forth, *Moffatt.*

20:22. The act of breathing is the act of living. By breathing or blowing, Jesus assured His disciples that He is a living being as surely as He did by eating before them (see verse 20 and Luke 24:42,43). He was preparing them for the outpouring of the Spirit on the Day of Pentecost.

While He breathed on them, He said, "Receive ye the Holy Ghost." What did this mean? It is clear that some sort of an experience took place. The word "receive" is an imperative verb, a command. They were to accept the gift of the Spirit. Surely some spiritual benefit occurred at that time. Some scholars believe this was a conversion experience, an actual reception of the Holy Spirit.

22. And when he had said this, he breathed on them: . . . he breathed strongly, *Rotherham* . . . He exhales, *Concordant* . . . He infused Himself into them, *Fenton.*

and saith unto them, Receive ye the Holy Ghost: Receive at once, *Wuest* . . . Receive ye the Holy Spirit, *ASV* . . . Get holy spirit! *Concordant* . . . Let the Holy Spirit come on you, *BB* . . . Take ye the Hooly Gost, *Wycliffe.*

20:23. Some commentators have given this statement an extreme interpretation. The prerogative of forgiving sins belongs only to God. Jesus had just commissioned His apostles. Their message was to be the same He had proclaimed. Those who heard had a choice, to accept or reject the message. The apostles could assure those who accepted that their sins had been forgiven, and those who rejected that they were still guilty.

23. Whose soever sins ye remit, they are remitted unto them: If you forgive any men's sins, they are forgiven, *Phillips* . . . If you expel sins from any, they will be free, *Fenton* . . . Any to whom you give forgiveness, will be made free from their sins, *BB* . . . forgyue, thei ben forgouun, *Wycliffe* . . . they have been previously forgiven them, *Wuest.*

and whose soever sins ye retain, they are retained: If you bind fast the sins for any, they remain bound, *Weymouth* . . . if you let people's sins fasten upon them, they will remain fastened upon them, *Williams* . . . If you subdue them, they shall be subdued, *Fenton.*

20:24. Thomas Didymus ("Twin") is an interesting character. Earlier (11:16), he showed that he loved his Master enough to be

24. But Thomas, one of the twelve, called Didymus, was not

24.a.**Txt:** 02A,017K,019L,032W,033X,036,037,038,1,13,etc.byz.Sod **Var:** p5,01א,03B,05D,Lach,Treg,Alf,Tisc,We/Ho,Weis,UBS/☆

840.1 prs-pron gen pl	**3616.1** conj	**2048.3** verb 3sing indic aor act	**3450.5** art sing masc	**2400.1** name nom masc	**2978.25** verb indic imperf act
αὐτῶν	ὅτε	ἦλθεν	⸂a ὁ ⸃	Ἰησοῦς.	**25.** ἔλεγον
autōn	*hote*	*ēlthen*	*ho*	*Iēsous*	*elegon*
them	when	came		Jesus.	Said

3631.1 conj	**840.4** prs-pron dat sing	**3450.7** art pl masc	**241.6** adj nom pl masc	**3073.5** noun nom pl masc	**3571.12** verb 1pl indic perf act
οὖν	αὐτῷ	οἱ	ἄλλοι	μαθηταί,	Ἑωράκαμεν
oun	*autō*	*hoi*	*alloi*	*mathētai*	*Heōrakamen*
therefore	to him	the	other	disciples,	We have seen

3450.6 art acc sing masc	**2935.4** noun acc sing masc	**3450.5** art sing masc	**1156.2** conj	**1500.5** verb 3sing indic aor act	**840.2** prs-pron dat pl
τὸν	κύριον.	Ὁ	δὲ	εἶπεν	αὐτοῖς,
ton	*kurion*	*Ho*	*de*	*eipen*	*autois*
the	Lord.	The	but	said	to them,

1430.1 partic	**3231.1** partic	**1481.8** verb 1sing subj aor act	**1706.1** prep	**3450.14** art dat pl fem	**5331.7** noun dat pl fem	**840.3** prs-pron gen sing
Ἐὰν	μὴ	ἴδω	ἐν	ταῖς	χερσὶν	αὐτοῦ
Ean	*mē*	*idō*	*en*	*tais*	*chersin*	*autou*
If	not	I see	in	the	hands	his

3450.6 art acc sing masc	**5020.2** noun acc sing masc	**3450.1** art gen pl	**2230.1** noun gen pl masc	**2504.1** conj	**900.12** verb 1sing subj aor act
τὸν	τύπον	τῶν	ἥλων,	καὶ	βάλω
ton	*tupon*	*tōn*	*hēlōn*	*kai*	*balō*
the	mark	of the	nails,	and	put

3450.6 art acc sing masc	**1142.3** noun acc sing masc	**1466.2** prs-pron gen 1sing	**1519.1** prep	**3450.6** art acc sing masc	**5020.2** noun acc sing masc
τὸν	δάκτυλόν	μου	εἰς	τὸν	⸂☆ τύπον
ton	*daktulon*	*mou*	*eis*	*ton*	*tupon*
the	finger	my	into	the	mark

25.a.**Txt:** 01א-corr,03B,05D,017K,019L,033X,036,037,etc.byz.We/Ho **Var:** 02A,038,Lach,Tisc Weis,UBS/☆

4964.4 noun acc sing masc	**3450.1** art gen pl	**2230.1** noun gen pl masc	**2504.1** conj	**900.12** verb 1sing subj aor act	**3450.12** art acc sing fem
[a τόπον]	τῶν	ἥλων,	καὶ	βάλω	⸂ τὴν
topon	*tōn*	*hēlōn*	*kai*	*balō*	*tēn*
[place]	of the	nails,	and	put	the

5331.4 noun acc sing fem	**1466.2** prs-pron gen 1sing	**1466.2** prs-pron gen 1sing	**3450.12** art acc sing fem	**5331.4** noun acc sing fem	**1519.1** prep
χεῖρα	μου	[☆ μου	τὴν	χεῖρα]	εἰς
cheira	*mou*	*mou*	*tēn*	*cheira*	*eis*
hand	my	[my	the	hand]	into

3450.12 art acc sing fem	**3985.1** noun acc sing fem	**840.3** prs-pron gen sing	**3620.3** partic	**3231.1** partic	**3961.17** verb 1sing act
τὴν	πλευρὰν	αὐτοῦ,	οὐ	μὴ	πιστεύσω.
tēn	*pleuran*	*autou*	*ou*	*mē*	*pisteusō*
the	side	his,	not	not	will I believe.

2504.1 conj	**3196.1** prep	**2232.1** noun fem	**3501.1** num card	**3687.1** adv	**1498.37** verb 3pl indic imperf act	**2059.1** prep gen
26. Καὶ	μεθ'	ἡμέρας	ὀκτὼ	πάλιν	ἦσαν	ἔσω
Kai	*meth'*	*hēmeras*	*oktō*	*palin*	*ēsan*	*esō*
And	after	days	eight	again	were	within

3450.7 art pl masc	**3073.5** noun nom pl masc	**840.3** prs-pron gen sing	**2504.1** conj	**2358.1** name nom masc	**3196.2** prep	**840.1** prs-pron gen pl
οἱ	μαθηταὶ	αὐτοῦ,	καὶ	Θωμᾶς	μετ'	αὐτῶν.
hoi	*mathētai*	*autou*	*kai*	*Thōmas*	*met'*	*autōn*
the	disciples	his,	and	Thomas	with	them.

willing to die for Him—which he did later. For some reason, unmentioned, he was not present when the resurrected Lord first appeared to the disciples.

with them when Jesus came: . . . called the twin, *Fenton, Murdock* . . . was about when Jesus, *ET.*

20:25. Thomas was naturally skeptical (see 11:16; 14:5). But then the other disciples also needed visual proof before they would believe (20:20). Merrill Tenney comments: "In spite of the repeated assurances of his colleagues that Jesus had risen (*elegon,* 'they kept saying,' is the imperfect tense of repeated action), Thomas was obstinate. He was so certain of the death of Jesus that he would not credit the report of his reappearance and insisted that he would not believe unless he could actually touch Jesus' body. Thomas would be satisfied by nothing less than material evidence. His incredulity is testimony to the fact that the resurrection appearances were not illusions induced by wishful thinking" (Tenney, *Expositor's Bible Commentary,* 9:195).

R.V.G. Tasker suggests adopting the variant reading for the second "print" (*tupon*). The text on the left shows this variant as *topon* ("place"). Tasker says: "Thomas wants not only to see the scar made by the nails in the hands, but also to put his finger into the place where the nails had been. *Thrust* is too strong a translation, as the word it translates (*ballō*) was often used at this time with a weaker significance; hence RV 'put' " (Tasker, *Tyndale New Testament Commentaries,* 4:226,227).

25. The other disciples therefore said unto him, We have seen the Lord: Accordingly the other disciples, *Montgomery* . . . kept telling him, *AmpB* . . . the Master, *Campbell.*

But he said unto them, Except I shall see in his hands the prints of the nails: Unless I see his hands with the mark of the nails, *Moffatt* . . . I see in His hands the imprint, *NASB* . . . the very scars of the nails, *ET* . . . the impression, *Fenton.*

and put my finger into the print of the nails: . . . and press my finger into the print, *Rotherham* . . . and put my finger into the wound, *Weymouth* . . . into the nail-holes, *Fenton.*

and thrust my hand into his side: . . . and press my hand into his side, *Rotherham.*

I will not believe: I refuse to believe it, *Moffatt* . . . I will not at all believe, *Berkeley* . . . I will never believe it, *SEB* . . . I will never have belief, *BB* . . . I will positively not believe, *Wuest* . . . I refuse to believe, *JB.*

20:26. By Jewish calculation (the first and last days being counted), this would be the following Lord's Day, meaning Sunday following the Resurrection Sunday. The first day of the week became the day for the disciples to gather in the Lord's name, and He blessed them by His presence. On the Resurrection Sunday and the next Sunday they gathered together.

"Came" (Greek, *erchetai*) is a present tense verb literally rendered "comes." It is a vivid action verb. The doors were "shut" meaning they had been locked (as in verse 19). How interesting that the Resurrection had made little impact on the Jews and the disciples after a week. The Jewish leaders were filled with wrath, and the disciples met behind locked doors because of the Jews. Where had Jesus been during that week? He had not appeared to the disciples. It is unwise to guess. The place for Jesus seems always to be "in the midst." "Midst" (Greek, *mesos*) means "in the middle of" or "midst of." He went through the "midst" of His enemies (8:59). He was on the middle cross. He is in "the midst" of the seven lampstands (Revelation 1:13). He comes "in the midst" of His disciples (20:19,26). He is in "the midst" of the elders (Revelation 5:6). He is in "the midst" of the throne of God (Revelation 7:17).

26. And after eight days again his disciples were within, and Thomas with them: A week later, *Berkeley, Montgomery* . . . were again indoors, *Norlie* . . . were again in the house, *Montgomery.*

2048.34 verb 3sing indic pres	**3450.5** art sing masc	**2400.1** name nom masc	**3450.1** art gen pl	**2351.6** noun gen pl fem	**2781.11** verb gen pl fem part perf pass
ἔρχεται	ὁ	Ἰησοῦς,	τῶν	θυρῶν	κεκλεισμένων,
erchetai	*ho*	*Iēsous*	*tōn*	*thurōn*	*kekleismenōn*
Comes		Jesus,	the	doors	having been shut,

2504.1 conj	**2449.3** verb 3sing indic aor act	**1519.1** prep	**3450.16** art sing neu	**3189.5** adj acc sing neu	**2504.1** conj	**1500.5** verb 3sing indic aor act
καὶ	ἔστη	εἰς	τὸ	μέσον	καὶ	εἶπεν,
kai	*estē*	*eis*	*to*	*meson*	*kai*	*eipen*
and	stood	in	the	midst	and	said,

1503.1 noun nom sing fem	**5050.3** prs-pron dat 2pl	**1520.1** adv	**2978.5** verb 3sing indic pres act	**3450.3** art dat sing	**2358.3** name dat masc
Εἰρήνη	ὑμῖν.	27. Εἶτα	λέγει	τῷ	Θωμᾷ,
Eirēnē	*humin*	*Eita*	*legei*	*tō*	*Thōma*
Peace	to you.	Then	he says	to	Thomas,

5179.6 verb 2sing impr pres act	**3450.6** art acc sing masc	**1142.3** noun acc sing masc	**4622.2** prs-pron gen 2sing	**5436.1** adv	**2504.1** conj
Φέρε	τὸν	δάκτυλόν	σου	ὧδε,	καὶ
Phere	*ton*	*daktulon*	*sou*	*hōde*	*kai*
Bring	the	finger	your	here,	and

1481.14 verb 2sing impr aor act	**3450.15** art acc pl fem	**5331.8** noun acc pl fem	**1466.2** prs-pron gen 1sing	**2504.1** conj	**5179.6** verb 2sing impr pres act
ἴδε	τὰς	χεῖράς	μου,	καὶ	φέρε
ide	*tas*	*cheiras*	*mou*	*kai*	*phere*
see	the	hands	my;	and	bring

3450.12 art acc sing fem	**5331.4** noun acc sing fem	**4622.2** prs-pron gen 2sing	**2504.1** conj	**900.16** verb 2sing impr aor act	**1519.1** prep	**3450.12** art acc sing fem
τὴν	χεῖρά	σου,	καὶ	βάλε	εἰς	τὴν
tēn	*cheira*	*sou*	*kai*	*bale*	*eis*	*tēn*
the	hand	your,	and	put	into	the

28.a.**Txt:** 02A,04C-corr, 017K,036,037,byz. **Var:** 01ℵ,03B,04C-org, 05D,019L,033X,038,it. sa.Gries,Lach,Treg,Alf, Word,Tisc,We/HoWeis, Sod,UBS/⋆

3985.1 noun acc sing fem	**1466.2** prs-pron gen 1sing	**2504.1** conj	**3231.1** partic	**1090.29** verb 2sing impr pres mid	**566.2** adj sing
πλευράν	μου·	καὶ	μὴ	γίνου	ἄπιστος,
pleuran	*mou*	*kai*	*mē*	*ginou*	*apistos*
side	my;	and	not	be	unbelieving,

28.b.**Txt:** 01ℵ,019L,33, Steph,Sod **Var:** 02A,03B,04C,05D, 017K,036,037,038,byz. Gries,Lach,Treg,AlfTisc, We/Ho,Weis,UBS/⋆

233.2 conj	**3964.2** adj nom sing masc	**2504.1** conj	**552.6** verb 3sing indic aor pass	**3450.5** art sing masc	**2358.1** name nom masc
ἀλλὰ	πιστός.	28. (a Καὶ \	ἀπεκρίθη	(b ὁ \	Θωμᾶς
alla	*pistos*	*Kai*	*apekrithē*	*ho*	*Thōmas*
but	believing.	And	answered		Thomas

2504.1 conj	**1500.5** verb 3sing indic aor act	**840.4** prs-pron dat sing	**3450.5** art sing masc	**2935.1** noun nom sing masc	**1466.2** prs-pron gen 1sing
καὶ	εἶπεν	αὐτῷ,	Ὁ	κύριός	μου
kai	*eipen*	*autō*	*Ho*	*kurios*	*mou*
and	said	to him,	The	Lord	my

2504.1 conj	**3450.5** art sing masc	**2296.1** noun nom sing masc	**1466.2** prs-pron gen 1sing	**2978.5** verb 3sing indic pres act	**840.4** prs-pron dat sing
καὶ	ὁ	θεός	μου.	29. Λέγει	αὐτῷ
kai	*ho*	*theos*	*mou*	*Legei*	*autō*
and	the	God	my.	Says	to him

29.a.**Txt:** Steph **Var:** 01ℵ,02A,03B,04C, 05D,017K,019L,036, 037,038,byz.Gries,Lach Treg,Alf,Tisc,We/Ho, Weis,Sod,UBS/⋆

3450.5 art sing masc	**2400.1** name nom masc	**3617.1** conj	**3571.10** verb 2sing indic perf act	**1466.6** prs-pron acc 1sing	**2358.2** name masc
ὁ	Ἰησοῦς,	Ὅτι	ἑώρακάς	με,	(a Θωμᾶ, \
ho	*Iēsous*	*Hoti*	*heōrakas*	*me*	*Thōma*
	Jesus,	Because	you have seen	me,	Thomas,

His greeting was the same as that stated in verse 19 and restated in verse 21. Jesus is forever the consoling Christ. "Peace" was the usual Jewish form of greeting; yet greetings often lose their significance by much use. Jesus is forever the answer to the prophecy of "Shiloh" (Genesis 49:10), and Micah's prediction of the One who was to be our peace (Micah 5:5), and the apostle Paul's declaration that He himself is our peace (Ephesians 2:14). All the blessings of God are summed up in this great comprehensive word, "peace."

then came Jesus, the doors being shut, and stood in the midst: . . . having been fastened, *Rotherham* . . . Although the doors were locked, *Fenton* . . . and stood there among them, *Montgomery* . . . in the middle, *BB.*

and said, Peace be unto you:

27. Then saith he to Thomas, Reach hither thy finger, and behold my hands: Look at my hands, put your finger here, *Moffatt* . . . Place your finger here, *Montgomery* . . . Bring your finger here, *Weymouth* . . . and examine My hands, *Norlie.*

and reach hither thy hand, and thrust it into my side: . . . and take your hand and put it in My side, *Beck* . . . place your hand here, *Montgomery* . . . bring your hand, *Weymouth.*

and be not faithless, but believing: You must not doubt, but believe, *Phillips* . . . Do not be a doubter, but a believer, *Norlie* . . . cease this unbelief and have faith, *ALBA* . . . You must not doubt, *Phillips* . . . Doubt no longer, *JB* . . . Stop your doubting, and believe! *TEV* . . . Stop doubting and start believing! *SEB* . . . and be not incredulous, *Campbell, Weymouth, Murdock* . . . call a halt to your progressive state of unbelief, *Wuest.*

20:27. Before Thomas could say what he had asserted to his fellows in verse 25, Jesus spoke to relieve his doubts. Jesus did not have to be told what Thomas had said; He knew. We cannot hide our doubts from Jesus. He knows the things we say, and He knows why we say them.

Thomas was invited, as the others were prior to this, to "reach," "reach . . . and thrust." Thomas' finger could feel the recesses of the gaping nail holes, and his hands could examine the gash made by the spear's thrust. Thomas accepted the evidence because he made the examination, though we are not told he actually touched Jesus. He could tell by looking. The Lord had no rebuke for His skeptical apostle. Jesus merely invited an investigation of the evidence. Truth is backed by facts, and facts will hold up in sincere inquiry.

Jesus rebuked Thomas' unbelief. The present imperative verb with the negative Greek word *mē* means "stop being faithless." "But believing" is the opposite of Thomas' faithless condition. The evidence changed Thomas from a faithless disciple to a faithful disciple.

28. And Thomas answered and said unto him, My Lord and my God: My Master, *TCNT.*

20:28. "My Lord" expressed Thomas' new condition, that of believing Jesus to be deity. He did not merely recognize Jesus as the Messiah, but grasped the great truth that Jesus is truly the "Word" of God. Thomas called Jesus his "God." No one in the New Testament has improved upon the great testimony to Jesus which Thomas asserted. To ascribe these two titles to Jesus Christ is the highest essence of worship.

29. Jesus saith unto him, Thomas, because thou hast seen me, thou hast believed: Have you believed because you have seen me? *RSV* . . . You believe because you have seen Me, *Norlie* . . . you have seen me you have found faith, *NEB.*

20:29. Jesus affirmed the evidence of what Thomas had experienced; yet He cautioned him that faith is not merely seeing and feeling, but taking Him at His word.

During the 40 days of Jesus' appearances, He did not seem to manifest himself to all who believed in Him. Some believed the

John 20:30

3961.38 verb 2sing indic perf act	3079.4 adj nom pl masc	3450.7 art pl masc	3231.1 partic	1481.17 verb nom pl masc part aor act
πεπίστευκας·	μακάριοι	οἱ	μὴ	ἰδόντες
pepisteukas	*makarioi*	*hoi*	*mē*	*idontes*
you have believed:	blessed	the	not	having seen

2504.1 conj	3961.31 verb nom pl masc part aor act	4044.17 adj pl neu	3173.1 conj	3631.1 conj	2504.1 conj
καὶ	πιστεύσαντες.	**30.** Πολλὰ	μὲν	οὖν	καὶ
kai	*pisteusantes*	*Polla*	*men*	*oun*	*kai*
and	having believed.	Many		therefore	also

241.15 adj pl neu	4447.2 noun pl neu	4020.24 verb 3sing indic aor act	3450.5 art sing masc	2400.1 name nom masc	1783.1 prep gen
ἄλλα	σημεῖα	ἐποίησεν	ὁ	Ἰησοῦς	ἐνώπιον
alla	*sēmeia*	*epoiēsen*	*ho*	*Iēsous*	*enōpion*
other	signs	did		Jesus	in presence

30.a.**Txt:** p66,01ℵ,04C,05D,019L,032W,036,038,1,13,byz.it.sa.bo. **Var:** 02A,03B,017K,037,Lach,Treg,Alf,Tisc,We/Ho,WeisSod,UBS/⋆

3450.1 art gen pl	3073.6 noun gen pl masc	840.3 prs-pron gen sing	3614.17 rel-pron pl neu	3620.2 partic	1498.4 verb 3sing indic pres act
τῶν	μαθητῶν	⸂a αὐτοῦ, ⸃	ἃ	οὐκ	ἔστιν
tōn	*mathētōn*	*autou*	*ha*	*ouk*	*estin*
of the	disciples	his,	which	not	are

1119.31 verb acc pl neu part perf	1706.1 prep	3450.3 art dat sing	968.3 noun dat sing neu	3642.5 dem-pron dat sing masc
γεγραμμένα	ἐν	τῷ	βιβλίῳ	τούτῳ.
gegrammena	*en*	*tō*	*bibliō*	*toutō*
having been written	in	the	book	this;

31.a.**Txt:** 01ℵ-corr,02A,04C,05D,017K,019L,032W,036,037,1,13,byz.Gries,LachTreg,Alf,Weis,Sod **Var:** p66,01ℵ-org,03B,038,892,Tisc,We/Ho,UBS/⋆

3642.18 dem-pron pl neu	1156.2 conj	1119.22 verb 3sing indic perf pass	2419.1 conj	3961.1 verb 2pl subj act
31. ταῦτα	δὲ	γέγραπται	ἵνα	⸂☆ πιστεύσητε
tauta	*de*	*gegraptai*	*hina*	*pisteusēte*
these	but	have been written	that	you may believe

31.b.**Txt:** Steph **Var:** 01ℵ,02A,03B,04C,05D,017K,019L,036,037,038,byz.Gries,Lach Treg,Alf,Word,Tisc,We/Ho,Weis,Sod,UBS/⋆

3961.8 verb 2pl subj pres act	3617.1 conj	3450.5 art sing masc	2400.1 name nom masc	1498.4 verb 3sing indic pres act	3450.5 art sing masc
[a πιστεύητε]	ὅτι	⸂b ὁ ⸃	Ἰησοῦς	ἐστιν	ὁ
pisteuēte	*hoti*	*ho*	*Iēsous*	*estin*	*ho*
[idem]	that		Jesus	is	the

5382.1 name nom masc	3450.5 art sing masc	5048.1 noun nom sing masc	3450.2 art gen sing	2296.2 noun gen sing masc	2504.1 conj
Χριστὸς	ὁ	υἱὸς	τοῦ	θεοῦ,	καὶ
Christos	*ho*	*huios*	*tou*	*theou*	*kai*
Christ	the	Son		of God,	and

2419.1 conj	3961.13 verb nom pl masc part pres act	2205.4 noun acc sing fem	2174.9 verb 2pl subj pres act	1706.1 prep	3450.3 art dat sing
ἵνα	πιστεύοντες	ζωὴν	ἔχητε	ἐν	τῷ
hina	*pisteuontes*	*zōēn*	*echēte*	*en*	*tō*
that	believing	life	you may have	in	the

3549.4 noun dat sing neu	840.3 prs-pron gen sing	3196.3 prep	3642.18 dem-pron pl neu	5157.3 verb 3sing indic aor act
ὀνόματι	αὐτοῦ.	**21:1.** Μετὰ	ταῦτα	ἐφανέρωσεν
onomati	*autou*	*Meta*	*tauta*	*ephanerōsen*
name	his.	After	these things	manifested

1.a.**Txt:** 01ℵ,02A,017K,019L,032W,036,037,038,1,byz.LachSod **Var:** 03B,04C,Treg,Tisc,We/HoWeis,UBS/⋆

1431.6 prs-pron acc 3sing masc	3687.1 adv	3450.5 art sing masc	2400.1 name nom masc	3450.4 art dat pl	3073.7 noun dat pl masc	1894.3 prep
ἑαυτὸν	πάλιν	⸂a ὁ ⸃	Ἰησοῦς	τοῖς	μαθηταῖς	ἐπὶ
heauton	*palin*	*ho*	*Iēsous*	*tois*	*mathētais*	*epi*
himself	again		Jesus	to the	disciples	at

witness of the other disciples. Multitudes through the centuries have not seen or handled the body of Christ. For these Jesus pronounced a special blessedness. "Blessed" means "happy" and "fortunate." Blessedness comes as a result of believing. The one who would be happy must be a seeker after the truth and a worshiper of Jesus as the embodiment of the reality of God. We are not to seek happiness, but we are to seek Him, whom to know is joy unspeakable and full of glory.

blessed are they that have not seen, and yet have believed: Spiritually prosperous are those, *Wuest* . . . Blessed are those who believe without seeing, *Berkeley* . . . Happy are those who have never seen me and yet have believed! *Phillips.*

20:30. The word "many" of this verse and "these" of the next verse are contrasted by the use of a strong pair of Greek conjunctions, *men* and *de.* These two words literally mean "on the one hand" many signs, "but on the other hand" these things were written. The Gospel of John does not record a full account of Jesus' "signs" (Greek, *sēmeia*). This is the word for miracles which Jesus performed that indicate who He is and His mission. The disciples were eyewitnesses of His glory (1:14). They learned who Jesus is and the revelation of God He came to bring. The disciples were commissioned to testify before others that which they had learned as His disciples. John's Gospel assures us that there was no scarcity of evidence. The life and ministry of Jesus were filled with many convincing proofs (Acts 1:3).

30. And many other signs truly did Jesus in the presence of his disciples, which are not written in this book: Jesus showed many more proofs from God in front of his followers, *SEB* . . . not recorded in this narrative, *Fenton.*

31. But these are written, that ye might believe that Jesus is the Christ, the Son of God: This selection has been written, *ALBA* . . . These proofs have been written, *SEB* . . . and are on record in order that, *Wuest* . . . so that you believe Jesus is the promised Savior, *Beck.*

and that believing ye might have life through his name: If you believe this, *SEB* . . . and so that, having this faith you may have life, *BB* . . . and that through believing you may have life, as bearers of His name, *Williams* . . . possessed of life by means of His power, *Fenton* . . . in the knowledge of him, *TCNT.*

20:31. The multitudes of signs of Jesus' personal identity and ministry were impossible to record. Therefore, John's Gospel records only certain facts and events.

In Jesus' own words we learn that the knowledge of Him is eternal life (17:3). The reverse is also true: not to know Him is to remain in the state of darkness and death (1 John 5:12). John's Gospel presents Jesus as the Son of God, the same One whom Thomas addressed as "My Lord and my God."

"Through his name" is the only origin of life. So often in this Gospel the term "eternal life" is used. "Through his name" refers to one's relationship with Him which secures eternal life. Eternal life is a present possession. "Life" is not a reward for good conduct to be given after death. It is a gift of God given in the name of Jesus when one accepts Christ as the revelation of God and commits his life to Him.

1. After these things Jesus shewed himself again to the disciples at the sea of Tiberias; and

21:1. The last chapter of John's Gospel is commonly called the epilogue because it appears after the conclusion of 20:30,31 as a

3450.10 art gen sing fem	2258.2 noun gen sing fem	3450.10 art gen sing fem	4933.1 name gen fem	5157.3 verb 3sing indic aor act
τῆς	θαλάσσης	τῆς	Τιβεριάδος·	ἐφανέρωσεν
tēs	*thalassēs*	*tēs*	*Tiberiados*	*ephanerōsen*
the	sea		of Tiberias.	He manifested

1156.2 conj	3643.1 adv	1498.37 verb 3pl indic imperf act	3537.1 adv	4468.1 name masc	3935.1 name nom masc
δὲ	οὕτως·	2. ἦσαν	ὁμοῦ	Σίμων	Πέτρος,
de	*houtōs*	*ēsan*	*homou*	*Simōn*	*Petros*
and	thus:	There were	together	Simon	Peter,

2504.1 conj	2358.1 name nom masc	3450.5 art sing masc	2978.30 verb nom sing masc part pres pass	1318.1 name nom masc	2504.1 conj
καὶ	Θωμᾶς	ὁ	λεγόμενος	Δίδυμος,	καὶ
kai	*Thōmas*	*ho*	*legomenos*	*Didumos*	*kai*
and	Thomas	the	being called	Didymus,	and

3345.1 name masc	3450.5 art sing masc	570.3 prep gen	2551.2 name fem	3450.10 art gen sing fem	1049.2 name gen sing fem
Ναθαναὴλ	ὁ	ἀπὸ	Κανὰ	τῆς	Γαλιλαίας,
Nathanaēl	*ho*	*apo*	*Kana*	*tēs*	*Galilaias*
Nathanael	the	from	Cana		of Galilee,

2504.1 conj	3450.7 art pl masc	3450.2 art gen sing	2181.1 name gen masc	2504.1 conj	241.6 adj nom pl masc	1523.2 prep gen
καὶ	οἱ	τοῦ	Ζεβεδαίου,	καὶ	ἄλλοι	ἐκ
kai	*hoi*	*tou*	*Zebedaiou*	*kai*	*alloi*	*ek*
and	the		of Zebedee,	and	others	of

3450.1 art gen pl	3073.6 noun gen pl masc	840.3 prs-pron gen sing	1411.3 num card	2978.5 verb 3sing indic pres act	840.2 prs-pron dat pl
τῶν	μαθητῶν	αὐτοῦ	δύο.	3. λέγει	αὐτοῖς
tōn	*mathētōn*	*autou*	*duo*	*legei*	*autois*
the	disciples	his	two.	Says	to them

4468.1 name masc	3935.1 name nom masc	5055.1 verb 1sing indic pres act	230.1 verb inf pres act	2978.3 verb 3pl pres act
Σίμων	Πέτρος,	Ὑπάγω	ἁλιεύειν,	Λέγουσιν
Simōn	*Petros*	*Hupagō*	*halieuein*	*Legousin*
Simon	Peter,	I go	to fish.	They say

840.4 prs-pron dat sing	2048.35 verb 1pl indic pres	2504.1 conj	2231.1 prs-pron nom 1pl	4713.1 prep dat	4622.3 prs-pron dat 2sing
αὐτῷ,	Ἐρχόμεθα	καὶ	ἡμεῖς	σὺν	σοί.
autō	*Erchometha*	*kai*	*hēmeis*	*sun*	*soi*
to him,	Come	also	we	with	you.

1814.1 verb indic aor act	2504.1 conj	303.14 verb 3pl indic aor act	1671.2 verb 3pl indic aor act	1519.1 prep
Ἐξῆλθον	καὶ	⸂ ἀνέβησαν	[[a]☆ ἐνέβησαν]	εἰς
Exēlthon	*kai*	*anebēsan*	*enebēsan*	*eis*
They went forth	and	went up	[embarked]	into

3450.16 art sing neu	4003.1 noun sing neu	2098.1 adv	2504.1 conj	1706.1 prep	1552.11 dem-pron dat sing fem
τὸ	πλοῖον	⸂[b] εὐθύς, ⸃	καὶ	ἐν	ἐκείνῃ
to	*ploion*	*euthus*	*kai*	*en*	*ekeinē*
the	boat	immediately,	and	during	that

3450.11 art dat sing fem	3433.3 noun dat sing fem	3945.3 verb 3pl indic aor act	3625.6 num card neu	4263.2 noun gen sing fem	1156.2 conj
τῇ	νυκτὶ	ἐπίασαν	οὐδέν.	4. πρωΐας	δὲ
tē	*nukti*	*epiasan*	*ouden*	*prōias*	*de*
the	night	they took	nothing.	Morning	and

3.a.**Txt:** 037,Steph
Var: 01א,02A,03B,04C,05D,017K,019L,024P,036,038,byz.Gries,Lach Treg,Alf,Word,Tisc,We/Ho,Weis,Sod,UBS/☆

3.b.**Txt:** 02A,04C-corr,017K,024P,036,byz.
Var: 01א,03B,04C-org,05D,019L,033X,037,038,33,it.bo.Lach,Treg,Alf,Tisc,We/Ho,WeisSod,UBS/☆

supplement to the meaning of the book. This chapter extends the message of Jesus' appearances by narrating this third appearance to the apostles. The epilogue forms a balance to the prologue.

"After these things" signifies what has been recorded concerning Jesus' last appearance.

This is the Gospel's fourth record of Jesus' appearances and the seventh appearance as recorded by the New Testament writers. According to verse 14 this is the third time Jesus appeared to His disciples (apostles). The second Lord's Day had passed and the disciples had returned to Galilee. The Sea of Tiberias was the Roman name for the Sea of Galilee. It is a freshwater lake about 14 miles long and 9 miles wide at its extremities. The Old Testament name was Chinnereth (Numbers 34:11). Several days must have intervened since Jesus last appeared to the apostles (20:26-31). "Manifested" is an aorist tense verb pointing out the historical fact of His appearance. Jesus did not lodge with the disciples after the Resurrection, but He did spend some time in their presence.

on this wise shewed he himself: Jesus manifests Himself, *Concordant* . . . Jesus showed many more proofs from God in front of his followers, *SEB* . . . now he manifested himself thus, *Rotherham* . . . made himself visible, *Wuest* . . . It happened in this way, *ALBA, Norlie* . . . The circumstances were as follows, *Weymouth* . . . And He appeared in this way, *Fenton* . . . this is the way He showed Himself, *Williams.*

2. There were together Simon Peter, and Thomas called Didymus, and Nathanael of Cana in Galilee, and the sons of Zebedee, and two other of his disciples: . . . the one from the town of Cana, *SEB* . . . were all together, *ET.*

21:2. This verse records a list of the apostles who were present at this appearance of the risen Christ. The "two other of his disciples" are the only unrecorded names. Philip the friend of Nathanael may have been one of the other disciples (see 1:45-51).

3. Simon Peter saith unto them, I go a fishing: Simon Peter told them, I go off fishing! *Berkeley* . . . I will go (and) catch fishes, *Murdock* . . . I am going off...to my former fishing business, *Wuest* . . . I am going away to fish, *Worrell* . . . I'm going out to fish, *NIV.*

They say unto him, We also go with thee: We will go with you, *Norlie* . . . And we are coming with you! *Berkeley* . . . we are coming also to join you, *Wuest.*

They went forth, and entered into a ship immediately: Off they went and embarked in the boat, *Moffatt* . . . So they started, *NEB* . . . got into the boat at once, *Norlie* . . . went on board their boat, *Weymouth.*

and that night they caught nothing: . . . and throughout that night, *AmpB, Montgomery* . . . but that night they took no fish, *BB* . . . thei tokun no thing, *Wycliffe* . . . not even one thing, *Wuest.*

21:3. Peter's statement is interesting, for the verb indicates that he was returning to his old occupation of fishing. The disciples were not well off (except perhaps John and James, see 19:27). They had lost many days of work. Probably they felt the financial necessity of fishing for their support. They had been fishermen all their lives. They knew little of earning a living except fishing. When Jesus asked them to follow Him, He seemingly asked a difficult thing of them. We do not know how many of these disciples had families to support. Very little is mentioned concerning their wives and children. We do know Peter had a wife. Nothing is said about Peter's having children. We do know that most of the apostles were poor. How could they support themselves and their families if they did not fish or earn a living in some way? Perhaps questions like this cannot be answered, yet they are very practical. The disciples had been in Jerusalem for some time prior to this event. Certainly their funds must have been low indeed!

Peter's influence affected the other six apostles. They said, "We also go with thee." John's Gospel very simply states what happened: "They caught nothing." Without Jesus their efforts were vain. He had told them, "For without me ye can do nothing" (15:5). Jesus

John 21:5

4.a.**Txt:** 01ℵ,04C-corr, 05D,017K,024P,032W, 036,037,038,1,13,byz. Lach
Var: 02A,03B,04C-org, 07E,019L,Treg,Tisc, We/Ho,Weis,Sod,UBS/☆

4.b.**Txt:** 017K,019L,036, 037,038,1,13,byz.
Var: 01ℵ,02A,03B,04C, 05D,024P,Lach,Treg, Alf,Tisc,We/HoWeis,Sod, UBS/☆

4.c.**Var:** 01ℵ,02A,05D, 019L,021M,030U,033X, 038,33,Lach,Tisc,Sod

2218.1 adv	**1090.57** verb gen sing fem part aor mid	**1090.75** verb gen sing fem part pres	**2449.3** verb 3sing indic aor act	**3450.5** art sing masc
ἤδη	⸂☆ γενομένης	[a γινομένης]	ἔστη	⸂b ὁ ⸃
ēdē	*genomenēs*	*ginomenēs*	*estē*	*ho*
already	being come	[becoming]	stood	

2400.1 name nom masc	**1519.1** prep	**1894.3** prep	**3450.6** art acc sing masc	**123.1** noun acc sing masc	**3620.3** partic	**3175.1** conj
Ἰησοῦς	⸂ εἰς	[c ἐπὶ]	τὸν	αἰγιαλόν·	οὐ	μέντοι
Iēsous	*eis*	*epi*	*ton*	*aigialon*	*ou*	*mentoi*
Jesus	on	[upon]	the	shore;	not	however

3471.13 verb 3pl indic plperf act	**3450.7** art pl masc	**3073.5** noun nom pl masc	**3617.1** conj	**2400.1** name nom masc	**1498.4** verb 3sing indic pres act
ᾔδεισαν	οἱ	μαθηταὶ	ὅτι	Ἰησοῦς	ἐστιν.
ēdeisan	*hoi*	*mathētai*	*hoti*	*Iēsous*	*estin*
had known	the	disciples	that	Jesus	it is.

5.a.**Txt:** 02A-corr,04C, 05D,017K,019L,024P, 032W,036,037,038,1,13, etc.byz.Lach,Weis,Sod
Var: 01ℵ,03B,Alf,Tisc, We/Ho,UBS/☆

2978.5 verb 3sing indic pres act	**3631.1** conj	**840.2** prs-pron dat pl	**3450.5** art sing masc	**2400.1** name nom masc	**3676.3** noun pl masc
5. λέγει	οὖν	αὐτοῖς	⸂a ὁ ⸃	Ἰησοῦς,	Παιδία,
legei	*oun*	*autois*	*ho*	*Iēsous*	*Paidia*
Says	therefore	to them		Jesus,	Little children,

3231.1 partic	**4948.10** indef-pron sing neu	**4229.1** noun acc sing neu	**2174.2** verb 2pl pres act	**552.8** verb 3pl indic aor pass
μή	τι	προσφάγιον	ἔχετε;	Ἀπεκρίθησαν
mē	*ti*	*prosphagion*	*echete*	*Apekrithēsan*
not	any	food	have you?	They answered

6.a.**Var:** 01ℵ-org,032W, sa.bo.Tisc

840.4 prs-pron dat sing	**3620.3** partic	**3450.5** art sing masc	**1156.2** conj	**1500.5** verb 3sing indic aor act	**2978.5** verb 3sing indic pres act
αὐτῷ,	Οὔ.	6. ⸂ Ὁ	δὲ	εἶπεν	[a λέγει]
autō	*Ou*	*Ho*	*de*	*eipen*	*legei*
him,	No.	The	and	said	[says]

840.2 prs-pron dat pl	**900.18** verb 2pl impr aor act	**1519.1** prep	**3450.17** art pl neu	**1182.3** adj	**3183.4** noun acc pl neu	**3450.2** art gen sing
αὐτοῖς,	Βάλετε	εἰς	τὰ	δεξιὰ	μέρη	τοῦ
autois	*Balete*	*eis*	*ta*	*dexia*	*merē*	*tou*
to them,	Cast	to	the	right	side	of the

4003.2 noun gen sing neu	**3450.16** art sing neu	**1344.1** noun sing neu	**2504.1** conj	**2128.28** verb 2pl indic fut act	**900.11** verb 3pl indic aor act
πλοίου	τὸ	δίκτυον,	καὶ	εὑρήσετε.	Ἔβαλον
ploiou	*to*	*diktuon*	*kai*	*heurēsete*	*Ebalon*
boat	the	net,	and	you shall find.	They cast

3631.1 conj	**2504.1** conj	**3620.2** partic	**2068.1** adv	**3629.1** adv	**840.15** prs-pron sing neu
οὖν,	καὶ	⸂ οὐκ	ἔτι	[☆ οὐκέτι]	αὐτὸ
oun	*kai*	*ouk*	*eti*	*ouketi*	*auto*
therefore,	and	no	longer	[no longer]	it

6.b.**Txt:** 02A,017K,024P, 032W,036,037,13,byz. Gries
Var: 01ℵ,03B,04C,05D, 019L,038,041,33,Lach, Treg,Alf,Tisc,We/Ho, Weis,Sod,UBS/☆

1657.5 verb inf aor act	**2453.10** verb 3pl indic aor act	**2453.13** verb 3pl indic imperf act	**570.3** prep gen	**3450.2** art gen sing
ἑλκύσαι	⸂ ἴσχυσαν	[b☆ ἴσχυον]	ἀπὸ	τοῦ
helkusai	*ischusan*	*ischuon*	*apo*	*tou*
to draw	were they able	[idem]	from	the

3988.2 noun gen sing neu	**3450.1** art gen pl	**2459.4** noun gen pl masc	**2978.5** verb 3sing indic pres act	**3631.1** conj	**3450.5** art sing masc
πλήθους	τῶν	ἰχθύων.	7. λέγει	οὖν	ὁ
plēthous	*tōn*	*ichthuōn*	*legei*	*oun*	*ho*
multitude	of the	fish.	Says	therefore	the

now asked them if they had caught any fish. After they acknowledged their failure, He directed them. When they followed His directions, they were successful. What a lesson in spiritual service!

4. But when the morning was now come: Now just as day was breaking, *Williams* . . . at the break of day, *Norlie* . . . Day had already dawned, *Berkeley* . . . It was light by now, *JB.*

Jesus stood on the shore: Jesus stood on the beach, *ASV, Wuest, Confraternity* . . . ihesus stood in the brynke, *Wycliffe.*

but the disciples knew not that it was Jesus: . . . had no idea that, *Phillips* . . . did not recognize that it was Jesus, *Montgomery* . . . failed to recognise, *Fenton.*

21:4. Jesus allowed them the entire night of futile efforts before appearing in the morning. He could have manifested himself during the night, yet He did not. The Lord respects man's own will no matter if it operates ineffectively or profitlessly.

This time He waited for the seven disciples to come to Him instead of appearing in one of the boats. He appeared on the shore at a most despondent moment for the disciples. They had not expected to see Him.

5. Then Jesus saith unto them, Children, have ye any meat?: Lads, you have no fish, have you, *Williams* . . . young men, *SEB* . . . have you got anything, *Moffatt* . . . Fellows, have you, *Norlie* . . . have you any food there? *Weymouth* . . . any thing to eat? *Murdock.*

They answered him, No:

21:5. "Children" is not the more affectionate term He used. The word is used here as a teacher addressing his disciples.

Jesus knew their failure in fishing, yet His question focused on their need. He asked as if He desired to be their guest and eat their fish, yet He knew that He would supply their food.

It was probably embarrassing for these fishermen to acknowledge they had not even caught enough for their food. When they admitted this fact, Jesus could reveal His grace, power, and provision.

6. And he said unto them, Cast the net on the right side of the ship, and ye shall find: Let out your net to the right of the boat and you will make a catch, *ALBA* . . . out to starboard, *JB* . . . and you'll have a catch, *Phillips.*

They cast therefore, and now they were not able to draw it for the multitude of fishes: They did so, *Norlie* . . . no longer did they have the strength to draw it, *Wuest* . . . could scarcely drag it along for the quantity of fish, *Weymouth* . . . There were so many fish that they were no longer able to pull the net into the boat, *SEB* . . . and they no longer had the strength to draw it, *Concordant* . . . owing to the quantity of fish, *Fenton* . . . for the mass of fish, *Moffatt.*

21:6. Thus far in the incident, Jesus was not recognized by the disciples, but the tone of His command impressed them. Jesus knew where the one fish was with a piece of money in its mouth (Matthew 17:27). He had asked the disciples to launch out into the deep to let down their nets for a draught (Luke 5:4). This time the boats were in the shallows. No matter to Him whether one fish or schools of fish, He knows where they are. He is the Lord of nature as well as the Lord of men.

Their obedience followed His command, and their catch was such that "they were not able to draw" it in because of the "multitude of fishes." The word "draw" refers to lifting the net full of fish into the boat. "Dragging" (verse 8) refers to pulling the net of fish through the water onto the shore. The latter was much easier. Their obedience to His promise brought success after the night of futile toil. Though they were fishermen, their knowledge was insufficient and their efforts were fruitless. But as they followed His directions and applied them to their skills, they were abundantly prosperous. The disciples doubtless recalled the lesson of fishing He had given them at another time (Luke 5:10).

John 21:8

3073.1 noun nom sing masc	1552.3 dem-pron nom sing masc	3614.6 rel-pron acc sing masc	25.26 verb 3sing indic imperf act	3450.5 art sing masc	2400.1 name nom masc
μαθητὴς	ἐκεῖνος	ὃν	ἠγάπα	ὁ	Ἰησοῦς
mathētēs	*ekeinos*	*hon*	*ēgapa*	*ho*	*Iēsous*
disciple	that	whom	loved		Jesus

3450.3 art dat sing	3935.3 name dat masc	3450.5 art sing masc	2935.1 noun nom sing masc	1498.4 verb 3sing indic pres act	4468.1 name masc
τῷ	Πέτρῳ,	Ὁ	κύριός	ἐστιν.	Σίμων
tō	*Petrō*	*Ho*	*kurios*	*estin*	*Simōn*
	to Peter,	The	Lord	it is.	Simon

3631.1 conj	3935.1 name nom masc	189.31 verb nom sing masc part aor act	3617.1 conj	3450.5 art sing masc	2935.1 noun nom sing masc
οὖν	Πέτρος,	ἀκούσας	ὅτι	ὁ	κύριός
oun	*Petros*	*akousas*	*hoti*	*ho*	*kurios*
therefore	Peter,	having heard	that	the	Lord

1498.4 verb 3sing indic pres act	3450.6 art acc sing masc	1888.1 noun acc sing masc	1235.2 verb 3sing indic aor mid	1498.34 verb sing indic imperf act
ἐστιν,	τὸν	ἐπενδύτην	διεζώσατο·	ἦν
estin	*ton*	*ependutēn*	*diezōsato*	*ēn*
it is,	the	upper garment	he girded on,	he was

1056.1 conj	1125.1 adj nom sing masc	2504.1 conj	900.10 verb 3sing indic aor act	1431.6 prs-pron acc 3sing masc	1519.1 prep	3450.12 art acc sing fem
γὰρ	γυμνός,	καὶ	ἔβαλεν	ἑαυτὸν	εἰς	τὴν
gar	*gumnos*	*kai*	*ebalen*	*heauton*	*eis*	*tēn*
for	naked,	and	cast	himself	into	the

2258.4 noun acc sing fem	3450.7 art pl masc	1156.2 conj	241.6 adj nom pl masc	3073.5 noun nom pl masc	3450.3 art dat sing
θάλασσαν.	**8.** οἱ	δὲ	ἄλλοι	μαθηταὶ	τῷ
thalassan	*hoi*	*de*	*alloi*	*mathētai*	*tō*
sea.	The	and	other	disciples	in the

4002.2 noun dat sing neu	2048.1 verb indic aor act	3620.3 partic	1056.1 conj	1498.37 verb 3pl indic imperf act	3084.1 adv
πλοιαρίῳ	ἦλθον·	οὐ	γὰρ	ἦσαν	μακρὰν
ploiariō	*ēlthon*	*ou*	*gar*	*ēsan*	*makran*
small boat	came,	not	for	were they	far

570.3 prep gen	3450.10 art gen sing fem	1087.2 noun gen sing fem	233.1 conj	233.2 conj	5453.1 conj
ἀπὸ	τῆς	γῆς,	(ἀλλ'	[☆ ἀλλὰ]	ὡς
apo	*tēs*	*gēs*	*all'*	*alla*	*hōs*
from	the	land,	but	[idem]	somewhere

570.3 prep gen	3944.2 noun gen pl masc	1244.1 num card gen masc	4803.3 verb nom pl masc part pres act	3450.16 art sing neu	1344.1 noun sing neu
ἀπὸ	πηχῶν	διακοσίων,	σύροντες	τὸ	δίκτυον
apo	*pēchōn*	*diakosiōn*	*surontes*	*to*	*diktuon*
about	cubits	two hundred,	dragging	the	net

3450.1 art gen pl	2459.4 noun gen pl masc	5453.1 conj	3631.1 conj	571.1 verb 3pl indic aor act	1519.1 prep
τῶν	ἰχθύων.	**9.** Ὡς	οὖν	ἀπέβησαν	εἰς
tōn	*ichthuōn*	*Hōs*	*oun*	*apebēsan*	*eis*
of the	fish.	When	therefore	they went up	on

3450.12 art acc sing fem	1087.4 noun acc sing fem	984.6 verb 3pl indic pres act	437.1 noun acc sing fem	2719.7 verb acc sing fem part pres
τὴν	γῆν	βλέπουσιν	ἀνθρακιὰν	κειμένην
tēn	*gēn*	*blepousin*	*anthrakian*	*keimenēn*
the	land	they see	a fire of coals	lying

21:7. "That disciple" refers to John, the inspired writer of this Gospel. How delicately and humbly John revealed himself as a participant and eyewitness in his narrative. "It is the Lord," he said to the other fishermen.

How characteristic of John and Simon Peter are their actions. John was thoughtful, retiring, and penetrating. Peter was verbose, forward, and impulsive. John was the first to recognize Jesus, but Peter was the first in zeal to reach Jesus on the shore. Our Lord needs both kinds of disciples; disciples of love and insight, and disciples of zeal and activity. Each fits and functions in the Kingdom to the glory of Jesus the Lord.

7. Therefore that disciple whom Jesus loved saith unto Peter, It is the Lord: That is our Lord, *Murdock.*

Now when Simon Peter heard that it was the Lord, he girt his fisher's coat unto him, (for he was naked,): . . . took his tunic, and girded his loins, *Murdock* . . . he fastened his coat, *TCNT* . . . girded on his outer garment, *HBIE* . . . he belted on his fisherman's coat, for he had taken it off, *Williams* . . . his fisherman's linen blouse, for he was only partially clad, *Wuest* . . . he was stripped, *Fenton, Norlie* . . . wrapped his work jacket around him, *Berkeley* . . . he was not clothed, *BB* . . . who had practically nothing on, *JB* . . . not having been dressed, *ALBA* . . . he was unclad, *HistNT.*

and did cast himself into the sea: . . . and plunged into the sea, *Norlie* . . . and sprang, *AmpB.*

21:8. Peter heard John say, "It is the Lord"; therefore, he put on his outer garment which he had removed so it did not hinder his work of fishing. Peter was not naked, but he had merely removed his long, flowing garments which were impediments to his labor. In his impulsiveness Peter threw his outer garment about him, placing the belt around his middle, and "cast himself into the sea" in an effort to reach his Lord. Peter did not wish to wait for the slow-moving boat to reach Jesus. Peter's eagerness to be in the immediate presence of the Lord is surely an incentive to all disciples. Peter could not wait calmly in the boat when Jesus was waiting on the shore!

Peter swam or waded and the other disciples managed to pull the net and row the boat about 100 yards. The miracle of the multitude of fish did not lessen the labors, but rather increased their toil as well as their joy. They needed the Lord to bring about this miracle; yet we should remember the Lord needed them also.

8. And the other disciples came in a little ship: The rest of the disciples came in the boat, *Montgomery* . . . in the punt, *Moffatt.*

(for they were not far from land, but as it were two hundred cubits,): . . . for they were only about a hundred yards from shore, *TCNT.*

dragging the net with fishes: . . . hauling in the net of fish, *Berkeley* . . . towing the net, *JB.*

21:9. As soon as the disciples came ashore, they saw the Lord's provisions. A charcoal fire was burning, with bread and fish placed upon it. Mention of a charcoal fire occurs only here and at 18:18 in the New Testament. A mystery surrounds the source of the bread and fish He had provided. It is obvious Jesus did not use the fish they had just caught. Were they provided by a miracle? Had Jesus caught the fish himself? We are not told. The Scriptures provide enough information to reinforce our faith, but they often do not satisfy our curiosity. It is unwise to speculate.

There were two kinds of provisions from His blessed hands. First, He supplied the fish in their nets for which they had to labor. The necessities of life were provided for them and their families. Second, they received personal provisions for which they exerted no energy. The grace of our Lord was never intended to produce lazy beggars. All the provisions of His grace come because of His love for His own, yet He does not hamper the maturing of believers by

9. As soon then as they were come to land, they saw a fire of coals there: As, then, they stepped off to the land, *Concordant* . . . they beheld a charcoal fire ready laid, *Montgomery* . . . they saw burning coals there, *Beck* . . . a charcoal fire, *Norlie.*

2504.1 conj	3659.1 noun acc sing neu	1930.3 verb acc sing neu part pres	2504.1 conj	735.4 noun acc sing masc	2978.5 verb 3sing indic pres act
καὶ	ὀψάριον	ἐπικείμενον,	καὶ	ἄρτον.	10. λέγει
kai	*opsarion*	*epikeimenon*	*kai*	*arton*	*legei*
and	fish	lying on,	and	bread.	Says

840.2 prs-pron dat pl	3450.5 art sing masc	2400.1 name nom masc	5179.16 verb 2pl impr aor act	570.3 prep gen	3450.1 art gen pl
αὐτοῖς	ὁ	Ἰησοῦς,	Ἐνέγκατε	ἀπὸ	τῶν
autois	*ho*	*Iēsous*	*Enenkate*	*apo*	*tōn*
to them		Jesus,	Bring	of	the

3659.2 noun gen pl neu	3614.1 rel-pron gen pl	3945.2 verb 2pl indic aor act	3431.1 adv	303.13 verb 3sing indic aor act
ὀψαρίων	ὧν	ἐπιάσατε	νῦν.	11. Ἀνέβη
opsariōn	*hōn*	*epiasate*	*nun*	*Anebē*
fish	which	you took	just now.	Went up

11.a.**Var:** 01א,03B,04C, 019L,032W,033X,038, 33,bo.Treg,Alf,We/Ho Sod

3631.1 conj	4468.1 name masc	3935.1 name nom masc	2504.1 conj	1657.2 verb 3sing indic aor act	3450.16 art sing neu
[a+ οὖν]	Σίμων	Πέτρος,	καὶ	εἵλκυσεν	τὸ
oun	*Simōn*	*Petros*	*kai*	*heilkusen*	*to*
[therefore]	Simon	Peter,	and	drew	the

11.b.**Txt:** 07E,017K, 021M,036,byz. **Var:** 01א,02A,03B,04C, 019L,024P,033X,037, 038,33,Lach,TregAlf, Tisc,We/Ho,Weis,Sod, UBS/☆

1344.1 noun sing neu	1894.3 prep	3450.10 art gen sing fem	1087.2 noun gen sing fem	1519.1 prep	3450.12 art acc sing fem	1087.4 noun acc sing fem
δίκτυον	⸂ ἐπὶ	τῆς	γῆς,	[b☆ εἰς	τὴν	γῆν]
diktuon	*epi*	*tēs*	*gēs*	*eis*	*tēn*	*gēn*
net	to	the	land,	[to	the	land]

3194.1 adj sing	2459.4 noun gen pl masc	3144.6 adj gen pl masc	1526.1 num card	3867.1 num card gen
μεστὸν	ἰχθύων	μεγάλων	ἑκατὸν	⸂ πεντήκοντατριῶν·
meston	*ichthuōn*	*megalōn*	*hekaton*	*pentēkontatriōn*
full	of fish	large	a hundred	fifty-three;

3866.1 num card	4980.2 num card gen	2504.1 conj	4965.4 dem-pron gen pl masc	1498.20 verb gen pl part pres act
[☆ πεντήκοντα	τριῶν·]	καὶ	τοσούτων	ὄντων
pentēkonta	*triōn*	*kai*	*tosoutōn*	*ontōn*
[a hundred fifty	three.]	and	so many	being

3620.2 partic	4829.4 verb 3sing indic aor pass	3450.16 art sing neu	1344.1 noun sing neu	2978.5 verb 3sing indic pres act	840.2 prs-pron dat pl
οὐκ	ἐσχίσθη	τὸ	δίκτυον.	12. Λέγει	αὐτοῖς
ouk	*eschisthē*	*to*	*diktuon*	*Legei*	*autois*
not	was torn	the	net.	Says	to them

12.a.**Txt:** 01א,02A,05D, 017K,019L,032W,038,1, 13,etc.byz.Lach,Tisc,Sod **Var:** 03B,04C,sa.Alf, We/HoWeis,UBS/☆

3450.5 art sing masc	2400.1 name nom masc	1199.1 adv	703.3 verb 2pl impr aor act	3625.2 num card nom masc	1156.2 conj
ὁ	Ἰησοῦς,	Δεῦτε	ἀριστήσατε.	οὐδεὶς	⸀a δὲ ⸌
ho	*Iēsous*	*Deute*	*aristēsate*	*oudeis*	*de*
	Jesus,	Come you,	dine.	None	but

4958.9 verb 3sing indic imperf act	3450.1 art gen pl	3073.6 noun gen pl masc	1816.2 verb inf aor act	840.6 prs-pron acc sing masc	4622.1 prs-pron nom 2sing
ἐτόλμα	τῶν	μαθητῶν	ἐξετάσαι	αὐτόν,	Σὺ
etolma	*tōn*	*mathētōn*	*exetasai*	*auton*	*Su*
ventured	of the	disciples	to ask	him,	You

4949.3 intr-pron nom sing	1498.3 verb 2sing indic pres act	3471.20 verb nom pl masc part perf act	3617.1 conj	3450.5 art sing masc	2935.1 noun nom sing masc
τίς	εἶ;	εἰδότες	ὅτι	ὁ	κύριός
tis	*ei*	*eidotes*	*hoti*	*ho*	*kurios*
who	are?	having known	that	the	Lord

cutting short their training. Thus He delights to perform both kinds of miracles.

and fish laid thereon, and bread: . . . and a little fish laid thereon, *Panin* . . . with fish cooking on it, and some bread, *Moffatt.*

21:10. "Of the fish" is literally "from the fish." It seems He asked them to contribute to the meal that which they by His direction had caught. The word for "fish" is the same as that used in verse 9; yet there the word is singular and here plural, so that they might choose the species of fish that suited their taste. This Greek word for "fish" (*opsariōn*) occurs only in John's Gospel (6:9,11; 21:9,10,13). John used the word "fish" (Greek, *ichthus*) three times (21:6,8,11). The former word seems to emphasize fish as food, and the latter does not signify the purpose of the fish.

This verse is a beautiful example of what Jesus promises in Revelation 3:20, "If any man hear my voice, and open the door, I will come in to him, and will sup with him, and he with me." He invites us to share with Him from the abundance which He supplies. What debtors we are to Him when we banquet at His table.

10. Jesus saith unto them, Bring of the fish which ye have now caught: Fetch some of the fish you have just caught, *Williams* . . . Get some of the fish which you have now taken, *BB* . . . you caught just now, *HistNT.*

21:11. After Simon Peter greeted his Lord, he went back to the water's edge to help drag in the net of fish. The miracle consisted partly in the fact that the catch was of large fish and partly in the great number of the catch. John's Gospel records the exact number: 153 large fish.

In the Luke 5:5 passage and in Matthew 4:18-22 Jesus associated their fishing occupation with their calling to be fishers of men. Jesus' miracles teach us great spiritual truths. First, Jesus himself directs the operations of spiritual fishing (cf. 21:6). Second, Jesus needs laborers in the boats and skillful toilers at the nets. Third, the great size and great number of fish caught are symbolic of the individual members of the multitude of the redeemed. Fourth, the sea is a troubled place and pictures the world from which men are rescued.

11. Simon Peter went up, and drew the net to land full of great fishes, an hundred and fifty and three: Peter climbed aboard and dragged the net ashore, *NIV* . . . and dragged the net to shore, *Montgomery* . . . full of huge fishes, *Murdock.*

and for all there were so many, yet was not the net broken: . . . and yet, although there were so many, the net had not been torn, *TCNT* . . . And with all this weight, *Murdock* . . . But in spite of the large number, *Phillips* . . . was not rent, *Rotherham* . . . not broken, *Douay* . . . was not split, *Wuest.*

21:12. It was early morning as is known from verse 4. As soon as the net was pulled to shore, Jesus invited them to eat. The morning meal provides strength for the day's activities. This is the meal which Jesus supplied for His disciples. They were to breakfast on His provisions. His grace supplies the strength for our daily needs. He prepares His workers for their day of labor. The kind of labors are indicated by the analogies of fishing and shepherding (verses 15-17).

They were convinced as to who He was, but the situation was so unusual that their reverence for Him restrained them from asking foolish questions. We may infer from their reticence there was

12. Jesus saith unto them, Come and dine: Come and break your fast, *ASV* . . . Come and have your breakfast, *Phillips* . . . Come and eat, *Norlie* . . . Here, have breakfast, *Wuest.*

And none of the disciples durst ask him, Who art thou?: Not one of the disciples ventured to ask him who he was, *TCNT, Weymouth* . . . Not one, however, of the disciples was venturing to draw from him, *Rotherham* . . . was daring to inquire of Him, *Wuest* . . . presumed to ask him, *Murdock* . . . were bold enough to ask Him, *Norlie.*

knowing that it was the Lord: . . . being conscious that it was the Lord, *BB.*

John 21:13

13.a.**Txt:** 02A,017K,036, 037,038,13,byz.Gries
Var: 03B,04C,05D, 032W,Lach,Treg,Alf, Tisc,We/Ho,UBS/⋆

1498.4 verb 3sing indic pres act	**2048.34** verb 3sing indic pres	**3631.1** conj	**3450.5** art sing masc	**2400.1** name nom masc	**2504.1** conj
ἐστιν·	**13.** ἔρχεται	⸂a οὖν	ὁ ⸃	Ἰησοῦς	καὶ
estin	*erchetai*	*oun*	*ho*	*Iēsous*	*kai*
it is.	Comes	therefore		Jesus	and

2956.4 verb 3sing indic pres act	**3450.6** art acc sing masc	**735.4** noun acc sing masc	**2504.1** conj	**1319.2** verb 3sing indic pres act	**840.2** prs-pron dat pl
λαμβάνει	τὸν	ἄρτον	καὶ	δίδωσιν	αὐτοῖς,
lambanei	*ton*	*arton*	*kai*	*didōsin*	*autois*
takes	the	bread	and	gives	to them,

2504.1 conj	**3450.16** art sing neu	**3659.1** noun acc sing neu	**3532.1** adv	**3642.17** dem-pron sing neu
καὶ	τὸ	ὀψάριον	ὁμοίως.	**14.** τοῦτο
kai	*to*	*opsarion*	*homoiōs*	*touto*
and	the	fish	in like manner.	This

14.a.**Txt:** 01ℵ,02A,017K, 019L,036,037,038,1,13, byz.Sod
Var: 03B,04C,05D,Lach Treg,Alf,Tisc,We/Ho, Weis,UBS/⋆

2218.1 adv	**4995.1** num ord sing	**5157.10** verb 3sing indic aor pass	**3450.5** art sing masc	**2400.1** name nom masc
ἤδη	τρίτον	ἐφανερώθη	⸂a ὁ ⸃	Ἰησοῦς
ēdē	*triton*	*ephanerōthē*	*ho*	*Iēsous*
now	the third time	was manifested		Jesus

14.b.**Txt:** 05D,017K, 033X,036,037,13,byz.
Var: 01ℵ,02A,03B,04C, 019L,038,33,Lach,Treg Alf,Word,Tisc,We/Ho, Weis,Sod,UBS/⋆

3450.4 art dat pl	**3073.7** noun dat pl masc	**840.3** prs-pron gen sing	**1446.25** verb nom sing masc part aor pass
τοῖς	μαθηταῖς	⸂b αὐτοῦ ⸃	ἐγερθεὶς
tois	*mathētais*	*autou*	*egertheis*
to the	disciples	his	having been raised

1523.2 prep gen	**3361.2** adj gen pl	**3616.1** conj	**3631.1** conj	**703.1** verb 3pl indic aor act
ἐκ	νεκρῶν.	**15.** Ὅτε	οὖν	ἠρίστησαν,
ek	*nekrōn*	*Hote*	*oun*	*ēristēsan*
from among	dead.	When	therefore	they had dined,

2978.5 verb 3sing indic pres act	**3450.3** art dat sing	**4468.3** name dat masc	**3935.3** name dat masc	**3450.5** art sing masc	**2400.1** name nom masc
λέγει	τῷ	Σίμωνι	Πέτρῳ	ὁ	Ἰησοῦς,
legei	*tō*	*Simōni*	*Petrō*	*ho*	*Iēsous*
says		to Simon	Peter		Jesus,

15.a.**Txt:** 02A,04C-corr, 017K,036,037,038,1,13, byz.
Var: (01-corr),(03), 04C-org,(05),019L,Alf, TiscSod,UBS/⋆

4468.1 name masc	**2468.2** name gen masc	**2464.2** name gen masc	**25.6** verb 2sing indic pres act	**1466.6** prs-pron acc 1sing
Σίμων	⸀ Ἰωνᾶ,	[a⋆ Ἰωάννου,]	ἀγαπᾷς	με
Simōn	*Iōna*	*Iōannou*	*agapas*	*me*
Simon	of Jona,	[of John,]	do you love	me

15.b.**Txt:** 02A,07E,017K, 036,037,byz.
Var: 01ℵ,03B,04C,05D, 019L,037,038,33,Lach, Treg,Alf,Tisc,We/Ho, Weis,Sod,UBS/⋆

3979.8 adj comp sing neu	**3979.9** adj comp acc sing neu	**3642.2** dem-pron gen pl	**2978.5** verb 3sing indic pres act	**840.4** prs-pron dat sing
⸀ πλεῖον	[b⋆ πλέον]	τούτων;	Λέγει	αὐτῷ,
pleion	*pleon*	*toutōn*	*Legei*	*autō*
more	[idem]	than these?	He says	to him,

3346.1 partic	**2935.5** noun voc sing masc	**4622.1** prs-pron nom 2sing	**3471.3** verb 2sing indic perf act	**3617.1** conj	**5205.1** verb 1sing pres act
Ναί,	κύριε,	σὺ	οἶδας	ὅτι	φιλῶ
Nai	*kurie*	*su*	*oidas*	*hoti*	*philō*
Yes,	Lord;	you	know	that	I love

4622.4 prs-pron acc 2sing	**2978.5** verb 3sing indic pres act	**840.4** prs-pron dat sing	**999.1** verb 2sing impr pres act	**3450.17** art pl neu	**715.4** noun acc pl neu
σε.	λέγει	αὐτῷ,	Βόσκε	τὰ	ἀρνία
se	*legei*	*autō*	*Boske*	*ta*	*arnia*
you.	He says	to him,	Feed	the	lambs

something different about Jesus after His resurrection. His followers could still recognize Him, but His deity was more pronounced.

13. Jesus then cometh, and taketh bread, and giveth them, and fish likewise:

21:13. Jesus was the gracious host for this breakfast on the beach. He was the One who gathered the fuel for the fire and the bread and fish to be cooked. Here we are told He took the place of a waiter, serving them with the food. What Jesus does, He does well.

14. This is now the third time that Jesus shewed himself to his disciples: . . . the third occasion, *Weymouth* . . . made himself visible to the disciples, *Wuest.*

after that he was risen from the dead: . . . raised out from among the dead, *Wuest.*

21:14. This is the third time Jesus appeared to His disciples after His resurrection. The two previous manifestations are recorded in 20:19-25 and 20:26-31. This is the seventh manifestation recorded in the New Testament, if we enumerate all His appearances. An eighth, in Galilee, is recorded by Matthew, Mark, and Paul (Matthew 28:16-20; Mark 15:15-18; 1 Corinthians 15:6). The ninth appearance was to James, the Lord's earthly brother (1 Corinthians 15:7). The 10th manifestation occurred in Jerusalem and is recorded in Luke 24:44-49 and Acts 1:3-8. The 11th appearance was at His ascension, which Mark and Luke record (Mark 16:19-20; Luke 24:50-53; Acts 1:9-12). The 12th and final appearance came to Paul the apostle as one born out of due season (Acts 9; 1 Corinthians 15:8).

15. So when they had dined: So when they had breakfasted, *HBIE.*

Jesus saith to Simon Peter, Simon, son of Jonas, lovest thou me more than these?: Simon Johnson, *Klingensmith* . . . do you love me more than these others do, *Montgomery, Norlie* . . . more devoted...to these things? *Williams* . . . are you My friend more than these? *Fenton* . . . is your love for me greater than the love of these others? *BB* . . . do you prize Me more dearly than these do? *Berkeley* . . . than these fish, *Wuest.*

He saith unto him, Yea, Lord; thou knowest that I love thee: . . . you know that I am your friend, *TCNT* . . . that you are dear to me, *Montgomery* . . . that I love You dearly, *Norlie* . . . I am fond, *Concordant* . . . I affectionately love thee, *Wilson* . . . I care for you, *Adams* . . . that I like you, *SEB* . . . I am a friend to you, *Sawyer.*

He saith unto him, Feed my lambs: Feed my lambs for me, *Murdock* . . . Look after my little ones, *ALBA* . . . Take care of, *TEV* . . . Pasture my young lambs, *Klingensmith* . . . Then give my lambs food, *BB* . . . Be grazing my lamb-kins, *Concordant* . . . my dear-lambs, *Rotherham.*

21:15. Verses 15-17 contain an interesting comparison of two Greek words for "love," *agapaō* and *phileō*. It seems that *agapaō*, with its noun *agapē*, usually means a higher quality of love than *phileō* (though the two words are sometimes used interchangeably in the New Testament, where sometimes *phileō* means God's love and *agapaō* man's love). However, the lexical meaning of the two words, and especially the context here, indicates that Jesus was calling for the higher kind of love, *agapaō/agapē*. See the *Greek-English Dictionary* for a fuller discussion.

By the word "these" Jesus means the other disciples. The word can mean "these things" since it is either masculine or neuter. If it is taken as a neuter, it would mean the boats, nets, and fish, but it is more likely that Jesus is referring to Peter's companions. Jesus used the word "these" to remind Peter of his wild boasts (Matthew 26:33).

Peter had gone through a critical period. He did not even dare claim that his love was equal to that of his brothers, certainly not greater.

Jesus strengthened Peter and reassured him of his ministry three times (verses 15,16,17). Jesus turned from the breakfast scene to

John 21:16

1466.2 prs-pron gen 1sing	2978.5 verb 3sing indic pres act	840.4 prs-pron dat sing	3687.1 adv	1202.8 num ord sing neu
μου.	16. Λέγει	αὐτῷ	πάλιν	δεύτερον,
mou	*Legei*	*autō*	*palin*	*deuteron*
my.	He says	to him	again	a second time,

16.a.**Txt:** 02A,04C-corr,017K,036,037,038,1,13,byz.
Var: 01ℵ,(03),04C-org,(05),Alf,Tisc,Sod,UBS/☆

4468.1 name masc	2468.2 name gen masc	2464.2 name gen masc	25.6 verb 2sing indic pres act	1466.6 prs-pron acc 1sing
Σίμων	ʼ Ἰωνᾶ,	[a☆ Ἰωάννου,]	ἀγαπᾷς	με;
Simōn	*Iōna*	*Iōannou*	*agapas*	*me*
Simon	of Jona,	[of John,]	do you love	me?

2978.5 verb 3sing indic pres act	840.4 prs-pron dat sing	3346.1 partic	2935.5 noun voc sing masc	4622.1 prs-pron nom 2sing
Λέγει	αὐτῷ,	Ναί,	κύριε,	σὺ
Legei	*autō*	*Nai*	*kurie*	*su*
He says	to him,	Yes,	Lord;	you

3471.3 verb 2sing indic perf act	3617.1 conj	5205.1 verb 1sing pres act	4622.4 prs-pron acc 2sing	2978.5 verb 3sing indic pres act
οἶδας	ὅτι	φιλῶ	σε.	λέγει
oidas	*hoti*	*philō*	*se*	*legei*
know	that	I love	you.	He says

16.b.**Txt:** 01ℵ,02A,05D,017K,036,037,038,1,13,byz.Gries,LachSod
Var: 03B,04C,Tisc,We/Ho,Weis,UBS/☆

840.4 prs-pron dat sing	4025.2 verb 2sing impr pres act	3450.17 art pl neu	4122.3 noun pl neu	4121.1 noun acc pl neu
αὐτῷ,	Ποίμαινε	τὰ	ʼ πρόβατά	[b☆ προβάτιά]
autō	*Poimaine*	*ta*	*probata*	*probatia*
to him,	Shepherd	the	sheep	[idem]

1466.2 prs-pron gen 1sing	2978.5 verb 3sing indic pres act	840.4 prs-pron dat sing	3450.16 art sing neu	4995.1 num ord sing
μου.	17. Λέγει	αὐτῷ	τὸ	τρίτον,
mou	*Legei*	*autō*	*to*	*triton*
my.	He says	to him	the	third time,

17.a.**Txt:** 02A,04C,017K,036,037,038,1,13,byz.
Var: 01ℵ,(03),(05),Alf,Tisc,Sod,UBS/☆

4468.1 name masc	2468.2 name gen masc	2464.2 name gen masc	5205.2 verb 2sing indic pres act	1466.6 prs-pron acc 1sing
Σίμων	ʼ Ἰωνᾶ,	[a☆ Ἰωάννου,]	φιλεῖς	με;
Simōn	*Iōna*	*Iōannou*	*phileis*	*me*
Simon	of Jona,	[of John,]	do you love	me?

3048.11 verb 3sing indic aor pass	3450.5 art sing masc	3935.1 name nom masc	3617.1 conj	1500.5 verb 3sing indic aor act	840.4 prs-pron dat sing
Ἐλυπήθη	ὁ	Πέτρος	ὅτι	εἶπεν	αὐτῷ
Elupēthē	*ho*	*Petros*	*hoti*	*eipen*	*autō*
Was grieved		Peter	because	he said	to him

3450.16 art sing neu	4995.1 num ord sing	5205.2 verb 2sing indic pres act	1466.6 prs-pron acc 1sing	2504.1 conj
τὸ	τρίτον,	Φιλεῖς	με;	καὶ
to	*triton*	*Phileis*	*me*	*kai*
the	third time,	Do you have affection for	me?	and

17.b.**Var:** 01ℵ,02A,05D,032W,033X,038,1,33,Tisc

1500.5 verb 3sing indic aor act	2978.5 verb 3sing indic pres act	840.4 prs-pron dat sing	2935.5 noun voc sing masc	4622.1 prs-pron nom 2sing	3820.1 adj
ʼ εἶπεν	[b λέγει]	αὐτῷ,	Κύριε,	ʼ σὺ	πάντα
eipen	*legei*	*autō*	*Kurie*	*su*	*panta*
said	[says]	to him,	Lord,	you	all things

3820.1 adj	4622.1 prs-pron nom 2sing	3471.3 verb 2sing indic perf act	4622.1 prs-pron nom 2sing	1091.2 verb 2sing indic pres act
[☆ πάντα	σὺ]	οἶδας·	σὺ	γινώσκεις
panta	*su*	*oidas*	*su*	*ginōskeis*
[all things	you]	know;	you	know

speak to Peter about shepherding the sheep. Lambs are young, tender sheep, and they speak of young, immature disciples. Young sheep need food for growth and health. "Feed" is a present active imperative verb. It indicates a continuing action: "keep feeding" my lambs. Especially close to Jesus' heart are the young ones in His flock.

21:16. A "second time" Jesus asked Peter the personal question. This time He did not refer to the love of the other disciples. Surely Peter was glad for the omission for the probe had touched a flaw in Peter's character. He had thought his devotion to Jesus far superior to that of any of his friends.

Jesus used Peter's old name, "Simon," in all three questions. The use of this name instead of "Peter" surely penetrated the heart of Peter. Jesus implied that in Peter's three denials the old nature of his character was at work. Simon had not yet become a solid rock.

The first question was connected to the comparison with the other disciples. Here the question is more personal. Again Jesus used the term *agapaō,* and again Peter used the word *phileō*. Peter's reply was the same as it was to the first question. He was not as boastful of his love as he had been before his three denials.

The Lord accepted Peter's response. He did not rebuke him for the weaker confession. "Feed my sheep" is another present active imperative verb meaning "keep on shepherding." This word is more inclusive of the shepherd's work than "feed" of verse 15. The lambs need feeding, but all the sheep need shepherding.

21:17. Here John brings us to the climax of this dramatic conversation. The first two times Jesus used the word *agapas* (from *agapaō*) when interrogating Peter about his love for the Master. Each time Peter had replied with *philō* (from *phileō*). Jesus now changes to the word Peter used, asking *phileis me* ("do you have an affection for me?"). It is as though the Lord is saying, "Do you only have affection for me? Can you not say you love me with the highest kind of love?"

Peter's response is very interesting. It reveals something about the change in his attitude. Possibly Jesus' thrice reiterated question reminded him of his bold statement earlier that he would never forsake Jesus, and also his threefold denial. If so, this explains why "Peter was grieved."

No longer would Peter be so bold in his declaration of loyalty and love. He had learned some things. He had not known himself very well when he said, "Though I should die with thee, yet will I not deny thee" (Matthew 26:35). He had learned not to trust his own evaluation of the degree of his love.

16. He saith to him again the second time, Simon, son of Jonas, lovest thou me?: Jesus asked again, *ET.*

He saith unto him, Yea, Lord; thou knowest that I love thee: Yes, Master, *ET* . . . you know that you are dear to me, *Weymouth, Montgomery* . . . you know that I am your friend, *Phillips* . . . Why, Lord, he said, you know I love you, *Moffatt* . . . that I fondly love Thee, *Worrell.*

He saith unto him, Feed my sheep: Shepherd my sheep, *HBIE* . . . Shepherd my flock, *ALBA* . . . Keep my sheep, *Alford* . . . Tend my sheep, *RSV, Campbell* . . . Care for my sheep, *Klingensmith* . . . Look after my sheep, *JB.*

17. He saith unto him the third time, Simon, son of Jonas, lovest thou me?: Simon, son of John, are you my friend, *TCNT* . . . Am I dear to you, *Weymouth* . . . do you love Me dearly? *Norlie* . . . Am I really dear to you? *Montgomery* . . . do you fondly love Me? *Worrell.*

Peter was grieved because he said unto him the third time, Lovest thou me?: Peter was sorie, *Geneva* . . . was deeply hurt, *Adams* . . . Peter was upset, *JB* . . . Now Peter was troubled in his heart because, *BB* . . . was vexed at being asked, *Moffatt.*

And he said unto him, Lord, thou knowest all things: Lord, you know everything, *Williams, Norlie* . . . thou understandest, *Murdock* . . . You can tell that, *TCNT* . . . all things intuitively, *Clementson.*

17.c.**Txt:** 02A,017K, 033X,036,037,038,13, byz.Weis,Sod
Var: 01ℵ,03B,04C,05D, 032W,1,33,Lach,Treg, Alf,TiscWe/Ho,UBS/☆

17.d.**Txt:** 01ℵ,05D,017K, 032W,036,037,038,1,13, byz.Gries,Lach,Sod
Var: 02A,03B,04C,Treg, AlfTisc,We/Ho,Weis, UBS/☆

3617.1 conj	**5205.1** verb 1sing pres act	**4622.4** prs-pron acc 2sing	**2978.5** verb 3sing indic pres act	**840.4** prs-pron dat sing	**3450.5** art sing masc	**2400.1** name nom masc
ὅτι	φιλῶ	σε.	Λέγει	αὐτῷ	(c ὁ)	Ἰησοῦς,
hoti	*philō*	*se*	*Legei*	*autō*	*ho*	*Iēsous*
that	I love	you.	Says	to him		Jesus,

999.1 verb 2sing impr pres act	**3450.17** art pl neu	**4122.3** noun pl neu	**4122.3** noun pl neu	**1466.2** prs-pron gen 1sing
Βόσκε	τὰ	(πρόβατά	[d☆ πρόβατά]	μου.
Boske	*ta*	*probata*	*probata*	*mou*
Feed	the	sheep	[idem]	my.

279.1 partic	**279.1** partic	**2978.1** verb 1sing pres act	**4622.3** prs-pron dat 2sing	**3616.1** conj	**1498.35** verb 2sing indic imperf act
18. ἀμὴν	ἀμὴν	λέγω	σοι,	ὅτε	ἦς
amēn	*amēn*	*legō*	*soi*	*hote*	*ēs*
Truly	truly	I say	to you,	When	you were

3365.4 adj comp nom sing masc	**2207.2** verb 2sing indic imperf act	**4427.4** prs-pron acc 2sing masc	**2504.1** conj	**3906.27** verb 2sing indic imperf act	**3562.1** adv
νεώτερος	ἐζώννυες	σεαυτὸν,	καὶ	περιεπάτεις	ὅπου
neōteros	*ezōnnues*	*seauton*	*kai*	*periepateis*	*hopou*
younger	you girded	yourself,	and	walked	where

2286.31 verb 2sing indic imperf act	**3615.1** conj	**1156.2** conj	**1088.2** verb 2sing subj aor act	**1601.6** verb 2sing indic fut act
ἤθελες·	ὅταν	δὲ	γηράσῃς	ἐκτενεῖς
ētheles	*hotan*	*de*	*gērasēs*	*ekteneis*
you did desire;	when	but	you shall be old	you shall stretch forth

3450.15 art acc pl fem	**5331.8** noun acc pl fem	**4622.2** prs-pron gen 2sing	**2504.1** conj	**241.4** adj nom sing masc	**4622.4** prs-pron acc 2sing
τὰς	χεῖράς	σου,	καὶ	ἄλλος	(☆ σε
tas	*cheiras*	*sou*	*kai*	*allos*	*se*
the	hands	your,	and	another	you

2207.1 verb 3sing indic fut act	**2207.1** verb 3sing indic fut act	**4622.4** prs-pron acc 2sing	**2504.1** conj	**5179.19** verb 3sing indic fut act	**3562.1** adv
ζώσει,	[ζώσει	σε]	καὶ	οἴσει	ὅπου
zōsei	*zōsei*	*se*	*kai*	*oisei*	*hopou*
shall gird,	[shall gird	you]	and	bring	where

3620.3 partic	**2286.2** verb 2sing indic pres act	**3642.17** dem-pron sing neu	**1156.2** conj	**1500.5** verb 3sing indic aor act	**4446.1** verb nom sing masc part pres act
οὐ	θέλεις.	**19.** Τοῦτο	δὲ	εἶπεν	σημαίνων
ou	*theleis*	*Touto*	*de*	*eipen*	*sēmainōn*
not	you desire.	This	but	he said	signifying

4029.2 intr-pron dat sing	**2265.3** noun dat sing masc	**1386.16** verb 3sing indic fut act	**3450.6** art acc sing masc	**2296.4** noun acc sing masc	**2504.1** conj
ποίῳ	θανάτῳ	δοξάσει	τὸν	θεόν.	καὶ
poiō	*thanatō*	*doxasei*	*ton*	*theon*	*kai*
by what	death	he should glorify		God.	And

3642.17 dem-pron sing neu	**1500.15** verb nom sing masc part aor act	**2978.5** verb 3sing indic pres act	**840.4** prs-pron dat sing	**188.3** verb 2sing impr pres act
τοῦτο	εἰπὼν	λέγει	αὐτῷ,	Ἀκολούθει
touto	*eipōn*	*legei*	*autō*	*Akolouthei*
this	having said	he says	to him,	Follow

20.a.**Txt:** 01ℵ,05D,017K, 036,037,038,041-corr,1, 13,byz.Gries
Var: 02A,03B,04C, 041-org,33,Lach,Treg, Alf,TiscWe/Ho,Weis,Sod, UBS/☆

1466.4 prs-pron dat 1sing	**1978.20** verb nom sing masc part aor pass	**1156.2** conj	**3450.5** art sing masc	**3935.1** name nom masc
μοι.	**20.** Ἐπιστραφεὶς	(a δὲ)	ὁ	Πέτρος
moi	*Epistrapheis*	*de*	*ho*	*Petros*
me.	Having turned	but		Peter

How would Peter answer? Would he use the *agapaō* term? No, once again Peter said *philcis se* ("I have an affection for you"). He prefaced his comment by saying, "Lord, thou knowest all things." He was willing to let the Son of God determine the depth of his love. In after years Peter showed he had risen to the *agapaō* level of love by the way he lived and the way he died, crucified head downwards at Rome.

thou knowest that I love thee: You must know that I love You dearly, *Norlie* . . . you know that you are dear to me, *Montgomery.*

Jesus saith unto him, Feed my sheep: Be grazing My little sheep, *Concordant* . . . Shepherd My sheep, *Fenton* . . . Look after my flock, *ALBA.*

21:18. Jesus took Peter through deep probings of his soul. The examination of Peter's self-confidence and pride indicated his lack of self-knowledge. Peter's relationship to his fellow disciples was probed as well. Peter realized now that his devotion to the Lord was not superior to the other disciples. There was no place for spiritual pride. Peter was also tested as to his love for Jesus. Now he realized his love was not strong enough. He sensed he must strive all his life toward a steadfast love for Jesus. Jesus knew Peter would live until he was "old." The Lord also knew the kind of death Peter would suffer.

Jesus told Peter he would carry out His threefold ministry until he died. Peter had denied the Lord, yet he would remain faithful until his death. To fail is not the end, for if it were, few if any disciples would arrive safely at the Father's house. The same grace Jesus extended to Peter is available to all.

"Thou girdedst" is an imperfect active verb used only here in the New Testament. It referred to Peter's customary action in doing as he pleased. If he wished to put his belt around his flowing robe so that his garments would not get in the way of his walk, he girded himself and went.

"But when thou shalt be old" is the contrast to "when thou wast young." Verse 19 explains what Jesus meant. "Thou shalt be old" (*gērasēs*) is from the Greek verb *gēraskō* which occurs only here and in Hebrews 8:13. Peter was told that in his old age he would be helpless. Others would determine for him the girding of his belt and the places he would go. The place they would bring him would be a cross. This is clear from the next verse.

18. Verily, verily, I say unto thee, When thou wast young, thou girdedst thyself: . . . when you were younger, you used to dress yourself, *Phillips* . . . whereas in your youth you dressed, *Norlie* . . . used to put on your own girdle, *TCNT* . . . you tied your own belt, *SEB.*

and walkedst whither thou wouldest: . . . and walk wherever you chose, *Weymouth* . . . and were free to go where you liked, *ALBA* . . . go anywhere you wanted to, *TEV* . . . whither it pleased thee, *Murdock.*

but when thou shalt be old, thou shalt stretch forth thy hands, and another shall gird thee: . . . but, whensoever thou mayest become aged, *Rotherham* . . . yet whenever you may be decrepit, *Concordant* . . . you will stretch out your hands for some one to gird you, *Montgomery* . . . and someone else will dress you, *Phillips* . . . someone else will tie you, *Beck, SEB* . . . and another will clothe you, *Adams.*

and carry thee whither thou wouldest not: . . . and you will be taken where you have no wish to go, *Moffatt* . . . and lead you where you won't like, *ALBA.*

21:19. According to the church father Tertullian, and Eusebius, the church historian, Peter was crucified at Rome in A.D. 67 or 68. This was a couple of years after the apostle Paul's martydom at Rome. Thus John's Gospel tells us the Lord's prophecy of Peter's manner of death.

Jesus' reassurance to Peter was followed by a renewal of full discipleship. "Follow me" means to "follow me now." This may indicate a personal word Jesus had for Peter (see verse 22). Yet,

19. This spake he, signifying by what death he should glorify God: . . . by what manner of death, *HBIE* . . . He said this to show by what kind of death, *Beck* . . . by which he would give God glory, *BB* . . . pay honour to God, *Fenton.*

And, when he had spoken this, he saith unto him, Follow me: Keep on following me! *Williams.*

984.4 verb 3sing indic pres act	3450.6 art acc sing masc	3073.4 noun acc sing masc	3614.6 rel-pron acc sing masc	25.26 verb 3sing indic imperf act
βλέπει	τὸν	μαθητὴν	ὃν	ἠγάπα
blepei	*ton*	*mathētēn*	*hon*	*ēgapa*
sees	the	disciple	whom	loved

3450.5 art sing masc	2400.1 name nom masc	188.7 verb acc sing masc part pres act	3614.5 rel-pron nom sing masc	2504.1 conj
ὁ	Ἰησοῦς	ἀκολουθοῦντα,	ὃς	καὶ
ho	*Iēsous*	*akolouthounta*	*hos*	*kai*
	Jesus	following,	who	also

375.1 verb 3sing indic aor act	1706.1 prep	3450.3 art dat sing	1168.3 noun dat sing neu	1894.3 prep	3450.16 art sing neu
ἀνέπεσεν	ἐν	τῷ	δείπνῳ	ἐπὶ	τὸ
anepesen	*en*	*tō*	*deipnō*	*epi*	*to*
reclined	at	the	supper	on	the

4589.1 noun acc sing neu	840.3 prs-pron gen sing	2504.1 conj	1500.5 verb 3sing indic aor act	2935.5 noun voc sing masc	4949.3 intr-pron nom sing
στῆθος	αὐτοῦ	καὶ	εἶπεν,	Κύριε,	τίς
stēthos	*autou*	*kai*	*eipen*	*Kurie*	*tis*
breast	his	and	said,	Lord,	who

1498.4 verb 3sing indic pres act	3450.5 art sing masc	3722.3 verb nom sing masc part pres act	4622.4 prs-pron acc 2sing	3642.6 dem-pron acc sing masc
ἐστιν	ὁ	παραδιδούς	σε;	21. Τοῦτον
estin	*ho*	*paradidous*	*se*	*Touton*
is it	the	delivering up	you?	This

21.a.Var: 01ℵ,03B,04C, 05D,33,Lach,Treg,Alf, Tisc,We/HoWeis,Sod, UBS/☆

3631.1 conj	1481.16 verb nom sing masc part aor act	3450.5 art sing masc	3935.1 name nom masc	2978.5 verb 3sing indic pres act
[a☆+ οὖν]	ἰδὼν	ὁ	Πέτρος	λέγει
oun	*idōn*	*ho*	*Petros*	*legei*
[therefore]	seeing		Peter	says

3450.3 art dat sing	2400.2 name masc	2935.5 noun voc sing masc	3642.4 dem-pron nom sing masc	1156.2 conj	4949.9 intr-pron sing neu
τῷ	Ἰησοῦ,	Κύριε,	οὗτος	δὲ	τί;
tō	*Iēsou*	*Kurie*	*houtos*	*de*	*ti*
	to Jesus,	Lord,	of this one	but	what;

2978.5 verb 3sing indic pres act	840.4 prs-pron dat sing	3450.5 art sing masc	2400.1 name nom masc	1430.1 partic	840.6 prs-pron acc sing masc
22. Λέγει	αὐτῷ	ὁ	Ἰησοῦς,	Ἐὰν	αὐτὸν
Legei	*autō*	*ho*	*Iēsous*	*Ean*	*auton*
Says	to him		Jesus,	If	him

2286.1 verb 1sing pres act	3176.15 verb inf pres act	2175.1 conj	2048.32 verb 1sing indic pres	4949.9 intr-pron sing neu	4242.1 prep
θέλω	μένειν	ἕως	ἔρχομαι,	τί	πρὸς
thelō	*menein*	*heōs*	*erchomai*	*ti*	*pros*
I want	to remain	till	I come,	what	to

4622.4 prs-pron acc 2sing	4622.1 prs-pron nom 2sing	188.3 verb 2sing impr pres act	1466.4 prs-pron dat 1sing	1466.4 prs-pron dat 1sing
σέ;	σύ	ʽ ἀκολούθει	μοι.	[☆ μοι
se	*su*	*akolouthei*	*moi*	*moi*
you?	You	follow	me.	[me

188.3 verb 2sing impr pres act	1814.3 verb 3sing indic aor act	3631.1 conj	3450.5 art sing masc	3030.1 noun nom sing masc
ἀκολούθει.]	23. Ἐξῆλθεν	οὖν	ʽ ὁ	λόγος
akolouthei	*Exēlthen*	*oun*	*ho*	*logos*
follow.]	Went out	therefore	the	word

the Gospel's meaning surely may be understood in the figurative sense, "follow me" to the martyr's death.

20. Then Peter, turning about, seeth the disciple whom Jesus loved following: Peter turned and saw the disciple whom Jesus loved following them, *Beck* . . . Peter turned round and saw that the favourite disciple, *Moffatt* . . . whom Jesus specially loved, *Williams.*

which also leaned on his breast at supper, and said, Lord, which is he that betrayeth thee?: . . . the one who had been sitting at the table very close to Jesus who asked, Lord, who is the one who is turning against, *SEB* . . . thy betrayer? *HistNT.*

21:20. Peter's response was indicative of his entire future walk with Christ. John is described as: (1) the one whom Jesus loved, (2) he who leaned on Jesus' breast, and (3) the one who asked Jesus of thc betrayer. He was an eyewitness to the event.

21. Peter seeing him saith to Jesus, Lord, and what shall this man do?: On catching sight of him, *Montgomery* . . . Lord, yet what of this one? *Concordant* . . . as for this man, what? *Murdock* . . . what, Lord, shall become of this man? *Campbell* . . . Lord, what will happen to him? *NEB* . . . And what about him, Lord, *Moffatt.*

21:21. Peter was the one addressed in verses 18-20; therefore, when he saw John following, he asked Jesus concerning John. We do not know if Peter asked because he felt John was intruding or if he had a genuine interest in John's welfare.

22. Jesus saith unto him, If I will that he tarry till I come: If I choose, *Montgomery* . . . If I desire him to remain till I come, *Weymouth* . . . If it is my wish, *Phillips* . . . that he remain until I come, *Rotherham* . . . I return, *Campbell* . . . If I were to choose that he should wait till I come, *TCNT* . . . If I want him to stay alive, *SEB.*

what is that to thee?: . . . what concern is that of yours, *Weymouth* . . . is it any concern of yours? *ALBA* . . . what does it concern you? *Norton* . . . is that your business, *Phillips* . . . what does that matter to you? *Moffatt.*

follow thou me: You follow Me! *Berkeley* . . . Your business is to follow Me, *Norlie* . . . Follow me yourself, *Weymouth.*

21:22. Jesus had already foretold John's suffering for His name, but He had not spoken of the apostle's death (see Matthew 20:23; Mark 10:39). "That he tarry" means to continue to live in the flesh. Long life was considered one of the greatest blessings from God. Surely Jesus implied His deity by claiming the authority to prolong John's life indefinitely. However, "if" puts the longevity of John as a possibility, not a prediction. "Till I come" refers to Jesus' second coming as He prophesied in 14:3. His promise was that all His disciples would be taken to be with Him at that time, but not all would live in the flesh until that time.

Jesus' words were a rebuke to Peter's interference between another disciple and Jesus. It is true that we are our brother's keeper and we are to love our neighbor as ourselves; but Jesus' rebuke safeguards each disciple against envy, jealousy, and curiosity concerning His dealings with other disciples.

The word "you" is emphatic indicating that Peter, as a believer, was solely responsible for his own conduct, not that of John or any other.

21:23. "This saying" refers to verse 22 according to the false interpretation which follows. "The brethren" is a beautiful designation for the disciples of Jesus the Lord. The term implies equality among believers, an equality based on family relationship with God as the Heavenly Father.

Some disciples inferred that John would not die until Jesus came

3642.4 dem-pron nom sing masc	3642.4 dem-pron nom sing masc	3450.5 art sing masc	3030.1 noun nom sing masc	1519.1 prep
οὗτος	[☆ οὗτος	ὁ	λόγος]	εἰς
houtos	houtos	ho	logos	eis
this	[this	the	word]	among

3450.8 art acc pl masc	79.9 noun acc pl masc	3617.1 conj	3450.5 art sing masc	3073.1 noun nom sing masc	1552.3 dem-pron nom sing masc
τοὺς	ἀδελφοὺς,	Ὅτι	ὁ	μαθητὴς	ἐκεῖνος
tous	adelphous	Hoti	ho	mathētēs	ekeinos
the	brothers,	That	the	disciple	that

23.a.**Txt:** 02A,05D,017K, 033X,036,037,038,1,13, byz.Gries,Lach,Tisc,Sod
Var: p59,01ℵ,03B,04C, 032W,33,Treg,We/Ho, Weis,UBS/☆

3620.2 partic	594.2 verb 3sing indic pres act	2504.1 conj	3620.2 partic	1500.5 verb 3sing indic aor act	3620.2 partic
οὐκ	ἀποθνῄσκει·	(καὶ	οὐκ	εἶπεν	[a☆ οὐκ
ouk	apothnēskei	kai	ouk	eipen	ouk
not	does die.	However	not	said	[not

1500.5 verb 3sing indic aor act	1156.2 conj	840.4 prs-pron dat sing	3450.5 art sing masc	2400.1 name nom masc	3617.1 conj	3620.2 partic
εἶπεν	δὲ]	αὐτῷ	ὁ	Ἰησοῦς,	ὅτι	οὐκ
eipen	de	autō	ho	Iēsous	hoti	ouk
said	but]	to him		Jesus,	That	not

594.2 verb 3sing indic pres act	233.1 conj	1430.1 partic	840.6 prs-pron acc sing masc	2286.1 verb 1sing pres act	3176.15 verb inf pres act
ἀποθνῄσκει·	ἀλλ',	Ἐὰν	αὐτὸν	θέλω	μένειν
apothnēskei	all'	Ean	auton	thelō	menein
he does die;	but,	If	him	I desire	to remain

23.b.**Txt:** 01ℵ-corr,02A, 03B,04C-org,(05),017K, 036,037,038,byz.Lach, We/Ho,Weis,UBS/☆
Var: 01ℵ-org,04C-corr,1, 565,Tisc,Sod

2175.1 conj	2048.32 verb 1sing indic pres	4949.9 intr-pron sing neu	4242.1 prep	4622.4 prs-pron acc 2sing	3642.4 dem-pron nom sing masc
ἕως	ἔρχομαι,	(b τί	πρὸς	σέ;)	24. Οὗτός
heōs	erchomai	ti	pros	se	Houtos
till	I come,	what	to	you?	This

1498.4 verb 3sing indic pres act	3450.5 art sing masc	3073.1 noun nom sing masc	3450.5 art sing masc	3113.7 verb nom sing masc part pres act	3875.1 prep
ἐστιν	ὁ	μαθητὴς	ὁ	μαρτυρῶν	περὶ
estin	ho	mathētēs	ho	marturōn	peri
is	the	disciple	the	bearing witness	concerning

24.a.**Var:** 03B,05D,it.sa. bo.Lach,Treg,Alf,We/Ho, Weis,UBS/☆

3642.2 dem-pron gen pl	2504.1 conj	3450.5 art sing masc	1119.13 verb nom sing masc part aor act	3642.18 dem-pron pl neu	2504.1 conj
τούτων,	καὶ	[a+ ὁ]	γράψας	ταῦτα·	καὶ
toutōn	kai	ho	grapsas	tauta	kai
these things,	and	[the]	having written	these things:	and

3471.5 verb 1pl indic perf act	3617.1 conj	225.2 adj nom sing	1498.4 verb 3sing indic pres act	3450.9 art nom sing fem	3114.1 noun nom sing fem
οἴδαμεν	ὅτι	ἀληθὴς	(ἐστίν	ἡ	μαρτυρία
oidamen	hoti	alēthēs	estin	hē	marturia
we know	that	true	is	the	witness

840.3 prs-pron gen sing	840.3 prs-pron gen sing	3450.9 art nom sing fem	3114.1 noun nom sing fem	1498.4 verb 3sing indic pres act
αὐτοῦ.	[☆ αὐτοῦ	ἡ	μαρτυρία	ἐστίν.]
autou	autou	hē	marturia	estin
his.	[his	the	witness	is.]

1498.4 verb 3sing indic pres act	1156.2 conj	2504.1 conj	241.15 adj pl neu	4044.17 adj pl neu	3607.8 rel-pron pl neu
25. Ἔστιν	δὲ	καὶ	ἄλλα	πολλὰ	(ὅσα
Estin	de	kai	alla	polla	hosa
There are	and	also	other things	many	whatever

back the second time (see 1 Corinthians 15:51; 1 Thessalonians 4:17). The longer John lived, the more logical it seemed to them that what Jesus meant was that Jesus would come before John died. This verse, therefore, corrects the fallacy.

"But" contrasts the interpretation with what Jesus actually said. The wish of the Lord is submission to His authority. Things are done according to His desires. But the "if" is conditional. He did not say it was His wish, but only "if" He did wish. This appeal to what Jesus said should be an incentive to all believers to rightly divide the Word of Truth. To add to or subtract from it can bring dishonor to Jesus and His kingdom.

23. Then went this saying abroad among the brethren, that that disciple should not die: This started the report, *Moffatt* . . . Consequently the report spread, *TCNT* . . . So the report got out, *Williams* . . . This started the report, *Moffatt* . . . Accordingly the report spread, *Montgomery* . . . The rumor then went out among the brothers that this disciple, *JB* . . . The Christian community got to know about this saying, and they took it to mean that that man would not die, *Barclay* . . . That saying of Jesus became current in the brotherhood, and was taken to mean that that disciple would not die, *NEB* . . . led to a general impression among the brothers, *Fenton* . . . a rumor spread, *ET* . . . went out to the brothers, *SEB* . . . the brotherhood, *Berkeley* . . . among the Christians and were taken to mean that, *ALBA* . . . would not undergo death, *BB*.

yet Jesus said not unto him, He shall not die:

but, If I will that he tarry till I come, what is that to thee?: . . . that he should survive until, *Barclay* . . . what business is it of yours? *SEB* . . . is it any concern of yours? *ALBA*.

21:24. These "things" refers to the entire Gospel of John. There is no reason to limit them to the last chapter. John assures us at the end of the Gospel that he was the inspired writer so that he might impress on them the validity of his witness. According to *BAGD*, p.556, the Greek phrase translated "we know that" is often used to introduce a fact that is well known and "generally accepted." Through the Church ages John's testimony has been used of the Spirit to bring multitudes into the Kingdom. This Gospel has furnished evidence to all believers as to the identity of the Son of God and His great redemptive work.

"We know" here indicates a knowledge which exceeds that of personal experience. This knowledge may be grounded on experience, yet it means a spiritual, intuitive certainty. The use of "we know" serves to reinforce John's witness as "true." John was aware that to validate any testimony it was necessary to strengthen one's witness by the addition of one or two others (Deuteronomy 17:6; 19:15; Matthew 13:16; 2 Corinthians 13:1). Therefore, he affirmed what is "true" by stating, "We know." "We" includes the other apostles and all others who knew the facts as John knew them. In 21:25 the personal, individual judgment of a disciple is only expressed as "I suppose." "I suppose" occurs only at 21:25 in the New Testament, but "we know" occurs many times in the Gospel of John and in John's epistles. John witnessed to that which he was assured of, not what he thought or supposed.

24. This is the disciple which testifieth of these things: It is this disciple who bears testimony to these facts, *Montgomery* . . . who attests these things, *Campbell* . . . who vouches for, *JB* . . . who guarantees the truth of these facts, *Barclay* . . . these events, *Fenton*.

and wrote these things: and we know that his testimony is true: It is in fact he who wrote it, *NEB* . . . he it was who wrote them down, *ALBA* . . . and has written this account, *Norton* . . . and who recorded them, *Montgomery* . . . We know that his witness is reliable, *Phillips* . . . is trustworthy, *TCNT*.

21:25. What is written in John's Gospel is to reveal that Jesus is Christ, the Son of God. Most of the material this Gospel relates is not found in the other Gospels. But John's Gospel harmonizes with the Synoptics and gives narrative not included in the other Gospels. It presents Jesus as God more clearly than does any other book of the New Testament, including the other Gospels.

"Many other things" which Jesus did refers to events not recorded in the Gospel of John. "If they should be written every one"

25. And there are also many other things which Jesus did, the

John 21:25

25.a.**Txt:** 02A,04C-corr, 05D,017K,032W,036, 037,038,1,13,byz.Lach **Var:** 01ℵ,03B,04C-org, 033X,33,Treg,Alf, We/Ho,WeisSod,UBS/⋆

25.b.**Txt:** 02A,04C-corr, 05D,017K,032W,036, 037,038,1,13,byz.Lach, Sod **Var:** 01ℵ-corr,03B, 04C-org,Treg,We/Ho, Weis,UBS/⋆

25.c.**Txt:** 07E,017K, 021M,033X,036,037, 038,13,byz. **Var:** 01ℵ,02A,03B,04C, 05D,33,Gries,Lach,Treg, Alf,We/HoWeis,Sod, UBS/⋆

25.d.**Var:** 03B,Treg

3614.17 rel-pron pl neu [a⋆ ἃ] *ha* [which]
4020.24 verb 3sing indic aor act ἐποίησεν *epoiēsen* did
3450.5 art sing masc ὁ *ho*
2400.1 name nom masc Ἰησοῦς, *Iēsous* Jesus,
3610.6 rel-pron nom pl neu ἅτινα *hatina* which
1430.1 partic ἐὰν *ean* if

1119.18 verb 3sing subj pres pass γράφηται *graphētai* they should be written
2567.2 prep καθ' *kath'* according
1518.9 num card neu ἕν, *hen* by one,
3624.1 adv ⸀ οὐδὲ *oude* not even
3624.2 adv [⋆ οὐδ'] *oud'* [idem]

840.6 prs-pron acc sing masc αὐτὸν *auton* it
3492.1 verb 1sing indic pres οἶμαι *oimai* I suppose
3450.6 art acc sing masc τὸν *ton* the
2862.4 noun acc sing masc κόσμον *kosmon* world
5397.7 verb inf aor act ⸀⋆ χωρῆσαι *chōrēsai* would contain

5397.8 verb inf fut act [b χωρήσειν] *chōrēsein* [idem]
3450.17 art pl neu τὰ *ta* the
1119.19 verb acc pl neu part pres pass γραφόμενα *graphomena* being written
968.4 noun pl neu βιβλία. *biblia* books.
279.1 partic ⸂c Ἀμήν. ⸃ *Amēn* Amen.

2567.3 prep [d+ Κατὰ *Kata* [According to
2464.5 name acc sing masc Ἰωάνην] *Iōanēn* John]

relates to 20:30. Even if an eyewitness desired to describe the full details of Jesus' deeds and utterances, he could not. It would be virtually impossible to express in totality and with finality the majestic greatness of God in Christ. God is infinite, and any full explanation of Him must be as infinite as He is. Therefore, "the world itself could not contain the books that should be written."

which, if they should be written every one: There were many other things that Jesus did, *JB* . . . many other activities...if they were all described in detail, *Berkeley* . . . also performed...to be severally related, *Campbell* . . . so many, indeed, that if every one were recorded, *Norlie* . . . vvhich if they vvere vvritten in particular, *Rheims* . . . written out with particularity, *Murdock* . . . to be written, one by one, *Rotherham* . . . if they were all described in detail, *Weymouth* . . . if each one were written down in detail, *Phillips* . . . if a detailed account of them were, *Barclay* . . . in detail, *Williams.*

I suppose that even the world itself could not contain the books that should be written: . . . it is my opinion, *BB* . . . I am surmising...the written scrolls, *Concordant* . . . the volumes there would be, *Campbell* . . . the universe, *Wuest* . . . the world would not have room for, *Beck* . . . would not receive the books, *Scarlett* . . . would not suffice for the books that would be written, *Murdock* . . . the written books, *Wilson.*

Amen.

Overview

The *Overview* is a significant section of the *Study Bible.* It offers important information describing the major incidents and themes of each book. Its background facts concerning history, customs, geography, economics, and politics provide a splendid backdrop for understanding the events which transpired on the first-century stage.

Prologue

The opening or "prologue" of the Gospel of John focuses upon the divine personality of Jesus Christ, the central character of the entire book. He is called *logos,* "the Word," and because the inspired writer assumed his readers understood what this meant, he offered no other further explanation. Logos, the Word, is the terminology of that day's literature—both Jewish and Greek—which in a natural way informs us of the writer's use of the language. For example, the Jewish philosopher Philo spoke of the Logos as the adopted Son of God, (Philo *De Sobr.* 56).

However, in the Gospel of John the term *logos* acquires a new depth of meaning: Christ. The expression was "purified" and removed from its heritage in pagan Gentile philosophy (cf. Psalm 12:6). The Logos of the Gospel contrasts Greek philosophical usage and breaks with traditional Jewish use of the Hebrew word, *dābar.* The developing understanding of *logos* as found in the Jewish synagogue now became crystal clear. Christ is the eternal Word of God to the world; He is the perfect expression of the nature of the Father. The Word become flesh is the total manifestation of God's nature; He is the totality of how God is to be known by humanity.

The *logos*-concept common in the thinking and writing of that time, however, surpassed all former understanding of the word. Although the vocabulary was the same, its meaning was completely different. John used *logos* solely to point to the Logos Person.

Nevertheless, the use of *logos* to describe the divine Person in John's Gospel derived from particular reasons. The *logos*-concept is essentially the only philosophical-religious expression that simultaneously resonates with both Jewish and Greek modes of thought. Thus it became a common point of contact for preaching the Messiah.

Apparently much of the background for the New Testament's *logos*-doctrine can be traced to the Jewish synagogue. The Old Testament used *logos* as the primary expression of God's revelation to mankind. The same can be said for the New Testament. In all likelihood, therefore, there is a definite link between the revelation of the Old Testament and that of the New. One need not travel outside the Scripture to discover the source of the *logos*-concept and its background in the New Testament.

At the same time, because the New Testament employs a term so well known in Greek philosophy, it is possible to assume there is an intrinsic relationship with the Greek usage, although it may not have been intentional on the writer's part. If that is indeed the case, examining the Hellenistic background of the term helps to assess how the concept was expanded by the New Testament.

The Greek Concept of Logos. Much of the data suggests that the Gospel of John was written in Ephesus during the last decade of the First Century A.D. It was Ephesus where the *logos*-concept first emerged. More than 500 years earlier, Heraclitus, a Greek philosopher (540-480 B.C.), lived there. His basic theory was that everything in the world is subject to change, "everything flows." Since existence is not in complete chaos, Heraclitus explained that a controlling factor, a basic pattern from which everything originated, kept the world in unity. This designing, determinative principle of existence, the rational and unchanging force that controlled life, was called *logos* by Heraclitus. This "law" or "force" he also termed "righteousness" or "harmony"; on a few occasions he called it "god." It is not known whether or not he envisioned a personal being in his use of that title (cf. Jaspers, pp.17-24).

Even the theory of Heraclitus was not without forerunners. The most ancient evidence of similar speculations found in the Egyptian *hu* and the Sumerian *enem* suggests that "word" was regarded as a "being" having its own existence (i.e., *hupostasis*). But the Hellenistic speculations about *logos* are of the most concern for our purposes, because the Hellenistic understanding became absorbed by the term itself, which was later used by the New Testament.

Clearly the *logos*-concept introduced by Heraclitus is one of the most vital concepts in Greek philosophy. The doctrine was never given up. Fascinated by the entire concept, the philosophers, especially the Stoics, developed and modified the concept for centuries to come. On one occasion Plato (427-347 B.C.) used *logos* to denote the divine power responsible for creating the world. The Greeks considered *logos* as the creative and controlling power of God, that is, the power which both created the world and kept it going.

Elsewhere *logos* is understood differently by different authors. Because of the dualistic tendencies that dominated Greek philosophy, and the Greek view that the divine (immaterial) could never come into contact with the material, *logos* was regarded as a mediator between God and His universe, a manifestation of the divine principle in the world. According to Stoic thought *logos* was divine thought as well as the light of reason that was dispersed in the world—the rational principle in the world.

Despite the errors and superstitions inherent in these speculations, the *logos*-concept nonetheless stands as one of the noblest thoughts in Greek philosophy. This concept—or at least this word, *logos*—was there, ready for John to use when he wrote his Gospel under the inspiration of the Spirit. Just as Paul related his message to the concept of "the unknown God" (Acts 17:23), John introduced his Gospel in the familiar language of Greek thought—*logos*. Jesus Christ is the Logos; the Word become flesh and living among men. He is the Creator of the world, the true Light that enlightens every person.

This should not be misinterpreted as saying that the *logos*-doctrine of the New Testament depends upon the Hellenistic concept of *logos* or that it merely develops that view. Just as the altar of the "unknown god" served as an altar of the idolatrous, likewise at its heart *logos* in Greek thought was essentially a pagan Gentile concept. The *logos* proclamation of the New Testament does not develop this pagan strain of thought. It contrasts with it. At the same time, the need of those who worshiped at the altar of the unknown god and of those who followed the teachings of the philosophers in search of truth could be redirected toward the revelation of God in Jesus Christ. He is the Word, the ultimate revelation of God to men.

In the Gospel of John use of the word *logos* picks up a common Greek term, but redresses it in new and exciting terms. It is doubtful that another term would have received as much immediate attention and interest as *logos*. Those truly seeking for the meaning of life would be intrigued to investigate the light and the life of the world.

Logos connotes the deepest mystery of the gospel—Jesus Christ himself. While the gospel is conveyed in the language of Greek thought of that day, John broke radically with the principal tenet of Greek thought. It was axiomatic to Greek philosophy that any deity was far removed from the physical universe and was relatively uninterested in human affairs, struggles, and joys. How starkly contrasting is the God who reveals himself in the *logos* of the Gospel of John! He does not isolate himself as an unaffected spectator: "And the Word was made flesh, and dwelt among us" (1:14).

Jewish Background in the Old Testament. While there was an earlier tendency in scholarship to regard the *logos*-doctrine of John as being derived only from Greek thought, it is now apparent that the concept was rooted more firmly in the Old Testament and Judaism.

The relationship between the prologue of John's Gospel and the Old Testament is clear. John's opening words "In the beginning was the Word" unquestionably allude to the phrase "and God said" repeated so often in the early chapters of Genesis. In the creation account we are confronted by the Word as the powerful, creative Word of God. The Hebrew text reads 'āmar, "to say" (literally, "God said"). Contained in 'āmar is the idea of "to command"; God "commands" through His powerful word (cf. 2 Corinthians 4:6). Together with the Spirit of God (cf. Genesis 1:2), the Word was the means of effecting creation. God spoke and it took place (cf. Psalm 33:9). By speaking that which did not exist God caused it to come into being (cf. Romans 4:17).

The ordinary term for "word" in the Old Testament is *dābar*, although *dābar* has a much broader meaning than simply "word." *Dābar* has three chief meanings and some variations of these: (1) "word, speech, saying for a reason"; (2) "thing or action"; (3) "reason, the reason for something."

The term is pivotal and central to the concept of salvation history and revelation. Its entire scope of meaning comes to bear here. Consequently, no true distinction can be drawn between God's "word" and God's "work." God speaks through His prophetic "word" as well as in the events of history. The prophetic word not only interprets history, it also creates and shapes it. All of salvation history recorded in the Holy Scriptures—both word and deed, message and history—is the "Word" God speaks to the world.

The word of the Lord is not merely "talk," or a "vain thing" (Deuteronomy 32:47); rather, it is a divine creative manifestation of God's power.

The word is intricately bound to the cause of the event; that "word" is tantamount to "work" from God's perspective. This is the word that creates and sustains all life (Deuteronomy 32:47; Isaiah 38:16). The word itself does not have this power, rather it is powerful because God is its source. It is His "word."

God reveals himself through His Word; He makes His will known and He gives knowledge and makes available the truth. The Word is the means of revelation. "The Lord spoke . . . " and "the word of the Lord came . . . " are frequent refrains of the Old Testament. The Word was perceived as "heard" from the Lord (cf. Isaiah 22:14); but on other occasions it could be "seen" (Isaiah 2:1; Amos 1:1), or it could come through visions or revelations (Jeremiah 1:11,12). It might also be accompanied by explanatory illustrations (Jeremiah 18:1f.) or by other confirmatory signs (Isaiah 7:10-14). The word of the Lord was revealed (1 Samuel 3:7) and that which was itself a revelation was understood through revelation.

The word of the Lord is that word He spoke to His prophets (Genesis 15:1; Exodus 6:2f.; Joshua 1:1f.); or, it could be the word spoken by the prophets, the word proclaimed in the name of the Lord (Exodus 4:30; 2 Kings 7:1; Isaiah 1:10f.; Amos 1:1f., and elsewhere). It could be spoken or written.

The knowledge revealed by the Word and the truth disclosed are not only knowledge and truth in the philosophical or historical sense of those terms. It is the truth of God. The Word not only affords insight into information or events. First and foremost it allows knowledge of God. The Word is the self- disclosure of God that unveils His essence and nature and reflects His glory. Chiefly the Word of God indicates God's desire to make himself known.

To the Hebrew mind the word involved more than the sound of words or a remark. The declared word was irrevocable. It was virtually an entity in itself. It probably extended beyond what we consider "words" and would be perceived as having a life of its own. Many times the Old Testament writers personified the Word in this way.

The Word is preexistent, eternal, and divine (Psalm 119:89). Therefore, God must send it (Psalm 107:20; 147:15). Having fulfilled its mission, it returns to God (Isaiah 55:11).

The same can be said for wisdom (Proverbs 8:25f.). Very often in the Old Testament the Word points to something more than a mere concept to something personal—or even to a person. The Word is the One who was to come to Israel with the long-awaited message of God.

Palestinian Judaism and Logos Doctrine. The trend towards personification of the "Word" found in the Old Testament was developed even further in the apocryphal literature. The Word, or "Wisdom," was considered preexistent; it was seen as a heavenly being who was revealed in judgment or salvation (Wisdom 10:15f.; Sirach 24:1f.). This concerned not simply a poetic personification but an actual person—a being with God and next to God, "the image itself of the goodness of God."

In the later Jewish Targums (Hebrew, *tigrēm* from the Akkadian word *targumanu*, "interpreter") there are fascinating examples of Jewish thought prevalent during the time of Jesus. These Aramaic paraphrases were developed for use in Scripture reading in the synagogues, because it was necessary to interpret the Hebrew text in the language of the people—Aramaic. Hebrew, for the most part, ceased to be a spoken language. A distinguishing feature of the Targums is their consistent messianic interpretation of many Old Testament texts.

Of particular interest are the Jewish *Memra* speculations, a typical characteristic of the Targums. The rabbis might employ *memra* ("word," from the same stem as 'āmar) as a circumlocution for God, i.e., another way of saying God without mentioning the ineffable name. Therefore *memra* often occurs in the Targums in texts whose Hebrew counterpart in the Old Testament reads "the Lord." The *Targum of Jonathan* contains more than three hundred such circumlocutions. It is especially used in those places where the Lord is depicted as manifesting himself to His people or speaking to them. The "Word" is said to have created the world. The Word spoke to Adam in Paradise and to Abraham. It judged Sodom and gave the Law at Mount Sinai. The Word spoke to Moses "face to face." The *Targum of Onkelos* records that Jacob gave his promise to the "Word" at Bethel (cf. Genesis 28:20; 31:13) (Etheridge, pp.254, 268). The *Targum of Jonathan* translates Isaiah 45:22 thus: "Turn ye to the Word and be saved."

This indicates that among God's chosen people of the Old Testament an understanding of the incarnate Word of God was beginning to be recognized. This clearly corresponds to the New Testament presentation of the Word made flesh. Studies of the *Dead Sea Scrolls* have led many interpreters to conclude that the background of John's *logos*-doctrine/concept is Jewish rather than Hellenistic.

In all likelihood, Jewish scribes attached different understandings to the expression "the Word of God." To some the function as a circumlocution for the name of God would have been understood. Others, however, would have adopted the concept that the Logos was a divine being. When John opened his Gospel by saying that the Word was God he was not misunderstood, since many had heard this application in the reading of the Scripture in the synagogue (cf. above on Isaiah 45:22).

Logos Doctrine in Hellenistic Judaism. The difference between the Hebraic and Hellenistic ways of thinking is reflected in the meanings of the terms *dābar* and *logos.* Whereas from a Hebrew point of view the word is intrinsically tied to something concrete or to an action, in the Greek mind "word" is primarily an abstract concept such as reason, thought. *Logos* is regarded as the rational principle or the impersonal force that orders and controls the universe. *Dābar,* however, denotes the medium of divine revelation for the Hebrew mind. *Dābar* is thus the instrument through which God carries out His purposes.

Judaism—particularly Diaspora Judaism—came in contact with Hellenistic thought and as a natural result was, to some extent, influenced by its concepts. Philo of Alexandria, a Jewish "philosopher" (ca. 30 B.C. to A.D. 50) represents such a tendency. Strongly affected by Hellenistic thought, Alexandrian Judaism attempted to synthesize the Greek concept of *logos* (as thought, reason, principle) with the Hebraic view of *dābar* (as word, message [in concrete actions]). In Philo's case, as well as Alexandrian Judaism as a whole, the union of Greek and Hebrew ideas occurred to such an extent that the image of God was itself distorted. The intent of those who merged the two world views was to present the Jewish religion of the Old Testament as the perfect Greek philosophy, which, if properly understood, would be the ultimate truth to which the Hellenistic thinkers aspired.

From Philo's point of view *logos* simultaneously expressed the word of God (i.e., "message") and the thought of God. *Logos* thus became the controlling principle of existence, the law that controlled everything, including the destiny of humanity.

But at the same time *logos* represented the will of God and the personification of His power. A variety of other powers, such as the angels of the Old Testament are subordinate to *logos.* These lesser powers supposedly embodied the "ideas" of Platonic thought and executed the will of God in the universe.

Philo adopted several images from the Hebrew to describe the Logos: The sword of the cherubim at the entrance to Paradise (*Cher.* 27-28); the cloud that guided Israel in the wilderness; the rock in the wilderness; the stream of living water; the bread from heaven, etc. (*De Fuga,* esp. 137-39 and 197-99). He also used expressions normally reserved for persons. *Logos* was the eldest or firstborn son of God. He was the man of God, the man from heaven, the immortal father of all good men (*Quod Deus* 31, *De Conf.* 62-3, and *De Spec. Leg.* 3.37 for examples). Sometimes *logos* was used to indicate the image of God and even "the second God" (*Leg. All.* 1.43,45,6). *Logos* was the mediator between God and men. He prayed for them and interceded on their behalf (*De Plant.* 9-10). He was the high priest, the messenger from heaven who revealed God to mankind (*Leg. All.* 3.177-78).

Although Philo employed *logos* no less than 1300 times in his writings, he did not say whether he understood this *logos* as a personal being or an impersonal object. When speaking of the *logos*, Philo remained ambiguous and figurative. He detected *logos* in the *Septuagint* and interpreted it there in light of Hellenistic philosophical concepts. Philo lived during the time of Christ, but there is no indication that he was aware of or believed in John's preaching of the Word become flesh. On the contrary, Philo believed that the life of God "never came down to us and has never been subject to the limitations of the body." (For a good discussion of Philo's *logos* concepts, see Dodd, pp.66-73, 276ff.)

Philo's *logos* was a personification but not a person. This Alexandrian thinker contributed to the development of the understanding of *logos* as the truth, and in a way he prepared the ground for the growth of understanding. However, he did not teach the apostles. He himself was unable to bring the truth to light. Human philosophy cannot disclose that which can only be known by divine revelation.

The Logos Person. Jews and Greeks alike perceived *logos* as the controlling force in the universe and as God's medium of expression. Consequently, when John used this term to introduce his Gospel he knew his readers had a basic awareness of the term.

From the many available Greek words the inspired writer used *logos*, rather than *rhēma*, which more closely stands for an articulate word, a statement or saying. *Logos* on the other hand, includes the message of the word or the thought it conveys. *Logos* differs from *muthos*, which also means "word," but in a false sense, such as a legend, myth, fable. *Logos* also differs from *nomos*, "law" (*tōrāh*) and the deification of the Law that became part of later Judaism. Grace and truth first came by Jesus Christ, not by the Law which was given by Moses (John 1:17).

Logos, the Word, is closely associated with the "gospel" of the New Testament, the contrast of "law." "The Word" denotes the Christian message (Mark 2:2) and that message is Christ (Acts 8:5). Paul wrote to the Corinthians, "We preach Christ" (1 Corinthians 1:23), which equals preaching "the cross" (1 Corinthians 1:18; cf. Galatians 3:1) or preaching "Christ Jesus the Lord" (2 Corinthians 4:5). He called Christ "the wisdom of God" (1 Corinthians 1:24), and he ascribed to Him the same qualities attributed to wisdom in the Old Testament (cf. Colossians 1:15-17).

John spoke of Christ the Word (John 1:1ff.), and the Word of God (Revelation 19:13). He further characterized Christ in terminology used to describe God's Word in the Old Testament. The opening words in Luke's Gospel which refer to those who "from the beginning were eyewitnesses, and ministers of the word" (Luke 1:2), closely approximate John's language in his prologue, where Jesus is called the Word. So John's application of Logos to Jesus is entirely in harmony with the rest of the New Testament. John did not introduce a foreign concept, although it was essentially a new presentation. Christ is one with the gospel. He is the personification of the Word itself. *Logos* in John's prologue is not an alien philosophical concept to the New Testament. Instead, it is an accurate expression of an authentic Christian tenet of faith. The *logos*-doctrine belongs to the central teaching of the New Testament describing the person and work of Jesus Christ.

John's Gospel emphasizes first and foremost that the Word is the principal means of God's self-disclosure. Jesus' sermons have a prominent place in the format of the Fourth Gospel, even when compared with the substantial amount of space which tells about His works. Consequently, as the Word, Jesus is the perfect manifestation of God. Because the Word expresses precisely God's thoughts and plans in concrete terms—both in word and deed—and because it does so in personal rather than impersonal terms (in Jesus), John's Gospel gives insight into the true character and nature of God. God reveals himself in His Son, the personification of His word.

The opening words of the Fourth Gospel clearly allude to the creation account. Echoed in the words "In the beginning was the Word" are the marvelous words of Genesis. "In the beginning God created . . . " (Genesis 1:1). Genesis depicts the creation as taking place through God's spoken word; John's Gospel picks up on this. However, it moves ahead and shows that the new creation is sustained by the Word. The death and darkness hanging over the fallen and lost creation of God can be dispelled only by the Life and the Light.

Verse 1 of the prologue presents three "was" declarations about the Word: (1) In the beginning "was," not "became," the Word. He was already, He was preexistent. (2) The Word was with God. He is an independent, divine Person in fellowship with the Father. He is "God with God." (3) The Word was God; He is not simply "divine," He is God ("God of God," cf. John

20:28, "My Lord and my God!"). Verse 1 gives the main theme of this Gospel—the proclamation of the deity of Jesus Christ.

These three monumental declarations stand beside one another. The first confirms Christ's preexistence. He was in the beginning. Since He himself was in the beginning, it follows that He is without beginning. The second declaration demonstrates two things: (1) the Logos is a distinct personality. The Son did not "begin" His existence at the Incarnation: the eternal Logos is the essence of the personality of Him whom the Scriptures call "the man Jesus Christ." (2) The Logos exists in eternal communion with God. He is not identical with the Father but is nevertheless one with God. Literally, the words imply that He was oriented towards God—face-to-face with God. He is the Son in the bosom of the Father (verse 18).

In the figurative language of the Old Testament this eternal fellowship between the Father and the Son is expressed thus: "I was daily his delight, rejoicing always before him" (Proverbs 8:30). Finite men and women lack the ability to grasp the depths of this eternal communion between persons in the Godhead. It would potentially be irreverent to inquire further into this, but Jesus' own words indicate that the fellowship and glory of this relationship was embedded so deeply in His personality that throughout His earthly ministry He constantly longed to return to the Father.

"And the Word was God" represents the third great, magnificent declaration of this verse. The entire verse moves toward this climax. Nothing can be said above this. "The Word was God." Jesus Christ is God. John declared not that Jesus is divine or that there is something divine in Him. Rather, he said Jesus *is* God. If John had wanted to indicate some divine aspect of Jesus' character, the Greek language had a very common term suitable for such purposes—the adjective *theios*, "divine." But *theios* does not adequately describe the divinity of Jesus Christ. He is not merely "divine." He is more than a creation with divine attributes. John was unable to say more than he did. Thus there is nothing to add, nothing to qualify: The Word was God.

The word "God" appears seven times in the prologue without the article (verses 1,2,6,12,13,18). E.C. Colwell seemingly satisfactorily explains the absence of the article. He demonstrates that as a general rule most definite predicate nouns precede the verb when they lack the article. He comments on John's opening verse in the Fourth Gospel: "The absence of the article does *not* make the predicate indefinite or qualitative when it precedes the verb; it is indefinite in this position only when the context demands it," (Colwell, "A Definite Rule for the use of the Article," p.21). He continues, "The context makes no such demand in the Gospel of John, for this statement cannot be regarded as strange in the prologue of the gospel . . . " (ibid.).

The absence of the article before the word "God" in this text emphasizes that *logos* alone does not comprise the Godhead. It suggests that the Godhead must include the other persons of the Father and Spirit.

After introducing this person of the Godhead, *logos*, and having reflected upon His preexistence with God, John began to describe the activity of *logos* in the creation. *Logos* mediates between creation and the Creator, not only as an instrumental force (cf. Colossians 1:16; Hebrew 1:2), but vital and having creative power himself. An instrument may be subordinate to what it fashions, but the same cannot be said for the creator. He must be superior. He who is without beginning, who is and always has been, created everything that has a beginning or which was brought into existence. The creative word is a powerful command from the Second Person of the Trinity—the Spoken Word, the Son.

It may seem strange that other passages in the New Testament attach such significance to the fact that Jesus Christ is the One who created and sustains the world. Without question we have a classic example of the paradox that truth cannot be precisely defined or identified. Although heretical Gnostic speculation probably was as yet not fully developed when the New Testament was written, evidently the concepts it later collected, systematized, and cataloged under the term *logos* were. Apparently the beginnings of this threat challenged the Church even during the apostolic period. Gnostic doctrine was actually not original. They collected material from sources old and ran in new. So there may be much to support the view that the opponents of John were indeed showing Gnostic tendencies.

A central concept in Gnosticism argued that matter always existed and that within it were the seeds of cruelty and corruption. From this evil matter the world was created by a "lesser or minor god," and "antigod." Thus creation itself was considered essentially evil in origin.

The Biblical view, in contrast, contends that the world was created "out of nothing." It was created by God in accordance with His divine purpose. Sin is what makes the world evil. Christ came in order to reestablish God's creation and to deliver mankind from the bondage of sin. Therefore the inspired New Testament writers—and significantly so—accented the point that the Redeemer of the world is also its Creator. John wrote, "He came to his 'own' "—to His "own" in the sense that it was "His" because He had created it. This world, despite its being fallen and corrupt, belongs to God. God demonstrated His love for His world by giving His Son, that the world through Him might be saved (cf. John 3:16,17).

Thus we note the significance of uniting creation and redemption in the prologue. The Word created the world. The Word came in the flesh and dwelt among us.

The Word Became Flesh. The Incarnation remains one of the deepest mysteries of the Christian faith. God manifest in human form is the mystery of godliness (1 Timothy 3:16). Furthermore, the fact that Christ came in the flesh is such an essential tenet of Christian faith that the one believing in this truth is born of God, but the one rejecting it has the spirit of antichrist (1 John 4:2,3).

Mankind was not granted the ability to grasp fully the depth of this mystery of the *Logos* clothed in humanity. It is impossible to understand the union of soul and flesh, let alone the mystery of God incarnate. Nevertheless, we cannot be indifferent to this mystery since our eternal salvation hinges to a great degree on what we believe about it.

The Word Became Flesh and Dwelt Among Us. The timeless eternal One entered time (Micah 5:2). The transcendent became immanent. He who is truly God became truly man. The invisible became visible: "That which was from the beginning, which we have heard, which we have seen with our eyes, which we have looked upon, and our hands have handled, of the Word of life; (for the life was manifested, and we have seen it, and bear witness, and show unto you that eternal life, which was with the Father, and was manifested unto us)" (1 John 1:1,2).

When the Word became flesh He did not do so in such a way as to cease being God. He may disguise His external majesty. He may cover His deity. He may hide His almighty character. But God cannot cease to be God. As He journeyed across the land, healing all those He touched, He left the footprint of God upon earth. When He died for the sin of the world it was at the cost of His own blood (Acts 20:28). (See Metzger, p.482 for a discussion of the variant reading in this text.) Through the Resurrection Jesus proved himself to be the only begotten Son of God (Romans 1:4).

The Incarnation does not imply that the Logos ceased being God. However, it does indicate that the almighty Second Person of the Godhead became the God-man. An ancient Latin saying expressed it thus: "I am what I am, that is God. I was not what I am, that is man. I am now called God as well as man." The Word became flesh not by exchanging one nature for another. He became God-man by uniting His two natures—the divine and human—in one Person. This union is a most sacred and deep mystery. It eludes all psychological inquiry, since no finite human knows the nature of the God-man. Only brief glimpses afforded by the revelation of Scripture allow any insight into this divine mystery.

Scripture is clear concerning Jesus' deity, just as it is Scripture which demonstrates His true humanity. This was anticipated by the Old Testament. The messianic prophecies speak of Messiah as simultaneously human and divine. He is the seed of the woman (Genesis 3:15); the descendant of Abraham, Isaac, and Jacob; the son of David (cf. Matthew 1:1). At the same time He is "mighty God, eternal Father" (Isaiah 9:6). His origins are from of old—from ancient times (Micah 5:2). "And the Lord, whom ye seek, shall suddenly come to his temple, even the messenger of the covenant, whom ye delight in: behold, he shall come, saith the Lord of hosts" (Malachi 3:1). These two statements of the prophetic Word resonate with John's declaration: "The Word became flesh." The ancient promises are fulfilled in Christ.

Jesus' humanity is equally as indisputable as His divinity. This is confirmed by the fact that He took on a true body. If John's Hellenistic readers would have reacted to anything, it would have been to the idea that a god would put on an earthly body. To the Greek mind the body was essentially evil and corruptible, a prison of the soul and an unbearable burden. Some Greek philosophers held that it was blasphemous—and terribly so—to involve God in the affairs of this world.

This attitude typified the ancient Christian heresy called Docetism. The Greek *dokein* ("to seem, to be apparent") is the term behind the concept. This heresy argued that Jesus' "body" was not really a body at all. Rather, it only "appeared" (*dokein*) to be. From their point of view the Son of God came in a spiritual body; He was thought to be a phantom or ghostlike figure, simply a bodiless spirit in a human form. Consequently, it was maintained that Jesus did not experience fatigue, pain, hunger, sorrow, or any of the other frailties common to mankind. This attitude undoubtedly emerged quite early, because Paul and John both strongly resisted such tendencies, as their letters make plain (e.g., Colossians; First John).

With this in mind it is very significant that John utilized not only "man" (*anthrōpos*) in writing of the incarnation of the Son of God, he also used the word "flesh" (*sarx*). This captures a thought central to the entire New Testament: the Saviour of the world came in the flesh. He had a human body.

Jesus spoke of this same phenomenon in His words about the temple of His body, which, if destroyed, would be rebuilt (John 2:21). This thought recurs vividly in the Synoptic accounts of the Last Supper. In words which later became confessional for the Church, Jesus called the elements of the supper His "body" and His "blood." He stated that His body "is given for you" and His blood "shed for many" (Mark 14:22-24). Jesus challenged those who had witnessed the miracle of the loaves with the words: "I tell you the truth, unless you eat the flesh of the Son of Man and drink his blood, you have no life in you" (John 6:53, NIV).

In his sermon on the Day of Pentecost Peter referred to Jesus' death as an important fulfillment of the prophetic word that "neither his flesh did see corruption" (Acts 2:31). Paul also stressed the importance of Christ's body. He referred to Him as "manifest in the flesh" (1 Timothy 3:16), and he said that Christ "was made of the seed of David according to flesh" (Romans 1:3), i.e., in accordance with the promises.

Paul tied the overall work of redemption with the body of Jesus. He stated that believers are reconciled to God not by a spiritual body or an "apparent" body, such as the Docetists would have maintained, but rather, "in his (Christ's) fleshly body by death." In this manner Jews as well as Gentiles are now both reconciled "in one body by the cross, having slain the enmity thereby" (Ephesians 2:15,16). Having been reconciled to God by "one body" (i.e., Christ's body), Jews as well as Gentiles can become a "new man" (i.e., the Church, that one body; cf. 1 Corinthians 10:17).

Christ, "having abolished in his flesh the enmity, even the law of commandments contained in ordinances" (Ephesians 2:15), has made believers "dead to the law by the body of Christ" (Romans 7:4). Paul rejected any attempt to "spiritualize" these events by asserting that blessing is found in Christ: "In him dwelleth all the fulness of the Godhead bodily" (Colossians 2:9).

The Epistle to the Hebrews spoke of the earthly life of Jesus as the "days of his flesh," at which time with loud cries, tears, and supplications He learned obedience from His sufferings. Consequently, "Once made perfect, he became the source of eternal salvation for all who obey him" (Hebrews 5:9, NIV). He partook of flesh and blood "that through death he might destroy him that had the power of death, that is, the devil" (Hebrews 2:14). In Hebrews 10:5-20 Jesus' nature is viewed as a fulfillment of messianic prophecies. God prepared a body for the Messiah, through whom the sacrificial system of the old covenant was abolished. Thus "we are sanctified through the offering of the body of Jesus Christ once for all" (Hebrews 10:10). Now believers can enter the Most Holy Place "by a new and living way," that is, "his flesh" (cf. Hebrews 10:20).

Peter also combined the work of redemption and Jesus' nature. He wrote of Christ, "Who his own self bare our sins in his own body on the tree, that we, being dead to sins, should live unto righteousness: by whose stripes ye were healed" (1 Peter 2:24). Concerning the death of Jesus his epistle says that Christ was "put to death in the flesh" (1 Peter 3:18).

The recognition of the centrality of the human nature of Jesus to the preaching of the New Testament—and to the doctrine of redemption—makes it transparently clear that the exalted, majestic declaration of John's Gospel prologue, "and the Word became flesh," captures one of the tremendous salvation truths of the gospel.

First of all, Jesus' humanity is closely tied to His messianic mission—to suffer and die for the sin of the world. As God He could not die. Therefore He had to become man "that he by the grace of God should taste death for every man" (Hebrews 2:9). Just as actual as His humanity, so too was His death. Jesus himself declared that His atoning death was His reason for coming. He came to give His life a ransom for the many (cf. Mark 10:45). For the sake of mankind He became man. Nevertheless, the Incarnation is founded upon the preincarnate relationship within the Godhead. Thus it is a mystery that the death of Jesus could "please" God (Isaiah 53:10). His sacrifice was a "sweet-smelling savor" to God (Ephesians 5:2). Just as His death is the ultimate proof of His love for His friends (15:13), likewise it is also the proof of His love for the Father (14:31). As the Son of Man—God incarnate—Jesus gave His Heavenly Father something He could not give while He existed in His body of glory.

Furthermore, Jesus' relationship to humanity is based upon His own humanity. "Because he is the Son of man" He will judge unbelieving mankind (5:27). Or, as Luke puts it, by One who is a "man" the world will be judged (Acts 17:31). One of humanity's own will have the last word in the final judgment.

Jesus' relationship to humanity is tremendously affected by His own humanity. He who demands obedience was himself obedient. He experienced temptation and trial. Thus He has compassion upon us in our weakness. The One who himself was tempted is the believers' help in times of temptation (Hebrews 2:18; 4:15). Jesus understands the human condition, not only as the all-knowing God, but as one who experienced it firsthand. He leaves us the example of the perfect man as guide for our own lives (1 Peter 2:21).

Therefore, "the Word became flesh" denotes the true humanity of Jesus. It does not mean that God lived in a man—it means that God became a man. He became like us in every way except for sin (Hebrews 4:15). Paul wrote that not only did Christ come in the flesh, He came "in the likeness of sinful flesh" (Romans 8:3). He arrived on the human scene in the midst of the consequences of its fall, not immune to the weaknesses and anxieties this implies. Yet He "knew no sin" (2 Corinthians 5:21). The devil had no hold on Him (14:30). He did not sin (1 Peter 2:22), and "in him is no sin" (1 John 3:5). Jesus was holy, spotless, undefiled, separate from sinners (Hebrews 7:26). The Incarnation of the Word of God did not become a sinful person. He came in the likeness of sinful flesh but He was not sinful. He was free from all sin in both His body and soul. Precisely because He himself knew no sin, He could bear our sins—be "made sin" for us.

The human nature adopted by the Logos-become-flesh was not different. He was born into full humanity, clothing himself with our humanity. As fully man, He was tried in every way, tempted by the devil, scorned by the accusations of sinners. As true man, He fulfilled the law of God as one "born under the Law." He submitted His human will to the will of His Father and was obedient unto the death of the cross.

The true extent of Jesus' humanity is such that He never stopped being a man. Even when He departed from this existence—having fulfilled His mission—to return to the Father and to reclaim the glory He had prior to His humility, Jesus retained His humanity. It is "the man Christ Jesus" who presently mediates between God and men (1 Timothy 2:5). As the believer's forerunner Jesus assumed His place in the heavenly realm (Hebrews 6:20). This is the eternal guarantee of God's love of mankind. The Son of God is man—the Word became flesh.

Though *logos* is the key term in the prologue to John's Gospel, nevertheless, many other great themes of this Gospel are present. Origen, an Early Church father, complained of the tendency of interpreters to be one-sided in their study of the prologue. But other expressions included in the prologue recur throughout the Gospel, and it is natural that they should be discussed here. *Logos*, on the other hand, occurs for the last time in verse 14 of the prologue: "And the Word was made flesh." Immediately after John began to refer to the Son by His name and messianic title: Jesus Christ. This is the name of the *Logos* who became a man. Those believing this are born of God (1:12,13).

The Johannine prologue concludes with a powerful declaration that it is Christ who reveals God. He is the only begotten Son in the bosom of the Father who testifies to the God no one has ever seen.

This is tied to *logos* as the broader concept of the prologue. God reveals himself through His *logos* just as man makes himself known by his words. Sight and touch add little to what can be learned about someone from their words. Words convey the essence of man's nature. Thus the *Logos* conveys the essence of God's character. He represents God's wisdom, will, and power in a tangible way. In Him God descended and revealed himself to men through a man— though more than man. Only God can disclose the character of God. The mediator of revelation is the God-man, the eternal Logos "come in the flesh."

Logos was the term selected by the most ardent monotheists to depict God's self-disclosure. But John utilized *logos* as a "bridge" between the strict monotheism of Judaism and the concept of the Triune God of the Christian faith (also strict monotheism). The eternal nature of God is revealed in the Son. In Christ's light we are given the light of the knowledge of the glory of God (cf. 2 Corinthians 4:6). He is the perfect and final revelation of God, the ultimate appearance.

As such, requests to see the Father are irrelevant: "He that hath seen me hath seen the Father" (14:8,9). Naturally, however, believers do not yet understand everything Jesus has told them about the Father. Only time and eternity will make this possible (16:25), even though Christ is the total expression of God. The glory Jesus has as the only begotten of the Father is the full measure of all God has and is.

Those things that afford the greatest insight into the nature and character of God are not the magnificent wonders of nature, cosmic wonders, isolated manifestations of power, or shining glory. No, it is simply God's love revealed in Jesus Christ.

Jesus' Seven Journeys to Judea

Whereas the Synoptic Gospels primarily describe Jesus' activity in Galilee and His final week in Jerusalem during Passover, John's Gospel mainly relates Jesus' ministry in Judea, although there are a few accounts of Jesus' Galilean ministry. In this way John's Gospel fills in many of the "blanks" left by the Synoptic accounts, which could otherwise be difficult to understand. When compared with John's Gospel the Synoptic Gospels become more clearly understandable.

It could be said that the Fourth Gospel is actually a record of Jesus' seven journeys into Judea with some accounts of His ministry in Galilee and Peraea interspersed. If one keeps the scheme of Jesus' journeys in mind, John's Gospel acquires a unique and distinct coloring.

Furthermore, the chronological order of Jesus' ministry is indirectly indicated in John's Gospel by seven chronological markers (see 2:13,23; 4:35; 5:1; 6:4; 7:2,37; 10:22; 12:1; 13:1). These, coupled with the Synoptic record, afford a much fuller picture of Jesus' ministry. These "markers" may be unintentional, that is, they may not have been designed as markers. However, they do provide a chronological basis for the public ministry of Jesus.

Six of these markers involve Jewish holidays during the period of time between Jesus' baptism and His crucifixion. Three are distinctly recalled as Passover holidays (2:23; 6:4; 12:1). John recorded that a portion of Jesus' ministry took place prior to the first of these Passover weeks. Apparently Jesus' ministry must have covered about 2½ years. However, it is possible that one other Jewish feast mentioned by John was also a Passover (cf. the unnamed feast in 5:1f.). If this was indeed a Passover then the span of Jesus' ministry would be approximately 3½ years, just as the most ancient church tradition maintains.

Based upon the holidays and feast pilgrimages mentioned in the Fourth Gospel, together with the chronological markers found there and the Synoptic chronologies, one can make the following reconstruction of Jesus' life and ministry:

Winter 6 B.C. to winter A.D. 26: The birth of Jesus in Bethlehem and His childhood in Nazareth recorded in the Synoptic Gospels but not in John.

Winter A. D. 26 to spring A.D. 27: The first journey of Jesus to Judea in order to be baptized by John the Baptist. Jesus made His first disciples and worked His first miracle in Galilee (1:19 to 2:12). This is only briefly mentioned in the Synoptic Gospels.

Spring to winter A.D. 27: The early ministry of Jesus in Judea (about 8 months). The second journey of Jesus to Judea; His first Passover in Jerusalem (first time note 2:13,23) takes place. For the second time (note 4:35) Jesus returned to Galilee. In December there were still "four months left until the harvest" (2:13 to 4:42). This is not mentioned in the Synoptic accounts.

Winter A.D. 27 to spring A.D. 29: The principal ministry of Jesus in Galilee (about 17 months). The Synoptic writers offer a detailed account of this. John mentioned that this period was broken by Jesus' third journey to Judea for the unnamed holiday (perhaps a Passover, His second; cf. 5:1). Apparently Jesus spent His third Passover in Galilee (fourth time; 6:4). John's Gospel speaks of these events in 4:43 to 6:71.

Spring to fall A.D. 29: Jesus once again ministered in Galilee (about 6 months). He traveled to Decapolis and the countryside of Caesarea Philippi. Both the Synoptics and John's Gospel record this (7:1).

Fall to winter A.D. 29: Jesus' later ministry in Judea (about 3 months), which is related to two journeys to feasts in Jerusalem. Jesus traveled for the fourth time through Judea and went to the Feast of Tabernacles in Jerusalem (note the fifth time; cf. 7:2,37). For a fifth time Jesus traveled to Judea; this time for the Feast of Dedication (Hanukkah; the sixth time, cf. 10:22,23). The Synoptic Gospels do not record this (7:2 to 10:39).

Winter A.D. 29 to A.D. 30: Jesus ministered in Peraea (about 4 months), but in the midst of this He returned to Judea—to Bethany—to raise Lazarus from the dead (10:40 to 11:57). The Synoptics do recall Jesus' activity in Peraea.

Spring A.D. 30: Jesus traveled to Judea for His final Passover week in Jerusalem (the seventh time, cf. 12:1). The suffering, death, and resurrection of Jesus are consistently recorded by all the Evangelists (chapters 12 to 21).

A great deal of evidence indicates that the chronological structure presented above is substantially correct. Without the chronological markers in John's Gospel, however, it would be impossible to reconstruct Jesus' ministry. This gives us some appreciation of the value of the Fourth Gospel as an historical document.

Because John provided so much data about Jesus' ministry in Judea that would otherwise be unknown, our portrait of Jesus is significantly enhanced. Of course, much of the basis for John's Gospel are his own recollections as Jesus' disciple.

With respect to Jesus' journeys in Judea and to Jerusalem—about which the Synoptics are largely silent—John's Gospel provides us with much needed data for reconstructing Jesus' life. The Gospel of John informs us that much of Jesus' ministry occurred in Judea. It is impossible to know precisely how many times Jesus and His disciples made the pilgrimage to Jerusalem, but John tells us of some of them. The seven journeys of Jesus to Judea recorded by John form a framework not only for the structure of John's Gospel, but also for the overall portrait of Jesus' whole gospel ministry.

(1) *Jesus' First Journey To Judea*

That John's Gospel should begin his account of Jesus' life with a detailed description of the events which took place during the first week of Jesus' public ministry is fascinating. The description of this first week of ministry may in fact parallel the creation week recorded in the first chapter of Genesis. God's work of redemption had begun! A new creation would appear. The One who spoke on the day of creation saw His word come to pass in speaking again. He was again creating on earth.

The first scene depicts the day when the Jewish leadership sent some priests and Levites from Jerusalem to interrogate John the Baptist about his identity. It may be the Jews respected John the Baptist much more than Jesus—at least they believed he could be Messiah.

John the Baptist, being from a priestly family, merited some of their respect, and his ascetic life-style would also have been admired. But Jesus, the apparent son of a carpenter, was a "nobody" in their eyes. The issue John addressed was whether John the Baptist ever pretended to be the Messiah. Martin Luther pointed out the temptation to seek personal glory that faced John, (cf. Pelikan, *Luther's Works*, 22:56f.,454). He also noted the humility and faith John demonstrated by rejecting any such thoughts. John the Baptist testified that he was neither the Messiah nor the prophet for whom people waited (cf. Deuteronomy 18:15-18). He furthermore denied that he was Elijah, who, according to Jewish expectation, was to reveal himself before the coming of the Messiah.

This last denial has caused problems for some, since Jesus himself referred to the Baptist as the Elijah who was to come. The explanation for this seeming inconsistency may be quite simply that John the Baptist was not aware that he was Elijah. In humility he denied his position, although Jesus afforded him this honor. Thus in the spiritual sense John was Elijah but not literally.

Many church fathers contended that the prophecy of Elijah's return would have a double fulfillment. Both Chrysostom and Augustine, for example, saw a relationship between John the Baptist and the prophet Elijah. They proposed that as John was the herald and forerunner of Jesus at His first coming, Elijah would appear before the second coming of Christ. John the Baptist came in the spirit and power of Elijah, but Elijah himself would come to proclaim Christ's return.

Thus John denied he was the Messiah. He contended that he was the messianic forerunner. He was to prepare the way of the Lord, to make known the arrival of the Messiah: "There standeth one among you, whom ye know not; he it is, who coming after me is preferred before me, whose shoe-latchet I am not worthy to unloose" (1:26,27).

The second day, following the questioning by the delegation from Jerusalem, John saw Jesus approaching. John declared to the people that Jesus was the Messiah he had announced. He declared that God gave him a sign at Jesus' baptism that God's Holy Spirit came upon Jesus. John's testimony climaxed with the words: "And I saw, and bare record that this is the Son of God" (1:34).

The next day John was standing with two of his disciples when he saw Jesus walking by. The Baptist repeated his testimony of the day before: "Behold the Lamb of God!" (1:36). The sinless One, although He had no sins to confess as He was baptized by John, bore the sins of the world—not only the sins of Israel but of all the peoples of the earth.

John's disciples understood that his work was preparatory and future-oriented. Two of them, John and Andrew, immediately recognized what they must do. They left John the Baptist and followed Jesus. This was entirely in keeping with John's mission: to prepare the way for others to come to Jesus. Moreover, when Jesus did come on the scene it was among the disciples of John that He found some of His closest followers.

On the same day Peter and John became disciples, and during the initial week five of the Galileans in Bethany followed Jesus. In all likelihood they too were former disciples of John the Baptist. As early as the first day Jesus gave Simon the name "Peter." The fact that the disciples became acquainted with Jesus during His initial week of ministry explains why they so willingly followed Him when He called them later by the Sea of Gennesaret (as the Synoptic Gospels record).

The fourth day—"the next day" (cf. 1:29,35,43)—two new disciples joined the band: Philip and Nathanael Bartholomew (Tolomeus' son). Each of these men accepted the witness of John the Baptist as to Jesus' divine Sonship, the Messiah of whom Moses and the Prophets promised (1:42,46,50).

Jesus' opening words to Nathanael, "Behold an Israelite indeed, in whom is no guile!" are apparently a clear reference to the story of Jacob who was renamed "Israel." Whereas Jacob means "usurper, supplanter," a characteristic of a true Israelite was that he be without "guile, deceit." Moreover, Jesus' words in the ensuing conversation about the ascending and descending angels upon the Son of Man that Nathanael would witness point back to Jacob's dream of the heavenly ladder. The relationship between heaven and earth was to be reestablished. The broken and fragmented parts of creation were to be reunited as one in Christ. These are the "greater things" Jesus promised Nathanael he would see. Verse 43 indicates that on this day Jesus "would go forth into Galilee." This verse marks the close of Jesus' first journey in Judea.

The fifth and sixth days of the first week of ministry, Jesus, along with His first disciples, spent traveling, as often would have been the case. The trip took 2 or 3 days. On the seventh day, the third day after leaving Bethany, Jesus and His disciples arrived in Cana in Galilee, Nathanael's hometown (cf. 21:2). Jesus' mother, Mary, was at a wedding to which Jesus and His disciples were also invited. There, on the last day of His first week of ministry, Jesus performed His first miracle: He changed the water into wine. "This beginning of miracles did Jesus in Cana of Galilee, and manifested forth his glory; and his disciples believed on him" (2:11). Jesus, accompanied by His mother, His brothers, and His disciples, then traveled to Capernaum and remained there for a few days.

(2) *Jesus' Second Journey to Judea*

This journey to Judea was a Passover pilgrimage to Jerusalem. The first Feast of Passover during Jesus' public ministry probably occurred during A.D. 27. We have some indication of this in the comment by the Jews that the building of the temple had taken 46 years (2:20). Herod the Great began his reign in 37 B.C. According to Josephus, Herod started construction on the temple in the 18th year of his administration (Josephus, *Antiquities* 15.11.1), approximately 20-19 B.C. In the spring of A.D. 27 the Jews would have said the work had taken 46 years. Since this first Passover Feast is the principal time marker of Jesus' public ministry, it is critical to be as precise as possible in fixing this date.

Jesus' first trip to Judea and His travels to the Jordan for baptism took place beforehand. This implies that Jesus' baptism took place in winter of A.D. 26. Next came the 40 days of temptation in the wilderness. Then He returned to Bethany, the headquarters of John. There John announced publicly that Jesus is the Messiah and Son of God. At this time Jesus won His first disciples from the ranks of John, whose groundwork had prepared them for the transition. Next He returned to Galilee. The time of these events can be narrowed to February through March of A.D. 27. Following a short stay in Capernaum He made the pilgrimage with His disciples to the Passover festival in Jerusalem.

This Passover marked the official start of the messianic mission of Jesus. Through His cleansing of the temple He revealed His authority and origin to the people.

This act has been the focus of much discussion because in the Fourth Gospel this is the first great messianic sign by Jesus. But in the Synoptic accounts the cleansing of the temple stands as His final, public appearance. Those who think that only one cleansing of the temple occurred contend that the Synoptic records are correct in their placement. John, they would say, had little concern for chronology. This argument, however, loses its strength, since John's account is chronological. Moreover, the statement of the Jews about the 46-year construction of the temple almost certainly proves that the cleansing took place in A.D. 27—the start of Jesus' ministry—not 3 years later.

Jesus was about 30 when He was baptized and He was born about the sixth year B.C. Jesus' words about destroying the temple appear in an altered form as an accusation of those at the High Court. However, it was impossible to determine precisely what Jesus had said. This seems odd if it were something Jesus had said earlier that week; but if He had made the statement about 3 years earlier, their lack of recollection makes more sense.

Nevertheless, it seems clear enough that Jesus did cleanse the temple at the close of His ministry. The simplest answer—and the most obvious—is that Jesus purged the temple twice: once at the start of His ministry and again at its close. Furthermore, in all probability He was reacting to a recurring evil. Even after the second cleansing it probably continued.

There are some slight variations in the accounts. Whereas on the first occasion Jesus objected that the house of God had become a house of merchandise, on the second occasion He lamented that they had changed it into a "den of thieves." Jesus' ensuing debate with the Jews also differs. The disagreement between Jesus and the Jewish authorities is now much sharper. Following the second cleansing they even attempted to kill Him.

What probably happened was that Jesus, upon entering the temple precincts, discovered that one of the outer courts of the temple, such as the Court of the Gentiles, had been changed into a veritable marketplace. Thus the only place in which God-fearers from other nations could worship was actually a noisy, crowded place of business. There was no place for proper, peaceful meditation and worship.

Those pilgrims traveling to Jerusalem for holy feasts needed sacrificial animals and proper currency in order to pay the temple tax. From this necessity Annas the high priest and his family saw the opportunity for making a large profit. They went even further than Tobias did in times past (Nehemiah 13:4-9). They exchanged money and sold sacrifices in the court of the temple. Theoretically, those making sacrifices were permitted to bring along their own livestock or animals for sacrifice. Practically, however, since the authorities of the temple had to approve the sacrifice, it was easier to buy one in the temple. This is how the high priest's family secured huge profits. If people bought their sacrifices from the temple precincts they could be assured that they were approved. This selling of sacrifices and exchanging of currency afforded many opportunities for extortion and cheating.

Jesus reacted to both the presence of the merchants in the temple and the fact that they disturbed the sanctity and peace of the temple. He was also enraged at the overall corrupt system that had converted God's house into a "den of thieves." In ardent wrath He constructed a whip from cords—which were in abundant supply with so many animals on hand—and drove the merchants and their animals out of the temple. Naturally it was more Jesus' moral power than His physical strength that forced them to flee the house of God. Nevertheless, there is no reason to think that Jesus reserved the whip for the livestock. For, in the second cleansing account, it is distinctly said that those selling and buying in the temple were driven out (Matthew 21:12).

Although Jesus was relatively unknown when He cleansed the temple for the first time, the implications of such action were clearly perceived as a messianic declaration. He called the temple "my Father's house," a totally unique action. His purging of the temple was itself a messianic sign, for as the prophet Malachi wrote, "the messenger of the covenant" would come to his temple (Malachi 3:1f.).

Jesus showed himself to be Messiah through His actions. Consequently, the Jewish authorities asked Jesus to prove His identity and authority with another sign. They elected to ignore the implications of the act itself.

How a mere man could clear out a whole area like this is difficult to explain from a natural standpoint. It suggests an unparalleled spiritual strength. The reaction of the authorities to Jesus revealed their own evil intent. They should have maintained the sanctity of the temple themselves. They magnified their crime of profaning the house of God by plotting to kill God's agent. This proves their deeply rooted stubbornness.

Jesus did not grant them the sign they demanded. Just as under similar circumstances He pointed to the 3 days of Jonah as a sign, now He pointed to the "three days" which would be their sign. "Destroy this temple, and in three days I will raise it up" (2:19). Whenever Jesus spoke of "three days" it suggested His death and resurrection. The Resurrection is the undeniable proof that Jesus is indeed the Son of God.

Jesus' words were a *māshal*, a "riddle" with a hidden meaning incapable of interpretation apart from careful thought. Jewish Scripture is replete with such sayings. They recognized this device quite plainly, but they elected to ignore the challenge of His enigmatic words by taking them literally. They asked, "Forty and six years was this temple in building, and wilt thou rear it up in three days?" (2:20), indicating they thought Jesus was making an absurd statement.

Actually, Jesus' words were full of meaning. John 2:21 explains: "But he spake of the temple of his body." The temple symbolized the one who "dwelt among us" (1:14). His opponents might destroy the temple of His body, but He would raise it up again in 3 days. It was only after Jesus had been raised from the dead that the disciples understood the import of His words.

The words of Jesus contained a double meaning, particularly the word "destroy" (2:19). This term, *luō*, literally means "to loosen," but it can be used for "destroying" a building—"tearing it down." Figuratively it can refer to the "killing" of a human being. The word for "temple," *naos* can refer to the whole temple or in a narrow sense to the "Holy of Holies" in the temple, i.e., the sanctuary. Elsewhere, the New Testament refers to man's body as the temple of God. "I will raise it up" are words which could be understood literally of the building, or they could describe restoring a man, i.e., "raising" him up (resurrection language).

Thus the twofold meaning includes the actual temple and the temple of Jesus' body. When the Jews destroyed His body they also destroyed the temple of stone, because through Christ's sacrifice the sacrificial system—vital to the life of the temple—was rendered obsolete. Upon His death "the first tabernacle" fell (Hebrews 9:8). The veil of the Holy of Holies was torn in two. But in 3 days Jesus raised the temple of His body. In their killing of the Lord of Glory the Jews effected the very signs they demanded. Additionally, Jesus established a new temple: the church of God, the church of the new covenant, the body of Christ. Thus the New Testament's temple imagery is built around the work of Christ. He superseded and abolished the sacrificial system of the old temple through the sacrifice of himself.

Interestingly, Jesus, through His first official act as Messiah, was challenged by the Jewish religiosity. From the outset He made His messiahship plain, and from the outset the custodians of God's holy covenant resisted and opposed Him.

Nevertheless, the inspired writer recalled that some did believe in Jesus because of the signs He did. Although John did not mention these signs, he indicated that Jesus continued to work miracles following the first sign in Cana. Still, John pointed out that Jesus did not entrust himself to those who followed and believed in Him simply because they saw signs. Jesus knew everyone's true heart. He knew that their faith was "rocky ground" faith. When trouble and hardship came they would turn away from the Faith.

One person affected by Jesus' mighty works was the Pharisee Nicodemus, a member of the Jewish council of rulers, who came to Jesus one night and said: "We know that thou art a teacher come from God: for no man can do these miracles that thou doest, except God be with him" (3:1f.). At this Jesus gave His first sermon on the new birth.

The Early Ministry of Jesus in Judea. John's Gospel provides us with some information not found in the Synoptics—namely,that after His baptism Jesus spent time ministering in Judea. "After these things came Jesus and his disciples into the land of Judea; and there he tarried with them, and baptized" (3:22). This effort took place simultaneously with John the Baptist's, which was soon overshadowed by the ministry of Jesus.

Passover Week in Jerusalem initiated an 8-month period of ministry in the rural districts of Judea (probably from spring to winter A.D. 27). Jesus, along with His disciples—probably the five mentioned in chapter 1—itinerated a great deal. Since they baptized many disciples in their ministry, they apparently spent a great deal of time around the Jordan River and around Jericho. John the Baptist was still active in the northern part of the Jordan Valley, not far from Bethany, his former place of ministry. Now he was on the west side of the Jordan near Salim, where there were seven great "springs" and plenty of water (3:23).

During this period of John's declining popularity he demonstrated his true greatness. His disciples bitterly complained that many were leaving him and going to Jesus. They apparently were so upset that they would not even say Jesus' name, calling Him instead "he that was with thee beyond Jordan, to whom thou barest witness" (3:26). Perhaps there was some slight sarcasm in this; they may have resented John's open reception of Jesus. It seems as if at least some of John's disciples who stayed with him following Jesus' arrival on the scene were unwilling to let John's ministry decline or be "swallowed up" by Jesus' preaching. The possibility exists that these were signs of a "John the Baptist movement" which can be traced into the early decades of the Church (cf. Acts 18:25f.; 19:3f.). John the Baptist, however, had no such plans. His ambitions were the most noble a man can have—"He (Jesus) must increase, but I must decrease" (3:30). These words reflected John the Baptist's final testimony of Jesus.

The apostle John was one of the Baptist's disciples who followed Jesus because of John's testimony. His Gospel portrays John the Baptist in such positive terms. The Synoptics afford him an important position as the forerunner of Jesus. They recall Jesus' words about John the Baptist being more than a prophet and being the greatest of those born of women (Matthew 11:9f.; Luke 7:26f.). But they comment little about the reason for John's greatness other than saying he was a fearless prophet who preached repentance from sin to both the high and low.

John the Baptist's understanding of Jesus' person and mission surfaces in the Fourth Gospel. When no one else knew Jesus' real identity, John recognized Jesus as God's Son, a revelation that only later became known by the disciples. John spoke of the preexistence of Jesus (1:15,30); he knew the love of the Father for the Son (3:35). John testified that Jesus is the Son of God (1:34) and he knew that Jesus came from above (3:31). He recognized Jesus as the Lamb of God who "taketh away the sin of the world" (1:29). He also preached that Jesus would baptize people in the Holy Spirit (1:33). Hc acknowledged that Jesus was the bridegroom who had the bride; he was satisfied with being a friend of the groom (3:29).

In his final testimony of Jesus John placed that faith in Jesus which is essential for salvation: "He that believeth on the Son hath everlasting life: and he that believeth not the Son shall not see life; but the wrath of God abideth on him" (3:36). John confirmed his message with his life. It is rightly said that no greater, no humbler human figure than John the Baptist has graced the pages of history in the Old or New Testaments.

The ministries of Jesus and John the Baptist paralleled one another for several months, and then John was imprisoned. Matthew recorded that John was literally "betrayed" or "deserted." Herod had John arrested (Luke 3:20), but since John had not preached in Galilee, Herod's jurisdiction, and since John was not a Galilean, in all probability the inhabitants of Judea handed John over to Herod. For the most part the Pharisees and/or other members of the religious establishment, such as the Sanhedrin, would have had the authority to do this. In reference to John, Jesus said: "They . . . have done to him everything they wished. In the same way the Son of Man is going to suffer at their hands" (Matthew 17:12, NIV). Thus the same group who handed John over to Herod in an effort to get rid of him also handed Jesus over to Pilate for crucifixion.

After John's arrest Jesus knew what to expect from the Pharisees. Now the crowds followed Jesus, the One whom John had proclaimed as Messiah. This forms the background for John 4:1-3: "When therefore the Lord knew how the Pharisees had heard that Jesus made and baptized more disciples than John, . . . he left Judea, and departed again into Galilee" (cf. Matthew 4:12).

Jesus left Judea because if he had remained it would have precipitated a conflict with Jewish religiosity much too early. Therefore, Jesus went to Galilee in order to distance himself from the leaders in Jerusalem. In Galilee He would be less of a threat to them.

Initially the Galileans received Jesus with interest and anticipation because of the miracles they had witnessed Him performing in Jerusalem during the feast days. Nevertheless, opposition soon grew to the point that His own countrymen tried to kill Him (Luke 4:28-30). After a brief period of startling success and reception in towns adjacent to the Sea of Gennesaret, Jesus was deserted by many of His followers (6:66).

John's Gospel gives a unique glimpse of an incident that took place on the road from Judea to Galilee. Jesus was traveling with His disciples through Samaria when they stopped in the small village of Sychar. There Jesus began to converse with a Samaritan woman. As a result of her conversion Jesus spent 2 days in Sychar where many believed in Him. This account gives the second time-marker in John. Jesus said, "Say not ye, There are yet four months, and then cometh harvest?" (4:35). The interim between sowing and harvesting in Palestine was 6 months. The most obvious understanding is that the time was around December or January and that there remained 4 months, i.e., until April or May, until harvest.

Following this brief stop, Jesus and His disciples traveled on to Galilee and arrived in Cana, the site of His first miracle, changing water into wine. In Cana in Galilee He performed His second sign, the healing of the Capernaum official's son.

With this act Jesus initiated the period called the great Galilean ministry. This is the period of ministry afforded the most space in the Synoptic Gospels. The passages in the Synoptics paralleling this include Matthew 4:12 to 15:20; Mark 1:14 to 7:23; Luke 4:14 to 9:17. John's Gospel records only the account of the healing of the Capernaum official's son and the feeding of the five thousand (John 6). But John records the account of a trip to Jerusalem that took place in the midst of this period that is not related by the Synoptics.

(3) *Jesus Third Journey to Judea*

Jesus' third journey to Judea was a festival pilgrimage to the "feast without a name" (5:1f.). While in Jerusalem Jesus healed on the Sabbath Day the lame man who was lying beside the pool of Bethesda. Related to this Jesus gave His great discourse on the divine authority of the Son.

Because of Jesus' actions on this feast day the enmity between Jesus and the religious leaders heightened. "The Jews sought the more to kill him" (5:18). Consequently, after the feast Jesus returned to Galilee, the setting of chapter 6 of this Gospel.

We would know more about how long Jesus ministered in Judea on this occasion if we knew what feast He had gone to celebrate. But in light of the available evidence much indicates that the unnamed feast in 5:1 was probably one of the chief feasts of A.D. 28—either Passover, the Feast of Tabernacles, or Pentecost. Apart from the question of which of these it was, the effect upon an understanding of the duration of Jesus' ministry in Judea is the same. In any case the Passover Feast of 6:4 may be dated in the year A.D. 29. This is supported by church tradition as well. Irenaeus is a chief example. Nevertheless, no opinion offers proof positive of the identity of the feast or its respective date.

The Third Passover Week of Jesus in Galilee. Having told of the opening signs of Jesus' ministry in Galilee (4:46), and having recounted one of Jesus' journeys to Jerusalem during this period, John next (chapter 6) recalled two of the greatest wonders taking place at the close of Jesus' Galilean ministry—the feeding of the five thousand in the wilderness and Jesus' walking on the Sea of Galilee. Related to the feeding of the five thousand Jesus gave His famous Bread of Life Discourse in Capernaum.

The multiplication of the loaves in only one of many of the great miracles of Jesus recorded in the Gospels. The Synoptics indicate that following this miracle Jesus withdrew from public view in order to give the disciples unique instruction about His upcoming suffering and death in Jerusalem. The reason for crossing to the other side of the Sea of Gennesaret was simply to be alone with His disciples. When the people followed, He fed the five thousand, but after this miracle many of Jesus' disciples took offense and no longer followed Him. As they left Jesus inquired of the Twelve, "Will ye also go away?" (6:67). Peter, on behalf of the other disciples responded, "Lord, to whom shall we go? thou hast the words of eternal life. And we believe and are sure that thou art that Christ, the Son of the living God" (6:68,69). A short time later Peter confessed at Caesarea Philippi, "Thou art the Christ, the Son of the living God" (Matthew 16:16). One week after that, on the Mount of Transfiguration, Jesus was glorified. The Synoptics give us the impression that during this time—from April to October—Jesus reduced His pace of ministry, choosing instead to teach His disciples.

(4) *Jesus' Fourth Journey to Judea*

This journey took place in October of A.D. 29. It was the final Feast of Tabernacles celebrated by Jesus during His earthly life. It was approximately one-half of a year prior to His return to the Father.

The opening words of chapter 7 tell us that it was dangerous for Jesus to appear publicly in Judea because the Jewish religious leaders were trying to kill Him. Jesus therefore had to exercise extreme caution when He decided to go to the Feast of Tabernacles. He did not travel with the other pilgrims, but chose instead to go secretly. John tells us that Jesus' brothers challenged Him to go to Jerusalem to demonstrate His power before the whole world. But Jesus would not oblige their request for such a showy display of power. His brothers did not believe in Him as the Christ and did not recognize that His means of victory would be His suffering and death on the cross. Some manuscripts record that Jesus said: "I will not go up to this feast." Others record His words as, "I will not yet go up." Waiting for His brothers to leave ahead of Him, Jesus delayed leaving until He could travel secretly from Galilee to Jerusalem. In this way He succeeded in eluding the Jewish authorities who were seeking to arrest Him.

In the midst of the Feast Jesus went up to the temple courts and began to teach the people. During the course of this feast and following it He delivered three of His great discourses: about the life-giving Spirit (7:14-52), about the Light of the World (8:12-59), and about the Good Shepherd (10:1-21). He also performed one of His most spectacular miracles when He healed a man who was born without sight.

During His stay in Jerusalem this time Jesus was almost stoned by the Jewish authorities, but He managed to hide himself. They were unable to arrest Him either, for His "hour was not yet come." The account of this Feast of Tabernacles extends over nearly four entire chapters. It concludes with the point that there was dissension among the people because of Jesus.

Jesus' final preaching journey was in Galilee, Samaria, and Peraea. Because of the hostile circumstances in Judea it was impossible for Jesus to minister openly there. Any appearance in public caused immediate, violent reactions. It is virtually certain that following the Feast of Tabernacles He returned to Galilee to engage in further ministry.

Jesus returned to His hometown on His final preaching effort before He went to Jerusalem. John tells nothing about this trip. Matthew and Mark provide only brief information. In the Gospel of Luke, however, there are no less than 10 chapters about this 2-month journey through southern Galilee, along the border of Samaria and across the Jordan River into Peraea (Matthew 19:1; Mark 10; Luke 9:51 to 19:27).

During this period Jesus apparently spent His time preaching and healing, debating with and refuting His opponents, and giving His disciples private instruction. Although He was deserted by many "disciples," many still continued to follow Him. During this period one particular urgency of Jesus apparently was to teach the Twelve. Luke also includes the information that Jesus chose 70 other disciples and sent them out ahead of Him into each town. He was limited in the amount of time He could spend in each place. From this group of disciples Jesus chose a body of men, who together with the 12 apostles, were sent to prepare the way for His coming.

Within a few months Jesus and His disciples undoubtedly arrived in Peraea. After being present at the Feast of Dedication at the temple Jesus again returned to the other side of the Jordan, where John the Baptist had first baptized (10:40). The expression used here implies that Jesus returned to the place He had been previously (cf. 14:3; 16:28). Thus it is unlikely that "again" refers to 1:28, the account of Jesus' baptism with John. Twice Jesus made trips from Peraea: one to Jerusalem and Bethany in December at the Feast of Dedication, and the other to Bethany in order to raise Lazarus from the dead (11:1-54).

(5) *Jesus' Fifth Journey to Judea*

Jesus made another appearance in Jerusalem at the dedication of the temple, a feast celebrated between the 10th and 20th of December. John noted that "it was winter" (10:22ff.). The controversy Jesus caused on this occasion was closely related to the preceding discourse on the Good Shepherd, which was His last discourse during His visit at the Feast of Tabernacles a few months earlier. The same phenomenon is recorded in chapter 7 (verses 21ff.) where it is noted that Jesus resumed His teaching about the Sabbath. This issue first arose during the unnamed feast (see chapter 5). For all practical purposes this was the continuation of the previous debate. This time Jesus addressed the issue from a different perspective. As the One sent from heaven He came to heal the whole man—even on the Sabbath. His authority over the Sabbath was interpreted by some of the people as a messianic claim.

Just as the Jews would later attempt to stone Jesus (8:59), so too, they now tried to kill Him. He escaped their clutches, however, for His "time had not yet come."

Jesus returned to Peraea on the other side of the Jordan. He was probably accompanied by many of those who followed Him throughout Galilee. This was the region in which John the Baptist had ministered. Many remembered John's recent proclamation that Jesus was the promised Messiah. The inhabitants of these regions now recognized that everything John had announced about Jesus was true. As a result many believed in Jesus.

(6) *Jesus' Sixth Journey to Judea*

Jesus' stay in Peraea was briefly interrupted by a side trip to Bethany (near Jerusalem) in order to raise Lazarus from the dead (11:1-44). This miracle caused a great stir among the people. It was at this time the Sanhedrin, under the direction of Caiaphas the high priest, formally decided to kill Jesus. They decreed that anyone knowing the whereabouts of Jesus must inform them so that they might arrest Him. But Jesus wisely withdrew from the public eye after He raised Lazarus from the dead.

Jesus traveled to Bethany after having spent some time in Peraea. But it was probably not long after His cleansing of the temple, since the disciples told their Master: "The Jews of late sought to stone thee" (11:8). It is reasonable to assume that Lazarus was raised sometime around January or February.

After visiting Bethany, Jesus went to the town of Ephraim in a region near the desert. He stayed there with His disciples up until the time of Passover (11:54). Both Jerome and Eusebius said Ephraim was located 20 Roman miles north-northeast of Jerusalem. Josephus said it was near Bethel. Many Old Testament texts tend to support that claim (cf. Joshua 15:9; 2 Samuel 13:23; 2 Chronicles 13:19).

Current scholarship tends to indicate that Ephraim was located on the present-day site of El-Tajibech, about 24 kilometers from Jericho along the road to Samaria east of the site of ancient Bethel and on the ancient road to Jericho. The nearness of the site to Jericho ties it to the Synoptic account of Jesus' last journey into Jerusalem (Matthew 20:29 to 21:1f.; Mark 10:46 to 11:1f.; Luke 19:1-40). Several weeks had probably elapsed since Lazarus was raised. Now, perhaps 2 months later, Passover was at hand. Quite possibly Jesus spent a good deal of this time in Ephraim. But it is equally possible that He may have returned to Peraea one more time. In any case He traveled down to Jericho in order to join His disciples as they made their way to the Feast of Passover in Jerusalem.

As the pilgrims to the Passover began to arrive in Jerusalem prior to Passover, they undoubtedly spoke among themselves about Jesus and wondered whether or not He would be present at the Feast (11:56). They apparently doubted that He would come. They probably thought He feared the decree of the Sanhedrin, which was an effort to incriminate those who knew where Jesus was and yet would not come forward.

(7) *Jesus Seventh Journey to Judea*

All four Gospels record Jesus' final journey to Jerusalem and His last Passover Week there. The account of the concluding days of Jesus' earthly life are given in such explicit detail that we are justified in saying the Gospels are themselves the Passion account with rich insights.

Six days prior to Passover, on the evening of the Sabbath, the Passion Week began. Jesus was anointed beforehand in anticipation of His burial. This took place in Bethany where Lazarus gave a feast in Jesus' honor. According to Oriental custom, Mary, Lazarus' sister, anointed the Lord. The costly spikenard she used was the equivalent of a worker's yearly wages. Some strongly criticized her actions as a "waste of the ointment." Judas is explicitly mentioned as an active critic, but the other disciples were also responsible. Their actions implied they thought this was too costly a gift to spend on Jesus. How deeply this must have hurt Him. How lonely and misunderstood He truly was during His life on earth.

On the following day the Passion procession started as a triumphant procession. On the colt of an ass Jesus rode into Jerusalem, accompanied by the shouts of acclaim and praise of the disciples and crowds. He was given a royal welcome by the people. However, He was not carried away by the glory of the moment. Jesus knew that as He drew near Jerusalem He was approaching His death upon the cross. Soon the shouts of "Hosanna" would be changed to

"Crucify!" As He neared the city, He wept over it.

A comparison of John's Gospel with the Synoptics permits one the following approximate reconstruction of Jesus' ministry and what confronted Him during that final Passover Week.

Palm Sunday: Jesus entered Jerusalem.

Monday: He cursed the unfruitful fig tree and cleansed the temple.

Tuesday: Greeks came wishing to see Jesus. Jesus was challenged by His opponents. He gave His last warning to the people. He pronounced the seven woes over the Pharisees. On the Mount of Olives Jesus spoke with the disciples about the end times.

Wednesday: Judas met with the high priest.

Thursday: Jesus and His disciples prepared for the final Passover meal. Jesus gave His farewell discourse to the disciples and went to Gethsemane. He was arrested.

Good Friday: Jesus appeared before the High Court, Pilate. Later He was crucified and died. He was buried by Joseph of Arimathea.

Saturday: (the Sabbath): The women prepared spices to anoint Jesus' body.

Sunday: Jesus was raised from the dead.

Material unique to John's Gospel, in addition to the passage on the Greeks who wished to see Jesus, includes chiefly Jesus' farewell discourse to His disciples and the washing of the disciples' feet. John's Gospel also records Jesus' appearing to Thomas and the rest of the disciples. John's Gospel adds another appearance of Jesus by the Sea of Tiberias and a meeting with His disciples following His resurrection.

Jesus instructed His disciples that He would meet them in Galilee following His resurrection. Matthew's Gospel tells of the climactic meeting on the mountain in Galilee. The Gospel of John, though, records that prior to this Jesus met seven of the disciples beside the Sea of Tiberias. They had just returned from an unsuccessful fishing expedition that night when Jesus appeared to them. At His instruction they received a supernatural, great catch of fish—just as they had once before when they met Jesus beside the sea and were called by Him to be His disciples. Jesus then ate with them on the shore.

The Fourth Gospel closes with the account of Jesus' discussion with Peter. Jesus gave Peter the responsibility of being a spiritual shepherd.

The Seven Signs

The miracles of Jesus were never designed for show. Satan challenged Jesus to turn stones into bread and to throw himself from the pinnacle of the temple. During His ministry Jesus was constantly challenged to give a "sign from heaven" He rebuked people for having such an attitude. Throughout the Passion narrative, the "sign-seekers," beginning with Herod and continuing through those who taunted Jesus to come down from the cross, were ever present. Jesus, however, never satisfied their demands, for they were asking in unbelief.

Although Jesus' miracles were powerful and spectacular, they were not designed to this end. Sensational wonders could never satisfy the fleshly minds of those sign-seekers. His miracles were not an end unto themselves. Neither were they designed to create a sensation. In fact, Jesus frequently tried to downplay or hide His miracles. The true purpose of the miracles was to meet the need of humanity. John's Gospel and the Synoptics agree wholeheartedly on this. At the same time, though, there are some differences between John's presentation of Jesus' miracles and those of the Synoptic Gospels. John spoke not of "miracles" but of "works." Apparently the intention was to say the "supernatural wonders" Jesus did were actually "natural" to Jesus!

John's Gospel refers to Jesus' miracles as "signs." The Synoptics also call Jesus' miracles "signs." They were His messianic credentials. But in John's Gospel the sign itself was primarily in focus. The miracles of Jesus point to something greater than the immediate relief He gave. Nor are they indicative only of Jesus' compassion. First and foremost they relate to the central theme of the overall Gospel: signs lead to faith in Jesus as the Messiah, the Son of God (20:30,31).

John did not record all of Jesus' miracles. Whereas Matthew recorded 20 of Jesus' miracles, Mark 18, and Luke 20, John's Gospel tells of only 7. But he distinctly recorded that the signs and wonders Jesus did were innumerable; so many that the world could not contain the books if they had been written down! (21:25). John's Gospel shows that these "signs" verified His messianic person and work.

Signs are one of the central ideas in the Fourth Gospel. The term *sign* (*sēmeion*) occurs 17 times in John. It is a technical term for the miracles of the Messianic Age. It is used in connection with the turning of water into wine at Cana (2:11); concerning the healing of the official's son (4:54); referring to healing miracles in general (6:2); concerning the miracle of the loaves (6:14-26); and referring to the raising of Lazarus (12:18). Nicodemus and the Pharisees described Jesus' mighty works as "signs" (3:2; 9:16). The Jews demanded that Jesus legitimize His messianic claims by doing signs (2:18; 6:30). The people pointed out that John the Baptist did not perform any signs (10:41). They noted that when Messiah came He would not perform any more signs than Jesus (7:31).

Jesus' miracles caused many to put their faith in Him. Although the miracle at Cana cannot, with all certainty, be determined as the basis for the disciples' faith, John's Gospel does maintain that many believed when they saw Jesus' mighty deeds (2:23; 12:11).

It is transparently clear that John did not present Jesus' signs as something He did to satisfy the fleshly desires of the people. They substantiated Jesus' messianic claims. They proved that the long-awaited Messianic Age had arrived.

Jesus rebuked the Jews (6:26) because they sought Him on the basis of being satisfied by the bread He gave them, rather than on the basis of having witnessed messianic signs. "Sign" here can be easily misinterpreted if viewed as some undefined miraculous work. The people who ate of the bread erroneously viewed the miracle of the loaves as simply a miracle. They did not recognize it as a miraculous messianic sign of the arrival of the age to come.

Such a superficial attitude toward the miracle and Jesus' work indicated unbelief. This is the unbelief for which Jesus rebuked them. The same criticism also resounds in 12:37, "But though he had done so many miracles before them, yet they believed not on him."

The signs invited men and women to believe in the messiahship of Jesus—His messianic glory. This is plainly seen in the phrase "and we beheld his glory" (1:14; cf. 2:11; 6:14; 7:31). The Fourth Gospel emphasizes the validity and testimony of these signs (20:30,31). In spite of witnessing signs, the Jewish religious establishment denied their own Messiah and condemned Him to die upon a cross.

Indeed, those signs that proved Jesus to be the Messiah became a stumbling block to the very ones they were designed to bring to faith. Eventually they even caused these rebellious men to plot to kill Him (5:18; 7:19,25; 8:37,40; 11:50). Because of their disbelief and stubbornness, and because of their rejection of Jesus, the Jewish religiosity became the greatest of all "signs" to which all others are subordinate—the death and resurrection of Jesus.

All of Jesus' miraculous signs acquire meaning and purpose only in light of the "work/sign" completed on the cross.
This is hinted as early as the first sign in Cana, which is tied thematically to Jesus' "hour" (2:4). In the raising of Lazarus there is a mighty portent of what will occur (chapter 11). The "sign of Jonah," the death of the Son of Man and His subsequent resurrection on the "third day," was the final validation that Jesus is indeed the Son of God.

Examination of the seven signs in John's Gospel will lead us toward this realization.

The First Sign: Turning Water into Wine (2:1-12)

John wrote that Jesus' first sign did not take place in Judea but in Cana of Galilee at a wedding. The substance of the miracle was His changing water into wine. Some critically suggest that this was an "unnecessary miracle" done as a luxury. Because of the circumstances the precise opposite, however, is the case. The lack of enough wine at the wedding clearly indicated that this involved poor people. The bridegroom provided as much as he could for the wedding in the hope that it would be sufficient. Jewish weddings might extend over the period of a week. Guests came and went as they wished and soon there was nothing left to drink at mealtime. The situation was more than awkward. Certain prescribed customs governed the wedding. Both the giving of gifts and the insuring of entertainment were carefully outlined. Legal action could even be undertaken if someone neglected his duty in these matters.

Jesus performed this first miracle to meet this need. Since Jesus' mother was giving orders to the servants she must have played some supervisory role in the affairs of the wedding. She may have been among the first to realize the problem. As she must have done before, she came to Jesus with the dilemma. She did not attempt to tell Him what to do, only what the problem was.

Jesus' response is intriguing: "Woman, what have I to do with thee?" (2:4). Although Jesus was neither rude nor unfriendly, this was an unusual way for a son to speak to his mother. There is no escaping the fact that Jesus was gently rebuking Mary. The time had come when she must no longer regard Jesus solely as her son; He is also her Lord.

Jesus' reply to her suggests that she had invited Him to demonstrate His power by performing a miracle. She, above anyone else, knew her son. As a virgin girl she had given birth to this divine child. The angel told her He would be the Son of God. The words of the Bethlehem shepherds lay treasured in her heart, just as did the words of Simeon, and the Wise Men from the East who traveled to worship Jesus.

She undoubtedly knew what occurred during His baptism in the Jordan, and she must have realized that His time to be manifested to Israel had arrived. This must have given her some sense of satisfaction after all those years of humiliation when Jesus was known as "the son of Mary," i.e., an illegitimate child (Mark 6:3).

Now Mary wanted Jesus to reveal himself fully. Jesus must have viewed her eagerness with the greatest of understanding and with the deepest of compassion. He knew the path of earthly glory would not be His route. He would go the ignominious way of the cross. For Mary this would be like piercing her soul with a sword (Luke 2:35). He realized what effect revealing His glory would have upon men. His miracles were the divine credentials that would reveal Him to Israel as being sent by God (cf. Acts 2:22). Nevertheless, these very miraculous works became the main reason that the Jews crucified Him.

Jesus recognized that in working His first miracle He moved himself from the peace of a private life to the chaos of public ministry. He would be ridiculed, scoffed at, falsely accused, abandoned by friends. After this, His whole life would be turned upside down. He would begin His trek to the Cross.

Thus Jesus associated this first sign with His "hour" that was "not yet come." Mary could only have understood Jesus' words as referring to some "delay" in His performing some miracle. She interpreted His words positively as a promise that He would help. Therefore, she went to the servants and instructed them to do precisely what Jesus told them. Jesus' words, though, have a far deeper meaning.

Of the seven times the reference to the "hour" for which Jesus came appears, all point to His hour of suffering.

(1) "Woman, what have I to do with thee? mine hour is not yet come" (2:4).

(2) "Then they sought to take him: but no man laid hands on him, because his hour was not yet come" (7:30).

(3) "These words spake Jesus in the treasury, as he taught in the temple: and no man laid hands on him; for his hour was not yet come" (8:20).

(4) "And Jesus answered them, saying, The hour is come, that the Son of man should be glorified. Verily, verily, I say unto you, Except a corn of wheat fall into the ground and die, it abideth alone: but if it die, it bringeth forth much fruit" (12:23,24).

(5) "Now is my soul troubled; and what shall I say? Father, save me from this hour: but for this cause came I unto this hour" (12:27).

(6) "Behold, the hour cometh, yea, is now come, that ye shall be scattered, every man to his own, and shall leave me alone: and yet I am not alone, because the Father is with me" (16:32).

(7) "These words spake Jesus, and lifted up his eyes to heaven, and said, Father, the hour is come; glorify thy Son, that thy Son also may glorify thee" (17:1).

Thus, the thought of the final "hour" of Jesus' death was in the back of His mind when He performed His first miracle.

Jesus' first miracle was critical for many reasons. It is significant that it was done not in the temple, nor in a synagogue, nor when the crowds were pressing upon Him. Rather, it was done in a private home during a wedding feast. In this setting Jesus was not some disinterested onlooker whose personality did not know human joy. No, here He stood as a true man capable of rejoicing in human fellowship. He shares our interests and joys. Truly He is "the happy Master of life from Cana!" Before He restored the divine worship in God's house by cleansing the temple, He shared in the establishment of a new home. God's first blessing to mankind was marriage (Genesis 1:28). Jesus gave His first blessing to the newly married couple in Cana by performing His first sign at their wedding feast.

In this miracle Jesus revealed His glory (2:11). Since His disciples already believed Him to be the Messiah and God's Son, this miracle must have been a powerful confirmation of their faith. Without a prayer—without even a word or gesture—Jesus worked the miracle. It was the presence of the almighty Creator himself in His creation and among His people that accomplished this great miracle. On behalf of His people, God elected to use His tremendous power.

Jesus' first sign provided a key for understanding all of His subsequent miracles. He worked these miracles in order to reveal His glory, but they were more than a demonstration of power. He was motivated by something more than a simple desire to show His power.

In the face of human need Jesus exercised His divine power to deliver men and women. But He never used this power to work miracles whose effect would be to overwhelm or subjugate those looking on. He did not desire followers who were not followers by their own choice and desire.

The Second Sign: Healing of the Official's Son (4:43-54)

The second sign John records was the healing of the son of a Capernaum official. The distinctive aspect of the miracle is the great distance between Jesus and the one He healed. He also did it only through the spoken word. This indicates that His words are as powerful as His presence. This sign, therefore, carries a unique message to later generations who lack the visible presence of Christ. Those lacking the undergirding visible presence of Jesus are encouraged to believe, even without having seen.

During His stay in Cana where He performed His first sign—turning water into wine—Jesus received a visit from an official of Capernaum whose son was deathly sick. Some have supposed this official was Chuza, the manager of Herod's household (Luke 8:3), or Manaen, who was brought up with Herod (Acts 13:1). It may seem strange that close associates of Herod would request Jesus' help, for according to John's Gospel such a high position would be an obstacle to confessing openly one's faith in Jesus (cf. 7:26,48; 12:42). But need forced this man of high standing to make the trip personally from Capernaum to Cana when he learned that Jesus was there.

Jesus regarded the man as typical of those whose faith in Him rested upon their having seen miracles. He gave him a discouraging reply when he asked Jesus to come to Capernaum: "Except ye see signs and wonders, ye will not believe" (4:48).

Jesus was not influenced by the man's status as a powerful and influential governmental official. He strictly made no effort to gain an audience with Herod's court. When the official refused to be denied and repeated his request humbly, Jesus obliged him in a totally unexpected way. He said, "Go thy way; thy son liveth" (4:50). The man's faith in Jesus was strengthened and purified; he believed Jesus' words. While he was still on his way home, servants came telling him that the child lived. He later discovered that the illness had left at precisely the same moment Jesus had spoken to him. Consequently the man and his whole household believed in Jesus.

The initial wavering and weak faith of the man, founded upon rumors of miraculous works, was transformed into a solid trust in Jesus' words and then into active faith in the person of Jesus. The passage is in keeping with the overall intent of the Gospel—to remind the readers that signs can lead to faith in Jesus as the Son of God.

The Third Sign: Healing the Lame Man at Bethesda (5:1-9)

Three of the seven signs recorded by John's Gospel took place in Judea: the healing of the lame man at Bethesda, the healing of the man born blind, and the raising of Lazarus. Each of these mighty miracles testify convincingly of the messianic glory and power of Jesus.

None of the healing miracles Jesus performed illustrated more clearly the unmerited nature of the healed person than does the healing of the man beside the pool of Bethesda. He was crippled and perhaps unwilling to receive help. He may even have been ungrateful. But Jesus, according to God's sovereign grace, chose to heal him.

The man's faith did not cause Jesus to heal him, because he did not know who Jesus was—not even His name. His hope for healing—if indeed he had any—was in the pool of Bethesda, not in Jesus. After 38 years of illness, his very will to be healthy seems to have deteriorated. When Jesus inquired whether or not he wished to be well, his response was vague. Instead, he began to reflect upon the hopelessness of his present situation. His soul as well as his body appeared to be paralyzed.

There is no indication that he was particularly devout or godly. In fact, Jesus' caution to him not to continue in sin because something worse might happen suggests that he lived in his sins, unpardoned.

In this way the man somewhat symbolizes the hopelessness of all of suffering humanity. If help were to come to him it could only be from an outside source. Even after his healing he appeared uninterested in Jesus. Upon learning Jesus' identity he went to Jesus' enemies.

There is only one explanation for this man's healing and it is found in Jesus' own words about it: "The Son quickeneth whom he will"

(5:21). The man was healed because of Jesus' gracious will, not the man's will to be healed. From the many sick and paralyzed in the colonnades at Bethesda Jesus chose the most hopeless and tragic example to confirm His divine power and grace.

The miracle at Bethesda is a miracle of grace—a testimony to Jesus as God coming in grace and truth. It is also a sign of God's love for sinners, for those unworthy of His favor, for those who have nothing to offer in exchange either in the present or in the future. God gives abundantly to those who do not deserve it.

There is another important aspect of this sign. It was done on the Sabbath. When Jesus instructed the lame man to take up his bed and walk, it led to an open dispute between Jesus and the Jewish leadership. Jesus, of course, was fully aware of the implications of His actions, but He refused to be party to the strict legalistic interpretations of the Law that the Jews advocated. His love and power were not capable of being reduced to a dead and callous set of rules. Jesus could not turn away from doing good on the Sabbath in order to satisfy the evil legalists. He came to do the work of the Father; His defense was simple: "My Father worketh hitherto, and I work" (5:17). Coupled with this sign we also have Jesus' great discourse about the authority of the Son (the third discourse in John's Gospel).

The Fourth Sign: The Miracle of the Loaves (6:1-15)

The feeding of the five thousand is the only miracle recorded in all four Gospels. That fact alone indicates the significance of this mighty manifestation of divine power.

The turning of water into wine at Cana and the feeding of the multitudes (miracle of the loaves) are unique miracles. These supernatural transformations of matter were creative acts and therefore testimonies that the Creator himself was at work in His creation.

Nevertheless, it should not be overlooked that these miracles, while so clearly supernatural, are at the same time patterned after the course of nature itself. The changing of water into wine is precisely what happens on the vine. Bread, similarly, is multiplied in fields where grain grows.

The same Lord who performed these supernatural miracles is also at work in the "natural" miracles of nature. These miracles are not in contrast to nature. Instead, they are supernatural signs that the Creator of everything is still "upholding all things by the word of his power" (Hebrews 1:3). Moreover, the Creator revealed himself in these miraculous acts, not as a stranger but as the mediator between creation and the Creator—the Son of God.

This miracle was witnessed by more people than any other miracle Jesus did. Whereas many of Jesus' works take place in a small group, in a home, or among His disciples, this was a public sign done before thousands of witnesses. Later He duplicated the miracle, feeding the four thousand. The thousands who ate of the loaves confirmed the reality of the miracle, and the remaining baskets full of fragments were tangible evidence.

Jesus interpreted the spiritual significance of the bread in His discourse on the Bread of Life. It not only symbolized His power and care, it also pointed to His own person—Messiah. The bread was not merely a gift to the hungry, it was a sign that He himself is the gift of God to those hungering and thirsting after righteousness.

The wine at the wedding in Cana and the bread the Lord broke for the hungry multitudes are symbols of the bread and wine of the Lord's Supper. Jesus plainly associated this with eating the flesh of the Son of Man and drinking His blood—an obvious reference to the Lord's Supper.

The event was more than simply a miracle. It was a "sign." The sign was designed "that ye might believe that Jesus is the Christ, the Son of God; and that believing ye might have life through his name" (20:30,31).

The Fifth Sign: Jesus Walks on the Water (6:16-21)

Following the narrative of Jesus' multiplication of the loaves and fish, John recorded how He came walking on the water to the disciples as they struggled against the wind and waves. Of the seven signs John recorded in his Gospel, three are miracles involving nature.

After the people had eaten the bread and fish, Jesus saw that in their excitement they were determined to make Him king—by force if necessary. They did not understand that this would have violated the purpose for which He came into the world.

The multitude believed that Jesus was "that Prophet that should come into the world" (verse 14). This very statement, however, showed how limited was their understanding of Him. They could accept Him as a prophet and even as a king, but they had not comprehended His teaching about faith and salvation. They honored Him with their lips but did not realize that He is not only prophet and king, but also priest. They were blind to the truth that as priest He must offer a sacrifice for their sins. The sacrifice was to be himself.

Jesus did not need men to make Him king, for He was born a king. His kingdom came from His Father, not from humans. In Daniel's prophecy, the clash of winds over the sea was a symbol of the rise of human kingdoms (Daniel 7:2,3). But the same chapter shows that the royal power of Christ was given Him by God the Father (Daniel 7:13,14). When Saul became Israel's first king it was because a rebellious people demanded a human ruler. If Jesus had allowed the frenzied multitude to force Him to become king, His throne would have had no better foundation than Saul's.

The enthusiasm of the crowd was carnal, and Jesus did not want His followers infected by such a spirit. It was an opportunity for Him to teach a lesson to His 12 disciples, so He ordered them to get into a boat and leave the scene while He hid himself on the mountainside. As Jesus continued in prayer all night, the disciples encountered a strong wind which made them forget any thoughts of earthly greatness. The headwind blowing against them was so strong that by the fourth watch of the night they had only reached the middle of the sea. What a change this was for them! During the day they had been in the center of exciting events, watching a fervent crowd clamor for Jesus to be their king. Now, just hours later, they could think only of their loneliness and danger while they battled the wind and waves.

In the fourth watch of the night Jesus came to them, walking on the rough sea. Thinking He was a spirit, they cried out in fear, but soon the familiar voice of their Master reached them through the storm: "It is I!" (literally, "I am!"). These words are among the "*egō eimi* words" of which there are so many in John's Gospel. It is possible this is an allusion to the name by which God identified himself to Moses (Exodus 3:14). Matthew's record of this event indicates that the miracle caused Jesus' disciples to recognize His divine nature, for "they worshipped him, saying, Of a truth thou art the Son of God" (Matthew 14:33).

The Sixth Sign: The Man Who Was Born Blind (9:1-7)

The healing of the paralyzed man at the pool of Bethesda and the miracle of the loaves and fish proclaimed that Jesus gives life to the world. The healing of the man who was born blind testified that Jesus is the Light of the World. This miracle is closely connected with Jesus' sermon on the Light of the World recorded in the preceding chapter. It is possible that the healing of this blind man was performed on the same day, immediately following the events recorded in chapter 8, since chapter 9 begins with the words, "And as Jesus passed by, he saw a man which was blind from his birth." The connection between these two chapters is Jesus' reference to himself in both as the Light of the World (8:12; 9:5). Chapter 8 is a sermon in words. Chapter 9 is a sermon in action—or as John usually called it, a sign.

The blind beggar was probably well known in Jerusalem. The disciples' knowledge of his condition led them to ask Jesus the reason for it. To the Jews there was a connection between affliction and sin. It was the same view held by Job's friends—that personal suffering was the result of personal sin. This was also the teaching of the rabbis: "There is no death without sin, and there is no suffering without mischief" (Rabbi Ammi, *Shabbath 55a*).

But which particular sin might result in a man's being born blind? Was he sufferring for his own sins? If so, when had he committed them? Two opinions prevailed among the Jews. Some thought that an individual afflicted from birth had sinned in his mother's womb. Others believed he had sinned in an earlier existence and now had to endure the consequences. These heathen ideas about the preexistence of the soul had become mixed with the Jewish religion from their contact with the Babylonians and from Greek philosophy. Believing such things made it difficult to have compassion for the sufferer who, after all, in their thinking was only getting what he deserved! It also promoted self-righteousness in those who enjoyed happy circumstances, for they considered themselves better than others.

Jesus rejected these ideas. His reply was simply, "Neither hath this man sinned, nor his parents" (9:3). Jesus did not mean to deny that there may be a connection between suffering and sin. Neither was He implying that either the blind beggar or his parents were sinless. He was making it clear that in this man's case no particular sins, committed by either him or his parents, had caused his blindness (cf. Luke 13:1-5).

Jesus pointed to the real reason this man had been born blind: "That the works of God should be made manifest in him." Jesus knew what others did not—that the man's affliction was connected with a divine plan. His blindness provided an opportunity for another sign that Jesus was the Messiah. He would heal the man as a further witness to that truth.

The Old Testament teaches that God himself can "open the eyes of the blind" (Psalm 146:8; cf. Exodus 4:11). Jews who waited for the Messiah believed this would be one of the signs that would accompany His coming into the world. Jesus did what only God can do. It is the Lord himself who opens the eyes of the blind (Isaiah 35:4,5; cf. Isaiah 29:18; 42:7). When Jesus opened the eyes of the blind it was a sign that He was God as well as Messiah.

John's Gospel gives many details of this healing because the purpose of his Gospel was to declare that Jesus is the Son of God. The healing of the blind was one of the signs Jesus told John the Baptist's disciples they should report to their leader (Matthew 11:5). The Bible does not record that anyone other than Jesus opened the eyes of the blind (besides the healing of Paul's temporary blindness), but the Scriptures tell us Jesus performed this miracle many times.

Jesus employed what may seem an unusual procedure. On two previous occasions He had used spit when He healed. This was when He healed a deaf man (Mark 7:33) and a blind man (Mark 8:23). In ancient times it was believed that spit had healing power. So there was nothing offensive in Jesus employing such a method. It was as acceptable then as anointing the sick with oil (which was also considered a medicine). Awareness of this background means there is no need to strain for some special "explanation" for this action of Jesus.

Mark 8:23 says Jesus spit in the eyes of another blind man. On this occasion John says He spit on the ground and formed what might be called a poultice which He put on the blind man's eyes. Then He told the man to go to the pool of Siloam and wash the mud off. Jesus did all of this without praying and without the man himself or anyone else praying.

If there was a symbolic meaning to Jesus' use of clay in this healing, it may be an allusion to the fact that in the beginning, man was created from the soil. A divine act of creation was necessary to bring life to the first man, and such an act took place when the man born blind received his sight.

However, it may have been that Jesus was only calling special attention to the sign He was performing. This miracle did not take place in private. It happened publicly while a multitude of pilgrims from outside Jerusalem were present for the Feast of Tabernacles. It was a sign to them and all the inhabitants of Jerusalem that Jesus was the Messiah. While He was preparing the clay poultice, a crowd gathered. As the man went to the pool of Siloam he was easy to distinguish from other people because his eyes were smeared with the mud. A large procession probably followed him to the pool to see what happened. During this time Jesus also had an opportunity to withdraw from the crowd. The situation had become tense because some of the Jews in the temple had just threatened to stone Him.

The healings of the paralyzed man and the man born blind were both connected with pools of water—Bethesda and Siloam. Since John's Gospel gives the meaning of the name "Siloam" ("sent"), it may be an indication there was symbolism here, i.e., that Jesus was the One sent from God, His true Messenger. "Bethesda" means "house of mercy," which certainly applies to the miracle Jesus performed at that pool.

When the man born blind returned from the pool completely healed, it caused a great commotion. The crowd began to discuss the possibility that he was not really the blind beggar who was so well known in the city. However, the man and his parents confirmed that he was the same man. The parents were rather guarded in their comments because they feared the religious leaders, but their son gave a distinct testimony to having been healed by Jesus.

The Pharisees then seemed to begin an official investigation of the incident as they questioned the man. They had to face the fact that a miracle had taken place, although some tried to deny that the man had actually been born blind (9:18). When this explanation failed, they demanded that God alone should be given the praise for the miracle. They insisted that because Jesus was a sinner, He should not be honored for what had happened. Their accusation was based on the fact that He had broken their Sabbath laws by this healing and therefore had sinned (9:24).

The Sabbath rules of the Jewish religion were detailed and rigorous. Many requirements had been added to the Law, even though God had forbidden either adding to or subtracting from it (Deuteronomy 4:2; 12:32). The Pharisees' interpretation gave a totally distorted concept of the Sabbath, which was actually God's gift to the people. Jesus purposely disregarded these "human commandments." In this instance He had broken the Pharisees' Sabbath rules in several ways. His forming the clay and lifting it from the ground was considered "work." In the eyes of the Pharisees Jesus had lifted a burden! They even forbade the wearing of sandals made with nails because to lift the nails was to carry a burden. However, they apparently did not consider that they themselves had lifted a burden when they picked up stones to throw at Jesus!

Jesus had also disregarded their rules by smearing the clay on the eyes of the blind man. Healing was forbidden on the Sabbath by the regulations the Pharisees had added to the Law. Only when saving a person's life was involved could medical help be given. Even then it must be only the kind which would keep the patient from getting worse, not any treatment which could make him better!

The messianic sign of the blind man's healing should have shown the Pharisees that Jesus was truly the One sent from God. However, they concluded that since the man's life had not been in danger and he became "better" after Jesus' help (being healed), the Sabbath law had been broken. This was, therefore, "proof" to them that Jesus was not from God (9:16).

However, this very reasoning created dissension among the Pharisees because it contradicted another of their Jewish interpretations of the Law—that God hears only the godly and does not listen to sinners. They held this belief as firmly as their rules about the kinds of activity that should be avoided on the Sabbath. Confusion was created among these leaders when someone asked, "How can a sinner do such signs?" Three times in the Gospel of John it is recorded that a division arose among the Jews because of Jesus (7:43; 9:16; 10:19).

When the man who had been born blind was questioned about his healing, he used the same logic about God hearing only the godly. He disagreed with the Pharisees' assertion that Jesus was a sinner. He said he had no knowledge of Jesus before this but could not accept their accusations. One thing he did know was that Jesus had opened his eyes, a miracle unheard of before. The man turned the Pharisees' logic back on them, declaring that Jesus could not have performed the miracle if He had not come from God (9:31-33). From the very beginning the man was convinced that Jesus was a prophet, and he did not try to hide this belief (9:17).

This beggar who had been born blind behaved like a true Israelite. Instead of allowing the Pharisees to intimidate him with their arguments he showed a strong and independent spirit. This was unusual because those leaders were accustomed to having everyone submit meekly to their opinions. This man soon let them know he was irritated and weary with their repeated questions, asking them sarcastically if all their investigation meant they intended to become Jesus' disciples themselves. This enraged the Pharisees, who then reviled him as one "born in sins." They were Moses' disciples, they said, but he was a disciple of Jesus. They recognized he was Jesus' disciple before he knew it himself!

Then they cast him out—literally. First they drove him from the house where the examination took place. Undoubtedly they also cast him out of membership in the synagogue. They had already decided that if anyone confessed Jesus as the Messiah he would be excommunicated from the worship privileges of other Israelites. This was a severe punishment for this new disciple and is the first direct persecution of Jesus' followers that John recorded.

When Jesus heard what had happened, He went looking for the man. He did not meet him accidentally, but "found" him and asked, "Dost thou believe on the Son of God?" (9:35). Some translations read, "Dost thou believe on the son of man?" This rendering has some support, but evidence for the former seems stronger. Actually there is little difference between these variations because if one believes on Jesus as the Son of Man he must believe in Him as the Son of God. The man worshiped Jesus (verse 38), so he must have believed He was the Son of God.

The healed beggar (9:8) first referred to Jesus as "a man that is called Jesus" (9:11). He continued to confess Jesus as "a prophet" (9:17), and finally he worshiped Him as the Son of God (9:38).

The blind man regained his sight in two ways—physically and spiritually. The Pharisees who claimed to see were blind to Him who is the Light of the World. Their spiritual blindness was as real as the man's physical blindness had been. Jesus declared that He had come to the world so the spiritually blind might receive their sight, while those like the Pharisees who boasted they could see would be made more blind (9:39; cf. 12:40).

The Seventh Sign: The Resurrection of Lazarus (11:1-44)

When John the Baptist in prison heard of the works of Christ, he wanted to hear more about them. Finally, he sent two of his disciples to ask Jesus if He was really the Messiah or if the Messiah was yet to come. Jesus' answer came through actions rather than words. He performed a series of miracles in view of John's disciples and made it clear to them these signs witnessed to the truth that He was the Messiah.

To John's disciples, Jesus spoke of signs He had performed in three areas. (1) Sicknesses and bodily defects: the lame were walking, the lepers were cleansed. (2) Afflictions involving the physical senses: the blind saw, the deaf heard. (3) Human life itself: the dead were raised (Matthew 11:4-6).

When John recorded Jesus' miracles in Jerusalem and Judea, he used a sign from each of these categories: (1) the healing of the paralyzed man at Bethesda; (2) the healing of the man born blind; (3) the raising of Lazarus from the dead. (See chapters 5,9,11.)

Prior to this, Jesus had raised the daughter of Jairus shortly after she died and raised the son of the widow of Nain when his body was enroute to the grave. But Lazarus was raised after having been in the grave 4 days and after his body had begun to experience corruption.

According to the Jewish point of view the condition of a corpse deteriorated so much in 3 days that after that it could not be identified. A rabbinic tradition held that the soul of one who had died stayed near the grave for 3 days, hoping to return to the body it had left. After 3 days, however, the body was in such a condition that the soul gave up all hope of returning and left. (See *Yerushalami Mo'ed Katan* 3, 82b, and *Shabbat* 152a.) These views are, of course, totally unscriptural, but were believed by many at the time of Jesus. For one to rise from the dead on the fourth day would thus be considered an unusually great sign. (C. Ginzburg, *The Legend of the Jews* 5:78.)

However, it was no more difficult for Jesus to raise the dead after 4 days than after 4 hours. Such a miracle involved bringing individuals back to life no matter how long they had been dead. Nothing in Scripture indicates that the raising of Lazarus was a miracle of higher order than the others Jesus raised from the dead. However, when a body that has already begun to decay is raised, there can be no doubt that death has really occurred. This makes the sign even more indisputable. Even Jesus' enemies could not deny this miracle.

During the Feast of Dedication the Jews challenged Jesus to say directly whether He was the Messiah (10:24). Jesus pointed them to the works He had been performing and asked them to believe those works even if they could not accept His word about himself (10:27,38). The raising of Lazarus was a final, mighty sign which should have provided the Jews one more indisputable proof that Jesus was the promised Messiah. This miracle was performed shortly after the Feast of Dedication and it happened before the eyes of the religious leaders—in Bethany just outside Jerusalem. After this sign these people had no reason to maintain they lacked convincing evidence that Jesus was who He claimed to be.

None of the miracles of Jesus are more fully confirmed than the raising of Lazarus. It was an event which took place in the light of full publicity, being witnessed by both friends and opponents of Jesus. Many of the Jews who came to Bethany to express their sympathy to Lazarus' sisters did not share their faith in Jesus, but many did believe when they saw this miracle.

Matthew, Mark, and Luke do not mention any of the miracles Jesus performed in Jerusalem, so the raising of Lazarus is not included in those three Gospels. They tell only of Jesus' works in Galilee. So there is no reason to search for artificial explanations about the raising of Lazarus not being included among the miracles in the Synoptics.

There is no indication that the raising of Lazarus was a miracle in a special class or that it was a climax to the miraculous works of Jesus. It was simply another raising of the dead, of which there were apparently others which are not specifically mentioned (Matthew 11:5; Luke 7:22). Even the disciples of Jesus were commanded by Him to raise the dead (Matthew 10:8). The raising of Jairus' daughter and the widow's son are given as examples of such miracles performed by Jesus. These were sufficient proof of His power. No more needed to be recorded. But it is safe to assume that there were more miracles of raising the dead by both Jesus and His apostles than are mentioned .

The record of Lazarus' raising in John 11 is clearly the testimony of an eyewitness concerning what he had "seen and heard." The account speaks for itself. It is lively and follows this Gospel's style of illuminating the story with personal observations and details. It draws a matchless picture of Jesus' personality.

The members of the family in Bethany were close friends of Jesus. Luke records that Martha had received Jesus in her house earlier. In John's Gospel, Martha is shown as the same energetic person engaged in her customary activities, and Mary as a more retiring, contemplative individual. Lazarus is not mentioned earlier.

The onset of Lazarus' sickness appears to have been sudden. When the two sisters saw his life might be in danger, they sent for Jesus. At that time He was a day's journey away on the other side of the Jordan. Although they did not directly ask Jesus to come to Bethany, their message was clearly a plea for help. When Jesus received the message He said, "This sickness is not unto death, but for the glory of God, that the Son of God might be glorified thereby" (11:4). Probably the messenger returned with these words, which must have been difficult for the sisters to understand because their brother apparently died shortly after they had sent for Jesus.

John's Gospel records that Jesus waited 2 days before starting for Bethany, but it also says, "Now Jesus loved Martha, and her sister, and Lazarus" (11:5). Thus it was not indifference or lack of love that motivated Jesus' delay.

John's Gospel tells of several events which show how Jesus constantly refused to be led by other people, including those who were close to Him. At the wedding in Cana His mother had said, "They have no wine"; but He answered, "Woman, what have I to do with thee?" (2:3,4). His Heavenly Father, not Mary, would determine when His earthly ministry would begin. When His brothers chided Him about making himself known to the world through His miracles, He replied in a similar way: "My time is not yet come" (7:6). From a human viewpoint, Jesus owed a debt of gratitude to the family in Bethany for their past hospitality. However, He would not allow mere sympathy to govern His behavior. The message from the sisters was restrained and it was beautiful: "Lord, behold, he whom thou lovest is sick" (11:3). But were they not implying that this was not just an ordinary sick person? It was one who was especially close to Jesus. Jesus loved Lazarus, but He would not discriminate among people who called on Him for help. By divine grace, the poorest beggar would receive the same help as Jesus' close friends. Anything Mary, Martha, and Lazarus received from Jesus would also be through divine grace, not special privilege. Jesus' delay seemed long to Martha and Mary, but it must have also seemed long to Jesus himself. However, He always waited for the Father's time to do His Father's works, so "he abode two days still in the same place where he was" (11:6).

Jesus knew Lazarus was already dead when He got the message of his sickness. When Jesus arrived in Bethany, Lazarus had been in his grave 4 days. On the first day the messenger came to the place where he knew Jesus could be found. During the next 2 days Jesus remained in that place. On the fourth day He traveled to Bethany. Martha and Mary were aware there would be some delay because of travel time, so their words to Jesus were not a reproach when each of them said, "Lord, if thou hadst been here, my brother had not died" (11:21,32). This was probably just what they had told each other over and over during those trying days.

When Martha was told that Jesus had come, she went to meet Him. Her conversation with Him is one of the high points of John's Gospel. Martha's confession of her faith in Jesus was strong: "Lord: I believe that thou art the Christ, the Son of God, which should come into the world" (11:27). She gave this testimony in one of the darkest hours of her life. It was at a time when Jesus' own actions were puzzling to her because she knew He could have prevented Lazarus' death.

Jesus had said previously that Lazarus' sickness was not unto death. Now He spoke to Martha the same way. He assured her that he who believes in Him shall never die and the one who believes in Him shall live even though he were dead.

Jesus assured Martha, "Thy brother shall rise again" (11:23). Martha's answer shows she knew he would rise in the resurrection at the last day, but Jesus explained, "I am the resurrection, and the life" (11:25). By this statement He reminded Martha that He is the only One who can call forth the dead in that future resurrection. But at that very moment He had the same power He will have in the last day. Martha seems to have wavered between faith and doubt, yet it seems evident she still had hope that a miracle would take place: "I know, that even now, whatsoever thou wilt ask of God, God will give it thee" (11:22).

When Mary came and fell down weeping before Jesus, He was disturbed in His spirit and was moved to tears himself. The words used to describe His emotion seem to express sorrow, compassion, and deep indignation. His own tears showed His sympathy. He weeps with those who weep. Jesus was showing not only human compassion, but divine love. At this moment the whole God-human personality of Jesus was expressing itself.

But Jesus' wrath is also expressed here. One of the words He used *embrimaomai* conveys a sense of a deep feeling of indignation. The word is used in 11:33, Matthew 9:30, and Mark 1:43, where it emphasizes that Jesus spoke very sternly.

Jesus felt grief as well as compassion when He stood before the grave in Bethany. He was deeply stirred because even those who believed in Him seemed to have allowed their sorrow to overshadow the joy they should have felt over a believer going home to his Father. Jesus expected His disciples to show such joy when He was summoned back to heaven himself (14:28). Lazarus' sisters and friends loved him enough to weep over his death, but that love was not strong enough for them to rejoice at his eternal happiness. Can we imagine what Jesus must have really felt when He recalled Lazarus from death—from the peace and happiness he was already enjoying?

Jesus also experienced a burning wrath toward death itself and toward the devil who had the power of death. The One who came into the world to destroy the works of Satan now showed His authority. Lazarus' raising was a forerunner of the final victory when all who are in their graves shall hear the voice of the Son of God.

Jesus' cry was a word of command: "Lazarus, come forth!" (11:43). And the dead one returned to life. Jesus thus showed His power and authority over both the material world and the spiritual world. To Him who can perform a miracle like raising the dead, nothing is impossible. He would soon rise from His own tomb as Victor over death and the grave.

The raising of Lazarus should have prepared the Jews for Jesus' own resurrection which would take place in a short time. What happened in Bethany proved indisputably that the power of God can raise from the dead a man who has been in the grave 4 days. When Jesus' tomb was found empty on the first Easter, the empty grave once occupied by Lazarus also bore witness: The Lord is surely risen!

The Main Theme of the Gospel of John

The Gospel of John has a distinct theological aim: to prove that Jesus is the Messiah and Son of God and by this truth to bring men to faith and spiritual life. The inspired writer himself declared this to be the purpose for the book (20:30-31).

Under the heading of this primary purpose there are a series of secondary purposes for the writing of John's Gospel. If proclaiming the deity of Jesus Christ is the primary motive, then combating distortions and deviations from this doctrine naturally becomes a secondary motive. In this Gospel there are distinct traces of a conscious intent to deal with early heresies which later became known as Gnosticism. This Gospel also presents a strong indictment of the Jewish leaders and their followers who rejected their Messiah. This Gospel also points to the errors of a group of John the Baptist's disciples who wanted to continue their own activities instead of following Jesus.

These secondary purposes are plainly subordinate to the great purpose of proclaiming Jesus as the Son of God. That is the message of this book, the gospel which must be preached.

An analysis of the Gospel of John in light of the book's central theme shows a whole series of proofs of Jesus' deity. None of the other Gospels and no New Testament epistle employs such a systematic, theological presentation of this foundational truth of Christianity.

What is unique about the Gospel of John is the presentation of testimony to the deity of Jesus rather than philosophical arguments. Instead of giving his interpretation of Jesus' ministry, the inspired writer recorded his testimony concerning Jesus' works. He spoke about events "which we have heard, which we have seen with our eyes, which we have looked upon, and our hands have handled" (1 John 1:1). The message of the Gospel of John is the self-revelation of Jesus in His words and works—His own testimony to himself.

We come very close to the person of Jesus in this Gospel. It is not merely a book *about* Him. His heart beats on every page. His thoughts, His words, and His mode of expression confront us constantly. Human imagination could not have created such a picture, for in the Gospel of John we truly meet the God-man. Furthermore, in meeting Him we worship Him as the One who identifies with us in all our needs.

Throughout the Gospel of John the testimony of Jesus as the Son of God is clear. Each miracle was a sign of His deity. He was the theme of His own sermons. A series of sevenfold testimonies from both heaven and earth supported His claim to be the Messiah. Jesus himself testified to His relationship with the Father. His testimony was expressed in seven similarities and reached its climax in the seven "*I AM* proclamations" and in the revelation of the Triune God in Jesus' farewell sermon. The following is a summary of this series of proofs of the deity of Christ.

The Seven Signs

These seven signs form a major part of the contents of John's Gospel. The following shows only how each of these seven signs contributed to the main theme of the book.

(1) *The sign of the water changed into wine (2:1-11).* Jesus showed His glory through a miracle of creation and transformation, which confirmed the disciples' faith in Him as the Son of God.

(2) *The sign of the healing of the nobleman's son (4:46-54).* Jesus showed the power in His word, which leads to faith in himself.

(3) *The sign of the healing of the paralyzed man at Bethesda (5:5-18).* Jesus showed His sovereign grace toward the unworthy and helpless.

(4) *The sign of the multiplication of bread and fish (6:1-15).* Jesus fed the 5000—a sign that He himself is the Bread of Life who gives life to the world.

(5) *The sign of walking on the water (6:16-21).* Jesus showed His power over nature and the disciples worshiped Him as the Son of God.

(6) *The sign of the healing of the man born blind (9:1-7).* Jesus showed He is the Light of the World by healing this man who worshiped Him as the Son of God.

(7) *The sign of Lazarus' raising from the dead (11:1-44).* By this sign Jesus revealed himself as the One who gives life to the world and has power over death.

The Seven Sermons

The seven sermons are treated rather thoroughly in the Gospel of John. The following summary highlights features which pertain particularly to the person and work of Christ.

(1) *The new birth (3:1-21).* During His conversation with Nicodemus, Jesus revealed himself as the One who gives life through His own sacrificial death. All who believe in Him have eternal life.

(2) *The Water of Life (4:1-42).* During His conversation with the Samaritan woman, Jesus revealed himself as the Messiah. He is the One who gives the Water of Life to the spiritually thirsty who call on Him.

(3) *Equality with the Father (5:19-47).* Jesus spoke in this passage of the seven resemblances of the Son to the Father—the fourfold testimony concerning Jesus' deity (treated especially in the following).

(4) *The Bread of Life (6:22-66).* Jesus declared himself the Bread of Life who gives life to the world.

(5) *The life-giving Spirit (7:1-52).* Jesus proclaimed himself the One who gives the Holy Spirit to those who believe in Him.

(6) *The Light of the World (8:12-59).* In connection with the healing of the man born blind, Jesus proclaimed himself the Light of the World.

(7) *The Shepherd (10:1-21).* Jesus proclaimed himself the Good Shepherd who gives His life for the sheep, thus announcing both His death and resurrection.

The seven sermons of Jesus recorded in the Gospel of John have many similarities to His sermons recorded in the Synoptic Gospels. All the sermons present the same messianic claims and the same teachings. Jesus often used symbols to illustrate spiritual truth. In John, His sermons are in the form of allegories more than actual parables, but this can be found in the other Gospels also. In His Judean sermons Jesus sometimes used a different form of presentation from the form used in the sermons He preached in Galilee. The great sermon in Capernaum on the Bread of Life is similar in form to the other sermons in John. During Jesus' last week, the record in the Synoptic Gospels of His discussions with His opponents is not basically different from His manner of address in the other sermons.

The difference between Jesus' sermons as recorded in John and the other Gospels is mainly in their form. In the Synoptics, Jesus' sermons consist of many brief statements. Jewish rabbis taught their disciples in this manner—expecting them to memorize these statements. Matthew, Mark, and Luke present Jesus as a rabbi using this same method.

In addition to the seven sermons John recorded, there is also Jesus' farewell sermon to the disciples. Of the seven sermons, two are private conversations—one with the Pharisee Nicodemus and one with the Samaritan woman by the well of Jacob. Five of the seven sermons were given in Jerusalem, one in Samaria, and one in Galilee.

Three of the seven sermons are clearly connected with three of the miracles John recorded. The sermon concerning the Son's divine authority and likeness to the Father was preached in answer to the Pharisees' criticism after Jesus had healed a paralyzed man on the Sabbath (chapter 5). The sermon on Jesus as the Bread of Life was given after the miracles of the loaves and fishes (chapter 6). His sermon on himself as the Light of the World was followed by the healing of the man born blind, and the connection between the sermon and the miracle seems to be clear in this instance also (chapters 8,9).

All seven of these sermons are messianic proclamations, like the seven signs which authenticated Jesus' claim to be the Messiah. Thus the sermons as well as the signs are connected with the main purpose of John's Gospel—to declare that Jesus is the Messiah and the Son of God.

The Seven Resemblances to the Father

When Jesus healed the sick man at Bethesda on the Sabbath and was criticized for it by the Jews, He defended His action by referring to His divine authority. The Jews then tried to kill Him, not only because He broke their Sabbath rules, but "said also that God was his Father, making himself equal with God" (5:18). Jesus proved His resemblance to the Father in the following ways.

(1) *Similar in work (5:19):* "What things soever he (the Father) doeth, these also doeth the Son likewise."

(2) *Similar in knowledge (5:20):* "The Father loveth the Son, and showeth him all things that himself doeth."

(3) *Similar in power to raise the dead (5:21):* "For as the Father raiseth up the dead, and quickeneth them; even so the Son quickeneth whom he will" (cf. 5:28,29).

(4) *Similar in judgment authority (5:22):* "The Father judgeth no man, but hath committed all judgment unto the Son" (cf. 5:27).

(5) *Similar in honor (5:23):* "All men should honor the Son, even as they honor the Father."

(6) *Similar in power to give eternal life (5:24):* "He that heareth my word, and believeth on him that sent me, hath everlasting life, and shall not come into condemnation; but is passed from death unto life" (cf. 5:25).

(7) *Similar in divine self-existence (5:26):* "As the Father hath life in himself; so hath he given to the Son to have life in himself."

The Seven Testimonies to the Deity of Jesus

In addition to the sermon concerning His resemblances to the Father, Jesus also gave a fourfold testimony to the fact that he is the Messiah (5:31-39). In the Gospel of John there are also three more testimonies of Jesus to this truth.

(1) *The testimony of the Father (5:34,37; 8:18).* The entire history of Israel was a preparation for the sending of the Son. When He appeared to the people of Israel, the Father's voice testified at His baptism that He is the Son of God. Even now the Father continues to testify of His Son, for the one who believes on the Son of God has the witness in himself. (Compare 1 John 5:9-11.)

(2) *Jesus' own testimony (8:14,18,37).* In 5:31 Jesus said, "If I bear witness of myself, my witness is not true." Actually He was saying, "Then my witness is not true in their opinion" (the opinion of His enemies). From 8:13 we see that this was exactly the attitude of the Pharisees toward Jesus' testimony. He rejected their objections, saying that even though He witnessed of himself, He knew where He came from and where He was going, so His testimony was true.

There may be a deeper meaning in Jesus' words in 5:31. Not all testimony to oneself is true because it might not be of God, which would render it invalid. In this connection Jesus referred to a false and seductive individual who comes "in his own name" (5:43). Such self-assertion is not at God's direction, so it is a lie. The words Jesus spoke about himself came from the Father just as His works did (17:8). Jesus' testimony about himself does not stand alone. What the Father spoke through the Son harmonized with what He spoke through the Spirit. It was "the Spirit of Christ" who testified of Him before He came to earth and even now testifies of Him and glorifies Him.

(3) *The testimony of the Holy Spirit (15:26; 16:13,14).* Since the beginning, the Holy Spirit has testified of Him who should come, His sufferings, and the glory that would follow (1 Peter 1:11). When the Spirit descended like a dove

and hovered over Jesus at His baptism, John recognized this was the sign that Jesus is the Son of God (1:32-34). Since Jesus went back to heaven the Spirit has continued to testify of Him (15:26). No one can say "Jesus is Lord" except by the Holy Spirit who reveals to the individual the deity of Jesus (1 Corinthians 12:3).

(4) *The testimony of the Scriptures (5:39-46).* What God spoke in the past He still speaks to all mankind because it is recorded in the Holy Scriptures. That word was originally entrusted to the Jews as part of their great privileges (cf. Romans 3:2). The Jews believed that through the Scriptures they had eternal life. In a sense they were correct because God's Word is the word of eternal life (cf. John 6:68; Acts 5:20). However, it is not enough to be only a hearer of the Word. There is life in the Scriptures because they testify of Christ, but only those who believe the Word and come to Jesus receive life. Jesus said of the Scriptures, "They . . . testify of me" (5:39). The prophecies, promises, and types of the Old Testament speak of God. Therefore, Jesus referred to the Scriptures as the great testimony of himself.

The events in Jesus' life were foretold centuries before they took place and stand as indisputable proof that He is the One He says He is. To believe in Jesus requires believing His own words as well as the prophecies about Him.

(5) *The testimony of the works (5:36; 10:25).* When the disciples of John the Baptist came to Jesus for His own confirmation that He was the Messiah, He referred to the works He had been performing (Matthew 11:4) Jesus also referred to His works as proof of His messiahship. He performed miracles that no one else had done (15:24). He appealed to His listeners to believe His works even if they did not believe His word (10:38; cf. 14:11).

Jesus attached the greatest importance to the evidence of the miracles He performed. They were a "greater witness" than the forerunner, John the Baptist (5;36), who had been entrusted with the mission of preparing the people for Christ's coming. In all of His work Jesus fulfilled the task the Father had given Him (cf. 3:35). Those works testified to His deity, showing that the Father was in Him and did the works through Him (14:10).

Today the miracles of Christ are given much too little importance as evidence of His deity. Some skeptics even deny that the miracles are signs of the truth of Christianity. So it is important to understand that Jesus himself attached great importance to these supernatural manifestations. The signs Jesus performed were so irrefutable that even His fiercest opponents could not deny they had happened. Even the Jewish Talmud confirms them. The only argument Jesus' enemies could find was to insist that His miracles were of satanic origin and so were not valid messianic signs. In making such charges they were sinning against the Holy Spirit (Matthew 12:24-32).

Note the following points concerning Jesus' miracles.

(a) *Proof:* This refers to concrete, material things one could see and observe and which stood the test of every kind of investigation.

(b) *Publicity:* Jesus' works were not done in a corner (cf. Acts 26:26). They were witnessed by His enemies as well as His friends. Sometimes thousands of people were present.

(c) *Number:* The miracles recorded in the Gospels are only a few that were selected by the Holy Spirit for the writers to tell about. John said the signs Jesus performed were so many that it would have been impossible to write about them all (cf. 20:30; 21:25).

(d) *Greatness:* Jesus performed miraculous healings, raisings of the dead, and miracles in nature which cannot have any "natural" explanation.

(e) *Character:* The miracles of Jesus were not empty demonstrations intended only to show His power. Almost all of them were acts of mercy that helped people—expressing Jesus' compassion, goodness, and love.

(6) *The testimony of John the Baptist (1:7,27,36; 5:33,35,36).* Jesus referred to John's testimony in addressing the delegation sent by the Jewish leaders. Actually, Jesus did not need testimony from any man. It was not necessary for John, or anyone else, to convince Him He was the Messiah. But to help the people believe and be saved, Jesus referred to John's testimony. John himself was now removed from the scene, but his words concerning Jesus were a lasting testimony (cf. 10:41).

(7) *The testimony of the disciples (15:27; 19:35).* "And ye also shall bear witness" (15:27). Jesus had called His disciples for this task. At their word men would believe in Him (cf. 17:20). Those who saw the glory of Jesus Christ—who witnessed His life, death, and resurrection—could not hold their peace about what they had

seen and heard. Obeying their Lord's command and the heavenly vision, they went forth to bring the message of Christ to the ends of the earth.

The Church is built on the foundation of the apostles and prophets (Ephesians 2:20). The prophetic messages of the Old Testament and the apostolic testimony in the New Testament stand as the foundation of faith to the end of time.

The Seven "I AM" Proclamations

Unique to the Gospel of John are the so-called *egō-eimi* words which Jesus used concerning himself and which allude to the name of God in the Old Testament: I AM. The Septuagint has *egō eimi* for I AM in Exodus 3:14 where the name of God is rendered "I AM THAT I AM" (*egō eimi ho ōn*). The form is emphatic and was not normally used in everyday speech. This mode of expression was used in many Old Testament passages where the Lord made known that He is the One who speaks. An example is Deuteronomy 32:39: "See now that I, even I, am he." Isaiah 43:10 is another: "Understand that I am he."

This unusual style expresses deity. Its usage is clearly stamped with the name of God. Therefore, it is remarkable that Jesus used such a style of expression as His own, thus connecting the I AM name with himself.

In the Gospel of John there are over 20 of these important "I AM" quotations from Jesus. In a few instances the *egō eimi* statements may seem only to convey information. But even in those cases Jesus' words seem to be more than the common usage employed merely to inform people of facts. The *egō eimi* words are a proclamation of Jesus' deity.

To the Samaritan woman who said she knew the Messiah would come (4:25), Jesus replied, "I that speak unto thee am he" (4:26). When the disciples were frightened at Jesus' walking toward them on the sea He cried, "It is I!" (6:20). To the Pharisees who attacked His self-testimony (8:13), He said, "I am one that bear witness of myself" (8:18). Three times in Gethsemane He said to those who came to arrest "Jesus of Nazareth," "I am he." Even in these instances, Jesus' words seem to be more than mere conveying of information about himself. *Egō eimi* is a proclamation of His deity and divine authority.

The second group consists of four *egō-eimi* words which are clearly divine self-proclamations. They cannot have any other meaning. Three of these words were uttered by Jesus during His last Feast of Tabernacles: "If ye believe not that I am he, ye shall die in your sins" (8:24). He said, "When ye have lifted up the Son of man, then shall ye know that I am he" (8:28). In both verses there is no predicate. The expression "I am" stands alone and can only be an allusion to the name of God. The first of these sayings is followed by the words that He is the One that he said He was "from the beginning" (8:25). This strongly emphasizes the eternal preexistence of Jesus and agrees with the words of John's prologue (1:1). The truth that Jesus is from the beginning is the very foundation of the Gospel of John.

In 8:58 we have the most unusual of all these *egō-eimi* words: "Verily, verily I say unto you, Before Abraham was, I am." By His "verily, verily," Jesus emphasized the importance of this statement and confirmed it with a Biblical oath. When Jesus maintained that He existed before Abraham was born, it can only be understood in one way. It is a claim for His deity. He proclaimed himself to be the great I AM, the eternal God. He did not say "even as it was before Abraham," but "before Abraham was, I am." He who speaks here is elevated over time itself. He is God revealed in flesh—the eternal Word who was in the beginning and who is himself the beginning of all which came into being. He was the Angel with the name of God (Exodus 23:20,21). This unique Angel of the Lord in the Old Testament is the Son of Man in the New Testament.

In 13:19 we have one more *egō-eimi* word without a predicate: "Now I tell you before it come, that when it is come to pass, ye may believe that I am he." Thus Jesus revealed the name of God to the disciples (cf. 17:26).

This third group of *egō-eimi* words connects "I am" to certain pictures of truth relating to salvation and the message of the gospel.

Here the "I am" proclamations of Jesus correspond in a remarkable way to the use of God's name in the Old Testament in passages where His name is connected with His redemptive work. God makes himself known in the Old Testament by at least seven such "Redeemer" names in the same way Jesus makes seven "I am" proclamations in the Gospel of John.

The seven Redeemer names of God in the Old Testament are: (1) The Lord sees (Genesis 22:14). (2) The Lord, our righteousness (Jeremiah 23:6). (3) The Lord is peace (Judges

6:24). (4) The Lord my shepherd (Psalm 23:1). (5) The Lord thy physician (Exodus 15:26). (6) Thc Lord my banner (Exodus 17:15). (7) The Lord is there (Ezekiel 48:35).

The seven "I AM" proclamations of Jesus are as follows:

(1) *"I am the Bread of Life" (6:35,41,48,51).* The Jews expected the miracle of the manna to be repeated in the last days. Such an expectation was fulfilled in Christ, but not as they imagined. He did feed the multitudes with physical bread, but above all He is the Bread of Life himself, giving life to the world. Jesus told the people that He alone satisfies the hunger and thirst of the soul. He does it by giving His flesh for food and His blood for drink (cf. 6:51-56). Christ is needed not only to save, but to sustain after an individual is saved. Without Him, life lacks the element which gives it reality and meaning. Jesus is the True Bread from heaven of which the manna in the wilderness was only a type.

(2) *"I am the Light of the World" (8:12).* When Jesus proclaimed himself the Light of the World He was alluding to God's command in the beginning: "Let there be light" (Genesis 1:3; cf. 2 Corinthians 4:6). The coming of light preceded everything else during creation, for light is necessary to all life in the world. Spiritually, Christ came to begin a new creation of which He is the Light required for complete and eternal life.

(3) *"I am the door" (10:2,7,9).* This statement is closely connected to Jesus' comparison of himself to Jacob's ladder (1:52). That ladder touched both heaven and earth, so the illustration is a good one for the Saviour who calls himself "the way" (14:6). In declaring himself to be the door, Jesus pointed to two aspects of this truth. First, He is the door where the shepherds have their admittance (verse 2). But He is also the "door of the sheep" where all who enter are saved (verses 7,9). There is only one door to the sheepfold, and both shepherds and sheep must come through it. In verse 7 the emphasis seems to be on shepherds. In verse 9 it is on the sheep and their salvation. Jesus is not *a* door; He is *the* door—the only admittance to salvation and the safety of the sheepfold.

All of these "I am" words concern the person of Jesus. He not only *gives* bread; He *is* himself the Bread of Life. He not only *holds* the light to shine on our pathway, He *is* the Light. He not only *points at* a door and a way, He himself *is* the Door and the Way. In His own person He is the gospel He preached. He redeems from sin (1 John 2:2) and is thcrcfore the believer's peace (Ephesians 2:14), life (Colossians 3:4), and hope (1 Timothy 1:1).

(4) *"I am the good shepherd" (10:11,14).* Jesus presented himself in this chapter under two pictures: the door to the sheepfold and the shepherd of the sheep. Both symbols refer to His provision for the salvation of sinners and their security after salvation. At the same time Jesus emphasized the contrast between himself and the false shepherds who are robbers and hirelings (verses 1,12). Jesus' sermon recorded in chapter 10 seems to be a continuation of His dispute with the Pharisees in chapter 9. They are blind leaders claiming to see. Therefore, they are blind guides who lead their followers astray. The fact that they will not enter into the sheepfold through the door, but climb up some other way, shows they are thieves and robbers. Jesus is the door, and they rejected Him. In this last public sermon recorded in the Gospel of John, Jesus warned against false shepherds and teachers in much the same way He did in His first and last public sermons recorded in Matthew—the Sermon on the Mount (Matthew 7:15) and the sermon concerning the woes coming on the Pharisees (Matthew 23). Over and over Jesus warned against seducers. The entire New Testament reflects an unceasing struggle against those who want to destroy God's sheep. The final test is always one's attitude toward Jesus Christ—His person, His Word, and His work.

Jesus said the sheep know the shepherd's voice. They will not follow a stranger because they do not know his voice. A true believer has spiritual instincts which enable him to tell the difference between true and false doctrine (cf. 1 John 2:20). God has given believers spiritual senses that must be exercised to discern between good and evil (Hebrews 5;14).

In a world full of danger the sheep need the Shepherd. Jesus' *egō-eimi* word here answers the question, "Who is the real Shepherd?" He says, in effect, "I am the Good Shepherd, the only real shepherd. I AM." This statement in addition to the solemn introduction, "verily, verily," emphasizes the importance of Jesus' teaching.

What is the main point of Jesus' proclamation that He is the only real shepherd of the flock? The relationship of the sheep to the Good Shepherd is noted by the fact that they listen to Him and follow Him. The flock is under the leadership and protection of the shepherd. This gives the sheep security, but it also demands their obedience. The flock does not wander aimlessly here and there. It is led by the will of the shepherd to places of pasture and rest. He plans each day where they will go. Each member of the flock is in intimate contact with the shepherd and with each other. The shepherd knows his sheep and calls them by name. It is evident that this is a picture of the Church gathered under its Lord's guidance and protection and being constantly on guard against "thieves" and "robbers."

The shepherd illustration must have been familiar to Jesus' listeners. In the Old Testament the Lord is often described as the shepherd and Israel as His flock (Genesis 48:18; Psalms 23:1 28:9; 77:21; 78:52; 80:2; 95:7; 100:3; Isaiah 40:11; Jeremiah 23:1; Ezekiel 34:11; Zechariah 11:4). In Zechariah 13:7 we read of the shepherd who is wounded while defending his flock: "Awake, O sword, against my shepherd, and against the man that is my fellow, saith the Lord of hosts: smite the shepherd and the sheep shall be scattered." Jesus undoubtedly had this prophecy in mind when He spoke of himself as the Good Shepherd who "giveth his life for the sheep" (John 10:11; cf. Matthew 26:31).

In John 10 Jesus used a shepherd's readiness to die for his flock (verse 15) as an illustration of His own willingness to lay down His life for His own (verses 17,18). Such a sacrifice does not show that the shepherd is weak. On the contrary, it emphasized His power over His own life: "I have power to lay it down, and I have power to take it again" (verse 18). Here we see a merging of Jesus' mission as both Shepherd and King. As the Messiah-King He wins and gathers His people through His death on the cross. As the Good Shepherd He gathers the flock by sacrificing His life for His own. Those already in the sheepfold and those who will be brought in later from the Gentile world will be gathered as one flock under one shepherd (verse 16; cf. 11:52).

While a Jewish shepherd might be willing to risk his life for his flock if it became unavoidable, Christ, the Good Shepherd, sacrificed His life willingly. The theme of the Shepherd-King's voluntary sacrifice of His life is emphasized throughout the Gospel of John and receives special emphasis in the treacherous events in Gethsemane (18:3-11). At that moment Judas was playing a rather passive role, and the soldiers fell to the ground. All the time Jesus kept the initiative and surrendered to His opponents only after the repeated proclamation, *Egō eimi.* "I AM!" The Good Shepherd is also the "great shepherd of the sheep" who arose from the dead (Hebrews 13;20). He is the "chief shepherd" who will be revealed in glory when He returns (1 Peter 5;4).

(5) *"I am the resurrection and the life" (11:25).* No prophet or apostle could use such words about himself. Only He who is truly God could say it. Jesus was more than a human teacher who taught about resurrection. He confirmed His word by raising Lazarus from the dead. He revealed himself as the source and origin of life (11:25). He is the One who brings the dead to life, who calls those things that are not as though they were (Romans 4:17). He is the fountain of all life because He himself is "life" (14:6). He has power and authority over death and is himself the Resurrection. He is "the resurrection and the life," the eternal "I AM." Because He is "the life," knowing Him is eternal life (17:3). Because He is the Resurrection, the one who believes in His name will live even if he dies (11:25).

"Life" is one of the main subjects in the Gospel of John. The Greek word is *zōē*, and it has implications connected with Hebrew thought. John presents life as a thoroughly spiritual matter, not a vague philosophical or metaphysical idea. When the Scripture speaks of death in contrast to life, it does not mean cessation of existence but an existence that is under the wrath of God: "He that believeth on the Son hath everlasting life: and he that believeth not the Son shall not see life; but the wrath of God abideth on him" (3:36). Death is not only the loss of life itself but loss of the possibilities which belong to life. Death is the state of desolation and emptiness which prevails when fellowship with God is broken.

The life which Christ *is*—this is the life He *gives.* He who is "the life, the eternal" (1 John 1:2) gives eternal life. He who manifests the life of God gives men a share in that life and its abundance (10:10). This includes the spiritual riches of power, understanding, and love which are in Christ himself. This is the "abundance" He gives to those who receive Him (1:16).

The Scripture uses three expressions to explain this picture of life—creation, birth, and resurrection. Creation refers to a coming into existence by the creative word of God (1:3). Birth speaks of the infusion of the life of God himself, a birth from above (3:3). Resurrection is the renewal of what was broken down by sin and death (5:24,25). All of this is wrought by Him who is "the resurrection and the life."

Christ is the Light of Life: "The life was the light of men" (1:4). Christ is the Water of Life: "Whosoever drinketh of the water that I shall give him shall never thirst" (4:14). Christ is the Bread of Life who gives eternal life. This means life which is possessed now but really belongs to the age to come. It is both present and future. The present is combined with the future by the term "resurrection." As the resurrection of Christ combines His earthly life with His eternal existence as the glorified Lord and makes both an indissoluble unity, so it is with the life believers have in Him.

Through the Resurrection, their life in this world is connected with life in the world to come in a unity where personality is retained. Man lives a real life, involving both body and soul—first here on earth, and later in eternity. The Gospel of John does not refer to spiritual life versus bodily life but, to living versus death. In Greek philosophy resurrection meant total discontinuance of the body. But in Christianity resurrection includes the redemption of the body. The resurrection and the life belong together.

The Gospel of John treats bodily death as almost nothing. It is still an enemy which even the believer must eventually meet, but the enemy's victory is only temporary, as it was in the case of our Lord's death. Because death is a conquered enemy, it cannot destroy the real life of the believer. It only brings a transfer to another sphere of existence because the life the believer has received through Christ is eternal. It is a life which cannot be separated from Christ himself. When Christ offers this life He offers himself because He is the One who is "the Resurrection and the Life."

(6) *"I am the way, the truth, and the life" (14:6).* This *egō-eimi* saying is close in meaning to the two statements mentioned earlier: "I am the door" (10:9) and "I am the resurrection and the life" (11:25). The new dimension now brought to our attention is this: "I am the truth."

Jesus was saying He is the starting point of all truth. Thomas complained that since the disciples did not know where their Lord was going they could not know the way either. Jesus answered: "I am the way." To this figurative expression He added the concrete statement: "I am the truth." Jesus is the way to God because He is the truth concerning God—the total and complete revelation of the Father (1:17,18). Because He is the Truth, He is also the Life which is in God. Eternal life consists of knowing the only true God and the One He sent, Jesus Christ (17:3).

None of the three expressions in this declaration is subordinate to the others. Each one stands beside the others and thus forms a complete statement. They illuminate and mutually reinforce each other. The fact that Jesus is the Truth is central because He is the embodiment of truth—the truth personally.

Truth is a major theme in the Gospel of John. Different forms of the word are used over 50 times; while Matthew, Mark, and Luke use them only a few times each. This does not mean that the subject of truth is unimportant in the other Gospels. It only shows how dominant it is in John's Gospel.

In Scripture, as elsewhere, truth has the usual meaning of being the contrast to that which is false. Truth is reality, not just something which merely appears to be. In both the Old Testament and the New, truth is connected with the revelation of God: "God is not a man that he should lie" (Numbers 23:19). "The word of the Lord is right" (Psalm 33:4). The New Testament also declares that "God is true" (John 3:33). He is "the true God" (1 John 5:20) who cannot lie (Hebrews 6:18). God in His very being is truth, and it is necessary to know Him in order to know what truth is. Only through the revelation of God can men know the truth. The result of worshiping false gods is to "change the truth of God into a lie" (Romans 1:25). Turning to God for salvation brings an individual to "the knowledge of the truth" (1 Timothy 2:4).

This divine truth came by Jesus Christ (1:17). The message is identified by the messenger. He is "full of grace and truth" (1:14) and can therefore say "I am the truth." He is the True Light (1:9), the True Food and Drink (6:55), the True Vine (15:1). The message concerning Him is the liberating truth (8:36), the saving word about Him who is the Saviour of the world. His message is the word concerning His death and resurrection.

(7) *"I am the vine" (15:1,5).* This is the last of the *egō-eimi* words that involve metaphors. This picture of the vine and branches empha-

sizes the close union between Jesus and those who believe in Him.

Jesus spoke of himself as "the true vine" in contrast to Israel, who in many Old Testament passages is compared to a vine (Psalm 80:8,9; Isaiah 5:1; Jeremiah 2:21; Ezekiel 15:1-6; 19:10; Hosea 10:1). The vine, like the fig and olive trees, was interpreted as a symbol of Israel. Coins have been found from the period of the Maccabees with an inscription representing Israel as a vine. When the Old Testament uses the vine as a symbol of Israel, the subject is Israel's failure and the resulting judgment lying ahead. The Messiah would be a shoot coming up from the stump of Israel (Isaiah 11:1), the One who would restore the holy remnant of Israel to their former place. He is "the true vine."

There may be a connection between the picture of the vine and "the tree of life" in Eden (Genesis 2:9). The test involving the tree of knowledge of good and evil resulted in man's fall, causing him to lose access to the tree of life (Genesis 3:24). Jesus is now "the tree of life" into which each believer is grafted.

By using the illustration of the vine and branches Jesus was telling His disciples that everything they did depended on their union with Him. In Him they had life and in Him they received power to bring forth fruit. "Without me ye can do nothing" (15:5). The parable is a serious admonition not to receive the grace of God in vain, but to bring forth the fruits of salvation (cf. Matthew 3:8). The branch which does not bear fruit will be taken away by the Father, who is the vinedresser. Such a branch will then wither and be thrown into the fire.

But the Father will prune and carefully tend each branch which brings forth fruit so it will bear even more fruit. As in other New Testament passages, the fruit mentioned here is Christian character, the fruit of walking in the light (Ephesians 5:8,9), the fruit of righteousness (Philippians 1:11), the fruit of the Spirit (Galatians 5:22,23; cf. Matthew 7:20; Romans 6:22). When followers of Christ bring forth good fruit the Father is glorified, and it is the Father's glory which is always uppermost with the Son. During His earthly life He glorified His Father by fulfilling the work the Father had given Him to do (17:4). He continues to glorify the Father by giving His disciples power to bring forth much fruit.

In this "I AM" word Jesus referred to himself as the source of life and the source of fruit. Those who are united with Him through the new birth manifest the Christian character which is the goal of sanctification. Thus Jesus once more placed himself at the center of His gospel, for without Him there will be no life, no fruit, no character, no sanctification.

The Farewell Sermon of Jesus

All four Gospels record Jesus' private meeting with His disciples the evening before His suffering. The Synoptics record this in connection with other details about the institution of the Lord's Supper. John's Gospel omits this, but gives a full summary of Jesus' farewell sermon and the prayer He prayed for His disciples (chapters 14-17). This sermon section is also connected with the main theme of John's Gospel—the proclamation of Jesus as the Son of God. His farewell sermon is a climax of the revelation of God—perhaps the strongest emphasis on the doctrine of the Trinity. The Biblical picture of God is probably not expressed more distinctly anywhere concerning the unity and personality of the Godhead—the Father, the Son, and the Holy Spirit.

It is difficult to survey the farewell sermon by dividing it into clear-cut sections. One section seems to overlap another. The following division and survey of the farewell sermon seems valid.

(1) *Reunion in the house of the Father (14:1-11).* Jesus began by saying: "Let not your heart be troubled: ye believe in God, believe also in me. In my Father's house are many mansions." This promise is the foundation for Jesus' words of comfort. He presented the final goal of redemption—the eternal reunion of believers with the Father. Jesus himself is the way to the Father's house. "I am the way, the truth, and the life: no man cometh unto the Father, but by me" (14:6). Jesus is the complete revelation of the Father's eternal being, His power and love. A special revelation of the Father—a theophany such as Philip asked for would not be as great as the revelation the disciples already had, for God was revealed in flesh in the person of His Son. That revelation was the basis of their faith in the Father and their faith in Christ.

(2) *The kingdom of God shall come (14:12-17).* How could the kingdom of God have come near when Jesus was going to leave them as He now said? Jesus comforted them in their confusion. The work He had begun would not be destroyed, for greater works would now take place. Jesus gave two reasons for this. First, He

himself will do whatever the disciples ask in His name (verses 12-14). Also, He will send another Paraclete, the Holy Spirit, who will be not merely *with* them but *in* them (verses 16-18). Through the Spirit, the kingdom of God will come in power (cf. Mark 9:1).

(3) *A deeper relationship (14:18-27).* The third basis of comfort Jesus gave the disciples was the promise that His departure would not break the relationship they had with Him. On the contrary, that relationship would be deepened. He promised to come to them himself, together with His Father (verses 18,23). By the Spirit of Truth (verse 26) He promised to dwell in believers. It was to be a relationship in which the Triune God and each disciple participated. The relationship would be even deeper and more real than the one they had been enjoying through their physical contact with Jesus (cf. 2 Corinthians 5:16).

(4) *The death of Jesus would take place according to the will of God (14:28-31).* The fourth basis of comfort Jesus gave His disciples was the assurance that His death would not take place because "the prince of this world," the devil, had any claims on Him. "He has nothing in me," declared the Lord. When the power of darkness reached its hour, it was because it was in the purpose and plan of God. The death of Jesus was not a catastrophe which befell Him. It took place according to the Father's will, and Jesus went willingly to death because of His love for the Father. He told the disciples ahead of time what would happen so that when it came to pass they would believe in Him. This is a basic principle of prophecy—especially messianic prophecies. If the disciples loved Jesus as they should, they would rejoice because He was now going to the Father where He would also prepare a place for them.

These are the main points in the sermon of comfort. The sermon also contains special instructions concerning the relationship between Jesus and the Father. This teaching about the Father included the following: (1) the Father's house (14:2,3); (2) the way to the Father (14:3-6); (3) the Father revealed in the Son (14:7-9); (4) the word of the Father (14:10,24); (5) the works of the Father (14:10-14); (6) the Spirit of the Father (14:15-18,26); and (7) the love of the Father (14:21). There is also further teaching about the relationship between Jesus and the Father: (1) Jesus sent from the Father (14:24); (2) Jesus' return to the Father (14:28); and (3) the love of Jesus for the Father (14:31).

Christian Relationships (Chapter 15)

(1) *The relationship of the disciples with Christ (15:1-11).* The deep relationship Christ mentioned in chapter 14 (verses 8-27) is further illustrated in His teaching about the vine and branches. He admonished the disciples seriously to remain in Him, to remain in His love. Probably the strongest words in the Bible about Christ's love for His own are found in this teaching: "As the Father hath loved me, so have I loved you" (15:9). This comparison exceeds all human imagination (cf. 17:24). Most amazing of all is that this love is mutual—the love God has for His Son is the measure of Christ's love for His people (17:26; cf. Romans 5:5).

(2) *The mutual relationship of the disciples (15:12-17).* Jesus' love for these who belong to Him is to be a pattern for their love for each other. Jesus' love is to be the inspiration for love among themselves (cf. 1 John 5:1). Jesus reminded them that His love is proved by the sacrifice of His life for His friends. Such a self-giving love is to be manifested among believers.

(3) *The disciples' relationship to the world (15:18-27).* The love of believers is a contrast to the hatred the world has for them. Jesus did not want His followers to have any illusions about this. The world which crucified their Lord would have a cross for them too. Believers should not expect sympathy from the world, but this should not concern them, because it was Jesus' own experience. The world's hatred of Christ and His followers is without cause. It is the reaction of darkness against the light.

In the Biblical sense, "the world" is humanity estranged from God—"our fallen earth with its fallen inhabitants." The world is a perversion of the creation God once pronounced "very good" (Genesis 1:31). This is what sin has brought on the human race.

The believer's relationship to the world is paradoxical, as the relationship of Jesus himself was. God loves the world and sent His Son that the world might be saved through Him (3:16,17). The believer testifies to the world of this but at the same time stands opposed to the world as Jesus did. The world which hated Him because He testified that its works are evil will for that same reason hate believers (cf. 7:7). Followers of Jesus must expect this and endure it. To seek friendship with the world is treachery against the Lord. James 4:4 says, "The friendship of the world is enmity with God." The hatred of the world is a sign the believer does not belong to it but is separated from it.

Warnings and Promises (Chapter 16)

(1) *Warning of persecution (16:1-4).* Jesus foretold that the world's opposition would result in frequent persecution. He was not referring here to casual opposition from individuals, but organized persecution from religious and public authorities. To be excluded from the synagogues included religious excommunication as well as exclusion from the public community. "The time cometh, that whosoever killeth you will think that he doeth God service" (16:2). Jesus warned the disciples of this so they would remember it when the time came. This is another example of the purpose of prophecy—trials will not come on believers unexpectedly. Jesus has prepared them for that which will take place, and His Word will be their strength for the time of trial. As long as He was with the disciples He did not have to say anything about this. But as His departure drew near it was necessary. (Compare Matthew 24:9 with parallel passages.)

(2) *The promise concerning the Spokesman (16:5-15).* The disciples were not, however, to believe they would suffer any loss at the departure of their Master. On the contrary, His going away would be for their benefit because then the Spokesman, the Holy Spirit, would come. Jesus then pointed to the works of the Holy Spirit in the world and among believers.

(a) The *paraclētos* and the world (16:8-11). "He will reprove the world of sin, and of righteousness, and of judgment." "Reprove" means that He indicts the world as guilty as well as awakening the individual conscience to its guilt. Normally the word *paraclētos* refers to one who defends the accused, which makes the term paradoxical as applied to the Holy Spirit. The Spirit is the one who cross-examines with the intent of convicting or conquering an opponent.

The Spirit's conviction is aimed first of all at the attitude the world has toward Jesus Christ. The world declares itself righteous (Luke 18:9), but sentenced Jesus as a sinner (John 9:24) and sent Him to the cross. The power behind such actions is that of "the princes of this world" (1 Corinthians 2:8), guided by Satan, the prince of this world. However, Jesus was now going to the Father. He who was revealed in flesh is "justified in Spirit" by God (1 Timothy 3:16), while the prince of this world is sentenced. Satan is conquered, not by an act of power alone, but by a just judgment, and the world is sentenced with its prince. Since this has taken place it is a matter of greater importance than ever that "he that believeth not is condemned already, because he hath not believed in the name of the only begotten Son of God" (3:18).

The work of the Spirit now is to convict of sin because the world does not believe. Unbelief is the sin which is characteristic of the world. It is the chief sin and the root sin which is the origin of all sin. The world looks on this unbelief not only as excusable but even lawful. The natural man thinks it is just as shocking that "he that believeth and is baptized shall be saved" as "he that believeth not shall be damned" (Mark 16:16). Only by the conviction of the Holy Spirit are men able to see that unbelief is sinful and brings them under condemnation.

(b) The *paraclētos* and believers (16:12-15). After Jesus had spoken of the convicting work of the Spirit in the world, He continued speaking of the Spirit's teaching work among the people of God. Jesus is the teacher of righteousness. In both works and words He is the perfect revelation of God. The disciples were His confidential friends and He said, "All things that I have heard of my Father I have made known unto you" (15:15). He had much to tell them which He could not share with them yet. This was not because of lack of confidence on Jesus' part but because the disciples were not yet ready for such teachings. These things the Holy Spirit would bring to them. Jesus promised that when He, the Spirit of Truth, came He would guide them into the total truth.

This does not mean that the Holy Spirit would put Jesus and His doctrine in a secondary role. On the contrary, He would glorify Jesus. He would remind the disciples of what Jesus had said. "He shall receive of mine, and shall show it unto you" (verse 14). All the Holy Spirit would teach them would be a further illumination of the person of Jesus, His work, and His Word. In Him are hid all the treasures of wisdom and knowledge (Colossians 2:3). The Spirit brings forth these hidden treasures when He teaches that "the truth is in Jesus" (Ephesians 4:21). All that leads to the total truth in the New Testament has its root and foundation in the words of Jesus himself.

Jesus also said that the Comforter would show believers "the things to come." This might be understood as doctrine which had not yet been revealed in its complete meaning. However, Jesus was referring especially to the fact that the Holy Spirit is the Spirit of prophecy. He reveals the eschatological truths concerning the future of the kingdom of God, such as those which are unveiled in the last book of the Bible.

(c) The seven Paraclete sayings. In His farewell sermon the teaching of Jesus about the Holy Spirit can be divided into four sections: 14:15-17, 14:26, 15:26, and 16:7-15. The content of this material may be subdivided into what is called the seven Paraclete sayings where the different aspects of the Spirit's work are emphasized: (1) He shall abide and remain in believers (14:17). (2) He shall teach the words of Jesus and remind believers of them (14:26). (3) He shall testify of Jesus (15:26). (4) He shall convince (convict) the world of sin (16:8). (5) He shall guide believers into all the truth by "receiv(ing) of mine, and . . . show(ing) it unto you" (16:13-15). (6) He shall glorify Jesus (16:14). (7) He shall preach the things to come (16:13).

(3) *The promise of meeting again (16:16-22).* Jesus ended His sermon the same way He began by promising the disciples He would be united with them once more. In the beginning He referred to the eternal gathering in His Father's house, but at the end He spoke of the joyous reunion that was going to take place with Him after His resurrection. As a woman naturally feels pain when the time of a birth is at hand, the disciples now felt sorrow when they thought of Jesus' departure. But what causes a woman pain at first becomes the reason for her greatest joy. Likewise, that which now caused the disciples to grieve would become the theme of their greatest joy when they saw Him again not many days later. Then no one would be able to take their joy from them.

Jesus continued speaking of the glory in this new, deepened relationship between himself and the disciples. They could pray for what they wanted in His name and He would freely speak to them concerning the Father. The words of Jesus here opened new perspectives—not only concerning the 40 days after the Resurrection and then the Age of the Spirit, but also the nearness of all believers to God in eternity. Jesus ended His sermon with the majestic proclamation, "I came forth from the Father, and am come into the world: again, I leave the world, and go to the Father" (16:28).

In addition to the disciples' remarks, Jesus added some final words of His own when He informed them He was fully aware of the fact that they would soon be scattered. Every man would be concerned about his own safety, and they would leave Him alone. However, to assure them they would have peace in Him despite their failure, He contrasted His own victory over the world with their distress. "In the world ye shall have tribulation: but be of good cheer; I have overcome the world" (16:33).

The High Priestly Prayer of Jesus (Chapter 17)

Only Jesus could pray like this! In such a way God speaks to God. The disciples here received (and all believers along with them) a glimpse into the eternal relationship of Deity itself. Therefore, the high priestly prayer of Jesus is the climax of the Bible's revelation. Believers are brought into the Holy of Holies to listen while the God-man speaks to His holy Father.

The prayer of John 17 is the high priestly prayer of Jesus. One of the main functions of the Old Testament high priest was to bear the name of Israel before God in prayer. Here the true High Priest prayed for His followers before the Father.

The unity of this prayer is apparent. In the first verses Jesus prayed for himself. In the following verses He prayed for His disciples. In the last section He prayed for those who would believe in Him because of the witness of the apostles. This refers to the true universal Church.

(1) *The prayer of Jesus for himself* (verses 1-5). When Jesus prayed for himself it was not a selfish prayer. He prayed that the Father would glorify the Son so the Son might glorify the Father. He said He had received from the Father the power to give eternal life to those the Father had given Him. It was the honor of the Father and the spiritual welfare of mankind that lay most heavily on the heart of Jesus when He prayed for himself.

It was the holy, sinless One who prayed here. That is why this prayer is totally different from the prayer He taught His disciples. The prayer of the disciples (called the Lord's Prayer because He taught it) contains a prayer for forgiveness of sins. In the high priestly prayer of Christ, however, there was the opposite—a frank confession that the Son had in every way fulfilled the will of the Father and finished His task.

The prayer of Jesus for glorification was not presumptuous. He prayed to receive again the glory He had with the Father before the world was created. It was glory He had laid aside for a time in order to become the Saviour of the lost. Jesus was about to take the last step on His road of humiliation. He was willing to go to death on a cross. But He knew that from this deep debasement He would be lifted up and glorified. The shame of the cross would be turned into eternal glory. Because He suffered death He was to be crowned with glory and honor (cf. Hebrews 2:9). Facing the cross with its agonizing death, Jesus lifted His eyes toward the glory that was waiting for Him (cf. Hebrews 12:2). Just a few more hours and He would be with His Father again.

(2) *The prayer of Jesus for His disciples* (verses 6-19). Having prayed for himself, Jesus prayed for His disciples. They were the ones who had been with Him during His time of rejection and had shared His trials. He began by "introducing" them to His Father, not that they were unknown to the Father. On the contrary, they belonged to Him from the beginning. He had given them to the Son. They had not ceased to belong to the Father. "They are thine. And all mine are thine, and thine are mine" (verses 9,10). This is something only the Son could say.

The disciples were not of the world, therefore the world hated them. However, Jesus did not ask that they be taken out of the world. On the contrary, He sent them into the world with His message. They had received the word He had preached to them and believed that God had sent Him. The Word was their message.

When He now sent them into the world He prayed that the Father would keep them from the evil of the world. Until then Jesus himself had been with them. Now He was leaving them. So He handed them over to the Father's protection.

(3) *The prayer of Jesus for all who believe* (verses 20-26). Next He prayed for those who would believe in Him because of the apostles' words. That for which Jesus prayed concerning His first disciples applies to all believers. It is a prayer for the universal Church. It applies to all in whom Jesus is glorified (verse 10) and to whom He has given His glory (verse 22)—glory that is full of grace and truth (cf. 1:14).

In addition to praying that the Father would keep the disciples from evil, Jesus prayed for the unity of believers (verses 20-23) and that they should at last be with Him in His eternal glory (verse 24).

The divine pattern for unity among believers is the unity between the Father and the Son. The foundation of unity is faith in Jesus, and this unity will point the world to faith in Jesus as the One sent from God. Once more the purpose of the Gospel of John was emphasized: to guide the lost to faith in Jesus as the Son of God (20:30,31). In the unity of believers the love of God himself is revealed to men. The love of Jesus for His own (15:9) reaches its highest expression by being compared with the Father's love for the Son. The Father's love for believers finds its highest expression when compared with His love for the Son: "Thou hast sent me, and hast loved them, as thou hast loved me" (17:23).

Jesus' words were filled with divine majesty when He said, "Father, I will that they also, whom thou hast given me, be with me where I am; that they may behold my glory" (17:24). That "will" is unshakable because it is based on the eternal counsel of God and the eternal love of God for men. The Son of God came into the world to redeem those who received Him in faith. Jesus ended this mighty prayer with an appeal to the Father's righteousness and love. The most wonderful of all sermons—the farewell sermon of Jesus—ended with the highest and most sublime prayer ever heard on earth: the high priestly prayer of Jesus.

The History of the Suffering of Christ

It has been said that the gospel is "passion history" with the rich beginnings. This is true of the Gospel of John. The record of Jesus' sufferings and the Resurrection forms the climax of the book. In preceding chapters, the inspired writer presented Jesus as the One who acts and teaches. Now he drew a picture of Him who endured suffering greater than anyone else ever experienced. It was from the viewpoint of an eyewitness. John's Gospel therefore supplements the record of the Synoptics with a series of new facts.

Many scholars emphasize the way the Passion account in John's Gospel shows Jesus' willingness—one could almost say His active assistance—in all that took place. To an even greater extent than the other Gospel writers, John's Gospel refers to the exaltation of Jesus, even as he pictured Him in His deepest humiliation. The humiliation itself was a glorification (cf. 12:23; 13:32; 17:5).

In John's Gospel the high priestly prayer of Jesus on His way to Gethsemane was a great doorway leading to the "passion history." The duties of the Old Testament priest involved teaching the people, praying for them, and offering sacrifices to God. When Christ had completed His teaching work, He fulfilled His earthly intercession ministry through this last great prayer. Then He presented himself as the sacrificial offering. He had said all He had to say as a prophet. He was ready to complete His priestly service.

(1) *Gethsemane*

Jesus went out of the city with His disciples and crossed the brook Kidron. It was a "winter brook" which was dried up most of the year and was probably dry at this time.

The Mount of Olives was separated from the city by a deep valley bearing the same name as the brook. "Kidron" probably means "the dark brook" or "the brook of the dark valley." The brook and the valley are mentioned frequently in the Old Testament. Many of the pious kings of Israel are mentioned in connection with this place. Asa, Josiah, and Hezekiah had burned idols and other unclean objects here.

One commentator mentions the Kidron Valley in connection with services in the temple. With a Jewish writer as his source, Lightfoot states that the blood from sacrifices flowed down to the valley of Kidron through a channel, (Lightfoot, *A Commentary on the New Testament* 3:413-14). The road Jesus followed out of the city may have been the same road where the scapegoat was led out into the desert on the Day of Atonement (Leviticus 16:8-10).

It was the road David followed when he left Jerusalem while fleeing from his son Absalom (2 Samuel 15:23). Now the Son of David was leaving Jerusalem, following David's footprints, rejected by His own people.

John's Gospel says Jesus and His disciples came to a garden, or olive grove. The Synoptics name the place—Gethsemane, which means "olive press." A number of commentators note here that man's fall took place in a garden, that the sufferings of Christ began in a garden, that there was a garden where Jesus was crucified, and that His grave was in a garden. The first Adam had everything good, all he could wish for, in the Garden of Eden, yet he fell. The last Adam had to endure everything heavy and painful in the Garden of Gethsemane, yet He won the victory.

It had been Jesus' custom to go out to the Mount of Olives from time to time, often resting there with His disciples during the night. John mentions particularly that Judas also knew the place where Jesus frequently spent the night. Jesus was aware of Judas' knowledge of the location and could expect that the traitor would lead the authorities to Him there. This olive grove seems also to have been where Jesus went for prayer. At this holy place, filled with sacred memories, Judas betrayed his Master.

John's Gospel omits Jesus' inner struggle in Gethsemane. The incident is well known from the other Gospels and forms the background of certain features in John's record (cf. 18:11).

John recorded that Judas brought the guard and servants from the high priest and Pharisees to the garden with him. This does not mean Judas was their leader. He was only there to show them the way. While the Synoptics speak of "a great multitude with swords and staves" (Matthew 26:47; Mark 14:43), John's Gospel says the Roman guard stationed at the fortress of Antonia also participated in the arrest of Jesus. A Roman cohort could consist of about 600 men. This was one-tenth of a legion and was divided again into 3 smaller operational groups of about 200 men each. The captain of the guard led the group that went out to arrest Jesus. It is unlikely that all the guard participated, but the Romans sometimes sent unusually large forces to perform such tasks (cf. Acts 23:23). The Roman guard must have been included in this operation at the order of Pilate. From Matthew 27:27-29 it is evident that Pilate knew about the turmoil over Jesus before He was brought before him. The Sanhedrin presented Jesus to Pilate as a political rebel, probably referring to His triumphal entry into Jerusalem on what is now called Palm Sunday. Part of the plan of Jesus' enemies was first to have Him arrested by the Romans so they could have Him sentenced by Pilate. The high priest probably did not trust his own servants, some of whom had previously returned without Jesus when they were sent to arrest Him. The temple police of the Levites and the private servants of the high priest also participated in the plan to have Jesus arrested. However, the Jewish authorities had asked for the assistance of the Romans, probably using the excuse that in arresting Jesus they would risk opposition, not only from Jesus' disciples but from many Galileans who had come to the feast and were also His followers. From the very beginning, the Jews and Gentiles worked together to have Jesus removed from the earthly scene (cf. Acts 4:26,27). Jesus knew what was going to happen to Him. He was destined for suffering from the beginning because this was why He came into the world. Each cross He saw erected reminded Him of His own cross. Each lamb He saw sacrificed in the temple was a reminder that He was himself the Lamb of God who was to be sacrificed for the sin of the world. In spite of this (or, more correctly, *because* of this), Jesus walked with firm steps toward His sacrificial death.

John's Gospel records that when the mixed multitude armed with swords and clubs and carrying torches came to the Garden of Gethsemane, Jesus met them and asked for whom they were looking. In reply to Jesus' question, many in the multitude said they were looking for Jesus of Nazareth. Evidently they could not imagine that the One who met them was He. Judas the betrayer stepped out from the crowd and kissed the Master—the sign he and the authorities had agreed upon. But the kiss was totally unnecessary because Jesus said, "I am the One!" or, literally, "I Am!" This was the language of Deity.

At Jesus' words the multitude drew back and fell to the earth. His appearance alone struck fear into them. They thought they had come to apprehend a fugitive, but He met them with a majesty that overwhelmed them. The divine nature of Jesus struck even His enemies with awe. For a time those who came to seize Him lay on the ground as though struck by lightning. This was an opportunity for Jesus and His disciples to slip away, if that was what He wanted to do. Earlier in His ministry Jesus had escaped the crowd in Nazareth when His enemies wanted to take His life (Luke 4:30). But not so now. He waited, for He knew His time had come. He repeated His question: "Whom seek ye?" (18:7).

They repeated their reply: "Jesus of Nazareth." Jesus then said, "I have told you that I am he: if therefore ye seek me, let these go their way" (verse 8). Jesus said this to fulfill what He declared in His prayer to the Father: "Those that thou gavest me I have kept, and none of them is lost, but the son of perdition" (17:12). Only a few hours earlier in the same night, Jesus had told Peter he would not be able to follow Him now, but that He should do so later (13:36). The disciples were not yet mature enough to be brought before Caiaphas and Pilate with their Master. Their faith would have failed totally. Jesus could not permit them to be tested above their ability to withstand.

Peter was not willing to use the opportunity Jesus had given him to insure his own safety. The disciples had secured two short swords (Luke 22:38). Peter carried one of these. Now he drew his sword and attacked Malchus, the servant of the high priest, who must have been in the front row among Jesus' enemies. John, who was known in the high priest's household, gives the servant's name. Probably Malchus dodged Peter's thrust in such a way that he was only wounded instead of being killed, although the loss of his ear was no small injury.

Jesus rebuked His disciple and ordered him to put the sword into its sheath. Jesus had already shown His power. His enemies had been prostrate at His feet. If He had wanted to defend himself He could have asked the Father for 12 legions of angels. Jesus said to Peter: "The cup which my Father hath given me, shall I not drink it?" (18:11). The other Gospels tell us that Jesus had just spoken of this cup in His prayer in Gethsemane (Matthew 26:39; Mark 14:36; Luke 22:42). The first prayer had been, "If it be possible, let this cup pass from me" (Matthew 26:39). In the next prayer He cried with holy submission, "O my Father, if this cup may not pass away from me, except I drink it, thy will be done" (Matthew 26:42). But after the struggle in Gethsemane was over, He declared: "The cup which my Father hath given me, shall I not drink it?" (18:11). Thus Jesus received the outward cup of suffering from the hand of the Father. What is implied in this picture is evident from Old Testament passages which connect the "cup" with suffering and with enduring the wrath of God: Psalm 75:8; Isaiah 51:17-22; Jeremiah 25:15; Ezekiel 23:31-33 (cf. Revelation 14:10; 16:19).

Now the disciples fled and Jesus' enemies seized Him and bound His hands. A moment before this they lay on their faces stricken with fear, but this had not changed their attitude toward Jesus. They had seen Him heal the severed ear of Malchus, but even this "surgical miracle" did not open their eyes to Jesus' real identity. So they led Him away.

(2) *The Examination by the High Priest*

At the captain's command, the soldiers seized Jesus (the Greek word for *seized* is simply a technical term for the arrest). They brought Him first to Annas the high priest, which shows it was the Jews who were the main force behind Jesus' arrest. If it had been the Romans, He would have been led directly to Pilate.

According to the Mosaic law, Annas was still the legitimate high priest, in spite of the fact that he had been removed from his office by the Roman ruler some 15 years earlier. However, his family had become a kind of high priestly dynasty, with five of his sons in turn succeeding him in the office. Presently his son-in-law Caiaphas was the one serving as high priest. In spite of the fact that Annas had lost his position, he was still called high priest (Luke 3:2; Acts 4:6) and with an even greater right to the title than many others who filled the office.

Annas had a strong influence in the leading religious circles of Jerusalem. He was very rich and he and his family were known for their greediness. Their main source of wealth seems to have been the business activity in the temple which Jesus attacked so fiercely. By charging high prices for the sacrificial animals and by shameless money exchanges, this family plundered the people who came to the temple to worship God. Jesus said they had changed the temple into a den of robbers.

Matthew's Gospel records that Jesus was led to Caiaphas the high priest after His arrest in Gethsemane. Mark and Luke say only that He was led to the high priest or the house of the high priest. It is John's Gospel that gives the supplementary information that Jesus was first presented to Annas. John's Gospel also tells about the more private examination before Annas, concerning which, all the Synoptics are silent.

The high priest began to examine Jesus about His disciples and His doctrine. This procedure was illegal according to the laws of the Jews. Those legal rules provided that the accused should not be questioned in such a way as to confirm the charges against him. It was the duty of the accusers to bring witnesses to prove their allegations.

However, it seems that Annas tried to lay the groundwork for an accusation of political rebellion against Jesus because this could be used before Pilate. Annas' inquiry about Jesus' disciples seems to indicate that he intended to accuse Him of forming a group for revolt. When he also asked about Jesus' doctrine it may have indicated that he intended to have some of Jesus' disciples testify against Him. Judas had already deserted his Master willingly.

Jesus recognized the high priest's strategy and would not play into his hand. As He did in Gethsemane, He defended His disciples now. First, He accepted the entire responsibility for all He had said: "I spake openly . . . I ever taught in the synagogue" (18:20). What He taught was done publicly. He had spoken freely to everybody, speaking in synagogues and in the temple where all Jews gathered. "In secret have I said nothing. Why askest thou me? ask them which heard me, what I have said unto them: behold, they know what I said" (18:20-21). The high priests had among their own servants those who had listened to Jesus, and their testimony was: "Never man spake like this man" (John 7:46).

When Jesus said He had not spoken anything in secret, this of course did not imply that He had not taught His disciples privately. Even then, however, He did so mostly to explain what He had preached publicly. He did not have two different kinds of teaching—one for the people and another that promoted rebellion in a smaller circle. His messiahship could not be linked with any kind of sectarianism, and He did not preach any esoteric doctrine. Jesus did indeed have a circle of disciples who were close to Him, but it was not a closed or separate group in the sense the high priest was trying to insinuate. Jesus had followers among all who had heard Him, whether they declared it publicly or kept it secret. When He rejected the high priest's attempts to discover more about His disciples, He defended them against being involved in His own trial.

Jesus refused to be trapped by the high priest's questions. He would not tell who His disciples were and He refused to explain His doctrine—suggesting to the high priest that he could examine those who had heard Him speak. It is evident that in reality Jesus rebuked the high priest for his illegal handling of the charges. Jesus' behavior was a complete contrast to the usual cringing demeanor of an accused individual.

One of the servants of the court accused Jesus of violating the high priest's authority and struck Him in the face, saying, "Answerest thou the high priest so?" (18:22). This indicates something about the decay of the Jew's judicial system. When a servant of the court could strike the accused in this manner, real justice had broken down. Acts 23:2 says that the high priest even ordered those who stood with him to strike Paul in the mouth. Paul, who did not know it was the high priest, told him, "God shall smite thee, thou whited wall: for sittest thou to judge me after the law, and commandest me to be smitten contrary to the law?" The same kind of unlawful action was perpetrated against Jesus.

It is interesting that in this situation, Jesus did not react by "turning His other cheek" literally (cf. Matthew 5:39). Instead, He was so bold and fearless that He might have received another blow. Patiently and with dignity Jesus corrected the servant: "If I have spoken evil, bear witness of the evil: but if well, why smitest thou me?" (18:23). Jesus' words are a commentary on one of His sayings in the Sermon on the Mount (Matthew 5:39). His behavior showed a submission to governmental authorities in spirit and not merely by acting according to the letter of the Law. Augustine has said regarding this incident: "Our Lord showed what needed to be shown, namely, that those great precepts of His are to be fulfilled not by bodily ostentation, but by the preparation of the heart. For it is possible that even an angry man may visibly hold out his other cheek. How much better, then, is it for one who is inwardly pacified to make a truthful answer, and with tranquil mind hold himself ready for the endurance of heavier sufferings to come?" (See Schaff, ed., *Nicene and Post-Nicene Fathers of the Christian Church*, 7:420.)

Annas then sent Jesus bound to Caiaphas the high priest. Jesus' fearlessness in the presence of His enemies had made it clear to Annas that he would accomplish nothing by continuing this preliminary examination. At this time also "all the elders and the scribes" had gathered with Caiaphas (Mark 14:53). John tells nothing about this second examination of Jesus during the night. Neither did he record anything about the official meeting held early in the morning (Mark 15:1) except to say that these men sent Jesus to the Roman governor Pilate after He had already been sentenced to death (John 18:31; 19:7). What John wrote about Annas' examination was as an eyewitness. Throughout the Gospel of John this unnamed disciple testified of that which he had seen and heard. Compare 18:15 with the four verses in John 10:2,3,4,8, which distinctly refer to John the apostle.

As in the Synoptics, the story of Peter's denial is woven into the description of the high priests' examinations. Jesus had predicted that in three different situations during the night, Peter would deny Him. In some of these instances Peter was challenged repeatedly by different persons, and he repeatedly denied any knowledge of Jesus. In what sequence these denials are to be "numbered" is not entirely certain from the text. Many attempts have been made to harmonize the accounts and there are several possibilities. If we follow the Synoptics, it seems that John's Gospel does not mention Peter's second denial, which took place shortly after the first one (Luke 22:58). It appears that all John recorded in 18:25-27 belongs to the same situation and must be counted as Peter's third denial. Perhaps at that same moment, Jesus was led across the courtyard from Annas to Caiaphas, and Peter met His glance, after which he went out and wept bitterly.

(3) *Jesus Before Pilate*

John's Gospel tells nothing of Jesus' examination and sentencing by the Sanhedrin. In his Gospel the judgment scene changes immediately to the residence of the Roman praetor where this official resided when he was in Jerusalem. The place may have been connected with the Antonia fortress of Herod's palace. John gives a thorough description of what took place during the Roman process.

Jesus was led to Pilate early in the morning. This expression may refer to the technical meaning—that this was during the last of the four night watches, i.e., between 3 and 6 a.m.—or it can simply mean it was early in the day. The latter interpretation seems most likely, since Luke 22:66 says that the official meeting of the Sanhedrin took place when it was daylight. Such meetings by the Romans usually started very early. In this instance there had probably been an agreement with the governor in advance.

The Jews would not enter the praetor's quarters. It would make them ritually unclean for 7 days, and this was immediately before the Passover Feast (cf. Acts 10:28). This is a grotesque example of how formal and external their service to God had become. While they were about to murder their Messiah, assisted by bribes and false witnesses, they scrupulously took care of their ceremonial purity (cf. Luke 11:39).

Pilate was governor of Judea during A.D. 26-36. The Roman historian Tacitus calls him a procurator, (Tacitus *Annals* XV,44). It is probably an anachronism, since officials in his position were given this title during Claudius' reign (A.D. 41-54). Before this time he would be called *praefectus* (prefect), as he is referred to on an inscription discovered later. History shows that Pilate's time in Judea was characterized by bribes, acts of violence, plunderings, oppressions, humiliations, unceasing executions without legal sentence, and investigations with an excessive, intolerable cruelty. After many unpleasant incidents Pilate's relationship with the

Jews was tense. Despite this, however, they had to approach him in order to have Jesus executed. The Sanhedrin was permitted to pass a death sentence, but after the period of Herod the Great it seems they had lost their right to execute such sentences.

Because of this the Jewish authorities were in a somewhat difficult situation. Where Jesus was concerned, they were unable to find an accusation that made Him subject to the death penalty by either the Jewish or Roman courts. The Sanhedrin sentenced Jesus to death because of "blasphemy," citing His claim to be the Son of God.

However, such an indictment would not carry weight in a Roman court which did not engage in controversial questions about religion (cf. Acts 18:14; 23:29; 25:18-20). When facing Pilate, the Jews had to use other points of accusation. Some of them would have been ridiculous before a Jewish court, e.g., "We found this fellow perverting the nation, and forbidding to give tribute to Caesar, saying that he himself is Christ a king" (Luke 23:2). It would not have been a popular sentence for a Jewish court to pass—to judge a man because he said it was not right to pay tribute to Caesar! Before Pilate, however, it was important to give the impression that Jesus was a rebel against the Roman occupation.

Evidently the Jews had counted on Pilate's confirming their sentence of death for Jesus without further procedure. He had just helped to get Him arrested. So they were astonished and indignant when it turned out that Pilate himself would investigate the matter and pass the sentence. In an injured tone they said, "If he were not a malefactor, we would not have delivered him up unto thee" (18:30). They had no definite unlawful action of Jesus to refer to, but they did insist He was obviously guilty and that Pilate must rely on their decision. Pilate, however, was not willing to serve them as executioner without further investigation. He knew they had delivered the Nazarene to him because of envy, and now he brought Jesus into the fortress to examine Him alone.

Pilate immediately took up the Jews' main point of accusation and asked Jesus, "Art thou the King of the Jews?" (18:33). Jesus answered with a question: "Sayest thou this thing of thyself, or did others tell it thee of me?" (18:34). By this question He forced Pilate to consider whether he would be satisfied to be a willing tool in a dark conspiracy or a just and unprejudiced judge. Had Pilate during his time as governor heard anything about Jesus as a leader of rebels or as a rebel against the Romans? Instead, he had probably heard rumors that Jesus was a prophet and miracle-worker! Was this why he asked this question or was it from personal interest?

Pilate rejected Jesus' suggestion with disdain. "Am I a Jew?" he asked. "Thine own nation and the chief priests have delivered thee unto me" (18:35). The only reason he was interested in Jesus was His claim to be king. It is evident that this question concerned Pilate. Roman authors tell us that at this time there was widespread expectation that a Jewish Messiah-king would arise to claim authority over the world. Pilate could not have been ignorant of these rumors and expectations. It was the question of Jesus' kingdom and kingship that dominated the strange discussion between the accused Man and His judge. It was as the king of the Jews that Jesus was examined by Pilate. He was sentenced to death as the king of the Jews. He hung on the cross under the inscription, "Jesus of Nazareth the King of the Jews" (19:19).

Jesus said to Pilate, "My kingdom is not of this world" (18:36). His kingdom is different from all governmental power in this world. This does not mean the world lies outside the domain of His authority, but His kingdom is not "of this world." It does not belong to or rely on the world. It does not have this world as its origin. One of the first steps in establishing a kingdom in this world is to recruit soldiers; but Pilate's own soldiers could confirm that Jesus had commanded His disciple to put the sword in its sheath. Jesus assured Pilate, "If my kingdom were of this world, then would my servants fight, that I should not be delivered to the Jews," (18:36). Jesus would have led the Jews in a revolt against the Romans if He had been determined to establish an earthly kingdom. However, it was the Jews who appeared before Pilate as His accusers. This shows how absurd their charges were.

From Jesus' reply, Pilate concluded that He claimed royal authority. "Art thou a king then?" (verse 37), he asked. With the same solemnity by which Jesus had assured the high priest He was the Son of God (Matthew 26:64), He now confirmed to Pilate that He is the Messiah-king: "Thou sayest that I am a king" (18:37; cf. 1 Timothy 6:13). "To this end was I born, and for this cause came I into the world, that I should bear witness unto the truth" (18:37).

Jesus did not explain to Pilate the spiritual character of His kingdom, but asserted its divine origin. He is not a king because His servants have fought for Him. He does not owe His royalty to any earthly power. He came into the world as the King. The truth He came to testify of is not truth as an abstract idea, but the divine truth about which the entire Gospel of John witnesses, and which is manifested in the person of Jesus Christ himself: "I am the truth" (14:6). He came into the world from another realm, from heaven (18:37). Jesus stated His preexistence here. He is the center of His message. He is not only the preacher of the truth, but the revelation of the truth in this world. He is Truth itself.

Jesus then added that the person who is of the truth hears His voice (cf. John 3:21). It was the King of truth who admonished Pilate to pay attention to His words, but Pilate would not listen. He left Jesus after a remark apparently intended to be more or less serious: "What is truth?" (18:38). After his conversation with Jesus, Pilate was at least convinced He was innocent of that which He had been accused. This he told the Jews when he went out to them. Luke's Gospel says the people were then even more fierce in their cries: "He stirreth up the people, teaching throughout all Jewry, beginning from Galilee to this place" (Luke 23:5).

When Pilate learned Jesus was from Galilee and belonged to Herod's jurisdiction, He saw a way to get rid of this unpleasant case. Herod was in Jerusalem at this time and Pilate sent Jesus to him so he could pass the sentence. "And when Herod saw Jesus, he was exceeding glad: for he was desirous to see him of a long season, because he had heard many things of him; and he hoped to have seen some miracle done by him. Then he questioned with him in many words; but he answered him nothing. And the chief priests and scribes stood and vehemently accused him" (Luke 23:8-10). When Herod did not see the magic performance for which he had hoped, he started to mock Jesus along with his soldiers. He was no more willing than Pilate to take the high priests' accusation seriously, but he was also just as unwilling as Pilate to give the Nazarene His freedom. Then the soldiers threw a robe around Jesus and sent Him back to the Roman governor.

At this time a multitude had gathered in Pilate's courtyard. Many of them had come to demand a prisoner's release, as was the custom at the Feast. They had probably agreed on what they should propose to Pilate. John's Gospel does not tell anything about the interlude with Herod, but continues to show how Pilate tried to rid himself of the case by using this custom—one confirmed in the Mishna tract *Pesachin*.

The Roman court provided two forms of amnesty: *abolitio*, the release of a prisoner who was not yet sentenced, and *indulgentia*, mercy shown to a sentenced prisoner. In Jesus' case the type of amnesty in question was *abolitio*. Pilate took this opportunity to release Jesus without acquitting Him. Thus he could repeal the sentence the Sanhedrin had passed but would not challenge the Jewish leaders as if he had ignored their judgment completely. He asked, "Ye have a custom, that I should release unto you one at the Passover: will you therefore that I release unto you the King of the Jews?" (18:39).

This proved to be a deadly mistake. While Pilate previously had only the members of the Sanhedrin to contend with, he now had all the people as his opponents. The priests passed through the crowd and persuaded the people to demand the release of Barabbas, a robber. In spite of his crimes, Barabbas was a popular man. He did not claim to be a messiah, but the Jews considered an individual like him closer to their Messiah ideal than the one Pilate was offering them. Soon the people were calling with one voice for Barabbas.

Pilate then ordered Jesus to be scourged. This Roman punishment was barbaric. They used a whip made of many leather straps knit around sharp bits of bone and pieces of lead. The prisoner was stripped of his clothes and bound to a pole or thrown on the ground. Then he was whipped until the flesh hung from his body in strips. Veins were broken to pieces. Sometimes the entrails became visible. Many died during the scourging. Usually those who were to be crucified were scourged first, and this hastened their death.

The soldiers had heard that Jesus was called "the King of the Jews," and now they began a vulgar masquerade to have fun at His expense. Their performance seems to have been some kind of "kingplay." Pictures of this kind of activity have been found carved into stones near Gabbatha. Among other things, the trappings of vassal kings consisted of the purple robe, the scepter, and the golden garland. Only a sovereign king was permitted to carry a diadem. Jesus was now dressed as a king. The soldiers threw a purple robe over His naked body, put a reed in His hand, then braided a crown of thorns which they pressed down on His head. Perhaps they let Him sit down then in order to receive their scornful homage. Marching toward Him in procession, they fell on their knees in front of Him and cried, "Hail, King of the Jews!" (19:3). Instead of the kiss of homage, they spit at Him and smote Him on the head with the reed.

No doubt the soldiers' scorn was toward the Jewish people as much as Jesus himself. In the Gentile world it was widely known that the Jews aspired to world domination. The soldiers considered Jesus a representative of this messianic hope. It was the idea of a kingdom ruled by Israel which they turned into ridicule. But the scene illustrates in a striking manner the two aspects of Christ's humiliation—the physical suffering and the disgrace.

Pilate then went out to the people and said, "I bring him forth to you, that ye may know that I find no fault in him" (19:4). Two other times during the process Pilate repeated these words (18:38; 19:4,6). "Then came Jesus forth, wearing the crown of thorns, and the purple robe. And Pilate saith unto them, Behold the man!" (19:5). He had the double intent of showing what a miserable and harmless king Jesus was and of awakening the people's sympathy. However, the high priests and their servants now began to cry, "Crucify!" Pilate simply repeated that he had found Jesus free of guilt.

For a time the Jews changed tactics. They realized their political accusation of high treason had not produced results. So they came out with their real accusation: "We have a law, and by our law he ought to die, because he made himself the Son of God" (19:7). The Romans were protectors of the Jews' temple and its services. Pilate himself had incurred the wrath of the emperor because he had not paid enough attention to the religious feelings of the Jews. Now they demanded that he lend them a helping hand in upholding the Jewish law to which they appealed.

Jesus' personality had already impressed Pilate deeply, and he was growing more unwilling to deliver Him to the cross. When he now learned that Jesus claimed to be the Son of God, Pilate became even more afraid than before. He was not a religious man and did not believe that Jesus' claim was true. But he was affected by a superstitious fear that he might be laying hands on one of the "sons of the gods" he knew so well from Gentile myths. He had been warned through his wife's dream not to have anything to do with this just One (Matthew 27:19), so he entered the judgment hall once more and asked Jesus, "Whence art thou?" He knew Jesus came from Galilee, but his question did not concern this matter. What he wanted to know was Jesus' origin, but Jesus did not give any reply. It was Jesus, the man from Nazareth, that Pilate was to sentence. If he could not release Him as man, he would not release Him as the Son of God.

In Jesus' silence there was actually a reply. When the Jews repeated His testimony about himself erroneously, it was His duty to correct their statements. But here was no misunderstanding to be corrected. Jesus had claimed deity, and the Jews had understood this. Jesus' silence confirmed it. Shocked and indignant, Pilate exclaimed, "Speakest thou not unto me? knowest thou not that I have power to crucify thee, and have power to release thee?" Then Jesus answered, "Thou couldest have no power at all against me, except it were given thee from above: therefore he that delivered me unto thee hath the greater sin" (19:10,11). What a strange situation! Here the Judge of the world was speaking with His judge. Pilate had to admit he did not find any guilt in Jesus, but Jesus declared Pilate guilty. At the same time He found extenuating circumstances. There are degrees of sin. He who judges righteously said so on this occasion. It was His last word to Pilate.

After this, Pilate still tried to release Jesus. The Jews, however, understood how close Pilate was to pronouncing acquittal, so they made use of their final weapon. They had felt reluctant to use it because it meant reducing themselves to servants of the emperor and indicated that they had renounced the Jewish messianic belief. But when they saw they had not accomplished anything by their new charges against Jesus for blasphemy, they brought up the political charges again. Now they used them as a threat against Pilate personally: "If thou let this man go, thou art not Caesar's friend: whosoever maketh himself a king speaketh against Caesar" (19:12).

When Pilate heard this he knew all hope of saving Jesus was gone. He was fully aware that the Jews were serious about their threat. They knew—and Pilate himself knew—how weak his position was and how badly his administration would fare under a close investigation. The Jews had lodged serious complaints about him previously. If he was accused now of having spared a rebel, he would lose his position. It would mean the end of his career and could even cost him his life if the suspicious emperor Tiberius should receive such information.

Pilate then ended his discussion with the Jews. There was nothing left to negotiate. "When Pilate saw that he could prevail nothing, but that rather a tumult was made, he took water, and washed his hands before the multitude, saying, I am innocent of the blood of this just person: see ye to it" (Matthew 27:24).

Then he had Jesus led out while he sat down on his judgment seat. John's Gospel emphasizes the importance of this moment by one of his characteristic references to time. He records that this took place on the day of the preparation of the Passover and that it was about the sixth hour. There is a difficulty here because Mark's Gospel says Jesus was crucified at the third hour (Mark 15:25). There have been many attempts to explain this, three of which should be mentioned. Some think Mark's Gospel indicates time according to Jewish reckoning—from 6 o'clock in the morning—while John's Gospel counts from midnight like the Romans. Another explanation, which goes all the way back to Augustine, is that John was not referring to the sixth hour of the day but the sixth hour of the preparation for Passover. Thus his starting point was the changing of the guard about 3 o'clock in the morning. A third solution is that the Jews divided the 12 hours of the day into 4 segments: from 6 to 9, from 9 to 12, from 12 to 3, and from 3 to 6. The three points which were marked in this way were the third, sixth, and ninth hours, that is, 9 o'clock, 12 o'clock, and 3 o'clock in the afternoon. At that time a trumpet was blown in the temple because it was "the hour of prayer."

Each point of time between these trumpet signals was given according to that part of the day to which it belonged. Between 6 and 9 it was the third hour; between 9 and 12 it was the sixth hour; between 12 and 3 it was the ninth hour. We may conclude then that the sentence as well as the crucifixion took place about 9 o'clock in the morning. Mark calls it the third hour because it was close to that point of time and the time of the trumpet signal. John called it the sixth hour because it is between 9 and 12 o'clock. It might be difficult for those who are accustomed to accurate expressions of times and dates to understand language which usually stated the figures only approximately. The third hour can mean simply late in the morning and the sixth hour can mean only that it was early in the forenoon—in other words, almost the same thing.

When Pilate brought Jesus out and sat on the judgment seat he said to the Jews (probably with great sarcasm): "Behold, your King!" This provoked Jesus' enemies and they shouted back, "Away with him, away with him, crucify him!" Pilate continued with the same tones of derision but also as a last appeal to their messianic hope: "Shall I crucify your King?" (19:14,15).

The high priest replied, "We have no king but Caesar" (19:15). They stood as representatives of God's Old Testament people who had God as their King (Judges 8:23; 1 Samuel 8:7), yet they declared publicly that Caesar was their only king. These religious leaders who should have preached the messianic hope to the people now publicly renounced the Messiah and declared themselves satisfied with Caesar. As they proclaimed this to the world they were unaware that the prophecy of Jacob was fulfilled. "The scepter had departed from Judah" (Genesis 49:10), and Messiah had come (Ryle, *Expository Thoughts*, 3:323).

Pilate had to admit they had defeated him. In return he had received the Jews' subjection to the Roman emperor, and this puzzling judgment scene ends with the words, "Then delivered he him therefore unto them to be crucified" (19:16). That which had to take place had taken place. When the Early Church summed up what had happened they did so in these words: "For of a truth against thy holy child Jesus, whom thou hast anointed, both Herod, and Pontius Pilate, with the Gentiles, and the people of Israel, were gathered together, for to do whatsoever thy hand and thy counsel determined before to be done" (Acts 4:27,28).

Manuscripts

Egyptian Papyri

Note: (a) designates the section of the New Testament on which the manuscript is based; (b) designates the century in which it is believed the manuscript was written (using the Roman numerals); (c) provides information on the present location of the manuscript.

p1 (a) Gospels; (b) III; (c) Philadelphia, University of Pennsylvania Museum, no. E2746.

p2 (a) Gospels; (b) VI; (c) Florence, Museo Archeologico, Inv. no. 7134.

p3 (a) Gospels; (b) VI, VII; (c) Vienna, Österreichische Nationalbibliothek, Sammlung Papyrus Erzherzog Rainer, no. G2323.

p4 (a) Gospels; (b) III; (c) Paris, Bibliothèque Nationale, no. Gr. 1120, suppl. 2°.

p5 (a) Gospels; (b) III; (c) London, British Museum, P. 782 and P. 2484.

p6 (a) Gospels; (b) IV; (c) Strasbourg, Bibliothèque de la Université, 351ʳ, 335ᵛ, 379, 381, 383, 384 copt.

p7 (a) Gospels; (b) V; (c) now lost, was in Kiev, library of the Ukrainian Academy of Sciences.

p8 (a) Acts; (b) IV; (c) now lost; was in Berlin, Staatliche Museen, P. 8683.

p9 (a) General Epistles; (b) III; (c) Cambridge, Massachusetts, Harvard University, Semitic Museum, no. 3736.

p10 (a) Paul's Epistles; (b) IV; (c) Cambridge, Massachusetts, Harvard University, Semitic Museum, no. 2218.

p11 (a) Paul's Epistles; (b) VII; (c) Leningrad, State Public Library.

p12 (a) General Epistles; (b) late III; (c) New York, Pierpont Morgan Library, no. G. 3.

p13 (a) General Epistles; (b) III, IV; (c) London, British Museum, P. 1532 (verso), and Florence, Biblioteca Medicea Laurenziana.

p14 (a) Paul's Epistles; (b) V (?); (c) Mount Sinai, St. Catharine's Monastery, no. 14.

p15 (a) Paul's Epistles; (b) III; (c) Cairo, Museum of Antiquities, no. 47423.

p16 (a) Paul's Epistles; (b) III, IV; (c) Cairo, Museum of Antiquities, no. 47424.

p17 (a) General Epistles; (b) IV; (c) Cambridge, England, University Library, gr. theol. f. 13 (P), Add. 5893.

p18 (a) Revelation; (b) III, IV; (c) London, British Museum, P. 2053 (verso).

p19 (a) Gospels; (b) IV, V; (c) Oxford, Bodleian Library, MS. Gr. bibl. d. 6 (P.).

p20 (a) General Epistles; (b) III; (c) Princeton, New Jersey, University Library, Classical Seminary AM 4117 (15).

p21 (a) Gospels; (b) IV, V; (c) Allentown, Pennsylvania, Library of Muhlenberg College, Theol. Pap. 3.

p22 (a) Gospels; (b) III; (c) Glasgow, University Library, MS. 2-x. 1.

p23 (a) General Epistles; (b) early III; (c) Urbana, Illinois, University of Illinois, Classical Archaeological and Art Museum, G. P. 1229.

p24 (a) Revelation; (b) IV; (c) Newton Center, Massachusetts, Library of Andover Newton Theological School.

p25 (a) Gospels; (b) late IV; (c) now lost, was in Berlin, Staatliche Museen, P. 16388.

p26 (a) Paul's Epistles; (b) c. 600; (c) Dallas, Texas, Southern Methodist University, Lane Museum.

p27 (a) Paul's Epistles; (b) III; (c) Cambridge, England, University Library, Add. MS. 7211.

p28 (a) Gospels; (b) III; (c) Berkeley, California, Library of Pacific School of Religion, Pap. 2.

p29 (a) Acts; (b) III; (c) Oxford, Bodleian Library, MS. Gr. bibl. g. 4 (P.).

p30 (a) Paul's Epistles; (b) III; (c) Ghent, University Library, U. Lib. P. 61.

p31 (a) Paul's Epistles; (b) VII; (c) Manchester, England, John Rylands Library, P. Ryl. 4.

p32 (a) Paul's Epistles; (b) c. 200; (c) Manchester England, John Rylands Library, P. Ryl. 5.

p33 (a) Acts; (b) VI; (c) Vienna, Österreichische Nationalbibliothek, no. 190.

p34 (a) Paul's Epistles; (b) VII; (c) Vienna, Österreichische Nationalbibliothek, no. 191.

p35 (a) Gospels; (b) IV (?); (c) Florence, Biblioteca Medicea Laurenziana.

p36 (a) Gospels; (b) VI; (c) Florence, Biblioteca Medicea Laurenziana.

p37 (a) Gospels; (b) III, IV; (c) Ann Arbor, Michigan, University of Michigan Library, Invent. no. 1570.

p38 (a) Acts; (b) c. 300; (c) Ann Arbor, Michigan, University of Michigan Library, Invent. no. 1571.

p39 (a) Gospels; (b) III; (c) Chester, Pennsylvania, Crozer Theological Seminary Library, no. 8864.

p40 (a) Paul's Epistles; (b) III; (c) Heidelberg, Universitätsbibliothek, Inv. Pap. graec. 45.

p41 (a) Acts; (b) VIII; (c) Vienna, Österreichische Nationalbibliothek, Pap. K.7541-8.

p42 (a) Gospels; (b)VII, VIII; (c) Vienna, Österreichische Nationalbibliothek, KG 8706.

p43 (a) Revelation; (b) VI, VII; (c) London, British Museum, Pap. 2241.

p44 (a) Gospels; (b) VI, VII; (c) New York, Metropolitan Museum of Art, Inv. 14-1-527.

p45 (a) Gospels, Acts; (b) III; (c) Dublin, Chester Beatty Museum; and Vienna, Osterreichische Nationalbibliothek, P. Gr. Vind. 31974.

p46 (a) Paul's Epistles; (b) c. 200; (c) Dublin, Chester Beatty Museum, and Ann Arbor, Michigan, University of Michigan Library, Invent. no. 6238.

p47 (a) Revelation; (b) late III; (c) Dublin, Chester Beatty Museum.

p48 (a) Acts; (b) late III; (c) Florence, Museo Medicea Laurenziana.

p49 (a) Paul's Epistles; (b) late III; (c) New Haven, Connecticut, Yale University Library, P. 415.

p50 (a) Acts; (b) IV, V; (c) New Haven, Connecticut, Yale University Library, P. 1543.

p51 (a) Paul's Epistles; (b) c. 400; (c) London British Museum.

p52 (a) Gospels; (b) early II; (c) Manchester, John Rylands Library, P. Ryl. Gr. 457.

p53 (a) Gospels, Acts; (b) III; (c) Ann Arbor, Michigan, University of Michigan Library, Invent. no. 6652.

p54 (a) General Epistles; (b) V, VI; (c) Princeton, New Jersey, Princeton University Library, Garrett Depos. 7742.

p55 (a) Gospels; (b) VI, VII; (c) Vienna, Österreichische Nationalbibliothek, P. Gr. Vind. 26214.

p56 (a) Acts; (b) V, VI; (c) Vienna, Österreichische Nationalbibliothek, P. Gr. Vind. 19918.

p57 (a) Acts; (b) IV, V; (c) Vienna, Österreichische Nationalbibliothek, P. Gr. Vind. 26020.

p58 (a) Acts; (b) VI; (c) Vienna, Österreichische Nationalbibliothek, P. Gr. Vind. 17973, 36133[54], and 35831.

p59 (a) Gospels; (b) VII; (c) New York, New York University, Washington Square College of Arts and Sciences, Department of Classics, P. Colt. 3.

p60 (a) Gospels; (b) VII; (c) New York, New York University, Washington Square College of Arts and Sciences, Department of Classics, P. Colt. 4.

p61 (a) Paul's Epistles; (b) c. 700; (c) New York, New York University, Washington Square College of Arts and Sciences, Department of Classics, P. Colt. 5.

p62 (a) Gospels; (b) IV; (c) Oslo, University Library.

p63 (a) Gospels; (b) c. 500; (c) Berlin, Staatliche Museen.

p64 (a) Gospels; (b) c. 200; (c) Oxford, Magdalen College Library.

p65 (a) Paul's Epistles; (b) III; (c) Florence, Biblioteca Medicea Laurenziana.

p66 (a) Gospels; (b) c. 200; (c) Cologny/Genève, Bibliothèque Bodmer.

p67 (a) Gospels; (b) c. 200; (c) Barcelona, Fundación San Lucas Evangelista, P. Barc. 1.

p68 (a) Paul's Epistles; (b) VII (?); (c) Leningrad, State Public Library, Gr. 258.

p69 (a) Gospels; (b) III; (c) place (?)

p70 (a) Gospels; (b) III; (c) place (?)

p71 (a) Gospels; (b) IV; (c) place (?)

p72 (a) General Epistles; (b) III, IV; (c) Cologny/Genève, Bibliothèque Bodmer.

p73 (a) Gospels; (b)—; (c) Cologny/Genève, Bibliothèque Bodmer.

p74 (a) Acts, General Epistles; (b) VII; (c) Cologny/Genève, Bibliothèque Bodmer.

p75 (a) Gospels; (b) early III; (c) Cologny/Genève, Bibliothèque Bodmer.

p76 (a) Gospels; (b) VI; (c) Vienna, Österreichische Nationalbibliothek, P. Gr. Vind. 36102.

Major Codices

01, aleph:	Sinaiticus
02, A:	Alexandrinus
03, B:	Vaticanus
04, C:	Ephraemi Rescriptus
05, D:	Bezae Cantabrigiensis
06, E:	Claromontanus

Majuscules

No.	Contents	Century
01, *aleph*	Total New Testament	4th
02, A	Total New Testament	5th
03, B	New Testament, Revelation	4th
04, C	Total New Testament	5th
05, D	Gospels, Acts	6th
06, D	Paul's Epistles	6th
07, E	Gospels	8th
08, E	Acts	6th
09, F	Gospels	9th
010, F	Paul's Epistles	9th
011, G	Gospels	9th
012, G	Paul's Epistles	9th
013, H	Gospels	9th
015, H	Paul's Epistles	6th
016, I	Paul's Epistles	5th
017, K	Gospels	9th
018, K	Acts, Paul's Epistles	9th
019, L	Gospels	8th
020, L	Acts, Paul's Epistles	9th
021, M	Gospels	9th
022, N	Gospels	6th
023, O	Gospels	6th
024, P	Gospels	6th
025, P	Acts, Paul's Epistles, Revelation	9th
026, Q	Gospels	5th
028, S	Gospels	10th
029, T	Gospels	9th
030, U	Gospels	9th
031, V	Gospels	9th
032, W	Gospels	5th
033, X	Gospels	10th
034, Y	Gospels	9th
036,	Gospels	10th
037,	Gospels	9th
038,	Gospels	9th
039,	Gospels	9th
040,	Gospels	6th-8th
041,	Gospels	9th
042,	Gospels	6th
043,	Gospels	6th
044,	Gospels, Acts, Paul's Epistles	8th-9th

In addition to these manuscripts identified by a letter (letter uncials), there are 200 other numbered majuscule manuscripts. Even though most of these manuscripts are very valuable, there is not enough room to list them all. Our apparatus gives the official numbers, 046, 047 etc.

Minuscules

There are about 2800 of these. A total classification of these is only possible in specialized literature dealing with textual criticism.

Early Versions

it	Itala, early Latin	II-IV
vul	Vulgate	IV-V
old syr	Old Syrian	II-III
syr pesh	"peshitta"	V
got	Gothic	IV
arm	Armenian	IV-V
geo	Georgian	V
cop	Coptic	VI
nub	Nubian	VI
eth	Ethiopian	VI

Early Church Fathers

Ambrosius, deacon of Alexandria, and intimate friend of Origen, died 250.

Athanasius, was bishop of Alexandria, 326; died in 373.

Athenagoras, a Christian philosopher of Athens, flourished in 178.

Augustine, 354-430.

Basil the Great, bishop of Caesarea, born in Cappadocia, 329; died 379.

Bede, the Venerable, born 673.

Chrysostom, bishop of Constantinople, born 344; died 407.

Clemens Alexandrinus, Clement of Alexandria, the preceptor of Origen, died 212.

Clemens Romanus, Clement of Rome, *supposed* to have been fellow laborer with Peter and Paul, and bishop of Rome, 91.

Cyprian, Bishop of Carthage, in 248; was martyred, 258.

Cyrillus Alexandrinus, this Cyril was patriarch of Alexandria 412; died 444.

Cyrillus Hierosolymitanus, Cyril, bishop of Jerusalem, was born 315; died 386.

Ephraim Syrus, Ephraim the Syrian, was deacon of Edessa; and died 373.

Eusebius of Caesarea, c.260-340.

Gregory the Great, bishop of Rome, flourished in 590.

Gregory Thaumaturgus, was a disciple of Origen, and bishop of Neocaesarea in 240.

Hippolytus, a Christian bishop, flourished 230; died 235.

Ignatius, bishop of Antioch, was martyred about 110.

Irenaeus, disciple of Polycarp; born in Greece about 140; martyred 202.

Jerome, also called Hieronymus, one of the most eminent of the Latin fathers; author of the translation of the Scriptures called the Vulgate; born about 342, died in 420.

Justin Martyr, a Christian philosopher, martyred 165.

Origen, one of the most eminent of the Greek fathers, 185-254.

Tertullian, a most eminent Latin father, died about 220.

Books of the New and Old Testament and the Apocrypha

New Testament Books

Matthew
Mark
Luke
John
Acts
Romans
1 Corinthians
2 Corinthians
Galatians
Ephesians
Philippians
Colossians
1 Thessalonians
2 Thessalonians
1 Timothy
2 Timothy
Titus
Philemon
Hebrews
James
1 Peter
2 Peter
1 John
2 John
3 John
Jude
Revelation

Old Testament Books

Genesis
Exodus
Leviticus
Numbers
Deuteronomy
Joshua
Judges
Ruth
1 Samuel
2 Samuel
1 Kings
2 Kings
1 Chronicles
2 Chronicles
Ezra
Nehemiah
Esther
Job
Psalms
Proverbs
Ecclesiates
Song of Solomon
Isaiah
Jeremiah
Lamentations
Ezekiel
Daniel
Hosea
Joel
Amos
Obadiah
Jonah
Micah
Nahum
Habakkuk
Zephaniah
Haggai
Zechariah
Malachi

Books of the Apocrypha

1 & 2 Esdras
Tobit
Judith
Additions to Esther
Wisdom of Solomon
Ecclesiasticus or the Wisdom of Jesus Son of Sirach
Baruch
Prayer of Azariah and the Song of the Three Holy Children
Susanna
Bel and the Dragon
The Prayer of Manasses
1–4 Maccabees

Bibliography

Modern Greek Texts.

Aland, K. et al. in cooperation with the Institute for New Testament Textual Research. *The Greek New Testament.* 2nd ed. London: United Bible Societies. 1968.

Aland, K. et al. in cooperation with the Institute for New Testament Textual Research. *The Greek New Testament.* 3rd ed. New York: United Bible Societies. 1975.

Nestle, E. and K. Aland. *Novum Testamentum Graece.* 25th ed. Stuttgart: Deutsche Bibelstiftung. 1963.

Nestle, E. and K. Aland. et al. *Novum Testamentum Graece.* 26th ed. Stuttgart: Deutsche Bibelstiftung. 1979.

General Reference Sources with Abbreviations.

BAGD
Bauer, W. *A Greek-English Lexicon of the New Testament and Other Early Christian Literature.* 2nd ed. Revised and augmented by F. Wilbur Gingrich and Frederick W. Danker from Walter Bauer's Fifth Edition, Chicago: University of Chicago Press. 1958.

NIDNTT
Brown, Colin. ed. *The New International Dictionary of New Testament Theology.* Grand Rapids: Zondervan. 1975.

TDNT
Kittel, G. and G. Friedrich. *Theological Dictionary of the New Testament.* Trans. G.W. Bromiley. Grand Rapids: Wm. B. Eerdmans. 1964-. Vols. I-IV were edited by G. Kittell (1933-42), and Vols. V-IX by G. Friedrich (1954-72).

LSJ
Lidell, H.G. and R. Scott. *A Greek-English Lexicon.* 9th ed., H. Stuart Jones and R. McKenzie. Oxford: Clarendon. 1940.

M-M
Moulton, J.H. and G. Milligan. *The Vocabulary of the Greek Testament Illustrated from the Papyri and Other Non-Literary Sources.* London: Hodder and Stoughton. 1914-30; Grand Rapids: Eerdmans. 1985.

General Bibliography

Albright, W. F. and D. N. Freedman, eds. *The Anchor Bible.* Vol. 29, *The Gospel According to John I-XII,* by Raymond E. Brown. Garden City: Doubleday & Company, Inc. 1966.

Blaney, Harvey J. S. *The Gospel According to John.* In *The Wesleyan Bible Commentaries.* Ed. by Charles Carter. Vol. 4, *Matthew-Acts.* Grand Rapids: William B. Eerdmans Publishing Company. 1964.

Bruce, F. F. *The Gospel of John.* Grand Rapids: William B. Eerdmans Publishing Company. 1983.

Bruce, F. F., ed. *The New International Commentary on the New Testament. The Gospel According to John,* by Leon Morris. Grand Rapids: William B. Eerdmans Publishing Company. 1981.

Bunyan, John. *The Pilgrim's Progress.* New York: Charles Scribner's Sons. N.d. Reprint. Grand Rapids: Baker Book House. 1984.

Clarke, Adam. *Clarke's Commentary.* Vol. 5, *Matthew-Acts.* Nashville: Abingdon Press. N.d.

Colwell, Ernest Cadman. "A Definite Rule for the Use of the Article in the Greek of the New Testament." *Journal of Biblical Literature.* 52 (Spring 1933). Pp.12-21.

Dodd, C. H. *The Interpretation of the Fourth Gospel.* Cambridge: Cambridge University Press. 1968.

Edersheim, Alfred. *The Life and Times of Jesus the Messiah.* 2 vols. Grand Rapids: William B. Eerdmans Publishing Company. 1959.

Ethridge, J. W. *The Targums of Onkelos and Jonathan Ben Uzziel on the Pentateuch.* New York: KTAV Publishing House, Inc. 1968.

Filson, Floyd, V. *Current Issues in New Testament Interpretation.* Ed. by W. Klassen and G. F. Snyder. New York: Harper & Row. 1962.

Ginzberg, Louis. *The Legends of the Jews.* Vol. 5, *From Creation to Exodus.* Philadelphia: The Jewish Publication Society of America. 1968.

Guthrie, Donald, gen. ed. *The New Bible Commentary.* 3d. ed. Grand Rapids: William B. Eerdmans Publishing Company. 1970.

Harner, Philip B. *The "I Am" of the Fourth Gospel.* Vol. 26 of *Facet Books Biblical Series.* Ed. by John Reumann. Philadelphia: Fortress Press. 1970.

Jaspers, Karl. *The Great Philosophers.* Ed. by Hannah Arendt. Trans. by Ralph Manheim. New York: Harcourt, Brace, & World, Inc. 1966.

Josephus, F. *The Complete Works of Flavius Josephus.* Trans. by William Whiston. Grand Rapids: Kregel Pulications. 1960.

Lightfoot, John. *A Commentary on the New Testament from the Talmud and Hebraica.* Vol. 3, *Luke-John.* Oxford: Oxford University Press. 1859. Reprint. Grand Rapids: Baker Book House. 1979.

Mayfield, Joseph H. *The Gospel According to John.* In *Beacon Bible Commentary.* Ed. by Ralph Earle. Vol. 7, *Matthew-Acts.* Kansas City: Beacon Hill Press. 1965.

Metzger, Bruce M. *A Textual Commentary on the Greek New Testament.* London: United Bible Societies. 1975.

Milton, John. *Paradise Lost: Book 1.* In *Complete Poetry and Major Prose.* Ed. by Merritt G. Hughes. Indianapolis: The Odyssey Press. 1980.

Pelikan, Jaroslav, ed. *Luther's Works.* Vol. 22, *Sermons on the Gospel of St. John.* Trans. by Martin H. Bertam. St. Louis: Concordia Publishing House. 1957.

Philo. Trans. by F. H. Colson and G. H. Whitaker. 12 vols. London: William Heinemann Ltd. 1971.

Ryle, John Charles. *Expository Thoughts on the Gospels.* Vol. 3, *St. John.* Greenwood, S.C.: The Attic Press, Inc. N.d.

Schnackenburg, Rudolf. *The Gospel According to St. John.* 3 vols. Trans. by Cecily Hastings, Francis McDonagh, David Smith, and Richard Foley. New York: Seabury Press. 1980.

Tacitus. Trans. by Alfred John Church and William Jackson Brodribb. *Great Books of the Western World,* vol. 15. Ed. by Robert Hutchins. Chicago: Encyclopedia Britannica, Inc. 1971.

Tasker, R. V. G., ed. *Tyndale New Testament Commentaries.* Vol. 4, *The Gospel According to St. John,* by R. V. G. Tasker. Grand Rapids: William B. Eerdmans Publishing Company. 1972.

Tenney, Merrill C. *The Gospel According to John.* In *The Expositor's Bible Commentary.* Ed. by Frank E. Gaebelein. Vol. 9, *John-Acts.* Grand Rapids: Zondervan Publishing House. 1981.

The Babylonian Talmud. Trans. by H. Freedman. *Shabbath.* 2 vols. London: The Soncino Press. 1938.

The Talmud of the Land of Israel. Trans. by Jacob Neusner. Vol. 20, *Hagigah and Moed Qatan.* Chicago: The University of Chicago Press. 1982.

Various Versions Acknowledgments

Scripture quotations found in Various Versions were taken from the following sources with special permssion as indicated. The sources listed may be found in one or all of the volumes of THE COMPLETE BIBLICAL LIBRARY.

AB

Fitzmyer, Joseph A., S. J., trans. *The Gospel According to Luke I-IX; (Anchor Bible).* New York: Doubleday & Company, Inc. 1985.
Reprinted with permission. ©1981, 1985.

ADAMS

Adams, Jay E. *The Christian Counselor's New Testament: a New Translation in Everyday English with Notations, Marginal References, and Supplemental Helps.* Grand Rapids, MI: Baker Book House. 1977.
Reprinted with permission. ©1977.

ALBA

Condon, Kevin. *The Alba House New Testament.* Staten Island, NY: Alba House, Society of St. Paul copublished with The Mercier Press Ltd. 1972.
Reprinted with permission. *The Mercier New Testament.* 4 Bridge Street. Cork, Ireland: The Mercier Press Ltd. ©1970.

ALFORD

Alford, Henry. *The New Testament of Our Lord and Saviour Jesus Christ: After the Authorized Version.* Newly compared with the original Greek, and revised. London: Daldy, Isbister. 1875.

AMPB

The Amplified Bible. Grand Rapids, MI: Zondervan Publishing House. 1958.
Reprinted with permission from the *Amplified New Testament.* © The Lockman Foundation. 1954, 1958.

ASV

(American Standard Version) The Holy Bible Containing the Old and New Testaments: Translated out of the original tongues, being the version set forth A.D. 1611, compared with the most ancient authorities and rev. A.D. 1881-1885. New York: Thomas Nelson Inc., Publishers. 1901, 1929.

BARCLAY

Barclay, William. *The New Testament: A New Translation.* Vol. 1, *The Gospels and the Acts of the Apostles.* London: William Collins Sons & Co. Ltd. 1968.
Reprinted with permission. ©1968.

BB

The Basic Bible: Containing the Old and New Testaments in Basic English. New York: Dutton. 1950.
Reprinted with permission. *The Bible In Basic English.* © Cambridge University Press. 1982.

BECK

Beck, William F. *The New Testament in the Language of Today.* St. Louis, MO: Concordia Publishing House. 1963.
Reprinted with permission. © Mrs. William Beck, *An American Translation.* Leader Publishing Company: New Haven, MO.

BERKELEY

The Holy Bible: the Berkeley Version in Modern English Containing the Old and New Testaments. Grand Rapids: Zondervan Publishing House. 1959. Used by permission. ©1945, 1959, 1969.

BRUCE

Bruce, F. F. *The Letters of Paul: An Expanded Paraphrase Printed in Parallel with the RV.* Grand Rapids: William B. Eerdmans Publishing Co. 1965.
Reprinted with permission. F. F. Bruce. *An Expanded Paraphrase of the Epistles of Paul.* The Paternoster Press: Exeter, England. ©1965, 1981.

CAMPBELL

Campbell, Alexander. *The Sacred Writings of the Apostles and Evangelists of Jesus Christ commonly styled the New Testament:* Translated from the original Greek by Drs. G. Campbell, J. Macknight & P. Doddridge with prefaces, various emendations and an appendix by A. Campbell. Grand Rapids: Baker Book House. 1951 reprint of the 1826 edition.

CKJB

The Children's 'King James' Bible: New Testament. Translated by Jay Green. Evansville, IN: Modern Bible Translations, Inc. 1960.

CLEMENTSON

Clementson, Edgar Lewis. *The New Testament: a Translation.* Pittsburg, PA: Evangelization Society of Pittsburgh Bible Institute. 1938.

CONCORDANT

Concordant Version: The Sacred Scriptures: Designed to put the Englished reader in possession of all the vital facts of divine revelation without a former knowledge of Greek by means of a restored Greek text. Los Angeles: Concordant Publishing Concern. 1931.
Reprinted with permission. *Concordant Literal New Testament.* Concordant Publishing Concern. 15570 Knochaven Road, Canyon Country, CA 91351. ©1931.

CONFRATERNITY

The New Testament of Our Lord and Savior Jesus Christ: Translated from the Latin Vulgate, a revision of the Challoner-Rheims Version edited by Catholic scholars under the patronage of the Episcopal Committee of the Confraternity Christian Doctrine. Paterson, NJ: St. Anthony Guild Press. 1941.
Reprinted with permission by the Confraternity of Christian Doctrine, Washington, DC. ©1941.

CONYBEARE

Conybeare, W. J. and Rev. J. S. Howson, D.D. *The Life and Epistles of St. Paul.* 2 vols. rev. ed. London: Longman, Green, Longman, and Roberts. 1862.

CRANMER

Cranmer or Great Bible. *The Byble in Englyshe,* . . . translated after the veryte of the Hebrue and Greke text, by ye dilygent studye of dyverse excellent learned men, expert in the forsayde tonges. Prynted by Richard Grafton & Edward Whitchurch. Cum privilegio ad Imprimendum solum. 1539.

DARBY

Darby, J. N. *The Holy Scriptures A New Translation from the Original Languages.* Lansing, Sussex, England: Kingston Bible Trust. 1975 reprint of the 1890 edition.

DOUAY

The Holy Bible containing the Old and New Testaments: Translated from the Latin Vulgate . . . and with the other translations diligently compared, with annotations, references and an historical and chronological index. New York: Kennedy & Sons. N.d.

ET

Editor's Translation. Gerard J. Flokstra, Jr., Ph.D.

FENTON

Fenton, Farrar. *The Holy Bible in Modern English.* London: A. & C. Black. 1944 reprint of the 1910 edition.

GENEVA

The Geneva Bible: a facsimile of the 1560 edition. Madison, WI: University of Wisconsin Press. 1969.

GOODSPEED

The Bible: An American Translation. Translated by Edgar J. Goodspeed. Chicago: The University of Chicago Press. 1935.

HBIE

The Holy Bible containing the Old and New Testaments: An improved edition (based in part on the Bible Union Version). Philadelphia: American Baptist Publication Society. 1913.

HISTNT

The Historical New Testament: Being the literature of the New Testament arranged in the order of its literary growth and according to the dates of the documents: a new translation by James Moffatt. Edinburgh: T & T Clark. 1901.

JB

The Jerusalem Bible. Garden City, NY: Darton, Longman & Todd, Ltd. and Doubleday and Co., Inc. 1966.
Reprinted by permission of the publisher. ©1966.

KLINGENSMITH

Klingensmith, Don J. *Today's English New Testament.* New York: Vantage Press. 1972.
Reprinted by permission of author. ©Don J. Klingensmith. 1972.

KNOX

Knox, R. A. *The New Testament of our Lord and Saviour Jesus Christ: a New Translation.* New York: Sheen and Ward. 1946.
Reprinted by permission of The Liturgy Commission.

LAMSA

Lamsa, George M. *The Holy Bible From Ancient Eastern Text:* Translated from original Aramaic sources. Philadelphia: Holman. 1957. From *The Holy Bible From Ancient Eastern Text* by George Lamsa. ©1933 by Nina Shabaz; renewed 1961 by Nina Shabaz. ©1939 by Nina Shabaz; renewed 1967 by Nina Shabaz. ©1940 by Nina Shabaz; renewed 1968 by Nina Shabaz. ©1957 by Nina Shabaz.
Reprinted by permission of Harper & Row, Publishers, Inc.

LATTIMORE

Lattimore, Richmond. *The Four Gospels and The Revelation:* Newly translated from the Greek. New York: Farrar, Straus, Giroux, Inc. 1979.
Reprinted by permission of the publisher. © Richmond Lattimore, 1962, 1979.

LIVB

The Living Bible: Paraphrased. Wheaton, IL: Tyndale House Publishers. 1973. Used by permission of the publisher. © Tyndale House Publishers. 1971.

LOCKE

Locke, John. *A Paraphrase and Notes on the Epistles of St. Paul to the Galatians, First and Second Corinthians, Romans, and Ephesians:* To which is prefixed an essay for the understanding of St. Paul's Epistles. Cambridge, England: Brown, Shattuck; Boston: Hilliard, Gray, and Co. 1832.

MACKNIGHT

Macknight, James. *New Literal Translation:* From the original Greek, of all the Apostolical Epistles, with a commentary, and notes, philological, critical, explanatory, and practical. Philadelphia: Wardkem. 1841.

MACKNIGHT

Macknight, James. *Harmony of the Four Gospels:* 2 vols. in which the natural order of each is preserved, with a paraphrase and notes. London: Longman, Hurst, Rees, Orme and Brown. 1819.

MOFFATT

The New Testament: A New Translation. New York: Harper and Row Publishers, Inc.; Kent, England: Hodder and Stoughton Ltd. c.1912.
Reprinted with permission.

MONTGOMERY

Montgomery, Helen Barrett. *The Centenary Translation of the New Testament:* Published to signalize the completion of the first hundred years of work of the American Baptist Publication Society. Philadelphia: American Baptist Publication Society. 1924. Used by permission of Judson Press. *The New Testament in Modern English* by Helen Barrett Montgomery. Valley Forge: Judson Press. 1924, 1952.

MURDOCK

Murdock, James. *The New Testament: The Book of the Holy Gospel of our Lord and Our God, Jesus the Messiah:* A literal translation from the Syriac Peshito version. New York: Stanford and Swords. 1851.

NASB

New American Standard Bible. Anaheim, CA: Lockman Foundation. 1960.
Reprinted with permission. © The Lockman Foundation 1960, 1962, 1963, 1968, 1971, 1972, 1973, 1975, 1977.

NEB

The New English Bible: New Testament. Cambridge, England: Cambridge University Press. 1970.
Reprinted by permission. ©The Delegates of the Oxford University Press and The Syndics of the Cambridge University Press 1961, 1970.

NIV

The Holy Bible: New International Version. Grand Rapids: Zondervan Publishing House. 1978. Used by permission of Zondervan Bible Publishers. ©1973, 1978, International Bible Society.

NKJB

The New King James Bible, New Testament. Nashville, TN: Royal Pub. 1979.
Reprinted from *The New King James Bible-New Testament.* ©1979, 1982, Thomas Nelson, Inc., Publishers.

NORLIE

Norlie, Olaf M. *Simplified New Testament: In plain English for today's reader. A new translation from the Greek.* Grand Rapids: Zondervan Publishing House. 1961. Used by permission. ©1961.

NORTON

Norton, Andrews. *A Translation of the Gospels with Notes.* Boston: Little, Brown. 1856.

NOYES

Noyes, George R. *The New Testament:* Translated from the Greek text of Tischendorf. Boston: American Unitarian Association. 1873.

PANIN

Panin, Ivan., ed. *The New Testament from the Greek Text as Established by Bible Numerics.* Toronto, Canada: Clarke, Irwin. 1935.

PHILLIPS

Phillips, J. B., trans. *The New Testament in Modern English.* Rev. ed. New York: Macmillan Publishing Company, Inc. 1958.
Reprinted with permission. ©J. B. Phillips, 1958, 1960, 1972.

PNT

A Plain Translation of the New Testament by a Student. Melbourne, Australia: McCarron, Bird. 1921.

RHEIMS

The Nevv Testament of Iesus Christ. Translated faithfully into English, out of the authentical Latin, . . . In the English College of Rhemes. Printed at Rhemes by Iohn Fogny. Cum privilegio. 1582.

RIEU

Rieu, E. V. *The Four Gospels.* London: Penguin Books Ltd. 1952.
Reprinted with permission. ©E. V. Rieu, 1952.

ROTHERHAM

Rotherham, Joseph B. *The New Testament:* Newly translated (from the Greek text of Tregelles) and critically emphasized, with an introduction and occasional notes. London: Samual Bagster. 1890.

RSV

Revised Standard Version; The New Covenant commonly called the New Testament of our Lord and Saviour Jesus Christ: Translated from the Greek being the version set forth A.D. 1611, revised A.D. 1881, A.D. 1901. New York: Thomas Nelson Inc. Publishers. 1953. Used by permission. ©1946, 1952, 1971, 1973 by the Division of Christian Education of the National Council of the Churches of Christ in the U.S.A.

RV

The New Testament of our Lord and Savior Jesus Christ: Translated out of the Greek . . . being the new version revised 1881. St. Louis, MO: Scammell. 1881.

SAWYER

Sawyer, Leicester Ambrose. *The New Testament: Translated from the original Greek,* with chronological arrangement of the sacred books, and improved divisions of chapters and verses. Boston: Walker, Wise. 1861.

SCARLETT

Scarlett, Nathaniel. *A translation of the New Testament from the original Greek:* humbly attempted. London: T. Gillett. 1798.

SEBNT

The Simple English ™ Bible, New Testament: American edition. New York: International Bible Translators, Inc. 1981. Used by permission from International Bible Translators, Inc.

TCNT

The Twentieth Century New Testament: a Translation into Modern English Made from the Original Greek: (Westcott & Hort's text). New York: Revell. 1900.

TEV

The Good News Bible, Today's English Version. New York: American Bible Society. 1976. Used by permission. © American Bible Society, 1966, 1971, 1976.

TORREY

Torrey, Charles Cutler. *The Four Gospels: A New Translation.* New York: Harper and Row Publishers Inc. 1933.
Reprinted by permission. ©1933.

TYNDALE

Tyndale, William. *The Newe Testament dylygently corrected and compared with the Greke.* and fynesshed in the yere of oure Lorde God anno M.D. and XXXIIII in the month of Nouember. London: Reeves and Turner. 1888.

WAY

Way, Arthur S., trans. *Letters of St. Paul: To seven churches and three friends with the letter to the Hebrews.* 8th ed. Chicago: Moody. 1950 reprint of the 1901 edition.

WESLEY

Wesley, John. *Explanatory notes upon the New Testament.* London: Wesleyan-Methodist Book-room. N.d.

WEYMOUTH

Weymouth, Richard Francis. *The New Testament in Modern Speech:* An idiomatic translation into everyday English from the text of the "Resultant Greek Testament." Revised by J. A. Robertson. London: James Clarke and Co. Ltd. and Harper and Row Publishers Inc. 1908. Reprinted by permission.

WILLIAMS

Williams, Charles B. *The New Testament: A Translation in the Language of the People.* Chicago: Moody Bible Institute of Chicago. 1957. Used by permission of Moody Press. Moody Bible Institute of Chicago. ©1937, 1966 by Mrs. Edith S. Williams.

WILSON

Wilson, Benjamin. *The Emphatic Diaglott containing the original Greek Text of what is commonly styled the New Testament* (according to the recension of Dr. F. F. Griesback) with interlineary word for word English translation. New York: Fowler & Wells. 1902 reprint edition of the 1864 edition.

WORRELL

Worrell, A. S. *The New Testament: Revised and Translated:* With notes and instructions; designed to aid the earnest reader in obtaining a clear understanding of the doctrines, ordinances, and primitive assemblies as revealed. Louisville, KY: A. S. Worrell. 1904.

WUEST

Wuest, Kenneth S. *The New Testament: An Expanded Translation.* Grand Rapids: Wm. B. Eerdmans Publishing Company. 1961. Used by permission of the publisher. ©1961.

WYCLIF

Wyclif(fe), John. *The Holy Bible containing the Old and New Testaments with the Apocryphal Books:* in the earliest English version made from the Latin Vulgate by John Wycliffe and his followers. London: Reeves and Turner. 1888.

YOUNG

Young, Robert. *Young's Literal Translation of the Holy Bible.* Grand Rapids: Baker Book House. 1953 reprint of the 1898 3rd edition.